THE SENATE INTELLIGENCE COMMITTEE REPORT ON TORTURE

THE SENATE INTELLIGENCE COMMITTEE REPORT ON TORTURE

COMMITTEE STUDY OF THE CENTRAL INTELLIGENCE AGENCY'S DETENTION AND INTERROGATION PROGRAM

SENATE SELECT COMMITTEE ON INTELLIGENCE

MELVILLE HOUSE
BROOKLYN • LONDON

THE SENATE INTELLIGENCE COMMITTEE REPORT ON TORTURE

FIRST MELVILLE HOUSE PRINTING: DECEMBER 2014

Melville House Publishing
145 Plymouth Street Brooklyn, NY 11201
&
8 Blackstock Mews
IslingtonLondon N4 2BT

mhpbooks.com facebook.com/mhpbooks @melvillehouse

ISBN: 978-1-61219-485-1

Printed in the United States of America
10 9 8 7 6 5 4 3 2 1

CONTENTS

FOREWORD

On April 3, 2014, the Senate Select Committee on Intelligence voted to send the Findings and Conclusions and the Executive Summary of its final Study on the CIA's Detention and Interrogation Program to the President for declassification and subsequent public release.

This action marked the culmination of a monumental effort that officially began with the Committee's decision to initiate the Study in March 2009, but which had its roots in an investigation into the CIA's destruction of videotapes of CIA detainee interrogations that began in December 2007.

The full Committee Study, which totals more than 6,700 pages, remains classified but is now an official Senate report. The full report has been provided to the White House, the CIA, the Department of Justice, the Department of Defense, the Department of State, and the Office of the Director of National Intelligence in the hopes that it will prevent future coercive interrogation practices and inform the management of other covert action programs.

As the Chairman of the Committee since 2009, I write to offer some additional views, context, and history.

I began my service on the Senate Intelligence Committee in January 2001. I remember testimony that summer from George Tenet, the Director of Central Intelligence, that warned of a possible major terrorist event against the United States, but without specifics on the time, location, or method of attack. On September 11, 2001, the world learned the answers to those questions that had consumed the CIA and other parts of the U.S. Intelligence Community.*

* For information on the events at the CIA prior to September 11, 2001, see the Final Report of the National Commission on Terrorist Attacks upon the United States (9/11 Commission) and Office of the Inspector General Report on Accountability With Respect to the 9/11 Attacks.

I recall vividly watching the horror of that day, to include the television footage of innocent men and women jumping out of the World Trade Center towers to escape the fire. The images, and the sounds as their bodies hit the pavement far below, will remain with me for the rest of my life.

It is against that backdrop—the largest attack against the American homeland in our history—that the events described in this report were undertaken.

Nearly thirteen years later, the Executive Summary and Findings and Conclusions of this report are being released. They are highly critical of the CIA's actions, and rightfully so. Reading them, it is easy to forget the context in which the program began—not that the context should serve as an excuse, but rather as a warning for the future.

It is worth remembering the pervasive fear in late 2001 and how immediate the threat felt. Just a week after the September 11 attacks, powdered anthrax was sent to various news organizations and to two U.S. Senators. The American public was shocked by news of new terrorist plots and elevations of the color-coded threat level of the Homeland Security Advisory System. We expected further attacks against the nation.

I have attempted throughout to remember the impact on the nation and to the CIA workforce from the attacks of September 11, 2001. I can understand the CIA's impulse to consider the use of every possible tool to gather intelligence and remove terrorists from the battlefield,* and CIA was encouraged by political leaders and the public to do whatever it could to prevent another attack.

The Intelligence Committee as well often pushes intelligence agencies to act quickly in response to threats and world events.

Nevertheless, such pressure, fear, and expectation of further terrorist plots do not justify, temper, or excuse improper actions taken by individuals or organizations in the name of national security. The major lesson of this report is that regardless of the pressures and the need to act, the Intelligence Community's actions must always reflect who we are as a nation, and adhere to our laws and standards. It is precisely at these times of national crisis that our government must be guided by the lessons of our history and subject decisions to internal and external review.

Instead, CIA personnel, aided by two outside contractors, decided to initiate a program of indefinite secret detention and the use

* It is worth repeating that covert action authorities approved by the President in September 2001 did not provide any authorization or contemplate coercive interrogations.

of brutal interrogation techniques in violation of U.S. law, treaty obligations, and our values.

This Committee Study documents the abuses and countless mistakes made between late 2001 and early 2009. The Executive Summary of the Study provides a significant amount of new information, based on CIA and other documents, to what has already been made public by the Bush and Obama Administrations, as well as non-governmental organizations and the press.

The Committee's full Study is more than ten times the length of the Executive Summary and includes comprehensive and excruciating detail. The Study describes the history of the CIA's Detention and Interrogation Program from its inception to its termination, including a review of each of the 119 known individuals who were held in CIA custody.

The full Committee Study also provides substantially more detail than what is included in the Executive Summary on the CIA's justification and defense of its interrogation program on the basis that it was necessary and critical to the disruption of specific terrorist plots and the capture of specific terrorists. While the Executive Summary provides sufficient detail to demonstrate the inaccuracies of each of these claims, the information in the full Committee Study is far more extensive.

I chose not to seek declassification of the full Committee Study at this time. I believe that the Executive Summary includes enough information to adequately describe the CIA's Detention and Interrogation Program, and the Committee's Findings and Conclusions cover the entirety of the program. Seeking declassification of the more than six thousand page report would have significantly delayed the release of the Executive Summary. Decisions will be made later on the declassification and release of the full 6,700-page Study.

In 2009, when this effort began, I stated (in a press release coauthored with the Vice Chairman of the Committee, Senator Kit Bond) that "the purpose is to review the program and to shape detention and interrogation policies in the future." The review is now done. It is my sincere and deep hope that through the release of these Findings and Conclusions and Executive Summary that U.S. policy will never again allow for secret indefinite detention and the use of coercive interrogations. As the Study describes, prior to the attacks of September 2001, the CIA itself determined from its own experience with coercive interrogations, that such techniques "do not produce intelligence," "will probably result in false answers," and had historically proven to be ineffective. Yet these conclusions were ignored. We cannot again allow history to be forgotten and grievous past mistakes to be repeated.

President Obama signed Executive Order 13491 in January 2009 to prohibit the CIA from holding detainees other than on a "short-term, transitory basis" and to limit interrogation techniques to those included in the Army Field Manual. However, these limitations are not part of U.S. law and could be overturned by a future president with the stroke of a pen. They should be enshrined in legislation.

Even so, existing U.S. law and treaty obligations should have prevented many of the abuses and mistakes made during this program. While the Office of Legal Counsel found otherwise between 2002 and 2007, it is my personal conclusion that, under any common meaning of the term, CIA detainees were tortured. I also believe that the conditions of confinement and the use of authorized and unauthorized interrogation and conditioning techniques were cruel, inhuman, and degrading. I believe the evidence of this is overwhelming and incontrovertible.

While the Committee did not make specific recommendations, several emerge from the Committee's review. The CIA, in its June 2013 response to the Committee's Study from December 2012, has also already made and begun to implement its own recommendations. I intend to work with Senate colleagues to produce recommendations and to solicit views from the readers of the Committee Study.

I would also like to take this opportunity to describe the process of this study.

As noted previously, the Committee approved the Terms of Reference for the Study in March 2009 and began requesting information from the CIA and other federal departments. The Committee, through its staff, had already reviewed in 2008 thousands of CIA cables describing the interrogations of the CIA detainees Abu Zubaydah and 'Abd al-Rahim al-Nashiri, whose interrogations were the subject of videotapes that were destroyed by the CIA in 2005.

The 2008 review was complicated by the existence of a Department of Justice investigation, opened by Attorney General Michael Mukasey, into the destruction of the videotapes and expanded by Attorney General Holder in August 2009. In particular, CIA employees and contractors who would otherwise have been interviewed by the Committee staff were under potential legal jeopardy, and therefore the CIA would not compel its workforce to appear before the Committee. This constraint lasted until the Committee's research and documentary review were completed and the Committee Study had largely been finalized.

Furthermore, given the volume and internal nature of relevant CIA documents, the CIA insisted that the Committee enter into an arrangement where our staff would review documents and conduct research at a CIA-leased facility █████ rather than at the Committee's offices on Capitol Hill.

From early 2009 to late 2012, a small group of Committee staff reviewed the more than six million pages of CIA materials, to include operational cables, intelligence reports, internal memoranda and emails, briefing materials, interview transcripts, contracts, and other records. Draft sections of the Study were prepared and distributed to the full Committee membership beginning in October 2011 and this process continued through to the Committee's vote to approve the full Committee Study on December 13, 2012.

The breadth of documentary material on which the Study relied and which the Committee Study cites is unprecedented. While the Committee did not interview CIA officials in the context of the Committee Study, it had access to and drew from the interviews of numerous CIA officials conducted by the CIA's Inspector General and the CIA Oral History program on subjects that lie at the heart of the Committee Study, as well as past testimony to the Committee.

Following the December 2012 vote, the Committee Study was sent to the President and appropriate parts of the Executive Branch for comments by February 15, 2013. The CIA responded in late June 2013 with extensive comments on the Findings and Conclusions, based in part on the responses of CIA officials involved in the program. At my direction, the Committee staff met with CIA representatives in order to fully understand the CIA's comments, and then incorporated suggested edits or comments as appropriate.

The Committee Study, including the now-declassified Executive Summary and Findings and Conclusions, as updated is now final and represents the official views of the Committee. This and future Administrations should use this Study to guide future programs, correct past mistakes, increase oversight of CIA representations to policymakers, and ensure coercive interrogation practices are not used by our government again.

Finally, I want to recognize the members of the staff who have endured years of long hours poring through the difficult details of one of the lowest points in our nation's history. They have produced the most significant and comprehensive oversight report in the Committee's history, and perhaps in that of the U.S. Senate, and their contributions should be recognized and praised.

Daniel Jones has managed and led the Committee's review effort from its inception. Dan has devoted more than six years to this effort, has personally written thousands of its pages, and has been integrally involved in every Study decision. Evan Gottesman, Chad Tanner, and Alissa Starzak have also played integral roles in the Committee Study and have spent considerable years researching and drafting specific sections of the Committee Study.

Other Committee staff members have also assisted in the review and provided valuable contributions at the direction of our Committee Members. They include, among others, Jennifer Barrett, Nick Basciano, Michael Buchwald, Jim Catella, Eric Chapman, John Dickas, Lorenzo Goco, Andrew Grotto, Tressa Guenov, Clete Johnson, Michael Noblet, Michael Pevzner, Tommy Ross, Caroline Tess, and James Wolfe. The Committee's Staff Director throughout the review, David Grannis, has played a central role in assisting me and guiding the Committee through this entire process. Without the expertise, patience, and work ethic of our able staff, our Members would not have been able to complete this most important work.

Dianne Feinstein

Chairman
Senate Select Committee on Intelligence

SENATE SELECT COMMITTEE ON INTELLIGENCE

COMMITTEE STUDY OF THE CENTRAL INTELLIGENCE AGENCY'S DETENTION AND INTERROGATION PROGRAM

FINDINGS AND CONCLUSIONS

Approved: December 13, 2012
Updated for Release: April 3, 2014
Declassification Revisions: December 3, 2014

THE COMMITTEE MAKES THE FOLLOWING FINDINGS AND CONCLUSIONS:

#1: The CIA's use of its enhanced interrogation techniques was not an effective means of acquiring intelligence or gaining cooperation from detainees.

The Committee finds, based on a review of CIA interrogation records, that the use of the CIA's enhanced interrogation techniques was not an effective means of obtaining accurate information or gaining detainee cooperation.

For example, according to CIA records, seven of the 39 CIA detainees known to have been subjected to the CIA's enhanced interrogation techniques produced no intelligence while in CIA custody.[1] CIA detainees who were subjected to the CIA's enhanced interrogation techniques were usually subjected to the techniques immediately after being rendered to CIA custody. Other detainees provided significant accurate intelligence prior to, or without having been subjected to these techniques.

While being subjected to the CIA's enhanced interrogation techniques and afterwards, multiple CIA detainees fabricated information, resulting in faulty intelligence. Detainees provided fabricated information on critical intelligence issues, including the terrorist threats which the CIA identified as its highest priorities.

At numerous times throughout the CIA's Detention and Interrogation Program, CIA personnel assessed that the most effective method for acquiring intelligence from detainees, including from detainees the CIA considered to be the most "high-value," was to confront the detainees with information already acquired by the Intelligence Community. CIA officers regularly called into question whether the CIA's enhanced interrogation techniques were effective, assessing that the use of the techniques failed to elicit detainee cooperation or produce accurate intelligence.

#2: The CIA's justification for the use of its enhanced interrogation techniques rested on inaccurate claims of their effectiveness.

The CIA represented to the White House, the National Security Council, the Department of Justice, the CIA Office of Inspector General, the Congress, and the public that the best measure of effectiveness of the CIA's enhanced interrogation techniques was examples of specific terrorist plots "thwarted" and specific terrorists captured as a result of the use of the techniques. The CIA used these examples to claim that its enhanced interrogation techniques were not only effective, but also necessary to acquire "otherwise unavailable" actionable intelligence that "saved lives."

The Committee reviewed 20 of the most frequent and prominent examples of purported counterterrorism successes that the CIA has attributed to the use of its enhanced interrogation techniques, and found them to be wrong in fundamental respects. In some cases, there was no relationship between the cited counterterrorism success and any information provided by detainees during or after the use of the CIA's enhanced interrogation techniques. In the remaining cases, the CIA inaccurately claimed that specific, otherwise unavailable information was acquired from a CIA detainee "as a result" of the CIA's enhanced interrogation techniques, when in fact the information was either: (1) corroborative of information already available to the CIA or other elements of the U.S. Intelligence Community from sources other than the CIA detainee, and was therefore not "otherwise unavailable"; or (2) acquired from the CIA detainee prior to the use of the CIA's enhanced interrogation techniques. The examples provided by the CIA included numerous factual inaccuracies.

In providing the "effectiveness" examples to policymakers, the Department of Justice, and others, the CIA consistently omitted the significant amount of relevant intelligence obtained from sources other than CIA detainees who had been subjected to the CIA's enhanced interrogation techniques—leaving the false impression the CIA was acquiring unique information from the use of the techniques.

Some of the plots that the CIA claimed to have "disrupted" as a result of the CIA's enhanced interrogation techniques were assessed by intelligence and law enforcement officials as being infeasible or ideas that were never operationalized.

#3: The interrogations of CIA detainees were brutal and far worse than the CIA represented to policymakers and others.

Beginning with the CIA's first detainee, Abu Zubaydah, and continuing with numerous others, the CIA applied its enhanced interrogation techniques with significant repetition for days or weeks at a time. Interrogation techniques such as slaps and "wallings" (slamming detainees against a wall) were used in combination, frequently concurrent with sleep deprivation and nudity. Records do not support CIA representations that the CIA initially used an "an open, nonthreatening approach,"[2] or that interrogations began with the "least coercive technique possible"[3] and escalated to more coercive techniques only as necessary.

The waterboarding technique was physically harmful, inducing convulsions and vomiting. Abu Zubaydah, for example, became "completely unresponsive, with bubbles rising through his open, full mouth."[4] Internal CIA records describe the waterboarding of Khalid Shaykh Mohammad as evolving into a "series of near drownings."[5]

Sleep deprivation involved keeping detainees awake for up to 180 hours, usually standing or in stress positions, at times with their hands shackled above their heads. At least five detainees experienced disturbing hallucinations during prolonged sleep deprivation and, in at least two of those cases, the CIA nonetheless continued the sleep deprivation.

Contrary to CIA representations to the Department of Justice, the CIA instructed personnel that the interrogation of Abu Zubaydah would take "precedence" over his medical care,[6] resulting in the deterioration of a bullet wound Abu Zubaydah incurred during his capture. In at least two other cases, the CIA used its enhanced interrogation techniques despite warnings from CIA medical personnel that the techniques could exacerbate physical injuries. CIA medical personnel treated at least one detainee for swelling in order to allow the continued use of standing sleep deprivation.

At least five CIA detainees were subjected to "rectal rehydration" or rectal feeding without documented medical necessity. The CIA placed detainees in ice water "baths." The CIA led several detainees to believe they would never be allowed to leave CIA custody alive, suggesting to one detainee that he would only leave in a coffin-shaped box.[7] One interrogator told another detainee that he would never go to court, because "we can never let the world know what I have done to you."[8] CIA officers also threatened at least three detainees with harm to their families—to include threats to harm the children of a detainee, threats to sexually abuse the mother of a detainee, and a threat to "cut [a detainee's] mother's throat."[9]

#4: The conditions of confinement for CIA detainees were harsher than the CIA had represented to policymakers and others.

Conditions at CIA detention sites were poor, and were especially bleak early in the program. CIA detainees at the COBALT detention facility were kept in complete darkness and constantly shackled in isolated cells with loud noise or music and only a bucket to use for human waste.[10] Lack of heat at the facility likely contributed to the death of a detainee. The chief of interrogations described COBALT as a "dungeon."[11] Another senior CIA officer stated that COBALT was itself an enhanced interrogation technique.[12]

At times, the detainees at COBALT were walked around naked or were shackled with their hands above their heads for extended periods of time. Other times, the detainees at COBALT were subjected to what was described as a "rough takedown," in which approximately five CIA officers would scream at a detainee, drag him outside of his cell, cut his clothes off, and secure him with Mylar tape. The detainee would then be hooded and dragged up and down a long corridor while being slapped and punched.

Even after the conditions of confinement improved with the construction of new detention facilities, detainees were held in total isolation except when being interrogated or debriefed by CIA personnel.

Throughout the program, multiple CIA detainees who were subjected to the CIA's enhanced interrogation techniques and extended isolation exhibited psychological and behavioral issues, including hallucinations, paranoia, insomnia, and attempts at self-harm and self-mutilation. Multiple psychologists identified the lack of human contact experienced by detainees as a cause of psychiatric problems.

#5: The CIA repeatedly provided inaccurate information to the Department of Justice, impeding a proper legal analysis of the CIA's Detention and Interrogation Program.

From 2002 to 2007, the Office of Legal Counsel (OLC) within the Department of Justice relied on CIA representations regarding: (1) the conditions of confinement for detainees, (2) the application of the CIA's enhanced interrogation techniques, (3) the physical effects of the techniques on detainees, and (4) the effectiveness of the techniques. Those representations were inaccurate in material respects.

The Department of Justice did not conduct independent analysis or verification of the information it received from the CIA. The department warned, however, that if the facts provided by the CIA were to change, its legal conclusions might not apply. When the CIA determined that information it had provided to the Department of Justice was incorrect, the CIA rarely informed the department.

Prior to the initiation of the CIA's Detention and Interrogation Program and throughout the life of the program, the legal justifications for the CIA's enhanced interrogation techniques relied on the CIA's claim that the techniques were necessary to save lives. In late 2001 and early 2002, senior attorneys at the CIA Office of General Counsel first examined the legal implications of using coercive interrogation techniques. CIA attorneys stated that "a novel application of the necessity defense" could be used "to avoid prosecution of U.S. officials who tortured to obtain information that saved many lives."[13]

Having reviewed information provided by the CIA, the OLC included the "necessity defense" in its August 1, 2002, memorandum to the White House counsel on *Standards of Conduct for Interrogation*. The OLC determined that "under the current circumstances, necessity or self-defense may justify interrogation methods that might violate" the criminal prohibition against torture.

On the same day, a second OLC opinion approved, for the first time, the use of 10 specific coercive interrogation techniques against Abu Zubaydah—subsequently referred to as the CIA's "enhanced interrogation techniques." The OLC relied on inaccurate CIA representations about Abu Zubaydah's status in al-Qa'ida and the interrogation team's "certain[ty]" that Abu Zubaydah was withholding information about planned terrorist attacks. The CIA's representations to the OLC about the techniques were also inconsistent with how the techniques would later be applied.

In March 2005, the CIA submitted to the Department of Justice various examples of the "effectiveness" of the CIA's enhanced interrogation techniques that were inaccurate. OLC memoranda signed on May 30, 2005, and July 20, 2007, relied on these representations, determining that the techniques were legal in part because they produced "specific, actionable intelligence" and "substantial quantities of otherwise unavailable intelligence" that saved lives.[14]

#6: The CIA has actively avoided or impeded congressional oversight of the program.

The CIA did not brief the leadership of the Senate Select Committee on Intelligence on the CIA's enhanced interrogation techniques until September 2002, after the techniques had been approved and used. The CIA did not respond to Chairman Bob Graham's requests for additional information in 2002, noting in its own internal communications that he would be leaving the Committee in January 2003. The CIA subsequently resisted efforts by Vice Chairman John D. Rockefeller IV, to investigate the program, including by refusing in 2006 to provide requested documents to the full Committee.

The CIA restricted access to information about the program from members of the Committee beyond the chairman and vice chairman until September 6, 2006, the day the president publicly acknowledged the program, by which time 117 of the 119 known detainees had already entered CIA custody. Until then, the CIA had declined to answer questions from other Committee members that related to CIA interrogation activities.[15]

Prior to September 6, 2006, the CIA provided inaccurate information to the leadership of the Committee. Briefings to the full Committee beginning on September 6, 2006, also contained numerous inaccuracies, including inaccurate descriptions of how interrogation techniques were applied and what information was obtained from CIA detainees. The CIA misrepresented the views of members of Congress on a number of occasions. After multiple senators had been critical of the program and written letters expressing concerns to CIA Director Michael Hayden, Director Hayden nonetheless told a meeting of foreign ambassadors to the United States that every Committee member was "fully briefed," and that "[t]his is not CIA's program. This is not the President's program. This is America's program."[16] The CIA also provided inaccurate information describing the views of U.S. senators about the program to the Department of Justice.

A year after being briefed on the program, the House and Senate Conference Committee considering the Fiscal Year 2008 Intelligence Authorization bill voted to limit the CIA to using only interrogation techniques authorized by the Army Field Manual. That legislation was approved by the Senate and the House of Representatives in February 2008, and was vetoed by President Bush on March 8, 2008.

#7: The CIA impeded effective White House oversight and decision-making.

The CIA provided extensive amounts of inaccurate and incomplete information related to the operation and effectiveness of the CIA's Detention and Interrogation Program to the White House, the National Security Council principals, and their staffs. This prevented an accurate and complete understanding of the program by Executive Branch officials, thereby impeding oversight and decision-making.

According to CIA records, no CIA officer, up to and including CIA Directors George Tenet and Porter Goss, briefed the president on the specific CIA enhanced interrogation techniques before April 2006. By that time, 38 of the 39 detainees identified as having been subjected to the CIA's enhanced interrogation techniques had already been subjected to the techniques.[17] The CIA did not inform the president or vice president of the location of CIA detention facilities other than Country ■.[18]

At the direction of the White House, the secretaries of state and defense—both principals on the National Security Council—were not briefed on program specifics until September 2003. An internal CIA email from July 2003 noted that ". . . the WH [White House] is extremely concerned [Secretary] Powell would blow his stack if he were to be briefed on what's been going on."[19] Deputy Secretary of State Armitage complained that he and Secretary Powell were "cut out" of the National Security Council coordination process.[20]

The CIA repeatedly provided incomplete and inaccurate information to White House personnel regarding the operation and effectiveness of the CIA's Detention and Interrogation Program. This includes the provision of inaccurate statements similar to those provided to other elements of the U.S. Government and later to the public, as well as instances in which specific questions from White House officials were not answered truthfully or fully. In briefings for the National Security Council principals and White House officials, the CIA advocated for the continued use of the CIA's enhanced interrogation techniques, warning that "[t]ermination of this program will result in loss of life, possibly extensive."[21]

#8: The CIA's operation and management of the program complicated, and in some cases impeded, the national security missions of other Executive Branch agencies.

The CIA, in the conduct of its Detention and Interrogation Program, complicated, and in some cases impeded, the national security missions of other Executive Branch agencies, including the Federal Bureau of Investigation (FBI), the State Department, and the Office of the Director of National Intelligence (ODNI). The CIA withheld or restricted information relevant to these agencies' missions and responsibilities, denied access to detainees, and provided inaccurate information on the CIA's Detention and Interrogation Program to these agencies.

The use of coercive interrogation techniques and covert detention facilities that did not meet traditional U.S. standards resulted in the FBI and the Department of Defense limiting their involvement in CIA interrogation and detention activities. This reduced the ability of the U.S. Government to deploy available resources and expert personnel to interrogate detainees and operate detention facilities. The CIA denied specific requests from FBI Director Robert Mueller III for FBI access to CIA detainees that the FBI believed was necessary to understand CIA detainee reporting on threats to the U.S. Homeland. Information obtained from CIA detainees was restricted within the Intelligence Community, leading to concerns among senior CIA officers that limitations on sharing information undermined government-wide counterterrorism analysis.

The CIA blocked State Department leadership from access to information crucial to foreign policy decision-making and diplomatic activities. The CIA did not inform two secretaries of state of locations of CIA detention facilities, despite the significant foreign policy implications related to the hosting of clandestine CIA detention sites and the fact that the political leaders of host countries were generally informed of their existence. Moreover, CIA officers told U.S. ambassadors not to discuss the CIA program with State Department officials, preventing the ambassadors from seeking guidance on the policy implications of establishing CIA detention facilities in the countries in which they served.

In two countries, U.S. ambassadors were informed of plans to establish a CIA detention site in the countries where they were serving after the CIA had already entered into agreements with the countries to host the detention sites. In two other countries where negotiations on hosting new CIA detention facilities were taking place,[22] the CIA told local government officials not to inform the U.S. ambassadors.[23]

The ODNI was provided with inaccurate and incomplete information about the program, preventing the director of national intelligence from effectively carrying out the director's statutory responsibility to serve as the principal advisor to the president on intelligence matters. The inaccurate information provided to the ODNI by the CIA resulted in the ODNI releasing inaccurate information to the public in September 2006.

#9: The CIA impeded oversight by the CIA's Office of Inspector General.

The CIA avoided, resisted, and otherwise impeded oversight of the CIA's Detention and Interrogation Program by the CIA's Office of Inspector General (OIG). The CIA did not brief the OIG on the program until after the death of a detainee, by which time the CIA had held at least 22 detainees at two different CIA detention sites. Once notified, the OIG reviewed the CIA's Detention and Interrogation Program and issued several reports, including an important May 2004 "Special Review" of the program that identified significant concerns and deficiencies.

During the OIG reviews, CIA personnel provided OIG with inaccurate information on the operation and management of the CIA's Detention and Interrogation Program, as well as on the effectiveness of the CIA's enhanced interrogation techniques. The inaccurate information was included in the final May 2004 Special Review, which was later declassified and released publicly, and remains uncorrected.

In 2005, CIA Director Goss requested in writing that the inspector general not initiate further reviews of the CIA's Detention and Interrogation Program until reviews already underway were completed. In 2007, Director Hayden ordered an unprecedented review of the OIG itself in response to the OIG's inquiries into the CIA's Detention and Interrogation Program.

#10: The CIA coordinated the release of classified information to the media, including inaccurate information concerning the effectiveness of the CIA's enhanced interrogation techniques.

The CIA's Office of Public Affairs and senior CIA officials coordinated to share classified information on the CIA's Detention and Interrogation Program to select members of the media to counter public criticism, shape public opinion, and avoid potential congressional action to restrict the CIA's detention and interrogation authorities and budget. These disclosures occurred when the program was a classified covert action program, and before the CIA had briefed the full Committee membership on the program.

The deputy director of the CIA's Counterterrorism Center wrote to a colleague in 2005, shortly before being interviewed by a media outlet, that "we either get out and sell, or we get hammered, which has implications beyond the media. [C]ongress reads it, cuts our authorities, messes up our budget . . . we either put out our story or we get eaten. [T]here is no middle ground."[24] The same CIA officer explained to a colleague that "when the [*Washington Post*]/[*New York T*]imes quotes 'senior intelligence official,' it's us . . . authorized and directed by opa [CIA's Office of Public Affairs]."[25]

Much of the information the CIA provided to the media on the operation of the CIA's Detention and Interrogation Program and the effectiveness of its enhanced interrogation techniques was inaccurate and was similar to the inaccurate information provided by the CIA to the Congress, the Department of Justice, and the White House.

#11: The CIA was unprepared as it began operating its Detention and Interrogation Program more than six months after being granted detention authorities.

On September 17, 2001, the President signed a covert action Memorandum of Notification (MON) granting the CIA unprecedented counterterrorism authorities, including the authority to covertly capture and detain individuals "posing a continuing, serious threat of violence or death to U.S. persons and interests or planning terrorist activities." The MON made no reference to interrogations or coercive interrogation techniques.

The CIA was not prepared to take custody of its first detainee. In the fall of 2001, the CIA explored the possibility of establishing clandestine detention facilities in several countries. The CIA's review identified risks associated with clandestine detention that led it to conclude that U.S. military bases were the best option for the CIA to detain individuals under the MON authorities. In late March 2002, the imminent capture of Abu Zubaydah prompted the CIA to again consider various detention options. In part to avoid declaring Abu Zubaydah to the International Committee of the Red Cross, which would be required if he were detained at a U.S. military base, the CIA decided to seek authorization to clandestinely detain Abu Zubaydah at a facility in Country ■—a country that had not previously been considered as a potential host for a CIA detention site. A senior CIA officer indicated that the CIA "will have to acknowledge certain gaps in our planning/preparations,"[26] but stated that this plan would be presented to the president. At a Presidential Daily Briefing session that day, the president approved CIA's proposal to detain Abu Zubaydah in Country ■.

The CIA lacked a plan for the eventual disposition of its detainees. After taking custody of Abu Zubaydah, CIA officers concluded that he "should remain incommunicado for the remainder of his life," which "may preclude [Abu Zubaydah] from being turned over to another country."[27]

The CIA did not review its past experience with coercive interrogations, or its previous statement to Congress that "inhumane physical or psychological techniques are counterproductive because they do not produce intelligence and will probably result in false answers."[28] The CIA also did not contact other elements of the U.S. Government with interrogation expertise.

In July 2002, on the basis of consultations with contract psychologists, and with very limited internal deliberation, the CIA requested approval from the Department of Justice to use a set of coercive interrogation techniques. The techniques were adapted from the training of U.S. military personnel at the U.S. Air Force Survival, Evasion, Resistance and Escape (SERE) school, which was designed to prepare U.S. military personnel for the conditions and treatment to which they might be subjected if taken prisoner by countries that do not adhere to the Geneva Conventions.

As it began detention and interrogation operations, the CIA deployed personnel who lacked relevant training and experience. The CIA began interrogation training more than seven months after taking custody of Abu Zubaydah, and more than three months after the CIA began using its "enhanced interrogation techniques." CIA Director George Tenet issued formal guidelines for interrogations and conditions of confinement at detention sites in January 2003, by which time 40 of the 119 known detainees had been detained by the CIA.

#12: The CIA's management and operation of its Detention and Interrogation Program was deeply flawed throughout the program's duration, particularly so in 2002 and early 2003.

The CIA's COBALT detention facility in Country ■ began operations in September 2002 and ultimately housed more than half of the 119 CIA detainees identified in this Study. The CIA kept few formal records of the detainees in its custody at COBALT. Untrained CIA officers at the facility conducted frequent, unauthorized, and unsupervised interrogations of detainees using harsh physical interrogation techniques that were not—and never became—part of the CIA's formal "enhanced" interrogation program. The CIA placed a junior officer with no relevant experience in charge of COBALT. On November ■, 2002, a detainee who had been held partially nude and chained to a concrete floor died from suspected hypothermia at the facility. At the time, no single unit at CIA Headquarters had clear responsibility for CIA detention and interrogation operations. In interviews conducted in 2003 with the Office of Inspector General, CIA's leadership and senior attorneys acknowledged that they had little or no awareness of operations at COBALT, and some believed that enhanced interrogation techniques were not used there.

Although CIA Director Tenet in January 2003 issued guidance for detention and interrogation activities, serious management problems persisted. For example, in December 2003, CIA personnel reported that they had made the "unsettling discovery" that the CIA had been "holding a number of detainees about whom" the CIA knew "very little" at multiple detention sites in Country ■.[29]

Divergent lines of authority for interrogation activities persisted through at least 2003. Tensions among interrogators extended to complaints about the safety and effectiveness of each other's interrogation practices.

The CIA placed individuals with no applicable experience or training in senior detention and interrogation roles, and provided inadequate linguistic and analytical support to conduct effective questioning of CIA detainees, resulting in diminished intelligence. The lack of CIA personnel available to question detainees, which the CIA inspector general referred to as "an ongoing problem,"[30] persisted throughout the program.

In 2005, the chief of the CIA's BLACK detention site, where many of the detainees the CIA assessed as "high-value" were held, complained that CIA Headquarters "managers seem to be selecting either problem, underperforming officers, new, totally inexperienced officers or whomever seems to be willing and able to deploy at any given time," resulting in "the production of mediocre or, I dare say, useless intelligence . . ."[31]

Numerous CIA officers had serious documented personal and professional problems—including histories of violence and records of abusive TREATMENT of others—that should have called into question their suitability to participate in the CIA's Detention and Interrogation Program, their employment with the CIA, and their continued access to classified information. In nearly all cases, these problems were known to the CIA prior to the assignment of these officers to detention and interrogation positions.

#13: Two contract psychologists devised the CIA's enhanced interrogation techniques and played a central role in the operation, assessments, and management of the CIA's Detention and Interrogation Program. By 2005, the CIA had overwhelmingly outsourced operations related to the program.

The CIA contracted with two psychologists to develop, operate, and assess its interrogation operations. The psychologists' prior experience was at the U.S. Air Force Survival, Evasion, Resistance and Escape (SERE) school. Neither psychologist had any experience as an interrogator, nor did either have specialized knowledge of al-Qa'ida, a background in counterterrorism, or any relevant cultural or linguistic expertise.

On the CIA's behalf, the contract psychologists developed theories of interrogation based on "learned helplessness,"[32] and developed the list of enhanced interrogation techniques that was approved for use against Abu Zubaydah and subsequent CIA detainees. The psychologists personally conducted interrogations of some of the CIA's most significant detainees using these techniques. They also evaluated whether detainees' psychological state allowed for the continued use of the CIA's enhanced interrogation techniques, including some detainees whom they were themselves interrogating or had interrogated. The psychologists carried out inherently governmental functions, such as acting as liaison between the CIA and foreign intelligence services, assessing the effectiveness of the interrogation program, and participating in the interrogation of detainees in held in foreign government custody.

In 2005, the psychologists formed a company specifically for the purpose of conducting their work with the CIA. Shortly thereafter, the CIA outsourced virtually all aspects of the program.

In 2006, the value of the CIA's base contract with the company formed by the psychologists with all options exercised was in excess of $180 million; the contractors received $81 million prior to the contract's termination in 2009. In 2007, the CIA provided a multi-year indemnification agreement to protect the company and its employees from legal liability arising out of the program. The CIA has since paid out more than $1 million pursuant to the agreement.

In 2008, the CIA's Rendition, Detention, and Interrogation Group, the lead unit for detention and interrogation operations at the CIA, had a total of ■■ positions, which were filled with ■ CIA staff officers and ■■ contractors, meaning that contractors made up 85% of the workforce for detention and interrogation operations.

#14: CIA detainees were subjected to coercive interrogation techniques that had not been approved by the Department of Justice or had not been authorized by CIA Headquarters.

Prior to mid-2004, the CIA routinely subjected detainees to nudity and dietary manipulation. The CIA also used abdominal slaps and cold water dousing on several detainees during that period. None of these techniques had been approved by the Department of Justice.

At least 17 detainees were subjected to CIA enhanced interrogation techniques without authorization from CIA Headquarters. Additionally, multiple detainees were subjected to techniques that were applied in ways that diverged from the specific authorization, or were subjected to enhanced interrogation techniques by interrogators who had not been authorized to use them. Although these incidents were recorded in CIA cables and, in at least some cases were identified at the time by supervisors at CIA Headquarters as being inappropriate, corrective action was rarely taken against the interrogators involved.

#15: The CIA did not conduct a comprehensive or accurate accounting of the number of individuals it detained, and held individuals who did not meet the legal standard for detention. The CIA's claims about the number of detainees held and subjected to its enhanced interrogation techniques were inaccurate.

The CIA never conducted a comprehensive audit or developed a complete and accurate list of the individuals it had detained or subjected to its enhanced interrogation techniques. CIA statements to the Committee and later to the public that the CIA detained fewer than 100 individuals, and that less than a third of those 100 detainees were subjected to the CIA's enhanced interrogation techniques, were inaccurate. The Committee's review of CIA records determined that the CIA detained at least 119 individuals, of whom at least 39 were subjected to the CIA's enhanced interrogation techniques.

Of the 119 known detainees, at least 26 were wrongfully held and did not meet the detention standard in the September 2001 Memorandum of Notification (MON). These included an "intellectually challenged" man whose CIA detention was used solely as leverage to get a family member to provide information, two individuals who were intelligence sources for foreign liaison services and were former CIA sources, and two individuals whom the CIA assessed to be connected to al-Qa'ida based solely on information fabricated by a CIA detainee subjected to the CIA's enhanced interrogation techniques. Detainees often remained in custody for months after the CIA determined that they did not meet the MON standard. CIA records provide insufficient information to justify the detention of many other detainees.

CIA Headquarters instructed that at least four CIA detainees be placed in host country detention facilities because the individuals did not meet the MON standard for CIA detention. The host country had no independent reason to hold the detainees.

A full accounting of CIA detentions and interrogations may be impossible, as records in some cases are non-existent, and, in many other cases, are sparse and insufficient. There were almost no detailed records of the detentions and interrogations at the CIA's COBALT detention facility in 2002, and almost no such records for the CIA's GRAY detention site, also in Country ■. At CIA detention facilities outside of Country ■, the CIA kept increasingly less-detailed records of its interrogation activities over the course of the CIA's Detention and Interrogation Program.

#16: The CIA failed to adequately evaluate the effectiveness of its enhanced interrogation techniques.

The CIA never conducted a credible, comprehensive analysis of the effectiveness of its enhanced interrogation techniques, despite a recommendation by the CIA inspector general and similar requests by the national security advisor and the leadership of the Senate Select Committee on Intelligence.

Internal assessments of the CIA's Detention and Interrogation Program were conducted by CIA personnel who participated in the development and management of the program, as well as by CIA contractors who had a financial interest in its continuation and expansion. An "informal operational assessment" of the program, led by two senior CIA officers who were not part of the CIA's Counterterrorism Center, determined that it would not be possible to assess the effectiveness of the CIA's enhanced interrogation techniques without violating "Federal Policy for the Protection of Human Subjects" regarding human experimentation. The CIA officers, whose review relied on briefings with CIA officers and contractors running the program, concluded only that the "CIA Detainee Program" was a "success" without addressing the effectiveness of the CIA's enhanced interrogation techniques.[33]

In 2005, in response to the recommendation by the inspector general for a review of the effectiveness of each of the CIA's enhanced interrogation techniques, the CIA asked two individuals not employed by the CIA to conduct a broader review of "the entirety of" the "rendition, detention and interrogation program."[34] According to one individual, the review was "heavily reliant on the willingness of [CIA Counterterrorism Center] staff to provide us with the factual material that forms the basis of our conclusions." That individual acknowledged lacking the requisite expertise to review the effectiveness of the CIA's enhanced interrogation techniques, and concluded only that "the program," meaning all CIA detainee reporting regardless of whether it was connected to the use of the CIA's enhanced interrogation techniques, was a "great success."[35] The second reviewer concluded that "there is no objective way to answer the question of efficacy" of the techniques.[36]

There are no CIA records to indicate that any of the reviews independently validated the "effectiveness" claims presented by the CIA, to include basic confirmation that the intelligence cited by the CIA was acquired from CIA detainees during or after the use of the CIA's enhanced interrogation techniques. Nor did the reviews seek to confirm whether the intelligence cited by the CIA as being obtained "as a result" of the CIA's enhanced interrogation techniques was unique and "otherwise unavailable," as claimed by the CIA, and not previously obtained from other sources.

#17: The CIA rarely reprimanded or held personnel accountable for serious and significant violations, inappropriate activities, and systemic and individual management failures.

CIA officers and CIA contractors who were found to have violated CIA policies or performed poorly were rarely held accountable or removed from positions of responsibility.

Significant events, to include the death and injury of CIA detainees, the detention of individuals who did not meet the legal standard to be held, the use of unauthorized interrogation techniques against CIA detainees, and the provision of inaccurate information on the CIA program did not result in appropriate, effective, or in many eases, any corrective actions. CIA managers who were aware of failings and shortcomings in the program but did not intervene, or who failed to provide proper leadership and management, were also not held to account.

On two occasions in which the CIA inspector general identified wrongdoing, accountability recommendations were overruled by senior CIA leadership. In one instance, involving the death of a CIA detainee at COBALT, CIA Headquarters decided not to take disciplinary action against an officer involved because, at the time, CIA Headquarters had been "motivated to extract any and all operational information" from the detainee.[37] In another instance related to a wrongful detention, no action was taken against a CIA officer because, "[t]he Director strongly believes that mistakes should be expected in a business filled with uncertainty," and "the Director believes the scale tips decisively in favor of accepting mistakes that over connect the dots against those that under connect them."[38] In neither case was administrative action taken against CIA management personnel.

#18: The CIA marginalized and ignored numerous internal critiques, criticisms, and objections concerning the operation and management of the CIA's Detention and Interrogation Program.

Critiques, criticisms, and objections were expressed by numerous CIA officers, including senior personnel overseeing and managing the program, as well as analysts, interrogators, and medical officers involved in or supporting CIA detention and interrogation operations.

Examples of these concerns include CIA officers questioning the effectiveness of the CIA's enhanced interrogation techniques, interrogators disagreeing with the use of such techniques against detainees whom they determined were not withholding information, psychologists recommending less isolated conditions, and Office of Medical Services personnel questioning both the effectiveness and safety of the techniques. These concerns were regularly overridden by CIA management, and the CIA made few corrective changes to its policies governing the program. At times, CIA officers were instructed by supervisors not to put their concerns or observations in written communications.

In several instances, CIA officers identified inaccuracies in CIA representations about the program and its effectiveness to the Office of Inspector General, the White House, the Department of Justice, the Congress, and the American public. The CIA nonetheless failed to take action to correct these representations, and allowed inaccurate information to remain as the CIA's official position.

The CIA was also resistant to, and highly critical of more formal critiques. The deputy director for operations stated that the CIA inspector general's draft Special Review should have come to the "conclusion that our efforts have thwarted attacks and saved lives,"[39] while the CIA general counsel accused the inspector general of presenting "an imbalanced and inaccurate picture" of the program.[40] A February 2007 report from the International Committee of the Red Cross (ICRC), which the CIA acting general counsel initially stated "actually does not sound that far removed from the reality,"[41] was also criticized. CIA officers prepared documents indicating that "critical portions of the Report are patently false or misleading, especially certain key factual claims . . ."[42] CIA Director Hayden testified to the Committee that "numerous false allegations of physical and threatened abuse and faulty legal assumptions and analysis in the [ICRC] report undermine its overall credibility."[43]

#19: The CIA's Detention and Interrogation Program was inherently unsustainable and had effectively ended by 2006 due to unauthorized press disclosures, reduced cooperation from other nations, and legal and oversight concerns.

The CIA required secrecy and cooperation from other nations in order to operate clandestine detention facilities, and both had eroded significantly before President Bush publicly disclosed the program on September 6, 2006. From the beginning of the program, the CIA faced significant challenges in finding nations willing to host CIA clandestine detention sites. These challenges became increasingly difficult over time. With the exception of Country ■■, the CIA was forced to relocate detainees out of every country in which it established a detention facility because of pressure from the host government or public revelations about the program. Beginning in early 2005, the CIA sought unsuccessfully to convince the U.S. Department of Defense to allow the transfer of numerous CIA detainees to U.S. military custody. By 2006, the CIA admitted in its own talking points for CIA Director Porter Goss that, absent an Administration decision on an "endgame" for detainees, the CIA was "stymied" and "the program could collapse of its own weight."[44]

Lack of access to adequate medical care for detainees in countries hosting the CIA's detention facilities caused recurring problems. The refusal of one host country to admit a severely ill detainee into a local hospital due to security concerns contributed to the closing of the CIA's detention facility in that country. The U.S. Department of Defense also declined to provide medical care to detainees upon CIA request.

In mid-2003, a statement by the president for the United Nations International Day in Support of Victims of Torture and a public statement by the White House that prisoners in U.S. custody are treated "humanely" caused the CIA to question whether there was continued policy support for the program and seek reauthorization from the White House. In mid-2004, the CIA temporarily suspended the use of its enhanced interrogation techniques after the CIA inspector general recommended that the CIA seek an updated legal opinion from the Office of Legal Counsel. In early 2004, the U.S. Supreme Court decision to grant certiorari in the case of *Rasul v. Bush* prompted the CIA to move detainees out of a CIA detention facility at Guantanamo Bay, Cuba. In late 2005 and in 2006, the Detainee Treatment Act and then the U.S. Supreme Court decision in *Hamdan v. Rumsfeld* caused the CIA to again temporarily suspend the use of its enhanced interrogation techniques.

By 2006, press disclosures, the unwillingness of other countries to host existing or new detention sites, and legal and oversight concerns had largely ended the CIA's ability to operate clandestine detention facilities.

After detaining at least 113 individuals through 2004, the CIA brought only six additional detainees into its custody: four in 2005, one in 2006, and one in 2007. By March 2006, the program was operating in only one country. The CIA last used its enhanced interrogation techniques on November 8, 2007. The CIA did not hold any detainees after April 2008.

#20: The CIA's Detention and Interrogation Program damaged the United States' standing in the world, and resulted in other significant monetary and non-monetary costs.

The CIA's Detention and Interrogation Program created tensions with U.S. partners and allies, leading to formal *demarches* to the United States, and damaging and complicating bilateral intelligence relationships.

In one example, in June 2004, the secretary of state ordered the U.S. ambassador in Country ■ to deliver a *demarche* to Country ■, "in essence demanding [Country ■ Government] provide full access to all [Country ■ ■] detainees" to the International Committee of the Red Cross. At the time, however, the detainees Country ■ was holding included detainees being held in secret at the CIA's behest.[45]

More broadly, the program caused immeasurable damage to the United States' public standing, as well as to the United States' longstanding global leadership on human rights in general and the prevention of torture in particular.

CIA records indicate that the CIA's Detention and Interrogation Program cost well over $300 million in non-personnel costs. This included funding for the CIA to construct and maintain detention facilities, including two facilities costing nearly $■ million that were never used, in part due to host country political concerns.

To encourage governments to clandestinely host CIA detention sites, or to increase support for existing sites, the CIA provided millions of dollars in cash payments to foreign government officials. CIA Headquarters encouraged CIA Stations to construct "wish lists" of proposed financial assistance to ■ [entities of foreign governments], and to "think big" in terms of that assistance.[46]

SENATE SELECT COMMITTEE ON INTELLIGENCE

COMMITTEE STUDY OF THE CENTRAL INTELLIGENCE AGENCY'S DETENTION AND INTERROGATION PROGRAM

EXECUTIVE SUMMARY

Approved: December 13, 2012
Updated for Release: April 3, 2014
Declassification Revisions: December 3, 2014

I. BACKGROUND ON THE COMMITTEE STUDY

On December 11, 2007, the Senate Select Committee on Intelligence ("the Committee") initiated a review of the destruction of videotapes related to the interrogations of CIA detainees Abu Zubaydah and 'Abd al-Rahim al-Nashiri after receiving a briefing that day on the matter by CIA Director Michael Hayden. At that briefing, Director Hayden stated that contemporaneous CIA operational cables were "a more than adequate representation of the tapes," and he agreed to provide the Committee with limited access to these cables at CIA Headquarters.

On February 11, 2009, after the Committee was presented with a staff-prepared summary of the operational cables detailing the interrogations of Abu Zubaydah and al-Nashiri, the Committee began considering a broader review of the CIA's detention and interrogation practices. On March 5, 2009, in a vote of 14 to 1, the Committee approved Terms of Reference for a study of the CIA's Detention and Interrogation Program.[1]

The *Committee Study of the CIA's Detention and Interrogation Program* is a lengthy, highly detailed report exceeding 6,700 pages, including approximately 38,000 footnotes. It is divided into three volumes:

I. **History and Operation of the CIA's Detention and Interrogation Program.** This volume is divided chronologically into sections addressing the establishment, development, and evolution of the CIA's Detention and Interrogation Program. It includes an addendum on *CIA Clandestine Deten-tion Sites and the Arrangements Made with Foreign Entities in Relation to the CIA's Detention and In-terrogation Program.*

II. **Intelligence Acquired and CIA Representations on the Effectiveness of the CIA's Enhanced Inter-rogation Techniques.** This volume addresses the intelligence the CIA attributed to CIA detainees and the use of the CIA's enhanced interrogation tech-niques, specifically focusing on CIA representations regarding the effectiveness of the CIA's enhanced in-terrogation techniques, as well as how the CIA's Detention and Interrogation Program was operated and managed. It includes sections on CIA represen-tations to the media, the Department of Justice, and the Congress.

III. **Detention and Interrogation of CIA Detainees.** This volume addresses the detention and interrogation of 119 CIA detainees, from the program's authori-zation on September 17, 2001, to its official end on January 22, 2009, to include information on their capture, detention, interrogation, and conditions of confinement. It also includes extensive information on the CIA's management, oversight, and day-to-day operation of its Detention and Interrogation Program.

On December 13, 2012, the Senate Select Committee on Intelligence approved the *Committee Study of the CIA's Detention and Interrogation Program* ("Committee Study") by a bipartisan vote of 9–6. The Committee Study included 20 findings and conclusions. The Committee requested that specific executive branch agencies review and provide comment on the Committee Study prior to Committee action to seek declassification and public release of the Committee Study. On June 27, 2013, the CIA provided a written response, which was followed by a series of meetings between the CIA and the Committee that concluded in September 2013. Following these meetings and the receipt of Minority views, the Committee revised the findings and conclusions and updated the Committee Study. On April 3, 2014, by a bipartisan vote of 11–3, the Committee agreed to send the revised findings and conclusions, and the updated Executive Summary of the Committee Study, to the President for declassification and public release.

The Committee's Study is the most comprehensive review ever conducted of the CIA's Detention and Interrogation Program. The CIA has informed the Committee that it has provided the Committee with all CIA records related to the CIA's Detention and Interrogation Program.[2] The document production phase lasted more than three years, produced more than six million pages of material, and was completed in July 2012. The Committee Study is based primarily on a review of these documents,[3] which include CIA operational cables, reports, memoranda, intelligence products, and numerous interviews conducted of CIA personnel by various entities within the CIA, in particular the CIA's Office of Inspector General and the

CIA's Oral History Program, as well as internal email[4] and other communications.[5]

The Executive Summary is divided into two parts. The first describes the establishment, development, operation, and evolution of the CIA's Detention and Interrogation Program. The second part provides information on the effectiveness of the CIA's Detention and Interrogation Program, to include information acquired from CIA detainees, before, during, and after the use of the CIA's enhanced interrogation techniques; as well as CIA representations on the effectiveness and operation of the CIA's Detention and Interrogation Program to the media, the Department of Justice, and the Congress. The Executive Summary does not include a description of the detention and interrogations of all 119 known CIA detainees. Details on each of these detainees are included in Volume III.

Throughout this summary and the entire report, non-supervisory CIA personnel have been listed by pseudonym. The pseudonyms for these officers are used throughout the report. To distinguish CIA officers in pseudonym from those in true name, pseudonyms in this report are denoted by last names in upper case letters. Additionally, the CIA requested that the names of countries that hosted CIA detention sites, or with which the CIA negotiated the hosting of sites, as well as information directly or indirectly identifying such countries, be redacted from the classified version provided to Committee members. The report therefore lists these countries by letter. The report uses the same designations consistently, so "Country J," for example, refers to the same country throughout the Committee Study. Further, the CIA requested that the Committee replace the original code names for CIA detention sites with new identifiers.[6]

II. OVERALL HISTORY AND OPERATION OF THE CIA'S DETENTION AND INTERROGATION PROGRAM

A. September 17, 2001, Memorandum of Notification (MON) Authorizes the CIA to Capture and Detain a Specific Category of Individuals

1. After Considering Various Clandestine Detention Locations, the CIA Determines That a U.S. Military Base Is the "Best Option": the CIA Delegates "Blanket" Detention Approvals to CIA Officers in ██████

On September 17, 2001, six days after the terrorist attacks of September 11, 2001, President George W. Bush signed a covert action Memorandum of Notification (MON) to authorize the director of central intelligence (DCI) to "undertake operations designed to capture and detain persons who pose a continuing, serious threat of violence or death to U.S. persons and interests or who are planning terrorist activities."[7] Although the CIA had previously been provided limited authorities to detain specific, named individuals pending the issuance of formal criminal charges, the MON provided unprecedented authorities, granting the CIA significant discretion in determining whom to detain, the factual basis for the detention, and the length of the detention.[8] The MON made no reference to interrogations or interrogation techniques.[9]

On September 14, 2001, three days before the issuance of the MON, the chief of operations of the CIA's ██████ based on an urgent requirement from the chief of the Counterterrorism Center (CTC), sent an email to CIA Stations in ███ seeking input on appropriate locations for potential CIA detention facilities.[10] Over the course of the next month, CIA officers considered at least four countries in ████ and one in ██████ as possible hosts for detention facilities and ████ at least three proposed site locations.[11]

On September 26, 2001, senior CTC personnel met to discuss the capture and detain authorities in the MON. On September 28, 2001, █████ CTC Legal, ████████, sent an email describing the meeting and a number of policy decisions. The email stated that covert facilities would be operated "in a manner consistent with, but not pursuant to, the formal provision of appropriately comparable Federal instructions for the operation of prison facilities and the incarceration of inmates held under the maximum lawful security mechanisms." ████'s email recognized the CIA's lack of experience in running detention facilities, and stated that the CIA would consider acquiring cleared personnel from the Department of Defense or the Bureau of Prisons with specialized expertise to assist the CIA in operating the facilities.[12] On September 27, 2001, CIA Headquarters informed CIA Stations that any future CIA detention facility would have to meet "U.S. POW Standards."[13]

In early November 2001, CIA Headquarters further determined that any future CIA detention facility would have to meet U.S. prison standards and that CIA detention and interrogation operations should be tailored to "meet the requirements of U.S. law and the federal rules of criminal procedure," adding that "[s]pecific methods of interrogation w[ould] be permissible so long as they generally comport with commonly accepted practices deemed lawful by U.S. courts."[14] The CIA's search for detention site locations was then put on hold and an internal memorandum from senior CIA officials explained that detention at a U.S. military base outside of the United States was the "best option."[15] The memorandum thus urged the DCI to "[p]ress the DOD and the US military, at highest levels, to have the US Military agree to host a long-term facility, and have them identify an agreeable location," specifically requesting that the DCI "[s]eek to have the US Naval Base at Guantanamo Bay designated as a long-term detention facility."[16]

Addressing the risks associated with the CIA maintaining a detention facility, the CIA memorandum warned that "[a]s captured terrorists may be held days, months, or years, the likelihood of exposure will grow over time," and that "[m]edia exposure could inflame public opinion against a host government and the U.S., thereby threatening the continued operation of the facility." The memorandum also anticipated that, "[i]n a foreign country, close cooperation with the host government will entail intensive negotiations."[17] The CIA memorandum warned that "any foreign country poses uncontrollable risks that could create incidents, vulnerability to the security of the facility, bilateral problems, and uncertainty over maintaining the facility."[18] The memorandum recommended the establishment of a "short-term" facility in which the CIA's role would be limited to "oversight, funding and responsibility." The CIA would "contract out all other requirements to other US Government organizations, commercial companies, and, as appropriate, foreign governments."[19]

On October 8, 2001, DCI George Tenet delegated the management and oversight of the capture and detention authorities provided by the MON to the CIA's deputy director for operations (DDO), James Pavitt, and the CIA's chief of the Counterterrorism Center, Cofer Black.[20] The DCI also directed that all requests and approvals for capture and detention be documented in writing. On December 17, 2001, however, the DDO rescinded these requirements and issued via a CIA cable "blanket approval" for CIA officers in ████ to "determine [who poses] the requisite 'continuing serious threat of violence or death to US persons and interests or who are planning terrorist activities.'"[21] By March 2002, CIA Headquarters had expanded the authority beyond the language of the MON and instructed CIA personnel that it would be appropriate to detain individuals who might not be high-value targets in their own right, but could provide information on high-value targets.[22]

On April 7, 2003, ████ CTC Legal, █████ sent a cable to CIA Stations and Bases stating that "at this stage in the war [we] believe there is sufficient opportunity in advance to document the key aspects of many, if not most, of our capture and detain operations.[23] ████'s cable also provided guidance as to who could be detained under the MON, stating:

> "there must be an articulable basis on which to conclude that the actions of a specific person whom we propose to capture and/or detain pose a 'continuing serious threat' of violence or death to U.S. persons or interests or that the person is planning a terrorist activity.
>
> ". . . We are not permitted to detain someone merely upon a suspicion that he or she has valuable information about terrorists or planned acts of terrorism . . . Similarly, the mere membership in a particular group, or the mere existence of a particular familial tie, does not necessarily connote that the threshold of 'continuing, serious threat' has been satisfied."[24]

2. The CIA Holds at Least 21 More Detainees Than It Has Represented; At Least 26 CIA Detainees Wrongly Detained

While the CIA has represented in public and classified settings that it detained "fewer than one hundred" individuals,[25] the Committee's review of CIA records indicates that the total number of CIA detainees was at least 119.[26] Internal CIA documents indicate that inadequate record keeping made it impossible for the CIA to determine how many individuals it had detained. In December 2003, a CIA Station overseeing CIA detention operations in Country ■ informed CIA Headquarters that it had made the "unsettling discovery" that the CIA was "holding a number of detainees about whom" it knew "very little."[27] Nearly five years later, in late 2008, the CIA attempted to determine how many individuals the CIA had detained. At the completion of the review, CIA leaders, including CIA Director Michael Hayden, were informed that the review found that the CIA had detained at least 112 individuals, and possibly more.[28] According to an email summarizing the meeting, CIA Director Hayden instructed a CIA officer to devise a way to keep the number of CIA detainees at the same number the CIA had previously briefed to Congress. The email, which the briefer sent only to himself, stated:

> "I briefed the additional CIA detainees that could be included in RDI[29] numbers. DCIA instructed me to keep the detainee number at 98—pick whatever date i [*sic*] needed to make that happen but the number is 98."[30]

While the CIA acknowledged to the House Permanent Select Committee on Intelligence (HPSCI) in February 2006 that it had wrongly detained five individuals throughout the course of its detention program,[31] a review of CIA records indicates that at least 21 additional individuals, or a total of 26 of the 119 (22 percent) CIA detainees identified in this Study, did not meet the MON standard for detention.[32] This is a conservative calculation and includes only CIA detainees whom the CIA itself determined did not meet the standard for detention. It does not include individuals about whom there was internal disagreement within the CIA over whether the detainee met the standard or not, or the numerous detainees who, following their detention and interrogation, were found not to "pose a continuing threat of violence or death to U.S. persons and interests" or to be "planning terrorist activities" as required by the September 17, 2001, MON.[33] With one known exception, there are no CIA records to indicate that the CIA held personnel accountable for the detention of individuals the CIA itself determined were wrongfully detained.[34]

On at least four occasions, the CIA used host country detention sites in Country ■ to detain individuals on behalf of the CIA who did not meet the MON standard for capture and detention. ALEC Station officers at CIA Headquarters explicitly acknowledged that these detainees did not meet the MON standard for detention, and recommended placing the individuals in host country detention facilities because they did not meet the standard. The host country had no independent reason to detain these individuals and held them solely at the behest of the CIA.[35]

B. The Detention of Abu Zubaydah and the Development and Authorization of the CIA's Enhanced Interrogation Techniques

1. Past Experience Led the CIA to Assess that Coercive Interrogation Techniques Were "Counterproductive" and "Ineffective"; After Issuance of the MON, CIA Attorneys Research Possible Legal Defense for Using Techniques Considered Torture; the CIA Conducts No Research on Effective Interrogations, Relies on Contractors with No Relevant Experience

At the time of the issuance of the September 17, 2001, MON—which, as noted, did not reference interrogation techniques—the CIA had in place long-standing formal standards for conducting interrogations. The CIA had shared these standards with the Committee. In January 1989, the CIA informed the Committee that "inhumane physical or psychological techniques are counterproductive because they do not produce intelligence and will probably result in false answers."[36] Testimony of the CIA deputy director of operations in 1988 denounced coercive interrogation techniques, stating, "[p]hysical abuse or other degrading treatment was rejected not only because it is wrong, but because it has historically proven to be ineffective."[37] By October 2001, CIA policy was to comply with the Department of the Army Field Manual "Intelligence Interrogation."[38] A CIA Directorate of Operations Handbook from October 2001 states that the CIA does not engage in "human rights violations," which it defined as: "Torture, cruel, inhuman, degrading treatment or punishment, or prolonged detention without charges or trial." The handbook further stated that "[i]t is CIA policy to neither participate directly in nor encourage interrogation which involves the use of force, mental or physical torture, extremely demeaning indignities or exposure to inhumane treatment of any kind as an aid to interrogation."[39]

The CIA did, however, have historical experience using coercive forms of interrogation. In 1963, the CIA produced the KUBARK

Counterintelligence Interrogation Manual, intended as a manual for Cold War interrogations, which included the "principal coercive techniques of interrogation: arrest, detention, deprivation of sensory stimuli through solitary confinement or similar methods, threats and fear, debility, pain, heightened suggestibility and hypnosis, narcosis and induced regression."[40] In 1978, DCI Stansfield Turner asked former CIA officer John Limond Hart to investigate the CIA interrogation of Soviet KGB officer Yuri Nosenko[41] using the KUBARK methods—to include sensory deprivation techniques and forced standing.[42] In Hart's testimony before the House Select Committee on Assassinations on September 15, 1978, he noted that in his 31 years of government service:

> "It has never fallen to my lot to be involved with any experience as unpleasant in every possible way as, first, the investigation of this case, and, second, the necessity of lecturing upon it and testifying. To me it is an abomination, and I am happy to say that . . . it is not in my memory typical of what my colleagues and I did in the agency during the time I was connected with it."[43]

Notwithstanding the Hart investigation findings, just five years later, in 1983, a CIA officer incorporated significant portions of the KUBARK manual into the Human Resource Exploitation (HRE) Training Manual, which the same officer used to provide interrogation training in Latin America in the early 1980s, and which was used to provide interrogation training to the ████████████████ in 198█.[44] CIA officer ████████ was involved in the HRE training and conducted interrogations. The CIA inspector general later recommended that he be orally admonished for inappropriate use of interrogation techniques.[45] In the fall of 2002, ██████ became the CIA's chief of interrogations in the CIA's Renditions Group,[46] the officer in charge of CIA interrogations.[47]

Despite the CIA's previous statements that coercive physical and psychological interrogation techniques "result in false answers"[48] and have "proven to be ineffective,"[49] as well as the aforementioned early November 2001 determination that "[s]pecific methods of interrogation w[ould] be permissible so long as they generally comport with commonly accepted practices deemed lawful by U.S. courts,"[50] by the end of November 2001, CIA officers had begun researching potential legal defenses for using interrogation techniques that were considered torture by foreign governments and a non-governmental organization. On November 26, 2001, attorneys in the CIA's Office of General Counsel circulated a draft legal memorandum describing the criminal prohibition on torture and a potential "novel" legal defense for CIA officers who engaged in torture. The memorandum stated that the "CIA could argue that the torture was necessary to prevent imminent, significant, physical harm to persons, where there is no other available means to prevent the harm," adding that "states may be very unwilling to call the U.S. to task for torture when it resulted in saving thousands of lives."[51] An August 1, 2002, OLC memorandum to the White House Counsel includes a similar analysis of the "necessity defense" in response to potential charges of torture.[52]

In January 2002, the National Security Council principals began to debate whether to apply the protections of the Geneva Convention Relative to the Treatment of Prisoners of War of August 12, 1949 ("Geneva") to the conflict with al-Qa'ida and the Taliban. A letter drafted for DCI Tenet to the president urged that the CIA be exempt from any application of these protections, arguing that application of Geneva would "significantly hamper the ability of CIA to obtain critical threat information necessary to save American lives."[53] On February 1, 2002—approximately two months prior to the detention of the CIA's first detainee—a CIA attorney wrote that if CIA detainees were covered by Geneva there would be "few alternatives to simply asking questions." The attorney concluded that, if that were the case, "then the optic becomes how legally defensible is a particular act that probably violates the convention, but ultimately saves lives."[54]

On February 7, 2002, President Bush issued a memorandum stating that neither al-Qa'ida nor Taliban detainees qualified as prisoners of war under Geneva, and that Common Article 3 of Geneva, requiring humane treatment of individuals in a conflict, did not apply to al-Qa'ida or Taliban detainees.[55]

From the issuance of the MON to early 2002, there are no indications in CIA records that the CIA conducted significant research to identify effective interrogation practices, such as conferring with experienced U.S. military or law enforcement interrogators, or with the intelligence, military, or law enforcement services of other countries with experience in counterterrorism and the interrogation of terrorist suspects.[56] Nor are there CIA records referencing any review of the CIA's past use of coercive interrogation techniques and associated lessons learned. The only research documented in CIA records during this time on the issue of interrogation was the preparation of a report on an al-Qa'ida manual that was initially assessed by the CIA to include strategies to resist interrogation. This report was commissioned by the CIA's Office of Technical Services (OTS) and drafted by two CIA contractors, Dr. Grayson SWIGERT and Dr. Hammond DUNBAR.[57]

Both SWIGERT and DUNBAR had been psychologists with the U.S. Air Force Survival, Evasion, Resistance and Escape (SERE) school, which exposes select U.S. military personnel to, among other things, coercive interrogation techniques that they might be subjected to if taken prisoner by countries that did not adhere to Geneva protections. Neither psychologist had experience as an interrogator, nor did either have specialized knowledge of al-Qa'ida, a background in terrorism, or any relevant regional, cultural, or linguistic expertise. SWIGERT had reviewed research on "learned helplessness," in which individuals might become passive and depressed in response to adverse or uncontrollable events.[58] He theorized that inducing such a state could encourage a detainee to cooperate and provide information.[59]

2. The CIA Renders Abu Zubaydah to a Covert Facility, Obtains Presidential Approval Without Inter-Agency Deliberation

In late March 2002, Pakistani government authorities, working with the CIA, captured al-Qa'ida facilitator Abu Zubaydah in a raid during which Abu Zubaydah suffered bullet wounds. At that time, Abu Zubaydah was assessed by CIA officers in ALEC Station, the office within the CIA with specific responsibility for al-Qa'ida, to possess detailed knowledge of al-Qa'ida terrorist attack plans. However, as is described in greater detail in the full Committee Study, this assessment significantly overstated Abu Zubaydah's role in al-Qa'ida and the information he was likely to possess.[60]

On the day that Abu Zubaydah was captured, CIA attorneys discussed interpretations of the criminal prohibition on torture that might permit CIA officers to engage in certain interrogation activities.[61] An attorney in CTC also sent an email with the subject line "Torture Update" to ████ CTC Legal ██████, listing, without commentary, the restrictions on interrogation in the Geneva Conventions, the Convention Against Torture, and the criminal prohibition on torture.[62]

In late March 2002, anticipating its eventual custody of Abu Zubaydah, the CIA began considering options for his transfer to CIA custody and detention under the MON. The CIA rejected U.S. military custody ████, in large part because of the lack of security and the fact that Abu Zubaydah would have to be declared to the International Committee of the Red Cross (ICRC).[63] The CIA's concerns about custody at Guantanamo Bay, Cuba, included the general lack of secrecy and the "possible loss of control to US military and/or FBI."[64] Rendition to Country ██ was rejected because of the perception that the results of that country's recent interrogations had been disappointing, as well as the intense interest in Abu Zubaydah from CIA leadership. As ALEC Station wrote, the CIA needed to participate directly in the interrogation, "[n]ot because we believe necessarily we can improve on [Country ██] performance, but because the reasons for the lack of progress will be transparent and reportable up the line."[65]

Over the course of four days, the CIA settled on a detention site in Country ██ because of that country's "████████████████████ █ ████████████████," and the lack of U.S. court jurisdiction. The only disadvantages identified by the CIA with detention in Country ██ were that it would not be a "USG-controlled facility" and that "diplomatic/policy decisions" would be required.[66] As a March 28, 2002, CIA document acknowledged, the proposal to render Abu Zubaydah to Country ██ had not yet been broached with that country's officials. The document also warned: "[w]e can't guarantee security. If AZ's presence does become known, not clear what the impact would be."[67]

The decision to detain Abu Zubaydah at a covert detention facility in Country ██ did not involve the input of the National Security Council Principals Committee, the Department of State, the U.S. ambassador, or the CIA chief of Station in Country ██.[68] On March 29, 2002, an email from the Office of the Deputy DCI stated that "[w]e will have to acknowledge certain gaps in our planning/preparations, but this is the option the DDCI will lead with for POTUS consideration."[69] That morning, the president approved moving forward with the plan to transfer Abu Zubaydah to Country ██.[70] During the same Presidential Daily Brief (PDB) session, Secretary of Defense Rumsfeld suggested exploring the option of putting Abu Zubaydah on a ship; however, CIA records do not indicate any further input from the principals.[71] That day, the CIA Station in Country ██ obtained the approval of Country ██'s ██████████████ officials for the CIA detention site.[72] The U.S. deputy chief of mission in Country ██, who was notified by the CIA Station after Country ██'s leadership, concurred in the absence of the ambassador, █████ ████████████████████.[73] Shortly thereafter, Abu Zubaydah was rendered from Pakistan to Country ██ where he was held at the first

CIA detention site, referred to in this summary as "DETENTION SITE GREEN."[74] CIA records indicate that Country ■ was the last location of a CIA detention facility known to the president or the vice president, as subsequent locations were kept from the principals as a matter of White House policy to avoid inadvertent disclosures of the location of the CIA detention sites.[75]

3. Tensions with Host Country Leadership and Media Attention Foreshadow Future Challenges

The day after the rendition of Abu Zubaydah to DETENTION SITE GREEN, the ■■■■■■■■, which was responsible for the security of the detention facility, linked its support for the CIA's detention site to a request for ■■■ support from the CIA ■■■■■■■■■■. The CIA eventually provided the requested ■■■ support, ■■■■■■■■ ■■■■■■■■■■.[76] According to CIA cables and internal documents, ■■■■■■■■■■■■■ ■■■■■■■ prompted ■■■■■■■■■■ to replace ■■■■■■■■■■■■■■■■■■■■ ■ individuals responsible for supporting the CIA's detention facility.[77] Those officials were replaced by different officials whom the CIA believed were not supportive of the CIA's detention site.[78] Despite considerable effort by the CIA's Station in Country ■ to retain support for DETENTION SITE GREEN from its new ■■ ■ partners, ■■■■ called for the closing of the CIA detention facility within three weeks.[79] Continued lobbying by the chief of Station, however, eventually led Country ■ to reverse this decision, allowing DETENTION SITE GREEN to remain operational.[80]

On April ■, 2002, the CIA Station in Country ■ attempted to list the number of Country ■ officers who, "[t]o the best of Station's knowledge," had "knowledge of the presence of Abu Zubaydah" in a specific city in Country ■. The list included eight individuals, references to "various" personnel ■■■■■ and the "staff" of ■■■■■■■■■, and concluded "[d]oubtless many others."[81] By April ■, 2002, a media organization had learned that Abu Zubaydah was in Country ■, prompting the CIA to explain to the media organization the "security implications" of revealing the information.[82] The CIA Station in Country ■ also expressed concern that press inquiries "would do nothing for our liaison and bilateral relations, possibly diminishing chances that [the ■■

■ of Country ■■] will permit [Abu Zubaydah] to remain in country or that he would accept other [Abu Zubaydah]-like renderees in the future."[83] In November 2002, after the CIA learned that a major U.S. newspaper knew that Abu Zubaydah was in Country ■■, senior CIA officials, as well as Vice President Cheney, urged the newspaper not to publish the information.[84] While the U.S. newspaper did not reveal Country ■■ as the location of Abu Zubaydah, the fact that it had the information, combined with previous media interest, resulted in the decision to close DETENTION SITE GREEN.[85]

4. FBI Officers Are the First to Question Abu Zubaydah, Who States He Intends to Cooperate; Abu Zubaydah is Taken to a Hospital Where He Provides Information the CIA Later Describes as "Important" and "Vital"

After Abu Zubaydah was rendered to DETENTION SITE GREEN on March ■■, 2002, he was questioned by special agents from the Federal Bureau of Investigation (FBI) who spoke Arabic and had experience interrogating members of al-Qa'ida. Abu Zubaydah confirmed his identity to the FBI officers, informed the FBI officers he wanted to cooperate, and provided background information on his activities. That evening, Abu Zubaydah's medical condition deteriorated rapidly and he required immediate hospitalization. Although Abu Zubaydah was largely unable to communicate because of a breathing tube, he continued to provide information to FBI and CIA officials at the hospital using an Arabic alphabet chart. According to records, the FBI officers remained at Abu Zubaydah's bedside throughout this ordeal and assisted in his medical care. When Abu Zubaydah's breathing tube was removed on April 8, 2002, Abu Zubaydah provided additional intelligence and reiterated his intention to cooperate.[86]

During an April 10, 2002, debriefing session, conducted in the hospital's intensive care unit, Abu Zubaydah revealed to the FBI officers that an individual named "Mukhtar" was the al-Qa'ida "mastermind" of the 9/11 attacks. Abu Zubaydah identified a picture of Mukhtar provided by the FBI from the FBI's Most Wanted list. The picture was of Khalid Shaykh Mohammad (KSM), who had been indicted in 1996 for his role in Ramzi Yousef's terrorist plotting to detonate explosives on 12 United States-flagged aircraft and destroy them mid-flight over the Pacific Ocean.[87] Abu Zubaydah told the interrogators that "Mukhtar" was related to Ramzi Yousef, whom Abu Zubaydah said was in an American jail (Yousef had been convicted for the aforementioned terrorist plotting and was involved in the 1993 World Trade Center terrorist attack).[88]

Zubaydah told the FBI officers that "Mukhtar" trained the 9/11 hijackers and also provided additional information on KSM's background, to include that KSM spoke fluent English, was approximately 34 years old, and was responsible for al-Qa'ida operations outside of Afghanistan.[89] Subsequent representations on the success of the CIA's Detention and Interrogation Program consistently describe Abu Zubaydah's identification of KSM's role in the September 11, 2001, attacks, as well as his identification of KSM's alias ("Mukhtar"), as being "important" and "vital" information.[90] A review of CIA records found that this information was corroborative of information already in CIA databases.[91]

5. While Abu Zubaydah is Hospitalized, CIA Headquarters Discusses the Use of Coercive Interrogation Techniques Against Abu Zubaydah

While Abu Zubaydah was still hospitalized, personnel at CIA Headquarters began discussing how CIA officers would interrogate Abu Zubaydah upon his return to DETENTION SITE GREEN. The initial CIA interrogation proposal recommended that the interrogators engage with Abu Zubaydah to get him to provide information, and suggested that a "hard approach," involving foreign government personnel, be taken "only as a last resort."[92] At a meeting about this proposal, ███████ CTC Legal, ███████████, recommended that a psychologist working on contract in the CIA's Office of Technical Services (OTS), Grayson SWIGERT, be used by CTC to "provide real-time recommendations to overcome Abu Zubaydah's resistance to interrogation."[93] SWIGERT had come to ██████'s attention through ██████████, who worked in OTS. Shortly thereafter, CIA Headquarters formally proposed that Abu Zubaydah be kept in an all-white room that was lit 24 hours a day, that Abu Zubaydah not be provided any amenities, that his sleep be disrupted, that loud noise be constantly fed into his cell, and that only a small number of people interact with him. CIA records indicate that these proposals were based on the idea that such conditions would lead Abu Zubaydah to develop a sense of "learned helplessness."[94] CIA Headquarters then sent an interrogation team to Country ██, including SWIGERT, whose initial role was to consult on the psychological aspects of the interrogation.[95]

DCI Tenet was provided an update on the Abu Zubaydah

interrogation plans on April 12, 2002. The update stated that the CIA team was preparing for Abu Zubaydah's transfer back to DETENTION SITEGREEN, and noted the CIA interrogation team intended to "set the stage" and increase control over Abu Zubaydah.[96] The update stated:

> "Our [CIA] lead interrogator will require Abu Zubaydah to reveal the most sensitive secret he knows we are seeking; if he dissembles or diverts the conversation, the interview will stop and resume at a later time . . . In accordance with the strategy, and with concurrence from FBI Headquarters, the two on-site FBI agents will no longer directly participate in the interview/debriefing sessions."[97]

The FBI special agents questioning Abu Zubaydah at the hospital objected to the CIA's plans. In a message to FBI Headquarters, an FBI special agent wrote that the CIA psychologists had acquired "tremendous influence."[98] The message further stated:

> "AZ's health has improved over the last two days and Agency [CIA] is ready to move [Abu Zubaydah] out of the hospital and back to ████ ████ on ████ in an elaborate plan to change AZ's environment. Agency [CIA] advised this day that they will be immediately changing tactics in all future AZ interviews by having only there [*sic*] [CIA officer] interact with AZ (there will be no FBI presence in interview room). This change contradicts all conversations had to date . . . They believe AZ is offering, 'throw away information' and holding back from providing threat information (It should be note [*sic*] that we have obtained critical information regarding AZ thus far and have now got him speaking about threat information, albeit from his hospital bed and not [an] appropriate interview environment for full follow-up (due to his health). Suddenly the psychiatric team here wants AZ to only interact with their [CIA officer, and the CIA sees this] as being the best way to get the threat information . . . We offered several compromise solutions . . . all suggestions were immediately declined without further discussion . . . This again is quite odd as all information obtained from AZ has come from FBI lead interviewers and questioning . . . I have spent an un-calculable amount of hours at [Abu Zubaydah's] bedside assisting with medical help, holding his hand and comforting him through various medical procedures, even assisting him in going [to] the bathroom . . . We have built tremendous report [*sic*] with AZ and now that we are on the eve of 'regular' interviews to get threat information, we have been 'written out' of future interviews."[99]

6. New CIA Interrogation Plan Focuses on Abu Zubaydah's "Most Important Secret"; FBI Temporarily Barred from the Questioning of Abu Zubaydah; Abu Zubaydah then Placed in Isolation for 47 Days Without Questioning

On April 13, 2002, while Abu Zubaydah was still at the hospital, the CIA implemented the "new interrogation program."[100] This initial meeting was held with just one interrogator in the room and lasted 11 minutes. A cable stated that the CIA interrogator was coached by the "psychological team."[101] The CIA interrogator advised Abu Zubaydah that he (Abu Zubaydah) "had a most important secret that [the interrogator] needed to know." According to the cable, Abu Zubaydah "amazingly" nodded in agreement about the secret, but "did not divulge any information, as [the interrogation team] expected."[102] A cable further explained that Abu Zubaydah indicated that he understood that the key question was about "impending future terrorist plans against the United States,"[103] and that the CIA officer told Abu Zubaydah to signal for him "when he decides to discuss that 'one key item he knows he is keeping from the [interrogator].'"[104] The FBI officers provided a similar account to FBI Headquarters, adding that: "We spent the rest of the day in the adjoining room with [the CIA officer] and one of the psychiatrists [REDACTED] waiting for [Abu Zubaydah] to signal he was ready to talk. [Abu Zubaydah] apparently went to sleep . . . they did not approach [Abu Zubaydah] the rest of the day."[105] In their communications with FBI Headquarters, the FBI officers wrote that they explained their rapport-building approaches to the CIA interrogation team and "tried to explain that we have used this approach before on other Al-Qaeda members with much success (al-Owhali,[106] KKM, Jandal, Badawi etc.). We tried to politely suggest that valuable time was passing where we could attempt to solicit threat information . . ."[107]

On April 15, 2002, per a scripted plan, the same CIA interrogator delivered what a CIA cable described as "the pre-move message" to Abu Zubaydah; that "time is running out," that his situation had changed, and that the interrogator was disappointed that Abu Zubaydah did not signal "to discuss the one thing he was hiding."[108] Abu Zubaydah was sedated and moved from the hospital to DETENTION SITE GREEN. When Abu Zubaydah awoke at 11:00 PM, four hours after his arrival, he was described as surprised and disturbed by his new situation. An April 16, 2002, cable states the "objective is to ensure that [Abu Zubaydah] is at his most vulnerable state."[109]

A cable described Abu Zubaydah's cell as white with no natural lighting or windows, but with four halogen lights pointed into the cell.[110] An air conditioner was also in the room. A white curtain separated the interrogation room from the cell. The interrogation cell had three padlocks. Abu Zubaydah was also provided with one of two chairs that were rotated based on his level of cooperation (one described as more comfortable than the other). Security officers wore all black uniforms, including boots, gloves, balaclavas, and goggles to keep Abu Zubaydah from identifying the officers, as well as to prevent Abu Zubaydah "from seeing the security guards as individuals who he may attempt to establish a relationship or dialogue with."[111] The security officers communicated by hand signals when they were with Abu Zubaydah and used hand-cuffs and leg shackles to maintain control. In addition, either loud rock music was played or noise generators were used to enhance Abu Zubaydah's "sense of hopelessness."[112] Abu Zubaydah was typically kept naked and sleep deprived.[113]

An April 16, 2002, cable explained that the interrogation strategy had shifted since Abu Zubaydah's medical condition prevented "total isolation as originally planned." According to the cable, a 24-hour interrogation strategy was now "deemed to be the best approach" for acquiring information. As a result, the FBI officers were once again allowed to question Abu Zubaydah.[114] On April 17, 2002, an FBI officer met with Abu Zubaydah for six hours.[115] FBI records state that Abu Zubaydah had "not seen the interviewing (FBI) agent" since April 11, 2002, but that Abu Zubaydah greeted the agent by name.[116] During the questioning Abu Zubaydah denied any knowledge related to specific targets for a pending attack and "advised that many of the brothers on the front lines (nfi) [no further information] talked about all types of attacks against America but that for the most part this was usually just talk and that [the United States] should not be concerned about this type of talk,"[117] Abu Zubaydah provided information on al-Qa'ida, KSM, his past travel to the United States, as well as general information on extremists in Pakistan.[118]

Abu Zubaydah continued to provide information to interrogators throughout April 2002, but not information on pending attacks against the United States. On the evening of April 20, 2002, Abu Zubaydah told the FBI officers about two men who approached him with a plan to detonate a uranium-based explosive device in the United States. Abu Zubaydah stated he did not believe the plan was viable and did not know the names of the two individuals, but provided physical descriptions of the pair.[119] This information was acquired after Abu Zubaydah was confronted with emails indicating that he had sent the two individuals to KSM.[120] The CIA would later represent that this information was acquired "as a result" of the use of the CIA's enhanced interrogation techniques, and that the information acquired resulted in the thwarting of the "Dirty Bomb Plot" and the capture of Jose Padilla.[121] However, the chief of the Abu Zubaydah Task Force stated that "AZ's info alone would never have allowed us to find them," while another CIA officer stated that the CIA was already "alert" to the threat posed by Jose Padilla, and that the CIA's "suspicion" was only "enhanced during the debriefings of Abu Zubaydah."[122] Additional information on the "Dirty Bomb Plot" and the capture of Jose Padilla is provided later in this summary.

During the month of April 2002, which included a period during which Abu Zubaydah was hospitalized, on life support, and unable to speak, the CIA disseminated 39 intelligence reports based on his interrogations.[123] At the end of April 2002, the DETENTION SITE GREEN interrogation team provided CIA Headquarters with three interrogation strategies. CIA Headquarters chose the most coercive interrogation option, which was proposed and supported by CIA contractor SWIGERT.[124] This coercive interrogation option—which included sensory deprivation—was again opposed by the FBI special agents at the detention site.[125] The interrogation proposal was to engage in "only a single-minded, consistent, totally focused questioning of current threat information."[126] Once implemented, this approach failed to produce the information CIA Headquarters believed Abu Zubaydah possessed: threats to the United States and information about al-Qa'ida operatives located in the United States. Nonetheless, Abu Zubaydah continued to provide other intelligence. In May 2002, the CIA disseminated 56 intelligence reports based on the interrogations.[127]

In early June 2002, the CIA interrogation team recommended that Abu Zubaydah spend several weeks in isolation while the interrogation team members departed the facility "as a means of keeping [Abu Zubaydah] off-balance and to allow the team needed time off for a break and to attend to personal matters █████," as well as to discuss "the endgame" of Abu Zubaydah █████ with officers from CIA Headquarters.[128] As a result, from June 18, 2002, through August 4, 2002, Abu Zubaydah spent 47 days in isolation without being asked any questions. Despite the fact that Abu Zubaydah was in isolation for nearly half of the month, the CIA disseminated 37 intelligence reports based on the interrogations of Abu Zubaydah in June 2002.[129] The CIA would later represent publicly—as well as in classified settings—that during the use of "established US Government interrogation techniques," Abu Zubaydah "stopped all cooperation" in June 2002, requiring the development of the CIA's enhanced interrogation techniques.[130] CIA records do not support this assertion.

Prior to Abu Zubaydah's 47-day isolation period, Abu Zubaydah provided information on al-Qa'ida activities, plans, capabilities, and relationships, in addition to information on its leadership structure, including personalities, decision-making processes, training, and tactics.[131] As described in more detail in the full Committee Study, Abu Zubaydah's inability to provide information on the next attack in the United States and operatives in the United States served as the basis for CIA representations that Abu Zubaydah was "uncooperative," as well as for the CIA's determination that Abu Zubaydah required the use of what would later be known as the CIA's "enhanced interrogation techniques" to become "compliant" and reveal the information the CIA believed he was withholding. Abu Zubaydah never provided this information, and CIA officers later concluded this was information Abu Zubaydah did not possess.[132]

After Abu Zubaydah was placed in isolation, the Abu Zubaydah interrogation team ■■■■■■■■■■ [departed Country ■ ■]. Security and medical personnel remained at the detention site. The FBI special agents did not return to DETENTION SITE GREEN.[133]

7. Proposal by CIA Contract Personnel to Use SERE-Based Interrogation Techniques Leads to the Development of the CIA's Enhanced Interrogation Techniques; The CIA Determines that "the Interrogation Process Takes Precedence Over Preventative Medical Procedures"

In early July 2002, CIA officers held several meetings at CIA Headquarters to discuss the possible use of "novel interrogation methods" on Abu Zubaydah.[134] During the course of those meetings SWIGERT proposed using techniques derived from the U.S. military's SERE (Survival, Evasion, Resistance and Escape) school.[135] SWIGERT provided a list of 12 SERE techniques for possible use by the CIA: (1) the attention grasp, (2) walling, (3) facial hold, (4) facial slap, (5) cramped confinement, (6) wall standing, (7) stress positions, (8) sleep deprivation, (9) waterboard, (10) use of diapers, (11) use of insects, and (12) mock burial.[136] SWIGERT also recommended that the CIA enter into a contract with Hammond DUNBAR, his co-author of the CIA report on potential al-Qa'ida interrogation resistance training, to aid in the CIA interrogation process.[137] Like SWIGERT, DUNBAR had never participated in a real-world interrogation. His interrogation experience was limited to the paper he authored with

SWIGERT and his work with U.S. Air Force personnel at the SERE school.[138]

In May 2003, a senior CIA interrogator would tell personnel from the CIA's Office of Inspector General that SWIGERT and DUNBAR's SERE school model was based on resisting North Vietnamese "physical torture" and was designed to extract "confessions for propaganda purposes" from U.S. airmen "who possessed little actionable intelligence." The CIA, he believed, "need[ed] a different working model for interrogating terrorists where confessions are not the ultimate goal."[139]

After the July 2002 meetings, the CIA's ████ CTC Legal, ██████, drafted a letter to Attorney General John Ashcroft asking the Department of Justice for "a formal declination of prosecution, in advance, for any employees of the United States, as well as any other personnel acting on behalf of the United States, who may employ methods in the interrogation of Abu Zubaydah that otherwise might subject those individuals to prosecution."[140] The letter further indicated that "the interrogation team had concluded" that "the use of more aggressive methods is required to persuade Abu Zubaydah to provide the critical information we need to safeguard the lives of innumerable innocent men, women and children within the United States and abroad." The letter added that these "aggressive methods" would otherwise be prohibited by the torture statute, "apart from potential reliance upon the doctrines of necessity or of self-defense."[141] This letter was circulated internally at the CIA, including to SWIGERT; however, there are no records to indicate it was provided to the attorney general.[142]

On July 13, 2002, ████ CTC Legal, ██████, and the CIA's acting general counsel, John Rizzo, met with attorneys from the National Security Council and the Department of Justice Office of Legal Counsel (OLC), as well as with Michael Chertoff, the head of the Department of Justice Criminal Division, and Daniel Levin, the chief of staff to the FBI director, to provide an overview of the CIA's proposed interrogation techniques and to ask for a formal, definitive DOJ opinion regarding the lawfulness of employing the specific CIA interrogation techniques against Abu Zubaydah.[143]

The CIA attorneys described the 12 proposed interrogation techniques and told the Department of Justice and National Security Council attorneys that Abu Zubaydah continued to withhold critical intelligence on the identities of al-Qa'ida personnel in the United States and planned al-Qa'ida attacks. The CIA attorneys also told the group that CIA officers were complemented by:

> "expert personnel retained on contract who possess extensive experience, gained within the Department of Defense, on the psychological and physical methods of interrogation and the resistance techniques employed as countermeasures to such interrogation."[144]

According to the CIA cable describing the meeting, the representatives from the OLC, including Deputy Assistant Attorney General John Yoo, advised that the criminal prohibition on torture would not prohibit the methods proposed by the interrogation team because of the absence of any specific intent to inflict severe physical or mental pain or suffering.[145] On July 13, 2002, Yoo sent an unclassified letter to the CIA's acting general counsel describing his interpretation of the statute.[146]

Despite the initial view expressed by Yoo that the use of the proposed CIA interrogation techniques would be lawful, on July 17, 2002, National Security Advisor Condoleezza Rice requested a delay in the approval of the interrogation techniques for Abu Zubaydah's interrogation until the attorney general issued an opinion.[147] The following day. Rice and Deputy National Security Advisor Stephen Hadley requested that the Department of Justice "delay the approval of the memo detailing the next phase of interrogations" until the CIA provided specific details on its proposed interrogation techniques and "an explanation of why the CIA is confident these techniques will not cause lasting and irreparable harm to Abu Zubaydah."[148] Rice asked the CIA to provide the OLC with a description of each of the planned interrogation techniques, and to "gather and provide any available empirical data on the reactions and likelihood of prolonged mental harm from the use of the 'water board' and the staged burial."[149]

On July 15, 2002, a cable providing details on the proposed interrogation phase stated that only the DETENTION SITE GREEN chief of Base would be allowed to interrupt or stop an interrogation in process, and that the chief of Base would be the final decision-making authority as to whether the CIA's interrogation techniques applied to Abu Zubaydah would be discontinued.[150] The CIA officers at the detention site added:

> "If [Abu Zubaydah] develops a serious medical condition which may involve a host of conditions including a heart attack or another catastrophic type of condition, all efforts will be made to ensure that proper medical care will be provided to [him]. In the event [Abu Zubaydah] dies, we need to be prepared to act accordingly, keeping in mind the liaison equities involving our hosts."[151]

To address these issues, the cable stated that if Abu Zubaydah were to die during the interrogation, he would be cremated.[152] The interrogation team closed the cable by stating:

> "regardless which [disposition] option we follow however, and especially in light of the planned psychological pressure techniques to be implemented, we need to get reasonable assurances that [Abu Zubaydah] will remain in isolation and incommunicado for the remainder of his life."[153]

Officers from the CIA's ALEC Station responded to the interrogation team's comments several days later. Their cable noted that the interrogation team was correct in its "understanding that the interrogation process takes precedence over preventative medical procedures."[154] ALEC Station further observed:

> "There is a fairly unanimous sentiment within HQS that [Abu Zubaydah] will never be placed in a siutation where he has any significant contact with others and/or has the opportunity to be released. While it is difficult to discuss specifics at this point, all major players are in concurrence that [Abu Zubaydah] should remain incommunicado for the remainder of his life. This may preclude [Abu Zubaydah] from being turned over to another country, but a final decision regarding his future incarceration condition has yet to be made."[155]

As a result of the request by National Security Advisor Rice for additional research on the CIA's proposed interrogation techniques, CIA and DOJ personnel contacted individuals at the Department of Defense's Joint Personnel Recovery Agency (JPRA), the agency that administers the SERE school, to gather information about the effects of using the techniques in training exercises.[156] According to CIA officer ███████████, who had █████ joined the CIA's OTS after ██ years at JPRA, an individual with SERE school experience commented that "information gleaned via harsh treatment may not be accurate, as the prisoner may say anything to avoid further pain," and that "[c]urrent doctrine for interrogations conducted in the permanent phase of capture may lean towards 'soft' or 'indirect' rounds of questioning."[157]

Pursuant to National Security Advisor Rice's request, CIA Headquarters personnel also requested information from the interrogation team—particularly SWIGERT and DUNBAR—about the psychological effects of the use of the waterboard and mock burial. The chief of Base at DETENTION SITE GREEN responded by cable noting that:

> "We are a nation of laws and we do not wish to parse words. A bottom line in considering the new measures proposed is that [Abu Zubaydah] is being held in solitary confinement, against his will, without legal

> representation, as an enemy of our country, our society and our people. Therefore, while the techniques described in Headquarters meetings and below are administered to student volunteers in the U.S. in a harmless way, with no measurable impact on the psyche of the volunteer, we do not believe we can assure the same here for a man forced through these processes and who will be made to believe this is the future course of the remainder of his life. Station, [DETENTION SITE GREEN chief of Base] and [DETENTION SITE GREEN] personnel will make every effort possible to insure [*sic*] that subject is not permanently physically or mental harmed but we should not say at the outset of this process that there is no risk."[158]

As former psychologists for the United States Air Force, SWIGERT and DUNBAR had no direct experience with the waterboard, as it was not used in Air Force SERE training. Nonetheless, they indicated that the waterboard—which they described as an "absolutely convincing technique"—was necessary to overwhelm Abu Zubaydah's ability to resist.[159] They also responded that they were aware that the Navy—which used the waterboard technique in training—had not reported any significant long-term consequences on individuals from its use. Unlike the CIA's subsequent use of the waterboard, however, the Navy's use of the technique was a single training exercise and did not extend to multiple sessions. SWIGERT and DUNBAR wrote:

> "any physical pressure applied to extremes can cause severe mental pain or suffering. Hooding, the use of loud music, sleep deprivation, controlling darkness and light, slapping, walling, or the use of stress positions taken to extreme can have the same outcome. The safety of any technique lies primarily in how it is applied and monitored."[160]

On July 24, 2002, the attorney general verbally approved the use of 10 interrogation techniques, which included: the attention grasp, walling, the facial hold, the facial slap (insult slap), cramped confinement, wall standing, stress positions, sleep deprivation, use of diapers, and use of insects.[161] The interrogation team, however, indicated that they intended to wait for the approval to use the waterboard before proceeding with their interrogation of Abu Zubaydah. On July 26, 2002, the attorney general verbally approved the use of the waterboard.[162] The OLC finalized its classified written legal opinion on August 1, 2002. The earlier CIA request to conduct a mock burial was not formally considered by the OLC. The approved interrogation techniques, along with other CIA interrogation techniques that were subsequently identified and used by the CIA, are referred to as the CIA's "enhanced interrogation techniques," or more commonly by the CIA as "EITs."

In the course of seeking approval to use the techniques, CIA Headquarters advised the Depaitment of Justice and the national security advisor that "countless more Americans may die unless we can persuade AZ to tell us what he knows." CIA Headquarters further represented that the DETENTION SITE GREEN interrogation team believed "Abu Zubaydah continues to withhold critical threat information," and "that in order to persuade him to provide" that information, "the use of more aggressive techniques is required."[163] The cable to DETENTION SITE GREEN from CIA Headquarters documenting the information CIA Headquarters had provided to the Department of Justice warned that "[t]he legal conclusions are predicated upon the determinations by the interrogation team that Abu Zubaydah continues to withhold critical threat information."[164] According to cables, however, the CIA interrogators at the detention site had not determined that "the use of more aggressive techniques was required" to "persuade" Abu Zubaydah to provide threat information. Rather, the interrogation team believed the objective of the coercive interrogation techniques was to confirm Abu Zubaydah did not have additional information on threats to the United States, writing:

> "Our assumption is the objective of this operation is to achieve a high degree of confidence that [Abu Zubaydah] is not holding back actionable information concerning threats to the United States beyond that which [Abu Zubaydah] has already provided."[165]

As is described in this summary, and in more detail in the full Committee Study, the interrogation team later deemed the use of the CIA's enhanced interrogation techniques a success, not because it resulted in critical threat information, but because it provided further evidence that Abu Zubaydah had not been withholding the aforementioned information from the interrogators.[166]

8. The CIA Obtains Legal and Policy Approval for Its Enhanced Interrogation Techniques: The CIA Does Not Brief the President

As described, CIA officers represented to National Security Advisor Rice that Abu Zubaydah was withholding information on pending attacks and operatives in the United States. On July 31, 2002, Rice informed Deputy DCI John McLaughlin that, in balancing the application of the CIA's enhanced interrogation techniques against the possible loss of American lives, she would not object to the CIA's enhanced interrogation techniques if the attorney general determined them to be legal.[167]

During the month of July 2002, the CIA anticipated that the president would need to approve the use of the CIA's enhanced interrogation techniques before they could be used. Therefore, in late July 2002, the CIA prepared talking points for a briefing of the president. These draft talking points indicated that the CIA was planning to use interrogation techniques beyond what was normally permitted by law enforcement, and included a brief description of the waterboard interrogation technique. On August 1, 2002, based on comments from White House Counsel Alberto Gonzales, the talking points were revised to eliminate references to the waterboard.[168] CIA records indicate, however, that the talking points were not used to brief the president. On August 2, 2002, the National Security Council legal advisor informed the DCI's chief of staff that "Dr. Rice had been informed that there would be no briefing of the President on this matter,"[169] but that the DCI had policy approval to employ the CIA's enhanced interrogation techniques.[170]

CIA records state that prior to the use of the CIA's enhanced interrogation techniques on Abu Zubaydah in 2002, the CIA did not brief Secretary of State Colin Powell or Secretary of Defense Donald Rumsfeld, two members of the National Security Council, on the techniques.[171] The Committee, including the chairman and vice chairman, was also not briefed on the CIA's enhanced interrogation techniques prior to their use.[172]

Approximately a year later, on July 31, 2003, senior CIA personnel believed the president had still not been briefed on the CIA's enhanced interrogation techniques.[173] In August 2003, DCI Tenet told the CIA Office of Inspector General that "he had never spoken to the President regarding the detention and interrogation program or EITs, nor was he aware of whether the President had been briefed by his staff."[174] The May 2004 CIA Inspector General Special Review included a recommendation for the DCI to:

> "Brief the President regarding the implementation of the Agency's detention and interrogation activities pursuant to the MON of 17 September 2001 or any other authorities, including the use of EITs and the fact that detainees have died. This Recommendation is significant."[175]

In transmitting the Special Review to the Committee, DCI Tenet responded to the recommendation, noting only that "[t]he DCI will determine whether and to what extent the President requires a briefing on the Program."[176] On April 6, 2006, CIA Inspector General Helgerson responded to a request from Committee Vice Chairman John D. Rockefeller IV on the status of corrective actions taken in response to the Special Review recommendations. With regard to a briefing for the president, Helgerson wrote: "Consistent with this recommendation, DCI Tenet, before he left office, and Director Goss, shortly after taking office, both advised me that they had made requests to brief the President."[177] Prepared "Questions and Answers" for the National Security Council principals in connection with the disclosure of the program in September 2006 and subsequent media outreach also suggest that the president was not briefed at the outset about the CIA's interrogation techniques. In response to the potential question: "What role did the President play . . . Was he briefed on the interrogation techniques, and if so when?" the proposed answer did not assert that the president was briefed, but rather that the "President was not of course involved in CIA's day to day operations—including who should be held by CIA and how they should be questioned—these decisions are made or overseen by CIA Directors."[178]

CIA records indicate that the first CIA briefing for the president on the CIA's enhanced interrogation techniques occurred on April 8, 2006.[179] CIA records state that when the president was briefed, he expressed discomfort with the "image of a detainee, chained to the ceiling, clothed in a diaper, and forced to go to the bathroom on himself."[180]

9. The CIA Uses the Waterboard and Other Enhanced Interrogation Techniques Against Abu Zubaydah

On August 3, 2002, CIA Headquarters informed the interrogation team at DETENTION SITE GREEN that it had formal approval to apply the CIA's enhanced interrogation techniques, including the waterboard, against Abu Zubaydah. According to CIA records, only the two CIA contractors, SWIGERT and DUNBAR, were to have contact with Abu Zubaydah. Other CIA personnel at DETENTION SITE GREEN—including CIA medical personnel and other CIA "interrogators with whom he is familiar"—were only to observe.[181]

From August 4, 2002, through August 23, 2002, the CIA subjected Abu Zubaydah to its enhanced interrogation techniques on a near 24-hour-per-day basis. After Abu Zubaydah had been in complete isolation for 47 days, the most aggressive interrogation phase began at approximately 11:50 AM on August 4, 2002.[182] Security personnel entered the cell, shackled and hooded Abu Zubaydah, and removed his towel (Abu Zubaydah was then naked). Without asking any questions, the interrogators placed a rolled towel around his neck as a collar, and backed him up into the cell wall (an interrogator later acknowledged the collar was used to slam Abu Zubaydah against a concrete wall).[183] The interrogators then removed the hood, performed an attention grab, and had Abu Zubaydah watch while a large confinement box was brought into the cell and laid on the floor.[184] A cable states Abu Zubaydah "was unhooded and the large confinement box was carried into the interrogation room and paced [*sic*] on the floor so as to appear as a coffin."[185] The interrogators then demanded detailed and verifiable information on terrorist operations planned against the United States, including the names, phone numbers, email addresses, weapon caches, and safe houses of anyone involved. CIA records describe Abu Zubaydah as appearing apprehensive. Each time Abu Zubaydah denied having additional information, the interrogators would perform a facial slap or face grab.[186] At approximately 6:20 PM, Abu Zubaydah was waterboarded for the first time. Over a two-and-a-half-hour period, Abu Zubaydah coughed, vomited, and had "involuntary spasms of the torso and extremities" during waterboarding.[187] Detention site personnel noted that "throughout the process [Abu Zubaydah] was asked and given the opportunity to respond to questions about threats" to the United States, but Abu Zubaydah continued to maintain that he did not have any additional information to provide.[188] In an email to OMS leadership entitled, "So it begins," a medical officer wrote:

> "The sessions accelerated rapidly progressing quickly to the water board after large box, walling, and small box periods. [Abu Zubaydah] seems very resistant to the water board. Longest time with the cloth over his face so far has been 17 seconds. This is sure to increase shortly. NO useful information so far . . . He did vomit a couple of times during the water board with some beans and rice. It's been 10 hours since he ate so this is surprising and disturbing. We plan to only feed Ensure for a while now. I'm head[ing] back for another water board session."[189]

The use of the CIA's enhanced interrogation techniques—including "walling, attention grasps, slapping, facial hold, stress positions, cramped confinement, white noise and sleep deprivation"—continued in "varying combinations, 24 hours a day" for 17 straight days, through August 20, 2002.[190] When Abu Zubaydah was left alone during this period, he was placed in a stress position, left on the waterboard with a cloth over his face, or locked in one of two confinement boxes. According to the cables, Abu Zubaydah was also subjected to the waterboard "2–4 times a day . . . with multiple iterations of the watering cycle during each application."[191]

The "aggressive phase of interrogation" continued until August

23, 2002.[192] Over the course of the entire 20 day "aggressive phase of interrogation," Abu Zubaydah spent a total of 266 hours (11 days, 2 hours) in the large (coffin size) confinement box and 29 hours in a small confinement box, which had a width of 21 inches, a depth of 2.5 feet, and a height of 2.5 feet. The CIA interrogators told Abu Zubaydah that the only way he would leave the facility was in the coffin-shaped confinement box.[193]

According to the daily cables from DETENTION SITE GREEN, Abu Zubaydah frequently "cried," "begged," "pleaded," and "whimpered," but continued to deny that he had any additional information on current threats to, or operatives in, the United States.[194]

By August 9, 2002, the sixth day of the interrogation period, the interrogation team informed CIA Headquarters that they had come to the "collective preliminary assessment" that it was unlikely Abu Zubaydah "had actionable new information about current threats to the United States."[195] On August 10, 2002, the interrogation team stated that it was "highly unlikely" that Abu Zubaydah possessed the information they were seeking.[196] On the same day, the interrogation team reiterated a request for personnel from CIA Headquarters to travel to the detention site to view the interrogations. A cable stated that the team believed that a "first-hand, on-the-ground look is best," but if CIA Headquarters personnel could not visit, a video teleconference would suffice.[197] DETENTION SITE GREEN personnel also informed CIA Headquarters that it was their assessment that the application of the CIA's enhanced interrogation techniques was "approach[ing] the legal limit."[198] The chief of CTC, Jose Rodriguez, responded:

> "Strongly urge that any speculative language as to the legality of given activities or, more precisely, judgment calls as to their legality vis-à-vis operational guidelines for this activity agreed upon and vetted at the most senior levels of the agency, be refrained from in written traffic (email or cable traffic). Such language is not helpful."[199]

DETENTION SITE GREEN cables describe Abu Zubaydah as "compliant," informing CIA Headquarters that when the interrogator "raised his eyebrow, without instructions," Abu Zubaydah "slowly walked on his own to the water table and sat down."[200] When the interrogator "snapped his fingers twice," Abu Zubaydah would lie flat on the waterboard.[201] Despite the assessment of personnel at the detention site that Abu Zubaydah was compliant, CIA Headquarters stated that they continued to believe that Abu Zubaydah was withholding threat information and instructed the CIA interrogators to continue using the CIA's enhanced interrogation techniques.[202]

At times Abu Zubaydah was described as "hysterical"[203] and "distressed to the level that he was unable to effectively communicate."[204] Waterboarding sessions "resulted in immediate fluid intake and involuntary leg, chest and arm spasms" and "hysterical pleas."[205] In at least one waterboarding session, Abu Zubaydah "became completely unresponsive, with bubbles rising through his open, full mouth."[206] According to CIA records, Abu Zubaydah remained unresponsive until medical intervention, when he regained consciousness and expelled "copious amounts of liquid." This experience with the waterboard was referenced in emails, but was not documented or otherwise noted in CIA cables.[207] When two CIA Headquarters officers later compared the Abu Zubaydah interrogation videotapes to the cable record, neither commented on this session. A review of the catalog of videotapes, however, found that recordings of a 21-hour period, which included two waterboarding sessions, were missing.[208]

CIA personnel at DETENTION SITE GREEN reported being disturbed by the use of the CIA's enhanced interrogation techniques against Abu Zubaydah. CIA records include the following reactions and comments by CIA personnel:

- August 5, 2002: "want to caution [medical officer] that this is almost certainly not a place he's ever been before in his medical career . . . It is visually and psychologically very uncomfortable."[209]
- August 8, 2002: "Today's first session . . . had a profound effect on all staff members present . . . it seems the collective opinion that we should not go much further . . . everyone seems strong for now but if the group has to continue . . . we cannot guarantee how much longer."[210]
- August 8, 2002: "Several on the team profoundly affected . . . some to the point of tears and choking up."[211]
- August 9, 2002: "two, perhaps three [personnel] likely to elect transfer" away from the detention site if the decision is made to continue with the CIA's enhanced interrogation techniques.[212]
- August 11, 2002: Viewing the pressures on Abu Zubaydah on video "has produced strong feelings of futility (and legality) of escalating or even maintaining the pressure." Per viewing the tapes, "prepare for something not seen previously."[213]

After the use of the CIA's enhanced interrogation techniques ended, CIA personnel at the detention site concluded that Abu Zubaydah had been truthful and that he did not possess any new terrorist threat information.[214]

As noted, CIA records indicate that Abu Zubaydah never provided the information for which the CIA's enhanced interrogation techniques were justified and approved: information on the next terrorist attack and operatives in the United States. Furthermore, as compared to the period prior to August 2002, the quantity and type of intelligence produced by Abu Zubaydah remained largely unchanged during and after the August 2002 use of the CIA's enhanced interrogation techniques.[215] Nonetheless, CIA Headquarters informed the National Security Council that the CIA's enhanced interrogation techniques used against Abu Zubaydah were effective and were "producing meaningful results."[216] A cable from DETENTION SITE GREEN, which CIA records indicate was authored by SWIGERT and DUNBAR, also viewed the interrogation of Abu Zubaydah as a success. The cable recommended that "the aggressive phase at [DETENTION SITE GREEN] should be used as a template for future interrogation of high value captives,"[217] not because the CIA's enhanced interrogation techniques produced useful information, but rather because their use confirmed that Abu Zubaydah did not possess the intelligence that CIA Headquarters had assessed Abu Zubaydah to have. The cable from the detention site stated:

> "Our goal was to reach the stage where we have broken any will or ability of subject to resist or deny providing us information (intelligence) to which he had access. We additionally sought to bring subject to the point that we confidently assess that he does not/not possess undisclosed threat information, or intelligence that could prevent a terrorist event."[218]

The cable further recommended that psychologists—a likely reference to contractors SWIGERT and DUNBAR—"familiar with interrogation, exploitation and resistance to interrogation should shape compliance of high value captives prior to debriefing by substantive experts."[219]

From Abu Zubaydah's capture on March 28, 2002, to his transfer to Department of Defense custody on September 5, 2006, information provided by Abu Zubaydah resulted in 766 disseminated intelligence reports.[220] According to CIA documents, Abu Zubaydah provided information on "al-Qa'ida activities, plans, capabilities, and relationships," in addition to information on "its leadership structure, including personalities, decision-making processes, training, and tactics."[221] As noted, this type of information was provided by Abu Zubaydah before, during, and after the use of the CIA's enhanced interrogation techniques. At no time during or after the use of the CIA's enhanced interrogation techniques did Abu Zubaydah provide information about operatives in, or future attacks against, the United States.[222]

10. A CIA Presidential Daily Brief Provides Inaccurate Information on the Interrogation of Abu Zubaydah

Although CIA personnel at DETENTION SITE GREEN agreed that Abu Zubaydah was compliant and cooperative, personnel at CIA Headquarters prepared a Presidential Daily Brief (PDB) in October 2002 that, according to a cable, "accurately reflect[ed] the collective HQS view of the information provided [by Abu Zubaydah] to date."[223] The October 2002 PDB stated Abu Zubaydah was still withholding "significant threat information," including information on operatives in the United States, and that Abu "Zubaydah resisted providing useful information until becoming more cooperative in early August, probably in the hope of improving his living conditions."[224] The PDB made no reference to the CIA's enhanced interrogation techniques or the counter-assessment from the detention site interrogation team indicating that Abu Zubaydah was cooperative and not withholding information.[225]

CIA documents identified the "key intelligence" acquired from Abu Zubaydah as information related to suspected terrorists Jose Padilla and Binyam Mohammad, information on English-speaking al-Qa'ida member Jaffar al-Tayyar, and information identifying KSM as the mastermind of the September 11, 2001, attacks who used the alias "Mukhtar."[226] All of this information was acquired by FBI special agents shortly after Abu Zubaydah's capture.[227]

The CIA has consistently represented that Abu Zubaydah stated that the CIA's enhanced interrogation techniques were necessary to gain his cooperation. For example, the CIA informed the OLC that:

> "As Zubaydah himself explained with respect to enhanced techniques, 'brothers who are captured and interrogated are permitted by Allah to provide information when they believe they have 'reached the limit of their ability to withhold it' in the face of psychological and physical hardships."[228]

As is described in greater detail in the full Committee Study, CIA records do not support the CIA representation that Abu Zubaydah made these statements.[229] CIA records indicate that Abu Zubaydah maintained that he always intended to talk and never believed he could withhold information from interrogators.[230] In February 2003, Abu Zubaydah told a CIA psychologist that he believed prior to his capture that every captured "brother" would talk in detention and that he told individuals at a terrorist training camp that "brothers should be able to expect that the organization will make adjustments to protect people and plans when someone with knowledge is captured."[231]

11. The CIA Does Not Brief the Committee on the Interrogation of Abu Zubaydah

In contrast to relatively open communications that the CIA had with the Committee following the issuance of the September 17, 2001, MON, the CIA significantly limited its communications with the Committee on its detention and interrogation activities after Abu Zubaydah's capture on March 28, 2002.[232] In responses to three different sets of Committee Questions for the Record addressed to the CIA regarding the MON authorities in the spring and summer of 2002, the CIA provided no indication that the CIA had established DETENTION SITE GREEN, or was using, or considering using, coercive interrogation techniques.[233]

On September 27, 2002, CIA officials provided a briefing on Abu Zubaydah's interrogation only to Committee Chairman Bob Graham, Vice Chairman Richard Shelby, and their staff directors. After this briefing Chairman Graham made multiple and specific requests for additional information on the CIA's Detention and Interrogation Program. Internal CIA emails include discussion of how the CIA could "get . . . off the hook on the cheap" regarding Chairman Graham's requests for additional information.[234] In the end, CIA officials simply did not respond to Graham's requests prior to his departure from the Committee in January 2003.

C. Interrogation in Country ■ and the January 2003 Guidelines

1. The CIA Establishes DETENTION SITE COBALT, Places Inexperienced First-Tour Officer in Charge

Plans for a specialized CIA detention facility Country ■ began in April 2002, with the intention that it would be "totally under [■■■■■■]/Station Control."[235] On June 6, 2002, CIA Headquarters approved more than $200,000 for the construction of the facility, identified in this summary as "DETENTION SITE COBALT."[236] In a 2003 interview with the CIA Office of Inspector General, Associate Deputy Director for Operations ■■■■■■■■ described his views of this facility and "stated that [DETENTION SITE COBALT] was opened because there needed to be a detention site in [Country ■] for those detainees enroute ■ to [DETENTION SITE GREEN]. It was not a place for the use of EITs."[237]

DETENTION SITE COBALT, constructed with CIA funding, opened in Country ■ in September 2002.[238] According to CIA records, the windows at DETENTION SITE COBALT were blacked out and detainees were kept in total darkness. The ■ ■ guards monitored detainees using headlamps and loud music was played constantly in the facility. While in their cells, detainees were shackled to the wall and given buckets for human waste. Four of the twenty cells at the facility included a bar across the top of the cell.[239] Later reports describe detainees being shackled to the bar with their hands above their heads, forcing them to stand, and therefore not allowing the detainees to sleep.[240]

The CIA officer in charge of DETENTION SITE COBALT, ■ [CIA OFFICER 1], was a junior officer on his first overseas assignment with no previous experience or training in handling prisoners or conducting interrogations. ■ [CIA OFFICER 1] was the DETENTION SITE COBALT manager during the period in which a CIA detainee died and numerous CIA detainees were subjected to unapproved coercive interrogation techniques.[241] A review of CIA records found that prior to ■ [CIA OFFICER 1's] deployment and assignment as the CIA's DETENTION SITE COBALT manager, other CIA officers recommended ■ [CIA OFFICER 1] not have continued access to classified information due to a "lack of honesty, judgment, and maturity."[242] According to records, "the chief of CTC told [■ [CIA OFFICER 1]] that he would not want [him] in his overseas station."[243] A supervising officer assessed that ■ [CIA OFFICER 1]:

> "has issues with judgment and maturity, [and his] potential behavior in the field is also worrisome. [The officer] further advised that [■ ■ [CIA OFFICER 1]] was only put into processing for an overseas position so that someone would evaluate all of the evidence of this situation all together. [The officer further noted that [■ [CIA OFFICER 1]] might not listen to his chief of station when in the field."[244]

2. CIA Records Lack Information on CIA Detainees and Details of Interrogations in Country ■

Detainees held in Country ■ were detained under the authority of the MON; however, CIA officers conducted no written assessment of whether these detainees "pose[d] a continuing, serious threat of violence or death to U.S. persons and interests or . . . [we]re planning terrorist activities." The CIA maintained such poor records of its detainees in Country ■■ during this period that the CIA remains unable to determine the number and identity of the individuals it detained. The full details of the CIA interrogations there remain largely unknown, as DETENTION SITE COBALT was later found to have not reported multiple uses of sleep deprivation, required standing, loud music, sensory deprivation, extended isolation, reduced quantity and quality of food, nudity, and "rough treatment" of CIA detainees.[245]

3. CIA Headquarters Recommends That Untrained Interrogators in Country ■■ Use the CIA's Enhanced Interrogation Techniques on Ridha al-Najjar

Ridha al-Najjar was the first CIA detainee to be held at DETENTION SITE COBALT. Al-Najjar, along with Hassan Muhammad Abu Bakr and number of other individuals, was arrested in Karachi, Pakistan, after raids conducted ■■■ by ■■■■■■ Pakistan ■■■ in late May 2002.[246] Al-Najjar was identified by the CIA as a former bodyguard for Usama bin Laden,[247] and was rendered with Abu Bakr to CIA custody at a Country ■■ ■■■■■ detention facility on June ■, 2002.[248] Ridha al-Najjar was transferred to DETENTION SITE COBALT on September ■, 2002.[249]

While the CIA was describing to the Department of Justice why it needed to use the CIA's enhanced interrogation techniques against Abu Zubaydah, a parallel internal discussion at the CIA was taking place regarding Ridha al-Najjar. An ALEC Station cable from a CTC officer stated that, on June 27, 2002:

> "ALEC/HQS held a strategy session regarding the interrogation of high priority ■■■■■ detainee Ridha Ahmed al-Najjar in [Country ■ ■]. The goal of the session was to review the progress of the interrogation to date and to devise a general plan as to how best to proceed once the new [Country ■■ ■■■] detention/debriefing facility [i.e., DETENTION SITE COBALT] is completed."[250]

The meeting participants included individuals who were also involved in discussions related to Abu Zubaydah's interrogation, including deputy chief of ALEC Station, ■■■■■■■, ■■■■ CTC Legal ■■■■■■■, and the chief of the ■■■ ■■■■■■■■■■■■■■■■■■■■.[251] A cable followed on July 16, 2002, to the CIA Station in Country ■■ suggesting possible interrogation techniques to use against Ridha al-Najjar, including:

- utilizing "Najjar's fear for the well-being of his family to our benefit," with the cable explicitly stating that interrogators could not "threaten his family with imminent death";
- using "vague threats" to create a "mind virus" that would cause al-Najjar to believe that his situation would continue to get worse until he cooperated;[252]
- manipulating Ridha al-Najjar's environment using a hood, restraints, and music; and
- employing sleep deprivation through the use of round-the-clock interrogations.[253]

The cable went on to note that the "possibility that [al-Najjar] may have current threat or lead information demands that we keep up the pressure on him."[254] With the exception of a brief mention of "diminished returns from the most recent interviews of al-Najjar," and references to the detainee's complaints about physical ailments, the cable offers no evidence al-Najjar was actively resisting CIA interrogators.[255]

Ten days later, on July 26, 2002, CIA officers in Country ■■, none of whom had been trained in the use of the CIA's enhanced interrogation techniques, proposed putting al-Najjar in isolation[256] and using "sound disorientation techniques," "sense of time deprivation," limited light, cold temperatures, and sleep deprivation.[257] The CIA officers added that they felt they had a "reasonable chance of breaking Najjar" to get "the intelligence and locator lead information on UBL and Bin Ladin's family."[258] The plan for al-Najjar was circulated to senior CIA officers as part of the Daily DCI Operations Update.[259]

On August 5, 2002, the day after Abu Zubaydah's interrogation using the CIA's enhanced interrogation techniques at DETENTION SITE GREEN began, CIA Headquarters authorized the proposed interrogation plan for al-Najjar, to include the use of loud music (at less than the level that would cause physical harm such as permanent hearing loss), worse food (as long as it was nutritionally adequate for sustenance), sleep deprivation, and hooding.[260]

More than a month later, on September 21, 2002, CIA interrogators described al-Najjar as "clearly a broken man" and "on the verge of complete breakdown" as result of the isolation.[261] The cable added that al-Najjar was willing to do whatever the CIA officer asked.[262]

In October 2002, officers from the U.S. military conducted a short debriefing of al-Najjar at DETENTION SITE COBALT and subsequently expressed an interest in a more thorough debriefing.[263] On November ■, 2002, a U.S. military legal advisor visited

DETENTION SITE COBALT and described it as a "CIA detention facility," noting that "while CIA is the only user of the facility they contend it is a [Country ██████] facility."[264] The U.S. military officer also noted that the junior CIA officer designated as warden of the facility "has little to no experience with interrogating or handling prisoners." With respect to al-Najjar specifically, the legal advisor indicated that the CIA's interrogation plan included "isolation in total darkness; lowering the quality of his food; keeping him at an uncomfortable temperature (cold); [playing music] 24 hours a day; and keeping him shackled and hooded." In addition, al-Najjar was described as having been left hanging—which involved handcuffing one or both wrists to an overhead bar which would not allow him to lower his arms—for 22 hours each day for two consecutive days, in order to "'break' his resistance." It was also noted al-Najjar was wearing a diaper and had no access to toilet facilities.[265]

The U.S. military legal advisor concluded that, because of al-Najjar's treatment, and the concealment of the facility from the ICRC, military participation in al-Najjar's interrogation would involve risks for the U.S. military █████. The legal advisor recommended briefing the CIA's detention and interrogation activities to U.S. ███ ████████ [combatant command] to alert the command of the risks prior to the U.S. military ██████ being involved in any aspect of the interrogation of al-Najjar.[266] According to the CIA inspector general, the detention and interrogation of Ridha al-Najjar "became the model" for handling other CIA detainees at DETENTION SITE COBALT.[267] The CIA disseminated one intelligence report from its detention and interrogation of Ridha al-Najjar.[268]

4. Death of Gul Rahman Leads CIA Headquarters to Learn of Unreported Coercive Interrogation Techniques at DETENTION SITE COBALT; CIA Inspector General Review Reveals Lack of Oversight of the Detention Site

In November 2002, ALEC Station officers requested that CIA contract interrogator Hammond DUNBAR, one of the two primary interrogators of Abu Zubaydah in August 2002, travel to DETENTION SITE COBALT to assess a detainee for the possible use of the CIA's enhanced interrogation techniques.[269] While DUNBAR was present at DETENTION SITE COBALT, he assisted █ ████████ [CIA OFFICER I] in the interrogations of Gul Rahman, a suspected Islamic extremist. As reported to CIA Headquarters, this interrogation included "48 hours of sleep deprivation, auditory overload, total darkness, isolation, a cold shower, and rough treatment." CIA Headquarters did not approve these interrogation techniques in advance. Upon receipt of these cables, however, officers at CIA Headquarters responded that they were "motivated to extract any and all operational information on al-Qa'ida and Hezbi Islami from Gul Rahman" and suggested that "enhanced measures" might be needed to gain Gul Rahman's compliance. CIA Headquarters also requested that a psychological assessment of Rahman be completed.[270] Prior to DUNBAR's departure from the detention site on November ■■, 2002, [a few days before the death of Gul Rahman] DUNBAR proposed the use of the CIA's enhanced interrogation techniques on other detainees and offered suggestions to ■■■■■■ [CIA OFFICER 1], the site manager, on the use of such techniques.[271]

On November ■■, 2002, ■■■■■■ [CIA OFFI-CER 1] ordered that Gul Rahman be shackled to the wall of his cell in a position that required the detainee to rest on the bare concrete floor. Rahman was wearing only a sweatshirt, as ■■■■■■ [CIA OFFICER 1] had ordered that Rahman's clothing be removed when he had been judged to be uncooperative during an earlier interrogation. The next day, the guards found Gul Rahman's dead body. An internal CIA review and autopsy assessed that Rahman likely died from hypothermia—in part from having been forced to sit on the bare concrete floor without pants.[272] ■■■■■■ [CIA OFFICER 1's] initial cable to CIA Headquarters on Rahman's death included a number of misstatements and omissions that were not discovered until internal investigations into Rahman's death.[273]

The death of Gul Rahman resulted in increased attention to CIA detention and interrogation activities in Country ■■ by CIA Headquarters. The CTC formally designated the CTC's Renditions Group[274] as the responsible entity for the management and maintenance of all CIA interrogation facilities, including DETENTION SITE COBALT, in early December 2002.[275] Despite this change, many of the same individuals within the CIA—including DUNBAR, officers at DETENTION SITE COBALT, and officers within ALEC Station who had recommended the use of the CIA's enhanced interrogation techniques against Gul Rahman—remained key figures in the CIA interrogation program and received no reprimand or sanction for Rahman's death. Instead, in March 2003, just four months after the death of Gul Rahman, the CIA Station in Country ■■ recommended that ■■■■■■■■ [CIA OFFICER 1] receive a "cash award" of $2,500 for his "consistently superior work."[276] ■■

█ [CIA OFFICER 1] remained in his position as manager of the detention site until July 2003 and continued to be involved in the interrogations of other CIA detainees. He was formally certified as a CIA interrogator in April 2003 after the practical portion of his training requirement was waived because of his past experience with interrogations at DETENTION SITE COBALT.[277]

Later investigations of DETENTION SITE COBALT conducted by the CIA inspector general and the deputy director of operations following the death of Gul Rahman found that the use of the CIA's enhanced interrogation techniques—and other coercive interrogation techniques—was more widespread than was reported in contemporaneous CIA cables. Specifically, the interrogation techniques that went unreported in CIA cables included standing sleep deprivation in which a detainee's arms were shackled above his head, nudity, dietary manipulation, exposure to cold temperatures, cold showers, "rough takedowns," and, in at least two instances, the use of mock executions.[278]

On November 18, 2002, the CIA's Office of Inspector General contacted █ CTC Legal, █, to indicate their interest in being briefed by CTC on the detention facility in Country █. At their meeting with the DDO and the chief of CTC on November █, 2002, the OIG staff explained that, while in that country on a separate matter, the staff had overheard a conversation that included references to "war crimes" and "torture" at a CIA detention facility and were therefore seeking to follow-up on this information. According to notes from the meeting, the DDO described the "most recent event concerning Gul Rahman"—his death, which occurred on November █, 2002.[279]

In January 2003, CIA Inspector General John Helgerson began a formal review of the death of Gul Rahman and began a separate review of the entire CIA Detention and Interrogation Program. The resulting Special Review of Counterterrorism Detention and Interrogation Activities ("Special Review") found that there were no guidelines for the use of the CIA's enhanced interrogation techniques at DETENTION SITE COBALT prior to December 2002, and that interrogators, some with little or no training, were "left to their own devices in working with detainees."[280]

The Inspector General's Special Review also revealed the lack of oversight of DETENTION SITE COBALT by CIA leadership. DCI Tenet stated that he was "not very familiar" with DETENTION SITE COBALT and "what the CIA is doing with medium value targets."[281] Associate Deputy Director of Operations ████ ████ stated that he was unaware that the CIA's enhanced interrogation techniques were being used there.[282] In August 2003, CIA General Counsel Scott Muller relayed that he was under the impression that DETENTION SITE COBALT was only a holding facility and that he had "no idea who is responsible for [COBALT]."[283] Senior Deputy General Counsel John Rizzo informed the OIG that he knew little about DETENTION SITE COBALT and that his focus was on DETENTION SITE GREEN and DETENTION SITE BLUE.[284] CTC Chief of Operations ██████████ stated that he had much less knowledge of operations at DETENTION SITE COBALT, and that the CIA's GREEN and BLUE detention sites were much more important to him.[285] Finally, Chief of CTC Jose Rodriguez stated that he did not focus on DETENTION SITE COBALT because he had "other higher priorities."[286]

5. The CIA Begins Training New Interrogators; Interrogation Techniques Not Reviewed by the Department of Justice Included in the Training Syllabus

The CIA's CTC Renditions Group began preparing for the first CIA interrogator training course in August 2002—during the period in which Abu Zubaydah was being interrogated using the CIA's enhanced interrogation techniques at DETENTION SITE GREEN. ██████, the CIA's chief of interrogations,[287] and ███████ ██, the CIA officer with OTS who had spent ██ years as a SERE Instructor with JPRA, led the interrogation training. The first interrogation training, conducted with the assistance of JPRA personnel, occurred from November 12, 2002, to November 18, 2002.[288] The class included eight students who were seeking to become CIA interrogators and three students seeking to support the CIA interrogation process.[289] The CIA training program involved 65 hours of instruction and training on the CIA's enhanced interrogation techniques, including at least two interrogation techniques whose legality had not been evaluated by the Department of Justice: the "abdominal slap" and the "finger press." Although a number of personnel at CIA Headquarters reviewed the training materials, there are no CIA records of any CIA officer raising objections to the techniques being included in the syllabus.[290]

6. Despite Recommendation from CIA Attorneys, the CIA Fails to

Adequately Screen Potential Interrogators in 2002 and 2003

On November ■, 2002, after the completion of the first formal training class, ■■■■■■ CTC Legal, ■■■■■■■■■■, asked CTC attorney ■■■■ ■■■■■ to "[m]ake it known that from now on, CTC/LGL must vet all personnel who are enrolled in, observing or teaching—or otherwise associated with—the class."[291] ■■■■■■ ■ added:

> "Moreover, we will be forced to DISapprove [*sic*] the participation of specific personnel in the use of enhanced techniques unless we have ourselves vetted them and are satisfied with their qualifications and suitability for what are clearly unusual measures that are lawful only when practiced correctly by personnel whose records clearly demonstrate their suitability for that role. The vetting process will not be that dissimilar from the checks that are provided by the OIG, OS, etc. in certain cases before individuals are promoted or receive awards, and the selection and training of aggressive interrogators certainly warrants a similar vetting process."[292]

The chief of CTC, Jose Rodriguez, objected to this approach, stating:

> "I do not think that CTC/LGL should or would want to get into the business of vetting participants, observers, instructors or others that are involved in this program. It is simply not your job. Your job is to tell all what are the acceptable legal standards for conducting interrogations per the authorities obtained from Justice and agreed upon by the White House."[293]

Contrary to statements later made by CIA Director Michael Hayden and other CIA officials that "[a]ll those involved in the questioning of detainees are carefully chosen and screened for demonstrated professional judgment and maturity,"[294] CIA records suggest that the vetting sought by ■■■■■■ did not take place. The Committee reviewed CIA records related to several CIA officers and contractors involved in the CIA's Detention and Interrogation Program, most of whom conducted interrogations. The Committee identified a number of personnel whose backgrounds include notable derogatory information calling into question their eligibility for employment, their access to classified information, and their participation in CIA interrogation activities. In nearly all cases, the derogatory information was known to the CIA prior to the assignment of the CIA officers to the Detention and Interrogation Program. This group of officers included individuals who, among other issues, had engaged in inappropriate detainee interrogations, had workplace anger management issues, and had reportedly admitted to sexual assault.[295]

7. Bureau of Prisons "WOW'ed" by Level of Deprivation at CIA's COBALT Detention Site

In December 2002, the CIA's Renditions Group sent a team of recently trained interrogators to DETENTION SITE COBALT to engage in interrogations. The interrogation plans proposed by that team for at least three detainees at DETENTION SITE COBALT included the use of interrupted sleep, loud music, and reduction in food quality and quantity. Less than a month after the death of Gul Rahman from suspected hypothermia, the plans also called for detainees' clothes to be removed in a facility that was described to be 45 degrees Fahrenheit. CIA Headquarters approved the proposals for these detainees, whom the CIA described as "Medium Value."[296]

Prior to this, in November 2002, a delegation of several officers from the Federal Bureau of Prisons conducted an assessment of DETENTION SITE COBALT. Following the November ■■, 2002, through November ■■, 2002, visit,[297] CIA officers in Country ■■ remarked that the Federal Bureau of Prisons assessments, along with recommendations and training, had "made a noticeable improvement on how the day to day operations at the facility are performed," and made the detention site a "more secure and safer working environment for ■■■■■■■■■■■■■■■■ officers."[298]

On December 4, 2002, officers at CIA Headquarters met with individuals from the Federal Bureau of Prisons to learn more about their inspection of DETENTION SITE COBALT and their training of ■■■■■■ security staff.[299] During that meeting, the Federal Bureau of Prisons personnel described DETENTION SITE COBALT and stated that there was "absolutely no talking inside the facility," that the guards do not interact with the prisoners, and that "[e]verything is done in silence and [in] the dark."[300] According to a CIA officer, the Federal Bureau of Prisons staff also commented that "they were 'WOW'ed'" at first by the facility, because:

> "They have never been in a facility where individuals are so sensory deprived, i.e., constant white noise, no talking, everyone in the dark, with the guards wearing a light on their head when they collected and escorted a detainee to an interrogation cell, detainees constantly being shackled to the wall or floor, and the starkness of each cell (concrete and bars). There is nothing like this in the Federal Bureau of Prisons. They then explained that they understood the mission and it was their collective assessment that in spite of all this sensory deprivation, the detainees were not being treated in humanely [*sic*]. They explained that the facility was sanitary, there was medical care and the guard force and our staff did not mistreat the detainee[s]."[301]

By the end of December 2002, the CIA Renditions Group that had visited DETENTION SITE COBALT had concluded that the detention facility's initial "baseline conditions" involved so much deprivation that any further deprivation would have limited impact on the interrogations. The team thus recommended that "experts and authorities other than the individuals who crafted the process" review the interrogation process and conditions, and that a legal review be conducted.[302] CIA Headquarters does not appear to have taken action on these recommendations.

8. The Places CIA Detainees in Country ███ Facilities Because They Did Not Meet the MON Standard for Detention

In the spring of 2003, the CIA continued to hold detainees at facilities in Country ███ who were known not to meet the MON standard for detention. CIA officer ██████████ [CIA OFFICER 1] described the arrangement he had with Country ███ officers in an email, writing:

> "██
> ███ They also happen to have 3 or 4 rooms where they can lock up people discretely [*sic*]. I give them a few hundred bucks a month and they use the rooms for whoever I bring over - no questions asked. It is very useful for housing guys that shouldn't be in [DETENTION SITE COBALT] for one reason or another but still need to be kept isolated and held in secret detention."[303]

CIA cables indicate that CIA officers transferred at least four detainees to these Country ███ facilities because they did not meet the standard for CIA detention under the MON.[304]

In total, four CIA detention facilities were established in Country ███. CIA records indicate that DETENTION SITE COBALT held a total of 64 detainees during the period of its operation between September 2002 and █████ 2004, while DETENTION SITE GRAY held eight detainees between ████████ 2003 and █████████ 2003. The CIA later established two other CIA facilities in Country ███: DETENTION SITE ORANGE, which held 34 detainees between █████ 2004 and ███████ 2006; and DETENTION SITE BROWN, which held 12 detainees between █████ 2006 and 2008.[305]

9. DCI Tenet Establishes First Guidelines on Detention Conditions and Interrogation; Formal Consolidation of Program Administration at CIA Headquarters Does Not Resolve Disagreements Among CIA Personnel

In late January 2003, in response to the death of CIA detainee Gul Rahman and the use of a gun and a drill in the CIA interrogations of 'Abd al-Rahim al-Nashiri (described later in this summary), DCI Tenet signed the first formal interrogation and confinement guidelines for the program.[306] In contrast to proposals from late 2001, when CIA personnel expected that any detention facility would have to meet U.S. prison standards, the confinement guidelines signed in January 2003 set forth minimal standards for a detention facility. The confinement guidelines required only that the facility be sufficient to meet basic health needs, meaning that even a facility like DETENTION SITE COBALT, in which detainees were kept shackled in complete darkness and isolation, with a bucket for human waste, and without notable heat during the winter months, met the standard.[307]

The guidelines also required quarterly assessments of the conditions at the detention facilities. The first quarterly review of detention facilities covered the period from January 2003 to April 2003, and examined conditions at DETENTION SITE COBALT, as well as at DETENTION SITE BLUE in a different country, Country ■.[308] At that time, DETENTION SITE BLUE, which was initially designed for two detainees, was housing five detainees. Nonetheless, the site review team found that conditions at DETENTION SITE BLUE—including the three purpose-built "holding units"—met "the minimum standards set by the CIA" in the January 2003 guidance. Detainees received bi-weekly medical evaluations, brushed their teeth once a day, washed their hands prior to each meal, and could bathe once a week. Amenities such as solid food, clothing (sweatshirts, sweatpants, and slippers), reading materials, prayer rugs, and Korans were available depending on the detainee's degree of cooperation with interrogators.[309]

The first quarter 2003 review also found that conditions at DETENTION SITE COBALT satisfied the January 2003 guidance, citing "significant improvements" such as space heaters and weekly medical evaluations. The review noted that a new facility was under construction in Country ■ to replace DETENTION SITE COBALT, and that this new detention facility, DETENTION SITE ORANGE, "will be a quantum leap forward" because "[it] will incorporate heating/air conditioning, conventional plumbing, appropriate lighting, shower, and laundry facilities."[310] DETENTION SITE ORANGE opened in ■■■ 2004. Although some of the cells at DETENTION SITE ORANGE included plumbing, detainees undergoing interrogation were kept in smaller cells, with waste buckets rather than toilet facilities.[311]

The DCI's January 2003 interrogation guidelines listed 12 "enhanced techniques" that could be used with prior approval of the director of CTC, including two—use of diapers for "prolonged periods" and the abdominal slap—that had not been evaluated by the OLC. The "enhanced techniques" were only to be employed by "approved interrogators for use with [a] specific detainee." The guidelines also identified "standard techniques"—including sleep deprivation up to 72 hours, reduced caloric intake, use of loud music, isolation, and the use of diapers "generally not to exceed 72 hours"—that required advance approval "whenever feasible," and directed that their use be documented. The "standard techniques" were described as "techniques that do not incorporate physical or substantial psychological pressure." The guidelines provided no description or further limitations on the use of either the enhanced or standard interrogation techniques.[312]

Although the DCI interrogation guidelines were prepared as a reaction to the death of Gul Rahman and the use of unauthorized interrogation techniques on 'Abd al-Rahim al-Nashiri, they did not reference all interrogation practices that had been employed at CIA detention sites. The guidelines, for example, did not address whether interrogation techniques such as the "rough take down,"[313] the use of cold water showers,[314] and prolonged light deprivation were prohibited. In addition, by requiring advance approval of "standard techniques" "whenever feasible," the guidelines allowed CIA officers a significant amount of discretion to determine who could be subjected to the CIA's "standard" interrogation techniques, when those techniques could be applied, and when it was not "feasible" to request advance approval from CIA Headquarters. Thus, consistent with the interrogation guidelines, throughout much of 2003, CIA officers (including personnel not trained in interrogation) could, at their discretion, strip a detainee naked, shackle him in the standing position for up to 72 hours, and douse the detainee repeatedly with cold water[315]—without approval from CIA Headquarters if those officers judged CIA Headquarters approval was not "feasible." In practice, CIA personnel routinely applied these types of interrogation techniques without obtaining prior approval.[316]

The DCI interrogation guidelines also included the first requirements related to recordkeeping, instructing that, for "each interrogation session in which an enhanced technique is employed," the field prepare a "substantially contemporaneous record . . . setting forth the nature and duration of each such technique employed, the identities of those present, and a citation to the required Headquarters approval cable."[317] In practice, these guidelines were not followed.[318]

There were also administrative changes to the program. As noted, on December 3, 2002, CTC's Renditions Group formally assumed responsibility for the management and maintenance of all CIA detention and interrogation facilities.[319] Prior to that time, the interrogation program was "joined at the hip" with CTC's ALEC Station, according to ██████ CTC Legal, although another CTC attorney who was directly involved in the program informed the CIA OIG that she "was never sure what group in CTC was responsible for interrogation activities."[320] Even after the formal designation of the CIA's Renditions Group,[321] tensions continued, particularly between CTC personnel who supported SWIGERT and DUNBAR's continued role, and the Renditions Group, which designated ████ ██ as the CIA's chief interrogator.[322] As late as June 2003, SWIGERT and DUNBAR, operating outside of the direct management of the Renditions Group, were deployed to DETENTION SITE BLUE to both interrogate and conduct psychological reviews of detainees.[323] The dispute extended to interrogation practices. The Renditions Group's leadership considered the waterboard, which Chief of Interrogations ██████ was not certified to use, as "life threatening," and complained to the OIG that some CIA officers in the Directorate of Operations believed that, as a result, the Renditions Group was "running a 'sissified' interrogation program."[324] At the same time, CIA CTC personnel criticized the Renditions Group and ████ for their use of painful stress positions, as well as for the conditions at DETENTION SITE COBALT.[325]

There were also concerns about possible conflicts of interest related to the contractors, SWIGERT and DUNBAR. On January 30, 2003, a cable from CIA Headquarters stated that "the individual at the interrogation site who administers the techniques is not the same person who issues the psychological assessment of record," and that "only a staff psychologist, not a contractor, could issue an assessment of record."[326] In June 2003, however, SWIGERT and DUNBAR were deployed to DETENTION SITE BLUE to interrogate KSM, as well as to assess KSM's "psychological stability" and "resistance posture."[327] As described later in this summary, the contractors had earlier subjected KSM to the waterboard and other CIA enhanced interrogation techniques. The decision to send the contract psychologists to DETENTION SITE BLUE prompted an OMS psychologist to write to OMS leadership that "[a]ny data collected by them from detainees with whom they previously interacted as interrogators will always be suspect."[328] OMS then informed the management of the Renditions Group that "no professional in the field would credit [SWIGERT and DUNBAR's] later judgments as psychologists assessing the subjects of their enhanced measures."[329] At the end of their deployment, in June 2003, SWIGERT and DUNBAR provided their assessment of KSM and recommended that he should be evaluated on a monthly basis by "an experienced interrogator known to him" who would assess how forthcoming he is and "remind him that there are differing consequences for cooperating or not cooperating."[330] In his response to the draft Inspector General Special Review, OMS noted that "OMS concerns about conflict of interest . . . were nowhere more graphic than in the setting in which the same individuals applied an EIT which only they were approved to employ, judged both its effectiveness and detainee resilience, and implicitly proposed continued use of the technique—at a daily compensation reported to be $1800/day, or four times that of interrogators who could not use the technique."[331]

D. The Detention and Interrogation of 'Abd al-Rahim al-Nashiri

7. CIA Interrogators Disagree with CIA Headquarters About Al-Nashiri's Level of Cooperation; Interrogators Oppose Continued Use of the CIA's Enhanced Interrogation Techniques

'Abd al-Rahim al-Nashiri,[332] assessed by the CIA to be an al-Qa'ida "terrorist operations planner" who was "intimately involved" in planning both the *USS Cole* bombing and the 1998 East Africa U.S. Embassy bombings, was captured in the United Arab Emirates in mid-October 2002.[333] He provided information while in the custody of a foreign government, including on plotting in the Persian Gulf,[334] and was then rendered by the CIA to DETENTION SITE COBALT in Country on November , 2002, where he was held for days before being transferred to DETENTION SITE GREEN on November , 2002.[335] At DETENTION SITE GREEN, al-Nashiri was interrogated using the CIA's enhanced interrogation techniques, including being subjected to the waterboard at least three times.[336] In December 2002, when DETENTION SITE GREEN was closed, al-Nashiri and Abu Zubaydah were rendered to DETENTION SITE BLUE.[337]

In total, al-Nashiri was subjected to the CIA's enhanced interrogation techniques during at least four separate periods, with each period typically ending with an assessment from on-site interrogators that al-Nashiri was compliant and cooperative.[338] Officers at CIA Headquarters disagreed with these assessments, with the deputy chief of ALEC Station, [redacted], commenting that DETENTION SITE BLUE interrogators should not make "sweeping statements" in cable traffic regarding al-Nashiri's compliance.[339] Officers at CIA Headquarters sought to reinstate the use of the CIA's enhanced interrogation techniques based on their belief that al-Nashiri had not yet provided actionable intelligence on imminent attacks.[340]

Shortly after al-Nashiri arrived at DETENTION SITE BLUE, CIA interrogators at the detention site judged al-Nashiri's cooperation and compliance by his engagement and willingness to answer questions, while CIA Headquarters personnel judged his compliance based on the specific actionable intelligence he had provided (or the lack thereof). For example, in December 2002, interrogators informed CIA Headquarters that al-Nashiri was "cooperative and truthful," and that the "consensus" at the detention site was that al-Nashiri was "a compliant detainee" who was not "withholding important threat information."[341] Officers from the CIA's ALEC Station at CIA Headquarters responded:

> "it is inconceivable to us that al-Nashiri cannot provide us concrete leads . . . When we are able to capture other terrorists based on his leads and to thwart future plots based on his reporting, we will have much more confidence that he is, indeed, genuinely cooperative on some level."[342]

Later, after multiple follow-up debriefings, DETENTION SITE BLUE officers again wrote that they had "reluctantly concluded" that al-Nashiri was providing "logical and rational explanations" to questions provided by CIA Headquarters and therefore they recommended "against resuming enhanced measures" unless ALEC Station had evidence al-Nashiri was lying.[343] A cable from the detention site stated:

> "without tangible proof of lying or intentional withholding, however, we believe employing enhanced measures will accomplish nothing except show [al-Nashiri] that he will be punished whether he cooperates or not, thus eroding any remaining desire to continue cooperating . . . [The] bottom line is that we think [al-Nashiri] is being cooperative, and if subjected to indiscriminate and prolonged enhanced measures, there is a good chance he will either fold up and cease cooperation, or suffer the

sort of permanent mental harm prohibited by the statute. Therefore, a decision to resume enhanced measures must be grounded in fact and not general feelings."[344]

2. CIA Headquarters Sends Untrained Interrogator to Resume Al-Nashiri's Interrogations; Interrogator Threatens al-Nashiri with a Gun and a Drill

After the DETENTION SITE BLUE chief of Base sent two interrogators back to the United States because of "prolonged absences from family" and the "fact that enhanced measures are no longer required for al-Nashiri," CIA Headquarters sent ████████ [CIA OFFICER 2], a CIA ██ officer who had not been trained or qualified as an interrogator, to DETENTION SITE BLUE to question and assess al-Nashiri.[345]

In late December 2002, following a meeting at CIA Headquarters to discuss resuming the use of the CIA's enhanced interrogation techniques against al-Nashiri, ████████, the chief of RDG[346]—the entity that managed the CIA's Detention and Interrogation Program—objected to sending ██████ [CIA OFFICER 2] to the detention site because he "had not been through the interrogation training" and because ██████ "had heard from some colleagues that [█████ [CIA OFFICER 2]] was too confident, had a temper, and had some security issues." █████ later learned from other CIA officials that "[CTC chief of operations ████████] wanted [██████ [CIA OFFICER 2]] at [DETENTION SITE BLUE] over the holidays." █████ told the Office of Inspector General that "his assessment is that the Agency management felt that the [RDG] interrogators were being too lenient with al-Nashiri and that [█████ [CIA OFFICER 2]] was sent to [DETENTION SITE BLUE] to 'fix' the situation."[347]

██████ [CIA OFFICER 2] arrived at DETENTION SITE BLUE on December ██, 2002, and the CIA resumed the use of its enhanced interrogation techniques on al-Nashiri shortly thereafter, despite the fact that ██████ [CIA OFFICER 2] had not been trained, certified, or approved to use the CIA's enhanced interrogation techniques. ██████ [CIA OFFICER 2] wrote in a cable to CIA Headquarters that "[al]-Nashiri responds well to harsh treatment" and suggested that the interrogators continue to administer "various degrees of mild punishment," but still allow for "a small degree of 'hope,' by introducing some 'minute rewards.'"[348]

It was later learned that during these interrogation sessions, ■ ■■■■■■ [CIA OFFICER 2], with the permission and participation of the DETENTION SITE BLUE chief of Base, who also had not been trained and qualified as an interrogator, used a series of unauthorized interrogation techniques against al-Nashiri. For example, ■ ■■■■■■ [CIA OFFICER 2] placed al-Nashiri in a "standing stress position" with "his hands affixed over his head" for approximately two and a half days.[349] Later, during the course of al-Nashiri's debriefings, while he was blindfolded, ■■■■■■ [CIA OFFICER 2] placed a pistol near al-Nashiri's head and operated a cordless drill near al-Nashiri's body.[350] Al-Nashiri did not provide any additional threat information during, or after, these interrogations.[351]

Based on a report from CTC, the CIA Office of Inspector General conducted a review of these interrogation incidents, and issued a report of investigation in the fall of 2003.[352] The Office of Inspector General later described additional allegations of unauthorized techniques used against al-Nashiri by ■■■■■■ [CIA OFFICER 2] and other interrogators, including slapping al-Nashiri multiple times on the back of the head during interrogations; implying that his mother would be brought before him and sexually abused; blowing cigar smoke in al-Nashiri's face; giving al-Nashiri a forced bath using a stiff brush; and using improvised stress positions that caused cuts and bruises resulting in the intervention of a medical officer, who was concerned that al-Nashiri's shoulders would be dislocated using the stress positions.[353] When interviewed by the Office of Inspector General, the DETENTION SITE BLUE chief of Base stated he did not object to using the gun and drill in the interrogations because he believed ■■■■■■ [CIA OFFICER 2] was sent from CIA Headquarters "to resolve the matter of al-Nashiri's cooperation" and that he believed ■■■■■■ [CIA OFFICER 2] had permission to use the interrogation techniques.[354] The chief of Base added that his own on-site approval was based on this and "the pressure he felt from Headquarters to obtain imminent threat information from al-Nashiri on 9/11-style attacks."[355] In April 2004, ■■■■■■ [CIA OFFICER 2] and the chief of Base were disciplined.[356]

3. CIA Contractor Recommends Continued Use of the CIA's Enhanced Interrogation Techniques Against Al-Nashiri; Chief Interrogator Threatens to Quit Because Additional Techniques Might "Push [Al-Nashiri] Over The Edge Psychologically," Refers to the CIA Program as a "Train Wreak [sic] Waiting to Happen"

On January ██, 2003, CIA contractor DUNBAR arrived at DETENTION SITE BLUE to conduct a "Psychological Interrogation Assessment" to judge al-Nashiri's suitability for the additional use of the CIA's enhanced interrogation techniques and develop recommendations for his interrogation. The resulting interrogation plan proposed that the interrogators would have the "latitude to use the full range of enhanced exploitation and interrogation measures," adding that "the use of the water board would require additional support from" fellow CIA contractor Grayson SWIGERT. According to the interrogation plan, once the interrogators had eliminated al-Nashiri's "sense of control and predictability" and established a "desired level of helplessness," they would reduce the use of the CIA's enhanced interrogation techniques and transition to a debriefing phase once again.[357]

After receiving the proposed interrogation plan for al-Nashiri on January 21, 2003, ██████, the CIA's chief of interrogations—whose presence had previously prompted al-Nashiri to tremble in fear[358]—emailed CIA colleagues to notify them that he had "informed the front office of CTC" that he would "no longer be associated in any way with the interrogation program due to serious reservation[s] [he had] about the current state of affairs" and would instead be "retiring shortly." In the same email, █████ wrote, "[t]his is a train wreak [*sic*] waiting to happen and I intend to get the hell off the train before it happens."[359] █████ drafted a cable for CIA Headquarters to send to DETENTION SITE BLUE raising a number of concerns that he, the chief of interrogations, believed should be "entered for the record." The CIA Headquarters cable—which does not appear to have been disseminated to DETENTION SITE BLUE—included the following:

> "we have serious reservations with the continued use of enhanced techniques with [al-Nashiri] and its long term impact on him. [Al-Nashiri] has been held for three months in very difficult conditions, both physically and mentally. It is the assessment of the prior interrogators that [al-Nashiri] has been mainly truthful and is not withholding significant information. To continue to use enhanced technique[s] without clear indications that he [is] withholding important info is excessive and may cause him to cease cooperation on any level. [Al-Nashiri] may come to the conclusion that whether he cooperates or not, he will continually be subjected to enhanced techniques, therefore, what is the incentive for continued cooperation. Also, both C/CTC/RG [Chief of CTC RDG ██████████████] and HVT Interrogator [████ ███] who departed [DETENTION SITE BLUE] in ██ January, believe continued enhanced methods may push [al-Nashiri] over the edge psychologically."[360]

The draft cable from ███ also raised "conflict of responsibility" concerns, stating:

> Another area of concern is the use of the psychologist as an interrogator. The role of the ops psychologist is to be a detached observer and serve as a check on the interrogator to prevent the interrogator from any unintentional excess of pressure which might cause permanent psychological harm to the subject. The medical officer is on hand to provide the same protection from physical actions that might harm the subject. Therefore, the medical officer and the psychologist should not serve as an interrogator, which is a conflict of responsibility. We note that [the proposed plan] contains a psychological interrogation assessment by █ ███ psychologist [DUNBAR] which is to be carried out by interrogator [DUNBAR]. We have a problem with him conducting both roles simultaneously."[361]

Rather than releasing the cable that was drafted by ███, CIA Headquarters approved a plan to reinstitute the use of the CIA's enhanced interrogation techniques against al-Nashiri, beginning with shaving him, removing his clothing, and placing him in a standing sleep deprivation position with his arms affixed over his head.[362] CIA cables describing subsequent interrogations indicate that al-Nashiri was nude and, at times, "put in the standing position, handcuffed and shackled."[363] According to cables, CIA interrogators decided to provide al-Nashiri clothes to "hopefully stabilize his physiological symptoms and prevent them from deteriorating,"[364] noting in a cable the next day that al-Nashiri was suffering from a head cold which caused his body to shake for approximately ten minutes during an interrogation.[365]

Beginning in June 2003, the CIA transferred al-Nashiri to five different CIA detention facilities before he was transferred to U.S. military custody on September 5, 2006.[366] In the interim, he was diagnosed by some CIA psychologists as having "anxiety" and "major depressive" disorder,[367] while others found no symptoms of either illness.[368] He was a difficult and uncooperative detainee and engaged in repeated belligerent acts, including attempts to assault CIA detention site personnel and efforts to damage items in his cell.[369] Over a period of years, al-Nashiri accused the CIA staff of drugging or poisoning his food, and complained of bodily pain and insomnia.[370] At one point, al-Nashiri launched a short-lived hunger strike that resulted in the CIA force feeding him rectally.[371]

In October 2004, 21 months after the final documented use of the CIA's enhanced interrogation techniques against al-Nashiri, an assessment by CIA contract interrogator DUNBAR and another CIA interrogator concluded that al-Nashiri provided "essentially no actionable information," and that "the probability that he has much more to contribute is low."[372] Over the course of al-Nashiri's detention and interrogation by the CIA, the CIA disseminated 145 intelligence reports based on his debriefings. Al-Nashiri provided information on past operational plotting, associates whom he expected to participate in plots, details on completed operations, and background on al-Qa'ida's structure and methods of operation.[373] Al-Nashiri did not provide the information that the CIA's ALEC Station sought and believed al-Nashiri possessed, specifically "perishable threat information to help [CIA] thwart future attacks and capture additional operatives."[374]

E. Tensions with Country ██ Relating to the CIA Detention Facility and the Arrival of New Detainees

According to CIA records, three weeks after ██████████ and political leadership of Country ██ agreed to host a CIA detention facility, the CIA informed the U.S. ambassador, because, as was noted in a cable, by not doing so, the CIA was "risking that he hear of this initiative" from Country ██ officials.[375] As was the case in other host countries, the ambassador in Country ██ was told by the CIA not to speak with any other State Department official about the arrangement.[376]

Prior to the opening of the CIA detention facility in Country ██, █████ CTC Legal, ███████, warned of possible legal actions against CIA employees in countries that "take a different view of the detention and interrogation practices employed by [the CIA]."[377] He further recommended the establishment of CIA facilities in countries that ████████████████ ██.[378] █████'s advice was not heeded and, in December 2002, the two individuals then being detained by the CIA in Country ██ (Abu Zubaydah and 'Abd al-Rahim al-Nashiri) were transferred to Country ██.[379]

The agreement to host a CIA detention facility in Country ██ created multiple, ongoing difficulties between Country ██ and the CIA. Country ██'s █████ proposed a written "Memorandum of Understanding" covering the relative roles and responsibilities of the CIA and ███████, which the CIA ultimately refused to sign.[380] Four months after the detention site began hosting CIA detainees, Country ██ rejected the transfer of ██████ ██, which included Khalid Shaykh Muhammad. The decision was

reversed only after the U.S. ambassador intervened with the political leadership of Country ██ on the CIA's behalf.[381] The following month, the CIA provided $██ million to Country ██'s ███████ █[382] after which ████████ officials, speaking for ██████ Country ██ political leadership, indicated that Country ██ was now flexible with regard to the number of CIA detainees at the facility and when the facility would eventually be closed.[383] The facility, which was described by the CIA as "over capacity," was nonetheless closed, as had been previously agreed, in ███████ [the fall of] 2003.[384]

According to CIA cables, years later, ████████ officials in Country █ reacted with "deep shock and regret" ██████████ ████████ which they acknowledged was "████████████ ████."[385] ████████████████████ [Country ██] officials were "extremely upset"[386] at the CIA's inability to keep secrets and were "deeply disappointed" in not having had more warning of President Bush's September 2006 public acknowledgment of the CIA program.[387] The CIA Station, for its part, described the ██████████ █████ as a "serious blow" to the bilateral relationship.[388]

F. The Detention and Interrogation of Ramzi Bin Al-Shibh

1. Ramzi Bin Al-Shibh Provides Information While in Foreign Government Custody, Prior to Rendition to CIA Custody

As early as September 15, 2001, Ramzi bin al-Shibh was assessed by the CIA to be a facilitator for the September 11, 2001, attacks and an associate of the 9/11 hijackers.[389] While targeting another terrorist, Hassan Ghul, ██████ Pakistani officials unexpectedly captured bin al-Shibh during raids in Pakistan on September 11, 2002.[390] On September ██, 2002, bin al-Shibh was rendered to a foreign government, ███████.[391] Approximately five months later, on February █, 2003, bin al-Shibh was rendered from the custody of ███████ to CIA custody, becoming the 41st CIA detainee.[392]

As with Abu Zubaydah and 'Abd al-Rahim al-Nashiri, personnel at CIA Headquarters—often in ALEC Station—overestimated the information bin al-Shibh would have access to within al-Qa'ida, writing that bin al-Shibh "likely has critical information on upcoming attacks and locations of senior al-Qa'ida operatives."[393] Later, after bin al-Shibh was interrogated using the CIA's enhanced interrogation techniques for an estimated 34 days, the CIA's ALEC Station concluded that bin al-Shibh was not a senior member of al-Qa'ida and was not in a position to know details about al-Qa'ida's plans for future attacks.[394] In another parallel, officers at CIA Headquarters requested and directed the continued use of the CIA's enhanced interrogation techniques against bin al-Shibh when CIA detention site personnel recommended ending such measures.[395]

Ramzi bin al-Shibh was initially interrogated by a foreign government.[396] While officers at CIA Headquarters were dissatisfied with the intelligence production from his five months of detention in foreign government custody, CIA officers in that country were satisfied with bin al-Shibh's reporting.[397] Those CIA officers wrote that bin al-Shibh had provided information used in approximately 50 CIA intelligence reports, including information on potential future threats, to include a potential attack on London's Heathrow Airport and al-Nashiri's planning for potential operations in the Arabian Peninsula. The CIA officers ████ [in-country] also noted that they found bin al-Shibh's information to be generally accurate and that they "found few cases where he openly/clearly misstated facts."[398] In a cable to CIA Headquarters, the CIA officers in █████ [the country where Ramzi bin al-Shibh was being held] concluded, "overall, he provided what was needed." The same cable stated that bin al-Shibh's interrogation was similar to other interrogations they had participated in, and that the most effective interrogation tool was having information available to confront him when he tried to mislead or provide incomplete information.[399] Personnel at CIA Headquarters concluded in 2005 that the most significant intelligence derived from bin al-Shibh was obtained during his detention in foreign government custody, which was prior to his rendition to CIA custody and the use of the CIA's enhanced interrogation techniques.[400]

2. Interrogation Plan for Ramzi Bin Al-Shibh Proposes Immediate Use of Nudity and Shackling with Hands Above the Head; Plan Becomes Template for Future Detainees

Despite the aforementioned assessments from CIA officers in ████ ██ concerning bin al-Shibh's cooperation, officers at CIA Headquarters decided the CIA should obtain ████ custody of bin al-Shibh and render him to DETENTION SITE BLUE in Country ██.[401] On February █, 2003, in anticipation of bin al-Shibh's arrival, interrogators at the detention site, led by the CIA's chief interrogator, ███ █████, prepared an interrogation plan for bin al-Shibh.[402] The plan became a template, and subsequent requests to CIA Headquarters to use the CIA's enhanced interrogation techniques against other detainees relied upon near identical language.[403]

The interrogation plan proposed that immediately following the psychological and medical assessments conducted upon his arrival, bin al-Shibh would be subjected to "sensory dislocation."[404] The proposed sensory dislocation included shaving bin al-Shibh's head and face, exposing him to loud noise in a white room with white lights, keeping him "unclothed and subjected to uncomfortably cool temperatures," and shackling him "hand and foot with arms outstretched over his head (with his feet firmly on the floor and not allowed to support his weight with his arms)."[405] Contrary to CIA representations made later to the Committee that detainees were always offered the opportunity to cooperate before being subjected to the CIA's enhanced interrogation techniques, the plan stated that bin al-Shibh would be shackled nude with his arms overhead in a cold room prior to any discussion with interrogators or any assessment of his level of cooperation.[406] According to a cable, only after the interrogators determined that his "initial resistance level [had] been diminished by the conditions" would the questioning and interrogation phase begin.[407]

The interrogation phase described in the plan included near constant interrogations, as well as continued sensory deprivation, a liquid diet, and sleep deprivation. In addition, the interrogation plan stated that the CIA's enhanced interrogation techniques would be used, including the "attention grasp, walling, the facial hold, the facial slap . . . the abdominal slap, cramped confinement, wall standing, stress positions, sleep deprivation beyond 72 hours, and the waterboard, as appropriate to [bin al-Shibh's] level of resistance."[408]

Based on versions of this interrogation plan, at least six detainees were stripped and shackled nude, placed in the standing position for sleep deprivation, or subjected to other CIA enhanced interrogation techniques prior to being questioned by an interrogator in 2003.[409] Five of these detainees were shackled naked in the standing position with their hands above their head immediately after their medical check.[410] These interrogation plans typically made no reference to the information the interrogators sought and why the detainee was believed to possess the information.[411]

3. CIA Headquarters Urges Continued Use of the CIA's Enhanced Interrogation Techniques, Despite Interrogators' Assessment That Ramzi Bin Al-Shibh Was Cooperative

When CIA interrogators at DETENTION SITE BLUE assessed that bin al-Shibh was cooperative and did not have additional knowledge of future attacks,[412] CIA Headquarters disagreed and instructed the interrogators to continue using the CIA's enhanced interrogation techniques, which failed to elicit the information sought by CIA Headquarters.[413] On February 11, 2003, interrogators asked CIA Headquarters for questions that ALEC Station was "85 percent certain [bin al-Shibh] will be able to answer," in order to verify bin al-Shibh's level of cooperation.[414] The interrogators stated that information from Abu Zubaydah and al-Nashiri suggested that bin al-Shibh would not have been given a new assignment or trusted with significant information given his high-profile links to the September 11, 2001, attacks.[415] They further stated that bin al-Shibh had "achieved substantial notoriety after 11 September," but was still unproven in al-Qa'ida circles and may have "been privy to information more as a bystander than as an active participant."[416]

The CIA's ALEC Station disagreed with the assessment of the detention site personnel, responding that it did not believe the portrayals of bin al-Shibh offered by Abu Zubaydah and al-Nashiri were accurate and that CIA Headquarters assessed that bin al-Shibh must have actionable information due to his proximity to KSM and CIA Headquarters' belief that bin al-Shibh had a history of withholding information from interrogators. ALEC Station wrote:

> "As base [DETENTION SITE BLUE] is well aware, Ramzi had long been deliberately withholding and/or providing misleading information to his interrogators in [a foreign government] . . . From our optic, it is imperative to focus Ramzi exclusively on two issues: 1) What are the next attacks planned for the US and 2) Who and where are the operatives inside the United States."[417]

The ALEC Station cable stated that bin al-Shibh had "spent extensive time with [KSM]," and "must have heard discussions of other targets." The cable added that "HQS strongly believes that Binalshibh was involved in efforts on behalf of KSM to identify and place operatives in the West." The February 13, 2003, cable concluded:

> "We think Binalshibh is uniquely positioned to give us much needed critical information to help us thwart large-scale attacks inside the United States, and we want to do our utmost to get it as soon as possible. Good luck."[418]

CIA officers at DETENTION SITE BLUE therefore continued to use the CIA's enhanced interrogation techniques against bin al-Shibh for approximately three additional weeks after this exchange, including sleep deprivation, nudity, dietary manipulation, facial holds, attention grasps, abdominal slaps, facial slaps, and walling.[419] Bin al-Shibh did not provide the information sought on "operatives inside the United States" or "large-scale attacks inside the United States."[420]

4. Information Already Provided by Ramzi Bin Al-Shibh in the Custody of a Foreign Government Inaccurately Attributed to CIA Interrogations; Interrogators Apply the CIA's Enhanced Interrogation Techniques to Bin Al-Shibh When Not Addressed as "Sir" and When Bin Al-Shibh Complains of Stomach Pain

CIA records indicate that the CIA interrogators at DETENTION SITE BLUE questioning Ramzi bin al-Shibh were unaware of the intelligence bin al-Shibh provided in foreign government custody, even though ████████████████████ and the intelligence from those interrogations had been disseminated by the CIA. On multiple occasions, personnel at the detention site drafted intelligence reports that contained information previously disseminated from interrogations of bin al-Shibh while he was in foreign government custody, under the faulty understanding that bin al-Shibh was providing new information.[421]

Ramzi bin al-Shibh was subjected to interrogation techniques and conditions of confinement that were not approved by CIA Headquarters. CIA interrogators used the CIA's enhanced interrogation techniques for behavior adjustment purposes, in response to perceived disrespect, and on several occasions, before bin al-Shibh had an opportunity to respond to an interrogator's questions or before a question was asked. The CIA's enhanced interrogation techniques were applied when bin al-Shibh failed to address an interrogator as "sir," when interrogators noted bin al-Shibh had a "blank stare" on his face, and when bin al-Shibh complained of stomach pain.[422] Further, despite CIA policy at the time to keep detainees under constant light for security purposes, bin al-Shibh was kept in total darkness to heighten his sense of fear."[423]

CIA psychological assessments of bin al-Shibh were slow to recognize the onset of psychological problems brought about, according to later CIA assessments, by bin al-Shibh's long-term social isolation and his anxiety that the CIA would return to using its enhanced interrogation techniques against him. The symptoms included visions, paranoia, insomnia, and attempts at self-harm.[424] In April 2005, a CIA psychologist stated that bin al-Shibh "has remained in social isolation" for as long as two and half years and the isolation was having a "clear and escalating effect on his psychological functioning." The officer continued, "in [bin al-Shibh's] case, it is important to keep in mind that he was previously a relatively high-functioning individual, making his deterioration over the past several months more alarming."[425] The psychologist wrote, "significant alterations to RBS'[s] detention environment must occur soon to prevent further and more serious psychological disturbance."[426] On September 5, 2006, bin al-Shibh was transferred to U.S. military custody at Guantanamo Bay, Cuba.[427] After his arrival, bin al-Shibh was placed on anti-psychotic medications.[428]

The CIA disseminated 109 intelligence reports from the CIA interrogations of Ramzi bin al-Shibh.[429] A CIA assessment, which included intelligence from his time in foreign government custody, as well as his reporting in CIA custody before, during, and after being subjected to the CIA's enhanced interrogation techniques,[430] concluded that:

> "Much of [bin al-Shibh's] statements on the 11 September attacks have been speculative, and many of the details could be found in media accounts of the attacks that appeared before he was detained. In the few instances where his reporting was unique and plausible, we cannot verify or refute the information . . . he has been sketchy on some aspects of the 9/11 plot, perhaps in order to downplay his role in the plot. His information on individuals is non-specific; he has given us nothing on the Saudi hijackers or others who played a role . . . The overall quality of his reporting has steadily declined since 2003."[431]

G. The Detention and Interrogation of Khalid Shaykh Muhammad

1. KSM Held in Pakistani Custody, Provides Limited Information; Rendered to CIA Custody at DETENTION SITE COBALT, KSM Is Immediately Subjected to the CIA's Enhanced Interrogation Techniques

The capture of KSM was attributable to a single CIA source who first came to the CIA's attention in the spring of 2001.[432] The source ████ ████████████ led the CIA and Pakistan authorities directly to KSM. KSM was held in Pakistani custody from the time of his capture on March 1, 2003, to March █, 2003, and was interrogated by CIA officers and Pakistani officials. According to CIA records, while in Pakistani custody, KSM was subjected to some sleep deprivation, but there are no indications of other coercive interrogation techniques being used.[433] While KSM denied knowledge of attack plans and the locations of Usama bin Laden and Ayman al-Zawahiri,[434] he did provide limited information on various al-Qa'ida leaders and operatives who had already been captured. KSM's willingness to discuss operatives when confronted with information about their capture—behavior noted by CIA officers on-site in Pakistan—was a recurring theme throughout KSM's subsequent detention and interrogation in CIA custody.[435]

Less than two hours after KSM's capture, anticipating KSM's arrival at DETENTION SITE COBALT, the chief of interrogations, ██████████, sent an email to CIA Headquarters with the subject line, "Let's roll with the new guy." The email requested permission to "press [KSM] for threat info right away."[436] Later that day, CIA Headquarters authorized ██████ to use a number of the CIA's enhanced interrogation techniques against KSM. The cable from CIA Headquarters did not require that non-coercive interrogation techniques be used first.[437] On March █, 2003, two days before KSM's arrival at the detention site, CIA Headquarters approved an interrogation plan for KSM.[438]

According to CIA records, interrogators began using the CIA's enhanced interrogation techniques at DETENTION SITE COBALT a "few minutes" after the questioning of KSM began. KSM was subjected to facial and abdominal slaps, the facial grab, stress positions, standing sleep deprivation (with his hands at or above head level), nudity, and water dousing.[439] Chief of Interrogations ████ ████ also ordered the rectal rehydration of KSM without a determination of medical need, a procedure that the chief of interrogations would later characterize as illustrative of the interrogator's "total control over the detainee."[440] At the end of the day, the psychologist on-site concluded that the interrogation team would likely have more success by "avoiding confrontations that allow [KSM] to transform the interrogation into battles of will with the interrogator."[441] KSM's reporting during his first day in CIA custody included an accurate description of a Pakistani/British operative, which was dismissed as having been provided during the initial "'throwaway' stage" of information collection when the CIA believed detainees provided false or worthless information.[442]

On March 5, 2003, and March 6, 2003, while he was still at DETENTION SITE COBALT, KSM was subjected to nudity and sleep deprivation. On March 5, 2003, KSM was also subjected to additional rectal rehydration,[443] which █████████OMS, █████ ████, described as helping to "clear a person's head" and effective in getting KSM to talk."[444] On March 6, 2003, ■■■■■ adopted a "'softer Mr. Rogers' persona" after the interrogation team concluded that the CIA's enhanced interrogation techniques had caused KSM to "clam up."[445] During this session KSM was described as "more cooperative," and the day's interrogation was deemed the "best session held to date" by the interrogation team.[446] During this period KSM fabricated information on an individual whom he described as the protector of his children.[447] That information resulted in the capture and CIA detention of two innocent individuals.[448]

2. The CIA Transfers KSM to DETENTION SITE BLUE, Anticipates Use of the Waterboard Prior to His Arrival

Within hours of KSM's capture, ALEC Station successfully argued that CIA contractors SWIGERT and DUNBAR should take over the interrogation of KSM upon KSM's arrival at DETENTION SITE BLUE.[449] On March 3, 2003, CIA Headquarters approved an interrogation plan indicating that KSM "will be subjected to immediate interrogation techniques," and that "the interrogation techniques will increase in intensity from standard to enhanced techniques commensurate with [KSM's] level of resistance, until he indicates initial cooperation."[450] On March ■, 2003, the day of KSM's arrival at DETENTION SITE BLUE, the on-site medical officer described the use of the waterboard on KSM as inevitable:

> "[T]he team here apparently looks to use the water board in two different contexts. One is as a tool of regression and control in which it is used up front and aggressively. The second is to vet information on an as needed basis. Given the various pressures from home vs what is happening on the ground, I think the team's expectation is that [KSM] will [be] getting treatment somewhere in between. I don't think they believe that it will be possible to entirely avoid the water board given the high and immediate threat to US and allied interests. It is an interesting dynamic because they are well aware of the toll it will take on the team vs. the detainee. The requirements coming from home are really unbelievable in terms of breadth and detail."[451]

Meanwhile, OMS completed draft guidelines on the use of the CIA's enhanced interrogation techniques, specifically addressing the waterboard interrogation technique. These guidelines were sent to the medical personnel at the detention site. The guidelines included a warning that the risk of the waterboard was "directly related to number of exposures and may well accelerate as exposures increase," that concerns about cumulative effects would emerge after three to five days, and that there should be an upper limit on the total number of waterboard exposures, "perhaps 20 in a week." CIA records indicate that, as of the day of KSM's arrival at DETENTION SITE BLUE, the interrogation team had not reviewed the draft OMS guidelines."[452]

KSM arrived at DETENTION SITE BLUE at approximately 6:00 PM local time on March ■, 2003, and was immediately stripped and placed in the standing sleep deprivation position.[453] At 6:38 PM, after the medical and psychological personnel who had traveled with KSM from DETENTION SITE COBALT cleared KSM for the CIA's enhanced interrogation techniques, the detention site requested CIA Headquarters' approval to begin the interrogation process.[454] The detention site received the approvals at 7:18 PM,[455] at which point the interrogators began using the CIA's enhanced interrogation techniques on KSM.[456]

Between March ■, 2003 and March 9, 2003, contractors SWIGERT and DUNBAR, and a CIA interrogator, ■■■■■, used the CIA's enhanced interrogation techniques against KSM, including nudity, standing sleep deprivation, the attention grab and insult slap, the facial grab, the abdominal slap, the kneeling stress position, and walling.[457] There were no debriefers present. According to the CIA interrogator, during KSM's first day at DETENTION SITE BLUE, SWIGERT and DUNBAR first began threatening KSM's children.[458] ■■■■■ CTC Legal, ■■■■■, later told the inspector general that these threats were legal so long as the threats were "conditional."[459] On March 9, 2003, KSM fabricated information indicating that Jaffar al-Tayyar and Jose Padilla were plotting together[460] because, as he explained on April 23, 2003, he "felt some pressure to produce information about operations in the United States in the initial phases of his interrogation."[461]

On March ■■, 2003, Deputy Chief of ALEC Station ■■■■■ ■■■■■, and a second ALEC Station officer, ■■■■■, arrived at DETENTION SITE BLUE to serve as debriefers. The detention site also reportedly received a phone call from CIA Headquarters conveying the views of the CIA's Deputy Director of Operations James Pavitt on the interrogation of KSM.[462] Pavitt later told the inspector general that he "did not recall specifically ordering that a detainee be waterboarded right away," but he "did not discount that possibility." According to records of the interview, "Pavitt did recall saying, 'I want to know what he knows, and I want to know it fast.'"[463] The on-site medical officer later wrote in an email that the CIA interrogators "felt that the [waterboard] was the big stick and that HQ was more or less demanding that it be used early and often."[464]

3. The CIA Waterboards KSM at Least 183 Times; KSM's Reporting Includes Significant Fabricated Information

On March 10, 2003, KSM was subjected to the first of his 15 separate waterboarding sessions. The first waterboarding session, which lasted 30 minutes (10 more than anticipated in the Office of Legal Counsel's August 1, 2002, opinion), was followed by the use of a horizontal stress position that had not previously been approved by CIA Headquarters.[465] The chief of Base, worried about the legal implications, prohibited the on-site medical officer from reporting on the interrogation directly to OMS outside of official CIA cable traffic.[466]

On March 12, 2003, KSM provided information on the Heathrow Airport and Canary Wharf plotting. KSM stated that he showed a sketch in his notebook of a building in Canary Wharf (a major business district in London) to Ammar al-Baluchi.[467] He also provided statements about directing prospective pilots to study at flight schools,[468] and stated that Jaffar al-Tayyar was involved in the Heathrow Plot.[469] KSM retracted all of this information later in his detention.[470] There are no CIA records indicating that these and other retractions were assessed to be false.

The March 12, 2003, reporting from KSM on the Heathrow Airport plotting was deemed at the time by CIA interrogators to be an effort by KSM to avoid discussion of plotting inside the United States and thus contributed to the decision to subject KSM to two waterboarding sessions that day.[471] During these sessions, KSM ingested a significant amount of water. CIA records state that KSM's "abdomen was somewhat distended and he expressed water when the abdomen was pressed."[472] KSM's gastric contents were so diluted by water that the medical officer present was "not concerned about regurgitated gastric acid damaging KSM's esophagus."[473] The officer was, however, concerned about water intoxication and dilution of electrolytes and requested that the interrogators use saline in future waterboarding sessions.[474] The medical officer later wrote to ██████ ██OMS that KSM was "ingesting and aspiration [*sic*] a LOT of water," and that "[i]n the new technique we are basically doing a series of near drownings."[475] During the day, KSM was also subjected to the attention grasp, insult slap, abdominal slap, and walling.[476]

On March 13, 2003, after KSM again denied that al-Qa'ida had operations planned for inside the United States, CIA interrogators decided on a "day of intensive waterboard sessions."[477] During the first of three waterboarding sessions that day, interrogators responded to KSM's efforts to breathe during the sessions by holding KSM's lips and directing the water at his mouth."[478] According to a cable from the detention site, KSM "would begin signaling by pointing upward with his two index fingers as the water pouring approached the established time limit." The cable noted that "[t]his behavior indicates that the subject remains alert and has become familiar with key aspects of the process."[479] CIA records state that KSM "yelled and twisted" when he was secured to the waterboard for the second session of the day, but "appeared resigned to tolerating the board and stated he had nothing new to say about terrorist plots inside the United States."[480]

Prior to the third waterboard session of that calendar day, the on-site medical officer raised concerns that the waterboard session—which would be the fourth in 14 hours—would exceed the limits included in draft OMS guidelines that had been distributed the previous afternoon.[481] Those draft guidelines stated that up to three waterboard sessions in a 24-hour period was acceptable.[482] At the time, KSM had been subjected to more than 65 applications of water during the four waterboarding sessions between the afternoon of March 12, 2003, and the morning of March 13, 2003. In response to a request for approval from the chief of Base, CTC attorney ███ ███████ assured detention site personnel that the medical officer "is incorrect that these guidelines have been approved and/or fully coordinated."[483] ███████ sent an email to the detention site authorizing the additional waterboarding session.[484] Despite indications from ██████ that the detention site personnel would receive a formal authorizing cable, no such authorization from CIA Headquarters was provided. At the end of the day, the medical officer wrote ███ ████OMS that "[t]hings are slowly evolving form [*sic*] OMS being viewed as the institutional conscience and the limiting factor to the ones who are dedicated to maximizing the benefit in a safe manner and keeping everyone's butt out of trouble." The medical officer noted that his communication with ███████OMS was no longer "viewed with suspicion."[485] On the afternoon of March 13, 2003, KSM was subjected to his third waterboard session of that calendar day and fifth in 25 hours. CIA records note that KSM vomited during and after the procedure.[486]

Shortly thereafter, CIA Headquarters began reevaluating

the use of the waterboard interrogation technique. According to a March 14, 2003, email from an interrogator who was not at DETENTION SITE BLUE, but was reviewing cable traffic, the "[o]verall view seems to be" that the waterboard "is not working in gaining KSM['s] compliance."[487] The deputy chief of the CIA interrogation program responded in agreement, adding that "[a]gainst KSM it has proven ineffective," and that "[t]he potential for physical harm is far greater with the waterboard than with the other techniques, bringing into question the issue of risk vs. gain . . ." The deputy chief further suggested that the waterboard was counterproductive, stating that "[w]e seem to have lost ground" with KSM since progress made at DETENTION SITE COBALT, and as a result, the CIA should "consider the possibility" that the introduction of the waterboard interrogation technique "may poison the well."[488] The email in which these sentiments were expressed was sent to ██████████, the CTC attorney overseeing the interrogation of KSM. Despite these reservations and assessments, the waterboarding of KSM continued for another 10 days.[489]

On March 15, 2003, KSM was waterboarded for failing to confirm references in signal intercepts on al-Qa'ida's efforts to obtain "nuclear suitcases."[490] Subsequent signals intercepts and information from a foreign government would later indicate that the nuclear suitcase threat was an orchestrated scam.[491] KSM was waterboarded a second time that day after failing to provide information on operations against the United States or on al-Qa'ida nuclear capabilities.[492] During the waterboarding sessions that day, the application of the interrogation technique further evolved, with the interrogators now using their hands to maintain a one-inch deep "pool" of water over KSM's nose and mouth in an effort to make it impossible for KSM to ingest all the water being poured.[493] At one point, SWIGERT and DUNBAR waited for KSM to talk before pouring water over his mouth.[494]

On the afternoon of March 17, 2003, and into the morning of March 18, 2003, ██████████, ████████OMS exchanged emails with the medical officer at DETENTION SITE BLUE on the waterboarding of KSM. According to ████████, the waterboard interrogation technique had "moved even further from the SERE model."[495] █ ████████ also wrote:

> "Truthfully, though, I don't recall that the WB [waterboard] produced anything actionable in AZ [Abu Zubaydah] any earlier than another technique might have. This may be different with KSM, but that is still as much a statement of faith as anything else - since we don't seem to

> study the question as we go . . . it's been many more days of constant WB repetitions, with the evidence of progress through most of them not being actionable intel but rather that 'he looks like he's weakening.' The WB may actually be the best; just don't like to base it on religion."[496]

On March 18, 2003, KSM was confronted with the reporting of Majid Khan, who was then in the custody of a foreign government,[497] regarding plotting against gas stations inside the United States, information that KSM had not previously discussed. In assessing the session, DETENTION SITE BLUE personnel noted that "KSM will selectively lie, provide partial truths, and misdirect when he believes he will not be found out and held accountable." On the other hand, they wrote that "KSM appears more inclined to make accurate disclosures when he believes people, emails, or other source material are available to the USG for checking his responses."[498]

The same day, KSM provided additional information on the Heathrow Airport plotting, much of which he would recant in 2004.[499] KSM also discussed Jaffar al-Tayyar again, prompting the detention site personnel to refer to the "all-purpose" al-Tayyar whom KSM had "woven . . . into practically every story, each time with a different role."[500] After KSM had included al-Tayyar in his discussion of Majid Khan's gas station plot, KSM debriefer ██████ wrote in an email that "[t]oday [al-Tayyar's] working with Majid Khan, yesterday the London crowd, the day before Padilla - you get the point."[501] Beginning the evening of March 18, 2003, KSM began a period of sleep deprivation, most of it in the standing position, which would last for seven and a half days, or approximately 180 hours.[502]

On March 19, 2003, the interrogators at the detention site decided to waterboard KSM due to KSM's inconsistent information about Jaffar al-Tayyar's passport.[503] According to CIA cables, after assuming his position on the waterboard, KSM "seemed to lose control" and appeared "somewhat frantic," stating that he "had been forced to lie, and ma[k]e up stories about" Jaffar al-Tayyar because of his interrogators.[504] KSM then stated that his reporting on al-Tayyar's role in Majid Khan's plotting was a "complete fabrication" and that al-Tayyar had been compromised as an operative and that as a result, al-Tayyar could not be used for a terrorist operation."[505] In response, the interrogators told KSM that they only wanted to hear him speak if he was revealing information on the next attack.[506] Deputy Chief of ALEC Station ██████████ later told the inspector general that it was around this time that contract interrogator DUNBAR stated that "he had not seen a 'resistor' [*sic*] like KSM, and was 'going to go to school on this guy.'"[507] According to CIA records, the interrogators then "devote[d] all measures to pressuring [KSM] on the single issue of the 'next attack on America,'" including attention grabs, insult slaps, walling, water dousing, and additional waterboard sessions.[508]

On March 20, 2003, KSM continued to be subjected to the CIA's enhanced interrogation techniques throughout the day, including a period of "intense questioning and walling."[509] KSM was described as "[t]ired and sore," with abrasions on his ankles, shins, and wrists, as well as on the back of his head."[510] He also suffered from pedal edema resulting from extended standing.[511] After having concluded that there was "no further movement" in the interrogation, the detention site personnel hung a picture of KSM's sons in his cell as a way to "[heighten] his imagination concerning where they are, who has them, [and] what is in store for them."[512]

The waterboarding of KSM on March 21, 2003, and March 22, 2003, was based on a misreading of intelligence provided by Majid Khan bv Deputy Chief of ALEC Station ██████. According to a cable from the CIA's █████, Khan, who was in foreign government custody, had stated that KSM wanted to use "two to three unknown Black American Muslim converts who were currently training in Afghanistan," to "conduct attacks" on gas stations in the United States, and that "KSM was interested in using anyone with US status to assist with this operation."[513] Upon receipt of this reporting, ████ wrote in an email "i love the Black American Muslim at AQ camps in Afghanuistan [*sic*] . . . Mukie [KSM] is going to be hatin' life on this one."[514] However, her subsequent questioning of KSM was not based on Khan's actual reporting, which was about potential operatives already in Afghanistan, but rather something Khan had not said—that KSM directed him to make contact with African-American converts in the United States.[515] According to CIA records, in a "contentious" session that lasted for hours and involved the use of the CIA's enhanced interrogation techniques, KSM "flatly denied" any efforts to recruit African-American Muslim converts. KSM was then waterboarded.[516] Later in the day, facing the threat of a second waterboarding session, KSM "relented and said that maybe he had told Khan that he should see if he could make contact with members of the Black American Muslim convert community." The CIA interrogators then returned KSM to the standing sleep deprivation position without a second waterboarding session.[517]

The next day, March 22, 2003, interrogators subjected KSM to "intense" questioning and walling, but when KSM provided no new information on African-American Muslim converts or threats inside the United States, he was subjected to additional waterboarding.[518] An hour later, KSM stated that he was "ready to talk."[519] He told the CIA interrogators that he had sent Abu Issa al-Britani to Montana to recruit African-American Muslim converts, a mission he said had been prompted by discussions with a London-based shaykh whose bodyguards had families in Montana.[520] KSM also stated that he tasked Majid Khan with attending Muslim conferences in the United States to "spot and assess potential extremists" who would assist in the gas station plot.[521] In June 2003, KSM admitted that he fabricated the story about Abu Issa al-Britani and Montana, explaining that he was "under 'enhanced measures' when he made these claims and simply told his interrogators what he thought they wanted to hear."[522] In August 2003, KSM reiterated that he had no plans to recruit or use "black American Muslim" converts operationally.[523] In December 2005, he denied ever asking Majid Khan to recruit converts or attend Islamic conferences.[524]

On March 24, 2003, KSM underwent his fifteenth and final documented waterboarding session due to his "intransigence" in failing to identify suspected Abu Bakr al-Azdi operations in the United States, and for having "lied about poison and biological warfare programs."[525] KSM was described in the session as being "composed, stoic, and resigned."[526]

That evening, the detention site received two reports. The first recounted the reporting of Majid Khan, who was still in the custody of a foreign government, on Uzhair, who ran the New York branch of his father's Karachi-based import-export business, and on Uzhair's father.[527] According to Khan, his meetings with the two were facilitated by Ammar al-Baluchi.[528] The second report described the reporting of Iyman Faris, who was in FBI custody, on a plot to cut the suspension cables on the Brooklyn Bridge and exploration of plans to derail trains and conduct an attack in Washington, D.C.[529] KSM, whom detention site personnel described as "boxed in" by the new reporting,[530] then stated that Uzhair's father, Sayf al-Rahman Paracha, had agreed to smuggle explosives into the United States.[531] As described elsewhere in this summary, the purported parties to the agreement denied that such an agreement existed.[532] In confirming Faris's reporting, KSM exhibited what the Interagency Intelligence Committee on Terrorism would later describe as an effort to "stay obvious/general" and "provide little information that might enable the US to thwart attacks."[533]

With the exception of sleep deprivation, which continued for one more day, the use of the CIA's enhanced interrogation techniques against KSM stopped abruptly on March 24, 2003.[534] There are no CIA records directing the interrogation team to cease using the CIA's enhanced interrogation techniques against KSM, nor any contemporaneous documentation explaining the decision.[535]

4. After the Use of the CIA's Enhanced Interrogation Techniques Against KSM Ends, the CIA Continues to Assess That KSM Is Withholding and Fabricating Information

On April 3, 2003, the Interagency Intelligence Committee on Terrorism produced an assessment of KSM's intelligence entitled, "Precious Truths, Surrounded by a Bodyguard of Lies." The assessment concluded that KSM was withholding or lying about terrorist plots and operatives targeting the United States. It also identified contradictions between KSM's reporting on CBRN and other sources.[536]

On April 24, 2003, FBI Director Robert Mueller began seeking direct FBI access to KSM in order to better understand CIA reporting indicating threats to U.S. cities.[537] Despite personal commitments from DCI Tenet to Director Mueller that access would be forthcoming, the CIA's CTC successfully formulated a CIA position whereby the FBI would not be provided access to KSM until his anticipated transfer to Guantanamo Bay, Cuba. Neither the CIA nor the FBI knew at the time that the transfer would not occur until September 2006.[538]

Between April 2003 and July 2003, KSM frustrated the CIA on a number of fronts. On May 7, 2003, after more than two months of conflicting reporting, ALEC Station concluded that KSM "consistently wavers" on issues of UBL's location, protectors, and hosts, and that his information "conveniently lack[s] sufficient detail [to be] actionable intelligence.[539] On June 12, 2003, CIA Headquarters indicated that it "remain[ed] highly suspicious that KSM is withholding, exaggerating, misdirecting, or outright fabricating information on CBRN issues."[540] At the end of April 2003, KSM was shown pictures of the recently captured Ammar al-Baluchi and Khallad bin Attash, after which he provided additional information related to their plotting in Karachi.[541] ALEC Station wrote in a May 20, 2003, cable that "[w]e consider KSM's long-standing omission of [this] information to be a serious concern, especially as this omission may well have cost American lives had Pakistani authorities not been diligent in following up on unrelated criminal leads that led to the capture of

Ammar, bin Attash, and other probable operatives involved in the attack plans."[542]

In May and June 2003, Ammar al-Baluchi and Khallad bin Attash provided reporting that contradicted KSM's statements about the Heathrow Airport plotting and included information that KSM had not provided.[543] After KSM was confronted with this reporting, Deputy Chief of ALEC Station ██████████ wrote in an email, "OK, that's it . . . yet again he lies and ONLY ADMITS details when he knows we know them from someone else."[544] On April 19, 2003, KSM was questioned for the first time about summer 2002 reporting from Masran bin Arshad, who was in the custody of a foreign government, regarding the "Second Wave" plot. Informed that bin Arshad had been detained, KSM stated, "I have forgotten about him, he is not in my mind at all."[545] In response, ALEC Station noted that it "remain[e]d concerned that KSM's progression towards full debriefing status is not yet apparent where it counts most, in relation to threats to US interests, especially inside CONUS."[546] In June 2003, almost three months after the CIA had stopped using its enhanced interrogation techniques against KSM, senior ALEC Station and RDG officers met at least twice to discuss concerns about KSM's lack of cooperation.[547] As an ALEC Station cable noted at the time, "KSM's pattern of behavior over the past three months, trying to control his environment, lying and then admitting things only when pressed that others have been caught and have likely admitted the plot, is a cause for concern."[548] In an email, one CIA officer noted that "what KSM's doing is fairly typical of other detainees . . . KSM, Khallad [bin Attash], and others are doing what makes sense in their situation—pretend cooperation."[549]

In the fall of 2003, after KSM's explanations about how to decrypt phone numbers related to British operative Issa al-Britani (KSM did not identify the operative as "Issa al-Hindi," or by his true name, Dhiren Barot) yielded no results, and after KSM misidentified another individual, known not to be Issa, as Issa, Deputy Chief of ALEC Station ██████████ stated in an email that KSM was "obstructing our ability to acquire good information," noting that KSM "misidentifie[s] photos when he knows we are fishing" and "misleads us on telephone numbers."[550] Later, after KSM's transfer to DETENTION SITE BLACK, ALEC Station wrote that KSM "may never be fully forthcoming and honest" on the topic of UBL's whereabouts.[551] Despite repeated challenges, KSM maintained that he lacked information on UBL's location.[552]

KSM was transferred to DETENTION SITE ■■■ on ■■■ ■, 2005,[553] to DETENTION SITE BROWN on March ■■, 2006,[554] and to U.S. military detention at Guantanamo Bay, Cuba, on September 5, 2006.[555] The CIA disseminated 831 intelligence reports from the interrogations of KSM over a period of 3.5 years. While KSM provided more intelligence reporting than any other CIA detainee (nearly 15 percent of all CIA detainee intelligence reporting), CIA records indicate that KSM also received the most intelligence requirements and attention from CIA interrogators, debriefers, analysts, and senior CIA leadership. Further, as noted, a significant amount of the disseminated intelligence reporting from KSM that the CIA identified as important threat reporting was later identified as fabricated.[556]

H. The Growth of the CIA's Detention and Interrogation Program

1. Fifty-Three CIA Detainees Enter the CIA's Detention and Interrogation Program in 2003

While the CIA held detainees from 2002 to 2008, early 2003 was the most active period of the CIA's Detention and Interrogation Program. Of the 119 detainees identified by the Committee as held by the CIA, 53 were brought into custody in 2003, and of the 39 detainees the Committee has found to have been subjected to the CIA's enhanced interrogation techniques, 17 were subjected to such techniques between January 2003 and August 2003. The CIA's enhanced interrogations during that time were primarily used at DETENTION SITE COBALT and DETENTION SITE BLUE.[557] Other interrogations using the CIA's enhanced interrogation techniques took place at a CIA ■■■■ in Country ■■, at which at least one CIA detainee was submerged in a bathtub filled with ice water.[558]

In 2003, CIA interrogators sought and received approval to use the CIA's enhanced interrogation techniques against at least five detainees prior to their arrival at a CIA detention facility.[559] In two of those cases, CIA Headquarters approved the use of the CIA's enhanced interrogation techniques before they were requested by CIA personnel at the detention sites.[560]

2. The CIA Establishes DETENTION SITE BLACK in Country ■■ and DETENTION SITE VIOLET in Country ■■

The CIA entered into an agreement with the ■■■■■■■■ in Country ■■ to host a CIA detention facility in ■■■■■■ 2002.[561] In ■■■■■ 2003, CIA Headquarters invited the CIA Station in Country ■■ to identify ways to support the ■■■■■■■ in Country ■■ to "demonstrate to ■■■■■■ and the highest levels of the [Country ■■] government that we deeply appreciate their cooperation and support" for the detention program.[562] The Station responded with an $■ million "wish list" ■■■■■■■■■■■■■■■■■;[563] CIA Headquarters provided the Station with $■ million more than was requested for the purposes of the ■■■■ subsidy.[564] CIA detainees were transferred to DETENTION SITE BLACK in Country ■■ in the fall of 2003.[565]

In August 2003, the U.S. ambassador in Country ■■ sought to contact State Department officials to ensure that the State Department was aware of the CIA detention facility and its "potential impact on our policy vis-à-vis the [Country ■■] government."[566] The U.S. ambassador was told by the CIA Station that this was not possible, and that no one at the State Department, including the secretary of state, was informed about the CIA detention facility in Country ■■. Describing the CIA's position as "unacceptable," the ambassador then requested a signed document from "at least the President's National Security Advisor" describing the authorities for the program, including a statement that the CIA's interrogation techniques met "legal and human rights standards," and an explicit order to him not to discuss the program with the secretary of state.[567] CIA Headquarters then sought the intervention of Deputy Secretary of State Richard Armitage, who called the U.S. ambassador. Deputy Secretary Armitage told the CIA to keep him and the secretary of state informed so that they would not be caught unaware when an ambassador raised concerns.[568]

Nearly a year later, in May 2004, revelations about U.S. detainee abuses at the U.S. military prison in Abu Ghraib, Iraq, prompted the same U.S. ambassador in Country ■■ to seek information on CIA detention standards and interrogation methods.[569] In the fall of 2004, when ■■■■■ U.S. ambassador to Country ■■ sought documents authorizing the program, the CIA again sought the intervention of Deputy Secretary Armitage, who once again made "strong remarks" to the CIA about how he and the secretary of state were "cut out of the NSC [National Security Council] clearance/coordination process" with regard to the CIA program. According to CIA records, Armitage also questioned the efficacy of the program and the value of the intelligence derived from the program.[570] While it is unclear how the ambassador's concerns were resolved, he later joined the chief of Station in making a presentation to Country ██'s ████████ █ on the CIA's Detention and Interrogation Program. The presentation talking points did not describe the CIA's enhanced interrogation techniques, but represented that "[w]ithout the full range of these interrogation measures, we would not have succeeded in overcoming the resistance of [Khalid Shaykh Muhammad] and other equally resistant HVDs." The talking points included many of the same inaccurate representations[571] made to U.S. policymakers and others, attributing to CIA detainees critical information on the "Karachi Plot," the "Heathrow Plot," the "Second Wave Plot," and the "Guraba Cell"; as well as intelligence related to Issa al-Hindi, Abu Talha al-Pakistani, Hambali, Jose Padilla, Binyam Mohammed, Sajid Badat, and Jaffar al-Tayyar. The presentation also noted that the President of the United States had directed that he not be informed of the locations of the CIA detention facilities to ensure he would not accidentally disclose the information.[572]

In a separate country, Country ██, the CIA obtained the approval of the ████████████████████ and the political leadership to establish a detention facility before informing the U.S. ambassador.[573] As the CIA chief of Station stated in his request to CIA Headquarters to brief the ambassador, Country ██'s ████████████ ███████ and the ██████ probably would ask the ambassador about the CIA detention facility.[574] After ████████████████████████████ ██████████ delayed briefing the ██████████ for ██ months, to the consternation of the CIA Station, which wanted political approval prior to the arrival of CIA detainees.[575] The ████████████████████ Country ██ official outside of the █████████████████████████████ ██ aware of the facility, was described as "shocked," but nonetheless approved.[576]

By mid-2003 the CIA had concluded that its completed, but still unused "holding cell" in Country ██ was insufficient, given the growing number of CIA detainees in the program and the CIA's interest in interrogating multiple detainees at the same detention site. The CIA thus sought to build a new, expanded detention facility in the country.[577] The CIA also offered $█ million to the ████████ to "show appreciation" for the ██████ support for the program.[578] According to a CIA cable, however, the ██████████████████████ ██ █████████████████."[579] While the plan to construct the expanded facility was approved by the ████ of Country ██, the CIA and ██ ████████ developed complex mechanisms to ████ ████████████████ in order to provide the $█ million to the ████.[580] ████████████████████ █ in Country █ complicated the arrangements. ████ ████████████████ when the Country █ ███ requested an update on planning for the CIA detention site, he was told ████████—inaccurately—that the planning had been discontinued.[581] In ████, when the facility received its first CIA detainees, ███ informed the CIA ████ that the ████ of Country █ "probably has an incomplete notion [regarding the facility's] actual function, i.e., he probably believes that it is some sort of ████████ center."[582]

3. At Least 17 CIA Detainees Subjected to the CIA's Enhanced Interrogation Techniques Without CIA Headquarters Authorization

CIA cables from the spring of 2003 and afterwards describe multiple examples of interrogation practices at CIA detention sites that were inconsistent with the CIA's detention and interrogation guidelines. CIA officers at DETENTION SITE COBALT—led principally by Chief of Interrogations ████████—also described a number of interrogation activities in cables that were not approved by CIA Headquarters. CIA Headquarters failed to respond, inquire, or investigate:

- Cables revealing that the CIA's chief of interrogations used water dousing against detainees, including with cold water and/or ice water baths, as an interrogation technique without prior approval from CIA Headquarters;[583]
- Cables and records indicating that CIA detainees who were undergoing or had undergone the CIA's enhanced interrogation techniques were subjected to rectal rehydration, without evidence of medical necessity, and that others were threatened with it;[584]
- Cables noting that groups of four or more interrogators, who required practical experience to acquire their CIA interrogation "certification," were allowed to apply the CIA's enhanced interrogation techniques as a group against a single detainee;[585] and
- Cables revealing that the CIA's enhanced interrogation techniques were used at CIA ████ that were not designated as CIA detention sites.[586]

In the first half of 2003, the CIA interrogated four detainees with medical complications in their lower extremities: two detainees had a broken foot, one detainee had a sprained ankle, and one detainee had a prosthetic leg.[587] CIA interrogators shackled each of these detainees in the standing position for sleep deprivation for extended periods of time until medical personnel assessed that they could not maintain the position. The two detainees that each had a broken foot were also subjected to walling, stress positions, and cramped confinement, despite the note in their interrogation plans that these specific enhanced interrogation techniques were not requested because of the medical condition of the detainees.[588] CIA Headquarters did not react to the site's use of these CIA enhanced interrogation techniques despite the lack of approval.

Over the course of the CIA program, at least 39 detainees were subjected to one or more of the CIA's enhanced interrogation techniques.[589] CIA records indicate that there were at least 17 CIA detainees who were subjected to one or more CIA enhanced interrogation techniques without CIA Headquarters approval. This count includes detainees who were approved for the use of some techniques, but were subjected to unapproved techniques, as well as detainees for whom interrogators had no approvals to use any of the techniques. This count also takes into account distinctions between techniques categorized as "enhanced" or "standard" by the CIA at the time they were applied.[590] The 17 detainees who were subjected to techniques without the approval of CIA Headquarters were: Rafiq Bashir al-Hami,[591] Tawfiq Nasir Awad al-Bihandi,[592] Hikmat Nafi Shaukat,[593] Lufti al-Arabi al-Gharisi,[594] Muhammad Ahmad Ghulam Rabbani aka Abu Badr,[595] Gul Rahman,[596] Abd al-Rahim al-Nashiri,[597] Ramzi bin al-Shibh,[598] Asadallah,[599] Mustafa al-Hawsawi,[600] Abu Khalid,[601] Laid bin Duhman aka Abu Hudhaifa,[602] Abd al-Karim,[603] Abu Hazim,[604] Sayyid Ibrahim,[605] Abu Yasir al-Jaza'iri,[606] and Suleiman Abdullah.[607] In every case except al-Nashiri, the unauthorized interrogation techniques were detailed in CIA cables, but CIA Headquarters did not respond or take action against the CIA personnel applying the unauthorized interrogation techniques.[608]

This list does not include examples in which CIA interrogators were authorized to use the CIA's enhanced interrogation techniques, but then implemented the techniques in a manner that diverged from the authorization. Examples include Abu Zubair[609] and, as detailed, KSM, whose interrogators developed methods of applying the waterboard in a manner that differed from how the technique had previously been used and how it had been described to the Department of Justice. This count also excludes additional allegations of the unauthorized use of the CIA's enhanced interrogation techniques.[610]

Over the course of the CIA's Detention and Interrogation Program, numerous detainees were subjected to the CIA's enhanced interrogation techniques by untrained interrogators. As noted, the CIA did not conduct its first training course until November 2002, by which time at least nine detainees had already been subjected to the techniques.[611] The DCI's January 28, 2003, guidelines, which stated that the CIA's enhanced interrogation techniques "may be employed only by approved interrogators for use with specific detainees," raised the additional issue of approved techniques used by unapproved interrogators.[612] The January 28, 2003, DCI guidelines did not explicitly require CIA Headquarters to approve who could use the CIA's "standard" interrogation techniques, including techniques that were not previously considered "standard" and that would later be reclassified as "enhanced" interrogation techniques. Rather, the DCI guidelines required only that "all personnel directly engaged in the interrogation" be "appropriately screened," that they review the guidelines, and that they receive "appropriate training" in the implementation of the guidelines. [613]

4. CIA Headquarters Authorizes Water Dousing Without Department of Justice Approval; Application of Technique Reported as Approximating Waterboarding

CIA Headquarters approved requests to use water dousing, nudity, the abdominal slap, and dietary manipulation, despite the fact that the techniques had not been reviewed by the Department of Justice.[614] Interrogators used the water dousing technique in various ways. At DETENTION SITE COBALT, detainees were often held down, naked, on a tarp on the floor, with the tarp pulled up around them to form a makeshift tub, while cold or refrigerated water was poured on them.[615] Others were hosed down repeatedly while they were shackled naked, in the standing sleep deprivation position. These same detainees were subsequently placed in rooms with temperatures ranging from 59 to 80 degrees Fahrenheit.[616]

Other accounts suggest detainees were water doused while placed on a waterboard.[617] Although CIA Headquarters approved the use of the "water dousing" interrogation technique on several detainees, interrogators used it extensively on a number of detainees without seeking or obtaining prior authorization from CIA Headquarters.[618]

In interrogation sessions on April 5, 2003, and April 6, 2003, senior CIA interrogator ██████████ and another interrogator used the water dousing technique on detainee Mustafa al-Hawsawi at DETENTION SITE COBALT. Al-Hawsawi later described the session to a different CIA interrogator, ██████████, who wrote that al-Hawsawi might have been waterboarded or subjected to treatment that "could be indistinguishable from the waterboard."[619] An email from the interrogator stated that:

> "We did not prompt al-Hawsawi - he described the process and the table on his own. As you know, I have serious reservations about watering them in a prone position because if not done with care, the net effect can approach the effect of the water board. If one is held down on his back, on the table or on the floor, with water poured in his face I think it goes beyond dousing and the effect, to the recipient, could be indistinguishable from the water board.
>
> "I have real problems with putting one of them on the water board for 'dousing.' Putting him in a head down attitude and pouring water around his chest and face is just too close to the water board, and if it is continued may lead to problems for us."[620]

Several months later, the incident was referred to the CIA inspector general for investigation. A December 6, 2006, inspector general report summarized the findings of this investigation, indicating that water was poured on al-Hawsawi while he was lying on the floor in a prone position, which, in the opinion of at least one CIA interrogator quoted in the report, "can easily approximate waterboarding."[621] The OIG could not corroborate whether al-Hawsawi was strapped to the waterboard when he was interrogated at DETENTION SITE COBALT. Both of the interrogators who subjected al-Hawsawi to the CIA's enhanced interrogation techniques on April 6, 2003, said that al-Hawsawi cried out for God while the water was being poured on him and one of the interrogators asserted that this was because of the cold temperature of the water. Both of the interrogators also stated that al-Hawsawi saw the waterboard and that its purpose was made clear to him. The inspector general report also indicates that al-Hawsawi's experience reflected "the way water dousing was done at [DETENTION SITE COBALT]," and that this method was developed with guidance from CIA CTC attorneys and the CIA's Office of Medical Services.[622]

During the same time that al-Hawsawi claimed he was placed on the waterboard in April 2003, a CIA linguist claimed that CIA detainee Abu Hazim had also been water doused in a way that approximated waterboarding.[623] ██████████, a linguist in Country

█████ from █████, 2003, until █████, 2003, told the OIG that:

> "when water dousing was used on Abu Hazim, a cloth covered Abu Hazim's face, and [█████ [CIA OFFICER 1]] poured cold water directly on Abu Hazim's face to disrupt his breathing. [The linguist] said that when Abu Hazim turned blue, Physician's Assistant [█████ █████] removed the cloth so that Abu Hazim could breathe."[624]

This allegation was reported to the CIA inspector general on August 18, 2004. The CIA reported this incident as a possible criminal violation on September 10, 2004, to the U.S. Attorney's Office in the Eastern District of Virginia.[625] The inspector general report concluded that there was no corroboration of the linguist's allegation, stating, "[t]here is no evidence that a cloth was placed over Abu Hazim's face during water dousing or that his breathing was impaired."[626]

5. Hambali Fabricates Information While Being Subjected to the CIA's Enhanced Interrogation Techniques

In the summer of 2003, the CIA captured three Southeast Asian operatives: Zubair,[627] Lillie,[628] and Hambali. (These captures are discussed later in this summary in the section entitled, "The Capture of Hambali.")[629]

In August 2003, Hambali was captured and transferred to CIA custody.[630] Despite assessments that Hambali was cooperative in the interview process without "the use of more intrusive standard interrogation procedures much less the enhanced measures," CIA interrogators requested and obtained approval to use the CIA's enhanced interrogation techniques on Hambali approximately a month after his transfer to CIA custody.[631] In late 2003, Hambali recanted most of the significant information he had provided to interrogators during the use of the CIA's enhanced interrogation techniques, recantations CIA officers assessed to be credible.[632] According to a CIA cable:

> "he had provided the false information in an attempt to reduce the pressure on himself . . . and to give an account that was consistent with what [Hambali] assessed the questioners wanted to hear."[633]

CIA officers later suggested that the misleading answers and resistance to interrogation that CIA interrogators cited in their requests to use the CIA's enhanced interrogation techniques against Hambali and an associated CIA detainee, Lillie, may not have been resistance to interrogation, but rather the result of issues related to culture and their poor English language skills.[634]

6. After the Use of the CIA's Enhanced Interrogation Techniques, CIA Headquarters Questions Detention of Detainee and Recommends Release; Detainee Transferred to U.S. Military Custody and Held for An Additional Four Years

In October 2003, the CIA interrogated Arsala Khan, an Afghan national in his mid-fifties who was believed to have assisted Usama bin Laden in his escape through the Tora Bora Mountains in late 2001.[635] After 56 hours of standing sleep deprivation, Arsala Khan was described as barely able to enunciate, and being "visibly shaken by his hallucinations depicting dogs mauling and killing his sons and family." According to CIA cables, Arsala Khan "stated that [the interrogator] was responsible for killing them and feeding them to the dogs."[636]

Arsala Khan was subsequently allowed to sleep.[637] Two days later, however, the interrogators returned him to standing sleep deprivation. After subjecting Khan to 21 additional hours of sleep deprivation, interrogators stopped using the CIA's enhanced interrogation techniques "[d]ue to lack of information from [Arsala Khan] pinning him directly to a recent activity.[638] Three days after the reporting about Khan's hallucinations, and after the interrogators had already subjected Khan to the additional 21 hours of standing sleep deprivation (beyond the initial 56 hours), CIA Headquarters sent a cable stating that RDG and the Office of Medical Services believed that Arsala Khan should not be subjected to additional standing sleep deprivation beyond the 56 hours because of his hallucinations.[639]

After approximately a month of detention and the extensive use of the CIA's enhanced interrogation techniques on Arsala Khan, the CIA concluded that the "detainee Arsala Khan does not appear to be the subject involved in . . . current plans or activities against U.S. personnel or facilities," and recommended that he be released to his village with a cash payment.[640] CIA interrogators at DETENTION SITE COBALT instead transferred him to U.S. military custody, where he was held for an additional four years despite the development of significant intelligence indicating that the source who reported that Arsala Khan had aided Usama bin Laden had a vendetta against Arsala Khan's family.[641]

7. A Year After DETENTION SITE COBALT Opens, the CIA Reports "Unsettling Discovery That We Are Holding a Number of Detainees About Whom We Know Very Little"

In the fall of 2003, CIA officers began to take a closer look at the CIA detainees being held in Country ■, raising concerns about both the number and types of detainees being held by the CIA. CIA officers in Country ■ provided a list of CIA detainees to CIA Headquarters, resulting in the observation by CIA Headquarters that they had not previously had the names of all 44 CIA detainees being held in that country. At the direction of CIA Headquarters, the Station in Country ■ "completed an exhaustive search of all available records in an attempt to develop a clearer understanding of the [CIA] detainees." A December 2003 cable from the Station in Country ■ to CIA Headquarters stated that:

> In the process of this research, we have made the unsettling discovery that we are holding a number of detainees about whom we know very little. The majority of [CIA] detainees in [Country ■] have not been debriefed for months and, in some cases, for over a year. Many of them appear to us to have no further intelligence value for [the CIAl and should more properly be turned over to the [U.S. military], to [Country ■] authorities or to third countries for further investigation and possibly prosecution. In a few cases, there does not appear to be enough evidence to continue incarceration, and, if this is in fact the case, the detainees should be released."[642]

Records indicate that all of these CIA detainees had been kept in solitary confinement. The vast majority of these detainees were later released, with some receiving CIA payments for having been held in detention.[643]

8. CIA Detention Sites in Country ■ Lack Sufficient Personnel and Translators to Support the Interrogations of Detainees

Throughout 2003, the CIA lacked sufficient personnel and adequate translators to conduct debriefings and interrogations in Country ■. Because of this personnel shortage, a number of detainees who were transferred to CIA custody were not interrogated or debriefed by anyone for days or weeks after their arrival at CIA detention facilities in Country ■.[644] As noted in a cable from the CIA Station in Country ■, in April 2003:

> "Station is supporting the debriefing and/or interrogation of a large number of individuals . . . and is constrained by a lack of personnel which would allow us to fully process them in a timely manner."[645]

I. Other Medical, Psychological, and Behavioral Issues

1. CIA Interrogations Take Precedence Over Medical Care

While CIA Headquarters informed the Department of Justice in July 2002 "that steps will be taken to ensure that [Abu Zubaydah's] injury is not in any way exacerbated by the use of these [enhanced interrogation] methods,"[646] CIA Headquarters informed CIA interrogators that the interrogation process would take "precedence" over Abu Zubaydah's medical care.[647] Beginning on August 4, 2002, Abu Zubaydah was kept naked, fed a "bare bones" liquid diet, and subjected to the non-stop use of the CIA's enhanced interrogation techniques.[648] On August 15, 2002, medical personnel described how Abu Zubaydah's interrogation resulted in the "steady deterioration" of his surgical wound from April 2002.[649] On August 20, 2002, medical officers wrote that Abu Zubaydah's wound had undergone "significant" deterioration.[650] Later, after one of Abu Zubaydah's eyes began to deteriorate,[651] CIA officers requested a test of Abu Zubaydah's other eye, stating that the request was "driven by our intelligence needs vice humanitarian concern for AZ." The cable relayed, "[w]e have a lot riding upon his ability to see, read and write."[652]

In April 2003, CIA detainees Abu Hazim and Abd al-Karim each broke a foot while trying to escape capture and were placed in casts.[653] CIA cables requesting the use of the CIA's enhanced interrogation techniques on the two detainees stated that the interrogators would "forego cramped confinement, stress positions, walling, and vertical shackling (due to [the detainees'] injury)."[654] Notwithstanding medical concerns related to the injuries, both of these detainees were subjected to one or more of these CIA enhanced interrogation techniques prior to obtaining CIA Headquarters approval.[655]

In the case of Abu Hazim, on May 4, 2003, the CIA regional medical officer examined Abu Hazim and recommended that he avoid all weight bearing activities for an additional five weeks due to his broken foot.[656] In the case of Abd al-Karim, on April 18, 2003, a CIA physician assistant recommended that al-Karim avoid extended standing for "a couple of weeks."[657] Six days later, on April 24, 2003, CIA Headquarters reviewed x-rays of al-Karim's foot, diagnosing him with a broken foot, and recommending no weight bearing and the use of crutches for a total of three months.[658] Despite these recommendations, on May 10, 2003, CIA interrogators believed that both Hazim and al-Karim were "strong mentally and physically due to [their] ability to sleep in the sitting position."[659] On May 12, 2003, a different CIA physician assistant, who had not been involved in the previous examinations determining the need for the detainees to avoid weight bearing, stated that it was his "opinion" that Abu Hazim's and Abd al-Karim's injuries were "sufficiently healed to allow being placed in the standing sleep deprivation position."[660] He further reported that he had "consulted with [CIA's Office of Medical Services] via secure phone and OMS medical officer concurred in this assessment."[661] CIA Headquarters approved the use of standing sleep deprivation against both detainees shortly thereafter.[662] As a result, both detainees were placed in standing sleep deprivation. Abu Hazim underwent 52 hours of standing sleep deprivation from June 3-5, 2003,[663] and Abd al-Karim underwent an unspecified period of standing sleep deprivation on May 15, 2003.[664]

CIA detainee Asadallah was left in the standing sleep deprivation position despite a sprained ankle. Later, when Asadallah was placed in stress positions on his knees, he complained of discomfort and asked to sit. Asadallah was told he could not sit unless he answered questions truthfully.[665]

2. CIA Detainees Exhibit Psychological and Behavioral Issues

Psychological and behavioral problems experienced by CIA detainees, who were held in austere conditions and in solitary confinement, also posed management challenges for the CIA.[666] For example, later in his detention, Ramzi bin al-Shibh exhibited behavioral and psychological problems, including visions, paranoia, insomnia, and attempts at self-harm.[667] CIA psychologists linked bin al-Shibh's deteriorating mental state to his isolation and inability to cope with his long-term detention.[668] Similarly, 'Abd al-Rahim al-Nashiri's unpredictable and disruptive behavior in detention made him one of the most difficult detainees for the CIA to manage. Al-Nashiri engaged in repeated belligerent acts, including throwing his food tray,[669] attempting to assault detention site personnel,[670] and trying to damage items in his cell.[671] Over a period of years, al-Nashiri accused the CIA staff of drugging or poisoning his food and complained of bodily pain and insomnia.[672] As noted, at one point, al-Nashiri launched a short-lived hunger strike, and the CIA responded by force feeding him rectally.[673] An October 2004 psychological assessment of al-Nashiri was used by the CIA to advance its discussions with National Security Council officials on establishing an "endgame" for the program.[674] In July

2005, CIA Headquarters expressed concern regarding al-Nashiri's "continued state of depression and uncooperative attitude."[675] Days later a CIA psychologist assessed that al-Nashiri was on the "verge of a breakdown."[676]

Beginning in March 2004, and continuing until his rendition to U.S. military custody at Guantanamo Bay in September 2006, Majid Khan engaged in a series of hunger strikes and attempts at self-mutilation that required significant attention from CIA detention site personnel. In response to Majid Khan's hunger strikes, medical personnel implemented various techniques to provide fluids and nutrients, including the use of a nasogastric tube and the provision of intravenous fluids. CIA records indicate that Majid Khan cooperated with the feedings and was permitted to infuse the fluids and nutrients himself.[677] After approximately three weeks, the CIA developed a more aggressive treatment regimen "without unnecessary conversation."[678] Majid Khan was then subjected to involuntary rectal feeding and rectal hydration, which included two bottles of Ensure. Later that same day, Majid Khan's "lunch tray," consisting of hummus, pasta with sauce, nuts, and raisins, was "pureed" and rectally infused.[679] Additional sessions of rectal feeding and hydration followed.[680] In addition to his hunger strikes, Majid Klian engaged in acts of self-harm that included attempting to cut his wrist on two occasions,[681] an attempt to chew into his arm at the inner elbow,[682] an attempt to cut a vein in the top of his foot,[683] and an attempt to cut into his skin at the elbow joint using a filed toothbrush.[684]

J. The CIA Seeks Reaffirmation of the CIA's Detention and Interrogation Program in 2003

1. Administration Statements About the Humane Treatment of Detainees Raise Concerns at the CIA About Possible Lack of Policy Support for CIA Interrogation Activities

On several occasions in early 2003, CIA General Counsel Scott Muller expressed concern to the National Security Council principals, White House staff, and Department of Justice personnel that the CIA's program might be inconsistent with public statements from the Administration that the U.S. Government's treatment of detainees was "humane."[685] CIA General Counsel Muller therefore sought to verify with White House and Department of Justice personnel that a February 7, 2002, Presidential Memorandum requiring the U.S.

military to treat detainees humanely did not apply to the CIA.[686] Following those discussions in early 2003, the White House press secretary was advised to avoid using the term "humane treatment" when discussing the detention of al-Qa'ida and Taliban personnel.[687]

In mid-2003, CIA officials also engaged in discussions with the Department of Justice, the Department of Defense, and attorneys in the White House on whether representations could be made that the U.S. Government complied with certain requirements arising out of the Convention Against Torture, namely that the treatment of detainees was consistent with constitutional standards in the Fifth, Eighth, and Fourteenth Amendments.[688] In late June 2003, after numerous inter-agency discussions, William Haynes, the general counsel of the Department of Defense, responded to a letter from Senator Patrick Leahy stating that it was U.S. Policy to comply with these standards.[689] According to a memorandum from the CIA's ████ ███ CTC Legal, ████████████, the August 1, 2002, OLC opinion provided a legal "safe harbor" for the CIA's use of its enhanced interrogation techniques.[690] The August 1, 2002, opinion did not, however, address the constitutional standards described in the letter from William Haynes.

In July 2003, after the White House made a number of statements again suggesting that U.S. treatment of detainees was "humane," the CIA asked the national security advisor for policy reaffirmation of the CIA's use of its enhanced interrogation techniques. During the time that request was being considered, CIA Headquarters stopped approving requests from CIA officers to use the CIA's enhanced interrogation techniques.[691] Because of this stand-down, CIA interrogators, with CIA Headquarters approval, instead used repeated applications of the CIA's "standard" interrogation techniques. These "standard" techniques were coercive, but not considered to be as coercive as the CIA's "enhanced" interrogation techniques. At this time, sleep deprivation beyond 72 hours was considered an "enhanced" interrogation technique, while sleep deprivation under 72 hours was defined as a "standard" CIA interrogation technique. To avoid using an "enhanced" interrogation technique, CIA officers subjected Khallad bin Attash to 70 hours of standing sleep deprivation, two hours less than the maximum. After allowing him four hours of sleep, bin Attash was subjected to an additional 23 hours of standing sleep deprivation, followed immediately by 20 hours of seated sleep deprivation.[692]

Unlike during most of the CIA's interrogation program, during the time that CIA Headquarters was seeking policy reaffirmation, the CIA responded to infractions in the interrogation program as reported through CIA cables and other communications. Although ██████, the chief of the interrogations program in RDG, does not appear to have been investigated or reprimanded for training interrogators on the abdominal slap before its use was approved,[693] training significant numbers of new interrogators to conduct interrogations on potentially compliant detainees,[694] or conducting large numbers of water dousing on detainees without requesting or obtaining authorization;[695] the CIA removed his certification to conduct interrogations in late July 2003 for placing a broom handle behind the knees of a detainee while that detainee was in a stress position.[696] CIA Headquarters also decertified two other interrogators, ████████ [CIA OFFICER 1] and ██████, in the same period, although there are no official records of why those decertifications occurred.[697]

2. The CIA Provides Inaccurate Information to Select Members of the National Security Council, Represents that "Termination of This Program Will Result in Loss of Life, Possibly Extensive"; Policymakers Reauthorize Program

On July 29, 2003, DCI Tenet and CIA General Counsel Muller attended a meeting with Vice President Cheney, National Security Advisor Rice, Attorney General Ashcroft, and White House Counsel Gonzales, among others, seeking policy reaffirmation of its coercive interrogation program. The presentation included a list of the CIA's standard and enhanced interrogation techniques. CIA General Counsel Muller also provided a description of the waterboard interrogation technique, including the inaccurate representation that it had been used against KSM 119 times and Abu Zubaydah 42 times.[698] The presentation warned National Security Council principals in attendance that "termination of this program will result in loss of life, possibly extensive." The CIA officers further noted that 50 percent of CIA intelligence reports on al-Qaida were derived from detainee reporting, and that "major threats were countered and attacks averted" because of the use of the CIA's enhanced interrogation techniques. The CIA provided specific examples of "attacks averted" as a result of using the CIA's enhanced interrogation techniques, including references to the U.S. Consulate in Karachi, the Heathrow Plot, the Second Wave Plot, and Iyman Faris,[699] As described later in this summary, and in greater detail in Volume II, these claims were inaccurate. After the CIA's presentation, Vice President Cheney stated, and

National Security Advisor Rice agreed, that the CIA was executing Administration policy in carrying out its interrogation program.[700]

The National Security Council principals at the July 2003 briefing initially concluded it was "not necessary or advisable to have a full Principals Committee meeting to review and reaffirm the Program."[701] A CIA email noted that the official reason for not having a full briefing was to avoid press disclosures, but added that:

> "it is clear to us from some of the runup meetings we had with [White House] Counsel that the [White House] is extremely concerned [Secretary of State] Powell would blow his stack if he were to be briefed on what's been going on."[702]

National Security Advisor Rice, however, subsequently decided that Secretary of State Colin Powell and Secretary of Defense Donald Rumsfeld should be briefed on the CIA interrogation program prior to recertification of the covert action.[703] As described, both were then formally briefed on the CIA program for the first time in a 25 minute briefing on September 16, 2003.[704]

On September 4, 2003, CIA records indicate that CIA officials may have provided Chairman Roberts, Vice Chairman Rockefeller, and their staff directors a briefing regarding the Administration's reaffirmation of the program.[705] Neither the CIA nor the Committee has a contemporaneous report on the content of the briefing or any confirmation that the briefing occurred.

K. Additional Oversight and Outside Pressure in 2004: ICRC, Inspector General, Congress, and the U.S. Supreme Court

1. ICRC Pressure Leads to Detainee Transfers; Department of Defense Official Informs the CIA that the U.S. Government "Should Not Be in the Position of Causing People to Disappear"; the CIA Provides Inaccurate Information on CIA Detainee to the Department of Defense

In January 2004, the ICRC sent a letter to ████████████ indicating that it was aware that the United States Government was holding unacknowledged detainees in several facilities in Country ██ "incommunicado for extensive periods of time, subjected to unacceptable conditions of internment, to ill treatment and torture, while deprived of any possible recourse."[706] According to the CIA, the letter included a "fairly complete list" of CIA detainees to whom the ICRC had not had access.[707] This prompted CIA Headquarters to conclude that it was necessary to reduce the number of detainees in

CIA custody.[708] The CIA subsequently transferred at least 25 of its detainees in Country ■■ to the U.S. military and foreign governments. The CIA also released five detainees.[709]

The CIA provided a factually incorrect description to the Department of Defense concerning one of the 18 CIA detainees transferred to U.S. military custody in March 2004. The transfer letter described CIA detainee Ali Jan as "the most trusted bodyguard of Jaluluddin Haqqani (a top AQ target of the USG)" who was captured in the village of ■■■■■■ on June ■■, 2002.[710] Although there was an individual named Ali Jan captured in the village of ■■■■■■ on June ■■, 2002,[711] CIA records indicate that he was not the detainee being held by the CIA in the Country ■■■■■■■ facility. The Ali Jan in CIA custody was apprehended circa early August 2003, during the U.S. military operation ■■■■■■■■■■ in Zormat Valley, Paktia Province, Afghanistan.[712] CIA records indicate that Ali Jan was transferred to CIA custody after his satellite phone rang while he was in military custody, and the translator indicated the caller was speaking in Arabic.[713] After his transfer to U.S. military custody, Ali Jan was eventually released on July ■, 2004.[714]

In response to the ICRC's formal complaint about detainees being kept in Country ■■ without ICRC access. State Department officials met with senior ICRC officials in Geneva, and indicated that it was U.S. policy to encourage all countries to provide ICRC access to detainees, including Country ■■.[715] While the State Department made these official representations to the ICRC, the CIA was repeatedly directing the same country to deny the ICRC access to the CIA detainees. In June 2004, the secretary of state ordered the U.S. ambassador in that country to deliver a demarche, "in essence demanding [the country] provide full access to all [country ■■■■■ ■■■■] detainees," which included detainees being held at the CIA's behest.[716] These conflicting messages from the United States Government, as well as increased ICRC pressure on the country for failing to provide access, created significant tension between the United States and the country in question.[717]

Later that year, in advance of a National Security Council Principals Committee meeting on September 14, 2004, officials from the Department of Defense called the CIA to inform the CIA that Deputy Secretary of Defense Paul Wolfowitz would not support the CIA's position that notifying the ICRC of all detainees in U.S. Government custody would harm U.S. national security. According to an internal CIA email following the call, the deputy secretary of defense had listened to the CIA's arguments for nondisclosure, but believed that it was time for full notification. The email stated that the Department of Defense supported the U.S. Government's position that there should be full disclosure to the ICRC, unless there were compelling reasons of military necessity or national security. The email added that the Department of Defense did not believe an adequate articulation of military necessity or national security reasons warranting nondisclosure existed, that "DoD is tired of 'taking hits' for CIA 'ghost detainees,'" and that the U.S. government "should not be in the position of causing people to 'disappear.'"[718]

Despite numerous meetings and communications within the executive branch throughout 2004, the United States did not formally respond to the January 6, 2004, ICRC letter until June 13, 2005.[719]

2. CIA Leadership Calls Draft Inspector General Special Review of the Program "Imbalanced and Inaccurate," Responds with Inaccurate Information; CIA Seeks to Limit Further Review of the CIA's Detention and Interrogation Program by the Inspector General

The CIA's Office of the Inspector General (OIG) was first informed of the CIA's Detention and Interrogation Program in November 2002, nine months after Abu Zubaydah became the CIA's first detainee. As described, the information was conveyed by the DDO, who also informed the OIG of the death of Gul Rahman. In January 2003, the DDO further requested that the OIG investigate allegations of unauthorized interrogation techniques against 'Abd al-Rahim al-Nashiri. Separately, the OIG "received information that some employees were concerned that certain covert Agency activities at an overseas detention and interrogation site might involve violations of human rights," according to the OIG's Special Review.[720]

During the course of the OIG's interviews, numerous CIA officers expressed concerns about the CIA's lack of preparedness for the detention and interrogation of Abu Zubaydah.[721] Other CIA officers expressed concern about the analytical assumptions driving interrogations,[722] as well as the lack of language and cultural background among members of the interrogation teams.[723] Some CIA officers described pressure from CIA Headquarters to use the CIA's enhanced interrogation techniques, which they attributed to faulty analytical assumptions about what detainees should know.[724] As the chief of RDG, [redacted], stated to the OIG in a February 2003 interview:

> "CTC does not know a lot about al-Qa'ida and as a result, Headquarters analysts have constructed 'models' of what al-Qa'ida represents to them. [██████] noted that the Agency does not have the linguists or subject matter experts it needs. The questions sent from CTC/Usama bin Laden (UBL) to the interrogators are based on SIGINT [signals intelligence] and other intelligence that often times is incomplete or wrong. When the detainee does not respond to the question, the assumption at Headquarters is that the detainee is holding back and 'knows' more, and consequently. Headquarters recommends resumption of EITs. This difference of opinion between the interrogators and Headquarters as to whether the detainee is 'compliant' is the type of ongoing pressure the interrogation team is exposed to. [██████] believes the waterboard was used 'recklessly' - 'too many times' on Abu Zubaydah at [DETENTION SITE GREEN], based in part on faulty intelligence."[725]

One senior interrogator, ██████, informed the OIG that differences between CIA Headquarters and the interrogators at the CIA detention sites were not part of the official record. According to ██████, "all of the fighting and criticism is done over the phone and is not put into cables," and that CIA "[c]ables reflect things that are 'all rosy.'"[726]

As is described elsewhere, and reflected in the final OIG Special Review, CIA officers discussed numerous other topics with the OIG, including conditions at DETENTION SITE COBALT, specific interrogations, the video taping of interrogations, the administration of the program, and concerns about the lack of an "end game" for CIA detainees, as well as the impact of possible public revelations concerning the existence and operation of the CIA's Detention and Interrogation Program.[727]

In January 2004, the CIA inspector general circulated for comment to various offices within the CIA a draft of the OIG Special Review of the CIA's Detention and Interrogation Program. Among other matters, the OIG Special Review described divergences between the CIA's enhanced interrogation techniques as applied and as described to the Department of Justice in 2002, the use of unauthorized techniques, and oversight problems related to DETENTION SITE COBALT. The draft OIG Special Review elicited responses from the CIA's deputy director for operations, the deputy director for science and technology, the Office of General Counsel, and the Office of Medical Services. Several of the responses—particularly those from CIA General Counsel Scott Muller and CIA Deputy Director for Operations James Pavitt—were highly critical of the inspector general's draft Special Review. General Counsel Muller wrote that the OIG Special Review presented "an imbalanced and inaccurate picture of the Counterterrorism Detention and Interrogation Program," and claimed the OIG Special Review, "[o]n occasion," "quoted or summarized selectively and misleadingly" from CIA documents.[728] Deputy Director for Operations James Pavitt wrote that the OIG Special Review should have come to the "conclusion that our efforts have thwarted attacks and saved lives," and that "EITs (including the water board) have been indispensable to our successes." Pavitt attached to his response a document describing information the CIA obtained "as a result of the lawful use of EITs" that stated, "[t]he evidence points clearly to the fact that without the use of such techniques, we and our allies would [have] suffered major terrorist attacks involving hundreds, if not thousands, of casualties."[729] A review of CIA records found that the representations in the Pavitt materials were almost entirely inaccurate.[730]

In addition to conveying inaccurate information on the operation, management, and effectiveness of the CIA program, CIA leadership continued to impede the OIG in its efforts to oversee the program. In July 2005, Director Goss sent a memorandum to the inspector general to "express several concerns regarding the in-depth, multi-faceted review" of the CIA's CTC. The CIA director wrote that he was "increasingly concerned about the cumulative impact of the OIG's work on CTC's performance," adding that "I believe it makes sense to complete existing reviews . . . before opening new ones." Director Goss added, "[t]o my knowledge, Congress is satisfied that you are meeting its requirements" with regard to the CIA's Detention and Interrogation Program.[731] At the time, however, the vice chairman of the Senate Select Committee on Intelligence was seeking a Committee investigation of the CIA program, in part because of the aspects of the program that were not being investigated by the Office of Inspector General.[732] In April 2007, CIA Director Michael Hayden had his "Senior Councilor"—an individual within the CIA who was accountable only to the CIA director—conduct a review of the inspector general's practices. Defending the decision to review the OIG, the CIA told the Committee that there were "morale issues that the [CIA] director needs to be mindful of," and that the review had uncovered instances of "bias" among OIG personnel against the CIA's Detention and Interrogation Program.[733] In 2008, the CIA director announced the results of his review of the OIG to the CIA work force and stated that the inspector general had "chosen to take a number of steps to heighten the efficiency, assure the quality, and increase the transparency of the investigative process."[734]

3. The CIA Does Not Satisfy Inspector General Special Review Recommendation to Assess the Effectiveness of the CIA's Enhanced Interrogation Techniques

The final May 2004 OIG Special Review included a recommendation that the CIA's DDO conduct a study of the effectiveness of the CIA's interrogation techniques within 90 days. Prompted by the recommendation, the CIA tasked two senior CIA officers to lead "an informal operational assessment of the CIA detainee program." The reviewers were tasked with responding to 12 specific terms of reference, including an assessment of "the effectiveness of each interrogation technique and environmental deprivation" to determine if any techniques or deprivation should be "added, modified, or discontinued."[735] According to a CIA memorandum from the reviewers, their review was based on briefings by CTC personnel, "a discussion with three senior CTC managers who played key roles in running the CIA detainee program," and a review of nine documents, including the OIG Special Review and an article by the CIA contractors who developed the CIA's enhanced interrogation techniques, Hammond DUNBAR and Grayson SWIGERT.[736] As described in this summary, and in more detail in Volume II, these documents contained numerous inaccurate representations regarding the operation and effectiveness of the CIA program. There are no records to indicate the two senior CIA officers reviewed the underlying interrogation cables and intelligence records related to the representations. Their resulting assessment repeated information found in the documents provided to them and reported that the "CIA Detainee Program is a success, providing unique and valuable intelligence at the tactical level for the benefit of policymakers, war fighters, and the CIA's covert action operators." The assessment also reported that regulations and procedures for handling detainees were "adequate and clear," and that the program had responded swiftly, fairly, and completely to deviations from the structured program.[737] Nonetheless, the assessment came to the conclusion that detention and interrogations activities should not be conducted by the CIA, but by "experienced U.S. law enforcement officers," stating:

> "The Directorate of Operations (DO) should not be in the business of running prisons or 'temporary detention facilities,' The DO should focus on its core mission: clandestine intelligence operations. Accordingly, the DO should continue to hunt, capture, and render targets, and then exploit them for intelligence and ops leads once in custody. The management of their incarceration and interrogation should be conducted by appropriately experienced U.S. law enforcement

officers, because that is their charter and they have the training and experience."[738]

The assessment noted that the CIA program required significant resources at a time when the CIA was already stretched thin. Finally, the authors wrote that they "strongly believe" that the president and congressional oversight members should receive a comprehensive update on the program, "[g]iven the intense interest and controversy surrounding the detainee issue."[739]

On January 26, 2005, DCI Goss forwarded the senior officer review to Inspector General John Helgerson.[740] The DCI asked whether the review would satisfy the inspector general recommendation for an independent review of the program.[741] On January 28, 2005, the inspector general responded that the senior officer review would not satisfy the recommendation for an independent review.[742] The inspector general also responded to a concern raised by ██████ ██████ OMS that studying the results of CIA interrogations would amount to human experimentation, stating:

> "I fear there was a misunderstanding. OIG did not have in mind doing additional, guinea pig research on human beings. What we are recommending is that the Agency undertake a careful review of its experience to date in using the various techniques and that it draw conclusions about their safety, effectiveness, etc., that can guide CIA officers as we move ahead. We make this recommendation because we have found that the Agency over the decades has continued to get itself in messes related to interrogation programs for one overriding reason: we do not document and learn from our experience - each generation of officers is left to improvise anew, with problematic results for our officers as individuals and for our Agency. We are not unaware that there are subtleties to this matter, as the effectiveness of techniques varies among individuals, over time, as administered, in combination with one another, and so on. All the more reason to document these important findings."[743]

In November and December 2004, the CIA responded to National Security Advisor Rice's questions about the effectiveness of the CIA's enhanced interrogation techniques by asserting that an effectiveness review was not possible, while highlighting examples of "[k]ey intelligence" the CIA represented was obtained after the use of the CIA's enhanced interrogation techniques. The December 2004 memorandum prepared for the national security advisor entitled, "Effectiveness of the CIA Counterterrorist Interrogation Techniques," begins:

> "Action Requested: None, This memorandum responds to your request for an independent study of the foreign intelligence efficacy of using enhanced interrogation techniques. There is no way to conduct such a

> study. What we can do, however, if [*sic*] set forth below the intelligence the Agency obtained from detainees who, before their interrogations, were not providing any information of intelligence [value]."[744]

Under a section of the memorandum entitled, "Results," the CIA memo asserts that the "CIA's use of DOJ-approved enhanced interrogation techniques, as part of a comprehensive interrogation approach, has enabled CIA to disrupt terrorist plots [and] capture additional terrorists." The memorandum then lists examples of "[k]ey intelligence collected from HVD interrogations after applying interrogation techniques," which led to "disrupte[ed] terrorist plots" and the "capture [of] additional terrorists." The examples include: the "Karachi Plot," the "Heathrow Plot," "the 'Second Wave'" plotting, the identification of the "the Guraba Cell," the identification of "Issa al-Hindi," the arrest of Abu Talha al-Pakistani, "Hambali's Capture," information on Jaffar al-Tayyar, the "Dirty Bomb" plot, the arrest of Sajid Badat, and information on Shkai, Pakistan. CIA records do not indicate when, or if, this memorandum was provided to the national security advisor.[745]

A subsequent CIA memorandum, dated March 5, 2005, concerning an upcoming meeting between the CIA director and the national security advisor on the CIA's progress in completing the OIG recommended review of the effectiveness of the CIA's enhanced interrogation techniques states, "we [CIA] believe this study is much needed and should be headed up by highly respected national-level political figures with widely recognized reputations for independence and fairness."[746]

On March 21, 2005, the director of the CTC formally proposed the "establishment of an independent 'blue ribbon' commission . . . with a charter to study our EITs."[747] The CIA then began the process of establishing a panel that included ████████████ ██████ and ████████████████ ████████████. Both panelists received briefings and papers from CIA personnel who participated in the CIA's Detention and Interrogation Program. ██████ [the first panelist] wrote: "It is clear from our discussions with both DO and DI officers that the program is deemed by them to be a great success, and I would concur. The EITs, as part of the overall program, are credited with enabling the US to disrupt terrorist plots, capture additional terrorists, and collect a high volume of useful intelligence on al-Qa'ida (AQ) . . . There are accounts of numerous plots against the US and the West that were revealed as a result of HVD interrogations." He also observed, however, that "[n]either my background nor field of expertise particularly lend themselves to judging the effectiveness of interrogation techniques, taken individually or collectively."[748] ████ ████ [the second panelist] concluded that "there is no objective way to answer the question of efficacy," but stated it was possible to "make some general observations" about the program based on CIA personnel assessments of "the quality of the intelligence provided" by CIA detainees. Regarding the effectiveness of the CIA's enhanced interrogation techniques, he wrote: "here enters the epistemological problem. We can never know whether or not this intelligence could have been extracted though alternative procedures. Spokesmen from within the organization firmly believe it could not have been."[749]

4. The CIA Wrongfully Detains Khalid Al-Masri; CIA Director Rejects Accountability for Officer Involved

After the dissemination of the draft CIA Inspector General Special Review in early 2004, approvals from CIA Headquarters to use the CIA's enhanced interrogation techniques adhered more closely to the language of the DCI guidelines. Nonetheless, CIA records indicate that officers at CIA Headquarters continued to fail to properly monitor justifications for the capture and detention of detainees, as well as the justification for the use of the CIA's enhanced interrogation techniques on particular detainees.[750]

For example, on January ██, 2004, the CIA rendered German citizen Khalid al-Masri to a Country ██ facility used by the CIA for detention purposes. The rendition was based on the determination by officers in the CIA's ALEC Station that "al-Masri knows key information that could assist in the capture of other al-Qa'ida operatives that pose a serious threat of violence or death to U.S. persons and interests and who may be planning terrorist activities.[751] The cable did not state that Khalid al-Masri himself posed a serious threat of violence or death, the standard required for detention under the September 17, 2001, Memorandum of Notification (MON).

CIA debriefing cables from Country ██ on January 27, 2004, and January 28, 2004, note that Khalid al-Masri "seemed bewildered on why he has been sent to this particular prison,"[752] and was "adamant that [CIA] has the wrong person."[753] Despite doubts from CIA officers in Country ██ about Khalid al-Masri's links to terrorists, and RDG's concurrence with those doubts, different components within the CIA disagreed on the process for his release.[754] As later described by the CIA inspector general, officers in ALEC Station continued to think that releasing Khalid al-Masri would pose a threat to U.S. interests and that monitoring should be required, while those in the CIA's ████ Division did not want to notify the German government about the rendition of a German citizen.[755] Because of the significance of the dispute, the National Security Council settled the matter, concluding that al-Masri should be repatriated and that the Germans should be told about al-Masri's rendition.[756]

On May ██, 2004, Khalid al-Masri was transferred from Country ██ to ████.[757] After al-Masri arrived in ████, CIA officers released him and sent him toward a fake border crossing, where the officers told him he would be sent back to Germany because he had entered ████ illegally.[758] At the time of his release, al-Masri was provided 14,500 Euros,[759] as well as his belongings.[760]

On July 16, 2007, the CIA inspector general issued a Report of Investigation on the rendition and detention of Khalid al-Masri, concluding that "[a]vailable intelligence information did not provide a sufficient basis to render and detain Khalid al-Masri," and that the "Agency's prolonged detention of al-Masri was unjustified."[761] On October 9, 2007, the CIA informed the Committee that it "lacked sufficient basis to render and detain al-Masri," and that the judgment by operations officers that al-Masri was associated with terrorists who posed a threat to U.S. interests "was not supported by available intelligence." The CIA director nonetheless decided that no further action was warranted against ████████████, then the deputy chief of ALEC Station, who advocated for al-Masri's rendition, because "[t]he Director strongly believes that mistakes should be expected in a business filled with uncertainty and that, when they result from performance that meets reasonable standards, CIA leadership must stand behind the officers who make them." The notification also stated that "with regard to counterterrorism operations in general and the al-Masri matter in particular, the Director believes the scale tips decisively in favor of accepting mistakes that over connect the dots against those that under connect them."[762]

5. Hassan Ghul Provides Substantial Information—Including Information on a Key UBL Facilitator—Prior to the CIA's Use of Enhanced Interrogation Techniques

████████████████ foreign authorities captured Hassan Ghul in the Iraqi Kurdistan Region on January █, 2004.[763] After his identity was confirmed on January █, 2004,[764] Ghul was rendered from U.S. military custody to CIA custody at DETENTION

SITE COBALT on January ■■, 2004.[765] The detention site interrogators, who, according to CIA records, did not use the CIA's enhanced interrogation techniques on Ghul, sent at least 21 intelligence reports to CIA Headquarters based on their debriefings of Hassan Ghul from the two days he spent at the facility.[766]

As detailed in this summary, and in greater detail in Volume II, CIA records indicate that the most accurate CIA detainee reporting on the facilitator who led to Usama bin Laden (UBL) was acquired from Hassan Ghul—prior to the use of the CIA's enhanced interrogation techniques.[767] Ghul speculated that "UBL was likely living in [the] Peshawar area," and that "it was well known that he was always with Abu Ahmed [al-Kuwaiti]."[768] Ghul described Abu Ahmad al-Kuwaiti as UBL's "closest assistant,"[769] who couriered messages to al-Qa'ida's chief of operations, and listed al-Kuwaiti as one of three individuals likely with UBL.[770] Ghul further speculated that:

> "UBL's security apparatus would be minimal, and that the group likely lived in a house with a family somewhere in Pakistan . . . Ghul speculated that Abu Ahmed likely handled all of UBL's needs, including moving messages out to Abu Faraj [al-Libi] . . ."[771]

During this same period, prior to the use of the CIA's enhanced interrogation techniques, Ghul provided information related to Abu Musab al-Zarqawi, Abu Faraj al-Libi (including his role in delivering messages from UBL), Jaffar al-Tayyar, 'Abd al-Hadi al-Iraqi, Hamza Rabi'a, Shaik Sa'id al-Masri, Sharif al-Masri, Abu 'Abd al-Rahman al-Najdi, Abu Talha al-Pakistani, and numerous other al-Qa'ida operatives. He also provided information on the locations, movements, operational security, and training of al-Qa'ida leaders living in Shkai, Pakistan, as well as on the visits of other leaders and operatives to Shkai.[772] Ghul's reporting on Shkai, which was included in at least 16 of the 21 intelligence reports,[773] confirmed earlier reporting that the Shkai valley served as al-Qa'ida's command and control center after the group's 2001 exodus from Afghanistan.[774] Notwithstanding these facts, in March 2005, the CIA represented to the Department of Justice that Hassan Ghul's reporting on Shkai was acquired "*after*" the use of the CIA's enhanced interrogation techniques.[775]

After two days of questioning at DETENTION SITE COBALT and the dissemination of 21 intelligence reports, Ghul was transferred to DETENTION SITE BLACK.[776] According to CIA records, upon arrival, Ghul was "shaved and barbered, stripped, and placed in the standing position against the wall" with "his hands above his head" with plans to lower his hands after two hours.[777]

The CIA interrogators at the detention site then requested to use the CIA's enhanced interrogation techniques on Ghul, writing:

> "[the] interrogation team believes, based on [Hassan Ghul's] reaction to the initial contact, that his al-Qa'ida briefings and his earlier experiences with U.S. military interrogators have convinced him there are limits to the physical contact interrogators can have with him. The interrogation team believes the approval and employment of enhanced measures should sufficiently shift [Hassan Ghul's] paradigm of what he expects to happen. The lack of these increasd [*sic*] measures may limit the team's capability to collect critical and reliable information in a timely manner."[778]

CIA Headquarters approved the request the same day.[779] Following 59 hours of sleep deprivation,[780] Hassan Ghul experienced hallucinations, but was told by a psychologist that his reactions were "consistent with what many others experience in his condition," and that he should calm himself by telling himself his experiences are normal and will subside when he decides to be truthful.[781] The sleep deprivation, as well as other enhanced interrogations, continued,[782] as did Ghul's hallucinations.[783] Ghul also complained of back pain and asked to see a doctor,[784] but interrogators responded that the "pain was normal, and would stop when [Ghul] was confirmed as telling the truth." A cable states that "[i]nterrogators told [Ghul] they did not care if he was in pain, but cared only if he provided complete and truthful information.[785] A CIA physician assistant later observed that Hassan Ghul was experiencing "notable physiological fatigue," including "abdominal and back muscle pain/spasm, 'heaviness' and mild paralysis of arms, legs and feet [that] are secondary to his hanging position and extreme degree of sleep deprivation," but that Ghul was clinically stable and had "essentially normal vital signs," despite an "occasional premature heart beat" that the cable linked to Ghul's fatigue.[786] Throughout this period, Ghul provided no actionable threat information, and as detailed later in this summary, much of his reporting on the al-Qa'ida presence in Shkai was repetitive of his reporting prior to the use of the CIA's enhanced interrogation techniques. Ghul also provided no other information of substance on UBL facilitator Abu Ahmad al-Kuwaiti.[787] Nonetheless, on May 5, 2011, the CIA provided a document to the Committee entitled, "Detainee Reporting on Abu Ahmad al-Kuwaiti," which lists Hassan Ghul as a CIA detainee who was subjected to the CIA's enhanced interrogation techniques and who provided "Tier One" information "link[ing] Abu Ahmad to Bin Ladin."[788] Hassan Ghul was ███ ████████████████████, and later released.[789] █

███

██.[790]

6. Other Detainees Wrongfully Held in 2004; CIA Sources Subjected to the CIA's Enhanced Interrogation Techniques; CIA Officer Testifies that the CIA Is "Not Authorized" "to Do Anything Like What You Have Seen" in Abu Ghraib Photographs

In March 2004, the CIA took custody of an Afghan national who had sought employment at a U.S. military base because he had the same name (Gul Rahman) as an individual believed to be targeting U.S. military forces in Afghanistan.[791] During the period in which the Afghan was detained, the CIA obtained signals intelligence of their true target communicating with his associates. DNA results later showed conclusively that the Afghan in custody was not the target. Nonetheless, the CIA held the detainee in solitary confinement for approximately a month before he was released with a nominal payment.[792]

In the spring of 2004, after two detainees were transferred to CIA custody, CIA interrogators proposed, and CIA Headquarters approved, using the CIA's enhanced interrogation techniques on one of the two detainees because it might cause the detainee to provide information that could identify inconsistencies in the other detainee's story.[793] After both detainees had spent approximately 24 hours shackled in the standing sleep deprivation position, CIA Headquarters confirmed that the detainees were former CIA sources.[794] The two detainees had tried to contact the CIA on multiple occasions prior to their detention to inform the CIA of their activities and provide intelligence. The messages they had sent to the CIA ████ ██████████ were not translated until after the detainees were subjected to the CIA's enhanced interrogation techniques.[795]

During this same period in early 2004, CIA interrogators interrogated Adnan al-Libi, a member of the Libyan Islamic Fighting Group. CIA Headquarters did not approve the use of the CIA's enhanced techniques against al-Libi, but indicated that interrogators could use "standard" interrogation techniques, which included up to 48 hours of sleep deprivation.[796] CIA interrogators subsequently reported subjecting Adnan al-Libi to sleep deprivation sessions of 46.5 hours, 24 hours, and 48 hours, with a combined three hours of sleep between sessions.[797]

Beginning in late April 2004, a number of media outlets published photographs of detainee abuse at the Department of Defense-run Abu Ghraib prison in Iraq. The media reports caused members of the Committee and individuals in the executive branch to focus on detainee issues. On May 12, 2004, the Committee held a lengthy hearing on detainee issues with Department of Defense and CIA witnesses. The CIA used the Abu Ghraib abuses as a contrasting reference point for its detention and interrogation activities. In a response to a question from a Committee member, CIA Deputy Director McLaughlin said, "we are not authorized in [the CIA program] to do anything like what you have seen in those photographs."[798] In response, a member of the Committee said, "I understand," and expressed the understanding, consistent with past CIA briefings to the Committee, that the "norm" of CIA's interrogations was "transparent law enforcement procedures [that] had developed to such a high level . . . that you could get pretty much what you wanted." The CIA did not correct the Committee member's misunderstanding that CIA interrogation techniques were similar to techniques used by U.S. law enforcement.[799]

7. The CIA Suspends the Use of its Enhanced Interrogation Techniques, Resumes Use of the Techniques on an Individual Basis; Interrogations are Based on Fabricated, Single Source Information

In May 2004, the OLC, then led by Assistant Attorney General Jack Goldsmith, informed the CIA's Office of General Counsel that it had never formally opined on whether the use of the CIA's enhanced interrogation techniques in the CIA's program was consistent with U.S. constitutional standards.[800] Goldsmith also raised concerns about divergences between the CIA's proposed enhanced interrogation techniques, as described in the August 1, 2002, memorandum, and their actual application, as described in the CIA Inspector General's Special Review.[801] In late May 2004, DCI Tenet suspended the use of the CIA's "enhanced" and "standard" interrogation techniques, pending updated approvals from the OLC.[802] On June 4, 2004, DCI Tenet issued a formal memorandum suspending the use of the CIA's interrogation techniques, pending policy and legal review.[803] The same day, the CIA sought reaffirmation of the program from the National Security Council.[804] National Security Advisor Rice responded, noting that the "next logical step is for the Attorney General to complete the relevant legal analysis now in preparation."[805]

On June ■, 2004, a foreign government captured Janat Gul, an individual believed, based on reporting from a CIA source, to have information about al-Qa'ida plans to attack the United States prior to the 2004 presidential election.[806] In October 2004, the CIA source who provided the information on the "pre-election" threat and implicated Gul and others admitted to fabricating the information. However, as early as March 2004, CIA officials internally expressed doubts about the validity of the CIA source's information.[807]

On July 2, 2004, the CIA met with National Security Advisor Rice, other National Security Council officials, White House Counsel Alberto Gonzales, as well as the attorney general and the deputy attorney general, to seek authorization to use the CIA's enhanced interrogation techniques, specifically on Janat Gul.[808] The CIA represented that CIA "interrogations have saved American lives," that more than half of the CIA detainees would not cooperate until they were interrogated using the CIA's enhanced interrogation techniques,[809] and that "unless CIA interrogators can use a full range of enhanced interrogation methods, it is unlikely that CIA will be able to obtain current threat information from Gul in a timely manner."[810] Janat Gul was not yet in CIA custody.[811]

On July 6, 2004, National Security Advisor Rice sent a memorandum to DCI Tenet stating that the CIA was "permitted to use previously approved enhanced interrogation methods for Janat Gul, with the exception of the waterboard." Rice offered "to assist [the CIA] in obtaining additional guidance from the Attorney General and NSC Principals on an expedited basis" and noted the CIA's agreement to provide additional information about the waterboard technique in order for the Department of Justice to assess its legality. Rice's memorandum further documented that the CIA had informed her that "Gul likely has information about preelection terrorist attacks against the United States as a result of Gul's close ties to individuals involved in these alleged plots.[812]

In a meeting on July 20, 2004, National Security Council principals, including the vice president, provided their authorization for the CIA to use its enhanced interrogation techniques—again, with the exception of the waterboard—on Janat Gul. They also directed the Department of Justice to prepare a legal opinion on whether the CIA's enhanced interrogation techniques were consistent with the Fifth and Fourteenth Amendments to the U.S. Constitution.[813] On July 22, 2004, Attorney General John Ashcroft sent a letter to Acting DCI John McLaughlin stating that nine interrogation techniques (those addressed in the August 1, 2002, memorandum, with the exception of the waterboard) did not violate the U.S. Constitution or any statute or U.S. treaty obligations, in the context of the interrogation of Janat Gul.[814] For the remainder of 2004, the CIA used its enhanced interrogation techniques on three detainees—Janat Gul, Sharif al-Masri, and Ahmed Khalfan Ghailani—with individualized approval from the Department of Justice.[815]

After being rendered to CIA custody on July [redacted], 2004, Janat Gul was subjected to the CIA's enhanced interrogation techniques, including continuous sleep deprivation, facial holds, attention grasps, facial slaps, stress positions, and walling,[816] until he experienced auditory and visual hallucinations.[817] According to a cable, Janat Gul was "not oriented to time or place" and told CIA officers that he saw "his wife and children in the mirror and had heard their voices in the white noise."[818] The questioning of Janat Gul continued, although the CIA ceased using the CIA's enhanced interrogation techniques for several days. According to a CIA cable, "[Gul] asked to die, or just be killed."[819] After continued interrogation sessions with Gul, on August 19, 2004, CIA detention site personnel wrote that the interrogation "team does not believe [Gul] is withholding imminent threat information.[820] On August 21, 2004, a cable from CIA Headquarters stated that Janat Gul "is believed" to possess threat information, and that the "use of enhanced techniques is appropriate in order to obtain that information."[821] On that day, August 21, 2004, CIA interrogators resumed using the CIA's enhanced interrogation techniques against Gul.[822] Gul continued not to provide any reporting on the pre-election threat described by the CIA source.[823] On August 25, 2004, CIA interrogators sent a cable to CIA Headquarters stating that Janat Gul "may not possess all that [the CIA] believes him to know."[824] The interrogators added that "many issues linking [Gul] to al-Qaida are derived from single source reporting" (the CIA source).[825] Nonetheless, CIA interrogators continued to question Gul on the pre-election threat. According to an August 26, 2004, cable, after a 47-hour session of standing sleep deprivation, Janat Gul was returned to his cell, allowed to remove his diaper, given a towel and a meal, and permitted to sleep.[826] In October 2004, the CIA conducted a [redacted] of the CIA source who had identified Gul as having knowledge of attack planning for the pre-election threat. [redacted], the CIA source admitted to fabricating the information.[827] Gul was subsequently transferred to a foreign government. On [redacted] [redacted] informed the CIA that Janat Gul had been released.[828]

Janat Gul never provided the threat information the CIA originally told the National Security Council that Gul possessed. Nor did the use of the CIA's enhanced interrogation techniques against Gul produce the "immediate threat information that could save American lives," which had been the basis for the CIA to seek authorization to use the techniques. As described elsewhere in this summary, the CIA's justification for employing its enhanced interrogation techniques on Janat Gul—the first detainee to be subjected to the techniques following the May 2004 suspension—changed over time. After having initially cited Gul's knowledge of the pre-election threat, as reported by the CIA's source, the CIA began representing that its enhanced interrogation techniques were required for Gul to deny the existence of the threat, thereby disproving the credibility of the CIA source.[829]

On August 11, 2004, in the midst of the interrogation of Janat Gul using the CIA's enhanced interrogation techniques, CIA attorney ■■■■■■■■ wrote a letter to Acting Assistant Attorney General Dan Levin with "brief biographies" of four individuals whom the CIA hoped to detain. Given the requirement at the time that the CLA seek individual approval from the Department of Justice before using the CIA's enhanced interrogation techniques against a detainee, the CIA letter states, "[w]e are providing these preliminary biographies in preparation for a future request for a legal opinion on their subsequent interrogation in CIA control." Two of the individuals—Abu Faraj al-Libi and Hamza Rabi'a—had not yet been captured, and thus the "biographies" made no reference to their interrogations or the need to use the CIA's enhanced interrogation techniques. The third individual, Abu Talha al-Pakistani, was in foreign government custody. His debriefings by a foreign government, ■■■■■■■■ ■, were described in the letter as "only moderately effective" because Abu Talha was "distracting [those questioning him] with noncritical information that is truthful, but is not related to operational planning." The fourth individual, Ahmed Khalfan Ghailani, was also in foreign government custody and being debriefed by foreign government officials ■■■■■■■■. According to the letter, Ghailani's foreign government debriefings were "ineffective" because Ghailani had "denied knowledge of current threats." The letter described reporting on the pre-election threat—much of which came from the CIA source—in the context of all four individuals.[830] Ahmed Ghailani and Abu Faraj al-Libi were eventually rendered to CIA custody and subjected to the CIA's enhanced interrogation techniques.

On September ■■, 2004, after the CIA had initiated a counterintelligence review of the CIA source who had reported on the pre-election threat, but prior to the CIA source's ■■■■■, the CIA took custody of Sharif al-Masri, whom the CIA source had reported would also have information about the threat.[831] Intelligence provided by Sharif al-Masri while he was in foreign government custody resulted in the dissemination of more than 30 CIA intelligence reports.[832] After entering CIA custody, Sharif al-Masri expressed his intent to cooperate with the CIA, indicating that he was frightened of interrogations because he had been tortured while being interrogated in ■ ■■■■■■■■.[833] The CIA nonetheless sought approval to use the CIA's enhanced interrogation techniques against al-Masri because of his failure to provide information on the pre-election threat.[834]

After approximately a week of interrogating al-Masri using the CIA's enhanced interrogation techniques, including sleep deprivation that coincided with auditory hallucinations, CIA interrogators reported that al-Masri had been "motivated to participate" at the time of his arrival.[835] Despite al-Masri's repeated descriptions of torture in ■■■■, the CIA transferred al-Masri to that government's custody after approximately three months of CIA detention.[836]

As in the case of Janat Gul and Sharif al-Masri, the CIA's requests for OLC advice on the use of the CIA's enhanced interrogation techniques against Ahmed Khalfan Ghailani were based on the fabricated reporting on the pre-election threat from the same CIA source.[837] Like Janat Gul and Sharif al-Masri, Ghailani also experienced auditory hallucinations following sleep deprivation.[838] As described in this summary, after having opined on the legality of using the CIA's enhanced interrogation techniques on these three individual detainees, the OLC did not opine again on the CIA's enhanced interrogation program until May 2005.

8. Country ■■ Detains Individuals on the CIA's Behalf

Consideration of a detention facility in Country ■■ began in ■■■■ 2003, when the CIA sought to transfer Ramzi bin al-Shibh from the custody of a foreign government to CIA custody.[839] ■■■■■■■■ ■■■■■■■■■■■■■■■■, which had not yet informed the country's political leadership of the CIA's request to establish a clandestine detention facility in Country ■■, surveyed potential sites for the facility, while the CIA set aside $■ million for its construction.[840] In ■■■■ 2003, the CIA arranged for a "temporary patch" involving placing two CIA detainees (Ramzi bin al-Shibh and 'Abd al-Rahim al-Nashiri) within an already existing Country ■■ detention facility, until the CIA's own facility could be built.[841] That spring, as the CIA was offering millions of dollars in subsidies to ■■■■■■■■ in Countries ■■,

■■, and ■■,[842] CIA Headquarters directed the CIA Station in Country ■■ to "think big" about how CIA Headquarters could support Country ■■'s ■■■■■■■■■■■■■■■■.[843] After the Station initially submitted relatively modest proposals, CIA Headquarters reiterated the directive, adding that the Station should provide a "wish list."[844] In ■■■■ 2003, the Station proposed a more expansive $■ million in ■■■■■■■ subsidies.[845] ■■■■■ subsidy payments, intended in part as compensation for support of the CIA detention program, rose as high as $■ million.[846] By ■■■■■■■ 2003, after an extension of five months beyond the originally agreed upon timeframe for concluding CIA detention activities in Country ■■, both bin al-Shibh and al-Nashiri had been transferred out of Country ■■ to the CIA detention facility at Guantanamo Bay, Cuba.[847]

9. U.S. Supreme Court Action in the Case of Rasul v. Bush Forces Transfer of CIA Detainees from Guantanamo Bay to Country ■■

Beginning in September 2003, the CIA held a number of detainees at CIA facilities on the grounds of, but separate from, the U.S. military detention facilities at Guantanamo Bay, Cuba.[848] In early January 2004, the CIA and the Department of Justice began discussing the possibility that a pending U.S. Supreme Court case, *Rasul v. Bush*, might grant *habeas corpus* rights to the five CIA detainees then being held at a CIA detention facility at Guantanamo Bay.[849] Shortly after these discussions, CIA officers approached the ■■■■■■■■ in Country ■■ to determine if it would again be willing to host these CIA detainees, who would remain in CIA custody within an already existing Country ■■ facility.[850] By January ■■, 2004, the ■■■■■■■■ ■ in Country ■■ had agreed to this arrangement for a limited period of time.[851]

Meanwhile, CIA General Counsel Scott Muller asked the Department of Justice, the National Security Council, and the White House Counsel for advice on whether the five CIA detainees being held at Guantanamo Bay should remain at Guantanamo Bay or be moved pending the Supreme Court's decision.[852] After consultation with the U.S. solicitor general in February 2004, the Department of Justice recommended that the CIA move four detainees out of a CIA detention facility at Guantanamo Bay pending the Supreme Court's resolution of the case.[853] The Department of Justice concluded that a fifth detainee, Ibn Shaykh al-Libi, did not need to be transferred because he had originally been detained under military authority and had been declared to the ICRC.[854] Nonetheless, by April ■■, 2004, all five CIA detainees were transferred from Guantanamo Bay to other CIA detention facilities.[855]

Shortly after placing CIA detainees within an already existing Country ■■ facility for a second time, tensions arose between the CIA and ■■■■■ Country ■■ ■■■■■■■■■.[856] In ■■■■ 2004, CIA detainees in a Country ■■ facility claimed to hear cries of pain from other detainees presumed to be in the ■■■■■■■■■■■■■■■■■■■■ ■■■■■■■■■■ facility.[857] When the CIA chief of Station approached the ■■■■■■■■■■■■■■■■■■■■■■■■■■■■■■■■■ about the accounts of the CIA detainees, the ■■■■■ stated with "bitter dismay" that the bilateral relationship was being "tested."[858] There were also counterintelligence concerns relating to CIA detainee Ramzi bin al-Shibh, who had attempted to influence a Country ■■ officer.[859] These concerns contributed to a request from ■■■■■■■■■■■■ ■■■ in ■■■■■ 2004 for the CIA to remove all CIA detainees from Country ■■.[860]

In ■■■■■ 2004, when the chief of Station in Country ■■ again approached the ■■■■■■■■■■■■■■■■■■■■■■■■■■■ with allegations from CIA detainees about the mistreatment of Country ■ ■ detainees ■■■■■ in the facility, the chief of Station received an angry response that, as he reported to CIA Headquarters, "starkly illustrated the inherent challenges [of] ■■■■■■■■■■■■■■■■■■■ ■■■■■■■■■■■■■." According to the chief of Station, Country ■■ saw the CIA as "querulous and unappreciative recipients of their ■■■ ■■■■ cooperation."[861] By the end of 2004, relations between the CIA and Country ■■ deteriorated, particularly with regard to intelligence cooperation.[862] The CIA detainees were transferred out of Country ■ ■ in ■■■■■ 2005.[863]

Beginning in ■■■■ 2005, the ■■■■■■■■■■■■■■■■■■■■■■ ■■ in Country ■ insisted, over the CIA's opposition, to brief Country ■'s ■■■■■■■■ on the effort to establish a more permanent and unilateral CIA detention facility, which was under construction. A proposed phone call to the ■■■■■■■■■■ from Vice President Cheney to solidify support for CIA operations in Country ■ was complicated by the fact that Vice President Cheney had not been told about the locations of the CIA detention facilities. The CIA wrote that there was a "primary need" to "eliminate any possibility that [■■■■■■■■ ■■] could explicitly or implicitly refer to the existence of a black site in [the country]" during the call with the vice president.[864] There are no indications that the call occurred. The ■■■■■■■■■■ of Country

■ nonetheless approved the unilateral CIA detention facility, which cost $■ million, but was never used by the CIA.[865] By ■ 2006, the CIA was working with Country ■ to decommission what was described as the "aborted" project.[866]

L. The Pace of CIA Operations Slows; Chief of Base Concerned About "Inexperienced, Marginal, Underperforming" CIA Personnel; Inspector General Describes Lack of Debriefers as "Ongoing Problem"

In the fall of 2004, CIA officers began considering "end games," or the final disposition of detainees in CIA custody. A draft CIA presentation for National Security Council principals dated August 19, 2004, identified the drawbacks of ongoing indefinite detention by the CIA, including: the need for regular relocation of detainees, the "tiny pool of potential host countries" available "due to high risks," the fact that "prolonged detention without legal process increases likelihood of HVD health, psychological problems [and] curtails intel flow," criticism of the U.S. government if legal process were delayed or denied, and the likelihood that the delay would "complicate, and possibly reduce the prospects of successful prosecutions of these detainees.[867] CIA draft talking points produced a month later state that transfer to Department of Defense or Department of Justice custody was the "preferred endgame for 13 detainees currently in [CIA] control, none of whom we believe should ever leave USG custody.[868]

By the end of 2004, the overwhelming majority of CIA detainees—113 of the 119 identified in the Committee Study—had already entered CIA custody. Most of the detainees remaining in custody were no longer undergoing active interrogations; rather, they were infrequently questioned and awaiting a final disposition. The CIA took custody of only six new detainees between 2005 and January 2009: four detainees in 2005, one in 2006, and one—the CIA's final detainee, Muhammad Rahim—in 2007.[869]

In 2004, CIA detainees were being held in three countries: at DETENTION SITE BLACK in Country ■, at the ■ facility ■ ■ in Country ■, as well as at detention facilities in Country ■. DETENTION SITE VIOLET in Country ■ opened in early 2005.[870] On April 15, 2005, the chief of Base at DETENTION SITE BLACK in Country ■ sent the management of RDG an email expressing his concerns about the detention site and the program in general. He commented that "we have seen clear indications that various Headquarters elements are experiencing mission fatigue vis-à-vis their interaction with the program," resulting in a "decline in the overall quality and level of experience of deployed personnel," and a decline in "level and quality of requirements." He wrote that because of the length of time most of the CIA detainees had been in detention, "[the] detainees have been all but drained of actionable intelligence," and their remaining value was in providing "information that can be incorporated into strategic, analytical think pieces that deal with motivation, structure and goals." The chief of Base observed that, during the course of the year, the detention site transitioned from an intelligence production facility to a long-term detention facility, which raised "a host of new challenges." These challenges included the need to address the "natural and progressive effects of long-term solitary confinement on detainees" and ongoing behavioral problems.[871]

With respect to the personnel at DETENTION SITE BLACK, the chief of Base wrote:

> "I am concerned at what appears to be a lack of resolve at Headquarters to deploy to the field the brightest and most qualified officers for service at [the detention site]. Over the course of the last year the quality of personnel (debriefers and [security protective officers]) has declined significantly. With regard to debriefers, most are mediocre, a handfull [*sic*] are exceptional and more than a few are basically incompetent. From what we can determine there is no established methodology as to the selection of debriefers. Rather than look for their best, managers seem to be selecting either problem, underperforming officers, new, totally inexperienced officers or whomever seems to be willing and able to deploy at any given time. We see no evidence that thought is being given to deploying an 'A-Team.' The result, quite naturally, is the production of mediocre or, I dare say, useless intelligence . . .
>
> "We have seen a similar deterioration in the quality of the security personnel deployed to the site . . . If this program truly does represent one of the agency's most secret activities then it defies logic why inexperienced, marginal, underperforming and/or officers with potentially significant [counterintelligence] problems are permitted to deploy to this site. It is also important that we immediately inact [*sic*] some form of rigorous training program."[872]

A CIA OIG audit completed in June 2006 "found that personnel assigned to CIA-controlled detention facilities, for the most part, complied with the standards and guidelines in carrying out their duties and responsibilities." The OIG also found that, "except for the shortage of debriefers, the facilities were staffed with sufficient numbers and types of personnel." The lack of debriefers, however, was described as "an ongoing problem" for the program. According to the audit, there were extended periods in 2005 when the CIA's DETENTION SITE ORANGE in Country ■ had either one or no debriefers. At least twice in the summer of 2005, the chief of Station in that country requested additional debriefers, warning that intelligence collection could suffer. Months later, in January 2006, the chief of Base at the detention site advised CIA Headquarters that "the facility still lacked debriefers to support intelligence collection requirements, that critical requirements were 'stacking up,' and that gaps in the debriefing of detainees were impacting the quantity and quality of intelligence reporting and would make the work of future debriefers more difficult.[873]

M. Legal and Operational Challenges in 2005

1. Department of Justice Renews Approval for the Use of the CIA's Enhanced Interrogation Techniques in May 2005

On May 10, 2005, the new acting assistant attorney general for OLC, Steven Bradbury, issued two legal memoranda. The first analyzed whether the individual use of the CIA's 13 enhanced interrogation techniques—including waterboarding, as well as a number of interrogation techniques that had been used in 2003 and 2004, but had not been analyzed in the original August 1, 2002, OLC memorandum—were consistent with the criminal prohibition on torture.[874] The second memorandum considered the combined use of the CIA's enhanced interrogation techniques.[875] Both legal memoranda concluded that the use of the CIA's enhanced interrogation techniques did not violate the torture statute.

On May 26, 2005, the CIA inspector general, who had been provided with the two OLC memoranda, wrote a memo to the CIA director recommending that the CIA seek additional legal guidance on whether the CIA's enhanced interrogation techniques and conditions of confinement met the standard under Article 16 of the Convention Against Torture.[876] The inspector general noted that "a strong case can be made that the Agency's authorized interrogation techniques are the kinds of actions that Article 16 undertakes to prevent," adding that the use of the waterboard may be "cruel" and "extended detention with no clothing would be considered 'degrading' in most cultures, particularly Muslim." The inspector general further urged that the analysis of conditions was equally important, noting that the inspector general's staff had "found a number of instances of detainee treatment which arguably violate the prohibition on cruel, inhuman, and/or degrading treatment."[877]

On May 30, 2005, a third OLC memorandum examining U.S. obligations under the Convention Against Torture was completed.[878] The conclusions in this opinion were based largely on the CIA's representations about the effectiveness of the CIA interrogation program in obtaining unique and "otherwise unavailable actionable intelligence." As described later in this summary, and in more detail in Volume II, the CIA's effectiveness representations were almost entirely inaccurate.

2. Abu Faraj Al-Libi Subjected to the CIA's Enhanced Interrogation Techniques Prior to Department of Justice Memorandum on U.S. Obligations Under the Convention Against Torture; CIA Subjects Abu Faraj Al-Libi to the CIA's Enhanced Interrogation Techniques When He Complains of Hearing Problems

On May 2, 2005, when Abu Faraj al-Libi, al-Qa'ida's chief of operations, was captured in Pakistan, the OLC had not yet issued the three aforementioned May 2005 legal memoranda.[879] CIA officers described Abu Faraj al-Libi's capture as the "most important al-Qa'ida capture since Khalid Shaykh Muhammad.[880] Shortly after al-Libi's capture, the CIA began discussing the possibility that Abu Faraj al-Libi might be rendered to U.S. custody.[881]

On May ■■, 2005, four days before the rendition of Abu Faraj al-Libi to CIA custody, Director of CTC Robert Grenier asked CIA Director Porter Goss to send a memorandum to the national security advisor and the director of national intelligence "informing them of the CIA's plans to take custody of Abu Faraj al-Libi and to employ interrogation techniques if warranted and medically safe.[882] On May 24, 2005, the White House informed the CIA that a National Security Council Principals Committee meeting would be necessary to discuss the use of the CIA's enhanced interrogation techniques on Abu Faraj al-Libi, but the travel schedule of one of the principals was delaying such a meeting.[883] CIA Director Goss instructed CIA officers to proceed as planned, indicating that he would call the principals individually and inform them that, if Abu Faraj al-Libi was found not to be cooperating and there were no contraindications to such an interrogation, he would approve the use of all of the CIA's enhanced interrogation techniques other than the waterboard, without waiting for a meeting of the principals.[884] Abu Faraj al-Libi was rendered to CIA custody at DETENTION SITE ORANGE on

May ■ 2005,[885] and transferred to DETENTION SITE BLACK on May ■, 2005.[886]

On May ■, 2005, CIA Director Goss formally notified National Security Advisor Stephen Hadley and Director of National Intelligence (DNI) John Negroponte that Abu Faraj al-Libi would be rendered to the unilateral custody of the CIA.[887] Director Goss's memorandum stated:

> "[should Abu Faraj resist cooperating in CIA debriefings, and pending a finding of no medical or psychological contraindictations [*sic*], to interrogation, I will authorize CIA trained and certified interrogators to employ one or more of the thirteen specific interrogation techniques for which CIA recently received two signed legal opinions from the Department of Justice (DOJ), Office of Legal Counsel (OLC) that these techniques, both individually and used collectively, are lawful."[888]

The memorandum from Director Goss described Abu Faraj al-Libi as holding the third most important position in al-Qa'ida, and "play[ing] a leading role in directing al-Qa'ida's global operations, including attack planning against the US homeland." Abu Faraj al-Libi was also described as possibly overseeing al-Qa'ida's "highly compartmented anthrax efforts."[889]

On May ■, 2005, one day after al-Libi's arrival at DETENTION SITE BLACK, CIA interrogators received CIA Headquarters approval for the use of the CIA's enhanced interrogation techniques on Abu Faraj al-Libi.[890] CIA interrogators began using the CIA's enhanced interrogation techniques on Abu Faraj al-Libi on May 28, 2005, two days before the OLC issued its memorandum analyzing whether the techniques violated U.S. obligations under the Convention Against Torture.[891]

The CIA interrogated Abu Faraj al-Libi for more than a month using the CIA's enhanced interrogation techniques. On a number of occasions, CIA interrogators applied the CIA's enhanced interrogation techniques to Abu Faraj al-Libi when he complained of a loss of hearing, repeatedly telling him to stop pretending he could not hear well.[892] Although the interrogators indicated that they believed al-Libi's complaint was an interrogation resistance technique, Abu Faraj al-Libi was fitted for a hearing aid after his transfer to U.S. military custody at Guantanamo Bay in 2006.[893] Despite the repeated and extensive use of the CIA's enhanced interrogation techniques on Abu Faraj al-Libi, CIA Headquarters continued to insist throughout the summer and fall of 2005 that Abu Faraj al-Libi was withholding information and pressed for the renewed use of the techniques. The use of the CIA's enhanced interrogation techniques against Abu

Faraj al-Libi was eventually discontinued because CIA officers stated that they had no intelligence to demonstrate that Abu Faraj al-Libi continued to withhold information, and because CIA medical officers expressed concern that additional use of the CIA's enhanced interrogation techniques "may come with unacceptable medical or psychological risks."[894] After the discontinuation of the CIA's enhanced interrogation techniques, the CIA asked Abu Faraj al-Libi about UBL facilitator Abu Ahmad al-Kuwaiti for the first time.[895] Abu Faraj al-Libi denied knowledge of al-Kuwaiti.[896]

3. CIA Acquires Two Detainees from the U.S. Military

Another legal issue in late 2005 was related to the U.S. Department of Defense's involvement in CIA detention activities. In September 2005, the CIA and the Department of Defense signed a Memorandum of Understanding on this subject,[897] and the U.S. military agreed to transfer two detainees, Ibrahim Jan and Abu Ja'far al-Iraqi, to CIA custody.[898] Both were held by the U.S. military without being registered with the ICRC for over 30 days, pending their transfer to CIA custody. The transfer of Abu Ja'far al-Iraqi took place notwithstanding Department of State concerns that the transfer would be inconsistent with statements made by the secretary of state that U.S. forces in Iraq would remain committed to the law of armed conflict, including the Geneva Conventions.[899]

In late 2005, during the period the U.S. Senate was debating the Detainee Treatment Act barring "cruel, inhuman, or degrading treatment or punishment,"[900] the CIA subjected Abu Ja'far al-Iraqi to its enhanced interrogation techniques.[901] A draft Presidential Daily Brief (PDB) stated that Abu Ja'far al-Iraqi provided "almost no information that could be used to locate former colleagues or disrupt attack plots"—the type of information sought by the CIA, and the CIA's justification for the use of its enhanced interrogation techniques.[902] Later, the statement that Abu Ja'far al-Iraqi provided "almost no information that could be used to locate former colleagues or disrupt attack plots" was deleted from the draft PDB.[903] Abu Ja'far al-Iraqi remained in CIA custody until early September 2006, when he was transferred to U.S. military custody in Iraq.[904]

4. The CIA Seeks "End Game" for Detainees in Early 2005 Due to Limited Support From Liaison Partners

In early 2005, the CIA again sought an "endgame" policy for its detainees, citing its unstable relations with host governments and its difficulty in identifying additional countries to host CIA detention facilities.[905] Talking points prepared for the CIA director for a meeting with the national security advisor made the following appeal:

> "CIA urgently needs [the President of the United States] and Principals Committee direction to establish a long-term disposition policy for the 12 High-Value detainees (HVD)s we hold in overseas detention sites. Our liaison partners who host these sites are deeply concerned by [REDACTED][906] press leaks, and they are increasingly skeptical of the [U.S. government's] commitment to keep secret their cooperation . . . A combination of press leaks, international scrutiny of alleged [U.S. government] detainee abuse, and the perception that [U.S. government] policy on detainees lacks direction is eroding our partners' trust in U.S. resolve to protect their identities and supporting roles. If a [U.S. government] plan for long-term [detainee] disposition does not emerge soon, the handful of liaison partners who cooperate may ask us to close down our facilities on their territory. Few countries are willing to accept the huge risks associated with hosting a CIA detention site, so shrinkage of the already small pool of willing candidates could force us to curtail our highly successful interrogation and detention program. Fear of public exposure may also prompt previously cooperative liaison partners not to accept custody of detainees we have captured and interrogated. Establishment of a clear, publicly announced [detainee] 'endgame'—one sanctioned by [the President of the United States] and supported by Congress—will reduce our partners' concerns and rekindle their enthusiasm for helping the US in the War on Terrorism."[907]

In March 2005, talking points prepared for the CIA director for a discussion with the National Security Council Principals Committee stated that it was:

> "only a matter of time before our remaining handful of current blacksite hosts concludes that [U.S. government] policy on [detainees] lacks direction and . . . [the blacksite hosts] ask us to depart from their soil . . . Continuation of status quo will exacerbate tensions in these very valuable relationships and cause them to withdraw their critical support and cooperation with the [U.S. government]."[908]

During this period, the U.S. solicitor general, however, expressed concern that if CIA detainees were transferred back to Guantanamo Bay, Cuba, they might be entitled to file a habeas petition and have access to an attorney.[909] Meanwhile, the National Security Council continued to discuss a public roll-out, and as described later in this summary, the CIA engaged the media directly in order to defend and promote the program.[910]

The question of what to do with the remaining detainees in

CIA custody remained unresolved throughout 2005, during which time the CIA pursued agreements with additional countries to establish clandestine CIA detention facilities.[911] The Detainee Treatment Act was passed by Congress on December 23, 2005, as part of the National Defense Authorization Act for Fiscal Year 2006. That day, the CIA suspended its interrogation program again.[912] As described later in this summary, in February 2006, the CIA informed the National Security Council principals that the CIA would not seek continued use of all of the CIA's enhanced interrogation techniques.[913]

5. Press Stories and the CIA's Inability to Provide Emergency Medical Care to Detainees Result in the Closing of CIA Detention Facilities in Countries ██ and ██

In October 2005, the CIA learned that *Washington Post* reporter Dana Priest had information about the CIA's Detention and Interrogation Program, ████████████████. The CIA then conducted a series of negotiations with the *Washington Post* in which it sought to prevent the newspaper from publishing information on the CIA's Detention and Interrogation Program.[914] Fearful that ████ ████████████████████████, the CIA recommended the immediate transfer of CIA detainees to Department of Defense custody.[915] When the Department of Defense rejected the proposal, the National Security Council directed the CIA to prepare other options.[916] Meanwhile, two U.S. ambassadors, one in █ ████ and another in █████, inquired whether Secretary of State Rice had been briefed on the impending *Washington Post* article and sought to speak to the secretary herself to ensure that the CIA program was authorized. According to CIA documents, Secretary Rice was not aware of the specific countries where the CIA detention facilities were located.[917] In lieu of a phone call from Secretary Rice, the CIA recommended that the State Department's Counterterrorism Coordinator and former CTC DDO, Henry Crumpton, call the ambassadors.[918] The *Washington Post* published an article about CIA detention sites on November 2, 2005.[919]

The publication of the *Washington Post* article resulted in a demarche to the United States from ██████, which also suggested that ██████ contribution ██████████ could be in jeopardy.[920] The United States also received a demarche from ████ ██.[921] According to a CIA cable, U.S. representatives to ████ ████ "if another shoe were to drop," there would be considerable ramifications for U.S. relations with ████████ on a number of issues that depended on U.S. credibility in the area of human rights. The representatives also "questioned whether the gravity of this potential problem is fully appreciated in Washington."[922]

The CIA catalogued how the *Washington Post* story created tensions in its bilateral counterterrorism relations with allies and determined that:

> "[t]he article is prompting our partners to reassess the benefits and costs of cooperating with the [U.S. government] and CIA. These services have conducted aggressive, high-impact operations with CIA against . . . targets, including . We no longer expect the services to be as aggressive or cooperative."[923]

In April 2006, informed CIA officers that press stories on the CIA's Detention and Interrogation Program led the government to prohibit from providing "information that could lead to the rendition or detention of al-Qa'ida or other terrorists to U.S. Government custody for interrogation, including CIA and the Department of Defense."[924]

Media leaks also created tensions with countries that had hosted or continued to host CIA detention facilities. For example, leaks prompted Country officials to convey their intent to communicate directly with the Departments of Justice and State. They then formally demarched the U.S. government.[925] As late as 2009, the Country raised with CIA Director Panetta the "problem of the secret detention facility" that had "tested and strained" the bilateral partnership. The of Country also stated that assurances were needed that future cooperation with the CIA would be safeguarded.[926]

After publication of the *Washington Post* article, Country demanded the closure of DETENTION SITE BLACK within hours.[927] The CIA transferred the remaining CIA detainees out of the facility shortly thereafter.[928]

,[929] . In Country officers refused to admit CIA detainee Mustafa Ahmad al-Hawsawi to a local hospital despite earlier discussions with country representatives about how a detainee's medical emergency would be handled.[930] While the CIA understood the officers' reluctance to place a CIA detainee in a local hospital given media reports, CIA Headquarters also questioned the "willingness of to participate as originally agreed/

planned with regard to provision of emergency medical care."[931] After failing to gain assistance from the Department of Defense,[932] the CIA was forced to seek assistance from three third-party countries in providing medical care to al-Hawsawi and four other CIA detainees with acute ailments. Ultimately, the CIA paid the ████████ ███ more than $███ million for the treatment of ████████ and ███ ██████;[933] paid the ████████████ approximately $██████ for the treatment of ██████████;[934] and made arrangements for █████████ ███ and ██████████ to be treated in ██████.[935] The medical issues resulted in the closing of DETENTION SITE VIOLET in Country ███ in █████ 2006.[936] The CIA then transferred its remaining detainees to DETENTION SITE BROWN. At that point, all CIA detainees were located in Country ███.[937]

Meanwhile, the pressures on the CIA's Detention and Interrogation Program brought about by the *Washington Post* story prompted the CIA to consider new options among what it called the "[d]windling pool ██████ partners willing to host CIA Blacksites."[938] The CIA thus renewed earlier efforts to establish a detention facility in Country ███. The CIA had earlier provided $███ million to Country ███'s ██████████ in preparation for a potential CIA detention site, prompting the chief of Station to comment, "Do you realize you can buy [Country ███] for $██████?"[939] On December ███, 2005, the chief of Station in Country ███ met with the ███████████, who was not concerned about the CIA's detention of terrorists in his country, but wanted assurances that the CIA interrogation program did not include the use of torture.[940] In providing his approval, the ████████ █████ agreed to a request from the chief of Station not to inform the U.S. ambassador in Country ███.[941] The CIA also reached an agreement with another country, Country ███, to establish a CIA detention facility in that country and arranged with the leadership of Country █ █ not to inform the U.S. ambassador there.[942] The CIA ultimately did not detain individuals in either county.

In late October 2005, days before the publication of the *Washington Post* article, the CIA asked a separate country, Country ███, to temporarily house ███ CIA detainees.[943] The chief of Station briefed the U.S. ambassador in Country ███, who requested that the National Security Council and the White House be briefed on the plan.[944] There are no CIA records to indicate the briefing occurred. Country ███'s █████████ then provided approval, while seeking assurances that the CIA would develop a contingeny plan in case the detention site was exposed in the press.[945] While the CIA Station and

the █████ considered █████ █ in Country ███, CIA Headquarters directed that a long-term CIA detention facility be established in the country. Country ███'s █████ █████ approved a plan to build a CIA detention facility █████ █████, but noted his ongoing concerns about the lack of a CIA "exit strategy."[946]

The lack of emergency medical care for detainees, the issue that had forced the closing of DETENTION SITE VIOLET in Country ███, was raised repeatedly in the context of the construction of the CIA detention facility in Country ███. On March ███, 2006, CIA Headquarters requested that the CIA Station in Country ███ ask Country ███ to arrange discreet access to the nearest hospital and medical staff. The cable stated that the CIA "look[s] forward to a favorable response, prior to commencing with the construction of our detention facility."[947] Construction nonetheless began on the facility without the issue of emergency medical care having been resolved. In █████ 2006, after the deputy chief of the CIA Station in Country █ █, the deputy chief of RDG, and an OMS officer met with █████ █████ officers, the Station reported that the establishment of emergency medical care proximal to the site was "not tenable."[948] In July 2006, an OMS representative informed the chief of █████ █████ at CIA Headquarters that the facility in Country ███ "should not be activated without a clear, committed plan for medical provider coverage.[949]

By the time a CIA team visited the Country ███ detention site in late 2006, the CIA had already invested $█████ million in the new facility. Describing the absence of adequate emergency medical care options as "unacceptable," the chief of RDG recommended in a draft memo that construction efforts be abandoned for this reason.[950] The following day, an edited version of the same memo described the issue as a "challenge," but did not recommend that the CIA cease construction of the facility.[951] The resulting CIA detention facility, which would eventually cost $█████ million, was never used by the CIA. Press reports about the CIA's Detention and Interrogation Program that appeared in █████ and █████ eventually forced the CIA to pass possession of the unused facility to the Country ███ government.[952]

In early January 2006, officials at the Department of Defense informed CIA officers that Secretary of Defense Rumsfeld had made a formal decision not to accept any CIA detainees at the U.S. military base at Guantanamo Bay, Cuba.[953] At the time, the CIA was holding

28 detainees in its two remaining facilities, DETENTION SITE VIOLET, in Country ■■, and DETENTION SITE ORANGE, in Country ■■.[954] In preparation for a meeting with Secretary of Defense Rumsfeld on January 6, 2006, CIA Director Goss was provided a document indicating that the Department of Defense's position not to allow the transfer of CIA detainees to U.S. military custody at Guantanamo Bay "would cripple legitimate end game planning" for the CIA.[955] The talking points for that meeting suggested that Director Goss tell Secretary Rumsfeld that the:

> "only viable 'endgame' for continued US Government custody of these most dangerous terrorists is a transfer to GTMO . . . [a]bsent the availability of GTMO and eventual DoD custody, CIA will necessarily have to begin transferring those detainees no longer producing intelligence to third countries, which may release them, or [the CIA itself may need to] outright release them."[956]

After Secretary Rumsfeld declined to reconsider his decision not to allow the transfer of CIA detainees to U.S. military custody at Guantanamo Bay, CIA officers proposed elevating the issue to the president. CIA officers prepared talking points for Director Goss to meet with the president on the "Way Forward" on the program on January 12, 2006.[957] The talking points recommended that the CIA director "stress that absent a decision on the long-term issue (so called 'endgame') we are stymied and the program could collapse of its own weight."[958] There are no records to indicate whether Director Goss made this presentation to the president.

In 2005 and 2006, the CIA transferred detainees from its custody to at least nine countries, including ■■■■■■■■■■■■■■■■ ■■■■■■■■■■■■■■■■■■■■■■■■■■■■ ■■■, as well as to the U.S. military in Iraq. Many of these detainees were subsequently released.[959] By May 2006, the CIA had 11 detainees whom it had identified as candidates for prosecution by a U.S. military commission. The remaining detainees were described as having "repatriation options open."[960]

6. The CIA Considers Changes to the CIA Detention and Interrogation Program Following the Detainee Treatment Act, Hamdan v. Rumsfeld

Following the passage of the Detainee Treatment Act in December 2005, the CIA conducted numerous discussions with the National Security Council principals about modifications to the program that would be acceptable from a policy and legal standpoint. In February 2006, talking points prepared for CIA Director Goss noted that

National Security Advisor Stephen Hadley:

> "asked to be informed of the criteria CIA will use before accepting a detainee into its CIA Counterterrorist Rendition, Detention, and Interrogation Program, stating that he believed CIA had in the past accepted detainees it should not have."[961]

The CIA director proposed future criteria that would require not only that CIA detainees meet the standard in the MON, but that they possess information about threats to the citizens of the United States or other nations, and that detention in a CIA facility was appropriate for intelligence exploitation.[962] A few months later, CTC Legal, , wrote to Acting Assistant Attorney General Steven Bradbury suggesting a modified standard for applying the CIA's enhanced interrogation techniques. The suggested new standard was that "the specific detainee is believed to possess critical intelligence of high value to the United States." While the proposed modification included the requirement that a detainee have "critical intelligence of high value," it represented an expansion of CIA authorities, insofar as it covered the detention and interrogation of an individual with information that "would assist in locating the most senior leadership of al-Qa'ida of [*sic*] an associated terrorist organization," even if that detainee was not assessed to have knowledge of, or be directly involved in, imminent terrorist threats.[963]

Discussions with the National Security Council principals also resulted in a March 2006 CIA proposal for an interrogation program involving only seven of the CIA's enhanced interrogation techniques: sleep deprivation, nudity, dietary manipulation, facial grasp, facial slap, abdominal slap, and the attention grab.[964] This proposal was not acted upon at the time. The proposal for sleep deprivation of up to 180 hours, however, raised concerns among the National Security Council principals.[965]

In April 2006, the CIA briefed the president on the "current status" of the CIA's Detention and Interrogation Program. According to an internal CIA review, this was the first time the CIA had briefed the president on the CIA's enhanced interrogation techniques.[966] As previously noted, the president expressed concern at the April 2006 briefing about the "image of a detainee, chained to the ceiling, clothed in a diaper, and forced to go to the bathroom on himself."[967]

On June 29, 2006, the Supreme Court issued its decision in the case of *Hamdan v. Rumsfeld*, concluding that the military commission convened to try Salim Hamdan, a detainee at Guantanamo Bay, was inconsistent with statutory requirements and Common Article 3 of the Geneva Conventions. The implication of the decision was that treating a detainee in a manner inconsistent with the requirements of Common Article 3 would constitute a violation of federal criminal law. CIA attorneys analyzed the *Hamdan* decision, noting that it could have a significant impact on "current CIA interrogation practices."[968] Their memorandum also referenced that Acting Assistant Attorney General Steven Bradbury had the "preliminary view . . . that the opinion 'calls into real question' whether CIA could continue its CT interrogation program involving enhanced interrogation techniques," as the CIA's enhanced interrogation techniques "could be construed as inconsistent with the provisions of Common Article 3 prohibiting 'outrages upon personal dignity' and violence to life and person."[969]

The case of *Hamdan v. Rumsfeld* prompted the OLC to withdraw a draft memorandum on the impact of the Detainee Treatment Act on the CIA's enhanced interrogation techniques.[970] The CIA did not use its enhanced interrogation techniques again until July 2007, by which time the OLC had interpreted the Military Commissions Act, signed by the president on October 17, 2006, in such a way as to allow the CIA to resume the use of the techniques.[971]

N. The Final Disposition of CIA Detainees and the End of the CIA's Detention and Interrogation Program

1. President Bush Publicly Acknowledges the Existence of the CIA's Detention and Interrogation Program

After significant discussions throughout 2006 among the National Security Council principals, the Department of Defense ultimately agreed to accept the transfer of a number of CIA detainees to U.S. military custody.[972]

On September 6, 2006, President George W. Bush delivered a public speech acknowledging that the United States had held al-Qa'ida operatives in secret detention, stating that the CIA had employed an "alternative set of procedures" in interrogating these detainees, and describing information obtained from those detainees while in CIA custody.[973] As described later in this summary, the speech, which was based on CIA information and vetted by the CIA, contained significant inaccurate statements, especially regarding the significance of information acquired from CIA detainees and the effectiveness of the CIA's interrogation techniques.[974]

In the speech, the president announced the transfer of 14 detainees to Department of Defense custody at Guantanamo Bay and the submission to Congress of proposed legislation on military commissions.[975] As all other detainees in the CIA's custody had been transferred to other nations, the CIA had no detainees in its custody at the time of the speech.[976]

2. The International Committee of the Red Cross (ICRC) Gains Access to CIA Detainees After Their Transfer to U.S. Military Custody in September 2006

After the 14 CIA detainees arrived at the U.S. military base at Guantanamo Bay, they were housed in a separate building from other U.S. military detainees and remained under the operational control of the CIA.[977] In October 2006, the 14 detainees were allowed meetings with the ICRC and described in detail similar stories regarding their detention, treatment, and interrogation while in CIA custody. The ICRC provided information on these claims to the CIA.[978] Acting CIA General Counsel John Rizzo emailed the CIA director and other CIA senior leaders, following a November 8, 2006, meeting with the ICRC, stating:

> "[a]s described to us, albeit in summary form, what the detainees allege actually does not sound that far removed from the reality . . . the ICRC, for its part, seems to find their stories largely credible, having put much stock in the fact that the story each detainee has told about his transfer, treatment and conditions of confinement was basically consistent, even though they had been incommunicado with each other throughout their detention by us."[979]

In February 2007 the ICRC transmitted to the CIA its final report on the "Treatment of Fourteen 'High Value Detainees' in CIA Custody." The ICRC report concluded that "the ICRC clearly considers that the allegations of the fourteen include descriptions of treatment and interrogation techniques—singly or in combination—that amounted to torture and/or cruel, inhuman or degrading treatment."[980] Notwithstanding Rizzo's comments, the CIA disagreed with a number of the ICRC's findings, provided rebuttals to the ICRC in writing, and informed the Committee that "numerous false allegations of physical or threatened abuses and faulty legal assumptions and analysis in the report undermine its overall credibility."[981] The ICRC report was acquired by *The New York Review of Books* and posted on the *Review*'s website in April 2009.[982] The Committee found the ICRC report to be largely consistent with information contained in CIA interrogation records.[983]

3. The CIA Considers Future of the Program Following the Military Commissions Act

As noted, in June 2006, the U.S. Supreme Court case of *Hamdan v. Rumsfeld* prompted the OLC to withdraw a draft legal memorandum on the impact of the Detainee Treatment Acton the CIA's enhanced interrogation techniques.[984] The administration determined that the CIA would need new legislation to continue to use the CIA's enhanced interrogation techniques.[985] The Military Commissions Act addressed the issues raised by the *Hamdan* decision and provided the president the authority to issue an Executive Order detailing permissible conduct under Common Article 3 of the Geneva Conventions. The bill passed the Senate on September 28, 2006, and the House of Representatives the following day.[986]

On November ■, 2006, when Abd Kadi al-Iraqi was rendered to CIA custody, the draft Executive Order and an updated OLC memorandum had not yet been prepared.[987] Although Abdal-Hadi al-Iraqi was consistently assessed as being cooperative, interrogators also believed he was withholding information on operational plots and the locations of high-value targets.[988] The CIA believed his ■■■ ■■■■■■■ in February 2007 supported this conclusion,[989] prompting discussions at CIA Headquarters about the possible use of the CIA's enhanced interrogation techniques against him. By the end of the month, however, the CIA had determined there was "insufficient intelligence . . . that [Abd al-Hadi al-Iraqi] possesses actionable information . . . to justify the use of" the CIA's enhanced interrogation techniques.[990]

In October 2006, a panel of CIA interrogators recommended that four CIA enhanced interrogation techniques—the abdominal slap, cramped confinement, nudity, and the waterboard—be eliminated, but that the remainder of the interrogation techniques be retained.[991] Under this proposal, the CIA would have been authorized to subject detainees to dietary manipulation, sleep deprivation, the facial slap, the facial grasp, the attention grab, walling, stress positions, and water dousing. There are few CIA records describing the panel's deliberations, or the CIA's response to its recommendations. The panel proposed dropping two of the CIA's enhanced interrogation techniques—nudity and the abdominal slap—that the CIA director had proposed retaining in March 2006, while recommending that the CIA retain three other techniques—walling, stress positions, and water dousing—that had not otherwise been requested for retention.[992]

4. The CIA Develops Modified Enhanced Interrogation Program After Passage of the Military Commissions Act

In the spring of 2007, the OLC completed a draft of a legal opinion concluding that the use of the CIA's seven proposed enhanced interrogation techniques—sleep deprivation, nudity, dietary manipulation, facial grasp, facial slap, abdominal slap, and the attention grab—would be consistent with the requirements of Common Article 3 of the Geneva Conventions and the Military Commissions Act. This draft generated significant disagreement between the State Department's legal advisor, John Bellinger, and the Acting Assistant Attorney General Steven Bradbury, resulting in Secretary of State Rice refusing to concur with the proposed Executive Order.[993]

In June 2007, in an effort to gain Secretary Rice's support, the CIA asked CIA contractors SWIGERT and DUNBAR to brief Secretary Rice on the CIA's interrogation program. During that briefing, Secretary Rice expressed her concern about the use of nudity and a detainee being shackled in the standing position for the purpose of sleep deprivation. According to CIA records, in early July 2007, after the capture of Muhammad Rahim, Secretary Rice indicated that she would not concur with an interrogation program that included nudity, but that she would not continue to object to the CIA's proposed interrogation program if it was reduced to six of the enhanced interrogation techniques listed in the draft OLC memorandum: (1) sleep deprivation, (2) dietary manipulation, (3) facial grasp, (4) facial slap, (5) abdominal slap, and (6) the attention grab.[994]

5. Muhammad Rahim, the CIA's Last Detainee, is Subjected to Extensive Use of the CIA's Enhanced Interrogation Techniques, Provides No Intelligence

On June 25, 2007, al-Qa'ida facilitator Muhammad Rahim was captured in Pakistan.[995] Based on reports of debriefings of Rahim in foreign government custody and other intelligence, CIA personnel assessed that Rahim likely possessed information related to the location of Usama bin Laden and other al-Qa'ida leaders.[996] On July 3, 2007, Acting CIA General Counsel John Rizzo informed Acting Assistant Attorney General Steven Bradbury that the CIA was anticipating a "new guest," and that the CIA "would need the signed DOJ opinion 'in a matter of days.'"[997]

Muhammad Rahim was rendered to CIA custody at DETENTION SITE BROWN in Country ■ on ■ July ■ ■, 2007.[998] Upon his arrival, CIA interrogators had a single discussion with Rahim during which he declined to provide answers to questions about threats to the United States and the locations of top al-Qa'ida leaders.[999] Based on this interaction, CIA interrogators reported that Rahim was unlikely to be cooperative. As a result, CIA Director Michael Hayden sent a letter to the president formally requesting that the president issue the Executive Order interpreting the Geneva Conventions in a manner to allow the CIA to interrogate Rahim using the CIA's enhanced interrogation techniques. A classified legal opinion from OLC concluding that the use of the CIA's six enhanced interrogation techniques proposed for use on Rahim (sleep deprivation, dietary manipulation, facial grasp, facial slap, abdominal slap, and the attention grab) did not violate applicable laws was issued on July 20, 2007. The accompanying unclassified Executive Order was issued the same day.[1000] Although Rahim had been described by the CIA as "one of a handful of al-Qa'ida facilitators working directly for Bin Ladin and Zawahiri,"[1001] Rahim remained in a CIA cell without being questioned for a week, while CIA interrogators waited for approval to use the CIA's enhanced interrogation techniques against him.[1002]

CIA interrogators initially expressed optimism about their ability to acquire information from Rahim using the CIA's enhanced interrogation techniques. A cable sent from the CIA detention site stated:

> "Senior interrogators on site, with experience in almost every HVD [high-value detainee] interrogation conducted by [CIA], believe the employment of interrogation with measures would likely provide the impetus to shock [Rahim] from his current resistance posture and provide an opportunity to influence his behavior to begin truthful participation."[1003]

Four CIA interrogators present at the CIA detention site began applying the CIA's enhanced interrogation techniques on July 21, 2007.[1004] According to CIA records, the interrogators "employed interrogation measures of facial slap, abdominal slap, and facial hold, and explained to [Rahim] that his assumptions of how he would be treated were wrong."[1005] The interrogators emphasized to Rahim that "his situation was the result of his deception, he would stay in this position until interrogators chose to remove him from it, and he could always correct a previous misstatement."[1006] According to the cable describing the interrogation, Rahim then threatened to fabricate information:

> "[Rahim] reiterated several times during the session that he would make up information if interrogators pressured him, and that he was at the complete mercy of the interrogators and they could even kill him if they wanted. Interrogators emphasized to [Rahim] that they would not allow him to die because then he could not give them information, but that he would, eventually, tell interrogators the truth."[1007]

During the interrogation of Rahim using the CIA's enhanced interrogation techniques, Rahim was subjected to eight extensive sleep deprivation sessions,[1008] as well as to the attention grasp, facial holds, abdominal slaps, and the facial slap.[1009] During sleep deprivation sessions, Rahim was usually shackled in a standing position, wearing a diaper and a pair of shorts.[1010] Rahim's diet was almost entirely limited to water and liquid Ensure meals.[1011] CIA interrogators would provide Rahim with a cloth to further cover himself as an incentive to cooperate. For example, a July 27, 2007, cable from the CIA detention site states that when Rahim showed a willingness to engage in questioning about "historical information," he was "provided a large towel to cover his torso" as a "subtle reward."[1012] CIA interrogators asked Rahim a variety of questions during these interrogations, seeking information about the current location of senior al-Qa'ida leaders, which he did not provide.[1013]

On September 8, 2007, CIA Director Hayden approved an extension of MuJiammad Rahim's CIA detention.[1014] The Director of the National Clandestine Service Jose Rodriguez disagreed with the approved extension, writing:

> "I did <u>not</u> sign because I do not concur with extending Rahim's detention for another 60 days. I do not believe the tools in our tool box will allow us to overcome Rahim's resistance techniques. J.A.R."[1015]

Shortly after the September 2007 extension, CIA personnel were directed to stop the use of the CIA's enhanced interrogation techniques on Rahim. Rahim was then left in his cell with minimal contact with CIA personnel for approximately six weeks.[1016] On September 10, 2007, Rahim's interrogators reported to CIA Headquarters that Rahim had "demonstrated that the physical collective measures available to HVDIs[1017] have become predictable and bearable."[1018] The use of the CIA's enhanced interrogation techniques on Rahim resumed on November 2, 2007, with a sleep deprivation session that lasted until November 8, 2007, for a total of 138.5 hours. This sleep deprivation session, the longest to which Rahim had been subjected, was his eighth and final session. Rahim was also subjected to dietary manipulation during this period.[1019]

According to CIA records, intermittent questioning of Rahim continued until December 9, 2007, when all questioning of Rahim ceased for nearly three weeks. During this time, CIA detention site personnel discussed and proposed new ways to encourage Rahim's cooperation. These new proposals included suggestions that Rahim could be told that audiotapes of his interrogations might be passed to his family, or that ████████████████████████████ ████████████████ Rahim was cooperating with U.S. forces. On December 18, 2007, CIA Headquarters directed the detention site to stand down on the proposals.[1020]

The CIA's detention and interrogation of Mohammad Rahim resulted in no disseminated intelligence reports.[1021] On March ██, 2008, Muhammad Rahim was ██████ by the CIA to ██████████ █, where ████████ took custody of Rahim. The ██████ government immediately transferred Rahim to the custody of ██████, at which point Rahim was transferred back to CIA custody and rendered by the CIA to U.S. military custody at Guantanamo Bay.[1022]

6. CIA After-Action Review of Rahim Interrogation Calls for Study of Effectiveness of Interrogation Techniques and Recommends Greater Use of Rapport-Building Techniques in Future CIA Interrogations

On April 21, 2008, and April 22, 2008, the CIA's RDG convened an after-action review of the CIA's interrogation of Muhammad Rahim. According to summary documents, the CIA review panel attempted to determine why the CIA had been unsuccessful in acquiring useful information from Rahim. The summary documents emphasized that the primary factors that contributed to Rahim's unresponsiveness were the interrogation team's lack of knowledge of Rahim, the decision to use the CIA's enhanced interrogation techniques immediately after the short "neutral probe" and subsequent isolation period, the lack of clarity about whether the non-coercive techniques described in the Army Field Manual were permitted, the team's inability to confront Rahim with incriminating evidence, and the use of multiple improvised interrogation approaches despite the lack of any indication that these approaches might be effective.[1023] The summary documents recommended that future CIA interrogations should incorporate rapport-building techniques, social interaction, loss of predictability, and deception to a greater extent.[1024] The documents also recommended that the CIA conduct a survey of interrogation techniques used by other U.S. government agencies and other countries in an effort to develop effective interrogation methods.[1025]

Muhammad Rahim was the last CIA detainee in the CIA's Detention and Interrogation Program.[1026]

7. CIA Contracting Expenses Related to Company Formed by SWIGERT and DUNBAR

CIA contractors SWIGERT and DUNBAR, who played a central role in the development of the CIA's enhanced interrogation techniques in the summer of 2002, and then used the techniques as contract interrogators, formed a company in 2005 ████ ["Company Y"].[1027] In addition to providing interrogators for the CIA's interrogation program, Company Y was granted a sole source contract to provide operational psychologists, debriefers, and security personnel at CIA detention sites.[1028] Under the contract, Company Y was tasked with conducting ongoing conversations with CIA detainees to learn about the terrorist mind set (this project was named the "Terrorist Think Tank" or "T^3"), developing ██████ strategies, and writing the history of the CIA's Detention and Interrogation Program.[1029] Later descriptions of their services note that—on behalf of the CIA—Company Y officers participated in the interrogations of detainees held in foreign government custody and served as intermediaries between entities of those governments and the CIA.[1030]

By 2006, the value of the base contract for their company, with all options exercised, was in excess of $180 million.[1031] As of May 2007, Company Y had hired ███ former CIA staff officers, many of whom had previously been involved with the CIA's Detention and Interrogation Program. Company Y's chief operating officer was the former chief of ████████, the division of the CIA supervising the Renditions and Detention Group. In addition, Company Y hired at least ██ CIA security protective officers to work on Company Y's CIA contracts. In March 2006, a list of projected staff and contractors within CIA's Renditions and Detention Group included ███ separate positions.[1032] Of those ███ positions, ███ [73%] were for contractors, the majority of whom were contractors from Company Y.[1033] By June 2007, RDG reported having ██ staff officers and ████ contractors.[1034] By 2008, RDG had a total of ███ positions, with ██ staff officers and ███ [85%] contractors, according to the CIA.[1035]

The CIA's contract with Company Y was terminated in

mid-2009. From the time of the company's creation in 2005 through the close-out of its contract in 2010, the CIA paid Company Y more than $75 million for services in conjunction with the CIA's Detention and Interrogation Program.[1036] The CIA also certified Company Y's office in ██████████, as a Secure Compartmented Information Facility (SCIF), which required a CIA officer to be detailed to ████, and provided Company Y access to CIA internal computer networks at its facility. In 2008, the CIA authorized an additional payment to Company Y of approximately $570,000, after Company Y indicated that it had incurred costs for conducting countersurveillance of its officers when ██████████ appeared in the press in conjunction with the program. The CIA agreed to a $5 million indemnification contract for the company that covered, among other expenses, criminal prosecution.[1037] Company Y hired a prominent █ █████ law firm for representation in 2007,[1038] and billed the CIA $1.1 million for legal expenses from 2007 through 2012 per its indemnification agreement.[1039] Part of these expenses included legal presentation at a Committee staff briefing by SWIGERT and DUNBAR on November ██, 2008.[1040] Under the CIA's indemnification contract, the CIA is obligated to pay Company Y's legal expenses through 2021.[1041]

8. The CIA's Detention and Interrogation Program Ends

On December 5, 2007, fewer than nine months after Director Hayden told the European Union that the CIA's Detention and Interrogation Program was not a CIA program, but "America's program," the House-Senate conference for the Fiscal Year 2008 Intelligence Authorization Act voted to include an amendment that banned coercive interrogation techniques and established the Army Field Manual on Human Intelligence Collector Operations as the interrogation standard for all U.S. government interrogations.[1042] The conference report passed both the House and the Senate with bipartisan majorities.[1043]

On March 8, 2008, President Bush vetoed the Intelligence Authorization Act for Fiscal Year 2008 that banned coercive interrogations. In a radio address explaining the decision, the president stated "[t]he bill Congress sent me would take away one of the most valuable tools in the war on terror—the CIA program to detain and question key terrorist leaders and operatives." Addressing the use of the CIA's enhanced interrogation techniques, President Bush stated that the "main reason" the CIA program "has been effective is that it allows the CIA to use specialized interrogation procedures to question a small number of the most dangerous terrorists under careful supervision." The president stated that the CIA program had a "proven track record," and that the CIA obtained "critical intelligence" as a result of the CIA's enhanced interrogation techniques related to the Camp Lemonier plotting, the Karachi plotting, the Second Wave plotting, and the Heathrow Airport plotting. The president then repeated a warning the CIA had previously provided to the White House, that to "restrict the CIA to [interrogation] methods in the [Army] Field Manual," "could cost American lives."[1044] As is described in this summary, and detailed more extensively in the full Committee Study, the CIA's representations to the White House regarding the role of the CIA's enhanced interrogation techniques in the thwarting of the referenced plots were inaccurate.

On March 11, 2008, by a vote of 225–188, the House of Representatives failed to override the presidential veto.[1045]

In December 2008 and January 2009, CIA officers briefed the transition team for President-elect Barack Obama on the CIA's Detention and Interrogation Program. CIA Director Hayden prepared a statement that relayed, "despite what you have heard or read in a variety of public fora, these [enhanced interrogation] techniques and this program did work."[1046] The prepared materials included inaccurate information on the operation and management of the CIA's Detention and Interrogation Program, as well as the same set of examples of the "effectiveness" of the CIA's enhanced interrogation techniques that the CIA had provided to policymakers over several years.[1047] The examples provided were nearly entirely inaccurate.

On January 22, 2009, President Obama issued Executive Order 13491, which required the CIA to "close as expeditiously as possible any detention facilities that it currently operates and . . . not operate any such detention facility in the future." The Executive Order prohibited any U.S. government employee from using interrogation techniques other than those in the Army Field Manual 2-22.3 on Human Intelligence Collector Operations.[1048]

III. INTELLIGENCE ACQUIRED AND CIA REPRESENTATIONS ON THE EFFECTIVENESS OF THE CIA'S ENHANCED INTERROGATION TECHNIQUES TO MULTIPLE CONSTITUENCIES

A. Background on CIA Effectiveness Representations

From 2002 through 2009, in order to obtain policy authorizations and legal approvals, the CIA made a series of representations to officials at the White House,[1049] the Department of Justice, and the Congress, asserting that the CIA's enhanced interrogation techniques were uniquely effective and necessary to produce otherwise unavailable intelligence that the U.S. government could not obtain from other sources.[1050] The CIA further represented that the CIA's enhanced interrogation techniques "saved lives" and "enabled the CIA to disrupt terrorist plots, capture additional terrorists, and collect a high volume of critical intelligence on al-Qa'ida."[1051] The Department of Justice used these representations of effectiveness to assess whether the CIA's enhanced interrogation techniques were legal;[1052] policymakers at the White House used these representations—and the legal analysis by the Department of Justice—to assess whether the CIA interrogation program should be approved as a matter of policy;[1053] and members of Congress relied on the CIA representations in overseeing and assessing the program, providing funding, and crafting related legislation.[1054]

In CIA presentations to the executive and legislative branches, the CIA represented that other parties had consented to, or endorsed, the CIA's interrogation program. As an example, during a policy review of the CIA's enhanced interrogation techniques in July 2003, the CIA informed a subset of the National Security Council principals that the use of the CIA's enhanced interrogation techniques was "approved by the attorney general," and was "fully disclosed to the SSCI and HPSCI leadership." In the same presentation, the CIA represented that the CIA interrogation program "had produced significant intelligence information that had, in the view of CIA professionals, saved lives." The CIA then provided examples of "attacks averted" as a direct result of the CIA interrogation program, and warned policymakers that "[t]ermination of this program will resultin loss of life, possibly extensive."[1055]

When the CIA was asked by White House officials to review and provide further evidence for the effectiveness of the CIA's enhanced interrogation techniques in 2004, the CIA responded that it was "difficult, if not impossible" to conduct such a review, but assured White House officials that "this program works," "the techniques are effective," and the program produces "results."[1056] The "results" provided by the CIA consisted of the "disruption" of specific terrorist plots and the capture of specific terrorists. The CIA further represented that the information acquired as a result of the CIA's enhanced interrogation techniques was unique and "otherwise unavailable."[1057] These specific CIA claims played an especially important role in the Department of Justice's legal review of the CIA's enhanced interrogation techniques.[1058] Department of Justice documents stated that an analysis of the legality of the CIA's enhanced interrogation techniques was a "highly context-specific, fact-dependent question" and highlighted the importance of the CIA representation that the CIA's enhanced interrogation techniques produced "substantial quantities of otherwise unavailable actionable intelligence," and were "largely responsible for preventing a subsequent attack within the United States."[1059]

B. Past Efforts to Review the Effectiveness of the CIA's Enhanced Interrogation Techniques

During the period in which the CIA's Detention and Interrogation Program was operational, from 2002 to 2009, there were three reviews that addressed the effectiveness of the CIA's enhanced interrogation techniques: (1) the CIA Office of Inspector General Special Review, released in May 2004; (2) an internal review conducted by two senior CIA officers in 2004; and (3) a 2005 "Blue Ribbon" panel consisting of two individuals not employed by the CIA. According to CIA records, as of the spring of 2007, the CIA had not "conducted any other studies on the effectiveness of interrogation techniques."[1060]

Each of the previous reviews relied on interviews with CIA personnel involved in the program, as well as documents prepared by CIA personnel, which represented that the CIA interrogation program was effective, and that the use of the CIA's enhanced interrogation techniques had "enabled the CIA to disrupt terrorist plots, capture additional terrorists, and collect a high-volume of critical intelligence on al-Qa'ida."[1061] CIA personnel represented: "[t]his is information that CTC could not have gotten any other way."[1062]

There are no indications in CIA records that any of the past reviews attempted to independently validate the intelligence claims related to the CIA's use of its enhanced interrogation techniques that were presented by CIA personnel in interviews and in documents. As such, no previous review confirmed whether the specific intelligence cited by the CIA was acquired from a CIA detainee during or after being subjected to the CIA's enhanced interrogation techniques, or if the intelligence acquired was otherwise unknown to the United States government ("otherwise unavailable"), and therefore uniquely valuable.

C. The Origins of CIA Representations Regarding the Effectiveness of the CIA's Enhanced Interrogation Techniques as Having "Saved Lives," "Thwarted Plots," and "Captured Terrorists"

Before the CIA took custody of its first detainee, CIA attorneys researched the limits of coercive interrogations and the legal definitions of torture. On November 26, 2001, CIA Office of General Counsel (OGC) attorneys circulated a draft legal memorandum entitled "Hostile Interrogations: Legal Considerations for CIA Officers."[1063] The memorandum listed interrogation techniques considered to be torture by a foreign government and a specific nongovernmental organization, including "cold torture," "forced positions," "enforced physical exhaustion," "sensory deprivation," "perceptual deprivation," "social deprivation," "threats and humiliation," "conditioning techniques," and "deprivation of sleep."[1064] The draft memorandum described various prohibitions on torture and the potential use of "necessity" as a legal defense against charges of torture, stating:

> "[i]t would, therefore, be a novel application of the *necessity* defense to avoid prosecution of U.S. officials who tortured to obtain information

that *saved many lives* . . . A policy decision must be made with regard to U.S. use of torture in light of our obligations under international law, with consideration given to the circumstances and to international opinion on our current campaign against terrorism—states may be very unwilling to call the U.S. to task for torture when it resulted in *saving thousands of lives*."[1065]

On February 1, 2002, a CTC attorney researched the impact of the application of the Geneva Conventions (GC) on future CIA interrogation activities.[1066] The attorney wrote:

> "If the detainee is a POW and enjoys GC coverage, then the optic becomes how legally defensible is a particular act that probably violates the convention, but ultimately saves lives. I believe that [a named CIA attorney]'s papers reflecting on *necessity and anticipatory self defense* are the two most obvious defenses available."[1067]

The Department of Justice Office of Legal Counsel (OLC) included the "necessity defense" in its August 1, 2002, memorandum to the White House Counsel, determining, among other things, that "under the current circumstances, necessity or self-defense may justify interrogation methods that might violate" the criminal prohibition against torture.[1068] The OLC memorandum states:

> "It appears to us that under the current circumstances the *necessity defense* could be successfully maintained in response to an allegation of a Section 2340A violation . . . Under these circumstances, a detainee may possess information that could enable the United States to prevent attacks that potentially could equal or surpass the September 11 attacks in their magnitude. Clearly, any harm that might occur during an interrogation would pale to insignificance compared to the harm avoided by preventing such an attack, which could take hundreds or thousands of lives."[1069]

According to a report by the Department of Justice Office of Professional Responsibility (OPR), released in July 2009, Deputy Assistant Attorney General John Yoo "acknowledged that the CIA may have indirectly suggested the new sections [related to Commander-in-Chief authority and possible defenses, including the necessity defense] by asking him what would happen in a case where an interrogator went 'over the line' and inadvertently violated the statute." Yoo also told the OPR that he drafted those relevant sections. Another senior Department of Justice lawyer at the time, Patrick Philbin, informed the OPR that when he told Yoo that the sections were superfluous and should be removed, Yoo responded, "They want it in there." The CIA's former Deputy General Counsel John Rizzo told the OPR that the CIA did not request the addition of the sections.[1070] In his response to the OPR report, Assistant Attorney General Jay Bybee stated that the "ticking time bomb" that could justify the necessity defense was, in fact, a "real world" scenario. According to Bybee, "the OLC attorneys working on the [August 1, 2002] Memo had been briefed on the apprehension of Jose Padilla on May 8, 2002. Padilla was believed to have built and planted a dirty bomb."[1071] The August 1, 2002, memorandum states that the "[i]nterrogation of captured al Qaida operatives allegedly allowed U.S. intelligence and law enforcement agencies to track Padilla and to detain him upon his entry into the United States."[1072] This information was inaccurate.[1073]

With the issuance on August 1, 2002, of a second OLC memorandum specific to Abu Zubaydah,[1074] the CIA initiated the use of its enhanced interrogation techniques. After the CIA subjected Abu Zubaydah and other CIA detainees to the techniques, the CIA made increasingly stronger assertions about the effectiveness of the CIA's interrogation program, eventually asserting that the CIA interrogation program "saved lives,"[1075] and that the use of the CIA's enhanced interrogation techniques was necessary, as the intelligence obtained could not have been acquired in any other way.[1076]

Many of the representations made by the CIA about the effectiveness of the CIA's enhanced interrogation techniques were first made in the spring of 2003 and evolved over the course of the year and into early 2004. In April 2003, CIA officers told the CIA's Office of Inspector General (OIG) that KSM, who had been subjected to the techniques between March ■, 2003, and March 25, 2003, was still not fully cooperative. For example, on April 3, 2003, more than a week after the CIA had discontinued the use of its enhanced interrogation techniques on KSM, the deputy chief of ALEC Station, ████████ ████, informed the OIG that KSM had made "remarkable progress," but there was "a lot more to be done." ██████ did not cite any specific intelligence obtained from KSM in this context.[1077]

On June 27, 2003, more than three months after the CIA had ceased using its enhanced interrogation techniques against KSM, CTC Chief of Operations ██████████ told the OIG that he was convinced that KSM "knows more and is just waiting for us to ask the right questions."[1078] ██████████ then provided two examples of information that KSM had not provided until he was asked specifically about the matters by CIA interrogators: information on the "tallest building in California" plot (also known as the "Second Wave" plot), and the inclusion of a building in Canary Wharf as a target in the plotting against Heathrow Airport.[1079] Asked if he could think of any instances in which information from CIA detainees had led to the arrest of a terrorist, ██████████ stated only that Majid Khan provided information that led to the arrest of Iyman Faris by the FBI.[1080] This information was inaccurate, as Majid Khan was not in CIA custody when he provided information on Iyman Faris.[1081]

█████████ represented to the OIG that the CIA's interrogation program was "very effective," and that the intelligence obtained from CIA detainees was "the main criteria for judging the success of the program; specifically, intelligence that has allowed CTC to take other terrorists off the street and to prevent terrorist attacks." ████ ████ also told the OIG that the information obtained from CIA interrogations was "information that CTC could not have gotten any other way."[1082]

On June 26, 2003, President Bush issued a statement for the United Nations International Day in Support of Victims of Torture. That statement—referenced in multiple news articles—relayed that the:

> "United States is committed to the world-wide elimination of torture and we are leading this fight by example. I call on all governments to join with the United States and the community of law-abiding nations in prohibiting, investigating, and prosecuting all acts of torture and in undertaking to prevent other cruel and unusual punishment."[1083]

The following day, after the *Washington Post* published an article on the Administration's detainee policy, CIA Deputy General Counsel John Rizzo called John Bellinger, the legal advisor to the National Security Council. According to an email from Rizzo to other senior CIA officers, Rizzo called Bellinger to:

> "express our surprise and concern at some of the statements attributed to the Administration in the piece, particularly the Presidential statement on the UN International Day in Support of Victims of Torture as well as a quote from the Deputy White House Press Secretary Scott McClellan that all prisoners being held by the USG are being treated 'humanely.'"[1084]

While Rizzo expressed the view that the presidential statement did not appear to contain anything "we can't live with," Rizzo conveyed to senior CIA leaders that it "might well be appropriate for us to seek written reaffirmation by some senior White House official that the Agency's ongoing practices . . . are to continue."[1085]

On July 3, 2003, DCI George Tenet sent a memorandum to National Security Advisor Condoleezza Rice seeking reaffirmation of the Administration's support for the CIA's detention and interrogation policies and practices. The memorandum stated that the reaffirmation was sought because:

> "recent Administration responses to inquiries and resulting media reporting about the Administration's position have created the impression that these [interrogation] techniques are not used by U.S. personnel and are no longer approved as a policy matter."[1086]

While the CIA was preparing to meet with the White House on the reaffirmation of the CIA interrogation program, CIA personnel provided additional inaccurate information about the "effectiveness" of the CIA's enhanced interrogation techniques to the OIG, as well as to senior CIA leadership. These inaccurate representations described the "thwarting" of specific plots and the capture of specific terrorists attributed to the interrogation of CIA detainees and the use of the CIA's enhanced interrogation techniques.

On July 16, 2003, Deputy Chief ALEC Station ██████ █ was interviewed again by the OIG. In this interview █████ asserted that KSM "provided information that helped lead to the arrest of Iyman Faris, Uzhair Paracha, Saleh al-Marri, Majid Khan, and Ammar al-Baluchi.[1087] These representations were almost entirely inaccurate.[1088]

█████ also informed the OIG that information from CIA detainees "provided a wealth of information about Al-Qa'ida plots," including: a terrorist plot in Saudi Arabia against Israel; a plot against the U.S. Consulate in Karachi, Pakistan; a plot against Heathrow Airport and Canary Wharf; a plot to derail trains; a plot against subways; a gas station plot; a plot against the "tallest building" in California; a plot against suspension bridges; and a plot to poison water supplies.[1089] Much of this information was inaccurate.[1090] According to OIG records, "[o]n the question of whether actual plots had been thwarted, [█████] opined that since the operatives involved in many of the above plots had been arrested, [CTC had], in effect, thwarted the operation[s]." █████ provided a list to the OIG of terrorists captured and the plots with which they were associated. None of the individuals listed by █████ were captured as a result of reporting from CIA detainees.[1091]

During this same period in 2003, CIA officers were compiling similar information for CIA leadership. On July 18, 2003, the chief of ALEC Station, ████████, wrote an email to ALEC Station officers requesting information on the "value and impact" of CIA detainee information on behalf of the CIA Renditions Group (RDG),[1092] which he stated was being compiled for senior CIA leadership.[1093] █████ wrote that "[o]ne way to assist now is to provide input to RDG on highlights of intel and ops reporting from the detainees," in particular "reporting that helped reveal or stop plots, reporting that clinched the identity of terrorist suspects, etc."[1094] The first portion of the response compiled by ALEC Station, was drafted by Deputy Chief of ALEC Station ████████, who wrote that CIA detainee reporting "plays a key role in our ability to identify and capture al-Qa'ida terrorists, including those who were planning to attack inside the United States." In an email, ██████ wrote that "[t]he ability of the detainees to identify many operatives previously unknown to us or to the FBI resulted in the successful capture/detention of several terrorists," and that the use of the CIA's enhanced interrogation techniques was "key" to acquiring this information on these operatives. As examples of operatives "previously unknown" to the CIA and the FBI and identified by CIA detainees, ██████ cited Jose Padilla, Binyam Mohammed, Majid Khan, Iyman Faris, and Sayf al-Rahman Paracha.[1095] These representations were inaccurate.[1096] ██████ email concluded:

> "Simply put, detainee information has *saved countless American lives* inside the US and abroad. We believe there is no doubt al-Qa'ida would have succeeded in launching additional attacks in the US and that the information obtained from these detainees *through the use of enhanced measures* was *key to unlocking this information*. It is our assessment that if CIA loses the ability to interrogate and use enhanced measures in a responsible way, we will not be able to effectively prosecute this war."[1097]

The information relayed from ALEC Station to RDG in July 2003 for CIA leadership also included information from a CIA assessment entitled "Significant Detainee Reporting."[1098] That document included information that was largely congruent with CIA records. It stated that KSM provided details on the Heathrow Airport Plot and the Karachi Plots only after being confronted with the capture of Khallad bin Attash and Ammar al-Baluchi;[1099] that with regard to plots inside the United States, KSM had only admitted to plots that had been abandoned or already disrupted; that KSM fabricated information in order to tell CIA interrogators "what he thought they wanted to hear"; and that KSM generally only provided information when "boxed in" by information already known to CIA debriefers.[1100] This information was not included in CIA representations to policymakers later that month.

On July 29, 2003, as a result of DCI Tenet's July 3, 2003, request seeking reaffirmation of the CIA's detention and interrogation policies and practices, Tenet and CIA General Counsel Scott Muller conducted a briefing for a subset of the National Security Council principals.[1101] According to a CIA memorandum, Muller represented that CIA "detainees subject to the use of Enhanced Techniques of one kind or another had produced significant intelligence information that had, in the view of CIA professionals, saved lives."[1102]

The CIA briefing provided the "results" of using the CIA's enhanced interrogation techniques in briefing slides with the heading: "RESULTS: MAJOR THREAT INFO." The slides represented that KSM provided information on "[a]ttack plans against US Capitol, other US landmarks"; "[a]ttacks against Chicago, New York, Los Angeles; against towers, subways, trains, reservoirs, Hebrew centers, Nuclear power plants"; and the "Heathrow and Canary Wharf Plot." The slides also represented that KSM identified Iyman Faris, the "Majid Khan family," and Sayf al-Rahman Paracha.[1103] These representations were largely inaccurate.[1104]

The CIA slides represented that "major threat" information was obtained from the use of the CIA's enhanced interrogation techniques on CIA detainee 'Abd al-Rahim al-Nashiri regarding "US Navy Ships in the Straits of Hormuz." This representation was inaccurate and omitted material facts.[1105] The CIA slides further indicated that "major threat" information was obtained from the use of the CIA's enhanced interrogation techniques against CIA detainee Ramzi bin al-Shibh—specifically that bin al-Shibh "[i]dentified Hawsawi" and provided "major threat" information on "[a]ttacks against Nuclear Power Plants, Hebrew Centers." This representation was inaccurate and omitted material facts.[1106]

In the context of "[m]ajor threats [that] were countered and attacks averted," the CIA slides represented that "major threat" information was obtained from the use of the CIA's enhanced interrogation techniques against Khallad bin Attash on an "[a]ttack against U.S. Consulate in Karachi." This representation was inaccurate.[1107] The CIA slides further represented that "major threat" information was obtained from the use of the CIA's enhanced interrogation techniques on CIA detainee Abu Zubaydah, resulting in the "[i]dentification of [Jose] Padilla, Richard Reid," as well as information on "[a] ttacks on banks, subways, petroleum and aircraft industries." These representations were inaccurate.[1108]

The briefing slides, which contained additional inaccuracies detailed in Volume II of the Committee Study, were used, at least in part, for CIA briefings for Secretary of State Powell and Secretary of Defense Rumsfeld,[1109] as well as for Assistant Attorney General Jack Goldsmith.[1110]

In subsequent interviews of CIA personnel, the OIG received information that contradicted other CIA representations about the

CIA's Detention and Interrogation Program. The chief of the ■ ■ Branch of the UBL Group at CTC described at length how the arrests of Majid Khan and Iyman Faris were unrelated to reporting from CIA detainees.[1111] The deputy director for law enforcement for the FBI's Counterterrorism Division told the OIG how Uzhair Paracha and FBI operational activities were ultimately responsible for the capture of Sayf al-Rahman Paracha.[1112] The chief of targeting and special requirements for CTC's al-Qa'ida Department and former chief of the Abu Zubaydah Task Force, ■■■■■, told the OIG that "the often-cited example of Zubaydah identifying Padilla is not quite accurate."[1113] According to ■■■■, "[n]ot only did [Abu Zubaydah] not tell us who Padilla was, his information alone would never have led us to Padilla." ■■■■ stated that the Pakistanis had told the CIA about Jose Padilla and his partner prior to Abu Zubaydah providing any information on the pair, relaying, "[i]n essence, CTC got lucky."[1114]

At the same time, however, CIA personnel provided inaccurate examples of the effectiveness of the CIA's enhanced interrogation techniques to the OIG. The deputy chief of the Al-Qa'ida Department of CTC told the OIG that "KSM gave us Majid Khan and Uzair Paracha."[1115] Deputy DCI John McLaughlin told the OIG that information from KSM "led to the capture" of Majid Khan, which in turn led to the capture of Hambali. McLaughlin also represented that "the capture of Richard Reid was a result of modus operandi information obtained from [Abu] Zubaydah."[1116] These representations were inaccurate.[1117]

In addition to these specific inaccurate examples, CIA leadership made additional general claims to the OIG about the effectiveness of the CIA interrogation program that highlighted the "critical threat information" that could only be acquired by using the CIA's enhanced interrogation techniques against CIA detainees. Jose Rodriguez, then CTC director, told the CIA OIG that "the use of EITs has saved lives and prevented terrorist operations from occurring."[1118] Deputy DCI McLaughlin told the OIG that he "believes the use of EITs has proven critical to CIA's efforts in the war on terrorism."[1119] DDO Pavitt stated that the program was "invaluable to U.S. national security," that "American lives have been saved as a result of information received from detainees," and that the CIA "has been able to obtain information that would not have been obtained without the use of EITs."[1120] According to OIG records, DCI Tenet stated he "firmly believes that the interrogation program, and specifically the use of EITs, has saved many lives." Tenet added that the use of the CIA's enhanced interrogation techniques was "extremely valuable" in obtaining "enormous amounts of critical threat information," and that he did not believe that the information could have been gained any other way.[1121]

On January 2, 2004, CIA Inspector General John Helgerson provided a draft of the OIG Special Review, entitled "Counterterrorism Detention and Interrogation Program," to senior CIA officials for comment. The draft Special Review, which was based on numerous interviews of CIA personnel, as well as additional research by the OIG, described the origins of the CIA's Detention and Interrogation Program, the detention sites that were operational at the time of the review, and the guidance that had been provided on both interrogation and detention. The draft also identified a number of unauthorized interrogation techniques that had been used,[1122] and concluded that, in a number of cases, CIA interrogations went "well beyond what was articulated in the written DOJ legal opinion of 1 August 2002."[1123] The draft report repeated the inaccurate examples of the "effectiveness" of the CIA's enhanced interrogation techniques that had been conveyed by CIA officers to OIG personnel,[1124] but nonetheless concluded:

> "[w]ith the capture of some of the operatives for the above-mentioned plots, it is not clear whether these plots have been thwarted or if they remain viable or even if they were fabricated in the first place. This Review did not uncover any evidence that these plots were imminent."[1125]

After reviewing the draft Special Review, including the OIG's qualified conclusions about the effectiveness of the CIA's enhanced interrogation techniques, the CIA's CTC began preparing a highly critical response. In preparation for that response, █████ CTC Legal, ███████, requested additional information that could be used as evidence for the effectiveness of the CIA's enhanced interrogation techniques from CTC personnel. █████ sent an email seeking "a list of specific plots that have been thwarted by the use of detainee reporting that we acquired following the use of enhanced techniques." █████ noted that he would compile the information, "emphasizing that hundreds or thousands of innocent lives have been saved as a result of our use of those techniques . . ."[1126] In a separate email, █████ emphasized that it was "critical" that the information "establish direct links between the application of the enhanced interrogation techniques and the production of intelligence that directly enabled the saving of innocent lives," that the intelligence obtained after the use of the CIA's enhanced interrogation techniques be "significantly different in nature from the intelligence acquired before the use of the enhanced techniques," and that the information be "absolutely ironclad" and "demonstrably supported by cable citations, analytical pieces, or what have you."[1127] ██████ further noted that "[w]e can expect to need to present these data to appropriately cleared personnel at the IG and on the Hill, to the Attorney General, and quite possibly to the President at some point, and they must be absolutely verifiable." He concluded, "[i]t is not an exaggeration to say that the future of the program, and the consequent saving of innocent lives, may depend substantially upon the input you provide."[1128]

Responding to the request for information, Deputy Chief of ALEC Station █████ sent an email describing intelligence from KSM in which she wrote, "let's be forward [*sic*] leaning."[1129] The content of █████'s email would serve as a template on which future justifications for the CIA program and the CIA's enhanced interrogation techniques were based.[1130] █████'s email stated that "Khalid Shaykh Muhammad's information alone has saved at least several hundred, possibly thousands, of lives." She then wrote that KSM "identified" Iyman Faris, "who is now serving time in the US for his support to al-Qa'ida," and "identified a photograph" of Saleh al-Marri, "whom the FBI suspected of some involvement with al-Qa'ida, but against whom we had no concrete information," adding that al-Marri "is now being held on a material witness warrant." █████'s email stated that KSM "provided information" on Majid Khan, who "is now in custody," "identified a mechanism for al-Qa'ida to smuggle explosives into the US," and "identified" Jaffar al-Tayyar.[1131] █████'s email also represented that "[a]fter the use of enhanced [interrogation techniques], [Abu Zubaydah] grew into what is now our most cooperative detainee," and that Abu Zubaydah's information "produced concrete results that helped saved [*sic*] lives."[1132] These representations were almost entirely inaccurate.[1133] As she had in an interview with the OIG, ████████, former chief of the Abu Zubaydah Task Force, refuted this view, writing in an email that Abu Zubaydah "never really gave 'this is the plot' type of information," that Abu Zubaydah discussed Jose Padilla prior to the use of the CIA's enhanced interrogation techniques, and that "he never really gave us actionable intel to get them."[1134] Separately, Deputy Chief of ALEC Station ██████ ■ forwarded additional inaccurate information from CIA personnel in ALEC Station to CTC Legal related to KSM,[1135] al-Nashiri,[1136] and Hambali.[1137]

On February 27, 2004, DDO Pavitt submitted his formal response to the OIG draft Special Review in the form of a memorandum to the inspector general. Pavitt urged the CIA OIG not to "shy away from the conclusion that our efforts have thwarted attacks and saved lives," and to "make it clear as well that the EITs (including the waterboard) have been indispensable to our successes."[1138] Pavitt's memorandum included an attachment describing the "Successes of CIA's Counterterrorism Detention and Interrogation Activities," and why the CIA's enhanced interrogation techniques were necessary. The attachment stated:

> "Information we received from detained terrorists as a result of the lawful use of enhanced interrogation techniques ('EITs') has almost certainly saved countless American lives inside the United States and abroad. The evidence points clearly to the fact that without the use of such techniques, we and our allies would [have] suffered major terrorist attacks involving hundreds, if not thousands, of casualties."[1139]

The attachment to Pavitt's memorandum repeated much of the inaccurate information contained in Deputy Chief of ALEC Station [redacted]'s email about KSM and Abu Zubaydah, as well as the additional information ALEC Station personnel provided on KSM, al-Nashiri, and Hambali. In Pavitt's memorandum, every intelligence success claim was preceded with some version of the phrase, "as a result of the lawful use of EITs."[1140] Inaccurate information provided to the OIG during interviews and in the Pavitt memorandum was included in the final version of the OIG's Special Review.[1141] The relevant portion of the Special Review, including much of the inaccurate information, has been declassified.[1142]

As [redacted] CTC Legal [redacted] anticipated in his February 10, 2004, email, much of the information provided to the inspector general on the "effectiveness" of the CIA's enhanced interrogation techniques was later provided to policymakers and the Department of Justice as evidence for the effectiveness of the CIA's enhanced interrogation techniques.[1143]

In late 2004, as the National Security Council was considering "endgame" options for CIA detainees, the CIA proposed a public relations campaign that would include disclosures about the "effectiveness" of the CIA program. CIA talking points prepared in December 2004 for the DCI to use with National Security Council principals stated that "[i]f done cleverly, selected disclosure of intelligence results could heighten the anxiety of terrorists at large about the sophistication of USG methods and underscore the seriousness of American commitment to prosecute aggressively the War on Terrorism."[1144]

The following month, the CIA proposed that the public information campaign include details on the "intelligence gained and lives saved in HVD interrogations."[1145] There was no immediate decision by the National Security Council about an "endgame" for CIA detainees or the proposed public information campaign.

In early April 2005, ■■■■■■■■, chief of ALEC Station, asked that information on the success of the CIA's Detention and Interrogation Program be compiled in anticipation of interviews of CIA personnel by Tom Brokaw of NBC News. The first draft included effectiveness claims relating to the "Second Wave" plotting, the Heathrow Airport plotting, the Karachi plotting, and the identification of a second shoe bomber.[1146] A subsequent draft sought to limit the information provided to what was already in the public record and included assertions about Issa al-Hindi, Iyman Faris, and Sajid Badat.[1147] That day, Deputy Director of CTC Philip Mudd told ■■■■■ ■ that "we either get out and sell, or we get hammered, which has implications beyond the media. [C]ongress reads it, cuts our authorities, messes up our budget."[1148] The following day, the draft was cleared for release to the media.[1149]

On April 20, 2005, the same examples were circulated as part of an anticipated official public campaign to promote the "effectiveness" of the still-classified CIA program.[1150] In response, ■■■■■ ■ CTC Legal, ■■■■■■■■, expressed concern that "the examples cited, while true, and perhaps as far as we can go, are not nearly the most striking examples of lives saved." Referencing KSM's reporting on Iyman Faris, noted that "we risk making ourselves look silly if the best we can do is the Brooklyn Bridge—perhaps we should omit specific examples rather than 'damn ourselves with faint praise.'" ■ ■■■■■, who offered the Heathrow Airport plot as an example, made the following suggestion: "Can [Office of Public Affairs] be more strongly declarative—'while we can't provide details' (or maybe we can) 'the program has produced intelligence that has directly saved 100's/1000's of American and other innocent lives'?" ■■■■■■ then attached claims originally compiled in February 2004 for the purpose of responding to the draft OIG Special Review which, he wrote, described "some of the actionable intelligence acquired as a result of the Program and the lawful use of such techniques."[1151] The examples were inaccurate.[1152]

On June 24, 2005, *Dateline NBC* aired a program, accompanied by several online articles, which quoted CIA Director Goss and Deputy Director of CTC Mudd, as well as anonymous "top American intelligence officials." Among other claims, NBC reported that the capture of Ramzi bin al-Shibh "le[d] ultimately" to the captures of KSM and Khallad bin Attash.[1153] This information was inaccurate.[1154]

At the end of 2005, congressional concerns about the treatment of detainees again spurred interest at the CIA for public disclosures on the "effectiveness" of the CIA's enhanced interrogation techniques. Specifically, congressional action on the Detainee Treatment Act (the "McCain amendment") prompted a CIA attorney working at the Office of the Director of National Intelligence to express concern that legislative support was needed for the CIA to continue to use its enhanced interrogation techniques, and that a public information campaign would be required to garner that support. The CIA attorney described the "striking" similarities between the public debate surrounding the McCain amendment and the situation in Israel in 1999, in which the Israeli Supreme Court had "ruled that several . . . techniques were possibly permissible, but require some form of legislative sanction," and that the Israeli government "ultimately got limited legislative authority for a few specific techniques."[1155] The CIA attorney then wrote:

> "Once this became a political reality here, it became incumbent on the Administration to publicly put forth some facts, if it wanted to preserve these powers. Yet, to date, the Administration has refused to put forth any specific examples of significant intelligence it adduced as a result of using any technique that could not reasonably be construed as cruel, inhuman or degrading. Not even any historical stuff from three or four years ago. What conclusions are to be drawn from the utter failure to offer a specific justification: That no such proof exists? That the Administration does not recognize the legitimacy of the political process on this issue? Or, that need to reserve the right to use these techniques really is not important enough to justify the compromise of even historical intelligence?"[1156]

As described in more detail in the full Committee Study, the Administration sought legislative support to continue the CIA's Detention and Interrogation Program, and chose to do so by publicly disclosing the program in a 2006 speech by President Bush. The speech, which was based on CIA-provided information and vetted by the CIA, included numerous inaccurate representations about the CIA program and the effectiveness of the CIA's enhanced interrogation techniques. The CIA's vetting of the speech is detailed in CIA "validation" documents, which include CIA concurrence and citations to records to support specific passages of the speech. For example, the CIA "Validation of Remarks" document includes the following:

"'. . . *questioning the detainees in this program has given us information that has saved innocent lives by helping us to stop new attacks—here in the United States and across the world.*'

"**CIA concurs with this assessment.** Information from detainees prevented—among others—the West Coast airliner plot, a plot to blow up an apartment building in the United States, a plot to attack various targets in the United Kingdom, and plots against targets in Karachi and the Arabian Gulf. These attacks would undoubtedly have killed thousands."[1157]

Multiple iterations of the CIA "validation" documents reflect changes to the speech as it was being prepared. One week before the scheduled speech, a passage in the draft speech made inaccurate claims about the role played by Abu Zubaydah in the capture of Ramzi bin al-Shibh and the role of Abu Zubaydah and Ramzi bin al-Shibh in the capture of KSM, but did not explicitly connect these claims to the use of the CIA's enhanced interrogation techniques. In an August 31, 2006, email exchange, CIA officers proposed the following language for the speech:

"That same year, information from Zubaydah led the CIA to the trail of one of KSM's accomplices, Ramzi bin al Shibh. Information from Zubaydah together with information from Shibh gave the CIA insight into al-Qa'ida's 9/11 attack planning and the importance of KSM. With the knowledge that KSM was the 'mastermind,' ████████ Pakistani partners planned and mounted an operation that resulted in his eventual capture and detention."[1158]

The August 31, 2006, email exchange included citations to CIA cables to support the proposed passage; however, neither the cables, nor any other CIA records, support the assertions.[1159]

Within a few days, the passage in the draft speech relating to the captures of Ramzi bin al-Shibh and KSM was modified to connect the use of the CIA's enhanced interrogation techniques against Abu Zubaydah to the capture of Ramzi bin al-Shibh. The updated draft now credited information from Abu Zubaydah and Ramzi bin al-Shibh with "help[ing] in the planning and execution of the operation that captured Khalid Sheikh Mohammed." The updated draft speech stated:

"Zubaydah [zoo-BAY-da] was questioned using these [interrogation] procedures, and he soon began to provide information on key al-Qaida operatives—including information that helped us find and capture more of those responsible for the attacks of Nine-Eleven. For example, Zubaydah [zoo-BAY-da] identified one of KSM's accomplices in the Nine-Eleven attacks—a terrorist named Ramzi bin al Shibh [SHEEB]. The information Zubaydah [zoo-BAY-da] provided helped lead to the capture of bin al Shibh. And together these two terrorists provided information that helped in the planning and execution of the operation that captured Khalid Sheikh Mohammed."[1160]

An updated CIA "validation" document concurring with the proposed passage provided a modified list of CIA cables as "sources" to support the passage. Cable citations to Abu Zubaydah's reporting prior to the use of the CIA's enhanced interrogation techniques were removed.[1161] Like the previous version, the CIA's updated "validation" document did not cite to any cables demonstrating that information from Abu Zubaydah "helped lead to the capture of [Ramzi] bin al-Shibh."[1162] Similarly, none of the cables cited to support the passage indicated that information from Abu Zubaydah and Ramzi bin al-Shibh (who was in foreign government custody when he provided the information cited by the CIA) "helped in the planning and execution of the operation that captured [KSM]."[1163] As described elsewhere in this summary, there are no CIA records to support these claims.[1164]

The CIA documents validating the president's speech addressed other passages that were likewise unsupported by the CIA's cited cables. For example, the speech included an inaccurate claim regarding KSM that had been part of the CIA's representations on the effectiveness of the CIA's enhanced interrogation techniques since 2003. The speech stated:

> "Once in our custody, KSM was questioned by the CIA using these procedures, and he soon provided information that helped us stop another planned attack on the United States. During questioning, KSM told us about another al Qaeda operative he knew was in CIA custody—a terrorist named Majid Khan. KSM revealed that [Majid] Khan had been told to deliver $50,000 to individuals working for a suspected terrorist leader named Hambali, the leader of al Qaeda's Southeast Asian affiliate known as 'J-I.' CIA officers confronted Khan with this information. Khan confirmed that the money had been delivered to an operative named Zubair, and provided both a physical description and contact number for this operative. Based on that information, Zubair was captured in June of 2003, and he soon provided information that helped lead to the capture of Hambali."[1165]

As support for this passage, the CIA cited a June 2003 cable describing a CIA interrogation of Majid Khan in which Majid Khan discussed Zubair.[1166] The CIA "validation" document did not include cable citations from March 2003 that would have revealed that Majid Khan provided this information while in foreign government custody, prior to the reporting from KSM.[1167]

On September 6, 2006, President Bush delivered the speech based on the CIA-vetted information.[1168] On September 8, 2006, the chief of the ██████ Department in CTC, ████████, who had participated in the CIA's validation of the speech, distributed the "final validation document" for possible updates or changes. In an email, ██████ urged the recipients to "[p]lease look very carefully, as this is going to be a very important document."[1169]

On September 11, 2006, a CIA officer responded, questioning the passage in the speech related to the capture of KSM, as well as the relevance of the CIA cables cited in the validation document to support the passage. The CIA officer questioned whether a CIA cable describing Ramzi bin al-Shibh's identification of "Ammar" supported the claim that bin al-Shibh's reporting helped lead to the capture of KSM. The officer wrote:

> "I presume the information in this cable that supports the statement is Ramzi's admission regarding Ammar?? Did that actually help lead us to KSM?? not sure who did this section, but we may want to double-check this and provide additional cables on how this actually 'assisted us'. This also seems to be a point critics in the press seem to be picking on, I will do some digging on my own as well."[1170]

There are no CIA records to indicate that the CIA officer's comments about the inadequate sourcing were further addressed. As described in this summary, and in more detail in Volume II, there are no CIA records to support the passage in the speech related to the capture of KSM.

After the speech, press accounts challenging aspects of the speech became the subject of internal discussion among some CIA officers. On September 7, 2006, the chief of the ██████ Department in CTC, ████████, sent an email stating: "The NY Times has posted a story predictably poking holes in the President's speech." Defending the passage in the speech asserting that, after the use of the CIA's enhanced interrogation techniques, Abu Zubaydah provided information "that helped lead to the capture of bin al-Shibh," ██████ explained:

> ". . . we knew Ramzi bin al-Shibh was involved in 9/11 beforeAZ was captured; however, AZ gave us information on his recent activities that—when added into other information—helped us track him. Again, on this point, we were very careful and the speech is accurate in what it says about bin al-Shibh."[1171]

███████'s statement, that Abu Zubaydah provided "information on [bin al-Shibh's] recent activities" that "helped [CIA] track him," was not supported by the cables cited in the CIA's "validation" document, or any other CIA record. ███████'s email did not address the other representation in the president's speech—that Abu Zubaydah "identified" Ramzi bin al-Shibh.[1172]

The *New York Times* article also challenged the representation in the speech that Abu Zubaydah "disclosed" that KSM was the "mastermind behind the 9/11 attacks and used the alias 'Mukhtar,'" and that "[t]his was a vital picce of the puzzle that helped our intelligence community pursue KSM." As the *New York Times* article noted, the 9/11 Commission had pointed to a cable from August 2001 that identified KSM as "Mukhtar." In her email, ███ acknowledged the August 2001 report identifying KSM as "Mukhtar" and provided additional information on the drafting of the speech:

> "[O]n 28 August, 2001, in fact, [CIA's] ███ [database] does show a report from [a source] stating that Mohammad Rahim's brother Zadran told him that KSM was now being called 'Mukhtar.' Moreover, we were suspicious that KSM might have been behind 9/11 as early as 12 Sept 2001, and we had some reporting indicating he was the mastermind. We explained this latter fact to the White House, although the 28 August report escaped our notice."[1173]

In her email, ███ stated that "[t]he fact that the 9/11 commission, with 20-20 hindsight, thinks we should have known this in August 2001 does not alter the fact that we didn't."[1174]

In addition to the *New York Times* article, the CIA was concerned about an article by Ron Suskind in *Time Magazine* that also challenged the assertions in the speech about the capture of Ramzi bin al-Shibh and KSM.[1175] In a September 11, 2006, email, the chief of the ███ Department in CTC, ███, wrote "[w]e are not claiming [Abu Zubaydah] provided exact locational information, merely that he provided us with information that helped in our targeting efforts." ███'s email did not address the representations in the president's speech that Abu Zubaydah "identified" Ramzi bin al-Shibh and that the information from Abu Zubaydah "helped lead to the capture" of bin al-Shibh. With regard to the capture of KSM, ███'s email acknowledged that Suskind's assertion that "the key was a cooperative source" was "correct as far as it goes, but the priority with which we pursued KSM changed once AZ conclusively identified him as the mastermind of 9/11."[1176] ███'s email did not address the representation in the president's speech that Abu Zubaydah, along with Ramzi bin al-Shibh, "helped in the planning and execution of the operation that captured Khalid Sheikh Mohammed." ███'s statements about the captures of Ramzi bin al-Shibh and KSM are not supported by CIA records.[1177]

The president's September 6, 2006, speech, which was based on CIA-provided information and vetted by the CIA, was the first detailed, formal public representation about the effectiveness of the

CIA's enhanced interrogation techniques.[1178] The inaccurate representations in the speech have been repeated in numerous articles, books, and broadcasts. The speech was also relied upon by the OLC in its July 20, 2007, memorandum on the legality of the CIA's enhanced interrogation techniques, specifically to support the premise that the use of the techniques was effective in "producing substantial quantities of otherwise unavailable intelligence."[1179]

D. CIA Representations About the Effectiveness of Its Enhanced Interrogation Techniques Against Specific CIA Detainees

While the CIA made numerous general representations about the effectiveness of its enhanced interrogation techniques, CIA representations on specific detainees focused almost exclusively on two CIA detainees, Abu Zubaydah, detained on March 28, 2002, and KSM, detained on March 1, 2003.[1180]

1. Abu Zubaydah

As described in greater detail in the full Committee Study, the CIA provided significant information to policymakers and the Department of Justice on the CIA's decision to use the newly developed CIA "enhanced interrogation techniques" on Abu Zubaydah and the effects of doing so. These representations were provided by the CIA to the CIA OIG,[1181] the White House,[1182] the Department of Justice,[1183] Congress,[1184] and the American public.[1185] The representations include that: (1) Abu Zubaydah told the CIA he believed "the general US population was 'weak,' lacked resilience, and would be unable to 'do what was necessary' ";[1186] (2) Abu Zubaydah stopped cooperating with U.S. government personnel using traditional interrogation techniques;[1187] (3) Abu Zubaydah's interrogation team believed the use of the CIA's enhanced interrogation techniques would result in critical information on terrorist operatives and plotting;[1188] and (4) the use of CIA's enhanced interrogation techniques on Abu Zubaydah was effective in eliciting critical intelligence from Abu Zubaydah.[1189] These representations are not supported by internal CIA records.

The CIA representation that Abu Zubaydah "expressed [his] belief that the general US population was 'weak,' lacked resilience, and would be unable to 'do what was necessary' to prevent the terrorists from succeeding in their goals" is not supported by CIA records.[1190] On August 30, 2006, a CIA officer from the CIA's al-Qa'ida Plans and Organization Group wrote: "we have no records that 'he declared that America was weak, and lacking in resilience and that our society did not have the will to 'do what was necessary' to prevent the terrorists from succeeding in their goals.' "[1191] In a CIA Sametime communication that same day, a CIA ALEC Station officer wrote, "I can find no reference to AZ being deifant [*sic*] and declaring America weak . . . in fact everything I have read indicated he used a non deifiant [*sic*] resistance strategy." In response, the chief of the ████ Department in CTC, ████████, wrote: "I've certainly heard that said of AZ for years, but don't know why . . ." The CIA ALEC Station officer replied, "probably a combo of [deputy chief of ALEC Station, ██████] and [████] . . . I'll leave it at that." The chief of the ████ Department completed the exchange, writing "yes, believe so . . . and agree, we shall pass over in silence."[1192]

The CIA representation that Abu Zubaydah stopped cooperating with debriefers using traditional interrogation techniques is also not supported by CIA records.[1193] In early June 2002, Abu Zubaydah's interrogators recommended that Abu Zubaydah spend several weeks in isolation while the interrogation team members traveled ███ "as a means of keeping [Abu Zubaydah] off-balance and to allow the team needed time off for a break and to attend to matters ███," as well as to discuss "the endgame" for Abu Zubaydah ███ with officers from CIA Headquarters.[1194] As a result, Abu Zubaydah spent much of June 2002, and all of July 2002, 47 days in total, in isolation. When CIA officers next interrogated Abu Zubaydah, they immediately used the CIA's enhanced interrogation techniques, including the waterboard.[1195] Prior to this isolation period, Abu Zubaydah provided information on al-Qa'ida activities, plans, capabilities, and relationships, in addition to information on its leadership structure, including personalities, decision-making processes, training, and tactics.[1196] Abu Zubaydah provided the same type of information prior to, during, and after the use of the CIA's enhanced interrogation techniques.[1197] Abu Zubaydah's inability to provide information on the next attack in the United States—and operatives in the United States—provided the basis for CIA representations that Abu Zubaydah was "uncooperative," as well as for the CIA's determination that Abu Zubaydah required the use of the CIA's enhanced interrogation techniques to become "compliant" and reveal the information that CIA Headquarters believed he was withholding. The CIA further stated that Abu Zubaydah could stop the application of the CIA's enhanced interrogation techniques, like the waterboard, by providing the names of operatives in the United States or information to stop the next attack.[1198] At no point during or after the use of the CIA's enhanced interrogation techniques did Abu Zubaydah provide this type of information.[1199]

The CIA representation that Abu Zubaydah's interrogation team believed the use of the CIA's enhanced interrogation techniques would result in new information on operatives in the United States and terrorist plotting is also incongruent with CIA records. While Abu Zubaydah was in isolation in July 2002, CIA Headquarters informed the Department of Justice and White House officials that Abu Zubaydah's interrogation team believed Abu Zubaydah possessed information on terrorist threats to, and al-Qa'ida operatives in, the United States.[1200] The CIA officials further represented that the interrogation team had concluded that the use of more aggressive methods "is required to persuade Abu Zubaydah to provide the critical information needed to safeguard the lives of innumerable innocent men, women, and children within the United States and abroad," and warned "countless more Americans may die unless we can persuade AZ to tell us what he knows."[1201] However, according to CIA cables, the interrogation team at the detention site had not determined that the CIA's enhanced interrogation techniques were required for Abu Zubaydah to provide such threat information. Rather, the interrogation team wrote "[o]ur assumption is the objective of this operation is to achieve a high degree of confidence that [Abu Zubaydah] is not holding back actionable information concerning threats to the United States beyond that which [Abu Zubaydah] has already provided."[1202]

The CIA representation that the use of the CIA's enhanced interrogation techniques on Abu Zubaydah was effective in producing critical threat information on terrorists and terrorist plotting against the United States is also not supported by CIA records. Abu Zubaydah did not provide the information for which the CIA's enhanced interrogation techniques were justified and approved—information on the next attack and operatives in the United States.[1203] According to CIA records, Abu Zubaydah provided information on "al-Qa'ida activities, plans, capabilities, and relationships," in addition to information on "its leadership structure, including personalities, decision-making processes, training, and tactics."[1204] This type of information was provided by Abu Zubaydah prior to, during, and after the use of the CIA's enhanced interrogation techniques.[1205] At no point during or after the use of the CIA's enhanced interrogation techniques did Abu Zubaydah provide information on al-Qa'ida cells in the United States or operational plans for terrorist attacks against the United States.[1206] Further, a quantitative review of Abu Zubaydah's intelligence reporting indicates that more intelligence reports were disseminated from Abu Zubaydah's first two months of interrogation, before the use of the CIA's enhanced interrogation techniques and when FBI special agents were directly participating, than were derived during the next two-month phase of interrogations, which included the non-stop use of the CIA's enhanced interrogation techniques 24 hours a day for 17 days.[1207] Nonetheless, on August 30, 2002, the CIA informed the National Security Council that the CIA's enhanced interrogation techniques were effective and "producing meaningful results."[1208] Shortly thereafter, however, in October 2002, CIA records indicate that President Bush was informed in a Presidential Daily Brief (PDB) that "Abu Zubaydah resisted providing useful information until becoming more cooperative in early August, probably in the hope of improving his living conditions." The PDB made no reference to the CIA's enhanced interrogation techniques.[1209] Subsequently, the CIA represented to other senior policymakers and the Department of Justice that the CIA's enhanced interrogation techniques were successfully used to elicit critical information from Abu Zubaydah.[1210] For example, in a March 2, 2005, CIA memorandum to the Department of Justice, the CIA represented that information obtained from Abu Zubaydah on the "Dirty Bomb Plot" and Jose Padilla was acquired only "*after* applying [enhanced] interrogation techniques."[1211] This CIA representation was repeated in numerous CIA communications with policymakers and the Department of Justice.[1212] The information provided by the CIA was inaccurate. On the evening of April 20, 2002, prior to the use of the CIA's enhanced interrogation techniques, Abu Zubaydah provided this information to FBI officers who were using rapport building interrogation techniques.[1213]

2. Khalid Shaykh Muhammad (KSM)

As described in more detail in the full Committee Study, the CIA provided significant inaccurate information to policymakers on the effectiveness of the CIA's enhanced interrogation techniques in the interrogation of KSM. These representations were provided by the CIA to the OIG,[1214] the White House,[1215] the Department of Justice,[1216] the Congress,[1217] and the American public.[1218] The representations include that: (1) KSM provided little threat information or actionable intelligence prior to the use of the CIA's enhanced interrogation techniques;[1219] (2) the CIA overcame KSM's resistance through the use of the CIA's enhanced interrogation techniques;[1220] (3) the CIA's waterboard interrogation technique was particularly effective in eliciting information from KSM;[1221] (4) KSM "recanted little of the information" he had provided, and KSM's information was "generally accurate" and "consistent";[1222] (5) KSM made a statement to CIA personnel—"soon, you will know"—indicating an attack was imminent upon his arrest; and (6) KSM believed "the general US population was 'weak,' lacked resilience, and would be unable to 'do what was necessary.'"[1223] These representations are not supported by internal CIA records.

While the CIA represented to multiple parties that KSM provided little threat information or actionable intelligence prior to the use of the CIA's enhanced interrogation techniques, CIA records indicate that KSM was subjected to the CIA's enhanced interrogation techniques within "a few minutes" of first being questioned by CIA interrogators.[1224] This material fact was omitted from CIA representations.

The CIA represented that the CIA overcame KSM's resistance to interrogation by using the CIA's enhanced interrogation techniques.[1225] CIA records do not support this statement. To the contrary, there are multiple CIA records describing the ineffectiveness of the CIA's enhanced interrogation techniques in gaining KSM's cooperation. On March 26, 2003, the day after the CIA last used its enhanced interrogation techniques on KSM, KSM was described as likely lying and engaged in an effort "to renew a possible resistance stance."[1226] On April 2, 2003, the Interagency Intelligence Committee on Terrorism (IICT) produced an assessment of KSM's intelligence entitled, "Precious Truths, Surrounded by a Bodyguard of Lies." The assessment concluded that KSM was withholding information or lying about terrorist plots and operatives targeting the United States.[1227] During and after the use of the CIA's enhanced interrogation techniques, the CIA repeatedly expressed concern that KSM was lying and withholding information in the context of CBRN (Chemical, Biological, Radiological, and Nuclear) programs,[1228] plotting against U.S. interests in Karachi, Pakistan,[1229] plotting against Heathrow Airport,[1230] Abu Issa al-Britani,[1231] as well as the "Second Wave" plotting against the "tallest building in California," which prompted the CIA's ALEC Station to note in a cable dated April 22, 2003, that it "remain[e]d concerned that KSM's progression towards full debriefing status is not yet apparent where it counts most, in relation to threats to US interests, especially inside CONUS."[1232]

The CIA repeatedly represented that the CIA's waterboard interrogation technique was particularly effective in eliciting information from KSM.[1233] This representation is not supported by CIA records. Numerous CIA personnel, including members of KSM's interrogation team, expressed their belief that the waterboard interrogation technique was ineffective on KSM. The on-site medical officer told the inspector general that after three or four days it became apparent that the waterboard was ineffective and that KSM "hated it but knew he could manage."[1234] KSM debriefer and Deputy Chief of ALEC Station ████ told the inspector general that KSM "figured out a way to deal with [the waterboard],[1235] and she relayed in a 2005 Sametime communication that "we broke KSM . . . using the Majid Khan stuff . . . and the emails"; in other words by confronting KSM with information from other sources.[1236] ████ █CTC Legal, ████, told the inspector general that the waterboard "was of limited use on KSM."[1237] A KSM interrogator told the inspector general that KSM had "beat the system,"[1238] and assessed that KSM responded to "creature comforts and sense of importance" and not to "confrontational" approaches.[1239] The interrogator later wrote in a Sametime communication that KSM and Abu Zubaydah "held back" despite the use of the CIA's enhanced interrogation techniques, adding "I'm ostracized whenever I suggest those two did not tell us everything. How dare I think KSM was holding back."[1240] In April 2003, ███OMS told the inspector general that the waterboard had "not been very effective on KSM." He also "questioned how the repeated use of the waterboard was categorically different from 'beating the bottom of my feet,' or from torture in general."[1241]

The CIA repeatedly represented that KSM had "recanted little of the information" he had provided, and that KSM's information was "generally accurate" and "consistent."[1242] This assertion is not supported by CIA records. Throughout the period during which KSM was subjected to the CIA's enhanced interrogation techniques, KSM provided inaccurate information, much of which he would later acknowledge was fabricated and recant. Specifically, KSM's fabrications and recantations covered his activities immediately before his capture,[1243] the identity of an individual whom he described as the protector of his children,"[1244] plotting against a U.S. aircraft carrier, a meeting with Abu Faraj al-Libi, and the location of Hassan Ghul.[1245] KSM fabricated significant information, which he would later recant, related to Jaffar al-Tayyar, stating that al-Tayyar and Jose Padilla were plotting together,[1246] linking al-Tayyar to Heathrow Airport plotting[1247] and to Majid Khan's plotting,[1248] and producing what CIA officials described as an "elaborate tale" linking al-Tayyar to an assassination plot against former President Jimmy Carter.[1249] KSM later explained that "he had been forced to lie" about al-Tayyar due to the pressure from CIA interrogators.[1250] KSM recanted other information about the Heathrow Airport plotting, including information regarding the targeting,[1251] additional operatives, and the tasking of prospective pilots to study at flight schools.[1252] KSM provided significant information on Abu Issa al-Britani (Dhiren Barot) that he would later recant, including linking Abu Issa al-Britani to Jaffar al-Tayyar and to the Heathrow Airport plot.[1253] Under direct threat of additional waterboarding,[1254] KSM told CIA interrogators that he had sent Abu Issa al-Britani to Montana to recruit African-American Muslim converts.[1255] In June 2003, KSM stated he fabricated the story because he was "under 'enhanced measures' when he made these claims and simply told his interrogators what he thought they wanted to hear."[1256] KSM also stated that he tasked Majid Khan with recruiting Muslims in the United States,[1257] which he would later recant.[1258] On May 3, 2003, CIA officers recommended revisiting the information KSM had provided "during earlier stages of his interrogation process," noting that "he has told us that he said some things during this phase to get the enhanced measures to stop, therefore some of this information may be suspect."[1259]

The CIA also repeatedly referred to a comment made by KSM while he was still in Pakistani custody as indicating that KSM had information on an imminent attack. In reports to the inspector general,[1260] the national security advisor,[1261] and the Department of Justice,[1262] among others, the CIA represented that:

> "When asked about future attacks planned against the United States, he coldly replied 'Soon, you will know.' In fact, soon we did know—after we initiated enhanced measures."[1263]

Contrary to CIA representations, CIA records indicate that KSM's comment was interpreted by CIA officers with KSM at the time as meaning that KSM was seeking to use his future cooperation as a "bargaining chip" with more senior CIA officers.[1264]

Finally, the CIA attributed to KSM, along with Abu Zubaydah, the statement that "the general US population was 'weak,' lacked resilience, and would be unable to 'do what was necessary' to prevent the terrorists from succeeding in their goals."[1265] There are no CIA operational or interrogation records to support the representation that KSM or Abu Zubaydah made these statements.

E. CIA Effectiveness Claims Regarding a "High Volume of Critical Intelligence"

The CIA represented that the CIA's enhanced interrogation techniques resulted in the collection of "a high volume of critical intelligence[1266] on al-Qa'ida."[1267] The Committee evaluated the "high volume" of intelligence collected by compiling the total number of sole source and multi-source disseminated intelligence reports from the 119 known CIA detainees.[1268]

The CIA informed the Committee that its interrogation program was successful in developing intelligence and suggested that all CIA detainees produced disseminated intelligence reporting. For example, in September 2006, CIA Director Michael Hayden provided the following testimony to the Committee:

> **SENATOR BAYH**: "I was impressed by your statement about how effective the [CIA's enhanced interrogation] techniques have been in eliciting important information to the country, at one point up to 50 percent of our information about al-Qa'ida. I think you said 9000 different intelligence reports?"
>
> **DIRECTOR HAYDEN**: "Over 8000, sir."
>
> **SENATOR BAYH**: "And yet this has come from, I guess, only thirty individuals."
>
> **DIRECTOR HAYDEN**: "No, sir, 96, all 96."[1269]

In April 2007, CIA Director Hayden testified that the CIA's interrogation program existed "for one purpose—intelligence," and that it is "the most successful program being conducted by American intelligence today" for "preventing attacks, disabling al-Qa'ida."[1270] At this hearing Director Hayden again suggested that the CIA interrogation program was successful in obtaining intelligence from all CIA detainees.[1271] A transcript of that hearing included the following exchange:

> **SENATOR SNOWE**: "General Hayden. Of the 8000 intelligence reports that were provided, as you said, by 30 of the detainees."
>
> **DIRECTOR HAYDEN**: "By all 97, ma'am."[1272]

The suggestion that all CIA detainees provided information that resulted in intelligence reporting is not supported by CIA records. CIA records reveal that 34 percent of the 119 known CIA detainees produced no intelligence reports, and nearly 70 percent produced fewer than 15 intelligence reports. Of the 39 detainees who were, according to CIA records, subjected to the CIA's enhanced interrogation techniques, nearly 20 percent produced no intelligence reports, while 40 percent produced fewer than 15 intelligence reports. While the CIA's Detention and Interrogation Program did produce significant amounts of disseminated intelligence reporting (5,874 sole-source intelligence reports), this reporting was overwhelmingly derived from a small subset of CIA detainees. For example, of the 119 CIA detainees identified in the Study, 89 percent of all disseminated intelligence reporting was derived from 25 CIA detainees. Five CIA detainees produced more than 40 percent of all intelligence reporting from the CIA's Detention and Interrogation Program. CIA records indicate that two of the five detainees were not subjected to the CIA's enhanced interrogation techniques.[1273]

F. The Eight Primary CIA Effectiveness Representations—The Use of the CIA's Enhanced Interrogation Techniques "Enabled the CIA to Disrupt Terrorist Plots" and "Capture Additional Terrorists"

From 2003 through 2009,[1274] the CIA consistently and repeatedly represented that its enhanced interrogation techniques were effective and necessary to produce critical intelligence that "enabled the CIA to disrupt terrorist plots, capture additional terrorists, and collect a high-volume of critical intelligence on al-Qa'ida." The CIA further stated that the information acquired as a result of the use of the CIA's enhanced interrogation techniques could not have been acquired by the U.S. government in any other way ("otherwise unavailable").[1275] The CIA also represented that the best measure of effectiveness of the CIA's enhanced interrogation techniques was examples of specific terrorist plots "thwarted" and specific terrorists captured as a result of the use of the CIA's techniques.

For example, in a December 2004 CIA memorandum prepared

for the national security advisor, the CIA wrote that there was "no way to conduct" an "independent study of the foreign intelligence efficacy of using enhanced interrogation techniques," but stated, "[t]he Central Intelligence Agency can advise you that this program works and the techniques are effective in producing foreign intelligence." To illustrate the effectiveness of the CIA's interrogation techniques, the CIA provided 11 examples of "[k]ey intelligence collected from HVD interrogations *after* applying interrogation techniques," nine of which referenced specific terrorist plots or the capture of specific terrorists.[1276] Similarly, under the heading, "Plots Discovered as a Result of EITs," a CIA briefing prepared for President Bush in November 2007 states, "reporting statistics alone will not provide a fair and accurate measure of the effectiveness of EITs." Instead, the CIA provided eight "examples of key intelligence collected from CIA detainee interrogations after applying the waterboard along with other interrogation techniques," seven of which referenced specific terrorist plots or the capture of specific terrorists.[1277]

The Committee selected 20 CIA documents that include CIA representations about the effectiveness of the CIA's enhanced interrogation techniques from 2003 through 2009. The 20 CIA documents, which were consistent with a broader set of CIA representations made during this period, include materials the CIA prepared for the White House, the Department of Justice, the Congress, the CIA Office of Inspector General, as well as incoming members of President Obama's national security team, and the public. The Committee selected the following 20 CIA documents:

1. July and September 2003: CIA Briefing Documents Seeking Policy Reaffirmation of the CIA Interrogation Program from White House Officials, "Review of Interrogation Program."[1278]
2. February 2004: The CIA's Response to the Draft Inspector General Special Review, CIA "Comments to Draft IG Special Review, 'Counterterrorism Detention and Interrogation Program,'" and attachment, "Successes of CIA's Counterterrorism Detention and Interrogation Activities."[1279]
3. July 2004: CIA Intelligence Assessment, "Khalid Shaykh Muhammad: Preeminent Source on Al-Qa'ida."[1280]
4. December 2004: CIA Memorandum for the President's National Security Advisor, "Effectiveness of the CIA Counterterrorist Interrogation Techniques."[1281]
5. March 2005: CIA Memorandum for the Office of Legal

Counsel, "Effectiveness of the CIA Counterterrorist Interrogation Techniques."[1282]

6. March 2005: CIA "Briefing for Vice President Cheney: CIA Detention and Interrogation Program."[1283]
7. March 2005: CIA Talking Points for the National Security Council, "Effectiveness of the High-Value Detainee Interrogation (HVDI) Techniques."[1284]
8. April 2005: CIA "Briefing Notes on the Value of Detainee Reporting" provided to the Department of Justice for the OLC's assessment of the legality of the CIA's enhanced interrogation techniques.[1285]
9. April 2005: CIA "Materials of KSM and Abu Zubaydah" and additional CIA documents provided to the Department of Justice for the OLC's assessment of the legality of the CIA's enhanced interrogation techniques.[1286]
10. June 2005: CIA Intelligence Assessment, "Detainee Reporting Pivotal for the War Against Al-Qa'ida."[1287]
11. December 2005: CIA Document entitled, "Future of CIA's Counterterrorist Detention and Interrogation Program," with the attachment, "Impact of the Loss of the Detainee Program to CT Operations and Analysis," from CIA Director Porter Goss to Stephen Hadley, Assistant to the President/National Security Advisor, Frances Townsend, Assistant to the President/Homeland Security Advisor, and Ambassador John Negroponte, the Director of National Intelligence.[1288]
12. May 2006: CIA Briefing for the President's Chief of Staff, "CIA Rendition, Detention and Interrogation Programs," on the effectiveness of the CIA's enhanced interrogation techniques.[1289]
13. 13. July 2006: CIA Memorandum for the Director of National Intelligence, "Detainee Intelligence Value Update."[1290]
14. September 2006: CIA documents supporting the President's September 6, 2006, speech, including representations on the effectiveness of the CIA's interrogation program, including: "DRAFT Potential Public Briefing of CIA's High-Value Terrorist Interrogations Program," "CIA Validation of Remarks on Detainee Policy," and "Summary of the High Value Terrorist Detainee Program."[1291]
15. April 2007: CIA Director Michael Hayden's Testimony to the Senate Select Committee on Intelligence describing the effectiveness of the CIA's interrogation program.[1292]
16. October 2007: CIA Talking Points for the Senate Appropriations Committee, addressing the effectiveness of the CIA's Detention and Interrogation Program, entitled, "Talking

Points Appeal of the $███ Million Reduction in CIA/CTC's Rendition and Detention Program."[1293]

17. November 2007: CIA Director Talking Points for the President, entitled, "Waterboard 06 November 2007," on the effectiveness of the CIA's waterboard interrogation technique.[1294]
18. January 2009: CIA Briefing for President-elect Obama's National Security Transition Team on the value of the CIA's "Renditions, Detentions, and Interrogations (RDI)."[1295]
19. February 2009: CIA Briefing for CIA Director Leon Panetta on the effectiveness of the CIA's enhanced interrogation techniques, including "DCIA Briefing on RDI Program—18FEB.2009," "Key Intelligence and Reporting Derived from Abu Zubaydah and Khalid Shaykh Muhammad (KSM)," "EITs and Effectiveness," "Key Intelligence Impacts Chart: Attachment (AZ and KSM)," "Background on Key Intelligence Impacts Chart: Attachment," and "Background on Key Captures and Plots Disrupted," among other CIA documents.[1296]
20. March 2009: CIA Memorandum for the Chairman of the Senate Select Committee on Intelligence, including representations on the "Key Captures and Disrupted Plots Gained from HVDs in the RDI Program."[1297]

From the 20 CIA documents, the Committee identified the CIA's eight most frequently cited examples of "thwarted" plots and captured terrorists that the CIA attributed to information acquired from the use of the CIA's enhanced interrogation techniques (see chart on next page).

The Committee sought to confirm that the CIA's representations about the most frequently cited examples of "thwarted" plots and captured terrorists were consistent with the more than six million pages of CIA detention and interrogation records provided to the Committee. Specifically, the Committee assessed whether the CIA's representations that its enhanced interrogation techniques produced unique, otherwise unavailable intelligence[1298] that led to the capture of specific terrorists and the "thwarting" of specific plots were accurate.[1299] The Committee found the CIA's representations to be inaccurate and unsupported by CIA records.

Below are the summaries of the CIA's eight most frequently cited examples of "thwarted" plots and captured terrorists, as well as a description of the CIA's claims and an explanation for why the CIA representations were inaccurate and unsupported by CIA records.[1300]

	Eight Most Frequently Cited Examples of Plots "Thwarted" and Terrorists Captured Provided by the CIA as Evidence for the Effectiveness of the CIA's Enhanced Interrogation Techniques	Referenced X Number of Times in the 20 CIA Documents
1.	The Thwarting of the Dirty Bomb/Tall Buildings Plot and the Capture of Jose Padilla	17/20
2.	The Thwarting of the Karachi Plots	17/20
3.	The Thwarting of the Second Wave Plot and the Discovery of the al-Ghuraba Group	18/20
4.	The Thwarting of the United Kingdom Urban Targets Plot and The Capture of Dhiren Barot, aka Issa al-Hindi	17/20
5.	The Identification, Capture, and Arrest of Iyman Faris	7/20
6.	The Identification, Capture, and Arrest of Sajid Badat	17/20
7.	The Thwarting of the Heathrow Airport and Canary Wharf Plotting	20/20
8.	The Capture of Hambali	18/20

1. The Thwarting of the Dirty Bomb/Tall Buildings Plot and the Capture of Jose Padilla

SUMMARY: The CIA represented that its enhanced interrogation techniques were effective and necessary to produce critical, otherwise unavailable intelligence, which enabled the CIA to disrupt terrorist plots, capture terrorists, and save lives. Over a period of years, the CIA provided the thwarting of terrorist plotting associated with, and the capture of, Jose Padilla, as evidence for the effectiveness of the CIA's enhanced interrogation techniques. These CIA representations were inaccurate. The CIA first received reporting on the terrorist threat posed by Jose Padilla from a foreign government. Eight days later, Abu Zubaydah provided information on the terrorist plotting of two individuals, whom he did not identify by true name, to FBI special agents. Abu Zubaydah provided this information in April 2002, prior to the commencement of the CIA's enhanced interrogation techniques in August 2002. The plots associated with Jose Padilla were assessed by the Intelligence Community to be infeasible.

FURTHER DETAILS: The Dirty Bomb/Tall Buildings plotting refers to terrorist plotting involving U.S. citizen Jose Padilla. Padilla and his associate, Binyam Mohammed, conceived the "Dirty Bomb Plot" after locating information, derived from what the CIA described as "a satirical internet article" entitled "How to Make an H-bomb," on a computer at a Pakistani safe house in early 2002.[1301] The article instructed would-be bomb makers to enrich uranium by placing it "in a bucket, attaching it to a six foot rope, and swinging it around your head as fast as possible for 45 minutes.[1302] Padilla and Mohammed approached Abu Zubaydah in early 2002, and later KSM, with their idea to build and use this device in the United States.[1303] Neither Abu Zubaydah nor KSM believed the plan was viable,[1304] but KSM provided funding for, and tasked Padilla to conduct, an operation using natural gas to create explosions in tall buildings in the United States,[1305] later known as the "Tall Buildings Plot."[1306]

The capture of, and the thwarting of terrorist plotting associated with Jose Padilla, is one of the eight most frequently cited examples provided by the CIA as evidence for the effectiveness of the CIA's enhanced interrogation techniques. Over a period of years, CIA documents prepared for and provided to senior policymakers, intelligence officials, and the Department of Justice represent the identification and/or the capture of Jose Padilla, and/or the disruption of the "Dirty Bomb," and/or the "Tall Buildings" plotting, as examples of how "[k]ey intelligence collected from HVD interrogations *after* applying interrogation techniques" had "enabled CIA to disrupt terrorist plots" and "capture additional terrorists."[1307] The CIA further represented that the intelligence acquired from the CIA's enhanced interrogation techniques was "otherwise unavailable" and "saved lives."[1308]

For example, a document prepared for Vice President Cheney in advance of a March 8, 2005, National Security Council principals meeting states, under a section entitled "INTERROGATION RESULTS," that:

> "Use of DOJ-authorized *enhanced interrogation techniques*, as part of a comprehensive interrogation approach, has *enabled* us to disrupt terrorist plots . . .
>
> ". . . Dirty Bomb Plot: Operatives Jose Padilla and Binyam Mohammed planned to build and detonate a 'dirty bomb' in the Washington DC area. *Plot disrupted.* Source: Abu Zubaydah."[1309]

Likewise, the July 20, 2007, Department of Justice Office of Legal Counsel (OLC) memorandum on the CIA's enhanced interrogation techniques used CIA provided information on Jose Padilla to describe the threat posed by al-Qa'ida and the success of the CIA's enhanced interrogation techniques to date. The July 20, 2007, OLC memorandum states:

> "The CIA interrogation program—and, in particular, its use of enhanced interrogation techniques—is intended to serve this paramount interest [security of the Nation] by *producing substantial quantities of otherwise unavailable intelligence.* The CIA believes that this program 'has been a key reason why al-Qa'ida has failed to launch a spectacular attack in the West since 11 September 2001' . . . We understand that use of enhanced techniques has produced significant intelligence that the Government has used to keep the Nation safe. As the President explained [in his September 6, 2006 speech], '*by giving us information about terrorist plans we could not get anywhere else, the program has saved innocent lives*' . . . For example, we understand that enhanced interrogation techniques proved particularly crucial in the interrogations of Khalid Shaykh Muhammad and Abu Zubaydah . . . *Interrogations of Zubaydah—again, once enhanced techniques were employed—revealed two al-Qaeda operatives already in the United States*[1310] *and planning to destroy a high rise apartment building and to detonate a radiological bomb in Washington, D.C.*"[1311]

On April 21, 2009, a CIA spokesperson confirmed the accuracy of the information in the OLC memorandum in response to the partial declassification of this and other memoranda.[1312]

The CIA provided similar inaccurate representations regarding the thwarting of the Dirty Bomb plotting, the thwarting of the Tall Buildings plotting, and/or the capture of Jose Padilla in 17 of the 20 documents provided to policymakers and the Department of Justice between July 2003 and March 2009.[1313]

A review of CIA operational cables and other CIA records found that the use of the CIA's enhanced interrogation techniques played no role in the identification of "Jose Padilla" or the thwarting of the Dirty Bomb or Tall Buildings plotting. CIA records indicate that: (1) there was significant intelligence in CIA databases acquired prior to—and independently of—the CIA's Detention and Interrogation Program to fully identify Jose Padilla as a terrorist threat and to disrupt any terrorist plotting associated with him;[1314] (2) Abu Zubaydah provided information on the terrorist plotting of two individuals who proposed an idea to conduct a "Dirty Bomb" attack, but did not identify their true names; (3) Abu Zubaydah provided this information to FBI special agents who were using rapport-building techniques,[1315] in April 2002, more than three months prior to the CIA's "use of DOJ-approved enhanced interrogation techniques";[1316] and (4) the Intelligence Community internally assessed that the "Dirty Bomb"[1317] and "Tall Buildings"[1318] plots were infeasible as envisioned.[1319]

Prior to the capture of Abu Zubaydah on March 28, 2002, the CIA was alerted to the threat posed by Jose Padilla. In early 2001, U.S. government records indicated that a Jose Padilla came to the U.S. Consulate in Karachi to report a lost passport. These records indicated that Jose Padilla provided a "sketchy" story about overstaying his Pakistani visa and that he was "allegedly studying Islamic law in Egypt." A search of the State Department's Consular Lookout and Support System was conducted at the time, which resulted in "multiple" hits for "Jose Padilla."[1320] State Department records confirmed that Jose Padilla had sought a new passport at the U.S. Consulate in Karachi in February 2001, and was subsequently provided with a replacement on March 21, 2001.[1321]

On December 15, 2001, the CIA provided the FBI with documents obtained in Afghanistan from a purported al-Qa'ida-related safe house. Included in the binder were 180 terrorist training camp application forms entitled, "Mujahideen Identification Form / New Applicant Form." An application form for a then 33-year-old individual with the alias "Abu Abdullah al-Muhajir" from "America" was among the forms. "Al-Muhajir's" form—dated July 24, 2000—listed other identifying information, to include a "10/18/70" date of birth; language skills to include English, Spanish, and Arabic; travels to Egypt, Saudi Arabia, and Yemen; and the individual's marital status.[1322]

On April 10, 2002, the CIA disseminated a cable with intelligence derived from the exploitation of documents obtained during the raids in which Abu Zubaydah was captured. Included in the CIA cable is a translation of a letter from mid-March 2002 that references a 33-year-old English-speaking individual. The cable states that the CIA believed this individual might be involved in "a martyrdom operation." The translation disseminated states: "There is a brother from Argentina, he speaks Spanish, English and Arabic, he is 33 years old, he is married and has two little children. He is a great brother. He knows business and studies English language. He trains [in] self defense, he is a good looking man."[1323]

The next day, April 11, 2002, the CIA was provided with information from Pakistani officials on a 33-year-old U.S. citizen named "Jose Padilla," with a date of birth of October 18, 1970, who was briefly detained by Pakistani officials on April 4, 2002. The Pakistani government provided a copy of Jose Padilla's U.S. passport and relayed that Jose Padilla had overstayed his travel visa, and that there were inconsistencies with Jose Padilla's appearance and accent. The CIA's ■■ ■■■ wrote that they would provide the information on "Jose Padilla" to the State Department's Regional Security Officer, and "would follow-up with [Pakistani officials] on this matter."[1324] The date of birth and travel information included with Jose Padilla's passport matched information on the "Mujahideen Identification Form" (33-year-old

"American" referenced as "Abu Abdullah al-Muhajir") the CIA had provided to the FBI on December 15, 2001.[1325]

On April 12, 2002, Pakistani officials provided additional information to the CIA's ▬▬, specifically that they had detained a U.S. passport holder named Jose Padilla and a British passport holder named "Fouad Zouaoui" (later identified as Binyam Muhammad), who had suspiciously attempted to depart Pakistan. According to the CIA cable, Pakistani authorities provided the information on the pair "due to concerns about possible terrorist activity."[1326] The cable noted that Pakistani authorities had to release Padilla, but that Padilla's associate remained in detention.[1327] (When questioned further, the Pakistani authorities stated that they suspected Jose Padilla of being "an al-Qa'ida member.")[1328] The information identifying Jose Padilla and "Fouad Zouaoui" as potential terrorists had been provided by the CIA's ▬▬ to CIA Headquarters, several CIA Stations, and the State Department's Regional Security Officer (RSO) in Karachi by April 12, 2002.[1329] Using the identifying information in Jose Padilla's passport, provided by the Pakistani government, the CIA's ▬ ▬▬ requested that CIA Headquarters and the CIA's ▬ Station conduct "▬▬" (a database search) using the name "Jose Padilla" and the other identifying information provided.[1330] The CIA's ▬▬ requested that CIA Headquarters and the CIA's ▬ Station do the same for Padilla's associate, Fouad Zouaoui.[1331] As a result, by April 12, 2002, the CIA was already alerted that a named U.S. citizen, "Jose Padilla," had spent significant time in Pakistan and was engaged in "possible terrorist activity."[1332]

Eight days after the CIA was informed that U.S. citizen Jose Padilla was engaged in "possible terrorist activity," on the evening of April 20, 2002, Abu Zubaydah told FBI special agents about two men who approached him with a plan to detonate a uranium-based explosive device in the United States (the "dirty bomb"). Abu Zubaydah stated he did not believe the plan was viable and did not know the true names of the two individuals, but did provide physical descriptions of the pair.[1333] This information was acquired after Abu Zubaydah was confronted with emails that indicated Abu Zubaydah had sent two individuals to KSM.[1334] The FBI special agents who acquired this information from Abu Zubaydah believed it was provided as a result of rapport-building interrogation techniques.[1335] Abu Zubaydah would not be subjected to the "use of DOJ-approved enhanced interrogation techniques" until August 2002, more than three months later.[1336]

Within two hours of the dissemination of this information, CIA officers [redacted] sent cables to CIA Headquarters and select CIA Stations calling attention to the similarities between Abu Zubaydah's reporting and their request from April 12, 2002, for information on Jose Padilla and Fouad Zouaoui, which had not yet been acted upon by the receiving offices.[1337] A travel alert was then initiated for Jose Padilla based on the previous information provided by the Pakistani government. Padilla was located and unknowingly escorted back to the United States by an FBI special agent on May 8, 2002.[1338] Upon his arrival in the United States Padilla was found to be carrying $10,526 in U.S. currency, an amount he failed to report.[1339] Padilla was interviewed and taken into FBI custody on a material witness warrant.[1340] The exploitation of Jose Padilla's pocket litter[1341] and phone revealed significant connections to known terrorists, including subjects of FBI terrorism investigations in the United States.[1342]

In separate debriefings, Padilla and his associate, Binyam Mohammed, maintained they had no intention of engaging in terrorist plotting, but proposed the "Dirty Bomb" plot in order to depart Pakistan, avoid combat in Afghanistan, and return home.[1343]

Over several years CIA officers identified errors in the CIA's representations concerning the "effectiveness" of the CIA's enhanced interrogation techniques in relation to the Abu Zubaydah reporting pertaining to Jose Padilla and Padilla's alleged plotting. In response to one such representation, the chief of the Abu Zubaydah Task Force wrote to [redacted] CTC Legal in 2002 that "AZ's info alone would never have allowed us to find [Jose Padilla and Binyam Mohammed]."[1344] In 2004, she sought to correct inaccurate CIA representations again, telling colleagues:

> "AZ never really gave 'this is the plot' type of information. He claimed every plot/operation he had knowledge of and/or was working on was only preliminary. (Padilla and the dirty bomb plot was prior to enhanced and he never really gave us actionable intel to get them)."[1345]

In October 2005, the chief of CTC's CBRN (Chemical, Biological, Radiological, and Nuclear) Group wrote, under the heading, "Don't Put All Your Uranium in One Bucket":

> "Jose Padilla: we'll never be able to successfully expunge Padilla and the 'dirty bomb' plot from the lore of disruption, but once again I'd like to go on the record that Padilla admitted that the only reason he came up with so-called 'dirty bomb' was that he wanted to get out of Afghanistan and figured that if he came up with something spectacular, they'd finance him. Even KSM says Padilla had a screw loose. He's a petty criminal who is well-versed in US criminal justice (he's got a rap sheet as

long as my arm). Anyone who believes you can build an IND or RDD by 'putting uranium in buckets and spinning them clockwise over your head to separate the uranium' is not going to advance al-Qa'ida's nuclear capabilities."[1346]

CIA and other U.S. government assessments also called into question the "Tall Buildings" plotting, which was loosely based on attacks that were conducted in Moscow in September 1999 using conventional explosives. The "Tall Buildings" plotting did not envision the use of conventional explosives.[1347] Instead, the plotting envisioned using natural gas to destroy high-rise residential buildings. As planned, the Intelligence Community assessed the plotting was not viable.[1348] An August 4, 2008, U.S. government assessment stated: "On the surface, the idea is simplistic, if not amateurish . . . the probability of an efficient fuel air explosion is low."[1349]

Jose Padilla was detained on a material witness warrant from May 8, 2002, to June 9, 2002, when he was transferred to U.S. military custody and designated an "enemy combatant." On January 3, 2006, Jose Padilla was transferred to U.S. law enforcement custody and tried in federal court. On August 16, 2007, Jose Padilla and two co-defendants, Adham Hassoun and Kifah Jayyousi, were found guilty of three criminal offenses relating to terrorist support activities from October 1993 to November 1, 2001.[1350] The case against Jose Padilla centered on his attendance at a terrorist training camp in Afghanistan in the fall of 2000—specifically, the terrorist training camp application form acquired by the CIA and provided to the FBI in December 2001. The form was found to have Jose Padilla's fingerprints, as well as identifying data to include his date of birth, languages spoken, and travels.[1351] On January 22, 2008, Jose Padilla was sentenced to 17 years in prison. On September 19, 2011, the U.S. 11th Circuit Court of Appeals ruled the sentence was too lenient in part because it did not take in account Jose Padilla's prior criminal offenses.[1352]

After being detained in Pakistan, Jose Padilla's associate Binyam Mohammad was rendered by the CIA ■■■■■ on July ■, 2002, where he was held by the ■■■■■ government. On January ■, 2004, Binyam Mohammad was rendered to CIA custody.[1353] On May ■ , 2004, Binyam Mohammad was transferred to the custody of the U.S. military in Bagram, Afghanistan.[1354] On September 21, 2004, he was transferred to Guantanamo Bay, Cuba.[1355] Binyam Mohammad was then transferred from U.S. military custody to the United Kingdom on February 23, 2009. ■■■■■■■■■■■■■■■■.[1356] Lawyers representing Binyam Mohammad sued the government of the United Kingdom to compel the release of documents relating to his whereabouts and treatment after his initial detention in April 2002.[1357] In February 2010, a British court compelled the release "of a summary of the torture" to which Binyam Mohammed was subjected during his detention. In the fall of 2010, the British government awarded Binyam Mohammed a reported £1 million in compensation.[1358]

2. The Thwarting of the Karachi Plots

SUMMARY: The CIA represented that its enhanced interrogation techniques were effective and necessary to produce critical, otherwise unavailable intelligence, which enabled the CIA to disrupt terrorist plots, capture terrorists, and save lives. Over a period of years, the CIA provided the thwarting of the Karachi Plot(s) as evidence for the effectiveness of the CIA's enhanced interrogation techniques. These CIA representations were inaccurate. The Karachi Plot(s) was dismpted with the confiscation of explosives and the airests of Ammar al-Baluchi and Khallad bin Attash in April 2003. The operation and arrests were conducted unilaterally by Pakistani authorities and were unrelated to any reporting from the CIA's Detention and Interrogation Program.

FURTHER DETAILS: The Karachi Plot(s) refers to terrorist plotting that targeted a variety of U.S. and Western interests in the Karachi area, to include the U.S. Consulate, named hotels near the airport and beach, U.S. vehicles traveling between the Consulate and the airport, U.S. diplomatic housing, U.S. personnel subject to potential sniper attacks, as well as Pakistan's Faisal Army Base.[1359] CIA records indicate the CIA became aware of the initial plotting as early as September 2002, and that it was disrupted in April 2003, when the remaining plot leaders were arrested in a unilateral operation by Pakistani authorities.[1360] While the plot leaders were captured in the process of procuring explosives, they maintained that they were still in the process of locating vehicles, a safe house, and suicide operatives at the time of their arrest.[1361]

The thwarting of the Karachi Plot(s) is one of the eight most frequently cited examples provided by the CIA as evidence for the effectiveness of the CIA's enhanced interrogation techniques.[1362] Over a period of years, CIA documents prepared for and provided to senior policymakers, intelligence officials, and the Department of Justice represent the Karachi Plot(s) as an example of how "[k]ey intelligence collected from HVD interrogations *after* applying interrogation techniques" had "enabled CIA to disrupt terrorist plots" and capture additional terrorists.[1363] The CIA further represented that the intelligence acquired from the CIA's enhanced interrogation techniques was "otherwise unavailable" and "saved lives."[1364]

For example, in November 2007, the CIA prepared and provided a set of talking points to the CIA director for an "upcoming meeting with the President regarding the Waterboard Enhanced Interrogation Technique."[1365] The document includes a section entitled, "Plots Discovered as a Result of EITs," which states "reporting statistics alone will not provide a fair and accurate measure of the effectiveness of EITs." The document then provides a list of "Key Intelligence Derived through use of EITs," stating:

> "CIA's use of DOJ-approved enhanced interrogation techniques, as part of a comprehensive interrogation approach, has enabled CIA to disrupt terrorist plots . . . The following are examples of key intelligence collected from CIA detainee interrogations *after applying the waterboard* along with other interrogation techniques: . . . The Karachi Plot: This plan to conduct attacks against the US Consulate and other US interests in Pakistan was *uncovered during the initial interrogations of Khallad Bin Attash and Ammar al-Baluchi and later confirmed by KSM.*"[1366]

Likewise, a CIA-prepared briefing for Vice President Cheney on the CIA's enhanced interrogation techniques in March 2005, under a section of the briefing called, "INTERROGATION RESULTS," asserts:

> "Use of DOJ-authorized *enhanced interrogation techniques*, as part of a comprehensive interrogation approach, has enabled us to disrupt terrorist plots, capture additional terrorists . . . The Karachi Plot: Plan to conduct attacks against the US Consulate and other US interests in Pakistan. *Plot disrupted.* Sources: Khallad Bin Attash, Ammar al-Baluchi. KSM also provided info on the plot after we showed him capture photos of Ammar and Khallad."[1367]

The CIA provided similar inaccurate representations regarding the thwarting of the Karachi Plot(s) in 17 of the 20 documents provided to policymakers and the Department of Justice between July 2003 and March 2009.[1368]

A review of CIA operational cables and other documents found that the CIA's enhanced interrogation techniques—to include the waterboard—played no role in the disruption of the Karachi Plot(s). CIA records indicate that the Karachi Plot(s) was thwarted by the arrest of operatives and the interdiction of explosives by Pakistani authorities, specifically ██████████████████████.[1369]

The CIA had information regarding the Karachi terrorist plotting as early as September 11, 2002.[1370] On that day, a ██ raid conducted by ▬▬ Pakistani authorities ▬▬▬▬▬▬, of an al-Qaida safe house in Karachi, Pakistan, uncovered the "perfume letter," named as such because the term "perfumes" is used as a code word. The letter, written in May 2002, was from KSM to Hamza al-Zubayr, a known al-Qa'ida member who was killed in the raids.[1371] KSM's letter to al-Zubayr states, "Dear Brother, we have the green light for the hotels," and suggests "making it three instead of one."[1372] By early October 2002, the CIA had completed a search of the names identified in the "perfume letter" in its databases and found many of the individuals who "had assigned roles in support of the operation" were arrested by Pakistani authorities during the raids.[1373] At least one person in the letter, Khallad bin Attash, a known al-Qa'ida operative, remained at large.[1374]

What remained of the Karachi plotting was disrupted unilaterally by Pakistani authorities as a result of a criminal lead. On April ■, 2003, Pakistani authorities, specifically ▬▬▬▬▬, received a report that explosives and weapons were to be transported in a pickup truck to a specific location in Karachi.[1375] Pakistani authorities made arrangements to intercede, and, on April 29, 2003, they intercepted the vehicle and confiscated explosives, detonators, and ammunition. The driver of the vehicle provided the location where the explosives were being delivered, leading to the capture of several operatives, including Ammar al-Baluchi and Khallad bin Attash, as well as to the discovery of another explosives cache. A third captured individual stated that the explosives had belonged to Hamza al-Zubayr, the known and now deceased al-Qa'ida operative, as well as others residing in the home raided on September 11, 2002, where the "perfume letter" was discovered.[1376]

While being arrested, Ammar al-Baluchi was asked by a Pakistani officer about his intentions regarding the seized explosives. Al-Baluchi responded that he was planning to attack the U.S. Consulate in Karachi.[1377] In foreign government custody—and prior to being rendered to CIA custody and subjected to the CIA's enhanced interrogation techniques—Ammar al-Baluchi continued to provide information about the Karachi plotting to a foreign government officer who was using rapport-building interrogation techniques.[1378] The information provided by Ammar al-Baluchi on the plotting included the surveillance conducted, the envisioned targets, and the exact method of attack that was considered for the U.S. Consulate in Karachi and other hard targets. Ammar al-Baluchi discussed the use of a motorcycle with a bomb to breach the perimeter wall of the consulate and then how the operatives would seek to exploit that breach with a vehicle filled with explosives.[1379] Ammar al-Baluchi and Khallad bin Attash remained in foreign government custody for approximately ■■ weeks, with Ammar al-Baluchi—and to a lesser extent bin Attash[1380]—responding to questions on a variety of matters, including the Karachi plotting.[1381]

On May ■, 2003, Ammar al-Baluchi and Khallad bin Attash were rendered to CIA custody and immediately subjected to the CIA's enhanced interrogation techniques.[1382] The next day, the CIA disseminated two intelligence reports on the Karachi Plot(s) from the interrogations of Ammar al-Baluchi and Khallad bin Attash.[1383] The reporting relayed that: (1) al-Qa'ida was targeting Western interests in Karachi, including the U.S. Consulate and Western housing in a specific neighborhood of Karachi; and (2) the attack could have occurred as early as "late May/early June 2003," but the plotters were still in the process of finding vehicles, a safe house, and the suicide operatives at the time of their arrest.[1384] These disseminated intelligence reports were used to support CIA representations in finished intelligence products,[1385] talking points, briefing documents, and President Bush's September 6, 2006, speech that the Karachi Plot(s) was "thwarted," "disrupted," or "uncovered" as a result of the CIA's enhanced interrogation techniques. However, within 24 hours of the dissemination of these intelligence reports, CIA personnel in Karachi responded in an official cable that the information acquired from the CIA detainees and disseminated was already known to the CIA and U.S. Consulate officials. The cable stated:

> "[w]hile reporting from both [al-Baluchi and bin Attash] was chilling- [CIA officers] had become aware of most of this reporting either through previous information or through interviews of al-Baluchi and [Khallad bin] Attash prior to their transfer out of Karachi."[1386]

The CIA personnel in Karachi reassured addressees that, in December 2002, ■■■■■■■■ the U.S. Consulate in Karachi took increased steps to protect U.S. Consulate personnel based on similar terrorist threat reporting. According to the cable, Americans in the referenced housing area had already been vacated from the "area for several months," the potential for "attacks targeting Americans at the airport" had been "recognized several months ago," and new procedures and security measures had been put in place to minimize the risks associated with the potential terrorist attacks.[1387]

As noted, in November 2007, the CIA prepared and provided a set of talking points to the CIA director for an "upcoming meeting with the President regarding the Waterboard Enhanced Interrogation Technique." Under a section entitled, "Plots Discovered as a Result of EITs," the document lists the "Karachi Plot," stating the disruption was the result of "key intelligence collected from CIA detainee interrogations *after applying the waterboard* along with other interrogation techniques," and that the plotting was "*uncovered* during the initial interrogations of Khallad Bin Attash and Ammar al-Baluchi and later confirmed by KSM."[1388] While Ammar al-Baluchi and Khallad bin Attash were subjected to the CIA's enhanced interrogation techniques, there are no CIA records to indicate that either was ever subjected to the CIA's waterboard interrogation technique. KSM did provide information on the plotting, but was assessed by CIA personnel to be withholding information on the plotting, more than a month after the CIA stopped using its enhanced interrogation techniques against KSM. In late April 2003, CIA interrogators confronted KSM with photographs demonstrating that Ammar al-Baluchi and Khallad bin Attash had been captured. When the CIA interrogators asked what Ammar al-Baluchi and Khallad bin Attash were "up to" in Karachi, KSM provided information regarding potential targets in Karachi.[1389] KSM's belated reporting prompted the CIA's ALEC Station to write a cable stating:

> "We were disappointed to see that KSM only made these new admissions of planned attacks in Pakistan after seeing the capture photographs of Ammar al-Baluchi and Khallad. We consider KSM's long-standing omission of [this] information to be a serious concern, especially as this omission may well have cost American lives had Pakistani authorities not been diligent in following up on unrelated criminal leads that led to the capture of Ammar, bin Attash, and other probable operatives involved in the attack plans . . . Simply put, KSM has had every opportunity to come clean on this threat and, from our optic, he deliberately withheld the information until he was confronted with evidence that we already knew about it, or soon would know about it from Ammar and Khallad . . . KSM's provision of the Pakistan threat reporting—only after he was made aware of the capture of the attack planners—is viewed as a clear illustration of continued and deliberate withholding of threat information which he believed had not yet been compromised."[1390]

Ammar al-Baluchi, Khallad bin Attash, and KSM remained in CIA custody until their transfer to U.S. military custody at Guantanamo Bay, Cuba, in September 2006.[1391] All three remain in U.S. military custody.

3. The Thwarting of the Second Wave Plot and the Discovery of the Al-Ghuraba Group

SUMMARY: The CIA represented that its enhanced interrogation techniques were effective and necessary to produce critical, otherwise unavailable intelligence, which enabled the CIA to disrupt terrorist plots, capture terrorists, and save lives. Over a period of years, the CIA provided the "discovery" and/or "thwarting" of the Second Wave plotting and the "discovery" of the al-Ghuraba group as evidence for the effectiveness of the CIA's enhanced interrogation techniques. These representations were inaccurate. The Second Wave plotting was disrupted with the arrest and identification of key individuals. The arrests and identifications were unrelated to any reporting acquired during or after the use of the CIA's enhanced interrogation techniques against CIA detainees. Likewise, the al-Ghuraba group was identified by a detainee who was not in CIA custody. CIA detainees subjected to the CIA's enhanced interrogation techniques provided significant fabricated information on both the Second Wave plotting and the al-Ghuraba group.

FURTHER DETAILS: Al-Qa'ida's "Second Wave" plotting refers to two efforts by KSM to strike the West Coast of the United States with airplanes using non-Arab passport holders. While intelligence reporting often conflated the "Second Wave" plotting, KSM viewed the plotting as two separate efforts.[1392] Neither of the two efforts was assessed to be imminent, as KSM was still engaged in the process of identifying suicide operatives and obtaining pilot training for potential participants when each effort was disrupted through the arrest or identification of the suspected operatives and operational planners.[1393]

The al-Ghuraba student group was established in late 1999 by Jemaah Islamiyah (JI) leaders primarily to educate the sons of jailed JI leaders and to groom the students for potential leadership and operational roles in JI. Some members of the al-Ghuraba group reportedly completed militant training in Afghanistan and Pakistan while enrolled at Islamic universities in Karachi.[1394] Despite CIA representations to the contrary, intelligence and open source reporting indicate the group was not "tasked with," witting, or involved in any aspect of KSM's Second Wave plotting.[1395]

The "discovery" and disruption of the "Second Wave Plot" (also known as the "West Coast Plot" and the "Tallest Building Plot"),[1396] along with the associated identification, discovery, and capture of the al-Ghuraba "cell," is one of the eight most frequently cited examples provided by the CIA as evidence for the effectiveness of CIA's enhanced interrogation techniques.[1397] Over a period of years, CIA documents prepared for and provided to senior policymakers, intelligence officials, and the Department of Justice represent the thwarting and discovery of the "Second Wave" plotting and the identification, discovery, or arrest of the al-Ghuraba group members as an example of how "[k]ey intelligence collected from HVD interrogations *after* applying interrogation techniques" had "enabled CIA to disrupt terrorist plots" and "capture additional terrorists."[1398] The CIA further represented that the intelligence acquired from the CIA's enhanced interrogation techniques was "otherwise unavailable" and "saved lives."[1399]

For example, in November 2007, the CIA prepared a briefing for President Bush. Under a section entitled, "Plots Discovered as a Result of EITs," the CIA represented that the CIA "*learned*" about the "Second Wave" plotting and the al-Ghuraba group only "after applying the waterboard along with other interrogation techniques."[1400]

Likewise, on March 2, 2005, the CIA provided the Department of Justice Office of Legal Counsel (OLC) with a document entitled, "Effectiveness of the CIA Counterterrorist Interrogation Techniques." The CIA memorandum stated that the "Central Intelligence Agency can advise you that this program works and the techniques are effective in producing foreign intelligence."[1401] The CIA stated that "enhanced interrogation techniques . . . [have] enabled CIA to disrupt plots" and "capture additional terrorists." The document then listed 11 examples of "key intelligence collected from HVD interrogations *after* applying interrogation techniques,"[1402] including:

> "The 'Second Wave': This was a KSM plot to use East Asian operatives to crash a hijacked airliner into the tallest building on the US West Coast (Los Angeles) as a follow-on to 9/11. *We learned this during the initial interrogation of KSM* and later confirmed it through the interrogation of Hambali and Khallad.
>
> ". . . The Guraba Cell: *We learned of this 17-member Jemaah Islamiyah cell from Hambali*, who confirmed that some of the cell's operatives were identified as candidates to train as pilots as part of KSM's 'second wave' attack against the US . . ."[1403]

The ensuing May 30, 2005, OLC memorandum, now declassified and publicly available, states:

> "[The CIA has] informed us that the interrogation of KSM—once [enhanced] interrogation techniques were employed—led to the *discovery* of a KSM plot, the 'Second Wave' . . . and the *discovery* of the Ghuraba Cell, a 17-member Jemaah Islamiyah cell *tasked with executing the 'Second Wave.'*"[1404]

The CIA provided similar inaccurate representations regarding the "discovery" and thwarting of the Second Wave plotting and/or the "discovery" of the al-Ghuraba Group in 18 of the 20 documents provided to senior policymakers and the Department of Justice between July 2003 and March 2009.[1405]

A review of CIA operational cables and other documents found that the CIA's enhanced interrogation techniques played no role in the "discovery" or thwarting of either "Second Wave" plot. Likewise, records indicate that the CIA's enhanced interrogation techniques played no role in the "discovery" of a 17-member "cell tasked with executing the 'Second Wave.'"[1406]

Intelligence Community records indicate that the initial "Second Wave" effort began in parallel with the planning for the September 11, 2001, attacks and included two operatives who were tasked with seeking pilot training. The thwarting of this plotting was unrelated to the use of the CIA's enhanced interrogation techniques. The two operatives, Zacarias Moussaoui and Faruq al-Tunisi (aka Abderraouf Jdey), were known to be engaged in terrorist activity prior to any reporting from CIA detainees.[1407] On August 16, 2001, Zacarias Moussaoui, a French citizen, was arrested on immigration charges by the FBI in Minnesota.[1408] At the time of his arrest, the FBI informed the CIA that the FBI considered Moussaoui to be a "suspected airline suicide attacker."[1409] On January 17, 2002, the FBI publicly released a statement identifying Faruq al-Tunisi, aka Abderraouf Jdey, a Canadian citizen, as an al-Qa'ida operative possibly "prepared to commit future suicide terrorist attacks."[1410] Intelligence indicates that al-Tunisi, who remains at large, withdrew from participating in al-Qa'ida operations.[1411] His whereabouts remain unknown.[1412]

The subsequent "Second Wave" effort began with KSM's tasking of several Malaysian nationals—led by Masran bin Arshad—in late 2001 to attack the "tallest building in California" using shoe-bomb explosive devices to gain access to a plane's cockpit.[1413] The thwarting of this plotting was also unrelated to the use of the CIA's enhanced interrogation techniques. This plot was disrupted with the arrest of Masran bin Arshad in January 2002. This arrest was unrelated to CIA detainee reporting.[1414] Bin Arshad claimed the effort had "not advanced beyond the initial planning stages" when KSM "shelve[d] the plan" in December 2001 when Richard Reid exposed the "shoe bomb" explosive method.[1415] Beginning in July 2002, while in the custody of a foreign government, and after the extensive use of rapport-building interrogation techniques,[1416] bin Arshad provided detailed information on this "Second Wave" plotting, the Malaysian operatives (details on Affifi, Lillie, and "Tawfiq"), and the proposed method of attack.[1417] This information would later be corroborated by other intelligence collection, including, to a limited extent, reporting from CIA detainees in the spring of 2003.[1418] Another Malaysian national associated with Masran bin Arshad, Zaini Zakaria, was identified by a foreign government as a potential operative seeking pilot training as early as July 2002.[1419] Zakaria was tasked with obtaining such training by al-Qa'ida, but failed to follow through with the tasking.[1420] Zakaria turned himself in to Malaysian authorities on December 18, 2002. Malaysian authorities released Zakaria in February 2009.[1421] In 2006, in a White House briefing on the "West Coast Terrorist Plot," the Assistant to the President for Homeland Security and Counterterrorism announced that the plot had been disrupted with the arrest of the cell leader, Masran bin Arshad.[1422]

Contrary to CIA representations, the use of the CIA's enhanced interrogation techniques against KSM did not result in the "discovery" of KSM's "Second Wave" plotting. On March 1, 2003, KSM was captured. He was rendered to CIA custody on March ■, 2003, and was immediately subjected to the CIA's enhanced interrogation techniques. While being subjected to the CIA's enhanced interrogation techniques, and in the weeks afterwards, KSM did not discuss the "Second Wave" plotting.[1423] On April 19, 2003—24 days after the use of the CIA's enhanced interrogation techniques had ceased—interrogators questioned KSM about Masran bin Arshad and his role in developing a cell for the "Second Wave" attacks. After being told that Masran bin Arshad had been arrested, KSM told his interrogators, "I have forgotten about him, he is not in my mind at all." KSM also denied that "he knew anything about a plot to take out the 'tallest building' in California."[1424] KSM's reporting prompted ALEC Station to write in a cable that "we remain concerned that KSM's progression towards full debriefing status is not yet apparent where it counts most, in relation to threats to US interests, especially inside CONUS."[1425]

According to a CIA cable, on May 5, 2003, KSM "eventually admitted to tasking Masran bin Arshad to target the tallest building in California."[1426] KSM continued, however, to deny aspects of the plotting—such as denying the use of shoe-bombs in the operation, only to confirm the planned use of shoe-bombs in later interrogations.[1427] On June 23, 2003, an ALEC Station officer wrote that "[g]iven that KSM only admitted knowledge of this operation upon learning of Masran's detention, we assess he is not telling all he knows, but rather is providing information he believes we already possess."[1428] KSM was asked about detained Malaysian national Zaini Zakaria for the first time on July 3, 2003. During the interrogation, the CIA debriefer stated that there was information suggesting that Zakaria was funded by al-Qa'ida to take flight lessons in September 2001.[1429] KSM denied knowing the name Zaini Zakaria, but later described "Mussa." The CIA suspected this was an alias for Zakaria. CIA officers at the detention site where KSM was being interrogated then wrote in a cable, "[t]he core problem, once again, is the appearance that KSM gave up this critical information only after being presented with the idea that we might already know something about it."[1430]

With regard to the al-Ghuraba group, contrary to CIA representations, a wide body of intelligence reporting indicates that the al-Ghuraba group was not "discovered" as a result of reporting from KSM or Hambali, nor was the al-Ghuraba group "tasked" with, or witting of, any aspect of KSM's "Second Wave" plotting.[1431] Rather, while in foreign government custody, Hambali's brother, Gun Gun Ruswan Gunawan, identified "a group of Malaysian and Indonesian students in Karachi" witting of Gunawan's affiliation with Jemaah Islamiyah.[1432] CIA records indicate that Gunawan stated that the students were in Karachi "at the request of Hambali."[1433] In a cable conveying this information, CIA officers recalled intelligence reporting indicating KSM planned to use Malaysians in the "next wave of attacks," and stated Gunawan had just identified "a group of 16 individuals, most all of whom are Malaysians."[1434] The cable closed by stating, "we need to question Hambali if this collection is part of his 'next wave' cell."[1435] (From July through December 2002, foreign government reporting described KSM's use of Malaysians in the "next wave attacks." The reporting included Masran bin Arshad's information, provided while he was in foreign government custody, on his four-person Malaysian cell tasked by KSM[1436] to be part of an operation targeting the West Coast of the United States, as well as July 2002 reporting on Malaysian national Zaini Zakaria seeking pilot training.[1437])

Contrary to CIA representations, the use of the CIA's enhanced interrogation techniques against Hambali did not result in the "discovery" of "the Guraba Cell" that was "tasked with executing the 'Second Wave'" plotting. As noted, in foreign government custody, Hambali's brother, Gun Gun Ruswan Gunawan, identified "a group of Malaysian and Indonesian students in Karachi" witting of Gunawan's affiliation with Jemaah Islamiyah.[1438] The cable conveying this information recommended "confronting Hambali" with this information.[1439] While being subjected to the CIA's enhanced interrogation techniques, Hambali was questioned about the al-Ghuraba group and KSM's effort to use airplanes to attack the United States. Hambali told his CIA interrogators "that some of the members of [the al-Ghuraba group] were destined to work for al-Qa'ida if everything had gone according to plan," that one member of the group had "ambitions to become a pilot," that he (Hambali) was going to send three individuals to KSM in response to KSM's "tasking to find pilot candidates, but never got around to asking these people," and that "KSM told him to provide as many pilots as he could.[1440] Months later, on November 30, 2003, after three weeks of being questioned by a debriefer "almost entirely in Bahasa Indonesia," Hambali admitted to fabricating a number of statements during the period he was being subjected to the CIA's enhanced interrogation techniques, including information on efforts to locate pilots for KSM. Specifically, Hambali stated "he lied about the pilot because he was constantly asked about it and under stress, and so decided to fabricate." According to a cable, Hambali said he fabricated these claims "in an attempt to reduce the pressure on himself," and "to give an account that was consistent with what [Hambali] assessed the questioners wanted to hear."[1441] The November 30, 2003, cable noted that CIA personnel "assesse[d] [Hambali]'s admission of previous fabrication to be credible."[1442] Hambali then consistently described "the al-Ghuraba organization" as a "development camp for potential future JI operatives and leadership, vice a JI cell or an orchestrated attempt by JI to initiate JI operations outside of Southeast Asia."[1443] This description was corroborative of other intelligence reporting.[1444]

An October 27, 2006, CIA cable states that "all of the members of the JI al-Ghuraba cell have been released,"[1445] while an April 18, 2008, CIA intelligence report focusing on the Jemaah Islamiyah and referencing the al-Ghuraba group makes no reference to the group serving as potential operatives for KSM's "Second Wave" plotting.[1446]

4. The Thwarting of the United Kingdom Urban Targets Plot and the Capture of Dhiren Barot, aka Issa al-Hindi

SUMMARY: The CIA represented that its enhanced interrogation techniques were effective and necessary to produce critical, otherwise unavailable intelligence, which enabled the CIA to disrupt terrorist plots, capture terrorists, and save lives. Over a period of years, the CIA provided the capture of Dhiren Barot, aka Issa al-Hindi, and the thwarting of Barot's United Kingdom Urban Targets Plot as evidence for the effectiveness of the CIA's enhanced interrogation techniques. These representations were inaccurate. The operation that resulted in the identification of a U.K.-based "Issa," the identification of "Issa" as Dhiren Barot, Dhiren Barot's arrest, and the thwarting of his plotting, resulted from the investigative activities of U.K. government authorities. Contrary to CIA representations, KSM did not provide the first reporting on a U.K.-based "Issa," nor are there records to support the CIA representation that reporting from CIA detainees subjected to the CIA's enhanced interrogation techniques resulted in Dhiren Barot's arrest. After the arrest of Dhiren Barot, CIA officers prepared a document for U.K. authorities which stated: "while KSM tasked al-Hindi to go to the US to surveil targets, he was not aware of the extent to which Barot's planning had progressed, who Issa's co-conspirators were, or that Issa's planning had come to focus on the UK." The plotting associated with Dhiren Barot was assessed by experts to be "amateurish," "defective," and unlikely to succeed.

FURTHER DETAILS: Dhiren Barot, aka Issa al-Hindi,[1447] met with al-Qa'ida leaders in Pakistan in early 2004 to discuss potential terrorist attacks against targets in the United Kingdom.[1448] Intelligence reporting indicates that Barot spent February and March 2004 in Pakistan with senior al-Qa'ida explosives expert 'Abd al-Rahman al-Muhajir, likely refining plans to use vehicle-based bombs against U.K. targets.[1449] In July 2004, casing reports associated with "Issa" were recovered in a raid in Pakistan associated with the capture of Abu Talha al-Pakistani.[1450] During questioning in foreign government custody, "Abu Talha stated the U.S. casing reports were from Abu Issa."[1451] Further debriefings of Abu Talha revealed that Issa, aka Dhiren Barot, was the "operational manager" for al-Qa'ida in the United Kingdom.[1452] Additional information about Dhiren Barot's U.K. plotting was recovered from the hard drives confiscated during the raid that resulted in the arrest of Dhiren Barot. A document describing the plotting was divided into two parts. The first part included "the Gas Limos project," which envisioned parking explosives-laden courier vans or limousines in underground garages. The second part, the "radiation (dirty bomb) project," proposed using 10,000 smoke detectors as part of an explosive device to spread a radioactive element contained in the detectors. Dhiren Barot's plotting was referred to as the United Kingdom Urban Targets Plot.[1453] The U.K. Urban Targets Plot was disrupted when Dhiren Barot and his U.K.-based associates were detained in the United Kingdom in early August 2004.[1454] On August 24, 2004, U.K. authorities informed the CIA that the criminal charges against Barot and his co-conspirators "were mainly possible owing to the recovery of terrorist-related materials during searches of associated properties and vehicles following their arrests."[1455] In September 2004, an Intelligence Community assessment stated that Dhiren Barot was "in an early phase of operational planning at the time of his capture," and that there was no evidence to indicate that Barot had acquired the envisioned materials for the attacks.[1456] In December 2005, an FBI assessment stated, "the main plot presented in the Gas Limos Project is unlikely to be as successful as described," concluding, "we assess that the Gas Limos Project, while ambitious and creative, is far-fetched.[1457] On November 7, 2006, Dhiren Barot was sentenced to life in prison. On May 16, 2007, Barot's sentence was reduced from life in prison to 30 years after a British Court of Appeal found that expert assessments describing the plot as "amateurish," "defective," and unlikely to succeed were not provided to the sentencing judge.[1458]

The thwarting of the United Kingdom Urban Targets Plot and the identification and/or capture of Dhiren Barot, aka Issa al-Hindi, is one of the eight most frequently cited examples provided by the CIA as evidence for the effectiveness of the CIA's enhanced interrogation techniques. Over a period of years, CIA documents prepared for and provided to senior policymakers, intelligence officials, and the Department of Justice represent the identification and/or arrest of Dhiren Barot, and/or the disruption of his U.K. plotting, as an example of how "[k]ey intelligence collected from HVD interrogations *after* applying interrogation techniques" had "enabled CIA to disrupt terrorist plots" and "capture additional terrorists."[1459] In at least one document prepared for the president, the CIA specifically highlighted the waterboard technique in enabling the "disruption of [Dhiren Barot's] sleeper cell."[1460] The CIA further represented that the intelligence acquired from the CIA's enhanced interrogation techniques was "otherwise unavailable" and "saved lives."[1461]

For example, documents prepared in February 2009 for CIA Director Leon Panetta on the effectiveness of the CIA's enhanced interrogation techniques state that the "CIA assesses . . . the techniques were effective in producing foreign intelligence," and that "most, if not all, of the timely intelligence acquired from detainees in this program would not have been discovered or reported by other means." The document provides examples of "some of the key captures, disrupted plots, and intelligence" attributed to CIA interrogations. The document includes the following:

> "Key Captures from HVD Interrogations: . . . *arrest of Dhiren Barot (aka Issa al-Hindi) in the United Kingdom.*"[1462]

The materials for Director Panetta also include a chart entitled, "Key Intelligence and Reporting Derived from Abu Zubaydah and Khalid Shaykh Muhammad," that identifies two pieces of "key intelligence" acquired from KSM, one related to Majid Khan[1463] and the other to Dhiren Barot:

> "KSM reports on an unidentified UK-based operative, Issa al-Hindi, which touches off an intensive CIA, FBI and [United Kingdom] manhunt."[1464]

Likewise, a December 2004 CIA memorandum prepared for National Security Advisor Condoleezza Rice responded to a request "for an independent study of the foreign intelligence efficacy of using enhanced interrogation techniques." The CIA responded, "[t]here is no way to conduct such a study," but stated that the "CIA's use of DOJ-approved enhanced interrogation techniques, as part of a comprehensive interrogation approach, has enabled CIA to disrupt terrorist plots, capture additional terrorists, and collect a high volume of critical intelligence on al-Qa'ida." The document then provides examples of "[k]ey intelligence collected from HVD interrogations *after* applying interrogation techniques,"[1465] including:

> "Issa al-Hindi: KSM first[1466] identified Issa al-Hindi as an operative he sent to the US prior to 9/11 to case potential targets in NYC and Washington. When shown surveillance photos provided by ███████ ███████ [foreign partner authorities], HVDs confirmed al-Hindi's identity. Al-Hindi's capture by the British resulted in the disruption of a sleeper cell and led to the arrest of other operatives."[1467]

Similarly, CIA Director Michael Hayden represented to the Committee on April 12, 2007, that "KSM also provided the first lead to an operative known as 'Issa al-Hindi,' with other detainees giving additional identifying information."[1468]

The CIA provided similar inaccurate representations regarding the thwarting of the United Kingdom Urban Targets Plot and the identification and/or arrest of Dhiren Barot, aka Abu Issa al-Hindi, in 17 of the 20 documents provided to policymakers and the Department of Justice between July 2003 and March 2009.[1469]

A review of CIA operational cables and other documents found that the CIA's enhanced interrogation techniques did not result in the unique intelligence that the CIA represented led to the arrest of

Dhiren Barot or the thwarting of his plotting.[1470] The review found that the intelligence that alerted security officials to: (1) the potential terrorist threat posed by one or more U.K.-based operatives with the alias "Issa"; (2) Issa's more common alias, "Issa al-Hindi"; (3) Issa al-Hindi's location; (4) Issa al-Hindi's true name, Dhiren Barot; and (5) information on Dhiren Barot's U.K. plotting, all came from intelligence sources unrelated to the CIA's Detention and Interrogation Program.[1471] Contrary to CIA representations, reporting from CIA detainees subjected to the CIA's enhanced interrogation techniques did not lead to the arrest of Dhiren Barot or the thwarting of the United Kingdom Urban Targets Plot, nor did KSM provide the first reporting on a U.K.-based "Issa." Rather, the disruption of the United Kingdom Urban Targets Plot and the identification and arrest of Dhiren Baro (aka Issa al-Hindi) was attributable to the efforts of U.K. law enforcement ████, as well as ████ ████ [a review of computer hard drives], ████ ████ [collected communications], and reporting from detainees in the custody of the U.S. Department of Justice, the U.S. military, and a foreign government. While records indicate KSM did provide the initial information on "Issa's" tasking to conduct casings in the United States prior to the September 11, 2001, attacks,[1472] as well as information on an email address related to Issa,[1473] this information was provided within a larger body of fabricated reporting KSM provided on Issa. The CIA was unable to distinguish between the accurate and inaccurate reporting, and KSM's varied reporting led CIA officers to conclude that KSM was "protecting" Issa[1474] and "obstructing [the CIA's] ability to acquire good information" on the U.K.-based operative well after the CIA ceased using enhanced interrogation techniques against KSM.[1475]

According to information provided to the CIA by the United Kingdom, Dhiren Barot, aka Issa al-Hindi, appeared in ████ ████ reporting related to "terrorist training" and participation "in jihad in occupied Kashmir, Pakistan, Afghanistan, and Malaysia throughout the 1990s."[1476] Information concerning a book written by Dhiren Barot (under the alias "Esa al-Hindi") on jihad in Kashmir appeared in ████ and CIA intelligence records as early as December 1999.[1477] At that time U.K. authorities had a number of U.K.-based extremists under investigation, including Moazzem Begg.[1478] Begg's Maktabah al-Ansar bookstore was described as "a known jihadist gathering place."[1479] According to intelligence reports, in 1999, ████ "████ 'Abu Issa' stayed with

Moazzem Begg[1480] at the Maktabah al-Ansar bookstore in Birmingham, U.K.," and that this "Issa" was in contact with other U.K. extremists.[1481] According to reporting, Begg was associated with two "al-Qa'ida operatives" arrested in 1999 for their involvement in terrorist plotting and later released.[1482] A report from August 1, 2000, stated that U.K. authorities raided Begg's bookstore and found an invoice for 5000 copies of a book entitled, "The Army of Madina in Kashmir."[1483] A search of computers associated with the two aforementioned "al-Qa'ida operatives" described the book as their "project" written by "a brother from England who was a Hindu and became a Muslim." According to the reporting, the U.K.-based author of the book "got training in Afghanistan" before fighting jihad in Kashmir.[1484] (The book advocates for "worldwide jihad" and the author is listed on the cover of the book as "Esa al-Hindi."[1485]) Additional reporting on "Issa" appeared in CIA records again in July 2001. At that time the FBI reported that Ahmed Ressam, who was in a U.S. federal prison (arrested by U.S. border patrol with explosives in his vehicle in December 1999), reported that a U.K. national named "Issa" attended a terrorist training camp associated with al-Qa'ida in Afghanistan.[1486]

In February 2002, Moazzem Begg was arrested at an al-Qa'ida safe house in Islamabad, Pakistan, and subsequently transferred to U.S. military custody at Guantanamo Bay, Cuba.[1487] While still in Pakistani custody, Begg provided reporting on U.K.-based extremists in the context of terrorist training camps, including information on an individual who would play a key role in "Issa's" identification and capture, "Sulayman" (variant Sulyman).[1488] In May 2002, the CIA was seeking to learn more about "Sulyman."[1489] ████ [foreign partner] authorities informed the CIA that Sulyman was a person of interest to U.K. authorities for his connections to U.K. extremists and his suspected travel to Kashmir multiple times for terrorist activity. The ████ [foreign partner] further reported that Sulyman may have been involved ████████████████████. The same intelligence report provided by ████ [foreign partner] included Sulyman's likely true name, Nisar Jilal, as well as his date of birth and place of employment.[1490]

Beginning in mid-2002, there was increasing intelligence reporting on one or more U.K.-based individuals referred to as "Issa" who were connected to KSM and possibly planning attacks in the United Kingdom.[1491] This reporting resulted in efforts by U.K. authorities to identify and locate this "Issa."[1492] In August 2002,[1493] and again in October 2002, ████ [foreign partner] informed the CIA that it was seeking to identify a U.K.-based "Abu Issa" who was reportedly "an English speaker and trusted [terrorist] operative."[1494]

In September 2002, an email address ("Lazylozy") was recovered during raids related to the capture of Ramzi bin al-Shibh that would later be found to be in contact with 'Issa." Information on the email address was disseminated in intelligence reporting.[1495] The same email address was found on March 1, 2003, during the raids that led to the capture of KSM. CIA records indicate that ■■■■■ sought ■ ■■ coverage for the email account.[1496] Within days, the Intelligence Community was collecting information from the account and had reported that the user of the account was in contact with other covered accounts and that the message content was in English.[1497]

KSM was captured on March 1, 2003. On March ■, 2003, KSM was rendered to CIA custody and immediately subjected to the CIA's enhanced interrogation techniques including at least 183 applications of the waterboard interrogation technique—until March 25, 2003.[1498] During the month of March 2003, KSM provided information on a variety of matters, including on a U.K.-based Abu Issa al-Britani. The information provided by KSM on "Issa" included both accurate and inaccurate information. At the time, the CIA was unable to discern between the two. During interrogation sessions in March 2003, KSM first discussed an "Issa al-Britani" among a list of individuals who were connected to KSM's Heathrow Airport plotting.[1499] On March 17, 2003, KSM stated that, prior to the September 11, 2001, attacks, he tasked Issa to travel to the United States to "collect information on economic targets." On March 21, 2003, KSM was waterboarded for failing to confirm interrogators' suspicions that KSM sought to recruit individuals from among the African American Muslim community. KSM then stated that he had talked with Issa about contacting African American Muslim groups prior to September 11, 2001.[1500] The next day KSM was waterboarded for failing to provide more information on the recruitment of African American Muslims. One hour after the waterboarding session, KSM stated that he tasked Issa "to make contact with black U.S. citizen converts to Islam in Montana," and that he instructed Issa to use his ties to Shaykh Abu Hamza al-Masri, a U.K.-based Imam, to facilitate his recruitment efforts.[1501] KSM later stated that Issa's mission in the United States was to surveil forests to potentially ignite forest fires.[1502] During this period, KSM was confronted with a series of emails that the aforementioned "Lazylozy" email account and another email account ("■ ■■■■■■■"). KSM confirmed that the emails were established for communication between Issa al-Britani and Ammar al-Baluchi and stated that Issa used the "Lazylozy" account, and that al-Baluchi used the "█████████" account.[1503] (A month later the CIA reported that Issa did not use the "Lazylozy" email address, but the other email address.)[1504] Over the next six months, KSM retracted or provided conflicting reporting on Issa. On June 22, 2003, CIA interrogators reported that "[KSM] nervously explained to debriefer that he was under 'enhanced measures' when he made these claims" about terrorist recruitment in Montana, and "simply told his interrogators what he thought they wanted to hear."[1505] A CIA Headquarters response cable stated that the CIA's ALEC Station believed KSM's fabrication claims were "another resistance/manipulation ploy" and characterized KSM's contention that he "felt 'forced' to make admissions" under enhanced interrogation techniques as "convenient excuses." As a result, ALEC Station urged CIA officers at the detention site to get KSM to reveal "who is the key contact person in Montana?"[1506] By June 30, 2005, ALEC Station had concluded that KSM's reporting about African American Muslims in Montana was "an outright fabrication."[1507]

On April 4, 2003, the CIA provided reporting to the U.K. on "Issa," stating that "we realize that Abu Issa is a target of interest to your service." The information compiled by the CIA included an August 2002 report (unrelated to the CIA's Detention and Interrogation Program) that stated that a U.K. national "Abu Issa Al-Pakistani" was slated by al-Qa'ida for "terrorist operations against foreign targets."[1508] On April 18, 2003, a ███ cable the U.K. relayed that the correct email for Abu Issa al-Britani is ("█████"). It further noted that "the Abu Issa account" is "under ███ coverage, and ██████████████████████████████."

The same cable notes that KSM had changed his reporting on Issa's background. According to the cable, KSM originally stated Issa was of Pakistani origin, but now claimed that Issa was of Indian origin. The CIA wrote that KSM's reporting:

> "tracks with reporting from another detainee. As you are aware, Feroz Abbasi and other detainees at Guantanmo [*sic*] Bay have described an Abu Issa that worked for the al-Qa'ida media Committee run by KSM . . . Abassi [at] one time related that Abu Issa described himself as Indian."[1509]

On May 11, 2003, █████ cable noted that the email address associated with Abu Issa ("█████") was used and tracked to a specific address in Wembley, a suburb of London.[1510]

On May 28, 2003, a CIA cable documented intelligence obtained by the FBI from interviews of James Ujaama (aka Bilal Ahmed), who was in FBI custody. Ujaama, who had spent time in the U.K. extremist community, reported on an "Issa" in the U.K. who was known as "Issa al-Hindi" and was "good friends with a Pakistani male named Sulyman."[1511] ████ had already disseminated intelligence indicating that Sulyman was likely Nisar Jalal, based on reporting from U.S military detainee Moazzem Begg.[1512] Ujaama provided the FBI with the name of the U.K. law office where Sulyman (aka Nisar Jalal) worked, which matched reporting provided to the CIA by ██ [foreign partner] authorities in ████ 2002.[1513]

On June 2, 2003, KSM was shown a sketch of Issa al-Hindi provided to the CIA by the FBI and based on reporting by James Ujaama. KSM stated that the sketch did not look like anyone he knew.[1514]

A June 5, 2003, cable states that the FBI had "gleaned new clues about Issa in recent days from detainees, including [from Moazzem] Begg," who was in U.S. military custody. According to the cable, Begg told FBI special agents "that Issa is likely from Wembley, Alperton, or Sudbury." A ████ noted that ████████████████ [technical collection indicated that Issa was located in Wembley].[1515] U.K. officials highlighted that Issa's reported "good friend," Nisar Jilal (aka Sulyman), also had an address in Wembley.[1516]

On September 13, 2003, KSM explained a coding system for telephone numbers for Issa that produced no results.[1517] On October 16, 2003, KSM identified a picture of an individual known as "Nakuda," as Abu Issa al-Britani.[1518] CIA relayed this information to U.K. officials, who responded that this identification was "extremely unlikely."[1519] CIA detainee Khallad bin Attash was shown the same photograph and stated that the photo "definitely" was not Issa.[1520] CIA officers wrote that KSM "is obstructing our ability to acquire good information" on Issa and noting that KSM has "misidentified photos when he knows we are fishing" and "misleads us on telephone numbers."[1521] A cable from the CIA's ALEC Station stated that "KSM appears to have knowingly led us astray on this potentially important, albeit historical, lead [the phone numbers] to one of our most hotly pursued targets."[1522]

In October 2003, CIA officers wrote:

> "even with all we have learned from our on-going partnership with [the United Kingdom] and various detainees, we have not been able to obtain

> accurate locational information, including confirmed phone numbers and timely information on email addresses. Our latest information, based on [foreign partner reporting] and a detainee's assessment [Moazzem Begg in U.S. military custody], is that Issa is believed to currently be located in Wembley, a suburb of London."[1523]

In January 2004, ████ urged ███ [foreign partner] officials to ████████ interview Nisar Jilal (aka Sulyman) "in light of Ujaama's reporting" from the FBI confirming a relationship between Issa al-Hindi and Nisar Jilal.[1524] Instead, ███ [foreign partner] officials began planning an operation ████████████████.[1525] █ ██ ██ ██ ██ ████████████████████. One individual ████████ personally saw Issa al-Hindi on June ■, 2003, in the Wembley area of South London. Based on the FBI reporting and the email coverage, U.K. authorities continuously surveilled Nisar Jilal (aka Sulyman) and photographed his associates.[1526] A specific series of photographs was passed by ████ [foreign partner] officials to CIA officials ████ ███ depicting an individual whom CIA officials wrote "bears a striking resemblance" to the Issa al-Hindi sketch provided by Moazzem Begg, the detainee in U.S. military custody.[1527] The CIA would later write that Moazzem Begg's "description and resulting sketch of U.K. contact Issa al-Hindi" was "compared to a still shot of an unidentified man taken from a surveillance video of UK extremists," and the comparison "revealed that the man in the video probably [was] the elusive Issa al-Hindi."[1528]

With the suspicion that the photo was Issa al-Hindi, the CIA's ████████ requested the photo be "shown to detainees" and requested "immediate feedback."[1529] According to a CIA cable dated June 17, 2004, the suspected Issa al-Hindi photograph was shown to KSM, who "confirmed that the unidentified photo depicts al-Hindi."[1530]

By July 2, 2004, ███ [foreign partner] authorities had informed the CIA that they felt "confident" that Issa's true name was "Dhiren Barot." According to ███ reporting, while under surveillance, Issa was observed talking for an extended period of time ██████ ████████████████████████ in the vicinity where James Ujaama (in FBI custody) had placed Issa.[1531] ███ [foreign partner] authorities observed that Issa drove ██████ to a residence in Wembley. A record search of the address in Wembley by U.K. authorities identified a passport application with a photograph that matched the Issa under surveillance. The name on the passport application was Issa's true name, Dhiren Barot.[1532]

Once identified, Dhiren Barot remained under U.K. surveillance as the U.K. collected additional information on Dhiren Barot and his activities. On July ██, 2004, an al-Qa'ida associate named Abu Talha al-Pakistani was arrested and detained by Pakistani officials.[1533] CIA records indicate that the arrest occurred after ██████ ██████████████████████ identified when and where Abu Talha al-Pakistani would be at ████████████.[1534] On July ██, 2004, after Abu Talha's capture, Pakistani authorities conducted a series of raids and seized a laptop computer that was shared with the U.S. government.[1535] The computer was suspected of belonging to senior al-Qa'ida member, Hamza Rabi'a,[1536] and contained a series of undated, Enghsh-language casing reports. In all, the computer contained over 500 photographs, maps, sketches, and scanned documents associated with apparent casings.[1537]

On July 31, 2004, KSM was questioned about the casing reports. KSM stated that he did not know of any al-Qa'ida plans by Abu Talha or anyone else to target the Citigroup/Citibank building. Prudential Group building, or the United Nations building in described in the documents.[1538] On the same day, Abu Talha, who was in the custody of a foreign government, stated the "U.S. casing reports were from Abu Issa."[1539] Issa, aka Dhiren Barot, was still under surveillance by U.K. authorities at this time.[1540]

On August 1, 2004, Abu Talha was shown a photograph of Dhiren Barot and "immediately identified him as Issa." Abu Talha—who was cooperating with foreign government authorities—described Issa's visit to Pakistan from February to April 2004, during which he stated "Issa" (aka Dhiren Barot) met with Hamza al-Rabi'a on multiple occasions to "discuss operations in the United Kingdom and targets already cased in the United States." Abu Talha stated that Issa believed his activities and identity were not known to the authorities.[1541]

An August 3, 2004, cable stated that "analysis of information on [the] hard drive" of the computer seized "revealed a document . . . that is a detailed study on the methodologies to affect a terrorist attack." According to the cable, "the study describes the operational and logistics environment in the UK." The document is divided into two main parts. The first part includes seven chapters on the topic entitled "rough presentation for gas limo project." The second part is entitled "rough presentation for radiation (dirty bomb) project." The "gas limo project" section concludes that the most feasible option would be to use a limousine to deliver explosives, while the "dirty bomb" project section states that smoke detectors could be used to deliver the radioactive substance americium-147. The document proposes to use 10,000 smoke detectors as part of an explosive device to spread this radioactive element. In addition, the document discusses the vulnerabilities of trains and the possibilities of hijacking and utilizing gasoline tankers to conduct a terrorist attack.[1542]

On the same day the analysis was disseminated, August 3, 2004, U.K. authorities arrested Dhiren Barot and 12 other individuals, and seized "over 100 hard-drives."[1543] On August 7, 2004, the U.K. shared ████████████ associated with Dhiren Barot with the U.S. government. The ███ [information provided] included copies of casing reports related to the United States and the United Kingdom.[1544] On August 17, 2004, U.K. authorities charged nine individuals in relation to the Dhiren Barot, aka Issa al-Hindi, investigation.[1545] U.K. authorities informed the CIA that "[d]espite intelligence about the activities of the network, the recent charges of the individuals involved or linked to this planning were mainly possible owing to the recovery of terrorist-related materials during searches of associated properties and vehicles following their arrests."[1546]

On August 23, 2004, the CIA received an update from ███ [foreign partner] authorities that noted the "research conducted by the [Barot] network into central London hotels and railway stations [is] likely to be exploratory rather than representing a detailed operational plan."[1547] A report from the ███ [foreign partner] stated:

> "material that is emerging from [the United Kingdom] investigation, combined with detainee reporting from senior al-Qa'ida members [an apparent reference to Abu Talha al-Palistani's reporting on U.K. targeting in Pakistani custody], strongly suggests that Barot's cell was planning a terrorist attack in the U.K., what is not yet clear is how close the cell was to mounting an attack or what, if any, targets had been finalized."[1548]

On August 30, 2004, talking points on the Dhiren Barot case were prepared by CIA officers. A CIA officer wrote that KSM's reporting on contact numbers for Issa was "a dead end" and "that it appears KSM was protecting al-Hindi."[1549] The talking points highlighted the cyber capabilities enabled by the USA PATRIOT Act in the investigation of Dhiren Barot, stating:

> "Probably the most important intelligence tool we used in breaking this [Dhiren Barot] case was our cyber capability enabled by the USA Patriot Act. From beginning to end cyber played a role, but it was not the only

> tool that was used. HUMINT and SIGINT threads were followed and contributed to our understanding of the cyber messages and also in finding new cyber leads. Exploitation of computers and other information obtained in raids before and during the case also contributed significantly, as did surveillance. However, none of these tools are stand-alones. Good old fashioned hard targeting and analysis of these maddeningly vague and disparate and incomplete threads of information was the glue that put it all together."[1550]

On September 10, 2004, the Interagency Intelligence Committee on Terrorism (IICT) disseminated a report entitled, "Homeland: Reappraising al-Qa'ida's Election Threat," which states:

> "We do not know the projected timeframe for any attacks Issa was planning to execute in the UK, but it is unlikely he would have been ready to strike in the near term. Upon returning to the UK in mid-2004, Issa attempted to gather materials to build explosives for future attacks in the UK . . . [U.K.] authorities have been unable to locate any explosives precursors, and it is possible he had not yet acquired the necessary materials at the time of his detention. The detainee [Abu Talha al-Pakistani] also noted that some of Issa's operatives required further training—most likely in explosives—and that [Issa] intended to send an associate to Pakistan for three months to receive instruction from senior al-Qa'ida explosives experts."[1551]

The assessment adds, "Issa appears to have been in an early phase of operational planning at the time of his capture."[1552]

In November 2004, ▇▇▇▇ authorities informed the CIA that "it was largely through the investigation of Nisar Jalal's associates that [the U.K.] was able to identify Dhiren Barot as being [identifiable] with Issa al-Hindi."[1553]

A December 14, 2004, FBI Intelligence Assessment entitled, "The Gas Limos Project: An al-Qa'ida Urban Attack Plan Assessment," evaluated "the feasibility and lethality of this plot" based on "documents captured during raids" against "al-Qa'ida operatives in Pakistan and the United Kingdom in July and August 2004, and on custodial interviews conducted in the weeks following these raids." The FBI concluded that "the main plot presented in the Gas Limos Project is unlikely to be as successful as described." The report continued: "We assess that the Gas Limos Project, while ambitious and creative, is far-fetched."[1554]

On December 12, 2005, the CIA assessed that "while KSM tasked al-Hindi to go to the US to surveil targets, he was not aware of the extent to which Barot's planning had progressed, who Issa's co-conspirators were, or that Issa's planning had come to focus on the UK."[1555]

On November 7, 2006, Dhiren Barot was sentenced to life imprisonment in the United Kingdom. On May 16, 2007, Dhiren Barot's sentence was reduced to 30 years after a British Court of Appeal found that expert assessments describing the plot as "amateurish," "defective," and unlikely to succeed were not provided to the sentencing judge.[1556]

5. *The Identification, Capture, and Arrest of Iyman Faris*

SUMMARY: The CIA represented that its enhanced interrogation techniques were effective and produced critical, otherwise unavailable intelligence, which thwarted plots and saved lives. Over a period of years, the CIA provided the "identification," "arrest," "capture," "investigation," and "prosecution" of Iyman Faris as evidence for the effectiveness of the CIA's enhanced interrogation techniques. These representations were inaccurate. Iyman Faris was identified, investigated, and linked directly to al-Qa'ida prior to any mention of Iyman Faris by KSM or any other CIA detainee. When approached by law enforcement, Iyman Faris voluntarily provided information and made self-incriminating statements. On May 1, 2003, Iyman Faris pled guilty to terrorism-related charges and admitted "to casing a New York City bridge for al Qaeda, and researching and providing information to al Qaeda regarding the tools necessary for possible attacks on U.S. targets."

FURTHER DETAILS: Iyman Faris was an Ohio-based truck driver tasked by KSM with procuring "tools and devices needed to collapse suspension bridges," as well as tools that could be used to derail trains.[1557] Faris had met KSM through his self-described "best friend," Maqsood Khan,[1558] who was a Pakistan-based al-Qa'ida facilitator and Majid Khan's uncle.[1559]

The identification and arrest of Iyman Faris is one of the eight most frequently cited examples provided by the CIA as evidence for the effectiveness of the CIA's enhanced interrogation techniques. Over a period of years, CIA documents prepared for and provided to senior policymakers, intelligence officials, and the Department of Justice represent the identification, capture, and/or arrest of Iyman Faris as an example of how "[k]ey intelligence collected from HVD interrogations *after* applying interrogation techniques" had "enabled CIA to disrupt terrorist plots" and "capture additional terrorists."[1560] The CIA further represented that the intelligence acquired from the CIA's enhanced interrogation techniques was "otherwise unavailable" and "saved lives."[1561]

For example, in a July 2003 CIA briefing for White House officials on the CIA interrogation program, the CIA represented that "[m]ajor threats were countered and attacks averted," and that "[t]ermination of this [CIA] program will result in loss of life, possibly extensive." The CIA further represented that "the use of the [CIA's enhanced interrogation] techniques has produced significant results" and "saved lives."[1562] Under the heading, "RESULTS: MAJOR THREAT INFO," a briefing slides states:

> "KSM: Al-Qa'ida Chief of Operations . . . - *Identification of Iyman Faris*"[1563]

Similarly, on February 27, 2004, DDO James Pavitt responded to the CIA Inspector General's draft Special Review and included a representation related to Iyman Faris. Pavitt stated that the Inspector General's Special Review should have come to the "conclusion that our efforts have thwarted attacks and saved lives," and that "EITs (including the water board) have been indispensable to our successes."[1564] Pavitt provided materials to the OIG that stated:

> "Specifically, as a result of the lawful use of EITs, KSM identified a truck driver who is now serving time in the United States for his support to al-Qa'ida."[1565]

The final CIA Inspector General Special Review, "Counterterrorism Detention and Interrogation Program," published in May 2004, states:

> "Khalid Shaykh Muhammad's information also *led to the investigation and prosecution Iyman Faris*, the truck driver arrested in early 2003 in Ohio.[1566]

This passage in the CIA Inspector General Special Review was declassified and publicly released on August 24, 2009.[1567]

Likewise, information prepared by the CIA for CIA Director Leon Panetta in February 2009 on the effectiveness of the CIA's enhanced interrogation techniques states that the "CIA assesses . . . the techniques were effective in producing foreign intelligence," and that "most, if not all, of the timely intelligence acquired from detainees in this program would not have been discovered or reported by other means." The document provides examples of "some of the key captures, disrupted plots, and intelligence gained from HVDs interrogated," including the "*arrest* of Iyman Faris."[1568] In March 2009, the CIA provided a three-page document to the chairman of the Committee stating, "CIA assesses that most, if not all, of the timely intelligence acquired from detainees in this program would not have been discovered or reported by any other means," before listing "Iyman Faris" as one of the "key captures" resulting from the CIA interrogation program.[1569]

The CIA provided similar inaccurate representations regarding the identification and capture of Iyman Faris in nine of the 20 documents and briefings provided to policymakers and the Department of Justice between July 2003 and March 2009.[1570]

A review of CIA operational cables and other records found that the CIA's Detention and Interrogation Program and the CIA's enhanced interrogation techniques played no role in the identification and capture of Iyman Faris.[1571]

CIA records indicate that Iyman Faris was known to the U.S. Intelligence Community prior to the attacks of September 11, 2001. On March ■■, 2001, the FBI opened an international terrorism investigation targeting Iyman Faris.[1572] According to CIA records, the "predication of the [FBI] Faris investigation was information provided by [foreign] authorities that [revealed] Faris' telephone number had been called by Islamic extremists operating in France, Belgium, Turkey and Canada," including "millennium bomber" Ahmad Ressam.[1573] Ressam, currently serving a 65-year U.S. prison term, was arrested on December 14, 1999, en route to Los Angeles International Airport with explosives in the trunk of his car. According to CIA records, as "a result of a post 9/11 lead," the FBI interviewed Iyman Faris shortly after the attacks of September 11, 2001.[1574] On November ■■, 2001, the FBI closed its investigation of Iyman Faris for unknown reasons.[1575]

On March 5, 2003, Majid Khan was taken into Pakistani custody.[1576] That same day, FISA coverage of Majid Khan's residence in Maryland indicated that Majid Khan's ■■■■■■■■ made a suspicious phone call to an individual at a residence associated with Iyman Faris.[1577] The call included discussion of Majid Khan's possible arrest and potential FBI surveillance of ■■■■■■, who asked the individual in Ohio if he had been approached and questioned.[1578] ■■■■■■ warned the Ohio-based individual not to contact anyone using his phone.[1579] That same day, ■■■■■■ informed FBI special agents that the other party to the intercepted conversation was Iyman Faris.[1580] By March 6, 2003, the FBI had officially reopened its international terrorism investigation of Iyman Faris.[1581]

While U.S. law enforcement investigations of Iyman Faris

moved forward, Majid Khan, in foreign government custody, was being questioned by foreign government interrogators. According to CIA records, the interrogators were using rapport-building techniques, confronting Khan with inconsistencies in his story and obtaining information on Majid Khan's al-Qa'ida connections.[1582] On March 11, 2003, Majid Khan identified a photo of Iyman Faris.[1583] Majid Khan stated that he knew Faris as "Abdul Raof," and claimed Faris was a 35-year-old truck driver of Pakistani origin who was a "business partner of his father."[1584] In addition to describing business deals Iyman Faris was involved in with Khan's family, Majid Khan stated that Faris spoke Urdu and excellent English and had a "colorful personality."[1585] The next day, while still in foreign government custody, Majid Khan stated that Iyman Faris was "an Islamic extremist."[1586] According to CIA cables, on March 14, 2003, Majid Khan provided "more damning information" on Iyman Faris, specifically that Faris was a "mujahudden during the Afghan/Soviet period" and was a close associate of his uncle, Maqsood Khan. Maqsood was a known al-Qa'ida associate whom Majid Khan had already admitted was in contact with senior al-Qa'ida members. Majid Khan told foreign government interrogators that it was Maqsood who provided the money for Majid Khan's al-Qa'ida-related travels.[1587] Majid Khan further stated that "after the KSM arrest became public knowledge," Iyman Faris contacted Majid Khan's family and requested the family pass a message to Maqsood Khan regarding the status of KSM.[1588] This information on Iyman Faris was acquired prior to—and independently of—any reporting from the CIA's Detention and Interrogation Program.[1589]

On March 10, 2003, in response to a requirements cable from CIA Headquarters reporting that al-Qa'ida was targeting U.S. suspension bridges,[1590] KSM stated that any such plans were "theoretical" and only "on paper." He also stated that no one was currently pursuing such a plot.[1591] KSM repeated this assertion on March 16, 2003,[1592] noting that, while UBL officially endorsed attacks against suspension bridges in the United States, he "had no planned targets in the US which were pending attack and that after 9/11 the US had become too hard a target."[1593] On neither occasion did KSM reference Iyman Faris.

On March 15, 2003, deputy chief of ALEC Station, ███ ███ ███, who was reading the intelligence from the foreign government interrogations of Majid Khan, requested a photograph of Majid Khan and additional information to use with KSM.[1594] In response, CIA

Headquarters sent the detention site photographs of Majid Khan's family and associates, including Iyman Faris.[1595]

On March 17, 2003, eleven days after the FBI officially reopened its investigation of Iyman Faris, KSM was shown photographs of both Iyman Faris and Majid Khan.[1596] According to CIA cables, KSM was also asked detailed questions based on email communications, which a cable stated served as "an effective means to convey to [KSM] the impression that the USG already possessed considerable information and that the information would be used to check the accuracy of his statements."[1597] In this context, KSM identified the photograph of Iyman Faris as a "truck driver" and a relative of Majid Khan. KSM claimed that he could not remember the truck driver's name. KSM described the "truck driver" as a "colorful character who liked to drink and have girlfriends and was very interested in business.[1598] The next day, March 18, 2003, KSM stated that in February 2002 he tasked the "truck driver" to procure specialized machine tools that would be useful to al-Qa'ida to loosen the nuts and bolts of suspension bridges in the United States. According to KSM, in March 2002, the "truck driver" asked Mansour Khan [son of Maqsood Khan][1599] to inform KSM that he (the "truck driver") could not find such tools. KSM stated that he made no further requests of the "truck driver."[1600]

According to a CIA cable, on the evening of March 20, 2003, the FBI informed the CIA that "Ohio police had been following [Iyman] Faris for 'some time,' and had stopped him and questioned him about his relationship to Shoukat Ali Khan [Majid Khan's father] of Baltimore."[1601] According to a CIA officer, "[w]hen the FBI approached Faris he talked voluntarily."[1602] Records indicate that Faris "initially claimed to know Shoukat All Khan though the gas station business" and agreed to take a polygraph examination. According to FBI records, prior to the polygraph, Faris admitted to being associated with KSM and provided details on his relationships with al-Qa'ida members in Pakistan.[1603] Specifically, Iyman Faris told FBI and Ohio police that he had met KSM twice and had been "tasked with procuring items." Faris detailed how KSM had a plan "to cut the suspension cables on the Brooklyn Bridge to cause its collapse using gas cutters.[1604] Faris maintained that he "thought that the task to take down the bridge was impossible"[1605] and did not take further action.[1606]

Over several weeks Iyman Faris continued to voluntarily cooperate with law enforcement officials and engaged in efforts to assist in the capture of Maqsood Khan.[1607] Faris provided additional details on his activities related to the Khan family, KSM, his meeting with UBL, and two extremists in the United States who had discussed wanting "to kill Americans in a Columbus area shopping mall with a Kalashnikov automatic rifle."[1608] On April 22, 2003, "Faris had accepted a plea agreement"[1609] and continued to cooperate, including by sending email messages to al-Qa'ida members in Pakistan for the purposes of intelligence collection.[1610] On May 1, 2003, Faris was transported from Quantico, Virginia, where he was voluntarily residing and working with the FBI, to a federal court in Alexandria, Virginia, where he pled guilty to material support to terrorism charges.[1611] He was subsequently sentenced to 20 years in prison.[1612]

On April 3, 2003, the Interagency Intelligence Committee on Terrorism (IICT) assessed that the use of tools to loosen the bolts of suspension bridges were "methods that appear to be unrealistic."[1613]

6. *The Identification, Capture, and Arrest of Sajid Badat*

SUMMARY: The CIA represented that its enhanced interrogation techniques were effective and produced critical, otherwise unavailable intelligence, which thwarted plots and saved lives. Over a period of years, the CIA provided the identification, discovery, capture, and arrest of Sajid Badat as evidence for the effectiveness of the CIA's enhanced interrogation techniques. These representations were inaccurate. U.K. domestic investigative efforts, reporting from foreign intelligence services, international law enforcement efforts, and U.S. military reporting resulted in the identification and arrest of Sajid Badat.

FURTHER DETAILS: Sajid Badat[1614] was selected by al-Qa'ida leaders, including Abu Hafs al-Masri and Sayf al-'Adl, to carry out an attack against a Western airliner with Richard Reid using a shoe bomb explosive device in December 2001.[1615] Sajid Badat returned to the United Kingdom in late 2001 and sent a message to his al-Qa'ida handler, Ammar al-Baluchi, stating that he was withdrawing from the operation.[1616] On December 22, 2001, Richard Reid attempted to detonate a shoe bomb on a flight from Paris, France, to Miami, Florida. The plane was diverted to Boston, Massachusetts, and Reid was taken into custody.[1617]

The discovery, identification, capture, and arrest of Sajid Badat, "the shoe bomber," is one of the eight most frequently cited examples provided by the CIA as evidence for the effectiveness of the CIA's enhanced interrogation techniques. Over a period of years,

CIA documents prepared for and provided to senior policymakers, intelligence officials, and the Department of Justice represent the discovery, identification, capture, and/or arrest of Sajid Badat as an example of how "[k]ey intelligence collected from HVD interrogations *after* applying interrogation techniques" had "enabled CIA to disrupt terrorist plots" and "capture additional terrorists."[1618] In at least one CIA document prepared for the president, the CIA specifically highlighted the waterboard interrogation technique in enabling the CIA to learn "that Sajid Badat was the operative slated to launch a simultaneous shoe bomb attack with Richard Reid in 2001."[1619] The CIA further represented that the intelligence acquired from the CIA's enhanced interrogation techniques was "otherwise unavailable" and "saved lives."[1620]

As an example, on October 26, 2007, the CIA faxed a document to the Senate Appropriations Committee appealing a proposed elimination of funding for the CIA's Rendition and Detention Program. The CIA appeal states that "[m]ost, if not all, of the intelligence acquired from high-value detainees in this program would likely not have been discovered or reported in any other way." Representing the success of the CIA interrogation program, the document states:

> "Detainees have . . . permitted discovery of terrorist cells, key individuals and the interdiction of numerous plots, including . . . the *discovery* of an operative who was preparing another attack[1621] like that attempted by 'shoe bomber' Richard Reid."[1622]

Similarly, in early March 2005, the CIA compiled talking points on the effectiveness of the CIA's enhanced interrogation techniques for use in a meeting with the National Security Council. The document states, "[t]he Central Intelligence Agency can advise you that this program works and the techniques are effective in producing foreign intelligence." The document states that "*after* applying interrogation techniques," the CIA "learned from KSM and Ammar that Sajid Badat was the operative slated to launch a simultaneous shoe bomb attack with Richard Reid in December 2001."[1623] A month later, on April 15, 2005, the CIA faxed an eight-page document to the Department of Justice's Office of Legal Counsel entitled, "Briefing Notes on the Value of Detainee Reporting" which contained similar information.[1624] The Office of Legal Counsel used the information to support its May 30, 2005, legal opinion on whether certain "enhanced interrogation techniques" were consistent with United States obligations under Article 16 of the United Nations Convention Against

Torture and Other Cruel, Inhumane or Degrading Treatment or Punishment.[1625] The CIA-provided document states:

> ***"Identifying the 'other' shoe bomber.*** Leads provided by KSM in November 2003 led directly to the arrest of shoe bomber Richard Reid's one-time partner Sajid Badat in the UK. KSM had volunteered the existence of Badat—whom he knew as 'Issa al-Pakistani'[1626]—as the operative who was slated to launch a simultaneous shoe bomb attack with Richard Reid in December 2001."[1627]

The CIA provided similar inaccurate representations regarding the purported role of KSM and Ammar al-Baluchi[1628] in the discovery, identification, capture, and arrest of Sajid Badat in 16 of the 20 documents provided to policymakers and the Department of Justice between July 2003 and March 2009.[1629] However, in an additional case, a March 4, 2005, CIA briefing for Vice President Cheney, the CIA credited Abu Zubaydah with identifying Sajid Badat,[1630] despite a lack of any reporting on Sajid Badat from Abu Zubaydah.[1631]

Contrary to CIA representations, a review of CIA operational cables and other documents found that the CIA's enhanced interrogation techniques did not result in otherwise unavailable intelligence leading to the discovery, identification, capture, or arrest of Sajid Badat. According to CIA records and the U.K.'s own investigative summary,[1632] the investigation of Sajid Badat was a United Kingdom-led operation, and the intelligence that alerted security officials to: (1) a U.K.-based "Issa" (aka, Sajid Badat); (2) a potential second "shoe bomber" related to Richard Reid;[1633] (3) a suspected U.K. terrorist named "Sajid Badat";[1634] (4) Sajid Badat's connection to Richard Reid; (5) Sajid Badat's physical description; (6) Sajid Badat's location; and (7) the initial identification of a U.K. surveillance photo of Sajid Badat, the "shoe bomber,"[1635] was unrelated to information acquired from CIA detainees during or after the use of the CIA's enhanced interrogation techniques. CIA records indicate that the information that led to Sajid Badat's arrest and U.K. criminal prosecution was also not derived from the CIA's Detention and Interrogation Program.[1636]

Prior to any reporting from CIA detainees, and as early as January 14, 2002, the FBI informed the CIA that Richard Reid "had an unidentified partner who allegedly backed out of the operation at the last minute."[1637] This information was later corroborated by a credible CIA source prior to any reporting from the CIA's Detention and Interrogation Program.[1638] In July 2002, a foreign government reported that pre-paid phone cards recovered by the FBI from Richard Reid upon his arrest were used by an individual named Sajid Badat to call a known terrorist, Nizar Trabelsi.[1639] FBI interviews of

Trabelsi—officially relayed to the CIA in July 2002—reported that "L. Badad Sajid" was "involved in operations targeting American interests."[1640] The CIA highlighted in a July 2002 cable that this information matched previous reporting from a European government that identified a "Saajid Badat," of Gloucester, United Kingdom, with a date of birth of March 28, 1979, as a person suspected of being involved in terrorist activity.[1641] Additional analysis of the phone card connecting Badat and Reid—as well as other intelligence—placed Sajid Badat and Richard Reid together in Belgium in September 2001.[1642]

According to ■■■■■■■■, Sajid Badat was linked to other well-known extremists in the United Kingdom who were already under investigation. Specifically, Badat was known to ■■■■■■■■ ■■■ as "a member of Babar Ahmad's group," and was a "particularly close associate of Mirza Beg." ■■■ reporting also determined that Badat had attended a jihad training camp in Afghanistan.[1643]

Concurrent with the emergence of information linking Sajid Badat to Richard Reid, there was an ongoing international effort to identify one or more U.K.-based al-Qa'ida operatives known as "Issa."[1644] As early as June 2002, CIA records indicate that an individual in the custody of a foreign government, Abu Zubair al-Ha'ili, repeatedly referenced an "Abu Issa al-Pakistani" as a British-born Pakistani associated with Richard Reid and engaged in plotting in the United Kingdom at the behest of KSM.[1645] This information was corroborative of other intelligence reporting.[1646] In May 2003, this detainee met with CIA officers to produce several sketches that were described as having "achieved a 95% likeness" of this individual.[1647] On August 17, 2003, CIA officers noted that a photograph of Sajid Badat provided by ■■■■■■■■ [foreign partner] looked "an awful lot like the sketches" of the Richard Reid associate made with the assistance of the detainee in foreign government custody.[1648]

CIA Headquarters requested that the photograph be shown to CIA detainees. According to CIA records, on August 18, 2003, "KSM viewed the picture for a while, but said he did not recognize the person in the photo." When KSM was asked if Issa's name could be Sajid Badat, "KSM shrugged and said that the Badat name was not the name he recalled." Pressed further, KSM stated, "he was confident that the name Sajid Badat was not Issa's name.[1649] On August 22, 2003, emails among CIA officers stated that "CTC believes that Abu Issa's true name is Sajid Badat . . . KSM says that Badat is not Abu Issa—but he might be lying."[1650] On August 23, 2003, the detailed sketches derived from interviews of the detainee in foreign custody, Abu Zubair al-Ha'ili—the sketches CIA officers stated so closely resembled the ▬▬ [foreign partner]-provided photos of Sajid Badat—were shown to KSM. KSM stated he did not recognize the individual in the sketches.[1651]

Meanwhile, on August 21, 2003, a CIA cable noted that the ▬ ▬ [foreign partner] had informed the CIA that joint interviews by the FBI and ▬▬ [foreign partner] authorities of an individual in FBI custody, James Ujaama, led investigators in the U.K. to a home "formerly occupied by both Mirza [Beg] and Sajid [Badat]."[1652] The ▬▬ [foreign partner] authorities relayed to the CIA that "at least one of these men was known by the alias Issa," and that the subjects were related to a separate ongoing terrorism investigation.[1653] On September 2, 2003, ▬▬ [foreign partner] authorities informed the CIA that "secret and reliable" reporting indicated that Sajid Badat is the Richard Reid associate and shoe bomber. According to the ▬ ▬ [foreign partner] report, ▬▬▬▬ [foreign partner information] linked Badat to a larger ▬▬▬▬▬ network in the United Kingdom, which was part of the ▬▬ [foreign partner] investigation.[1654]

On September 9, 2003, a detainee in U.S. military custody at Guantanamo Bay, Cuba, identified a photograph of Sajid Badat to a visiting U.K. official as Abu Issa the "shoe bomber."[1655] The next day, KSM identified a photograph of Sajid Badat as "Issa al-Britani, aka Issa Richard"—the associate of Richard Reid. Other detainees in U.S. military custody subsequently identified the same photograph of Sajid Badat as "Abu Issa" the "shoebomber."[1656]

After conducting extensive surveillance of Sajid Badat, U.K. authorities arrested Badat on November 27, 2003.[1657] Badat immediately cooperated with U.K. investigators and confirmed he withdrew from a shoe bomb operation with Richard Reid in December 2001.[1658] On November 28, 2003, the United Kingdom provided a detailed account to the CIA on how investigative efforts in the United Kingdom led to the identification of Sajid Badat, noting that "key aspects" of reporting acquired from CIA, U.S. military, and foreign government detainees matched those of a "▬▬▬▬▬▬" [specific U.K. intelligence collection on Sajid Badat]. The "▬▬▬▬▬▬" [specific U.K. intelligence collection on Sajid Badat] was not previously referenced in U.K. investigative updates to the CIA.[1659]

After pleading guilty in a U.K. court on February 28, 2005, to terrorism-related charges, Sajid Badat was sentenced to 13 years in prison. ▬▬▬▬▬ Sajid "Badat was voluntarily cooperative throughout much of his pre-sentencing incarceration."[1660] On November 13, 2009, Sajid Badat's 13-year prison sentence was reduced to 11 years. In March 2010, approximately five years after his sentencing, Sajid Badat was released under an agreement whereby Badat became a cooperating witness for U.S. and U.K. authorities.[1661] The legal agreement came to light when Sajid Badat testified against Adis Medunjanin, a U.S. terrorism suspect on trial in New York, via a video-link from the United Kingdom in April 2012.[1662]

7. The Thwarting of the Heathrow Airport and Canary Wharf Plotting

SUMMARY: The CIA represented that its enhanced interrogation techniques were effective and produced critical, otherwise unavailable intelligence, which thwarted plots and saved lives. Over a period of years, the CIA provided the identification and thwarting of the Heathrow Airport Plot as evidence for the effectiveness of the CIA's enhanced interrogation techniques. These representations were inaccurate. A review of records indicates that the Heathrow Airport and Canary Wharf plotting had not progressed beyond the initial planning stages when the operation was fully disrupted with the detentions of Ramzi bin al-Shibh, KSM, Ammar-al-Baluchi, and Khallad bin Attash. None of these individuals were captured as a result of reporting obtained during or after the use of the CIA's enhanced interrogation techniques against CIA detainees.

FURTHER DETAILS: After the September 11, 2001, attacks against the United States, KSM sought to target the United Kingdom using hijacked aircraft and surmised that Heathrow Airport and a building in Canary Wharf, a major business district in London, were powerful economic symbols.[1663] The initial plan was for al-Qa'ida operatives to hijack multiple airplanes departing Heathrow Airport, turn them around, and crash them into the airport itself. Security was assessed to be too tight at Heathrow Airport and the plan was altered to focus on aircrafts departing from mainly Eastern European airports to conduct attacks against Heathrow Airport. Al-Qa'ida was unable to locate pilots to conduct these attacks.[1664] Once KSM was detained in Pakistan on March 1, 2003, responsibility for the planning was passed to Ammar al-Baluchi and Khallad bin Attash, who were at the time focused on carrying out attacks against Western interests in Karachi, Pakistan.[1665]

The thwarting of the Heathrow Airport and Canary Wharf plotting is one of the eight most frequently cited examples provided by the CIA as evidence for the effectiveness of the CIA's enhanced interrogation techniques. Over a period of years, CIA documents prepared for and provided to senior policymakers, intelligence officials, and the Department of Justice represent the Heathrow Airport and Canary Wharf plotting as an example of how "[k]ey intelligence collected from HVD interrogations after applying interrogation techniques" had "enabled CIA to disrupt terrorist plots" and "capture additional terrorists."[1666] The CIA further represented that the intelligence acquired from the CIA's enhanced interrogation techniques was "otherwise unavailable" and "saved lives."[1667]

For example, on December 23, 2005, CIA Director Porter Goss explained in a letter to National Security Advisor Stephen Hadley, Homeland Security Advisor Frances Townsend, and Director of National Intelligence John Negroponte, that he was suspending the use of the CIA's enhanced interrogation techniques because of the passage of the Detainee Treatment Act (the "McCain amendment"). The letter stated:

> ". . . only 29 [CIA detainees] have undergone an interrogation that used one or more of the 13 [CIA enhanced interrogation] techniques.[1668] These interrogations produced intelligence that allowed the U.S., and its partners, to disrupt attacks such as 911-style attacks planned for the U.S. West Coast and *for Heathrow airport*. I can inform you with confidence that this program has allowed the U.S. to *save hundreds, if not thousands, of lives*."[1669]

Similarly, the CIA informed the CIA inspector general on February 27, 2004, that:

> "As a result of the lawful use of EITs, *KSM also provided information on an al-Qa'ida plot for suicide airplane attacks outside of the United States that would have killed thousands of people in the United Kingdom* . . . Of note, even after KSM reported that al-Qa'ida was planning to target Heathrow, he at first repeatedly denied there was any other target than the airport. *Only after the repeated lawful use of EITs did he stop lying and admit that the sketch of a beam labeled Canary Wharf in his notebook was in fact an illustration that KSM the engineer drew himself in order to show another AQ operative that the beams in the Wharf*—like those in the World Trade Center would likely melt and collapse the building, killing all inside . . . We are still debriefing detainees and following up on leads to destroy this cell, but *at a minimum the lawful use of EIT's on KSM provided us with critical information that alerted us to these threats* . . ."[1670]

The CIA provided similar inaccurate representations regarding the Heathrow and Canary Wharf Plotting in 20 of the 20 documents provided to policymakers and the Department of Justice between July 2003 and March 2009.[1671]

A review of CIA operational cables and other documents found that contrary to CIA representations, information acquired during or after the use of the CIA's enhanced interrogation techniques played no role in "alert[ing]" the CIA to the threat to—or "disrupt[ing]" the plotting against—Heathrow Airport and Canary Wharf.[1672]

Prior to the detention and interrogation of the CIA detainees credited by the CIA with providing information on the plot, the CIA and other intelligence agencies were already "alerted" to al-Qa'ida's efforts to target Heathrow Airport. Specifically, the CIA knew that: (1) KSM and al-Qa'ida were targeting "a national symbol in the United Kingdom" and that this symbol was the "Heathrow airport";[1673] (2) the attack plan called for hijacking commercial aircraft and crashing them directly into Heathrow airport;[1674] (3) no pilots had been identified by al-Qa'ida and the planned attack was not imminent;[1675] (4) KSM, Ammar al-Baluchi, and Ramzi bin al-Shibh were involved in or knowledgeable about the plotting;[1676] (5) al-Qa'ida was seeking to recruit numerous operatives, but potentially already had two operatives in place in the United Kingdom named "Abu Yusif" and "Abu Adel," although the two operatives were unwitting of the plot;[1677] and (6) KSM was seeking Saudi and British passport holders over the age of 30 for the attack.[1678]

A review of records indicates that the Heathrow Airport plotting had not progressed beyond the initial planning stages when the operation was fully disrupted with the detentions of Ramzi bin al-Shibh (detained on September 11, 2002),[1679] KSM (detained on March 1, 2003),[1680] Ammar-al-Baluchi (detained on April 29, 2003), and Khallad bin Attash (detained on April 29, 2003,).[1681] There are no CIA records to indicate that any of the individuals were captured as a result of CIA detainee reporting. A draft National Terrorism Bulletin from March 2006 states: "the [Heathrow Airport] operation was disrupted mid-cycle, around the spring of 2003, when several of the key plotters, including KSM, were detained."[1682] Foreign government intelligence analysis came to the same conclusion.[1683]

While each of these four detainees provided information on the plotting during their detentions, none of this information played any role in the disruption of the plot. A wide body of intelligence reporting indicated that no operatives were informed of the plot, no pilots were ever identified by al-Qa'ida for the attacks, and only schedules of potential flights were collected for review.[1684]

CIA detainee records indicate that reporting from CIA detainees on aspects of the Heathrow plotting was often unreliable and not believed by CIA officers. For example, KSM retracted information he provided while being subjected to the CIA's enhanced interrogation techniques, including information linking Jaffar al-Tayyar to the Heathrow Plot.[1685] On May 20, 2003, nearly two months after the CIA ceased using its enhanced interrogation techniques against KSM, a CIA analyst wrote that KSM had provided three different stories related to the Heathrow plotting, writing to CIA colleagues: "Bottom Line: KSM knows more about this plot than he's letting on."[1686] By late June 2004, KSM had retracted much of the varied reporting he had provided on the Heathrow plotting, most importantly the information KSM provided on tasking potential operatives to obtain flight training.[1687] KSM stated that during March 2003—when he was being subjected to the CIA's enhanced interrogation techniques—"he may have given false information," and that, in many cases, the information he provided was "just speculation."[1688] The value of other CIA detainee reporting was also questioned by CIA officers.[1689] In July 2003, a cable from the CIA's ALEC Station stated that "HQS/ALEC remains concerned with what we believe to be paltry information coming from detainees about operations in the U.K."[1690]

In addition, KSM withheld information linking Abu Talha al-Pakistani to the Heathrow plotting. According to CIA interrogation records, KSM discussed Canary Wharf the first time he was shown his notebook, in which the words "Canary Wharf' were written.[1691] KSM stated, however, that he had drawn the sketch for Ammar al-Baluchi. In June 2003, after being confronted with contradictory reporting from Ammar al-Baluchi, KSM admitted that he had actually shown the sketch to "Talha," whom KSM had not previously mentioned.[1692]

8. The Capture of Hambali

SUMMARY: The CIA represented that its enhanced interrogation techniques were effective and produced critical, otherwise unavailable intelligence, which thwarted plots and saved lives. Over a period of years, the CIA provided the capture of Hambali as evidence for the effectiveness of the CIA's enhanced interrogation techniques. Specifically, the CIA consistently represented that, as a result of the CIA's enhanced interrogation techniques, KSM provided the "*first*" information on a money transfer by Majid Khan that eventually led to Hambali's capture. These CIA representations were inaccurate. Majid Khan, who was in foreign government custody, provided this information prior to any reporting from KSM. CIA records indicate that the intelligence that led to Hambali's capture in Thailand was based on signals intelligence, a CIA source, and Thai investigative activities.

FURTHER DETAILS: Riduan bin Isomuddin, aka Hambali, was a senior member of Jemaah Islamiyah (JI), a Southeast Asia-based terrorist group, and served as an interface between the JI and al-Qa'ida. Hambali was linked to terrorist activity prior to the September 11, 2001, attacks. Shortly after those attacks, Hambali was described as the CIA's "number one target" in Southeast Asia.[1693] When the October 12, 2002, terrorist attacks occurred on the Indonesian island of Bali, killing more than 200 individuals, Hambali was immediately suspected of being the "mastermind" of the attacks and was further described as "one of the world's most wanted terrorists."[1694]

The capture of Hambali is one of the eight most frequently cited examples provided by the CIA as evidence for the effectiveness of the CIA's enhanced interrogation techniques. Over a period of years, CIA documents prepared for and provided to senior policy makers, intelligence officials, and the Department of Justice represent the capture of Hambali as an example of how "[k]ey intelligence collected from HVD interrogations after applying interrogation techniques" had "enabled CIA to disrupt terrorist plots" and "capture additional terrorists."[1695] The CIA further represented that the intelligence acquired from the CIA's enhanced interrogation techniques was "otherwise unavailable" and "saved lives."[1696]

As an example, in a briefing prepared for the president's chief of staff, Josh Bolten, on May 2, 2006, the CIA represented that the "[u]se of the DOJ-authorized *enhanced interrogation techniques*, as part of a comprehensive interrogation approach, has enabled us to disrupt terrorist plots, capture additional terrorists, and collect a high volume of critical intelligence on al-Qa'ida."[1697] The briefing document represents that "[a]ssessing the effectiveness of individual interrogation techniques is difficult," but provides 11 specific examples of "Key Intelligence Collected from HVD Interrogations," including:

> "Hambali's Capture: During KSM's interrogation we acquired information that led to the capture of Hambali in August 2003 and to the partial dismantling of the Jemaah Islamiyah leadership in SE Asia. *KSM first told us* about Majid Khan's role in delivering $50,000 to Hambali operatives for an attack KSM believed was imminent. *We then confronted Khan with KSM's admission* and [signals intelligence] confirming the money

> transfer and Khan's travel to Bangkok. Khan admitted he delivered the money to an operative named 'Zubair,' whom we subsequently identified and captured. Zubair's capture led to the identification and subsequent capture of an operative named Lilie who was providing forged passports to Hambali. Lilie identified the house in Bangkok where Hambali was hiding."[1698]

Similarly, on July 13, 2004, the CIA disseminated an Intelligence Assessment entitled, "Khalid Shaykh Muhammad: Preeminent Source on Al-Qa'ida."[1699] On April 2005, the paper, as well as other materials on CIA detainee reporting, was faxed from ██████ CTC Legal, to the Office of Legal Counsel at the Department of Justice, to support the OLC's legal review of the CIA's enhanced interrogation techniques.[1700] The document states:

> ". . . information that KSM provided on Majid Khan in the spring of 2003 was the *crucial first link* in the chain that led us to the capture of prominent JI leader and al-Qa'ida associate Hambali in August 2003, and more than a dozen Southeast Asian operatives slated for attacks against the US homeland. KSM told us about [Majid] Khan's role in delivering $50,000 in December 2002 to operatives associated with Hambali . . . [Majid] Khan—who had been detained in Pakistan in early 2003—was confronted with KSM's information about the money and acknowledged that he delivered the money to an operative named 'Zubair.' . . . Based on that information, Zubair was captured in June 2003."[1701]

On August 24, 2009, this document was declassified with redactions and publicly released with the inaccurate information unredacted.[1702]

The CIA provided similar inaccurate representations regarding the capture of Hambali in 18 of the 20 documents provided to policymakers and the Department of Justice between July 2003 and March 2009.[1703] In these representations, the CIA consistently asserted that "*after applying*" the CIA's enhanced interrogation techniques, KSM provided "*the crucial first link*" that led to the capture of Hambali.[1704]

A review of CIA operational cables and other records found that information obtained from KSM during and after the use of the CIA's enhanced interrogation techniques played no role in the capture of Hambali. A review of CIA records further found that prior to reporting from CIA detainees subjected to the CIA's enhanced interrogation techniques, the CIA had intelligence on: (1) Hambali's role in the Jemaah Islamiyah; (2) funding by al-Qa'ida and KSM of Hambali's terrorist activities; (3) the operative to whom Majid Khan delivered the money, Zubair, and Zubair's links to terrorism, Jemaah Islamiyah, and Hambali; and (4) Majid Khan's $50,000 money transfer from al-Qa'ida to Zubair in December 2002. CIA records indicate that the intelligence that led to Hambali's capture was based on signals intelligence, a CIA source, and Thai investigative activities in Thailand.[1705]

Prior to his capture, Hambali was known to have played a supporting role in the KSM and Ramzi Yousef "Bojinka Plot," an effort in early 1995 to place explosives on 12 United States-flagged aircraft and destroy them mid-flight.[1706] By the end of 2001, Hambali was suspected of playing a supporting role in the September 11, 2001, terrorist attacks, as well as helping to enroll Zacarias Moussaoui in flight school.[1707] By early 2002, a body of intelligence reporting unrelated to the CIA's Detention and Interrogation Program indicated that KSM was providing Hambali with funding to conduct terrorist operations in Southeast Asia.[1708] In March 2002, Hambali was described as the CIA's "number one target" in Southeast Asia.[1709] That same month, the FBI provided information to the CIA stating that foreign government detainee reporting indicated that KSM reimbursed terrorism-related expenditures made by Hambali for the JI.[1710] By June of 2002, the CIA had entered into discussions with representatives of the ████ government regarding their willingness to accept custody of Hambali once he was captured.[1711] On September 25, 2002, the CIA reported that an individual in FBI custody since May 2002, Mohammed Mansour Jabarah, reported that in November 2001, he collected $50,000 from KSM for a Hambali-directed terrorist operation targeting U.S. interests, as well as at least one other $10,000 payment.[1712] On the same day, September 25, 2002, a CIA cable stated that Masran bin Arshad, while in the custody of a foreign government, had detailed his connections to Abu Ahmad al-Kuwaiti and KSM.[1713] According to bin Arshad, after KSM's "Second Wave" plotting was "abandoned" in late 2001, bin Arshad was tasked by KSM to meet with Abu Ahmad al-Kuwaiti in Pakistan and to deliver $50,000 to Hambali for terrorist operations. Bin Arshad stated he was unable to deliver the money.[1714] When the October 12, 2002, terrorist attacks occurred on the Indonesian island of Bali, killing more than 200 individuals, Hambali was immediately suspected of being the "mastermind" of the attacks and was further described as "one of the world's most wanted terrorists."[1715] Open source information in October 2002 identified the funding for the Bali bombings as flowing through Hambali from al-Qa'ida leadership in Pakistan. Through November 2002, news reports highlighted links between senior al-Qa'ida leadership—including KSM—and JI in the context of the Bali bombings. Hambali continued to be identified as a potential mastermind of the bombing and likely residing in Thailand. These same reports identified a Malaysian named "Zubair" as one of three individuals sought by security officials for the Hambali-linked Bali bombings.[1716]

In early January 2003, coverage of a known al-Qa'ida email account uncovered communications between that account and the account of a former Baltimore, Maryland, resident, Majid Khan. The communications indicated that Majid Khan traveled to Bangkok, Thailand, in December 2002 for terrorist support activities and was in contact there with a "Zubair."[1717] By this time, the CIA had significant information—prior to KSM's capture—indicating that a "Zubair" played a central supporting role in the JI, was affiliated with al-Qa'ida figures like KSM, had expertise in ████████ Southeast Asia, and was suspected of playing a role in Hambali's October 12, 2002, Bali bombings.[1718] This information was derived from traditional intelligence collection, open source reporting, and FBI debriefings of Abu Zubaydah (prior to Abu Zubaydah being subjected to the CIA's enhanced interrogation techniques).[1719] On March 4, 2003, the day before Majid Khan's capture, the FBI requested additional information from the CIA on the "Zubair" referenced in Majid Khan's emails.[1720]

On March 6, 2003, the day after Majid Khan was captured in Pakistan, and while being questioned by foreign government interrogators using rapport-building techniques,[1721] Majid Khan described how he traveled to Bangkok in December 2002 and provided $50,000 USD to "Zubair" at the behest of al-Qa'ida. Khan also stated that he updated KSM's nephew, Ammar al-Baluchi, via email about the money exchange. Majid Khan's physical description of Zubair matched previous intelligence reporting already collected on Zubair.[1722] On March 10, 2003, the CIA ██████ requested that information about Majid Khan's travel to Thailand and his delivery of money to "Zubair" be shared with Thai authorities, along with the physical description and a phone number for "Zubair" provided by Majid Khan. CIA ██████ proposed that it inform the Thais that "[w]e are very concerned that the money mentioned may be funding terrorist activities, as well as the individuals in question," and that ████ request the Thai government "provide any details regarding these individuals and phone numbers."[1723]

On March 11, 2003, after being confronted with information that confirmed KSM's financial support to Hambali, KSM admitted to providing Hambali with $50,000 to conduct a terrorist attack "in approximately November 2002." KSM made no reference to Majid Khan or Zubair.[1724] On March 17, 2003, after being confronted with Majid Khan's reporting and a photograph of Majid Khan, KSM confirmed that Majid Khan—whom he stated he knew only as "Yusif"—was involved in the money transfer to Hambali.[1725] KSM denied knowing Zubair—who would be the critical link to Hambali's capture—or any other Hambali representative in Thailand.[1726]

By May 2003, the CIA had learned that a source the CIA had been developing ■■■■■■■■■■, received a call from a phone number associated with Zubair. When the source was contacted by the CIA, he described a Malaysian man ■■■■■■■■■■ ■■■■■■■■■■.[1727] CIA officers suspected this individual was the "Zubair" associated with Hambali and Majid Khan.[1728] ■■■ ■ later, the source alerted the CIA that the person suspected of being Zubair would be ■■■■■■. When Zubair arrived at ■■■ ■■■■■■■■, he was photographed and followed by Thai authorities.[1729] A detainee in foreign government custody confirmed the individual in the surveillance photo was Zubair.[1730] On June 8, 2003, Zubair was detained by the government of Thailand.[1731] While still in Thai custody, Zubair was questioned about his efforts to obtain fraudulent ■■■ documents, as well as his phone contact with ■ ■■■■■■■■■■■■■■■ [Business Q].[1732] Zubair admitted to seeking illegal ■■■ documents on behalf of Hambali, as well as using ■■■■ [Business Q] ■■■■■■.[1733] Signals intelligence had alerted the CIA that a phone number associated with Zubair had been in frequent contact with ■■■■■ [Business Q].[1734] After being transferred to CIA custody and rendered to the CIA's COBALT detention site, Zubair was immediately subjected to the CIA's enhanced interrogation techniques.[1735] Days later, Zubair was asked about his efforts to obtain illegal ■■■ documents for Hambali, at which point he again acknowledged ■■■■■■■■■ [Business Q] ■■■■ ■.[1736] When Thai authorities unilaterally approached a "contact" at ■ ■■■■■ [Business Q], they obtained ■■■■■■■■■■■■■■■ ■■■■■.[1737] An operation targeting ■■■■■■■■■ was developed that focused on surveillance of ■■■■■ [Business Q]. As a result of this surveillance, and the cooperation of ■■■■■, Hambali associate Amer was arrested on August 11, 2003.[1738] Amer was immediately cooperative and assisted in an operation that led to the arrest of Lillie, aka Bashir bin Lap, that same day.[1739] Lillie was found to have a key fob in his possession imprinted with an address of an apartment building in Ayutthaya, Thailand. In response to questioning, "within minutes of capture," Lillie admitted that the address on the key fob was the address where Hambali was located. Fewer than four hours later, an operation successfully led to Hambali's capture at the address found on the key fob.[1740]

On November 28, 2005, the chief of the CTC's Southeast Asia Branch explained how Hambali was captured in an interview with the CIA's Oral History Program, stating:

> "Frankly, we stumbled onto Hambali. We stumbled onto the [the source] ... picking up the phone and calling his case officer to say there's ██████ ██████ [related to Zubair] ... we really stumbled over it. It wasn't police work, it wasn't good targeting, it was we stumbled over it and it yielded up Hambali. What I tell my people is you work really, really hard to be in a position to get lucky."[1741]

Hambali was rendered to CIA custody on August ██, 2003, and almost immediately subjected to the CIA's enhanced interrogation techniques.[1742] On September 4, 2006, he was transferred to U.S. military custody.[1743]

G. CIA Secondary Effectiveness Representations—Less Frequently Cited Disrupted Plots, Captures, and Intelligence that the CIA Has Provided as Evidence for the Effectiveness of the CIA's Enhanced Interrogation Techniques

In addition to the eight most frequently cited "thwarted" plots and terrorists captured, the Committee examined 12 other less frequently cited intelligence successes that the CIA has attributed to the effectiveness of its enhanced interrogation techniques.[1744] These representations are listed below:

Additional Inteligence the CIA Has Attributed to the Effectiveness of the CIA's Enhanced Interrogation Techniques	
1.	The Identification of Khalid Shaykh Mohammad (KSM) as the Mastermind of the September 11, 2001, Attacks
2.	The Identification of KSM's "Mukhtar" Alias
3.	The Capture of Ramzi bin al-Shibh
4.	The Capture of KSM
5.	The Capture of Majid Khan
6.	The Thwarting of the Camp Lemonier Plotting
7.	The Assertion That Enhanced Interrogation Techniques Help Validate Sources
8.	The Identification and Arrests of Uzhair and Saifullah Paracha
9.	Critical Intelligence Alerting the CIA to Jaffar al-Tayyar
10.	The Identification and Arrest of Saleh al-Marri
11.	The Collection of Critical Tactical Intelligence on Shkai, Pakistan
12.	Information on the Facilitator That Led to the UBL Operation

1. The Identification of Khalid Shaykh Mohammad (KSM) as the Mastermind of the September 11, 2001, Attacks

The CIA represented that CIA detainee Abu Zubaydah provided "important" and "vital" information by identifying Khalid Shaykh Mohammed (KSM) as the mastermind behind the attacks of September 11, 2001.[1745] CIA Director Hayden told the Committee on April 12, 2007, that:

> ". . . it was Abu Zubaydah, early in his detention, who identified KSM as the mastermind of 9/11. Until that time, KSM did not even appear in our chart of key al-Qa'ida members and associates."[1746]

On at least two prominent occasions, the CIA represented, inaccurately, that Abu Zubaydah provided this information after the use of the CIA's enhanced interrogation techniques. On May 30, 2005, the Office of Legal Counsel wrote in a now-declassified memorandum:

> "Interrogations of [Abu] Zubaydah—again, once enhanced interrogation techniques were employed—furnished detailed information regarding al Qaeda's 'organization structure, key operatives, and modus operandi' and identified KSM as the mastermind of the September 11 attacks."[1747]

The OLC memorandum cited a document provided by the CIA to support the statement.[1748] The OLC memorandum further stated that the CIA's enhanced interrogation techniques provide the U.S. government with "otherwise unavailable actionable intelligence," that "ordinary interrogation techniques had little effect on . . . Zubaydah," and that the CIA had "reviewed and confirmed the accuracy of [the OLC's] description of the interrogation program, including its purposes, methods, limitations, and results."[1749]

In November 2007, the CIA prepared a set of documents and talking points for the CIA director to use in a briefing with the president on the effectiveness of the CIA's waterboard interrogation technique. The documents prepared assert that Abu Zubaydah identified KSM as the "mastermind" of the September 11, 2001, attacks after the use of the CIA's enhanced interrogation techniques.[1750]

While Abu Zubaydah did provide information on KSM's role in the September 11, 2001, attacks, this information was corroborative of information already in CIA databases and was obtained prior to the use of the CIA's enhanced interrogation techniques. There is no evidence to support the statement that Abu Zubaydah's information—obtained by FBI interrogators prior to the use of the CIA's enhanced interrogation techniques and while Abu Zubaydah was hospitalized—was uniquely important in the identification of KSM as the "mastermind" of the 9/11 attacks.

The following describes information available to the CIA prior to the capture of Abu Zubaydah:

- Both the Congressional Joint Inquiry Into the Intelligence Community Activities Before and After the Terrorist Attacks of September 11, 2001, and the CIA Office of the Inspector General Report on CIA Accountability With Respect to the 9/11 Attacks include lengthy chronologies of the Intelligence Community's interest in KSM prior to the attacks of September 11, 2001. The timelines begin in 1995, when the United States determined that KSM was linked to the 1993 bombing of the World Trade Center, leading to the determination by the National Security Council's Policy Coordination Group that KSM was a top priority target for the United States.[1751] The Congressional Joint Inquiry further noted that information obtained prior to the September 11, 2001, attacks "led the CIA to see KSM as part of Bin Ladin's organization."[1752] There was also CIA reporting in 1998 that KSM was "very close" to UBL.[1753] On June 12, 2001, it was reported that "Khaled" was actively recruiting people to travel outside Afghanistan, including to the United States where colleagues were reportedly already in the country to meet them, to carry out terrorist-related activities for UBL. According to the 9/11 Commission Report, the CIA presumed this "Khaled" was KSM.[1754]
- On September 12, 2001, a foreign government source, described as a member of al-Qa'ida, stated "the 11 September attacks had been masterminded from Kabul by three people," to include "Shaykh Khalid," who was related to Ramzi Yousef.[1755]
- Also on September 12, 2001, a CIA officer familiar with KSM wrote a cable stating that "[o]ne of the individuals who has the capability to organize the kind of strikes we saw in the World Trade Center and the Pentagon is Khalid Shaykh Mohammad."[1756]
- On September 15, 2001, a CIA officer wrote to a number of senior CTC officers, "I would say the percentages are pretty high that Khalid Sheikh Mohammad is involved [in the September 11, 2001, attacks]."[1757]
- On October 16, 2001, an email from a CTC officer who had been tracking KSM since 1997, stated that although more proof was needed, "I believe KSM may have been the mastermind behind the 9-11 attacks.[1758]
- A foreign government informed the CIA that in late December 2001, ■ ■ source, ■, provided information on the attacks of September, 11, 2001, and stated, "Khalid Shayk Muhammad, the maternal uncle of Ramzi [Yousef] . . . was the person who supervised the 'final touches' of the operation."[1759]
- Other reporting prior to the capture of Abu Zubaydah stated that KSM was: "one of the individuals considered the potential mastermind";[1760] "one of the top candidates for having been involved in the planning for the 11 September attacks" and one of "the masterminds";[1761] and "one

of the leading candidates to have been a hands-on planner in the 9/11 attacks."[1762]

2. *The Identification of KSM's "Mukhtar" Alias*

The CIA represented that CIA detainee Abu Zubaydah provided "important" and "vital" information by identifying Khalid Shaykh Mohammed's (KSM) alias, "Mukhtar."[1763] In at least one instance in November 2007, in a set of documents and talking points for the CIA director to use in a briefing with the president on the effectiveness of the CIA's waterboard interrogation technique, the CIA asserted that Abu Zubaydah identified KSM as "Mukhtar" after the use of the CIA's enhanced interrogation techniques.[1764]

While Abu Zubaydah did provide information on KSM's alias, this information was provided by Abu Zubaydah to FBI interrogators prior to the initiation of the CIA's enhanced interrogation techniques—and while Abu Zubaydah was still in the intensive care unit of a ██████ hospital recovering from a gunshot wound incurred during his capture. Further, the information was corroborative of information already in CIA databases.[1765] Prior to the information provided by Abu Zubaydah, the CIA had intelligence, including a cable from August 28, 2001, indicating that KSM was now being called "Mukhtar."[1766]

3. *The Capture of Ramzi bin al-Shibh*

The CIA has represented that information acquired from CIA detainee Abu Zubaydah, as a result of the CIA's enhanced interrogation techniques, led to the capture of Ramzi bin al-Shibh. This CIA representation was included in President Bush's September 6, 2006, speech on the CIA's Detention and Interrogation Program. The speech, which was based on CIA information and vetted by the CIA, stated that the intelligence provided by CIA detainees "cannot be found any other place," and that the nation's "security depends on getting this kind of information."[1767] The speech included the following:

> "Zubaydah *was questioned using these procedures* [the CIA's enhanced interrogation techniques], and soon he began to provide information on key al-Qa'ida operatives, including information that helped us find and capture more of those responsible for the attacks on September the 11th.[1768] For example, Zubaydah *identified* one of KSM's accomplices in the 9/11 attacks, a terrorist named Ramzi bin al-Shibh. *The information Zubaydah provided helped lead to the capture of bin al-Shibh.* And together these two terrorists provided information that helped in the

> planning and execution of the operation that captured Khalid Sheikh Mohammed."[1769]

While the speech provided no additional detail on the capture of bin al-Shibh, an internal email among senior CIA personnel provided additional background for why the CIA included "the capture of Ramzi bin ai-Shibh" in the president's speech as an example of the effectiveness of the CIA's enhanced interrogation techniques. After the speech, the chief of the ████ Department in CTC, ██████, sent an email to the chief of CTC, ██████, ██████ CTC Legal, ██████, and two officers in the CIA Office of Public Affairs, among others. The email addressed press speculation that the intelligence successes attributed to CIA detainees and the CIA's enhanced interrogation techniques in the president's speech were not accurate. Defending the accuracy of the speech, the chief of the ██████ Department in CTC wrote: "The NY Times has posted a story predictably poking holes in the President's speech." Regarding the CIA assertion that Abu Zubaydah provided information after the use of the CIA's enhanced interrogation techniques that led to the capture of Ramzi bin al-Shibh, the chief explained:

> ". . . we knew Ramzi bin al-Shibh was involved in 9/11 before AZ was captured; however, AZ gave us information on his recent activities that—when added into other information—helped us track him. Again, on this point, we were very careful and the speech is accurate in what it says about bin al-Shibh."[1770]

In addition, on February 17, 2007, the deputy chief of the ████ Department in CTC, ██████ testified to the Senate Select Committee on Intelligence that Abu Zubaydah "led us to Ramzi bin al-Shibh, who in kind of [*sic*] started the chain of events" that led to the capture of KSM.[1771]

A review of CIA records found no connection between Abu Zubaydah's reporting on Ramzi bin al-Shibh and Ramzi bin al-Shibh's capture. CIA records indicate that Ramzi was captured unexpectedly—on September 11, 2002, when Pakistani authorities, ████ ████, were conducting raids targeting Hassan Ghul in Pakistan.[1772]

While CIA records indicate that Abu Zubaydah provided information on Ramzi bin al-Shibh, there is no indication in CIA records that Abu Zubaydah provided information on bin al-Shibh's whereabouts. Further, while Abu Zubaydah provided information on bin al-Shibh while being subjected to the CIA's enhanced interrogation techniques, he provided similar information to FBI special agents prior to the initiation of the CIA's enhanced interrogation techniques.[1773] Prior to the application of the CIA's enhanced interrogation techniques, during interrogation sessions on May 19, 2003, and May 20, 2003, Abu Zubaydah reviewed photographs of individuals known by his interrogators to be associated with the bombing of the *USS Cole*, as well as the September 11, 2001, attacks. Abu Zubaydah identified a picture of Ramzi bin al-Shibh as "al-Shiba" and "noted that he is always with" KSM.[1774] Another record of this interrogation stated that showing Abu Zubaydah the photos:

> "was done to gauge his willingness to cooperate and provide details about people, the last times he saw them, where they were going, etc. He appeared to be very cooperative, provided details on people that we expected him to know, the collective groups when they departed Afghanistan, where he thinks they may now be, etc."[1775]

Shortly thereafter, on June 2, 2002, an FBI special agent showed Abu Zubaydah the FBI "PENTTBOM photobook"[1776] which contained photographs numbered 1–35. A cable states that Abu Zubaydah was volunteering information and was "forthcoming and respond[ing] directly to questioning." Abu Zubaydah, who was not asked any "preparatory questions regarding these photographs," identified photograph #31, known to the interrogators as Ramzi bin al-Shibh, as a man he knew as al-Shiba, and stated al-Shiba was with KSM in Qandahar circa December 2001. Abu Zubaydah stated that al-Shiba spoke Arabic like a Yemeni and noted that al-Shiba was in the media after the September 11, 2001, attacks.[1777]

In early June 2002, Abu Zubaydah's interrogators recommended that Abu Zubaydah spend several weeks in isolation while the interrogation team members traveled ████ "as a means of keeping [Abu Zubaydah] off-balance and to allow the team needed time off for a break and to attend to personal matters ██████," as well as to discuss "the endgame" of Abu Zubaydah ██████ with officers from CIA Headquarters.[1778] As a result, on June 18, 2002, Abu Zubaydah was placed in isolation.[1779] Abu Zubaydah spent the remainder of June 2002 and all of July 2002, 47 days in total, in solitary detention without being asked any questions. During this period, Abu Zubaydah's interrogators ██████████. The FBI special agents never returned to the detention site.[1780]

When CIA officers next interrogated Abu Zubaydah, on August 4, 2002, they immediately used the CIA's enhanced interrogation techniques on Abu Zubaydah, including the waterboard.[1781] On August 21, 2002, while Abu Zubaydah was still being subjected to the CIA's enhanced interrogation techniques, a CIA cable noted that Abu Zubaydah was shown several photographs and "immediately recognized the photograph of Ramzi bin al-Shibh."[1782] Abu Zubaydah described bin al-Shibh as having "very dark, almost African looking" skin and noted that he first met bin al-Shibh after the 9/11 attacks in Kandahar, but added that he "did not have in-depth conversations with him."[1783] A cable stated that, after being shown the photograph of bin al-Shibh, Abu Zubaydah told interrogators that he was told bin al-Shibh stayed at the same safe house that KSM "had established for the pilots and others destined to be involved in the 9/11 attacks."[1784] An accompanying intelligence cable stated that Abu Zubaydah informed interrogators that he did not know—and did not ask—whether bin al-Shibh had been involved in the attacks of September 11, 2001, but did state that he believed that bin al-Shibh was "one of the operatives working for Mukhtar aka Khalid Shaykh Mohammad."[1785]

The information Abu Zubaydah provided while being subjected to the CIA's enhanced interrogation techniques was described by CIA interrogators as "significant new details."[1786] However, the information provided by Abu Zubaydah was similar to information Abu Zubaydah provided prior to the application of the CIA's enhanced interrogation techniques, or was otherwise already known to the CIA. CIA records indicate that as early as September 15, 2001, Ramzi bin al-Shibh was identified as an associate of the September 11, 2001, hijackers who attempted to obtain flight training in Florida.[1787] A July 27, 2002, cable from the CIA's ALEC Station provided "background information" on bin al-Shibh and stated that he was "suspected of being the original '20th hijacker,' whose participation in the 11 September attacks was thwarted by his inability to obtain a visa to enter the United States."[1788] Ramzi bin al-Shibh was also identified as "a member of the Hamburg cell that included hijacker Mohammed Atta,"[1789] and bin al-Shibh was featured in one of "five suicide testimonial videos found in December 2001 at the residence of former UBL [Usama bin Ladin] lieutenant Mohammad Atef in Afghanistan."[1790]

None of the above information resulted in Ramzi bin al-Shibh's capture. As detailed below, Ramzi bin al-Shibh was captured unexpectedly during raids in Pakistan on September 11, 2002, targeting Hassan Ghul.[1791]

Prior to Abu Zubaydah's capture, the CIA considered Hassan Ghul a "First Priority Raid Target," based on reporting that:

> "Ghul has been a major support player within the al-Qa'ida network and has assisted al-Qa'ida and Mujahadin operatives by facilitating their travel. He is a senior aide to Abu Zubaydah who was heavily involved in fund raising for a terrorist operation in spring 2001."[1792]

Additional reporting noted that Hassan Ghul's phone number had been linked to a terrorist operative who "was ready to conduct a 'surgical operation' at any time,"[1793] while other reporting indicated that Hassan Ghul was working on a "program" believed to be related to terrorist activity.[1794]

According to CIA cables, once captured, and prior to the initiation of the CIA's enhanced interrogation techniques, Abu Zubaydah confirmed that Hassan Ghul was a high-level al-Qa'ida facilitator who had contact with senior al-Qa'ida members, including Hamza Rabi'a and Abu Musab al-Zarqawi.[1795] Abu Zubaydah also corroborated intelligence in CIA databases that Ghul was involved in al-Qa'ida fundraising efforts.[1796] During this same period, the CIA continued to receive additional intelligence on Ghul from foreign governments, including that Ghul was responsible for facilitating the movement of Saudi fighters through Pakistan.[1797] As noted, on June 18, 2002, Abu Zubaydah was placed in isolation and was not asked any questions for 47 days.[1798]

In early July 2002, Pakistani authorities and the CIA were continuing their efforts to locate and capture Hassan Ghul. A detainee in Pakistani custody, ■■■■■■■■, ■■■■■■■■■■■■■■■■, was providing detailed information to Pakistani authorities on Hassan Ghul.[1799] ■■■■■ [the detainee in Pakistani custody] had been arrested with ■■■■■■■ in ■■■■■■■■, on May ■■, 2002, during ■■ ■■■■■■■ government raids on multiple residences thought to be associated with al-Qa'ida.[1800] During interviews with Pakistani authorities concerning how to locate and capture Hassan Ghul, ■■■■ ■■■■■■ [the detainee in Pakistani custody] identified ■■■■■■■ [a well-known associate of Hassan Ghul] and the location of the ■■■■ ■■■■ [well-known associate's] home.[1801]

On July ■, 2002, seeking to capture Hassan Ghul, Pakistani authorities ■■■■■■■ raided the home of ■■■■■■■■■■■■■■■■ ■■■ [the well-known associate of Hassan Ghul]. When the raid occurred, present at the home was ■■■■■■■■■■■■■ [the well-known associate], ■■■■■■■■■■■■■■■■■■■■ [and family members of the well-known associate]. A ■■■■■■■ providing details on the raid states that "■■■■■ [the well-known associate] was interviewed on the spot and was fully cooperative with [Pakistani authorities]." ■■ ■■■■■■■■ [the well-known associate] stated that he had not seen

Hassan Ghul or ████████ since June 3, 2002, but that he believed they were still in Karachi. According to ████ [the well-known associate], he had already informed Pakistani authorities that Hassan Ghul was an al-Qa'ida member. According to a cable ██ ██████ [the well-known associate] stated that, as a result of his reporting on Ghul to Pakistani officials, he received "a death threat from Hassan Ghul," causing Ghul to "cease coming to the ██ ████ [the well-known associate's] house."[1802]

CIA records indicate that Pakistani authorities continued to interview the ████ [the well-known associate] in an effort to acquire information and capture Hassan Ghul. A CIA cable dated July █, 2002, states that the Pakistani government "is keying on any information which could get ██ closer to bagging [Hassan] Ghul," specifically "through ongoing interviews of ████████ ███ [the well-known associate of Hassan Ghul]." According to the cable, during one of the interviews, ████ [the well-known associate] told Pakistani authorities about an address where Hassan Ghul used to reside circa December 2001. ████ [the well-known associate] sent ███ with the Pakistani officers to identify the home.[1803] The CIA officers wrote that the location "is extremely close to (if not an exact match)" to a location where KSM once resided, according to a June 18, 2002, report from the FBI.[1804] The identified home was raided, but found empty. The CIA wrote "██ are hitting the right places [safe houses], albeit at the wrong time. Our efforts have got us closer than even to at least Hassan Ghul."[1805] During the meetings between the Pakistani authorities and ████ [the well-known associate], ████ [the well-known associate] provided the Pakistani authorities with a copy of a ████ "reportedly belonging to Hassan Ghul" ██████████." In the same cable, the CIA reported that ████ [the well-known associate] had "approached the police for assistance in retrieving █████," who was █████ [a specific family member of the well known associate].[1806]

On July █, 2002, CTC officers at CIA Headquarters wrote that they were reading the cables from the CIA █████, noting they were "particularly interested in the in the interview of raid target ██ ████ [the well-known associate of Hassan Ghul], who admitted ████████ to his knowledge of Ghul's involvement in al-Qa'ida activities." The cable stated:

> "[r]ecognize that ████ [the well-known associate] claims his contact with Ghul stopped approximately one month ago, when he reported

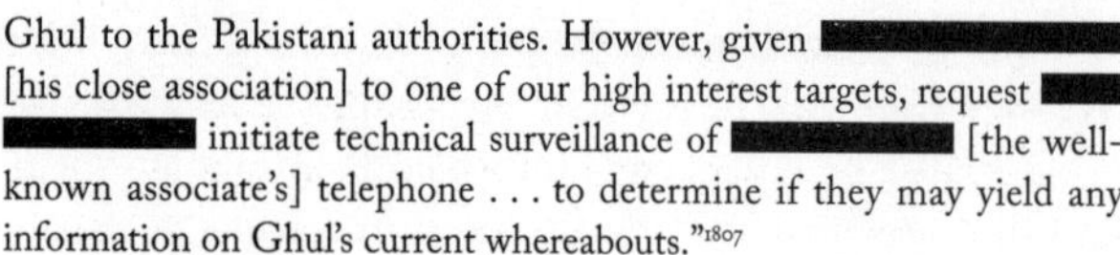
Ghul to the Pakistani authorities. However, given ■■■■■■ [his close association] to one of our high interest targets, request ■■■ ■■■■■ initiate technical surveillance of ■■■■■■ [the well-known associate's] telephone . . . to determine if they may yield any information on Ghul's current whereabouts."[1807]

CIA records do not indicate if "technical surveillance" of ■■■ ■■■ [the well-known associate's] telephone was conducted.[1808]

According to CIA records, once captured, and prior to the initiation of the CIA's enhanced interrogation techniques, Abu Zubaydah confirmed that Hassan Ghul was a high-level al-Qa'ida facilitator who had contact with senior al-Qa'ida members, including Hamza Rabi'a and Abu Musab al-Zarqawi. Abu Zubaydah also corroborated intelligence in CIA databases that Ghul was involved in al-Qa'ida fundraising efforts.[1809] As noted, on June 18, 2002, Abu Zubaydah was placed in isolation and therefore was not questioned on the July 2002 raids on ■■■■■■■■ [the well known associate's] home or the information acquired from the interviews of ■■■■■ [the well-known associate] conducted by Pakistani authorities.[1810] On August 4, 2002, after Abu Zubaydah spent 47 days in isolation, CIA interrogators entered his cell and immediately began subjecting Abu Zubaydah to the CIA's enhanced interrogation techniques, including the waterboard.[1811] As he had before the use of the CIA's enhanced interrogation techniques, when asked questions, Abu Zubaydah continued to provide intelligence, including on Hassan Ghul. On August 20, 2002—while still being subjected to the CIA's enhanced interrogation techniques—Abu Zubaydah was asked specifically how he would find Hassan Ghul. There are no records indicating that Abu Zubaydah had previously been asked this question. In response, Abu Zubaydah provided corroborative reporting: that Hassan Ghul could possibly be located through ■■■■■ [the well-known associate of Hassan Ghul].[1812] There are no CIA records indicating that Abu Zubaydah provided information on the location of ■■■■■ [the well-known associate's] home, which, as noted, had been raided weeks earlier, on July ■, 2002, and was already known to the CIA and Pakistani authorities.[1813]

Nine days after Abu Zubaydah referenced ■■■■■■ [the well-known associate of Hassan Ghul], on August 29, 2002, CIA Headquarters asked ■■■■■ to request that Pakistani authorities "reinterview ■■■■ [the well-known associate] for additional intelligence on Hassan Ghul."[1814] The next day, August 30, 2002, ■■ ■■■ informed CIA Headquarters that Pakistani authorities were "in contact with the ■■■■ [the well-known associate]," but that ■

███ would nonetheless ask the Pakistani authorities to question ███ [the well-known associate] again about Hassan Ghul's location.[1815] On August 31, 2002, ███ relayed that Pakistani authorities and ███ believed it was possible that ███ [the well-known associate] was not being fully truthful in his interviews with Pakistani authorities.[1816] On September 3, 2002, ███ reported that Pakistani authorities had re-interviewed ███ [the well-known associate] an unknown number of times, and that the Pakistani authorities noted that at times ███ [the well-known associate] contradicted himself.[1817] Approximately one week later, on September 9, 2002, Pakistani authorities returned again to ███ [the well-known associate's] home and interviewed ███ [a specific family member of the well-known associate], who had recently returned to ███ [the well-known associate's home].[1818]

In interviews with Pakistani authorities, ███ [the specific family member of the well-known associate] was cooperative and told the Pakistani authorities where Hassan Ghul's last apartment was located.[1819] Based on the information provided on Ghul's apartment, Pakistani authorities conducted a raid, but found the apartment empty.[1820]

Pakistani authorities then located and interviewed ███ [a third individual at the apartment complex]. From the interview [of the third individual], Pakistani authorities learned that while Hassan Ghul had vacated the apartment, he was scheduled to return to the complex ███. Based on this information, Pakistani authorities placed the complex under surveillance and waited for Hassan Ghul to return.[1821] On September 10, 2002, Pakistani authorities arrested two individuals believed to be Hassan Ghul and his driver outside of the apartment complex.[1822] A CIA cable noted that "Ghul had returned to the apartment to ███, however, he got more than he bargained for."[1823] Another CIA cable stated:

> "Interestingly, he denies being Hassan Ghul—claiming Hassan Ghul is someone else. While ███ are fairly certain we do in fact have Hassan Ghul in custody, we would like to make every effort to verify."[1824]

By September 11, 2002, it was determined that an individual named Muhammad Ahmad Ghulam Rabbani, aka Abu Badr, and his driver were arrested, not Hassan Ghul.[1825] Abu Badr's driver, Muhammad Madni, was immediately cooperative and told the arresting officers that Abu Badr was a "major al-Qa'ida [facilitator]." He then proceeded to provide Pakistani authorities with information about al-Qa'ida-affiliated residences and safe houses in Karachi.[1826]

Based on the information provided by Muhammad Madni, Pakistani authorities ■■■■■■■■ conducted ■■■■■■■■ raids in Karachi over the next two days.[1827] Raids of the initial sites resulted in the recovery of "a number of modified electrical switch type mechanisms, modified circuit and 'game' boards and other miscellaneous wires with alligator clips and battery attachments."[1828] On September 11, 2002, additional raids resulted in the arrest of 11 individuals, including Ramzi bin al-Shibh.[1829] According to CIA records, bin al-Shibh initially identified himself as 'Umar Muhammad 'Abdullah ba-'Amr, aka "Abu 'Ubyadah," but the CIA noted:

> "This individual strongly resembled pictures of Ramzi bin al-Shibh. When asked if he was videotaped in al-Qa'ida videos, he answered yes."[1830]

Shortly thereafter the CIA confirmed Ramzi bin al-Shibh was the individual in Pakistani custody.[1831]

Hassan Ghul was ultimately captured by foreign authorities in the Iraqi Kurdistan Region, on January ■, 2004.[1832] Hassan Ghul's capture was unrelated to any reporting from the CIA's Detention and Interrogation Program.[1833]

4. The Capture of Khalid Shaykh Mohammad (KSM)

On September 6, 2006, President Bush delivered a speech based on information provided by the CIA, and vetted by the CIA, that included the following statement:

> "Zubaydah *was questioned using these procedures* [the CIA's enhanced interrogation techniques], and soon he began to provide information on key al-Qa'ida operatives, including information that helped us find and capture more of those responsible for the attacks on September the 11th. For example, Zubaydah identified one of KSM's accomplices in the 9/11 attacks, a terrorist named Ramzi bin al-Shibh. The information Zubaydah provided helped lead to the capture of bin al-Shibh. *And together these two terrorists provided information that helped in the planning and execution of the operation that captured Khalid Sheikh Mohammed.*"[1834]

Contrary to CIA representations, there are no CIA records to support the assertion that Abu Zubaydah, Ramzi bin al-Shibh, or any other CIA detainee played any role in the "the planning and execution of the operation that captured Khalid Sheikh Mohammed." CIA records clearly describe how the capture of KSM was attributable to a unilateral CIA asset ("ASSET X"[1835]) who gained access to KSM through ████████, with whom the CIA asset had prior independent connections. ASSET X's possible access to KSM through ████████ was apparent to the CIA as early as the fall of 2001, prior to his formal recruitment. The CIA had multiple opportunities to exploit ASSET X's access to KSM's ████████ in 2001, and in 2002, after he was recruited, but did not. In February–March 2003, ASSET X led the CIA directly to KSM. The contemporaneous documentary record of this narrative is supported by numerous after-action interviews conducted by the CIA's Oral History Program. As the CIA officer who "handled" ASSET X and who was directly involved in the capture of KSM stated, "[t]he op[eration] was a HUMINT op pretty much from start to finish."[1836]

Within days after the attacks of September 11, 2001, CTC officers suspected KSM of playing a key role in the September 11, 2001, terrorist attacks.[1837] Shortly thereafter, CTC officers also noted the "striking similarities" between the September 11, 2001, attacks, and the 1993 World Trade Center bombing by KSM's nephew, Ramzi Yousef, ████████.[1838] On September 26, 2001, the CIA's ALEC Station issued a cable on KSM and Ramzi Yousef that described extensive derogatory information on ████████.[1839] The CIA officer who drafted the September 26, 2001, cable wrote an email that ████████ were "associated with terrorists," and that ████████ "probably is a close associate of KSM."[1840] In a separate email, the CIA officer wrote that, "at a minimum, we should go after" ████████. Both emails were sent to CIA officers who, a few days later, would consider ████████ ASSET X, a potential CIA source whose access to KSM through ████████ was readily apparent.[1841]

ASSET X came to the CIA's attention in the spring of 2001 ████████. However, CIA officers did not meet with ASSET X until after the September 11, 2001, attacks.[1842] On September 28, 2001, ALEC Station sent a cable ████████, noting that "[g]iven the events of 11 September . . . [w]e are very interested in exploring whatever information [ASSET X] may have with regard to terrorist plans by [UBL]."[1843] The CIA held its first meeting with ASSET X on ████████, 2001, at which time ASSET X indicated that he knew ████████.[1844] The cable describing the first meeting states that "[ASSET X's] knowledge ████████ appears to check out and demonstrates some degree of access/knowledge ████."[1845] On ████, 2001, the cable describing the first meeting with ASSET X was forwarded by the drafter of the September 26, 2001, cable on the derogatory information concerning ████ to a number of CTC officers in an email with the subject line: "Re: [ASSET X] Information Re ████."[1846] The following day, the cable was forwarded again to CTC officers with the subject line: "Access to Khalid Shaykh Muhammad."[1847]

On ████, 2001, ASSET X held his second meeting with CIA officers, who described ASSET X as "very willing to clandestinely assist the USG as directed."[1848] At the same meeting, ASSET X identified a photograph ████.[1849] On ████ ████, 2001, CIA Headquarters wrote that the CIA would be "keenly interested" if ASSET X "can dig into the [KSM] ████ ████."[1850]

In ████ 2001, ASSET X proposed multiple times to the CIA that CIA that he use his contacts to locate KSM through ████ ████—the same approach that would lead the CIA to KSM more than 15 months later.[1851] ASSET X also argued for "a more aggressive and proactive approach ████," but was eventually convinced by CIA officers to ████ ████, instead.[1852] After ALEC Station rejected the CIA case officer's recommended financial compensation for ASSET X, ASSET X declined to work with the CIA as a CIA source.[1853] Over the next nine months, the CIA continued to believe that ASSET X had the potential to develop information on KSM and his location, and sought, but was unable to reestablish contact with ASSET X.[1854] During this time, the CIA continued to collect intelligence on KSM's ████ ████,[1855] and sought other opportunities to gain access to KSM through ████.[1856] In July 2002, a detainee in foreign government custody provided extensive information on KSM's ████ and confirmed that KSM was "very close" to ████ who "should know how to contact KSM."[1857]

When the CIA finally located and met again with ASSET X on ████, 2002, ASSET X stated that "he could ████ ████ within a few weeks," and was "willing to travel ████ ████ to locate ████."[1858] ASSET X was recruited as a source by the CIA, but, despite his offer to track KSM's ████ ████, ASSET X was dispatched by the CIA to ████ ████ ████

[redacted].[1859] [redacted]
[redacted].[1860]

By the time ASSET X returned to [redacted] 2002,[1861] his previous CIA case officer "handler" there had departed for another CIA assignment [redacted]. ASSET X was thus handled by a new CIA officer who was unfamiliar with ASSET X's potential utility in tracking KSM.[1862] Seeking guidance on how to proceed with ASSET X, the new CIA case officer sent several cables to CIA Headquarters, which he later described as disappearing into a "black hole." According to an interview of a CIA officer involved in the operation, the cables were being sent to a special compartment at CIA Headquarters which had been previously used by the team [redacted] [redacted]. With the dispersal of that CIA team, however, the compartment was idle and no one at CIA Headquarters was receiving and reading the cables being sent to the special compartment.[1863] When the CIA case officer received no response to the cables he was sending to CIA Headquarters, he made preparations to terminate the CIA's relationship with ASSET X. According to interviews, in [redacted] [redacted] 2002, the CIA officer [redacted] and was on his way to meet ASSET X to terminate the asset's relationship with the CIA. By chance, a CIA officer who had previously handled ASSET X [redacted] was visiting [redacted]. This visiting CIA officer overheard the discussion between the chief of Base and the CIA case officer concerning the CIA's termination of ASSET X as a CIA source. The discussion included names that ASSET X had been discussing with the case officer [redacted]—names that the visiting officer recognized [redacted]. The visiting CIA officer interceded and recommended that the CIA Base delay the termination of ASSET X as a CIA source.[1864] At the next meeting ASSET X again demonstrated that he had direct access to KSM's [redacted] [redacted].[1865] As a result, the CIA decided not to terminate ASSET X's work as a CIA source.[1866]

Shortly thereafter, in [redacted] 2003, ASSET X traveled on his own volition, and without prior discussion with the CIA, to [redacted] [redacted], and [redacted] a face-to-face meeting with KSM. When ASSET X later informed CIA officers about his trip, [redacted] direct access to KSM [redacted]
[redacted]
[redacted]

.[1868]

.[1869]
The internal debate within the CIA continued, however, with the , and ASSET X and his CIA handlers urging the CIA to delay action and wait for an opportunity for ASSET X to locate KSM.[1870] ALEC Station initially supported immediate action to capture any KSM associate ASSET X could lead them to, before reversing its position on February , 2003.[1871] The next day, ASSET X arrived in Islamabad . , where he was surprised to find KSM. , ASSET X sent a text message to his CIA handler stating: "I M W KSM."[1872]

.[1873] .[1874] , ASSET X contacted the CIA and conveyed what had just occurred.[1875]

.[1876] In an interview with the CIA's Oral History Program, the CIA case officer described what had happened:

> "We went around, you know, . [ASSET X] turns around to me and says, look I don't know, I guess I'm nervous, . I said, 'Look brother there are twenty five million frigging reasons why you need to find .' That's what the reward was. He looks at me and says, 'I understand. I understand.'"[1877]

Shortly thereafter, ASSET X found and, in the early morning hours of March 1, 2003, Pakistani authorities conducted a raid and captured KSM.[1878] On March , 2003, KSM was rendered to CIA custody.[1879]

5. *The Capture of Majid Khan*

The CIA represented that intelligence derived from the use of the

CIA's enhanced interrogation techniques against CIA detainee KSM led to the capture of Majid Khan. These representations were inaccurate.

In multiple interviews with the CIA Office of Inspector General, CIA officers stated that "information from KSM led to the capture of [Majid] Kahn [*sic*]," and that "KSM gave us Majid Khan."[1880] The deputy chief of ALEC Station and former KSM debriefer ■■ ■■■■ represented that KSM "provided information that helped lead to the arrest of . . . Majid Khan, an operative who could get into the U.S. easily."[1881] The draft OIG Special Review repeated the representations of ■■■■ and others, stating that KSM "provided information that helped lead to the arrests of terrorists including . . . Majid Khan, an operative who could enter the United States easily and was tasked to research attacks against U.S. water reservoirs."[1882] On February 27, 2004, DDO James Pavitt submitted the CIA's formal response to the draft Inspector General Special Review. Pavitt's submission represented that Majid Khan was in custody "because of the information we were able lawfully to obtain from KSM."[1883] The final, and now declassified, CIA Inspector General Special Review states that KSM "provided information that helped lead to the arrests of terrorists including . . . Majid Khan, an operative who could enter the United States easily and was tasked to research attacks . . . ."[1884] In its analysis of the legality of the CIA's enhanced interrogation techniques, the OLC relied on passages of the Inspector General's Special Review that included this inaccurate representation.[1885]

On July 29, 2003, CIA leadership met with select members of the National Security Council to obtain reaffirmation of the CIA interrogation program. The CIA stated that "detainees subject[ed] to the use of Enhanced Techniques of one kind or another had produced significant intelligence information that had, in the view of CIA professionals, saved lives."[1886] Briefing slides provided by the CIA stated that "major threat" information was acquired, providing the "Identification of . . . the Majid Khan Family" by KSM as an example.[1887] The same slides were used, at least in part, for subsequent briefings.[1888] On September 16, 2003, a briefing was conducted for Secretary of State Colin Powell and Secretary of Defense Donald Rumsfeld, the content of which was described as "virtually identical" to the July 29, 2003, briefing.[1889] The slides were also used in an October 7, 2003, briefing for Assistant Attorney General Jack Goldsmith.[1890]

CIA records indicate that Majid Khan was identified and located prior to any reporting from KSM, There is no indication in CIA records that reporting from KSM—or any other CIA detainee—played any role in the identification and capture of Majid Khan.[1891]

On January 10, 2003, the FBI's Baltimore Field Office opened a full field international terrorism investigation on the email account "BobDesi(@)hotmail.com." According to FBI investigative records, the investigation was "predicated upon information received through the Central Intelligence Agency (CIA) concerning" a known al-Qa'ida email account that was already "under FTSA coverage ▬▬."[1892] Six days later, on January 16, 2003, open source research related to the "BobDesi" email account "revealed a personal website for the user, Majid Khan."[1893] In February 2003, ▬▬ was tracking Majid Khan's Internet activity and was confident he was located at his brother's house in Karachi, Pakistan.[1894] On March 4, 2003, ALEC Station noted that activity on an al-Qa'ida email account—associated with Khallad bin Attash—that was in contact with Majid Khan, had been dormant. ALEC Station recommended that ▬▬▬▬▬▬ ▬ move to capture Majid Khan in the hope that Majid Khan could lead CIA officers to Khallad bin Attash.[1895] The following morning, March 5, 2003, officers from Pakistan ▬▬▬ carried out a raid on Majid Khan's brother's house, detaining Majid Khan.[1896]

On March 15, 2003, Deputy Chief of ALEC Station ▬▬ ▬▬ sent an email to CIA Headquarters noting that she had read the reporting from Majid Khan's foreign government interrogations and was requesting photographs of Majid Khan and his associates to use in the KSM interrogations.[1897] CIA Headquarters provided the photographs the same day.[1898] On March 17, 2003, KSM was shown the photograph of Majid Khan and discussed the person he stated he knew as "Yusif," for the first time.[1899]

6. The Thwarting of the Camp Lemonier Plotting

The CIA represented that intelligence derived from the use of the CIA's enhanced interrogation techniques thwarted plotting against the U.S. military base. Camp Lemonier, in Djibouti. These representations were inaccurate.

In the September 6, 2006, speech, acknowledging the CIA's Detention and Interrogation Program, which was based on CIA-provided information and vetted by the CIA, President George W. Bush stated:

> "This is intelligence that cannot be found any other place. And our

security depends on getting this kind of information."

The speech continued:

> "These are some of the plots that have been stopped because of information from this vital program. Terrorists held in CIA custody have also provided information that helped stop the planned strike on U.S. Marines at Camp Lemonier in Djibouti."[1900]

An Office of the Director of National Intelligence public release accompanying the September 6, 2006, speech, states that "the CIA designed a new interrogation program that would be safe, effective, and legal." The document asserts: "In early 2004, *shortly after his capture*, al-Qa'ida facilitator Gouled Hassan Dourad *revealed* that in mid-2003 al-Qa'ida East Africa cell leader Abu Talha al-Sudani sent him from Mogadishu to Djibouti to case the US Marine base Camp Lemonier, as part of a plot to send suicide bombers with a truck bomb."[1901]

Similarly, in a prepared briefing for the chairman of the House Defense Appropriations Subcommittee, John Murtha, on October 30, 2007, the CIA represented that the CIA could not conduct its detention operations at Guantanamo Bay, Cuba, because "interrogations conducted on US military installations must comply with the Army Field Manual." The CIA presentation stated that the CIA program was "critical to [the CIA's] ability to protect the American homeland and US forces and citizens abroad from terrorist attack," that "[m]ost, if not all, of the intelligence acquired from high-value detainees in this [CIA] program would Likely not have been discovered or reported in any other way," that the CIA program "is in no way comparable to the detainee programs run by our military," and that the CIA used information derived from the program "to disrupt terrorist plots—**including against our military**."[1902] The CIA presentation then stated:

> "[A CIA detainee] informed us[1903] of an operation underway to attack the U.S. military at Camp Lemonier in Djibouti. We believe our understanding of this plot helped us to prevent the attack."[1904]

A review of CIA records found that: (1) the detainee to whom the CIA's representations refer—Guleed (variant, Gouled) Hassan Dourad—was not subjected to the CIA's enhanced interrogation techniques; (2) the CIA was aware of and reported on the terrorist threat to Camp Lemonier prior to receiving any information from CIA detainees;[1905] (3) Guleed provided corroborative reporting on the threat prior to being transferred to CIA custody; and (4) contrary to CIA representations, the plotting did not "stop" because of information acquired from CIA detainee Guleed in 2004, but rather, continued well into 2007.[1906]

On March 4, 2004, Guleed was captured in Djibouti based on information obtained from a foreign government and a CIA source.[1907] Prior to entering CIA custody, Guleed was confronted with information acquired from signals intelligence, and he confirmed that he cased Camp Lemonier for a potential terrorist attack.[1908] CIA sought to render Guleed to CIA custody in order to question Guleed about senior al-Qa'ida East Africa members Abu Talha al-Sudani and Saleh ali Saleh Nabhan. A CIA cable states:

> "Guleed represents the closest we have come to an individual with first hand, face-to-face knowledge of Abu Talha [al-Sudani] and Nabhan, and our hope is that Guleed will provide key intelligence necessary for the capture of these senior al-Qa'ida members."[1909]

Prior to Guleed's rendition to CIA custody, he provided detailed information on his casing of Camp Lemonier to CIA officers.[1910] On March ■, 2004, Guleed was rendered to CIA custody.[1911] There are no records to indicate that Guleed was subjected to the CIA's enhanced interrogation techniques, nor are there any CIA records to indicate that Guleed provided the information that was the basis for his rendition to CIA custody—information leading to the capture of Abu Talha al-Sudani or Saleh ali Saleh Nabhan.

While in CIA custody, Guleed continued to provide information on his targeting of Camp Lemonier. Guleed stated that Abu Talha al-Sudani had not yet picked the operatives for the attack against Camp Lemonier,[1912] that the attack was "on hold while they raised the necessary funds via the bank robbery operation,"[1913] and that "he [Guleed] was not informed of the operational plan."[1914]

Neither the detention of Guleed, nor the information he provided, thwarted terrorist plotting against Camp Lemonier; and CIA records indicate that attack planning against Camp Lemonier continued well after Guleed's capture in March 2004, to include a time period beyond the president's September 6, 2006, speech. In March 2005, the CIA sought approval to render an associate of Guleed whom the CIA stated was "planning terrorist attacks on U.S. targets in East Africa, particularly against Camp Lemonier in Djibouti."[1915] In October 2005, a cable stated, "a body of reporting indicates that East Africa al-Qa'ida network operatives are currently planning attacks on U.S. interests in the region, particularly . . . the U.S. military base Camp Lemonier in Djibouti."[1916] In April 2007, the continued terrorist threat reporting against Camp Lemonier resulted in a request for the Camp to further "alter their security practices."[1917]

In October 2007, in light of the ongoing threat reporting related to Camp Lemonier, CIA officer ■■■■■ attempted to explain the CIA-validated statement in the president's September 6, 2006, speech that "[t]errorists held in CIA custody "helped stop the planned strike on U.S. Marines at Camp Lemonier in Djibouti."[1918] ■■■■, who was involved in vetting of the speech, wrote to a CIA colleague tracking the ongoing threats to Camp Lemonier that:

> "The reasoning behind [the CIA] validation of the language in the speech—and remember, we can argue about whether or not 'planning' consistitutes [*sic*] a 'plot' and about whether anything is ever disrupted—was that the detainee reporting increased our awareness of attack plotting against the base, leading to heightened security."[1919]

A review of CIA records, however, found no indication that CIA detainee reporting from Guleed, or any other CIA detainee, alerted the CIA or the U.S. military to increased terrorist targeting of Camp Lemonier. To the contrary, CIA records indicate that the CIA was in possession of substantial threat reporting demonstrating that Camp Lemonier in Djibouti was being targeted by al-Qa'ida and al-Qa'ida affiliated extremists prior to the detention of Guleed on March 4, 2004.[1920] For example, on January 28, 2003, a foreign government report disseminated by the CIA stated that al-Qa'ida operatives were planning "to ram an explosives-laden truck into a military base, probably Camp Lemonier."[1921] On March 10, 2003, a "Terrorist Advisory" was issued, which stated that "U.S. forces stationed at Camp Lemonier in Djibouti . . . could be targeted."[1922] Similar reporting continued thimgh 2003, and by the end of the year, the CIA had ■ ■ coverage[1923] indicating that Guleed and other identified operatives were being directed by Abu Talha al-Sudani to target Camp Lemonier.[1924] By the end of December 2003, Djiboutian authorities confirmed that Guleed had cased Camp Lemonier and that Guleed appeared to have "formulate[d] a complete targeting package, which included an escape route."[1925] It was this reporting that led ■■■ to capture Guleed on March 4, 2004.[1926]

7. *The Assertion that CIA Detainees Subjected to Enhanced Interrogation Techniques Help Validate CIA Sources*

In addition to CIA claims that information produced during or after the use of CIA's enhanced interrogation techniques led to the disruption of terrorist plots and the capture of specific terrorists, the

CIA also represented that its enhanced interrogation techniques were necessary to validate CIA sources. The claim was based on one CIA detainee—Janat Gul—contradicting the reporting of one CIA asset.

The CIA repeatedly represented to policymakers that information acquired after the use of the CIA's enhanced interrogation techniques helped to "validate" CIA sources. For example, CIA Director Michael Hayden provided testimony to the Committee on April 12, 2007, that:

> "Detainee information is a key tool for validating clandestine sources. In fact, in one case, the detainee's information proved to be the accurate story, and the clandestine source was confronted and subsequently admitted to embellishing or fabricating some or all [of] the details in his report."[1927]

Similarly, in January 2009, the CIA compiled a detailed briefing book for a planned three-hour briefing of the CIA's Detention and Interrogation Program for President-elect Obama's national security staff. Included in the materials was a document that stated, "[k]ey intelligence [was] collected from HVD interrogations *after* applying [the CIA's enhanced] interrogation techniques." After this statement, the CIA provided examples, including that the "most significant reporting" acquired from CIA detainee Janat Gul after applying the CIA's enhanced interrogation techniques was information that helped the CIA "validate a CIA asset."[1928] The document states:

> "Pakistan-based facilitator *Janat Gul's most significant reporting* helped us validate a CIA asset who was providing information about the 2004 pre election threat. The asset claimed that Gul had arranged a meeting between himself and al-Qa'ida's chief of finance, Shaykh Sa'id, a claim that Gul vehemently denied. Gul's reporting was later matched with information obtained from Sharif al-Masri and Abu Talha al-Pakistani, captured after Gul. With this reporting in hand, CIA the asset, who subsequently admitted to fabricating his reporting about the meeting."[1929]

The CIA representation that the CIA's enhanced interrogation techniques produced information that allowed the CIA to identify the reporting of a CIA asset as fabricated lacked critical contextual information. The CIA representations did not describe how the CIA asset's reporting was already doubted by CIA officers prior to the use of the CIA's enhanced interrogation techniques against Gul. Nor did the CIA representations acknowledge that the asset's fabricated reporting was the reason that Janat Gul was subjected to the techniques in the first place. The CIA concluded that Janat Gul was not a high-level al-Qa'ida figure and did not possess threat information, but this conclusion was not included in CIA representations.

In March 2004, the CIA received reporting from a CIA asset, "ASSET Y"[1930] that Janat Gul was planning with senior al-Qa'ida leaders to conduct attacks inside the United States. The attacks were reportedly planned to occur prior to the U.S. elections in November 2004.[1931] ASSET Y, who cited Janat Gul as the source of the information, stated that Gul was going to facilitate a meeting between Abu Faraj al-Libi and ASSET Y in support of the operation.[1932] As noted, CIA officers expressed doubts about ASSET Y's reporting at the time it was received.[1933] A senior CIA officer, ██████, who formerly served as chief of the Bin Ladin Unit, raised questions about the reliability of the asset's reporting on March ██, 2004, stating that the reporting was "vague" and "worthless in terms of actionable intelligence," and that al-Qa'ida "loses nothing" by disclosing the information. He further stated that, given an al-Qa'ida statement emphasizing a lack of desire to strike before the U.S. election, and al-Qa'ida's knowledge that "threat reporting causes panic in Washington" and "leaks soon after it is received," the report "would be an easy way [for al-Qa'ida] to test" ASSET Y.[1934] ALEC Station officer ██████ expressed similar doubts about the source's reporting in response to the email.[1935]

Less than three months later, Janat Gul was captured in ████ █ on June ██, 2004.[1936] On June ██, 2004, CIA's ██████ proposed that Gul be rendered to CIA custody, citing ASSET Y's reporting.[1937] During this period, however, the use of the CIA's enhanced interrogation techniques had been suspended by the CIA director.[1938] On June 29, 2004, a draft memorandum from DCI Tenet to National Security Adviser Rice sought special approval from the National Security Council Principals Committee to use the CIA's enhanced interrogation techniques against Janat Gul to learn more about the threat reporting from ASSET Y.[1939] The memorandum referenced ASSET Y's reporting and stated that if the CIA could use the techniques, "the Agency would be in an optimum position to obtain from Gul critical intelligence necessary to save American lives by disrupting the pre-election plot, locating senior al-Qa'ida leaders still at large, and learning how Usama Bin Laden communicates with his operatives." The memorandum further stated that "[g]iven the magnitude of the danger posed by the pre-election plot, and [Janat] Gul's almost certain knowledge of any intelligence about that plot, I request the fastest possible resolution of the above issues."[1940]

On July 2, 2004, the day that CIA Headquarters approved the rendition of Janat Gul to CIA custody,[1941] the CIA represented to select members of the National Security Council that Janat Gul was one of the "most senior radical Islamic facilitators in Pakistan," and noted that he was "assessed by a key source on [the] pre-election plot to be involved in or [to] have information on the plot."[1942] On July 15, 2004, based on the reporting of ASSET Y, the CIA represented to the chairman and vice chairman of the Committee that Janat Gul was associated with a pre-election plot to conduct an attack in the United States.[1943] On July 20, 2004, select National Security Council principals met again, and according to CIA records, agreed that, "[g]iven the current threat and risk of delay, CIA was authorized and directed to utilize the techniques with Janat Gul as necessary."[1944] On July 22, 2004, Attorney General Ashcroft approved the use of the CIA's enhanced interrogation techniques against Janat Gul based on ASSET Y's reporting.[1945]

Janat Gul was rendered to CIA custody on July ■■, 2004.[1946] On August 2, 2004, Janat Gul denied knowledge of any imminent threats against the United States homeland. Gul's denial was deemed a "strong resistance posture" by CIA detention site personnel.[1947] Janat Gul was then subjected to the CIA's enhanced interrogation techniques from August 3, 2004, to August 10, 2004, and then again from August 21, 2004, to August 25, 2004.[1948]

On August 19, 2004, CIA personnel wrote that the interrogation "team does not believe [Gul] is withholding imminent threat information."[1949] On August 25, 2004, CIA interrogators sent a cable to CIA Headquarters stating that Janat Gul "may not possess all that [the CIA] believes him to know." The interrogators added that the interrogation "team maintains a degree of caution in some areas, as many issues linking [Gul] to al-Qaida are derived from single source reporting," a reference to the CIA source, ASSET Y.[1950]

That same day, August 25, 2004, the CIA's associate general counsel provided a letter to the DOJ seeking approval to use additional CIA enhanced interrogation techniques against Janat Gul: dietary manipulation, nudity, water dousing, and the abdominal slap. The letter asserted that Janat Gul had information concerning "imminent threats to the United States" and "information that might assist in locating senior al-Qa'ida operatives whose removal from the battlefield could severely disrupt planned terrorist attacks against the United States." The letter stated:

"In addition, CIA understands that before his capture, Gul had been

> working to facilitate a direct meeting between the ████ CIA ████ ████ source reporting on the pre-election threat [ASSET Y] and Abu Faraj himself; Gul had arranged a previous meeting between [ASSET Y] and al-Qa'ida finance chief Shaykh Sa'id at which elements of the pre-election threat were discussed."[1951]

The letter from the CIA's associate general counsel asserted that Janat Gul's "resistance increases when questioned about matters that may connect him to al-Qa'ida or evidence he has direct knowledge of operational terrorist activities."[1952] The letter stated that the CIA sought approval to add four enhanced interrogation techniques to Janat Gul's interrogation plan "in order to reduce markedly Gul's strong resistance posture and provide an opportunity for the interrogation team to obtain his cooperation."[1953] On August 26, 2004, Acting Assistant Attorney General Dan Levin informed CIA Acting General Counsel Rizzo that the use of the four additional enhanced interrogation techniques did not violate any U.S. statutes, the U.S. Constitution, or U.S. treaty obligations. Levin's letter stated that "[w]e understand that [Janat] Gul is a high-value al Qaeda operative who is believed to possess information concerning an imminent terrorist threat to the United States."[1954]

On August 27, 2004, Gul's CIA interrogators reported that "in terms of overt indications of resistance, [Gul's] overall resistance is currently judged to be minimal."[1955] Nonetheless, on August 31, 2004, the CIA interrogators asked CIA Headquarters to approve an extension of all CIA enhanced interrogation techniques against Janat Gul.[1956] The CIA's associate general counsel objected, writing:

> "In the end, its [*sic*] going to be an operational call. I just want to be sure that the record is clear that we're not acting precipitously and are taking into consideration everything we're learning about this guy. We open ourselves up to possible criminal liability if we misuse the interrogation techniques. I reflect again on the cable or cables from the interrogation team that opines that physical EITs (facial slap, walling, etc.) do not work on him. I would strongly encourage, then, HQS not to approval [*sic*] the use of physical interrogation techniques because if they don't work, then our motives are questionable. If our motives might be questioned, then we get ourselves in trouble." [1957]

Despite these concerns, on September 3, 2004, CIA Headquarters released a cable extending approval for sleep deprivation for 30 days. CIA records indicate, however, that Gul was not subjected to sleep deprivation, or any other enhanced interrogation technique, following this approval.[1958]

On September 7, 2004, more than a month after Janat Gul was rendered to CIA custody, a CIA officer who had observed the interrogations of Gul prepared a memorandum for the leadership of the CIA's Renditions, Detentions, and Interrogations Group, stating:

> "The definition of an HVD has probably become blurred over the past year as [CIA] began to render a higher number of MVDs [medium value detainees], but [Janat Gul] would not be considered an HVD when compared to Abu Zubaydah, KSM, and similar level HVDs. [Janat Gul] should likewise not be considered an operational planner or even an operator. It is very likely that [Janat Gul] came into contact with operational information, but we lack credible information that ties him to pre-election threat information or direct operational planning against the United States, at home or abroad. Likewise, we lack any substantive information that connects [Janat Gul] to UBL, Zawahiri, and Abu Faraj Al-Libi."[1959]

On September 16, 2004, CIA detention site personnel wrote that Janat Gul's reporting directly contradicted information from ASSET Y from March 2004, and stated that, "[m]uch of our derogatory information on [Gul] came from [ASSET Y] reporting, as did much of our pre-election threat information."[1960]

On September 17, 2004, following the reports about the discrepancies between the comments made by Janat Gul and ASSET Y, as well as similar denials from Sharif al-Masri, who was in foreign government custody, the CIA undertook a counterintelligence review of ASSET Y to assess the validity of ASSET Y's reporting.[1961]

On October ■, 2004, and October ■, 2004, CIA officers provided a ■■■■■■ assessment of ASSET Y. That ■■■■■■ assessment indicated that ASSET Y was deceptive in response to questions regarding his alleged meeting with a senior al-Qa'ida official, Shaykh Sa'id, at which ASSET Y claimed to have learned about the pre-election threat. ASSET Y then admitted to having fabricated the information about the meeting.[1962]

Despite the recantation of reporting from ASSET Y, officers from the CIA's ALEC Station continued to assess that Janat Gul "was one of the highest-ranking facilitators in Pakistan with long-standing access to senior leaders in al-Qa'ida" and other groups.[1963] This assessment was not shared by CIA personnel involved in Gul's interrogation. On November 10, 2004, the CIA's chief of Base at DETENTION SITE BLACK, the CIA detention site hosting Gul, wrote that the words used by ALEC Station to describe Janat Gul:

> ". . . fly in the face of what is now a rather long history of debriefings which, I would assert, paint a very different picture of him. While [Janat Gul] was certainly a facilitator, describing him as 'highest-ranking' gives him a stature which is undeserved, overblown and misleading. Stating that he had 'long standing access to senior leaders in al-Qa'ida' is simply

> wrong. . . . To put it simply, [Janat Gul] is not the man we thought he was. While he no doubt had associations and interactions with people of interest, [Janat Gul] is not the pivotal figure our pre-detention descriptions of him suggest. We do a disservice to ourselves, the mission and even [Janat Gul] by allowing misperceptions of this man to persist."[1964]

On November 22, 2004, a CIA officer noted the discrepancy between the CIA's description of Janat Gul as a "potential source of intelligence information regarding an attack by al-Qa'ida" in a draft OLC memorandum and the current assessment of Janat Gul.[1965] In an email, the CIA officer indicated that he had spoken to the CIA's associate general counsel, ██████, who had informed him that "the state of our knowledge about Gul had evolved since he was captured." The email noted that, "[a]t first, we believed he had attack information of a more imminent nature," but "[n]ow it appears that he does not have such information." The email indicated that ████ would talk to personnel at OLC about the issue to "[amend] the draft opinion to reflect the state of our knowledge."[1966] The OLC memorandum was not updated.

On December 19, 2004, CIA detention site personnel wrote again that Janat Gul was "not/not the man [CIA Headquarters] made him out to be," and that "[h]e is a very simple man who, no doubt, did a capable job as a facilitator but he is not the link to senior AQ leaders that [CIA Headquarters] said he was/is."[1967]

On April 6, 2005, as the OLC approached completion of its analysis of the legality of the CIA's enhanced interrogation techniques, the OLC asked the CIA about the interrogation of Gul using the CIA's enhanced interrogation techniques, specifically, "what [the CIA] got from Janat Gul, was it valuable, [and] did it help anything. . . ."[1968] The CIA did not immediately respond to this request and the CIA's Associate General Counsel ███████ noted that OLC personnel had "taken to calling [him] daily" for information.[1969] On April 14, 2005, a CIA officer emailed ████ talking points stating that:

> "Pakistan-based facilitator Janat Gul's most significant reporting helped us validate a CIA asset who was providing information about the 2004 pre-election threat. The asset claimed that Gul had arranged a meeting between himself and al-Qa'ida's chief of finance, Shaykh Sa'id, a claim that Gul vehemently denied.
>
> "Gul's reporting was later matched with information obtained from Sharif al-Masri and Abu Talha, captured after Gul. With this reporting in hand, CIA ██████ the asset, who subsequently admitted to fabricating his reporting about the meeting."[1970]

On May 10, 2005, the OLC issued a formal memorandum that

included a discussion of the legality of the use of the CIA's enhanced interrogation techniques against Janat Gul.[1971] Citing information provided in the CIA's August 25, 2004, letter, the OLC memorandum stated:

> "You asked for our advice concerning these interrogation techniques in connection with their use on a specific high value al Qaeda detainee named Janat Gul. You informed us that the CIA believed Gul had information about al Qaeda's plans to launch an attack within the United States. According to CIA's information, Gul had extensive connections to various al Qaeda leaders, members of the Taliban, and the al-Zarqawi network, and had arranged meetings between an associate and al Qaeda's finance chief to discuss such an attack. . . . Our conclusions depend on these assessments."[1972]

On May 30, 2005, the OLC issued a memorandum concluding that the use of the CIA's enhanced interrogation techniques against CIA detainees did not violate Article 16 of the Convention Against Torture.[1973] In the memorandum, Principal Deputy Assistant Attorney General Steven G. Bradbury used the example of Janat Gul as a detainee who was "representative of the high value detainees on whom enhanced techniques have been, or might be, used."[1974]

Citing information from the CIA's August 25, 2004, letter, Bradbury wrote:

> "the CIA believed [that Janat Gul] had actionable intelligence concerning the pre-election threat to the United States . . . Gul had extensive connections to various al Qaeda leaders, members of the Taliban, and the al-Zarqawi network, and intelligence indicated that 'Gul had arranged a . . . meeting between [a ████ source] and al-Qa'ida finance chief Shaykh Sa'id at which elements of the pre-election threat were discussed."[1975]

As noted, the CIA had represented that the use of the CIA's enhanced interrogation techniques was necessary for Janat Gul to provide information on an imminent threat to the United States, the pre-election threat. As further noted, Gul did not provide this information and records indicate that the threat was based on fabricated CIA source reporting. When the OLC requested the results of using the CIA's enhanced interrogation techniques against Janat Gul, the CIA represented that "Gul has provided information that has helped the CIA with validating one of its key assets reporting on the pre-election threat." This information was included in the May 30, 2005, OLC memorandum, which also stated that Gul's information "contradicted the asset's contention that Gul met with Shaykh Sa'id," and that, "[a]nned with Gul's assertions, the CIA ████ the asset, who then admitted that he had lied about the meeting."[1976] There are no indications in the memorandum that the CIA informed the OLC that CIA officers had concluded that Gul had no information about the pre-election threat and had determined that Gul was "not the man we thought he was."[1977] As noted, after the May 30, 2005, OLC memorandum, the CIA continued to represent that the use of the CIA's enhanced interrogation techniques allowed the CIA to validate sources.[1978]

8. The Identification and Arrests of Uzhair and Saifullah Paracha

The CIA represented that information obtained through the use of the CIA's enhanced interrogation techniques produced otherwise unavailable intelligence that led to the identification and/or arrest of Uzhair Paracha and his father Saifullah Paracha (aka, Sayf al-Rahman Paracha). These CIA representations include inaccurate information and omit significant material information—specifically a body of intelligence reporting acquired prior to CIA detainee reporting that linked the Parachas to al-Qa'ida-related activities.

CIA representations also credit the use of the CIA's enhanced interrogation techniques with the identification of a plot to smuggle explosives into the United States involving the Parachas.[1979] CIA records indicate that the plotting was denied by the supposed participants, and that at least one senior CIA counterterrorism official questioned the plausibility of the explosives smuggling plot given the relative ease of acquiring explosive material in the United States.[1980]

The CIA provided information to the CIA Office of Inspector General that "EITs (including the water board) have been indispensable to our successes," and stated that the CIA OIG Special Review should have come to the "conclusion that our efforts have thwarted attacks and saved lives."[1981] The CIA further represented to the OIG that KSM "provided information that helped lead to the arrest of . . . Uzair Paracha, a smuggler,"[1982] and that "as a result of the lawful use of EITs":

> "KSM identified a mechanism for al-Qa'ida to smuggle explosives into the US via a Pakistani businessman and textile merchant who shipped his material to the US. The businessman had agreed to use this method to help al-Qa'ida smuggle in explosives for follow-on attacks to 9/11."[1983]

Similarly, on July 29, 2003, the CIA made a presentation to a select group of National Security Council principals, including Vice President Cheney, seeking policy reaffirmation of the CIA interrogation program. The CIA briefing materials state that "the use of the [CIA interrogation] techniques has produced significant results," and warned that "[t]ermination of this [CIA] program will result in loss of life, possibly extensive." The CIA conveyed that "[m]ajor threats were countered and attacks averted," and under a briefing slide entitled "RESULTS: MAJOR THREAT INFO," represented that information obtained from KSM after the use of the CIA's enhanced interrogation techniques led to the "identification" of Saifullah Paracha.[1984]

A widely disseminated CIA Intelligence Assessment, entitled "Detainee Reporting Pivotal for the War Against Al-Qa'ida," that was described in internal CIA emails as being "put together using past assessments" and initially intended for the White House only, with "marching orders" to "throw everything in it,"[1985] states:

> "Since 11 September 2001, detainee reporting has become a crucial pillar of US counterterrorism efforts, aiding . . . operations to capture additional terrorists, helping to thwart terrorist plots . . . *KSM's revelation in March 2003 that he was plotting with Sayfal-Rahman Pamcha—who also used the name Saifullah al-Rahman Paracha—to smuggle explosives into the United States for a planned attack in New York prompted the FBI to investigate Paracha's business ties in the United States.*"[1986]

CIA representations related to the "identification" of the Parachas and/or the arrest of Uzair Paracha—as well as the identification of an explosives smuggling plot—omit significant information acquired by the Intelligence Community prior to any reporting from CIA detainees. Specifically, prior to KSM's reporting, the Intelligence Community had already collected and acted upon significant information related to the Paracha family's connections to al-Qa'ida and international terrorism:

- Information on Saifullah Paracha was found in documents seized during a March 28, 2002, raid against al-Qa'ida targets associated with Hassan Ghul, which resulted in the capture of Abu Zubaydah. The documents identified "Saifullah Piracha" (the spelling found in the document seized during the raid) and phone numbers, which would be associated with his Karachi-based business. International Merchandise Pvt Ltd, as early as April 2002. An address associated with the business was also identified.[1987]
- The name "Saifullah Piracha" was provided to Pakistani officials by the CIA in December 2002. The CIA wrote: "Information below leads us to believe that the following individual and phone numbers may have a connection to al-Qa'ida and international terrorism. . . . We request your assistance in investigating this individual to determine if he is involved in terrorist activity." The request included three phone numbers found in the documents seized on March 28, 2002, one of which was

associated with Saifullah Paracha's Karachi-based company, International Merchandise Pvt Ltd.[1988]

- In April 2002, the FBI opened an investigation on another ████████ ████████, at a New York-based business associated with Saifullah Paracha. During the course of the investigation, the FBI interviewed an employer at a New York address and acquired additional information on the business and the Parachas. ████████ business card, identifying him as an employee of International Merchandise Limited, was found among documents seized during the April 2002 Karachi raid.[1989]
- Months later, financial documents seized during the September 11, 2002, raids that resulted in the capture of Ramzi bin al-Shibh identified an email address attributed to International Merchandise Pvt Ltd., with the same contact—Saifullah A. Paracha—as well as the same address and phone number as the business identified after the March 2002 raid.[1990]
- Based on the information obtained during the September 2002 raids, the CIA informed the FBI, the NSA, and the Department of Treasury that they suspected "Saifullah Paracha" was engaged in terrorist financing activities, specifically for al-Qa'ida. The cable included detailed information on Saifullah Paracha and International Merchandise Pvt Ltd in Karachi, and noted the CIA's ongoing interest in, and analysis of, the information.[1991]
- FBI investigative activity of terrorism subject Iyman Faris found that Faris was linked to Paracha Imports via his Ohio-based housemates.[1992]
- Majid Khan, who was in foreign government custody, provided reporting that "Uzhair" ran the New York branch of his father's Karachi-based import-export business. According to the reporting, Uzhair was assisting Majid Khan and Ammar al-Baluchi in their efforts to resettle Majid Khan in the United States for terrorism-related purposes. Khan provided a detailed physical description of both Uzhair and his father.[1993]

KSM was captured on March 1, 2003. On March ■, 2003, KSM was rendered to CIA custody and immediately subjected to the CIA's enhanced interrogation techniques.[1994] A CIA interrogation report from March 24, 2003, states that during the afternoon, KSM continued to be subjected to the CIA's enhanced interrogation techniques, including the waterboard, for failing to provide information on operations in the United States and for having "lied about poison and biological warfare programs."[1995] That evening, KSM's interrogators received reports on information being provided by Majid Khan,[1996] who was in foreign government custody and being interviewed by FBI special agents and foreign government officers. The information included details on a U.S.-based individual associated with al-Qa'ida named Uzhair. According to Khan, this Uzhair ran the New York branch of his father's Karachi-based import-export business.[1997] CIA cables describe KSM as being "boxed in" by reporting from Majid Khan[1998] before providing the following information on the Parachas and a smuggling plot:

- KSM corroborated reporting from Majid Khan that Ammar al-Baluchi and Majid Khan approached Uzhair Paracha for assistance in resettling Majid Khan in the United States.[1999]
- KSM stated that he was close to Uzhair's father, Sayf al-Rahman Paracha, who provided assistance through his business and by helping to find safe houses in Karachi.[2000]
- KSM claimed that Ammar al-Baliichi and Majid Khan approached Sayf al-Rahman Paracha with a plan to use Sayf al-Rahman Paracha's textile business to smuggle explosives into the United States. KSM stated that Paracha agreed to this plan and was arranging the details with Ammar al-Baluchi and Majid Khan at the time of his (KSM's) capture.[2001] A later CIA cable provided additional background, stating: "KSM did not volunteer [the explosives plot] information on Paracha. He provided this reporting only when confronted with details on his role and other information on the plot, which had been provided by detainee Majid Khan," who was in foreign government custody.[2002]

According to CIA records, on March 28, 2003, at a FBI field office, Uzhair Paracha provided significant information to interviewing FBI special agents on his father's links to al-Qa'ida and his own efforts to assist Majid Khan's reentry to the United States. Uzhair denied knowing anything about an explosives smuggling plot.[2003]

On April 29, 2003, Ammar al-Baluchi was detained by Pakistani authorities as a result of reporting unrelated to the CIA's Detention and Interrogation Program. Records indicate Ammar al-Baluchi provided significant information prior to being transferred to CIA custody.[2004] On May ███, 2003, Ammar al-Baluchi was rendered to CIA custody and immediately subjected to the CIA's enhanced interrogation techniques.[2005] The CIA stopped using the CIA's enhanced interrogation techniques on Ammar al-Baluchi on May 20, 2003.[2006] A June 18, 2003, cable states that Ammar al-Baluchi denied that he and Sayf al-Rahman Paracha agreed to smuggle explosives into the United States. Ammar al-Baluchi stated he only asked Sayf al-Rahman Paracha questions and made inquiries about how explosives shipping could be done. Ammar al-Baluchi maintained that he did not take any action based on the discussion.[2007]

On July 5, 2003, Saifullah Paracha was detained in ███████, in an operation orchestrated by the FBI.[2008] Shortly thereafter, Saifullah Paracha was rendered to U.S. military custody at Bagram Air Force Base.[2009] At Bagram, Saifullah Paracha was questioned by an FBI special agent.[2010] A CIA cable from July 17, 2003, relays that Saifullah Paracha stated that Ammar al-Baluchi had asked if he knew a forwarding agent who could ship garments and "materials" to Europe, which Saifullah Paracha inferred were either explosives or chemicals. Paracha stated he had no information to provide to Ammar al-Baluchi on this topic and that no further action was taken on the matter.[2011]

With regards to the explosives smuggling reporting, a senior CIA counterterrorism official commented:

> "again, another ksm op worthy of the lamentable knuckleheads . . . why 'smuggle' in explosives when you can get them here? neither fertilizer for bombs or regular explosives are that hard to come by. ramzi yousef came to conus with a suitcase and hundred bucks and got everything he needed right here, this may be true, but it just seems damn odd to me."[2012]

9. Critical Intelligence Alerting the CIA to Jajfar al-Tayyar

The CIA made repeated claims that the use of the CIA's enhanced interrogation techniques resulted in "key intelligence" from Abu Zubaydah and KSM on an operative named Jaffar al-Tayyar,[2013] later identified as Adnan el-Shukrijumah.[2014] These CIA representations frequently asserted that information obtained from KSM after the use of the CIA's enhanced interrogation techniques resulted in an FBI investigation that prompted al-Tayyar to flee the United States. These representations were inaccurate. KSM was captured on March 1, 2003. Jaffar al-Tayyar departed the United States in May 2001.[2015]

CIA representations also omitted key contextual facts, including that: (1) the Intelligence Community was interested in the Florida-based Adnan el-Shukiijumah prior to the detention of the CIA's first detainee;[2016] (2) CIA detainee Abu Zubaydah provided a description and information on a KSM associate named Jaffar al-Tayyar to FBI special agents in May 2002, prior to being subjected to the CIA's enhanced interrogation techniques;[2017] (3) CIA personnel distrusted KSM's reporting on Jaffar al-Tayyar—stating that KSM fabricated information and had inserted al-Tayyar "into practically every story, each time with a different role";[2018] (4) other CIA detainee reporting differed from KSM's reporting in significant ways;[2019] and (5) CIA records indicate that KSM did not identify al-Tayyar's true name and that it was Jose Padilla—in military custody and being questioned by the FBI—who provided al-Tayyar's true name as Adnan el-Shukrijumah.[2020] Finally, the CIA attributed to KSM the characterization of al-Tayyar as the "next Mohammed Atta," despite clarifications from KSM to the contrary.[2021]

For example, in a March 2, 2005, CIA memorandum with the subject line, "Effectiveness of the CIA Counterterrorist Interrogation Techniques," the CIA responded to a request from the Office of Legal Counsel "for the intelligence the Agency obtained from detainees who, before their interrogations, were not providing any information of intelligence [value]." Under a section entitled, "Results," the CIA stated:

> "CIA's use of DOJ-approved enhanced interrogation techniques, as part of a comprehensive interrogation approach, has enabled CIA to disrupt terrorist plots, capture additional terrorists, and collect a high volume of critical intelligence on al-Qa'ida. We believe that intelligence acquired from these interrogations has been a key reason why al-Qa'ida has failed to launch a spectacular attack in the West since 11 September 2001. Key intelligence collected from HVD interrogations after applying interrogation techniques:"[2022]

The CIA then listed "Jafaar al-Tayyar" as one of 11 examples, stating:

> "Jafaar al-Tayyar: Tayyar is an al-Qa'ida operative who was conducting casing in the US for KSM prior to 9/11, according to KSM and other HVDs. KSM confirmed that he recruited Tayyar—who is still at large—to conduct a major operation against US interests. KSM described Tayyar as the next Muhammad Atta. Tayyar's family is in Florida and we have identified many of his extremist contacts. Acting on this information, the FBI quickly publicized Tayyar's true name and aggressively followed up with his family and friends in the United States, causing Tayyar to flee the United States. ▇▇▇▇▇▇▇▇ and we are actively pursuing his capture. ▇▇▇▇▇▇▇▇▇▇▇▇▇▇▇▇▇▇▇▇▇▇▇▇▇▇▇▇▇▇▇▇▇▇▇▇▇▇.[2023]

In January 2009, the CIA compiled a detailed briefing book—CIA Director Hayden produced his own prepared remarks—for a three-hour briefing on the CIA's Detention and Interrogation Program for President-elect Obama's national security staff.[2024] Included in the materials was a document entitled, "Key Impacts," which states:

> **"<u>Results</u>:** CIA's use of DOJ-approved enhanced interrogation techniques, as part of a comprehensive interrogation approach, has enabled CIA to disrupt terrorist plots, capture additional terrorists, and collect a high volume of critical intelligence on al-Qa'ida. We believe that intelligence acquired from these interrogations has been a key reason why al-Qa'ida has failed to launch a spectacular attack in the West since 11 September 2001. Key intelligence collected from HVD interrogations ***after*** applying interrogation techniques:[2025] . . . <u>Jafaar al-Tayyar:</u> Tayyar is an al-Qa'ida operative who was conducting casing in the US for KSM prior to 9/11, according to KSM and other HVDs. KSM confirmed that he recruited Tayyar—who is still at large—to conduct a major operation

> against US interests. KSM described Tayyar as the next Muhammad Atta. Tayyar's family is in Florida and we have identified many of his extremist contacts. Acting on this information, the FBI quickly publicized Tayyar's true name and aggressively followed up with his family and friends in the United States, causing Tayyar to flee the United States.[2026] ████████ and we are actively pursuing his capture. ████████ ████████.[2027]

Prior to receiving information from the CIA's Detention and Interrogation Program, the U.S. Intelligence Community was interested in Adnan el-Shukrijumah. According to CIA and open source records, the FBI interviewed the parents of Adnan el-Shukrijumah several times between September 2001 and October 2002 concerning their son and his suspected contact with a known extremist. The family provided no significant information on their son, except to alert the FBI that he had departed the United States circa May 2001.[2028]

CIA representations that Jaffar al-Tayyar fled the United States in 2003 in response to an investigation prompted by reporting from KSM were incongruent with CIA records at the time of the representations, which indicated that al-Tayyar had already relocated to Pakistan. In March 2003, when Jose Padilla identified Jaffar al-Tayyar as Adnan al-Shukrijumah, he stated that he had last seen al-Tayyar at a KSM safehouse in Karachi, Pakistan, in March 2002.[2029] Other reporting indicated al-Tayyar's presence in Pakistan in 2002 and 2003, as well. For example, KSM consistently reported that al-Tayyar was not in the United States and noted during a 2004 interrogation that al-Tayyar "would not return to the United States because his name was known to U.S. authorities."[2030] Further, ████████ ████████.[2031]

On May 20, 2002, prior to the initiation of the CIA's enhanced interrogation techniques—and while being questioned by FBI special agents—CIA detainee Abu Zubaydah provided information on "Abu Jafar al-Tayer" in the context of discussing associates of KSM. Abu Zubaydah provided a detailed description of "Abu Jafar al-Tayer" and stated that he was an English speaker who had studied in the United States. Abu Zubaydah stated that he first met "Abu Jafar al-Tayer" in Birmal, Afghanistan, circa January 2002, and that "Abu Jafar al-Tayer" was at that time seeking to travel to Pakistan. Abu Zubaydah repeated that "Abu Jafar al-Tayer" spoke "very good English" and was "short and stocky with black hair and dark skin."[2032] Abu Zubaydah did not provide significant additional information on Abu Jaffar al-Tayyar after the CIA used its enhanced interrogation techniques against him in August 2002.[2033]

On September 11, 2002, Ramzi bin al-Shibh was captured in Karachi, Pakistan.[2034] During the capture operation, a letter referencing Jaffar al-Tayyar was seized. According to a translation of the letter, it stated "tell an unidentified pilot named Ja'far that he should be ready for travel."[2035] Shortly after his capture, bin al-Shibh was rendered to foreign government custody.[2036] In November 2002, while still in foreign government custody, bin al-Shibh was questioned on "Ja'far the Pilot" and provided a physical description of "Ja'far."[2037]

On March 1, 2003, KSM was captured. A notebook associated with KSM retrieved during the capture operation included the name "Jafar al-TAYYAR."[2038] After his capture, KSM was rendered to CIA custody, and immediately subjected to the CIA's enhanced interrogation techniques.[2039]

On March 7, 2003, CIA Headquarters sent information on Jaffar al-Tayyar to the CIA's DETENTION SITE BLUE, where KSM was located, for use in the interrogation of KSM.[2040] The documents included the following:

- a "targeting study" on Jaffar al-Tayyar completed by the CIA in January 2003;[2041]
- a letter from KSM to bin al-Shibh referencing "Jafar the Pilot" and indicating that "Jafar" "ought to prepare himself to smuggle himself from Mexico into an unspecified country;
- a letter from Jaffar al-Tayyar to Ramzi bin al-Shibh asking for clarification of KSM's letter; and
- additional background and reporting information on Jaffar al-Tayyar.[2042]

The requirements cable from CIA Headquarters to the detention site included numerous specific questions, relying on the information already known about Jaffar al-Tayyar.[2043]

According to CIA records, on March 9, 2003—while KSM was being interrogated using the CIA's enhanced interrogation techniques, but before he was subjected to the waterboard interrogation technique—the CIA interrogation team used two letters referencing al-Tayyar as the "interrogation vehicle" to elicit information from KSM on Jaffar al-Tayyar.[2044] CIA cables state that KSM did not provide—and claimed not to know—Jaffar al-Tayyar's true name. However, KSM stated that Jaffar al-Tayyar's father lived in Florida and was named "Shukri Sherdil."[2045] This information was not accurate. Open source reporting indicates that Jaffar al-Tayyar's father's true name was "Gulshair El Shukrijumah."[2046]

Over the course of the next two weeks, during the period when

KSM was being subjected to the CIA's enhanced interrogation techniques—including the waterboard—KSM referred to Jaffar al-Tayyar as being engaged in multiple terrorist operations. As a result, the CIA's detention site began describing Jaffar as the "all-purpose" al-Tayyar whom KSM had "woven . . . into practically every story, each time with a different role."[2047] CIA records confirm that KSM made numerous statements about Jaffar al-Tayyar's terrorist plotting that were deemed not to be credible by CIA personnel,[2048] including, but not limited to, statements that:

- al-Tayyar was engaged in terrorist plotting with Jose Padilla;[2049]
- al-Tayyar was engaged in terrorist plots against Heathrow Airport;[2050]
- al-Tayyar was involved in terrorist plotting with Majid Khan;[2051] and
- al-Tayyar was engaged in an assassination plot against former President Jimmy Carter.[2052]

On March 12, 2003, when KSM was confronted with a page in his notebook about al-Tayyar, KSM stated that he "considered al-Tayyar to be the 'next 'emir' for an attack against the US, in the same role that Muhammad Atta had for 11 September."[2053] On March 16, 2003, KSM stated that the only comparison between Atta and al-Tayyar was their education and experience in the West.[2054]

An email exchange the afternoon of March 18, 2003, between CIA personnel expressed the views of interrogators and officers at CIA Headquarters with regard to KSM and Jaffar al-Tayyar. The email from KSM debriefer ████████████████ stated:

> "we've finally gotten [KSM] to admit that al-Tayyar is meant for a plan in the US, but I'm still not sure he's fessing up as to what Jafar's role/plan really is. Today he's working with Majid Khan, yesterday the London crowd, the day before Padilla - you get the point. Anyway, I'm still worried he might be misdirecting us on Jafar."[2055]

An officer from CIA Headquarters responded, "I agree . . . KSM is yanking our chain about Jafar . . . really trying hard to throw us off course . . . suggesting whatever Jafar really is up to must be baaaad [*sic*]." The officer noted that "[a]nother big hole is Jafar's true name," and relayed that KSM's use of "another Abu name . . . Abu Arif . . . doesn't get us far."[2056] When KSM was confronted with the reporting he had provided on Jaffar al-Tayyar, KSM claimed that he had been forced to lie about al-Tayyar because of the pressure he was under from his CIA interrogators, who had been subjecting KSM to the CIA's enhanced interrogation techniques since his rendition to CIA custody.[2057]

Additional CIA records from this period indicate that, while

KSM claimed not to know Jaffar al-Tayyar's true name, KSM suggested that Jose Padilla, then in U.S. military custody, would know his name. According to CIA records, the "FBI began participating in the military debriefings [of Jose Padilla] in March 2003, after KSM reported Padilla might know the true name of a US-bound al-Qa'ida operative known at the time only as Jaffar al-Tayyar. Padilla confirmed Jaffar al-Tayyar's true name as Adnan El Shukrijumah."[2058]

In March 2003, a senior CTC officer noted differences between KSM's reporting and reporting from Ramzi binal-Shibh.[2059] In April 2003, an Intelligence Community assessment concluded, based on comments from other detainees—including those not in CIA custody—that "[i]t seemed obvious that KSM was lying with regard to Jaffar al-Tayyar."[2060] In July 2003, after Ammar al-Baluchi stated that Jaffaral-Tayyar was not suited to be an operative and was "not doing much of anything," the deputy chairman of the Community Counterterrorism Board warned:

> "If [KSM] has pulled off focusing us on a person who is actually no threat, it would mean that our interrogation techniques have not/not broken down his resistance to any appreciable extent—and that we will have to doubt even more strongly anything he says."[2061]

In December 2005, an NCTC Red Team report, entitled "Ja'far al-Tayyar: An Unlikely Al-Qa'ida Operational Threat," highlighted the possibility that the information provided by KSM on al-Tayyar's capabilities and terrorist plotting was simply "deception." The report described a large body of other detainee reporting—from Abu Faraj al-Libi, Abu Talha al-Pakistani, 'Abd al-Rahim Ghulam Rabbani, and Ammar al-Baluchi—consisting of largely dismissive statements about Jaffar al-Tayyar's capabilities and role in al-Qa'ida.[2062]

10. The Identification and Arrest of Saleh al-Marri

The CIA represented to the CIA Office of Inspector General that as a result of the lawful use of EITs,"[2063] KSM "provided information that helped lead to the arrests of terrorists including ... Saleh Almari, a sleeper operative in New York."[2064] This information was included in the final version of the OIG's May 2004 Special Review under the heading, "Effectiveness."[2065] This CIA representation is inaccurate. KSM was captured on March 1, 2003.[2066] Saleh al-Marri was arrested in December 2001.[2067]

The inaccurate statements about al-Marri to the OIG began with the July 16, 2003, OIG interview of Deputy Chief of ALEC

Station ████████,[2068] and were repeated in DDO Pavitt's formal response to the draft OIG Special Review.[2069] The inaccurate statements were then included in the final May 2004 Special Review.[2070] The "Effectiveness" section of the Special Review was used repeatedly as evidence for the effectiveness of the CIA's enhanced interrogation techniques, including in CIA representations to the Department of Justice. The passage in the OIG Special Review that includes the inaccurate CIA representation that KSM provided information helping to lead to the arrest of al-Marri was referenced in the May 30, 2005, OLC memorandum analyzing the legality of the CIA's enhanced interrogation techniques.[2071] The portion of the Special Review discussing al-Marri has been declassified, as has the OLC memorandum.[2072]

The CIA also represented, in Pavitt's formal response to the OIG, that prior to reporting from KSM, the CIA possessed "no concrete information" on al-Marri.[2073] This representation is incongruent with CIA records. CIA records indicate that prior to the CIA's detention of KSM, the CIA possessed significant information on al-Marri, who was arrested after making attempts to contact a telephone number associated with al-Qa'ida member and suspected 9/11 facilitator, Mustafa al-Hawsawi.[2074] CIA records indicate that al-Marri had suspicious information on his computer upon his arrest,[2075] that al-Marri's brother had travelled to Afghanistan in 2001 to join in jihad against the United States,[2076] and that al-Marri was directly associated with KSM, as well as with al-Hawsawi.[2077]

The FBI also had extensive records on al-Marri. On March 26, 2002, a year before any reporting from KSM, the FBI provided the Committee with biographical and derogatory information on al-Marri, including al-Marri's links to Mustafa al-Hawsawi, suspicious information found on al-Marri's computer, and al-Marri's connections to other extremists.[2078]

11. The Collection of Critical Tactical Intelligence on Shkai, Pakistan

In the context of the effectiveness of the CIA's enhanced interrogation techniques, the CIA represented to policymakers over several years that "key intelligence" was obtained from the use of the CIA's enhanced interrogation techniques that revealed Shkai, Pakistan, to be "a major al-Qa'ida hub in the tribal areas," and resulted in "tactical intelligence ████████████████ in Shkai, Pakistan."[2079] These CIA representations were based on the CIA's experience with one CIA detainee, Hassan Ghul. While CIA records indicate that

Hassan Ghul did provide information on Shkai, Pakistan, a review of CIA records found that: (1) the vast majority of this information, including the identities, activities, and locations of senior al-Qa'ida operatives in Shkai, was provided prior to Hassan Ghul being subjected to the CIA's enhanced interrogation techniques; (2) CIA's ██████ ██████ assessed that Ghul's reporting prior to the use of the CIA's enhanced interrogation techniques contained sufficient detail to press the Pakistani ████████████████; and (3) the CIA assessed that the information provided by Ghul corroborated earlier reporting that the Shkai valley of Pakistan served as al-Qa'ida's command and control center after the group's 2001 exodus from Afghanistan.[2080]

As an example of one of the CIA's representations on Shkai, Pakistan, and the effectiveness of the CIA's enhanced interrogation techniques, on March 2, 2005, the CIA responded to a request from the OLC "for the intelligence the Agency obtained from detainees who, before their interrogations, were not providing any information of intelligence [value]." The resulting CIA memorandum, with the subject line "Effectiveness of the CIA Counterterrorist Interrogation Techniques," included the following under the heading, "Results":

> "CIA's use of DOJ-approved enhanced interrogation techniques, as part of a comprehensive interrogation approach, has enabled CIA to disnipt terrorist plots, capture additional terrorists, and collect a high volume of critical intelligence on al-Qa'ida. We believe that intelligence acquired from these interrogations has been a key reason why al-Qa'ida has failed to launch a spectacular attack in the West since 11 September 2001. Key intelligence collected from HVD interrogations after applying interrogation techniques:"[2081]

The CIA then listed "Shkai, Pakistan" as an example, stating:

> "Shkai, Pakistan: The interrogation of Hassan Ghul provided detailed tactical intelligence showing that Shkai, Pakistan was a major Al-Qa'ida hub in the tribal areas. Through use of ████████████████████ during the Ghul interrogation, we mapped out and pinpointed the residences of key AQ leaders in Shkai. This intelligence was provided ███ ██ ██████████████████████████████."[2082]

The CIA representation that the use of the CIA's enhanced interrogation techniques produced otherwise unavailable tactical intelligence related to Shkai, Pakistan, was provided to senior policymakers and the Department of Justice between 2004 and 2009.[2083]

Hassan Ghul was captured on January ██, 2004, by foreign authorities in the Iraqi Kurdistan Region.[2084] Ghul was reportedly first interrogated by ███████,[2085] then transferred to U.S. military custody and questioned, and then rendered to CIA custody on January ■, 2004.[2086] Hassan Ghul spent two days at DETENTION SITE COBALT before being transferred to the CIA's DETENTION SITE BLACK on January ■, 2004. Prior to his capture, the CIA assessed that Ghul possessed substantial knowledge of al-Qa'ida facilities and procedures in Wana and Shkai, Pakistan.[2087]

During Hassan Ghul's two days at DETENTION SITE COBALT, CIA interrogators did not use the CIA's enhanced interrogation techniques on Ghul. Instead, CIA cables state that upon his arrival at the CIA detention site, Hassan Ghul was "examined, and placed in a cell, given adequate clothing, bedding, water and a waste bucket."[2088] During this two-day period (January 2004, and January 2004),[2089] Ghul provided information for at least 21 intelligence reports.[2090] As detailed below, Ghul's reporting on Shkai, Pakistan, and al-Qa'ida operatives who resided in or visited Shkai, was included in at least 16 of these intelligence reports.[2091] The reports included information on the locations, movements, and operational security and training of senior al-Qa'ida leaders living in Shkai, Pakistan, as well as the visits of leaders and operatives to the area. The information provided by Ghul included details on various groups operating in Shkai, Pakistan, and conflicts among the groups. Hassan Ghul also identified and decoded phone numbers and email addresses contained in a notebook seized with him, some of which were associated with Shkai-based operatives.[2092]

Hassan Ghul described the origins of al-Qa'ida's presence in Shkai, including how Abd al-Hadi al-Iraqi became the original group's military commander and its al-Qa'ida representative.[2093] He discussed tensions between al-Hadi and others in Shkai, the mediating role of Abu Faraj al-Libi, and the role of Khalid Habib.[2094] Hassan Ghul explained how he moved to Shkai due to concerns about Abu Musa'b al-Baluchi's contacts with ■■■■■■, how he traveled to Shkai to make contact with Abd al-Hadi al-Iraqi, and how Abu Faraj mediated between Ghul and Hamza Rabi'a.[2095] Ghul stated that he last saw Abu Faraj in the summer of 2003, when Ghul was seeking Abu Faraj's assistance in moving money from Saudi Arabia to deliver to al-Hadi for support of their community in Shkai.[2096]

According to Hassan Ghul, Abd al-Hadi al-Iraqi moved periodically among various houses within the village, including that of Abu Hussein and ■■■■■, whom he described as "senior media people for al-Qa'ida."[2097] Elaborating on al-Hadi's location, Hassan Ghul described the importance of both a *madrassa* and a guesthouse in Shkai known as the "bachelor house," where unaccompanied men stayed. Ghul stated that he last saw al-Hadi in December 2003 when al-Hadi came to the "bachelor house" to visit with other Arabs.[2098] Ghul also identified other permanent and transient residents of the "bachelor house."[2099] He stated that al-Hadi, who he believed was seeking another safehouse in Shkai at which to hold meetings, had approximately 40 to 50 men under his command. Hassan Ghul also identified a phone number used to contact al-Hadi.[2100]

According to Hassan Ghul, as of December 2003, approximately 60 Arab males and between 150 and 200 Turkic/Uzbek males were living in Shkai, along with a "significant population" of Baluchis who assisted the Arabs and Uzbeks.[2101] Ghul described al-Qa'ida training, including an electronics course taught in the fall of 2003 by Abu Bakr al-Suri at the house of Hamza Rabi'a where, he believed, individuals were being trained for an ongoing operation.[2102] Ghul discerned from the training and Rabi'a's statements that al-Qa'ida operatives in Shkai were involved in an assassination attempt against Pakistani President Pervez Musharraf.[2103] Ghul stated Hamza Rabi'a was also likely planning operations into Afghanistan, but had no specifics.[2104]

Hassan Ghul elaborated on numerous other al-Qa'ida operatives he said resided in or visited Shkai, Pakistan, including Shaikh Sa'id al-Masri,[2105] Sharif al-Masri,[2106] Abu Maryam,[2107] Janat Gul,[2108] Khalil Deek,[2109] Abu Talha al-Pakistani,[2110] Firas,[2111] and others.[2112]

Finally, Hassan Ghul described his interactions with Abu Mus'ab al-Zarqawi, which also related to al-Qa'ida figures in Shkai, in particular Abd al-Hadi al-Iraqi.[2113] Ghul described al-Zarqawi's request to al-Hadi for money, explosive experts, and electronic experts, and provided details of his own trip to Iraq on behalf of al-Hadi.[2114] Hassan Ghul identified four email addresses for contacting al-Zarqawi directly,[2115] and described a phone code he would use to communicate with al-Zarqawi.[2116] Ghul also described his conversations with al-Zarqawi, interpreted the notes he had taken of the last of his conversations with al-Zarqawi, identified operatives whom al-Zarqawi and al-Hadi agreed to send to Iraq,[2117] and discussed strategic differences between al-Zarqawi and al-Hadi related to Iraq.[2118]

On January ■■, 2004, after two days at DETENTION SITE COBALT, during which Hassan Ghul provided the aforementioned information about al-Qa'ida activities in Shkai and other matters, Ghul was transferred to the CIA's DETENTION SITE BLACK.[2119] Ghul was immediately, and for the first time, subjected to the CIA's enhanced interrogation techniques. He was "shaved and barbered, stripped, and placed in the standing position."[2120] According to a CIA cable, Hassan Ghul provided no new information during this period and was immediately placed in standing sleep deprivation with his hands above his head, with plans to lower his hands after two hours.[2121] In their request to use the CIA's enhanced interrogation techniques on Ghul, CIA detention site personnel wrote:

> "The interrogation team believes, based on [Hassan Ghul's] reaction to the initial contact, that his al-Qa'ida briefings and his earlier experiences with U.S. military interrogators have convinced him there are limits to the physical contact interrogators can have with him. The interrogation team believes the approval and employment of enhanced measures should sufficiently shift [Hassan Ghul's] paradigm of what he expects to happen. The lack of these increasd [*sic*] measures may limit the team's capability to collect critical and reliable information in a timely manner."[2122]

CIA Headquarters approved the use of the CIA's enhanced interrogation techniques against Hassan Ghul in order to "sufficiently shift [Ghul's] paradigm of what he can expect from the interrogation process, and to increase base's capability to collect critical and reliable threat information in a timely manner."[2123] CIA records do not indicate that information provided by Ghul during this period, or after, resulted in the identification or capture of any al-Qa'ida leaders. After his arrival at DETENTION SITE BLACK, Ghul was asked to identify locations on ██████████ and line drawings of Shkai provided to him, for the first time, by interrogators.[2124]

Hassan Ghul's reporting on Shkai prior to the use of the CIA's enhanced interrogation techniques was compiled by the CIA for passage to the Pakistani government. On January 28, 2004, ███████ issued a cable stating that the information on Shkai provided by Hassan Ghul prior to the use of the CIA's enhanced interrogation techniques, combined with reporting unrelated to the CIA's Detention and Interrogation Program, "moved Shkai to the forefront ████ █," and that "[a]s a result, Station is currently revising its Shkai ███ ████████████████."[2125] On January 29, 2004, ALEC Station proposed that ███████ initiate a discussion with the Pakistanis on "possible Arabs in Shkai," and concurred with a tear-line that requests that Pakistan "undertake to verify" the presence of "a large number of Arabs" in Shkai "as soon as possible."[2126]

On January 31, 2004, CIA's ██████████ drafted with an extensive "tear-line" for Pakistan, much of it related to Shkai. The cable from ███████ referenced nine cables describing Hassan Ghul's reporting prior to the use of the CIA's enhanced interrogation techniques,[2127] and no cables describing Ghul's reporting after the use

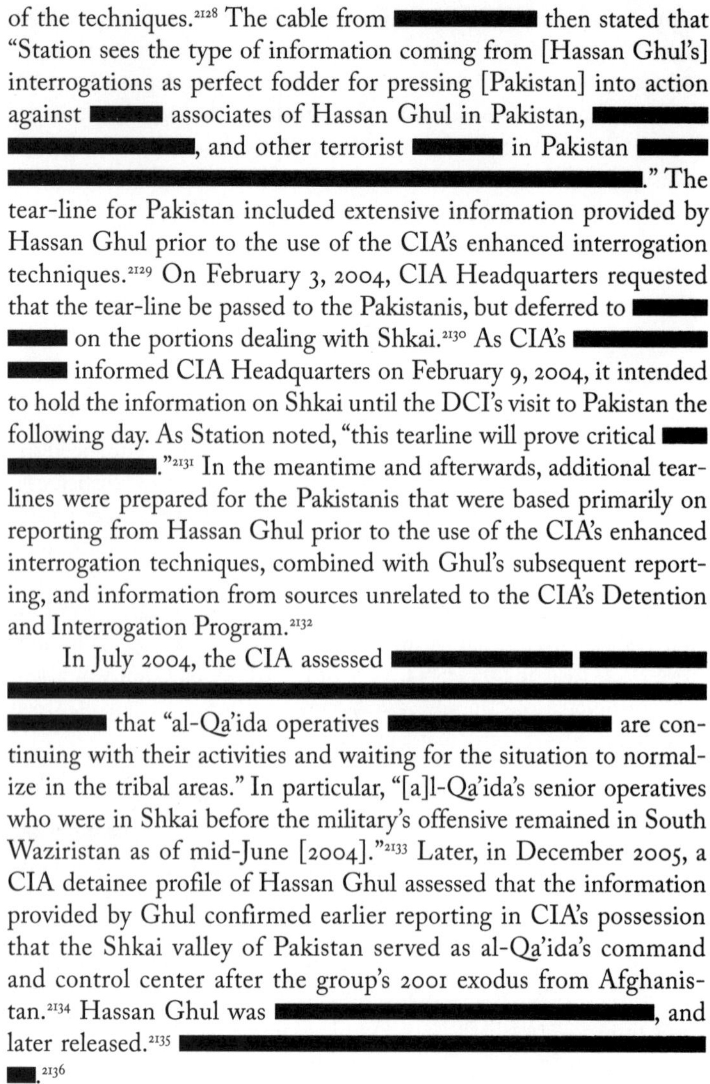

of the techniques.[2128] The cable from then stated that "Station sees the type of information coming from [Hassan Ghul's] interrogations as perfect fodder for pressing [Pakistan] into action against associates of Hassan Ghul in Pakistan, , and other terrorist in Pakistan ." The tear-line for Pakistan included extensive information provided by Hassan Ghul prior to the use of the CIA's enhanced interrogation techniques.[2129] On February 3, 2004, CIA Headquarters requested that the tear-line be passed to the Pakistanis, but deferred to on the portions dealing with Shkai.[2130] As CIA's informed CIA Headquarters on February 9, 2004, it intended to hold the information on Shkai until the DCI's visit to Pakistan the following day. As Station noted, "this tearline will prove critical ."[2131] In the meantime and afterwards, additional tear-lines were prepared for the Pakistanis that were based primarily on reporting from Hassan Ghul prior to the use of the CIA's enhanced interrogation techniques, combined with Ghul's subsequent reporting, and information from sources unrelated to the CIA's Detention and Interrogation Program.[2132]

In July 2004, the CIA assessed that "al-Qa'ida operatives are continuing with their activities and waiting for the situation to normalize in the tribal areas." In particular, "[a]l-Qa'ida's senior operatives who were in Shkai before the military's offensive remained in South Waziristan as of mid-June [2004]."[2133] Later, in December 2005, a CIA detainee profile of Hassan Ghul assessed that the information provided by Ghul confirmed earlier reporting in CIA's possession that the Shkai valley of Pakistan served as al-Qa'ida's command and control center after the group's 2001 exodus from Afghanistan.[2134] Hassan Ghul was , and later released.[2135] .[2136]

12. Information on the Facilitator that Led to the UBL Operation

Shortly after the raid on the Usama bin Ladin (UBL) compound on May 1, 2011, which resulted in UBL's death, CIA officials described the role of reporting from the CIA's Detention and Interrogation Program in the operation—and in some cases connected the reporting to the use of the CIA's enhanced interrogation techniques.[2137] The vast majority of the documents, statements, and testimony highlighting information obtained from the use of the CIA's enhanced interrogation techniques, or from CIA detainees more generally, was inaccurate and incongruent with CIA records.

CIA records indicate that: (1) the CIA had extensive reporting on Abu Ahmad al-Kuwaiti (variant Abu Ahmed al-Kuwaiti),[2138] the UBL facilitator whose identification and tracking led to the identification of UBL's compound and the operation that resulted in UBL's death, prior to and independent of information from CIA detainees; (2) the most accurate information on Abu Ahmad al-Kuwaiti obtained from a CIA detainee was provided by a CIA detainee who had not yet been subjected to the CIA's enhanced interrogation techniques; and (3) CIA detainees who were subjected to the CIA's enhanced interrogation techniques withheld and fabricated information about Abu Ahmad al-Kuwaiti.

Within days of the raid on UBL's compound, CIA officials represented that CIA detainees provided the "tip off"[2139] information on Abu Ahmad al-Kuwaiti.[2140] A review of CIA records found that the initial intelligence obtained, as well as the information the CIA identified as the most critical—or the most valuable—on Abu Ahmad al-Kuwaiti,[2141] was not related to the use of the CIA's enhanced interrogation techniques.[2142]

The CIA did not receive any information from CIA detainees on Abu Ahmad al-Kuwaiti until 2003. Nonetheless, by the end of 2002, the CIA was actively targeting Abu Ahmad al-Kuwaiti and had collected significant reporting on Abu Ahmad al-Kuwaiti—to include reporting on Abu Ahmad al-Kuwaiti's close links to UBL. CIA records indicate that prior to receiving any information from CIA detainees, the CIA had collected:

- *Reporting on Abu Ahmad al-Kuwaiti's Telephonic Activity:* A phone number associated with Abu Ahmad al-Kuwaiti was under U.S. government intelligence collection as early as January 1, 2002.[2143] In March 2002, this phone number would be found in Abu Zubaydah's address book under the heading "Abu Ahmad K."[2144] In April 2002, the same phone number was found to be in contact with UBL family members.[2145] In June 2002, a person using the identified phone number and believed at the time to be "al-Kuwaiti" called a number associated with KSM.[2146] All of this information was acquired in 2002, prior to any reporting on Abu Ahmad al-Kuwaiti from CIA detainees.

- *Reporting on Abu Ahmad al-Kuwaiti's Email Communications:* In July 2002, the CIA had obtained an email address believed to be associated with Abu Ahmad al-Kuwaiti.[2147] As early as August 24, 2002, the CIA was collecting and tracking al-Kuwaiti's email activity. A cable from that day states that an email account associated with KSM "intermediary Abu Ahmed al-Kuwaiti" remained active in Karachi.[2148] On September 17, 2002, the CIA received reporting on al-Kuwaiti's email address from a detainee in the custody of a foreign government. The detainee reported that al-Kuwaiti shared an email address with Ammar al-Baluchi, and that al-Kuwaiti was "coordinating martyrdom operations."[2149] When KSM was captured on March 1, 2003, an email address associated with al-Kuwaiti was found on a laptop believed to be used by KSM.[2150] All of this information was acquired prior to any reporting on Abu Ahmad al-Kuwaiti from CIA detainees.

- *A Body of Intelligence Reporting on Abu Ahmad al-Kuwaiti's Involvement in Operational Attack Planning with KSM—Including Targeting of the United States:* On June 10, 2002, the CIA received reporting from a detainee in the custody of a foreign government indicating that Abu Ahmad al-Kuwaiti was engaged in operational attack planning with KSM.[2151] On June 25, 2002, the CIA received reporting from another detainee in the custody of a foreign government corroborating information that al-Kuwaiti was close with KSM, as well as reporting that al-Kuwaiti worked on "secret operations" with KSM prior to the September 11, 2001, terrorist attacks.[2152] By August 9, 2002, the CIA had received reporting from a third detainee in the custody of a foreign government indicating that Abu Ahmad al-Kuwaiti was supporting KSM's operational attack planning targeting the United States.[2153] By October 20, 2002, the CIA had received reporting from a fourth detainee in the custody of a foreign government indicating that a known terrorist—Hassan Ghul—"received funding and instructions primarily from Abu Ahmad, a close associate of KSM."[2154] All of this information was acquired in 2002, prior to any reporting on Abu Ahmad al-Kuwaiti from CIA detainees.

- *Significant Corroborative Reporting on Abu Ahmad al-Kuwaiti's Age, Physical Description, and Family—Including Information the CIA Would Later Cite As Pivotal:* In September 2001, the CIA received reporting on al-Kuwaiti's family that the CIA would later cite as pivotal in identifying al-Kuwaiti's true name.[2155] From January 2002 through October 2002, the CIA received significant corroborative reporting on al-Kuwaiti's age, physical appearance, and family from detainees held in the custody of foreign governments and the U.S. military.[2156] All of this information was acquired prior to any reporting on Abu Ahmad al-Kuwaiti from CIA detainees.

- *Multiple Reports on Abu Ahmad al-Kuwaiti's Close Association with UBL and His Frequent Travel to See UBL.*[2157] As early as April 2002, CIA had signals intelligence linking a phone number associated with al-Kuwaiti with UBL's family, specifically al-Qa'ida member Sa'ad Bin Ladin.[2158] On June 5, 2002, the CIA received reporting from a detainee in the custody of a foreign government indicating that "Abu Ahmad" was one of three al-Qa'ida associated individuals—to include Sa'ad bin Ladin and KSM—who visited him. The detainee—Ridha al-Najjar—was a former UBL caretaker.[2159] On June 25, 2002, the CIA received reporting

> from another detainee in the custody of a foreign government—Riyadh the Facilitator—suggesting al-Kuwaiti may have served as a courier for UBL. Riyadh the Facilitator highlighted that al-Kuwaiti was "actively working in secret locations in Karachi, but traveled frequently" to "meet with Usama bin Ladin."[2160] Months earlier the CIA disseminated signals intelligence indicating that Abu Ahmad al-Kuwaiti and Riyadh the Facilitator were in phone contact with each other.[2161] In August 2002, another detainee in the custody of a foreign government with known links to al-Kuwaiti[2162]—Abu Zubair al-Ha'ili—reported that al-Kuwaiti "was one of a few close associates of Usama bin Ladin."[2163] All of this information was acquired in 2002, prior to any reporting on Abu Ahmad al-Kuwaiti from CIA detainees.[2164]

Within a day of the UBL operation, the CIA began providing classified briefings to Congress on the overall operation and the intelligence that led to the raid and UBL's death.[2165] On May 2, 2011, CIA officials, including CIA Deputy Director Michael Morell, briefed the Committee. A second briefing occurred on May 4, 2011, when CIA Director Leon Panetta and other CIA officials briefed both the Senate Select Committee on Intelligence and the Senate Armed Services Committee. Both of these briefings indicated that CIA detainee information—and the CIA's enhanced interrogation techniques—played a substantial role in developing intelligence that led to the UBL operation. The testimony contained significant inaccurate information.

For example, in the May 2, 2011, briefing, the CIA informed the Senate Select Committee on Intelligence that:

> "However, there remained one primary line of investigation that was proving the most difficult to run to ground, and that was the case of a courier named Abu Ahmed al-Kuwaiti. Abu Ahmed had totally dropped off our radar in about the 2002–2003 time frame *after several detainees in our custody* had highlighted him as a key facilitator for bin Ladin."[2166]

The information above is not fully congruent with CIA records. As described, the CIA was targeting Abu Ahmad al-Kuwaiti prior to any reporting from CIA detainees. Al-Kuwaiti was identified as early as 2002 as an al-Qa'ida member engaged in operational planning who "traveled frequently" to see UBL.[2167] No CIA detainee provided reporting on Abu Ahmad al-Kuwaiti in 2002. While CIA detainees eventually did provide some information on Abu Ahmad al-Kuwaiti beginning in the spring of 2003, the majority of the accurate intelligence acquired on Abu Ahmad al-Kuwaiti was collected outside of the CIA's Detention and Interrogation Program, either from detainees not in CIA custody, or from other intelligence sources and methods unrelated to detainees, to include human sources and foreign partners.[2168] The most accurate CIA detainee-related intelligence was obtained in early 2004, from a CIA detainee who had not yet been subjected to the CIA's enhanced interrogation techniques.[2169] That detainee—Hassan Ghul—listed Abu Ahmed al-Kuwaiti as one of three individuals likely to be with UBL,[2170] stated that "it was well known that [UBL] was always with Abu Ahmed [al-Kuwaiti],"[2171] and described al-Kuwaiti as UBL's "closest assistant,"[2172] who "likely handled all of UBL's needs."[2173] The detainee further relayed that he believed "UBL's security apparatus would be minimal, and that the group likely lived in a house with a family somewhere in Pakistan."[2174]

In the May 4, 2011, briefing, CIA Director Leon Panetta provided the following statement to the Senate Select Committee on Intelligence and the Senate Armed Services Committee (which mirrored similar statements by a "senior administration official" in a White House Press Briefing from May 2, 2011)[2175]:

> "*The detainees* in the post-9/11 period flagged for us that there were individuals that provided direct support to bin Ladin . . . *and one of those identified was a courier who had the nickname Abu Ahmad al-Kuwaiti. That was back in 2002.*"[2176]

As previously detailed, no CIA detainees provided information on Abu Ahmad al-Kuwaiti in 2002. As such, for the statement to be accurate, it can only be a reference to detainees in foreign government custody who provided information in 2002.[2177] As noted, prior to any reporting from CIA detainees, the CIA was targeting Abu Ahmad al-Kuwaiti—to include al-Kuwaiti's phone number and email address.[2178] Further, prior to 2003, the CIA possessed a body of intelligence reporting linking Abu Ahmad al-Kuwaiti to KSM and UBL and to operational targeting of the United States, as well as reporting that Abu Ahmad al-Kuwaiti was "one of a few close associates of Usama bin Ladin"[2179] and "traveled frequently" to "meet with Usama bin Ladin."[2180]

In the same May 4, 2011, briefing, a CIA officer elaborated on the previously provided statements and provided additional detail on how "a couple of early detainees" "identi[fied]" Abu Ahmad al-Kuwaiti as someone close to UBL:

> "I think the clearest way to think about this is, in 2002 *a couple of early detainees, Abu Zubaydah and an individual, Riyadh the Facilitator, talked about the activities of an Abu Ahmed al-Kuwaiti.* At this point we don't have his true name. *And they identify him as somebody involved with AQ and facilitation and some potential ties to bin Ladin.*"[2181]

This testimony is inaccurate. There are no CIA records of Abu

Zubaydah discussing Abu Ahmad al-Kuwaiti in 2002.[2182] The first reference to Abu Zubaydah providing information related to al-Kuwaiti is on July 7, 2003, when Abu Zubaydah denied knowing the name.[2183] CIA records indicate that the information in 2002 that the CIA has represented as the initial lead information on Abu Ahmad al-Kuwaiti was not obtained from the CIA's Detention and Interrogation Program, but was collected by the CIA from other intelligence sources, including from detainees in foreign government custody. Riyadh the Facilitator provided substantial information on Abu Ahmad al-Kuwaiti in 2002, including information suggesting al-Kuwaiti may have served as a courier, as al-Kuwaiti reportedly "traveled frequently" to see UBL.[2184] Consistent with the testimony, CIA records indicate that the information provided by Riyadh the Facilitator was important information; however, Riyadh the Facilitator was not in CIA custody in 2002, but was in the custody of a foreign government.[2185] Riyadh the Facilitator was not transferred to CIA custody until January ■, 2004.[2186] As noted, in 2002, the CIA received additional reporting from another detainee in the custody of a foreign government, Abu Zubair al-Ha'ili, that "Ahmad al-Kuwaiti" was "one of a few close associates of Usama bin Ladin."[2187]

At the May 4, 2011, briefing, a Senator asked, "I guess what we're trying to get at here, or certainly I am, was any of this information obtained through [enhanced] interrogation measures?" A CIA officer replied:

> "Senator, *these individuals were in our program and were subject to some form of enhanced interrogation*. Because of the time involved and the relationship to the information and the fact that I'm not a specialist on that program, I would ask that you allow us to come back to you with some detail."[2188]

The information above is not fully congruent with CIA records. As is detailed in the intelligence chronology in Volume II, the vast majority of the intelligence acquired on Abu Ahmad al-Kuwaiti was originally acquired from sources unrelated to the CIA's Detention and Interrogation Program, and the most accurate information acquired from a CIA detainee was provided prior to the CIA subjecting the detainee to the CIA's enhanced interrogation techniques.[2189] As detailed in CIA records, and acknowledged by the CIA in testimony, information from CIA detainees subjected to the CIA's enhanced interrogation techniques—to include CIA detainees who had clear links to Abu Ahmad al-Kuwaiti based on a large body of intelligence reporting—provided fabricated, inconsistent, and generally unreliable information on Abu Ahmad al-Kuwaiti throughout their detention.[2190]

At the May 4, 2011, briefing, a Senator asked, "of the people that you talked about as detainees that were interrogated, which of those were *waterboarded* and *did they provide unique intelligence* in order to make this whole mission possible?"[2191] CIA Director Panetta responded:

> "I want to be able to get back to you with specifics, but right now we think there were about *12 detainees that were interviewed,*[2192] *and about three of them were probably subject to the waterboarding process.*[2193] Now what came from those interviews, how important was it, I really do want to stress the fact that we had a lot of streams of intelligence here that kind of tipped us off there, but we had imagery, we had assets on the ground, we had information that came from a number of directions in order to piece this together. *But clearly the tipoff*[2194] *on the couriers came from those interviews.*"[2195]

As previously detailed, the "tipoff" on Abu Ahmad al-Kuwaiti in 2002 did not come from the interrogation of CIA detainees and was obtained prior to any CIA detainee reporting. The CIA was already targeting Abu Ahmad al-Kuwaiti and collecting intelligence on at least one phone number and an email address associated with al-Kuwaiti in 2002.[2196] No CIA detainee provided information on Abu Ahmad al-Kuwaiti in 2002, and prior to receiving any information from CIA detainees, the CIA possessed a body of intelligence reporting linking Abu Ahmad al-Kuwaiti to KSM and UBL and to operational targeting of the United States, as well as reporting that Abu Ahmad al-Kuwaiti was "one of a few close associates of Usama bin Ladin"[2197] and "traveled frequently" to "meet with Usama bin Ladin."[2198]

The day after the classified briefing, on May 5, 2011, the CIA provided the Committee with a six-page chart entitled, "Detainee Reporting on Abu Ahmad al-Kuwaiti," which accompanied a one-page document compiled by the CIA's CTC, entitled "Background Detainee Information on Abu Ahmad al-Kuwaiti."[2199] In total, the CIA chart identifies 25 "mid-value and high-value detainees" who "discussed Abu Ahmad al-Kuwaiti's long-time membership in al-Qa'ida and his historic role as courier for Usama Bin Ladin." The 25 detainees are divided into two categories. The chart prominently lists 12 detainees—all identified as having been in CIA custody—"who linked Abu Ahmad to Bin Ladin," which the CIA labeled as the most important, "Tier 1" information. The document states that nine of the 12 (9/12: 75 percent) CIA detainees providing "Tier 1" information were subjected to the CIA's enhanced interrogation techniques, and that of those nine detainees, two (2/9: 20 percent) were subjected to the CIA's waterboard interrogation technique. The chart then includes a list of 13 detainees "who provided general information on Abu Ahmad," labeled as "Tier 2" information. The CIA document states that four of the 13 (4/13: 30 percent) "Tier 2" detainees were in CIA custody and that all four (4/4: 100 percent) "CIA detainees" were subjected to the CIA's enhanced interrogation techniques.[2200]

On October 3, 2012, the CIA provided the Committee with a document entitled, "Lessons for the Hunt for Bin Ladin," completed in September 2012 by the CIA's Center for the Study of Intelligence. The CIA Lessons Learned document states, "[i]n sum, 25 detainees provided information on Abu Ahmad al-Kuwaiti, his al-Qa'ida membership, and his historic role as a courier for Bin Ladin." The CIA document then states that 16 of the 25 detainees who reported on Abu Ahmad al-Kuwaiti were in CIA custody, and that "[o]f the 16 held in CIA custody, all but three [13] had given information *after* being subjected to enhanced interrogation techniques (EITs)," before noting that "only two (KSM and Abu Zubaydah) had been waterboarded."[2201]

A review of CIA records found that these CIA documents contained inaccurate information and omitted important and material facts.

- *The May 5, 2011, CIA chart represents that all 12 detainees (12/12: 100 percent) providing "Tier 1" intelligence—information that "linked Abu Ahmad to Bin Ladin"[2202]—were detainees in CIA custody.* A review of CIA records found that the CIA document omitted the fact that five of the 12 listed detainees (5/12: 41 percent) provided intelligence on Abu Ahmad al-Kuwaiti prior to entering CIA custody.[2203] In addition, other detainees—not in CIA custody—provided information that "linked Abu Ahmad to Bin Ladin," but were not included in the CIA list. For example, the first detainee-related information identified in CIA records indicating a close relationship between UBL and Abu Ahmad al-Kuwaiti was acquired in July 2002, from a detainee in the custody of a foreign government, Abu Zubair al-Ha'ili (Zubair). According to CIA records, Zubair provided a detailed physical description of Abu Ahmad al-Kuwaiti, information on Abu Ahmad's family, his close connection to KSM, and that "Ahmad al-Kuwaiti: was a one of a few close associates of Usama bin Ladin."[2204] This information would be used to question other detainees, but was omitted in the CIA's "Detainee Reporting on Abu Ahmed al-Kuwaiti" chart.
- *The May 5, 2011, CIA chart also states that nine of the 12 (9/12: 75 percent) "CIA detainees" providing "Tier 1" intelligence were subjected to the CIA's enhanced interrogation techniques.* A review of CIA records found that of

the nine detainees the CIA identified as having been subjected to the CIA's enhanced interrogation techniques and providing "Tier 1" information on links between Abu Ahmad al-Kuwaiti and UBL, five of the 9 (5/9: 55 percent) provided information on Abu Ahmad al-Kuwaiti prior to being subjected to the CIA's enhanced interrogation techniques.[2205] This information was omitted from the CIA document. Of the remaining four detainees who did not provide information on Abu Ahmad al-Kuwaiti until after being subjected to the CIA's enhanced interrogation techniques, three were not substantially questioned on any topic prior to the CIA's use of enhanced interrogation techniques.[2206] All three provided information the CIA assessed to be fabricated and intentionally misleading.[2207] The fourth, Abu Zubaydah, who was detained on March 28, 2002, and subjected to the CIA's enhanced interrogation techniques in August 2002, to include the waterboard technique, did not provide information on Abu Ahmad al-Kuwaiti until August 25, 2005, intelligence that was described by CIA officers at the time as "speculative."[2208] These relevant details were omitted from the CIA documents.[2209]

- *The May 5, 2011, CIA chart also states that of the 13 detainees "who provided general information on Abu Ahmad," labeled as "Tier II" information, four of the 13 (4/13: 30 percent) detainees were in CIA custody and that all four (4/4:100 percent) were subjected to the CIA's enhanced interrogation techniques.*[2210] A review of CIA records found the CIA document omitted that two of the four (2/4; 50 percent) "CIA detainees" who were described as subjected to the CIA's enhanced interrogation techniques provided intelligence on Abu Ahmad al-Kuwaiti *prior* to entering CIA custody, and therefore *prior* to being subjected to the CIA's enhanced interrogation techniques.[2211] Finally, there were additional detainees in foreign government custody "who provided general information on Abu Ahmad" that were not included in the list of 13 detainees. For example, in January 2002, the CIA received reporting from a detainee in the custody of a foreign government who provided a physical description of a Kuwaiti named Abu Ahmad who attended a terrorist training camp.[2212]

- *The October 3, 2012, "Lessons for the Hunt for Bin Ladin" document states that "[i]n sum, 25 detainees provided information on Abu Ahmad al-Kuwaiti, his al-Qa'ida membership, and his historic role as a courier for Bin Ladin."* This is incorrect. As described, additional detainees—not in CIA custody—provided information on Abu Ahmad al-Kuwaiti, including 2002 reporting that al-Kuwaiti "was one of a few close associates of Usama bin Ladin."[2213]

- *The October 3, 2012, "Lessons for the Hunt for Bin Ladin" document also states that 16 of the 25 (16/25: 65 percent) detainees who reported on Abu Ahmad al-Kuwaiti were in CIA custody.* This is incorrect. At least seven of the 16 detainees (7/16: 45 percent) that the CIA listed as detainees in CIA custody provided reporting on Abu Ahmad al-Kuwaiti prior to being transferred to CIA custody.[2214]

- *The October 3, 2012, "Lessons for the Hunt for Bin Ladin" document also states that "[o]f the 16 held in CIA custody, all but three [13] had given information after being subjected to enhanced interrogation techniques (EITs)."*[2215]

This is incorrect. Seven of the 13 detainees that the CIA listed as having been subjected to the CIA's enhanced interrogation techniques provided information on Abu Ahmad al-Kuwaiti *prior* to being subjected to the CIA's enhanced interrogation techniques.[2216] Of the remaining six detainees who did not provide information on Abu Ahmad al-Kuwaiti until *after* being subjected to the CIA's enhanced interrogation techniques, five were not substantially questioned on any topic prior to the CIA's use of enhanced interrogation techniques.[2217] (Of the five detainees, three provided information the CIA assessed to be fabricated and intentionally misleading.[2218] The remaining two provided limited, non-unique, corroborative reporting.[2219]) The sixth, Abu Zubaydah, who was detained on March 28, 2002, and subjected to the CIA's enhanced interrogation techniques in August 2002, did not provide information on Abu Ahmad al-Kuwaiti until August 25, 2005, intelligence that, as noted, was described by CIA officers at the time as "speculative."[2220]

- *The October 3, 2012, "Lessons for the Hunt for Bin Ladin" document also states that "only two [detainees] (KSM and Abu Zubaydah) had been waterboarded. Even so, KSM gave false information about Abu Ahmad. . . ."*[2221] *The CIA's May 5, 2011, Chart, "Reporting on Abu Ahmad al-Kuwaiti," states that Abu Zubaydah and KSM provided "Tier 1" intelligence that "linked Abu Ahmad to Bin Ladin."* CIA records indicate that both detainees denied any significant connection between al-Kuwaiti and UBL. CIA records further indicate that Abu Zubaydah and KSM, who were both subjected to the CIA's waterboard interrogation technique, withheld information on Abu Ahmad al-Kuwaiti:

- Abu Zubaydah: "Abu Ahmad K." and a phone number associated with Abu Ahmad al-Kuwaiti was found on page 8 of a 27-page address book captured with Abu Zubaydah on March 28, 2002. In July 2003, Abu Zubaydah stated that he was not familiar with the name Abu Ahmad al-Kuwaiti, or the description provided to him by CIA officers. In April 2004, Abu Zubaydah again stated that he did not recognize the name "Abu Ahmad al-Kuwaiti."[2222] According to a CIA cable, in August 2005, Abu Zubaydah provided information on "an individual whose name he did not know, but who might be identifiable with Abu Ahmad al-Kuwaiti, aka Abu Ahmad al-Pakistani." According to the cable, Abu Zubaydah speculated that this individual knew UBL and al-Zawahiri, but did not think their relationship would be close. Days later a CIA cable elaborated that Abu Zubaydah had speculated on a family of brothers from Karachi that may have included Abu Ahmad.[2223]

- KSM: When KSM was captured on March 1, 2003, an email address associated with Abu Ahmad al-Kuwaiti was found on a laptop believed to be used by KSM. As detailed in this review, KSM first acknowledged Abu Ahmad al-Kuwaiti in May 2003, after being confronted with reporting on Abu Ahmad al-Kuwaiti from a detainee who was not in CIA custody. KSM provided various reports on Abu Ahmad that the CIA described as "pithy." In August 2005, KSM claimed that al-Kuwaiti was not a courier, and that he had never heard of Abu Ahmad transporting letters for UBL. In May 2007, the CIA reported that the denials of KSM and another detainee, combined with conflicting reporting from

> other detainees, added to the CIA's belief that Abu Ahmad al-Kuwaiti was a significant figure.[2224]

The CIA detainee who provided the most accurate "Tier 1" information linking Abu Ahmad al-Kuwaiti to UBL, Hassan Ghul, provided the information prior to being subjected to the CIA's enhanced interrogation techniques.[2225] Hassan Ghul was captured on January ■ ■, 2004, by foreign authorities in the Iraqi Kurdistan Region.[2226] Ghul was reportedly first interrogated by ■■■■, then transferred to U.S. military custody and questioned, and then rendered to CIA custody at DETENTION SITE COBALT on January ■■, 2004.[2227] From January ■■, 2004, to January ■■ 2004, Hassan Ghul was questioned by the CIA at DETENTION SITE COBALT. During this period the CIA disseminated 21 intelligence reports based on Ghul's reporting.[2228] A CIA officer told the CIA Office of Inspector General that Hassan Ghul "opened up right away and was cooperative from the outset."[2229] During the January ■■, 2004, to January ■■, 2004, sessions, Ghul was questioned on the location of UBL. According to a cable, Ghul speculated that "UBL was likely living in Peshawar area," and that "it was well known that [UBL] was always with Abu Ahmed [al-Kuwaiti]."[2230] Ghul described Abu Ahmad al-Kuwaiti as UBL's "closest assistant"[2231] and listed him as one of three individuals likely to be with UBL.[2232] Ghul further speculated that:

> "UBL's security apparatus would be minimal, and that the group likely lived in a House with a family somewhere in Pakistan. Ghul commented that after UBL's bodyguard entourage was apprehended entering Pakistan following the fall of Afghanistan, UBL likely has maintained a small security signature of circa one or two persons. Ghul speculated that Abu Ahmed likely handled all of UBL's needs, including moving messages out to Abu Faraj [al-Libi] . . ."[2233]

The next day, January ■■, 2004, Hassan Ghul was transferred to the CIA's DETENTION SITE BLACK.[2234] Upon arrival, Ghul was "shaved and barbered, stripped, and placed in the standing position against the wall" with "his hands above his head" for forty minutes.[2235] The CIA interrogators at the detention site immediately requested permission to use the CIA's enhanced interrogation techniques against Ghul, writing that, during the forty minutes, Ghul did not provide any new information, did not show the fear that was typical of other recent captures, and "was somewhat arrogant and self important." The CIA interrogators wrote that they "judged" that Ghul "has the expectation that in U.S. hands, his treatment will not be severe."[2236] The request to CIA Headquarters to use the CIA's enhanced interrogation techniques further stated:

> "The interrogation team believes, based on [Hassan Ghul's] reaction to the initial contact, that his al-Qa'ida briefings and his earlier experiences with U.S. military interrogators have convinced him there are limits to the physical contact interrogators can have with him. The interrogation team believes the approval and employment of enhanced measures should sufficiently shift [Hassan Ghul's] paradigm of what he expects to happen. The lack of these increasd [*sic*] measures may limit the team's capability to collect critical and reliable information in a timely manner."[2237]

CIA Headquarters approved the request the same day, stating that the use of the CIA's enhanced interrogation techniques would "increase base's capability to collect critical and reliable threat information in a timely manner."[2238] During and after the use of the CIA's enhanced interrogation techniques Ghul provided no other information of substance on al-Kuwaiti.[2239] Hassan Ghul was ██████ ██████ later released.[2240] ██████ ██████.[2241] The fact that Hassan Ghul provided the detailed information linking Abu Ahmad al-Kuwaiti to UBL prior to the use of the CIA's enhanced interrogation techniques was omitted from CIA documents and testimony.[2242]

While CIA documents and testimony highlighted reporting that the CIA claimed was obtained from CIA detainees—and in some cases from CIA detainees subjected to the CIA's enhanced interrogation techniques—the CIA internally noted that reporting from CIA detainees—specifically CIA detainees subjected to the CIA's enhanced interrogation techniques—was insufficient, fabricated, and/or unreliable.

A September 1, 2005, CIA report on the search for UBL states:

> "Bin Ladin Couriers: Low-level couriers who wittingly or unwittingly facilitate communications between Bin Ladin and his gatekeepers remain largely invisible to us until a detainee reveals them.[2243]" Even then, *detainees provide few actionable leads, and we have to consider the possibility that they are creating fictitious characters to distract us or to absolve themselves of direct knowledge about Bin Ladin.* We nonetheless continue the hunt for Abu Ahmed al-Kuwaiti—an alleged courier between Bin Ladin and KSM—and Abu 'Abd al Khaliq Jan, who[m] Abu Faraj identified as his go-between with Bin Ladin since mid-2003, in order to get one step closer to Bin Ladin."[2244]

A May 20, 2007, CIA "targeting study" for Abu Ahmad al-Kuwaiti states:

> "Khalid Shaykh Muhammad (KSM) *described Abu Ahmad as a relatively minor figure and Abu Faraj al-Libi denied all knowledge of Abu Ahmad. Station assesses that KSM and Abu Faraj's reporting is not credible* on this topic, and their attempts to downplay Abu Ahmad's importance or deny knowledge of Abu Ahmad are likely part of an effort to withhold

information on UBL or his close associates. These denials, combined with reporting from other detainees"[2245] indicating that Abu Ahmad worked closely with KSM and Abu Faraj, add to our belief that Abu Ahmad is an HVT courier or facilitator."[2246]

Additional CIA documents contrasted the lack of intelligence obtained from CIA detainees subjected to the CIA's enhanced interrogation techniques with the value of intelligence obtained from other sources. A November 23, 2007, CIA intelligence product, "Al-Qa'ida Watch," with the title, "Probable Identification of Suspected Bin Ladin Facilitator Abu Ahmad al-Kuwaiti," details how a:

"review of 2002 debriefings of a [foreign government] detainee who claimed to have traveled in 2000 from Kuwait to Afghanistan with an 'Ahmad al-Kuwaiti' provided the breakthrough leading to the likely identification of Habib al-Rahman as Abu Ahmad. The [foreign government] subsequently informed [the CIA] that Habib al-Rahman currently is living in Pakistan, probably in the greater Peshawar area—according to our analysis of a body of reporting."[2247]

This CIA intelligence product highlighted how reporting from Abu Faraj al-Libi, who was subjected to the CIA's enhanced interrogation techniques and denied knowing Abu Ahmad, differed from that of Hassan Ghul, who—prior to the application of the CIA's enhanced interrogation techniques—stated that "Bin Ladin was always with Abu Ahmad," and that Abu Ahmad had delivered a message to senior al-Qa'ida leaders in late 2003, "probably through Abu Faraj." The document further states that KSM "has consistently maintained that Abu Ahmad 'retired' from al-Qa'ida work in 2002." The CIA document states that the CIA will be working with ███████ and the █████ government, as well as utilizing a database of ███ ███ to follow-up on an individual traveling within Pakistan with a similar name and date of birth.[2248]

CIA cable records from early 2008 highlight how the discovery and exploitation of phone numbers associated with al-Kuwaiti ███ ███ had been critical in collecting intelligence and locating the target,[2249] and state:

"*. . . debriefings of the senior most detainees who were involved in caring for bin Ladin have produced little locational information*, and it is the final nugget that detainees hold on to in debriefings (over threat info and even Zawahiri LOCINT) given their loyalty to the al-Qa'ida leader. We assess that Abu Ahmad would likely be in the same category as Khalid Shaykh Muhammad and Abu Faraj al-Libi, so we advocate building as much of a targeting picture of where and when Habib/Abu Ahmad travels to flesh out current leads to bin Ladin."[2250]

On May 1, 2008, a CIA Headquarters cable entitled, "targeting efforts against suspected UBL facilitator Abu Ahmad al-Kuwaiti," documents that the CIA had a number of collection platforms established to collect intelligence on Abu Ahmad al-Kuwaiti in order to locate UBL. The cable closes by stating:

> "although we want to refrain from addressing endgame strategies, HQS judges that detaining Habib should be a last resort, since we have had no/no success in eliciting actionable intelligence on bin Ladings location from any detainees."[2251]

While the aforementioned CIA assessments highlight the unreliability of reporting from senior al-Qa'ida leaders in CIA custody, specifically "that KSM and Abu Faraj's reporting" was assessed to be "not credible"—and that their denials "add[ed] to [the CIA's] belief that Abu Ahmad is an HVT courier or facilitator"[2252]—the CIA assessments also highlight that "reporting from other detainees indicating that Abu Ahmad worked closely with KSM and Abu Faraj" was useful.[2253] As documented, the initial detainee-related information linking Abu Ahmad to UBL and KSM did not come from CIA detainees, but from detainees who were not in CIA custody.[2254]

IV. OVERVIEW OF CIA REPRESENTATIONS TO THE MEDIA WHILE THE PROGRAM WAS CLASSIFIED

A. The CIA Provides Information on the Still-Classified Detention and Interrogation Program to Journalists Who Then Publish Classified Information; CIA Does Not File Crimes Reports in Connection with the Stories

In seeking to shape press reporting on the CIA's Detention and Interrogation Program, CIA officers and the CIA's Office of Public Affairs (OPA) provided unattributed background information on the program to journalists for books, articles, and broadcasts, including when the existence of the CIA's Detention and Interrogation Program was still classified.[2255] When the journalists to whom the CIA had provided background information published classified information, the CIA did not, as a matter of policy, submit crimes reports. For example, as described in internal emails, the CIA's ███ ████████████████████████ never opened an investigation related to Ronald Kessler's book *The CIA at War*, despite the inclusion of classified information, because "the book contained no first time disclosures," and because "OPA provided assistance with the book."[2256] Senior Deputy General Counsel John Rizzo wrote that the CIA made the determination because the CIA's cooperation with Kessler had been "blessed" by the CIA director.[2257] In another example, CIA officers and the House Permanent Select Committee on Intelligence raised concerns that an article by Douglas Jehl in the *New York Times* contained significant classified information.[2258] ████████ CTC Legal wrote in an email that "part of this article was based on 'background' provided by OPA. That, essentially, negates any use in making an unauthorized disclosure [report]."[2259]

Both the Kessler book and the Jehl article included inaccurate claims about the effectiveness of CIA interrogations, much of it consistent with the inaccurate information being provided by the CIA to policymakers at the time. For example, Kessler's book stated that the FBI arrest of Iyman Faris was "[b]ased on information from the CIA's interrogation of [KSM]," and that the arrest of Khallad bin Attash was the "result" of CIA interrogations of KSM.[2260] The Jehl article stated that a "secret program to transfer suspected terrorists to foreign countries for interrogation has been carried out by the Central Intelligence Agency . . . according to current and former government officials." The article stated that a "senior United States official" had "provid[ed] a detailed description of the program," and quoted the official as claiming that "[t]he intelligence obtained by those rendered, detained and interrogated ha[d] disrupted terrorist operations." The senior official added, "[it] has saved lives in the United States and abroad, and it has resulted in the capture of other terrorists.[2261]

B. Senior CIA Officials Discuss Need to "Put Out Our Story" to Shape Public and Congressional Opinion Prior to the Full Committee Being Briefed

In early April 2005, [redacted], chief of ALEC Station, asked CTC officers to compile information on the success of the CIA's Detention and Interrogation Program preparation for interviews of CIA officers by Tom Brokaw of NBC News.[2262] As [redacted] remarked in a Sametime communication with Deputy CTC Director Philip Mudd, during World War II, the Pentagon had an Office of War Information (OWI), whereas the CIA's predecessor, the Office of Strategic Services (OSS), did not. [redacted] then noted that "we need an OWI, at least every now and then . . ."[2263] According to Mudd, concerns within the CIA about defending the CIA's Detention and Interrogation Program in the press were misplaced:[2264]

> "maybe people should know we're trying to sell their program, if they complain, they should know that we're trying to protect our capability to continue, we're not just out there to brag . . . they don't realize that we have few options here. we either get out and sell, or we get hammered, which has implications beyond the media. congress reads it, cuts our authorities, messes up our budget. we need to make sure the impression of what we do is positive . . . we must be more aggressive out there. we either put out our story or we get eaten. there is no middle ground."[2265]

Mudd counseled not to "advertise" the discussions between CIA personnel and the media with the CIA "workforce," because "they'd misread it."[2266] After [REDACTED] promised to keep the media outreach "real close hold," Mudd wrote:

> "most of them [CIA personnel] do not know that when the w post/ ny times quotes 'senior intel official,' it's us . . . authorized and directed by opa."[2267]

[REDACTED] sent a draft compilation of plot disruptions to [REDACTED] CTC Legal to determine whether the release of the information would pose any "legal problems."[2268] According to CIA attorneys, information on Issa al-Britani posed no problems because it was sourced to the 9/11 Commission. They also determined that information about lyman Faris and Sajid Badat that was sourced to press stories posed no legal problems because Faris had already pled guilty and Badat was not being prosecuted in the United States.[2269] On April 15, 2005, a CIA officer expressed concerns in an email to several CIA attorneys about the CIA releasing classified information to the media. There are no CIA records indicating a response to the CIA officer's email.[2270]

That day, April 15, 2005, the National Security Council Principals Committee discussed a public campaign for the CIA's Detention and Interrogation Program. After the meeting, ALEC Station personnel informed [REDACTED] CTC Legal that scheduled interviews with NBC News of Director Porter Goss and Deputy CTC Director Philip Mudd should not proceed so that "we don't get a head [*sic*] of ourselves . . ."[2271] On June 24, 2005, however, *Dateline NBC* aired a program that included on-the-record quotes from Goss and Mudd, as well as quotes from "top American intelligence officials."[2272] The program and *Dateline NBC*'s associated online articles included classified information about the capture and interrogation of CIA detainees and quoted "senior U.S. intelligence analysts" stating that intelligence obtained from CIA interrogations "approaches or surpasses any other intelligence on the subject of al-Qaida and the construction of the network."[2273] The *Dateline NBC* articles stated that "Al-Qaida leaders suddenly found themselves bundled onto a CIA Gulfstream V or Boeing 737 jet headed for long months of interrogation," and indicated that Abu Zubaydah, KSM, Ramzi bin al-Shibh, and Abu Faraj al-Libi were "picked up and bundled off to interrogation centers." The articles also stated that the capture of bin al-Shibh led to the captures of KSM and Khallad bin Attash.[2274] This information was inaccurate.[2275] There are no CIA records to indicate that there was any investigation or crimes report submitted in connection with the *Dateline NBC* program and its associated reporting.

C. CIA Attorneys Caution that Classified Information Provided to the Media Should Not Be Attributed to the CIA

After the April 15, 2005, National Security Council Principals Committee meeting, the CIA drafted an extensive document describing the CIA's Detention and Interrogation Program for an anticipated media campaign. CIA attorneys, discussing aspects of the campaign involving off-the-record disclosures, cautioned against attributing the information to the CIA itself. One senior attorney stated that the proposed press briefing was "minimally acceptable, but only if not attributed to a CIA official." The CIA attorney continued: "This should be attributed to an 'official knowledgeable' about the program (or some similar obfuscation), but should not be attributed to a CIA or intelligence official." Referring to CIA efforts to deny Freedom of Information Act (FOIA) requests for previously acknowledged information, the attorney noted that, "[o]ur Glomar figleaf is getting pretty thin."[2276] Another CIA attorney noted that the draft "makes the [legal] declaration I just wrote about the secrecy of the interrogation program a work of fiction . . ."[2277] ████████ CTC Legal urged that CIA leadership needed to "confront the inconsistency" between CIA court declarations "about how critical it is to keep this information secret" and the CIA "planning to reveal darn near the entire program."[2278]

D. The CIA Engages with Journalists and Conveys an Inaccurate Account of the Interrogation of Abu Zubaydah

In late 2005, the CIA decided to cooperate again with Douglas Jehl of the *New York Times*, despite his intention to publish information about the program. A CIA officer wrote about Jehl's proposed article, which was largely about the CIA's detention and interrogation of Abu Zubaydah, "[t]his is not necessarily an unflattering story."[2279] Jehl, who provided the CIA with a detailed outline of his proposed story, informed the CIA that he would emphasize that the CIA's enhanced interrogation techniques worked, that they were approved through an inter-agency process, and that the CIA went to great lengths to ensure that the interrogation program was authorized by the White House and the Department of Justice.[2280] CIA records indicate that the CIA decided not to dissuade Jehl from describing the

CIA's enhanced interrogation techniques because, as ▇▇▇ CTC Legal ▇▇▇▇▇ noted, "[t]he EITs have already been out there."[2281] The CIA's chief of ALEC Station, ▇▇▇▇▇▇, who wondered whether cooperation with Jehl would be "undercutting our complaint against those leakers," nonetheless suggested informing Jehl of other examples of CIA "detainee exploitation success."[2282]

While the *New York Times* did not publish Jehl's story, on September 7, 2006, the day after President Bush publicly acknowledged the program, David Johnston of the *New York Times* called the CIA's OPA with a proposed news story about the interrogation of Abu Zubaydah. In an email with the subject line, "We Can't Let This Go Unanswered," the CIA's director of public affairs in OPA, Mark Mansfield, described Johnston's proposed narrative as "bullshit" and biased toward the FBI, adding that "we need to push back."[2283] While it is unclear if Mansfield responded to Johnston's proposed story, Mansfield later wrote in an email that there was "[n]o need to worry."[2284] On September 10, 2006, the *New York Times* published an article by Johnston, entitled, "At a Secret Interrogation, Dispute Flared Over Tactics," that described "sharply contrasting accounts" of the interrogation of Abu Zubaydah. The article cited officials "more closely allied with law enforcement," who stated that Abu Zubaydah "cooperated with F.B.I, interviewers," as well as officials "closely tied to intelligence agencies," who stated that Abu Zubaydah "was lying, and things were going nowhere," and that "[i]t was clear that he had information about an imminent attack and time was of the essence." The article included the frequent CIA representation that, after the use of "tougher tactics," Abu Zubaydah "soon began to provide information on key Al Qaeda operators to help us find and capture those responsible for the 9/11 attacks."[2285] This characterization of Abu Zubaydah's interrogation is incongruent with CIA interrogation records.[2286] CTC stated that the article resulted in questions to the CIA from the country ▇▇▇▇▇▇▇▇▇▇▇▇, and assessed that "[disclosures of this nature could adversely [have an] impact on future joint CT operations with . . . ▇▇▇▇ partners."[2287] There are no indications that the CIA filed a crimes report in connection with the article.[2288]

In early 2007, the CIA cooperated with Ronald Kessler again on another book. According to CIA records, the purpose of the cooperation was to "push back" on Kessler's proposed accounts of intelligence related to the attacks of September 11, 2001, and the interrogation of Abu Zubaydah,[2289] which a CIA officer noted "give undue credit to the FBI for CIA accomplishments."[2290] After another CIA officer drafted information for passage to Kessler,[2291] █████ CTC Legal, ████ ██, wrote, "[o]f course being the lawyer, I would recommend not telling Kessler anything." █████ then wrote that if, "for policy reasons," the CIA decided to cooperate with the author, there was certain information that should not be disclosed. █████ then suggested that "if we are going to do this," the CIA could provide information to Kessler that would "undercut the FBI agents," who █████ stated had "leaked that they would have gotten everything anyway" from Abu Zubaydah.[2292]

After Kessler provided a draft of his book to the CIA and met with CIA officers, the CIA's director of public affairs, Mark Mansfield, described what he viewed as the problems in Kessler's narrative. According to Mansfield, Kessler was "vastly overstating the FBI's role in thwarting terrorism and, frankly, giving other USG agencies—including CIA—short shrift." Moreover, "[t]he draft also didn't reflect the enormously valuable intelligence the USG gleaned from CIA's interrogation program" and "had unnamed FBI officers questioning our methods and claiming their own way of eliciting information is much more effective." According to Mansfield, the CIA "made some headway" in its meeting with Kessler and that, as a result of the CIA's intervention, his book would be "more balanced than it would have been."[2293]

Later, in an email to Mansfield, Kessler provided the "substantive changes" he had made to his draft following his meeting with CIA officials. The changes included the statement that Abu Zubaydah was subjected to "coercive interrogation techniques" after he "stopped cooperating." Kessler's revised text further stated that "the CIA could point to a string of successes and dozens of plots that were rolled up because of coercive interrogation techniques." The statements in the revised text on the "successes" attributable to the CIA's enhanced interrogation techniques were similar to CIA representations to policymakers and were incongruent with CIA records.[2294]

Kessler's "substantive changes" made after his meeting with CIA officials included the statement that many members of Congress and members of the media "have made careers for themselves by belittling and undercutting the efforts of the heroic men and women who are trying to protect us," Kessler's revised text contended that, "[w]ithout winning the war being waged by the media against our own government, we are going to lose the war on terror because the tools that are needed will be taken away by a Congress swayed by a misinformed public and by other countries unwilling to cooperate with the CIA or FBI because they fear mindless exposure by the press." Finally, Kessler's changes, made after his meeting with CIA officers, included the statement that "[t]oo many Americans are intent on demonizing those who are trying to protect us."[2295]

V. REVIEW OF CIA REPRESENTATIONS TO THE DEPARTMENT OF JUSTICE

A. August 1, 2002, OLC Memorandum Relies on Inaccurate Information Regarding Abu Zubaydah

The office of Legal Counsel (OLC) in the Department of Justice wrote several legal memoranda and letters on the legality of the CIA's Detention and Interrogation Program between 2002 and 2007. The OLC requested, and relied on, information provided by the CIA to conduct the legal analysis included in these memoranda and letters. Much of the information the CIA provided to the OLC was inaccurate in material respects. On August 1, 2002, the OLC issued a memorandum advising that the use of the CIA's enhanced interrogation techniques against Abu Zubaydah would not violate prohibitions against torture found in Section 2340A of Title 18 of the United States Code.[2296] The techniques were: (1) attention grasp, (2) walling, (3) facial hold, (4) facial slap (insult slap), (5) cramped confinement, (6) wall standing, (7) stress positions, (8) sleep deprivation, (9) insects placed in a confinement box, and (10) the waterboard. The memorandum relied on CIA representations about Abu Zubaydah's status in al-Qa'ida, his role in al-Qa'ida plots, his expertise in interrogation resistance training, and his withholding of information on pending terrorist attacks.[2297] The OLC memorandum included the following statement about OLC's reliance on information provided by the CIA:

> "Our advice is based upon the following facts, which you have provided to us. We also understand that you do not have any facts in your possession contrary to the facts outlined here, and this opinion is limited to these facts. If these facts were to change, this advice would not necessarily apply."[2298]

The facts provided by the CIA, and relied on by the OLC to support its legal analysis, were cited in the August 1, 2002, memorandum, and many were repeated in subsequent OLC memoranda on the CIA's enhanced interrogation techniques. Much of the information provided by the CIA to the OLC was unsupported by CIA records. Examples include:

- *Abu Zubaydah's Status in Al-Qa'ida*: The OLC memorandum repeated the CIA's representation that Abu Zubaydah was the "third or fourth man" in al-Qa'ida.[2299] This CIA assessment was based on single-source reporting that was recanted prior to the August 1, 2002, OLC legal memorandum. This retraction was provided to several senior CIA officers, including ██████████ CTC Legal, to whom the information was emailed on July 10, 2002, three weeks prior to the issuance of the August 1, 2002, OLC memorandum.[2300] The CIA later concluded that Abu Zubaydah was not a member of al-Qa'ida.[2301]

- *Abu Zubaydah's Role in Al-Qa'ida Plots*: The OLC memorandum repeated the CIA's representation that Abu Zubaydah "has been involved in every major terrorist operation carried out by al Qaeda,"[2302] and that Abu Zubaydah "was one of the planners of the September 11 attacks."[2303] CIA records do not support these claims.

- *Abu Zubaydah's Expertise in Interrogation Resistance Training*: The OLC memorandum repeated the CIA's representation that Abu Zubaydah was "well-versed" in resistance to interrogation techniques, and that "it is believed Zubaydah wrote al Qaeda's manual on resistance techniques."[2304] A review of CIA records found no information to support these claims. To the contrary, Abu Zubaydah later stated that it was his belief that all individuals provide information in detention, and that captured individuals should "expect that the organization will make adjustments to protect people and plans when someone with knowledge is captured."[2305]

- *Abu Zubaydah's Withholding of Information on Pending Terrorist Attacks*: The OLC memorandum repeated CIA representations stating that "the interrogation team is certain" Abu Zubaydah was withholding information related to planned attacks against the United States, either within the U.S. homeland or abroad.[2306] CIA records do not support this claim. Abu Zubaydah's interrogation team was not "certain" that Abu Zubaydah was withholding "critical threat information." To the contrary, the interrogation team wrote to CIA Headquarters: "[o]ur assumption is the objective of this operation [the interrogation of Abu Zubaydah] is to achieve a high degree of confidence that [Abu Zubaydah] is not holding back actionable information concerning threats to the United States beyond that which [Abu Zubaydah] has already provided."[2307]

B. The CIA Interprets the August 1, 2002, Memorandum to Apply to Other Detainees, Despite Language of the

Memorandum; Interrogations of Abu Zubaydah and Other Detainees Diverge from the CIA's Representations to the OLC

The CIA broadly interpreted the August 1, 2002, OLC memorandum to allow for greater operational latitude. For example, the memorandum stated that the legal advice was specific to the interrogation of Abu Zubaydah and the specific CIA representations about Abu Zubaydah; however, the CIA applied its enhanced interrogation techniques to numerous other CIA detainees without seeking additional formal legal advice from the OLC. As detailed elsewhere, the other detainees subjected to the CIA's enhanced interrogation techniques varied significantly in terms of their assessed role in terrorist activities and the information they were believed to possess. CIA records indicate that it was not until July 29, 2003, almost a year later, that the attorney general stated that the legal principles of the August 1, 2002, memorandum could be applied to other CIA detainees.[2308]

The August 1, 2002, OLC memorandum also included an analysis of each of the CIA's proposed enhanced interrogation techniques with a description of how the CIA stated the techniques would be applied.[2309] However, in the interrogations of Abu Zubaydah and subsequent CIA detainees, the CIA applied the techniques in a manner that a Department of Justice attorney concluded "was quite different from the [description] presented in 2002."[2310] As reported by the CIA's inspector general, the CIA used the waterboarding technique against Abu Zubaydah, and later against KSM, in a manner inconsistent with CIA representations to the OLC, as well as the OLC's description of the technique in the August 1, 2002, memorandum. In addition, the CIA assured the OLC that it would be "unlikely" that CIA detainees subjected to sleep deprivation would experience hallucinations, and that if they did, medical personnel would intervene.[2311] However, multiple CIA detainees subjected to prolonged sleep deprivation experienced hallucinations, and CIA interrogation teams did not always discontinue sleep deprivation after the detainees had experienced hallucinations.[2312] The CIA further represented to the OLC that Abu Zubaydah's recovery from his wound would not be impeded by the use of the CIA's enhanced interrogation techniques.[2313] However, prior to the OLC memorandum, DETENTION SITE GREEN personnel stated, and CIA Headquarters had confirmed, that the interrogation process would take precedence over preventing Abu Zubaydah's wound from becoming infected.[2314] Other CIA detainees were also subjected to the CIA's enhanced interrogation techniques, notwithstanding concerns that the interrogation techniques could exacerbate their injuries.[2315] The CIA also repeatedly used interrogation techniques beyond those provided to the OLC for review, including water dousing, nudity, abdominal slaps, and dietary manipulation.[2316]

At the July 29, 2003, meeting of select National Security Council principals, Attorney General John Ashcroft expressed the view that "while appropriate caution should be exercised in the number of times the waterboard was administered, the repetitions described do not contravene the principles underlying DOJ's August 2002 opinion."[2317] Records do not indicate that the attorney general opined on the manner (as opposed to the frequency) with which the waterboard was implemented, or on interrogation techniques not included in the August 2002 opinion. The differences between the CIA's enhanced interrogation techniques, as described by the CIA to the OLC in 2002, and the actual use of the techniques as described in the CIA Inspector General May 2004 Special Review, prompted concerns at the Department of Justice. On May 27, 2004, Assistant Attorney General Jack Goldsmith sent a letter to the CIA general counsel stating that the Special Review "raises the possibility that, at least in some instances and particularly early in the program, the actual practice may not have been congruent with all of these assumptions and limitations." In particular, Goldsmith's letter highlighted the statement in the Special Review that the use of the waterboard in SERE training was "so different from subsequent Agency usage as to make it almost irrelevant."[2318]

C. Following Suspension of the Use of the CIA's Enhanced Interrogation Techniques, the CIA Obtains Approval from the OLC for the Interrogation of Three Individual Detainees

Inspector General Special Review recommended that the CIA's general counsel submit in writing a request for the Department of Justice to provide the CIA with a "formal, written legal opinion, revalidating and modifying, as appropriate, the guidance provided" in the August 1, 2002, memorandum. It also recommended that, in the absence of such a written opinion, the DCI should direct that the CIA's enhanced interrogation techniques "be implemented only within the parameters that were mutually understood by the Agency and DoJ on 1 August 2002."[2319] After receiving the Special Review, Assistant Attorney General Jack Goldsmith informed the CIA that the OLC had never formally opined on whether the CIA's enhanced interrogation techniques would meet constitutional standards.[2320] On May 24, 2004, DCI Tenet, Deputy Director John McLaughlin, General Counsel Scott Muller, and others met to discuss the Department of Justice's comments, after which DCI Tenet directed that the use of the CIA's enhanced interrogation techniques, as well as the use of the CIA's "standard" techniques, be suspended.[2321] On June 4, 2004, DCI Tenet issued a formal memorandum suspending the use of the techniques, pending policy and legal review.[2322]

As described in this summary, on July 2, 2004, Attorney General Ashcroft and Deputy Attorney General James Comey attended a meeting of select National Security Council principals, the topic of which was the proposed CIA interrogation of Janat Gul.[2323] According to CIA records, the attorney general stated that the use of the CIA's enhanced interrogation techniques against Gul would be consistent with U.S. law and treaty obligations, although Ashcroft made an exception for the waterboard, which he stated required further review, "primarily because of the view that the technique had been employed in a different fashion than that which DOJ initially approved."[2324] On July 20, 2004, Ashcroft, along with Patrick Philbin and Daniel Levin from the Department of Justice, attended a National Security Council Principals Committee meeting at which Ashcroft stated that the use of the CIA's enhanced interrogation techniques described in the August 1, 2002, OLC memorandum, with the exception of the waterboard, would not violate U.S. statutes, the U.S. Constitution, or U.S. treaty obligations. The attorney general was then "directed" to prepare a written opinion addressing the constitutional issues, and the CIA was directed to provide further information to the Department of Justice with regard to the waterboard.[2325] On July 22, 2004, Attorney General Ashcroft sent a letter to Acting DCI John McLaughlin stating that nine interrogation techniques (those addressed in the August 1, 2002, memorandum, with the exception of the waterboard) did not violate the U.S. Constitution or any statute or U.S. treaty obligations, in the context of the CIA interrogation of Janat Gul.[2326]

On July 30, 2004, anticipating the interrogation of Janat Gul, the CIA provided the OLC for the first time a description of dietary manipulation, nudity, water dousing, the abdominal slap, standing sleep deprivation, and the use of diapers, all of which the CIA described as a "supplement" to the interrogation techniques outlined in the August 1, 2002, memorandum.[2327] The CIA's descriptions of the interrogation techniques were incongruent with how the CIA had applied the techniques in practice. The CIA description of a minimum calorie intake was incongruent with the history of the program, as no minimum calorie intake existed prior to May 2004 and the March 2003 draft OMS guidelines allowed for food to be withheld for one to two days.[2328] The CIA represented to the OLC that nude detainees were "not wantonly exposed to other detainees or detention facility staff," even though nude detainees at the CIA's DETENTION SITE COBALT were "kept in a central area outside the interrogation room" and were "walked around" by guards as a form of humiliation.[2329] The CIA's description of water dousing made no mention of cold water immersion, which was used on CIA detainees and taught in CIA interrogator training.[2330] The CIA representation describing a two-hour limit for the shackling of detainees' hands above their heads is incongruent with records of CIA detainees whose hands were shackled above their heads for extended periods, as well as the draft March 2003 OMS guidelines permitting such shackling for up to four hours.[2331] The CIA further represented to the OLC that the use of diapers was "for sanitation and hygiene purposes," whereas CIA records indicate that in some cases, a central "purpose" of diapers was "[t]o cause humiliation" and "to induce a sense of helplessness."[2332]

On August 13, 2004, CIA attorneys, medical officers, and other personnel met with Department of Justice attorneys to discuss some of the techniques for which the CIA was seeking approval, in particular sleep deprivation, water dousing, and the waterboard. When asked about the possibility that detainees subjected to standing sleep deprivation could suffer from edema, OMS doctors informed the Department of Justice attorneys that it was not a problem as the CIA would "adjust shackles or [the] method of applying the technique as necessary to prevent edema, as well as any chafing or over-tightness from the shackles." With regard to water dousing, CIA officers represented that "water is at normal temperature; CIA makes no effort to 'cool' the water before applying it." With respect to the waterboard, CIA officers indicated that "each application could not last more than 40 seconds (and usually only lasted about 20 seconds)."[2333] As detailed in the full Committee Study, each of these representations was incongruent with the operational history of the CIA program.

On August 25, 2004, the CIA's Associate General Counsel ■ ■■■■■■■■■■ sent a letter to the OLC stating that Janat Gul, who had been rendered to CIA custody on July ■, 2004, had been subjected to the attention grasp, walling, facial hold, facial slap, wall standing, stress positions, and sleep deprivation. The letter further stated that CIA interrogators "assess Gul not to be cooperating, and to be using a sophisticated counterinterrogation strategy," and that the further use of the same enhanced interrogation techniques would be "unlikely to move Gul to cooperate absent concurrent use" of dietary manipulation, nudity, water dousing, and the abdominal slap. The letter referenced the reporting from a CIA source,[2334] stating: "CIA understands that before his capture, Gul had been working to facilitate a direct meeting between the CIA source reporting on the pre-election threat and Abu Faraj [al-Libi] himself."[2335]

The following day, August 26, 2004, Acting Assistant Attorney General Daniel Levin informed CIA Acting General Counsel John Rizzo that the use of the four additional interrogation techniques did not violate any U.S. statutes, the U.S. Constitution, or U.S. treaty obligations. Levin's advice relied on the CIA's representations about Gul, including that "there are no medical and psychological contraindications to the use of these techniques as you plan to employ them on Gul."[2336] At the time, CIA records indicated: (1) that standing sleep deprivation had already caused significant swelling in Gul's legs; (2) that standing sleep deprivation continued despite Gul's visual and auditory hallucinations and that Gul was "not oriented to time or place";[2337] (3) that CIA interrogators on-site did not believe that "escalation to enhanced pressures will increase [Gul's] ability to produce timely accurate locational and threat information";[2338] and (4) that CIA interrogators did not believe that Gul was "withholding imminent threat information."[2339]

Levin's August 26, 2004, letter to Rizzo was based on the premise that "[w]e understand that [Janat] Gul is a high-value al Qaeda operative who is believed to possess information concerning an imminent terrorist threat to the United States."[2340] Levin's understanding was based on the CIA's representation that "Gul had been working to facilitate a direct meeting between the CIA source reporting on the pre-election threat and Abu Faraj [al-Libi]."[2341] This information later proved to be inaccurate. As detailed elsewhere in this summary, the threat of a terrorist attack to precede the November 2004 U.S. election was found to be based on a CIA source whose information was questioned by senior CTC officials at the time.[2342] The same CIA source admitted to fabricating the information after a in October 2004.[2343] In November 2004, after the use of the CIA's enhanced interrogation techniques on Janat Gul, CIA's chief of Base at DETENTION SITE BLACK, where Janat Gul was interrogated, wrote that "describing [Gul] as 'highest ranking' gives him a stature which is undeserved, overblown and misleading." The chief of Base added that "[s]tating that [Gul] had 'long standing access to senior leaders in al-Qa'ida' is simply wrong."[2344] In December 2004, CIA officers concluded that Janat Gul was "not the link to senior AQ leaders that [CIA Headquarters] said he was/is,"[2345] and in April 2005 CIA officers wrote that "[t]here simply is no 'smoking gun' that we can refer to that would justify our continued holding of [Janat Gul]."[2346]

By April 2005, as the OLC neared completion of a new memorandum analyzing the legality of the CIA's enhanced interrogation techniques, the OLC sought information from the CIA on "what [the CIA] got from Janat Gul, was it valuable, [and] did it help anything . . ." The CIA did not immediately respond to this request, and the CIA's Associate General Counsel noted that DOJ personnel had "taken to calling [him] daily" for additional information."[2347] Subsequently, on April 15, 2005, the CIA informed the OLC that "during most of Gul's debriefings, he has sought to minimize his knowledge of extremist activities and has provided largely non-incriminating information about his involvement in their networks."[2348] On May 10, 2005, the OLC issued a memorandum that stated, "[y]ou informed us that the CIA believed Gul had information about al Qaeda's plans to launch an attack within the United States . . . [o]ur conclusions depend on these assessments." The OLC referenced [redacted]'s August 25, 2004, letter on Gul and the pre-election threat.[2349] In a May 30, 2005, memorandum, the OLC referred to Janat Gul as "representative of the high value detainees on whom enhanced techniques have been, or might be used," and wrote that "the CIA believed [that Janat Gul] had actionable intelligence concerning the pre-election threat to the United States."[2350] In the same memorandum, the OLC conveyed a new CIA representation describing the effectiveness of the CIA's enhanced interrogation techniques on Janat Gul, which stated:

> "Gul has provided information that has helped the CIA with validating one of its key assets reporting on the pre-election threat."[2351]

There are no indications in the memorandum that the CIA informed the OLC that it had concluded that Gul had no information about the pre-election threat, which was the basis on which the OLC had approved the use of the CIA's enhanced interrogation techniques against Gul in the first place, or that CIA officers had determined that Gul was "not the man we thought he was." In September 2004, the OLC advised the CIA that the use of the CIA's enhanced interrogation techniques against Ahmed Khalfan Ghailani and Sharif al-Masri was also legal, based on the CIA representations that the two detainees were al-Qa'ida operatives involved in the "operational planning" of the pre-election plot against the United States.[2352] This CIA assessment was based on the same fabrications from the same CIA questions from the same CIA source.[2353] Like Janat Gul, Ghailani and al-Masri were subjected to extended sleep deprivation and experienced hallucinations.[2354]

D. May 2005 OLC Memoranda Rely on Inaccurate Representations from the CIA Regarding the Interrogation Process, the CIA's Enhanced Interrogation Techniques, and the Effectiveness of the Techniques

On May 4, 2005, Acting Assistant Attorney General Steven Bradbury faxed to CIA Associate General Counsel ████████████ ███ questions related to the CIA's enhanced interrogation techniques, in which Bradbury referenced medical journal articles. The following day, ██████████ sent a letter to Bradbury stating that the CIA's responses had been composed by the CIA's Office of Medical Services (OMS). The CIA response stated that any lowering of the threshold of pain caused by sleep deprivation was "not germane" to the program, because studies had only identified differences in sensitivity to heat, cold, and pressure, and the CIA's enhanced interrogation techniques "do not involve application of heat, cold, pressure, any sharp objects (or indeed any objects at all)."[2355] With regard to the effect of sleep deprivation on the experience of water dousing, the CIA response stated that "at the temperatures of water we have recommended for the program the likelihood of induction of pain by water dousing is very low under any circumstances, and not a phenomenon we have seen in detainees subject to this technique."[2356] In response to Bradbury's query as to when edema or shackling would become painful as a result of standing sleep deprivation, the CIA responded, "[w]e have not observed this phenomenon in the interrogations performed to date, and have no reason to believe on theoretical grounds that edema or shackling would be more painful," provided the shackles are maintained with "appropriate slack" and "interrogators follow medical officers' recommendation to end standing sleep deprivation and use an alternate technique when the medical officer judges that edema is significant in any way." The CIA response added that the medical officers' recommendations "are always followed," and that "[d]etainees have not complained about pain from edema." Much of this information was inaccurate.[2357]

Bradbury further inquired whether it was "possible to tell reliably (e.g. from outward physical signs like grimaces) whether a detainee is experiencing severe pain."The CIA responded that "all pain is subjective, not objective,"[2358] adding:

> "Medical officers can monitor for evidence of condition or injury that most people would consider painful, and can observe the individual for outward displays and expressions associated with the experience of pain. Medical officer [*sic*] can and do ask the subject, after the interrogation session has concluded, if he is in pain, and have and do provide analgesics, such as Tylenol and Aleve, to detainees who report headache and other discomforts during their interrogations. We reiterate, that an interrogation session would be stopped if, in the judgment of the interrogators or medical personnel, medical attention was required."[2359]

As described elsewhere, multiple CIA detainees were subjected to the CIA's enhanced interrogation techniques despite their medical conditions.[2360]

Bradbury's fax also inquired whether monitoring and safeguards "will effectively avoid severe physical pain or suffering for detainees," which was a formulation of the statutory definition of torture under consideration. Despite concerns from OMS that its assessments could be used to support a legal review of the CIA's enhanced interrogation techniques,[2361] the CIA's response stated:

> "[i]t is OMS's view that based on our limited experience and the extensive experience of the military with these techniques, the program in place has effectively avoided severe physical pain and suffering, and should continue to do so. Application of the thirteen techniques[2362] has not to date resulted in any severe or permanent physical injury (or any injury other than transient bruising), and we do not expect this to change."[2363]

In May 2005, Principal Deputy Assistant Attorney General Steven Bradbury signed three memoranda that relied on information provided by the CIA that was inconsistent with CIA's operational records. On May 10, 2005, Bradbury signed two memoranda analyzing the statutory prohibition on torture with regard to the CIA's enhanced interrogation techniques and to the use of the interrogation techniques in combination.[2364] On May 30, 2005, Bradbury signed another memorandum examining U.S. obligations under the Convention Against Torture.[2365] The memoranda approved 13 techniques: (1) dietary manipulation, (2) nudity, (3) attention grasp, (4) walling, (5) facial hold, (6) facial slap or insult slap, (7) abdominal slap, (8) cramped confinement, (9) wall standing, (10) stress positions, (11) water dousing, (12) sleep deprivation (more than 48 hours), and (13) the waterboard. The three memoranda relied on numerous CIA representations that, as detailed elsewhere, were incongruent with CIA records, including: (1) the CIA's enhanced interrogation techniques would be used only when the interrogation team "considers them necessary because a detainee is withholding important, actionable intelligence or there is insufficient time to try other techniques," (2) the use of the techniques "is discontinued if the detainee is judged to be consistently providing accurate intelligence or if he is no longer believed to have actionable intelligence," (3) the "use of the techniques usually ends after just a few days when the detainee begins participating," (4) the interrogation techniques "would not be used on a detainee not reasonably thought to possess important, actionable intelligence that could not be obtained otherwise," and (5) the interrogation process begins with "an open, non-threatening approach" to discern if the CIA detainee would be cooperative.[2366]

The OLC memoranda also relied on CIA representations regarding specific interrogation techniques that were incongruent with the operational history of the program. For example, the CIA informed the OLC that it maintained a 75 degree minimum room temperature for nude detainees as "a matter of policy," with a minimum of 68 degrees in the case of technical problems. This information was inconsistent with CIA practice both before and after the CIA's representations to the OLC.[2367] The OLC relied on the CIA representation that standing sleep deprivation would be discontinued in the case of significant swelling of the lower extremities (edema), whereas in practice the technique was repeatedly not stopped when edema occurred.[2368] The OLC also repeated CIA representations that constant light was necessary for security, even though the CIA had subjected detainees to constant darkness.[2369] Additional CIA representations accepted by the OLC—and found to be inconsistent with CIA practice—related to: (1) the exposure of nude detainees to other detainees and detention facility staff,[2370] (2) the use of water dousing—specifically the inaccurate representation that the technique did not involve immersion, (3) the use of shackles in standing sleep deprivation, (4) the likelihood of hallucinations during sleep deprivation, (5) the responsibility of medical personnel to intervene when standing sleep deprivation results in hallucinations, and (6) the purpose and the use of diapers on CIA detainees.[2371]

The OLC repeated the CIA's representations that "the effect of the waterboard is to induce a sensation of drowning," that "the detainee experiences this sensation even if he is aware that he is not actually drowning," and that "as far as can be determined, [Abu Zubaydah and KSM] did not experience physical pain or, in the professional judgment of doctors, is there any medical reason to believe they would have done so." The OLC further accepted that physical sensations associated with waterboarding, such as choking, "end when the application ends."[2372] This information is incongruent with CIA records. According to CIA records, Abu Zubaydah's waterboarding sessions "resulted in immediate fluid intake and involuntary leg, chest and arm spasms" and "hysterical pleas."[2373] A medical officer who oversaw the interrogation of KSM stated that the waterboard technique had evolved beyond the "sensation of drowning" to what he described as a "series of near drownings."[2374] Physical reactions to waterboarding did not necessarily end when the application of water was discontinued, as both Abu Zubaydah and KSM vomited after being subjected to the waterboard.[2375] Further, as previously described, during at least one waterboard session, Abu Zubaydah "became completely unresponsive, with bubbles rising through his open, full mouth." He remained unresponsive after the waterboard was rotated upwards. Upon medical intervention, he regained consciousness and expelled "copious amounts of liquid."[2376] The CIA also relayed information to the OLC on the frequency with which the waterboard could be used that was incongruent with past operational practice.[2377]

The May 10, 2005, memorandum analyzing the individual use of the CIA's enhanced interrogation techniques accepted the CIA's representations that CIA interrogators are trained for "approximately four weeks," and that "all personnel directly engaged in the interrogation of persons detained... have been appropriately screened (from the medical, psychological and security standpoints)."[2378] The CIA representations about training and screening were incongruent with the operational history of the CIA program. CIA records indicate that CIA officers and contractors who conducted CIA interrogations in 2002 did not undergo any interrogation training. The first interrogator training course did not begin until November 12, 2002, by which time at least 25 detainees had been taken into CIA custody.[2379] Numerous CIA interrogators and other CIA personnel associated with the program had either suspected or documented personal and professional problems that raised questions about their judgment and CIA employment. This group of officers included individuals who, among other issues, had engaged in inappropriate detainee interrogations, had workplace anger management issues, and had reportedly admitted to sexual assault.[2380]

Finally, the OLC accepted a definition of "High Value Detainee" conveyed by the CIA[2381] that limited the use of the CIA's enhanced interrogation techniques to "senior member[s]" of al-Qa'ida or an associated terrorist group who have "knowledge of imminent terrorist threats" or "direct involvement in planning and preparing" terrorist actions. However, at the time of the OLC opinion, the CIA had used its enhanced interrogation techniques on CIA detainees who were found neither to have knowledge of imminent threats nor to have been directly involved in planning or preparing terrorist actions. Some were not senior al-Qa'ida members,[2382] or even members of al-Qa'ida.[2383] Others were never suspected of having information on, or a role in, terrorist plotting and were suspected only of having information on the location of UBL or other al-Qa'ida figures,[2384] or were simply believed to have been present at a suspected al-Qa'ida guesthouse.[2385] A year later, ██████████ CTC Legal wrote to Acting Assistant Attorney General Steven Bradbury suggesting a new standard that more closely reflected actual practice by allowing for the CIA detention and interrogation of detainees to be based on the belief that the detainee had information that could assist in locating senior al-Qa'ida leadership.[2386] The OLC modified the standard in a memorandum dated July 20, 2007.[2387] By then, the last CIA detainee, Muhammad Rahim, had already entered CIA custody.[2388]

The May 30, 2005, OLC memorandum analyzing U.S. obligations under the Convention Against Torture relied heavily on CIA representations about the intelligence obtained from the program. Many of these representations were provided in a March 2, 2005, CIA memorandum known as the "Effectiveness Memo," in which the CIA advised that the CIA program "works and the techniques are effective in producing foreign intelligence." The "Effectiveness Memo" stated that "[w]e assess we would not have succeeded in overcoming the resistance of Khalid Shaykh Muhammad (KSM), Abu Zubaydah, and other equally resistant high-value terrorist detainees without applying, in a careful, professional and safe manner, the full range of interrogation techniques."[2389] The CIA "Effectiveness Memo" further stated that "[p]rior to the use of enhanced techniques against skilled resistors [*sic*] like KSM and Abu Zubaydah—the two most prolific intelligence producers in our control—CIA acquired little threat information or significant actionable intelligence information." As described in this summary, the key information provided by Abu Zubaydah that the CIA attributed to the CIA's enhanced interrogation techniques was provided prior to the use of the CIA's enhanced interrogation techniques. KSM was subjected to CIA's enhanced interrogation techniques within minutes of his questioning, and thus had no opportunity to divulge information prior to their use. As described elsewhere, CIA personnel concluded the waterboard was not an effective interrogation technique against KSM.[2390]

Under a section entitled, "Results," the CIA "Effectiveness Memo" represented that the "CIA's use of DOJ-approved enhanced interrogation techniques, as part of a comprehensive interrogation approach, has enabled CIA to disrupt terrorist plots, capture additional terrorists, and collect a high volume of critical intelligence on al-Qa'ida." It then listed 11 examples of "critical intelligence" acquired "after applying enhanced interrogation techniques":[2391] the "Karachi Plot," the "Heathrow Plot," the "Second Wave," the "Guraba Cell," "Issa al-Hindi," "Abu Talha al-Pakistani," "Hambali's Capture," "Jafaar al-Tayyar," the "Dirty Bomb Plot," the "Shoe Bomber," and intelligence obtained on "Shkai, Pakistan." These representations of "effectiveness" were almost entirely inaccurate and mirrored other inaccurate information provided to the White House, Congress, and the CIA inspector general.[2392] In addition, on April 15, 2005, the CIA provided the OLC with an eight-page document entitled, "Briefing Notes on the Value of Detainee Reporting." The CIA "Briefing Notes" document repeats many of the same CIA representations in the "Effectiveness Memo," but added additional inaccurate information related to the capture of Iyman Faris.[2393]

The OLC's May 30, 2005, memorandum relied on the CIA's inaccurate representations in the "Effectiveness Memo" and the "Briefing Notes" document in determining that the CIA's enhanced interrogation techniques did not violate the Fifth Amendment's prohibition on executive conduct that "shocks the conscience," indicating that this analysis was a "highly context-specific and fact-dependent question." The OLC also linked its analysis of whether the use of the CIA's enhanced interrogation techniques was "constitutionally arbitrary" to the representation by the CIA that its interrogation program produced "substantial quantities of otherwise unavailable actionable intelligence."[2394] The CIA's representations to the OLC that it obtained "otherwise unavailable actionable intelligence" from the use of the CIA's enhanced interrogation techniques were inaccurate.[2395]

The OLC memorandum repeated specific inaccurate CIA representations, including that the waterboard was used against Abu Zubaydah and KSM "only after it became clear that standard interrogation techniques were not working"; that the information related to the "Guraba Cell" in Karachi was "otherwise unavailable actionable intelligence"; that Janat Gul was a "high value detainee"; and that information provided by Hassan Ghul regarding the al-Qa'ida presence in Shkai, Pakistan, was attributable to the CIA's enhanced interrogation techniques.[2396] Citing CIA information, the OLC memorandum also stated that Abu Zubaydah was al-Qa'ida's "third or fourth highest ranking member" and had been involved "in every major terrorist operation carried out by al Qaeda," and that "again, once enhanced techniques were employed," Abu Zubaydah "provided significant information on two operatives... who planned to build and detonate a 'dirty bomb' in the Washington DC area." The OLC repeated additional inaccurate information from the CIA related to KSM's reporting, including representations about the "Second Wave" plotting, the Heathrow Airport plotting, and the captures of Hambali, Iyman Paris, and Sajid Badat.[2397] The OLC relied on CIA representations that the use of the CIA's enhanced interrogation techniques against 'Abd al-Rahim al-Nashiri produced "notable results as early as the first day," despite al-Nashiri providing reporting on the same topics prior to entering CIA custody. The OLC also repeated inaccurate CIA representations about statements reportedly made by Abu Zubaydah and KSM.[2398]

Finally, the May 30, 2005, OLC memorandum referenced the CIA Inspector General May 2004 Special Review, stating; "we understand that interrogations have led to specific, actionable intelligence as well as a general increase in the amount of intelligence regarding al Qaeda and its affiliates."[2399] The OLC memorandum cited pages in the Special Review that included inaccurate information provided by CIA personnel to the CIA's OIG, including representations related to Jose Padilla and Binyam Muhammad, Hambali and the "Al-Qa'ida cell in Karachi," the Parachas, Iyman Paris, Saleh al-Marri, Majid Khan, the Heathrow Airport plotting, and other "plots".[2400]

E. After Passage of the Detainee Treatment Act, OLC Issues Opinion on CIA Conditions of Confinement, Withdraws Draft Opinion on the CIA's Enhanced Interrogation Techniques After the U.S. Supreme Court Case of *Hamdan v. Rumsfeld*

On December 19, 2005, anticipating the passage of the Detainee Treatment Act, Acting CIA General Counsel John Rizzo requested that the OLC review whether the CIA's enhanced interrogation techniques, as well as the conditions of confinement at CIA detention facilities, would violate the Detainee Treatment Act.[2401] In April 2006, attorneys at OLC completed initial drafts of two legal memoranda addressing these questions.[2402] In June 2006, however, the U.S. Supreme Court case of *Hamdan v. Rumsfeld* prompted the OLC to withdraw its draft memorandum on the impact of the Detainee Treatment Act on the CIA's enhanced interrogation techniques. As ██████████ CTC Legal explained, the OLC would prepare "a written opinion 'if we want'... but strongly implied we shouldn't seek it."[2403] As described in a July 2009 report of the Department of Justice Office of Professional Responsibility, the Administration determined that, after the Hamdan decision, it would need new legislation to support the continued use of the CIA's enhanced interrogation techniques.[2404]

Even as it withdrew its draft opinion on the CIA's enhanced interrogation techniques, the OLC continued to analyze whether the CIA's conditions of confinement violated the Detainee Treatment Act. To support this analysis, the CIA asserted to the OLC that loud music and white noise, constant light, and 24-hour shackling were all for security purposes, that shaving was for security and hygiene purposes and was conducted only upon intake and not as a "punitive step," that detainees were not exposed to an "extended period" of white noise, and that CIA detainees had access to a wide array of amenities.[2405] This information is incongruent with CIA records. Detainees were routinely shaved, sometimes as an aid to interrogation; detainees who were "participating at an acceptable level" were permitted to grow their hair and beards.[2406] The CIA had used music at decibels exceeding the representations to the OLC. The CIA had also used specific music to signal to a detainee that another interrogation was about to begin.[2407] Numerous CIA detainees were subjected to the extended use of white noise.[2408] The CIA further inaccurately represented that "[m]edical personnel will advise ending sleep deprivation in the event the detainee appears to be experiencing hallucinations, transient or not."[2409] In a May 18, 2006, letter, ██████████ CTC Legal, ██████████, wrote to the Department of Justice that "some of these conditions provide the additional benefit of setting a detention atmosphere conducive to continued intelligence collection from the detainee." While the letter referred generally to "constant light in the cells, use of white noise, use of shackles, hooding, and shaving/barbering," it described an intelligence collection purpose only for shaving, which "allows interrogators a clear view of the terrorist-detainee's facial clues."[2410]

On August 31, 2006, the OLC finalized two legal analyses on the conditions of confinement at CIA detention sites. The first was a memorandum that evaluated whether six detention conditions in the CIA's detention program were consistent with the Detainee Treatment Act.[2411] The second, provided in the form of a letter, concluded that those same six conditions did not violate the requirements of Common Article 3 of the Geneva Conventions.[2412] The OLC relied on the CIA's representations related to conditions of confinement for its analysis.[2413] The OLC wrote that "underlying our analysis of all these methods [conditions of confinement] is our understanding that the CIA provides regular and thorough medical and psychological care to the detainees in its custody."[2414] As detailed in this summary, the lack of emergency medical care for CIA detainees was a significant challenge for the CIA.[2415]

The August 31, 2006, OLC memorandum applying the terms of the Detainee Treatment Act to the conditions of confinement at CIA detention facilities stated that "over the history of the program, the CIA has detained a total of 96 individuals." This was based on a representation made by ██████████ CTC Legal on April 23, 2006."[2416] As of the date of the OLC memorandum, the CIA had detained at least 118 individuals. The OLC memorandum also stated that "we understand that, once the CIA assesses that a detainee no longer possesses significant intelligence value, the CIA seeks to move the detainee into alternative detention arrangements." CIA records indicate that detainees had remained in CIA custody long after the CIA had determined that they no longer possessed significant intelligence. Finally, the OLC memorandum repeated a number of earlier inaccurate CIA representations on the effectiveness of the program, citing both the CIA's "Effectiveness Memo" and its own May 30, 2005, memorandum. Notably, the August 31, 2006, OLC memorandum repeated the same inaccurate representation, which first appeared in an August 2002 OLC memorandum, that Abu Zubaydah was al-Qa'ida's "third or fourth highest ranking member" and had been involved "in every major terrorist operation carried out by al Qaeda." As described, CIA records as early as 2002 did not support these representations, and two weeks prior to the issuance of the August 2006 memorandum, the CIA had published an intelligence assessment stating that Abu Zubaydah had been rejected by al-Qa'ida and explaining how the CIA had come to "miscast Abu Zubaydah as a 'senior al-Qa'ida lieutenant.'"[2417]

F. July 2007 OLC Memorandum Relies on Inaccurate CIA Representations Regarding CIA Interrogations and the Effectiveness of the CIA's Enhanced Interrogation Techniques; CIA Misrepresents Congressional Views to the Department of Justice

On July 20, 2007, the OLC issued a memorandum applying the War Crimes Act, the Detainee Treatment Act, and Common Article 3 of the Geneva Conventions to the CIA's enhanced interrogation techniques. The memorandum noted that, while the *Hamdan* decision "was contrary to the President's prior determination that Common Article 3 does not apply to an armed conflict across national boundaries with an international terrorist organization such as al Qaeda," this challenge to the CIA program was resolved by the Military Commissions Act, which "left responsibility for interpreting the meaning and application of Common Article 3, except for the grave breaches defined in the amended War Crimes Act, to the President."[2418]

The OLC memorandum determined that six proposed interrogation techniques were legal: dietary manipulation, extended sleep deprivation, the facial hold, the attention grasp, the abdominal slap, and the insult (or facial) slap. The memorandum accepted the CIA's representation that, over the life of the program, the CIA had detained 98 individuals, of whom 30 had been subjected to the CIA's enhanced interrogation techniques.[2419] At the time of the OLC memorandum the CIA had detained at least 119 individuals, of whom at least 38 had been subjected to the CIA's enhanced interrogation techniques.[2420] The inaccurate statistics provided by the CIA to the OLC were used to support OLC's conclusion that the program was "proportionate to the government interest involved," as required by the "shocks the conscience" test. The OLC also noted that "careful screening procedures are in place to ensure that enhanced techniques will be used only in the interrogations of agents or members of al Qaeda or its affiliates who are reasonably believed to possess critical intelligence that can be used to prevent future terrorist attacks against the United States and its interests."[2421] In practice, numerous individuals had been detained by the CIA and subjected to the CIA's enhanced interrogation techniques, despite doubts and questions surrounding their knowledge of terrorist threats and the location of senior al-Qa'ida leadership. Examples include, among others: Asadullah,[2422] Mustafa al-Hawsawi,[2423] Abu Hudhaifa,[2424] Arsala Khan,[2425] ABU TALHA AL-MAGREBI and ABU BAHAR AL-TURKI,[2426] Janat Gul,[2427] Ahmed Ghailani,[2428] Sharif al-Masri,[2429] and Sayyid Ibrahim.[2430]

The July 20, 2007, OLC memorandum also stated that the CIA's enhanced interrogation techniques "are not the first option for CIA interrogators confronted even with a high value detainee."[2431] As described in this summary, numerous CIA detainees were subjected to the CIA's enhanced or "standard" interrogation techniques on their first day of CIA custody,[2432] while other detainees provided significant information prior to the use of the CIA's enhanced interrogation techniques. The OLC memorandum also accepted the CIA representation that "[t]he CIA generally does not ask questions during the administration of the techniques to which the CIA does not already know the answers," that the CIA "asks for already known information" during the administration of the CIA's enhanced interrogation techniques, and that when CIA personnel believe a detainee will cooperate, "the CIA would discontinue use of the techniques and debrief the detainee regarding matters on which the CIA is not definitely informed." As the memorandum concluded, "[t]his approach highlights the intended psychological effects of the techniques and reduces the ability of the detainee to provide false information solely as a means to discontinue their application."[2433] This description of the program was inaccurate. As described in this summary, and in more detail in the full Committee Study, CIA interrogators always questioned detainees during the application of the CIA's enhanced interrogation techniques seeking new information to which the CIA did not have answers, and numerous detainees fabricated information while being subjected to the interrogation techniques.

The July 20, 2007, OLC memorandum repeated CIA representations that "many, if not all, of those 30 detainees" who had been subjected to CIA's enhanced interrogation techniques received counter interrogation training, and that "al Qaeda operatives believe that they are morally permitted to reveal information once they have reached a certain limit of discomfort."[2434] Neither of these representations is supported by CIA records.

The memorandum also repeated CIA representations that interrogators were "highly trained in carrying out the techniques," and "psychologically screened to minimize the risk that an interrogator might misuse any technique." These presumptions were central to the OLC's determination that the limitations on interrogations contained in the Army Field Manual were not "dispositive evidence" that the CIA's interrogation program fell outside "traditional executive behavior and contemporary practice," an analysis required as part of the substantive due process inquiry. Specifically, the OLC distinguished

U.S. military interrogations from the CIA program by stating that the CIA program "will be administered only by trained and experienced interrogators who in turn will apply the techniques only to a subset of high value detainees."[2435] As described in this summary, and in greater detail in the full Committee Study, the CIA's representations to the OLC were incongruent with the history of the CIA's Detention and Interrogation Program with regard to the training, screening, and experience of interrogators, and the detainees against whom the CIA used its enhanced interrogation techniques.

The July 2007 OLC memorandum based its legal analysis related to the six interrogation techniques under consideration on CIA representations that were incongruent with the operational history of the program. In reviewing whether standing sleep deprivation was consistent with the War Crimes Act, the OLC noted that its understanding that the technique would be discontinued "should any hallucinations or significant declines in cognitive functioning be observed" was "crucial to our analysis." The memorandum repeated CIA representations that diapers employed during standing sleep deprivation "are used solely for sanitary and health reasons and not to humiliate the detainee," and that, more generally, "[t]he techniques are not intended to humiliate or to degrade."[2436] The OLC's understanding, which, as described, was not consistent with the operational history of the CIA program, was part of its analysis related to the prohibition on "outrages upon personal dignity" under Common Article 3.

As in the May 30, 2005 OLC memorandum, the July 20, 2007, OLC memorandum conducted an analysis of the "shocks the conscience" test under the Fifth Amendment of the U.S. Constitution, emphasizing the fact-specific nature of the analysis. Citing both the CIA's March 2005 "Effectiveness Memo" and the president's September 6, 2006, speech describing the interrogation program, the July 2007 OLC memorandum repeated the CIA assertion that the CIA's enhanced interrogation techniques produced "otherwise unavailable intelligence." It also repeated CIA representations related to KSM's reporting on the "Second Wave" plotting and Abu Zubaydah's reporting on Jose Padilla, both of which were inaccurate.[2437] The OLC memorandum also stated that the use of the CIA's enhanced interrogation techniques had "revealed plots to blow up the Brooklyn Bridge and to release mass biological agents in our Nation's largest cities."'[2438]

Finally, the July 20, 2007, OLC memorandum asserted—based on CIA representations—that members of Congress supported the CIA interrogation program, and that, by subsequently voting for the

Military Commissions Act, those members effectively endorsed an interpretation of the Act that would be consistent with the continued use of the CIA's enhanced interrogation techniques. This interpretation of congressional intent also supported the OLC's constitutional analysis, which stated that there could be "little doubt" that the Act "reflected an endorsement" from Congress that the CIA program "was consistent with contemporary practice, and therefore did not shock the conscience."[2439] Specifically, the OLC memorandum noted that according to CIA representations, prior to the passage of the Military Commissions Act, "several Members of Congress, including the full memberships of the House and Senate Intelligence Committees and Senator McCain, were briefed by General Michael Hayden, director of the CIA, on the six techniques," and that "in those classified and private conversations, none of the Members expressed the view that the CIA interrogation program should be stopped, or that the techniques at issue were inappropriate."[2440] This representation was inaccurate. For example, according to CIA records, during a briefing on September 11, 2006, Senator John McCain informed the CIA that he believed the CIA's enhanced interrogation techniques, including sleep deprivation and the waterboard, were "torture."[2441] On September 27, 2006 Senator Dianne Feinstein, a member of the Senate Select Committee on Intelligence, wrote a letter to CIA Director Hayden stating that she was "unable to understand why the CIA needs to maintain this program."[2442] On September 6, 2006, when the CIA provided its first and only briefing to the full Committee on the CIA program prior to the vote on the Military Commissions Act, Committee staff access was limited to the two Committee staff directors.[2443] In May 2007, shortly after the CIA allowed additional Committee staff to be briefed on the program, other members of the Committee prepared and provided letters to Director Hayden. On May 1, 2007, Senator Russ Feingold wrote that "I cannot support the program on moral, legal or national security grounds."[2444] On May 11, 2007, Senators Chuck Hagel, Dianne Feinstein, and Ron Wyden wrote a letter expressing their long-standing concerns with the program and their "deep discomfort with the use of EITs."[2445]

VI. REVIEW OF CIA REPRESENTATIONS TO THE CONGRESS

A. After Memorandum of Notification, the CIA Disavows Torture and Assures the Committee Will Be Notified of Every Individual Detained by the CIA

Following the September 11, 2001, terrorist attacks and the signing of the September 17, 2001, Memorandum of Notification (MON), the Senate Select Committee on Intelligence ("the Committee") held a series of hearings and briefings on CIA covert actions, including the new authority to detain terrorists. At a November 13, 2001, briefing for Committee staff, ███████████ CTC Legal, ████████ ████, described the CIA's new detention authorities as "terrifying" and expressed the CIA's intent to "find a cadre of people who know how to run prisons, because we don't."[2446] Deputy Director of Operations (DDO) James Pavitt assured the Committee that it would be informed of each individual who entered CIA custody. Pavitt disavowed the use of torture against detainees while stating that the boundaries on the use of interrogation techniques were uncertain—specifically in the case of having to identify the location of a hidden nuclear weapon.[2447]

In meetings with the CIA in February 2002, the month before the capture and detention of Abu Zubaydah, Committee staff expressed concern about the lack of any legal review of the CIA's new detention authorities. ████████████████ noted that the discussion with Committee staff was "the only peer review" the CIA lawyers had engaged in with regard to the MON authorities, and that the discussion helped refine the CIA's understanding of what MON-authorized activity was in fact legally permissible and appropriate.[2448]

B. The CIA Notifies Committee of the Detention of Abu Zubaydah, but Makes No Reference to Coercive Interrogation Techniques; the CIA Briefs Chairman and Vice Chairman After the Use of the CIA's Enhanced Interrogation Techniques; the CIA Discusses Strategy to Avoid the Chairman's Request for More Information

On April 18, 2002, the CIA informed the Committee that it "has no current plans to develop a detention facility."[2449] At the time of this representation, the CIA had already established a CIA detention site in Country ████ and detained Abu Zubaydah there. On April 24, 2002, the CIA notified the Committee about the capture of Abu Zubaydah with the understanding that the location of Abu Zubaydah's detention was among the "red lines" not to be divulged to the Committee.[2450] The notification and subsequent information provided to the Committee included representations that Abu Zubaydah was a "member of Bin Ladin's inner circle" and a "key al-Qa'ida lieutenant."[2451] These representations were inaccurate. Briefings to the Committee in the spring of 2002 emphasized the expertise of FBI and CIA interrogators engaged in the Abu Zubaydah interrogations and provided no indication that coercive techniques were being used or considered, or that there was significant disagreement between the CIA and the FBI on proposed interrogation approaches.[2452] In early August 2002, after the Department of Justice determined that the use of the CIA's enhanced interrogation techniques on Abu Zubaydah would be legal, the CIA considered briefing the Committee on the CIA's interrogation techniques, but did not.[2453]

In early September 2002, the CIA briefed the House Permanent Select Committee on Intelligence (HPSCI) leadership about the CIA's enhanced interrogation techniques. Two days after, the CIA's ████████████ CTC Legal, ████████████████, excised from a draft memorandum memorializing the briefing indications that the HPSCI leadership questioned the legality of the program by deleting the sentence: "HPSCI attendees also questioned the legality of these techniques if other countries would use them."[2454] After ████████████████ blind-copied Jose Rodriguez on the email in which he transmitted the changes to the memorandum, Rodriguez responded to ████████████'s email with: "short and sweet."[2455] The first briefing for Senate Select Committee on Intelligence Chairman Bob Graham and Vice Chairman Richard Shelby—and their staff directors—occurred on September 27, 2002, nearly two months after the CIA first began subjecting Abu Zubaydah to the CIA's enhanced interrogation techniques. The only record of the briefing is a one-paragraph CIA memorandum stating that the briefing occurred.[2456] The Committee does not have its own records of this briefing.

Shortly thereafter, in late 2002, Chairman Graham sought to expand Committee oversight of the CIA's Detention and Interrogation Program, including by having Committee staff visit CIA interrogation sites and interview CIA interrogators.[2457] The CIA rejected this request. An internal CIA email from ██████ CTC Legal ████████████ indicated that the full Committee would not be told about "the nature and scope of the interrogation process," and that even the chairman and vice chairman would not be told in which country or "region" the CIA had established its detention facilities.[2458] Other emails describe efforts by the CIA to identify a "strategy" for limiting the CIA's responses to Chairman Graham's requests for more information on the CIA's Detention and Interrogation Program, specifically seeking a way to "get off the hook on the cheap."[2459] The CIA eventually chose to delay its next update for the Committee leadership on the CIA's program until after Graham had left the Committee.[2460] At the same time, the CIA rejected a request for the Committee staff to be "read-in" and provided with a briefing on the CIA program.[2461]

C. No Detailed Records Exist of CIA Briefings of Committee Leadership; the CIA Declines to Answer Questions from Committee Members or Provide Requested Materials

On February 4, 2003, the CIA briefed the new chairman, Senator Pat Roberts, and the two staff directors. Vice Chairman John D. Rockefeller IV was not present. The only record of the briefing, a two-page CIA memorandum, states that CIA officers:

> "described in great detail the importance of the information provided by [Abu] Zubayda[h] and ['Abd al-Rahim al-] Nashiri, both of whom had information of on-going terrorist operations, information that might well have saved American lives, the difficulty of getting that information from them, and the importance of the enhanced techniques in getting that information."[2462]

As described in this summary, and in greater detail in the full Committee Study, Abu Zubaydah and al-Nashiri did not provide actionable intelligence on ongoing plotting, and provided significant reporting prior to the use of the CIA's enhanced interrogation techniques. The CIA declined to provide information pursuant to a request from Chairman Roberts on the location of the CIA's detention site. Finally, the CIA memorandum states that Chairman Roberts "gave his assent" to the destruction of interrogation videotapes; however, this account in the CIA memorandum was later disputed by Chairman Roberts.[2463] The Committee has no independent record of this briefing.

Throughout 2003, the CIA refused to answer questions from Committee members and staff about the CIA interrogations of KSM and other CIA detainees.[2464] The CIA produced talking points for a September 4, 2003, briefing on the CIA interrogation program exclusively for Committee leadership; however, there are no contemporaneous records of the briefing taking place. The CIA talking points include information about the use of the CIA's enhanced interrogation techniques, their effectiveness, and various abuses that occurred in the program.[2465] Many of the CIA representations in the talking points were inaccurate.[2466] The CIA continued to withhold from the Committee, including its leadership, any information on the location of the CIA's detention facilities. On more than one occasion the CIA directed CIA personnel at Guantanamo Bay, Cuba, not to brief a visiting Committee member about the CIA detention facility there, including during a July 2005 visit by Chairman Roberts.[2467]

In 2004, the Committee conducted two hearings on the CIA's role in interrogating U.S. military detainees at Abu Ghraib prison in Iraq. CIA witnesses stressed that the CIA was more limited in its interrogation authorities than the Department of Defense, but declined to respond to Committee questions about the interrogation of KSM or press reports on CIA detention facilities.[2468] During the first briefing, on May 12, 2004, Committee members requested Department of Justice memoranda addressing the legality of CIA interrogations. Despite repeated subsequent requests, limited access to the memoranda was not granted until four years later, in June 2008, by which time the CIA was no longer detaining individuals.[2469]

While the CIA continued to brief the Committee leadership on aspects of the CIA's Detention and Interrogation Program, there are no transcripts of these briefings. One briefing, on July 15, 2004, discussed the detention of Janat Gul.[2470] An email from ████████ ████████CTC Legal stated that the "only reason" the chairman and vice chairman were informed of the detention of Janat Gul was that the notification could serve as "the vehicle for briefing the committees on our need for renewed legal and policy support" for the CIA's Detention and Interrogation Program.[2471] At the July 2004 briefing, the minority staff director requested full Committee briefings and expanded Committee oversight, including visits to CIA detention sites and interviews with interrogators—efforts that had been sought by former Chairman Graham years earlier. This request was denied.[2472]

D. Vice Chairman Rockefeller Seeks Committee Investigation

On February 3, 2005, Vice Chairman Rockefeller began a formal effort to conduct a comprehensive Committee investigation of the CIA's detention, interrogation and rendition activities, including a review of the legality and effectiveness of CIA interrogations.[2473] On March 3, 2005, a CIA official wrote that Vice Chairman Rockefeller was "convinced that we're hiding stuff from him" and that the CIA had planned a detailed briefing to "shut Rockefeller up."[2474] The only Committee records of this briefing, which took place on March 7, 2005, are handwritten notes written by Vice Chairman Rockefeller and the minority staff director.[2475] Shortly after this briefing, the vice chairman reiterated his call for a broad Committee investigation of the CIA's Detention and Interrogation Program, which he and the ranking member of the HPSCI, Jane Harman, described in a letter to Vice President Cheney.[2476] There is no Committee record of a response to the letter.

On April 13, 2005, the day before an anticipated Committee vote on the chairman's proposed investigation of the CIA program, the chief of ALEC Station, ████████████ and the deputy chief of CTC, Philip Mudd, discussed a press strategy to shape public and congressional views of the program. As previously detailed, Mudd wrote:

> "we either get out and sell, or we get hammered, which has implications beyond the media, congress reads it, cuts our authorities, messes up our budget, we need to make sure the impression of what we do is positive."[2477]

The next day, CIA Inspector General John Helgerson briefed several members of the Committee on limited aspects of the CIA's Detention and Interrogation Program. According to Helgerson, Chairman Roberts' "motive was to have a presentation that made clear that CIA IG is looking at all appropriate detention and interrogation issues, as (he told me privately beforehand) the Committee will be voting today on whether to launch their own inquiry." Helgerson added that "Roberts said 'I know how that vote is going to come out, but I want the minority to go away knowing this is in good hands.'"[2478] The proposed investigation was not approved by the Committee. The Committee nonetheless subsequently approved legislation requiring CIA reports on renditions and plans for the disposition of high-value CIA detainees, as well as requesting expanded Committee staff access to the program beyond the Committee staff directors.[2479] In addition, Vice Chairman Rockefeller requested full Committee access to over 100 documents related to the May 2004 Inspector General Special Review.[2480] On January 5, 2006, after multiple rounds of negotiations with the CIA for the documents, the chief of staff to Director of National Intelligence John Negroponte wrote a letter rejecting the request. The letter had been prepared by the former ██████████CTC Legal, ██████████████████ ██, who was by then serving as a CIA detailee in the Office of the Director of National Intelligence.[2481]

E. In Response to Detainee Treatment Act, the CIA Briefs Senators Not on the Committee; Proposal from Senator Levin for an Independent Commission Prompts Renewed Calls Within the CIA to Destroy Interrogation Videotapes

In October and November 2005, after the Senate passed its version of the Detainee Treatment Act, the CIA, directed by the Office of the Vice President, briefed specific Republican senators, who were not on the Select Committee on Intelligence, on the CIA's Detention and Interrogation Program. (The full membership of the Committee had not yet been briefed on the CIA interrogation program.)[2482] The briefings, which were intended to influence conference negotiations,[2483] were provided to Senator McCain;[2484] Senators Ted Stevens and Thad Cochran, the chairmen of the Appropriations Committee and Defense Appropriations Subcommittee;[2485] Majority Leader Bill Frist;[2486] and Senator John Cornyn (CIA records state that Cornyn was not briefed on the CIA's specific interrogation techniques).[2487] Meanwhile, a proposal from Senator Carl Levin to establish an independent commission to investigate U.S. detention policies and allegations of detainee abuse resulted in concern at the CIA that such a commission would lead to the discovery of videotapes documenting CIA interrogations. That concern prompted renewed interest at the CIA to destroy the videotapes.[2488] Senator Levin's amendment to establish the commission failed on November 8, 2005.[2489] The CIA destroyed the CIA interrogation videotapes the following day.[2490]

F. CIA Director Goss Seeks Committee Support for the Program After the Detainee Treatment Act; CIA Declines to Answer Questions for the Record

In March 2006, three months after passage of the Detainee Treatment Act, the CIA provided a briefing for five Committee staffers that included limited information on the interrogation process, as well as the effectiveness of the CIA interrogation program.[2491] The briefings did not include information on the CIA's enhanced interrogation techniques or the location of CIA detention sites.[2492] A week later, on March 15, 2006, CIA Director Porter Goss briefed the full Committee on CIA detention matters, but did not provide the locations of the CIA's detention facilities, or a list or briefing on the CIA's enhanced interrogation techniques.[2493] At this hearing Director Goss explained to the Committee that "we cannot do it by ourselves," and that"[w]e need to have the support of our oversight committee."[2494] Goss then described challenges to the CIA's Detention and Interrogation Program as a result of the Detainee Treatment Act, as well as strained relations with countries hosting CIA detention sites after significant press revelations.[2495] Director Goss described the program as follows:

> "This program has brought us incredible information. It's a program that could continue to bring us incredible information. It's a program that could continue to operate in a very professional way. It's a program that I think if you saw how it's operated you would agree that you would be proud that it's done right and well, with proper safeguards."[2496]

Contrasting the CIA program to the abuse of prisoners in U.S. military detention at the Abu Ghraib prison in Iraq, Director Goss stated that the CIA program:

> "is a professionally-operated program that we operate uniquely . . . We are not talking military, and I'm not talking about anything that a contractor might have done . . . in a prison somewhere or beat somebody or hit somebody with a stick or something. That's not what this is about."[2497]

Addressing CIA interrogations. Director Goss testified that "we only bring in certain selected people that we think can give us intelligence information, and we treat them in certain specific ways" such that "they basically become psychologically disadvantaged to their interrogator." Explaining that the key to a successful interrogation was "getting a better psychological profile and knowing what makes someone tick," Director Goss stated, "just the simplest thing will work, a family photograph or something." Goss then represented that the CIA's interrogation program is "not a brutality. It's more of an art or a science that is refined."[2498]

After the hearing, the Committee submitted official Questions for the Record related to the history, legality, and the effectiveness of the CIA's Detention and Interrogation Program. The CIA did not respond.[2499]

In May 2006, the Committee approved legislation requiring the CIA to provide reports on the CIA's detention facilities (including their locations), the CIA's interrogation techniques, the impact of the Detainee Treatment Act on the CIA program, CIA renditions, and the CIA's plans for the disposition of its detainees. The legislation also called for full Committee access to the CIA May 2004 Inspector General Special Review, as well as expanded member and Committee staff access to information on the CIA's Detention and Interrogation Program.[2500] In July 2006, the new CIA director. General Michael Hayden, provided a briefing for the chairman and vice chairman in which he described the Detainee Treatment Act as a "safehaven" that potentially permitted the CIA to use its enhanced interrogation techniques.[2501]

G. Full Committee First Briefed on the CIA's Interrogation Program Hours Before It Is Publicly Acknowledged on September 6, 2006

On September 6, 2006, President Bush publicly acknowledged the CIA program and the transfer of 14 CIA detainees to U.S. military custody at Guantanamo Bay, Cuba. Hours prior to the announcement, CIA Director Hayden provided the first briefing on the CIA's "enhanced interrogation" program for all members of the Committee, although the CIA limited staff attendance to the Committee's two staff directors.[2502] Due to the impending public acknowledgment of the program, the briefing was abbreviated. At the briefing, the CIA's enhanced interrogation techniques were listed, but not described. Director Hayden stated that the techniques were developed at the Department of Defense SERE school and were "used against American service personnel during their training." He testified that "once [a detainee] gets into the situation of sustained cooperation," debriefings are "not significantly different than what you and I are doing right now." Hayden sought "legislative assistance" in interpreting Common Article 3, stated that he had not asked for an opinion from the Department of Justice, and represented that he had been informed informally that seven interrogation techniques "are viewed by the

Department of Justice to be consistent with the requirements of the Detainee Treatment Act."[2503] Director Hayden declined to identify the locations of the CIA's detention facilities to the members and stated that he personally had recommended not expanding Committee staff access beyond the two staff directors already briefed on the CIA's Detention and Interrogation Program.[2504]

There were no other Committee briefings or hearings on the CIA's Detention and Interrogation Program prior to the Senate's September 28, 2006, vote on the Military Commissions Act. As described, the Department of Justice later concluded that the CIA's enhanced interrogation techniques were consistent with the Military Commissions Act in part because, according to the CIA, "none of the Members [briefed on the CIA program] expressed the view that the CIA interrogation program should be stopped, or that the techniques at issue were inappropriate."[2505] However, prior to the vote, Senator McCain—who had been briefed on the CIA program—told CIA officials that he could not support the program and that sleep deprivation, one of the interrogation techniques still included in the program, as well as waterboarding, were torture.[2506] Members of the Committee also expressed their views in classified letters to the CIA. Senator Dianne Feinstein informed the CIA that Hayden's testimony on the CIA program was "extraordinarily problematic" and that she was "unable to understand why the CIA needs to maintain this program."[2507] In May 2007, shortly after additional Committee staff gained access to the program. Senator Russ Feingold expressed his opposition to the program, while Senators Feinstein, Ron Wyden, and Chuck Hagel described their concerns about the CIA program and their "deep discomfort" with the use of the CIA's enhanced interrogation techniques.[2508]

On November 16, 2006, CIA Director Hayden briefed the Committee.[2509] The briefing included inaccurate information, including on the CIA's use of dietary manipulation and nudity, as well as the effects of sleep deprivation.[2510] Before speaking about the CIA's enhanced interrogation techniques, however, Director Hayden asked to brief the Committee on the recent capture of the CIA's newest detainee, Abdul Hadi al-Iraqi, who was not subjected to the CIA's enhanced interrogation techniques. Vice Chairman Rockefeller and two other members of the Committee expressed frustration at the briefing that Director Hayden's description of Hadi al-Iraqi's capture was preventing what was expected to be an in-depth discussion of the CIA's enhanced interrogation techniques.[2511]

On February 14, 2007, during a hearing on CIA renditions, Director Hayden provided inaccurate information to the Committee, to include inaccurate information on the number of detainees held by the CIA. ████████████, the deputy chief of the ████████ Department in CTC and the previous deputy chief of ALEC Station, provided examples of information obtained from the CIA Detention and Interrogation Program.[2512] After providing the examples, ██████ closed her testimony with the statement that "[t]here's no question, in my mind, that having that detainee information has saved hundreds, conservatively speaking, of American lives."[2513]

On March 15, 2007, in a speech to a gathering of ambassadors to the United States from the countries of the European Union, Director Hayden stated that congressional support for the CIA's Detention and Interrogation Program assured the continuity of the program:

> "I mentioned earlier that it would be unwise to assume that there will be a dramatic change in the American approach to the war on terror in 2009. CIA got the legislation it needed to continue this program in the Military Commissions Act passed by our Congress last fall. And let me remind you that every member of our intelligence committees, House and Senate, Republican and Democrat, is now fully briefed on the detention and interrogation program. This is not CIA's program. This is not the President's program. This is America's program."[2514]

H. The CIA Provides Additional Information to the Full Committee and Staff, Much of It Inaccurate; Intelligence Authorization Act Passes Limiting CIA Interrogations to Techniques Authorized by the Army Field Manual

On April 12, 2007, CIA Director Hayden testified at a lengthy hearing that was attended by all but one committee member, and for the first time, the CIA allowed most of the Committee's staff to attend. The members stated that the Committee was still seeking access to CIA documents and information on the CIA's Detention and Interrogation Program, including Department of Justice memoranda and the location of the CIA's detention facilities.[2515] Director Hayden's Statement for the Record included extensive inaccurate information with regard to Abu Zubaydah, CIA interrogators, abuses identified by the ICRC, and the effectiveness of the CIA's enhanced interrogation techniques.[2516] Director Hayden's Statement for the Record also listed five examples of captures and four examples of plots "thwarted" purportedly resulting from information acquired from CIA detainees, all of which included significant inaccurate information.[2517][2517]

Director Hayden's Statement for the Record further included the following representation with regard to the effects of legislation that would limit interrogations to techniques authorized by the Army Field Manual:

> "The CIA program has proven to be effective . . . should our techniques be limited to the [Army] field manual, we are left with very little offense and are relegated to rely primarily on defense. Without the approval of EITs . . . we have severely restricted our attempts to obtain timely information from HVDs who possess information that will help us save lives and disrupt operations. Limiting our interrogation tools to those detailed in the [Army] field manual will increase the probability that a determined, resilient HVD will be able to withhold critical, time-sensitive, actionable intelligence that could prevent an imminent, catastrophic attack."[2518]

At the April 12, 2007, hearing, Director Hayden verbally provided extensive inaccurate information on, among other topics: (1) the interrogation of Abu Zubaydah, (2) the application of Department of Defense survival school practices to the program, (3) detainees' counterinterrogation training, (4) the backgrounds of CIA interrogators, (5) the role of other members of the interrogation teams, (6) the number of CIA detainees and their intelligence production, (7) the role of CIA detainee reporting in the captures of terrorist suspects, (8) the interrogation process, (9) the use of detainee reporting, (10) the purported relationship between Islam and the need to use the CIA's enhanced interrogation techniques, (11) threats against detainees' families, (12) the punching and kicking of detainees, (13) detainee hygiene, (14) denial of medical care, (15) dietary manipulation, (16) the use of waterboarding and its effectiveness, and (17) the injury and death of detainees. In addition, the chief of CTC's ■■■■ ■■■■ Department provided inaccurate information on the CIA's use of stress positions, while Acting General Counsel John Rizzo provided inaccurate information on the legal reasons for establishing CIA detention facilities overseas.[2519] A detailed comparison of Director Hayden's testimony and information in CIA records related to the program is included in an appendix to this summary.

In responses to official Committee Questions for the Record, the CIA provided inaccurate information related to detainees transferred from U.S. military to CIA custody.[2520] The Committee also requested a timeline connecting intelligence reporting obtained from CIA detainees to the use of the CIA's enhanced interrogation techniques. The CIA declined to provide such a timeline, writing that "[t]he value of each intelligence report stands alone, whether it is collected before, during, immediately after or significantly after the use of [the CIA's enhanced interrogation techniques].[2521]

In May 2007, the Committee voted to approve the Fiscal Year 2008 Intelligence Authorization bill, which required reporting on CIA compliance with the Detainee Treatment Act and Military Commissions Act. In September 2007, John Rizzo withdrew his nomination to be CIA general counsel amid Committee concerns related to his role in the CIA's Detention and Interrogation Program. On August 2, 2007, the Committee conducted a hearing that addressed the interrogation of Muhammad Rahim, who would be the CIA's last detainee, as well as the president's new Executive Order, which interpreted the Geneva Conventions in a manner to allow the CIA to use its enhanced interrogation techniques against Muhammad Rahim. At that hearing, the CIA's director of CTC, [redacted], provided inaccurate information to the Committee on several issues, including how the CIA conducts interrogations.[2522] Members again requested access to the Department of Justice memoranda related to the CIA program, but were denied this access.[2523]

On December 5, 2007, the conference committee considering the Fiscal Year 2008 Intelligence Authorization bill voted to restrict the CIA's interrogation techniques to those authorized by the Army Field Manual. Opponents of the provision referenced Director Hayden's testimony on the effectiveness of the CIA's enhanced interrogation techniques in acquiring critical information.[2524] On December 6, 2007, the *New York Times* revealed that the CIA had destroyed videotapes of CIA interrogations in 2005.[2525] The CIA claimed that the Committee had been told about the destruction of the videotapes at a hearing in November 2006.[2526] A review of the Committee's transcript of its November 16, 2006, hearing found that the CIA's claim of notification was inaccurate. In fact, CIA witnesses testified at the hearing that the CIA did not videotape interrogations, while making no mention of past videotaping or the destruction of videotapes.[2527]

At the CIA briefing to the Committee on December 11, 2007, Director Hayden testified about: (1) the information provided to the White House regarding the videotapes, (2) what the tapes revealed, (3) what was not on the tapes, (4) the reasons for their destruction, (5) the legal basis for the use of the waterboard, and (6) the effectiveness of the CIA's waterboard interrogation technique. Much of this testimony was inaccurate or incomplete. Director Hayden also testified that what was on the destroyed videotapes was documented in CIA cables, and that the cables were "a more than adequate representation of the tapes." Director Hayden committed the CIA to providing the Committee with access to the cables.[2528]

On February 5, 2008, after the House of Representatives passed the conference report limiting CIA interrogations to techniques authorized by the Army Field Manual, Director Hayden testified in an open Committee hearing against the provision. Director Hayden also stated, inaccurately, that over the life of the CIA program, the CIA had detained fewer than 100 people.[2529] On February 13, 2008, the Senate passed the conference report.[2530]

I. President Vetoes Legislation Based on Effectiveness Claims Provided by the CIA; CIA Declines to Answer Committee Questions for the Record About the CIA Interrogation Program

On March 8, 2008, President Bush vetoed the Intelligence Authorization bill. President Bush explained his decision to veto the bill in a radio broadcast that repeated CIA representations that the CIA interrogation program produced "critical intelligence" that prevented specific terrorist plots. As described in this summary, and in greater detail in Volume II, the statement reflected inaccurate information provided by the CIA to the president and other policymakers in CIA briefings."[2531] Three days later, the House of Representatives failed to override the veto.[2532] On May 22, 2008, the CIA informed the Committee that the vetoed legislation "has had no impact on CIA policies concerning the use of EITs."[2533] As noted, CIA Director Goss had previously testified to the Committee that "we cannot do it by ourselves," and that "[w]e need to have the support of our oversight committee."[2534] As further noted, the OLC's 2007 memorandum applying the Military Commissions Act to the CIA's enhanced interrogation techniques relied on the CIA's representation that "none of the Members expressed the view that the CIA interrogation program should be stopped, or that the techniques at issue were inappropriate."[2535]

In June 2008, the CIA provided information to the Committee in response to a reporting requirement in the Fiscal Year 2008 Intelligence Authorization Act. The CIA response stated that all of the CIA's interrogation techniques "were evaluated under the applicable U.S. law during the time of their use and were found by the Department of Justice to comply with those legal requirements." This was inaccurate. Diapers, nudity, dietary manipulation, and water dousing were used extensively by the CIA prior to any Department of Justice review. As detailed in the full Committee Study, the response included additional information that was incongruent with the history of the program.[2536]

On June 10, 2008, the Committee held a hearing on the Department of Justice memoranda relating to the CIA's Detention and Interrogation Program, to which the Committee had recently been provided limited access.[2537] At the hearing, [REDACTED] CTC Legal provided inaccurate information on several topics, including the use of sleep deprivation and its effects.[2538] Acting Assistant Attorney General Steven Bradbury also testified, noting that the Department of Justice deferred to the CIA with regard to the effectiveness of the CIA interrogation program.[2539] The Committee then submitted official Questions for the Record on the CIA's enhanced interrogation techniques and on the effectiveness of the program, including how the CIA assessed the effectiveness of its interrogation techniques for purposes of representations to the Department of Justice.[2540] The CIA prepared responses that included an acknowledgment that [REDACTED] CTC Legal, [REDACTED], had provided inaccurate information with regard to the "effectiveness" of the CIA's enhanced interrogation techniques.[2541] The prepared responses were never provided to the Committee. Instead, on October 17, 2008, the CIA informed the Committee that it would not respond to the Committee's Questions for the Record and that instead, the CIA was "available to provide additional briefings on this issue to Members as necessary."[2542] In separate letters to Director Hayden, Chairman Rockefeller and Senator Feinstein referred to this refusal to respond to official Committee questions as "unprecedented and . . . simply unacceptable,"[2543] and "appalling."[2544]

VII. CIA DESTRUCTION OF INTERROGATION VIDEOTAPES LEADS TO COMMITTEE INVESTIGATION; COMMITTEE VOTES 14–1 FOR EXPANSIVE TERMS OF REFERENCE TO STUDY THE CIA'S DETENTION AND INTERROGATION PROGRAM

The Committee's scrutiny of the CIA's Detention and Interrogation Program continued through the remainder of 2008 and into the 111th Congress, in 2009. On February 11, 2009, the Committee held a business meeting at which Committee staff presented a memorandum on the content of the CIA operational cables detailing the interrogations of Abu Zubaydah and 'Abd al-Rahim al-Nashiri in 2002.[2545] CIA Director Hayden had allowed a small number of Committee staff to review the cables at CIA Headquarters, and as noted, had testified that the cables provided "a more than adequate representation" of what was on the destroyed CIA interrogation videotapes.[2546] The chairman stated that the Committee staff memorandum represented "the most comprehensive statement on the treatment of these two detainees, from the conditions of their detention and the nature of their interrogations to the intelligence produced and the thoughts of CIA officers and contractors in the field and Headquarters."[2547] After the staff presentation, the vice chairman expressed his support for an expanded Committee investigation, stating, "we need to compare what was briefed to us by the Agency with what we find out, and we need to determine whether it was within the guidelines of the OLC, the MON, and the guidelines published by the Agency."[2548] Other members of the Committee added their support for an expanded investigation, with one member stating, "these are extraordinarily serious matters and we ought to get to the bottom of it . . . to look at how it came to be that these techniques were used, what the legal underpinnings of these techniques were all about, and finally what these techniques meant in terms of effectiveness."[2549]

The Committee held two subsequent business meetings to consider and debate the terms of the Committee's proposed expanded review of the CIA's Detention and Interrogation Program. The first, on February 24, 2009, began with bipartisan support for a draft Terms of Reference.[2550] The Committee met again on March 5, 2009, to consider a revised Terms of Reference, which was approved by a vote of 14–1.[2551]

On December 13, 2012, after a review of more than six million pages of records, the Committee approved a 6,300-page Study of the CIA's Detention and Interrogation Program.[2552] On April 3, 2014, by a bipartisan vote of 11–3, the Committee agreed to send the revised findings and conclusions, and an updated Executive Summary of the Committee Study to the president for declassification and public release.

VIII. APPENDIX 1: TERMS OF REFERENCE

Terms of Reference

Senate Select Committee on Intelligence Study of the Central Intelligence Agency's Detention and Interrogation Program

Adopted March 5, 2009

The Senate Select Committee on Intelligence's study of the Central Intelligence Agency's (CIA) detention and interrogation program consists of these terms of reference:

- A review of how the CIA created, operated, and maintained its detention and interrogation program, including a review of the locations of the facilities and any arrangements and agreements made by the CIA or other Intelligence Community officials with foreign entities in connection with the program.
- A review of Intelligence Community documents and records, including CIA operational cables, relating to the detention and interrogation of CIA detainees.
- A review of the CIA's assessments that particular detainees possessed relevant information and how the assessments were made.
- An evaluation of the information acquired from the detainees including the periods during which enhanced interrogation techniques (EITs) were administered.
- An evaluation of whether information provided to the Committee by the Intelligence Community adequately and accurately described the CIA's detention and interrogation program as it was carried out in practice, including conditions of detention, such as personal hygiene and medical needs, and their effect on the EITs as applied.

- An evaluation of the information provided by the CIA to the Department of Justice Office of Legal Counsel (OLC), including whether it accurately and adequately described:
    a. the implementation, effectiveness and expected effects of EITs;
    b. the value of information obtained through the use of EITs; and
    c. the threat environment at the time the EITs were being used or contemplated for use on CIA detainees.
- An evaluation of whether the CIA's detention and interrogation program complied with:
    a. the authorizations in any relevant Presidential Findings and Memoranda of Notification;
    b. all relevant policy and legal guidance provided by the CIA; and
    c. the opinions issued by the OLC in relation to the use of EITs.
- A review of the information provided by the CIA or other Intelligence Community officials involved in the program about the CIA detention and interrogation program, including the location of facilities and approved interrogation techniques, to U.S. officials with national security responsibilities.

The Committee will use those tools of oversight necessary to complete a thorough review including, but not limited to, document reviews and requests, interviews, testimony at closed and open hearings, as appropriate, and preparation of findings and recommendations.

IX. APPENDIX 2: CIA DETAINEES FROM 2002–2008

#	CIA Detainees	Date of Custody	Days in Custody
1.	**Abu Zubaydah**	█ 2002	1,59█
2.	Zakariya	█2002	36█
3.	Jamal Eldin Boudran	█2002	62█
4.	Abbar al-Hawari, aka Abu Sufiyan	█2002	36█
5.	Hassan Muhammad Abu Bakr Qa'id	█2002	51█
6.	**Ridha Ahmad Najar, aka Najjar**	█2002	69█
7.	Ayub Marshid Ali Salih	█2002	4█
8.	Bashir Nasir Ali al-Marwalali	█2002	4█
9.	Ha'il Aziz Ahmad al-Mithali	█2002	4█
10.	Hassan bin Attash	█2002	59█
11.	Musab Umar Ali al-Mudwani	█2002	4█
12.	Said Saleh Said, aka Said Salih Said	█2002	4█
13.	Shawqi Awad	█2002	4█
14.	Umar Faruq, aka Abu al-Faruq al-Kuwaiși	█2002	41█
15.	Abd al-Salam al-Hilah	█2002	59█
16.	*Karini, aka Asai Sar Jan*	█2002	6█
17.	*Akbar Zakaria, aka Zakai ia Zeineddin*	█2002	5█
18.	***Rafiq bin Bashir bin Halul al-Hami***	█2002	5█
19.	***Tawfiq Nasir Awad al Bihani***	█2002	5█
20.	**Lutfi al-Arabi al-Gharisi**	█2002	38█
21.	***Dr. Hikmat Nafi Shaukat***	█2002	7█
22.	*Yaqub al-Baluchi aka Abu Talha*	█2002	8█
23.	Abd al-Rahim Rhulam Rabbani	█2002	54█
24.	**Gul Rahman**	█2002	1█

KEY

Bold Text: Detainees in bold text were subjected to the CIA's enhanced interrogation techniques.

Italic Text: Detainees in italics have not been previously acknowledged by the CIA to the SSCI.

#: Detainee number on main detainee spreadsheet; based on date of CIA custody. Number is based on a designation made by the Committee, not the CIA.

Note on Redaction: The last digit of days in CIA custody is redacted.

#	CIA Detainees	Date of Custody	Days in Custody
25.	**Ghulam Rabbani aka Abu Badr**	■ 2002	54■
26.	**Abd al-Rahim al-Nashiri**	■ 2002	1,37■
27.	*Haji Ghalgi*	■ 2002	18■
28.	*Nazar Ali*	■ 2002	8■
29.	*Juma Gul*	■ 2002	6■
30.	*Wafti bin Ali aka Abdullah*	■ 2002	8■
31.	*Adel*	■ 2002	6■
32.	*Qari Mohib Ur Relman*	■ 2002	6■
33.	*Shah Wali Khan*	■ 2002	2■
34.	*Hayatullah Haqqani*	■ 2002	8■
35.	Bisher al-Rawi	■ 2002	■
36.	Jamil el-Banna, aka Abu Anas	■ 2002	■
37.	**Ghairat Bahir**	■ 2002	51■
38.	Pacha Wazir	■ 2002	33■
39.	Muhammad Amein al-Bakri	■ 2003	49■
40.	Abdullah Midhat Mursi	■ 2003	11■
41.	**Ramzi bin al-Shibh**	■ 2003	128■
42.	Ibn Shaykh al-Libi	■ 2003	114■
43.	**Muhammad Uraar 'Abd al-Rahman, aka Asadallah**	■ 2003	15■
44.	***Abu Khalid***	■ 2003	2■
45.	**Khalid Shaykh Mohammad**	■ 2003	126■
46.	**Mustafa Ahmad al-Hawsawi**	■ 2003	126■
47.	**Abu Yasir al-Jaza'iri**	■ 2003	124■
48.	**Suleiman Abdullah**	■ 2003	43■
49.	Hamid Aich	■ 2003	4■
50.	Sayed Habib	■ 2003	49■
51.	**Abu Hazim, aka Abu Hazim al-Libi**	■ 2003	72■
52.	**Al-Shara'iya, aka Abd al-Karim**	■ 2003	48■

SOURCE INFORMATION: CIA Fax to SSCI Committee Staff, entitled, "15 June Request for Excel Spreadsheet," June 17, 2009 (DTS #2009-2529); CIA detainee charts provided to the Committee on April 27, 2007; document in Committee records entitled, "Briefing Charts provided to committee Members from CIA Director Michael Hayden at the closed Hearing on April 12, 2007, concerning EITs used with CIA detainees, and a list of techniques" (DTS #2007-1594, hearing transcript at DTS #2007-3158); and CIA operational cables and other records produced for the Committee's Study of the CIA's Detention and Interrogation Program.

**Gul Rahman, listed as detainee 24, was the subject of a notification to the Senate Select Committee on Intelligence following his death at DETENTION SITE COBALT; however, he has not appeared on lists of CIA detainees provided to Committee.

#	CIA Detainees	Date of Custody	Days in Custody
53.	Muhammad Khan (son of Suhbat)	█2003	38█
54.	*Ibrahim Haqqani*	█2003	█
55.	**Ammar al-Baluchi**	█2003	118█
56.	**Khallad bin Attash**	█2003	118█
57.	**Laid Ben Dohman Saidi, aka Abu Hudhaifa**	█2003	46█
58.	**Majid Khan**	█2003	118█
59.	Mohammad Dinshah	█2003	26█
60.	Muhammad Jafar Jamal al-Qahtani	█2003	34█
61.	Abu Naeim al-Tunisi	█2003	37█
62.	**Mohd Farik bin Amin, aka Abu Zubair**	█2003	115█
63.	Zarmein	█2003	19█
64.	Hiwa Abdul Rahman Rashul	█2003	11█
65.	Adel Abu Redwan Ben Hamlili	█2003	30█
66.	Shaistah Habibullah Khan	█2003	21█
67.	**Samr Hilmi Abdul Latif al-Barq**	█2003	8█
68.	Ali Jan	█2003	34█
69.	Muhammad Khan (son of Amir)	█2003	1█
70.	Modin Nik Muhammad	█2003	20█
71.	Abdullah Ashami	█2003	27█
72.	**Bashir bin Lap, aka Lillie**	█2003	110█
73.	**Riduan bin Isomuddin, aka Hambali**	█2003	128█
74.	Sanad 'Ali Yislam al-Kazimi	█2003	26█
75.	Salah Nasir Salim Ali, aka Muhsin	█2003	59█
76.	Abd Qudra Allah Mala Azrat al-Hadi	█2003	8█
77.	Bismullah	█2003	█
78.	Sa'id Allam	█2003	8█
79.	Sa'ida Gul	█2003	8█
80.	Shah Khan Wali	█2003	8█
81.	Yahya, aka Rugollah	█2003	8█
82.	Zakariya 'abd al-Rauf	█2003	8█
83.	Zamarai Nur Muhammad Juma Khan	█2003	8█
84.	*Abdullah Salim al-Qahtani*	█2003	3█
85.	*Awwad Sabhan al-Shammari*	█2003	3█
86.	Noor Jalal	█2003	23█
87.	**Majid Bin Muhammad Bin Sulayman Khayil, aka Arsala Khan**	█2003	5█
88.	*Aso Hawleri*	█2003	2█
89.	Mohd al-Shomaila	█2003	54█
90.	Ali Saeed Awadh	█2003	17█
91.	**Adnan al-Libi**	█2003	23█
92.	Muhammad Abdullah Saleh	█2004	48█
93.	**Riyadh the Facilitator**	█2004	12█
94.	Abu Abdallah al-Zulaytini	█2004	21█
95.	Binyam Ahmed Mohamed	█2004	11█
96.	Firas al-Yemeni	█2004	95█
97.	**Hassan Ghul**	█2004	94█
98.	Khalid 'Abd al-Razzaq al-Masri	█2004	12█

#	CIA Detainees	Date of Custody	Days in Custody
99.	**Muhammad Qurban Sayyid Ibrahim**	■ 2004	26■
100.	Saud Memon	■ 2004	74■
101.	*Gul Rahman (2).*	■ 2004	3■
102.	Hassan Ahmed Guleed	■ 2004	90■
103.	Abu 'Abdallah	■ 2004	87■
104.	**ABU BAHAR AL-TURKI**	[REDACTED] 2004	13■
105.	**ABU TALHA AL-MAGREBI**	[REDACTED] 2004	13■
106.	Abd al-Bari al-Filistini	2004	77■
107.	Ayyub al-Libi	■ 2004	30■
108.	Marwan al-Jabbur	■ 2004	77■
109.	Qattal al-Uzbeki	■ 2004	80■
110.	**Janat Gul**	■ 2004	92■
111.	**Ahmed Khalfan Ghailani**	■ 2004	73■
112.	**Sharif al-Masri**	■ 2004	81■
113.	Abdi Rashid Samatar	■ 2004	65■
114.	Abu Farj al-Libi	■ 2004	46■
115.	Abu Munthir al-Magrebi	■ 2005	46■
116.	Ibrahim Jan	■ 2005	31■
117.	**Abu Ja'far al-Iraqi**	■ 2005	28■
118.	Abd al-Hadi al-Iraqi	■ 2006	17■
119.	**Muhammad Rahim**	■ 2007	24■

X. APPENDIX 3: EXAMPLE OF INACCURATE CIA TESTIMONY TO THE COMMITTEE—APRIL 12, 2007[2553]

CIA TESTIMONY	SAMPLING OF INFORMATION IN CIA RECORDS

THE INTERROGATION OF ABU ZUBAYDAH

CIA testimony:

DIRECTOR HAYDEN: "Now in June, after about four months of interrogation, Abu Zubaydah *reached a point where he refused to cooperate and he shut down*. He would not talk at all to the FBI interrogators and although he was still talking to CIA interrogators *no significant progress was being made in learning anything of intelligence value*. He was, to our eye, employing classic resistance to interrogation techniques and employing them quite effectively. And it was clear to us that we were unlikely to be able to overcome those techniques without some significant intervention."

Sampling of information in CIA records:

Abu Zubaydah was rendered to CIA custody on March ■, 2002. The CIA representation that Abu Zubaydah stopped cooperating with debriefers who were using traditional interrogation techniques is not supported by CIA records. In early June 2002, Abu Zubaydah's interrogators recommended that Abu Zubaydah spend several weeks in isolation from interrogation while the interrogation team members traveled ■ "as a means of keeping [Abu Zubaydah] off-balance and to allow the team needed time off for a break and to attend to personal matters ■," as well as to discuss "the endgame" for Abu Zubaydah ■ ■ with officers from CIA Headquarters. As a result, Abu Zubaydah spent much of June 2002 and all of July 2002, 47 days in total, in isolation. When CIA officers next interrogated Abu Zubaydah, they immediately used the CIA's enhanced interrogation techniques, including the waterboard.

Prior to the 47 day isolation period, Abu Zubaydah provided information on al-Qa'ida activities, plans, capabilities, and relationships, in addition to information on its leadership structure, including personalities, decision-making processes, training, and tactics. Abu Zubaydah provided this type of information prior to, during, and after the utilization of the CIA's enhanced interrogation techniques.[2554]

Abu Zubaydah's inability to provide information on the next attack in the United States and operatives in the United States was the basis for CIA representations that Abu Zubaydah was "uncooperative," and for the CIA's determination that Abu Zubaydah required the use of the CIA's enhanced interrogation techniques to become "compliant" and reveal the information the CIA believed he was withholding. At no point during or after the use of the CIA's enhanced interrogation techniques did Abu Zubaydah provide the information sought.[2555]

CIA testimony:

DIRECTOR HAYDEN: "This really began in the spring of 2002 with the capture of Abu Zubaydah. At that time we deployed a psychologist who had been under contract to CIA [Dr. SWIGERT], to provide

Sampling of information in CIA records:

The CIA testimony that SWIGERT was deployed to "overcome what seemed to be Abu Zubaydah's very strong resistance to interrogation" is not supported by internal CIA records. Rather, CIA records indicate that CIA CTC officers anticipated Abu Zubaydah would resist providing information and contracted with SWIGERT real-time recommendations to help us overcome what seemed to be Abu Zubaydah's very strong resistance to interrogation . . . We also made arrangements for [Dr. DUNBAR]. [Dr. DUNBAR] was the ████ psychologist for the Department of Defense's SERE program, DOD's Survival, Escape, Recovery and Evasion program, the program of training we put our troops, particularly our airmen, through so that they can withstand a hostile environment."

prior to any meaningful assessment of Abu Zubaydah and his level of cooperation.

- On April 1, 2002, at a meeting on the interrogation of Abu Zubayah, ████CTC Legal ████████ █ recommended that SWIGERT—who was working under contract in the CIA's OTS—be brought in to "provide real-time recommendations to overcome Abu Zubaydah's resistance to interrogation." (Abu Zubaydah had been in CIA custody for ████.) That evening, SWIGERT, and the CIA OTS officer who had recommended SWIGERT to ████, prepared a cable with suggestions for the interrogation of Abu Zubaydah. SWIGERT had monitored the U.S. Air Force's Survival, Evasion, Resistance, and Escape (SERE) training. SWIGERT, who had never conducted an actual interrogation, encouraged the CIA to focus on developing "learned helplessness" in CIA detainees.[2556]
- Following the suggestion of ████CTC Legal, CTC contracted with SWIGERT to assist in the interrogation of Abu Zubaydah.
- As described in the Abu Zubaydah detainee review in Volume III, almost immediately after Abu Zubaydah's transfer to CIA custody on March █, 2002, Abu Zubaydah's medical condition deteriorated and Abu Zubaydah was transferred to the intensive care unit of a ████ hospital in Country █. During this time, FBI personnel continued to collect significant intelligence from Abu Zubaydah. According to an FBI report, during the period when Abu Zubaydah was still "connected to the intubator" at the hospital and unable to speak, he "indicated that he was willing to answer questions of the interviewers via writing in Arabic." While in the intensive care unit of the hospital, Abu Zubaydah first discussed "Mukhtar" (KSM) and identified a photograph of KSM.
- When Abu Zubaydah was discharged from the █ ████ hospital and returned to the CIA's DETENTION SITE GREEN on April 15, 2002, he was kept naked, sleep deprived, and in a cell with bright lights with white noise or loud music playing. The FBI personnel objected to the coercive aspects of Abu Zubaydah's interrogation at this time, as they believed they were making substantial progress building rapport with Abu Zubaydah and developing intelligence without these measures. (During their questioning of Abu Zubaydah, the FBI officers provided a towel for Abu Zubaydah to cover himself and continued to use rapport building techniques with the detainee.[2557])

DIRECTOR HAYDEN: "We wanted [SWIGERT's and DUNBAR's] ideas about what approaches might be useful to get information from people like Abu Zubaydah and *other uncooperative al-Qa'ida detainees that we judged were withholding time-sensitive, perishable intelligence.* Keep in mind, as a backdrop for all

The representation that the "requirement to be in the CIA detention program is knowledge of [an] attack against the United States or its interests or knowledge about the location of Usama bin Ladin or Ayman al-Zawahiri" is inconsistent with how the CIA's Detention and Interrogation Program operated from its inception.[2558] As detailed elsewhere, numerous individuals had been detained and subjected to the CIA's enhanced interrogation techniques, despite doubts and questions surrounding of this, this wasn't interrogating a snuffy that's picked up on the battlefield. The *requirement to be in the CIA detention program is knowledge of [an] attack against the United States or its interests or knowledge about the location of Usama bin Ladin or Ayman al-Zawahiri.*"

their knowledge of terrorist threats and the location of senior al-Qa'ida leadership.

DIRECTOR HAYDEN: "We began in 2002, in the spring of 2002. We had one very high value detainee, Abu Zubaydah. *We knew he knew a lot. He would not talk. We were going nowhere with him.* The decision was made, we've got to do something. We've got to have an intervention here. What is it we can do?"

The representation that Abu Zubaydah "would not talk" is incongruent with CIA interrogation records. The CIA representation that the CIA "knew [Abu Zubaydah] knew a lot" reflected an inaccurate assessment of Abu Zubaydah from 2002, prior to his capture, and did not represent the CIA's assessment of Abu Zubaydah as of the April 2007 testimony.

- Prior to Abu Zubaydah's capture, the CIA had intelligence stating that Abu Zubaydah was the "third or fourth" highest ranking al-Qa'ida leader. This information was based on single-source reporting that was retracted in July 2002—prior to Abu Zubaydah being subjected to the CIA's enhanced interrogation techniques. Other intelligence in CIA databases indicated that Abu Zubaydah was not a senior member of al-Qa'ida, but assisted al-Qa'ida members in acquiring false passports and other travel documents. Still other reporting indicated that, while Abu Zubaydah served as an administrator at terrorist training camps, he was not the central figure at these camps.
- After Abu Zubaydah was subjected to the CIA's enhanced interrogation techniques in August 2002, the chief of Base at DETENTION SITE GREEN wrote: "I do not believe that AZ was as wired with al-Qa'ida as we believed him to be prior to his capture."[2559]
- In August 2006, the CIA published an assessment that concluded that "misconceptions" about Afghanistan training camps with which Abu Zubaydah was associated had resulted in reporting that "miscast Abu Zubaydah as a 'senior al-Qa'ida lieutenant.'" The assessment concluded that "al-Qa'ida rejected Abu Zubaydah's request in 1993 to join the group."[2560]

CIA representations that interrogators "were going nowhere with [Abu Zubaydah]" prior to the use of the CIA's enhanced interrogation techniques are also incongruent with CIA records.

- Prior the use of the CIA's enhanced interrogation techniques, Abu Zubaydah provided information on al-Qa'ida activities, plans, capabilities, relationships, leadership structure, personalities, decision-making processes, training, and tactics. Abu Zubaydah provided this type of information prior to, during, and after the utilization of the CIA's enhanced interrogation techniques.
- A quantitative review of Abu Zubaydah's disseminated intelligence reporting indicates that more intelligence reports were disseminated from Abu Zubaydah's first two months of interrogation—prior to the use of the CIA's enhanced interrogation

techniques—than were derived during the two-month period during and after the use of the CIA's enhanced interrogation techniques.[2561]

CIA'S ENHANCED INTERROGATION TECHNIQUES AND THE SERE SCHOOL

DIRECTOR HAYDEN: "After lengthy discussion, [Dr. SWIGERT] suggested that we might use the interrogation approaches that had been, for years, safely used at the DOD survival school—in other words, the interrogation techniques that we were training our airmen to resist. Those techniques have been used for about 50 years, with no significant injuries."
VICE CHAIRMAN BOND: "And the techniques you are using are boiled down, is it true, from the SERE school?"
DIRECTOR HAYDEN: "All of them are techniques that have been used in the SERE school, that's right, Senator."

The CIA consistently represented that the CIA's enhanced interrogation techniques were the same as the techniques used in the U.S. Department of Defense SERE school. However, CIA interrogation records indicate there were significant differences in how the techniques were used against CIA detainees. For example, a letter from the assistant attorney general to the CIA general counsel highlighted the statement in the Inspector General Special Review that the use of the waterboard in SERE training was "so different from subsequent Agency usage as to make it almost irrelevant."[2562] Prior to the use of the CIA's enhanced interrogation techniques against Abu Zubaydah, the chief of Base at the detention site identified differences between how the SERE techniques were applied in training, and how they would be applied to Abu Zubaydah:

> "while the techniques described in Headquarters meetings and below are administered to student volunteers in the U.S. in a harmless way, with no measurable impact on the psyche of the volunteer, we do not believe we can assure the same here for a man forced through these processes and who will be made to believe this is the future course of the remainder of his life . . . personnel will make every effort possible to insure [*sic*] that subject is not permanently physically or mental harmed but we should not say at the outset of this process that there is no risk."[2563]

DEPARTMENT OF JUSTICE APPROVAL

DIRECTOR HAYDEN: "This list of recommended techniques then went to the Department of Justice for their opinion regarding whether or not the techniques were lawful. DOJ returned a legal opinion that the 13 techniques were lawful, didn't constitute torture, and hence could be employed for CIA interrogations."[2564]

As described in this summary, the August 1, 2002, Department of Justice OLC memorandum relied on inaccurate information provided by the CIA concerning Abu Zubaydah's position in al-Qa'ida and the interrogation team's assessment of whether Abu Zubaydah was withholding information about planned terrorist attacks.

The OLC memorandum, which stated that it was based on CIA-provided facts and would not apply if facts were to change, was also specific to Abu Zubaydah. The CIA nonetheless used the OLC memorandum as the legal basis for applying its enhanced interrogation techniques against other CIA detainees.[2565]

RESISTANCE TRAINING

VICE CHAIRMAN BOND: "How far down the line [does al-Qa'ida] train [its] operatives for interrogation resistance?"
DIRECTOR HAYDEN: "I'm getting a nod from the experts,[2567] Senator, that it's rather broadly-based."

A review of CIA records on this topic identified no records to indicate that al-Qa'ida had conducted "broadly-based" interrogation resistance training. The CIA repeatedly represented that Abu Zubaydah "wrote al Qaeda's manual on resistance techniques."[2566] This representation is also not supported by CIA records. When asked about interrogation resistance training, Abu Zubaydah stated:

VICE CHAIRMAN BOND: "So even if you captured the al-Qa'ida facilitator, probably the army field manual stuff are things that he's already been trained on and he knows that he doesn't have to talk."
DIRECTOR HAYDEN: "We would expect that, yes, Senator."

> "... both Khaldan camp and Faruq [terrorist training] camp at least periodically included instruction in how to manage captivity. He explained that in one instance, Khaldan had an Egyptian who had collected and studied information from a variety of sources (including manuals and people who had been in 'different armies'). This Egyptian 'talked to the brothers about being strong' and 'not talking.' Abu Zubaydah's response to this was to take him aside—out of the view of the brothers—and explain to him that it was more important to have a 'super plan—not expect a superman.'"[2568]

Abu Zubaydah explained that he informed trainees at the training camp that "'no brother' should be expected to hold out for an extended time," and that captured individuals will provide information in detention. For that reason, the captured individuals, he explained, should "expect that the organization will make adjustments to protect people and plans when someone with knowledge is captured."[2569]

CIA INTERROGATORS, U.S. MILITARY INTERROGATORS, AND THE ARMY FIELD MANUAL

DIRECTOR HAYDEN: "All those involved in the questioning of detainees have been *carefully chosen and carefully screened*.[2570] The average age of our officers interrogating detainees is 43. Once they are selected, they must complete more than 250 hours of specialized training for this program before they are allowed to come face-to-face with a terrorist. And we require additional field work under the direct supervision of an experienced officer before a new interrogator can direct an interrogation."

DIRECTOR HAYDEN: "The Army field manual was also written to guide the conduct of a much larger, much younger force that trains primarily to detain large numbers of enemy prisoners of war. That's not what the CIA program is."

DIRECTOR HAYDEN: "[The Army Field Manual has] got to be done by hundreds and hundreds of teenagers in battlefield tactical situations."
SENATOR JOHN WARNER: "Without the benefit of a tenth of the training of your professionals."
DIRECTOR HAYDEN: "Exactly."[2573]

This CIA testimony is incongruent with internal CIA records and the operational history of the program.

- On November ■, 2002, after the completion of the first formal interrogation training class, ■■■ CTC Legal, ■■■■, asked CTC attorney ■■■■ to "[m]ake it known that from now on, CTC/LGL must vet all personnel who are enrolled in, observing or teaching—or otherwise associated with—the class."[2571] The chief of CTC, Jose Rodriguez, objected to this approach, stating: "I do not think that CTC/LGL should or would want to get into the business of vetting participants, observers, instructors or others that are involved in this program. It is simply not your job. Your job is to tell all what are the acceptable legal standards for conducting interrogations per the authorities obtained from Justice and agreed upon by the White House."[2572] Contrary to CIA Director Hayden's comments and Statement for the Record that "[a]ll those involved in the questioning of detainees are carefully chosen and screened for demonstrated professional judgment and maturity," CIA records suggest that the vetting sought by ■■■■ did not take place. The Committee reviewed CIA records related to several CIA officers and contractors involved in the CIA's Detention and Interrogation Program, most of whom conducted interrogations. The Committee identified a number of personnel whose backgrounds include notable derogatory information calling into question their eligibility for employment, their access to classified information, and their participation in CIA interrogation activities. In nearly all cases, the derogatory information was known to the CIA prior to the assignment of the CIA officers to the Detention and Interrogation Program. This group of officers included individuals who, among other issues, had engaged in inappropriate detainee interrogations, had workplace anger management issues, and had reportedly admitted to sexual assault.[2574]

- Director Hayden's testimony on the required hours of training for CIA interrogators is inconsistent with the early operational history of the program. Records indicate that CIA officers and contractors who conducted CIA interrogations in 2002 did not undergo any interrogation training. The first interrogator training course, held in November 2002, required approximately 65 hours of classroom and operational instruction.[2575] The initial training was designed and conducted by ██████, who had been sanctioned for using abusive interrogation techniques in the 1980s, and ██████, who had never been trained in, or conducted interrogations. In April 2003, ██████ [CIA OFFICER 1] was certified as an interrogator after only a week of classroom training.[2576] In 2003, interrogator certification required only two weeks of classroom training (a maximum of 80 hours) and 20 additional hours of operational training and/or actual interrogations.[2577]

OTHER MEMBERS OF THE INTERROGATION TEAM

DIRECTOR HAYDEN: "All interrogation sessions in which one of these lawful procedures is authorized for use has to be *observed by nonparticipants* to ensure the procedures are applied appropriately and safely. *Any observer can call 'knock it off' at any time.* They are authorized to terminate an interrogation immediately should they believe anything unauthorized is occurring."
SENATOR SNOWE: "So you also mentioned that there are nonparticipants who are observing the interrogation process. Who are these non-participants?"
DIRECTOR HAYDEN: "They could be other interrogators, medical personnel, chief of base, debriefers, analysts."
SENATOR SNOWE: "Do they ever raise concerns during this process, during these interrogations?"
DIRECTOR HAYDEN: "Everybody watching has—every individual has an absolute right to stop the procedure just by saying 'stop.'"
SENATOR SNOWE: "Did it happen? It's never happened?"
DIRECTOR HAYDEN: "No, we're not aware. I'm sorry. John [Rizzo] and [██████] point out it's just not the ability to stop it; it is an obligation to stop it if they believe something is happening that is unauthorized."

This testimony is incongruent with CIA records, for example:

- During the interrogation of Abu Zubaydah, CIA personnel at DETENTION SITE GREEN objected to the continued use of the CIA's enhanced interrogation techniques against Abu Zubaydah, stating that it was "highly unlikely" Abu Zubaydah possessed the threat information CIA Headquarters was seeking.[2578] When the interrogation team made this assessment, they stated that the pressures being applied to Abu Zubaydah approached "the legal limit."[2579] CIA Headquarters directed the interrogation team to continue to use the CIA's enhanced interrogation techniques and instructed the team to refrain from using "speculative language as to the legality of given activities" in CIA cables.[2580]

- During the KSM interrogation sessions, the CIA chief of Base directed that the medical officer at the detention site not directly contact CIA Headquarters via the CIA's classified internal email system, to avoid establishing "grounds for further legal action." Instead, the chief of Base stated that any information on KSM's interrogations would be first reviewed by the chief of Base before being released to CIA Headquarters."[2581] Prior to KSM's third waterboard session of March 13, 2003, the on-site medical officer raised concerns that the session would exceed the limits of draft OMS guidelines for the waterboard.[2582] The waterboard session was conducted after an approval email from a CTC attorney at CIA Headquarters.[2583] The medical officer would later write that "[t]hings are slowly evolving form [*sic*] [medical officers] being viewed as the institutional conscience and the limiting factor to the ones who are dedicated to maximizing the benefit in a safe manner and keeping everyone's butt out of trouble."[2584]

- As was the case with several other CIA detainees, 'Abd al-Rahim al-Nashiri was repeatedly subjected to the CIA's enhanced interrogation techniques at the direction of CIA Headquarters, despite opposition from CIA interrogators.[2585]
- The CIA Inspector General Special Review states that CIA "psychologists objected to the use of on-site psychologists as interrogators and raised conflict of interest and ethical concerns." According to the Special Review, this was "based on a concern that the on-site psychologists who were administering the [CIA's enhanced interrogation techniques] participated in the evaluations, assessing the effectiveness and impact of the [CIA's enhanced interrogation techniques] on the detainees.[2586] In January 2003, CIA Headquarters requested that at least one other psychologist be present who was not physically participating in the administration of the CIA's enhanced interrogation techniques. According to ███ ███OMS, however, the problem still existed because "psychologist/interrogators continue to perform both functions."[2587]

SENATOR SNOWE: "Did any CIA personnel express reservations about being engaged in the interrogation or these techniques that were used?"
DIRECTOR HAYDEN: "I'm not aware of any. These guys are more experienced. No."

This statement is incongruent with CIA records. For example, from August 4, 2002, through August 23, 2002, the CIA subjected Abu Zubaydah to its enhanced interrogation techniques on a near 24-hour-per-day basis. The non-stop use of the CIA's enhanced interrogation techniques was disturbing to CIA personnel at DETENTION SITE GREEN. These CIA personnel objected to the continued use of the CIA's enhanced interrogation techniques against Abu Zubaydah, but were instructed by CIA Headquarters to continue using the techniques. The interrogation using the CIA's enhanced techniques continued more than two weeks after CIA personnel on site questioned the legality "of escalating or even maintaining the pressure" on Abu Zubaydah. CIA records include the following reactions of CIA personnel expressing "reservations about being engaged in the interrogations" and the use of the techniques:

- August 5, 2002: "want to caution [medical officer] that this is almost certainly not a place he's ever been before in his medical career . . . It is visually and psychologically very uncomfortable."[2588]
- August 8, 2002: "Today's first session . . . had a profound effect on all staff members present . . . it seems the collective opinion that we should not go much further . . . everyone seems strong for now but if the group has to continue . . . we cannot guarantee how much longer."[2589]
- August 8, 2002: "Several on the team profoundly affected . . . some to the point of tears and choking up."[2590]
- August 9, 2002: "two, perhaps three [personnel] likely to elect transfer" away from the detention site if the decision is made to continue with the enhanced interrogation techniques.[2591]
- August 11, 2002: Viewing the pressures on Abu Zubaydah on video "has produced strong feelings

of futility (and legality) of escalating or even maintaining the pressure." With respect to viewing the interrogation tapes, "prepare for something not seen previously."[2592]

The chief of CTC, Jose Rodriguez—via email—instructed the CIA interrogation team to not use "speculative language as to the legality of given activities" in CIA cable traffic.[2593] Shortly thereafter, circa December 2002, the CIA general counsel had a "real concern" about the lack of details in cables of what was taking place at CIA detention sites, noting that "cable traffic reporting was becoming thinner," and that "the agency cannot monitor the situation if it is not documented in cable traffic."[2594] The CIA's chief of interrogations—who provided training to CIA interrogators—expressed his view that there was "excess information" in the Abu Zubaydah interrogation cables."[2595]

REPORTING ABUSES

DIRECTOR HAYDEN: "Any *deviations from approved procedures and practices that are seen are to be immediately reported and immediate corrective action taken*, including referring to the CIA Office of Inspector General and to the Department of Justice, as appropriate."

This testimony is not supported by CIA records, for example:

- Multiple individuals involved in the interrogation of CIA detainee 'Abd al-Rahim al-Nashiri failed to report inappropriate activity. With regard to the unauthorized use of a handgun and power drill to threaten al-Nashiri, one CIA interrogator stated he did not report the incidents because he believed they fell below the reporting threshold for the CIA's enhanced interrogation techniques, while noting he did not receive guidance on reporting requirements. The chief of Base stated he did not report the incidents because he assumed the interrogator had CIA Headquarters' approval and because two senior CIA officials had instructed him to scale back on reporting from the detention site to CIA Headquarters. The inappropriate activity was discovered during a chance exchange between recently arrived CIA Headquarters officials and security officers.[2596]

- There were significant quantitative and qualitative differences between the waterboarding of KSM, as applied, and the description of the technique provided to the Department of Justice. Neither CIA interrogators nor CIA attorneys reported these deviations to the inspector general or the Department of Justice at the time.

- Additionally, CIA records indicate that at least 17 detainees were subjected to CIA enhanced interrogation techniques for which they were not approved.[2597]

DETAINEE STATISTICS

DIRECTOR HAYDEN: "What you have there is a matrix. On the lefthand side of the matrix are the names of the 30 *individuals in the CIA program who have had any EITs*

This testimony is inaccurate. At the time of this testimony, there had been least 118 CIA detainees. CIA records indicate at least 38 of the detainees had been subjected to the CIA's enhanced interrogation techniques.[2598]

used against them. Mr. Chairman and Vice Chairman and Members, you've heard me say this before. In the history of the program, *we've had 97 detainees.* Thirty of the detainees have had EITs used against them."

LEGAL BASIS FOR CIA DETENTION AND INTERROGATION

DIRECTOR HAYDEN: "The Army field manual is designed for the folks at Guantanamo to interrogate a rifleman that was in the employ of Gulbuddin Hekmatyar. That guy never gets into our program. The *ticket into this program is knowledge of threat to the homeland or the interests of the United States or knowledge of location of 1 or 2.*"

This testimony is incongruent with CIA detention and interrogation records. For example, numerous individuals had been detained and subjected to the CIA's enhanced interrogation techniques, despite doubts and questions surrounding their knowledge of terrorist threats and the location of senior al-Qa'ida leadership. They include Asadullah,[2599] Mustafa al-Hawsawi,[2600] Abu Hudhaifa,[2601] Arsala Khan,[2602] ABU TALHA AL-MAGREBI[2603] and ABU BAHAR AL-TURKI,[2604] Janat Gul,[2605] Ahmed Ghailani,[2606] Sharif al-Masri,[2607] and Sayyid Ibrahim.[2608]

The CIA represented to the OLC that the CIA would only use its enhanced interrogation techniques against detainees who had knowledge of imminent threats or direct involvement in planning and preparing of terrorist actions. Not until July 20, 2007, more than three months after this testimony, did the OLC approve the use of the CIA's enhanced interrogation techniques against detainees based on their suspected knowledge of the locations of UBL or Ayman al-Zawahiri.[2609] Prior to July 20, 2007, in the case of at least six CIA detainees, the use of the CIA's enhanced interrogation techniques was nonetheless predicated on the assessment that the detainees possessed "locational information" on senior HVTs, to include UBL or Ayman al-Zawahiri.[2610]

INTELLIGENCE REPORTING FROM OVERALL DETAINEE POPULATION

DIRECTOR HAYDEN: "Since we began this in the summer of 2002, the 97 detainees have helped us by their testimony create 8,000 intelligence reports."
SENATOR SNOWE: "Of the 8,000 intelligence reports that were provided, as you said, by 30 of the detainees—"
DIRECTOR HAYDEN: "By all 97, ma'am."[2611]

CIA representations suggesting that every CIA detainee provided intelligence reporting are not supported by CIA records. A detailed reporting chart is provided in Volume II. CIA reporting records indicate that 34 percent of all CIA detainees produced no intelligence reports, and nearly 70 percent produced fewer than 15 intelligence reports. Of the 39 detainees who were, according to CIA records, subjected to the CIA's enhanced interrogation techniques, nearly 20 percent produced no intelligence reports, while 40 percent produced fewer than 15 intelligence reports.

CIA DETAINEE REPORTING AND CAPTURES OF TERRORISTS

DIRECTOR HAYDEN: "Detainee reporting has played a role in nearly every capture of key al-Qa'ida members and associates since 2002."

The CIA consistently represented that the interrogation of CIA detainees using the CIA's enhanced interrogation techniques resulted in critical and otherwise unavailable intelligence that led to the capture of specific terrorists, to include, among others: KSM, Majid Khan, Ramzi bin al-Shibh, Iyman Paris, Saleh al-Marri, Ammar al-Baluchi, Khallad bin Attash, Sajid Badat, and Dhiren Barot.[55] These representations were inaccurate.

THE CIA'S DETENTION AND INTERROGATION PROGRAM LED TO THE CAPTURE OF HAMBALI AND THE KARACHI "CELL"

DIRECTOR HAYDEN: "March 2003, KSM gives us information about an al-Qa'ida operative, Majid Khan . . . KSM was aware that Majid had been recently captured. KSM, *possibly believing that Khan was talking*, admitted to having tasked Majid with delivering $50,000 to some of Hambali's operatives in December 2002 . . . So now we go to [Majid] Khan and we tell him, hey, your uncle just told us about the money. *He acknowledged that he delivered the money to an operative named Zubair. He provided Zubair's physical description and phone number. Based on that* ███ *captured Zubair in June.*"

The chronology provided in this testimony, which is consistent with other CIA representations, is inaccurate. Prior to KSM's capture, in early January 2003, coverage of a known al-Qa'ida email account uncovered communications between the account and a former Baltimore, Maryland, resident, Majid Khan. The communications indicated that Majid Khan traveled to Bangkok for terrorist support activities and was in contact there with a "Zubair."[2613] By this time, the CIA had significant intelligence indicating that a "Zubair" played a central supporting role in Jemaah Islamiyah (JI), was affiliated with al-Qa'ida figures like KSM, had expertise in ███ in Southeast Asia, and was suspected of playing a role in Hambali's October 12, 2002, Bali bombings.[2614] On March 6, 2003, the day after Majid Khan was captured (the capture was unrelated to CIA detainee reporting), and while being questioned by foreign government interrogators using rapport-building techniques, Majid Khan described how he traveled to Bangkok and provided $50,000 USD to Zubair at the behest of al-Qa'ida.[2615] Majid Khan's physical description of Zubair matched previous intelligence reporting already collected on Zubair.[2616]

When confronted with this information, KSM confirmed the reporting, but denied knowing Zubair.[2617]

By May 2003, the CIA learned that a source the CIA had been developing, ███, received a call from a phone number associated with Zubair. When the source was contacted by the CIA, he described a Malaysian man ███ ███.[2618] ███ later, the source alerted the CIA that Zubair would be ███. Acting on this information, Thai authorities, ███, captured Zubair on June 8, 2003.

DIRECTOR HAYDEN: "*Zubair enters the program.* During debriefing, Zubair reveals he worked directly for Hambali. He provides information on ███ Hambali and a company ███."

This testimony is incongruent with CIA records. Prior to entering the CIA's Detention and Interrogation Program, while still in foreign government custody, Zubair was questioned about his efforts to obtain fraudulent ███ documents, as well as his phone contact with ███ [Business Q] ███.[2619] Zubair admitted to seeking illegal ███ documents on behalf of Hambali, as well as using ███ [Business Q] ███ ███.[2620] CIA detention records do not state what immediate investigative steps the CIA or Thai authorities took with regard to ███ [Business Q], although signals intelligence had indicated that Zubair had been in frequent contact with the company.[2621]

After being rendered to CIA custody, Zubair was immediately subjected to the CIA's enhanced interrogation techniques.[2622] After days of being questioned about other matters, Zubair was asked about his efforts to obtain ███ documents for Hambali, at which point he again acknowledged using ███ [Business Q] ███ ███.[2623] When Thai authorities approached "a contact" at ███ [Business Q], they were provided

█████████████████████████ █.[2624]

DIRECTOR HAYDEN: "Working with [an entity of a foreign government], we used that information to capture another Hambali lieutenant, a fellow named Lillie—who is also on your list [of CIA detainees]—who provided the location of Hambali. And that location information led us to his capture."

In an operation that included surveillance of ████ [Business Q], Hambali associate Amer was arrested on August 11, 2003.[2625] Amer was immediately cooperative and assisted in the arrest of Lillie hours later at approximately 6:00 PM.[2626] During his arrest, Lillie was found to have a key fob in his possession imprinted with an address of an apartment building in Ayutthaya, Thailand. In response to questioning, "within minutes of capture," Lillie admitted that the address on the key fob was the address where Hambali was located. Less than four hours later, Hambali was captured at the address found on the key fob.[2627]

According to the chief of the CTC's Southeast Asia Branch:

> "[The CIA] stumbled onto Hambali. We stumbled onto the [source] . . . picking up the phone and calling his case officer to say there's ████ . . . we really stumbled over it. It wasn't police work, it wasn't good targeting, it was we stumbled over it and it yielded up Hambali."[2628]

KSM, HAMBALI, AND THE KARACHI "CELL" (THE AL-GHURABA GROUP)

DIRECTOR HAYDEN: "Bringing this story full circle, 'Abdul al-Hadi then identifies a cell of JI operatives whom Hambali had sent to Karachi for another al-Qa'ida operation. We take this information from Abdul Hadi to his brother, Hambali. Hambali then admits that he was grooming members of the cell for a U.S. operation, at the guidance of KSM—remember, this is where this started—and we're almost certain these were the guys trying to implement KSM's plot to fly hijacked planes into the tallest buildings on the west coast of the United States."

CIA Director Hayden's reference to "the guys trying to implement KSM's plot to fly hijacked planes into the tallest buildings on the west coast of the United States," is a reference to the al-Ghuraba student group and KSM's "Second Wave" plotting detailed in this summary and in greater detail in Volume II.[2629]

A review of CIA records found that contrary to CIA representations, Hambali's brother, 'Abdul al-Hadi, aka Gunawan, who was in foreign government custody, did not identify a "cell of JI operatives whom Hambali had sent to Karachi for another al-Qa'ida operation." He identified "a group of Malaysian and Indonesian students in Karachi" who were witting of his affiliation with Jemaah Islamiyah.[2630] CIA officers on site recalled other intelligence reporting indicating that KSM planned to use Malaysians in the "next wave of attacks," connected it to Gunawan's statements about Malaysian students, and reported that Gunawan had just identified "a group of 16 individuals, most all of whom are Malaysians."[2631] Records indicate that it was this initial analysis that led the CIA to consider the group a KSM "cell" for the "next wave of attacks."

While Hambali was being subjected to the CIA's enhanced interrogation techniques, he was confronted about KSM's efforts to find pilots, as well as information on the al-Ghuraba group—which the CIA assessed was a KSM "cell." Hambali told his CIA interrogators "that some of the members of [the al-Ghuraba group] were destined to work for al-Qa'ida if everything had gone according to plan," and that "KSM told him to provide as many pilots as he could.[2632]

Months later, on November 30, 2003, after three weeks of being questioned by a debriefer "almost entirely in Bahasa

Indonesia," Hambali admitted to fabricating information during the period he was being subjected to the CIA's enhanced interrogation techniques. According to Hambali, he fabricated these claims "in an attempt to reduce the pressure on himself" and "to give an account that was consistent with what [Hambali] assessed the questioners wanted to hear."[2633] A November 30, 2003, cable noted that CIA personnel "assesse[d] [Hambali]'s admission of previous fabrication to be credible." Hambali then consistently described "the al-Ghuraba organization" as a "development camp for potential future JI operatives and leadership, vice a JI cell or an orchestrated attempt by JI to initiate JI operations outside of Southeast Asia." This description was consistent and corroborative of other intelligence reporting.[2634]

A wide body of intelligence reporting indicates that, contrary to CIA representations, the al-Ghuraba group was not "tasked" with, or witting, of any aspect of the "Second Wave" plotting.[2635]

While KSM's reporting varied, KSM stated "he did not yet view the group as an operational pool from which to draft operatives."[2636] An October 27, 2006,CIA cable stated that "all of the members of the JI al-Ghuraba cell have been released,"[2637] while an April 18, 2008, CIA intelligence report referencing the al-Ghuraba group makes no reference to the group serving as potential operatives for KSM's "Second Wave" plotting.[2638]

THE INTERROGATION PROCESS

DIRECTOR HAYDEN: "As before, with these seven [enhanced interrogation techniques] we use the least coercive measures to create cooperation at a predictable, reliable, sustainable level. They are used to create a state of cooperation. Once the state of cooperation is created, we simply productively debrief the detainee. On average, we get to that state of cooperation in a period measured by about one to two weeks."

"When we're asking him questions during that period of increased stress, when we're being more rather than less coercive, *we are generally asking him questions for which we know the answers*. Otherwise, how do we know we have moved him from a spirit of defiance into a spirit of cooperation? And only after we have moved him into this second stage do we then begin to ask him things we really think he knows but we don't."

This testimony is incongruent with CIA records. As is detailed throughout the Committee Study, CIA detainees were frequently subjected to the CIA's enhanced interrogation techniques immediately after being rendered to CIA custody.[2639] CIA interrogators asked open-ended questions of CIA detainees, to which the CIA did not know the answers, while subjecting detainees to the CIA's enhanced interrogation techniques. This approach began with Abu Zubaydah, whose interrogation focused on him being told to provide "the one thing you don't want me to know,"[2640] and remained a central feature of the program. Numerous CIA detainees were determined never to have reached a "state of cooperation." Several detainees, when subjected to the CIA's enhanced interrogation techniques, transitioned to normal debriefing, and were then subjected to one or more additional periods of being subjected to the techniques.[2641]

USE OF DETAINEE REPORTING

DIRECTOR HAYDEN: "Nothing that we get from the program, however, is used in isolation. It's a data point that then has to be rubbed up against all the other data points we have available to us."

The CIA regularly disseminated intelligence reports based on uncorroborated statements from CIA detainees. The reports, some of which included fabricated or otherwise inaccurate information, required extensive FBI investigations.[2642] For example, the CIA disseminated information that KSM had sent Abu Issa al-Britani to Montana to recruit African-American Muslim converts.[2643] In June 2003, KSM stated he fabricated the information because he was "under 'enhanced measures' when he made these claims and simply told his interrogators what he thought they wanted to hear."[2644] Other KSM fabrications led the CIA to capture and detain suspected terrorists who were later found to be innocent.[2645]

THE RELIGIOUS FOUNDATION FOR COOPERATION

DIRECTOR HAYDEN: "This proposed program you have in front of you has been informed by our experience and it has been informed by the comments of our detainees. It's built on the particular psychological profile of the people we have and expect to get—al-Qa'ida operatives. Perceiving themselves true believers in a religious war, detainees believe they are morally bound to resist until Allah has sent them a burden too great for them to withstand. At that point—and that point varies by detainee—their cooperation in their own heart and soul becomes blameless and they enter into this cooperative relationship with our debriefers."

DIRECTOR HAYDEN: "Number one, we use the enhanced interrogation techniques at the beginning of this process, and it varies how long it takes, but I gave you a week or two as the normal window in which we actually helped this religious zealot to get over his own personality and put himself in a spirit of cooperation."

VICE CHAIRMAN BOND: "Once you get past that time period, once you have convinced them that Allah gives them the green light, that's when you get the 8,000 intelligence reports."

DIRECTOR HAYDEN: "That's correct, Senator, when we get the subject into this zone of cooperation. I think, as you know, in two-thirds of the instances we don't need to use any of the techniques to get the individual into the zone of cooperation."

The CIA made a similar representation to the Department of Justice in the context of Abu Zubaydah.[2646] CIA records do not indicate that CIA detainees described a religious basis for cooperating in association with the CIA's enhanced interrogation techniques.[2647]

The CIA has referred only to Abu Zubaydah in the context of this representation. As detailed, Abu Zubaydah referenced religion in the context of his cooperation prior to being subjected to the CIA's enhanced interrogation techniques. On May 14, 2002, more than two months before Abu Zubaydah began his August 2002 enhanced interrogation period, Abu Zubaydah told interrogators that "if he possessed any more information on future threats, then he would provide this information to us to help himself, claiming that 'the sharia' gives him permission to do so in his current situation."[2648] Abu Zubaydah also made a similar statement to his interrogators approximately a week later—again, prior to the use of the CIA's enhanced interrogation techniques—stating that he had "prayed his 'Istikharah' (seeking God's guidance) and was now willing to tell what he really knew," and "that he had received guidance from God" to cooperate to "prevent his captured brothers from having a difficult time."[2649] Further, Abu Zubaydah maintained that he always intended to provide information and never believed he could withhold information from interrogators.[2650] In February 2003, he told a CIA psychologist that he believed every captured "brother" would talk in detention, and that these "brothers should be able to expect that the organization will make adjustments to protect people and plans when someone with knowledge is captured."[2651] Abu Zubaydah stated he conveyed this perspective to trainees at a terrorist training camp.[2652]

SENATOR NELSON: "How do you suspect that al-Qa'ida operatives are training in order to counter your techniques?"
DIRECTOR HAYDEN: "You recall the policy on which this is based, that we're going to give him a burden that Allah says is too great for you to bear, so they can put the burden down."[2653]

THREATS RELATED TO SODOMY, ARREST OF FAMILY

DIRECTOR HAYDEN: "Many assertions [in the ICRC report] regarding physical or threatened abuse are egregious and are simply not true. On their face, they aren't even credible. Threats of acts of sodomy, the arrest and rape of family members, the intentional infection of HIV or any other diseases have never been and would never be authorized. There are no instances in which such threats or abuses took place."

This testimony is incongruent with CIA interrogation records.

- As documented in the May 2004 Inspector General Special Review and other CIA records, interrogators threatened 'Abd al-Rahim al-Nashiri, KSM, and Abu Zubaydah with harm to their families.[2654]
- Rectal exams were standard operating procedure for security purposes. A June 2002 cable noted that Abu Zubaydah was mildly "tense," "likely an anticipatory reaction given his recent unexpected rectal exam" the previous day.[2655]
- At least five detainees were subjected to rectal rehydration or rectal feeding. There is at least one record of Abu Zubaydah receiving "rectal fluid resuscitation" for "partially refusing liquids."[2656] According to CIA records, Majid Khan was "very hostile" to rectal feeding and removed the rectal tube as soon as he was allowed to.[2657] KSM was subjected to rectal rehydration without a determination of medical need, a procedure that KSM interrogator and chief of interrogations, [REDACTED], would later characterize as illustrative of the interrogator's "total control over the detainee."[2658] Marwan al-Jabbur was subjected to what was originally referred to in a cable as an "enema," but was later acknowledged to be rectal rehydration.[2659] Both al-Nashiri[2660] and Majid Khan were subjected to rectal feeding.[2661]
- Three detainees, Ramzi bin al-Shibh, Khallad bin Attash and Adnan al-Libi, were threatened with rectal rehydration.[2662]

PUNCHES AND KICKS

DIRECTOR HAYDEN: "Punches and kicks are not authorized and have never been employed."[2663]

This testimony is incongruent with CIA records. Interviews conducted for two CIA internal reviews related to Gul Rahman's death provided details on CIA interrogations at the CIA's DETENTION SITE COBALT. In an interview report, CIA contractor DUNBAR described the "hard" or "rough" takedown used at DETENTION SITE COBALT. According to the interview report of DUNBAR, "there were approximately five CIA officers from the renditions team ... they opened the door of Rahman's cell and rushed in screaming and yelling for him to 'get down.' They dragged him outside, cut off his clothes and secured him with Mylar tape. They covered his head with a hood and ran him up and down a long corridor adjacent to his cell. They slapped him and punched him several times. [DUNBAR] stated that although it was obvious they were not trying to hit him as hard as they could, a couple of times the punches were forceful. As they ran him along the corridor, a couple of times he fell and they dragged him through the dirt (the floor outside of the cells is dirt). Rahman did acquire a number of abrasions on his face, legs, and hands, but nothing that required medical attention. (This may account for the abrasions found on Rahman's body after his death. Rahman had a number of surface abrasions on his shoulders, pelvis, arms, legs, and face.)"[2664]

The use of the "hard" or "rough" takedown, as used on Gul Rahman, was described by the CIA officer in charge of the CIA's DETENTION SITE COBALT as "employed often in interrogations at [DETENTION SITE COBALT] as 'part of the atmospherics.'"[2665]

HYGIENE

DIRECTOR HAYDEN: "Detainees have never been denied the means—at a minimum, they've always had a bucket—to dispose of their human waste."

This testimony is incongruent with CIA records. CIA detainees, particularly those subjected to standing sleep deprivation, were routinely placed in diapers. Waste buckets were not always available. In the interrogation of Abu Hazim, a waste bucket was removed from his cell for punishment. According to a CIA cable, Abu Hazim "requested a bucket in which he could relieve himself, but was told all rewards must be earned."[2666]

MEDICAL PERSONNEL AND MEDICAL CARE

DIRECTOR HAYDEN: "The medical section of the ICRC report concludes that the association of CIA medical officers with the interrogation program is 'contrary to international standards of medical ethics.' That is just wrong. The role of CIA medical officers in the detainee program is and always has been and always will be to ensure the safety and the well-being of the detainee. The placement of medical officers during the interrogation techniques represents an extra measure of caution. Our medical officers do not recommend the employment or continuation of any procedures or techniques."

CIA records detail how throughout the program, CIA medical personnel cleared detainees for the use of the CIA's enhanced interrogation techniques and played a central role in deciding whether to continue, adjust, or alter the use of the techniques against detainees. For example:

- Prior to the initiation of the CIA's enhanced interrogation techniques against Abu Zubaydah, CIA Headquarters, with medical personnel participation, stated that the "interrogation process takes precedence over preventative medical procedures."[2667]
- Abu Ja'far al-Iraqi was provided medication for swelling in his legs to allow for continued standing sleep deprivation.[2668]

DIRECTOR HAYDEN: "The allegation in the report that a CIA medical officer threatened a detainee, stating that medical care was conditional on cooperation is blatantly false. Health care has always been administered based upon detainee needs. It's neither policy nor practice to link medical care to any other aspect of

This testimony is incongruent with CIA records. For example, as CIA interrogators prepared for the August 2002 "enhanced interrogation" phase of Abu Zubaydah's interrogation, the CIA's DETENTION SITE GREEN noted, and CIA Headquarters confirmed, that the interrogation process would take precedence over preventing Abu Zubaydah's wounds from becoming infected.[2669] DETENTION SITE GREEN personnel also stated that delaying a medical session for 72 hours after the start the detainee program."

SENATOR HATCH: "Has there been any use of any kind of drug or withholding of any kind of drug or medication?"

DIRECTOR HAYDEN: "No, absolutely not."

of the new phase of interrogation would convey to Abu Zubaydah that his level of medical care was contingent upon his cooperation.[2670] On August 10, 2002, the medical officer at DETENTION SITE GREEN stated that, under the model of medical intervention that the detention site was following during the most aggressive interrogation phase, Abu Zubaydah's medical status was likely to deteriorate to an "unacceptable level" over the next two weeks.[2671] On August 25, 2002, the Base stated that the "combination of a lack of hygiene, sub-optimal nutrition, inadvertent trauma to the wound secondary to some of the stress techniques utilized at that stage, and the removal of formal obvious medical care to further isolate the subject had an overall additive effect on the deterioration of the wound."[2672]

Abu Zubaydah lost his left eye while in CIA custody. In October 2002, DETENTION SITE GREEN recommended that the vision in his right eye be tested, noting that "[w]e have a lot riding upon his ability to see, read and write." DETENTION SITE GREEN stressed that "this request is driven by our intelligence needs vice humanitarian concern for AZ."[2673]

CIA detainees Abu Hazim and Abd al-Karim each broke a foot while trying to escape capture and were placed in casts; Abd al-Karim's medical evaluation upon entry into CIA custody included a recommendation that he not be subjected to "extended standing for a couple of weeks," which was then extended to three months.[2674] A cable describing the CIA enhanced interrogation techniques to be used on the two detainees stated that the interrogator would "forego cramped confinement, stress positions, walling, and vertical shackling (due to [the detainees'] injury)."[2675] Abd al-Karim was nonetheless subjected to two 45-minute sessions of cramped confinement,[2676] repeated walling, and a stress position that involved placing his "head on [the] wall, bent at waist, shuffled backwards to a safe, yet uncomfortable position."[2677] As part of sleep deprivation, he was also "walked for 15 minutes every half-hour through the night and into the morning."[2678] A few days later, a cable stated that, even given the best prognosis, Abd al-Karim would have arthritis and limitation of motion for the rest of his life.[2679] Meanwhile, Abu Hazim was subjected to repeated walling.[2680]

Subsequently, and despite the aforementioned recommendation related to Abd al-Karim and a recommendation from a regional medical officer that Abu Hazim avoid any weight-bearing activities for five weeks,[2681] interrogators sought and received approval to use standing sleep deprivation on al-Karim and Abu Hazim.[2682]

Abu Hazim underwent 52 hours of standing sleep deprivation,[2683] and Abd al-Karim underwent an unspecified period of standing sleep deprivation.[2684]

Interrogators left Asadullah, a detainee with a sprained ankle, in the standing sleep deprivation position. When Asadullah was subsequently placed in a stress position on his knees, he complained of discomfort and asked to sit.

He was told he could not sit unless he answered questions truthfully.[2685]

Due to a lack of adequate medical care at CIA detention sites and the unwillingness of host governments to make hospital facilities available, CIA detainees had care delayed for serious medical issues. See, for example, the detainee reviews for Janat Gul, Hassan Guleed, Mustafa al-Hawsawi, Ramzi bin al-Shibh, and Firas al-Yemeni in Volume III.

DIETARY MANIPULATION

DIRECTOR HAYDEN: "And, in the section [of the ICRC report] on medical care, the report omits key contextual facts. For example, Abu Zubaydah's statement that he was given only Ensure and water for two to three weeks fails to mention the fact that *he was on a liquid diet [was] quite appropriate because he was recovering from abdominal surgery at the time.*"

This testimony is inaccurate. CIA records detail how Abu Zubaydah was fed solid food shortly after being discharged from the hospital in April 2002.[2686] In August 2002, as part of the CIA's enhanced interrogation techniques, Abu Zubaydah was placed on a liquid diet of Ensure and water as both an interrogation technique, and as a means of limiting vomiting during waterboarding.[2687] In planning for the interrogation of subsequent detainees, the CIA determined that it would use a "liquid diet."[2688] At least 30 CIA detainees were fed only a liquid diet of Ensure and water for interrogation purposes.[2689]

WATERBOARDING AND ITS EFFECTIVENESS

SENATOR HATCH: "So this is not tipping the board and putting his head underneath the water."
DIRECTOR HAYDEN: "No. It's slightly inclined, cloth, pouring of water under the rules I just laid out, Senator."

This testimony is incongruent with CIA interrogation records. As described in the Study, the waterboarding of KSM involved interrogators using their hands to maintain a one-inch deep "pool" of water over KSM's nose and mouth in an effort to make it impossible for KSM to ingest all the water being poured on him.[2690] According to the attending medical officer, the technique became a "series of near drownings."[2691]

DIRECTOR HAYDEN: "[W]aterboarding *cannot take place any more than five days out of a total of 30 days.* There *cannot be more than two sessions per day.* A session is described as being strapped to the board. No session can last longer than two hours. In any session, *there can be no more than six pourings of the water greater than ten seconds in duration. Under no circumstances can any detainee be under the pouring of the water a total of more than twelve minutes in any 24-hour period*, and one pouring cannot exceed, one application cannot exceed 40 seconds."

This testimony is incongruent with CIA interrogation records. For example, KSM was waterboarded on nine separate days over a two-week period. On March 13, 2003, KSM was subjected to three waterboard sessions in one day. Over March 12–13, 2003, he was subjected to five waterboard sessions in 25 hours. During that same period, he was subjected to the pouring of water for more than twelve minutes during a 24-hour period.[2692]

In regard to the description of "pouring," a CIA record related to Abu Zubaydah states that:

> "Each iteration of the watering cycle consisted of four broad steps: 1) demands for information interspersed with the application of the water just short of blocking his airway 2) escalation of the amount of water applied until it blocked his airway and he started to have involuntary spasms 3) raising the waterboard to clear subject's airway 4) lowering of the water-board and return to demands for information."[2693]

SENATOR NELSON: "On KSM, was it waterboarding that you were able to get the information from

This testimony is incongruent with CIA interrogation records. CIA personnel—including members of KSM's interrogation team—believed that the waterboard

him?"
DIRECTOR HAYDEN: "Yes, sir, *it was*."
SENATOR NELSON: "Although it took you a long time to break him?"
DIRECTOR HAYDEN: "He had nine separate days in which waterboarding took place. He also was subject[ed] to sleep deprivation and I believe his deprivation was the longest of any detainee's, at one stretch, and I think that may be what Senator Hatch was referring to by that 180 number. That's the number of hours at one stretch."

interrogation technique was ineffective on KSM.[2694] The on-site medical officer told the inspector general that, after three or four days, it became apparent that the waterboard was ineffective, and that KSM "hated it but knew he could manage."[2695] KSM interrogator [REDACTED] told the inspector general that KSM had "beat the system,"[2696] and assessed two months after the discontinuation of the waterboard that KSM responded to "creature comforts and sense of importance" and not to "confrontational" approaches.[2697] KSM debriefer and Deputy Chief of ALEC Station [REDACTED] told the inspector general that KSM "figured out a way to deal with [the waterboard]."[2698] [REDACTED] CTC Legal, [REDACTED], told the inspector general that the waterboard "was of limited use on KSM."[2699] CIA records indicate that KSM was subjected to the waterboard interrogation technique at least 183 times.

INJURIES AND DEATHS

DIRECTOR HAYDEN: "The most serious injury that I'm aware of—and I'll ask the experts to add any color they want, Senator—is bruising as a result of shackling."

This testimony is incongruent with CIA interrogation records. CIA records indicate that CIA detainees suffered physical injuries beyond bruising from shackling, as well as psychological problems:

- During a waterboard session, Abu Zubaydah "became completely unresponsive, with bubbles rising through his open, full mouth." He remained unresponsive after the waterboard was rotated upwards and only regained consciousness after receiving a "xyphoid thrust."[2700]

- Multiple CIA detainees subjected to prolonged sleep deprivation experienced hallucinations, and CIA interrogation teams did not always discontinue sleep deprivation after the detainees had experienced hallucinations.[2701]

- Some detainees exhibited significant bruising and swelling unrelated to shackling. For example, a medical officer noted that, in addition to the swelling of his ankles and wrists, Ramzi bin al-Shibh had a bruise on his brow.[2702]

- During the application of the CIA's enhanced interrogation techniques, KSM was described as "[t]ired and sore," with abrasions on his ankles, shins, and wrists, as well as on the back of his head.[2703] He also suffered from pedal edema[2704] resulting from extended standing.[2705]

- At the CIA's DETENTION SITE COBALT, CIA interrogators used "rough takedowns," described as taking a naked detainee outside of his cell, placing a hood over his head, and dragging him up and down a long corridor while slapping and punching him. Gul Rahman, after his death, was found to have surface abrasions on his shoulders, pelvis, arms, legs, and face.[2706]

SENATOR LEVIN: "Did anybody die?"
DIRECTOR HAYDEN: "No."

This testimony is incongruent with CIA records.

- Gul Rahman died in CIA custody at the CIA's DETENTION SITE COBALT after being rendered

SENATOR LEVIN: "Not one person?"
DIRECTOR HAYDEN: "No one. The Committee is aware that there was an individual who died in CIA custody prior to the initiation of this program."
SENATOR LEVIN: "Prior to the initiation of what?"
DIRECTOR HAYDEN: "This program. In fact, the discipline of this program is a product of or result of the undisciplined activity that took place earlier."

DIRECTOR HAYDEN: "[Gul Rahman] was not part of this program, but I understand it was in CIA custody."

there on November ■, 2002. At the time, DETENTION SITE COBALT was described as a place where the CIA could detain suspected terrorists for the purposes of "intense interrogations" by CIA officers.[2707] DDO James Pavitt told the inspector general that "there were some who say that [DETENTION SITE COBALT] is not a CIA facility, but that is 'bullshit.'"[2708]

- CIA records reveal that Gul Rahman was subjected to what the CIA chief of interrogations described as "coercive techniques without authorization."[2709] At ALEC Station's request, CIA contractor Hammond DUNBAR conducted an assessment of Gul Rahman to determine which CIA enhanced interrogation techniques should be used on him.[2710] While the CIA's enhanced interrogation techniques were never authorized, DUNBAR interrogated Rahman, once employing the "insult slap" enhanced interrogation technique without CIA Headquarters approval.[2711] On November ■, 2002, Gul Rahman was shackled to the wall of his cell in a short chain position,[2712] which required him to sit on the bare concrete.[2713] Rahman was wearing a sweatshirt, but was nude from the waist down. On November ■, 2002, the guards at DETENTION SITE COBALT found Gul Rahman's dead body.[2714] Although a CIA employee tried to perform CPR, Gul Rahman remained unresponsive and was declared dead.[2715] An autopsy report by the CIA found that the cause of Gul Rahman's death was "undetermined," but that the clinical impression of the medical officer who conducted the autopsy was that the cause of death was hypothermia.[2716]

STRESS POSITIONS

SENATOR LEVIN: [Reading a SSCI staff document, "Summary Notes of the Februaiy 14, 2007 ICRC Report"] "Prolonged stress standing position, naked, armed chained above the head [?]"
DIRECTOR HAYDEN: "Not above the head. Stress positions are part of the EITs, and nakedness were part of the EITs, Senator."

This testimony is inaccurate.

There are multiple descriptions of CIA detainees being forced to stand with their arms shackled above their heads for extended periods of time at the CIA's DETENTION SITE COBALT.[2717] In one example, a U.S. military legal advisor observed the technique known as "hanging," involving handcuffing one or both wrists to an overhead horizontal bar. The legal advisor noted that one detainee was apparently left hanging for 22 hours each day for two consecutive days to "break" his resistance.[2718]

CIA records indicate that multiple detainees were shackled with their hands above their heads at other CIA detention sites. For example, see detainee reviews in Volume III, to include 'Abd al-Rahim al-Nashiri,[2719] Hassan Ghul,[2720] and KSM.[2721] According to CIA cables, Abu Zubaydah was handcuffed "high on the bars."[2722]
Draft OMS guidelines on interrogations, noted that detainees could be shackled with their arms above their heads for "roughly two hours without great concern," and that the arms could be elevated for between two and four hours if the detainee was monitored for "excessive distress."[2723]

LEGAL REASONS FOR OVERSEAS DETENTION

SENATOR WHITEHOUSE: "Has there been any consideration at any point within the Agency that the purpose in locating facilities overseas is either to avoid liability under American statutes or to avoid the ability of any court to claim jurisdiction because they would not know where these took place? Is there an element of providing legal defense to the participants in these applications?"

MR. RIZZO: "Well, certainly not the first."

Mr. Rizzo's testimony is incongruent with CIA records. After the capture of Abu Zubaydah, ■■CTCLegal, ■■ ■■■■, prepared a PowerPoint presentation laying out the "pros" and "cons" of six detention options. The pros for detention in Country ■, where Abu Zubaydah would be rendered, included "[n]o issues of possible U.S. [court] jurisdiction." The cons for a CIA facility in the United States included "[c]an't foreclose ability of U.S. [courts] considering Habeas Corpus petition.[2724]

In late 2003 and early 2004, the U.S. Supreme Court's decision to accept certiorari in the case of *Rasul v. Bush* prompted a decision by the CIA, in coordination with the Department of Justice, to transfer five CIA detainees held at Guantanamo to other CIA detention facilities.[2725]

NOTES

FINDINGS AND CONCLUSIONS

1. As measured by the number of disseminated intelligence reports. Therefore, zero intelligence reports were disseminated based on information provided by seven of the 39 detainees known to have been subjected to the CIA's enhanced interrogation techniques.
2. May 30, 2005, Memorandum for John A. Rizzo, Senior Deputy General Counsel, Central Intelligence Agency, from Steven G. Bradbury, Principal Deputy Assistant Attorney General, Office of Legal Counsel, Department of Justice, re: Application of United States Obligations Under Article 16 of the Convention Against Torture to Certain Techniques that May Be Used in the Interrogation of High Value al Qaeda Detainees.
3. Transcript of Senate Select Committee on Intelligence briefing, September 6, 2006.
4. This episode was not described in CIA cables, but was described in internal emails sent by personnel in the CIA Office of Medical Services and the CIA Office of General Counsel. A review of the videotapes of the interrogations of Abu Zubaydah by the CIA Office of Inspector General (OIG) did not note the incident. A review of the catalog of videotapes, however, found that recordings of a 21-hour period, which included two waterboarding sessions, were missing.
5. April 10, 2003 email from to ; cc: ; re: More. Throughout the Committee Study, last names in all capitalized letters are pseudonyms.
6. ALEC (182321Z JUL 02).
7. At the time, confining a detainee in a box with the dimensions of a coffin was an approved CIA enhanced interrogation technique.
8. [REDACTED] 1324 (161750Z SEP 03), referring to Hambali.
9. Interview of , by [REDACTED] and [REDACTED], Office of the Inspector General, June 17, 2003.
10. In one case, interrogators informed a detainee that he could earn a bucket if he cooperated.
11. Interview Report, 2003-7123-IG, Review of Interrogations for Counterterrorism Purposes, , April 7, 2003, p. 12.
12. Interview Report, 2003-7123-IG, Review of Interrogations for Counterterrorism Purposes, , May 8, 2003, p. 9.
13. November 26, 2001, Draft of Legal Appendix, Paragraph 5, "Hostile Interrogations: Legal Considerations for CIA Officers," at 1.
14. May 30, 2005, Memorandum for John A. Rizzo, Senior Deputy General Counsel, Central Intelligence Agency, from Steven G. Bradbury, Principal Deputy Assistant Attorney General, Office of Legal Counsel, Department of Justice, re: Application of United States Obligations Under Article 16 of the Convention Against Torture to Certain Techniques that May Be Used in the Interrogation of High Value al Qaeda Detainees. July 20, 2007, Memorandum for John A. Rizzo, Acting General Counsel, Central Intelligence Agency, from Steven G. Bradbury, Principal Deputy Assistant Attorney General, Office of Legal Counsel, Department of Justice, re: Application of War Crimes Act, the Detainee Treatment Act, and Common Article 3 of the Geneva Conventions to Certain Techniques that May be Used by the CIA in the Interrogation of High Value al Qaeda Detainees.
15. The CIA's June 27, 2013, Response to the Committee Study of the CIA's Detention and Interrogation Program states that these limitations were dictated by the White House. The CIA's June 2013 Response then acknowledges that the CIA was "comfortable" with this decision.
16. DIRECTOR (152227Z MAR 07).
17. The Committee's conclusion is based on CIA records, including statements from CIA Directors George Tenet and Porter Goss to the CIA inspector general, that the directors had not briefed the president on the CIA's

interrogation program. According to CIA records, when briefed in April 2006, the president expressed discomfort with the "image of a detainee, chained to the ceiling, clothed in a diaper, and forced to go to the bathroom on himself." The CIA's June 2013 Response does not dispute the CIA records, but states that "[w]hile Agency records on the subject are admittedly incomplete, former President Bush has stated in his autobiography that he discussed the program, including the use of enhanced techniques, with then-DCIA Tenet in 2002, prior to application of the techniques on Abu Zubaydah, and personally approved the techniques." A memoir by former Acting CIA General Counsel John Rizzo disputes this account.

18. CIA records indicate that the CIA had not informed policymakers of the presence of CIA detention facilities in Countries █, █, █, and █. It is less clear whether policymakers were aware of the detention facilities in Country █ and at Guantanamo Bay, Cuba. The CIA requested that country names and information directly or indirectly identifying countries be redacted. The Study therefore lists the countries by letter. The Study uses the same designations consistently, so "Country J," for example refers to the same country throughout the Study.
19. July 31, 2003, email from John Rizzo to █████ re Rump PC on interrogations.
20. Lotus Notes message from Chief of The CIA Station in Country █ to D/CTC, COPS; copied in: email from █████, to [REDACTED], [REDACTED], cc: [REDACTED], █████, █████ █████, █████, subj: ADCI Talking Points for Call to DepSec Armitage, date 9/23/2004, at 7:40:43 PM.
21. Briefing slides, CIA Interrogation Program, July 29, 2003
22. No CIA detention facilities were established in these two countries.
23. U.S. law (22 U.S.C. § 3927) requires that chiefs of mission "shall be kept fully and currently informed with respect to all activities and operations of the Government within that country," including the activities and operations of the CIA.
24. Sametime communication, between John P. Mudd and █████, April 13, 2005.
25. Sametime communication, between John P. Mudd and █████, April 13, 2005.
26. March 29, 2002, email from █████ to █████, re A-Z Interrogation Plan.
27. ALEC █████ (182321Z JUL 02).
28. January 8, 1989, Letter from John L. Helgerson, Director of Congressional Affairs, to Vice Chairman William S. Cohen, Senate Select Committee on Intelligence, re: SSCI Questions on █████, at 7-8.
29. [REDACTED] 1528 (191903Z DEC 03).
30. Report of Audit, CIA-controlled Detention Facilities Operated Under the 17 September 2001 Memorandum of Notification, Report No. 2005-0017-AS, June 14, 2006.
31. April 15, 2005, email from [REDACTED] (Chief of Base of DETENTION SITE BLACK), to █████ █████, █████, █████, re: General Comments.
32. "Learned helplessness" in this context was the theory that detainees might become passive and depressed in response to adverse or uncontrollable events, and would thus cooperate and provide information. Memo from Grayson SWIGERT, Ph.D., February 1, 2003, "Qualifications to provide special mission interrogation consultation."
33. They also concluded that the CIA "should not be in the business of running prisons or 'temporary detention facilities.'" May 12, 2004, Memorandum for Deputy Director for Operations from █████, Chief, Information Operations Center, and Henry Crumpton, Chief, National Resources Division via Associate Deputy Director for Operations, with the subject line, "Operational Review of CIA Detainee Program."
34. March 21, 2005, Memorandum for Deputy Director for Operations from Robert L. Grenier, Director DCI Counterterrorism Center, re: Proposal for Full-Scope Independent Study of the CTC Rendition, Detention, and Interrogation Programs.
35. September 2, 2005, Memorandum from █████ to Director Porter Goss, CIA, "Assessment of EITs Effectiveness."
36. September 23, 2005, Memorandum from █████ to The Honorable Porter Goss, Director, Central Intelligence Agency, "Response to request from Director for Assessment of EIT effectiveness."
37. February 10, 2006, Memorandum for [█████ CIA OFFICER 1], CounterTerrorist Center, National Clandestine Service, from Executive Director re: Accountability Decision.
38. Congressional notification, CIA Response to OIG Investigation Regarding the Rendition and Detention of German Citizen Khalid al-Masri, October 9, 2007.
39. Memorandum for Inspector General; from: James Pavitt, Deputy Director for Operations; subject: re: Comments to Draft IG Special Review, "Counterterrorism Detention and Interrogation Program" (2003-7123-IG); date: February 27, 2004; attachment: February 24, 2004, Memorandum re: Successes of CIA's Counterterrorism Detention and Interrogation Activities.
40. February 24, 2004, Memorandum from Scott W. Muller, General Counsel, to Inspector General re: Interrogation Program Special Review (2003-7123-IG).
41. November 9, 2006, email from John A. Rizzo, to Michael V. Hayden, Stephen R. Kappes, cc: Michael Morell, █████, █████, █████, Subject: Fw: 5 December 2006 Meeting with ICRC Rep.

42. CIA Comments on the February 2007 ICRC Report on the Treatment of Fourteen "High Value Detainees" in CIA Custody."
43. Senate Select Committee on Intelligence hearing transcript for April 12, 2007.
44. DCIA Talking Points for 12 January 2006 Meeting with the President, re: Way Forward on Counterterrorist Rendition, Detention and Interrogation Program.
45. HEADQUARTERS [REDACTED] (071742Z JUN 04).
46. [REDACTED] 5759 ([REDACTED] 03); ALEC [REDACTED] ([REDACTED] 03); ALEC [REDACTED] ([REDACTED] 03).

EXECUTIVE SUMMARY

1. See Appendix 1: "Terms of Reference, Senate Select Committee on Intelligence Study of the Central Intelligence Agency's Detention and Interrogation Program."
2. The Committee did not have access to approximately 9,400 CIA documents related to the CIA's Detention and Interrogation Program that were withheld by the White House pending a determination and claim of executive privilege. The Committee requested access to these documents over several years, including in writing on January 3, 2013, May 22, 2013, and December 19, 2013. The Committee received no response from the White House.
3. From January 2, 2008, to August 30, 2012, the Department of Justice conducted a separate investigation into various aspects of the CIA's Detention and Interrogation Program, with the possibility of criminal prosecutions of CIA personnel and contractors. On October 9, 2009, the CIA informed the Committee that it would not compel CIA personnel to participate in interviews with the Committee due to concerns related to the pending Department of Justice investigations. (See DTS #2009-4064.) While the Committee did not conduct interviews with CIA personnel during the course of this review, the Committee utilized previous interview reports of CIA personnel and CIA contractors conducted by the CIA's Office of the Inspector General and the CIA's Oral History Program. In addition to CIA materials, the Committee reviewed a much smaller quantity of documents from the Department of Justice, the Department of Defense, and the Department of State, as well as documents that had separately been provided to the Committee outside of this review. Inconsistent spellings found within the Committee Study reflect the inconsistencies found in the underlying documents reviewed.
4. The CIA informed the Committee that due to CIA record retention policies, the CIA could not produce all CIA email communications requested by the Committee. As a result, in a few cases, the text of an email cited in the Study was not available in its original format, but was embedded in a larger email chain. For this reason, the Committee, in some limited cases, cites to an email chain that contains the original email, rather than the original email itself.
5. The report does not review CIA renditions for individuals who were not ultimately detained by the CIA, CIA interrogation of detainees in U.S. military custody, or the treatment of detainees in the custody of foreign governments, as these topics were not included in the Committee's Terms of Reference.
6. On April 7, 2014, the Executive Summary of the Committee Study of the CIA's Detention and Interrogation Program was provided to the executive branch for declassification and public release. On August 1, 2014, the CIA returned to the Committee the Executive Summary with its proposed redactions. Over the ensuing months, the Committee engaged in deliberations with the CIA and the White House to ensure that the Committee's narrative—and support for the Committee's findings and conclusions—remained intact. Significant alterations have been made to the Executive Summary in order to reach agreement on a publicly releasable version of the document. For example, the CIA requested that in select passages, the Committee replace specific dates with more general time frames. The Committee also replaced the true names of some senior non-undercover CIA officials with pseudonyms. The executive branch then redacted all pseudonyms for CIA personnel, and in some cases the titles of positions held by the CIA personnel. Further, while the classified Executive Summary and full Committee Study lists specific countries by letter (for example "Country J"), and uses the same letter to designate the specific country throughout the Committee Study, the letters have been redacted by the executive branch for this public release.
7. September 17, 2001, Memorandum of Notification, for Members of the National Security Council, re: [REDACTED] (DTS #2002-0371). at paragraph 4. [REDACTED].
8. Attachment 5 to May 14, 2002, letter from Stanley Moskowitz, CIA Office of Congressional Affairs, to Al Cumming, Staff Director, Senate Select Committee on Intelligence, transmitting the [REDACTED] Memoranda of Notification (DTS #2002-2175).
9. September 17, 2001, Memorandum of Notification, for Members of the National Security Council, re: [REDACTED] (DTS #2002-0371), at paragraph 4.
10. DIRECTOR [REDACTED] ([REDACTED]); email from: [REDACTED]; to: [REDACTED]; subject: Cable

re: Country ▇; date: January 29, 2009.

11. Memorandum for DCI from J. Cofer Black, Director of Counterterrorism, via Deputy Director of Central Intelligence, General Counsel, Executive Director, Deputy Director for Operations and Associate Director of Central Intelligence/Military Support, entitled, "Approval to Establish a Detention Facility for Terrorists."
12. Email from: ▇▇▇▇▇; to: [REDACTED]; subject: EYES ONLY- Capture and Detention; date: September 28, 2001, at 09:29:24 AM.
13. DIRECTOR ▇▇▇ (272119Z SEP 01).
14. November 7, 2001, Draft of Legal Appendix, "Handling Interrogation." *See also* Volume I.
15. Memorandum for DCI from J. Cofer Black, Director of Counterterrorism, via Deputy Director of Central Intelligence, General Counsel, Executive Director, Deputy Director for Operations and Associate Director of Central Intelligence/Military Support, entitled, "Approval to Establish a Detention Facility for Terrorists."
16. Memorandum for DCI from J. Cofer Black, Director of Counterterrorism, via Deputy Director of Central Intelligence, General Counsel, Executive Director, Deputy Director for Operations and Associate Director of Central Intelligence/Military Support, entitled, "Approval to Establish a Detention Facility for Terrorists."
17. Memorandum for DCI from J. Cofer Black, Director of Counterterrorism, via Deputy Director of Central Intelligence, General Counsel, Executive Director, Deputy Director for Operations and Associate Director of Central Intelligence/Military Support, entitled, "Approval to Establish a Detention Facility for Terrorists."
18. Memorandum for DCI from J. Cofer Black, Director of Counterterrorism, via Deputy Director of Central Intelligence, General Counsel, Executive Director, Deputy Director for Operations and Associate Director of Central Intelligence/Military Support, entitled, "Approval to Establish a Detention Facility for Terrorists."
19. Memorandum for DCI from J. Cofer Black, Director of Counterterrorism, via Deputy Director of Central Intelligence, General Counsel, Executive Director, Deputy Director for Operations and Associate Director of Central Intelligence/Military Support, entitled, "Approval to Establish a Detention Facility for Terrorists."
20. Memorandum from George Tenet, Director of Central Intelligence, to Deputy Director for Operations, October 8, 2001, Subject: (U) Delegations of Authorities.
21. DIRECTOR ▇▇▇ (171410Z DEC 01).
22. WASHINGTON ▇▇▇ (272040Z MAR 02).
23. DIRECTOR ▇▇▇ (072216Z APR 03).
24. DIRECTOR ▇▇▇ (072216Z APR 03). In a later meeting with Committee staff, ▇▇▇ CTC Legal, ▇ ▇▇▇ stated that the prospect that the CIA "could hold [detainees] forever" was "terrifying," adding, "[n] o one wants to be in a position of being called back from retirement in however many years to go figure out what do you do with so and so who still poses a threat." See November 13, 2001, Transcript of Staff Briefing on Covert Action Legal Issues (DTS #2002-0629).
25. CIA Director Hayden typically described the program as holding "fewer than a hundred" detainees. For example, in testimony before the Committee on February 4, 2008, in response to a question from Chairman Rockefeller during an open hearing, Hayden stated, "[i]n the life of the CIA detention program we have held fewer than a hundred people." (See DTS #2008-1140.) Specific references to "98" detainees were included in a May 5, 2006, House Permanent Select Committee on Intelligence (HPSCI) report on Renditions, Detentions and Interrogations. *See also* Memorandum for John A. Rizzo, Acting General Counsel, Central Intelligence Agency, from Steven G. Bradbury, Principal Deputy Assistant Attorney General, Office of Legal Counsel, July 20, 2007, Re: Application of the War Crimes Act, the Detainee Treatment Act, and Article 3 of the Geneva Conventions to Certain Techniques that May Be Used by the CIA in the Interrogation of High Value al Qaeda Detainees. Other examples of this CIA representation include a statement by CTC officer ▇▇▇ ▇▇▇ to the HPSCI on February 15, 2006, and a statement by ▇▇▇ CTC Legal ▇▇▇ to the SSCI on June 10, 2008. See DTS #2008-2698.
26. The Committee's accounting of the number of CIA detainees is conservative and only includes individuals for whom there is clear evidence of detention in CIA custody. The Committee thus did not count, among the 119 detainees, six of the 31 individuals listed in a memo entitled "Updated List of Detainees attached to a March 2003 email sent by DETENTION SITE COBALT site manager ▇▇▇ [CIA OFFICER 1], because they were not explicitly described as CIA detainees and because they did not otherwise appear in CIA records. (*See* email from: ▇▇▇ [CIA OFFICER 1]; to: ▇▇▇ ▇▇▇, ▇▇▇ subject: ▇▇▇ DETAINEES; date: March 13, 2003.) An additional individual is the subject of CIA cables describing a planned transfer from U.S. military to CIA custody at DETENTION SITE COBALT. He was likewise not included among the 119 CIA detainees because of a lack of CIA records confirming either his transfer to, or his presence at, DETENTION SITE COBALT. As detailed in this summary, in December 2008, the CIA attempted to identify the total number of CIA detainees. In a graph prepared for CIA leadership, the CIA represented the number of CIA detainees as "112+ ?" *See* ▇▇▇ 12417 (101719Z OCT 02); ALEC ▇▇▇ (232056Z OCT 02); ▇▇▇ 190159 (240508Z OCT 02); and ALEC ▇▇▇ (301226Z OCT 02).
27. ▇▇▇ 1528 ▇▇▇.
28. As of June 27, 2013, when the CIA provided its Response to the Committee Study of the CIA's Detention and Interrogation Program (hereinafter, the "CIA's June 2013 Response"), the CIA had not yet made an

independent determination of the number of individuals it had detained. The CIA's June 2013 Response does not address the number of detainees determined by the Committee to be held by the CIA, other than to assert that the discrepancy between past CIA representations, that there were fewer than 100 detainees, and the Committee's determination of there being at least 119 CIA detainees, was not "substantively meaningful." The CIA's June 2013 Response states that the discrepancy "does not impact the previously known scale of the program," and that "[i]t remains true that approximately 100 detainees were part of the program; not 10 and not 200." The CIA's June 2013 Response also states that, "[t]he *Study* leaves unarticulated what impact the relatively small discrepancy might have had on policymakers or Congressional overseers." The CIA's June 2013 Response further asserts that, at the time Director Hayden was representing there had been fewer than 100 detainees (2007-2009), the CIA's internal research "indicate[d] the total number of detainees could have been *as high as* 112," and that "uncertainty existed within CIA about whether a group of additional detainees were actually part of the program, partially because some of them had passed through [DETENTION SITE COBALT] prior to the formal establishment of the program under CTC auspices on 3 December 2002" (emphasis added). This June 27, 2013, CIA statement is inaccurate: the CIA's determination at the time was that there had been *at least* 112 CIA detainees and that the inclusion of detainees held prior to December 3, 2002, would make that number higher. On December 20, 2008, a CTC officer informed the chief of CTC that "112 were detained by CIA since September 11, 2001," noting "[t]hese revised statistics do not include any detainees at [DETENTION SITE COBALT] (other than Gul Rahman) who departed [DETENTION SITE COBALT] prior to RDG assuming authority of [DETENTION SITE COBALT] as of 03 December 2002." (*See* " numbers brief.doc," attached to the email from: ; to: , [REDACTED], , ; subject: Revised Rendition and Detention Statistics; date: December 20, 2008.) By December 23, 2008, CTC had created a graph that identified the total number of CIA detainees, excluding Gul Rahman, "Post 12/3/02" as 111. The graph identified the total number including Gul Rahman, but *excluding* other detainees "pre-12/3/02" as "112+ ?." (See CIA-produced PowerPoint Slide, RDG Numbers, dated December 23, 2008.) With regard to the Committee's inclusion of detainees held at DETENTION SITE COBALT prior to December 3, 2002, the CIA does not dispute that they were held by the CIA pursuant to the same MON authorities as detainees held after that date. Moreover, the CIA has regularly counted among its detainees a number of individuals who were held solely at DETENTION SITE COBALT prior to December 3, 2002, as well as several who were held exclusively at Country facilities on behalf of the CIA. In discussing the role of DETENTION SITE COBALT in the CIA's Detention and Interrogation Program, then Deputy Director of Operations James Pavitt told the CIA Office of Inspector General in August 2003 that "there are those who say that [DETENTION SITE COBALT] is not a CIA facility, but that is 'bullshit.'" (See Interview Report, 2003-7123-IG, Review of Interrogations for Counterterrorism Purposes, James Pavitt, August 21, 2003.).

29. The "Renditions and Interrogations Group," is also referred to as the "Renditions Group," the "Rendition, Detention, and Interrogation Group," "RDI," and "RDG" in CIA records.

30. Email from: to: [Himself]; subject: Meeting with DCIA; date: January 5, 2009. According to the CIA's June 2013 Response, "Hayden did not view the discrepancy, if it existed, as particularly significant given that, if true, it would increase the total number by just over 10 percent."

31. They include Sayed Habib, who was detained due to fabrications made by KSM while KSM was being subjected to the CIA's enhanced interrogation techniques (1281 (130801Z JUN 04); 3031 ; 3015 ; 2817); Ali Saeed Awadh, the subject of mistaken identity (ALEC ; 1871 ; 2024 ; 2022 ; 14322); Modin Nik Muhammed, whom the CIA determined had been purposefully misindentified by a source due to a blood feud (43701 ; DIRECTOR ; 52893 ( ); Khalid al-Masri, whose "prolonged detention" was determined by the CIA Inspector General to be "unjustified" (CIA Office of Inspector General, Report of Investigation, The Rendition and Detention of German Citizen Khalid al-Masri (2004-7601-IG), July 16, 2007, at 83); and Zarmein, who was one of "a number of detainees about whom" the CIA knew "very little" (1528 .

32. They include Abu Hudhaifa, who was subjected to ice water baths and 66 hours of standing sleep deprivation before being released because the CIA discovered he was likely not the person he was believed to be (WASHINGTON ; 51303); Muhammad Khan, who, like Zarmein, was among detainees about whom the CIA acknowledged knowing "very little" (1528); Gul Rahman, another case of mistaken identity (HEADQUARTERS); Shaistah Habibullah Khan, who, like his brother, Sayed Habib, was the subject of fabrications by KSM (HEADQUARTERS); Haji Ghalgi, who was detained as "useful leverage" against a family member (33678); Nazir Ali, an "intellectually challenged" individual whose taped crying was used as leverage against his family member (13065 ; , ;

13147 ; 29864 ( ); Juma Gul, who was released with a payment of $ and [other currency] (150822Z ; 33693 ; 33265 ; 33693); Hayatullah Haqqani, whom the CIA determined "may have been in the wrong place at the wrong time" (33322); Ali Jan, who was detained for using a satellite phone, traces on which "revealed no derogatory information" (1542); two individuals —Mohammad al-Shomaila and Salah Nasir Salim Ali—on whom derogatory information was "speculative" (email from: [REDACTED]; to: [REDACTED], [REDACTED], and [REDACTED]; subject: Backgrounders; date: April 19, 2006; 17411 ; ALEC ; undated document titled, "Talking Points for HPSCI about Former CIA Detainees"); two individuals who were discovered to be foreign government sources prior to being rendered to CIA custody, and later determined to be former CIA sources (2185 ([REDACTED]); ALEC ([REDACTED]); HEADQUARTERS ([REDACTED])); seven individuals thought to be travelling to Iraq to join al-Qa'ida who were detained based on claims that were "thin but cannot be ignored" (email from [REDACTED]; to: [REDACTED|; cc: [REDACTED], [REDACTED], , [REDACTED], , [REDACTED], [REDACTED], [REDACTED]; subject: Request Chief/CTC Approval to Apprehend and Detain Individuals Departing Imminently for Iraq to Fight Against US Forces; date: September 16, 2003); and Bismullah, who was mistakenly arrested and later released with $ and told not to speak about his experience (46620).

33. For example, the Committee did not include among the 26 individuals wrongfully detained: Dr. Hikmat Nafi Shaukat, even though it was determined that he was not involved in CBRN efforts and his involvement with al-Qa'ida members was limited to personal relationships with former neighbors (30414 ; DIRECTOR); Karim, aka Asat Sar Jan, about whom questions were raised within the CIA about whether he may have been slandered by a rival tribal faction (27931 ; [REDACTED] Memo, SUBJECT: getting a handle on detainees); Arsala Khan, who suffered disturbing hallucinations after 56 hours of standing sleep deprivation, after which the CIA determined that he does not appear to be the subject involved in . . . current plans or activities against U.S. personnel or facilities" (1393 (201006Z OCT 03); HEADQUARTERS ( ); and Janat Gul, who also suffered "frightful" hallucinations following sleep deprivation and about whom the chief of the detention facility wrote, "[t]here simply is no 'smoking gun' that we can refer to that would justify our continued holding of [Janat Gul] at a site such as [DETENTION SITE BLACK]" (1530 04); 1537 04); 1542 04); email from: [REDACTED] (COB [DETENTIONSITEBLACK]); to: cc: , , ; subject: re: date: April 30, 2005).

34. The CIA's June 2013 Response "acknowledge[s] that there were cases in which errors were made," but points only to the case of Khalid al-Masri, whose wrongful detention was the subject of an Inspector General review. The CIA's June 2013 Response does not quantify the number of wrongfully detained individuals, other than to assert that it was "far fewer" than the 26 documented by the Committee. The CIA's June 2013 Response acknowledges that "the Agency frequently moved too slowly to release detainees," and that "[o]f the 26 cases cited by the Study, we adjudicated only three cases in less than 31 days. Most took three to six months. CIA should have acted sooner." As detailed in the Study, there was no accountability for personnel responsible for the extended detention of individuals determined by the CIA to have been wrongfully detained.

35. ALEC (; DIRECTOR ; DIRECTOR ; ALEC . Despite the CIA's conclusion that these individuals did not meet the standard for detention, these individuals were included in the list of 26 wrongfully detained if they were released, but not if they were transferred to the custody of another country. The list thus does not include Hamid Aich, although CIA Headquarters recognized that Aich did not meet the threshold for unilateral CIA custody, and sought to place him in Country custody where the CIA could still debrief him. (See DIRECTOR)). Hamid Aich was transferred to Country custody on April , 2003, and transferred to [another country's] custody more than a month later. (See 36682 ; 38836). The list also does not include Mohammad Dinshah, despite a determination prior to his capture that the CIA "does not view Dinshah as meeting the 'continuing serious threat' threshold required for this operation to be conducted pursuant to [CIA] authority," and a determination, after his capture, that "he does not meet the strict standards required to go to [DETENTION SITE COBALT]." (See DIRECTOR ; HEADQUARTERS). Dinshah was transferred to custody. See HEADQUARTERS ; 41204 ; 60937 .

36. January 8, 1989, Letter from John L. Helgerson, Director of Congressional Affairs, to Vice Chairman William

S. Cohen, Senate Select Committee on Intelligence, re: SSCI Questions on [REDACTED], at 7-8 (DTS #1989-0131).

37. Senate Select Committee on Intelligence, Transcript of Richard Stolz, Deputy Director for Operations, Central Intelligence Agency (June 17, 1988), p. 15 (DTS #1988-2302).
38. Attachment to Memorandum entitled, "Approval to Establish a Detention Facility for Tenorists," CTC: 1026(138)/01 from J. Cofer Black, Director of DCI Counterterrorist Center, to Director of Central Intelligence via multiple parties, October 25, 2001; Draft of Legal Appendix, "Handling Interrogations."
39. Directorate of Operations Handbook, 50-2, Section XX(1)(a), updated October 9, 2001.
40. KUBARK Counterintelligence Interrogation, July 1963, at 85.
41. According to public records, in the mid-1960s, the CIA imprisoned and interrogated Yuri Nosenko, a Soviet KGB officer who defected to the U.S. in early 1964, for three years (April 1964 to September 1967). Senior CIA officers at the time did not believe Nosenko was an actual defector and ordered his imprisonment and interrogation. Nosenko was confined in a specially constructed "jail," with nothing but a cot, and was subjected to a series of sensory deprivation techniques and forced standing.
42. Among other documents, see CIA "Family Jewels" Memorandum, 16 May 1973, pp. 5, 23–24, available at www.gwu.edu/~nsarchiv/NSAEBB/NSAEBB222/family_jewels_full_ocr.pdf.
43. "Investigation of the Assassination of President John F. Kennedy," Hearings before the Select Committee on Assassinations of U.S. House of Representatives, 95th Congress, Second Session, September 11–15, 1978. Testimony of John Hart, pp. 487–536 (September 15, 1978) (DTS #Q04761).
44. Transcript of Committee Hearing on [REDACTED] Interrogation Manual, June 17, 1988, pp. 3–4 (DTS #1988-2302).
45. April 13, 1989, Memorandum from CIA Inspector General William F. Donnelly to Jim Currie and John Nelson, SSCI Staff, re: Answers to SSCI Questions on, [REDACTED], attachment M to Memorandum to Chairman and Vice Chairman, re: Inquiry into [REDACTED] Interrogation Training, July 10, 1989 (DTS # 1989-0675). *See also* [REDACTED] 1984, Memorandum for Inspector General from [REDACTED], Inspector, via Deputy Inspector General, re: [REDACTED], IG-[REDACTED]84.
46. As noted, the Renditions Group was also known during the program as the "Renditions and Interrogations Group," as well as the "Rendition, Detention, and Interrogation Group," and by the initials, "RDI" and "RDG."
47. December 4, 2002, Training Report, Revised Version, High Value Target Interrogation and Exploitation (HVTIE) Training Seminar 12-18 Nov 02 ("[[REDACTED]] was recently assigned to the CTC/RG to manage the HVT Interrogation and Exploitation (HVTIE) mission, assuming the role as HVT interrogator/Team Chief.").
48. January 8, 1989, Letter from John L. Helgerson, Director of Congressional Affairs to Vice Chairman William S. Cohen, Senate Select Committee on Intelligence re: SSCI Questions on [REDACTED], at 7-8 (DTS #1989-0131).
49. Senate Select Committee on Intelligence, Transcript of Richard Stolz, Deputy Director for Operations, Central Intelligence Agency (June 17, 1988), at 15 (DTS #1988-2302).
50. November 7, 2001, Draft of Legal Appendix, "Handling Interrogation." *See also* Volume I.
51. November 26, 2001, Draft of Legal Appendix, "Hostile Interrogations: Legal Considerations for CIA Officers." The draft memo cited the "Israeli example" as a possible basis for arguing that "torture was necessary to prevent imminent, significant, physical harm to persons, where there is no other available means to prevent the harm."
52. Memorandum for Alberto R. Gonzales, Counsel to the President, re: Standards of Conduct for Interrogation under 18 U.S.C. §§ 2340-2340A. Like the November 26, 2001, draft memo, the OLC memorandum addressed the Israeli example.
53. Email from [REDACTED]; to: [REDACTED] cc: [REDACTED], [REDACTED], [REDACTED], Jose Rodiguez, [REDACTED], [REDACTED], [REDACTED], [REDACTED], [REDACTED], [REDACTED], [REDACTED]; subject: For OOB Wednesday - Draft Letter to the President; date: January 29, 2002. No records have been identified to indicate that this letter was or was not sent.
54. Email from: [REDACTED]; to: [REDACTED] and [REDACTED]; subject: POW's and Questioning; date: February 1, 2002, at 01:02:12 PM.
55. February 7, 2002, Memorandum for the Vice President, the Secretary of State, the Secretary of Defense, the Attorney General, chief of staff to the President, Director of Central Intelligence, Assistant to the President for National Security Affairs, and Chairman of the Joint Chiefs of Staff, re: Humane Treatment of al Qaeda and Taliban Detainees.
56. After the CIA was unsuccessful in acquiring information from its last detainee, Muhammad Rahim, using the CIA's enhanced interrogation techniques, an after-action review in April 2008 suggested that the CIA conduct a survey of interrogation techniques used by other U.S. government agencies and other countries in an effort to develop effective interrogation techniques. See undated CIA Memorandum, titled [REDACTED] After-Action Review, author [REDACTED], and undated CIA Memorandum, titled [Rahim] After Action Review: HVDI Assessment, with attached addendum, [Rahim] Lessons Learned Review Panel Recommendations Concerning the Modification of Sleep Deprivation and Reinstatement of Walling as an EIT. For

additional information, see Volume I.

57. Grayson SWIGERT and Hammond DUNBAR, Recognizing and Developing Countermeasures to Al Qaeda Resistance to Interrogation Techniques: A Resistance Training Perspective (undated). *See also* Memorandum for the Record, November 15, 2007, SSCI Staff Briefing with Grayson SWIGERT and Hammond DUNBAR (DTS #2009-0572).
58. See, for example, [REDACTED], Memo from Grayson SWIGERT, [REDACTED], subject, "Qualifications to provide special mission interrogation consultation"; Undated, untitled memo stating: "The following information was obtained by a telephone conversation with [REDACTED], [REDACTED] [REDACTED]; [REDACTED], Interrogator Training, Lesson Plan, Title: A Scientific Approach to Successful Interrogation; DIR [REDACTED] (031227Z APR 02).
59. See, for example, Memo from Grayson SWIGERT, [REDACTED], subject: "Qualifications to provide special mission interrogation consultation."
60. See detainee review of Abu Zubaydah in Volume III. *See also* CIA Intelligence Assessment, August 16, 2006, "Countering Misconceptions About Training Camps in Afghanistan, 1990-2001." The document states: "Khaldan Not Affiliated With Al-Qa'ida. A common misperception in outside articles is that Khaldan camp was run by al-Qa'ida. Pre-11 September 2001 reporting miscast Abu Zubaydah as a 'senior al-Qa'ida lieutenant,' which led to the inference that the Khaldan camp he was administering was tied to Usama bin Laden. The group's flagship camp, al-Faruq, reportedly was created in the late 1980s so that bin Laden's new organization could have a training infrastructure independent of 'Abdullah Azzam's Maktab al-Khidamat, the nongovernmental organization that supported Khaldan. Al-Qa'ida rejected Abu Zubaydah's request in 1993 to join the group and Khaldan was not overseen by bin Laden's organization. There were relations between the al-Qa'ida camps and Khaldan. Trainees, particularly Saudis, who had finished basic training at Khaldan were referred to al-Qa'ida camps for advanced courses, and Khaldan staff observed al-Qa'ida training. The two groups, however, did not exchange trainers."
61. March 29, 2002, email from [REDACTED] to [REDACTED], cc: John Rizzo, [REDACTED], [REDACTED], [REDACTED], subject, NEW INFO: A-Z Interrogation Plan ("I have thought about the 18 USC sect. 2340 issues we briefly discussed yesterday.").
62. Email from: [REDACTED]; to: [REDACTED]; subject: Torture Update; date: March 28, 2002, at 11:28:17 AM.
63. [REDACTED] 19595 (281106Z MAR 02). PowerPoint presentation, Options for Incarcerating Abu Zubaydah, March 27, 2002.
64. PowerPoint presentation, Options for Incarcerating Abu Zubaydah, March 27, 2002. PowerPoint presentation, Options for Incarcerating Abu Zubaydah, March 28, 2002.
65. ALEC [REDACTED] (282105Z MAR 02).
66. PowerPoint presentation, Options for Incarcerating Abu Zubaydah, March 27, 2002.
67. PowerPoint presentation. Options for Incarcerating Abu Zubaydah, March 28, 2002.
68. Email from: [REDACTED] [REDACTED]; James Pavitt; subject: DCI Decision on [DETENTION SITE GREEN] Briefing for Armitage; date: September 26 2002; DIRECTOR [REDACTED] ([REDACTED] MAR 02).
69. Email from: [REDACTED]; to: [REDACTED]; subject: A-Z Interrogation Plan; date: March 29, 2002. POTUS is an abbreviation for President of the United States.
70. Email from: [REDACTED]; to: [REDACTED]; subject: NEW INFO: A-Z Interrogation Plan; date: March 29, 2002.
71. Email from: [REDACTED]; to: [REDACTED], [REDACTED]; subject: A-Z Interrogation Plan; email from: [REDACTED] [REDACTED]; to: James Pavitt; subject: DCI Decision on [DETENTION SITE GREEN] Briefing for Armitage; date: September 26, 2002. After the PDB session, the assistant secretary of state [REDACTED] was briefed. The assistant secretary indicated that he would brief the secretary and deputy secretary of state. An internal CIA email stated that at the NSC, only National Security Advisor Rice and Deputy National Security Advisor Hadley were briefed. See DIRECTOR [REDACTED] ([REDACTED] MAR 02); email from: [REDACTED] [REDACTED]; to: James Pavitt; date: September 26, 2002.
72. [REDACTED] 69132 ([REDACTED] MAR 02).
73. [REDACTED] 69132 ([REDACTED] MAR 02).
74. For additional information on the rendition of Abu Zubaydah and the establishment of DETENTION SITE GREEN, see Volume I.
75. HEADQUARTERS [REDACTED] [REDACTED]; HEADQUARTERS [REDACTED] [REDACTED]. CIA records indicate that the CIA had not informed policymakers of the presence of CIA detention facilities in Countries [REDACTED], [REDACTED], [REDACTED] and [REDACTED]. It is less clear whether policymakers were aware of the detention facilities in Country [REDACTED] and at Guantanamo Bay, Cuba.
76. See, for example, [REDACTED] 70240 (300614Z APR 02); [REDACTED] 70112 (250929Z APR 02); [REDACTED] 70459 (080545Z MAY 02); Congressional Notification: Intelligence Support to [REDACTED] [REDACTED] Operation, [REDACTED], 2002 (DTS #2002-2932); and MEMORANDUM FOR: Director of Central Intelligence; FROM: [REDACTED] [REDACTED]; SUBJECT: Your meeting with [REDACTED]

, 2002; cover page dated 2002. |

77. See, for example. [REDACTED] 74636 .
78. [REDACTED] 76975 .
79. [REDACTED] 77115 .
80. [REDACTED] 77281 . The CIA's June 2013 Response states that "[i]t was only as leaks detailing the program began to emerge that foreign partners felt compelled to alter the scope of their involvement." As described, however, the tensions with Country were unrelated to public revelations about the program.
81. [REDACTED] 69626 .
82. Email from: William Harlow, Director of the CIA Office of Public Affairs; to: John McLaughlin, Buzzy Krongard, John Moseman, John Rizzo, James Pavitt, [REDACTED], Stanley Moskowitz; subject: [REDACTED] call Re: Abu Zubaydah; date: April 25, 2002, 12:06:33 PM.
83. [REDACTED] 701681 .
84. ALEC ; April 6, 2006, Interview, , Chief, Renditions and Detainees Group.
85. DIRECTOR .
86. 10005 (092316Z APR 02). See Abu Zubaydah detainee review in Volume HI for additional information.
87. See United States Court of Appeals, August Term, 2001, *U.S. v Ramzi Ahmed Yousef*, and DIRECTOR JAN 02). *See also* CIA MAR 02).
88. 10022 (121216Z APR 02). CIA records include the variant spelling, "Muhktar." KSM was placed on the FBI's public "Most Wanted Terrorist" list on October 10, 2001. *See also* U.S. Department of Justice materials related to Ramzi Ahmed Yousef.
89. 10022 (121216Z APR 02); 18334 (261703Z MAR 02).
90. See, for example. President Bush's September 6, 2006, speech, based on CIA information and vetted by the CIA, which stated that Abu Zubaydah provided "quite important" information and "disclosed Khalid Sheikh Mohammed, or KSM, was the mastermind behind the 9/11 attacks and used the alias Mukhtar. This was a vital piece of the puzzle that helped our intelligence community pursue KSM."
91. See information later in this summary and Volume II for additional details.
92. Attachment to email from: [REDACTED] [REDACTED]; to: ; subject: Interrogation Strategy, Powerpoint on [Abu Zubaydah] Interrogation Strategy, 01 April 2002; date: March 31, 2002.
93. Email from [REDACTED] to [REDACTED], cc: , April 1, 2002, re: POC for [Grayson SWIGERT]- consultant who drafted al-Qa'ida resistance to interrogation backgrounder (noting that CTC/LGL would reach out to SWIGERT). According to the email, after the meeting, CTC Legal, , provided SWIGERT's contact information to ALEC Station officers, noting that it was SWIGERT who composed an OTS assessment on al-Qa'ida resistance techniques.
94. On the evening of April 1, 2002, "at the request of CTC/OPS and ALEC" Station, a cable from OTS with a proposed interrogation strategy was sent to Country (178955 (012236Z APR 02). The information in this cable was consistent with a subsequent cable, which was coordinated with SWIGERT, that proposed "several environmental modifications to create an atmosphere that enhances the strategic interrogation process." The cable noted, "[t]he deliberate manipulation of the environment is intended to cause psychological disorientation, and reduced psychological wherewithal for the interrogation," as well as "the deliberate establishment of psychological dependence upon the interrogator," and "an increased sense of learned helplessness." (See [REDACTED] 69500 (070009Z APR 02).) For detailed information, see Volume I and the Abu Zubaydah detainee review in Volume III.
95. DIRECTOR APR 02).
96. CIA Sensitive Addendum "Update on the Abu Zubaydah Operation," dated 12 April 2002, "1630 Hours."
97. CIA Sensitive Addendum "Update on the Abu Zubaydah Operation," dated 12 April 2002, "1630 Hours."
98. Federal Bureau of Investigation documents pertaining "to the interrogation of detainee Zayn Al Abideen Abu Zabaidah" and provided to the Senate Select Committee on Intelligence by cover letter dated July 20, 2010 (DTS #2010-2939).
99. Federal Bureau of Investigation documents pertaining "to the interrogation of detainee Zayn Al Abideen Abu Zabaidah" and provided to the Senate Select Committee on Intelligence by cover letter dated July 20, 2010 (DTS #2010-2939).
100. 10026 (131233Z APR 02).
101. 10026 (131233Z APR 02).
102. 10026 (131233Z APR 02).
103. 10029 (131505Z APR 02).
104. 10029 (131505Z APR 02).
105. Federal Bureau of Investigation documents pertaining "to the interrogation of detainee Zayn Al Abideen Abu Zabaidah" and provided to the Senate Select Committee on Intelligence by cover letter dated July 20,

2010 (DTS #2010-2939).

106. See Intelligence Science Board "Intelligence Interviewing: Teaching Papers and Case Studies" for additional details on the FBI's interrogation of Mohamed Rashed Daoud al-Owhali.

107. Federal Bureau of Investigation documents pertaining "to the interrogation of detainee Zayn Al Abideen Abu Zabaidah" and provided to the Senate Select Committee on Intelligence by cover letter dated July 20, 2010 (DTS #2010-2939).

108. ████ 10043 (151614Z APR 02).

109. ████ 10047 (161406Z APR 02).

110. ████ 10116 (250731Z APR 02).

111. ████ 10053 (162029Z APR 02).

112. ████ 10116 (250731Z APR 02). CIA records indicate Abu Zubaydah was nude, but given a towel to cover himself when interrogated. See, for example ████ 10080 (200735Z APR 02).

113. ████ 10053 (162029Z APR 02); ████ 10094 (211905Z APR 02). As detailed in Volume III, the FBI Special Agents only questioned Abu Zubaydah when he was covered with a towel. Sleep deprivation during this period also differed from how sleep deprivation was implemented after the Department of Justice approved the CIA's enhanced interrogation techniques in August 2002. Rather than being placed in a stress position during sleep deprivation, Abu Zubaydah was kept awake by being questioned nearly non-stop by CIA and FBI interrogators. Records further indicate that during breaks in the interrogations at this time, Abu Zubaydah was allowed to briefly sleep. See, for example, ████ 10116 (250731Z APR 02).

114. ████ 10047 (161406Z APR 02).

115. ████ 10058 (171904Z APR 02).

116. Federal Bureau of Investigation documents pertaining "to the interrogation of detainee Zayn Al Abideen Abu Zabaidah" and provided to the Senate Select Committee on Intelligence by cover letter dated July 20, 2010 (DTS #2010-2939).

117. ████ 10058 (171904Z APR 02).

118. See Abu Zubaydah detainee review in Volume III for additional information.

119. ████ 10090 (210703Z APR 02). As described in more detail in Volume II, Abu Zubaydah did provide *kunyas* for the pair.

120. ████ 10063 (180515Z APR 02). As described in detail in Volume II and Volume III, as well as more briefly in this summary, Abu Zubaydah provided this information after being allowed to sleep.

121. See information in this summary and Volume II for additional details on the CIA's representations on the effectiveness of the CIA's enhanced interrogation techniques to policy makers and the Department of Justice.

122. CIA email from: ████; to: ████; subject: AZ information; date: July 10, 2002, at 01:18:50 PM. The email states: "The only way we put this together is that Paki liaison mentioned to ████ the arrest of two individuals (one being an American) and ████ put two and two together. Therefore, AZ's info alone would never have allowed us to find them." *See also* SSCI Transcript "Detention of Jose Padilla," dated June 12, 2002 (DTS #2002-2603), in which a CIA officer states, "the Pakistani liaison felt it was important to bring [Padilla] to our attention, given the recent raids . . . there was enough information indicating that his travel was suspicious, to put us on alert. This suspicion was enhanced during the debriefings of Abu Zubaydah, which occurred on 21 April."

123. See analysis provided to the Committee on April 18, 2011, by the CIA, based on CIA searches in 2011 of the ████ database. The titles of specific intelligence reports resulting from information provided by Abu Zubaydah are listed in the Abu Zubaydah detainee review in Volume III.

124. ALEC ████ ████ MAY 02).

125. See email exchange from: [REDACTED]; to [REDACTED]; with multiple ccs; subject: Turning Up the Heat in the AZ Interrogations; date: April 30, 2002, at 12:02:47 PM.

126. See email exchange from: [REDACTED]; to [REDACTED]; with multiple ccs; subject: Turning Up the Heat in the AZ Interrogations; date: April 30, 2002, at 12:02:47 PM.

127. See analysis provided to the Committee on April 18, 2011, by the CIA, based on CIA searches in 2011 of the ████ database. The titles of specific intelligence reports resulting from information provided by Abu Zubaydah are listed in the Abu Zubaydah detainee review in Volume III.

128. ████ 10424 (070814Z JUN 02).

129. See analysis provided to the Committee on April 18, 2011, by the CIA, based on CIA searches in 2011 of the ████ database. The titles of specific intelligence reports resulting from information provided by Abu Zubaydah are listed in the Abu Zubaydah detainee review in Volume III of the Committee Study.

130. See Presidential Speech on September 6, 2006, based on CIA information and vetted by CIA personnel. *See also* ODNI September 2006 Unclassified Public Release: "During initial interrogation, Abu Zubaydah gave some information that he probably viewed as nominal. Some was important, however, including that Khalid Shaykh Mohammad (KSM) was the 9/11 mastermind and used the moniker 'Mukhtar.' This identification allowed us to comb previously collected intelligence for both names, opening up new leads to this terrorist plotter—leads that eventually resulted in his capture. It was clear to his interrogators that Abu Zubaydah possessed a great deal of information about al-Qa'ida; however, he soon stopped all cooperation. Over the

ensuing months, the CIA designed a new interrogation program that would be safe, effective, and legal." *See also* CIA Director Michael Hayden, Classified Statement for the Record, Hearing on the Central Intelligence Agency Detention and Interrogation Program, April 12, 2007 (DTS #2007-1563) ("... FBI and CIA continued unsuccessfully to try to glean information from Abu Zubaydah using established US Government interrogation techniques ....").

131. See reporting charts in Abu Zubaydah detainee review in Volume III, as well as CIA paper entitled "Abu Zubaydah," dated March 2005. The same information is included in an "Abu Zubaydah Bio" document "Prepared on 9 August 2006."
132. See Abu Zubaydah detainee review in Volume III for additional details.
133. See Abu Zubaydah detainee review in Volume III for additional details.
134. See CIA document dated, July 3, 2002, 1630 Hours, titled, "CIA Operational Update Memorandum for CIA Leadership, SENSITIVE ADDENDUM: Update on the Abu Zubaydah Operation and ████ Raid ██ ██."
135. For more information on the SERE program, see the Senate Armed Services Committee Inquiry into the Treatment of Detainees in U.S. Custody, December 2008. *See also* statement of Senator Carl Levin on the inquiry, December 11, 2008; "SERE training is intended to be used to teach our soldiers how to resist interrogation by enemies that refuse to follow the Geneva Conventions and international law. In SERE school, our troops who are at risk of capture are exposed in a controlled environment with great protections and caution—to techniques adapted from abusive tactics used against American soldiers by enemies such as the Communist Chinese during the Korean War. SERE training techniques include stress positions, forced nudity, use of fear, sleep deprivation and, until recently, the Navy SERE school used the waterboard. These techniques were designed to give our students a taste of what they might be subjected to if captured by a ruthless, lawless enemy so that they would be better prepared to resist. The techniques were never intended to be used against detainees in U.S. custody. As one [Joint Personnel Recovery Agency (JPRA)] instructor explained, SERE training is based on illegal exploitation (under the rules listed in the 1949 Geneva Convention Relative to the Treatment of Prisoners of War) of prisoners over the last 50 years."
136. Email from: ████; to: ████; subject: Description of Physical Pressures; date: July 8, 2002, at 04:15:15 PM.
137. ALEC ██ (051724Z JUL 02).
138. See Resume, Hammond DUNBAR, submitted to the CIA in March 2003. In a section on "Interrogation and Debriefing Experience," DUNBAR's 2003 resume noted that he had been a "debriefer for all USG DOD and Civilian ████████████████████████████████ ██ ████████████████████████.)." All other experience in the section related to his interrogation experience as a contractor for the CIA beginning in 2002. DUNBAR's resume did state that he had participated in an interrogation training course in ████ in 1992, and that he had taken a one-week Defense Interrogation Course at some point in 2002, although his resume does not indicate whether this was prior to, or after, the interrogation of Abu Zubaydah. The CIA's June 2013 Response states that the Committee Study was "incorrect ... in asserting that the contractors selected had no relevant experience." The CIA's June 2013 Response notes SWIGERT and DUNBAR's experience at the Department of Defense SERE school, and SWIGERT's "academic research" and "research papers" on "such topics as resistance training, captivity familiarization, and learned helplessness—all of which were relevant to the development of the program." The CIA's June 2013 Response does not describe any experience related to actual interrogations or counterterrorism, or any relevant cultural, geographic, or linguistic expertise. The CIA's June 2013 Response provides the following explanation: "Drs. [SWIGERT] and [DUNBAR] had the closest proximate expertise CIA sought at the beginning of the program, specifically in the area of ***non-standard means of interrogation***. Experts on traditional interrogation methods did not meet this requirement. Non-standard interrogation methodologies were not an area of expertise of CIA officers or of the US Government generally. We believe their expertise was so unique that we would have been derelict had we not sought them out when it became clear that CIA would be heading into the uncharted territory of the program" (italics and emphasis in original). As noted above, the CIA did not seek out SWIGERT and DUNBAR after a decision was made to use coercive interrogation techniques; rather, SWIGERT and DUNBAR played a role in convincing the CIA to adopt such a policy.
139. Interview of ████, by [REDACTED] and [REDACTED], Office of the Inspector General, October 22, 2003. The senior interrogator had participated in the use of the CIA's enhanced interrogation techniques with SWIGERT and DUNBAR.
140. Email from: ████; to: ████; subject: EYES ONLY – DRAFT; date: July 8, 2002.
141. Email from: ████; to: ████; subject: EYES ONLY – DRAFT; date: July 8, 2002.
142. Email from: ████; to: ████; subject: EYES ONLY – DRAFT; date: July 8, 2002.
143. DIRECTOR ██ (031357Z AUG 02).
144. DIRECTOR ██ (031357Z AUG 02).
145. DIRECTOR ██ (031357Z AUG 02).

146. July 13, 2002, Letter from John Yoo, Deputy Assistant Attorney General to John Rizzo, Acting General Counsel, CIA.
147. Memorandum for the Record from John H. Moseman, Chief of Staff, re: NSC Weekly Meeting, July 17, 2002.
148. July 19, 2002, 1630 Hours, CIA Operational Update Memorandum for CIA Leadership, SENSITIVE ADDENDUM: Update on the Abu Zubaydah Operation and ███ Raid ███.
149. July 21, 2002, 1630 Hours, CIA Operational Update Memorandum for CIA Leadership, SENSITIVE ADDENDUM: Update on the Abu Zubaydah Operation and ███ Raid ███.
150. ██████ 10536 (151006Z JUL 02).
151. ██████ 10536 (151006Z JUL 02).
152. ██████ 10536 (151006Z JUL 02).
153. ██████ 10536 (151006Z JUL 02).
154. ALEC █████ (182321Z JUL 02).
155. ALEC █████ (182321Z JUL 02).
156. Email from: ██████; to: [REDACTED]; subject: Request for JPRA information; date: July 19, 2002; July 24, 2002, fax from █████ to John Yoo and [REDACTED] providing information from the OTS/OAD psychologists; email from: █████; to: █████, [REDACTED], [REDACTED], █████; subject: Discussion with JPRA Chief of Staff; date: July 24, 2002.
157. Email from: ██████; to: [REDACTED]; subject: Request for JPRA information; date: July 19, 2002. Records indicate that ████'s notes were not provided to the Department of Justice. In November 2002, ██ ██ along with Chief of Interrogations █████, led the first CIA interrogator training course.
158. [REDACTED] 73208 (231043Z JUL 02).
159. ████ 10568 (261101Z JUL 02).
160. [REDACTED] 73208 (231043Z JUL 02).
161. DIRECTOR ███ (251609Z AUG 02).
162. Email from: ██████; to: Jose Rodriguez, [REDACTED], ██████, [REDACTED], subject: EYES ONLY—Where we stand re: Abu Zubaydah; date: July 26, 2002. *See also* ████ 10568 (261101Z JUL 02).
163. DIRECTOR ███ (031357Z AUG 02).
164. DIRECTOR ███ (031357Z AUG 02).
165. [REDACTED] 73208 (231043Z JUL 02) and email from: ██████; to: [REDACTED], [REDACTED], and █████; subject: Addendum from [DETENTION SITE GREEN], [REDACTED] 73208 (231043Z JUL 02); date: July 23, 2002, at 07:56:49 PM.
166. ████ 10644 (201235Z AUG 02).
167. Memorandum for the Record from John Moseman, Chief of Staff, re: NSC Weekly Meeting, July 31, 2002.
168. July 26, 2001, DCI Talking Points with the President- Next Phase of the Abu Zubaydah Interrogation; July 31, 2001, DCI Talking Points with the President- Next Phase of the Abu Zubaydah Interrogation. Note that the draft document lists the incorrect year.
169. CIA records do not indicate who informed National Security Advisor Rice "that there would be no briefing of the President on this matter."
170. Email from: John Moseman; to: John McLaughlin, Jose Rodriguez, [REDACTED], John Rizzo, [REDACTED]; subject: Abu-Z Interrogation; date: August 2, 2002.
171. Email from: John Rizzo; to: ██████; subject: Rump PC on interrogations; date: July 31, 2003.
172. See Volume II for additional information on congressional briefings.
173. An email from CIA Senior Deputy General Counsel John Rizzo stated that "the President will be briefed as part of the regular annual [covert action] review. Briefing (by Rice or VP or Counsel to the President or some combination thereof) will describe the interrogation program, the fact that some aggressive but AG-approved techniques have been used, but will not apparently get into the details of the techniques themselves." See email from: John Rizzo; to: █████; subject: Rump PC on interrogations; date: July 31, 2003.
174. Office of General Counsel Comments on Counterterrorism Detention and Interrogation Program Special Review, at 23 ("[i]n August 2003, the DCI advised OIG . . ."); CIA Office of Inspector General, Interview of George Tenet, memorandum dated 8 September 2003, subject: 2003-7123-IG, Review of Interrogation for Counterterrorism Purposes.
175. Inspector General, Special Review, Counterterrorism Detention and Interrogation Activities (September 2001–October 2003), May 7, 2004 (DTS #2004-2710).
176. Letter from George J. Tenet to Chairman Pat Roberts, June 22, 2004 (DTS #2004-2710).
177. Helgerson then added, "Additionally, public disclosure of many of these activities ensured wide awareness. In light of these developments, I consider the matter closed." The Helgerson letter does not indicate to whom Directors Tenet and Goss, who met regularly with the President, submitted requests to brief the President about the program. See letter from John L. Helgerson to Vice Chairman John D. Rockefeller IV, April 5, 2006 (DTS #2006-1564). The CIA's June 2013 Response does not dispute these records. It states, however, that "[w]hile Agency records on the subject are admittedly incomplete, former President Bush has stated in his autobiography that he discussed the program, including the use of enhanced techniques, with DCIA Tenet in 2002, prior to application of the techniques on Abu Zubaydah, and personally approved the techniques."

A subsequent memoir by former CIA Acting General Counsel John Rizzo (published January 7, 2014) states, "The one senior U.S. Government national security official during this time—from August 2002 through 2003—who I did not believe was knowledgeable about the E.I.T.s was President Bush himself. He was not present at any of the Principal Committee meetings . . . and none of the principals at any of the E.I.T. sessions during this period ever alluded to the President knowing anything about them."

178. Included in the packet of CIA information was the following: "Question: 'What role did the President play in authorizing this program? Did he select detainees held by CIA or direct their interrogation? Was he briefed on the interrogation techniques, and if so when?' Answer: 'In the days after 9/11, the President directed that all the instruments of national power, including the resources of our intelligence, military, and law enforcement communities, be employed to fight and win the war against al Qaeda and its affiliates, within the bounds of the law. This included important, new roles for CIA in detaining and questioning terrorists. [He was periodically updated by CIA Directors on significant captures of terrorists, and information obtained that helped stop attacks and led to capture of other terrorists.] [The President was not of course involved in CIA's day to day operations—including who should be held by CIA and how they should be questioned—these decisions are made or overseen by CIA Directors].'" See Draft Questions and Proposed Answers, attached to Memorandum from National Security Advisor Stephen J. Hadley; for: the Vice President, Secretaries of State and Defense, the Attorney General, Director of National Intelligence and Chairman of the Joint Chiefs of Staff; cc: chief of staff to the President, Counsel to the President, Assistant to the President for National Security, White House Spokesman, dated September 2, 2006. Brackets in the original.

179. See April 16, 2008, CIA "Backgrounder: Chronology of Interrogation Approvals, 2001–2003" (noting that "CIA documentation and discussions with Presidential briefers and individuals involved with the interrogation program at the time suggest that details on enhanced interrogation techniques (EITs) were not shared with the President" in the 2001–2003 timeframe); CIA Q&A, Topic: Waterboarding ("The information we have indicates the President was not briefed by CIA regarding the specific interrogation techniques until April 2006, and at that time DCIA Goss briefed him on the seven EITs proposed at that time for the post-Detainee Treatment Act CIA interrogation program."). As described, in the April 2006 briefing the President "expressed discomfort" with the "image of a detainee, chained to the ceiling, clothed in a diaper, and forced to go to the bathroom on himself." See email from: Grayson SWIGERT; to: [REDACTED]; cc: ██████; subject: Dr. SWIGERT's 7 June meeting with DCI; date: June 7, 2006.

180. Email from: Grayson SWIGERT; to: [REDACTED]; cc: ██████; subject: Dr. SWIGERT's 7 June meeting with DCI; date: June 7, 2006.

181. Increased Pressure in the Next Phase of the Abu Zubaydah Interrogations, Attachment to email from: [REDACTED]; to: [REDACTED]; cc: ██████, [REDACTED], ██████, [REDACTED], [REDACTED]; subject: Increased Pressure Phase – for DCI Sensitive Addendum; date: July 10, 2002.

182. ████ 10586 (041559Z AUG 02).

183. See email from: [REDACTED]; to: ████; subject: Subject detainee allegation—per our telcon of today; date: March 28, 2007, at 04:42 PM, which states Abu Zubaydah claims "a collar was used to slam him against a concrete wall. While we do not have a record that this occurred, one interrogator at the site at the time confirmed that this did indeed happen. For the record, a plywood 'wall' was immediately constructed at the site after the walling on the concrete wall."

184. ████ 10644 (201235Z AUG 02).

185. ████ 10586 (041559Z AUG 02).

186. ████ 10586 (041559Z AUG 02); ████ 10644 (201235Z AUG 02).

187. ████ 10644 (201235Z AUG 02).

188. ████ 10586 (041559Z AUG 02). CIA contractor DUNBAR later told the CIA OIG that "[t]heir instructions from [chief of Base] were to focus on only one issue, that is, Zubaydah's knowledge of plans to attack the U.S." According to the OIG's record of the interview, "[DUNBAR] and [SWIGERT] could ask that question in a number of ways, but it was the only theme they were authorized by [chief of Base] to use with [Abu] Zubaydah." (See February 10, 2003, interview report of Hammond DUNBAR, Office of the Inspector General.) The acting chief of Station in Country ██, in an interview with the CIA OIG, stated that "there were days at [DETENTION SITE GREEN] when the team had no requirements from Headquarters," and that CTC did not give the chief of Base (COB) the "flexibility as COB to ask other questions" besides those related to threats to the United States. (See May 28, 2003, interview report of ██████, Office of the Inspector General.) The chief of Support Services at the CIA Station stated that "[SWIGERT] and [DUNBAR] were frustrated that they kept beating Zubaydah up on the same question while getting the same physiologic response from him." (See May 21, 2003, interview report of ██████, Office of the Inspector General.) Other interviewees described how analytical assumptions about Abu Zubaydah drove the interrogation process. (See May 22, 2003, interview report of ██████, Office of the Inspector General; and February 27, 2003, interview report of ██████, Office of the Inspector General.) Chief of CTC, Jose Rodriguez, told the OIG that "CTC subject matter experts" pointed to intelligence that they said indicated that Abu Zubaydah knew more than he was admitting and thus disagreed with the assessment from DETENTION SITE GREEN that Abu Zubaydah was "compliant." According to the OIG's record of the Jose Rodriguez interview,

"disagreement between the analysts and interrogators can be healthy, but in this case Rodriguez believes that the analysts were wrong." (See interview of Jose Rodriguez, Office of the Inspector General, March 6, 2003.).

189. Emphasis in the original. Email from: [REDACTED]; to: ■■■■■ and [REDACTED]; subject: Re: So it begins; date: August 4, 2002, at 09:45:09 AM. CIA Director Hayden informed the Committee in 2007 that "in the section [of the ICRC report] on medical care, the report omits key contextual facts. For example, Abu Zubaydah's statement that he was given only Ensure and water for two to three weeks fails to mention the fact that he was on a liquid diet quite appropriate because he was recovering from abdominal surgery at the time."
190. ■■■■■ 10644 (201235Z AUG 02). For the first 17 days, the CIA's enhanced interrogation techniques were used against Abu Zubaydah in "varying combinations, 24 hours a day." The "aggressive phase," as defined by the CIA, continued for an additional three days. The CIA continued to use its enhanced interrogation techniques against Abu Zubaydah until August 30, 2002.
191. ■■■■■ 10644 (201235Z AUG 02).
192. ■■■■■ 10672 (231206Z AUG 02); ■■■■■ 10667 (240229Z AUG 02).
193. ■■■■■ 10615 (120619Z AUG 02).
194. ■■■■■ 10644 (201235Z AUG 02).
195. ■■■■■ 10604 (091624Z AUG 02).
196. ■■■■■ 10607 (100335Z AUG 02).
197. ■■■■■ 10607 (100335Z AUG 02). On August ■, 2002, a video-conference between DETENTION SITE GREEN and CIA Headquarters occurred, which included an interrogation video described by the interrogation team as "quite graphic" and possibly "disturbing to some viewers." After the video-conference, CIA Headquarters instructed DETENTION SITE GREEN to continue the use of the CIA's enhanced interrogation techniques against Abu Zubaydah, but agreed to send two CIA Headquarters officers to the detention site to observe the interrogations first-hand. On August ■, 2002, a team from CIA Headquarters, including ■■■■■ CTC Legal ■■■■■ and Deputy Chief of ALEC Station ■■■■■, visited DETENTION SITE GREEN and observed the use of the CIA's enhanced interrogation techniques, including waterboarding. The "aggressive phase of interrogation" ended ■■ days after the arrival of the officers from CIA Headquarters. See ■■■■■ 10616 (■■■ AUG 02); ALEC ■■■ (■■■■■ AUG 02); ■■■■■ 10643 (■■■ AUG 02); ■■■■■ 10667 (231206Z AUG 02); and ■■■■■ 10672 (240229Z AUG 02).
198. ■■■■■ 10607 (100335Z AUG 02).
199. Email from: Jose Rodriguez; to: [REDACTED]; subject: [DETENTION SITE GREEN]; date: August 12, 2002, with attachment of earlier email from: [REDACTED]; to: [REDACTED].
200. ■■■■■ 10614 (111633Z AUG 02).
201. ■■■■■ 10614 (111633Z AUG 02).
202. See, for example, ALEC ■■■■■ (101728 AUG 02); ALEC ■■■■■ (130034Z AUG 02); ALEC ■■■■■ AUG 02); and ■■■■■ 10700 (280820Z AUG 02).
203. ■■■■■ 10644 (201235Z AUG 02).
204. ■■■■■ 10643 (191518Z AUG 02).
205. ■■■■■ 10643 (191518Z AUG 02).
206. The description of the episode stated that "on being righted, he failed to respond until the interrogators gave him a xyphoid thrust (with our medical folks edging toward the room)." This passage was included in multiple emails, to include emails from the ■■■■■ OMS, ■■■■■. See email from: ■■■■■; to: [DETENTION SITE BLUE] and [REDACTED]; subject: Re: Departure; date: March 6, 2003, at 7:11:59 PM; email from ■■■■■, OMS; to: [REDACTED] and [REDACTED] subject: Re: Acceptable lower ambient temperatures; date: March 7, 2003, at 8:22 PM; email from: ■■■■■ OMS; to: [REDACTED] and [REDACTED]; subject: Re: Talking Points for review and comment; date: August 13, 2004, at 10:22 AM; and email from ■■■■■; to: [REDACTED], [REDACTED], [REDACTED], [REDACTED], and [REDACTED]; subject: Discussion with Dan Levin – AZ; date: October 26, 2004, at 6:09 PM.
207. Email from: ■■■■■, OMS; to: [REDACTED] and [REDACTED]; subject: Re: Acceptable lower ambient temperatures; date; March 7, 2003, at 8:22 PM; email from: ■■■■■ OMS; to: [REDACTED] and [REDACTED]; subject: Re: Talking Points for review and comment; date: August 13, 2004, at 10:22 AM; email from: ■■■■■; to: [REDACTED], [REDACTED], [REDACTED], [REDACTED], [REDACTED], and [REDACTED]; subject: Re: Discussions with Dan Levin—AZ; date: October 26, 2004, at 6:09 PM.
208. CIA Inspector General's Special Review on Counterterrorism Detention and Interrogation Activities issued on May 7, 2004.
209. Email from: [REDACTED]; to: ■■■■■ and [REDACTED]; subject: Re: Monday; date: August 5, 2002, at 05:35AM.
210. Email from: [REDACTED]; to: [REDACTED], ■■■■■, and [REDACTED]; subject: Update; date: August 8, 2002, at 06:50 AM.
211. Email from: [REDACTED]; to: [REDACTED], ■■■■■, and [REDACTED]; subject: Update; date: August 8, 2002, at 06:50 AM.
212. Email from: [REDACTED]; to: ■■■■■ and [REDACTED]; subject: Re: August 9, 2002, at 10:44:16

PM.

213. Email from: [REDACTED]; to: ████ and [REDACTED]; subject: Greetings; date: August 11, 2002, at 09:45AM.

214. See, for example, ████ 10672 (240229Z AUG 02).

215. See Abu Zubaydah detainee review in Volume III for details on Abu Zubaydah's intelligence production. As noted, Abu Zubaydah was taken into CIA custody on March █, 2002, and was hospitalized until April 15, 2002. During the months of April and May 2002, which included a period during which Abu Zubaydah was on life support and unable to speak, the interrogations of Abu Zubaydah produced 95 intelligence reports. Abu Zubaydah spent much of June 2002 and all of July 2002 in isolation, without being asked any questions. The CIA reinstituted contact with Abu Zubaydah on August 4, 2002, and immediately began using the CIA's enhanced interrogation techniques—including the waterboard. During the months of August and September 2002, Abu Zubaydah produced 91 intelligence reports, four fewer than the first two months of his CIA detention. CIA records indicate that the type of intelligence Abu Zubaydah provided remained relatively constant prior to and after the use of the CIA's enhanced interrogation techniques. According to CIA records, Abu Zubaydah provided information on "al-Qa'ida activities, plans, capabilities, and relationships," in addition to information on "its leadership structure, including personalities, decision-making processes, training, and tactics." *See also* CIA paper entitled "Abu Zubaydah," dated March 2005, as well as "Abu Zubaydah Bio" Document, "Prepared on 9 August 2006."

216. On August 30, 2002, ████ CTC Legal, ████ met with NSC Legal Adviser John Bellinger to discuss Abu Zubaydah's interrogation. See email from: John Rizzo; to: John Moseman; subject: Meeting with NSC Legal Adviser; date: August 30, 2002; ALEC ████ (052227Z SEP 02). In his email documenting the meeting, ████ "noted that we had employed the walling techniques, confinement box, waterboard, along with some of the other methods which also had been approved by the Attorney General," and "reported that while the experts at the site and at Headquarters were still assessing the product of the recent sessions, it did appear that the current phase was producing meaningful results." (See email from: John Rizzo; to: John Moseman; subject: Meeting with NSC Legal Adviser; date: August 30, 2002.) The email did not provide any additional detail on what was described to Bellinger with respect to either the use of the techniques or the "results" of the interrogation. It is unclear from CIA records whether the CIA ever informed the NSC Legal Adviser or anyone else at the NSC or the Department of Justice that Abu Zubaydah failed to provide information about future attacks against the United States or operatives tasked to commit attacks in the U.S. during or after the use of the CIA's enhanced interrogation techniques. According to CIA records, on September 27, 2002, the CIA briefed the chairman and the vice chairman of the Committee, Senators Graham and Shelby, as well as the Committee staff directors, on Abu Zubaydah's interrogation. The CIA's memorandum of the briefing indicates that the chairman and vice chairman were briefed on "the enhanced techniques that had been employed," as well as "the nature and quality of reporting provided by Abu Zubaydah." See (DIRECTOR ████ (252018Z OCT 02).

217. ████ 10644 (201235Z AUG 02).

218. ████ 10644 (201235Z AUG 02).

219. ████ 10644 (201235Z AUG 02).

220. The Committee uses sole-source intelligence reporting in this summary. While CIA multi-source intelligence reports are included in the full Committee Study, the focus of the Committee analysis on sole-source intelligence reporting, as these reports were deemed to more accurately reflect useful reporting from individual CIA detainees. As background, multi-source intelligence reports are reports that contain data from multiple detainees. For example, a common multi-source report would result from the CIA showing a picture of an individual to all CIA detainees at a specific CIA detention site. A report would be produced regardless if detainees were or were not able to identify or provide information on the individual. As a specific example, see HEADQUARTERS ████ (202255Z JUN 06), which states that from January 1, 2006–April 30, 2006, information from Hambali was "used in the dissemination of three intelligence reports, two of which were non-recognitions of Guantanamo Bay detainees," and the third of which "detailed [Hambali's] statement that he knew of no threats or plots to attack any world sporting events." Sole-source reports, by contrast, are based on specific information provided by one CIA detainee.

221. CIA paper entitled, "Abu Zubaydah," dated March 2005. Same information included in an "Abu Zubaydah Bio" document "Prepared on 9 August 2006."

222. See Abu Zubaydah detainee review in Volume III for additional details.

223. ALEC ████ (181439Z OCT 02).

224. ALEC ████ (181439Z OCT 02).

225. Among other documents, see ████ 10667 (231206Z AUG 02); ████ 10672 (240229Z AUG 02); and email from: [REDACTED] (████ chief of Base at DETENTION SITE GREEN); to: CIA Headquarters; subject: "Assessment to Date" of Abu Zubaydah; date: October 6, 2002, at 05:36:46 AM.

226. See "Key Intelligence and Reporting Derived from Abu Zubaydah and KSM," dated February 2008, updated for briefings on several dates, including for a 2009 briefing to Director Leon Panetta, as well as the "Effectiveness Memo" provided to the Department of Justice, testimony provided by CIA Director Michael

Hayden, and other documents discussed in detail in Volume II. For example, see ODNI September 2006 press release stating: "During initial interrogation, Abu Zubaydah gave some information that he probably viewed as nominal. Some was important, however, including that Khalid Shaykh Mohammad (KSM) was the 9/11 mastermind and used the moniker 'Mukhtar.' This identification allowed us to comb previously collected intelligence for both names, opening up new leads to this terrorist plotter—leads that eventually resulted in his capture. It was clear to his interrogators that Abu Zubaydah possessed a great deal of information about al-Qa'ida; however, he soon stopped all cooperation. Over the ensuing months, the CIA designed a new interrogation program that would be safe, effective, and legal."

227. See Abu Zubaydah detainee review in Volume III for additional details.
228. Memorandum for John A. Rizzo, Senior Deputy General Counsel, Central Intelligence Agency, from Steven G. Bradbury, Principal Deputy Assistant Attorney General, Office of Legal Counsel, May 30, 2005, Re: Application of United States Obligations Under Article 16 of the Convention Against Torture to Certain Techniques that May be Used in the Interrogation of High Value Al Qaeda Detainees (DTS #2009-1810, Tab 11). This OLC memorandum cites CIA memorandum for Steve Bradbury at the Department of Justice, dated March 2, 2005, from ████ ███, ██ Legal Group, DCI Counterterrorist Center, subject "Effectiveness of the CIA Counterterrorist Interrogation Techniques."
229. While there are no records of Abu Zubaydah making these statements, the deputy chief of ALEC Station, █ ███, told the Inspector General on July 17, 2003, that the "best information [the CIA] received on how to handle the [CIA] detainees came from a walk-in [a source ████████ to volunteer information to the CIA] after the arrest of Abu Zubaydah. He told us we were underestimating Al-Qa'ida. The detainees were happy to be arrested by the U.S. because they got a big show trial. When they were turned over to [foreign governments], they were treated badly so they talked. Allah apparently allows you to talk if you feel threatened. The [CIA] detainees never counted on being detained by us outside the U.S. and being subjected to methods they never dreamed of." See ████, Memorandum for the Record; subject: Meeting with deputy chief, Counterterrorist Center ALEC Station; date: 17 July 2003.
230. ███ 10496 (162014Z FEB 03). For more information, see a March 7, 2005, cable describing Abu Zubaydah's explanations more fully (██ 2166 (070647Z MAR 05)).
231. ███ 10496 (162014Z FEB 03). For additional details on this matter, see Volume II, specifically the section on information provided by the CIA to the Department of Justice.
232. The information provided by the CIA to the Committee on the CIA's Detention and Interrogation Program is summarized later in this document, and described in greater detail in Volume II.
233. See Volume II, specifically the section on CIA representations to Congress.
234. Email from: Stanley Moskowitz; to: John H. Moseman; cc: Scott Muller and James Pavitt; subject: [attached document] Re: Graham request on interrogations; date: December 9, 2002, at 05:46:11 PM.
235. By June 2002 the CIA had taken custody of five detainees who were captured outside of Country █ and placed these CIA detainees in Country ███ detention facilities. The detainees were held at the Country █ facilities at the request of the CIA and the CIA had unlimited access to them. See █████ 21147 █████.
236. DIRECTOR ███ (062212Z JUN 02).
237. Interview Report, 2003-7123-IG, Review of Interrogations for Counterterrorism Purposes, █████, September 9, 2003.
238. For additional information on DETENTION SITE COBALT, see Volume I and Volume III. The specific date has been generalized at the request of the CIA.
239. █████ 28246 ███.
240. For additional information on DETENTION SITE COBALT, see Volume I and Volume III, and among other documents: ████ 31118 ████; DIRECTOR ███ █████; email from: [REDACTED]; to: [REDACTED], [REDACTED], [REDACTED], █████, [REDACTED]; subject: Meeting with SO & Federal Bureau of Prisons; date: December 4, 2002; email from: [REDACTED]; to: [REDACTED]; subject: Meeting with SO & Federal Bureau of Prisons; date: December 5, 2002; Special Review, Counterterrorism Detention and Interrogation Activities (September 2001–October 2003) (2003-7123-IG), May 7, 2004; Memorandum for Deputy Director of Operations, from █████, January 28, 2003, Subject: Death Investigation - Gul RAHMAN; and CIA Inspector General, Report of Investigation, Death of a █████ (2003-7402-IG), April 27, 2005. One senior interrogator, █████, told the CIA OIG that "literally, a detainee could go for days or weeks without anyone looking at him," and that his team found one detainee who, " 'as far as we could determine,' had been chained to the wall in a standing position for 17 days." According to the CIA interrogator, some of the CIA detainees at DETENTION SITE COBALT "'literally looked like a dog that had been kenneled.' When the doors to their cells were opened, 'they cowered.'" [See Interview Report, 2003-7123-IG, Review of Interrogations for Counterterrorism Purposes, █ ██, April 30, 2003.) The chief of interrogations, █████, told the CIA OIG that "[DETENTION SITE COBALT] is good for interrogations because it is the closest thing he has seen to a dungeon, facilitating the displacement of detainee expectations." (See Interview Report, 2003-7123-IG, Review of Interrogations for Counterterrorism Purposes, █████, April 7, 2003.) An analyst who conducted interrogations at

DETENTION SITE COBALT told the CIA OIG that "[DETENTION SITE COBALT] is an EIT." (See Interview Report, 2003-7123-IG, Review of Interrogations for Counterterrorism Purposes, , May 8, 2003.).

241. See April 27, 2005, CIA Inspector General, Report of Investigation: Death of a Detainee April 7, 2005, Memorandum for John Helgerson, Inspector General, from Robert Grenier, Subject: Comments on Draft Report of Investigation: Death of a Detainee (2003-7402-IG).

242. , Subject: [CIA OFFICER 1]. .

243. [CIA OFFICER 1] .

244. [CIA OFFICER 1] .

245. The full Committee Study includes a CIA photograph of a waterboard at DETENTION SITE COBALT. While there are no records of the CIA using the waterboard at COBALT, the waterboard device in the photograph is surrounded by buckets, with a bottle of unknown pink solution (filled two thirds of the way to the top) and a watering can resting on the wooden beams of the waterboard. In meetings between the Committee Staff and the CIA in the summer of 2013, the CIA was unable to explain the details of the photograph, to include the buckets, solution, and watering can, as well as the waterboard's presence at COBALT.

246. 11357 ; 11443 .

247. 178155 .

248. 11542 .

249. 27054 .

250. ALEC (162135Z JUL 02). Although the plans at the time were for DETENTION SITE COBALT to be owned and operated by the Country government, the detention site was controlled and overseen by the CIA and its officers from the day it became operational in September 2002.

251. ALEC (162135Z JUL 02). The deputy chief of ALEC Station, , and CTC Legal, would later travel to DETENTION SITE GREEN to observe the use of the CIA's enhanced interrogation techniques against Abu Zubaydah.

252. The term "mind virus" first appeared in the interrogations of Abu Zubaydah. See 10086 (201900Z APR 02).

253. Referenced July 16, 2002, cable is ALEC (162135Z JUL 02).

254. ALEC (162135Z JUL 02).

255. ALEC (162135Z JUL 02).

256. At this time, July 26, 2002, Abu Zubaydah was in isolation at DETENTION SITE GREEN. Abu Zubaydah was placed in isolation on June 18, 2002, and remained in isolation for 47 days, until the CIA began subjecting him to its enhanced interrogation techniques on August 4, 2002.

257. 25107 (260903Z JUL 02).

258. 25107 (260903Z JUL 02).

259. Email from: [REDACTED]; to: Buzzy Krongard, John O. Brennan, [REDACTED], [REDACTED], John H. Moseman, [REDACTED] , [REDACTED], [REDACTED], [REDACTED], [REDACTED], [REDACTED], [REDACTED], , , Jose Rodriguez, , John P. Mudd, , [REDACTED], [REDACTED], [REDACTED], [REDACTED], , [REDACTED]; subject: ABU ZUBAYDAH - SENSITIVE ADDENDUM TO DCI DAILY 1630 OPS UPDATE - 26 JULY; date: July 26, 2002.

260. DIRECTOR (052309Z AUG 02). The OLC opinion that reviewed and approved the use of CIA's enhanced interrogation techniques, signed on August 1, 2002, was specific to Abu Zubaydah. The Office of Legal Counsel did not produce legal opinions for al-Najjar or other detainees held by or for the CIA until August 2004.

261. [REDACTED] 27297 (210713Z SEP 02).

262. [REDACTED] 27297 (210713Z SEP 02).

263. November 2002, Memorandum for . Subject: Legal Analysis of Personnel Participating in Interrogation at the CIA Detention Facility in [REDACTED] (aka "[DETENTION SITE COBALT]").

264. November 2002, Memorandum for . Subject: Legal Analysis of Personnel Participating in Interrogation at the CIA Detention Facility in [REDACTED] (aka "[DETENTION SITE COBALT]").

265. November 2002, Memorandum for . Subject: Legal Analysis of Personnel Participating in Interrogation at the CIA Detention Facility in [REDACTED] (aka "[DETENTION SITE COBALT]").

266. November 2002, Memorandum for . Subject: Legal Analysis of

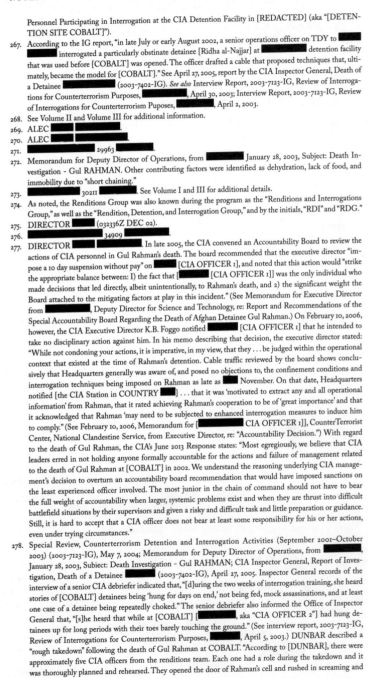

Personnel Participating in Interrogation at the CIA Detention Facility in [REDACTED] (aka "[DETENTION SITE COBALT]").

267. According to the IG report, "in late July or early August 2002, a senior operations officer on TDY to [REDACTED] interrogated a particularly obstinate detainee [Ridha al-Najjar] at [REDACTED] detention facility that was used before [COBALT] was opened. The officer drafted a cable that proposed techniques that, ultimately, became the model for [COBALT]." See April 27, 2005, report by the CIA Inspector General, Death of a Detainee [REDACTED] (2003-7402-IG). *See also* Interview Report, 2003-7123-IG, Review of Interrogations for Counterterrorism Purposes, [REDACTED], April 30, 2003; Interview Report, 2003-7123-IG, Review of Interrogations for Counterterrorism Puposes, [REDACTED], April 2, 2003.
268. See Volume II and Volume III for additional information.
269. ALEC [REDACTED] [REDACTED].
270. ALEC [REDACTED] [REDACTED].
271. [REDACTED] 29963 [REDACTED].
272. Memorandum for Deputy Director of Operations, from [REDACTED] January 28, 2003, Subject: Death Investigation - Gul RAHMAN. Other contributing factors were identified as dehydration, lack of food, and immobility due to "short chaining."
273. [REDACTED] 30211 [REDACTED]. See Volume I and III for additional details.
274. As noted, the Renditions Group was also known during the program as the "Renditions and Interrogations Group," as well as the "Rendition, Detention, and Interrogation Group," and by the initials, "RDI" and "RDG."
275. DIRECTOR [REDACTED] (032336Z DEC 02).
276. [REDACTED] 34909 [REDACTED].
277. DIRECTOR [REDACTED] [REDACTED]. In late 2005, the CIA convened an Accountability Board to review the actions of CIA personnel in Gul Rahman's death. The board recommended that the executive director "impose a 10 day suspension without pay" on [REDACTED] [CIA OFFICER 1], and noted that this action would "strike the appropriate balance between: I) the fact that [[REDACTED] [CIA OFFICER 1]] was the only individual who made decisions that led directly, albeit unintentionally, to Rahman's death, and 2) the significant weight the Board attached to the mitigating factors at play in this incident." (See Memorandum for Executive Director from [REDACTED], Deputy Director for Science and Technology, re: Report and Recommendations of the Special Accountability Board Regarding the Death of Afghan Detainee Gul Rahman.) On February 10, 2006, however, the CIA Executive Director K.B. Foggo notified [REDACTED] [CIA OFFICER 1] that he intended to take no disciplinary action against him. In his memo describing that decision, the executive director stated: "While not condoning your actions, it is imperative, in my view, that they . . . be judged within the operational context that existed at the time of Rahman's detention. Cable traffic reviewed by the board shows conclusively that Headquarters generally was aware of, and posed no objections to, the confinement conditions and interrogation techniques being imposed on Rahman as late as [REDACTED] November. On that date, Headquarters notified [the CIA Station in COUNTRY [REDACTED]] . . . that it was 'motivated to extract any and all operational information' from Rahman, that it rated achieving Rahman's cooperation to be of 'great importance' and that it acknowledged that Rahman 'may need to be subjected to enhanced interrogation measures to induce him to comply." (See February 10, 2006, Memorandum for [[REDACTED] CIA OFFICER 1]], CounterTerrorist Center, National Clandestine Service, from Executive Director, re: "Accountability Decision.") With regard to the death of Gul Rahman, the CIA's June 2013 Response states: "Most egregiously, we believe that CIA leaders erred in not holding anyone formally accountable for the actions and failure of management related to the death of Gul Rahman at [COBALT] in 2002. We understand the reasoning underlying CIA management's decision to overturn an accountability board recommendation that would have imposed sanctions on the least experienced officer involved. The most junior in the chain of command should not have to bear the full weight of accountability when larger, systemic problems exist and when they are thrust into difficult battlefield situations by their supervisors and given a risky and difficult task and little preparation or guidance. Still, it is hard to accept that a CIA officer does not bear at least some responsibility for his or her actions, even under trying circumstances."
278. Special Review, Counterterrorism Detention and Interrogation Activities (September 2001–October 2003) (2003-7123-IG), May 7, 2004; Memorandum for Deputy Director of Operations, from [REDACTED], January 28, 2003, Subiect: Death Investigation - Gul RAHMAN; CIA Inspector General, Report of Investigation, Death of a Detainee [REDACTED] (2003-7402-IG), April 27, 2005. Inspector General records of the interview of a senior CIA debriefer indicated that, "[d]uring the two weeks of interrogation training, she heard stories of [COBALT] detainees being 'hung for days on end,' not being fed, mock assassinations, and at least one case of a detainee being repeatedly choked." The senior debriefer also informed the Office of Inspector General that, "[s]he heard that while at [COBALT] [[REDACTED], aka "CIA OFFICER 2"] had hung detainees up for long periods with their toes barely touching the ground." (See interview report, 2003-7123-IG, Review of Interrogations for Counterterrorism Purposes, [REDACTED], April 5, 2003.) DUNBAR described a "rough takedown" following the death of Gul Rahman at COBALT. "According to [DUNBAR], there were approximately five CIA officers from the renditions team. Each one had a role during the takedown and it was thoroughly planned and rehearsed. They opened the door of Rahman's cell and rushed in screaming and

yelling for him to 'get down.' They dragged him outside, cut off his clothes and secured him with Mylar tape. They covered his head with a hood and ran him up and down a long corridor adjacent to his cell. They slapped him and punched him several times. [DUNBAR] stated that although it was obvious they were not trying to hit him as hard as they could, a couple of times the punches were forceful. As they ran him along the corridor, a couple of times he fell and they dragged him through the dirt (the floor outside of the cells is dirt). Rahman did acquire a number of abrasions on his face, legs, and hands, but nothing that required medical attention. (This may account for the abrasions found on Rahman's body after his death. Rahman had a number of surface abrasions on his shoulders, pelvis, arms, legs, and face.) At this point, Rahman was returned to his cell and secured. [DUNBAR] stated that [[CIA OFFICER 1]] [the CIA officer in charge of DETENTION SITE COBALT] may have spoken to Rahman for a few moments, but he did not know what [[CIA OFFICER 1]] said. [DUNBAR] stated that after something like this is done, interrogators should speak to the prisoner 'to give them something to think about.'" (See Memorandum for Deputy Director of Operations, from January 28, 2003, Subject: Death Investigation - Gul RAHMAN, pp. 21–22.).

279. See Notes of November, 2002, meeting D/IG [REDACTED].
280. See Office of Inspector General Special Review of Counterterrorism Detention and Interrogation Activities (September 2001–October 2003), May 7, 2004, p. 52. According to an OIG interview with an analyst who conducted interrogations at DETENTION SITE COBALT, "indicative of the lack of interrogators was the fact that [[CIA OFFICER 1]] enlisted a [REDACTED] case officer friend . . . to conduct interrogations at [DETENTION SITE COBALT] after he completed his [REDACTED] business in ." (See Interview Report, 2003-7123-IG, Review of Interrogations for Counterterrorism Purposes , May 8, 2003.) Inspector General records of an interview with a senior CIA debriefer indicate that the debriefer, "heard prior to taking the [interrogator] training that people at [COBALT] had debriefed detainees on their own, sometimes going out to the site at night." (See Interview Report, 2003-7123-IG, Review of Interrogations for Counterterrorism Purposes, , April 5, 2003.) As described elsewhere, DCI Tenet issued formal interrogation guidelines for the program on January 28, 2003. (See Guidelines on Interrogations Conducted Pursuant to the Presidential Memorandum of Notification of 17 September 2001, signed by George Tenet, Director of Central Intelligence, January 28, 2003.).
281. Interview of George Tenet, by [REDACTED], [REDACTED], Office of the Inspector General, memorandum dated, September 8, 2003.
282. Interview , Office of the Inspector General, September 9, 2003.
283. Interview of Scott Muller, by [REDACTED], [REDACTED], and [REDACTED], Office of the Inspector General, August 20, 2003.
284. Interview of John Rizzo, by [REDACTED], [REDACTED], and [REDACTED], Office of the Inspector General, August 14, 2003.
285. Interview of , Office of the Inspector General, February 11, 2003.
286. Interview of Jose Rodriguez, by [REDACTED] and [REDACTED], Office of the Inspector General, August 12, 2003.
287. December 4, 2002, Training Report, High Value Target Interrogation and Exploitation (HVTIE) Training Seminar 12-18 Nov 02 (pilot running) at 4. *See also* email from: ; to: [REDACTED], [REDACTED], ; subject: Formation of a High Value Target Interrogation team (describing initial training plan and requirements); date: August 30, 2002, at 8:30 AM.
288. December 4, 2002, Training Report, High Value Target Interrogation and Exploitation (HVTIE) Training Seminar 12-18 Nov 02 (pilot running).
289. December 4, 2002, Training Report, High Value Target Interrogation and Exploitation (HVTIE) Training Seminar 12-18 Nov 02 (pilot running), at 15.
290. See, for example, email from: to: , [REDACTED]; subject: HVT training; date: October 10, 2002; email from: [REDACTED]; to: ; cc: , , [REDACTED], [REDACTED], [REDACTED]; subject: HVT traininhg; date: October 10, 2002; November 1, 2002, Memorandum for: Director, DCI Counterterrorist Center, from , Chief, Renditions Group, CTC, re: Request for use of Military Trainers in Support of Agency Interrogation Course, REFERENCE: Memo for D/CTC from C/RG/CTC, dtd 26 Aug 02, Same Subject.
291. Email from: , CTC/LGL; to: [REDACTED]; cc: Jose Rodriguez, [REDACTED], [REDACTED], ; subject: EYES ONLY; date: November , 2002, at 03:13:01 PM. As described above, Gul Rahman likely froze to to death at DETENTION SITE COBALT sometime in the morning of November , 2002. 's email, however, appears to have been drafted before the guards had found Gul Rahman's body and before that death was reported to CIA Headquarters. See [REDACTED] 30211 describing the guards observing Gul Rahman alive in the morning of November, 2002. Gul Rahman's death appeared in cable traffic at least after 's email. No records could be identified to provide the impetus for 's email.
292. Email from: , CTC/LGL; to: [REDACTED], cc: Jose Rodriguez, [REDACTED], [REDACTED], ; subject: EYES ONLY; date: November , 2002, at 03:13:01 PM.
293. Email from: Jose Rodriguez; to: , CTC/LGL; cc: [REDACTED], [REDACTED],

[REDACTED], ; subject: EYES ONLY; date: November , 2002, at 04:27 PM.

294. Transcript of hearing, April 12, 2007 (DTS #2007-1563).
295. The information is described at length in the Committee Study in Volume III.
296. 3118 ; DIRECTOR .
297. CIA detainee Gul Rahman died at DETENTION SITE COBALT at the end of the Federal Bureau of Prisons visit to the CIA detention site.
298. [REDACTED] 30589 (271626Z NOV 02).
299. Email from: [REDACTED]; to: [REDACTED], [REDACTED], [REDACTED], , [REDACTED]; subject: Meeting with SO & Federal Bureau of Prisons; date: December 4, 2002.
300. Email from: [REDACTED]; to: [REDACTED], [REDACTED], [REDACTED], , [REDACTED]; subject: Meeting with SO & Federal Bureau of Prisons; date: December 4, 2002.
301. Email from: [REDACTED]; to: [REDACTED]; subject: Meeting with SO & Federal Bureau of Prisons; date: December 5, 2002.
302. CIA document entitled Renditions Group Interrogation Team (RGIT), Baseline assessment for MVT, Detainee/Prisoner management, December 30, 2002. The CIA does not appear to have taken action on this recommendation.
303. Email from [CIA OFFICER 1]; to: [REDACTED]; subject: Thanks and Query re: List of DETAINEES; date: March 14, 2003.
304. The cables did not explain any legal basis for detaining individuals who did not meet the detention requirements of the September 17, 2001, MON. HEADQUARTERS ( ) 36682 ( ); 38836 ( ); HEADQUARTERS ; 41204 ( ); ALEC ( ).
305. See Volume III for additional information.
306. Guidelines on Interrogations Conducted Pursuant to the Presidential Memorandum of Notification of 17 September 2001, signed by George Tenet, Director of Central Intelligence, January 28, 2003.
307. Guidelines on Interrogations Conducted Pursuant to the Presidential Memorandum of Notification of 17 September 2001, signed by George Tenet, Director of Central Intelligence, January 28, 2003.
308. CIA document titled, Quarterly Review of Confinement Conditions for CIA Detainees, 1/28/03–4/30/03, May 22, 2003.
309. CIA document titled, Quarterly Review of Confinement Conditions for CIA Detainees, 1/28/03–4/30/03, May 22, 2003.
310. CIA document titled, Quarterly Review of Confinement Conditions for CIA Detainees, 1/28/03–4/30/03, May 22, 2003.
311. 3741 .
312. Guidelines on Interrogations Conducted Pursuant to the Presidential Memorandum of Notification of 17 September 2001, signed by George Tenet, Director of Central Intelligence, January 28, 2003.
313. For a description of the "rough takedown," see Memorandum for Deputy Director of Operations, from , January 28, 2003, Subject: Death Investigation - Gul RAHMAN, pp. 21–22.
314. One cold water shower was described by a CIA linguist; "Rahman was placed back under the cold water by the guards at [[CIA OFFICER 1]]'s direction. Rahman was so cold that he could barely utter his alias. According to [the on-site linguist], the entire process lasted no more than 20 minutes. It was intended to lower Rahman's resistance and was not for hygienic reasons. At the conclusion of the shower, Rahman was moved to one of the four sleep deprivation cells where he was left shivering for hours or over night with his hands chained over his head." See CIA Inspector General, Report of Investigation, Death of a Detainee (2003-7402-IG), April 27, 2005.
315. Water dousing was not designated by the CIA as a "standard" interrogation technique until June 2003. In January 2004 water dousing was recategorized by the CIA as an "enhanced" interrogation technique.
316. See Volume III for additional information.
317. DIRECTOR (302126Z JAN 03); DIRECTOR (311702Z JAN 03). Despite the formal record keeping requirement, the CIA's June 2013 Response argues that detailed reporting on the use of the CIA's enhanced interrogation techniques at CIA detention sites was not necessary, stating: "First, the decline in reporting over time on the use of enhanced techniques, which the *Study* characterizes as poor or deceptive record keeping, actually reflects the maturation of the program. In early 2003, a process was put in place whereby interrogators requested permission in advance for interrogation plans. The use of these plans for each detainee obviated the need for reporting in extensive detail on the use of specific techniques, unless there were deviations from the approved plan." As detailed in the Study, the process put in place by the CIA in early 2003 explicitly required record keeping, including "the nature and duration of each such technique employed, the identities of those present, and a citation to the required Headquarters approval cable." That requirement was never revised.
318. Subsequent to the January 2003 guidance, many cables reporting the use of the CIA's enhanced interrogation techniques listed the techniques used on a particular day, but did not describe the frequency with which those

techniques were employed, nor did they integrate the specific techniques into narratives of the interrogations. As the CIA interrogation program continued, descriptions of the use of the CIA's enhanced interrogation techniques were recorded in increasingly summarized form, providing little information how or when the techniques were applied during an interrogation. There are also few CIA records detailing the rendition process for detainees and their transportation to or between detention sites. CIA records do include detainee comments on their rendition experiences and photographs of detainees in the process of being transported. Based on a review of the photographs, detainees transported by the CIA by aircraft were typically hooded with their hands and feet shackled. The detainees wore large headsets to eliminate their ability to hear, and these headsets were typically affixed to a detainee's head with duct tape that ran the circumference of the detainee's head. CIA detainees were placed in diapers and not permitted to use the lavatory on the aircraft. Depending on the aircraft, detainees were either strapped into seats during the flights, or laid down and strapped to the floor of the plane horizontally like cargo. See CIA photographs of renditions among CIA materials provided to the Committee pursuant to the Committee's document requests, as well as CIA detainee reviews in Volume III for additional information on the transport of CIA detainees.

319. DIRECTOR (032336Z DEC 03).
320. Interview of , by [REDACTED], [REDACTED] and [REDACTED], Office of the Inspector General, August 20, 2003. Interview of , by [REDACTED] and [REDACTED], Office of the Inspector General, February 14, 2003. CTC Chief of Operations told the Inspector General that the program was handled by the Abu Zubaydah Task Force. See February 11, 2003, interview report of Office of the Inspector General.
321. As noted, the CIA's Rendition Group is variably known as the "Renditions Group," the "Renditions and Detainees Group," the "Renditions, Detentions, and Interrogations Group," and by the initials, "RDI" and "RDG."
322. Interview of [ ], by [REDACTED] and [REDACTED], Office of the Inspector General, April 3, 2003. February 21, 2003, interview report, , Office of the Inspector General. Hammond DUNBAR told the Office of Inspector General that there was "intrigue" between the RDG and him and SWIGERT, and "there were emails coming to [DETENTION SITE BLUE] that questioned [his] and [SWIGERT]'s qualifications." See Interview of Hammond DUNBAR, by [REDACTED] and [REDACTED], Office of the Inspector General, February 4, 2003.
323. Email from: ; to: ; cc: , , , , ; subject: Re: RDG Tasking for IC Psychologists [DUNBAR] and [SWIGERT]; date: June 20, 2003, at 5:23:29 PM. OMS expressed concern that "no professional in the field would credit [SWIGERT and DUNBAR's] later judgments as psychologists assessing the subjects of their enhanced measures." (See email from: ; to: ; cc: , , , , ; subject: Re: RDG Tasking for IC Psychologists DUNBAR and SWIGERT; date: June 20, 2003, at 2:19:53 PM.) The CIA's June 2013 Response states that CIA "Headquarters established CTC's Renditions and Detentions Group CTC/RDG as the responsible entity for all CIA detention and interrogation sites in December 2002, removing any latent institutional confusion."
324. Interview of , by [REDACTED] and [REDACTED], Office of the Inspector General, February 21, 2003. The chief of interrogations, , told the Inspector General that the waterboard was overused with Abu Zubaydah and KSM and was ineffective in the interrogations of KSM. (See Interview of , by [REDACTED] and [REDACTED] of the Office of the Inspector General, March 27, 2003.) One doctor involved in CIA interrogations using the waterboard interrogation technique stated that "has a huge bias against the waterboard b/c he's not approved to use it. The reverse is the contract psy guys [SWIGERT and DUNBAR] who have a vested interest in favor of it." See email from: ; to ; cc: [REDACTED]; subject: re: More; date: April 11, 2003, at 08:11:07 AM.
325. March 10, 2003, interview report of , Office of the Inspector General. Interview of , by [REDACTED] and [REDACTED], Office of the Inspector General, February 27, 2003. Interview of , by [REDACTED] and [REDACTED], Office of the Inspector General, April 3, 2003. March 24, 2003, interview report of , Office of the Inspector General.
326. DIRECTOR (301835Z JAN 03).
327. 12168 (301822Z JUN 03).
328. The email, which expressed concern that SWIGERT and DUNBAR would interfere with on-site psychologists, stated that, "[a]lthough these guys believe that their way is the only way, there should be an effort to define roles and responsibilities before their arrogance and narcissism evolve into unproductive conflict in the field." See email from: ; to: cc: , , ; subject: RDG Psychologists DUNBAR and SWIGERT; date: June 16, 2003, at 4:54:32 PM.
329. Email from: to: ; cc: , , , , ; subject: Re: Tasking for IC Psychologists DUNBAR and SWIGER; date: June 20, 2003, at 2:19:53 PM.
330. 12168 (301822Z JUN 03). The CIA's June 2013 Response states: "In practice, by April 2003, [CIA]

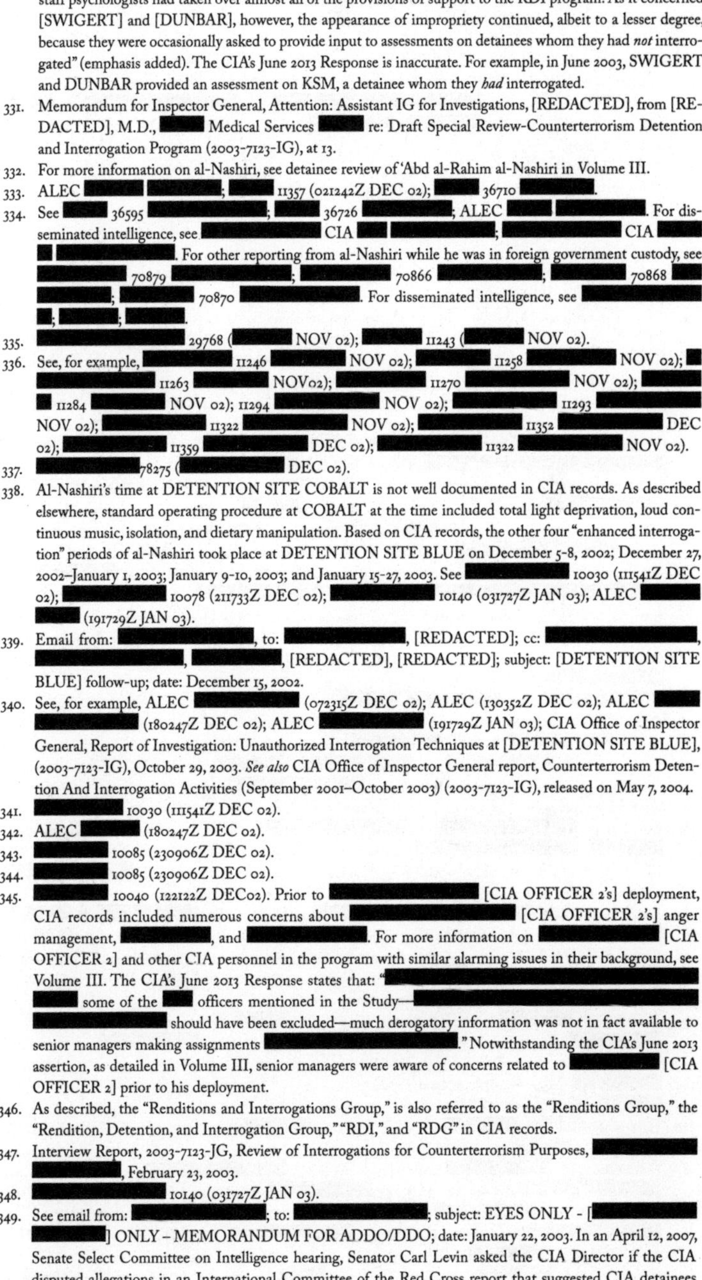

staff psychologists had taken over almost all of the provisions of support to the RDI program. As it concerned [SWIGERT] and [DUNBAR], however, the appearance of impropriety continued, albeit to a lesser degree, because they were occasionally asked to provide input to assessments on detainees whom they had *not* interrogated" (emphasis added). The CIA's June 2013 Response is inaccurate. For example, in June 2003, SWIGERT and DUNBAR provided an assessment on KSM, a detainee whom they *had* interrogated.

331. Memorandum for Inspector General, Attention: Assistant IG for Investigations, [REDACTED], from [REDACTED], M.D., Medical Services re: Draft Special Review-Counterterrorism Detention and Interrogation Program (2003-7123-IG), at 13.
332. For more information on al-Nashiri, see detainee review of 'Abd al-Rahim al-Nashiri in Volume III.
333. ALEC ; 11357 (021242Z DEC 02); 36710 .
334. See 36595 ; 36726 ; ALEC . For disseminated intelligence, see CIA ; CIA . For other reporting from al-Nashiri while he was in foreign government custody, see 70879 ; 70866 ; 70868 ; 70870 . For disseminated intelligence, see ; ; .
335. 29768 (NOV 02); 11243 (NOV 02).
336. See, for example, 11246 NOV 02); 11258 NOV 02); 11263 NOV02); 11270 NOV 02); 11284 NOV 02); 11294 NOV 02); 11293 NOV 02); 11322 NOV 02); 11352 DEC 02); 11359 DEC 02); 11322 NOV 02).
337. 78275 (DEC 02).
338. Al-Nashiri's time at DETENTION SITE COBALT is not well documented in CIA records. As described elsewhere, standard operating procedure at COBALT at the time included total light deprivation, loud continuous music, isolation, and dietary manipulation. Based on CIA records, the other four "enhanced interrogation" periods of al-Nashiri took place at DETENTION SITE BLUE on December 5-8, 2002; December 27, 2002–January 1, 2003; January 9-10, 2003; and January 15-27, 2003. See 10030 (111541Z DEC 02); 10078 (211733Z DEC 02); 10140 (031727Z JAN 03); ALEC (191729Z JAN 03).
339. Email from: , to: , [REDACTED]; cc: , , , [REDACTED], [REDACTED]; subject: [DETENTION SITE BLUE] follow-up; date: December 15, 2002.
340. See, for example, ALEC (072315Z DEC 02); ALEC (130352Z DEC 02); ALEC (180247Z DEC 02); ALEC (191729Z JAN 03); CIA Office of Inspector General, Report of Investigation: Unauthorized Interrogation Techniques at [DETENTION SITE BLUE], (2003-7123-IG), October 29, 2003. *See also* CIA Office of Inspector General report, Counterterrorism Detention And Interrogation Activities (September 2001–October 2003) (2003-7123-IG), released on May 7, 2004.
341. 10030 (111541Z DEC 02).
342. ALEC (180247Z DEC 02).
343. 10085 (230906Z DEC 02).
344. 10085 (230906Z DEC 02).
345. 10040 (122122Z DEC02). Prior to [CIA OFFICER 2's] deployment, CIA records included numerous concerns about [CIA OFFICER 2's] anger management, , and . For more information on [CIA OFFICER 2] and other CIA personnel in the program with similar alarming issues in their background, see Volume III. The CIA's June 2013 Response states that: " some of the officers mentioned in the Study— should have been excluded—much derogatory information was not in fact available to senior managers making assignments ." Notwithstanding the CIA's June 2013 assertion, as detailed in Volume III, senior managers were aware of concerns related to [CIA OFFICER 2] prior to his deployment.
346. As described, the "Renditions and Interrogations Group," is also referred to as the "Renditions Group," the "Rendition, Detention, and Interrogation Group," "RDI," and "RDG" in CIA records.
347. Interview Report, 2003-7123-JG, Review of Interrogations for Counterterrorism Purposes, , February 23, 2003.
348. 10140 (031727Z JAN 03).
349. See email from: ; to: ; subject: EYES ONLY - [ ] ONLY – MEMORANDUM FOR ADDO/DDO; date: January 22, 2003. In an April 12, 2007, Senate Select Committee on Intelligence hearing, Senator Carl Levin asked the CIA Director if the CIA disputed allegations in an International Committee of the Red Cross report that suggested CIA detainees were placed in "[p]rolonged stress standing position, naked, arm[s] chained above the head . . . ." The CIA

Director responded, "Not above the head. Stress positions are part of the EITs, and nakedness were part of the EITs, Senator." See Senate Select Committee on Intelligence Hearing Transcript, dated April 12, 2007 (DTS #2007-3158).

350. See, for example, CIA Office of Inspector General, Report of Investigation: Unauthorized Interrogation Techniques at [DETENTION SITE BLUE], (2003-7123-IG), October 29, 2003; email from: [DETENTION SITE BLUE] COB ███; to: ███; subject: EYES ONLY - [███] ONLY -- MEMO FOR ADDO/DDO; date: January 22, 2003.

351. For additional details, see Volume III.

352. CIA Office of Inspector General, Report of Investigation: Unauthorized Interrogation Techniques at [DETENTION SITE BLUE], (2003-7123-IG), October 29, 2003.

353. CIA Office of Inspector General, Special Review – Counterterrorism Detention and Interrogation Program, (2003-7123-IG), May 2004.

354. CIA Office of Inspector General, Report of Investigation: Unauthorized Interrogation Techniques at [DETENTION SITE BLUE], (2003-7123-IG), October 29, 2003.

355. CIA Office of Inspector General, Report of Investigation: Unauthorized Interrogation Techniques at [DETENTION SITE BLUE], (2003-7123-IG), October 29, 2003.

356. ███ [CIA OFFICER 2] received a one-year Letter of Reprimand, was suspended for five days without pay, and was prohibited from promotions, within-grade step increases, quality step increases, or permanent salary increases during that one-year period. The decision did not affect ███ [CIA OFFICER 2's] eligibility to receive Exceptional Performance Awards, bonuses, or non-monetary forms of recognition. See ███. ███ [CIA OFFICER 2] retired from the CIA on ███, 2004. (See ███.) On June 20, 2005, the CIA director of transnational issues, aware of ███ [CIA OFFICER 2's] problematic background, approved ███ [CIA OFFICER 2's] employment on a CIA contract because the project was "mission critical" and "no other contractor with the needed skills was available." (See ███.) The chief of Base received a two-year Letter of Reprimand and a ten-day suspension without pay, and was prohibited from receiving any bonus awards from the CIA during the period of reprimand. On ███, 2003, prior to the implementation of the prohibitions, this individual retired from the CIA. See ███.

357. ███ 10267 ███.

358. According to a December 12, 2002, CIA cable, al-Nashiri "visibly and markedly trembles with fear every time he sees [███]." See ███ 10038 (122119Z DEC 02).

359. Email from: ███; to: ███; cc: [REDACTED]; subject: Re: date: January 22, 2003. Despite this notification ███ did not immediately resign from the interrogation program.

360. Email from: ███; to: ███, [REDACTED], ███, ███, [REDACTED], [REDACTED]; subject: CONCERNS OVER REVISED INTERROGATION PLAN FOR NASHIRI; date: January 22, 2003. ███, referenced in the passage as a "HVT Interrogator," was the chief of interrogations.

361. Email from: ███; to: ███, [REDACTED], ███, ███, [REDACTED], [REDACTED]; subject: CONCERNS OVER REVISED INTERROGATION PLAN FOR NASHIRI; date: January 22, 2003. As noted above, personnel from CIA's Office of Medical Services raised the same concerns about medical and psychological personnel serving both to assess the health of a detainee and to participate in the interrogation process.

362. DIRECTOR ███ (201659Z JAN 03); DIRECTOR ███ (230008Z JAN 03).

363. ███ 10289 (241203Z JAN 03); ███ 10296 (251113Z JAN 03), ███ 10306 (261403Z JAN 03).

364. ███ 10309 (261403Z JAN 03).

365. ███ 10312 (270854Z JAN 03).

366. HEADQUARTERS ███ (031945Z SEP 06); ███ 1242 (050744Z SEP 06); HEADQUARTERS ███ (051613Z SEP 06).

367. See, for example, ███ 11247 (141321Z APR 03); ███ 1959 (111700Z DEC 04); ███ 2038 (211558Z JAN 05); ███ 2169 (251133Z MAR 05); ███ 11701 (191640Z MAY 03); ███ 1756 (190800Z SEP 03).

368. ███ 1502 (021841Z AUG 04); ███ 2709 (271517Z APR 06); ███ 3910 (241852Z JAN 06); ███ 2709 (271517Z APR 06).

369. See, for example, ███ 1029 (291750Z JUN 06); ███ 1142 (041358Z AUG 06); ███ 1543 (111600Z AUG 04); ███ 1716 (180742Z SEP 04); ███ 3051 (301235Z SEP 05); ███

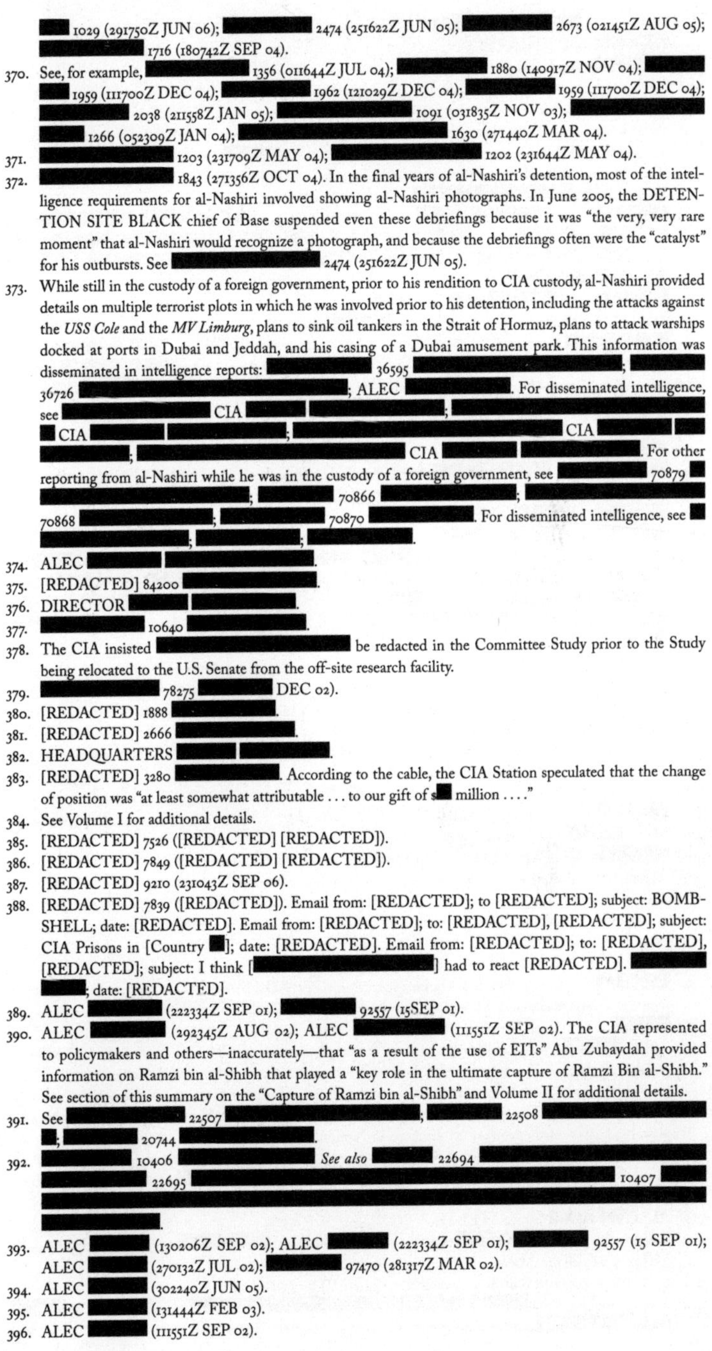

1029 (291750Z JUN 06); 2474 (251622Z JUN 05); 2673 (021451Z AUG 05); 1716 (180742Z SEP 04).

370. See, for example, 1356 (011644Z JUL 04); 1880 (140917Z NOV 04); 1959 (111700Z DEC 04); 1962 (121029Z DEC 04); 1959 (111700Z DEC 04); 2038 (211558Z JAN 05); 1091 (031835Z NOV 03); 1266 (052309Z JAN 04); 1630 (271440Z MAR 04).

371. 1203 (231709Z MAY 04); 1202 (231644Z MAY 04).

372. 1843 (271356Z OCT 04). In the final years of al-Nashiri's detention, most of the intelligence requirements for al-Nashiri involved showing al-Nashiri photographs. In June 2005, the DETENTION SITE BLACK chief of Base suspended even these debriefings because it was "the very, very rare moment" that al-Nashiri would recognize a photograph, and because the debriefings often were the "catalyst" for his outbursts. See 2474 (251622Z JUN 05).

373. While still in the custody of a foreign government, prior to his rendition to CIA custody, al-Nashiri provided details on multiple terrorist plots in which he was involved prior to his detention, including the attacks against the *USS Cole* and the *MV Limburg*, plans to sink oil tankers in the Strait of Hormuz, plans to attack warships docked at ports in Dubai and Jeddah, and his casing of a Dubai amusement park. This information was disseminated in intelligence reports: 36595 ; 36726 ; ALEC . For disseminated intelligence, see CIA ; CIA ; CIA ; CIA . For other reporting from al-Nashiri while he was in the custody of a foreign government, see 70879 ; 70866 ; ; 70868 ; 70870 . For disseminated intelligence, see ; ; .

374. ALEC .

375. [REDACTED] 84200 .

376. DIRECTOR .

377. 10640 .

378. The CIA insisted be redacted in the Committee Study prior to the Study being relocated to the U.S. Senate from the off-site research facility.

379. 78275 DEC 02).

380. [REDACTED] 1888 .

381. [REDACTED] 2666 .

382. HEADQUARTERS .

383. [REDACTED] 3280 . According to the cable, the CIA Station speculated that the change of position was "at least somewhat attributable . . . to our gift of $ million . . . ."

384. See Volume I for additional details.

385. [REDACTED] 7526 ([REDACTED] [REDACTED]).

386. [REDACTED] 7849 ([REDACTED] [REDACTED]).

387. [REDACTED] 9210 (231043Z SEP 06).

388. [REDACTED] 7839 ([REDACTED]). Email from: [REDACTED]; to [REDACTED]; subject: BOMBSHELL; date: [REDACTED]. Email from: [REDACTED]; to: [REDACTED], [REDACTED]; subject: CIA Prisons in [Country]; date: [REDACTED]. Email from: [REDACTED]; to: [REDACTED], [REDACTED]; subject: I think [ ] had to react [REDACTED]. ; date: [REDACTED].

389. ALEC (222334Z SEP 01); 92557 (15SEP 01).

390. ALEC (292345Z AUG 02); ALEC (111551Z SEP 02). The CIA represented to policymakers and others—inaccurately—that "as a result of the use of EITs" Abu Zubaydah provided information on Ramzi bin al-Shibh that played a "key role in the ultimate capture of Ramzi Bin al-Shibh." See section of this summary on the "Capture of Ramzi bin al-Shibh" and Volume II for additional details.

391. See 22507 ; 22508 ; 20744 .

392. 10406 *See also* 22694 22695 10407 .

393. ALEC (130206Z SEP 02); ALEC (222334Z SEP 01); 92557 (15 SEP 01); ALEC (270132Z JUL 02); 97470 (281317Z MAR 02).

394. ALEC (302240Z JUN 05).

395. ALEC (131444Z FEB 03).

396. ALEC (111551Z SEP 02).

397. DIRECTOR DEC 02).
398. 22888 (240845Z FEB 03).
399. 22888 (240845Z FEB 03).
400. According to a 2005 CIA assessment, the "most significant" reporting from Ramzi bin al-Shibh on potential future attacks was background information related to al-Qa'ida's plans to attack Heathrow Airport. According to the CIA, Ramzi bin al-Shibh provided "useful intelligence," including an "overview of the plot" that was then used in the interrogation of other detainees. (See ALEC (302240Z JUN 05).) Ramzi bin al-Shibh provided the majority of this information in mid-October 2002, while in foreign government custody. See CIA .
401. 10406 . *See also* 22694 22695 10407 .
402. 10361 .
403. This included Khaled Shaykh Mohammed (10654 (030904Z MAR 03)); Hambali 1310 (101825Z SEP 03)); Abu Yasir al-Jaza'iri (10990); Abd al-Latif al-Barq 12348); Hambali and Lillie (1243 (152049Z AUG 03)); Hassan Ghul (1267 (JAN 04)); Adnan al-Libi 1758 ; and AL-TURKI 2179 .
404. 10361 .
405. 10361 .
406. 10361 . See Volume II for detailed information on CIA representations to Congress.
407. 10361 .
408. 10361 .
409. This included Asadullah (DIRECTOR (FEB 03)); Abu Yasir al-Jaza'iri 35558 (MAR 03)); Suleiman Abdullah 35787 (MAR 03); 36023 (APR 03)); Abu Hudhaifa 38576 (MAY 03)); Hambali 1241 (151912Z AUG 03)); and Majid Khan (46471 (241242Z MAY 03); 39077 (27179Z MAY 03)).
410. For additional information, see Volume III. In an April 12, 2007, Senate Select Committee on Intelligence hearing, Senator Levin asked the CIA Director if the CIA disputed allegations in an International Committee of the Red Cross report that suggested CIA detainees were placed in "[p]rolonged stress standing position, naked, arm[s] chained above the head . . ." The CIA Director responded, "Not above the head. Stress positions are part of the EITs, and nakedness were part of the EITs, Senator." Senate Select Committee on Intelligence, Hearing Transcript, dated April 12, 2007 (DTS #2007-3158).
411. See Volume III for additional information.
412. 10452 (121723Z FEB 03).
413. ALEC (131444Z FEB 03).
414. 10446 (111754Z FEB 03). The Committee was informed that the CIA's standard practice during coercive interrogations was to ask questions to which interrogators already knew the answers in order to assess the detainee's level of cooperation. The Committee was further informed that only after detainees were assessed to be cooperative did interrogators ask questions whose answers were unknown to the CIA. See, for example, Transcript of SSCI Hearing, April 12, 2007 (testimony of CIA Director Michael Hayden) (DTS #2007-3158).
415. 10452 (121723Z FEB 03). In June 2002, Ramzi bin al-Shibh participated with KSM in an interview with the al-Jazeera television network on the 9/11 attacks. DIRECTOR (112136Z SEP 02).
416. 10452 (121723Z FEB 03).
417. ALEC (131444Z FEB 03). Contrary to the statement in the CIA cable, as described, CIA officers in the country where Ramzi bin al-Shibh was held prior to being rendered to CIA custody wrote that Ramzi bin al-Shibh had provided information used in approximately 50 CIA intelligence reports, including information on potential future threats, to include a potential attack on London's Heathrow airport and al-Nashiri's planning for potential operations in the Arabian Peninsula. The CIA officers in that country also noted that they found Ramzi bin al-Shibh's information to be generally accurate, and that they "found few cases where he openly/clearly misstated facts." The CIA officers in concluded, "overall, [Ramzi bin al-Shibh] provided what was needed." See 22888 (240845Z FEB 03).
418. ALEC (131444Z FEB 03).
419. See, for example, 10525 (200840Z FEB 03) and 10573 (241143Z FEB 03). For further detail, see the detainee review of Ramzi bin al-Shibh in Volume III.
420. See detainee review of Ramzi bin al-Shibh in Volume III for additional information.
421. See, for example, CIA 20817 (describing the foreign government's interrogators' "plan to ask Binalshibh to clarify his

statements that Mohamed Atta, Marwan el-Shehhi, and Ziad Jarrah could not agree on the wisdom of targeting nuclear facilities"); [REDACTED] 10568 (231514Z FEB 03); [REDACTED] 20817 [REDACTED]; CIA [REDACTED]; CIA [REDACTED].

422. [REDACTED] 10582 (272026Z FEB 03); [REDACTED] 10627 (281949Z FEB 03).

423. [REDACTED] 10521 (191750Z FEB 03). The cable referred to keeping bin al-Shibh in darkness as a "standard interrogation technique." The same cable states that during the night of February 18, 2003, the light went out in bin al-Shibh's cell and that "[w]hen security personnel arrived to replace the bulb, bin al-Shibh was cowering in the corner, shivering. Security personnel noted that he appeared relieved as soon as the light was replaced."

424. [REDACTED] 1759 (021319Z OCT 04); HEADQUARTERS [REDACTED] (040023Z NOV 05); [REDACTED] 1890 (171225Z NOV 04); [REDACTED] 1878 (140915Z NOV 04); [REDACTED] 1930 (061620Z DEC 04); [REDACTED] 2207 (111319Z APR 05); [REDACTED] (141507Z APR 05); [REDACTED] 2535 (051805Z JUL 05); [REDACTED] 2589 (120857Z JUL 05); [REDACTED] 2830 (291304Z AUG 05); [REDACTED] 1890 (171225Z NOV 04); [REDACTED] 1893 (200831Z NOV 04); CIA document entitled, "Detainee Talking Points for ICRC Rebuttal, [REDACTED]"; 2210 (141507Z APR 05); [REDACTED] 2535 (0518005Z JUL 05); [REDACTED] 2210 (141507Z APR 05); [REDACTED] 2535 (051805Z JUL 05); [REDACTED] 2830 (291304Z AUG 05); [REDACTED] 1930 (061620Z DEC 04); [REDACTED] 2210 (141507Z APR 05).

425. [REDACTED] 2210 (141507Z APR 05).

426. [REDACTED] 2210 (141507Z APR 05).

427. HEADQUARTERS [REDACTED] (031945Z SEP 06).

428. [REDACTED] SITE DAILY REPORT – 24 MAY 07: [REDACTED] 8904 (182103Z APR 08).

429. See Volume II for additional information.

430. Ramzi bin al-Shibh was immediately subjected to the CIA's enhanced interrogation techniques at DESTINATION SITE BLUE.

431. ALEC [REDACTED] (302240Z JUN 05).

432. For more details, see section of this summary on the capture of KSM and additional information in Volume II.

433. [REDACTED] 41403 (020949Z MAR 03).

434. [REDACTED] 41484 (031315Z MAR 03).

435. [REDACTED] 41564 (041307Z MAR 03); [REDACTED] 41592 (051050Z MAR 03). For details on KSM's detention in Pakistani custody, see the KSM detainee review in Volume III.

436. Email from: [REDACTED]; to: [REDACTED], [REDACTED]; subject: Let's Roll with the new guy; date: March 1, 2003, at 03:43:12 AM.

437. DIRECTOR [REDACTED] (012240Z MAR 03).

438. [REDACTED] 35354 ([REDACTED] MAR 03); DIRECTOR [REDACTED] ([REDACTED] MAR 03).

439. [REDACTED] 34491 (051400Z MAR 03).

440. [REDACTED] 34491 (051400Z MAR 03); Interview of [REDACTED], by [REDACTED] and [REDACTED], Office of the Inspector General, 27 March 2003.

441. [REDACTED] 34575 [REDACTED].

442. "Khalid Shaykh Muhammad's Threat Reporting – Precious Truths, Surrounded by a Bodyguard of Lies," IICT, April 3, 2003. KSM also named three individuals who, he said, worked on an al-Qa'ida anthrax program that was still in its "earliest stages." They were led, he said, by "Omar" who had been arrested in the country of [REDACTED]. The group also included Abu Bakr al-Filistini. (See [REDACTED] 34475 [REDACTED].) KSM would later state that "Yazid" led al-Qa'ida's anthrax efforts. (See [REDACTED] 10769 (120937Z MAR 03).) Yazid Sufaat, who had been in [REDACTED] [foreign government] custody since 2001, had long been suspected of participating in al-Qa'ida chemical and biological activities. (See email from: [REDACTED]; to: [REDACTED], [REDACTED], [REDACTED] cc: [REDACTED], [REDACTED], [REDACTED], [REDACTED], [REDACTED], [REDACTED], [REDACTED]; subject: FOR COORD by noon please: Yazid Sufaat PDB; date: March 14, 2003, at 09:05 AM; email from: [REDACTED]; to: [REDACTED]; subject: Re: [REDACTED] RESPONSE – INDIVIDUALS CONNECTED TO USAMA BIN LADIN ASSOCIATE YAZID SUFAAT; date: March 6, 2003, at 12:50:27 PM; [REDACTED]; email from: [REDACTED]; to: [REDACTED]; SUBJECT: Re: KSM on WMD; date: March 12, 2003, at 08:28:31 AM.) A draft PDB prepared on March 17, 2003, states that "Sufaat's own claims to [REDACTED] [foreign government] authorities and personal background tracks with KSM's assertions." (See "KSM Guarding Most Sensitive Information," labeled "For the President Only 18 March 2003," stamped 0319 ksmupdate.doc 17 March 2003.) On April 3, 2003, an IICT analysis stated that KSM "likely judges that information related to Sufaat already has been compromised since his arrest." (See "Khalid Shaykh Muhammad's Threat Reporting – Precious Truths, Surrounded by a Bodyguard of Lies," IICT, April 3, 2003.) CIA analysis from 2005 stated that "[REDACTED] [a foreign government holding Sufaat] was likely to have known details of Yazid's involvement in al-Qa'ida's anthrax program by early 2002," although that information was not provided at the time to the CIA. (See CIA Directorate of Intelligence; "Al-Qa'ida's Anthrax Program; Cracks Emerge in a Key Reporting Stream; New Insights into Yazid Sufaat's Credibility

" (DTS #2005-3264).) Al-Filistini was later captured and detained by the CIA. While being subjected to the CIA's enhanced interrogation techniques he changed his description of al-Qa'ida's anthrax efforts multiple times. On August 1, 2003, Abu Bakr al-Filistini, also known as Samr al-Barq, told CIA interrogators that "we never made anthrax." At the time, he was being subjected to the CIA's enhanced interrogation techniques and was told that the harsh treatment would not stop until he "told the truth." According to cables, crying, al-Barq then said "I made the anthrax." Asked if he was lying, al-Barq said that he was. After CIA interrogators "demonstrated the penalty for lying," al-Barq again stated that "I made the anthrax" and then immediately recanted, and then again stated that he made anthrax. (See 1015 (012057Z AUG 03).) Two days later, al-Barq stated that he had lied about the anthrax production "only because he thought that was what interrogators wanted." See 1017 (030812Z AUG 03).

443. 34573 .
444. Email from: ; to: [REDACTED]; cc: [REDACTED], ; subject: Re: Departure; date: March 6, 2003, at 7:11:59 PM; email from: ; to: [REDACTED]; cc: ; subject: Re: Update; date: March 6, 2003, at 4:51:32 PM.
445. 34573 (061751Z MAR 03); 34614 (071551Z MAR 03).
446. 34573 (061751Z MAR 03); 34614 (071551Z MAR 03).
447. In June 2004, KSM described his reporting as "all lies." 34569 (061722Z MAR 03); 1281 (130801Z JUN 04).
448. The two individuals, Sayed Habib and Shaistah Habibullali Khan, entered CIA custody in April and July 2003 respectively, and were released in August and February 2004, respectively. (See 5712 ; email from: ; to: , [REDACTED], [REDACTED]; subject: planned release of [DETENTION SITE ORANGE] detainee Syed Habib; ; and CIA document, "Additional Details for DCIA on Sayed Habib's Arrest and Detention.") The CIA's June 2013 Response states that the detention of the two individuals "can only be considered 'wrongful' after the fact, not in the light of credible information available at the time and in a context in which plot disruption was deemed an urgent national priority." The CIA's June 2013 Response further states that KSM's reporting on March 6, 2003, was "credible" because, at the time, "[CIA] assessed that Khalid Shaykh Muhammad (KSM) had moved to a more cooperative posture as his interrogation progressed." A review of CIA records indicates that the CIA subjected KSM to the CIA's enhanced interrogation techniques the following day. The use of the techniques continued until March 25, 2003, and included 183 applications of the waterboard. See 10711 .
449. Interview of , by [REDACTED] and [REDACTED] Office of the Inspector General, April 3, 2003. Email to: , ; from: ; cc: [REDACTED], [REDACTED], , , , , [REDACTED], [REDACTED], , [REDACTED]; subject: KSM planning; date: March 1, 2003, at 07:07:33 AM.
450. 10654 (030904Z MAR 03); DIRECTOR (041444Z MAR 03). The initial approval was for SWIGERT and CIA interrogator . The authorization was extended to DUNBAR on March , 2003. DIRECTOR .
451. Email from: [REDACTED]; to: ; cc: ; subject: Technique; date: March , 2003, at 3:51:09 AM.
452. Email from: [REDACTED]; to: ; cc: ; subject: Re: Technique; date: March , 2003, at 3:22:45 PM.
453. 10711 .
454. 10705 .
455. DIRECTOR .
456. 107011 .
457. 10711 ; 10725 ; 10732 ; 10731 ; 10741 (100917Z MAR 03).
458. Interview of , by [REDACTED] and [REDACTED], Office of the Inspector General, April 30, 2003. Interview of by [REDACTED] and [REDACTED], Office of the Inspector General, October 22, 2003.
459. CIA Inspector General, Special Review, Counterterrorism Detention and Interrogation Program (2003-7123-IG), January 2004.
460. 10740 (092308Z MAR 03), disseminated as ; 10741 (100917Z MAR 03).
461. 11377 (231943Z APR 03), disseminated as .
462. Interview of , by [REDACTED] and [REDACTED], Office of the Inspector General, 30 April 2003.

463. Interview of James Pavitt, by [REDACTED] and [REDACTED], Office of the Inspector General, August 21, 2003.
464. Email from: [REDACTED]; to: [REDACTED]; cc: [REDACTED]; subject: More; date: April 10, 2003, at 5:59:27 PM.
465. [REDACTED] 10752 (102320Z MAR 03).
466. Email from: [REDACTED]; to: [REDACTED]; cc: [REDACTED]; subject: Re: MEDICAL SITREP 3/10; date: March 11, 2003, at 8:10:39 AM.
467. [REDACTED] 10798 (131816Z MAR 03), disseminated as [REDACTED].
468. [REDACTED] 10778 (121549Z MAR 03), disseminated as [REDACTED].
469. [REDACTED] 10778 (121549Z MAR 03), disseminated as [REDACTED].
470. [REDACTED] 12141 (272231Z JUN 03); [REDACTED] 22939 (031541Z JUL 04); [REDACTED] 10883 (182127Z MAR 03), disseminated as [REDACTED].
471. [REDACTED] 10787 (130716Z MAR 03). The CIA would later represent that the information KSM provided on the Heathrow plotting was an example of the effectiveness of the waterboard interrogation technique, listing the Heathrow Plot as one of the "plots discovered as a result of EITs" in a briefing on the waterboard for the President in November 2007. See document entitled, "DCIA Talking Points: Waterboard 06 November 2007," dated November 6, 2007, with the notation the document was "sent to DCIA Nov. 6 in preparation for POTUS meeting."
472. [REDACTED] 10800 (131909Z MAR 03).
473. Interview of [REDACTED], by [REDACTED] and [REDACTED], Office of the Inspector General, May 15, 2003.
474. [REDACTED] 10800 (131909Z MAR 03); Interview of [REDACTED], by [REDACTED] and [REDACTED], Office of the Inspector General, May 15, 2003.
475. Email from: [REDACTED] to: [REDACTED]; cc: [REDACTED]; subject: More; date: April 10, 2003, at 5:59:27 PM. Emphasis in the original.
476. [REDACTED] 10787 (130716Z MAR 03).
477. [REDACTED] 10804 (140710Z MAR 03); [REDACTED] 10790 (130946Z MAR 03).
478. Interview of [REDACTED], by [REDACTED] and [REDACTED], Office of the Inspector General, April 30, 2003. The interviewee was a CIA interrogator for KSM at the CIA detention site.
479. [REDACTED] 10790 (130946Z MAR 03).
480. [REDACTED] 10791 (131229Z MAR 03).
481. Email from: [REDACTED]; to: [REDACTED]; cc: [REDACTED], [REDACTED], Jose Rodriguez; subject: re: Eyes Only – Legal and Political Quand[]ry; date: March 13, 2003, at 11:28:06 AM.
482. Email from: [REDACTED]; to: [REDACTED]; cc: [REDACTED]; subject: Re: MEDICAL SITREP 3/10; date: March 12, 2003, at 2:09:47 PM.
483. Email from: [REDACTED]; to: [REDACTED]; cc: [REDACTED], [REDACTED], Jose Rodriguez; subject: Re: EYE ONLY - Legal and Political Quandary; date: MMarch 13, 2003, at 8:01:12 AM.
484. Email from: [REDACTED]; to: [REDACTED]; cc: Jose Rodriguez, [REDACTED], [REDACTED], [REDACTED], [REDACTED]; subject: EYES ONLY - Use of Water Board; date: March 13, 2003, at 08:28 AM.
485. Email from: [REDACTED]; to: [REDACTED]; cc: [REDACTED]; subject: Re: State cable; date: March 13, 2003, at 1:43:17 PM. The previous day, the medical officer had written that "I am going the extra mile to try to handle this in a non confrontational manner." Email from: [REDACTED]; to: [REDACTED]; cc: [REDACTED]; subject: Re: MEDICAL SITREP 3/10; date: March 12, 2003, at 5:17:07 AM.
486. [REDACTED] 10803 (131929Z MAR 03).
487. Email from: [REDACTED]; to [REDACTED]; cc: [REDACTED]; [REDACTED], [REDACTED], [REDACTED]; subject: re: Summary of KSM Waterboard Sessions - As of 1000 HRS 14 Mar 03; date: March 14, 2003, at 10:44:12 AM.
488. Email from: [REDACTED]; to: [REDACTED]; cc: [REDACTED], [REDACTED], [REDACTED], [REDACTED], [REDACTED]; subject: re: Summary of KSM Waterboard Sessions - As of 1000 HRS 14 MAR 03; date: March 14, 2003, at 02:02:42 PM.
489. See detailed review of these sessions in Volume III.
490. [REDACTED] 10831 (151510Z MAR 03); [REDACTED] 10841 (152007Z MAR 03); [REDACTED] 10849 (161058Z MAR 03); Interview of [REDACTED], by [REDACTED] and [REDACTED], Office of the Inspector General, May 15, 2003.
491. The original reporting, that al-Qa'ida had purchased nuclear suitcases in Yemen, was later determined to be based on an effort by unknown Yemenis to sell "suitcase weapons" to al-Qa'ida. Al-Qa'ida operatives concluded that the offer was a scam. See [REDACTED] 74492 (250843Z JUL 03), disseminated as [REDACTED]; and HEADQUARTERS [REDACTED] (092349Z DEC 04).
492. [REDACTED] 10841 (152007Z MAR 03); [REDACTED] 10831 (151510Z MAR 03).
493. Email from: [REDACTED]; to: [REDACTED]; cc: [REDACTED]; subject: Re: Sitrep as of AM 3/15; date: March 15, 2003, at 3:52:54 A.M. Interview of [REDACTED], by [REDACTED] and

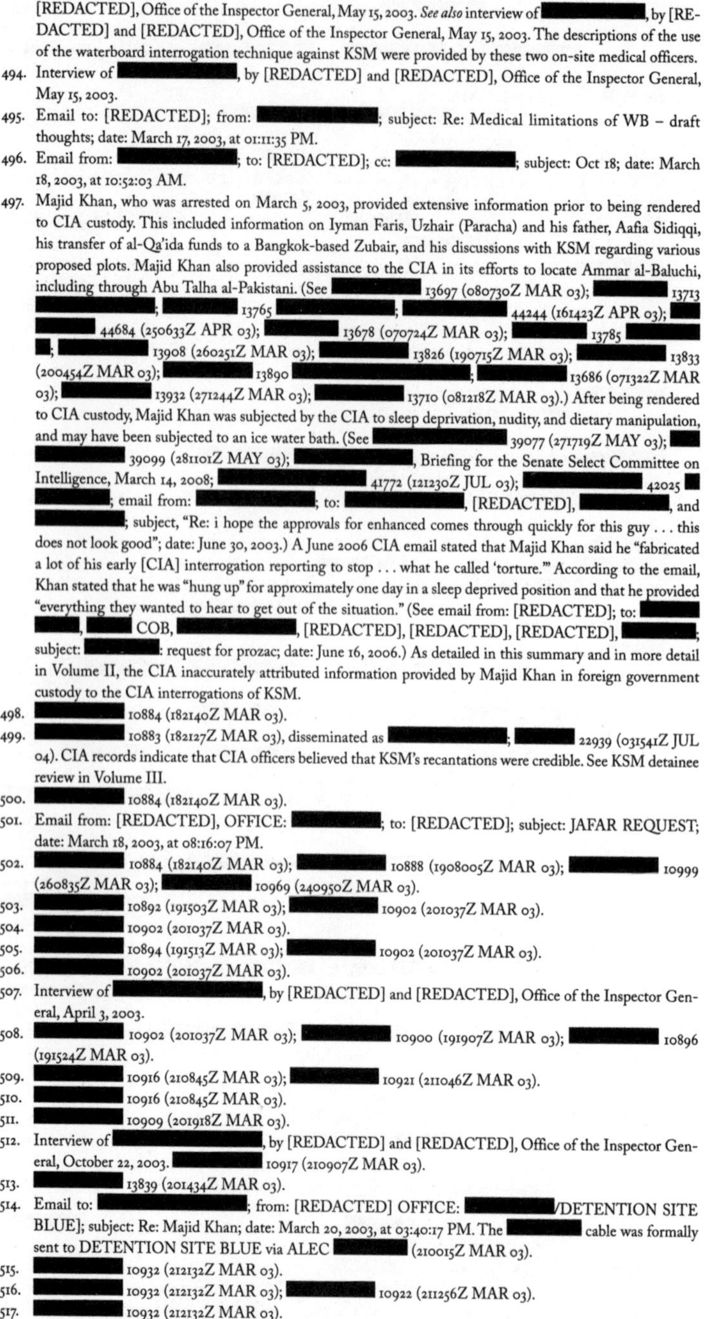

[REDACTED], Office of the Inspector General, May 15, 2003. *See also* interview of , by [REDACTED] and [REDACTED], Office of the Inspector General, May 15, 2003. The descriptions of the use of the waterboard interrogation technique against KSM were provided by these two on-site medical officers.

494. Interview of , by [REDACTED] and [REDACTED], Office of the Inspector General, May 15, 2003.
495. Email to: [REDACTED]; from: ; subject: Re: Medical limitations of WB – draft thoughts; date: March 17, 2003, at 01:11:35 PM.
496. Email from: ; to: [REDACTED]; cc: ; subject: Oct 18; date: March 18, 2003, at 10:52:03 AM.
497. Majid Khan, who was arrested on March 5, 2003, provided extensive information prior to being rendered to CIA custody. This included information on Iyman Faris, Uzhair (Paracha) and his father, Aafia Sidiqqi, his transfer of al-Qa'ida funds to a Bangkok-based Zubair, and his discussions with KSM regarding various proposed plots. Majid Khan also provided assistance to the CIA in its efforts to locate Ammar al-Baluchi, including through Abu Talha al-Pakistani. (See 13697 (080730Z MAR 03); 13713 ; 13765 ; 44244 (161423Z APR 03); 44684 (250633Z APR 03); 13678 (070724Z MAR 03); 13785 ; 13908 (260251Z MAR 03); 13826 (190715Z MAR 03); 13833 (200454Z MAR 03); 13890 ; 13686 (071322Z MAR 03); 13932 (271244Z MAR 03); 13710 (081218Z MAR 03).) After being rendered to CIA custody, Majid Khan was subjected by the CIA to sleep deprivation, nudity, and dietary manipulation, and may have been subjected to an ice water bath. (See 39077 (271719Z MAY 03); 39099 (281101Z MAY 03); , Briefing for the Senate Select Committee on Intelligence, March 14, 2008; 41772 (121230Z JUL 03); 42025 ; email from: ; to: , [REDACTED], , and ; subject, "Re: i hope the approvals for enhanced comes through quickly for this guy . . . this does not look good"; date: June 30, 2003.) A June 2006 CIA email stated that Majid Khan said he "fabricated a lot of his early [CIA] interrogation reporting to stop . . . what he called 'torture.'" According to the email, Khan stated that he was "hung up" for approximately one day in a sleep deprived position and that he provided "everything they wanted to hear to get out of the situation." (See email from: [REDACTED]; to: , COB, , [REDACTED], [REDACTED], [REDACTED], ; subject: : request for prozac; date: June 16, 2006.) As detailed in this summary and in more detail in Volume II, the CIA inaccurately attributed information provided by Majid Khan in foreign government custody to the CIA interrogations of KSM.
498. 10884 (182140Z MAR 03).
499. 10883 (182127Z MAR 03), disseminated as ; 22939 (031541Z JUL 04). CIA records indicate that CIA officers believed that KSM's recantations were credible. See KSM detainee review in Volume III.
500. 10884 (182140Z MAR 03).
501. Email from: [REDACTED], OFFICE: ; to: [REDACTED]; subject: JAFAR REQUEST; date: March 18, 2003, at 08:16:07 PM.
502. 10884 (182140Z MAR 03); 10888 (1908005Z MAR 03); 10999 (260835Z MAR 03); 10969 (240950Z MAR 03).
503. 10892 (191503Z MAR 03); 10902 (201037Z MAR 03).
504. 10902 (201037Z MAR 03).
505. 10894 (191513Z MAR 03); 10902 (201037Z MAR 03).
506. 10902 (201037Z MAR 03).
507. Interview of , by [REDACTED] and [REDACTED], Office of the Inspector General, April 3, 2003.
508. 10902 (201037Z MAR 03); 10900 (191907Z MAR 03); 10896 (191524Z MAR 03).
509. 10916 (210845Z MAR 03); 10921 (211046Z MAR 03).
510. 10916 (210845Z MAR 03).
511. 10909 (201918Z MAR 03).
512. Interview of , by [REDACTED] and [REDACTED], Office of the Inspector General, October 22, 2003. 10917 (210907Z MAR 03).
513. 13839 (201434Z MAR 03).
514. Email to: ; from: [REDACTED] OFFICE: /DETENTION SITE BLUE]; subject: Re: Majid Khan; date: March 20, 2003, at 03:40:17 PM. The cable was formally sent to DETENTION SITE BLUE via ALEC (210015Z MAR 03).
515. 10932 (212132Z MAR 03).
516. 10932 (212132Z MAR 03); 10922 (211256Z MAR 03).
517. 10932 (212132Z MAR 03).

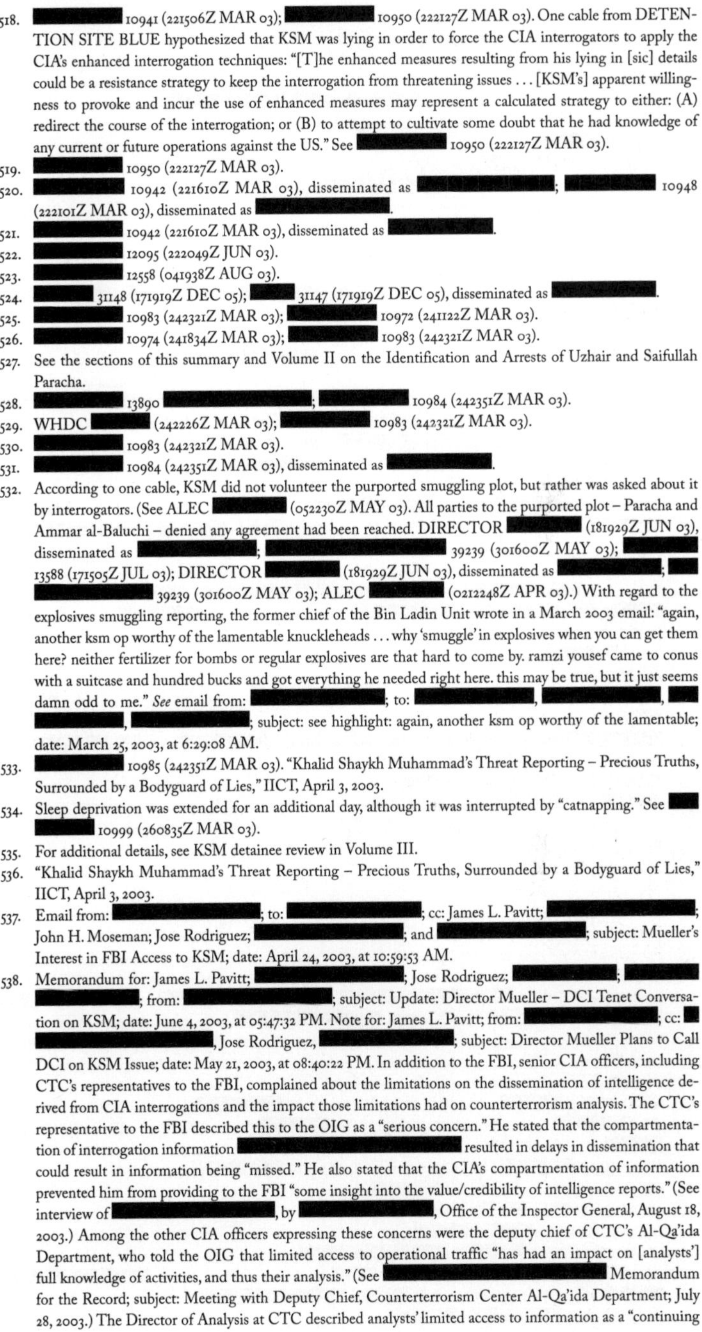

518. 10941 (221506Z MAR 03); 10950 (222127Z MAR 03). One cable from DETENTION SITE BLUE hypothesized that KSM was lying in order to force the CIA interrogators to apply the CIA's enhanced interrogation techniques: "[T]he enhanced measures resulting from his lying in [sic] details could be a resistance strategy to keep the interrogation from threatening issues . . . [KSM's] apparent willingness to provoke and incur the use of enhanced measures may represent a calculated strategy to either: (A) redirect the course of the interrogation; or (B) to attempt to cultivate some doubt that he had knowledge of any current or future operations against the US." See 10950 (222127Z MAR 03).
519. 10950 (222127Z MAR 03).
520. 10942 (221610Z MAR 03), disseminated as ; 10948 (222101Z MAR 03), disseminated as .
521. 10942 (221610Z MAR 03), disseminated as .
522. 12095 (222049Z JUN 03).
523. 12558 (041938Z AUG 03).
524. 31148 (171919Z DEC 05); 31147 (171919Z DEC 05), disseminated as .
525. 10983 (242321Z MAR 03); 10972 (241122Z MAR 03).
526. 10974 (241834Z MAR 03); 10983 (242321Z MAR 03).
527. See the sections of this summary and Volume II on the Identification and Arrests of Uzhair and Saifullah Paracha.
528. 13890 ; 10984 (242351Z MAR 03).
529. WHDC (242226Z MAR 03); 10983 (242321Z MAR 03).
530. 10983 (242321Z MAR 03).
531. 10984 (242351Z MAR 03), disseminated as .
532. According to one cable, KSM did not volunteer the purported smuggling plot, but rather was asked about it by interrogators. (See ALEC (052230Z MAY 03). All parties to the purported plot – Paracha and Ammar al-Baluchi – denied any agreement had been reached. DIRECTOR (181929Z JUN 03), disseminated as ; 39239 (301600Z MAY 03); 13588 (171505Z JUL 03); DIRECTOR (181929Z JUN 03), disseminated as ; 39239 (301600Z MAY 03); ALEC (0212248Z APR 03).) With regard to the explosives smuggling reporting, the former chief of the Bin Ladin Unit wrote in a March 2003 email: "again, another ksm op worthy of the lamentable knuckleheads . . . why 'smuggle' in explosives when you can get them here? neither fertilizer for bombs or regular explosives are that hard to come by. ramzi yousef came to conus with a suitcase and hundred bucks and got everything he needed right here. this may be true, but it just seems damn odd to me." *See* email from: ; to: , , , ; subject: see highlight: again, another ksm op worthy of the lamentable; date: March 25, 2003, at 6:29:08 AM.
533. 10985 (242351Z MAR 03). "Khalid Shaykh Muhammad's Threat Reporting – Precious Truths, Surrounded by a Bodyguard of Lies," IICT, April 3, 2003.
534. Sleep deprivation was extended for an additional day, although it was interrupted by "catnapping." See 10999 (260835Z MAR 03).
535. For additional details, see KSM detainee review in Volume III.
536. "Khalid Shaykh Muhammad's Threat Reporting – Precious Truths, Surrounded by a Bodyguard of Lies," IICT, April 3, 2003.
537. Email from: ; to: ; cc: James L. Pavitt; ; John H. Moseman; Jose Rodriguez; ; and ; subject: Mueller's Interest in FBI Access to KSM; date: April 24, 2003, at 10:59:53 AM.
538. Memorandum for: James L. Pavitt; ; Jose Rodriguez; ; ; from: ; subject: Update: Director Mueller – DCI Tenet Conversation on KSM; date: June 4, 2003, at 05:47:32 PM. Note for: James L. Pavitt; from: ; cc: , Jose Rodriguez, ; subject: Director Mueller Plans to Call DCI on KSM Issue; date: May 21, 2003, at 08:40:22 PM. In addition to the FBI, senior CIA officers, including CTC's representatives to the FBI, complained about the limitations on the dissemination of intelligence derived from CIA interrogations and the impact those limitations had on counterterrorism analysis. The CTC's representative to the FBI described this to the OIG as a "serious concern." He stated that the compartmentation of interrogation information resulted in delays in dissemination that could result in information being "missed." He also stated that the CIA's compartmentation of information prevented him from providing to the FBI "some insight into the value/credibility of intelligence reports." (See interview of , by , Office of the Inspector General, August 18, 2003.) Among the other CIA officers expressing these concerns were the deputy chief of CTC's Al-Qa'ida Department, who told the OIG that limited access to operational traffic "has had an impact on [analysts'] full knowledge of activities, and thus their analysis." (See Memorandum for the Record; subject: Meeting with Deputy Chief, Counterterrorism Center Al-Qa'ida Department; July 28, 2003.) The Director of Analysis at CTC described analysts' limited access to information as a "continuing

problem." (See August 18, 2003, Memorandum for the Record, meeting with Counterterrorism Center, Director of Analysis, Office of the Inspector General.) The CIA's Deputy Director of Intelligence told the OIG that limitations on the dissemination of operational information prevented the "full cadre of analysts" from reviewing the intelligence and that, as a result, "we're losing analytic ability to look at [foreign intelligence] in a timely manner." See interview of ████████, by [REDACTED] and [REDACTED], Office of the Inspector General, September 12, 2003.

539. ALEC ████ (072002Z MAY 03).
540. DIRECTOR ████ (121550Z JUN 03).
541. ████ 11454 (301710Z APR 03); ████ 11448 (301141Z APR 03).
542. ALEC ████ (022012Z MAY 03). See information in this summary and Volume II on the "Karachi Plot" for additional information.
543. See detainee reviews for Ammar al-Baluchi and Khallad bin Attash in Volume III for additional information on the reporting the detainees provided.
544. Memorandum for: ████; ████; ████; from: ████; subject: Action detainee branch; date: June 12, 2003 (emphasis in the original).
545. ████ 11319 (191445Z APR 03), disseminated as ████.
546. ALEC ████ (222153Z APR 03).
547. Email from: ████; to: ████; cc: ████, ████, [REDACTED], ████, ████, [REDACTED], [REDACTED], [REDACTED], ████, ████, [REDACTED]; subject: Khallad & KSM Detainee Case Discussion; date: June 18, 2003, at 10:09 AM; ALEC ████ (302258Z JUN 03).
548. ALEC ████ (302258Z JUN 03).
549. Email from: ████; to: ████; cc: [REDACTED], [REDACTED], ████, ████, ████, ████, ████, ████, [REDACTED], ████, [REDACTED]; subject: Re: KSM's passive restraint – please let me know if you have comments for a memo to the DCI; date: June 24, 2003, at 1:27:06 PM.
550. Email from: ████; to: ████, ████, ████, ████, ████, ████, ████, [REDACTED]; CC: ████; subject: KSM and Khallad Issues; date: October 16, 2003, at 5:25:13 PM.
551. ALEC ████ (111932Z NOV 03).
552. ████ 10400 (161754Z NOV 03). KSM, who was with Ayman al-Zawahiri the day before March 1, 2003, capture, first informed the CIA of this fact more than a month later, on April 3, 2003. See ████ 11139 (051956Z APR 03).
553. ████ 7847 ████; ████ 2218 ████; HEADQUARTERS ████ ████.
554. ████ 2441 ████.
555. ████ 1079 ████; ████ 2214 (050539Z SEP 06).
556. See KSM detainee review in Volume III.
557. For more information, see detainee reviews and reports in Volume III for Ramzi bin al-Shibh, Muhammad Umar 'Abd al-Rahman aka Asadallah, Abu Khalid, Khalid Shaykh Mohammad, Mustafa Ahmad al-Hawsawi, Abu Yasir al-Jaza'iri, Suleiman Abdullah, Abu Hazim, Al-Shara'iya aka Abd al-Karim, Ammar al-Baluchi, Khallad bin Attash, Laid Ben Dohman Saidi aka Abu Hudhaifa, Majid Khan, Mohd Farik bin Amin aka Abu Zubair, Samr Hilmi Abdul Latif al-Barq, Bashir bin Lap aka Lillie, and Riduan bin Isomuddin aka Hambali.
558. For example, Abu Hudhaifa was subjected to this technique at the safehouse. [*See* email from: [REDACTED]; to: [REDACTED]; subject: Memo; date: March 15, 2004.) The incident was reported to the CIA inspector general. See email from: ████; to: ████; cc: [REDACTED], ████, ████, ████; subject: our telcon; at: March 17, 2004, at 11:24 AM. *See also* claims related to the treatment of Majid Khan. *See* ████, Briefing for the Senate Select Committee on Intelligence, Implementation of Central Intelligence Agency Secret Detention and Interrogation Program, March 14, 2008.
559. DIRECTOR ████ (012214Z MAR 03); DIRECTOR ████ (040049Z MAR 03); DIRECTOR ████ (252003Z MAR 03); DIRECTOR ████ (162224Z MAY 03); HEADQUARTERS ████ (102352Z SEP 03).
560. DIRECTOR ████ (012214Z MAR 03); DIRECTOR ████ (040049Z MAR 03).
561. [REDACTED] 60040 ████.
562. HEADQUARTERS ████ ████.
563. [REDACTED] 5759 ████ 03).
564. HEADQUARTERS ████ ████.
565. According to a cable from CIA Headquarters, ████ detainees arrived in Country ████ ████, 2003. HEADQUARTERS ████ ████.
566. [REDACTED] ████ ████.

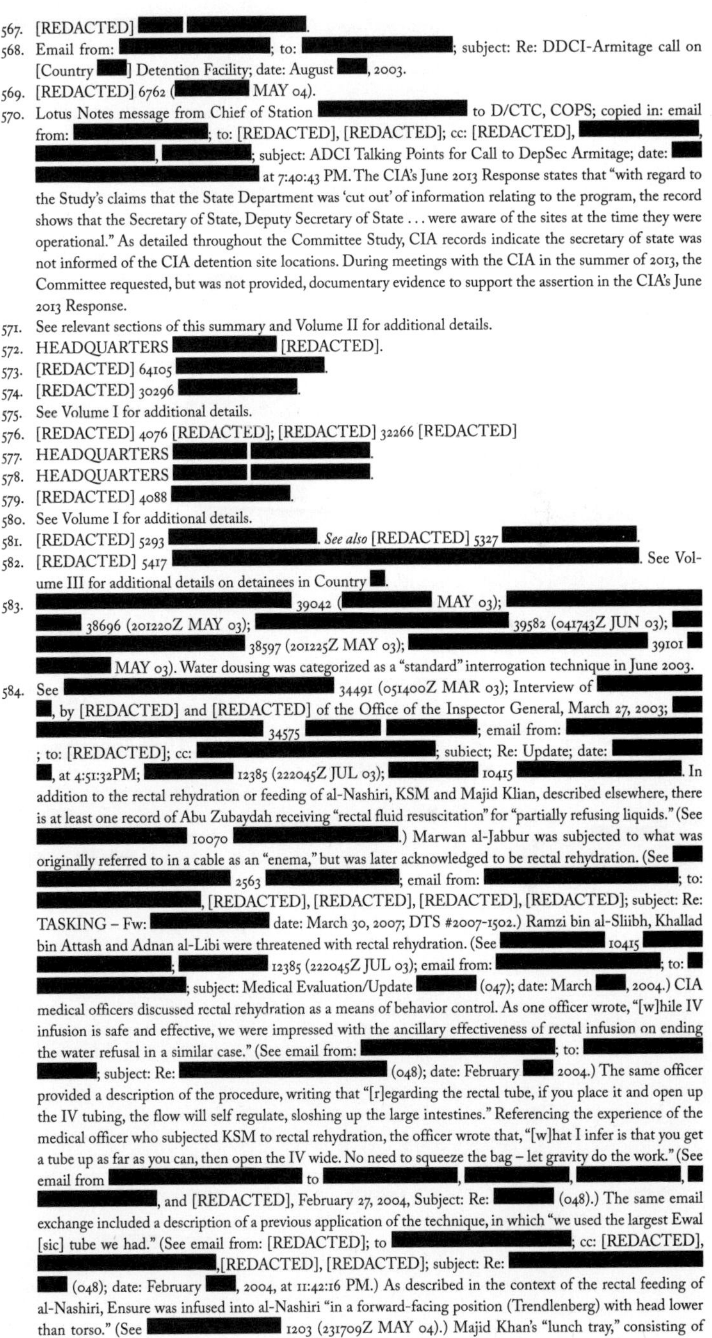

567. [REDACTED] .
568. Email from: ; to: ; subject: Re: DDCI-Armitage call on [Country] Detention Facility; date: August , 2003.
569. [REDACTED] 6762 (MAY 04).
570. Lotus Notes message from Chief of Station to D/CTC, COPS; copied in: email from: ; to: [REDACTED], [REDACTED]; cc: [REDACTED], , , ; subject: ADCI Talking Points for Call to DepSec Armitage; date: at 7:40:43 PM. The CIA's June 2013 Response states that "with regard to the Study's claims that the State Department was 'cut out' of information relating to the program, the record shows that the Secretary of State, Deputy Secretary of State . . . were aware of the sites at the time they were operational." As detailed throughout the Committee Study, CIA records indicate the secretary of state was not informed of the CIA detention site locations. During meetings with the CIA in the summer of 2013, the Committee requested, but was not provided, documentary evidence to support the assertion in the CIA's June 2013 Response.
571. See relevant sections of this summary and Volume II for additional details.
572. HEADQUARTERS [REDACTED].
573. [REDACTED] 64105 .
574. [REDACTED] 30296 .
575. See Volume I for additional details.
576. [REDACTED] 4076 [REDACTED]; [REDACTED] 32266 [REDACTED]
577. HEADQUARTERS .
578. HEADQUARTERS .
579. [REDACTED] 4088 .
580. See Volume I for additional details.
581. [REDACTED] 5293 . *See also* [REDACTED] 5327 .
582. [REDACTED] 5417 . See Volume III for additional details on detainees in Country .
583. 39042 (MAY 03); 38696 (201220Z MAY 03); 39582 (041743Z JUN 03); 38597 (201225Z MAY 03); 39101 MAY 03). Water dousing was categorized as a "standard" interrogation technique in June 2003.
584. See 34491 (051400Z MAR 03); Interview of , by [REDACTED] and [REDACTED] of the Office of the Inspector General, March 27, 2003; 34575 ; email from: ; to: [REDACTED]; cc: ; subiect; Re: Update; date: , at 4:51:32PM; 12385 (222045Z JUL 03); 10415 . In addition to the rectal rehydration or feeding of al-Nashiri, KSM and Majid Klian, described elsewhere, there is at least one record of Abu Zubaydah receiving "rectal fluid resuscitation" for "partially refusing liquids." (See 10070 .) Marwan al-Jabbur was subjected to what was originally referred to in a cable as an "enema," but was later acknowledged to be rectal rehydration. (See 2563 ; email from: ; to: , [REDACTED], [REDACTED], [REDACTED], [REDACTED]; subject: Re: TASKING – Fw: date: March 30, 2007; DTS #2007-1502.) Ramzi bin al-Sliibh, Khallad bin Attash and Adnan al-Libi were threatened with rectal rehydration. (See 10415 ; 12385 (222045Z JUL 03); email from: ; to: ; subject: Medical Evaluation/Update (047); date: March , 2004.) CIA medical officers discussed rectal rehydration as a means of behavior control. As one officer wrote, "[w]hile IV infusion is safe and effective, we were impressed with the ancillary effectiveness of rectal infusion on ending the water refusal in a similar case." (See email from: ; to: ; subject: Re: (048); date: February 2004.) The same officer provided a description of the procedure, writing that "[r]egarding the rectal tube, if you place it and open up the IV tubing, the flow will self regulate, sloshing up the large intestines." Referencing the experience of the medical officer who subjected KSM to rectal rehydration, the officer wrote that, "[w]hat I infer is that you get a tube up as far as you can, then open the IV wide. No need to squeeze the bag – let gravity do the work." (See email from to , , , , and [REDACTED], February 27, 2004, Subject: Re: (048).) The same email exchange included a description of a previous application of the technique, in which "we used the largest Ewal [sic] tube we had." (See email from: [REDACTED]; to ; cc: [REDACTED], ,[REDACTED], [REDACTED]; subject: Re: (048); date: February , 2004, at 11:42:16 PM.) As described in the context of the rectal feeding of al-Nashiri, Ensure was infused into al-Nashiri "in a forward-facing position (Trendlenberg) with head lower than torso." (See 1203 (231709Z MAY 04).) Majid Khan's "lunch tray," consisting of

hummus, pasta with sauce, nuts, and raisins was "pureed" and rectally infused. (See 3240 (231839Z SEP 04).) The CIA's June 2013 Response does not address the use of rectal feeding with CIA detainees, but defends the use of rectal rehydration as a "well acknowledged medical technique." CIA leadership, including General Counsel Scott Muller and DDO James Pavitt, was also alerted to allegations that rectal exams were conducted with "excessive force" on two detainees at DETENTION SITE COBALT. CIA attorney was asked to follow up, although CIA records do not indicate any resolution of the inquiry. CIA records indicate that one of the detainees, Mustafa al-Hawsawi, was later diagnosed with chronic hemorrhoids, an anal fissure, and symptomatic rectal prolapse. See email from: [REDACTED]; to [REDACTED]; cc: , , [REDACTED]; subject: ACTIONS from the GC Update this morning, date: , at 12:15 PM; email from: to: [REDACTED]; cc: , [REDACTED], [REDACTED], [REDACTED], subject: ACTIONS from the GC Update this Mornjng, date: , at 1:23:31 PM; email from: ; to: [REDACTED]; cc: , [REDACTED]; subject: Re: ACTIONS from the GC Update this Morning REQUEST FOR STATUS UPDATE; date: December, 2003, at 10:47:32 AM; 3223 ; HEADQUARTERS .

585. See, for example, 38130 (121722Z MAY 03); 38584 (201133Z MAY 03); 38127 (121714Z MAY 03); 38161 (131326Z MAY 03); 38595 (201216Z MAY 03); 38126 (121709Z MAY 03).

586. See, for example, 35341 ; 39098 : 39042 (MAY 03); email from: [REDACTED] to: [REDACTED]; subject: Memo; date: ; 2005-8085-IG; 39101 MAY 03); 37708 (051225Z MAY 03); 39077 (271719Z MAY 03); 39099 (281101Z MAY 03).

587. For more details, see detainee reviews for Muhammad Umar 'Abd al-Rahman aka Asadallah; Abu Hazim al-Libi; Al-Shara'iya aka Abd al-Karim; and Khallad bin Attash.

588. The two detainees were Abu Hazim al-Libi and Al-Shara'iya aka Abd al-Karim.

589. This is a conservative estimate. CIA records suggest that the CIA's enhanced interrogation techniques may have also been used against five additional detainees at DETENTION SITE COBALT in 2002, which would bring the number of CIA detainees subjected to the CIA's enhanced interrogation techniques to 44. Those additional detainees were [DETAINEE R], who was approved for the CIA's enhanced interrogation techniques, but whose records do not refer to the use of the techniques (ALEC ( )); Ayub Murshid Ali Salih and Ha'il Aziz Ahmad Al-Maythali whose records refer to a lack of sleep, but not the application of sleep deprivation (28132 (101143Z OCT 02); 27964 (071949Z OCT 02)); Bashir Nasir Ali al-Marwalah, who later told debriefers that, when he was first captured, he "had to stand up for five days straight and answer questions" and "was also forced to strip naked and stand in front of a female interrogator" (14353 (231521Z APR 03)); and Sa'id Salili Sa'id, who later told debriefers that he was "mistreated and beaten by Americans while blind-folded and stripped down to his underwear in ." *See* 13386 (090154Z JAN 03)). *See also* detainee reviews in Volume III for more information.

590. The CIA's June 2013 Response objects to the Committee's count, arguing that "[n]o more than seven detainees received enhanced techniques prior to written Headquarters approval." The CIA's June 2013 Response then asserts that "the *Study* miscounts because it confuses the use of standard techniques that did not require prior approval at the time they were administered with enhanced techniques that did." This statement in the CIA's June 2013 Response is inaccurate. First, prior to January 2003, the CIA had not yet designated any technique as a "standard" technique. Because sleep deprivation was included in the August 1, 2002, OLC memorandum approving the use of the CIA's enhanced interrogation techniques on Abu Zubaydah, the Committee included, among the 17, CIA detainees subjected to sleep deprivation without CIA Headquarters authorization prior to January 2003. In January 2003, sleep deprivation under a specific time limit was categorized as a "standard" CIA interrogation technique. Second, the January 2003 guidelines state that advance CIA Headquarters approval was required for "standard" techniques "whenever feasible." For this reason, the Committee did not include cases where CIA interrogators failed to obtain authorization in advance, but did acquire approval within several days of initiating the use of the "standard" techniques. Finally water dousing was not characterized as a "standard" technique until June 2003. (See DIRECTOR (211518Z JUN 03); DIRECTOR (302126Z JAN 03); DIRECTOR (311702Z JAN 03); 39582 (041743Z JUN 03).) In numerous cases prior to June 2003, water dousing was explicitly described in CIA cables as an "enhanced" interrogation technique. (See, for example, DIRECTOR (101700Z FEB 03).) The Committee thus included, among the 17, CIA detainees subjected to water dousing prior to June 2003 without CIA Headquarters authorization. The distinction between standard and enhanced interrogation techniques, which began in January 2003, was eliminated by CIA leadership in 2005. See Volume I and Volume III for additional details.

591. Rafiq Bashir al-Hami was subjected to 72 hours of sleep deprivation between his arrival at DETENTION SITE COBALT and his October [REDACTED], 2002, interrogation. See [REDACTED] 28297 [REDACTED].

592. Tawfiq Nasir Awad al-Bihani was subjected to 72 hours of sleep deprivation between his arrival at DETENTION SITE COBALT and his October [REDACTED], 2002, interrogation. See [REDACTED] 28462 [REDACTED].

593. CIA cables from October 2002 noted that Shaukat was "tired from his regimen of limited sleep deprivation." See [REDACTED] 29381 [REDACTED].

594. Lufti al-Arabi al-Gharisi underwent at least two 48-hour sessions of sleep deprivation in October 2002. See [REDACTED] 29036 [REDACTED]; and [REDACTED] 29352 [REDACTED].

595. Abu Badr was subjected to forced standing, attention grasps, and cold temperatures without blankets in November 2002. *See* [REDACTED] 29963 [REDACTED].

596. CIA interrogators used sleep deprivation, facial slap, use of cold (including cold cells and cold showers), "hard takedowns," dietary manipulation, nudity, and light deprivation on Gul Rahman. See [REDACTED] 29520 [REDACTED]; [REDACTED] 29520 [REDACTED]; [REDACTED] 29770 [REDACTED]; [REDACTED] interview of [REDACTED] [CIA OFFICER 1], December 19, 2002; [REDACTED] Interview of Hammond DUNBAR, January 9, 2003; Memorandum for Deputy Director of Operations, from [REDACTED] January 28, 2003, Subiect: Death Investigation - Gul RAHMAN; CIA Inspector General, Report of Investigation, Death of a Detainee [REDACTED] (2003-7402-IG), April 27, 2005; and CIA Inspector General, Special Review, Counterterrorism Detention And Interrogation Activities (September 2001–October 2003), May 7, 2004.

597. Abd al-Raliira al-Nashiri was subjected to unapproved nudity and approximately two-and-a-half days of sleep deprivation in December 2002, with his arms shackled over his head for as long as 16 hours. *See* email from: [DETENTION SITE BLUE] [REDACTED]; to: [REDACTED]; subject: EYES ONLY - [[REDACTED]] ONLY -- MEMO FOR ADDO/DDO; date: January 22, 2003.

598. The facial hold was used against Ramzi bin al-Shibh multiple times without approval. *See* [REDACTED] 10415 [REDACTED]; [REDACTED] 10429 (101215Z FEB 03); [REDACTED] 10573 (241143Z FEB 03); [REDACTED] 10582 (242026Z FEB 03); [REDACTED] 10591 (252002Z FEB 03); [REDACTED] 10602 (262020Z FEB 03); [REDACTED] 10633 (011537Z MAR 03); and [REDACTED] 10704 (071239Z MAR 03).

599. Interrogators used water dousing, nudity, and cramped confinement on Asadallah without having sought or received authorization from CIA Headquarters. Bathing detainees did not require authorization by CIA Headquarters; however, as described in CIA cables, the application of "bathing" in the case of Asadallalh was done punitively and was used as an interrogation technique. Nudity was also used in conjunction with water dousing/bathing and later as an interrogation technique, without approval from CIA Headquarters. See [REDACTED] 34241 [REDACTED]; and [REDACTED] 34310 [REDACTED].

600. Mustafa al-Hawsawi was subjected to water dousing without approval from CIA Headquarters. See [REDACTED] (081207Z APR 03).

601. Interrogators used sleep deprivation against Abu Khalid prior to seeking authorization from CIA Headquarters, and then failed to obtain such authorization. See [REDACTED] 35193 [REDACTED]; and [REDACTED] 35341 [REDACTED]. Abu Khalid had been in CIA custody for 17 days prior to the use of the technique. Advance authorization from CIA Headquarters was therefore "feasible," and thus required under the guidelines.

602. Abu Hudhaifa was subjected to baths in which ice water was used, standing sleep deprivation for 66 hours that was discontinued due to a swollen leg attributed to prolonged standing, nudity, and dietary manipulation. (See email from: [REDACTED] to: [REDACTED], [REDACTED], [REDACTED], [REDACTED], and [REDACTED]; subject: our telecom; date: March [REDACTED], 2004; CIA Office of Inspector General Report; 2005-8085-IG; [REDACTED] 39098 [REDACTED] 39042 [REDACTED] MAY 03); and [REDACTED] 39101 [REDACTED] MAY 03).). No request or approval for the use of standard or enhanced interrogation techniques could be located in CIA records.

603. Abd al-Karim, who suffered from a foot injury incurred during his capture, was subjected to cramped confinement, stress positions, and walling despite CIA Headquarters having not approved their use. See DIRECTOR [REDACTED] [REDACTED] MAY 03); and DIRECTOR [REDACTED] [REDACTED].

604. Abu Hazim, who also had a foot injury incurred during his capture, was subject to walling, despite CIA Headquarters having not approved its use. (See [REDACTED] 36908 [REDACTED]; and [REDACTED] 37410 (291828Z APR 03).) Nudity, dietary manipulation, and facial grasp were used on Abu Hazim at least 13 days prior to receiving approval. See [REDACTED] 37411 (291829Z APR 03); [REDACTED] 37410 (291828Z APR 03); [REDACTED] 37493 [REDACTED]; DIRECTOR [REDACTED] [REDACTED] MAY 03).

605. CIA cables indicate that Sayyid Ibraliim was subjected to sleep deprivation from January 27, 2004, to January 30, 2004, which exceeded the 48 hours approved by CIA Headquarters. See HEADQUARTERS (272155Z JAN 04); 1303 JAN 04); 1298 JAN 04); 1303 JAN 04); 1311 JAN 04).

606. During March 2003 interrogations at DETENTION SITE COBALT, Abu Yasir al-Jaza'iri was "bathed," a term used to describe water dousing, which was considered at the time to be an enhanced interrogation technique. (See 35558 MAR 03).) Water dousing had not been approved, and the subsequent request, by DETENTION SITE BLUE, to use the CIA's enhanced interrogation techniques on al-Jaza'iri, did not include water dousing. See 10990 .

607. Interrogators requested approvals to use the CIA's enhanced interrogation techniques on Suleiman Abdullah, including water dousing. CIA Headquarters then approved other techniques, but not water dousing. (*See* 36559 ; DIRECTOR .) Suleiman Abdullah was nonetheless subjected to water dousing. See 37117 .

608. The CIA's June 2013 Response states that the CIA "conducted at least 29 investigations of RDI-related conduct, plus two wide-ranging reviews of the program . . . one involved the death of an Afghan national who was beaten by a contractor. The individual involved was prosecuted by the Department of Justice and convicted of a felony charge. Another case involved a contractor who slapped, kicked, and struck detainees while they were in military custody. . . . [T]he contractor was terminated from the CIA, had his security clearances revoked, and was placed on a contractor watch list." However, the two specific examples provided in the CIA's June 2013 Response refer to detainees who were never part of the CIA's Detention and Interrogation Program. On November 6, 2013, the CIA provided a list of "IG Investigations Concerning Detention, Interrogations, and Renditions." The list of 29 included 14 investigations that were directly related to the CIA's Detention and Interrogation Program. Four additional investigations were related to detainees who claimed they had been subjected to abuse in transit from CIA custody to U.S. military custody at Guantanamo Bay. The remaining 11 investigations were unrelated to the CIA's Detention and Interrogation Program. See DTS #2013-3250.

609. CIA chief of interrogations, , placed a broomstick behind the knees of Zubair when Zubair was in a stress position on his knees on the floor. Although stress positions had been approved for Zubair, the use of the broomstick was not approved. See April 7, 2005, Briefing for Blue Ribbon Panel, CIA Rendition, Detention, and Interrogation Programs, at 22.

610. Majid Khan has claimed that, in May 2003, he was subjected to immersion in a tub that was filled with ice and water. (See , Briefing for the Senate Select Committee on Intelligence, Implementation of Central Intelligence Agency Secret Detention and Interrogation Program, dated March 14, 2008.) While CIA cables do not confirm bathing or water dousing, Chief of Interrogations , subjected Abu Hudhaifa to an (unauthorized) "icy water" bath at the same where Majid Khan was held. (See email from: ; to: [REDACTED], [REDACTED], , , and ; subject: our telecon; date: ; and email from: [REDACTED] ; to: ; subject: Memo; date: .) Ayub Murshid Ali Salih and Ha'il Aziz Ahmad al-Maythali were described as not having slept, although it is unclear from CIA records whether CIA interrogators kept them awake. (See 28132 (101143Z OCT 02) and 27964 (071949Z OCT 02).) Bashir Nasri Ali al-Marwalah told debriefers at Guantanamo Bay that he was "tortured" at DETENTION SITE COBALT with five days of continual standing and nudity. (See 14353 (231521Z APR 03).) Sa'id Salih Sa'id likewise informed debriefers at Guantanamo that he was "beaten" while blind-folded in CIA custody. (See 13386 (090154Z JAN 03).) Sixteen other detainees were held at DETENTION SITE COBALT between September and December 2002, a period during which exposure to the CIA's enhanced interrogation techniques such as sleep deprivation and nudity cannot be determined based on the lack of details in CIA cables and related documents.

611. December 4, 2002, Training Report, High Value Target Interrogation and Exploitation (HVTIE) Training Seminar 12-18 Nov 02 (pilot running).

612. DIRECTOR (302126Z JAN 03); DIRECTOR (311702Z JAN 03). For example, on May , 2003, CIA interrogator applied three facial attention grabs, five facial insult slaps, and three abdominal slaps to Abd al-Karim, under the supervision of CIA interrogator [CIA OFFICER 1]. (See 37821 .) had not been approved by CIA Headquarters to employ the CIA's enhanced interrogation techniques on al-Karim; approval had only been provided for [CIA OFFICER 1] to use the CIA's enhanced interrogation techniques. (See DIRECTOR .) On , CIA interrogator , under the supervision of conducted an interrogation of Abd al-Karim in which interrogators used the facial attention grab, facial insult slap, and abdominal slap against al-Karim. (See 38583 .) had not approved by CIA Headquarters to employ the CIA's enhanced interrogation techniques against Abd al-Karim. In another example, on DETENTION SITE COBALT requested approval for certified interrogators

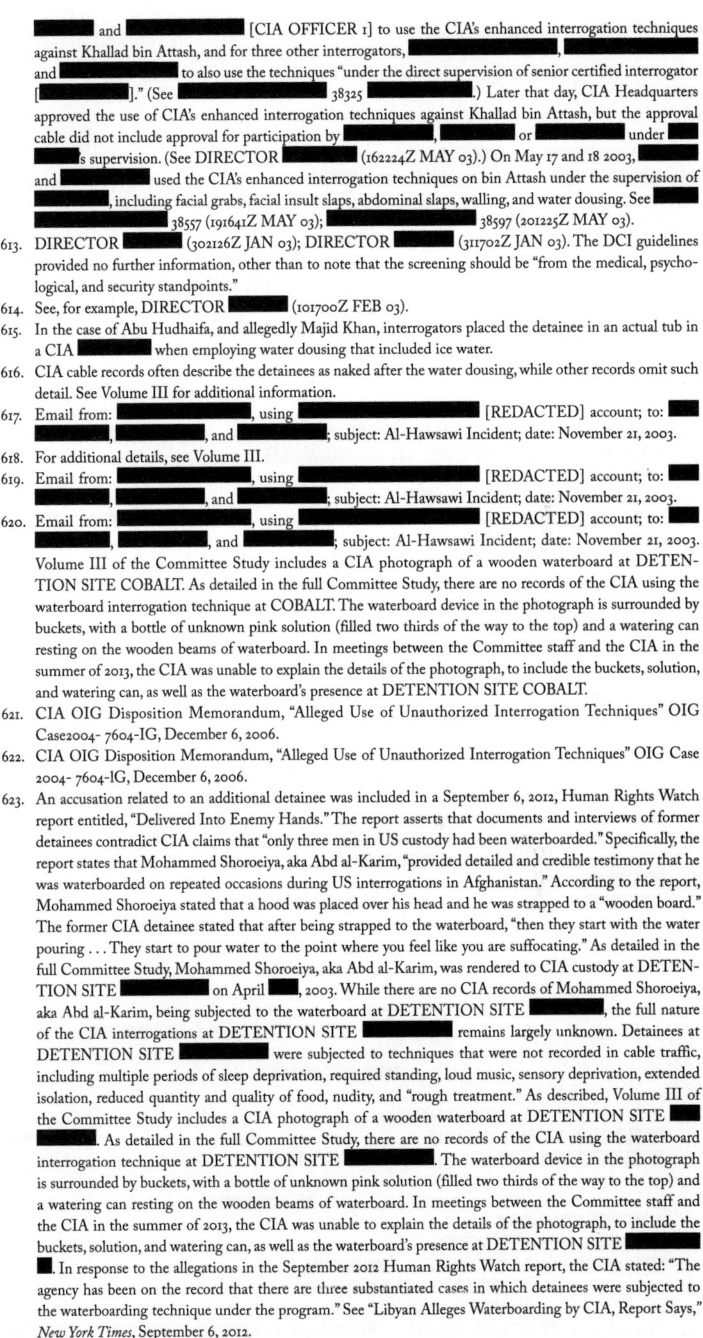

███ and ███ [CIA OFFICER 1] to use the CIA's enhanced interrogation techniques against Khallad bin Attash, and for three other interrogators, ███, ███ and ███ to also use the techniques "under the direct supervision of senior certified interrogator [███]." (See ███ 38325 ███.) Later that day, CIA Headquarters approved the use of CIA's enhanced interrogation techniques against Khallad bin Attash, but the approval cable did not include approval for participation by ███, ███ or ███ under ███ ███'s supervision. (See DIRECTOR ███ (162224Z MAY 03).) On May 17 and 18 2003, ███ and ███ used the CIA's enhanced interrogation techniques on bin Attash under the supervision of ███, including facial grabs, facial insult slaps, abdominal slaps, walling, and water dousing. See ███ ███ 38557 (191641Z MAY 03); ███ 38597 (201225Z MAY 03).

613. DIRECTOR ███ (302126Z JAN 03); DIRECTOR ███ (311702Z JAN 03). The DCI guidelines provided no further information, other than to note that the screening should be "from the medical, psychological, and security standpoints."
614. See, for example, DIRECTOR ███ (101700Z FEB 03).
615. In the case of Abu Hudhaifa, and allegedly Majid Khan, interrogators placed the detainee in an actual tub in a CIA ███ when employing water dousing that included ice water.
616. CIA cable records often describe the detainees as naked after the water dousing, while other records omit such detail. See Volume III for additional information.
617. Email from: ███, using ███ [REDACTED] account; to: ███ ███, ███, and ███; subject: Al-Hawsawi Incident; date: November 21, 2003.
618. For additional details, see Volume III.
619. Email from: ███, using ███ [REDACTED] account; to: ███ ███, ███, and ███; subject: Al-Hawsawi Incident; date: November 21, 2003.
620. Email from: ███, using ███ [REDACTED] account; to: ███ ███, ███, and ███; subject: Al-Hawsawi Incident; date: November 21, 2003. Volume III of the Committee Study includes a CIA photograph of a wooden waterboard at DETENTION SITE COBALT. As detailed in the full Committee Study, there are no records of the CIA using the waterboard interrogation technique at COBALT. The waterboard device in the photograph is surrounded by buckets, with a bottle of unknown pink solution (filled two thirds of the way to the top) and a watering can resting on the wooden beams of waterboard. In meetings between the Committee staff and the CIA in the summer of 2013, the CIA was unable to explain the details of the photograph, to include the buckets, solution, and watering can, as well as the waterboard's presence at DETENTION SITE COBALT.
621. CIA OIG Disposition Memorandum, "Alleged Use of Unauthorized Interrogation Techniques" OIG Case2004- 7604-IG, December 6, 2006.
622. CIA OIG Disposition Memorandum, "Alleged Use of Unauthorized Interrogation Techniques" OIG Case 2004- 7604-IG, December 6, 2006.
623. An accusation related to an additional detainee was included in a September 6, 2012, Human Rights Watch report entitled, "Delivered Into Enemy Hands." The report asserts that documents and interviews of former detainees contradict CIA claims that "only three men in US custody had been waterboarded." Specifically, the report states that Mohammed Shoroeiya, aka Abd al-Karim, "provided detailed and credible testimony that he was waterboarded on repeated occasions during US interrogations in Afghanistan." According to the report, Mohammed Shoroeiya stated that a hood was placed over his head and he was strapped to a "wooden board." The former CIA detainee stated that after being strapped to the waterboard, "then they start with the water pouring . . . They start to pour water to the point where you feel like you are suffocating." As detailed in the full Committee Study, Mohammed Shoroeiya, aka Abd al-Karim, was rendered to CIA custody at DETENTION SITE ███ on April ███, 2003. While there are no CIA records of Mohammed Shoroeiya, aka Abd al-Karim, being subjected to the waterboard at DETENTION SITE ███, the full nature of the CIA interrogations at DETENTION SITE ███ remains largely unknown. Detainees at DETENTION SITE ███ were subjected to techniques that were not recorded in cable traffic, including multiple periods of sleep deprivation, required standing, loud music, sensory deprivation, extended isolation, reduced quantity and quality of food, nudity, and "rough treatment." As described, Volume III of the Committee Study includes a CIA photograph of a wooden waterboard at DETENTION SITE ███ ███. As detailed in the full Committee Study, there are no records of the CIA using the waterboard interrogation technique at DETENTION SITE ███. The waterboard device in the photograph is surrounded by buckets, with a bottle of unknown pink solution (filled two thirds of the way to the top) and a watering can resting on the wooden beams of waterboard. In meetings between the Committee staff and the CIA in the summer of 2013, the CIA was unable to explain the details of the photograph, to include the buckets, solution, and watering can, as well as the waterboard's presence at DETENTION SITE ███ ███. In response to the allegations in the September 2012 Human Rights Watch report, the CIA stated: "The agency has been on the record that there are three substantiated cases in which detainees were subjected to the waterboarding technique under the program." See "Libyan Alleges Waterboarding by CIA, Report Says," *New York Times*, September 6, 2012.

624. CIA IG Disposition Memo, "Alleged Use of Unauthorized Techniques," dated December 6, 2006. 2004-77717-16.
625. CIA IG Disposition Memo, "Alleged Use of Unauthorized Techniques," dated December 6, 2006. 2004-77717-16.
626. CIA IG Disposition Memo, "Alleged Use of Unauthorized Techniques," dated December 6, 2006. 2004-77717-16.
627. [redacted] 84854 [redacted].
628. [redacted] 87617 [redacted]; [redacted] 87426 (111223Z AUG 03). Lillie was subjected to the CIA's enhanced interrogation techniques almost immediately upon his arrival at DETENTION SITE COBALT, on August [redacted], 2003. He was "stripped of his clothing," and "placed in a cell in the standing sleep deprivation position, in darkness." (See [redacted] 1242 (151914 ZAUG03).) A day later an interrogation plan for Lillie, including the use of the CIA's enhanced interrogation techniques, was submitted to CIA Headquarters on August [redacted], 2003. (See [redacted] 1243 (152049Z AUG 03).) CIA Headquarters approved the use of the CIA's enhanced interrogation techniques on Lillie on the following day, August [redacted], 2003. (See HEADQUARTERS [redacted] ([redacted] AUG 03).) As described, the Committee's count of detainees subjected to unauthorized techniques did not include detainees such as Lillie, who were subjected to the CIA's "standard" techniques prior to authorization from CIA Headquarters, but for whom authorization from CIA Headquarters was acquired shortly thereafter. As noted, the January 2003 guidelines required advance approval of such techniques "whenever feasible."
629. [redacted] 9515 [redacted]; [redacted] 87617 [redacted]; [redacted] 87414 [redacted] [redacted]; [redacted] "Hambali Capture." For additional details, see Volume II.
630. [redacted] 87617 [redacted].
631. [redacted] 1271 [redacted] AUG 03); [redacted] 1267 [redacted] AUG 03). The cable also noted that CIA contractor Hammond DUNBAR had arrived at the detention site and was participating in Hambali's interrogations as an interrogator. The "psychological assessment" portion of the cable was attributed to a CIA staff psychologist, however, and not to DUNBAR.
632. CIA officers interrogating Hambali in November 2003 wrote about Hambali's "account of how, through statements read to him and constant repetition of questions, he was made aware of what type of answers his questioners wanted. [Hambali] said he merely gave answers that were similar to what was being asked and what he inferred the interrogator or debriefer wanted, and when the pressure subsided or he was told that the information he gave was okay, [Hambali] knew that he had provided the answer that was being sought." The cable states, "Base assesses [Hambali]'s admission of previous fabrication to be credible. [Hambali]'s admission came after three weeks of daily debriefing sessions with [the case officer] carried out almost entirely in Bahasa Indonesia. [Hambali] has consistently warmed to [the case officer's] discussions with him, and has provided to [the case officer] additional information that he had avoided in the past . . . More tellingly, [Hambali] has opened up considerably to [the case officer] about his fears and motivations, and has taken to trusting [the case officer] at his word. [Hambali] looks to [the case officer] as his sole confidant and the one person who has [Hambali]'s interest in mind . . ." *See* [redacted] 1142 (301055Z NOV 03). This cable appears to have been retransmitted the following day as [redacted] 1144 (010823Z DEC 03).
633. [redacted] 1142 (301055Z NOV 03).
634. [redacted] 1072 (110606Z OCT 03); [redacted] 1075 (111828Z OCT 03); [redacted] 1142 (301055Z NOV 03); [redacted] 1158 (081459Z DEC 03); [redacted] 1604 (191232Z JAN 04). After an Indonesian speaker was deployed to debrief Hambali, the debriefer "got the distinct impression [Hambali] was just responding 'yes' in the typical Indonesian cultural manner when they [sic] do not comprehend a question." The CIA cable then noted that, "[j]ust to clarify, [the Indonesian speaking debriefer] then posed the same question in Indonesian," and "[w]ithout pause, [Hambah] replied with a direct contradiction, claiming that on 20 September 2001, he was in Karachi, not Qandahar." (See [redacted] 1075 (111828Z OCT 03).) A January 2004 cable stated that "Lillie is of limited value," adding that "[h]is English is very poor, and we do not have a Malay linguist." *See* [redacted] 1604 (191232Z JAN 04). *See also* detainee reviews in Volume III for additional information.
635. WASHINGTON [redacted] [redacted].
636. [redacted] 1393 (201006Z OCT 03). The information was also released in [redacted] [redacted] 48122 [redacted]. CIA records indicate that the CIA's interrogations of Arsala Khan resulted in one disseminated intelligence report derived from information Khan provided the day he experienced the hallucinations. See [redacted], via CIA WASHINGTON DC [redacted] [redacted] [redacted].
637. [redacted] 1393 (201006Z OCT 03).
638. [redacted] 1396 [redacted].
639. HEADQUARTERS [redacted] [redacted].
640. HEADQUARTERS [redacted] [redacted].
641. *See*, for example, [redacted] 1407 [redacted]; [redacted] 1407 [redacted]

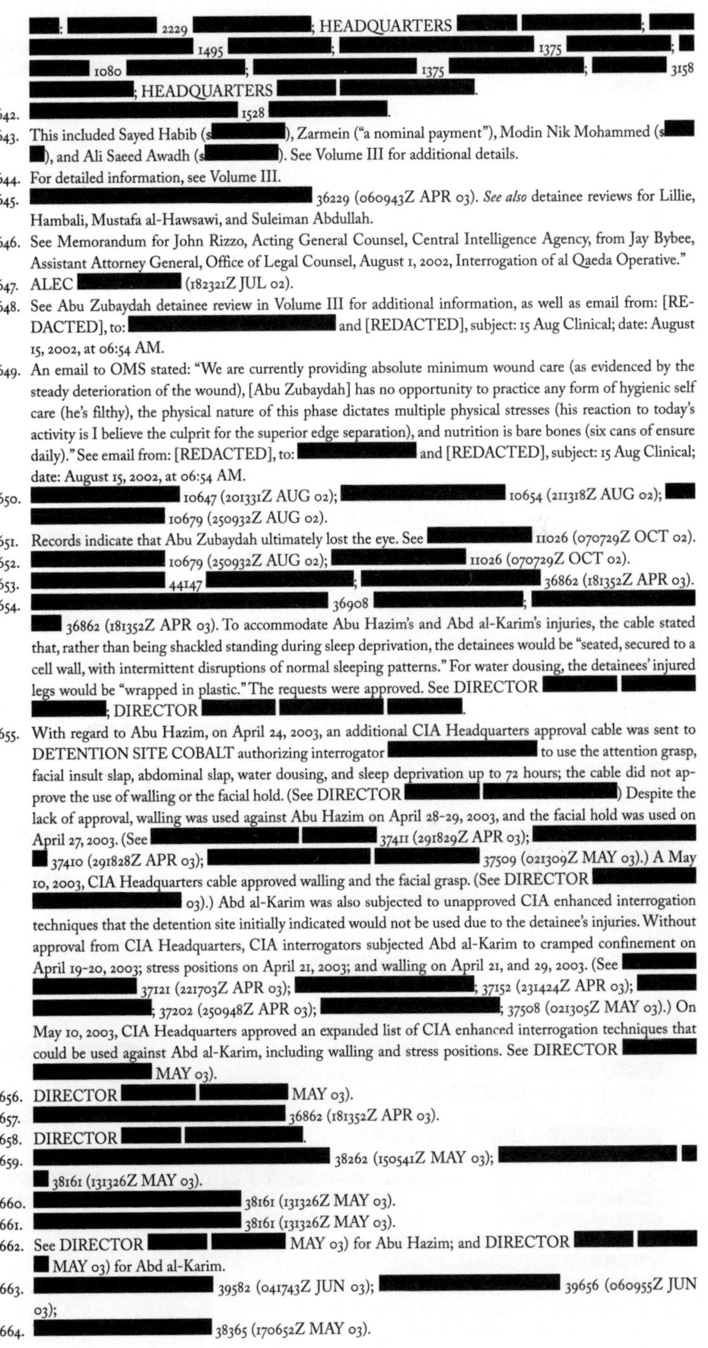

: 2229 ; HEADQUARTERS ; 1495 ; 1375 ; 1080 ; 1375 ; 3158 ; HEADQUARTERS .

642. 1528 .

643. This included Sayed Habib ($), Zarmein ("a nominal payment"), Modin Nik Mohammed ($), and Ali Saeed Awadh ($). See Volume III for additional details.

644. For detailed information, see Volume III.

645. 36229 (060943Z APR 03). *See also* detainee reviews for Lillie, Hambali, Mustafa al-Hawsawi, and Suleiman Abdullah.

646. See Memorandum for John Rizzo, Acting General Counsel, Central Intelligence Agency, from Jay Bybee, Assistant Attorney General, Office of Legal Counsel, August 1, 2002, Interrogation of al Qaeda Operative."

647. ALEC (182321Z JUL 02).

648. See Abu Zubaydah detainee review in Volume III for additional information, as well as email from: [REDACTED], to: and [REDACTED], subject: 15 Aug Clinical; date: August 15, 2002, at 06:54 AM.

649. An email to OMS stated: "We are currently providing absolute minimum wound care (as evidenced by the steady deterioration of the wound), [Abu Zubaydah] has no opportunity to practice any form of hygienic self care (he's filthy), the physical nature of this phase dictates multiple physical stresses (his reaction to today's activity is I believe the culprit for the superior edge separation), and nutrition is bare bones (six cans of ensure daily)." See email from: [REDACTED], to: and [REDACTED], subject: 15 Aug Clinical; date: August 15, 2002, at 06:54 AM.

650. 10647 (201331Z AUG 02); 10654 (211318Z AUG 02); 10679 (250932Z AUG 02).

651. Records indicate that Abu Zubaydah ultimately lost the eye. See 11026 (070729Z OCT 02).

652. 10679 (250932Z AUG 02); 11026 (070729Z OCT 02).

653. 44147 ; 36862 (181352Z APR 03).

654. 36908 ; 36862 (181352Z APR 03). To accommodate Abu Hazim's and Abd al-Karim's injuries, the cable stated that, rather than being shackled standing during sleep deprivation, the detainees would be "seated, secured to a cell wall, with intermittent disruptions of normal sleeping patterns." For water dousing, the detainees' injured legs would be "wrapped in plastic." The requests were approved. See DIRECTOR ; DIRECTOR .

655. With regard to Abu Hazim, on April 24, 2003, an additional CIA Headquarters approval cable was sent to DETENTION SITE COBALT authorizing interrogator to use the attention grasp, facial insult slap, abdominal slap, water dousing, and sleep deprivation up to 72 hours; the cable did not approve the use of walling or the facial hold. (See DIRECTOR) Despite the lack of approval, walling was used against Abu Hazim on April 28-29, 2003, and the facial hold was used on April 27, 2003. (See 37411 (291829Z APR 03); 37410 (291828Z APR 03); 37509 (021309Z MAY 03).) A May 10, 2003, CIA Headquarters cable approved walling and the facial grasp. (See DIRECTOR 03).) Abd al-Karim was also subjected to unapproved CIA enhanced interrogation techniques that the detention site initially indicated would not be used due to the detainee's injuries. Without approval from CIA Headquarters, CIA interrogators subjected Abd al-Karim to cramped confinement on April 19-20, 2003; stress positions on April 21, 2003; and walling on April 21, and 29, 2003. (See 37121 (221703Z APR 03); ; 37152 (231424Z APR 03); ; 37202 (250948Z APR 03); ; 37508 (021305Z MAY 03).) On May 10, 2003, CIA Headquarters approved an expanded list of CIA enhanced interrogation techniques that could be used against Abd al-Karim, including walling and stress positions. See DIRECTOR MAY 03).

656. DIRECTOR MAY 03).

657. 36862 (181352Z APR 03).

658. DIRECTOR .

659. 38262 (150541Z MAY 03); 38161 (131326Z MAY 03).

660. 38161 (131326Z MAY 03).

661. 38161 (131326Z MAY 03).

662. See DIRECTOR MAY 03) for Abu Hazim; and DIRECTOR MAY 03) for Abd al-Karim.

663. 39582 (041743Z JUN 03); 39656 (060955Z JUN 03);

664. 38365 (170652Z MAY 03).

665. Asadallah was also placed in a "small isolation box" for 30 minutes, without authorization and without discussion of how the technique would affect his ankle. (See 34098 ; 34294 34310 .) While CIA records contain information on other detainee medical complaints (see Volume III), those records also suggest that detainee medical complaints could be underreported in CIA medical records. For example, CIA medical records consistently report that CIA detainee Ramzi bin al-Shibh had no medical complaints. However, CIA interrogation records indicate that when bin al-Shibh had previously complained of ailments to CIA personnel, he was subjected to the CIA's enhanced interrogation techniques and told by CIA interrogators that his medical condition was not of concern to the CIA. (See 10591 (252002Z FEB 03); 10627 (281949Z FEB 03).) In testimony on April 12, 2007, CIA Director Michael Hayden referenced medical care of detainees in the context of the ICRC report on CIA detentions. Hayden testified to the Committee: "The medical section of the ICRC report concludes that the association of CIA medical officers with the interrogation program is 'contrary to international standards of medical ethics.' That is just wrong. The role of CIA medical officers in the detainee program is and always has been and always will be to ensure the safety and the well-being of the detainee. The placement of medical officers during the interrogation techniques represents an extra measure of caution. Our medical officers do not recommend the employment or continuation of any procedures or techniques. The allegation in the report that a CIA medical officer threatened a detainee, stating that medical care was conditional on cooperation is blatantly false. Health care has always been administered based upon detainee needs. It's neither policy nor practice to link medical care to any other aspect of the detainee program." This testimony was incongruent with CIA records.

666. For additional details, see Volume III.

667. 1759 (021319Z OCT 04); HEADQUARTERS (040023Z NOV 05); 1890 (171225Z NOV 04); 1878 (140915ZNOV 04); 1930 (061620Z DEC 04); 2207 (111319Z APR 05) 2210 (141507Z APR 05); 2535 (051805Z JUL 05); 2589 (120857Z JUL 05); 2830 (291304Z AUG 05); 1890 (171225Z NOV 04); 1893 (200831Z NOV 04); CIA document entitled, "Detainee Talking Points for ICRC Rebuttal, 12 April 2007"; 2210 (141507Z APR 05); 2535 (051805Z JUL 05); 2210 (141507Z APR 05); 2535 (051805Z JUL 05); 2830 (291304Z AUG 05); 1930 (061620Z DEC 04); 2210 (141507Z APR 05).

668. 2210 (141507Z APR 05); 2535 (051805Z JUL 05); 2830 (291304Z AUG 05).

669. 1691 (081609Z SEP 04); 1716 (180742Z SEP 04); 1998 (020752Z JAN 05); 2023 (151735Z JAN 05); 2515 (301946Z JUN 05); 1150 (282019Z NOV 03).

670. 1029 (291750Z JUN 06); 1142 (041358Z AUG 06); 1543 (111600Z AUG 04); 1716 (180742Z SEP 04); 3051 (301235Z SEP 05); 1029 (291750Z JUN 06).

671. See, for example, 2474 (251622Z JUN 05); 2673 (021451Z AUG 05); 1716 (180742Z SEP 04).

672. See, for example, 1356 (011644Z JUL 04); 1880 (140917Z NOV 04); 1959 (111700Z DEC 04); 1962 (121029Z DEC 04); 1959 (111700Z DEC 04); 2038 (211558Z JAN 05); 1091 (031835Z NOV 03); 1266 (052309Z JAN 04); 1630 (271440Z MAR 04).

673. 1203 (231709Z MAY 04); 1202 (231644Z MAY 04). CIA records indicate that at least five detainees were subjected to rectal rehydration or rectal feeding: Abu Zubaydah, Abd al-Rahim al-Nashiri, Khalid Shaykh Mohammad, Majid Khan, and Marwan al-Jabbur. See Volume III for additional details.

674. Email from: ; to: . [DETENTION SITE BLACK cc: ; subject: Interrogator Assessments/Request for Endgame Views; date: October 30, 2004.

675. HEADQUARTERS (282217Z JUL 05).

676. CIA Sametime exchange, dated 29/JUL/05 08:01:51–08:50:13; between and .

677. 3183 (161626Z SEP 04); 3184 (161628Z SEP 04); 3190 (181558Z SEP 04); 3196 (201731Z SEP 04); ; 3197 (201731Z SEP 04); ; 3206 (211819Z SEP 04); 3135 (120625Z SEP04); 3181 (161621Z SEP 04).

678. 3237 (230552Z SEP 04).

679. 3240 (231839Z SEP 04).

680. 3259 (261734Z SEP 04). The CIA's June 2013 Response states that "rectal rehydration" is a "well acknowledged medical technique to address pressing health issues." A follow-up CIA document provided on October 25, 2013 (DTS #2013-3152), states that "[f]rom a health perspective, Majid

Khan became uncooperative on 31 August 2004, when he initiated a hunger strike and before he underwent rectal rehydration ... CIA assesses that the use of rectal rehydration is a medically sound hydration technique ...." The assertion that Majid Khan was "uncooperative" prior to rectal rehydration and rectal feeding is inaccurate. As described in CIA records, prior to being subjected to rectal rehydration and rectal feeding, Majid Khan cooperated with the nasogastric feedings and was permitted to infuse the fluids and nutrients himself.

681. 3694 (301800Z NOV 04); 4242 (191550Z MAR 05); 4250 (221213Z MAR 05).
682. 3724 (031723Z DEC 04).
683. 3835 (260659Z DEC 04).
684. 4614 (071358Z JUN 05).
685. February 12, 2003, MFR from Scott Muller, Subject: "Humane" treatment of CIA detainees; March 7, 2003, Memorandum for DDCIA from Muller, Subject: Proposed Response to Human Rights Watch Letter.
686. January 9, 2003, Draft Memorandum for Scott Mueller [sic], General Counsel of the Central Intelligence Agency, from John C. Yoo, Deputy Assistant Attorney General, Office of Legal Counsel, re: Application of the President's February 7, 2002, Memorandum on the Geneva Convention (III) of 1949 to the Release of an al Qaeda Detainee to the Custody of the CIA. The memorandum stated that neither al-Qa'ida nor Taliban detainees qualified as prisoners of war under Geneva, and that Common Article 3 of Geneva, requiring humane treatment of individuals in a conflict, did not apply to al-Qa'ida or Taliban detainees
687. March 18, 2003, Memorandum for the Record from , Subject: meeting with DOJ and NSC Legal Adviser.
688. See, for example, March 18, 2003, email from: ; to: Scott Muller; subject: Memorandum for the Record - Telcon with OLC; date: March 13, 2003; email from: Scott W. Muller; to: Stanley M. Moskowitz, John H. Moseman; cc: , John A. Rizzo, ; subject: Interrogations; date: April 1, 2003, at 1:18:35 PM; email from: ; to: Scott Muller; cc: John Rizzo, [REDACTED], [REDACTED], [REDACTED]; subject: Black letter law on Interrogations; Legal Principles Applicable to CIA Detention and Interrogation of Captured Al-Qa'ida Personnel; date: April 17, 2003.
689. June 25, 2003, Letter from William J. Haynes, II, General Counsel of the Department of Defense to Patrick Leahy, United States Senate.
690. June 30, 2003, Memorandum for the Record from , Subject: White House Meeting on Enhanced Techniques (DTS #2009-2659).
691. See, for example, email from: to: [REDACTED] and [REDACTED]; subject: FYI - Draft Paragraphs for the DCI on the Legal Issues on Interrogation, as requested by the General Counsel; date: March 14, 2003; June 26, 2003, Statement by the President, United Nations International Day in Support of Victims of Torture, http://www.whitehouse.gov/news/releases/2003/06/20030626-3.htm; email from: John Rizzo; to: John Moseman, ; cc: Buzzy Krongard, Scott Muller, William Harlow; subject: Today's Washington Post Piece on Administration Detainee Policy; date: June 27, 2003; July 3, 2003, Memorandum for National Security Advisor from Director of Central Intelligence George J. Tenet, Subject: Reaffirmation of the Central Intelligence Agency's Interrogation Program.
692. Bin Attash has one leg, which swelled during standing sleep deprivation, resulting in the transition to seated sleep deprivation. He was also subjected to nudity and dietary manipulation during this period. See 12371 (212121Z JUL 03); 12385 (222045Z JUL 03); and 12389 (232040Z JUL 03).
693. HVT Training and Curriculum, November 2, 2002, at 17.
694. HVT Training and Curriculum, November 2, 2002, at 17.
695. See, for example, 10168 (092130Z JAN 03); Interview Report, 2003-7123-IG, Review of Interrogations for Counterterrorism Purposes, , April 7, 2003; CIA Office of Inspector General, Special Review: Counterterrorism Detention and Interrogation Activities (September 2001–October 2003) (2003- 7123-IG), May 7, 2004; 10168 (092130Z JAN 03); 34098 : 31479 (262200Z FEB 03); 34294 ; 34310 : 34757 (101742Z MAR 03); and 35025 (161321Z MAR 03).
696. April 7, 2005, Briefing for Blue Ribbon Panel: CIA Rendition, Detention, and Interrogation Programs at 22; Memorandum for Chief, , via CTC Legal from Chief, CTC/RDG, July 28, 2003, Subject: Decertification of former Interrogator. Document not signed by because he was not "available for signature."
697. *See* Memorandum for Chief, via CTC Legal from Chief, CTC/RDG, July 28, 2003, Subject: Decertification of former Interrogator, signed by [CIA OFFICER 1] on July 29, 2003; and April 7, 2005, Briefing for Blue Ribbon Panel: CIA Rendition, Detention, and Interrogation Programs at 22; Memorandum for Chief, , via CTC Legal from Chief, CTC/RDG, July 28, 2003, Subject: Decertification of former Interrogator.

698. CIA records indicate that KSM received at least 183 applications of the waterboard technique, and that Abu Zubaydah received at least 83 applications of the waterboard technique. In April 2003, CIA Inspector General John Helgerson asked General Counsel Scott Muller about the repetitious use of the waterboard. In early June 2003, White House Counsel Alberto Gonzales and the Vice President's Counsel, David Addington, who were aware of the inspector general's concerns, asked Muller whether the number of waterboard repetitions had been too high in light of the OLC guidance. This question prompted Muller to seek information on the use of the waterboard on Abu Zubaydah and KSM. (See interview of Scott Muller, by [REDACTED], [REDACTED], [REDACTED] and [REDACTED], Office of the Inspector General, August 20, 2003; and email from: Scott Muller; to: John Rizzo; cc: ██████████, ██████████, [REDACTED], ██████████, [REDACTED]; subject: "Report from Gitmo trip (Not proofread, as usual)"; date: June ██, 2003, 05:47 PM.) As Muller told the OIG, he could not keep up with cable traffic from CIA detainee interrogations and instead received monthly briefings. According to OIG records of the interview, Muller "said he does not know specifically how [CIA guidelines on interrogations] changed because he does not get that far down into the weeds," and "each detainee is different and those in the field have some latitude." (See interview of Scott Muller, Office of the Inspector General, August 20, 2003.) Despite this record and others detailed in the full Committee Study, the CIA's June 2013 Response asserts that the CIA's "confinement conditions and treatment of high profile detainees like Abu Zubaydah were closely scrutinized at all levels of management from the outset."

699. August 5, 2003 Memorandum for the Record from Scott Muller, Subject: Review of Interrogation Program on 29 July 2003; Briefing slides, CIA Interrogation Program, July 29, 2003.

700. August 5, 2003, Memorandum for the Record from Scott Muller, Subject: Review of the Interrogation Program on 29 July 2003. A briefing slide describing the "Pros" and "Cons" associated with the program listed the following under the heading "Con": (1) "Blowback due to public perception of 'humane treatment,'" (2) "ICRC continues to attack USG policy on detainees," and (3) "Congressional inquiries continue." See Volume II for additional details.

701. August 5, 2003, Memorandum for the Record from Scott Muller, Subject: Review of Interrogation Program, July 29, 2003.

702. Email from: John Rizzo; to: ██████████ subject: Rump PC on interrogations; date: July 31, 2003.

703. August 5, 2003, Memorandum for the Record from Scott Muller, Subject: Review of Interrogation Program, July 29, 2003.

704. September 26, 2003, CIA Memorandum for the Record from Muller, Subject: CIA Interrogation Program.

705. September 4, 2003, CIA Memorandum for the Record, Subject: Member Briefing.

706. January 6, 2004, Letter from ██████████ ██████████ ██████████.

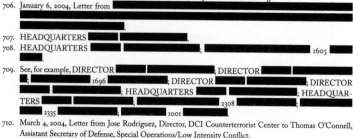

707. HEADQUARTERS ██████ ██████████.

708. HEADQUARTERS ██████ ██████████; ██████████ 1603 ██████ ██████.

709. See, for example, DIRECTOR ██████ ██████████; DIRECTOR ██████ ██████████ ██; ██████████ 1696 ██████████; DIRECTOR ██████ ██████████; DIRECTOR ██████ ██████████; HEADQUARTERS ██████ ██████████; HEADQUARTERS ██████ ██████████; ██████████ 2308 ██████████; ██████████ ██████ 2335 ██████████; ██████████ 1001 ██████████.

710. March 4, 2004, Letter from Jose Rodriguez, Director, DCI Counterterrorist Center to Thomas O'Connell, Assistant Secretary of Defense, Special Operations/Low Intensity Conflict.

711. See ██████ 180219 ██████████.

712. ██████████ 2296 (101709Z ██████ 04).

713. ██████████ 2296 (101709Z ██████ 04).

714. Details in June 13, 2005, Letter to ICRC, responding to 2004 ICRC *note verbale*.

715. ██████████ 2348 ██████████.

716. HEADQUARTERS ██████ ██████████. During this same period, countries whose nationals were in CIA custody were issuing demarches. ██████████ issued a demarche to Country ██ in ██████ 2004, and ██████ issued a demarche to the U.S. in ██████ 2004. See ██████████ 2274 ██████ ██████; ██████ 92037, and 93291 ██████████.

717. For more information, see Volume I.

718. Email from: [REDACTED]; to: John Rizzo, [REDACTED]; cc: [REDACTED], ██████████, [REDACTED], [REDACTED], [REDACTED], [REDACTED], ██████████, Jose Rodriguez, John P. Mudd, [REDACTED], [REDACTED], [REDACTED]; subject: DoD's position on ICRC notification; date: September 13, 2004.

719. June 13, 2005, Letter to ICRC, responding to 2004 ICRC *note verbale*.

720. Special Review, Counterterrorism Detention and Interrogation Activities (September 2001–October 2003) (2003-7123-IG), 7 May 2004, (DTS #2004-2710).

721. The chief of Station in the country that hosted the CIA's first detention site told the OIG that "[t]he Reports Officers did not know what was required of them, analysts were not knowledgeable of the target, translators were not native Arab speakers, and at least one of the [chiefs of Base] had limited field experience." See Interview report of [REDACTED], Office of the Inspector General, May 20, 2003. According to of CTC Legal, there was no screening procedure in place for officers assigned to DETENTION SITE GREEN. See interview of , by [REDACTED] and [REDACTED], Office of the Inspector General, February 14, 2003. *See also* interview of , Office of the Inspector General, March 24, 2003.

722. In addition to the statements to the OIG described above, regarding the interrogation of Abu Zubaydah, CIA officers expressed more general concerns. As noted, the assumptions at CIA Headquarters that Abu Zubaydah "knew everything about Al-Qa'ida, including details of the next attack" reflected how "the 'Analyst vs. Interrogator' issue ha[d] been around from 'day one.'" (See interview of Office of the Inspector General, February 27, 2003.) According to Chief of Interrogations , subject matter experts often provided interrogation requirements that were "not valid or well thought out," providing the example of Mustafa al-Hawsawi. (See interview of , Office of the Inspector General, April 7, 2003.) Senior CIA interrogator told the OIG that interrogators "suffered from a lack of substantive requirements from CIA Headquarters," and that "in every case so far, Headquarters' model of what the detainee should know is flawed." told the OIG that "I do not want to beat a man up based on what Headquarters says he should know," commenting that, "I want my best shot on something he (the detainee) knows, not a fishing expedition on things he should know." (See interview of , Office of the Inspector General, April 30, 2003.) Two interviewees told the OIG that requirements were sometimes based on inaccurate or improperly translated intercepts. See interview of interrogator , Office of the Inspector General, March 24, 2003; Interview of [former chief of Station in the country that hosted the CIA's first detention site], Office of the Inspector General, May 29, 2003.

723. One interviewee noted that several interrogators with whom he had worked insisted on conducting interrogations in English to demonstrate their dominance over the detainee. (See interview report of , Office of the Inspector General, March 17, 2003.) The CIA's June 2013 Response acknowledges that "[t]he program continued to face challenges in identifying sufficient, qualified staff -- particularly language-qualified personnel -- as requirements imposed by Agency involvement in Iraq increased."

724. According to of CTC Legal, "[t]he seventh floor [CIA leadership] can complicate the process because of the mindset that interrogations are the silver bullet [and CIA leadership is] expecting immediate results." (See interview of , Office of the Inspector General, February 14, 2003.) Senior Interrogator provided the example of Khallad bin Attash, who, he told the OIG, was determined by the chief of Base at DETENTION SITE BLUE not to "warrant" the CIA's enhanced interrogation techniques. According to , debriefer called ALEC Station and told them to "go to the mat" in advocating for the use of the CIA's enhanced interrogation techniques, claiming that bin Attash was holding back information. (See interview of , Office of the Inspector General, April 30, 2003.) described the "inherent tension that occasionally exists between officers at the interrogation facilities and those at Headquarters who view the detainees are withholding information." provided the example of Abu Yassir al-Jaza'iri. (See interview of , Office of the Inspector General, May 8, 2003.) also described disagreements on whether to subject detainees to the CIA's enhanced interrogation techniques as a "field versus Headquarters issue." (See interview of , Office of the Inspector General, August 18, 2003.) As described, interviewees also described pressure from CIA Headquarters related to the interrogations of KSM and Abu Zubaydah.

725. Interview of , Office of the Inspector General, February 21, 2003.

726. Interview of , Office of the Inspector General, April 30, 2003.

727. DDO Pavitt described possible public revelations related to the CIA's Detention and Interrogation Program as "the CIA's worst nightmare." Interview of James Pavitt, Office of the Inspector General, September 21, 2003. According to OIG records of an interview with DCI Tenet, "Tenet believes that if the general public were to find out about this program, many would believe we are torturers." Tenet added, however, that his "only potential moral dilemma would be if more Americans die at the hands of terrorists and we had someone in our custody who possessed information that could have prevented deaths, but we had not obtained such information." See interview of George Tenet, Office of the Inspector General, memorandum dated, September 8, 2003.

728. See CIA Memorandum from Scott W. Muller, General Counsel, to Inspector General re Interrogation Program Special Review, dated February 24, 2004 (2003-7123-IG).

729. Memorandum to the Inspector General from James Pavitt, CIA's Deputy Director for Operations, dated February 27, 2004, with the subject line, "Comments to Draft IG Special Review, 'Counterterrorism Detention and Interrogation Program' (2003-7123-IG)," Attachment, "Successes of CIA's Counterterrorism Detention and Interrogation Activities," dated February 24, 2004.

730. For additional information, see Volume II.

731. July 21, 2005, Memorandum for Inspector General from Porter J. Goss, Director, Central Intelligence Agency

re: New IG Work Impacting the CounterTerrorism Center.

732. Transcript of business meeting, April 14, 2005 (DTS #2005-2810).

733. Committee Memorandum for the Record, "Staff Briefing with Bob Deitz on his Inquiry into the Investigative Practices of the CIA Inspector General," October 17, 2007 (DTS #2007-4166); Committee Memorandum for the Record, "Notes from Meetings with John Helgerson and Bob Deitz in late 2007 and early 2008" (DTS #2012-4203); Committee Memorandum for the Record, "Staff Briefing with CIA Inspector General John Helgerson" (DTS #2007- 4165).

734. Letter from DCIA Michael Hayden to Senator John D. Rockefeller IV, January 29, 2008 (DTS#2008-0606).

735. May 12, 2004, Memorandum for Deputy Director for Operations from [REDACTED], Chief, Information Operations Center, and Henry Crumpton, Chief, National Resources Division, via Associate Deputy Director for Operations, with the subject line, "Operational Review of CIA Detainee Program."

736. May 12, 2004, Memorandum for Deputy Director for Operations from [REDACTED], Chief, Information Operations Center, and Henry Crumpton, Chief, National Resources Division, via Associate Deputy Director for Operations, with the subject line, "Operational Review of CIA Detainee Program." The CIA's June 2013 Response states, "[w]e acknowledge that the Agency erred in permitting the contractors to assess the effectiveness of enhanced techniques. They should not have been considered for such a role given their financial interest in continued contracts from CIA."

737. May 12, 2004, Memorandum for Deputy Director for Operations from [REDACTED], Chief, Information Operations Center, and Henry Crumpton, Chief, National Resources Division, via Associate Deputy Director for Operations re Operational Review of CIA Detainee Program. For additional information, see Volume II.

738. May 12, 2004, Memorandum for Deputy Director for Operations from [REDACTED], Chief, Information Operations Center, and Henry Crumpton, Chief, National Resources Division, via Associate Deputy Director for Operations re Operational Review of CIA Detainee Program.

739. May 12, 2004 Memorandum for Deputy Director for Operations from [REDACTED], Chief, Information Operations Center, and Henry Crumpton, Chief, National Resources Division, via Associate Deputy Director for Operations re Operational Review of CIA Detainee Program.

740. See Volume I for additional information.

741. Email from: John Helgerson; to: Porter Goss, [REDACTED]; cc: Jose Rodriguez, John Rizzo, [REDACTED], [REDACTED]; subject: DCI Question Regarding OIG Report; date: January 28, 2005.

742. Email from: John Helgerson; to: Porter Goss, [REDACTED]; cc: Jose Rodriguez, John Rizzo, [REDACTED], [REDACTED]; subject: DCI Question Regarding OIG Report; January 28, 2005.

743. Email from: John Helgerson; to: Porter Goss, [REDACTED]; cc: Jose Rodriguez, John Rizzo, [REDACTED], [REDACTED]; subject: DCI Question Regarding OIG Report; date: January 28, 2005. The CIA's June 2013 Response maintains that "[a] systematic study over time of the effectiveness of the techniques would have been encumbered by a number of factors," including "Federal policy on the protection of human subjects and the impracticability of establishing an effective control group."

744. December 2004 CIA Memorandum to "National Security Advisor," from "Director of Central Intelligence," Subject: "Effectiveness of the CIA Counterterrorist Interrogation Techniques."

745. December 2004 CIA Memorandum to "National Security Advisor," from "Director of Central Intelligence," Subject: "Effectiveness of the CIA Counterterrorist Interrogation Techniques." Italics in original.

746. March 5, 2005, Talking Points for Weekly Meeting with National Security Advisor re CIA Proposal for Independent Study of the Effectiveness of CTC Interrogation Program's Enhanced Interrogation Techniques.

747. March 21, 2005, Memorandum for Deputy Director for Operations from Robert L. Grenier, Director DCI Counterterrorism Center, re: Proposal for Full-Scope Independent Study of the CTC Rendition, Detention, and Interrogation Programs.

748. September 2, 2005 Memorandum from [REDACTED] to Director Porter Goss, CIA re: Assessment of EITs Effectiveness. For additional information, see Volume II.

749. September 23, 2005 Memorandum from [REDACTED] to the Honorable Porter Goss, Director, Central Intelligence Agency re: Response to Request from Director for Assessment of EIT Effectiveness. For additional information, see Volume II.

750. For additional information, see Volume III.

751. [REDACTED] 1658 [REDACTED] JAN 04); ALEC [REDACTED] [REDACTED] JAN 04).

752. [REDACTED] 54305 [REDACTED].

753. [REDACTED] 54301 [REDACTED].

754. [REDACTED] [REDACTED] 1871 [REDACTED]; HEADQUARTERS [REDACTED] (022341Z APR 04).

755. CIA Office of Inspector General, Report of Investigation, The Rendition and Detention of German Citizen Khalid al-Masri (2004-7601-IG), July 16, 2007.

756. CIA Office of Inspector General, Report of Investigation, The Rendition and Detention of German Citizen Khalid al-Masri (2004-7601-IG), July 16, 2007.

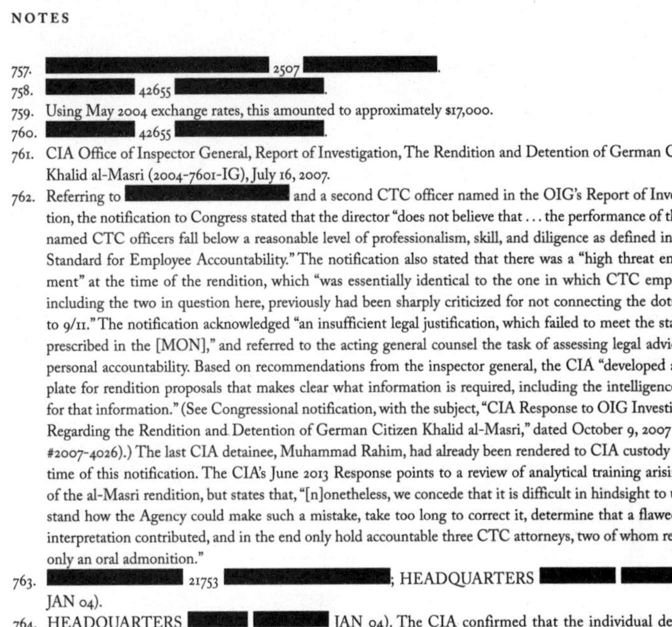

757. 2507 .
758. 42655 .
759. Using May 2004 exchange rates, this amounted to approximately $17,000.
760. 42655 .
761. CIA Office of Inspector General, Report of Investigation, The Rendition and Detention of German Citizen Khalid al-Masri (2004-7601-IG), July 16, 2007.
762. Referring to and a second CTC officer named in the OIG's Report of Investigation, the notification to Congress stated that the director "does not believe that . . . the performance of the two named CTC officers fall below a reasonable level of professionalism, skill, and diligence as defined in CIA's Standard for Employee Accountability." The notification also stated that there was a "high threat environment" at the time of the rendition, which "was essentially identical to the one in which CTC employees, including the two in question here, previously had been sharply criticized for not connecting the dots prior to 9/11." The notification acknowledged "an insufficient legal justification, which failed to meet the standard prescribed in the [MON]," and referred to the acting general counsel the task of assessing legal advice and personal accountability. Based on recommendations from the inspector general, the CIA "developed a template for rendition proposals that makes clear what information is required, including the intelligence basis for that information." (See Congressional notification, with the subject, "CIA Response to OIG Investigation Regarding the Rendition and Detention of German Citizen Khalid al-Masri," dated October 9, 2007 (DTS #2007-4026).) The last CIA detainee, Muhammad Rahim, had already been rendered to CIA custody by the time of this notification. The CIA's June 2013 Response points to a review of analytical training arising out of the al-Masri rendition, but states that, "[n]onetheless, we concede that it is difficult in hindsight to understand how the Agency could make such a mistake, take too long to correct it, determine that a flawed legal interpretation contributed, and in the end only hold accountable three CTC attorneys, two of whom received only an oral admonition."

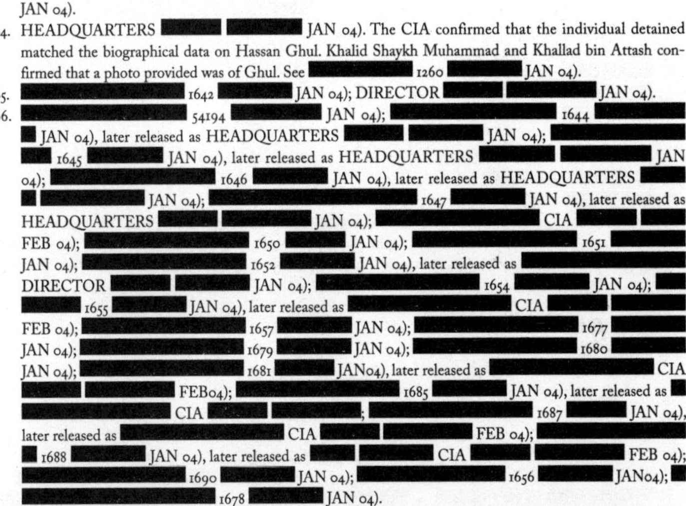

763. 21753 ; HEADQUARTERS JAN 04).
764. HEADQUARTERS JAN 04). The CIA confirmed that the individual detained matched the biographical data on Hassan Ghul. Khalid Shaykh Muhammad and Khallad bin Attash confirmed that a photo provided was of Ghul. See 1260 JAN 04).
765. 1642 JAN 04); DIRECTOR JAN 04).
766. 54194 JAN 04); 1644 JAN 04), later released as HEADQUARTERS JAN 04); 1645 JAN 04), later released as HEADQUARTERS JAN 04); 1646 JAN 04), later released as HEADQUARTERS JAN 04); 1647 JAN 04), later released as HEADQUARTERS JAN 04); CIA FEB 04); 1650 JAN 04); 1651 JAN 04); 1652 JAN 04), later released as DIRECTOR JAN 04); 1654 JAN 04); 1655 JAN 04), later released as CIA FEB 04); 1657 JAN 04); 1677 JAN 04); 1679 JAN 04); 1680 JAN 04); 1681 JAN04), later released as CIA FEB04); 1685 JAN 04), later released as CIA ; 1687 JAN 04), later released as CIA FEB 04); 1688 JAN 04), later released as CIA FEB 04); 1690 JAN 04); 1656 JAN04); 1678 JAN 04).
767. As the dissemination of 21 intelligence reports suggests, information in CIA records indicates Hassan Ghul was cooperative prior to being subjected to the CIA's enhanced interrogation techniques. In an interview with the CIA Office of Inspector General, a CIA officer familiar with Ghul's initial interrogations stated, "He sang like a tweetie bird. He opened up right away and was cooperative from the outset." (See December 2, 2004, interview with [REDACTED], Chief, DO, CTC UBL Department, .) CIA records reveal that Ghul's information on Abu Ahmad al-Kuwaiti was disseminated while Ghul was at DETENTION SITE COBALT, prior to the initiation of the CIA's enhanced interrogation techniques. On April 16, 2013, the Council on Foreign Relations hosted a forum in relation to the screening of the film, "Manhunt." The forum included former CIA officer Nada Bakos, who states in the film that Hassan Ghul provided the critical information on Abu Ahmad al-Kuwaiti to Kurdish officials prior to entering CIA custody. When asked about the interrogation techniques used by the Kurds, Bakos stated: ". . . honestly, Hassan Ghul . . . when he was being debriefed by the Kurdish government, he literally was sitting there having tea. He was in a safe house. He wasn't locked up in a cell. He wasn't handcuffed to anything. He was—he was having a free flowing

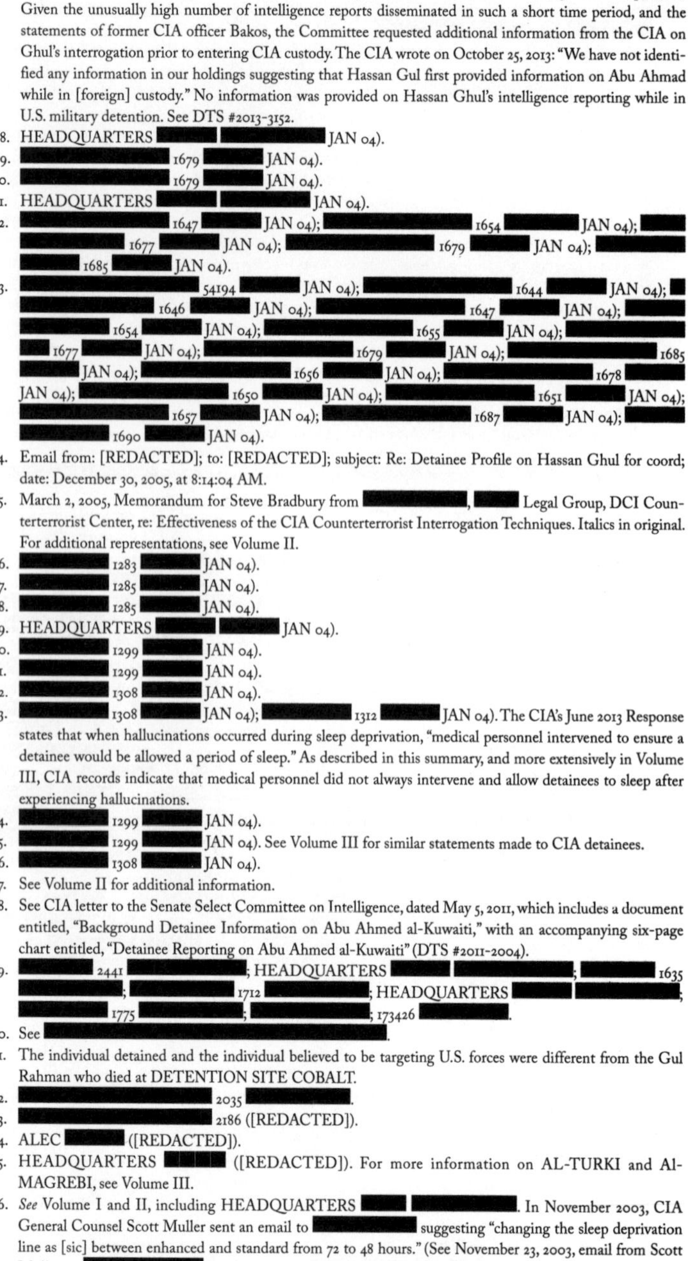

conversation. And there's—you know, there's articles in Kurdish papers about sort of their interpretation of the story and how forthcoming he was." (See www.cfr.org/counterterrorism/film-screening-manhunt/p30560.) Given the unusually high number of intelligence reports disseminated in such a short time period, and the statements of former CIA officer Bakos, the Committee requested additional information from the CIA on Ghul's interrogation prior to entering CIA custody. The CIA wrote on October 25, 2013: "We have not identified any information in our holdings suggesting that Hassan Gul first provided information on Abu Ahmad while in [foreign] custody." No information was provided on Hassan Ghul's intelligence reporting while in U.S. military detention. See DTS #2013-3152.

768. HEADQUARTERS JAN 04).
769. 1679 JAN 04).
770. 1679 JAN 04).
771. HEADQUARTERS JAN 04).
772. 1647 JAN 04); 1654 JAN 04); 1677 JAN 04); 1679 JAN 04); 1685 JAN 04).
773. 54194 JAN 04); 1644 JAN 04); 1646 JAN 04); 1647 JAN 04); 1654 JAN 04); 1655 JAN 04); 1677 JAN 04); 1679 JAN 04); 1685 JAN 04); 1656 JAN 04); 1678 JAN 04); 1650 JAN 04); 1651 JAN 04); 1657 JAN 04); 1687 JAN 04); 1690 JAN 04).
774. Email from: [REDACTED]; to: [REDACTED]; subject: Re: Detainee Profile on Hassan Ghul for coord; date: December 30, 2005, at 8:14:04 AM.
775. March 2, 2005, Memorandum for Steve Bradbury from , Legal Group, DCI Counterterrorist Center, re: Effectiveness of the CIA Counterterrorist Interrogation Techniques. Italics in original. For additional representations, see Volume II.
776. 1283 JAN 04).
777. 1285 JAN 04).
778. 1285 JAN 04).
779. HEADQUARTERS JAN 04).
780. 1299 JAN 04).
781. 1299 JAN 04).
782. 1308 JAN 04).
783. 1308 JAN 04); 1312 JAN 04). The CIA's June 2013 Response states that when hallucinations occurred during sleep deprivation, "medical personnel intervened to ensure a detainee would be allowed a period of sleep." As described in this summary, and more extensively in Volume III, CIA records indicate that medical personnel did not always intervene and allow detainees to sleep after experiencing hallucinations.
784. 1299 JAN 04).
785. 1299 JAN 04). See Volume III for similar statements made to CIA detainees.
786. 1308 JAN 04).
787. See Volume II for additional information.
788. See CIA letter to the Senate Select Committee on Intelligence, dated May 5, 2011, which includes a document entitled, "Background Detainee Information on Abu Ahmed al-Kuwaiti," with an accompanying six-page chart entitled, "Detainee Reporting on Abu Ahmed al-Kuwaiti" (DTS #2011-2004).
789. 2441 ; HEADQUARTERS ; 1635 ; 1712 ; HEADQUARTERS ; 1775 ; ; 173426 .
790. See .
791. The individual detained and the individual believed to be targeting U.S. forces were different from the Gul Rahman who died at DETENTION SITE COBALT.
792. 2035 .
793. 2186 ([REDACTED]).
794. ALEC ([REDACTED]).
795. HEADQUARTERS ([REDACTED]). For more information on AL-TURKI and Al-MAGREBI, see Volume III.
796. *See* Volume I and II, including HEADQUARTERS . In November 2003, CIA General Counsel Scott Muller sent an email to suggesting "changing the sleep deprivation line as [sic] between enhanced and standard from 72 to 48 hours." (See November 23, 2003, email from Scott Muller to , cc: John Rizzo, Subject: Al-Hawsawi Incident.) On January 10, 2004, CIA

Headquarters informed CIA detention sites of the change, stating that sleep deprivation over 48 hours would now be considered an "enhanced" interrogation technique. See HEADQUARTERS [REDACTED] (101713Z JAN 04).

797. [REDACTED] 1888 (091823Z MAR 04); [REDACTED] 1889 (091836Z MAR 04). There is no indication in CIA records that CIA Headquarters addressed the repeated use of "standard" sleep deprivation against Adnan al-Libi. For more information, see Volume III detainee report for Adnan al-Libi.

798. Transcript of Senate Select Committee on Intelligence hearing, May 12, 2004 (DTS #2004-2332).

799. Transcript of Senate Select Committee on Intelligence hearing, May 12, 2004 (DTS #2004-2332).

800. May 25, 2004, Talking Points for DCI Telephone Conversation with Attorney General: DOJ's Legal Opinion re CIA's Counterterrorist Program (CT) Interrogation. Letter from Assistant Attorney General Jack L. Goldsmith III to Director Tenet, June 18, 2004 (DTS #2004-2710).

801. May 27, 2004, letter from Assistant Attorney General Goldsmith to General Counsel Muller.

802. May 24, 2003, Memorandum for the Record from [REDACTED], subject: Memorandum of Meeting with the DCI Regarding DOJ's Statement that DOJ has Rendered No Legal Opinion on Whether CIA's Use of Enhanced Interrogation Techniques would meet Constitutional Standards. Memorandum for Deputy Director for Operations from Director of Central Intelligence, June 4. 2004, re: Suspension of Use of Interrogation Techniques.

803. June 4, 2004, Memorandum for Deputy Director for Operations from Director of Central Intelligence, re: Suspension of Use of Interrogation Techniques. On June 2, 2004, George Tenet informed the President that he intended to resign from his position on July 11, 2004. The White House announced the resignation on June 3, 2004.

804. June 4, 2004, Memorandum for the National Security Advisor from DCI George Tenet, re: Review of CIA Interrogation Program.

805. June 2004, Memorandum for the Honorable George J. Tenet, Director of Central Intelligence from Condoleezza Rice, Assistant to the President for National Security Affairs, re: Review of CIA's Interrogation Program.

806. [REDACTED] 39254 [REDACTED]; ALEC [REDACTED] [REDACTED]; [REDACTED] 3121 [REDACTED] [REDACTED]; [REDACTED] 3121 [REDACTED].

807. The former chief of the CIA's Bin Ladin Unit wrote in a March [REDACTED], 2004, email that the reporting was "vague" and "worthless in terms of actionable intelligence." He suggested that the reporting "would be an easy way [for al-Qa'ida] to test" the loyalty of the source, given al-Qa'ida's knowledge that leaked threat reporting "causes panic in Washington." (See email from: [REDACTED]; to: [REDACTED], [REDACTED], [REDACTED], [REDACTED], [REDACTED]; subject: could AQ be testing [ASSET Y] and [source name REDACTED]?; date: March [REDACTED], 2004, at 06:55 AM.) ALEC Station officer [REDACTED] expressed similar doubts in response to the email. See email from: [REDACTED]; to: [REDACTED]; cc: [REDACTED], [REDACTED] [REDACTED], [REDACTED], [REDACTED] subject: Re: could AQ be testing [ASSET Y] and [source name REDACTED]?; date: March [REDACTED], 2004, at 07:52:32 AM). *See also* [REDACTED] 1411 ([REDACTED] 04).

808. July 2, 2004, CIA Memorandum re Meeting with National Adviser Rice in the White House Situation Room, re: Interrogations and Detainee Janat Gul, July 2, 2004.

809. At the time of this CIA representation, the CIA had held at least 109 detainees and subjected at least 33 of them (30 percent) to the CIA's enhanced interrogation techniques.

810. July 6, 2004, Memorandum from Condoleezza Rice, Assistant to the President for National Security Affairs, to the Honorable George Tenet, Director of Central Intelligence, re Janat Gul. CIA Request for Guidance Regarding Interrogation of Janat Gul, July 2, 2004.

811. For additional details, see Volume III.

812. July 6, 2004, Memorandum from Condoleezza Rice, Assistant to the President for National Security Affairs, to the Honorable George Tenet, Director of Central Intelligence, re Janat Gul.

813. July 29, 2004, Memorandum for the Record from CIA General Counsel Scott Muller, "Principals Meeting relating to Janat Gul on 20 July 2004."

814. The one-paragraph letter did not provide legal analysis or substantive discussion of the interrogation techniques. Letter from Attorney General Ashcroft to Acting DCI McLaughlin, July 22, 2004 (DTS #2009-1810, Tab 4).

815. See Volume III for additional details.

816. [REDACTED] 1512 [REDACTED] 04); [REDACTED] 1519 [REDACTED] 04); [REDACTED] 1521 [REDACTED] [REDACTED] 04); [REDACTED] 1530 [REDACTED] 04); [REDACTED] 1537 [REDACTED] 04); [REDACTED] 1541 [REDACTED] 04); [REDACTED] 1542 [REDACTED] 04).

817. [REDACTED] 1541 [REDACTED] 04).

818. [REDACTED] 1541 [REDACTED] 04).

819. [REDACTED] 1567 [REDACTED] 04).

820. [REDACTED] 1574 [REDACTED] 04).

821. HEADQUARTERS [REDACTED] [REDACTED] 04).

822. 1603 04).
823. 1603 04).
824. 1622 04).
825. 1622 04).
826. 1622 04).
827. 1411 04). See Volume III for additional information.
828. 3398 ; 5492 .
829. Memorandum for John A. Rizzo, Senior Deputy General Counsel, Central Intelligence Agency, from Steven G. Bradbury, Principal Deputy Assistant Attorney General, Office of Legal Counsel, May 30, 2005, Re: Application of United States Obligations Under Article 16 of the Convention Against Torture to Certain Techniques that May Be Used in the Interrogation of High Value al Qaeda Detainees, at 11. See section of this summary and Volume II entitled, "The Assertion that CIA Detainees Subjected to Enhanced Interrogation Techniques Help Validate CIA Sources."
830. Letter from , Assistant General Counsel, to Dan Levin, Acting Assistant Attorney General, , 2004.
831. WASHINGTON 04); 19045 MAR 04). See HEADQUARTERS 04); 4267 04).
832. See, for example, ; ; ; ; and 24611 .
833. 3191 ; 3192 .
834. 3194 ; HEADQUARTERS .
835. 3289 . For more information, see Volume III, detainee report for Sharif al-Masri.
836. HEADQUARTERS ; 3802 .
837. *See* letter from , Associate General Counsel, CIA, to Dan Levin, Acting Assistant Attorney General, August 25, 2004 (DTS #2009-1809). Note: At various times during this period is identified as both CIA associate general counsel and CTC Legal). *See also* a letter from , Assistant General Counsel, to Dan Levin, Acting Assistant Attorney General, September 5, 2004 (DTS #2009-1809). A CIA email sent prior to the CIA's request for advice from the OLC indicated that the judgment that Ghailani had knowledge of terrorist plotting was speculative: "Although Ghailani's role in operational planning is unclear, his respected role in al-Qa'ida and presence in Shkai as recently as October 2003 may have provided him some knowledge about ongoing attack planning against the United States homeland, and the operatives involved." (*See* email from: , CTC/UBLD (formerly ALEC ; to: [REDACTED], [REDACTED], [REDACTED], [REDACTED]; subject: derog information for ODDO on Talha, Ghailani, Hamza Rabi'a and Abu Faraj; date: August 10, 2004.) Ghailani was rendered to CIA custody on September 2004. (See 3072 .) The CIA began using its enhanced interrogation techniques on Ghailani on September 17, 2004, as the CIA was initiating its counterintelligence review of the source who provided the false reporting on the pre-election threat. See 3189 (181558Z SEP 04); HEADQUARTERS 04); 4267 04).
838. [REDACTED] 3221 .
839. [REDACTED] 22343 .
840. HEADQUARTERS .
841. HEADQUARTERS .
842. While CIA Headquarters offered $ million to Country for hosting a CIA detention facility, precluded the opening of the facility. Only $ million was made available to the CIA Station for support to the although CIA Headquarters asked the CIA Station to "advise if additional funds may be needed to keep [the facility] viable over the coming year and beyond." CIA Headquarters added, "we cannot have enough blacksite hosts, and we are loathe to let one we have slip away." Country never hosted CIA detainees. See HEADQUAR ; [REDACTED] 5298 ; HEADQUAR .
843. ALEC 03). In an interview on the CIA program, noted that the program had "more money than we could possibly spend we thought, and it turned out to be accurate." In the same interview, he stated that "in one case, we gave $,000,000 . Myself and José [Rodriguez] . We never counted it. I'm not about to count that kind of money for a receipt." The boxes contained one hundred dollar bills. did not identify the recipient of the $ million. See transcript of Oral History Interview, Interviewee: (RJ) – October 13, 2006, Interviewer: [REDACTED] and [REDACTED].
844. ALEC 03).
845. ALEC .

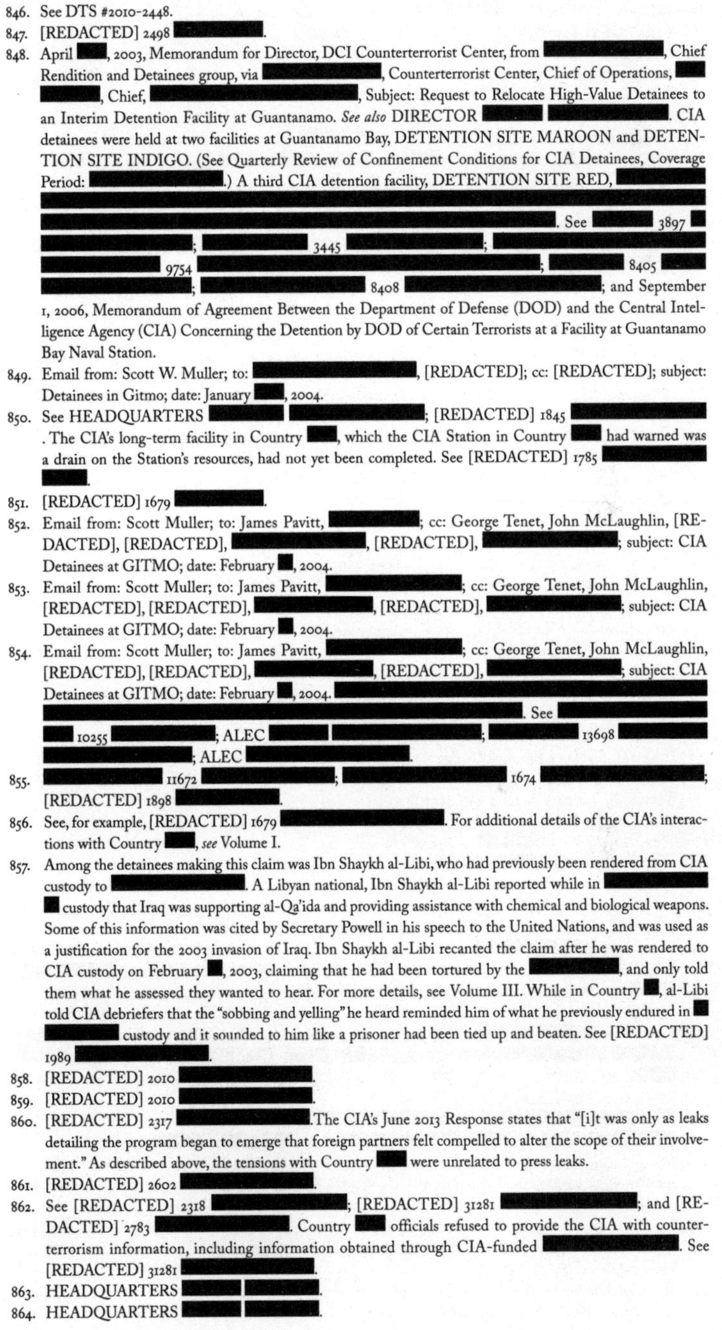

846. See DTS #2010-2448.
847. [REDACTED] 2498 .
848. April , 2003, Memorandum for Director, DCI Counterterrorist Center, from , Chief Rendition and Detainees group, via , Counterterrorist Center, Chief of Operations, , Chief, , Subject: Request to Relocate High-Value Detainees to an Interim Detention Facility at Guantanamo. *See also* DIRECTOR . CIA detainees were held at two facilities at Guantanamo Bay, DETENTION SITE MAROON and DETENTION SITE INDIGO. (See Quarterly Review of Confinement Conditions for CIA Detainees, Coverage Period: .) A third CIA detention facility, DETENTION SITE RED, . See 3897 ; 3445 ; 9754 ; 8405 ; 8408 ; and September 1, 2006, Memorandum of Agreement Between the Department of Defense (DOD) and the Central Intelligence Agency (CIA) Concerning the Detention by DOD of Certain Terrorists at a Facility at Guantanamo Bay Naval Station.
849. Email from: Scott W. Muller; to: , [REDACTED]; cc: [REDACTED]; subject: Detainees in Gitmo; date: January , 2004.
850. See HEADQUARTERS ; [REDACTED] 1845 . The CIA's long-term facility in Country , which the CIA Station in Country had warned was a drain on the Station's resources, had not yet been completed. See [REDACTED] 1785 .
851. [REDACTED] 1679 .
852. Email from: Scott Muller; to: James Pavitt, ; cc: George Tenet, John McLaughlin, [REDACTED], [REDACTED], , [REDACTED], ; subject: CIA Detainees at GITMO; date: February , 2004.
853. Email from: Scott Muller; to: James Pavitt, ; cc: George Tenet, John McLaughlin, [REDACTED], [REDACTED], , [REDACTED], ; subject: CIA Detainees at GITMO; date: February , 2004.
854. Email from: Scott Muller; to: James Pavitt, ; cc: George Tenet, John McLaughlin, [REDACTED], [REDACTED], , [REDACTED], ; subject: CIA Detainees at GITMO; date: February , 2004. . See 10255 ; ALEC ; 13698 ; ALEC .
855. 11672 ; 1674 ; [REDACTED] 1898 .
856. See, for example, [REDACTED] 1679 . For additional details of the CIA's interactions with Country , *see* Volume I.
857. Among the detainees making this claim was Ibn Shaykh al-Libi, who had previously been rendered from CIA custody to . A Libyan national, Ibn Shaykh al-Libi reported while in custody that Iraq was supporting al-Qa'ida and providing assistance with chemical and biological weapons. Some of this information was cited by Secretary Powell in his speech to the United Nations, and was used as a justification for the 2003 invasion of Iraq. Ibn Shaykh al-Libi recanted the claim after he was rendered to CIA custody on February , 2003, claiming that he had been tortured by the , and only told them what he assessed they wanted to hear. For more details, see Volume III. While in Country , al-Libi told CIA debriefers that the "sobbing and yelling" he heard reminded him of what he previously endured in custody and it sounded to him like a prisoner had been tied up and beaten. See [REDACTED] 1989 .
858. [REDACTED] 2010 .
859. [REDACTED] 2010 .
860. [REDACTED] 2317 . The CIA's June 2013 Response states that "[i]t was only as leaks detailing the program began to emerge that foreign partners felt compelled to alter the scope of their involvement." As described above, the tensions with Country were unrelated to press leaks.
861. [REDACTED] 2602 .
862. See [REDACTED] 2318 ; [REDACTED] 31281 ; and [REDACTED] 2783 . Country officials refused to provide the CIA with counterterrorism information, including information obtained through CIA-funded . See [REDACTED] 31281 .
863. HEADQUARTERS .
864. HEADQUARTERS .

865. [REDACTED] and CTC ████ RDG, "Evolution of the Program."
866. [REDACTED] 3706 ([REDACTED] [REDACTED]).
867. CIA PowerPoint Presentation, CIA Detainees: Endgame Options and Plans, dated August 19, 2004.
868. September 17, 2004, DRAFT Talking Points for the ADCI: Endgame Options and Plans for CIA Detainees.
869. The CIA took custody of Abu Faraj al-Libi, Abu Munthir al-Magrebi, Ibrahim Jan, and Abu Ja'far al-Iraqi in 2005, and Abd al-Hadi al-Iraqi in 2006.
870. The first detainees arrived in Country ██ in ██████ 2003. CIA detainees were held within an existing Country ██ facility in Country ██ from ███ to ██████ 2003, and then again beginning in ████ 2004. For additional information, see Volume I.
871. Email from: [REDACTED] (COB DETENTION SITE BLACK); to: ██████, ██████ █, █████; subject: General Comments; date: April 15, 2005.
872. Email from: [REDACTED] (COB DETENTION SITE BLACK); to: ██████, ██████ █, █████; subject: General Comments; date: April 15, 2005.
873. Report of Audit, CIA-controlled Detention Facilities Operated Under the 17 September 2001 Memorandum of Notification, Report No. 2005-0017-AS, June 14, 2006, at DTS # 2006-2793. As further described in the Committee Study, the Inspector General audit described how the CIA's detention facilities were not equipped to provide detainees with medical care. The audit described unhygienic food preparation, including at a facility with a "rodent infestation," and noted that a physician assistant attributed symptoms of acute gastrointestinal illness and giardiasis experienced by six staff and a detainee to food and water contamination. The audit further identified insufficient guidelines covering possible detainee escape or the death of a detainee.
874. See Memorandum for John A. Rizzo, Senior Deputy General Counsel, Central Intelligence Agency, from Steven G. Bradbury, Principal Deputy Assistant Attorney General, Office of Legal Counsel, May 10, 2005, Re: Application of 18 U.S.C. §§ 2340-2340A to Certain Techniques That May Be Used in the Interrogation of High Value al Qaeda Detainees.
875. See Memorandum for John A. Rizzo, Senior Deputy General Counsel, Central Intelligence Agency, from Steven G. Bradbury, Principal Deputy Assistant Attorney General, Office of Legal Counsel, May 10, 2005, Re: Application of 18 U.S.C. §§ 2340-2340A to the Combined Use of Certain Techniques That May Be Used in the Interrogation of High Value al Qaeda Detainees.
876. May 26, 2005, Memorandum for Director, Central Intelligence Agency, from John Helgerson, Inspector General, re: Recommendation for Additional Approach to Department of Justice Concerning Legal Guidance on Interrogation Techniques.
877. May 26, 2005, Memorandum for Director, Central Intelligence Agency, from John Helgerson, Inspector General, re: Recommendation for Additional Approach to Department of Justice Concerning Legal Guidance on Interrogation Techniques.
878. See Memorandum for John A. Rizzo, Senior Deputy General Counsel, Central Intelligence Agency, from Steven G. Bradbury, Principal Deputy Assistant Attorney General, Office of Legal Counsel, May 30, 2005, Re: Application of United States Obligations Under Article 16 of the Convention Against Torture to Certain Techniques that May Be Used in the Interrogation of High Value al Qaeda Detainees.
879. For more information on Abu Faraj al-Libi's detention and interrogation, see Volume III.
880. HEADQUARTERS ████ (251840Z MAY05).
881. See, for example, ██████ 1085 (describing meetings on May 6 and 7, 2005).
882. May, ██, 2005, Memorandum for Director, Central Intelligence Agency, via Acting Deputy Director, Central Intelligence Agency, Executive Director, Deputy Director for Operations from Robert Grenier, Director, DCI Counterterrorist Center re: Interrogation Plan for Abu Faraj al-Libi.
883. Email from: █████; to: Robert Grenier, John Mudd, [REDACTEDl, [REDACTED], ██ ███, █████, [REDACTED], █████, ██████; cc: █████ ███, [REDACTED], [REDACTED], [REDACTED]; subject: Possible significant delay in EITs for AFAL; date: May 24, 2005.
884. Email from: █████; to: Robert Grenier, John Mudd, [REDACTEDl, [REDACTED], ██ ███, █████, [REDACTED], █████, ██████; cc: █████ ███, [REDACTED], [REDACTED], [REDACTED]; subject: Possible significant delay in EITs for AFAL; date: May 24, 2005.
885. ██████ 4526 ██████.
886. ██████ 6131 █████; ████ 2319 ██████.
887. Memorandum for Assistant to the President for National Security Affairs, Director of National Intelligence, from Porter Goss, Director, Central Intelligence Agency, May █, 2005, re: Interrogation Plan for Abu Faraj al-Libi.
888. Memorandum for Assistant to the President for National Security Affairs, Director of National Intelligence, from Porter Goss, Director, Central Intelligence Agency, May ██, 2005, re: Interrogation Plan for Abu Faraj al-Libi.
889. Memorandum for Assistant to the President for National Security Affairs, Director of National Intelligence, from Porter Goss, Director, Central Intelligence Agency, May ██, 2005, re: Interrogation Plan for Abu

Faraj al-Libi.

890. HEADQUARTERS ███ ███.

891. ███ 2336 (282003Z MAY 05).

892. ███ 2499 (262123Z JUN 05).

893. ███.

894. Email from: ███; to: ███; cc: [REDACTED], [REDACTED], ███, ███, [REDACTED], [REDACTED] ███, [REDACTED], ███; subject: ███ Response to DDO Tasking of 7 July on Abu Faraj Interrogation; date: July 8, 2005, at 06:16 PM.

895. DIRECTOR ███ (121847Z JUL 05); HEADQUARTERS ███ ███ JAN 04); ███ 20361 (291232Z JAN 04); DIRECTOR ███ (040522Z MAY 04).

896. ███ 29454 (131701Z JUL 05).

897. Memorandum of Understanding Concerning DOD Support to CIA with Sensitive Capture and Detention Operations in the War on Terrorism.

898. See email from: [REDACTED], ███; to: ███, [REDACTED], [REDACTED]; cc: ███, [REDACTED], [REDACTED], [REDACTED], [REDACTED], [REDACTED]; subject: DoD Request for a list of HVTs not to be issued ISN numbers. The email stated: "In conjunction with discussions between CIA and DoD over the weekend regarding our request to have the military render Ibraliim Jan to our custody and NOT issuing him an ISN number, DoD has requested CIA provide a list of HVTs to whom, if captured, the military should NOT issue ISN numbers" (emphasis in original). See ███ 1505 ███ OCT 05).

899. July ███, 2005 Memorandum for Joint Staff (███) from ███, re: Interim Guidance Regarding (███).

900. Email from: [REDACTED]; to: ███, [REDACTED], [REDACTED]; cc: ███ [REDACTED], [REDACTED]; Subject: McCain Amendment on Detainee Treatment; date: October 6, 2005, at 12:37 PM.

901. According to CIA records, Abu Ja'far al-Iraqi was subjected to nudity, dietary manipulation, insult slaps, abdominal slaps, attention grasps, facial holds, walling, stress positions, and water dousing with 44 degree Fahrenheit water for 18 minutes. He was shackled in the standing position for 54 hours as part of sleep deprivation, and experienced swelling in his lower legs requiring blood thinner and spiral ace bandages. He was moved to a sitting position, and his sleep deprivation was extended to 78 hours. After the swelling subsided, he was provided with more blood thinner and was returned to the standing position. The sleep deprivation was extended to 102 hours. After four hours of sleep, Abu Ja'far al-Iraqi was subjected to an additional 52 hours of sleep deprivation, after which CIA Headquarters informed interrogators that eight hours was the minimum rest period between sleep deprivation sessions exceeding 48 hours. In addition to the swelling, Abu Ja'far al-Iraqi also experienced an edema on his head due to walling, abrasions on his neck, and blisters on his ankles from shackles. See ███ 1810 ███ DEC 05); ███ 1813 ███ DEC 05); ███ 1819 ███ DEC 05); ███ 1847 ███ DEC 05); ███ 1848 ███ DEC 05); HEADQUARTERS ███ ███ DEC 05). See additional information on Abu Ja'far al-Iraqi in Volume III.

902. PDB Draft titled: ███, Date: December 13, 2005, ALT ID#: -2132586. Director Goss notified the national security advisor that he had authorized the use of the CIA's enhanced interrogation techniques on Abu Ja'far al-Iraqi because "CIA believes that Abu Ja'far possesses considerable operational information about Abu Mu'sab al-Zarqawi." See December 1, 2005, Memorandum for the National Security Advisor, Director of National Intelligence, from Porter Goss, Central Intelligence Agency, subject, "Counterterrorist Interrogation Techniques."

903. PDB Draft titled: ███, Date: December 16 2005, ALT ID: 20051217 PDB on Abu Jafar al-Iraqi. Urging the change to the draft PDB, one of the interrogators involved in Abu Ja'far al-Iraqi's interrogation wrote, "If we allow the Director to give this PDB, as it is written, to the President, I would imagine the President would say, 'You asked me to risk my presidency on your interrogations, and now you give me this that implies the interrogations are not working. Why do we bother?' We think the tone of the PDB should be tweaked. Some of the conclusions, based on our experts' observations, should be amended. The glass is half full, not half empty, and is getting more full every day." See email from: [REDACTED] ███; to: [REDACTED], [REDACTED], [REDACTED]; cc: [REDACTED], [REDACTED], [REDACTED]; subject: PDB on [Abu Ja'far al-Iraqi]; date: December 15, 2005, at 12:25 AM.

904. ███ 2031 ███. In June 2007, inaccurate information about the effectiveness of the CIA's enhanced interrogation techniques on Abu Ja'far al-Iraqi was provided to the Committee. See CIA Response to Senate Select Committee on Intelligence Questions for the Record, June 18, 2007 (DTS #2007-2564); ███ 32732 ███ OCT 05); ███ 32707 ███

OCT 05); 32726 OCT 05); 32810 OCT 05); 32944 OCT 05).

905. The CIA's June 2013 Response states that an "important factor" contributing to the slower pace of CIA detention operations was al-Qa'ida's relocation to the FATA, which "made it significantly more challenging [for the Pakistani government] to mount capture operations resulting in renditions and detentions by the RDI program." A review of CIA records by the Committee found that legal, policy, and other operational concerns dominated internal deliberations about the program. In 2005, CIA officers asked officials to render two detainees to CIA one and one . neither detainee was transferred to CIA custody. CIA officers noted that obtaining custody of detainees held by a foreign government during this period was becoming increasingly difficult, highlighting that ." In March 2006, Director Goss testified to the Committee that lack of space was the limiting factor in taking custody of additional detainees. See HEADQUARTERS ; HEADQUARTERS ; email from: [REDACTED], ; to: ; cc: [REDACTED], [REDACTED], , [REDACTED], [REDACTED], [REDACTED], [REDACTED], [REDACTED]; subject: for coord, pls: D/CIA talking points re: rendition of 6702 ; HEADQUARTERS ; and transcript of Senate Select Committee on Intelligence briefing, March 15, 2006 (DTS #2006-1308).

906. Text redacted by the CIA prior to provision to Committee members at the U.S. Senate.

907. See CIA document dated, January 12, 2005, entitled, "DCI Talking Points for Weekly Meeting with National Security Advisor."

908. See CIA Talking Points for Principals Committee Meeting on Long-Term Disposition of High-Value Detainees, 8 March 2005.

909. See email from: to: John Rizzo; subject: Meeting this am with WH counsel on endgame planning; date: January 14, 2005.

910. Email from: ; to: ; cc: [REDACTED], , [REDACTED], John A. Rizzo, , , ; subject: Re: Brokaw interview; Take one; date: April 14, 2005, at 9:22:32 AM. In 2006, Vice President Cheney expressed reservations about any public release of information regarding the CIA program. See CIA Memorandum for the Record from [REDACTED], C/CTC , subject, "9 March 2006 Principals Committee Meeting on Detainees."

911. Negotiations with Countries and to host CIA detention facilities are described in this summary, and in greater detail in Volume I.

912. HEADQUARTERS (232040Z DEC 05).

913. DDCIA Talking Points for 10 February 2006 Un-DC re: Future of the CIA Counterterrorist Rendition, Detention, and Interrogation Program - Interrogation Techniques.

914. HEADQUAR ; HEADQUAR ; HEADQUARTERS .

915. The other options put forward by the CIA were transfer of CIA detainees , which the CIA anticipated would release the detainees after a short period. The CIA also proposed its own outright release of the detainees. See CIA document entitled D/CIA Talking Points for use at Principals Meeting (2005).

916. HEADQUARTERS .

917. Talking Points for Dr. J.D. Crouch for telephone calls to Ambassadors in [REDACTED] regarding possibility of forthcoming Dana Priest press article; email from: ; to: [REDACTED], [REDACTED], [REDACTED]; cc: [REDACTED], [REDACTED]; subject: Phone Call with State/L re: Ambassadors who want to speak to the SecState; date: , at 06:45 PM.

918. Email from: ; to: [REDACTED], [REDACTED], [REDACTED]; cc: [REDACTED], [REDACTED]; subject: Phone Call with State/L re: Ambassadors who want to speak to the SecState; date: October 24, 2005, at 06:45 PM; email from: [REDACTED]; to: [REDACTED]; cc: , [REDACTED], [REDACTED], [REDACTED], [REDACTED], [REDACTED], [REDACTED]; subject: Phone call from S/CT Amb. Hank Crumpton to Ambassador in ; date: November 1, 2005, at 6:13:21 PM. After the subsequent press revelations, the U.S. ambassador in Country asked again about whether the secretary of state had been briefed, prompting the CIA Station in Country to note in a cable that briefing U.S. officials outside of the CIA "would be a significant departure from current policy." See [REDACTED] [REDACTED].

919. ." See "CIA Holds Terror Suspects in Secret Prisons," the *Washington Post*, November 2, 2005.

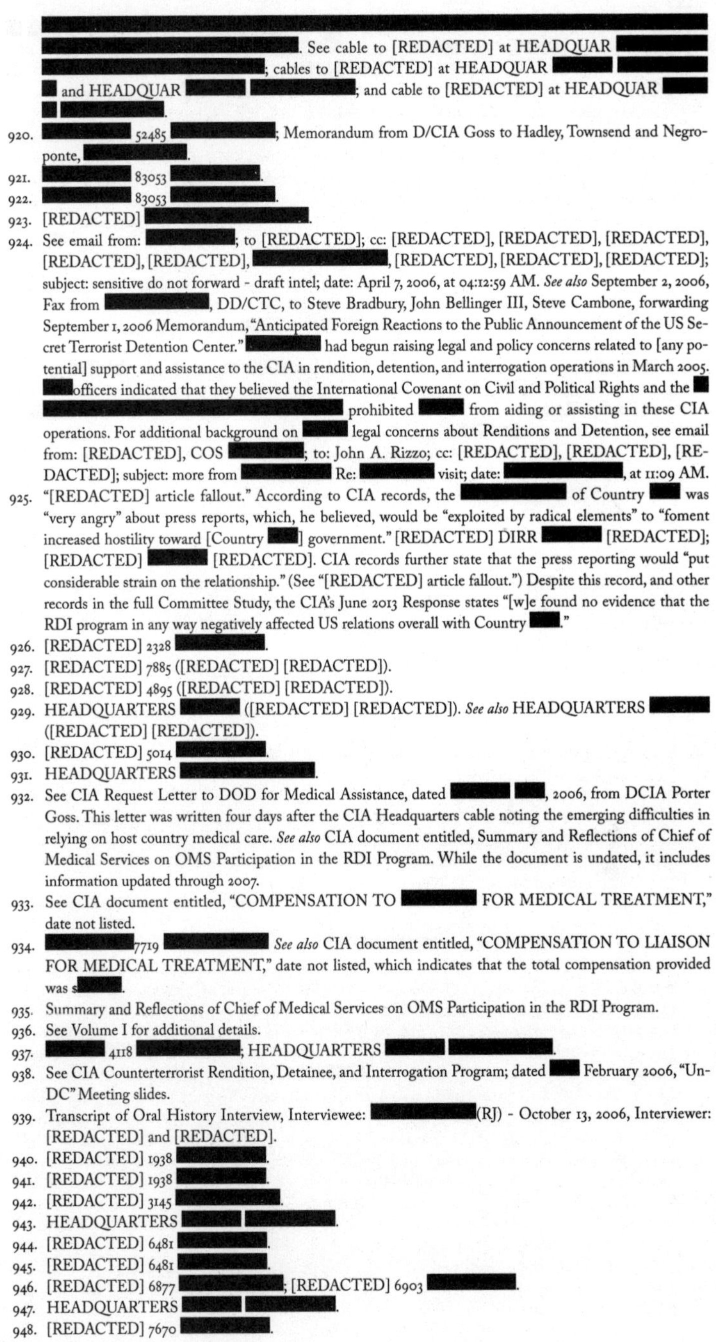

. See cable to [REDACTED] at HEADQUAR ; cables to [REDACTED] at HEADQUAR and HEADQUAR ; and cable to [REDACTED] at HEADQUAR .

920. 52485 ; Memorandum from D/CIA Goss to Hadley, Townsend and Negroponte, .

921. 83053 .

922. 83053 .

923. [REDACTED] .

924. See email from: ; to [REDACTED]; cc: [REDACTED], [REDACTED], [REDACTED], [REDACTED], [REDACTED], , [REDACTED], [REDACTED], [REDACTED]; subject: sensitive do not forward - draft intel; date: April 7, 2006, at 04:12:59 AM. *See also* September 2, 2006, Fax from , DD/CTC, to Steve Bradbury, John Bellinger III, Steve Cambone, forwarding September 1, 2006 Memorandum, "Anticipated Foreign Reactions to the Public Announcement of the US Secret Terrorist Detention Center." had begun raising legal and policy concerns related to [any potential] support and assistance to the CIA in rendition, detention, and interrogation operations in March 2005. officers indicated that they believed the International Covenant on Civil and Political Rights and the prohibited from aiding or assisting in these CIA operations. For additional background on legal concerns about Renditions and Detention, see email from: [REDACTED], COS ; to: John A. Rizzo; cc: [REDACTED], [REDACTED], [REDACTED]; subject: more from Re: visit; date: , at 11:09 AM.

925. "[REDACTED] article fallout." According to CIA records, the of Country was "very angry" about press reports, which, he believed, would be "exploited by radical elements" to "foment increased hostility toward [Country] government." [REDACTED] DIRR [REDACTED]; [REDACTED] [REDACTED]. CIA records further state that the press reporting would "put considerable strain on the relationship." (See "[REDACTED] article fallout.") Despite this record, and other records in the full Committee Study, the CIA's June 2013 Response states "[w]e found no evidence that the RDI program in any way negatively affected US relations overall with Country ."

926. [REDACTED] 2328 .

927. [REDACTED] 7885 ([REDACTED] [REDACTED]).

928. [REDACTED] 4895 ([REDACTED] [REDACTED]).

929. HEADQUARTERS ([REDACTED] [REDACTED]). *See also* HEADQUARTERS ([REDACTED] [REDACTED]).

930. [REDACTED] 5014 .

931. HEADQUARTERS .

932. See CIA Request Letter to DOD for Medical Assistance, dated , 2006, from DCIA Porter Goss. This letter was written four days after the CIA Headquarters cable noting the emerging difficulties in relying on host country medical care. *See also* CIA document entitled, Summary and Reflections of Chief of Medical Services on OMS Participation in the RDI Program. While the document is undated, it includes information updated through 2007.

933. See CIA document entitled, "COMPENSATION TO FOR MEDICAL TREATMENT," date not listed.

934. 7719 *See also* CIA document entitled, "COMPENSATION TO LIAISON FOR MEDICAL TREATMENT," date not listed, which indicates that the total compensation provided was $.

935. Summary and Reflections of Chief of Medical Services on OMS Participation in the RDI Program.

936. See Volume I for additional details.

937. 4118 ; HEADQUARTERS .

938. See CIA Counterterrorist Rendition, Detainee, and Interrogation Program; dated February 2006, "Un-DC" Meeting slides.

939. Transcript of Oral History Interview, Interviewee: (RJ) - October 13, 2006, Interviewer: [REDACTED] and [REDACTED].

940. [REDACTED] 1938 .

941. [REDACTED] 1938 .

942. [REDACTED] 3145 .

943. HEADQUARTERS .

944. [REDACTED] 6481 .

945. [REDACTED] 6481 .

946. [REDACTED] 6877 ; [REDACTED] 6903 .

947. HEADQUARTERS .

948. [REDACTED] 7670 .

949. See email from: [REDACTED]; to: [REDACTED], [REDACTED], [REDACTED]; cc: [REDACTED]; subject: [REDACTED] CTC [REDACTED] meeting re: [REDACTED]; date: [REDACTED], at 4:57:29 PM. The June discussion is also referenced in [REDACTED]; Memorandum for the Record; to: C/CTC [REDACTED]; from: C/CTC [REDACTED]/RDG; subject: Site Visit to [REDACTED] and Recommendations. As described, in June 2006, the CIA inspector general issued an audit that concluded that while CIA detention facilities lacked sufficient debriefers, they "were constructed, equipped, and staffed to securely and safely contain detainees and prompt intelligence exploitation of detainees." The audit further determined that the facilities "are not equipped to provide medical treatment to detainees who have or develop serious physical or mental disorders, and operable plans are not in place to provide inpatient care for detainees," and concluded that CIA detention facilities were not equipped to provide emergency medical care to detainees. The audit team did not visit the facility in Country [REDACTED], but stated, with regard to another country, Country [REDACTED], that "CIA funds have been wasted in constructing and equipping a medical facility that was later determined not to be a viable option for providing inpatient care for detainees." See Report of Audit, CIA-controlled Detention Facilities Operated Under the 17 September 2001 Memorandum of Notification, Report No. 2005-0017-AS, June 14, 2006, at DTS # 2006-2793. The CIA's [REDACTED] supervised the CIA's Renditions and Detention Group.

950. [REDACTED] 2006, Memorandum for the Record, to: C/CTC [REDACTED], from: C/CTC [REDACTED]/RDG, re: Site Visit to [REDACTED] and Recommendations.

951. See [REDACTED] 2006, Memorandum for the Record, to: C/CTC [REDACTED], from: C/CTC [REDACTED]/RDG, re: Site Visit to [REDACTED] and Recommendations (2).

952. Congressional Notification: Central Intelligence Agency Response to Host Country Government Order to Vacate an Inactive Blacksite Detention Facility, [REDACTED] (DTS #2009-3711); SSCI Memorandum for the Record, [REDACTED]; CIA Document, RDI Program Background Brief for Leon Panetta, 2009.

953. DCIA Talking Points for 6 January 2006 Breakfast with Secretary of Defense, re: SecDef Refusal to Take CIA Detainees on GTMO.

954. See CIA Memo, "As of 01 January 2006, there were 28 HVDs in CIA custody." As noted above, DETENTION SITE VIOLET in Country [REDACTED] would be closed in 2006.

955. DCIA Talking Points for 6 January 2006 Breakfast with Secretary of Defense, re: SecDef Refusal to Take CIA Detainees on GTMO.

956. DCIA Talking Points for 6 January 2006 Breakfast with Secretary of Defense, re: SecDef Refusal to Take CIA Detainees on GTMO.

957. DCIA Talking Points for 12 January 2006 Meeting with the President, re: Way Forward on Counterterrorist Rendition, Detention and Interrogation Program.

958. DCIA Talking Points for 12 January 2006 Meeting with the President, re: Way Forward on Counterterrorist Rendition, Detention and Interrogation Program.

959. See Volume I for additional details.

960. May 18, 2006, Deputies Committee (Un-DC) Meeting, Preliminary Detainee End Game Options. For additional information, see Volume I.

961. DCIA Talking Points for 9 February 2006 Un-DC, re: Future of the CIA Counterterrorist Rendition, Detention, and Interrogation Program - Detainees.

962. DCIA Talking Points for 9 February 2006 Un-DC, re: Future of the CIA Counterterrorist Rendition, Detention, and Interrogation Program - Detainees.

963. Letter from [REDACTED] CTC Legal [REDACTED] to Acting Assistant Attorney General Bradbury, May 23, 2006. (DTS#2009-1809); Memorandum for John A. Rizzo, Senior Deputy General Counsel, Central Intelligence Agency, from Steven G. Bradbury, Principal Deputy Assistant Attorney General, Office of Legal Counsel, May 10, 2005, Re: Application of 18 U.S.C. Sections 2340-2340A to Certain Techniques That May be Used in the Interrogation of a High Value al Qaeda Detainee (DTS #2009-1810, Tab 9), citing Fax for Daniel Levin, Acting Assistant Attorney General, Office of Legal Counsel, from [REDACTED], Assistant General Counsel, CIA (Jan. 4, 2005) ('January 4 [[REDACTED]] Fax'); Memorandum for John A. Rizzo, Senior Deputy General Counsel, Central Intelligence Agency, from Steven G. Bradbury, Principal Deputy Assistant Attorney General, Office of Legal Counsel, May 10, 2005, Re: Application of 18 U.S.C. Sections 2340-2340A to the Combined Use of Certain Techniques in the Interrogation of High Value al Qaeda Detainees (DTS #2009-1810, Tab 10); Memorandum for John A. Rizzo, Senior Deputy General Counsel, Central Intelligence Agency, from Steven G. Bradbury, Principal Deputy Assistant Attorney General, Office of Legal Counsel, May 30, 2005, Re: Application of United States Obligations Under Article 16 of the Convention Against Torture to Certain Techniques that May be Used in the Interrogation of High Value Al Qaeda Detainees (DTS #2009-1810, Tab 11).

964. DCIA Talking Points for 9 March 2006 Principals Committee Meeting.

965. Memorandum for the Record from [REDACTED], C/CTC [REDACTED], re: 9 March 2006 Principals Committee Meeting on Detainees.

966. See CIA document entitled, "DCIA Meeting with the President/dated April 8, 2006.

967. Email from: Grayson SWIGERT; to: [REDACTED]; cc: [REDACTED]; subject: Dr. [SWIGERT's] 7 June meeting with DCI; date: June 7, 2006.
968. CIA memorandum from the CIA's Office of General Counsel, circa June 2006, entitled, "Hamdan v. Rumsfeld."
969. CIA memorandum from the CIA's Office of General Counsel, circa June 2006, entitled, "Hamdan v. Rumsfeld."
970. Email from: [REDACTED]; to: [REDACTED]; cc: [REDACTED]; John Rizzo; subject: FW: Summary of *Hamdan* Decision; date: June 30, 2006, at 4:44 PM. Department of Justice Office of Professional Responsibility; Report, Investigation into the Office of Legal Counsel's Memoranda Concerning Issues Relating to the Central Intelligence Agency's Use of 'Enhanced Interrogation Techniques' on Suspected Terrorists, July 29, 2009 (DTS #2010-1058).
971. Memorandum for John A. Rizzo, Acting General Counsel, Central Intelligence Agency, from Steven G. Bradbury, Principal Deputy Acting Attorney General, Office of Legal Counsel, July 20, 2007, Re: Application of the War Crimes Act, the Detainee Treatment Act, and Common Article 3 of the Geneva Conventions to Certain Techniques that May Be Used by the CIA in the Interrogation of High Value al Qaeda Detainees.
972. See Volume I for details on these discussions.
973. September 6, 2006, The White House, President Discusses Creation of Military Commissions to Try Suspected Terrorists.
974. See Volume I and Volume II for additional information.
975. September 6, 2006, The White House, President Discusses Creation of Military Commissions to Try Suspected Terrorists.
976. See Volume III for additional information.
977. CIA Background Memo for CIA Director visit to Guantanamo, December [REDACTED], 2006, entitled Guantanamo Bay High-Value Detainee Detention Facility.
978. Email from: [REDACTED], [REDACTED] CTC/LGL; to: John Rizzo, [REDACTED], [REDACTED], [REDACTED], [REDACTED], [REDACTED], [REDACTED], [REDACTED], [REDACTED], [REDACTED], [REDACTED], [REDACTED], [REDACTED]; cc: [REDACTED]; subject: 8 November 2006 Meeting with ICRC reps; date: November 9, 2006, at 12:25 PM.
979. Email from: John A. Rizzo; to: Michael V. Hayden, Stephen R. Kappes, Michael J. Morell; cc: [REDACTED], [REDACTED], [REDACTED]; subject: Fw: 8 November 2006 Meeting with ICRC Reps; date: November 9, 2006, at 12:25 PM.
980. February 14, 2007, Letter to John Rizzo, Acting General Counsel, from [REDACTED] [REDACTED], International Committee of the Red Cross, [REDACTED].
981. CIA Comments on the February 2007 ICRC Report on the Treatment of Fourteen "High Value Detainees" in CIA Custody. At a Committee Hearing on April 12, 2007, CIA Director Hayden emphasized the close relationship the CIA had with the ICRC ("I believe our contacts with the ICRC have been very useful. I have met with [REDACTED] [REDACTED], the [REDACTED] for the Red Cross, on several occasions at CIA. It appears that [REDACTED] [REDACTED] is a runner and he's promised to bring his gear with him next time he comes to Langley so that we can jog on the compound."), but emphasized the errors in the ICRC report, stating: "While CIA appreciates the time, effort, and good intentions of the ICRC in forming its report, numerous false allegations of physical or threatened abuses and faulty legal assumptions and analysis in the report undermine its overall credibility." (See SSCI Hearing Transcript, dated April 12, 2007 (DTS# 2007-3158).) As is described in more detail in Volume II, Director Hayden's statements to the Committee regarding the ICRC report included significant inaccurate information.
982. See Assets/nybooks.com/media/doc/2010/04/022/icrc—report.pdf and detainee reviews and reports in Volume III.
983. CIA officers in RDG and OMS prepared a number of documents disputing the ICRC allegations. See document entitled, "CIA Comments on the February 2007 ICRC Report on the Treatment of Fourteen 'High Value Detainees' in CIA Custody." See Volumes I and III for additional information.
984. Email from: [REDACTED]; to: [REDACTED]; cc: [REDACTED] John Rizzo; subject: FW: Summary of *Hamdan* Decision; date: June 30, 2006, at 4:44 PM.
985. Acting Assistant Attorney General Bradbury told the Department of Justice's Office of Professional Responsibility (OPR) that officials from the Departments of State, Defense, and Justice met with the president and officials from the CIA and the NSC to consider the impact of the *Hamdan* decision, and that it was clear from the outset that legislation would have to be enacted to address the application of Common Article 3 and the War Crimes Act to the CIA interrogation program. As the OPR report noted, "*Hamdan* directly contradicted OLC's January 22, 2002 opinion to the White House and the Department of Defense, which had concluded that Common Article 3 did not apply to captured members of al Qaeda." See Department of Justice Office of Professional Responsibility; Report, Investigation into the Office of Legal Counsel's Memoranda Concerning Issues Relating to the Central Intelligence Agency's Use of Enhanced Interrogation Techniques on Suspected Terrorists, July 29, 2009 (DTS #2010-1058).
986. S. 3930 passed the Senate by a vote of 65-34 (Record Vote Number: 259) and the House by a vote of 250-170

(Roll no. 508). It was signed into law on October 17, 2006.

987. [REDACTED] 6361 [REDACTED].

988. See, for example, [REDACTED] 1335 (021946Z NOV 06); [REDACTED] 1340 (041114Z NOV 06); [REDACTED] 1343 (041805Z NOV 06); [REDACTED] 1370 (071318Z NOV 06); [REDACTED] 1574 (230910Z NOV 06); [REDACTED] 1624 (271250Z NOV 06); [REDACTED] 1703 (040918Z DEC 06); [REDACTED] 1860 (181622Z DEC 06); [REDACTED] 1931 (081606Z JAN 07; [REDACTED] 1956 (151211Z JAN 07); [REDACTED] 2007 (251057Z JAN 07).

989. [REDACTED] 2065 (081633Z FEB 07).

990. Email from: [REDACTED], [REDACTED]CTC/LGL; to: [REDACTED], [REDACTED], [REDACTED], [REDACTED] [REDACTED]; subject: What needs to occur before we ask for EITs on [REDACTED]; HEADQUARTERS [REDACTED] (272015Z FEB 07); date: February 9, 2007.

991. See October 23, 2006, Memorandum for Director, CIA from [REDACTED], Chief, [REDACTED] [REDACTED].

992. See October 23, 2006, Memorandum for Director, CIA from [REDACTED] Chief, [REDACTED] [REDACTED] [REDACTED] and DCIA Talking Points for 9 March 2006 Principals Committee Meeting.

993. February 9, 2007, letter from John B. Bellinger III, Legal Adviser, Department of State, to Steven G. Bradbury, Acting Assistant Attorney General, Office of Legal Counsel, Department of Justice. At the time, there were internal disagreements within the CIA about whether the CIA should have a detention and interrogation program. An April 2007 Sametime communication between the chief of CTC and another senior CIA leader described these disagreements and how CIA leadership responded to them. According to [REDACTED] [REDACTED], "[REDACTED] was carping to [REDACTED] and Jose [Rodiguez] last Friday . . . that he and [Michael] Sulick (!) had a long talk and agree the CIA is off the track and rails . . . that we should not be doing detention, rendition, interrogation." Referring to a CIA leadership meeting that day in which the Committee's April 12, 2007, hearing would be discussed, [REDACTED] stated that: "I want to take that [criticism] on by letting all know how importan [sic] this [hearing] is . . . and what the leaderships [sic] position is from hayden, kappes and jose . . . in case there is some corrosive, bullshit mumbling and rumblings among comopennt [sic – "competent"] chiefs, some of which i am seeing." Sametime communication between [REDACTED] and [REDACTED] [REDACTED], 12/Apr/07, 09:50:54 to 09:56:57.

994. Email from: [REDACTED]; to: Jose Rodriguez, John Rizzo etc.; subject: EIT briefing for SecState on June 22, 2007; date: June 22, 2007; July 3, 2007, Steven Bradbury, Handwritten Notes, "John Rizzo"; email from: John A. Rizzo; to: [REDACTED]; cc: [REDACTED], [REDACTED]; subject: Conversation with Bradbury; date: July 3, 2007.

995. [REDACTED] 1199 (251634Z JUN 07); [REDACTED] 6439 [REDACTED]; [REDACTED] [REDACTED] 7516 [REDACTED].

996. CIA memorandum titled, CTC/RDG Planning for Possible Rendition of Mohammed Rahim - 19 June 2007. The document was unsigned, and the author is unknown. A subsequent version, with identical text, was titled CTC/RDG Planning for Possible Rendition of Mohammad Rahim - 25 June 2007. *See also* [REDACTED] [REDACTED] 2463 (201956Z JUL 07).

997. Email from: John A. Rizzo; to: [REDACTED]; cc: [REDACTED], [REDACTED]; subject: Conversation with Bradbury; date: July 3, 2007.

998. [REDACTED] 6439 [REDACTED]; [REDACTED] 7516 [REDACTED].

999. [REDACTED] 2432 [REDACTED]JUL 07).

1000. July 16, 2007, letter from Michael Hayden, Director of the Central Intelligence Agency, to President George W. Bush; Executive Order 13440, July 20, 2007; and Memorandum for John A. Rizzo, Acting General Counsel, Central Intelligence Agency, from Steven G. Bradbury, Principal Deputy Acting Attorney General, Office of Legal Counsel, July 20, 2007, Re: Application of the War Crimes Act, the Detainee Treatment Act, and Common Article 3 of the Geneva Conventions to Certain Techniques that May Be Used by the CIA in the Interrogation of High Value al Qaeda Detainees.

1001. CIA memorandum titled, "CTC/RDG Planning for Possible Rendition of Mohammed Rahim - 19 June 2007." The document was unsigned, and the author is unknown. A subsequent version, with identical text, was titled "CTC/RDG Planning for Possible Rendition of Mohammad Rahim - 25 June 2007."

1002. [REDACTED] 2445 (181104Z JUL 07); [REDACTED] 2463 (201956Z JUL 07); [REDACTED] 2467 (211341Z JUL 07).

1003. [REDACTED] 2463 (201956Z JUL 07).

1004. [REDACTED] 2467 (211341Z JUL 07).

1005. [REDACTED] 2467 (211341Z JUL 07).

1006. [REDACTED] 2467 (211341Z JUL 07).

1007. [REDACTED] 2467 (211341Z JUL 07).

1008. Rahim was subjected to 104.5 hours of sleep deprivation from July 21, 2007, to July 25, 2007. Sleep deprivation was stopped when Rahim "described visual and auditory hallucinations." After Rahim was allowed to sleep for eight hours and the psychologist concluded that Rahim had been faking his symptoms, Rahim was subjected to another 62 hours of sleep deprivation. A third, 13 hour session, was halted due to a limit of 180 hours of sleep deprivation during a 30 day period. See [REDACTED] 2486 (251450Z JUL 07); [REDACTED] 2491 (261237Z JUL 07); [REDACTED] 2496 (261834Z JUL 07); [REDACTED] 2501 (271624Z JUL 07); [REDACTED] 2502 (281557Z JUL 07); and [REDACTED]

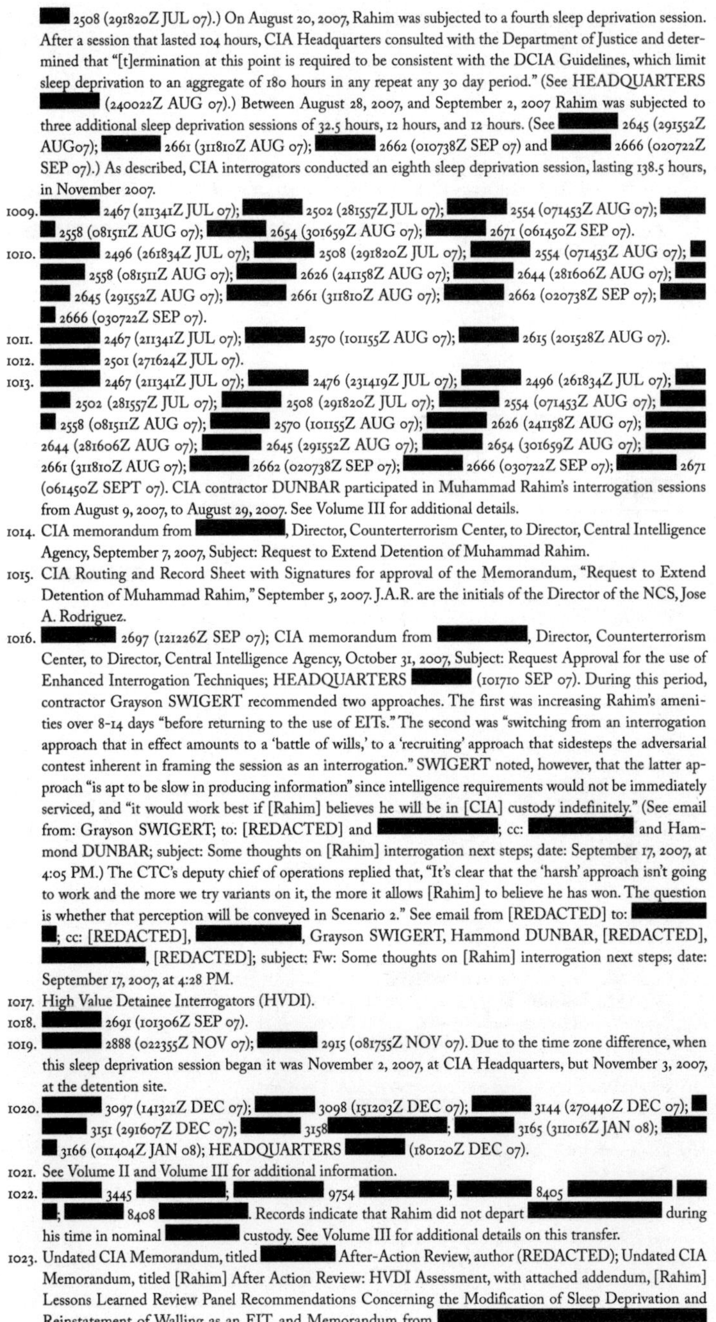

2508 (291820Z JUL 07).) On August 20, 2007, Rahim was subjected to a fourth sleep deprivation session. After a session that lasted 104 hours, CIA Headquarters consulted with the Department of Justice and determined that "[t]ermination at this point is required to be consistent with the DCIA Guidelines, which limit sleep deprivation to an aggregate of 180 hours in any repeat any 30 day period." (See HEADQUARTERS (240022Z AUG 07).) Between August 28, 2007, and September 2, 2007 Rahim was subjected to three additional sleep deprivation sessions of 32.5 hours, 12 hours, and 12 hours. (See 2645 (291552Z AUG07); 2661 (311810Z AUG 07); 2662 (010738Z SEP 07) and 2666 (020722Z SEP 07).) As described, CIA interrogators conducted an eighth sleep deprivation session, lasting 138.5 hours, in November 2007.

1009. 2467 (211341Z JUL 07); 2502 (281557Z JUL 07); 2554 (071453Z AUG 07); 2558 (081511Z AUG 07); 2654 (301659Z AUG 07); 2671 (061450Z SEP 07).

1010. 2496 (261834Z JUL 07); 2508 (291820Z JUL 07); 2554 (071453Z AUG 07); 2558 (081511Z AUG 07); 2626 (241158Z AUG 07); 2644 (281606Z AUG 07); 2645 (291552Z AUG 07); 2661 (311810Z AUG 07); 2662 (020738Z SEP 07); 2666 (030722Z SEP 07).

1011. 2467 (211341Z JUL 07); 2570 (101155Z AUG 07); 2615 (201528Z AUG 07).

1012. 2501 (271624Z JUL 07).

1013. 2467 (211341Z JUL 07); 2476 (231419Z JUL 07); 2496 (261834Z JUL 07); 2502 (281557Z JUL 07); 2508 (291820Z JUL 07); 2554 (071453Z AUG 07); 2558 (081511Z AUG 07); 2570 (101155Z AUG 07); 2626 (241158Z AUG 07); 2644 (281606Z AUG 07); 2645 (291552Z AUG 07); 2654 (301659Z AUG 07); 2661 (311810Z AUG 07); 2662 (020738Z SEP 07); 2666 (030722Z SEP 07); 2671 (061450Z SEPT 07). CIA contractor DUNBAR participated in Muhammad Rahim's interrogation sessions from August 9, 2007, to August 29, 2007. See Volume III for additional details.

1014. CIA memorandum from , Director, Counterterrorism Center, to Director, Central Intelligence Agency, September 7, 2007, Subject: Request to Extend Detention of Muhammad Rahim.

1015. CIA Routing and Record Sheet with Signatures for approval of the Memorandum, "Request to Extend Detention of Muhammad Rahim," September 5, 2007. J.A.R. are the initials of the Director of the NCS, Jose A. Rodriguez.

1016. 2697 (121226Z SEP 07); CIA memorandum from , Director, Counterterrorism Center, to Director, Central Intelligence Agency, October 31, 2007, Subject: Request Approval for the use of Enhanced Interrogation Techniques; HEADQUARTERS (101710 SEP 07). During this period, contractor Grayson SWIGERT recommended two approaches. The first was increasing Rahim's amenities over 8-14 days "before returning to the use of EITs." The second was "switching from an interrogation approach that in effect amounts to a 'battle of wills,' to a 'recruiting' approach that sidesteps the adversarial contest inherent in framing the session as an interrogation." SWIGERT noted, however, that the latter approach "is apt to be slow in producing information" since intelligence requirements would not be immediately serviced, and "it would work best if [Rahim] believes he will be in [CIA] custody indefinitely." (See email from: Grayson SWIGERT; to: [REDACTED] and ; cc: and Hammond DUNBAR; subject: Some thoughts on [Rahim] interrogation next steps; date: September 17, 2007, at 4:05 PM.) The CTC's deputy chief of operations replied that, "It's clear that the 'harsh' approach isn't going to work and the more we try variants on it, the more it allows [Rahim] to believe he has won. The question is whether that perception will be conveyed in Scenario 2." See email from [REDACTED] to: ; cc: [REDACTED], , Grayson SWIGERT, Hammond DUNBAR, [REDACTED], , [REDACTED]; subject: Fw: Some thoughts on [Rahim] interrogation next steps; date: September 17, 2007, at 4:28 PM.

1017. High Value Detainee Interrogators (HVDI).

1018. 2691 (101306Z SEP 07).

1019. 2888 (022355Z NOV 07); 2915 (081755Z NOV 07). Due to the time zone difference, when this sleep deprivation session began it was November 2, 2007, at CIA Headquarters, but November 3, 2007, at the detention site.

1020. 3097 (141321Z DEC 07); 3098 (151203Z DEC 07); 3144 (270440Z DEC 07); 3151 (291607Z DEC 07); 3158 ; 3165 (311016Z JAN 08); 3166 (011404Z JAN 08); HEADQUARTERS (180120Z DEC 07).

1021. See Volume II and Volume III for additional information.

1022. 3445 ; 9754 ; 8405 ; 8408 . Records indicate that Rahim did not depart during his time in nominal custody. See Volume III for additional details on this transfer.

1023. Undated CIA Memorandum, titled After-Action Review, author (REDACTED); Undated CIA Memorandum, titled [Rahim] After Action Review: HVDI Assessment, with attached addendum, [Rahim] Lessons Learned Review Panel Recommendations Concerning the Modification of Sleep Deprivation and Reinstatement of Walling as an EIT, and Memorandum from to Director, CTC, May 9, 2008, Subject: Results of After-Action Review of [Rahim] Interrogation. A document drafted by one of the participants prior to the review suggested that "intense legal/policy scrutiny" was also a negative factor; however, this point was not mentioned in any of the post-review summaries, except in the context of discussing confusion over whether particular interrogation methods were legal. The summary documents state that CIA officers devised and implemented several different strategies, one after another. According to one of the documents, "[t]hese varied strategies were implemented due to frustration and concern regarding the lack of intelligence production."

1024. Undated CIA Memorandum, titled [REDACTED] After-Action Review, author (REDACTED), Undated CIA Memorandum, titled [Rahim] After Action Review: HVDI Assessment, with attached addendum, [Rahim] Lessons Learned Review Panel Recommendations Concerning the Deprivation and Reinstatement of Walling and Memorandum from [REDACTED] to Director, CTC, May 9, 2008, Subject: Results of After-Action Review of [Rahim] Interrogation.
1025. Undated CIA Memorandum, titled [REDACTED] After-Action Review, author (REDACTED), Undated CIA Memorandum, titled [Rahim] After Action Review: HVDI Assessment, with attached addendum, [Rahim] Lessons Learned Review Panel Recommendations Concerning the Modification of Sleep Deprivation and Reinstatement of Walling as an EIT.
1026. See Volume III for additional information.
1027. For more information on CIA contracting with [Company Y], see Volume I.
1028. Letter to [REDACTED] [Company Y], attn: Hammond DUNBAR from [REDACTED], Contracting Officer, re: Confirmation of Verbal Authorization to Proceed Not to Exceed (ATP/NTE); email from: [REDACTED]; to: [REDACTED]; cc: [REDACTED], [REDACTED], [REDACTED]; [REDACTED]; subject: Next Contractual Steps with SWIGERT& DUNBAR; date: March 2, 2005; March 18, 2005, Letter from [REDACTED], Chief, to [REDACTED] [Company Y], re: Letter Contract [REDACTED].
1029. Email from: [REDACTED]; to: [REDACTED]; subject: [REDACTED]; date: June 17, 2005, at 11:08:22 AM; email from: [REDACTED] to: [REDACTED], [REDACTED], [REDACTED]; cc: [REDACTED]. [REDACTED], [REDACTED], [REDACTED]; subject: PCS CTC officer to [Company Y location] ("One of the primary functions is to develop and set-up what we call the 'Terrorist Think Tank' (previously briefed to the DDO and ADDO) which will be critical as we develop our [REDACTED]); date: July 12, 2005, at 10:25:48 AM; Justification Date: 28 February 2006, Justification For Other Than Full And Open Competition, Contractor: [Company Y].
1030. See, for example, [Company Y] Monthly report, February 2006; [Company Y] Monthly Report, March 2006; [Company Y] Quarterly, 01 Jan - 31 March 2007.
1031. Justification Date: 25 July 2006, Justification For Other Than Full and Open Competition, Contractor: [Company Y].
1032. DO/CTC[REDACTED]/RDG Projected Staff & Contractors, updated as of March 15, 2006.
1033. DO/CTC/[REDACTED]/RDG Projected Staff & Contractors, updated as of March 15, 2006.
1034. June 4, 2007, RDG, Mission Summary.
1035. CTC confirmation, received by telephone on November 16, 2012.
1036. DTS #2009-1258; DTS #2012-4008. CIA paid Company Y $612,000 in 2010 for contract close-out costs. In a March 2009 notification, the CIA also informed the Committee that, in addition to payments to Company Y, Grayson SWIGERT and Hammond DUNBAR had received $1.5 million and $1.1 million, respectively, as individuals. As noted elsewhere, the notification includes inaccurate representations about the effectiveness of the CIA program. See Congressional Notification, March 18, 2009 (DTS#2009-1258).
1037. Email from: [REDACTED], CTC[REDACTED]; to: Hammond DUNBAR, Grayson SWIGERT; cc: [REDACTED], [REDACTED], [REDACTED], [REDACTED], [REDACTED], [REDACTED]; subject: Copy of Signed Indemnification Agreement; date: July 13, 2007, at 02:22 PM; email from: [REDACTED], Chief, Contract Law Division; to: [REDACTED]; cc: [REDACTED], [REDACTED], [REDACTED], [REDACTED], [REDACTED], [REDACTED]; subject: Fw: Modified Indemnification Agmt . . . New AR 7-17 Waiver Memo, Too?; date: November 13, 2007, at 10:32 AM.
1038. Email from: [REDACTED]; to: [REDACTED] subject: [REDACTED] Billing, May-December 2007; date: August 12, 2008, at 06:42 PM.
1039. Response from the CIA regarding Contract Costs for [Company Y], October 15, 2012 (DTS#2012-4008).
1040. See DTS #2009-0572.
1041. Response from the CIA regarding Contract Costs for [Company Y], October 15, 2012 (DTS #2012-4008).
1042. DIRECTOR [REDACTED] (152227Z MAR 07); House Report 110-478 - Intelligence Authorization Act for Fiscal Year 2008, 110th Congress (2007-2008), Section 327.
1043. H.R. 2082 passed the House of Representatives on December 13, 2007, by a vote of 222-197 (Roll No: 1160) and passed the Senate on February 13, 2008, by a vote of 51-45 (Record Vote Number: 22).
1044. See "Text: Bush on Veto of Intelligence Bill," *The New York Times*, dated March 8, 2008. Located, among other places, at www.nytimes.com/2008/03/08/washington/08cnd-ptext.html. For an example of a previous

CIA briefing to the White House with similar assertions, see CIA Memorandum for the Record, "Review of Interrogation Program on 29 July 2003," prepared by CIA General Counsel Scott Muller, dated August 5, 2003; with briefing slides entitled, "*CIA Interrogation Program*," dated July 29, 2003. The CIA document provided to the participants states, "Termination of this program will result in loss of life, possibly extensive." For additional commentary, see "Veto of Bill on CIA Tactics Affirms Bush's Legacy," *The New York Times*, dated March 9, 2008.

1045. U.S. House of Representatives Roll Call Vote 117 of the 110th Congress, Second Session, March 11, 2008, 7:01 PM.

1046. CIA Briefing for Obama National Security Team - "Renditions, Detentions, and Interrogations (RDI)" including "Tab 7," named "RDG Copy- Briefing on RDI Program 09 Jan. 2009." Referenced materials attached to cover memorandum with the title, "D/CIA Conference Room Seating Visit by President-elect Barrack [sic] Obama National Security Team Tuesday, 13 January 2009; 8:30–11:30 a.m." The briefing book includes the previously mentioned, "Briefing Notes on the Value of Detainee Reporting," dated 15 May 2006, which provided the same intelligence claims found in the document of the same name, but dated April 15, 2005.

1047. For detailed information, see Volume II.

1048. The Executive Order also stated that the FBI and "other Federal law enforcement agencies" could "continu[e] to use authorized, non-coercive techniques of interrogation that are designed to elicit voluntary statements and do not involve the use of force, threats, or promises." (See Executive Order 13491, "Ensuring Lawful Interrogation," January 22, 2009.) [redacted].

1049. These representations were also made by the CIA to other elements of the executive branch, to include the Office of the Director of National Intelligence. As described in this Study, the Department of Justice first approved the use of the CIA's enhanced interrogation techniques on August 1, 2002.

1050. From 2003 through 2009, the CIA's representations regarding the effectiveness of the CIA's enhanced interrogation techniques provided a specific set of examples of terrorist plots "disrupted" and terrorists captured that the CIA attributed to information obtained from the use of its enhanced interrogation techniques. CIA representations further asserted that the intelligence obtained from the use of the CIA's enhanced interrogation techniques was unique, otherwise unavailable, and resulted in "saved lives." Among other CIA representations, see: (1) CIA representations in the Department of Justice Office of Legal Counsel Memorandum, dated May 30, 2005, which relied on a series of highly specific CIA representations on the type of intelligence acquired from the use of the CIA's enhanced interrogation techniques to assess their legality. The CIA representations referenced by the OLC include that the use of the CIA's enhanced interrogation techniques was "necessary" to obtain "critical," "vital," and "otherwise unavailable actionable intelligence" that was "essential" for the U.S. government to "detect and disrupt" terrorist threats. The OLC memorandum further states that "[the CIA] ha[s] informed [the OLC] that the CIA believes that this program is largely responsible for preventing a subsequent attack within the United States." See Memorandum for John A. Rizzo, Senior Deputy General Counsel, Central Intelligence Agency, from Steven G. Bradbury, Principal Deputy Assistant Attorney General, Office of Legal Counsel, May 30, 2005, Re: Application of United States Obligations Under Article 16 of the Convention Against Torture to Certain Techniques that May Be Used in the Interrogation of High Value al Qaeda Detainees.) (2) CIA representations in the Department of Justice Office of Legal Counsel Memorandum dated July 20, 2007, which also relied on CIA representations on the type of intelligence acquired from the use of the CIA's enhanced interrogation techniques. Citing CIA documents and the President's September 6, 2006, speech describing the CIA's interrogation program (which was based on CIA-provided information), the OLC memorandum states: "The CIA interrogation program—and, in particular, its use of enhanced interrogation techniques—is intended to serve this paramount interest [security of the Nation] by producing substantial quantities of otherwise unavailable intelligence. . . . As the President explained [on September 6, 2006], 'by giving us information about terrorist plans we could not get anywhere else, the program has saved innocent lives.'" (See Memorandum for John A. Rizzo, Acting General Counsel, Central Intelligence Agency, from Steven G. Bradbury, Principal Deputy Assistant Attorney General, Office of Legal Counsel, July 20, 2007, Re: Application of the War Crimes Act, the Detainee Treatment Act, and Common Article 3 of the Geneva Conventions to Certain Techniques that May Be Used by the CIA in the Interrogation of High Value al Qaeda Detainees.) (3) CIA briefings for members of the National Security Council in July and September 2003 represented that "the use of Enhanced Techniques of one kind or another had produced significant intelligence information that had, in the view of CIA professionals, saved lives," and which warned policymakers that "[t]ermination of this program will result in loss of life, possibly extensive." See August 5, 2003 Memorandum for the Record from Scott Muller, Subject: Review of Interrogation Program on 29 July 2003; Briefing slides, CIA Interrogation Program, July 29, 2003; September 4, 2003, CIA Memorandum for the Record, Subject: Member Briefing; and September 26, 2003, Memorandum for the Record from Muller, Subject: CIA Interrogation Program.) (4) The CIA's response to the Office of Inspector General draft Special Review of the CIA program, which asserts: "Information [the CIA] received . . . as a result of the lawful use of enhanced interrogation techniques ('EITs') has almost certainly saved countless American lives inside the United States and abroad. The evidence points clearly to the fact that without the use of such techniques, we and our allies would [have] suffered major terrorist attacks involving hundreds, if not thousands, of casualties." (See Memorandum for: Inspector General; from: James Pavitt, Deputy Director for Operations; subject: re: (S) Comments to Draft IG Special Review, "Counterterrorism Detention and Interrogation Program" 2003-7123-IG; date: February 27, 2004; attachment: February 24, 2004, Memorandum re: Successes of CIA's Counterterrorism Detention and Interrogation Activities.) (5) CIA briefing documents for CIA Director Leon Panetta in February 2009, which state that the "CIA assesses that the RDI program worked and the [enhanced interrogation] techniques were effective in producing foreign intelligence," and that "[m]ost, if not all, of the timely intelligence acquired from detainees in this program would not have been discovered or reported by other means." (See CIA briefing documents for Leon Panetta, entitled, "Tab 9: DCIA Briefing on RDI Program- 18FEB.2009" and graphic attachment, "Key Intelligence and Reporting Derived from Abu Zubaydah and Khalid Shaykh Muhammad (KSM)," including "DCIA Briefing on RDI Program" agenda, CIA document "EITs and Effectiveness," with associated documents, "Key Intelligence Impacts Chart: Attachment (AZ and KSM)," "Background on Key Intelligence Impacts Chart: Attachment," and "supporting references," to include "Background on Key Captures and Plots Disrupted.") (6) CIA document faxed to the Senate Select Committee on Intelligence on March 18, 2009, entitled, "[SWIGERT] and [DUNBAR]" (DTS #2009-1258), which provides a list of "some of the key captures and disrupted plots" that the CIA had attributed to the use of the CIA's enhanced interrogation techniques, and states: "CIA assesses that most, if not all, of the timely intelligence acquired from detainees in this program would not have been discovered or reported by any other means." See Volume II for additional CIA representations asserting that the CIA's enhanced interrogation techniques enabled the CIA to obtain unique, otherwise unavailable intelligence that "saved lives."

1051. Among other documents that contain the exact, or similar CIA representations, see: (1) CIA memorandum for the Record, "Review of Interrogation Program on 29 July 2003," prepared by CIA General Counsel Scott Muller, dated August 5, 2003; briefing slides entitled, "*CIA Interrogation Program*," dated July 29, 2003, presented to senior White House officials with additional briefings using the slides as documented in September 4, 2003, CIA Memorandum for the Record, Subject: Member Briefing; and September 26, 2003, Memorandum for the Record from Scott Muller, Subject: CIA Interrogation Program. (2) CIA memorandum to the CIA Inspector General from James Pavitt, CIA's Deputy Director for Operations, dated February 27, 2004, with the subject line, "Comments to Draft IG Special Review, 'Counterterrorism Detention and Interrogation Program' (2003-7123-IG)," Attachment, "Successes of CIA's Counterterrorism Detention and Interrogation Activities," dated February 24, 2004. (3) CIA Directorate of Intelligence, "Khalid Shaykh Muhammad: Preeminent Source on Al-Qa'ida," dated July 13, 2004; fax to the Department of Justice, April 22, 2005, entitled, "██████, Materials on KSM and Abu Zubaydah. ██████." This report was widely disseminated in the Intelligence Community and a copy of this report was provided to the Senate Select Committee on Intelligence on July 15, 2004. On March 31, 2009, former Vice President Cheney requested the declassification of this Intelligence Assessment, which was publicly released with redactions on August 24, 2009. (4) CIA memorandum to "National Security Advisor," from "Director of Central Intelligence," Subject: "Effectiveness of the CIA Counterterrorist Interrogation Techniques," included in email from: ██████████; to: ██████████, ██████████████, and ██████████; subject: "paper on value of interrogation techniques"; date: December 6, 2004, at 5:06:38 PM. The email references the attached "information paper to Dr. Rice explaining the value of the interrogation techniques." (5) CIA Memorandum for Steve Bradbury at Office of Legal Counsel, Department of Justice, dated March 2, 2005, from ██████████, ██████ Legal Group, DCI Counterterrorist Center, subject: "Effectiveness of the CIA Counterterrorist Interrogation Techniques," (6) CIA briefing for Vice President Cheney, dated March 4, 2005, entitled, "Briefing for Vice President Cheney: CIA Detention and Interrogation Program." (7) CIA Talking Points entitled, "Talking Points for 10 March 2005 DCI Meeting PC: Effectiveness of the High-Value Detainee Interrogation (HVDI) Techniques." (8) CIA "Briefing Notes on the Value of Detainee Reporting" faxed from the CIA to the Department of Justice on April 15, 2005, at 10:47AM. (9) CIA fax to DOJ Command Center, dated April 22, 2005, for ██████████, Office of Legal Counsel, U.S. Department of Justice, from ██████████, ██████ Legal Group, DCI Counterterrorist Center, re: ██████, Materials of KSM and Abu Zubaydah, included CIA Intelligence Assessment "Khalid Shaykh Muhammad: Preeminent Source on Al-Qa'ida," and CIA document, "Materials of KSM and Abu Zubaydah.; (10) CIA Intelligence Assessment, "Detainee Reporting Pivotal for the War Against Al-Qa'ida," June 2005, which CIA records indicate was provided to White House officials on June 1, 2005. The Intelligence Assessment at the SECRET// NOFORN classification level was more broadly disseminated on June 3, 2005. On March 31, 2009, former Vice President Cheney requested the declassification of this Intelligence Assessment, which was publicly released with redactions on August 24, 2009. (11) CIA memorandum entitled, "Future of CIA's Counterterrorist Detention and Interrogation Program," dated December 23, 2005, from CIA Director Porter Goss to Stephen J. Hadley, Assistant to the President/National Security Advisor, Frances F. Townsend, Assistant to the President/Homeland Security Advisor, and Ambassador John D. Negroponte, the Director of National Intelligence, Attachment, "Impact of the Loss of the Detainee Program to CT Operations and Analysis." (12) CIA briefing document dated May 2, 2006, entitled, "BRIEFING FOR CHIEF OF STAFF TO THE PRESIDENT 2 May 2006 Briefing for Chief of Staff to the President Josh Bolten: CIA Rendition, Detention and Interrogation Programs." (13) CIA briefing document entitled, "Detainee Intelligence Value Update," dated 11 July 2006, internal document saved within CIA records as, "DNI Memo Intel Value July 11 2006 . . . TALKING POINTS FOR DCI MEETING." (14) CIA document dated July 16, 2006, entitled, "DRAFT Potential Public Briefing of CIA's High-Value Terrorist Interrogations Program," and "CIA Validation of Remarks on Detainee Policy," drafts supporting the September 6, 2006, speech by President George W. Bush acknowledging and describing the CIA's Detention and Interrogation Program, as well as an unclassified Office of the Director of National Intelligence release, entitled, "Summary of the High Value Terrorist Detainee Program." (15) CIA classified statement for the record. Senate Select Committee on Intelligence, provided by General Michael V. Hayden, Director, Central Intelligence Agency, 12 April 2007, and accompanying Senate Select Committee on Intelligence hearing transcript, entitled, "Hearing on Central Intelligence Agency Detention and Interrogation Program." (16) CIA fax from CIA employee [REDACTED] to U.S. Senate Committee on Appropriations, Subcommittee on Defense, with fax cover sheet entitled, "Talking points," sent on October 26, 2007, at 5:39:48 PM, entitled, "Talking Points Appeal of the $██ Million reduction in CIA/CTC's Rendition and Detention Program." (17) "DCIA Talking Points: Waterboard 06 November 2007," dated November 6, 2007, with the notation the document was "sent to DCIA Nov. 6 in preparation for POTUS meeting." (18) CIA Briefing for Obama National Security Team- "Renditions, Detentions, and Interrogations (RDI)" including "Tab 7," named "RDG Copy- Briefing on RDI Program 09 Jan. 2009," prepared "13 January 2009." (19) CIA briefing documents for Leon Panetta, entitled, "Tab 9: DCIA Briefing on RDI Program- 18FEB.2009" and graphic attachment, "Key Intelligence and Reporting Derived from Abu Zubaydah and Khalid Shaykh Muhammad (KSM)." The documents include "DCIA Briefing on RDI Program" agenda, CIA document "EITs and Effectiveness," with associated documents, "Key Intelligence Impacts Chart: Attachment (AZ and KSM)," "Background on Key Intelligence Impacts Chart: Attachment," and "supporting references," to include "Background on Key Captures and Plots Disrupted." (20) CIA document faxed to the Senate Select Committee on Intelligence on March 18, 2009, at 3:46PM, entitled, "[SWIGERT] and [DUNBAR]" (DTS #2009-1258). *See also* CIA representations detailed in OLC memorandum for John A. Rizzo, Senior Deputy General Counsel, Central Intelligence Agency, from Steven G. Bradbury, Principal Deputy Assistant Attorney General, Office of Legal Counsel, May 30, 2005, Re: Application of United States Obligations Under Article 16 of the Convention Against Torture to Certain Techniques that May Be Used in the Interrogation of High Value al Qaeda Detainees; and OLC memorandum for John A. Rizzo, Acting General Counsel, Central Intelligence Agency, from Steven G. Bradbury, Principal Deputy Assistant Attorney General, Office of Legal Counsel, July 20, 2007, Re: Application of the War Crimes Act, the Detainee Treatment Act, and Common Article 3 of the Geneva Conventions to Certain Techniques that May Be Used by the CIA in the Interrogation of High Value al Qaeda Detainees.

1052. See section of this summary addressing representations to the Department of Justice, as well as Memorandum for John Rizzo, Acting General Counsel, Central Intelligence Agency, from Jay Bybee, Assistant Attorney General, Office of Legal Counsel, August 1, 2002, Interrogation of al Qaeda Operative; Memorandum for John A. Rizzo, Senior Deputy General Counsel, Central Intelligence Agency, from Steven G. Bradbury, Principal Deputy Assistant Attorney General, Office of Legal Counsel, May 30, 2005, Re: Application of United States Obligations Under Article 16 of the Convention Against Torture to Certain Techniques that May be Used in the Interrogation of High Value Al Qaeda Detainees; and Memorandum for John A. Rizzo, Acting General Counsel, Central Intelligence Agency, from Steven G. Bradbury, Principal Deputy Assistant Attorney General, Office of Legal Counsel, July 20, 2007, Re: Application of the War Crimes Act, the Detainee Treatment Act, and Common Article 3 of the Geneva Conventions to Certain Techniques that May be Used by the CIA in the Interrogation of High Value Al Qaeda Detainees.

1053. Among other documents, see the August 5, 2003, CIA Memorandum for the Record from Scott Muller from a July 29, 2003, National Security Council Principals Meeting with the subject, "Review of Interrogation Program on 29 July 2003," as well as the accompanying briefing slides, "CIA Interrogation Program, July 29, 2003"; March 4, 2005, Briefing for Vice President Cheney: CIA Detention and Interrogation Program. CIA document, dated March 4, 2005, entitled, "Briefing for Vice President Cheney: CIA Detention and Interrogation Program"; CIA document, dated May 2, 2006, entitled, BRIEFING FOR CHIEF OF STAFF TO THE PRESIDENT 2 May 2006 Briefing for Chief of Staff to the President Josh Bolten: CIA Rendition, Detention and Interrogation Programs; CIA document entitled, "DCIA Talking Points: Waterboard 06 November 2007," dated November 6, 2007, with the notation the document was "sent to DCIA Nov. 6 in preparation for POTUS meeting"; and CIA Briefing for Obama National Security Team- "Renditions, Detentions, and Interrogations (RDI)" including "Tab 7," named "RDG Copy- Briefing on RDI Program 09 Jan. 2009," prepared "13 January 2009."

1054. Among other documents, see: (1) CIA testimony to the Senate Select Committee on Intelligence (SSCI) on April 24, 2002, regarding Abu Zubaydah's initial interrogation; (2) CIA written answers to Committee Questions for the Record, dated August 15, 2002, regarding results of Abu Zubaydah's interrogations; (3) CIA testimony to SSCI on September 5, 2002, regarding covert detention facilities and results of Abu Zubaydah's interrogation; (4) CIA cable documenting September 27, 2002, briefing to Chairman Bob Graham and Vice Chairman Richard Shelby and their staff directors regarding the CIA's enhanced interrogation techniques in the interrogations of Abu Zubaydah; (5) CIA Memorandum for the Record documenting February 4, 2003, briefing to SSCI Chairman Pat Roberts and Committee staff directors regarding the CIA's Detention and Interrogation Program; (6) CIA testimony to SSCI on March 5, 2003, regarding the capture and initial interrogation of KSM; (7) CIA witness testimony to SSCI on March 19, 2003, regarding KSM's interrogation; (8) CIA witness testimony to SSCI on April 1, 2003, regarding KSM's capture; (9) April 3, 2003, Intelligence Community Terrorist Threat Assessment regarding KSM threat reporting, entitled "Khalid Shaykh Muhammad's Threat Reporting—Precious Truths, Surrounded by a Bodyguard of Lies," provided to the SSCI on April 7, 2003; (10) CIA testimony to SSCI on April 30, 2003, regarding detainee reporting; (11) CIA testimony to SSCI on June 25, 2003, regarding KSM interrogation; (12) CIA testimony to SSCI on July 30, 2003, regarding CIA detainee threat reporting; (13) CIA testimony to SSCI on September 3, 2003, regarding [REDACTED] authorities, including CIA detention authorities; (14) CIA prepared briefing for Chairman Pat Roberts and Vice Chairman John D. Rockefeller IV entitled, "CIA Interrogation Program: DDO Talking Points, 04 September 2003"; (15) CIA witness testimony to SSCI on May 12, 2004, regarding CIA role in abuses at Abu Ghraib prison; (16) SSCI staff notes for July 15, 2004, CIA briefing to Chairman Pat Roberts and Vice Chairman John D. Rockefeller IV regarding the status of the CIA interrogation programs; (17) CIA testimony to SSCI on September 13, 2004, regarding CIA and the abuses at Abu Ghraib prison; (18) Hand-written notes of Vice Chairman John D. Rockefeller IV recording a briefing by Jose Rodriguez on March 7, 2005; (19) CIA Memorandum for the Record, Subject: Sensitive Issue -Counterterrorism, October 31, 2005, regarding briefing for Senate Majority Leader Bill Frist regarding the Detainee Treatment Act, and email exchanges between John Rizzo, [REDACTED], [REDACTED], subject: "Re: Immediate Re: Sen. Frist required for briefing on impact of McCain Amendment"; date: October 31, 2005, and associated records concerning CIA briefings for Senators John McCain, Thad Cochran, Ted Stevens, and John Cornyn; (20) SSCI Memorandum for the Record, March 8, 2006, documenting CIA briefing of March 7, 2006, to staff on status of the CIA's Detention and Interrogation Program; (21) CIA Director Porter Goss testimony to the SSCI on March 15, 2006, regarding the status of the CIA's Detention and Interrogation Program; (22) CIA Director Michael Hayden testimony to the SSCI on September 6, 2006, regarding the CIA's Detention and Interrogation Program, prior to Senate consideration of the Military Commissions Act of 2006; (23) CIA Director Michael Hayden testimony to the SSCI on November 16, 2006, regarding the CIA's Detention and Interrogation Program, following passage of the Military Commissions Act of 2006; (24) CIA Director Michael Hayden testimony to the SSCI on April 12, 2007, regarding the CIA's Detention and Interrogation Program and a report of the International Committee of the Red Cross; (25) CIA fax from CIA employee [REDACTED] to U.S. Senate Committee on Appropriations, Subcommittee on Defense, with fax cover sheet entitled, "Talking points," sent on October 26, 2007, at 5:39:48 PM. Document faxed entitled, "Talking Points Appeal of the $[REDACTED] Million reduction in CIA/CTC's Rendition and Detention Program"; (26) CIA Director Michael Hayden testimony to the SSCI on December 11, 2007, regarding the public revelation of the CIA's destruction of videotapes of the interrogations of Abu Zubaydah and 'Abd al-Rahim al-Nashiri; (27) CIA Director Michael Hayden public testimony to the SSCI on February 5, 2008, regarding waterboarding and CIA interrogations, prior to Senate vote on February 13, 2008, on the Fiscal Year 2008 Intelligence Authorization Act that would have prohibited any member of the U.S. Intelligence Community from using interrogation techniques not authorized by the U.S. Army Field Manual.

1055. Memorandum for the Record: "Review of Interrogation Program on 29 July 2003." Memorandum prepared by CIA General Counsel Scott Muller, dated August 5, 2003, and briefing slides entitled, "*CIA Interrogation Program*," dated July 29, 2003, presented to senior White House officials. Those attending the meeting included the director of the CIA, George Tenet; the CIA general counsel, Scott Muller; Vice President Cheney; National Security Advisor Condoleezza Rice; White House Counsel Alberto Gonzales; Attorney General John Ashcroft; Acting Assistant Attorney General, Office of Legal Counsel, Patrick Philbin; and counsel to the National Security Council, John Bellinger.

1056. CIA talking points for the National Security Council entitled, "Talking Points for 10 March 2005 DCI Meeting PC: Effectiveness of the High-Value Detainee Interrogation (HVDI) Techniques," dated March 4, 2005, for a March 8, 2005, meeting. *See also* CIA Memorandum for National Security Advisor Rice entitled, "Effectiveness of the CIA Counterterrorist Interrogation Techniques," dated December 2004.

1057. From 2003 through 2009, the CIA's representations regarding the effectiveness of the CIA's enhanced interrogation techniques provided a specific set of examples of terrorist plots "disrupted" and terrorists captured that the CIA attributed to information obtained from the use of its enhanced interrogation techniques. CIA representations further asserted that the intelligence obtained from the use of the CIA's enhanced interrogation techniques was unique, otherwise unavailable, and resulted in "saved lives." Among other CIA representations, see: (1) CIA representations in the Department of Justice Office of Legal Counsel Memorandum, dated May 30, 2005, which relied on a series of highly specific CIA representations on the type of intelligence acquired from the use of the CIA's enhanced interrogation techniques to assess their legality. The

CIA representations referenced by the OLC include that the use of the CIA's enhanced interrogation techniques was "necessary" to obtain "critical," "vital," and "otherwise unavailable actionable intelligence" that was "essential" for the U.S. government to "detect and disrupt" terrorist threats. The OLC memorandum further states that "[the CIA] ha[s] informed [the OLC] that the CIA believes that this program is largely responsible for preventing a subsequent attack within the United States." (See Memorandum for John A. Rizzo, Senior Deputy General Counsel, Central Intelligence Agency, from Steven G. Bradbury, Principal Deputy Assistant Attorney General, Office of Legal Counsel, May 30, 2005, Re: Application of United States Obligations Under Article 16of the Convention Against Torture to Certain Techniques that May Be Used in the Interrogation of High Value al Qaeda Detainees.) (2) CIA representations in the Department of Justice Office of Legal Counsel Memorandum dated July 20, 2007, which also relied on CIA representations on the type of intelligence acquired from the use of the CIA's enhanced interrogation techniques. Citing CIA documents and the President's September 6, 2006, speech describing the CIA's interrogation program (which was based on CIA-provided information), the OLC memorandum states: 'The CIA interrogation program—and, in particular, its use of enhanced interrogation techniques—is intended to serve this paramount interest [security of the Nation] by producing substantial quantities of otherwise unavailable intelligence. . . . As the President explained [on September 6, 2006], 'by giving us information about terrorist plans we could not get anywhere else, the program has saved innocent lives.'" See Memorandum for John A. Rizzo, Acting General Counsel, Central Intelligence Agency, from Steven G. Bradbury, Principal Deputy Assistant Attorney General, Office of Legal Counsel, July 20, 2007, Re: Application of the War Crimes Act, the Detainee Treatment Act, and Common Article 3 of the Geneva Conventions to Certain Techniques that May Be Used by the CIA in the Interrogation of High Value al Qaeda Detainees.) (3) CIA briefings for members of the National Security Council in July and September 2003, which represented that "the use of Enhanced Techniques of one kind or another had produced significant intelligence information that had, in the view of CIA professionals, saved lives," and which warned policymakers that "[t]ermination of this program will result in loss of life, possibly extensive." (See August 5, 2003 Memorandum for the Record from Scott Muller, Subject: Review of Interrogation Program on 29 July 2003; Briefing slides, CIA Interrogation Program, July 29, 2003; September 4, 2003, CIA Memorandum for the Record, Subject: Member Briefing; and September 26, 2003, Memorandum for the Record from Muller, Subject: CIA Interrogation Program.) (4) The CIA's response to the Office of Inspector General draft Special Review of the CIA program, which asserts: "Information [the CIA] received . . . as a result of the lawful use of enhanced interrogation techniques ('EITs') has almost certainly saved countless American lives inside the United States and abroad. The evidence points clearly to the fact that without the use of such techniques, we and our allies would [have] suffered major terrorist attacks involving hundreds, if not thousands, of casualties." (See Memorandum for: Inspector General; from: James Pavitt, Deputy Director for Operations; subject: re: (S) Comments to Draft IG Special Review, "Counterterrorism Detention and Interrogation Program" 2003-7123-IG; date; February 27, 2004; attachment: February 24, 2004, Memorandum re: Successes of CIA's Counterterrorism Detention and Interrogation Activities.) (5) CIA briefing documents for CIA Director Leon Panetta in February 2009, which state that the "CIA assesses that the RDI program worked and the [enhanced interrogation] techniques were effective in producing foreign intelligence," and that "[m]ost, if not all, of the timely intelligence acquired from detainees in this program would not have been discovered or reported by other means." (See CIA briefing documents for Leon Panetta, entitled, "Tab 9: DCIA Briefing on RDI Program- 18FEB.2009" and graphic attachment, "Key Intelligence and Reporting Derived from Abu Zubaydah and Khalid Shaykh Muhammad (KSM)," including "DCIA Briefing on RDI Program" agenda, CIA document "EITs and Effectiveness," with associated documents, "Key Intelligence Impacts Chart: Attachment (AZ and KSM)," "Background on Key Intelligence Impacts Chart: Attachment," and "supporting references," to include "Background on Key Captures and Plots Disrupted.") (6) CIA document faxed to the Senate Select Committee on Intelligence on March 18, 2009, entitled, "[SWIGERT] and [DUNBAR]" (DTS #2009-1258), which provides a list of "some of the key captures and disrupted plots" that the CIA had attributed to the use of the CIA's enhanced interrogation techniques, and states: "CIA assesses that most, if not all,of the timely intelligence acquired from detainees in this program would not have been discovered or reported by any other means." See Volume II for additional CIA representations asserting that the CIA's enhanced interrogation techniques enabled the CIA to obtain unique, otherwise unavailable intelligence that "saved lives."

1058. See Volume II for detailed information. The OLC's May 30, 2005, memorandum relied on the CIA's representations in determining that the CIA's enhanced interrogation techniques did not violate the Fifth Amendment's prohibition on executive conduct that "shocks the conscience," indicating that this analysis was a "highly context-specific and fact-dependent question." The OLC also linked its analysis of whether the use of the CIA's enhanced interrogation techniques was "constitutionally arbitrary" to the representation by the CIA that the program produced "substantial quantities of otherwise unavailable actionable intelligence." (See Memorandum for John A. Rizzo, Senior Deputy General Counsel, Central Intelligence Agency, from Steven G. Bradbury, Principal Deputy Assistant Attorney General, Office of Legal Counsel, re: Application of United States Obligations Under Article 16 of the Convention Against Torture to Certain Techniques that May be Used in the Interrogation of High Value Al Qaeda Detainees.) The CIA provided examples of the purported effectiveness of the CIA enhanced interrogation techniques in response to a request from the OLC. According to an email from CTC Legal , Principal Deputy Assistant Attorney General Steven Bradbury explained that "because the standards under Article 16 [of the Convention Against Torture] require a balancing of the government's need for the information, it would be quite helpful if we had any case studies or examples to demonstrate the value of information produced by the program." See email from: to: , , , ; cc: , [REDACTED], [REDACTED], [REDACTED]; date: March 2, 2005, 2:32 PM.

1059. Among other documents, see Department of Justice Office of Legal Counsel memoranda dated May 30, 2005, and July 20, 2007. The May 30, 2005, OLC memorandum repeats additional CIA representations, including that "enhanced interrogation techniques remain essential to obtaining vital intelligence necessary to detect and disrupt such emerging threats" and that the use of the techniques "led to specific, actionable intelligence." The July 20, 2007, OLC memorandum states that the ". . .use of enhanced interrogation techniques is intended to service this paramount interest [security of the Nation] by producing substantial quantities of otherwise unavailable intelligence," citing CIA representations to the President that the CIA's enhanced interrogation techniques produced information "we could not get anywhere else," and that "the use of such techniques saved American lives by revealing information about planned terrorist plots."

1060. See CIA draft response to Questions for the Record submitted by the Senate Select Committee on Intelligence after an April 12, 2007, hearing on the CIA's Detention and Interrogation Program. The CIA draft response states the CIA Blue Ribbon Panel, consisting of two outside reviewers, was the only independent review of the effectiveness of the CIA's enhanced interrogation techniques, and that "CIA had not conducted any other studies on the effectiveness of [the] interrogation techniques." The final CIA response to the Committee states: "The 2004 CIA Office of the Inspector General report that reviewed CIA's counterterrorism detention and interrogation activities recommended a non-CIA independent experts' review of the effectiveness of each of the authorized EFT and a determination regarding the necessity for the continued use of each technique. As a result, CIA sought and obtained the agreement of Mr. and Mr. to conduct an independent review, which is also known as the Blue-Ribbon Panel report. Their individual reports are provided at Tabs A and B."

1061. See: (1) CIA Office of Inspector General, Special Review - Counterterrorism Detention and Interrogation Program, (2003-7123-IG), May 2004; (2) May 12, 2004, Memorandum for Deputy Director for Operations from , Chief, Information Operations Center, and Henry Crumpton, Chief, National Resources Divisions via Associate Deputy Director for Operations, with the subject line, "Operational Review of CIA Detainee Program"; and (3) Blue Ribbon Panel Review, including a September 2, 2005, Memorandum from to Director Porter Goss, CIA, entitled "Assessment of EITs Effectiveness," and a September 23, 2005, Memorandum from to the Honorable Porter Goss, Director, Central Intelligence Agency, entitled, "Response to request from Director for Assessment of EIT effectiveness."

1062. See, among other examples, a June 27, 2003, Inspector General interview with CTC's Chief of Operations, . The record of that interview (2003-7123-IG) states: "[ ] stated that the Agency's Al-Qa'ida program has been very effective. . . . [ ] views the intelligence as the main criteria for judging the success of the program; specifically, intelligence that has allowed CTC to take other terrorists off the street and to prevent terrorist attacks. This is information that CTC could not have gotten any other way."

1063. November 26, 2001, Draft of Legal Appendix, Paragraph 5, "Hostile Interrogations: Legal Considerations for CIA Officers." This document includes information regarding Paragraph 4.

1064. November 26, 2001, Draft of Legal Appendix, Paragraph 5, "Hostile Interrogations: Legal Considerations for CIA Officers." See Volume I for additional information.

1065. Italics added. November 26, 2001, Draft of Legal Appendix, Paragraph 5, "Hostile Interrogations: Legal Considerations for CIA Officers," at 1. The CIA would later repeat both claims, representing to senior officials and the Department of Justice that the use of the CIA's enhanced interrogation techniques produced intelligence that "saved lives," and that this intelligence was otherwise unavailable. Further, on August 1, 2002, OLC issued an unclassified, but non-public opinion, in the form of a memorandum to White House Counsel Alberto Gonzales, analyzing whether certain interrogation methods would violate 18 U.S.C. §§ 2340-2340A. The memorandum provides a similar rationale for the necessity defense, stating, "certain justification defenses might be available that would potentially eliminate criminal liability. Standard criminal law defenses of necessity and self-defense could justify interrogation methods needed to elicit information to prevent a direct and imminent threat to the United States and its citizens." The memorandum later concludes: "even if an interrogation method might violate Section 2340A, necessity or self-defense could provide justifications that would eliminate any criminal liability."

1066. Email from: [REDACTED]; to: and [REDACTED]; subject: "POW's and Questioning"; date: February 1, 2002.

1067. Italics added. Email from: [REDACTED]; to: and [REDACTED]; subject: "POW's and Questioning"; date: February 1, 2002. In response to a request from the Department of Justice's Office of Professional Responsibility (OPR), the CIA provided two memoranda—one dated November 7, 2001, the other undated—neither of which discussed the necessity defense. The OPR report states: "Although the CIA Office of General Counsel (OGC) told us that these were the only CIA memoranda in its possession on interrogation policy, some of the information we obtained from the CIA suggested otherwise. In an internal email message dated February 1, 2002, from CTC attorney [REDACTED] to [REDACTED], [REDACTED] referred to '[CIA Attorney [REDACTED]] papers reflecting on necessity and anticipatory self defense.'" See Department of Justice, Office of Professional Responsibility, Report. Investigation into the Office of Legal Counsel's Memoranda Concerning Issues Relating to the Central Intelligence Agency's Use of 'Enhanced Interrogation Techniques' on Suspected Terrorists, July 29, 2009, pp. 31–32.

1068. Memorandum for Alberto R. Gonzales, Counsel to the President, from Jay C. Bybee, Assistant Attorney General, Office of Legal Counsel, August 1, 2002, "Re Standards of Conduct for Interrogation under 18 U.S.C 2340-2340A," the U.S. Federal Torture Statute.

1069. Italics added. Memorandum for Alberto R. Gonzales, Counsel to the President, Re: Standards of Conduct for Interrogation under 18 U.S.C. §§ 2340-2340A, pp. 39–41. On December 30, 2004, the OLC issued a new memorandum superseding the August 1, 2002, memorandum in its entirety. The OLC wrote that "[b]ecause the discussion in [the August 1, 2002] memorandum concerning the President's Commander-in-Chief power and the potential defenses to liability was—and remains—unnecessary, it has been eliminated from the analysis that follows. Consideration of the bounds of any such authority would be inconsistent with the President's unequivocal directive that United States personnel not engage in torture." (See Memorandum for James B. Comey, Deputy Attorney General, Re: Legal Standards Applicable Under 18 U.S.C. §§ 2340-2340A). No CIA detainees were subjected to the CIA's enhanced interrogation techniques between the issuance of the December 2004 memorandum and May 2005, when the OLC opined on the application of the federal prohibition on torture to the techniques.

1070. Department of Justice, Office of Professional Responsibility, Report, Investigation into the Office of Legal Counsel's Memoranda Concerning Issues Relating to the Central Intelligence Agency's Use of 'Enhanced Interrogation Techniques' on Suspected Terrorists, July 29, 2009, p. 51.

1071. Bybee response, at 74, n. 6, cited in the OPR Report at fn. 171. Department of Justice, Office of Professional Responsibility, Report, Investigation into the Office of Legal Counsel's Memoranda Concerning Issues Relating to the Central Intelligence Agency's Use of 'Enhanced Interrogation Techniques' on Suspected Terrorists, July 29, 2009.

1072. Memorandum for Alberto R. Gonzales, Counsel to the President, Re: Standards of Conduct for Interrogation under 18 U.S.C. §§ 2340-2340A.

1073. See section of this summary and Volume II on the Thwarting of the Dirty Bomb/Tall Buildings Plot and the Capture of Jose Padilla.

1074. Memorandum for John Rizzo, Acting General Counsel, Central Intelligence Agency, from Jay Bybee, Assistant Attorney General, Office of Legal Counsel, August 1, 2002, Interrogation of al Qaeda Operative (DTS #2009-1810, Tab 1).

1075. Among other documents, see CIA memorandum for the Record, "Review of Interrogation Program on 29 July 2003," prepared by CIA General Counsel Scott Muller, dated August 5, 2003; briefing slides entitled, "CIA Interrogation Program," dated July 29, 2003, presented to senior White House officials; Memorandum to the Inspector General from James Pavitt, CIA's Deputy Director for Operations, dated February 27, 2004, with the subject line, "Comments to Draft IG Special Review, 'Counterterrorism Detention and Interrogation Program' (2003-7123-IG)," Attachment, "Successes of CIA's Counterterrorism Detention and Interrogation Activities," dated February 24, 2004; and the September 6, 2006, CIA-vetted speech by the President on the CIA's Detention and Interrogation Program.

1076. See, among other examples, interview of James Pavitt, by and [REDACTED], Office of the Inspector General, August 21, 2003; Memorandum for: Inspector General; from: James Pavitt, Deputy Director for Operations; subject: re: Comments to Draft IG Special Review, "Counterterrorism Detention and Interrogation Program" 2003-7123-IG; date: February 27, 2004; attachment: February 24, 2004, Memorandum re: Successes of CIA's Counterterrorism Detention Interrogation Activities; and a June 27, 2003, Inspector General interview of the Chief of Operations CTC, . The record of that interview states: "[ ] stated that the Agency's Al-Qa'ida program has been very effective. . . .[ ] views the intelligence as the main criteria for judging the success of the program; specifically, intelligence that has allowed CTC to take other terrorists off the street and to prevent terrorist attacks. This is information that CTC could not have gotten any other way."

1077. Interview of , by [REDACTED] and [REDACTED], Office of the Inspector General, April 3, 2003. On April 2003, a CTC analyst told the IG that KSM "has not provided anything significant to date." See interview of , by [REDACTED] and [REDACTED], Office of the Inspector General, April 21, 2003.) On April 30, 2003, one of KSM's interrogators pointed to "information on hijackings, bridges in New York, and nuclear plants," and information on hidden uranium, which was never found. See interview of , by [REDACTED] and [REDACTED], Office of the Inspector General, April 30, 2003.

1078. told the OIG that KSM was asked about the plan to hijack an airplane in Malaysia and fly

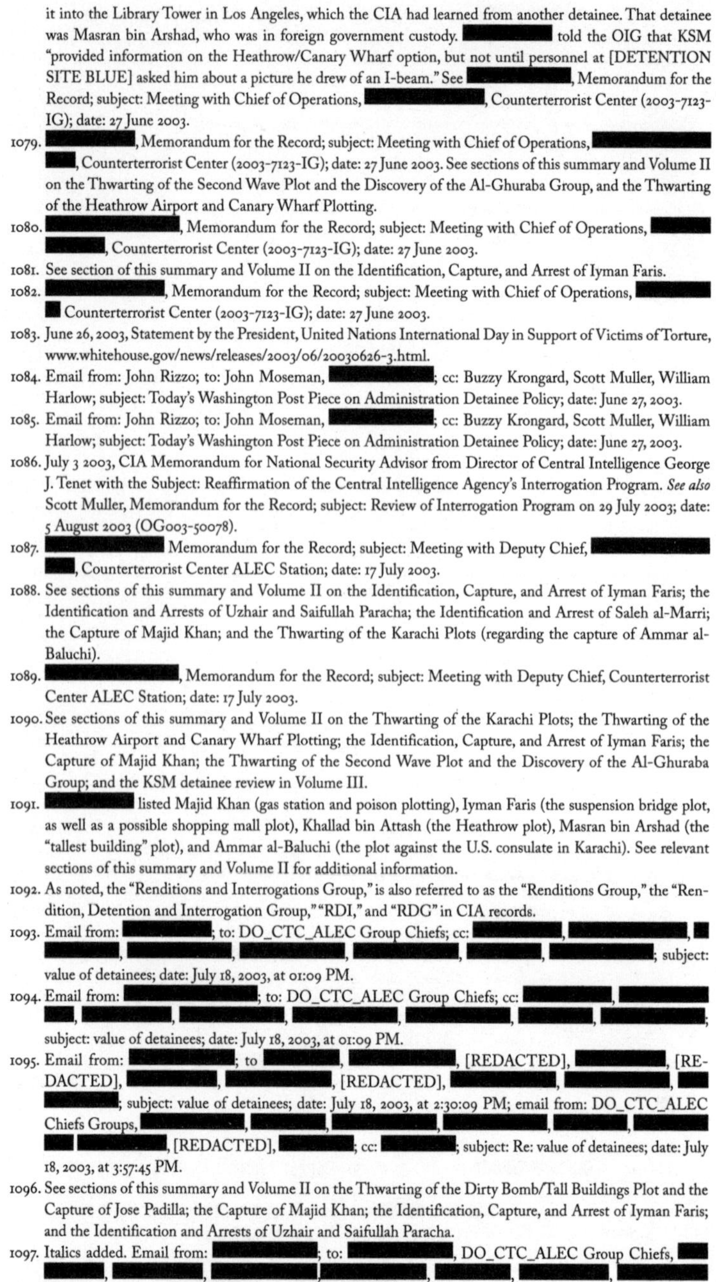

it into the Library Tower in Los Angeles, which the CIA had learned from another detainee. That detainee was Masran bin Arshad, who was in foreign government custody. told the OIG that KSM "provided information on the Heathrow/Canary Wharf option, but not until personnel at [DETENTION SITE BLUE] asked him about a picture he drew of an I-beam." See , Memorandum for the Record; subject: Meeting with Chief of Operations, , Counterterrorist Center (2003-7123-IG); date: 27 June 2003.

1079. , Memorandum for the Record; subject: Meeting with Chief of Operations, , Counterterrorist Center (2003-7123-IG); date: 27 June 2003. See sections of this summary and Volume II on the Thwarting of the Second Wave Plot and the Discovery of the Al-Ghuraba Group, and the Thwarting of the Heathrow Airport and Canary Wharf Plotting.

1080. , Memorandum for the Record; subject: Meeting with Chief of Operations, , Counterterrorist Center (2003-7123-IG); date: 27 June 2003.

1081. See section of this summary and Volume II on the Identification, Capture, and Arrest of Iyman Faris.

1082. , Memorandum for the Record; subject: Meeting with Chief of Operations, Counterterrorist Center (2003-7123-IG); date: 27 June 2003.

1083. June 26, 2003, Statement by the President, United Nations International Day in Support of Victims of Torture, www.whitehouse.gov/news/releases/2003/06/20030626-3.html.

1084. Email from: John Rizzo; to: John Moseman, ; cc: Buzzy Krongard, Scott Muller, William Harlow; subject: Today's Washington Post Piece on Administration Detainee Policy; date: June 27, 2003.

1085. Email from: John Rizzo; to: John Moseman, ; cc: Buzzy Krongard, Scott Muller, William Harlow; subject: Today's Washington Post Piece on Administration Detainee Policy; date: June 27, 2003.

1086. July 3 2003, CIA Memorandum for National Security Advisor from Director of Central Intelligence George J. Tenet with the Subject: Reaffirmation of the Central Intelligence Agency's Interrogation Program. *See also* Scott Muller, Memorandum for the Record; subject: Review of Interrogation Program on 29 July 2003; date: 5 August 2003 (OG003-50078).

1087. Memorandum for the Record; subject: Meeting with Deputy Chief, , Counterterrorist Center ALEC Station; date: 17 July 2003.

1088. See sections of this summary and Volume II on the Identification, Capture, and Arrest of Iyman Faris; the Identification and Arrests of Uzhair and Saifullah Paracha; the Identification and Arrest of Saleh al-Marri; the Capture of Majid Khan; and the Thwarting of the Karachi Plots (regarding the capture of Ammar al-Baluchi).

1089. , Memorandum for the Record; subject: Meeting with Deputy Chief, Counterterrorist Center ALEC Station; date: 17 July 2003.

1090. See sections of this summary and Volume II on the Thwarting of the Karachi Plots; the Thwarting of the Heathrow Airport and Canary Wharf Plotting; the Identification, Capture, and Arrest of Iyman Faris; the Capture of Majid Khan; the Thwarting of the Second Wave Plot and the Discovery of the Al-Ghuraba Group; and the KSM detainee review in Volume III.

1091. listed Majid Khan (gas station and poison plotting), Iyman Faris (the suspension bridge plot, as well as a possible shopping mall plot), Khallad bin Attash (the Heathrow plot), Masran bin Arshad (the "tallest building" plot), and Ammar al-Baluchi (the plot against the U.S. consulate in Karachi). See relevant sections of this summary and Volume II for additional information.

1092. As noted, the "Renditions and Interrogations Group," is also referred to as the "Renditions Group," the "Rendition, Detention and Interrogation Group," "RDI," and "RDG" in CIA records.

1093. Email from: ; to: DO_CTC_ALEC Group Chiefs; cc: , , , , , , , ; subject: value of detainees; date: July 18, 2003, at 01:09 PM.

1094. Email from: ; to: DO_CTC_ALEC Group Chiefs; cc: , , , , , , , ; subject: value of detainees; date: July 18, 2003, at 01:09 PM.

1095. Email from: ; to , , [REDACTED], , [REDACTED], , , [REDACTED], , , ; subject: value of detainees; date: July 18, 2003, at 2:30:09 PM; email from: DO_CTC_ALEC Chiefs Groups, , , , , , , [REDACTED], ; cc: ; subject: Re: value of detainees; date: July 18, 2003, at 3:57:45 PM.

1096. See sections of this summary and Volume II on the Thwarting of the Dirty Bomb/Tall Buildings Plot and the Capture of Jose Padilla; the Capture of Majid Khan; the Identification, Capture, and Arrest of Iyman Faris; and the Identification and Arrests of Uzhair and Saifullah Paracha.

1097. Italics added. Email from: ; to: , DO_CTC_ALEC Group Chiefs, , , , , , , , [REDACTED], ; cc: ; subject: Re: value of detainees; date: July 18, 2003, at 3:57:45 PM.

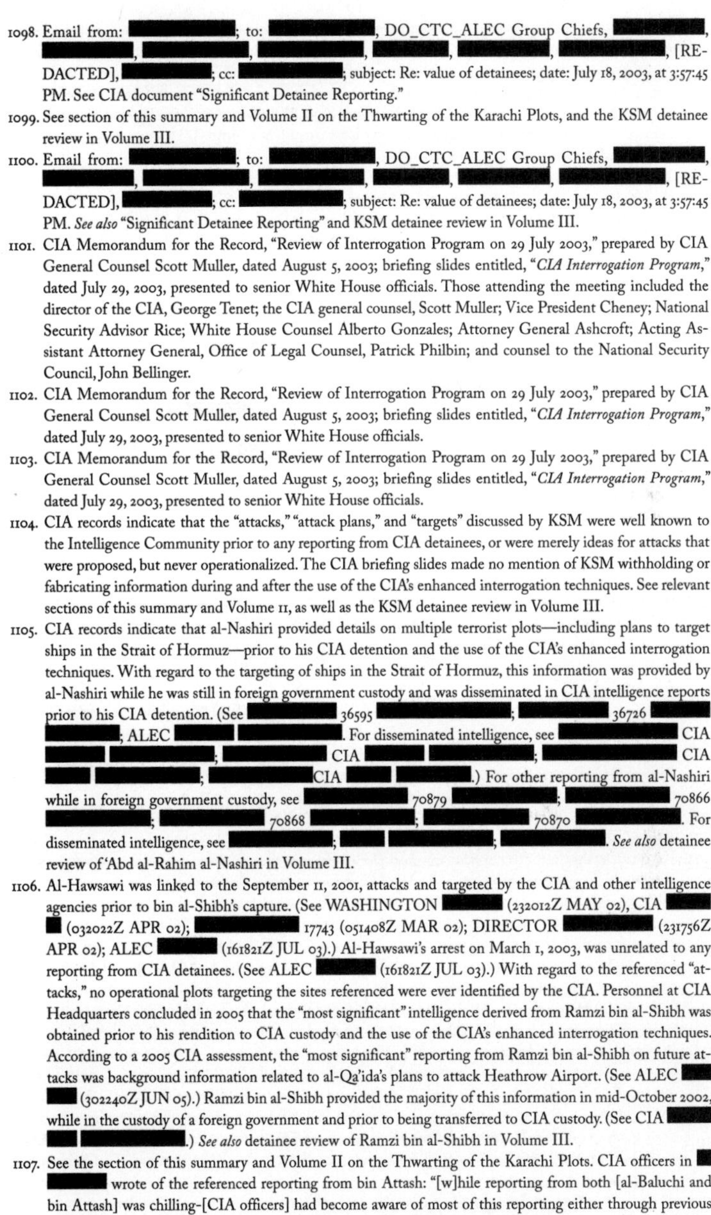

1098. Email from: ; to: , DO_CTC_ALEC Group Chiefs, , , , , , , , [REDACTED], ; cc: ; subject: Re: value of detainees; date: July 18, 2003, at 3:57:45 PM. See CIA document "Significant Detainee Reporting."

1099. See section of this summary and Volume II on the Thwarting of the Karachi Plots, and the KSM detainee review in Volume III.

1100. Email from: ; to: , DO_CTC_ALEC Group Chiefs, , , , , , , , [REDACTED], ; cc: ; subject: Re: value of detainees; date: July 18, 2003, at 3:57:45 PM. *See also* "Significant Detainee Reporting" and KSM detainee review in Volume III.

1101. CIA Memorandum for the Record, "Review of Interrogation Program on 29 July 2003," prepared by CIA General Counsel Scott Muller, dated August 5, 2003; briefing slides entitled, "*CIA Interrogation Program*," dated July 29, 2003, presented to senior White House officials. Those attending the meeting included the director of the CIA, George Tenet; the CIA general counsel, Scott Muller; Vice President Cheney; National Security Advisor Rice; White House Counsel Alberto Gonzales; Attorney General Ashcroft; Acting Assistant Attorney General, Office of Legal Counsel, Patrick Philbin; and counsel to the National Security Council, John Bellinger.

1102. CIA Memorandum for the Record, "Review of Interrogation Program on 29 July 2003," prepared by CIA General Counsel Scott Muller, dated August 5, 2003; briefing slides entitled, "*CIA Interrogation Program*," dated July 29, 2003, presented to senior White House officials.

1103. CIA Memorandum for the Record, "Review of Interrogation Program on 29 July 2003," prepared by CIA General Counsel Scott Muller, dated August 5, 2003; briefing slides entitled, "*CIA Interrogation Program*," dated July 29, 2003, presented to senior White House officials.

1104. CIA records indicate that the "attacks," "attack plans," and "targets" discussed by KSM were well known to the Intelligence Community prior to any reporting from CIA detainees, or were merely ideas for attacks that were proposed, but never operationalized. The CIA briefing slides made no mention of KSM withholding or fabricating information during and after the use of the CIA's enhanced interrogation techniques. See relevant sections of this summary and Volume II, as well as the KSM detainee review in Volume III.

1105. CIA records indicate that al-Nashiri provided details on multiple terrorist plots—including plans to target ships in the Strait of Hormuz—prior to his CIA detention and the use of the CIA's enhanced interrogation techniques. With regard to the targeting of ships in the Strait of Hormuz, this information was provided by al-Nashiri while he was still in foreign government custody and was disseminated in CIA intelligence reports prior to his CIA detention. (See 36595 ; 36726 ; ALEC . For disseminated intelligence, see CIA ; CIA ; CIA ; CIA .) For other reporting from al-Nashiri while in foreign government custody, see 70879 ; 70866 ; 70868 ; 70870 . For disseminated intelligence, see ; ; . *See also* detainee review of 'Abd al-Rahim al-Nashiri in Volume III.

1106. Al-Hawsawi was linked to the September 11, 2001, attacks and targeted by the CIA and other intelligence agencies prior to bin al-Shibh's capture. (See WASHINGTON (232012Z MAY 02), CIA (032022Z APR 02); 17743 (051408Z MAR 02); DIRECTOR (231756Z APR 02); ALEC (161821Z JUL 03).) Al-Hawsawi's arrest on March 1, 2003, was unrelated to any reporting from CIA detainees. (See ALEC (161821Z JUL 03).) With regard to the referenced "attacks," no operational plots targeting the sites referenced were ever identified by the CIA. Personnel at CIA Headquarters concluded in 2005 that the "most significant" intelligence derived from Ramzi bin al-Shibh was obtained prior to his rendition to CIA custody and the use of the CIA's enhanced interrogation techniques. According to a 2005 CIA assessment, the "most significant" reporting from Ramzi bin al-Shibh on future attacks was background information related to al-Qa'ida's plans to attack Heathrow Airport. (See ALEC (302240Z JUN 05).) Ramzi bin al-Shibh provided the majority of this information in mid-October 2002, while in the custody of a foreign government and prior to being transferred to CIA custody. (See CIA .) *See also* detainee review of Ramzi bin al-Shibh in Volume III.

1107. See the section of this summary and Volume II on the Thwarting of the Karachi Plots. CIA officers in wrote of the referenced reporting from bin Attash: "[w]hile reporting from both [al-Baluchi and bin Attash] was chilling-[CIA officers] had become aware of most of this reporting either through previous information or through interviews of al-Baluchi and Ba Attash prior to their transfer out of Karachi." This cable also stated, "[a]s noted in several previous cables, in December 2002 Consulate became aware of the threat to Consulate officials." See 14510 .

1108. For information on the "[i]dentification of [Jose] Padilla," see the section of this summary and Volume II on the Thwarting of the Dirty Bomb/Tall Buildings Plot and the Capture of Jose Padilla. Richard Reid was arrested in December 2001, prior to Abu Zubaydah's capture. See multiple open source reporting and

Department of Justice materials, including, *United States v. Richard Reid* Indictment, U.S. District Court, District of Massachusetts, January 16, 2002. Abu Zubaydah provided information on potential places al-Qa'ida might target, including banks and subways, shortly after his capture to FBI interrogators, months prior to the use of the CIA's "enhanced interrogation techniques" in August 2002. See Federal Bureau of Investigation documents pertaining "to the interrogation of detainee Zayn Al Abideen Abu Zabaidah" and provided to the Senate Select Committee on Intelligence by cover letter dated July 20, 2010 (DTS #2010-2939). *See also* Abu Zubaydah detainee review in Volume III.

1109. Memorandum for the Record; subject: CIA Interrogation Program; September 27, 2003 (OGC-FO-2003-50088). Slides, CIA Interrogation Program, 16 September 2003. The Memorandum for the Record drafted by John Bellinger refers to a "detailed handout" provided by the CIA. See John B. Bellinger, III, Senior Associate Counsel to the President and Legal Advisor, National Security Council; Memorandum for the Record; subject: Briefing of Secretaries Powell and Rumsfeld regarding Interrogation of High-Value Detainees; date: September 30, 2003.

1110. Scott W. Muller; Memorandum for the Record; Interrogation briefing for Jack Goldsmith; date: 16 October 2003 (OGC-FO-2003-50097).

1111. Interview of chief of the Branch of the UBL Group, by , Office of the Inspector General, July 30, 2003.

1112. Interview of , by , Office of the Inspector General, August 5, 2003.

1113. August 19, 2003, Memorandum for the Record, meeting with , Office of the Inspector General.

1114. August 19, 2003, Memorandum for the Record, meeting with , Office of the Inspector General. This information was not included in the IG Special Review.

1115. , Memorandum for the Record; subject: Meeting with Deputy Chief, Counterterrorist Center Al-Qa'ida Department; date: 28 July 2003.

1116. Interview of John E. McLaughlin, by [REDACTED] and [REDACTED], Office of the Inspector General, September 5, 2003. This information was included in the CIA's July 2003 briefing slides. Richard Reid was arrested in December 2001, prior to the capture of Abu Zubaydah.

1117. See the section in this summary and in Volume II on the Capture of Majid Khan; the Capture of Hambali; and the Identification and Arrests of Uzhair and Saifullah Paracha. *See also* the KSM detainee review in Volume III. Richard Reid was arrested prior to the capture of Abu Zubaydah.

1118. Interview of Jose E. Rodriguez, by [REDACTED] and [REDACTED], Office of the Inspector General, August 12, 2003.

1119. Interview of John E. McLaughlin, by [REDACTED] and [REDACTED], Office of the Inspector General, September 5, 2003.

1120. Pavitt also stated that by "September, October and November" of 2002, "they saw a clear benefit" to the use of CIA's enhanced interrogation techniques on Abu Zubaydah (Interview of James Pavitt, by and [REDACTED], Office of the Inspector General, August 21, 2003).

1121. Interview of George Tenet, by [REDACTED], [REDACTED], Office of the Inspector General, 8 September, 2003.

1122. For example, the draft described interrogators placing pressure on a detainee's artery, conducting mock executions, blowing cigarette or cigar smoke into a detainee's face, using cold water to interrogate detainees, and subjecting a detainee to a "hard takedown." In an interview conducted after Gul Rahman's death at DETENTION SITE COBALT, Dr. DUNBAR described a "rough takedown." The interview report stated: "According to [DUNBAR], there were approximately five CIA officers from the renditions team. Each one had a role during the takedown and it was thoroughly planned and rehearsed. They opened the door of [a detainee] cell and rushed in screaming and yelling for him to 'get down.' They dragged him outside, cut off his clothes and secured him with Mylar tape. They covered his head with a hood and ran him up and down a long corridor adjacent to his cell. They slapped him and punched him several times. [DUNBAR] stated that although it was obvious they were not trying to hit him as hard as they could, a couple of times the punches were forceful. As they ran him along the corridor, a couple of times he fell and they dragged him through the dirt (the floor outside of the cells is dirt). [The detainee] did acquire a number of abrasions on his face, legs, and hands, but nothing that required medical attention." DUNBAR stated that after "something like this is done, interrogators should speak to the prisoner to 'give them something to think about.'" See Memorandum for Deputy Director of Operations, from January 28, 2003, Subject: Death Investigation - Gul Rahman, pp. 21–22, paragraph 34.

1123. CIA Inspector General, Special Review, Counterterrorism Detention and Interrogation Program (2003-7123-IG), January 2004.

1124. The Special Review draft stated that KSM "provided information that helped lead to the arrests" of Sayf al-Rahman Paracha, Uzhair Paracha, Saleh al-Marri, and Majid Khan, and that KSM's information "led to the investigation and prosecution" of Iyman Faris. The draft Special Review also stated that information from Abu Zubaydah "helped lead to the identification" of Jose Padilla and Binyam Muhammad. Finally, the draft included the "plots" described by Deputy Chief of ALEC Station during her July 16,

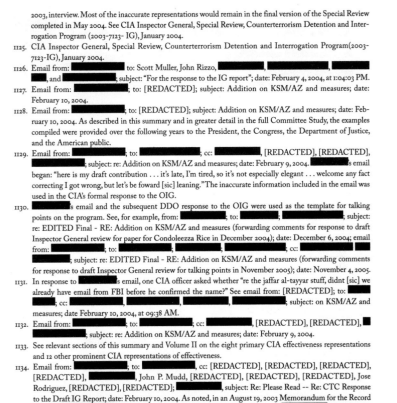

2003, interview. Most of the inaccurate representations would remain in the final version of the Special Review completed in May 2004. See CIA Inspector General, Special Review, Counterterrorism Detention and Interrogation Program (2003-7123- IG), January 2004.

1125. CIA Inspector General, Special Review, Counterterrorism Detention and Interrogation Program(2003-7123-IG), January 2004.

1126. Email from: █████ to: Scott Muller, John Rizzo, █████, █████, █████ █████, and █████; subject: "For the response to the IG report"; date: February 4, 2004, at 1:04:03 PM.

1127. Email from: █████; to: [REDACTED]; subject: Addition on KSM/AZ and measures; date: February 10, 2004.

1128. Email from: █████; to: [REDACTED]; subject: Addition on KSM/AZ and measures; date: February 10, 2004. As described in this summary and in greater detail in the full Committee Study, the examples compiled were provided over the following years to the President, the Congress, the Department of Justice, and the American public.

1129. Email from: █████; to: █████; cc: █████, [REDACTED], [REDACTED], █████; subject: re: Addition on KSM/AZ and measures; date: February 9, 2004. █████s email began: "here is my draft contribution . . . it's late, I'm tired, so it's not especially elegant . . . welcome any fact correcting I got wrong, but let's be foward [sic] leaning." The inaccurate information included in the email was used in the CIA's formal response to the OIG.

1130. █████s email and the subsequent DDO response to the OIG were used as the template for talking points on the program. See, for example, from: █████; to: █████; █████; subject: re: EDITED Final - RE: Addition on KSM/AZ and measures (forwarding comments for response to draft Inspector General review for paper for Condoleezza Rice in December 2004); date: December 6, 2004; email from: █████; to: █████; █████; █████; cc: █████ █████ █████; subject: re: EDITED Final - RE: Addition on KSM/AZ and measures (forwarding comments for response to draft Inspector General review for talking points in November 2005); date: November 4, 2005.

1131. In response to █████s email, one CIA officer asked whether "re the jaffar al-tayyar stuff, didnt [sic] we already have email from FBI before he confirmed the name?" See email from: [REDACTED]; to: █████ █████; cc: █████, █████, █████, █████; subject: on KSM/AZ and measures; date February 10, 2004, at 09:38 AM.

1132. Email from: █████; to: █████; cc: █████, [REDACTED], [REDACTED], █████ █████; subject: re: Addition on KSM/AZ and measures; date: February 9, 2004.

1133. See relevant sections of this summary and Volume II on the eight primary CIA effectiveness representations and 12 other prominent CIA representations of effectiveness.

1134. Email from: █████; to: █████, cc: [REDACTED], [REDACTED], [REDACTED], [REDACTED], █████, John P. Mudd, [REDACTED], [REDACTED], [REDACTED], Jose Rodriguez, [REDACTED], [REDACTED]; █████, subject: Re: Please Read -- Re: CTC Response to the Draft IG Report; date: February 10, 2004. As noted, in an August 19, 2003 Memorandum for the Record detailing █████s interview with the Office of the Inspector General, █████ told the OIG that "the often-cited example of Zubaydah identifying Padilla is not quite accurate," and that "[n]ot only did [Abu Zubaydah] not tell us who Padilla was, his information alone would never have led us to Padilla." Noting that the Pakistani government had told the CIA about Jose Padilla and his partner prior to Abu Zubaydah providing any information on the pair, █████ stated, "[i]n essence, CTC got lucky." This information was not included in the draft or final OIG Special Review.

1135. The information forwarded by █████ was related to the Heathrow Airport plotting and stated that "[o]nly after enhanced measures" did KSM "admit that the sketch of a beam labeled Canary Wharf in his notebook was in fact an illustration that KSM the engineer drew himself to show another AQ operative that the beams in the Wharf like those in the World Trade Center - would likely melt and collapse the building, killing all inside." The email also stated that KSM "identified the leading operatives involved in both the UK and Saudi cells that would support the operation." These representations were inaccurate. See the section of this summary and Volume II on the Thwarting of the Heathrow Airport and Canary Wharf Plotting, and the KSM detainee review in Volume III.

1136. The information forwarded by █████ stated that, "subsequent to the application of enhanced measures," the CIA "learned more in-depth details" about operational planning, "to include ongoing operations against both the US and Saudi interests in Saudi Arabia." This representation omitted key information provided by al-Nashiri in foreign government custody and prior to the use of the CIA's enhanced interrogation techniques. See the 'Abd al-Rahimal-Nashiri detainee review in Volume III.

1137. The information forwarded by █████ stated that, "after the use of enhanced measures [Hambali] provided information that led to the wrap-up of an al-Qa'ida cell in Karachi, some of whose members were destined to be the second wave attack pilots inside the US after 911 . . . . [T]heir identification and subsequent detention saved hundreds of lives." This representation was inaccurate. See the section of this summary and Volume II on the Thwarting of the Second Wave Plot and the Discovery of the Al-Ghuraba Group. (See email from: █████; to █████, █████, █████; multiple cc's; subject:

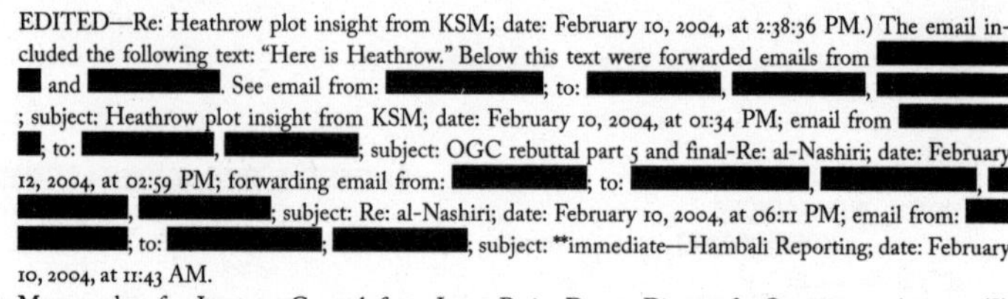
EDITED—Re: Heathrow plot insight from KSM; date: February 10, 2004, at 2:38:36 PM.) The email included the following text: "Here is Heathrow." Below this text were forwarded emails from and . See email from: ; to: , , ; subject: Heathrow plot insight from KSM; date: February 10, 2004, at 01:34 PM; email from ; to: , ; subject: OGC rebuttal part 5 and final-Re: al-Nashiri; date: February 12, 2004, at 02:59 PM; forwarding email from: ; to: , , , ; subject: Re: al-Nashiri; date: February 10, 2004, at 06:11 PM; email from: ; to: ; ; subject: **immediate—Hambali Reporting; date: February 10, 2004, at 11:43 AM.

1138. Memorandum for: Inspector General; from: James Pavitt, Deputy Director for Operations; subject: re (S) Comments to Draft IG Special Review, "Counterterrorism Detention and Interrogation Program" (2003-7123-IG); date: February 27, 2004; attachment: February 24, 2004, Memorandum re Successes of CIA's Counterterrorism Detention and Interrogation Activities.

1139. Memorandum for: Inspector General; from: James Pavitt, Deputy Director for Operations; subject: re (S) Comments to Draft IG Special Review, "Counterterrorism Detention and Interrogation Program" (2003-7123-IG); date: February 27, 2004; attachment: February 24, 2004, Memorandum re Successes of CIA's Counterterrorism Detention and Interrogation Activities.

1140. Memorandum for: Inspector General; from: James Pavitt, Deputy Director for Operations; subject: re (S) Comments to Draft IG Special Review, "Counterterrorism Detention and Interrogation Program" (2003-7123-IG); date: February 27, 2004; attachment: February 24, 2004, Memorandum re Successes of CIA's Counterterrorism Detention and Interrogation Activities.

1141. A review of CIA records found that almost all of the information in the Pavitt memorandum was inaccurate and unsupported by CIA interrogation and intelligence records. The CIA's June 2013 Response states that CIA officers "generally provided accurate information [to the Inspector General] on the operation and effectiveness of the program," and that "with rare exceptions, [CIA officers] provided accurate assessments to the OIG."

1142. The CIA Inspector General Special Review, "Counterterrorism Detention and Interrogation Program," was declassified with redactions in May 2008. On August 24, 2009, some portions of the Review that were redacted in May 2008 were unredacted and declassified.

1143. wrote in an email: "We can expect to need to present these data to appropriately cleared personnel at the IG and on the Hill, to the Attorney General and quite possibly to the President at some point, and they must be absolutely verifiable." (See email from: ; to: [REDACTED]; subject: Addition on KSM/AZ and measures; date: February 10, 2004.) As detailed in this Study, the CIA consistently used the same "effectiveness" case studies. The eight most frequently cited "thwarted" plots and captured terrorists are examined in this summary, and in greater detail in the full Committee Study, as are 12 other prominent examples that the CIA has cited in the context of the "effectiveness" of the CIA's enhanced interrogation techniques.

1144. Talking Points for the DCI: DOD Proposals to Move Forward on Transfer of HVDs to Guantanamo, 16 December 2004.

1145. DCI Talking Points for Weekly Meeting with National Security Advisor, 12 January 2005; included in email from: [REDACTED]; to: [REDACTED], ; cc: , John A. Rizzo, , , , , , ; subject: Re Coord on NSC Talkings for 1/14; date: January 11, 2005, at 03:33 PM.

1146. The draft stated that the "Second Wave" plotting "was uncovered during the initial debriefings of a senior al-Qa'ida detainee," that the Heathrow plotting "was also discovered as a result of detainee debriefings," that the Karachi plotting "was revealed during the initial debriefings of two senior al-Qa'ida detainees," and that the CIA "learned form [sic] detainee debriefings of the second shoe bomber. (See email from: ; to: [REDACTED], , , [REDACTED], [REDACTED], [REDACTED], , [REDACTED], , [REDACTED], , [REDACTED], [REDACTED]; cc: ; subject: FOR IMMEDIATE COORDINATION: summary of impact of detainee program; date: April 13, 2005, at 5:21:37 PM.) These claims were inaccurate. See relevant sections of this summary and Volume II.

1147. The draft discussed Issa al-Hindi, who had been referenced in the 9/11 Commission Report, stating that "[p]rior to KSM's reporting, the U.S. Government was not aware of Issa's casing activity, nor did we know his true identity." It added that "KSM's reporting was the impetus for an intense investigation, culminating in Issa's identification and arrest." The draft also included two examples that had not been in official public documents, but had been described in press stories. The first was that "KSM led U.S. investigators to an Ohio truck driver named Iyman Faris." The second was that "KSM's confessions were also instrumental in determining the identity of Saajid Badat," the second shoe bomber. (See email from: , Chief of Operations, ALEC Station; to: , , [REDACTED], [REDACTED], [REDACTED], , ,[REDACTED], [REDACTED], , , , [REDACTED], [REDACTED], , , ; cc: ,

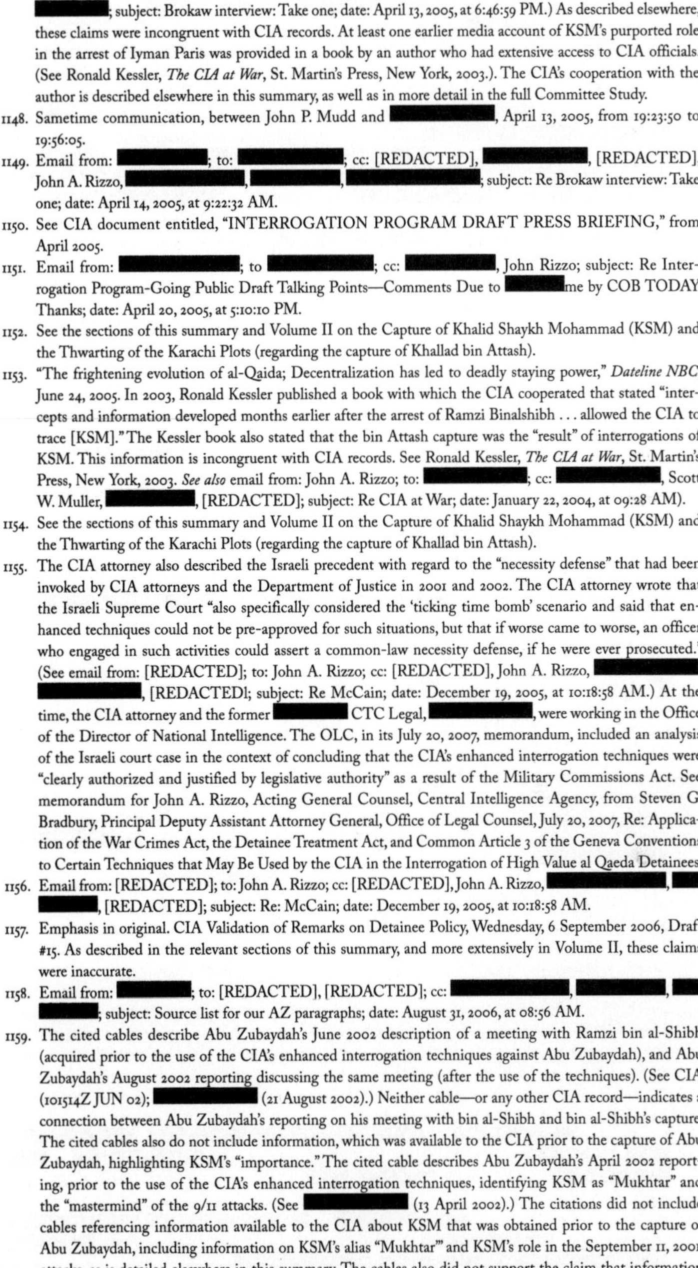

; subject: Brokaw interview: Take one; date: April 13, 2005, at 6:46:59 PM.) As described elsewhere, these claims were incongruent with CIA records. At least one earlier media account of KSM's purported role in the arrest of Iyman Paris was provided in a book by an author who had extensive access to CIA officials. (See Ronald Kessler, *The CIA at War*, St. Martin's Press, New York, 2003.). The CIA's cooperation with the author is described elsewhere in this summary, as well as in more detail in the full Committee Study.

1148. Sametime communication, between John P. Mudd and , April 13, 2005, from 19:23:50 to 19:56:05.

1149. Email from: ; to: ; cc: [REDACTED], , [REDACTED], John A. Rizzo, , , ; subject: Re Brokaw interview: Take one; date: April 14, 2005, at 9:22:32 AM.

1150. See CIA document entitled, "INTERROGATION PROGRAM DRAFT PRESS BRIEFING," from April 2005.

1151. Email from: ; to ; cc: , John Rizzo; subject: Re Interrogation Program-Going Public Draft Talking Points—Comments Due to me by COB TODAY Thanks; date: April 20, 2005, at 5:10:10 PM.

1152. See the sections of this summary and Volume II on the Capture of Khalid Shaykh Mohammad (KSM) and the Thwarting of the Karachi Plots (regarding the capture of Khallad bin Attash).

1153. "The frightening evolution of al-Qaida; Decentralization has led to deadly staying power," *Dateline NBC*, June 24, 2005. In 2003, Ronald Kessler published a book with which the CIA cooperated that stated "intercepts and information developed months earlier after the arrest of Ramzi Binalshibh . . . allowed the CIA to trace [KSM]." The Kessler book also stated that the bin Attash capture was the "result" of interrogations of KSM. This information is incongruent with CIA records. See Ronald Kessler, *The CIA at War*, St. Martin's Press, New York, 2003. *See also* email from: John A. Rizzo; to: ; cc: , Scott W. Muller, , [REDACTED]; subject: Re CIA at War; date: January 22, 2004, at 09:28 AM).

1154. See the sections of this summary and Volume II on the Capture of Khalid Shaykh Mohammad (KSM) and the Thwarting of the Karachi Plots (regarding the capture of Khallad bin Attash).

1155. The CIA attorney also described the Israeli precedent with regard to the "necessity defense" that had been invoked by CIA attorneys and the Department of Justice in 2001 and 2002. The CIA attorney wrote that the Israeli Supreme Court "also specifically considered the 'ticking time bomb' scenario and said that enhanced techniques could not be pre-approved for such situations, but that if worse came to worse, an officer who engaged in such activities could assert a common-law necessity defense, if he were ever prosecuted." (See email from: [REDACTED]; to: John A. Rizzo; cc: [REDACTED], John A. Rizzo, , , [REDACTEDl; subject: Re McCain; date: December 19, 2005, at 10:18:58 AM.) At the time, the CIA attorney and the former CTC Legal, , were working in the Office of the Director of National Intelligence. The OLC, in its July 20, 2007, memorandum, included an analysis of the Israeli court case in the context of concluding that the CIA's enhanced interrogation techniques were "clearly authorized and justified by legislative authority" as a result of the Military Commissions Act. See memorandum for John A. Rizzo, Acting General Counsel, Central Intelligence Agency, from Steven G. Bradbury, Principal Deputy Assistant Attorney General, Office of Legal Counsel, July 20, 2007, Re: Application of the War Crimes Act, the Detainee Treatment Act, and Common Article 3 of the Geneva Conventions to Certain Techniques that May Be Used by the CIA in the Interrogation of High Value al Qaeda Detainees.

1156. Email from: [REDACTED]; to: John A. Rizzo; cc: [REDACTED], John A. Rizzo, , , [REDACTED]; subject: Re: McCain; date: December 19, 2005, at 10:18:58 AM.

1157. Emphasis in original. CIA Validation of Remarks on Detainee Policy, Wednesday, 6 September 2006, Draft #15. As described in the relevant sections of this summary, and more extensively in Volume II, these claims were inaccurate.

1158. Email from: ; to: [REDACTED], [REDACTED]; cc: , , ; subject: Source list for our AZ paragraphs; date: August 31, 2006, at 08:56 AM.

1159. The cited cables describe Abu Zubaydah's June 2002 description of a meeting with Ramzi bin al-Shibh (acquired prior to the use of the CIA's enhanced interrogation techniques against Abu Zubaydah), and Abu Zubaydah's August 2002 reporting discussing the same meeting (after the use of the techniques). (See CIA (101514Z JUN 02); (21 August 2002).) Neither cable—or any other CIA record—indicates a connection between Abu Zubaydah's reporting on his meeting with bin al-Shibh and bin al-Shibh's capture. The cited cables also do not include information, which was available to the CIA prior to the capture of Abu Zubaydah, highlighting KSM's "importance." The cited cable describes Abu Zubaydah's April 2002 reporting, prior to the use of the CIA's enhanced interrogation techniques, identifying KSM as "Mukhtar" and the "mastermind" of the 9/11 attacks. (See (13 April 2002).) The citations did not include cables referencing information available to the CIA about KSM that was obtained prior to the capture of Abu Zubaydah, including information on KSM's alias "Mukhtar'" and KSM's role in the September 11, 2001, attacks, as is detailed elsewhere in this summary. The cables also did not support the claim that information provided by Abu Zubaydah or Ramzi bin al-Shibh led to the capture of KSM. One cited cable related to the identification by Ramzi bin al-Shibh, while bin al-Shibh was in foreign government custody, of Ali Abdul

Aziz Ali as "Ammar." [The cable was cited as 20700 . As determined later, the actual cable was 20790.] As described elsewhere in this summary, KSM was not captured as a result of information related to Ammar al-Baluchi. The email exchange listed two cables directly related to the capture of KSM. The first cable, from approximately a week before KSM's capture, described the CIA's operational use and value of the asset who led the CIA to KSM. The cable stated that the relationship between the asset and KSM's , through whom the asset gained access to KSM, was "based on ." The cable stated that CIA Headquarters "continues to be impressed with the evidence of [the asset's] access to KSM associates, ." (See DIRECTOR .) The second cable described KSM's capture, stating that it was "based on locational information" provided by the asset. (See 41351 .) Neither of the two cables cited to support the claim made any reference to Abu Zubaydah, Ramzi bin al-Shibh, or any other detainee in CIA or foreign government custody. The capture of KSM, including the role of the asset (referred to herein as "ASSET X") is detailed elsewhere in this summary and in greater detail in the full Committee Study. See email from: ; to: [REDACTED], [REDACTED]; cc: , , ; subject: Source list for our AZ paragraphs; date: August 31, 2006, at 08:56 AM.

1160. Pronunciation brackets in original draft. CIA Validation of Remarks on Detainee Policy, Wednesday, 6 September 2006, Draft #15.

1161. The document cited a cable on Abu Zubaydah's August 2002 description of his meeting with Ramzi bin al-Shibh, but not the previously cited June 2002 cable related to Abu Zubaydah's description of the same meeting Zubaydah was subjected to the CIA's enhanced interrogation techniques. See .

1162. The information included in the cable describing Abu Zubaydah's August 2002 reporting on his meeting with Ramzi bin al-Shibh was unrelated to the capture of Ramzi bin al-Shibh. (See .) The CIA document also cited as a "source" the capture of bin al-Shibh with no mention of Abu Zubaydah's reporting. (See .) The details of Ramzi bin al-Shibh's capture are described elsewhere in this summary and in greater detail in the full Committee Study.

1163. The CIA document included a previously cited cable relating to the capture of KSM that made no mention of reporting from CIA detainees. (See 41351 .) The CIA document also included the previously cited cable describing bin al-Shibh's identification of "Ammar." As described in the section of this summary, as well as in Volume II, on the Capture of KSM, KSM was not captured as a result of information related to Ammar al-Baluchi. (The document cited the cable as 20700, as noted, the actual cite was 20790.) The CIA cable also cited an analytical product whose relevance was limited to the connection between KSM and al-Aziz (Ammar al-Baluchi). (See DI Serial Flier CTC 2002-30086 CH: CIA analytic report, "Threat Threads: Recent Advances in Understanding 11 September.") Finally, the document included a cable that was unrelated to the content of the speech.

1164. See sections of this summary and Volume II on the Capture of Ramzi bin al-Shibh and the Capture of Khalid Shaykh Mohammad (KSM).

1165. Presidential Speech on September 6, 2006, based on CIA information and vetted by CIA personnel.

1166. CIA Validation of Remarks on Detainee Policy, Wednesday, 6 September 2006, Draft #15; .

1167. 13678 (070724Z MAR 03), disseminated as . Further, the June 2003 cable, DIRECTOR (122120Z JUN 03), cited by the CIA as validation, makes no reference to reporting from KSM. Khan was captured on March 5, 2003 and was in foreign government detention until being transferred to CIA custody on May 2003. See details on the detention and interrogation of Majid Khan in Volume III.

1168. On April 29, 2009, Marc Thiessen, the speechwriter responsible for President Bush's September 6, 2006, speech, wrote: "This was the most carefully vetted speech in presidential history - reviewed by all the key players from the individuals who ran the program all the way up to the director of national intelligence, who personally attested to the accuracy of the speech in a memo to the president. And just last week on Fox News, former CIA Director Michael Hayden said he went back and checked with the agency as to the accuracy of that speech and reported: "We stand by our story."" See Marc Thiessen, "The West Coast Plot: An 'Inconvenient Truth,'" *The National Review*, April 25, 2009.

1169. Email from: ; to: , , , , [REDACTED], [REDACTED], [REDACTED], m , [REDACTED], ; subject: THE MOMENT YOU MAY HAVE BEEN WAITING FOR!!! Please verify the attached; date: September 8, 2006, at 06:28 PM.

1170. Email from: [REDACTED]; to: ; cc: , , [REDACTED], [REDACTED], [REDACTED], [REDACTED], , , , ; subject: Re: THE MOMENT YOU MAY HAVE BEEN WAITING FOR!!! Please verify the Attached; date: September 11, 2006, at 9:16:15 AM; attachment Nl: CIA Validation of Remarks on Detainee Policy Final (Draft #15). The email also identified as unrelated one cable that had been cited as a source and corrected a transposed number of the cable describing Ramzi bin al-Shibh's identification of "Ammar."

1171. Email from: ; to , , , , Mark Mansfield, [REDACTED], [REDACTED]; cc: [REDACTED], , , [REDACTED], [REDACTED]; subject: Questions about Abu Zubaydah's identification of KSM as "Mukhtar"; date: September 7, 2006. A September 7, 2006, article (published September 8, 2006) in the *New York Times*, by Mark Mazzetti, entitled, "Questions Raised About Bush's Primary Claims of Secret Detention System" included comments by CIA officials defending the assertions in the President's speech. The article stated: "Mr. Bush described the interrogation techniques used on the C.I.A. prisoners as having been 'safe, lawful and effective,' and he asserted that torture had not been used . . . Mr. Bush also said it was the interrogation of Mr. Zubaydah that identified Mr. bin al-Shibh as an accomplice in the Sept. 11 attacks. American officials had identified Mr. bin al-Shibh's role in the attacks months before Mr. Zubaydah's capture."

1172. There are no CIA records to support these claims. See the section of this summary on the capture of Ramzi bin al-Shibh, as well as a more detailed account in Volume II.

1173. Email from: ; to , , , , Mark Mansfield, [REDACTED], [REDACTED]; cc: [REDACTED], , , [REDACTED], [REDACTED]; subject: Questions about Abu Zubaydah's identification of KSM as "Mukhtar"; date: September 7, 2006. There are no CIA records indicating what was "explained" to the White House. The CIA validation document provided officially concurred with the passage in the speech. See CIA Validation of Remarks on Detainee Policy, Wednesday, 6 September 2006, Draft #15: .

1174. Email from: ; to , , , , , Mark Mansfield, [REDACTED], [REDACTED]; cc: [REDACTED], , , [REDACTED], [REDACTED]; subject: Questions about Abu Zubaydah's identification of KSM as "Mukhtar"; date: September 7, 2006.

1175. The Unofficial Story of the al-Qaeda 14; Their torture by the CIA was wrong - in more ways than you might think, Ron Suskind, *Time*, 18 September 2006.

1176. Email from: to: [REDACTED], , [REDACTED], [REDACTED], [REDACTED], [REDACTED], [REDACTED]; subject: URGENT: FOR YOUR COMMENT: DCIA Questions on the Suskind Article; date: September 11, 2006, at 08:23 PM.

1177. See the section of this summary and Volume II on the Capture of Ramzi bin al-Shibh and the Capture of Khalid Shaykh Mohammad (KSM). In 2007, CIA officers also questioned the passage in the President's September 6, 2006, speech concerning the disruption of plotting against Camp Lemonier in Djibouti. See the section of this summary and Volume II on the Thwarting of the Camp Lemonier Plotting for additional information.

1178. President Bush made other public statements that relied on inaccurate information provided by the CIA. For example, as described elsewhere in this summary, on March 8, 2008, President Bush vetoed legislation that would have limited interrogations to techniques authorized by the Army Field Manual. The President's veto message to the House of Representatives stated that "[t]he CIA's ability to conduct a separate and specialized interrogation program for terrorists who possess the most critical information in the war on terror has helped the United States prevent a number of attacks, including plots to fly passenger airplanes into the Library Tower in Los Angeles and into Heathrow Airport or buildings in downtown London." (See message to the House of Representatives, President George W. Bush, March 8, 2008). The President also explained his veto in his weekly radio address, in which he referenced the "Library Tower," also known as the "Second Wave" plot, and the Heathrow plot, while representing that the CIA program "helped us stop a plot to strike a U.S. Marine camp in Djibouti, a planned attack on the U.S. consulate in Karachi . . ." (See President's Radio Address, President George W. Bush, March 8, 2008). As detailed in this summary, and described more fully in Volume II, CIA representations regarding the role of the CIA's enhanced interrogation techniques with regard to the Second Wave, Heathrow, Djibouti and Karachi plots were inaccurate.

1179. The OLC memorandum, along with other OLC memoranda relying on inaccurate CIA representations, has been declassified, as has the May 2004 OIG Special Review containing inaccurate information provided by CIA officers. Memorandum for John A. Rizzo, Acting General Counsel, Central Intelligence Agency, from Steven G. Bradbury, Principal Deputy Assistant Attorney General, Office of Legal Counsel, July 20, 2007, Re: Application of the War Crimes Act, the Detainee Treatment Act, and Common Article 3 of the Geneva Conventions to Certain Techniques that May Be Used by the CIA in the Interrogation of High Value al Qaeda Detainees (DTS#2009-1810, Tab14).

1180. See Volume II for additional information on CIA representations.

1181. Among other documents, see Memorandum for: Inspector General; from: James Pavitt, Deputy Director for Operations; subject: re (S) Comments to Draft IG Special Review, "Counterterrorism Detention and Interrogation Program" (2003-7123-IG); date: February 27, 2004; attachment: February 24, 2004, Memorandum re

Successes of CIA's Counterterrorism Detention and Interrogation Activities.

1182. Among other documents, see Memorandum for the Record: "Review of Interrogation Program on 29 July 2003." Memorandum prepared by CIA General Counsel Scott Muller, dated August 5, 2003, and briefing slides entitled, "CM Interrogation Program," dated July 29, 2003, presented to senior White House officials; and Briefing for Vice President Cheney: CIA Detention and Interrogation Program, CIA document dated March 4, 2005, entitled, "Briefing for Vice President Cheney: CIA Detention and Interrogation Program."

1183. Among other documents, see March 2, 2005, Memorandum for Steve Bradbury from [REDACTED], [REDACTED] Legal Group, DCI Counterterrorist Center re: Effectiveness of the CIA Counterterrorist Interrogation Techniques.

1184. Among other documents, see CIA classified statement for the record. Senate Select Committee on Intelligence, provided by General Michael V. Hayden, Director, Central Intelligence Agency, 12 April 2007; and accompanying Senate Select Committee on Intelligence hearing transcript for April 12, 2007, entitled, "Hearing on Central Intelligence Agency Detention and Interrogation Program." Director Hayden stated: "Now in June [2002], after about four months of interrogation, Abu Zubaydah reached a point where he refused to cooperate and he shut down. He would not talk at all to the FBI interrogators and although he was still talking to CIA interrogators no significant progress was being made in learning anything of intelligence value."

1185. For example, see CIA "Questions and Proposed Answers," 9/2/2006, Tab 2 of CIA Validation of Remarks on Detainee Policy, September 6, 2006.

1186. See, for example, March 2, 2005, CIA memorandum for Steve Bradbury from [REDACTED], [REDACTED] Legal Group, DCI Counterterrorist Center, "Effectiveness of the CIA Counterterrorist Interrogation Techniques."

1187. See, for example, ODNI September 2006 Unclassified Public Release: "During initial interrogation, Abu Zubaydah gave some information that he probably viewed as nominal. Some was important, however, including that Khalid Shaykh Mohammad (KSM) was the 9/11 mastermind and used the moniker 'Mukhtar.' This identification allowed us to comb previously collected intelligence for both names, opening up new leads to this terrorist plotter—leads that eventually resulted in his capture. It was clear to his interrogators that Abu Zubaydah possessed a great deal of information about al-Qa'ida; however, he soon stopped all cooperation. Over the ensuing months, the CIA designed a new interrogation program that would be safe, effective, and legal." *See also* Presidential Speech on September 6, 2006, based on CIA information and vetted by CIA personnel.

1188. As detailed in DIRECTOR [REDACTED] (031357Z AUG 02). *See also* Office of Legal Counsel Memorandum for John Rizzo, Acting General Counsel of the Central Intelligence Agency, dated August 1, 2002, and entitled "Interrogation of al Qaeda Operative," which states: "The interrogation team is certain [Abu Zubaydah] has additional information that he refuses to divulge. Specifically, he is withholding information regarding terrorist networks in the United States or in Saudi Arabia and information regarding plans to conduct attacks within the United States or against our interests overseas."

1189. Among other documents, see Office of the Director of National Intelligence, "Summary of the High Value Terrorist Detainee Program," September 6, 2006; and CIA Memorandum for Steve Bradbury at the Department of Justice, dated March 2, 2005, from [REDACTED], [REDACTED] Legal Group, DCI Counterterrorist Center, subject "Effectiveness of the CIA Counterterrorist Interrogation Techniques."

1190. See, for example, March 2, 2005, CIA memorandum for Steve Bradbury from [REDACTED], [REDACTED] Legal Group, DCI Counterterrorist Center, "Effectiveness of the CIA Counterterrorist Interrogation Techniques."

1191. Email from: [REDACTED]; to: [REDACTED], [REDACTED], and [REDACTED]; subject: "Suggested language change for AZ"; date: August 30, 2006, at 06:32 PM.

1192. Sametime communication, [REDACTED] and [REDACTED], 30/Aug/06 13:15:23 to 19:31:47.

1193. See ODNI September 2006 Unclassified Public Release: "During initial interrogation, Abu Zubaydah gave some information that he probably viewed as nominal. Some was important, however, including that Khalid Shaykh Mohammad (KSM) was the 9/11 mastermind and used the moniker 'Mukhtar.' This identification allowed us to comb previously collected intelligence for both names, opening up new leads to this terrorist plotter—leads that eventually resulted in his capture. It was clear to his interrogators that Abu Zubaydah possessed a great deal of information about al-Qa'ida; however, he soon stopped all cooperation. Over the ensuing months, the CIA designed a new interrogation program that would be safe, effective, and legal." *See also* Presidential Speech on September 6, 2006, based on CIA information and vetted by CIA personnel, that states: "We knew that Zubaydah had more information that could save innocent lives. But he stopped talking . . . And so, the CIA used an alternative set of procedures."

1194. [REDACTED] 10424 (070814Z JUN 02).

1195. See Abu Zubaydah detainee review in Volume IE, to include CIA email [REDACTED] dated March 28, 2007, 04:42PM, with the subject line, "Subject detainee allegation—per our telcon of today."

1196. See reporting charts in Abu Zubaydah detainee review, as well as CIA paper entitled "Abu Zubaydah" and dated March 2005. The same information was included in an "Abu Zubaydah Bio" document "Prepared on 9 August 2006."

1197. See reporting charts in the Abu Zubaydah detainee review in Volume III.

1198. See [REDACTED] 10586 (041559Z AUG 02), which states: "In truth, [Zubaydah] can halt the proceedings at any time by providing truthful revelations on the threat which may save countless lives."

1199. See Abu Zubaydah detainee review in Volume III.

1200. As detailed in DIRECTOR [REDACTED] (031357Z AUG 02). The CIA further represented: (1) that the enhanced interrogation phase of Abu Zubaydah's interrogation would likely last "no more than several days but could last up to thirty days," (2) "that the use of the [enhanced interrogation techniques] would be on an as-needed basis and that not all of these techniques will necessarily be used," (3) that the CIA expected "these techniques to be used in some sort of escalating fashion, culminating with the waterboard, though not necessarily ending with this technique," (4) "that although some of these techniques may be used more than once, that repetition will not be substantial because the techniques generally lose their effectiveness after several repetitions," and (5) "that steps will be taken to ensure that [Abu Zubaydah's] injury is not in any way exacerbated by the use of these methods." See the Abu Zubaydah detainee review for detailed information for how these statements proved almost entirely inaccurate. *See also* Memorandum for John Rizzo, Acting General Counsel, Central Intelligence Agency, from Jay Bybee, Assistant Attorney General, Office of Legal Counsel, August 1, 2002, Interrogation of al Qaeda Operative.

1201. DIRECTOR [REDACTED] (031357Z AUG 02).

1202. [REDACTED] 73208 (231043Z JUL 02); email from: [REDACTED]; to: [REDACTED], [REDACTED], and [REDACTED]; subject: Addendum from [DETENTION SITE GREEN]; date: July 23, 2002, at 07:56:49 PM; [REDACTED] 73208 (231043Z JUL 02). Additional assessments by the interrogation team that Abu Zubaydah was not withholding information are described in the Abu Zubaydah detainee review in Volume III.

1203. See Abu Zubaydah detainee review in Volume III. Participants in the interrogation of Abu Zubaydah also wrote that Abu Zubaydah "probably reached the point of cooperation even prior to the August institution of 'enhanced' measures -a development missed because of the narrow focus of the questioning. In any event there was no evidence that the waterboard produced time-perishable information which otherwise would have been unobtainable." See CIA Summary and Reflections of [REDACTED] Medical Services on OMS participation in the RDI program.

1204. CIA paper entitled "Abu Zubaydah" and dated March 2005. *See also* "Abu Zubaydah Bio" document "Prepared on 9 August 2006."

1205. See Abu Zubaydah detainee review in Volume III, and CIA paper entitled, "Abu Zubaydah," dated March 2005; as well as "Abu Zubaydah Bio" document "Prepared on 9 August 2006."

1206. See Abu Zubaydah detainee review in Volume III.

1207. Abu Zubaydah was taken into CIA custody on March [REDACTED], 2002, and was shortly thereafter hospitalized until April 15, 2002. Abu Zubaydah returned to DETENTION SITE GREEN on April 15, 2002. During the months of April and May 2002, which included a period during which Abu Zubaydah was on life support and unable to speak (Abu Zubaydah communicated primarily with FBI special agents in writing), Abu Zubaydah's interrogations resulted in 95 intelligence reports. In February 2008, the CIA identified the "key intelligence and reporting derived" from Abu Zubaydah. The three items identified by the CIA were all acquired in April and May of 2002 by FBI interrogators. Abu Zubaydah was placed in isolation from June 18, 2002, to August 4, 2002, without being asked any questions. After 47 days in isolation, the CIA reinstituted contact with Abu Zubaydah at approximately 11:50 AM on August 4, 2002, when CIA personnel entered the cell, shackled and hooded Abu Zubaydah, and removed his towel, leaving Abu Zubaydah naked. Without asking any questions, CIA personnel made a collar around his neck with a towel and used the collar "to slam him against a concrete wall." Multiple enhanced interrogation techniques were used non-stop until 6:30 PM, when Abu Zubaydah was strapped to the waterboard and subjected to the waterboard technique "numerous times" between 6:45 PM and 8:52 PM. The "aggressive phase of interrogation" using the CIA's enhanced interrogation techniques continued for 20 days. (See Abu Zubaydah treatment chronology in Volume III.) During the months of August and September 2002, Abu Zubaydah's reporting resulted in 91 intelligence reports, four fewer than the first two months of his CIA detention. (See Abu Zubaydah detainee review in Volume III.) Specifically, for information on Abu Zubaydah's initial walling, see CIA email dated March 28, 2007, at 04:42 PM, with the subject line, "Subject detainee allegation—per our telcon of today," which states that Abu Zubaydah claims "a collar was used to slam him against a concrete wall." The CIA officer wrote, "While we do not have a record that this occurred, one interrogator at the site at the time confirmed that this did indeed happen. For the record, a plywood 'wall' was immediately constructed at the site after the walling on the concrete wall." Regarding the CIA's assessment of the "key intelligence" from Abu Zubaydah, see CIA briefing documents for Leon Panetta entitled, "Tab 9: DCIA Briefing on RDI Program- 18FEB.2009" and graphic attachment, "Key Intelligence and Reporting Derived from Abu Zubaydah and Khalid Muhammad (KSM)" (includes "DCIA Briefing on RDI Program" agenda, CIA document "EITs and Effectiveness," with associated documents, "Key Intelligence Impacts Chart: Attachment (AZ and KSM)," "Background on Key Intelligence Impacts Chart: Attachment," and "supporting references," to include "Background on Key Captures and Plots Disrupted").

1208. On August 30, 2002, [REDACTED] CTC Legal, [REDACTED], met with NSC Legal Adviser John Bellinger to discuss Abu Zubaydah's interrogation. (See email from: John Rizzo; to: John Moseman; subject: Meeting with NSC Legal Adviser, 30 August 2002; date: September 3, 2002; ALEC [REDACTED], 052227Z SEP 02.) According to [REDACTED]'s email documenting the meeting, he "noted that we had employed the walling techniques, confinement box, waterboard, along with some of the other methods which also had been approved by the Attorney General," and "reported that while the experts at the site and at Headquarters were still assessing the product of the recent sessions, it did appear that the current phase was producing meaningful results." (See email from: John Rizzo; to: John Moseman; subject: Meeting with NSC Legal Adviser, 30 August 2002; date: September 3, 2002.) The email did not provide any additional detail on what was described to Bellinger with respect to either the use of the techniques or the "results" of the interrogation. It is unclear from CIA records whether the CIA ever informed the NSC legal adviser or anyone else at the NSC or the Department of Justice that Abu Zubaydah failed to provide information about future attacks against the United States or operatives tasked to commit attacks in the U.S., during or after the use of the CIA's enhanced interrogation techniques.

1209. ALEC ███ (181439Z OCT 02).

1210. These representations were eventually included in the President's September 6, 2006, speech, in which the President stated: "We knew that Zubaydah had more information that could save innocent lives, but he stopped talking . . . so the CIA used an alternative set of procedures . . . Zubaydah was questioned using these procedures, and soon he began to provide information on key al Qaeda operatives, including information that helped us find and capture more of those responsible for the attacks on September the 11th." These representations were also made to the Committee. On September 6, 2006, Director Hayden testified that, "faced with the techniques and with the prospects of what he did not know was coming, Abu Zubaydah decided that he had earned the burden as far as Allah had required him to carry it and that he could put the burden down and cooperate with his interrogators." (See transcript of briefing, September 6, 2006 (DTS#2007-1336).) Director Hayden's Statement for the Record for an April 12, 2007, hearing stated that: "[a]fter the use of these techniques, Abu Zubaydah became one of our most important sources of intelligence on al-Qa'ida." See statement for the Senate Select Committee on Intelligence from CIA Director Hayden, for April 12, 2007, hearing (DTS #2007-1563).

1211. Italics in original document. CIA Memorandum Bradbury at Office of Legal Counsel Department of Justice, dated March 2, 2005, from ███, ███ Legal Group, DCI Counterterrorist Center, subject "Effectiveness of the CIA Counterterrorist Interrogation Techniques."

1212. Among other documents, see Department of Justice Office of Legal Counsel Memoranda dated May 30, 2005, and July 20, 2007. The July 20, 2007, memorandum—now declassified—states (inaccurately) that: "Interrogations of Zubaydah—again, once enhanced techniques were employed—revealed two al Qaeda operatives already in the United States and planning to destroy a high rise apartment building and to detonate a radiological bomb in Washington, D.C." See Volume II, specifically the section on the "Thwarting of the Dirty Bomb/Tall Buildings Plot" and the capture of Jose Padilla, for additional details concerning the inaccuracies of this statement.

1213. ███ 10091 (210959Z APR 02). Despite requests by the Senate Select Committee on Intelligence, the CIA has never corrected the record on this assertion. On September 8, 2008, the Committee submitted Questions for the Record (QFRs) to the CIA from a hearing on the legal opinions issued by the Department of Justice's Office of Legal Counsel on the CIA's Detention and Interrogation Program. Because of time constraints, the CIA agreed "to take back several questions from Members that [the CIA was] unable to answer at the hearing." On the topic of the effectiveness of the CIA's enhanced interrogation techniques, the Committee asked "Why was this information [related to Padilla], which was not obtained through the use of EITs, included in the 'Effectiveness Memo?'" CIA records provided for this review contain completed responses to these Questions for the Record. The CIA's answer to this question was: "[███ CTC Legal ███] simply inadvertently reported this wrong. Abu Zubaydah provided information on Jose Padilla while being interrogated by the FBI (███ 10091)." The Committee never received this response, despite numerous requests. Instead, the CIA responded with a letter dated October 17, 2008, stating that the "CIA has responded to numerous written requests for information from SSCI on this topic [the CIA's Detention and Interrogation Program]," and that "[w]e are available to provide additional briefings on this issue to Members as necessary." In a letter to CIA Director Michael Hayden, Chairman Rockefeller wrote, "[t]he CIA's refusal to respond to hearing Questions for the Record is unprecedented and is simply unacceptable." Senator Feinstein wrote a separate letter to CIA Director Michael Hayden stating, "I want you to know that I found the October 17, 2008 reply . . . appalling." The CIA did not respond. (See: (1) Senate Select Committee on Intelligence Questions for the Record submitted to CIA Director Michael Hayden on September 8, 2008, with a request for a response by October 10, 2008 (DTS #2008-3522); (2) CIA document prepared in response to "Questions for the Record" submitted by the Senate Select Committee on Intelligence on September 8, 2008; (3) letter from Senate Select Committee on Intelligence Chairman John D. Rockefeller IV, dated October 29, 2008, to CIA Director Michael Hayden (DTS #2008-4217); (4) letter from Senate Select Committee on Intelligence Chairman John D. Rockefeller IV, dated October 29, 2008, to CIA Director Michael Hayden (DTS #2008-4217); and (5) letter from Senate Select Committee on Intelligence Committee member, Dianne Feinstein, dated October 30, 2008, to CIA Director Michael Hayden (DTS#2008-4235).) In February 2004, a senior CIA officer wrote: "AZ never really gave 'this is the plot' type of information. He claimed every plot/operation he had knowledge of and/or was working on was only preliminary. (Padilla and the dirty bomb plot was prior to enhanced and he never really gave actionable to get them)." See email from: ███; to: ███

, cc: [REDACTED], [REDACTED], [REDACTED], [REDACTED], , John P. Mudd, [REDACTED], [REDACTED], [REDACTED], [REDACTED], Jose Rodriguez, [REDACTED], [REDACTED], ; subject: Please Read—Re CTC Response to the Draft IG Report; date: February 10, 2004).

1214. Among other documents, see Memorandum for: Inspector General; from: James Pavitt, Deputy Director for Operations; subject: re (S) Comments to Draft IG Special Review, "Counterterrorism Detention and Interrogation Program" (2003-7123-IG); date: February 27, 2004; attachment: February 24, 2004, Memorandum re Successes of CIA's Counterterrorism Detention and Interrogation Activities.

1215. Among other documents, see Memorandum for the Record: "Review of Interrogation Program on 29 July 2003, "Memorandum prepared by CIA General Counsel Scott Muller, dated August 5, 2003, and briefing slides entitled, "CIA Interrogation Program," dated July 29, 2003, presented to senior White House officials; Briefing for Vice President Cheney: CIA Detention and Interrogation Program. CIA document dated March 4, 2005, entitled, "Briefing for Vice President Cheney: CIA Detention and Interrogation Program," and "DCIA Talking Points: Waterboard 06 November 2007," dated November 6, 2007, with the notation the document was "sent to DCIA Nov. 6 in preparation for POTUS meeting."

1216. Among other documents, see March 2, 2005, Memorandum for Steve Bradbury from , Legal Group, DCI Counterterrorist Center re: Effectiveness of the CIA Counterterrorist Interrogation Techniques.

1217. Among other documents, see CIA classified Statement for the Record, Senate Select Committee on Intelligence, provided by General Michael V. Hayden, Director, Central Intelligence Agency, 12 April 2007; and accompanying Senate Select Committee on Intelligence hearing transcript for April 12, 2007, entitled, "Hearing on Central Intelligence Agency Detention and Interrogation Program."

1218. See, for example, CIA "Questions and Proposed Answers" (related to the President's speech) 9/2/2006; Tab 2 of CIA Validation of Remarks on Detainee Policy, September 6, 2006; and speech by President Bush on September 6, 2006.

1219. CIA memorandum to "National Security Advisor," from "Director of Central Intelligence," Subject: "Effectiveness of the CIA Counterterrorist Interrogation Techniques," included in email from: ; to: , , and ; subject: "paper on value of interrogation techniques"; date: December 6, 2004, at 5:06:38 PM. CIA document dated March 4, 2005, entitled, "Briefing for Vice President Cheney: CIA Detention and Interrogation Program." CIA Talking Points entitled, "Talking Points for 10 March 2005 DCI Meeting PC: Effectiveness of the High-Value Detainee Interrogation (HVDI) Techniques." CIA briefing document dated May 2, 2006, entitled, "BRIEFING FOR CHIEF OF STAFF TO THE PRESIDENT 2 May 2006 Briefing for Chief of Staff to the President Josh Bolten: CIA Rendition, Detention and Interrogation Programs." March 2, 2005, Memorandum for Steve Bradbury from , Legal Group, DCI Counterterrorist Center re: Effectiveness of the CIA Counterterrorist Interrogation Techniques.

1220. CIA memorandum to "National Security Advisor," from "Director of Central Intelligence," Subject: "Effectiveness of the CIA Counterterrorist Interrogation Techniques," included in email from: ; to: , , and ; subject: "paper on value of interrogation techniques"; date: December 6, 2004, at 5:06:38 PM; CIA document dated March 4, 2005, entitled, "Briefing for Vice President Cheney: CIA Detention and Interrogation Program." CIA briefing document dated May 2, 2006, entitled, "BRIEFING FOR CHIEF OF STAFF TO THE PRESIDENT 2 May 2006 Briefing for Chief of Staff to the President Josh Bolten: CIA Rendition, Detention and Interrogation Programs."

1221. See, for example, transcript. Senate Select Committee on Intelligence, April 12, 2007 (DTS #2007-3158).

1222. "Khalid Shaykh Muhammad: Preeminent Source On Al-Qa'ida," authored by [REDACTED], CTC/UBLD/AQPO/AQLB; CIA Briefing for Obama National Security Team—"Renditions, Detentions, and Interrogations (RDI)" including "Tab 7," named "RDG Copy- Briefing on RDI Program 09 Jan. 2009," referenced materials attached to cover memorandum with the title, "D/CIA Conference Room Seating Visit by President-elect Banack [*sic*] Obama National Security Team Tuesday, 13 January 2009; 8:30 – 11:30 a.m."

1223. March 2, 2005, Memorandum for Steve Bradbury from , Legal Group, DCI Counterterrorist Center re: Effectiveness of the CIA Counterterrorist Interrogation Techniques.

1224. 34491 (051400Z MAR 03).

1225. CIA memorandum to "National Security Advisor," from "Director of Central Intelligence," Subject: "Effectiveness of the CIA Counterterrorist Interrogation Techniques," included in email from: ; to: , , and ; subject: "paper on value of interrogation techniques"; date: December 6, 2004, at 5:06:38 PM. CIA document dated March 4, 2005, entitled, "Briefing for Vice President Cheney: CIA Detention and Interrogation Program." CIA briefing document dated May 2, 2006, entitled, "BRIEFING FOR CHIEF OF STAFF TO THE PRESIDENT 2 May 2006 Briefing for Chief of Staff to the President Josh Bolten: CIA Rendition, Detention and Interrogation Programs."

1226. 11026 (271034Z MAR 03).

1227. "Khalid Shaykh Muhammad's Threat Reporting—Precious Truths, Surrounded by a Bodyguard of Lies," Interagency Intelligent Committee on Terrorism (IICT), April 3, 2003.

1228. DIRECTOR (121550Z JUN 03).

1229. ALEC (022012Z MAY 03).

1230. Memorandum for: ; ; ; from: ; subject: Action detainee

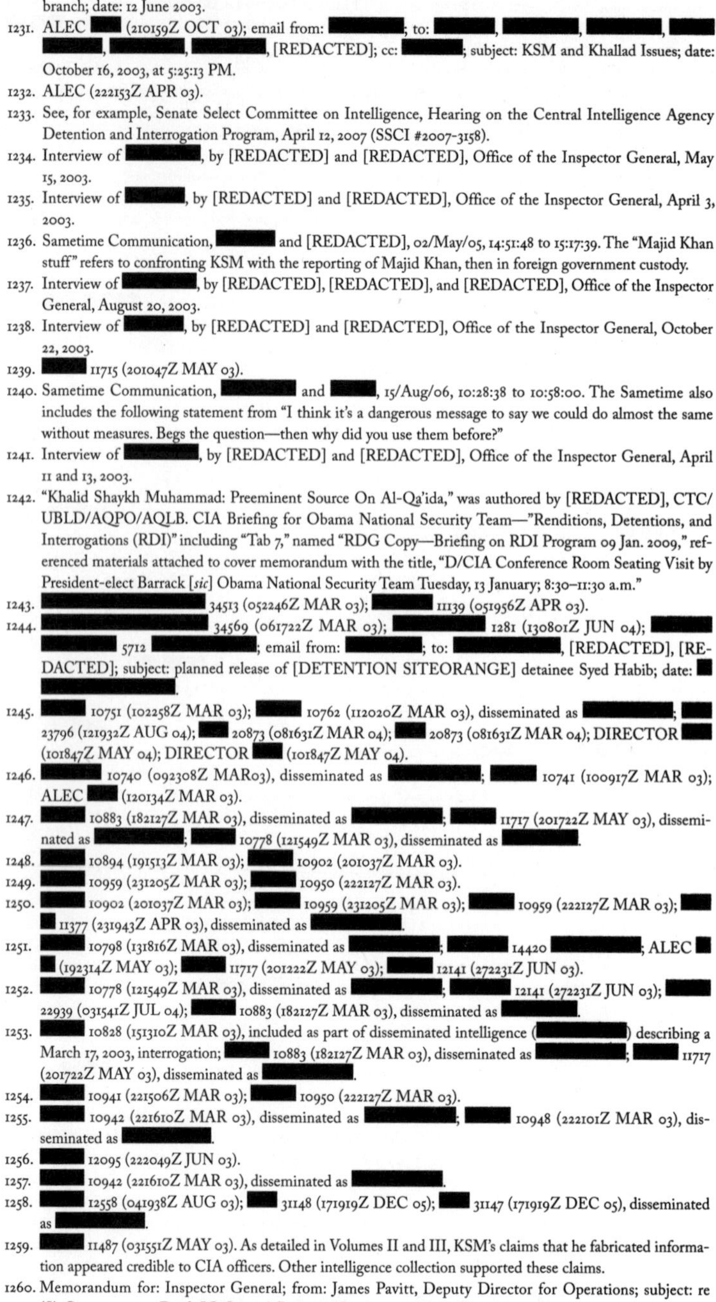

branch; date: 12 June 2003.

1231. ALEC (210159Z OCT 03); email from: ; to: , , , , , , [REDACTED]; cc: ; subject: KSM and Khallad Issues; date: October 16, 2003, at 5:25:13 PM.

1232. ALEC (222153Z APR 03).

1233. See, for example, Senate Select Committee on Intelligence, Hearing on the Central Intelligence Agency Detention and Interrogation Program, April 12, 2007 (SSCI #2007-3158).

1234. Interview of , by [REDACTED] and [REDACTED], Office of the Inspector General, May 15, 2003.

1235. Interview of , by [REDACTED] and [REDACTED], Office of the Inspector General, April 3, 2003.

1236. Sametime Communication, and [REDACTED], 02/May/05, 14:51:48 to 15:17:39. The "Majid Khan stuff" refers to confronting KSM with the reporting of Majid Khan, then in foreign government custody.

1237. Interview of , by [REDACTED], [REDACTED], and [REDACTED], Office of the Inspector General, August 20, 2003.

1238. Interview of , by [REDACTED] and [REDACTED], Office of the Inspector General, October 22, 2003.

1239. 11715 (201047Z MAY 03).

1240. Sametime Communication, and , 15/Aug/06, 10:28:38 to 10:58:00. The Sametime also includes the following statement from "I think it's a dangerous message to say we could do almost the same without measures. Begs the question—then why did you use them before?"

1241. Interview of , by [REDACTED] and [REDACTED], Office of the Inspector General, April 11 and 13, 2003.

1242. "Khalid Shaykh Muhammad: Preeminent Source On Al-Qa'ida," was authored by [REDACTED], CTC/UBLD/AQPO/AQLB. CIA Briefing for Obama National Security Team—"Renditions, Detentions, and Interrogations (RDI)" including "Tab 7," named "RDG Copy—Briefing on RDI Program 09 Jan. 2009," referenced materials attached to cover memorandum with the title, "D/CIA Conference Room Seating Visit by President-elect Barrack [*sic*] Obama National Security Team Tuesday, 13 January; 8:30–11:30 a.m."

1243. 34513 (052246Z MAR 03); 11139 (051956Z APR 03).

1244. 34569 (061722Z MAR 03); 1281 (130801Z JUN 04); 5712 ; email from: ; to: , [REDACTED], [REDACTED]; subject: planned release of [DETENTION SITEORANGE] detainee Syed Habib; date: .

1245. 10751 (102258Z MAR 03); 10762 (112020Z MAR 03), disseminated as ; 23796 (121932Z AUG 04); 20873 (081631Z MAR 04); 20873 (081631Z MAR 04); DIRECTOR (101847Z MAY 04); DIRECTOR (101847Z MAY 04).

1246. 10740 (092308Z MAR03), disseminated as ; 10741 (100917Z MAR 03); ALEC (120134Z MAR 03).

1247. 10883 (182127Z MAR 03), disseminated as ; 11717 (201722Z MAY 03), disseminated as ; 10778 (121549Z MAR 03), disseminated as .

1248. 10894 (191513Z MAR 03); 10902 (201037Z MAR 03).

1249. 10959 (231205Z MAR 03); 10950 (222127Z MAR 03).

1250. 10902 (201037Z MAR 03); 10959 (231205Z MAR 03); 10959 (222127Z MAR 03); 11377 (231943Z APR 03), disseminated as .

1251. 10798 (131816Z MAR 03), disseminated as ; 14420 ; ALEC (192314Z MAY 03); 11717 (201222Z MAY 03); 12141 (272231Z JUN 03).

1252. 10778 (121549Z MAR 03), disseminated as ; 12141 (272231Z JUN 03); 22939 (031541Z JUL 04); 10883 (182127Z MAR 03), disseminated as .

1253. 10828 (151310Z MAR 03), included as part of disseminated intelligence ( ) describing a March 17, 2003, interrogation; 10883 (182127Z MAR 03), disseminated as ; 11717 (201722Z MAY 03), disseminated as .

1254. 10941 (221506Z MAR 03); 10950 (222127Z MAR 03).

1255. 10942 (221610Z MAR 03), disseminated as ; 10948 (222101Z MAR 03), disseminated as .

1256. 12095 (222049Z JUN 03).

1257. 10942 (221610Z MAR 03), disseminated as .

1258. 12558 (041938Z AUG 03); 31148 (171919Z DEC 05); 31147 (171919Z DEC 05), disseminated as .

1259. 11487 (031551Z MAY 03). As detailed in Volumes II and III, KSM's claims that he fabricated information appeared credible to CIA officers. Other intelligence collection supported these claims.

1260. Memorandum for: Inspector General; from: James Pavitt, Deputy Director for Operations; subject: re (S) Comments to Draft IG Special Review, "Counterterrorism Detention and Interrogation Program"

(2003-7123-IG); date: February 27, 2004; attachment: February 24, 2004, Memorandum re Successes of CIA's Counterterrorism Detention and Interrogation Activities.

1261. CIA memorandum to "National Security Advisor," from "Director of Central Intelligence," Subject: "Effectiveness of the CIA Counterterrorist Interrogation Techniques," included in email from: ; to: , , and ; subject: "paper on value of interrogation techniques"; date: December 6, 2004, at 5:06:38 PM.

1262. March 2, 2005, Memorandum for Steve Bradbury from , Legal Group, DCI Counterterrorist Center re: Effectiveness of the CIA Counterterrorist Interrogation Techniques.

1263. Email from: ; to: ; cc: , [REDACTED], [REDACTED], ; subject: re Addition on KSM/AZ and measures; date: February 9, 2004. Memorandum for: Inspector General; from: James Pavitt, Deputy Director for Operations; subject: re (S) Comments to Draft IG Special Review, "Counterterrorism Detention and Interrogation Program" (2003-7123-IG); date: February 27, 2004; attachment: February 24, 2004, Memorandum re Successes of CIA's Counterterrorism Detention and Interrogation Activities.

1264. 41592 (051050Z MAR 03); 41627 (051329Z MAR 03).

1265. March 2, 2005, Memorandum for Steve Bradbury from , Legal Group, DCI Counterterrorist Center re: Effectiveness of the CIA Counterterrorist Interrogation Techniques.

1266. The "critical" description in this CIA representation is addressed in the section of this summary concerning the reported acquisition of actionable intelligence after the use of the CIA's enhanced interrogation techniques that the CIA represented as enabling the CIA to thwart terrorist plots and capture specific terrorists. See Volume II for additional information.

1267. Among other documents, see CIA Memorandum for the National Security Advisor (Rice) entitled, "Effectiveness of the CIA Counterterrorist Interrogation Techniques," December 2004; CIA Memorandum to the Office of Legal Counsel, entitled, "Effectiveness of the CIA Counterterrorist Interrogation Techniques," March 2, 2005; CIA briefing notes entitled, "Briefing for Vice President Cheney: CIA Detention and Interrogation Program," March 4, 2005; CIA talking points for the National Security Council entitled, "Talking Points for 10 March 2005 DCI Meeting PC: Effectiveness of the High-Value Detainee Interrogation (HVDI) Techniques," dated March 4, 2005; CIA briefing notes entitled, "Briefing for Chief of Staff to the President Josh Bolten: CIA Rendition, Detention, and Interrogation Programs," dated May 2, 2006; CIA briefing document, entitled, "DCIA Talking Points: Waterboard 06 November 2007," dated November 6, 2007, with the notation the document was "sent to DCIA Nov. 6 in preparation for POTUS meeting." Also included in additional briefing documents referenced and described in this summary.

1268. While CIA multi-source intelligence reports are included in the Committee Study, the quantitative analysis in this summary is based on sole-source intelligence reporting, as these reports best reflect reporting from CIA detainees. Multi-source intelligence reports are reports that contain data from multiple detainees. As described above, a common multi-source report would result from the CIA showing a picture of an individual to all CIA detainees at a specific CIA detention site. A report would be produced regardless if detainees were or were not able to identify or provide information on the individual. As a specific example, see HEADQUARTERS (202255Z JUN 06), which states that from January 1, 2006–April 30, 2006, information from Hambali was "used in the dissemination of three intelligence reports, two of which were non-recognitions of Guantanamo Bay detainees," while the third "detailed [Hambali's] statement that he knew of no threats or plots to attack any world sporting events." Sole-source reports, by contrast, are based on specific information provided by one CIA detainee.

1269. Senate Select Committee on Intelligence, Briefing by the Director, Central Intelligence Agency, on the Central Intelligence Agency Detention, Interrogation and Rendition Program, September 6, 2006 (SSCI #2007-1336). At the time this statement was made there had been at least 118 CIA detainees.

1270. Senate Select Committee on Intelligence, Hearing on the Central Intelligence Agency Detention and Interrogation Program, April 12, 2007 (DTS #2007-3158).

1271. Senate Select Committee on Intelligence, Hearing on the Central Intelligence Agency Detention and Interrogation Program, April 12, 2007 (DTS #2007-3158).

1272. Senate Select Committee on Intelligence, Hearing on the Central Intelligence Agency Detention and Interrogation Program, April 12, 2007 (DTS #2007-3158).

1273. See detainee intelligence reporting data in Volume II.

1274. The CIA represented in 2002 that the CIA's enhanced interrogation techniques were necessary and effective. The Committee analysis focuses on CIA representations between 2003 and 2009, during which time the CIA provided specific examples of counterterrorism "successes" the CIA attributed to the use of the CIA's enhanced interrogation techniques.

1275. See list of 20 CIA representations included in this summary. From 2003 through 2009, the CIA's representations regarding the effectiveness of the CIA's enhanced interrogation techniques included a specific set of examples of terrorist plots "disrupted" and terrorists captured that the CIA attributed to information obtained from the use of its enhanced interrogation techniques. CIA representations further asserted that the intelligence obtained from the use of the CIA's enhanced interrogation techniques was unique, otherwise unavailable, and resulted in "saved lives." Among other CIA representations, sec. (1) CIA representations in the Department of Justice Office of Legal Counsel Memorandum, dated May 30, 2005, which relied on a series of highly specific CIA representations on the type of intelligence acquired from the use of the CIA's enhanced interrogation techniques to assess their legality. The CIA representations referenced by the OLC include that the use of the CIA's enhanced interrogation techniques was "necessary" to obtain "critical," "vital," and "otherwise unavailable actionable intelligence" that was "essential" for the U.S. government to "detect and disrupt" terrorist threats. The OLC memorandum further states that "[the CIA] ha[s] informed [the OLC] that the CIA believes that this program is largely responsible for preventing a subsequent attack within the United States." (See Memorandum for John A. Rizzo, Senior Deputy General Counsel, Central Intelligence Agency, from Steven G. Bradbury, Principal Deputy Assistant Attorney General, Office of Legal Counsel, May 30, 2005, Re: Application of United States Obligations Under Article 16 of the Convention Against Torture to Certain Techniques That May Be Used in the Interrogation of High Value al Qaeda Detainees.) (2) CIA representations in the Department of Justice Office of Legal Counsel Memorandum dated July 20, 2007, which also relied on CIA representations on the type of intelligence acquired from the use of the CIA's enhanced interrogation techniques. Citing CIA documents and the President's September 6, 2006, speech describing the CIA's interrogation program (which was based on CIA-provided information), the OLC memorandum states: "The CIA interrogation program—and, in particular, its use of enhanced interrogation techniques—is intended to serve this paramount interest [security of the Nation] by producing substantial quantities of otherwise unavailable intelligence . . . As the President explained [on September 6, 2006], 'by giving us information about terrorist plans we could not get anywhere else, the program has saved innocent lives.'" (See Memorandum for John A. Rizzo, Acting General Counsel, Central Intelligence Agency, from Steven G. Bradbury, Principal Deputy Assistant Attorney General, Office of Legal Counsel, July 20, 2007, Re: Application of the War Crimes Act, the Detainee Treatment Act, and Common Article 3 of the Geneva Conventions to Certain Techniques That May Be Used by the CIA in the Interrogation of High Value al Qaeda Detainees.) (3) CIA briefings for members of the National Security Council in July and September 2003 represented that "the use of Enhanced Techniques of one kind or another had produced significant intelligence information that had, in the view of CIA professionals, saved lives," and warned policymakers that "[t]ermination of this program will result in loss of life, possibly extensive." (See August 5, 2003, Memorandum for the Record from Scott Muller, Subject: Review of Interrogation Program on 29 July 2003; Briefing slides, CIA Interrogation Program, July 29, 2003; September 4, 2003, CIA Memorandum for the Record, Subject: Member Briefing; and September 26, 2003, Memorandum for the Record from Muller, Subject: CIA Interrogation Program.) (4) The CIA's response to the Office of Inspector General Draft Special Review of the CIA program, which asserts: "Information [the CIA] received . . . as a result of the lawful use of enhanced interrogation techniques ('EITs') has almost certainly saved countless American lives inside the United States and abroad. The evidence points clearly to the fact that without the use of such techniques, we and our allies would [have] suffered major terrorist attacks involving hundreds, if not thousands, of casualties." (See Memorandum for: Inspector General; from: James Pavitt, Deputy Director for Operations; subject: re (S) Comments to Draft IG Special Review, "Counterterrorism Detention and Interrogation Program" 2003-7123-IG; date: February 27, 2004; attachment: February 24, 2004, Memorandum re Successes of CIA's Counterterrorism Detention and Interrogation Activities.) (5) CIA briefing documents for CIA Director Leon Panetta in February 2009, which state that the "CIA assesses that the RDI program worked and the [enhanced interrogation] techniques were effective in producing foreign intelligence," and that "[m]ost, if not all, of the timely intelligence acquired from detainees in this program would not have been discovered or reported by other means." (See CIA briefing documents for Leon Panetta, entitled, "Tab 9: DCIA Briefing on RDI Program—18FEB.2009" and graphic attachment, "Key Intelligence and Reporting Derived from Abu Zubaydah and Khalid Shaykh Muhammad (KSM)," including "DCIA Briefing on RDI Progiam" agenda, CIA document "EITs and Effectiveness," with associated documents, "Key Intelligence Impacts Chart: Attachment (AZ and KSM)," "Background on Key Intelligence Impacts Chart: Attachment," and "supporting references," to include "Background on Key Captures and Plots Disrupted.") (6) CIA document faxed to the Senate Select Committee on Intelligence on March 18, 2009, entitled, "[SWIGERT] and [DUNBAR]," located in Committee databases at DTS#2009-1258, which provides a list of "some of the key captures and disrupted plots" that the CIA had attributed to the use of the CIA's enhanced interrogation techniques, and stating: "CIA assesses that most, if not all, of the timely intelligence acquired from detainees in this program would not have been discovered or reported by any other means." See Volume II for additional CIA representations asserting that the CIA's enhanced interrogation techniques enabled the CIA to obtain unique, otherwise unavailable intelligence that "saved lives."

1276. Italics in original document. See CIA memorandum to "National Security Advisor," from "Director of Central Intelligence," Subject: "Effectiveness of the CIA Counterterrorist Interrogation Techniques," included in email from: ██████; to: ██████, ██████, and ██████; subject: "paper on value of interrogation techniques"; date: December 6, 2004, at 5:06:38 PM. The email references the attached "information paper to Dr. Rice explaining the value of the interrogation techniques." The document includes the following: The "Karachi Plot," "The Heathrow Plot," The "Second Wave," "The Guraba Cell," "Issa al-Hindi," "Abu Talha al-Pakistani," "Hambali's Capture," "Jafaar al-Tayyar," "Dirty Bomb Plot," "Shoe Bomber," and "Shkai, Pakistan."

1277. See CIA document entitled, "DCIA Talking Points: Waterboard 06 November 2007," dated November 6, 2007, with the notation the document was "sent to DCIA Nov. 6 in preparation for POTUS meeting." The document states, under the heading, "Plots Discovered as a Result of EITs," that "reporting statistics alone will not provide a fair and accurate measure of the effectiveness of EITs," and then provides a list of "examples of key intelligence collected from CIA detainee interrogations *after applying the waterboard* along with other interrogation techniques . . . The 'Second Wave' . . . Hambali's Capture . . . The Guraba Cell . . . Shoe Bomber . . . Issa al-Hindi . . . Jafaar al-Tayyar . . . The Karachi Plot . . . The Heathrow (italics added).

1278. CIA memorandum for the Record, "Review of Interrogation Program on 29 July 2003," prepared by CIA General Counsel Scott Muller, dated August 5, 2003; briefing slides entitled, "CIA Interrogation Program," dated July 29, 2003, presented to senior White House officials. Additional briefings are detailed in September 4, 2003, CIA Memorandum for the Record, Subject: Member Briefing; and September 26, 2003, Memorandum for the Record from Scott Muller, Subject: CIA Interrogation Program.

1279. CIA memorandum to the CIA Inspector General from James Pavitt, CIA's Deputy Director for Operations, dated February 27, 2004, with the subject line, "Comments to Draft IG Special Review, 'Counterterrorism Detention and Interrogation Program' (2003-7123-IG)," Attachment, "Successes of CIA's Counterterrorism Detention and Interrogation Activities," dated February 24, 2004.

1280. CIA Directorate of Intelligence, "Khalid Shaykh Muhammad; Preeminent Source on Al-Qa'ida," dated July 13, 2004; fax to the Department of Justice, April 22, 2005, entitled, "████, Materials on KSM and Abu Zubaydah. ████." This report was widely disseminated in the Intelligence Community, and a copy of this report was provided to the Senate Select Committee on Intelligence on July 15, 2004. On March 31, 2009, former Vice President Cheney requested the declassification of this Intelligence Assessment, which was publicly released with redactions on August 24, 2009.

1281. CIA memorandum to "National Security Advisor," from "Director of Central Intelligence," Subject: "Effectiveness of the CIA Counterterrorist Interrogation Techniques," included in email from: ████; to: ████, ████, and ████; subject: "paper on value of interrogation techniques"; date: December 6, 2004, at 5:06:38 PM. The email references the attached "information paper to Dr. Rice explaining the value of the interrogation techniques."

1282. CIA Memorandum for Steve Bradbury at Office of Legal Counsel, Department of Justice, from ████ ████, ████ Legal Group, DCI Counterterrorist Center, subject: "Effectiveness of the CIA Counterterrorist Interrogation Techniques."

1283. CIA briefing for Vice President Cheney, dated March 4, 2005, entitled, "Briefing for Vice President Cheney: CIA Detention and Interrogation Program."

1284. CIA Talking Points entitled, "Talking Points for 10 March 2005 DCI Meeting PC: Effectiveness of the High-Value Detainee Interrogation (HVDI) Techniques."

1285. CIA "Briefing Notes on the Value of Detainee Reporting" faxed from the CIA to the Department of Justice on April 15, 2005, at 10:47AM.

1286. CIA fax to DOJ Command Center, dated April 2, 2005, for ████, Office of Legal Counsel, U.S. Department of Justice, from ████, ████ Legal Group, DCI Counterterrorist Center, re: ████, Materials of KSM and Abu Zubaydah, included CIA Intelligence Assessment "Khalid Shaykh Muhammad: Preeminent Source on Al-Qa'ida," and CIA document, "Materials of KSM and Abu Zubaydah."

1287. CIA Intelligence Assessment, "Detainee Reporting Pivotal for the War Against Al-Qa'ida," June 2005, which CIA records indicate was provided to White House officials on June 1, 2005. The Intelligence Assessment at the SECRET//NOFORN classification level was more broadly disseminated on June 3, 2005. On March 31, 2009, former Vice President Cheney requested the declassification of this Intelligence Assessment, which was publicly released with redactions on August 24, 2009.

1288. CIA memorandum entitled, "Future of CIA's Counterterrorist Detention and Interrogation Program," dated December 23, 2005, from CIA Director Porter Goss to Stephen J. Hadley, Assistant to the President/National Security Advisor, Frances F. Townsend, Assistant to the President/Homeland Security Advisor, Ambassador John D. Negroponte, the Director of National Intelligence, Attachment, "Impact of the Loss of the Detainee Program to CT Operations and Analysis."

1289. CIA briefing document dated May 2, 2006, entitled, "BRIEFING FOR CHIEF OF STAFF TO THE PRESIDENT 2 May 2006 Briefing for Chief of Staff to the President Josh Bolten: CIA Rendition, Detention and Interrogation Programs."

1290. CIA briefing document entitled, "Detainee Intelligence Value Update," dated 11 July 2006, internal document saved within CIA records as, "DNI Memo Intel Value July 11 2006 . . . TALKING POINTS FOR DCI MEETING."

1291. CIA document dated July 16, 2006, entitled, "DRAFT Potential Public Briefing of CIA's High-Value Terrorist Interrogations Program," and "CIA Validation of Remarks on Detainee Policy," drafts supporting the September 6, 2006, speech by President George W. Bush acknowledging and describing the CIA's Detention and Interrogation Program, as well as an unclassified Office of the Director of National Intelligence release, entitled, "Summary of the High Value Terrorist Detainee Program."

1292. CIA classified Statement for the Record, Senate Select Committee on Intelligence, provided by General Michael V. Hayden, Director, Central Intelligence Agency, 12 April 2007; and accompanying Senate Select Committee on Intelligence heating transcript for April 12, 2007, entitled, "Hearing on Central Intelligence Agency Detention and Interrogation Program."

1293. CIA fax from CIA employee [REDACTED] to U.S. Senate Committee on Appropriations, Subcommittee on Defense, with fax cover sheet entitled, "Talking points," sent on October 26, 2007, at 5:39:48 PM. Document faxed entitled, "Talking Points Appeal of the $███ Million reduction in CIA/CTC's Rendition and Detention Program."

1294. "DCIA Talking Points: Waterboard 06 November 2007," dated November 6, 2007, with the notation the document was "sent to DCIA Nov. 6 in preparation for POTUS meeting."

1295. CIA Briefing for Obama National Security Team. "Renditions, Detentions, and Interrogations (RDI)" including "Tab 7," named "RDG Copy—Briefing on RDI Program 09 Jan. 2009," prepared "13 January 2009."

1296. CIA briefing documents for Leon Panetta, entitled, "Tab 9: DCIA Briefing on RDl Program—18FEB.2009" and graphic attachment, "Key Intelligence and Reporting Derived from Abu Zubaydah and Khalid Shaykh Muhammad (KSM)," Includes "DCIA Briefing on RDI Program" agenda, CIA document "EITs and Effectiveness," with associated documents, "Key Intelligence Impacts Chart: Attachment (AZ and KSM)," "Background on Key Intelligence Impacts Chart: Attachment," and "supporting references," to include "Background on Key Captures and Plots Disrupted."

1297. CIA document faxed to the Senate Select Committee on Intelligence on March 18, 2009, at 3:46 PM, entitled, "[SWIGERT] and [DUNBAR]," which includes "Key Captures and Disrupted Plots Gained From HVDs in the RDI Program" (DTS #2009-1258).

1298. From 2003 through 2009, the CIA's representations regarding the effectiveness of the CIA's enhanced interrogation techniques provided a specific set of examples of terrorist plots "disrupted" and terrorists captured that the CIA attributed to information obtained from the use of its enhanced interrogation techniques. CIA representations further asserted that the intelligence obtained from the use of the CIA's enhanced interrogation techniques was unique, otherwise unavailable, and resulted in "saved lives." Among other CIA representations, see: (1) CIA representations in the Department of Justice Office of Legal Counsel Memorandum, dated May 30, 2005, which relied on a series of highly specific CIA representations on the type of intelligence acquired from the use of the CIA's enhanced interrogation techniques to assess their legality. The CIA representations referenced by the OLC include that the use of the CIA's enhanced interrogation techniques was "necessary" to obtain "critic," "vital," and "otherwise unavailable actionable intelligence" that was "essential" for the U.S. government to "detect and disrupt" terrorist threats. The OLC memorandum further states that "[the CIA] ha[s] informed [the OLC] that the CIA believes that this program is largely responsible for preventing a subsequent attack within the United States." (See Memorandum for John A. Rizzo, Senior Deputy General Counsel, Central Intelligence Agency, from Steven G. Bradbury, Principal Deputy Assistant Attorney General, Office of Legal Counsel, May 30, 2005, Re: Application of United States Obligations Under Article 16 of the Convention Against Torture to Certain Techniques that May Be Used in the Interrogation of High Value al Qaeda Detainees.) (2) CIA representations in the Department of Justice Office of Legal Counsel Memorandum dated July 20, 2007, which also relied on CIA representations on the type of intelligence acquired from the use of the CIA's enhanced interrogation techniques. Citing CIA documents and the President's September 6, 2006, speech describing the CIA's interrogation program (which was based on CIA-provided information), the OLC memorandum states: "The CIA interrogation program—and, in particular, its use of enhanced interrogation techniques—is intended to serve this paramount interest [security of the Nation] by producing substantial quantities of otherwise unavailable intelligence . . . As the President explained [on September 6, 2006], 'by giving us information about terrorist plans we could not get anywhere else, the program has saved innocent lives.'" (See Memorandum for John A. Rizzo, Acting General Counsel, Central Intelligence Agency, from Steven G. Bradbury, Principal Deputy Assistant Attorney General, Office of Legal Counsel, July 20, 2007, Re: Application of the War Crimes Act, the Detainee Treatment Act, and Common Article 3 of the Geneva Conventions to Certain Techniques that May Be Used by the CIA in the Interrogation of High Value al Qaeda Detainees.) (3) CIA briefings for members of the National Security Council in July and September 2003 represented that "the use of Enhanced Techniques of one kind or another had produced significant intelligence information that had, in the view of CIA professionals, saved lives," and warned policymakers that "[t]ermination of this program will result in loss of life, possibly extensive." (See August 5, 2003, Memorandum for the Record from Scott Muller, Subject: Review of Interrogation Program on 29 July 2003; Briefing slides, CIA Interrogation Program, July 29, 2003; September 4, 2003, CIA Memorandum for the Record, Subject: Member Briefing; and September 26, 2003, Memorandum for the Record from Muller, Subject: CIA Interrogation Program.) (4) The CIA's response to the Office of Inspector General draft Special Review of the CIA program, which asserts: "Information [the CIA] received . . . as a result of the lawful use of enhanced interrogation techniques ('EITs') has almost certainly saved countless American lives inside the United States and abroad. The evidence points clearly to the fact that without the use of such techniques, we and our allies would [have] suffered major terrorist attacks involving hundreds, if not thousands, of casualties." (See Memorandum for: Inspector General; from: James Pavitt, Deputy Director for Operations; subject: re (S) Comments to Draft IG Special Review, "Counterterrorism Detention and Interrogation Program" 2003-7123-IG; date: February 27, 2004; attachment: February 24, 2004, Memorandum re Successes of CIA's Counterterrorism Detention and Interrogation Activities.) (5) CIA briefing documents for CIA Director Leon Panetta in February 2009, which state that the "CIA assesses that the RDI program worked and the [enhanced interrogation] techniques were effective in producing foreign intelligence," and that "[m]ost, if not all, of the timely intelligence acquired from detainees in this program would not have been discovered or reported by other means." (See CIA briefing documents for Leon Panetta, entitled, "Tab 9: DCIA Briefing on RDI Program—18FEB.2009" and graphic attachment, "Key Intelligence and Reporting Derived from Abu Zubaydah and Khalid Shaykh Muhammad (KSM)," including "DCIA Briefing on RDI Program" agenda, CIA document "EITs and Effectiveness," with associated documents, "Key Intelligence Impacts Chart: Attachment (AZ and KSM)," "Background on Key Intelligence Impacts Chart: Attachment," and "supporting references," to include "Background on Key Captures and Plots Disrupted.") (6) CIA document faxed to the Senate Select Committee on Intelligence on March 18, 2009, entitled, "[SWIGERT] and [DUNBAR]," located in Committee databases at DTS #2009-1258, which provides a list of "some of the key captures and disrupted plots" that the CIA had attributed to the use of the CIA's enhanced interrogation techniques, and stating: "CIA assesses that most, if not all, of the timely intelligence acquired from detainees in this program would not have been discovered or reported by any other means." See Volume II for additional CIA representations asserting that the CIA's enhanced interrogation techniques enabled the CIA to obtain unique, otherwise unavailable intelligence that "saved lives."

1299. The CIA has represented that it has provided the Senate Select Committee on Intelligence with all CIA records related to the CIA's Detention and Interrogation Program. This document production phase lasted more than three years and was completed in July 2012. The records produced include more than six million pages of material, including records detailing the interrogation of detainees, as well as the disseminated intelligence derived from the interrogation of CIA detainees. The CIA did not provide—nor was it requested to provide—intelligence records that were unrelated to the CIA Detention and Interrogation Program. In other words, this Study was completed without direct access to reporting from CIA HUMINT assets, foreign liaison assets, electronic intercepts, military detainee debriefings, law enforcement derived information, and other methods of intelligence collection. Insomuch as this material is included in the analysis herein, it was provided by the CIA within the context of documents directly related to the CIA Detention and Interrogation Program. For example, a requirements cable from CIA Headquarters to CIA interrogators at a CIA detention site could cite SIGNALS intelligence collected by NSA, or include a CIA HUMINT source report on a particular subject, with a request to question the CIA detainee about the reporting. While direct access to the NSA report, or the CIA HUMINT report, may not have been provided, it may still be included in this Study because it appeared in the CIA Headquarters requirements cable relating to the questioning of a CIA detainee. As such, there is likely significant intelligence related to the terrorist plots, terrorists captured, and other intelligence matters examined in this report, that is unrelated to the CIA's Detention and Interrogation Program and within the databases of the U.S. Intelligence Community, but which has not been identified or reviewed by the Select Committee on Intelligence for this Study. As is detailed in the near 6800-page Committee Study, the Committee found that there was significant intelligence in CIA databases to enable the capture of the terrorists cited, and "disrupt" the terrorist plots represented as "thwarted," without intelligence from the CIA interrogation program. Had the Committee been provided with access to all intelligence available in CIA and Intelligence Community databases, it is likely this finding would be strengthened further. Finally, as of March 2014, the White House had not yet provided approximately 9,400 documents related to the CIA's Detention and Interrogation Program—equivalent to less than .2 percent of CIA detention and interrogation records—pending an Executive Privilege determination. The Committee requested access to these documents in three letters dated January 3, 2013, May 22, 2013, and December 19, 2013. The White House did not respond to the requests.

1300. See Volume II for additional information and analysis.

1301. ███ 10090 (210703Z APR 02) and CIA Document, Subject: "CIA Statement Summarizing Significant Information About Jose Padilla (21:10 hrs.- 8 June 02)." For more information on the Internet article that recommended enriching uranium by "putting it into a bucket and twisting it around one's head to enrich it," see "How to Make an H-Bomb" and [REDACTED] 2281 (071658Z MAY 04). *See also* email from: [REDACTED], ███OTA/CTWG/CBRN Group; to: [REDACTED] and multiple ccs, including ███ ███; subject: "Re: [REDACTED]: Re: KSM homework on AQ nuke program"; date: April 22, 2003, at 03:30 PM, explaining CIA's CBRN group's position on Padilla and Mohammed's plotting. According to the email: "Padilla and Binyam/Zouaoui had pulled an article off a satirical web site called 'How to make an H-bomb' which is based on a 1979 Journal of Irreproducible Results article. The article was intended to be humorous and included instructions such as enriching uranium by placing liquid uranium hexaflouride in a bucket, attaching it to a six foot rope, and swinging it around your head as fast as possible for 45 minutes. While it appears that Padilla and Zouaoui took the article seriously, Zubaydah recommended that they take their (cockamamie) ideas to (I believe) KSM in Karachi. It was at that point that KSM told them to focus on bringing down apartment buildings with explosives. (in other words: keep your day jobs)." U.K. courts noted "that [ ]."

1302. Email from: [REDACTED], CTC/OTA/CBRNB; subject: "Note to Briefers Updating Zubaydah 'Uranium Device' Information"; date: April 23, 2002, at 08:25:40 PM. The email states, "CIA and Lawrence Livermore National Lab have assessed that the article is filled with countless technical inaccuracies which would likely result in the death of anyone attempting to follow the instructions, and would definitely not result in a nuclear explosive device." *See also* [REDACTED] 2281 (071658Z MAY 04).

1303. 10090 (210703Z APR 02).

1304. CIA (290925Z APR 02); 11086 (261140Z APR 02). *See also* Padilla statement noting Abu Zubaydah "chuckled at the idea," but sent Padilla and Muhammad to Karachi to present the idea to KSM. See fax from Pat Rowan, Department of Justice National Security Division, to [REDACTED], at CTC Legal, on August 15, 2007, with subject line: "Jose Padilla."

1305. DIRECTOR (041637Z). *See also* CIA (290925Z APR 02); 10091 (210959Z APR 02); [REDACTED] 2281 (071658Z MAY 04); and DIRECTOR (101725Z MAR 04).

1306. For additional background on the Dirty Bomb/Tall Buildings Plotting, see fax from Pat Rowan, Department of Justice National Security Division, to [REDACTED], at CTC Legal, on August 15, 2007, with subject line: "Jose Padilla." The document states: "Jose Padilla is a United States citizen who has been designated as an enemy combatant by the President and has been detained by the military since June 9, 2002. Padilla is commonly known as the 'dirty bomber' because early intelligence from a senior al Qaeda detainee [Abu Zubaydah] and Padilla's intended accomplice [Binyam Muhammad] indicated that he had proposed to senior al Qaeda leaders the use of a radiological dispersion device, or 'dirty bomb,' against United States targets, or interests, and he was detained by the military partly on that basis. Based on later and more complete intelligence, including Padilla's own statements during military detention, it now appears that Padilla re-entered the United States after he accepted a mission from al Qaeda leaders, specifically from Khalid Sheikh Mohammad ('KSM'), the emir of the attacks of September 11, to destroy one or more high-rise apartment buildings in the United States through the use of natural gas explosions triggered by timing devices, and had received training, equipment and money for that mission." *See also* other records that describe the plotting as targeting tall apartment buildings, without reference to a radiological or "dirty" bomb. For example, a July 15, 2004, CIA intelligence report titled, "Khalid Shaykh Muhammad: Preeminent Source on Al-Qa'ida," noted: "From late 2001 until early 2003, KSM also conceived several low-level plots, including an early 2002 plan to send al-Qa'ida operative and US citizen Jose Padilla to set off bombs in high-rise apartment buildings in an unspecified major US city." Similarly, an Intelligence Community report titled, "Khalid Shaykh Muhammad's Threat Reporting—Precious Truths, Surrounded by a Bodyguard of Lies," noted: "Binyam Muhammad stated during his debriefings that his and Padilla's objective was to topple a high-rise building with a gas explosion in Chicago." (See Community Counterterrorism Board, Intelligence Community Terrorist Threat Assessment, "Khalid Shaykh Muhammad's Threat Reporting—Precious Truths, Surrounded by a Bodyguard of Lies," Report Number IICT-2003-14, April 3, 2003.) The unclassified ODNI "Summary of the High Value Terrorist Detainee Program," released September 6, 2006, states that, "[w]orking with information from detainees, the US disrupted a plot to blow up tall buildings in the United States. KSM later described how he had directed operatives to ensure the buildings were high enough to prevent the people trapped above from escaping out of the windows, thus ensuring their deaths from smoke inhalation."

1307. Italics included in CIA Memorandum to the Office of Legal Counsel, entitled, "Effectiveness of the CIA Counterterrorist Interrogation Techniques," from March 2, 2005. *See also* CIA talking points for National Security Council entitled, "Talking Points for 10 March 2005 DCI Meeting PC: Effectiveness of the High-Value Detainee Interrogation (HVDI) Techniques," dated March 4, 2005, as well as multiple other CIA briefing records and memoranda described in Volume II.

1308. From 2003 through 2009, the CIA's representations regarding the effectiveness of the CIA's enhanced interrogation techniques provided a specific set of examples of terrorist plots "disrupted" and terrorists captured that the CIA attributed to information obtained from the use of its enhanced interrogation techniques. CIA representations further asserted that the intelligence obtained from the use of the CIA's enhanced interrogation techniques was unique, otherwise unavailable, and resulted in "saved lives." Among other CIA representations, see: (1) CIA representations in the Department of Justice Office of Legal Counsel Memorandum, dated May 30, 2005, which relied on a series of highly specific CIA representations on the type of intelligence acquired from the use of the CIA's enhanced interrogation techniques to assess their legality. The CIA representations referenced by the OLC include that the use of the CIA's enhanced interrogation techniques was "necessary" to obtain "critical," "vital," and "otherwise unavailable actionable intelligence" that was "essential" for the U.S. government to "detect and disrupt" terrorist threats. The OLC memorandum further states that "[the CIA] ha[s] informed [the OLC] that the CIA believes that this program is largely responsible for preventing a subsequent attack within the United States." (See Memorandum for John A. Rizzo, Senior Deputy General Counsel, Central Intelligence Agency, from Steven G. Bradbury, Principal Deputy Assistant Attorney General, Office of Legal Counsel, May 30, 2005, Re: Application of United States Obligations Under Article 16of the Convention Against Torture to Certain Techniques that May Be Used in the Interrogation of High Value al Qaeda Detainees.) (2) CIA representations in the Department of Justice Office of Legal Counsel Memorandum dated July 20, 2007, which also relied on CIA representations on the type of intelligence acquired from the use of the CIA's enhanced interrogation techniques. Citing CIA documents and the President's September 6, 2006, speech describing the CIA's interrogation program (which was based on CIA-provided information), the OLC memorandum states: "The CIA interrogation program—and, in particular, its use of enhanced interrogation techniques—is intended to serve this paramount interest [security of the Nation] by producing substantial quantities of otherwise unavailable intelligence . . . As the President explained [on September 6, 2006], 'by giving us information about terrorist plans we could not get anywhere else, the program has saved innocent lives.'" (See Memorandum for John A. Rizzo, Acting General Counsel, Central Intelligence Agency, from Steven G. Bradbury, Principal Deputy Assistant Attorney General, Office of Legal Counsel, July 20, 2007, Re: Application of the War Crimes Act, the Detainee Treatment Act, and Common Article 3 of the Geneva Conventions to Certain Techniques that May Be Used by the CIA in the Interrogation of High Value al Qaeda Detainees.) (3) CIA briefings for members of the National Security Council in July and September 2003 represented that "the use of Enhanced Techniques of one kind or another had produced significant intelligence information that had, in the view of CIA professionals, saved lives," and warned policymakers that "[t]ermination of this program will result in loss of life, possibly extensive." (See August 5, 2003 Memorandum for the Record from Scott Muller, Subject: Review of Interrogation Program on 29 July 2003; Briefing slides, CIA Interrogation Program, July 29, 2003; September 4, 2003, CIA Memorandum for the Record, Subject: Member Briefing; and September 26, 2003, Memorandum for the Record from Muller, Subject: CIA Interrogation Program.) (4) The CIA's response to the Office of Inspector General draft Special Review of the CIA program, which asserts: "Information [the CIA] received . . . as a result of the lawful use of enhanced interrogation techniques ('EITs') has almost certainly saved countless American lives inside the United States and abroad. The evidence points clearly to the fact that without the use of such techniques, we and our allies would [have] suffered major terrorist attacks involving hundreds, if not thousands, of casualties." (See Memorandum for: Inspector General; from: James Pavitt, Deputy Director for Operations; subject: re (S) Comments to Draft IG Special Review, "Counterterrorism Detention and Interrogation Program" 2003-7123-IG; date: February 27, 2004; attachment: February 24, 2004, Memorandum re Successes of CIA's Counterterrorism Detention and Interrogation Activities.) (5) CIA briefing documents for CIA Director Leon Panetta in February 2009, which state that the "CIA assesses that the RDI program worked and the [enhanced interrogation] techniques were effective in producing foreign intelligence," and that "[m]ost, if not all, of the timely intelligence acquired from detainees in this program would not have been discovered or reported by other means." (See CIA briefing documents for Leon Panetta, entitled, "Tab 9: DCIA Briefing on RDI Program—18FEB.2009" and graphic attachment, "Key Intelligence and Reporting Derived from Abu Zubaydah and Khalid Shaykh Muhammad (KSM)," including "DCIA Briefing on RDI Program" agenda, CIA document "EITs and Effectiveness," with associated documents, "Key Intelligence Impacts Chart: Attachment (AZ and KSM)," "Background on Key Intelligence Impacts Chart: Attachment," and "supporting references," to include "Background on Key Captures and Plots Disrupted.") (6) CIA document faxed to the Senate Select Committee on Intelligence on March 18, 2009, entitled, "[SWIGERT] and [DUNBAR]," located in Committee databases at DTS #2009-1258, which provides a list of "some of the key captures and disrupted plots" that the CIA had attributed to the use of the CIA's enhanced interrogation techniques, and stating: "CIA assesses that most, if not all, of the timely intelligence acquired from detainees in this program would not have been discovered or reported by any other means." See Volume II for additional CIA representations asserting that the CIA's enhanced interrogation techniques enabled the CIA to obtain unique, otherwise unavailable intelligence that "saved lives."

1309. CIA document dated March 4, 2005, entitled, "Briefing for Vice President Cheney: CIA Detention and Interrogation Program." The briefing document further represented that: (1) "Prior to the use of enhanced measures against skilled resistors [sic] like KSM and Abu Zubaydah—the two most prolific intelligence producers in our control—we acquired little threat information or significant actionable intelligence"; and (2) "[CIA] would not have succeeded in overcoming the resistance of KSM, Abu Zubaydah, and other equally resistant HVDs without the application of EITs."

1310. Italics added. CIA records indicate that Abu Zubaydah never provided information on "two operatives already in the United States." While neither Binyam Muhammad nor Jose Padilla was "already in the United States," the OLC description appears to be a reference to Jose Padilla and Binyam Mohammad, as the OLC then makes reference to the "Dirty Bomb" and "Tall Buildings" plotting.

1311. Italics added. See Memorandum for John A. Rizzo, Acting General Counsel, Central Intelligence Agency, from Steven G. Bradbury, Principal Deputy Assistant Attorney General, Office of Legal Counsel, July 20, 2007, Re: Application of the War Crimes Act, the Detainee Treatment Act, and Common Article 3 of the Geneva Conventions to Certain Techniques that May Be Used by the CIA in the Interrogation of High Value al Qaeda Detainees.

1312. See "Waterboarding Saved L.A.," *Washington Times*, April 25, 2009. The CIA's June 2013 Response asserts that it "took [the CIA] until 2007 to consistently stop referring to [Padilla's] 'Dirty Bomb' plot—a plan [the CIA] concluded early on was never operationally viable." As noted, the CIA continued to refer to the "Dirty Bomb" plotting through 2007 and confirmed the information publicly in 2009.

1313. See list of CIA prepared briefings and memoranda from 2003 through 2009 with representations on the effectiveness of the CIA's enhanced interrogation techniques referenced in this summary and described in detail in Volume II.

1314. See, for example, [REDACTED]; CIA document entitled, "CIA Statement Summarizing Significant Information About Jose Padilla (21:10 hrs.- 8 June 02)"; [REDACTED] 10972 (12031Z APR 02); ALEC [REDACTED] (231837Z APR 02); and [REDACTED] 10976 (120948Z APR 02); among other records.

1315. Federal Bureau of Investigation documents pertaining "to the interrogation of detainee Zayn Al Abideen Abu Zabaidah" and provided to the Select Committee on Intelligence by cover letter dated July 20, 2010 (DTS# 2010-2939). *See also* [REDACTED] 10092 (211031Z APR 02). While Abu Zubaydah was subjected to sleep deprivation and nudity prior to this date by the CIA, he had been allowed to sleep shortly prior to being questioned on this matter by the FBI special agents, who were exclusively using rapport-building interrogation techniques when the information was acquired from Abu Zubaydah (who was covered with a towel). The sleep deprivation and nudity as implemented during this period differed from how sleep deprivation and nudity were implemented after the CIA developed, and the Department of Justice approved, the CIA's "enhanced interrogation techniques" in August 2002. Rather than being placed in a stress position during sleep deprivation, Abu Zubaydah was kept awake by being questioned nearly non-stop by CIA and FBI interrogators. Records further indicate that during breaks in the interrogations, Abu Zubaydah was allowed to briefly sleep. *See also* [REDACTED] 10116 (250731Z APR 02), which describes this sleep deprivation as a period of "no sustained sleep" with "cat naps between interrogators." The cable further states: "Like many medical students, the subject appears to handle 76 plus hours of *limited sleep* with few problems" (italics added). The use of nudity during this period also differed from future uses of nudity, as Abu Zubaydah was covered when interrogated by the FBI. *See also* SSCI Staff interview of FBI Special Agent Ali Soufan, April 28, 2008, at 1:20 PM, Hart Senate Office Building (transcript at DTS #2008-2411). Ali Soufan described events prior to Abu Zubaydah's provision of information related to the "Dirty Bomb," stating: "He was injured, badly injured. He was dehydrated. I remember we were putting ice on his lips. And he didn't have any bowel control, so we were cleaning him. And the reason I'm telling you some of these disgusting things is because it helped build rapport with the guy in this short period of time." Later, Ali Soufan described the provision of information related to the Dirty Bomb plotting, stating: "When I was going in, he was totally naked. I refused to go and interview him naked. So I took a towel. And [REDACTED] and I and [REDACTED], every time we went in he had to be covered or I [wouldn't] go. It's as simple as that." *See also* section of transcript stating, "So we went back. And we start talking to him. We took some Coke, tea, and we start talking about different things. We flipped him about different things, [REDACTED] and I and [REDACTED]. And then he came back to his senses and he started cooperating again. And this is when he gave us Padilla." (Abu Zubaydah provided information concerning the Dirty Bomb plotting and Jose Padilla's *kunya*, but did not provide the name "Jose Padilla." As described in this summary, Jose Padilla's name had already been provided to the CIA by a foreign government that identified Padilla as a U.S. citizen suspected of being engaged in possible terrorist activity.) *See also* Abu Zubaydah detainee review in Volume III.

1316. The Department of Justice finalized its approval of the CIA's enhanced interrogation techniques, including walling, facial slaps, wall standing, stress positions, sleep deprivation, and the waterboard, as well as other techniques, on August 1, 2002. See Volume I and Volume III for additional details. Beginning on August 4, 2002, and extending through August 20, 2002, Abu Zubaydah was subjected to the non-stop concurrent use of the CIA's enhanced interrogation techniques, including at least 83 applications of the waterboard. CIA records indicate that the use of the CIA's enhanced interrogation techniques ceased on August 30, 2002, when Abu Zubaydah received clothing.

1317. See intelligence chronology in Volume II, to include: (1) email from: [REDACTED] [REDACTED] OTA/CTWG/CBRN Group; to: [REDACTED] and multiple ccs, including [REDACTED]; subject: "Re: [REDACTED]: Re: KSM homework on AQ nuke program"; date: April 22, 2003, at 03:30 PM, explaining CIA's CBRN group's position on Padilla and Mohammed's plotting; "Padilla and Binyam/Zouaoui had pulled an article off a satirical web site called 'How to make an H-bomb' which is based on a 1979 Journal of Irreproducible Results article. The article was intended to be humorous . . ."; (2) email from: [REDACTED], CTC/OTA/CBRNB; subject: "Note to Briefers Updating Zubaydah 'Uranium Device' Information"; date: April 23, 2003, at 08:25:40 PM; and (3) U.K. court records relaying that "[Binyam Mohammed] at the outset said there was no Dirty Bomb plot (a position he has consistently maintained to his defense lawyers)" (UK Judgment, at 39). According to U.K. legal records, "[Binyam Mohammed] said . . . that he had seen a file on a computer in Lahore and decided it was a joke—part of the instruction included adding bleach to uranium 238 in a bucket and rotating it around one's head for 45 minutes." (UK Judgment, at 11). On June 10, 2002, then–Attorney General John Ashcroft announced, "We have captured a known terrorist who was exploring a plan to build and explode a radiological dispersion device, or 'dirty bomb,' in the United States." The statement continued: "In apprehending Al Muhajir as he sought entry into the United States, we have disrupted an unfolding terrorist plot to attack the United States by exploding a radioactive 'dirty bomb.' Now, a radioactive 'dirty bomb' involves exploding a conventional bomb that not only kills victims in the immediate vicinity, but also spreads radioactive material that is highly toxic to humans and can cause mass death and injury. From information available to the United States government, we know that Abdullah Al Muhajir is an Al Qaeda operative and was exploring a plan to build and explode a radioactive dirty bomb. Let me be clear: We know from multiple independent and corroborating sources that Abdullah Al Muhajir was closely associated with Al Qaeda and that as an Al Qaeda operative he was involved in planning future terrorist attacks on innocent American civilians in the United States . . . I commend the FBI, the CIA and other agencies involved in capturing Abdullah Al Muhajir before he could act on his deadly plan." See Transcript of the Attorney General John Ashcroft Regarding the Transfer of Abdullah Al Muhajir (Born Jose Padilla) to the Department of Defense as an Enemy Combatant, on June 10, 2002.

1318. See Intelligence Community review of the Tall Buildings plotting included in CIA records with references to terrorist attacks in Russia in September 1999 against apartment buildings using traditional explosives and VBIEDs. *See also* U.S. Department of Justice Bureau of Alcohol, Tobacco, Firearms and Explosives report entitled, "Use of Natural Gas as a Terrorist Weapon in Apartment Buildings," dated August 4, 2008.

1319. The CIA's June 2013 Response acknowledges that the CIA "concluded early on" that the "dirty bomb" plot was "never operationally viable." The CIA's June 2013 Response states that "it took [the CIA] until 2007" to stop citing the "dirty bomb" plot in its representations about the effectiveness of the CIA's enhanced interrogation techniques. This is incorrect. The CIA referred to the disruption of this plotting in a representation to the Department of Justice in July 2007, in representations to Congress in late October 2007, and confirmed this information to the press in April 2009. See CIA fax from CIA employee [REDACTED] to U.S. Senate Committee on Appropriations, Subcommittee on Defense, with fax cover sheet entitled, "Talking points," sent on October 26, 2007, at 5:39:48 PM. Document faxed entitled, "Talking Points Appeal of the $[REDACTED] Million reduction in CIA/CTC's Rendition and Detention Program." *See also* the July 20, 2007, Office of Legal Counsel (OLC) memorandum, which states that "interrogations of Zubaydah—*again, once enhanced techniques were employed*—revealed two al-Qaeda operatives already in the United States and planning to destroy a high rise apartment building and to detonate a radiological bomb in Washington, D.C." (italics added). As described elsewhere in this summary and in the full Committee Study, on April 21, 2009, in response to the partial declassification of OLC memoranda that month, a CIA spokesperson confirmed the CIA stood by the "factual assertions" in the OLC memoranda. See "Waterboarding Saved L.A.," Washington Times, April 25, 2009. The CIA's June 2013 Response further states "[d]espite the imprecision of our language, we continue to assess it was a good example of the importance of intelligence derived from the detainee program." As described in this summary and throughout the full Committee Study, in its efforts to obtain legal authorization and policy approval for the CIA's enhanced interrogation techniques, the CIA represented that the intelligence referenced was obtained "as a result" of the CIA's enhanced interrogation techniques (not the "detainee program"), and that the information obtained was unique and otherwise unavailable.

1320. The Consular Lookout and Support System (CLASS) is used by State Department passport agencies, post, and border inspection agencies to perform name checks on visa and passport applicants to identify individuals who are ineligible for issuance or require other special action. Source: www.state.gov.

1321. A February 16, 2001, email entitled, "Lost passport case- Jose Padilla," states that a "Jose Padilla," with a date of birth of October 18, 1970, came to the U.S. Consulate in Karachi to report a lost passport. The email notes that "his story is really-sketchy-been traveling here long enough to overstay his Pakistani visa, but speaks no Urdu, and is allegedly studying Islamic law in Egypt." A March 5, 2001, email in CIA records, entitled, "The continuing Jose Padilla saga!" states that there are "multiple CLASS hits" (Consular Lookout and Support System) for a Jose Padilla. The author writes "[REDACTED] and I both agree there is something sketchy about the guy." On March 21, 2001, State Department records indicate that Jose Padilla was provided with a replacement passport. See documents included in materials provided by the CIA to the Senate Select Committee on Intelligence, including email from: [REDACTED]; to: [REDACTED]: cc: [REDACTED]; subject: "Lost passport case- Jose Padilla"; date: February 16, 2001, at 4:46 AM, included in materials provided by the CIA to the Senate Select Committee on Intelligence; second email from: [REDACTED]; to: [REDACTED]; cc: [REDACTED]; subject: "The continuing Jose Padilla saga!"; date: March 5, 2001, at 10:09AM; U.S. State Department travel records identified by the Department of Justice; letter from Paul Wolfowitz, U.S. Department of Defense, to James Comey, U.S. Department of Justice, dated May 28, 2004.

1322. Italics added. Jose Padilla's fingerprints would later be found on the forms. See Jose Padilla U.S. court documents, which include the pledge form and a translation of the pledge form. *See also* FBI Washington 101514Z (10 APR 07), "Summary Chronology of Intelligence on Jose Padilla," and email from: [REDACTED]; to: [REDACTED] [REDACTED]; subject: "Pakistan Raid Evidence- Meeting with FBI SA in Pakistan at the time"; date: July 17, 2007, at 01:07 PM, which notes the raids recovered a copy of "Padilla's Muj pledge form." *See also* numerous open source articles, to include, "CIA Officer Testifies He Was Given Qaeda 'Pledge Form' Said to be Padilla's," *New York Times*, dated May 16, 2007; "Key Padilla evidence got to CIA in Afghan pickup," *Associated Press*, March 28, 2007; and "Terror Suspect's Path from Streets to Brig," *New York Times*, dated April 24, 2004. The CIA's June 2013 Response states that the CIA could not locate information on this form in CIA databases. According to testimony of a CIA officer at Jose Padilla's federal trial, the binder and other material were provided by a CIA source to CIA officers in Kandahar, Afghanistan. The CIA officer testified at Jose

Padilla's trial that, after he sorted through the material, the blue binder was placed in a sealed box and provided to the FBI in Islamabad, Pakistan. See referenced open source reporting.

1323. ALEC ▮▮▮▮ (102327Z APR 02).

1324. ▮▮▮▮ 10972 (12031Z APR 02). As noted, the State Department already possessed information of concern related to Jose Padilla.

1325. See Jose Padilla U.S. court documents, which include the pledge form and a translation of the pledge form. *See also* FBI Washington 101514Z (10APR 07), "Summary Chronology of Intelligence on Jose Padilla," and email from: [REDACTED]; to: ▮▮▮▮; subject: "Pakistan Raid Evidence- Meeting with FBI SA in Pakistan at the time"; date: July 17, 2007, at 01:07 PM, which notes the raids recovered a copy of "Padilla's Muj pledge form"; and numerous open source articles, to include, "CIA Officer Testifies He Was Given Qaeda 'Pledge Form' Said to be Padilla's," *New York Times*, dated May 16, 2007.

1326. ▮▮▮▮ 10976 (120948Z APR 02). The official cable states that the Pakistani official and his office has "not received the full details, and he is passing this onto [the CIA] ▮▮▮▮ due to concerns about possible terrorist activity." The CIA's June 2013 Response states that the reporting from the Pakistani government that a Pakistan-based U.S. citizen named Jose Padilla was engaged in possible terrorist activity was "unremarkable at the time," and that the CIA viewed the report as a "routine 'illegal traveler'" report.

1327. ▮▮▮▮ 10972 (12031Z APR 02); ▮▮▮▮ 10976 (120948Z APR 02).

1328. See DIRECTOR ▮▮▮▮ (162003Z FEB 03), which details a follow-up exchange between ▮▮▮▮ personnel and Pakistani officials.

1329. ▮▮▮▮ 10972 (12031Z APR 02); ▮▮▮▮ 10976 (120948Z APR 02).

1330. There were no records identified to indicate that the CIA informed the FBI at this time that U.S. citizen "Jose Padilla" was engaged in "possible terrorist activity." As described in Volume 11, once alerted, the FBI identified links between Jose Padilla and FBI counterterrorism subjects, including an individual who reportedly paid for Jose Padilla's travel to Pakistan to attend a terrorist training camp.

1331. ▮▮▮▮ 10972 (12031Z APR 02); ▮▮▮▮ 10976 (120948Z APR 02).

1332. ▮▮▮▮ 10976 (120948Z APR 02). See additional reporting in the Volume II intelligence chronology.

1333. Abu Zubaydah provided the names of the individuals as Talha al-Kini and Abdallah al-Muhajir (▮▮▮▮ 10090 (210703Z APR 02)).

1334. ▮▮▮▮; ▮▮▮▮ 10063 (180515Z APR 02); ▮▮▮▮ 10096 (221545Z APR 02).

1335. See FBI communications to FBI Headquarters in April 2002, as well as May 13, 2009, Senate Judiciary Committee testimony of FBI Special Agent Ali Soufan on the interrogation of Abu Zubaydah. In the CIA's June 2013 Response, the CIA states the CIA's representation that Abu Zubaydah provided the information after the "use of DOJ-approved enhanced interrogation techniques" was accurate because, "Abu Zubaydah revealed this information after having been subjected to sleep deprivation, which would be categorized as an enhanced interrogation technique once the program was officially underway." As described in detail in the Abu Zubaydah detainee review in Volume III, when Abu Zubaydah was discharged from a hospital in Country ▮, the CIA sought to deprive Abu Zubaydah of sleep and to cease Abu Zubaydah's interaction with the FBI special agents who had been interviewing Abu Zubaydah and acquiring information from him at the hospital. Days later, after this new CIA approach was implemented, the CIA reversed this decision and the FBI was allowed to question Abu Zubaydah again. Further, the use of sleep deprivation during this period differed from future uses of sleep deprivation and had ceased by the time of the referenced FBI interview, as the CIA had determined that Abu Zubaydah's ability to focus on questions and provide coherent answers appeared compromised. (See ▮▮▮▮ 10071 (190827Z APR 02) and ▮▮▮▮ 10116 (250731Z APR02).) Ali Soufan testified that Abu Zubaydah provided information about the "Dirty Bomb" plot only after he (Soufan) re-initiated a more traditional interrogation approach with Abu Zubaydah, stating, "We then returned to using the Informed Interrogation Approach. Within a few hours, Abu Zubaydah again started talking and gave us important actionable intelligence. This included the details of Jose Padilla, the so-called 'dirty bomber.'" (See Senate Judiciary Testimony, transcript at: http://judiciary.senate.gov/hearings/testimony.cfm?id=38428wit_id=7906.) The assertion in the CIA's June 2013 Response is incongruent with additional CIA records. See senior CIA analyst comments on the draft CIA Inspector General Special Review from February 10, 2004, stating: "Padilla and the dirty bomb plot was prior to enhanced and he never really gave us actionable intel to get them"; CIA draft response to Committee Questions for the Record concerning an OLC memorandum suggesting that information on Jose Padilla was acquired from Abu Zubaydah after enhanced interrogation techniques, with the CIA response stating that the CIA's ▮▮▮▮ CTC Legal "[▮▮▮▮] simply inadvertently reported this wrong. Abu Zubaydah provided information on Jose Padilla while being interrogated by the FBI (▮▮▮▮ 10091)"; CIA testimony from CIA Director Hayden on April 12, 2007, stating, "In August 2002, CIA began using these few and lawful interrogation techniques in the interrogation of Abu Zubaydah"; and the CIA-vetted speech by President Bush on September 6, 2006. *See also* SSCI Staff interview of FBI Special Agent Ali Soufan, April 28, 2008, at 1:20 PM, Hart Senate Office Building (Ali Soufan: "So we went back. And we start talking to him. We took some Coke, tea, and we start talking about different things. We flipped him about different things, ▮▮▮▮ and I and [REDACTED]. And then he came back to his senses and he started cooperating again. And this is when he gave us Padilla.") (DTS #2008-2411).

1336. See Abu Zubaydah detainee review in Volume III that details how, after Department of Justice approval in August 2002, the CIA began using the CIA's enhanced interrogation techniques against Abu Zubaydah on August 4, 2002, including the waterboard. *See also* ██████ 10644 (201235Z AUG 02); and email from: [REDACTED]; to: ████████ and [REDACTED]; subject: "Re: So begins"; date; August 4, 2002, at 09:45 AM.

1337. ██████ 11036 (220348Z APR 02). *See also* ALEC ████ (220238Z APR 02); ██████ 11041 (220802Z APR 02); and ██████ 11042 (220921Z APR 02).

1338. Among other documents, see letter from the CIA addressed to SSCI Staff Director Al Cumming, dated June 24, 2002, and entitled, "Arrest of Jose Padilla." After being detained in Pakistan, Binyam Mohammad was rendered by the CIA ██████████ July █, 2002, where he was held ███████ government. On January █, 2004, Binyam Mohammad was transferred to CIA custody ███████ 30586 ██████████; ███████████ 1630 ████████.

1339. Fax from Pat Rowan, Department of Justice National Security Division to [REDACTED], at CTC Legal, on August 15, 2007 with subject line; "Jose Padilla," includes a Department of Justice memorandum that is based primarily on 29 IIRs of the joint FBI-military interrogations of Padilla disseminated from May 5, 2003, to July 9, 2003, a FBI document "Jose Padilla Debrief Summary, August 29, 2003," the FBI's 302s on Padilla (5/8/02) and Binyam Muhammad (6/4/02), an FBI EC on Padilla (5/14/02); a CIA Statement Summarizing Significant Information about Jose Padilla of 8 June 02 ['CIA Summary']; a DIA Info Memo from ████ █ (11/13/03); and an FBI LHM "Jose Padilla Debrief Status" (11/11/03). *See also* SSCI Transcript "Detention of Jose Padilla," dated June 12, 2002 (DTS #2002-2603).

1340. CIA Notification, "Arrest of Jose Padilla," dated June 24, 2002 (DTS #2002-2866); WHDC ████ (242226Z MAR 03). Discusses information obtained by FBI officials on March 20, 2003, and SSCI Transcript "Staff Briefing by the Federal Bureau of Investigation on the Detention of Jose Padilla," dated June 11, 2002 (DTS #2002-2598).

1341. Pocket litter refers to material acquired on a person upon a search and may include notes, identification cards, tickets, phone numbers, computer files, photographs, or any other material in the person's possession.

1342. See CIA Document, Subject "CIA Statement Summarizing Significant Information About Jose Padilla (21:10 hrs.- 8 June 02)," email from [REDACTED] to ████████ on August 2, 2002, at 3:54:17 PM, with the subject line: "Re: Padilla's travel history," and fax from Pat Rowan, Department of Justice National Security Division to [REDACTED], at CIA CTC Legal, on August 15, 2007, with subject line: "Jose Padilla." The fax includes a Department of Justice memorandum that is based primarily on 29 IIRs of the joint FBI-military interrogations of Padilla disseminated from May 5, 2003, to July 9, 2003, a FBI document "Jose Padilla Debrief Summary, August 29, 2003," the FBI's 302s on Padilla (5/8/02) and Binyam Muhammad (6/4/02), an FBI EC on Padilla (5/14/02); a CIA Statement Summarizing Significant Information about Jose Padilla of 8 June 02 ['CIA Summary']; a DIA Info Memo from ██████ (11/13/03); and an FBI LHM "Jose Padilla Debrief Status" (11/11/03). *See also* SSCI transcript "Detention of Jose Padilla," dated June 12, 2002 (DTS #2002-2603), in which the CIA informs the SSCI that, based on his address book confiscated in ██████, Padilla "did have connections to Islamic extremists, both within the United States and outside the U.S."

1343. See Department of Justice memorandum referenced in chronology in Volume II that is based primarily on 29 IIRs of the joint FBI-military interrogations of Padilla disseminated from May 5, 2003, to July 9, 2003; a FBI document "Jose Padilla Debrief Summary, August 29, 2003," the FBI's 302s on Padilla (5/8/02) and Binyam Muhammad (6/4/02), an FBI EC on Padilla (5/14/02); a CIA Statement Summarizing Significant Information about Jose Padilla of 8 June 02 ['CIA Summary']; a DIA Info Memo from ██████ (11/13/03); and an FBI LHM "Jose Padilla Debrief Status" (11/11/03).

1344. See CIA memorandum from: ███████; to: ███████; subject: "AZ information"; date: July 10, 2002, at 01:18:50 PM. *See also* February 10, 2004, email from: ████████; to: ███████; cc: [redacted], [redacted], [redacted], [redacted], ███████, John P. Mudd, [REDACTED], [REDACTED], [REDACTED], Jose Rodriguez, [REDACTED], [REDACTED], ███████; subject: Please Read -- Re CTC Response to the Draft IG Report; date: February 10, 2004. In a SSCI transcript dated June 12, 2002, entitled, "Detention of Jose Padilla" (DTS #2002-2603), the CIA acknowledged it had information on Jose Padilla prior to reporting from Abu Zubaydah. A CIA officer stated: "the Pakistani liaison felt it was important to bring [Padilla] to our attention, given the recent raids . . . there was enough information indicating that his travel was suspicious, to put us on alert. This suspicion was enhanced during the debriefings of Abu Zubaydah, which occurred on 21 April." This is the only known CIA representation that did not fully attribute information on Jose Padilla to CIA interrogations.

1345. Email from: ████████; to: ███████; cc: [REDACTED], [REDACTED], [REDACTED], [REDACTED], ███████, John P. Mudd, [REDACTED], [REDACTED], [REDACTED], Jose Rodriguez, [REDACTED], [REDACTED], █████████; subject: Please Read -- Re CTC Response to the Draft IG Report; date: February 10, 2004.

1346. See email from: [REDACTED] C/CTC/OTA/CBRNG/RNTB; to: multiple recipients; subject: "Re: Urgent: Unclassified Fact Sheet for David Shedd"; date: October 6, 2005, at 04:35 PM.

1347. See additional details in Volume II.

1348. See Intelligence Community review of the Tall Buildings plotting included in CIA records with references to terrorist attacks in Russia in September 1999 against apartment buildings using traditional explosives and VBIEDs.

1349. See Intelligence Community review of the Tall Buildings plotting included in CIA records with references to terrorist attacks in Russia in September 1999 against apartment buildings using traditional explosives and VBIEDs. *See also* U.S. Department of Justice Bureau of Alcohol, Tobacco, Firearms and Explosives report entitled, "Use of Natural Gas as a Terrorist Weapon in Apartment Buildings," dated August 4, 2008. The latter document states that: "If the idea of the plot is to cause death and destruction on the same scale as had occurred in Russia, then Padilla's methodology comes into question. The probability of causing this magnitude of death and destruction using natural gas [versus conventional explosives] would be considerably lower."

1350. ALEC ████ (May 17, 2002), with references to FBI WASH 150315Z, ████, and CIA reporting from 2001, ████. Upon Jose Padilla's arrest, Padilla was found to be in possession of the phone number of Adham Hassoun, ████ ████ ████ ████ ████ ████; and providing material support to terrorists. U.S. prosecutors focused on more than 70 intercepted phone calls between the defendants during the 1990s, but provided no information at the trial related to plotting in the United States. See U.S. District Criminal Court Docket, Florida Southern, for defendants, including Jose Padilla, as well as open source news reports, including "Without a plot, is Padilla guilty?," *Christian Science Monitor*, dated July 19, 2007; and "The others on trial in Padilla case," *Christian Science Monitor*, dated May 29, 2007.

1351. An Assistant U.S. Attorney involved in the prosecution stated, "The narrative is fairly clear that Padilla was recruited to go overseas to participate in jihad." See U.S. District Criminal Court Docket, Florida Southern, for defendants, including Jose Padilla, as well as open source news reports, including "Without a plot, is Padilla guilty?," *Christian Science Monitor*, dated July 19, 2007; and "The others on trial in Padilla case," *Christian Science Monitor*, dated May 29, 2007.

1352. See open sources, to include press articles such as, "Court Says Padilla Prison Sentence Too Lenient," *Reuters*, dated September 19, 2011.

1353. ████ 30586 ████; ████ 1630 ████.

1354. ████ 2335 ████.

1355. ████ 12520 (281655Z SEP 04).

1356. Terrorism Watch, March 10, 2009, *Guantanamo Detainee's Torture Claims Could Impact Bilateral Relationship with UK.*

1357. [REDACTED] 3174 (311725Z JUL 08).

1358. Among other open sources, see "Compensation to Guantanamo detainees 'was necessary,'" *BBC News UK*, November 16, 2010.

1359. See intelligence chronology in Volume II and ████ 11454 (3017102Z APR 03).

1360. ████ 33804 (190956Z SEP 02); [REDACTED] 34513 (052246Z MAR 03); ████ 45028 ████ ████; DIRECTOR ████ ████.

1361. See intelligence chronology in Volume II, including DIRECTOR ████ ████ MAY 03) and DIRECTOR ████ ████ MAY 03).

1362. The Karachi terrorist plots encompassed a variety of potential targets in the Karachi area associated with U.S. and Western interests. Although the plotting involved multiple targets, the plotting is most often referred to as the "Karachi Plot."

1363. Italics included in CIA Memorandum to the Office of Legal Counsel, entitled, "Effectiveness of the CIA Counterterrorist Interrogation Techniques," from March 2, 2005. *See also* CIA talking points for National Security Council entitled, "Talking Points for 10 March 2005 DCI Meeting PC: Effectiveness of the High-Value Detainee Interrogation (HVDI) Techniques," dated March 4, 2005.

1364. From 2003 through 2009, the CIA's representations regarding the effectiveness of the CIA's enhanced interrogation techniques provided a specific set of examples of terrorist plots "disrupted" and terrorists captured that the CIA attributed to information obtained from the use of its enhanced interrogation techniques. CIA representations further asserted that the intelligence obtained from the use of the CIA's enhanced interrogation techniques was unique, otherwise unavailable, and resulted in "saved lives." Among other CIA representations, see: (1) CIA representations in the Department of Justice Office of Legal Counsel Memorandum, dated May 30, 2005, which relied on a series of highly specific CIA representations on the type of intelligence acquired from the use of the CIA's enhanced interrogation techniques to assess their legality. The CIA representations referenced by the OLC include that the use of the CIA's enhanced interrogation techniques was "necessary" to obtain "critical," "vital," and "otherwise unavailable actionable intelligence" that was "essential" for the U.S. government to "detect and disrupt" terrorist threats. The OLC memorandum further states that "[the CIA] ha[s] informed [the OLC] that the CIA believes that this program is largely responsible for preventing a subsequent attack within the United States." (See Memorandum for John A. Rizzo, Senior Deputy General Counsel, Central Intelligence Agency, from Steven G. Bradbury, Principal Deputy Assistant Attorney General, Office of Legal Counsel, May 30, 2005, Re: Application of United States Obligations Under Article 16 of the Convention Against Torture to Certain Techniques that May Be Used in the Interrogation of High Value al Qaeda Detainees.) (2) CIA representations in the Department of Justice Office of Legal Counsel Memorandum dated July 20, 2007, which also relied on CIA representations on the type of intelligence acquired from the use of the CIA's enhanced interrogation techniques. Citing CIA documents and the President's September 6, 2006, speech describing the CIA's interrogation program (which was based on CIA-provided information), the OLC memorandum states: "The CIA interrogation program—and, in particular, its use of enhanced interrogation techniques—is intended to serve this paramount interest [security of the Nation] by producing substantial quantities of otherwise unavailable intelligence . . . As the President explained [on September 6, 2006], 'by giving us information about terrorist plans we could not get anywhere else, the program has saved innocent lives.'" (See Memorandum for John A. Rizzo, Acting General Counsel, Central Intelligence Agency, from Steven G. Bradbury, Principal Deputy Assistant Attorney General, Office of Legal Counsel, July 20, 2007, Re: Application of the War Crimes Act, the Detainee Treatment Act, and Common Article 3 of the Geneva Conventions to Certain Techniques that May Be Used by the CIA in the Interrogation of High Value al Qaeda Detainees.) (3) CIA briefings for members of the National Security Council in July and September 2003 represented that "the use of Enhanced Techniques of one kind or another had produced significant intelligence information that had, in the view of CIA professionals, saved lives," and warned policymakers that "[t]ermination of this program will result in loss of life, possibly extensive." (See August 5, 2003 Memorandum for the Record from Scott Muller, Subject: Review of Interrogation Program on 29 July 2003; Briefing slides, CIA Interrogation Program, July 29, 2003; September 4, 2003, CIA Memorandum for the Record, Subject: Member Briefing; and September 26, 2003, Memorandum for the Record from Muller, Subject: CIA Interrogation Program.) (4) The CIA's response to the Office of Inspector General draft Special Review of the CIA program, which asserts: "Information [the CIA] received . . . as a result of the lawful use of enhanced interrogation techniques ('EITs') has almost certainly saved countless American lives inside the United States and abroad. The evidence points clearly to the fact that without the use of such techniques, we and our allies would [have] suffered major terrorist attacks involving hundreds, if not thousands, of casualties." (See Memorandum for: Inspector General; from: James Pavitt, Deputy Director for Operations; subject: re (S) Comments to Draft IG Special Review, "Counterterrorism Detention and Interrogation Program" 2003-7123-IG; date: February 27, 2004; attachment: February 24, 2004, Memorandum re Successes of CIA's Counterterrorism Detention and Interrogation Activities.) (5) CIA briefing documents for CIA Director Leon Panetta in February 2009, which state that the "CIA assesses that the RDI program worked and the [enhanced interrogation] techniques were effective in producing foreign intelligence," and that "[m]ost, if not all, of the timely intelligence acquired from detainees in this program would not have been discovered or reported by other means." (See CIA briefing documents for Leon Panetta, entitled, "Tab 9: DCIA Briefing on RDI Program- 18FEB.2009" and graphic attachment, "Key Intelligence and Reporting Derived from Abu Zubaydah and Khalid Shaykh Muhammad (KSM)," including "DCIA Briefing on RDI Program" agenda, CIA document "EITs and Effectiveness," with associated documents, "Key Intelligence Impacts Chart: Attachment (AZ and KSM)," "Background on Key Intelligence Impacts Chart: Attachment," and "supporting references," to include "Background on Key Captures and Plots Disrupted.") (6) CIA document faxed to the Senate Select Committee on Intelligence on March 18, 2009, entitled, "[SWIGERT] and [DUNBAR]," located in Committee databases at DTS #2009-1258, which provides a list of "some of the key captures and disrupted plots" that the CIA had attributed to the use of the CIA's enhanced interrogation techniques, and stating: "CIA assesses that most, if not all, of the timely intelligence acquired from detainees in this program would not have been discovered or reported by any other means." See Volume II for additional CIA representations asserting that the CIA's enhanced interrogation techniques enabled the CIA to obtain unique, otherwise unavailable intelligence that "saved lives."

1365. On September 17, 2007, President Bush nominated Judge Michael Mukasey to be Attorney General of the United States. In October 2007, at his confirmation hearing before the Senate Judiciary Committee, Mukasey declined to say whether he believed waterboarding as an interrogation technique was unlawful. On October 30, 2007, Mukasey responded to written questions from the Senate Judiciary Committee on the issue of waterboarding, stating: "As described in your letter, these techniques seem over the line or, on a personal basis, repugnant to me, and would probably seem the same to many Americans. But hypotheticals are different from real life, and in any legal opinion the actual facts and circumstances are critical." (See October 30, 2007, Letter from Michael B. Mukasey, to Senators Patrick J. Leahy, Edward M. Kennedy, Joseph R. Biden, Jr., Herb Kohl, Dianne Feinstein, Russell D. Feingold, Charles E. Schumer, Richard J. Durbin, Benjamin L. Cardin, and Sheldon Whitehouse.) On November 6, 2007, days prior to a Senate vote to confirm Mukasey, the CIA provided a set of talking points to the CIA director for use with the President in a meeting about the CIA's use of the waterboard interrogation technique. See document entitled, "DCIA Talking Points: Waterboard 06 November 2007," dated November 6, 2007, with the notation the document was "sent to DCIA Nov. 6 in preparation for POTUS meeting."

1366. Italics added. See document entitled, "DCIA Talking Points: Waterboard 06 November 2007," dated November 6, 2007, with the notation the document was "sent to DCIA Nov. 6 in preparation for POTUS meeting."
1367. Italics added. CIA briefing for Vice President Cheney, dated March 4, 2005, entitled, "Briefing for Vice President Cheney: CIA Detention and Interrogation Program."
1368. See list of CIA prepared briefings and memoranda from 2003 through 2009 with representations on the effectiveness of the CIA's enhanced interrogation techniques referenced in this summary and described in detail in Volume II.
1369. ███ 45028 ███ and DIRECTOR ███ ███. The CIA's June 2013 Response concedes that the CIA "mischaracterized the impact of the reporting [the CIA] acquired from detainees on the Karachi plots," and acknowledges that the Karachi plotting was "thwarted by the arrest of the operatives and the interdiction of explosives by [Pakistani authorities]." The CIA does not dispute that Pakistani authorities arrested Ammar al-Baluchi and Khallad bin Attash independently, and that information from the CIA's Detention and Interrogation Program played no role in the arrests. The CIA's June 2013 Response states, however, that CIA detainee reporting "revealed ongoing attack plotting against the US official presence in Karachi that prompted the Consulate to take further steps to protect its officers." This statement is incongruent with CIA records. In response to the reporting cited by the CIA, CIA personnel in Karachi wrote: "[w]hile reporting from both [al-Baluchi and bin Attash] was chilling- [CIA officers] had become aware of most of this reporting either through previous information or through interviews of al-Baluchi and [Khallad bin] Attash prior to their transfer out of Karachi." The CIA personnel in Karachi further reassured addressees that, in December 2002, the U.S. Consulate in Karachi took increased steps to protect U.S. Consulate personnel. See Volume II for additional information.
1370. For detailed information, see Volume II.
1371. ALEC ███ (032142Z OCT 02).
1372. ███ 12535 (050557Z OCT 02); ███ 11050 (101207Z OCT 02); ███.
1373. ALEC ███ (0302054Z OCT 02). *See also* CIA paper dated January 11, 2002, entitled, "Threat Threads: Most 11 September Plotters Still Under the Radar."
1374. ALEC ███ (0302054Z OCT 02). *See also* CIA paper dated January 11, 2002, entitled, "Threat Threads: Most 11 September Plotters Still Under the Radar."
1375. ███ 45028 ███. CIA records indicate the interdiction was the result of criminal leads and was unrelated to any reporting from CIA detainees. ███ ███. See DIRECTOR ███.
1376. ███ 45028 ███; DIRECTOR ███ ███. The CIA's June 2013 Response maintains that KSM's reporting on the thwarted "perfume letter" plotting was separate from the "plots disrupted with the arrest and interrogation of Ammar and Khallad." Because CIA records did not make this distinction, and the fact that the operations, to at least some extent, shared targets, operatives, and the same set of explosives, the operations are linked in this Study.
1377. ███ 45028 ███; DIRECTOR ███ ███.
1378. Given the threat to U.S. interests, CIA officers sought to participate in the interrogations. A May 2, 2003, CIA cable (See ███ 14291) states that, because of Ammar al-Baluchi's "strong reticence towards the U.S.," CIA officers were observing the foreign government interrogations of Ammar al-Baluchi via video feed. The cable notes that a foreign government officer who had developed rapport with Ammar al-Baluchi was conducting all the questioning and obtaining intelligence from Ammar al-Baluchi on the plotting against U.S. interests in Pakistan, as well as other matters.
1379. The CIA's June 2013 Response claims that "Ammar and Khallad provided new information on other attack plans in Karachi after entering CIA custody and undergoing enhanced interrogation techniques," and that "[d]uring his first interrogation in CIA custody and after enhanced techniques commenced, [Ammar] revealed that the plan was to use a motorcycle bomb and a car bomb in a single, coordinated attack at the end of May or early June, and he pointed to the location on the Consulate's perimeter wall where the attack would occur." The information in the CIA's June 2013 Response is inaccurate. Ammar al-Baluchi provided the referenced information while in foreign government custody, prior to entering CIA custody and being subjected to the CIA's enhanced interrogation techniques. Given the threat to U.S. interests, CIA officers sought to participate in the interrogations. A May 2, 2003, CIA cable (███ 14291) states that, because of Ammar al-Baluchi's "strong reticence towards the U.S.," CIA officers were observing the foreign government interrogations of Ammar al-Baluchi via video feed. The cable notes that a foreign government officer who had developed rapport with Ammar al-Baluchi was conducting all the questioning and obtaining intelligence from Ammar al-Baluchi. This included information about the motorcycle-car bomb plotting against the U.S. Consulate, as well as information on plans to potentially target Westerners in a specific housing area in Karachi. According to the information obtained, surveillance by the plotters "had confirmed a U.S. presence significant enough to warrant such an attack." Ammar al-Baluchi further stated that he had considered carjacking a U.S. Consulate vehicle and loading it with explosives to target the Consulate, and elaborated on the initial idea to attack the U.S. Consulate with a helicopter, stating that he did not follow through with this idea because he believed it would take too long to train an operative for that type of attack (see ███

14291, May 2, 2003). Later, the foreign government officer described Ammar al-Baluchi as "more chatty" than Khallad bin Attash, and detailed how, while in foreign government custody Ammar al-Baluchi "acknowledged plans to attack U.S. Consulate officials at the airport, the Consul General's Residence and the Consulate itself." The foreign government officer explained that "both the Consulate and the CG's residence" required a "tiered attack of successive car bombs which would breach the perimeter" of the targets. The foreign government officer also stated that, based on Ammar al-Baluchi's comments on his casing efforts, it was inferred that Ammar al-Baluchi had sought totarget Americans at their residences in specific areas of Karachi. See [REDACTED] 19647 [REDACTED] APR 04).

1380. [REDACTED] 14282 [REDACTED]. Records indicate that Khallad bin Attash was less cooperative (Ammar al-Baluchi was described as "more chatty"), but nonetheless provided information in foreign government custody on the surveillance he conducted against United States government vehicles in Karachi, among other information.

1381. [REDACTED] 45028 ([REDACTED] APR 03); DIRECTOR [REDACTED] APR 03); [REDACTED] 14291 (May 2, 2003); [REDACTED] 19647 ([REDACTED] APR 04). CIA records indicate that Ammar al-Baluchi was providing significant information to the foreign government officer conducting the questioning who had developed rapport with Ammar al-Baluchi.

1382. [REDACTED] 38325 [REDACTED]; [REDACTED] 38389 [REDACTED].

1383. DIRECTOR [REDACTED] ([REDACTED] MAY 03); DIRECTOR [REDACTED] ([REDACTED] MAY 03).

1384. DIRECTOR [REDACTED] ([REDACTED] MAY 03); DIRECTOR [REDACTED] ([REDACTED] MAY 03). DIRECTOR [REDACTED] noted that Khallad bin Attash indicated that they had identified one suicide operative so far.

1385. See CIA speech validation efforts for the President's September 6, 2006, speech acknowledging the CIA's Detention and Interrogation Program. In the speech. President Bush stated that "Terrorists held in CIA custody . . . helped stop a planned attack on the U.S. consulate in Karachi using car bombs and motorcycle bombs." *See also*, among other documents, the June 2005 CIA Intelligence Assessment entitled, "Detainee Reporting Pivotal for the War Against Al-Qa'ida." CIA records indicate this document was provided to White House officials on June 1, 2005. A slightly modified version of this Intelligence Assessment was broadly disseminated within the Intelligence Community on June 3, 2005. On March 31, 2009, former Vice President Cheney requested the declassification of this Intelligence Assessment, which was publicly released with redactions on August 24, 2009. The assessment represents that "detainee reporting" resulted in the "[r]evealing of the Karachi Plots," stating: "When confronted with information provided by Ammar al-Baluchi, Khallad admitted during debriefings that al-Qa'ida was planning to attack the US Consulate in Karachi, Westerners at the Karachi Airport, and Western housing areas." The footnote for this claim cites the May [REDACTED], 2003, disseminated intelligence report detailing the admission made by Khallad bin Attash while being subjected to the CIA's enhanced interrogation techniques ([REDACTED]) as its source.

1386. [REDACTED] 14510 [REDACTED]. This cable also stated, "As noted in several previous cables, in December 2002 [REDACTED] Consulate became aware of the threat to Consulate officials."

1387. [REDACTED] 14510 [REDACTED].

1388. Italics added. See document entitled, "DCIA Talking Points; Waterboard 06 November 2007," dated November 6, 2007, with the notation the document was "sent to DCIA Nov. 6 in preparation for POTUS meeting."

1389. [REDACTED] 11448 (301141Z APR 03); [REDACTED] 11454 (301710Z APR 03). As described in detail in the intelligence chronology in Volume II, KSM was rendered to CIA custody on March [REDACTED], 2003, and was immediately subjected to the CIA's enhanced interrogation techniques. On March 5, 2003, he was "confronted" with the "perfume letter," at which point he discussed the letter and its recipient, Hamza al-Zubayr. KSM had not yet been subjected to the waterboard. As described, Hamza al-Zubayr was killed in a September 2002 raid against al-Qa'ida-related safe houses. KSM stated that Khallad bin Attash had been responsible for obtaining operatives for the Hamza al-Zubayr operation. At the time KSM provided this information, a separate cable stated that KSM "continued to deny that he has any [knowledge of] ongoing operations." See [REDACTED] 34513 (052246Z MAR 03); DIRECTOR [REDACTED] (062312Z MAR 02); [REDACTED] 34575 (061929Z MAR 03); [REDACTED] 34566 (061646Z MAR 03); [REDACTED] 34575 [REDACTED]; [REDACTED] 34513 (052246Z MAR03).

1390. ALEC [REDACTED] (022012Z MAY 03).

1391. [REDACTED] 3425 (050726Z SEP 06); [REDACTED] 1242 (050748Z SEP 06); [REDACTED] 2214 (050539Z SEP 06).

1392. See Second Wave / Al-Ghuraba Group intelligence chronology in Volume II, including, among other documents, DIRECTOR [REDACTED] (20211Z JUN 03) and cable note on "Draft Intel: KSM Details his Thinking on and Efforts to Target California," included as an attachment to an email from [REDACTED] to a distribution list for CIA OTA in the Directorate of Intelligence, dated June 30, 2003, at 06:25 PM.

1393. See intelligence chronology in Volume II for detailed information. *See also* statements by United States government officials, such as a February 9, 2006, White House briefing on "the West Coast Terrorist Plot by Frances Fragos Townsend, Assistant to the President for Homeland Security and Counterterrorism." At this briefing the White House emphasized how "collaboration with our international partners" had "disrupted terrorist networks around the world and serious al-Qaeda plots." Using the "West Coast" plot as an example, Townsend stated that: "Khalid Shaykh Mohammed was the individual who led this effort . . . The cell leader was arrested in February of 2002, and as we begin—at that point, the other members of the cell believed that the West Coast plot had been cancelled [and] was not going forward . . . the lead guy is arrested, which disrupts it in February of '02." When asked about whether this plotting could be accurately described as a disruption given the belief by some that "it never got far enough to be disrupted," Townsend stated, "there is no question in my mind that this is a disruption." *See also* May 23, 2007, White House Press Release, entitled, "Fact Sheet: Keeping America Safe From Attack," which states, "We Also Broke Up Other Post-9/11 Aviation Plots. In 2002, we broke up a plot by KSM to hijack an airplane and fly it into the tallest building on the West Coast." As described in the Study, KSM was not detained until March 1, 2003. The CIA's June 2013 Response acknowledges that "[t]he Study correctly points out that we erred when we represented that we 'learned' of the Second Wave plotting from KSM and 'learned' of the operational cell comprised of students from Hambali." The CIA's June 2013 Response describes the inaccurate representation as "imprecision" by the CIA, but nonetheless states that the CIA "continue(s) to assess this was a good example of the importance of intelligence derived from the detainee program"; and contends—for the first time—that Hambali's capture "was a critical factor in the disruption of al-Qa'ida's plan to conduct a 'Second Wave' attack." As described throughout the Committee Study, in its efforts to obtain legal authorization and policy approval for the CIA's enhanced interrogation techniques, the CIA represented that the intelligence referenced was obtained "as a result" of the CIA's enhanced interrogation techniques (not the "detainee program"), and that the information obtained was unique and otherwise unavailable. As detailed in this summary and in Volume II, the capture of Hambali was unrelated to the use of the CIA's enhanced interrogation techniques.

1394. Reporting indicates that the al-Ghuraba group was similar to the Pan Islamic Party of Malaysia (PAS)'s Masapakindo, aka Pakindo, organization. Masran bin Arshad was connected to Pakindo, and while in foreign government custody, explained that "in 1991, PAS [Pan Islamic Party of Malaysia] established a secret Malaysian Student Association known as 'Masapakindo' to help facilitate a steady pipeline of PAS religious and military trainees traveling from Malaysia to Pakistan, sometimes continuing on to Afghanistan, but ultimately returning to Malaysia. This student association for children of PAS members also was intended to serve as a general support structure for PAS students who were undergoing Islamic religious training in Pakistan and India. Masapakindo's headquarters was based in Karachi, Pakistan." *See also* February 27, 2004, Memorandum for CIA Inspector General from James L. Pavitt, CIA Deputy Director for Operations, entitled "Comments to Draft IG Special Review, Counterterrorism Detention and Interrogation Program," which contains a February 24, 2004, attachment entitled, "Successes of CIA's Counterterrorism Detention and Interrogation Activities." *See also* CIA Intelligence Product entitled, "Jemaah Islamiya: Counterterrorism Scrutiny Limiting Extremist Agenda in Pakistan," dated April 18, 2008. Although this report makes numerous references to the al-Ghuraba group, it does not reference the group's potential engagement in KSM's Second Wave attack. As described in this summary, and in greater detail in Volume II, contrary to CIA representations, a wide body of intelligence reporting indicates that the al-Ghuraba group was not "discovered" as a result of KSM's reporting, norwas the al-Ghuraba group "tasked" with, or witting of, any aspect of KSM's "Second Wave" plotting. *See also* KSM and Hambali reporting from October 2003, and the intelligence chronology in Volume II, to include [REDACTED] 45915 (141431Z SEP 03).

1395. Memorandum for John A. Rizzo, Senior Deputy General Counsel, Central Intelligence Agency, from Steven G. Bradbury, Principal Deputy Assistant Attorney General, Office of Legal Counsel, May 30, 2005, Re: Application of United States Obligations Under Article 16 of the Convention Against Torture to Certain Techniques that May be Used in the Interrogation of High Value Al Qaeda Detainees. The memorandum states: "Use of enhanced techniques, however, led to critical, actionable intelligence such as the discovery of the Guraba Cell, which was tasked with executing KSM's planned Second Wave attacks against Los Angeles."

1396. References to the "Second Wave" attacks appeared in public news reports shortly after September 11, 2001, sometimes in reference to Zacarias Moussaoui. See, for example, *The Washington Post*, "Suspected Planner of 9/11 Attacks Captured in Pakistan after Gunfight" (09/14/2002) ("Some investigators have theorized that Moussaoui, whose laptop computer contained information about crop dusting, may have been part of a second wave of terror attacks or a back-up plan instead."); *The New York Post*, "2nd Plot Tied to Moussaoui" (09/06/2002) ("French officials reportedly are claiming that Zacarias Moussaoui was never meant to be the '20th' hijacker' but was to be part of a 'second wave' of terror."); *The Los Angeles Times*, "Officials Skeptical as Detainees Say Sept. 11 was First in a Trio" (10/01/2002) ("The Sept. 11 attacks may have been planned as the first of three terrorist strikes in the United States, each progressively bigger and more devastating than the last, U.S. officials said Monday, citing recent interviews with captured Al Qaeda operatives . . . Since days after Sept. 11, authorities have said they were concerned about a possible 'second wave' of attacks."). Similarly, on May 6, 2006, an affidavit filed by Moussaoui stated, "I was part of another al-Qaeda plot which was to occur after September 11, 2001."

1397. A November 21, 2005, *Newsweek* article entitled, "The Debate Over Torture," referenced a member of the Senate Select Committee on Intelligence stating that "enhanced interrogation techniques" worked with KSM to thwart an al-Qa'ida terrorist plot, which the magazine indicated was the "Second Wave" plot. The article included the following: "A career CIA official involved with interrogation policy cautioned *Newsweek* not to put too much credence in such claims. 'Whatever briefing they got was probably not truthful,' said the official, who did not wish to be identified discussing sensitive matters."

1398. Italics in original. March 2, 2005, Memorandum for Steve Bradbury from [redacted], [redacted] Legal Group, DCI Counterterrorist Center, document entitled, "Effectiveness of the CIA Counterterrorist Interrogation Techniques."

1399. From 2003 through 2009, the CIA's representations regarding the effectiveness of the CIA's enhanced interrogation techniques provided a specific set of examples of terrorist plots "disrupted" and terrorists captured that the CIA attributed to information obtained from the use of its enhanced interrogation techniques. CIA representations further asserted that the intelligence obtained from the use of the CIA's enhanced interrogation techniques was unique, otherwise unavailable, and resulted in "saved lives." Among other CIA representations, see (1) CIA representations in the Department of Justice Office of Legal Counsel Memorandum, dated May 30, 2005, which relied on a series of highly specific CIA representations on the type of intelligence acquired from the use of the CIA's enhanced interrogation techniques to assess their legality. The CIA representations referenced by the OLC include that the use of the CIA's enhanced interrogation techniques was "necessary" to obtain "critical," "vital," and "otherwise unavailable actionable intelligence" that was "essential" for the U.S. government to "detect and disrupt" terrorist threats. The OLC memorandum further states that "[the CIA] ha[s] informed [the OLC] that the CIA believes that this program is largely responsible for preventing a subsequent attack within the United States." (See Memorandum for John A. Rizzo, Senior Deputy General Counsel, Central Intelligence Agency, from Steven G. Bradbury, Principal Deputy Assistant Attorney General, Office of Legal Counsel, May 30, 2005, Re: Application of United States Obligations Under Article 16 of the Convention Against Torture to Certain Techniques that May Be Used in the Interrogation of High Value al Qaeda Detainees.) (2) CIA representations in the Department of Justice Office of Legal Counsel Memorandum dated July 20, 2007, which also relied on CIA representations on the type of intelligence acquired from the use of the CIA's enhanced interrogation techniques. Citing CIA documents and the President's September 6, 2006, speech describing the CIA's interrogation program (which was based on CIA-provided information), the OLC memorandum states: "The CIA interrogation program—and, in particular, its use of enhanced interrogation techniques—is intended to serve this paramount interest [security of the Nation] by producing substantial quantities of otherwise unavailable intelligence . . . As the President explained [on September 6, 2006], 'by giving us information about terrorist plans we could not get anywhere else, the program has saved innocent lives.'" (See Memorandum for John A. Rizzo, Acting General Counsel, Central Intelligence Agency, from Steven G. Bradbury, Principal Deputy Assistant Attorney General, Office of Legal Counsel, July 20, 2007, Re: Application of the War Crimes Act, the Detainee Treatment Act, and Common Article 3 of the Geneva Conventions to Certain Techniques that May Be Used by the CIA in the Interrogation of High Value al Qaeda Detainees.) (3) CIA briefings for members of the National Security Council in July and September 2003 represented that "the use of Enhanced Techniques of one kind or another had produced significant intelligence information that had, in the view of CIA professionals, saved lives," and warned policymakers that "[t]ermination of this program will result in loss of life, possibly extensive." (See August 5, 2003 Memorandum for the Record from Scott Muller, Subject: Review of Interrogation Program on 29 July 2003; Briefing slides, CIA Interrogation Program, July 29, 2003; September 4, 2003, CIA Memorandum for the Record, Subject: Member Briefing; and September 26, 2003, Memorandum for the Record from Muller, Subject: CIA Interrogation Program.) (4) The CIA's response to the Office of Inspector General draft Special Review of the CIA program, which asserts: "Information [the CIA] received . . . as a result of the lawful use of enhanced interrogation techniques ('EITs') has almost certainly saved countless American lives inside the United States and abroad. The evidence points clearly to the fact that without the use of such techniques, we and our allies would [have] suffered major terrorist attacks involving hundreds, if not thousands, of casualties." (See Memorandum for: Inspector General; from: James Pavitt, Deputy Director for Operations; subject: re (S) Comments to Draft IG Special Review, "Counterterrorism Detention and Interrogation Program" 2003-7123-IG; date: February 27, 2004; attachment: February 24, 2004, Memorandum re Successes of CIA's Counterterrorism Detention and Interrogation Activities.) (5) CIA briefing documents for CIA Director Leon Panetta in February 2009, which state that the "CIA assesses that the RDI program worked and the [enhanced interrogation] techniques were effective in producing foreign intelligence," and that "[m]ost, if not all, of the timely intelligence acquired from detainees in this program would not have been discovered or reported by other means." (See CIA briefing documents for Leon Panetta, entitled, "Tab 9: DCIA Briefing on RDI Program- 18FEB.2009" and graphic attachment, "Key Intelligence and Reporting Derived from Abu Zubaydah and Khalid Shaykh Muhammad (KSM)," including "DCIA Briefing on RDI Program" agenda, CIA document "EITs and Effectiveness," with associated documents, "Key Intelligence Impacts Chart: Attachment (AZ and KSM)," "Background on Key Intelligence Impacts Chart: Attachment," and "supporting references," to include "Background on Key Captures and Plots Disrupted.") (6) CIA document faxed to the Senate Select Committee on Intelligence on March 18, 2009, entitled, "[SWIGERT] and [DUNBAR]," located in Committee databases at DTS #2009-1258, which provides a list of "some of the key captures and disrupted plots" that the CIA had attributed to the use of the CIA's enhanced interrogation techniques, and stating: "CIA assesses that most, if not all, of the timely intelligence acquired from detainees in this program would not have been discovered or reported by any other means." See Volume II for additional

CIA representations asserting that the CIA's enhanced interrogation techniques enabled the CIA to obtain unique, otherwise unavailable intelligence that "saved lives."

1400. Italics added. "DCIA Talking Points: Waterboard 06 November 2007," dated November 6, 2007, with the notation the document was "sent to DCIA Nov. 6 in preparation for POTUS meeting." CIA records indicate that Hambali was not subjected to the CIA's waterboard technique.

1401. March 2, 2005, Memorandum for Steve Bradbury from [REDACTED], [REDACTED] Legal Group, DCI Counterterrorist Center, document entitled, "Effectiveness of the CIA Counterterrorist Interrogation Techniques." Under a section entitled, "Results," the CIA "Effectiveness Memo" states that the "CIA's use of DOJ-approved enhanced interrogation techniques, aspart of a comprehensive interrogation approach, has enabled CIA to disrupt terrorist plots, capture additional terrorists, and collect a high volume of critical intelligence on al-Qa'ida. We believe that intelligence acquired from these interrogations has been a key reason why al-Qa'ida has failed to launch a spectacular attack in the West since 11 September 2001."

1402. Italics in original.

1403. Italics added. March 2, 2005, Memorandum for Steve Bradbury from [REDACTED], [REDACTED] Legal Group, DCI Counterterrorist Center, document entitled, "Effectiveness of the CIA Counterterrorist Interrogation Techniques." The same representation can be found in multiple documents, including "Briefing for Chief of Staff to the President Josh Bolten; CIA Rendition, Detention, and Interrogation Programs," dated May 2, 2006; as well as "Talking Points for 10 March 2005 DCI Meeting PC: Effectiveness of the High-Value Interrogation (HVDI) Techniques," dated March 2, 2005.

1404. Italics added. Memorandum for John A. Rizzo, Senior Deputy General Counsel, Central Intelligence Agency, from Steven G. Bradbury, Principal Deputy Assistant Attorney General, Office of Legal Counsel, May 30, 2005, Re: Application of United States Obligations Under Article 16 of the Convention Against Torture to Certain Techniques that Maybe Used in the Interrogation of High Value Al Qaeda Detainees. The memorandum states: "It is this paramount interest [the security of the nation] that the Government seeks to vindicate through the interrogation program. Indeed, the program, which the CIA believes 'has been a key reason why al-Qa'ida has failed to launch a spectacular attack in the West since 11 September 2001,' directly furthers that interest, producing substantial quantities of otherwise unavailable actionable intelligence. As detailed above, ordinary interrogation techniques had little effect on either KSM or Zubaydah. Use of enhanced techniques, however, led to critical, actionable intelligence such as the discovery of the Guraba Cell, which was tasked with executing KSM's planned Second Wave attacks against Los Angeles."

1405. See list of CIA prepared briefings and memoranda from 2003 through 2009 with representations on the effectiveness of the CIA's enhanced interrogation techniques referenced in this summary and described in detail in Volume II.

1406. Memorandum for John A. Rizzo, Senior Deputy General Counsel, Central Intelligence Agency, from Steven G. Bradbury, Principal Deputy Assistant Attorney General, Office of Legal Counsel, May 30, 2005, Re: Application of United States Obligations Under Article 16 of the Convention Against Torture to Certain Techniques that May be Used in the Interrogation of High Value Al Qaeda Detainees.

1407. See detailed reporting in the Second Wave / Al-Ghuraba Group intelligence chronology in Volume II of the Study, including [REDACTED] and [REDACTED].

1408. August 18, 2001, FBI Minneapolis Field Officer Memorandum referenced in Report of the Joint Inquiry into the Terrorist Attacks of September 11, 2001, by the House Permanent Select Committee on Intelligence and the Senate Select Committee on Intelligence. Zacarias Moussaoui was later convicted of terrorism-related offenses, and sentenced to life in prison. See Department of Justice, Office of the Inspector General, "A Review of the FBI's Handling of Intelligence Information Related to the September 11 Attacks," dated November 2004, and released publicly in June 2006, among other sources. *See also* other open source records, including November 20, 2007, *Associated Press* article entitled, "Judge in 9/11 Conspirator Moussaoui's Case Questions Government Evidence in Terrorism Trials." The article states: Judge "Brinkema said she no longer feels confident relying on those government briefs, particularly since prosecutors admitted last week that similar representations made in the Moussaoui case were false. In a letter made public Nov 13, [2007], prosecutors in the Moussaoui case admitted to Brinkema that the CIA had wrongly assured her that no videotapes or audiotapes existed of interrogations of certain high profile terrorism detainees. In fact, two such videotapes and one audio tape existed."

1409. August 25, 2001, CIA Headquarters cable referenced by the House Permanent Select Committee on Intelligence and the Senate Select Committee on Intelligence investigations, as well as the Twelfth Public Hearing on the "National Commission on Terrorist Attacks Upon the United States," June 16, 2004.

1410. January 17, 2002, Federal Bureau of Investigation public release.

1411. Zacarias Moussaoui was arrested on August 16, 2001. Intelligence indicates Faruq al-Tunisi withdrew from al-Qa'ida operations. Faruq al-Tunisi remains a fugitive [REDACTED].

1412. ALEC [REDACTED] (151618Z OCT 03); [REDACTED].

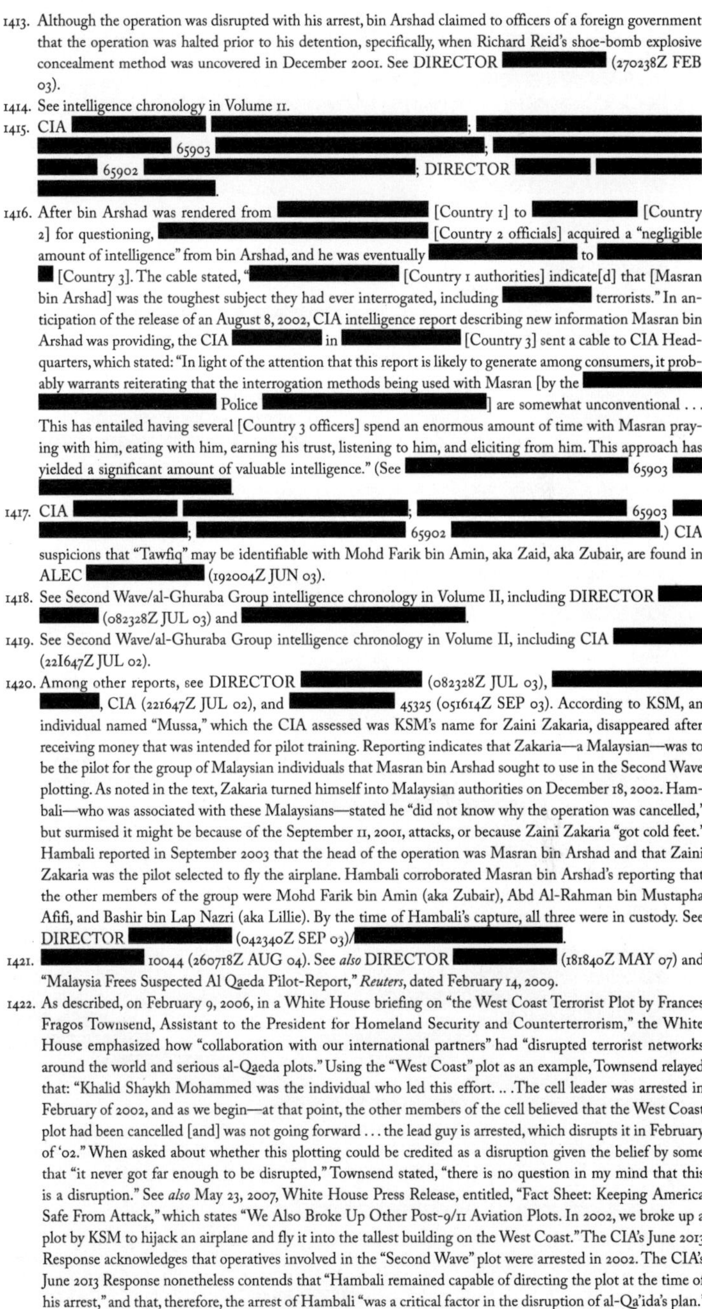

1413. Although the operation was disrupted with his arrest, bin Arshad claimed to officers of a foreign government that the operation was halted prior to his detention, specifically, when Richard Reid's shoe-bomb explosive concealment method was uncovered in December 2001. See DIRECTOR ██████ (270238Z FEB 03).

1414. See intelligence chronology in Volume II.

1415. CIA ██████ ██████; ██████ ██████ 65903 ██████; ██████ ██████ 65902 ██████; DIRECTOR ██████ ██████ ██████.

1416. After bin Arshad was rendered from ██████ [Country 1] to ██████ [Country 2] for questioning, ██████ [Country 2 officials] acquired a "negligible amount of intelligence" from bin Arshad, and he was eventually ██████ to ██████ █ [Country 3]. The cable stated, "██████ [Country 1 authorities] indicate[d] that [Masran bin Arshad] was the toughest subject they had ever interrogated, including ██████ terrorists." In anticipation of the release of an August 8, 2002, CIA intelligence report describing new information Masran bin Arshad was providing, the CIA ██████ in ██████ [Country 3] sent a cable to CIA Headquarters, which stated: "In light of the attention that this report is likely to generate among consumers, it probably warrants reiterating that the interrogation methods being used with Masran [by the ██████ ██████ Police ██████] are somewhat unconventional . . . This has entailed having several [Country 3 officers] spend an enormous amount of time with Masran praying with him, eating with him, earning his trust, listening to him, and eliciting from him. This approach has yielded a significant amount of valuable intelligence." (See ██████ 65903 ██████ ██████.

1417. CIA ██████ ██████; ██████ 65903 ██████ ██████; ██████ 65902 ██████.) CIA suspicions that "Tawfiq" may be identifiable with Mohd Farik bin Amin, aka Zaid, aka Zubair, are found in ALEC ██████ (192004Z JUN 03).

1418. See Second Wave/al-Ghuraba Group intelligence chronology in Volume II, including DIRECTOR ██████ ██████ (082328Z JUL 03) and ██████.

1419. See Second Wave/al-Ghuraba Group intelligence chronology in Volume II, including CIA ██████ (221647Z JUL 02).

1420. Among other reports, see DIRECTOR ██████ (082328Z JUL 03), ██████ ██████, CIA (221647Z JUL 02), and ██████ 45325 (051614Z SEP 03). According to KSM, an individual named "Mussa," which the CIA assessed was KSM's name for Zaini Zakaria, disappeared after receiving money that was intended for pilot training. Reporting indicates that Zakaria—a Malaysian—was to be the pilot for the group of Malaysian individuals that Masran bin Arshad sought to use in the Second Wave plotting. As noted in the text, Zakaria turned himself into Malaysian authorities on December 18, 2002. Hambali—who was associated with these Malaysians—stated he "did not know why the operation was cancelled," but surmised it might be because of the September 11, 2001, attacks, or because Zaini Zakaria "got cold feet." Hambali reported in September 2003 that the head of the operation was Masran bin Arshad and that Zaini Zakaria was the pilot selected to fly the airplane. Hambali corroborated Masran bin Arshad's reporting that the other members of the group were Mohd Farik bin Amin (aka Zubair), Abd Al-Rahman bin Mustapha Afifi, and Bashir bin Lap Nazri (aka Lillie). By the time of Hambali's capture, all three were in custody. See DIRECTOR ██████ (042340Z SEP 03)/██████.

1421. ██████ 10044 (260718Z AUG 04). See *also* DIRECTOR ██████ (181840Z MAY 07) and "Malaysia Frees Suspected Al Qaeda Pilot-Report," *Reuters*, dated February 14, 2009.

1422. As described, on February 9, 2006, in a White House briefing on "the West Coast Terrorist Plot by Frances Fragos Townsend, Assistant to the President for Homeland Security and Counterterrorism," the White House emphasized how "collaboration with our international partners" had "disrupted terrorist networks around the world and serious al-Qaeda plots." Using the "West Coast" plot as an example, Townsend relayed that: "Khalid Shaykh Mohammed was the individual who led this effort. .. .The cell leader was arrested in February of 2002, and as we begin—at that point, the other members of the cell believed that the West Coast plot had been cancelled [and] was not going forward . . . the lead guy is arrested, which disrupts it in February of '02." When asked about whether this plotting could be credited as a disruption given the belief by some that "it never got far enough to be disrupted," Townsend stated, "there is no question in my mind that this is a disruption." See *also* May 23, 2007, White House Press Release, entitled, "Fact Sheet: Keeping America Safe From Attack," which states "We Also Broke Up Other Post-9/11 Aviation Plots. In 2002, we broke up a plot by KSM to hijack an airplane and fly it into the tallest building on the West Coast." The CIA's June 2013 Response acknowledges that operatives involved in the "Second Wave" plot were arrested in 2002. The CIA's June 2013 Response nonetheless contends that "Hambali remained capable of directing the plot at the time of his arrest," and that, therefore, the arrest of Hambali "was a critical factor in the disruption of al-Qa'ida's plan." There are no CIA records indicating that Hambali took any action in furtherance of the plotting. Further, a

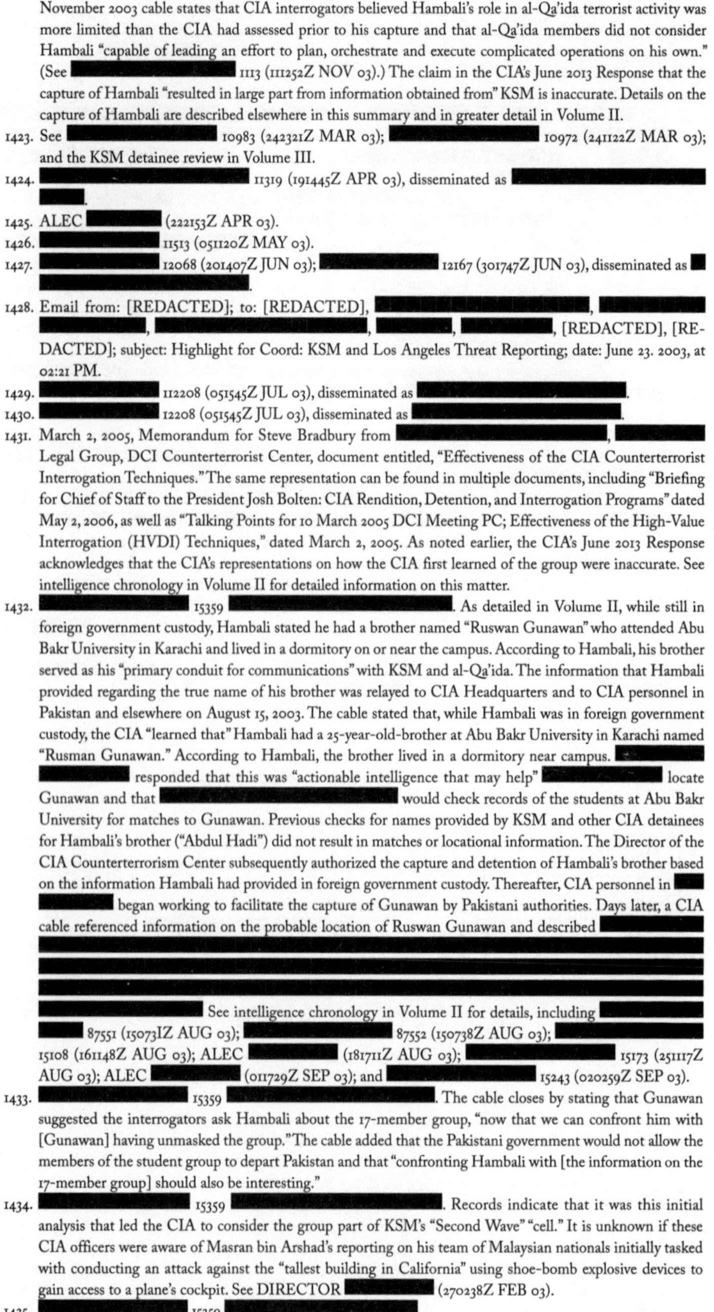

November 2003 cable states that CIA interrogators believed Hambali's role in al-Qa'ida terrorist activity was more limited than the CIA had assessed prior to his capture and that al-Qa'ida members did not consider Hambali "capable of leading an effort to plan, orchestrate and execute complicated operations on his own." (See 1113 (111252Z NOV 03).) The claim in the CIA's June 2013 Response that the capture of Hambali "resulted in large part from information obtained from" KSM is inaccurate. Details on the capture of Hambali are described elsewhere in this summary and in greater detail in Volume II.

1423. See 10983 (242321Z MAR 03); 10972 (241122Z MAR 03); and the KSM detainee review in Volume III.

1424. 11319 (191445Z APR 03), disseminated as .

1425. ALEC (222153Z APR 03).

1426. 11513 (051120Z MAY 03).

1427. 12068 (201407Z JUN 03); 12167 (301747Z JUN 03), disseminated as .

1428. Email from: [REDACTED]; to: [REDACTED], , , , , , [REDACTED], [REDACTED]; subject: Highlight for Coord: KSM and Los Angeles Threat Reporting; date: June 23. 2003, at 02:21 PM.

1429. 112208 (051545Z JUL 03), disseminated as .

1430. 12208 (051545Z JUL 03), disseminated as .

1431. March 2, 2005, Memorandum for Steve Bradbury from , Legal Group, DCI Counterterrorist Center, document entitled, "Effectiveness of the CIA Counterterrorist Interrogation Techniques." The same representation can be found in multiple documents, including "Briefing for Chief of Staff to the President Josh Bolten: CIA Rendition, Detention, and Interrogation Programs" dated May 2, 2006, as well as "Talking Points for 10 March 2005 DCI Meeting PC; Effectiveness of the High-Value Interrogation (HVDI) Techniques," dated March 2, 2005. As noted earlier, the CIA's June 2013 Response acknowledges that the CIA's representations on how the CIA first learned of the group were inaccurate. See intelligence chronology in Volume II for detailed information on this matter.

1432. 15359 . As detailed in Volume II, while still in foreign government custody, Hambali stated he had a brother named "Ruswan Gunawan" who attended Abu Bakr University in Karachi and lived in a dormitory on or near the campus. According to Hambali, his brother served as his "primary conduit for communications" with KSM and al-Qa'ida. The information that Hambali provided regarding the true name of his brother was relayed to CIA Headquarters and to CIA personnel in Pakistan and elsewhere on August 15, 2003. The cable stated that, while Hambali was in foreign government custody, the CIA "learned that" Hambali had a 25-year-old-brother at Abu Bakr University in Karachi named "Rusman Gunawan." According to Hambali, the brother lived in a dormitory near campus. responded that this was "actionable intelligence that may help" locate Gunawan and that would check records of the students at Abu Bakr University for matches to Gunawan. Previous checks for names provided by KSM and other CIA detainees for Hambali's brother ("Abdul Hadi") did not result in matches or locational information. The Director of the CIA Counterterrorism Center subsequently authorized the capture and detention of Hambali's brother based on the information Hambali had provided in foreign government custody. Thereafter, CIA personnel in began working to facilitate the capture of Gunawan by Pakistani authorities. Days later, a CIA cable referenced information on the probable location of Ruswan Gunawan and described See intelligence chronology in Volume II for details, including 87551 (150731Z AUG 03); 87552 (150738Z AUG 03); 15108 (161148Z AUG 03); ALEC (181711Z AUG 03); 15173 (251117Z AUG 03); ALEC (011729Z SEP 03); and 15243 (020259Z SEP 03).

1433. 15359 . The cable closes by stating that Gunawan suggested the interrogators ask Hambali about the 17-member group, "now that we can confront him with [Gunawan] having unmasked the group." The cable added that the Pakistani government would not allow the members of the student group to depart Pakistan and that "confronting Hambali with [the information on the 17-member group] should also be interesting."

1434. 15359 . Records indicate that it was this initial analysis that led the CIA to consider the group part of KSM's "Second Wave" "cell." It is unknown if these CIA officers were aware of Masran bin Arshad's reporting on his team of Malaysian nationals initially tasked with conducting an attack against the "tallest building in California" using shoe-bomb explosive devices to gain access to a plane's cockpit. See DIRECTOR (270238Z FEB 03).

1435. 15359 .

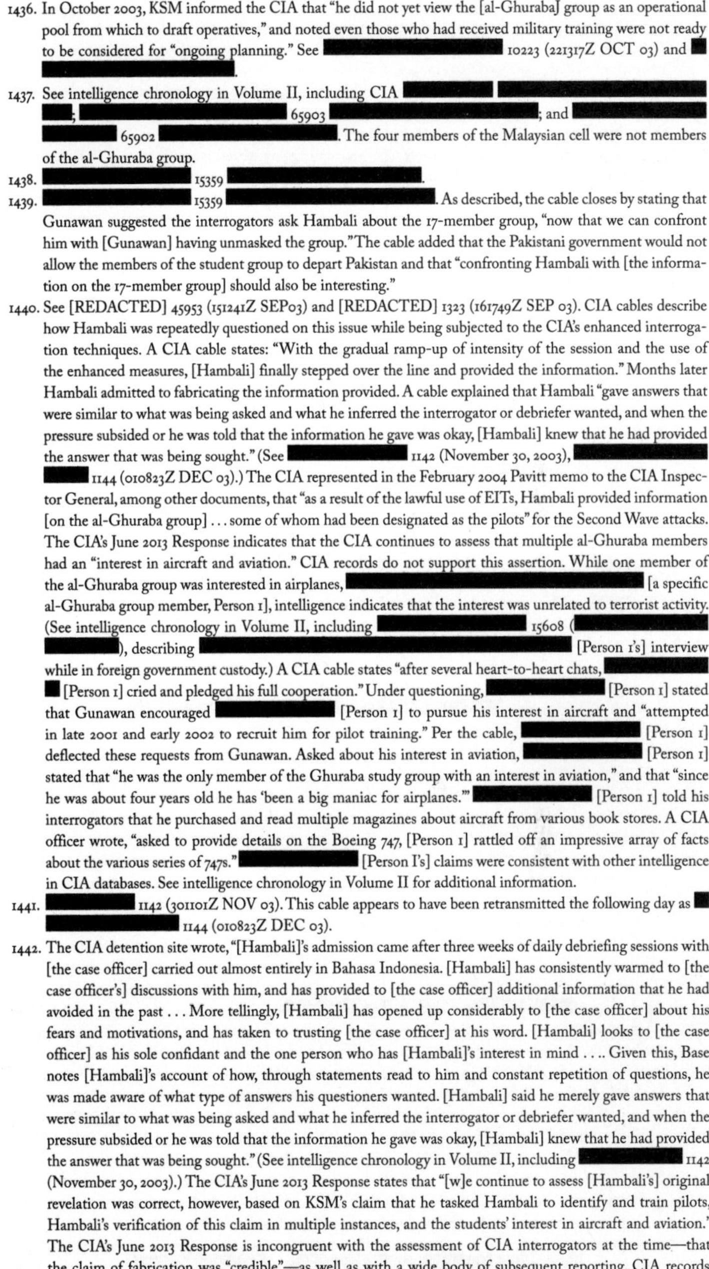

1436. In October 2003, KSM informed the CIA that "he did not yet view the [al-Ghuraba] group as an operational pool from which to draft operatives," and noted even those who had received military training were not ready to be considered for "ongoing planning." See [REDACTED] 10223 (221317Z OCT 03) and [REDACTED].

1437. See intelligence chronology in Volume II, including CIA [REDACTED]; [REDACTED] 65903 [REDACTED]; and [REDACTED] 65902 [REDACTED]. The four members of the Malaysian cell were not members of the al-Ghuraba group.

1438. [REDACTED] 15359 [REDACTED].

1439. [REDACTED] 15359 [REDACTED]. As described, the cable closes by stating that Gunawan suggested the interrogators ask Hambali about the 17-member group, "now that we can confront him with [Gunawan] having unmasked the group." The cable added that the Pakistani government would not allow the members of the student group to depart Pakistan and that "confronting Hambali with [the information on the 17-member group] should also be interesting."

1440. See [REDACTED] 45953 (151241Z SEP03) and [REDACTED] 1323 (161749Z SEP 03). CIA cables describe how Hambali was repeatedly questioned on this issue while being subjected to the CIA's enhanced interrogation techniques. A CIA cable states: "With the gradual ramp-up of intensity of the session and the use of the enhanced measures, [Hambali] finally stepped over the line and provided the information." Months later Hambali admitted to fabricating the information provided. A cable explained that Hambali "gave answers that were similar to what was being asked and what he inferred the interrogator or debriefer wanted, and when the pressure subsided or he was told that the information he gave was okay, [Hambali] knew that he had provided the answer that was being sought." (See [REDACTED] 1142 (November 30, 2003), [REDACTED] 1144 (010823Z DEC 03).) The CIA represented in the February 2004 Pavitt memo to the CIA Inspector General, among other documents, that "as a result of the lawful use of EITs, Hambali provided information [on the al-Ghuraba group] . . . some of whom had been designated as the pilots" for the Second Wave attacks. The CIA's June 2013 Response indicates that the CIA continues to assess that multiple al-Ghuraba members had an "interest in aircraft and aviation." CIA records do not support this assertion. While one member of the al-Ghuraba group was interested in airplanes, [REDACTED] [a specific al-Ghuraba group member, Person 1], intelligence indicates that the interest was unrelated to terrorist activity. (See intelligence chronology in Volume II, including [REDACTED] 15608 ([REDACTED]), describing [REDACTED] [Person 1's] interview while in foreign government custody.) A CIA cable states "after several heart-to-heart chats, [REDACTED] [Person 1] cried and pledged his full cooperation." Under questioning, [REDACTED] [Person 1] stated that Gunawan encouraged [REDACTED] [Person 1] to pursue his interest in aircraft and "attempted in late 2001 and early 2002 to recruit him for pilot training." Per the cable, [REDACTED] [Person 1] deflected these requests from Gunawan. Asked about his interest in aviation, [REDACTED] [Person 1] stated that "he was the only member of the Ghuraba study group with an interest in aviation," and that "since he was about four years old he has 'been a big maniac for airplanes.'" [REDACTED] [Person 1] told his interrogators that he purchased and read multiple magazines about aircraft from various book stores. A CIA officer wrote, "asked to provide details on the Boeing 747, [Person 1] rattled off an impressive array of facts about the various series of 747s." [REDACTED] [Person I's] claims were consistent with other intelligence in CIA databases. See intelligence chronology in Volume II for additional information.

1441. [REDACTED] 1142 (301101Z NOV 03). This cable appears to have been retransmitted the following day as [REDACTED] 1144 (010823Z DEC 03).

1442. The CIA detention site wrote, "[Hambali]'s admission came after three weeks of daily debriefing sessions with [the case officer] carried out almost entirely in Bahasa Indonesia. [Hambali] has consistently warmed to [the case officer's] discussions with him, and has provided to [the case officer] additional information that he had avoided in the past . . . More tellingly, [Hambali] has opened up considerably to [the case officer] about his fears and motivations, and has taken to trusting [the case officer] at his word. [Hambali] looks to [the case officer] as his sole confidant and the one person who has [Hambali]'s interest in mind . . .. Given this, Base notes [Hambali]'s account of how, through statements read to him and constant repetition of questions, he was made aware of what type of answers his questioners wanted. [Hambali] said he merely gave answers that were similar to what was being asked and what he inferred the interrogator or debriefer wanted, and when the pressure subsided or he was told that the information he gave was okay, [Hambali] knew that he had provided the answer that was being sought." (See intelligence chronology in Volume II, including [REDACTED] 1142 (November 30, 2003).) The CIA's June 2013 Response states that "[w]e continue to assess [Hambali's] original revelation was correct, however, based on KSM's claim that he tasked Hambali to identify and train pilots, Hambali's verification of this claim in multiple instances, and the students' interest in aircraft and aviation." The CIA's June 2013 Response is incongruent with the assessment of CIA interrogators at the time—that the claim of fabrication was "credible"—as well as with a wide body of subsequent reporting. CIA records indicate that CIA officers confused intelligence reporting on the Malaysians involved in the "Second Wave" plotting—an apparent reference to Masran bin Arshad, Zaini Zakaria, and three other Malaysians—with the al-Ghuraba Malaysian student group.

1443. Hambali elaborated that the al-Ghuraba group was similar to the Pan Islamic Party of Malaysia (PAS)'s Masapakindo, aka Pakindo, organization. Masran bin Arshad was connected to Pakindo, and, while in foreign government custody, explained that "in 1991, PAS [Pan Islamic Party of Malaysia] established a secret Malaysian Student Association known as 'Masapakindo' to help facilitate a steady pipeline of PAS religious and military trainees traveling from Malaysia to Pakistan, sometimes continuing on to Afghanistan, but ultimately returning to Malaysia. This student association for children of PAS members also was intended to serve as a general support structure for PAS students who were undergoing Islamic religious training in Pakistan and India. Masapakindo's headquarters was based in Karachi, Pakistan." See intelligence chronology in Volume II for additional information, including [REDACTED] 45915 (141431Z SEP 03) and CIA ███ ███ (160621Z DEC 02). See *also* February 27, 2004, Memorandum for CIA Inspector General from James L. Pavitt, CIA Deputy Director for Operations, entitled "Comments to Draft IG Special Review," "Counterterrorism Detention and Interrogation Program," which contains a February 24, 2004, attachment entitled, "Successes of CIA's Counterterrorism Detention and Interrogation Activities." See *also* CIA Intelligence Product entitled, "Jemaah Islamiya: Counterterrorism Scrutiny Limiting Extremist Agenda in Pakistan," dated April 18, 2008. See *also* KSM and Hambali reporting from October 2003.

1444. See intelligence chronology in Volume II. Although NSA signals intelligence was not provided for this Study, an April 2008 CIA intelligence report on the Jemaah Islamiya noted that the al-Ghuraba group "consisted of the sons of JI leaders, many of whom completed basic militant training in Afghanistan and Pakistan while enrolled at Islamic universities in Karachi," and that this assessment was based on "signals intelligence and other reporting." See CIA Intelligence Product entitled, "Jemaah Islamiya: Counterterrorism Scrutiny Limiting Extremist Agenda in Pakistan," dated April 18, 2008.

1445. WASHINGTON DC ███ (272113Z OCT 06).

1446. CIA Intelligence Product entitled, "Jemaah Islamiya: Counterterrorism Scrutiny Limiting Extremist Agenda in Pakistan," dated April 18, 2008.

1447. Dhiren Barot was referred to as "Issa," "Abu Issa," "Abu Issa al-Pakistani," and "Issa al-Britani." CIA records indicate that Dhiren Barot's most common alias, "Issa al-Hindi" (variant "Esa al-Hindi") – the name used to author the book, "The Army of Madinah in Kashmir" – was uncovered in May 2003 from FBI interviews of an individual in FBI custody, James Ujaama, aka Bilal Ahmed. Intelligence reporting indicated that Dhiren Barot's, aka Esa al-Hindi's, "The Army of Madinah in Kashmir" was a well-known book among the U.K. extremist community. Information on the book was prominently available online in 2002, on, among other internet sites, the website of the book store associated with Moazzem Begg, a U.K. extremist who was arrested and transferred to U.S. military custody at Guantanamo Bay, Cuba, in 2002. The cover of the book lists "Esa Al-Hindi" as the author (███ 280438Z (280746Z MAY 03)).

1448. Note on CIA records related to U.K.-based "Issas": Two United Kingdom-based al-Qa'ida associates, Dhiren Barot and Sajid Badat, were known by the same common aliases, Issa, Abu Issa, Abu Issa al-Britani ("[of] Britain") and/or Issa al-Pakistani. Both individuals were British Indians who had been independently in contact with senior al-Qa'ida leaders in Pakistan. Reporting indicated that the Issa(s) were located in the U.K. and engaged in terrorist targeting of the U.K. The investigation into their true identities was a U.K.-led operation. As a result, the CIA sometimes had limited insight into U.K.-based activities to identify and locate the Issas. Senior CIA personnel expressed frustration that the U.K. was not sharing all known information on its investigations, writing in August 2003 that "[the FBI is] clearly working closely with the [U.K. service] on these matters and [the CIA is] at the mercy" of what it is told. Until the arrest of one of the Issas, Sajid Badat, on November 27, 2003, the U.S. Intelligence Community and U.K. authorities often confused the two al-Qa'ida associates. As a result, the quality and clarity of detainee reporting on the Issas (including reporting from detainees in the custody of the CIA, U.S. military, Department of Justice, and foreign services) varied. CIA personnel ███ reported in September 2003 that there were "two (or three) Abu Issas" in intelligence reporting and that, because of their similarities, it was often "unclear which Issa the detainees [were] referring to at different stages." Once detained in the United Kingdom in November 2003, Sajid Badat (one of the Issas) cooperated with U.K. authorities and provided information about the other "Issa." Badat stated that "people often asked [Badat] about [the other] Issa, as they were both British Indians." According to Sajid Badat, "anyone who had been involved with jihad in Britain since the mid-90s" would know Issa al-Hindi (aka Dhiren Barot), to include Babar Ahmed, Moazzem Begg, Richard Reid, Zacarias Moussaoui, and KSM. Dhiren Barot (the other Issa), arrested on August 3, 2004, was found to have been especially well-known among the U.K. extremist community, having written a popular book in 1999 expounding the virtues of jihad in Kashmir under the alias, "Esa al-Hindi." CIA records include a reference to the book and a description of its author ("a brother from England who was a Hindu and became a Muslim . . . [who] got training in Afghanistan...") as early as December 1999. (See information disseminated by the CIA on 12/31/99 in ███.) ███ [A foreign partner] would later report that Dhiren Barot "frequently" appeared "in reporting of terrorist training" and "involvement in Jihad in occupied Kashmir, Pakistan, Afghanistan, and Malaysia, throughout the 1990s." As described, the Committee Study is based on more than six million pages of material related to the CIA's Detention and Interrogation Program provided by the CIA. Access was not provided to intelligence databases of the CIA, or any other U.S. or foreign intelligence or law enforcement agency. Insomuch as intelligence from these sources is included, it was, unless noted otherwise, found within the CIA's Detention and Interrogation Program material produced for this Study. It is likely that significant intelligence unrelated to the CIA's Detention and Interrogation Program on Sajid Badat and Dhiren Barot exists in U.S. intelligence and law enforcement records and databases. (See intelligence chronology in Volume II, including: ALEC ████ (112157Z JUN 03); ████ 19907 (231744Z APR 04); ████ 99093 (020931Z SEP 03); ALEC ████ (212117Z AUG 03); CIA WASHINGTON DC ████ (162127Z JUN 03); and a series of emails between ████ and ████ ████ (with multiple ccs) on August 22, 2003, at 9:24:43 AM.) In the context of the Capture/Identification of Sajid Badat, the CIA's June 2013 Response states that "KSM's reporting also clearly distinguished between, and thereby focused investigations of, two al-Qa'ida operatives known as Issa al-Britani." As detailed in the KSM detainee review in Volume III, KSM did discuss the two operatives, but he did not identify either by name (or, in the case of Dhiren Barot, by his more common *kunya*, Issa al-Hindi) and provided no actionable intelligence that contributed to the eventual identification and location of either "Issa."

1449. See email from: [REDACTED]; to: [REDACTED] at the Office of Director of National Intelligence; subject: "URGENT: Unclassified Fact Sheet for [REDACTED]"; date: October 6, 2005, at 2:39 PM.

1450. ████ 3924 ████ CIA WASHINGTON DC ████ ████. The CIA has represented that the use of the CIA's enhanced interrogation techniques resulted in the identification and arrest of "Abu Talha al-Pakistani." The CIA's June 2013 Response states that Abu Talha's arrest and debriefing was "invaluable to our overall understanding of Issa's activities and the threat he posed," and claims that Abu Talha's arrest "would not have happened if not for reporting from CIA-held detainees." CIA records do not support this statement. CIA records indicate that Abu Talha was identified and located independent of information from CIA detainees. Abu Talha al-Pakistani, a Pakistani with links to U.K. extremists, was identified through information derived from British ████ ████ [intelligence collection] and the U.K. investigation of U.K.-based extremist Baber Ahmed and his associates. These individuals were already under investigation by the ████ [foreign partner]. Further, Baber Ahmed was known to the U.S. intelligence and law enforcement authorities prior to any CIA detainee reporting. Foreign government authorities, relying on information provided by the United Kingdom and, to an extent, U.S. signals intelligence, ultimately located and arrested Abu Talha al-Pakistani. Because of the central role of U.K. authorities, CIA records do not include a comprehensive accounting of the investigation and operations that led to Abu Talha al-Pakistani's detention. CIA records indicate, however, that Abu Talha al-Pakistani was identified by two detainees in foreign government custody, shortly after their capture. (Both detainees would later be transferred to CIA custody and subjected to the CIA's enhanced interrogation techniques.) The first of these two detainees was Majid Khan, who on March 6, 2003, discussed Ammar al-Baluchi's Karachi-based assistant, "Talha." Majid Khan provided a phone number for Talha, and used that number at the request of his captors in an effort to locate and capture Ammar al-Baluchi through Talha. This reporting, which Majid Khan provided while he was in foreign government custody, preceded any reporting from CIA detainees. The other detainee who reported on Abu Talha was Ammar al-Baluchi, who described him as "Suliman" and stated that he had been dispatched to the United Kingdom to recruit operatives suitable for hijacking and suicide operations. Ammar al-Baluchi was also in foreign government custody at the time of this disclosure. KSM's failure to mention Abu Talha/"Suliman," more than a month after the CIA had ceased using its enhanced interrogation techniques against him, prompted one of KSM's debriefers to state that "KSM could be in trouble very soon." KSM also fabricated that he had shown a sketch related to the Heathrow Airport plot to Ammar al-Baluchi, rather than to Abu Talha, until confronted with Ammar al-Baluchi's denials, more than three months after the use of the CIA's enhanced interrogation techniques against KSM had ceased. See Volume II and the KSM detainee review in Volume III for additional information.

1451. Email from: ████; to: James Pavitt and others; subject: "Laptop docex from recent raid may yield pre-election threat information"; date: July ████, 2004, at 7:35 AM.

1452. ████ 3924 ████, disseminated as ████ ████; ████.

1453. See DIRECTOR ████ (032140Z AUG 04). See *also* intelligence chronology in Volume II, as well as email from: [REDACTED]; to: [REDACTED], at the Office of Director of National Intelligence; subject: "URGENT: Unclassified Fact Sheet for [REDACTED]"; date: October 6, 2005, at 02:39 PM. The email includes a CIA-coordinated fact sheet and states the following regarding Dhiren Barot and his U.K. attack planning: "Issa al-Hindi—who previously traveled to and cased a number of financial targets in the US—met with al-Qa'ida leaders in Pakistan in early 2004 to discuss attack planning against targets in the UK. Issa spent February and March 2004 in Shkai, Pakistan, with senior al-Qa'ida explosives expert 'Abd al-Rahman al-Muhajir, probably refining plans to use vehicle bombs against UK targets. Issa's reports, which were recovered in a raid in mid-2004, discussed ramming a fuel tanker into a target and parking explosives-laden courier vans or limousines in underground garages. Disruption: Issa and members of his cell were detained in the UK in early August 2004—soon after the arrest of key Hamza Rabi'a subordinate Abu Talha al-Pakistani in █████ Pakistan."

1454. CIA internal assessments concur with this analysis. See "disruption" text in an email from: [REDACTED]; to: [REDACTED], at the Office of Director of National Intelligence; subject: "URGENT: Unclassified Fact Sheet for [REDACTED]"; date: October 6, 2005, at 02:39 PM.

1455. CIA █████ (242144Z AUG 04).

1456. Disseminated intelligence product by the IICT, entitled, "Homeland: Reappraising al-Qa'ida's "Election Threat," dated September 10, 2004.

1457. FBI Intelligence Assessment, "The Gas Limos Project: An al-Qa'ida Urban Attack Plan Assessment," dated December 14, 2004.

1458. See Royal Courts of Justice Appeal, Barot v R [2007], EWCA Crim 1119 (16 May 2007). The expert assessments determined that the plotting involved "a professional-looking attempt from amateurs who did not really know what they were doing." See *also* June 15, 2007, *Bloomberg* news article entitled, "Terrorist Gang Jailed for Helping London and New York Bomb Plot."

1459. Italics included in CIA Memorandum to the Office of Legal Counsel, entitled, "Effectiveness of the CIA Counterterrorist Interrogation Techniques," from March 2, 2005. See *also* CIA talking points for National Security Council entitled, "Talking Points for 10 March 2005 DCI Meeting PC: Effectiveness of the High-Value Detainee Interrogation (HVDI) Techniques," dated March 4, 2005, as well as multiple other CIA briefing records and memoranda.

1460. See document entitled, "DCIA Talking Points: Waterboard 06 November 2007," dated November 6, 2007, with the notation the document was "sent to DCIA Nov. 6 in preparation for POTUS meeting."

1461. From 2003 through 2009, the CIA's representations regarding the effectiveness of the CIA's enhanced interrogation techniques provided a specific set of examples of terrorist plots "disrupted" and terrorists captured that the CIA attributed to information obtained from the use of its enhanced interrogation techniques. CIA representations further asserted that the intelligence obtained from the use of the CIA's enhanced interrogation techniques was unique, otherwise unavailable, and resulted in "saved lives." Among other CIA representations, see: (1) CIA representations in the Department of Justice Office of Legal Counsel Memorandum, dated May 30, 2005, which relied on a series of highly specific CIA representations on the type of intelligence acquired from the use of the CIA's enhanced interrogation techniques to assess their legality. The CIA representations referenced by the OLC include that the use of the CIA's enhanced interrogation techniques was "necessary" to obtain "critical," "vital," and "otherwise unavailable actionable intelligence" that was "essential" for the U.S. government to "detect and disrupt" terrorist threats. The OLC memorandum further states that "[the CIA] ha[s] informed [the OLC] that the CIA believes that this program is largely responsible for preventing a subsequent attack within the United States." (See Memorandum for John A. Rizzo, Senior Deputy General Counsel, Central Intelligence Agency, from Steven G. Bradbury, Principal Deputy Assistant Attorney General, Office of Legal Counsel, May 30, 2005, Re: Application of United States Obligations Under Article 16 of the Convention Against Torture to Certain Techniques that May Be Used in the Interrogation of High Value al Qaeda Detainees.) (2) CIA representations in the Department of Justice Office of Legal Counsel Memorandum dated July 20, 2007, which also relied on CIA representations on the type of intelligence acquired from the use of the CIA's enhanced interrogation techniques. Citing CIA documents and the President's September 6, 2006, speech describing the CIA's interrogation program (which was based on CIA-provided information), the OLC memorandum states: "The CIA interrogation program— and, in particular, its use of enhanced interrogation techniques—is intended to serve this paramount interest [security of the Nation] by producing substantial quantities of otherwise unavailable intelligence. . . . As the President explained [on September 6, 2006], 'by giving us information about terrorist plans we could not get anywhere else, the program has saved innocent lives.'" (See Memorandum for John A. Rizzo, Acting General Counsel, Central Intelligence Agency, from Steven G. Bradbury, Principal Deputy Assistant Attorney General, Office of Legal Counsel, July 20, 2007, Re: Application of the War Crimes Act, the Detainee Treatment Act, and Common Article 3 of the Geneva Conventions to Certain Techniques that May Be Used by the CIA in the Interrogation of High Value al Qaeda Detainees.) (3) CIA briefings for members of the National Security Council in July and September 2003 represented that "the use of Enhanced Techniques of one kind or another had produced significant intelligence information that had, in the view of CIA professionals, saved lives," and warned policymakers that "[t]ermination of this program will result in loss of life, possibly extensive." (See August 5, 2003 Memorandum for the Record from Scott Muller, Subject: Review of Interrogation Program on 29 July 2003; Briefing slides, CIA Interrogation Program, July 29, 2003; September 4, 2003, CIA Memorandum for the Record, Subject: Member Briefing; and September 26, 2003, Memorandum for the Record from Muller, Subject: CIA Interrogation Program.) (4) The CIA's response to the Office of Inspector General draft Special Review of the CIA program, which asserts: "Information [the CIA] received . . . as a result of the lawful use of enhanced interrogation techniques ('EITs') has almost certainly saved countless American lives inside the United States and abroad. The evidence points clearly to the fact that without the use of such techniques, we and our allies would [have] suffered major terrorist attacks involving hundreds, if not thousands, of casualties." (See Memorandum for: Inspector General; from: James Pavitt, Deputy Director for Operations; subject: re (S) Comments to Draft IG Special Review, "Counterterrorism Detention and Interrogation Program" 2003-7123-IG; date: February 27, 2004; attachment: February 24, 2004, Memorandum re Successes of CIA's Counterterrorism Detention and Interrogation Activities.) (5) CIA briefing documents for CIA Director Leon Panetta in February 2009, which state that the "CIA assesses that the RDI program worked and the [enhanced interrogation] techniques were effective in producing foreign intelligence," and that "[m]ost, if not all, of the timely intelligence acquired from detainees in this program would not have been discovered or reported by other means." (See CIA briefing documents for Leon Panetta, entitled, "Tab 9: DCIA Briefing on RDI Program- 18FEB.2009" and graphic attachment, "Key Intelligence and Reporting Derived from Abu Zubaydah and Khalid Shaykh Muhammad (KSM)," including "DCIA Briefing on RDI Program" agenda, CIA document "EITs and Effectiveness," with associated documents, "Key Intelligence Impacts Chart: Attachment (AZ and KSM)," "Background on Key Intelligence Impacts Chart: Attachment," and "supporting references," to include "Background on Key Captures and Plots Disrupted.") (6) CIA document faxed to the Senate Select Committee on Intelligence on March 18, 2009, entitled, "[SWIGERT] and [DUNBAR]," located in Committee databases (DTS #2009-1258), which provides a list of "some of the key captures and disrupted plots" that the CIA had attributed to the use of the CIA's enhanced interrogation techniques, and stating: "CIA assesses that most, if not all, of the timely intelligence acquired from detainees in this program would not have been discovered or reported by any other means." See Volume II for additional CIA representations asserting that the CIA's enhanced interrogation techniques enabled the CIA to obtain unique, otherwise unavailable intelligence that "saved lives."

1462. Italics added. CIA briefing documents for Leon Panetta, entitled, "Tab 9: DCIA Briefing on RDI Program-18FEB.2009" and graphic attachment, "Key Intelligence and Reporting Derived from Abu Zubaydah and Khalid Shaykh Muhammad (KSM)." The documents include "DCIA Briefing on RDI Program" agenda, CIA document "EITs and Effectiveness," with associated documents, "Key Intelligence Impacts Chart: Attachment (AZ and KSM)," "Background on Key Intelligence Impacts Chart: Attachment," and "supporting references," to include "Background on Key Captures and Plots Disrupted."

1463. The reference in the document to KSM's reporting related to Majid Khan is inaccurate. The document asserts: "When confronted with KSM's information, Majid admits he delivered the money to Zubair . . . ." As described in this summary, and more extensively in Volume II, Majid Khan provided information on the referenced money transfer while in foreign government custody, to an interrogator using rapport-building techniques, prior to any information from KSM.

1464. CIA briefing documents for Leon Panetta entitled, "Tab 9: DCIA Briefing on RDI Program- 18FEB.2009" and graphic attachment, "Key Intelligence and Reporting Derived from Abu Zubaydah and Khalid Shaykh Muhammad (KSM)." Includes "DCIA Briefing on RDI Program" agenda, CIA document "EITs and Effectiveness," with associated documents, "Key Intelligence Impacts Chart: Attachment (AZ and KSM)," "Background on Key Intelligence Impacts Chart: Attachment," and "supporting references," to include "Background on Key Captures and Plots Disrupted."

1465. Italics in original.

1466. The CIA's June 2013 Response states that the "CIA accurately represented that Khalid Shaykh Muhammad (KSM) provided the initial lead to a UK-based al-Qa'ida operative named Dhiren Barot, aka Issa al-Hindi, whom KSM had tasked to case US targets. That information [from KSM] allowed us to identify this Issa as Barot and ultimately led British authorities to arrest him." As is described in this summary, and in greater detail in Volume II, this CIA representation is not supported by internal CIA records.

1467. CIA memorandum to "National Security Advisor," from "Director of Central Intelligence," Subject: "Effectiveness of the CIA Counterterrorist Interrogation Techniques," included in email from: ; to: , , and ; subject: "paper on value of interrogation techniques"; date: December 6, 2004, at 5:06:38 PM. The email references the attached "information paper to Dr. Rice explaining the value of the interrogation techniques." The document includes references to the following: The Karachi Plot, the Heathrow Plot, the "Second Wave" plots, the Guraba Cell, Issa al-Hindi, Abu Talha al-Pakistani, Hambali's Capture, Jafaar al-Tayyar, the Dirty Bomb Plot, Sajid Badat, and Shkai, Pakistan. The document also asserts that "[p]rior to the use of enhanced measures" the CIA "acquired little threat information or significant actionable intelligence" from KSM. As detailed in the summary, KSM was subjected to the CIA's enhanced interrogation techniques immediately upon entering CIA custody.

1468. CIA classified statement for the record, Senate Select Committee on Intelligence, provided by General Michael V. Hayden, Director, Central Intelligence Agency, 12 April 2007; and accompanying Senate Select Committee on Intelligence hearing transcript for April 12, 2007, entitled, "Hearing on Central Intelligence Agency Detention and Interrogation Program" (DTS #2007-1563).

1469. See list of CIA prepared briefings and memoranda from 2003 through 2009 with representations on the effectiveness of the CIA's enhanced interrogation techniques referenced in this summary and described in detail in Volume II.

1470. CIA records indicate that CIA detainees largely provided corroborative reporting on Abu Issa, aka Dhiren Barot, and that CIA representations that "most, if not all, of the timely intelligence acquired from detainees in this program would not have been discovered or reported by other means," is not supported by CIA records. See intelligence chronology in Volume II for additional details.

1471. Dhiren Barot's arrest by U.K. authorities was also unrelated to reporting from the CIA's Detention and Interrogation Program. See information in this summary, as well as the intelligence chronology in Volume II.

1472. When Issa's U.S. casing reports were found on Abu Talha al-Pakistani's computer, KSM stated that he did not know of any al-Qa'ida plans, by Abu Talha or anyone else, to target the Citigroup/Citibank building, Prudential Group building, or the United Nations building in New York. (See [REDACTED] 1477 [REDACTED]) Nonetheless, KSM's reporting on Issa's travel to the U.S. was later corroborated by FBI reporting and individuals detained by foreign governments. See FBI IIR [REDACTED] (26 AUG 2004) and TTIC Special Analysis Report 2004-28H, entitled, "Homeland: Threat Assessment for IMF/World Bank Annual Meeting, 2-3 October 2004," dated September 28, 2004; and DIRECTOR [REDACTED] [REDACTED]. See *also* reissue, DIRECTOR [REDACTED] [REDACTED] [REDACTED].

1473. [REDACTED] 10948 (222101Z MAR 03).

1474. A CIA officer's comment on talking points prepared for "ADCI Tuesday Briefing of Kerry/Edwards" on Issa al-Hindi states that "KSM didn't decode the [phone] numbers for us (he just provided info on how he may have encoded the numbers—which when used didn't result in valid numbers) [an] address with the number didn't exist; it was a dead end, and it appears KSM was protecting [Issa] al-Hindi." See email from: [REDACTED]; to: [REDACTED],with multiple ccs; subject: "IMMEDIATE: al-Hindi TPs for ADCI Tuesday Briefing of Kerry/Edwards"; date: August 30, 2004, at 02:51 PM, which contains comments on previous drafts of talking points.

1475. Email from: [REDACTED]; to: [REDACTED], [REDACTED], [REDACTED], [REDACTED], [REDACTED] [REDACTED], [REDACTED], [REDACTED]; cc: [REDACTED] [REDACTED]; subject: KSM and Khallad Issues; date; October 16, 2003 at 5:25:13 PM. See *also* email from: [REDACTED] [REDACTED] to: [REDACTED], [REDACTED]; cc: [REDACTED] [REDACTED], [REDACTED], [REDACTED], [REDACTED]; subject: Some things to ping Mukie on--cable coming; date: April 11, 2003, at 5:00:12 PM; and ALEC [REDACTED] (222153Z APR 03).

1476. CIA [REDACTED] (242144Z AUG 04).

1477. [REDACTED].

1478. A June 25, 2004, CIA Serial Flyer entitled, "Guantanamo Bay Detainee Moazzem Begg's Links to Active Operatives," states that, after being captured in February 2002 and being held in U.S. military custody," Begg has been cooperative in debriefings and has provided background information and descriptions of a number of his past associates that have helped shed light on the extent of the Islamic extremist network in the United Kingdom and its ties to al-Qa'ida." According to the CIA report, in June 2004, Begg's "description and resulting sketch of UK contact Issa al-Hindi"—whose true identity was then unknown—"was compared to a still shot of an unidentified man taken from a surveillance video of UK extremists." The comparison "revealed that the man in the video probably [was] the elusive Issa al-Hindi." Begg co-owned the Maktabah al-Ansar bookshop in Birmingham, United Kingdom, that would later be found to have published a book written by "Esa al-Hindi" that was well known among U.K. extremists, "The Army of Madinah in Kashmir."

1479. See [REDACTED] 72330 [REDACTED] "Guantanamo Bay Detainee Moazzem Begg's Links to Active Operatives," June 2004 for intelligence referencing earlier reporting. See also open source reporting on U.K. raids of the bookstore in the year 2000, as well as subsequent raids, including. "Bookshop linked to Bin Laden's 'General,'" *The Telegraph* February 1, 2007.

1480. On April [REDACTED] 2004, [REDACTED] relayed information acquired from Sajid Badat, the other U.K. "Issa." Badat stated that "anyone who had been involved with jihad in Britain since the mid-90s" would know the other Issa, naming among other individuals, Moazzem Begg. See [REDACTED] 19907 (231744Z APR 04).

1481. CIA [REDACTED] (262213Z SEP 03) (cable referencing information collected in 1999).

1482. [REDACTED] 49612 (281213Z JUL03).

1483. [REDACTED] 72330 [REDACTED] (table discusses historical reporting). See *also* "Bookshop linked to Bin Laden's 'General,'" *The Telegraph*, dated February 1, 2007.

1484. [REDACTED].

1485. The CIA's June 2013 Response states that the "Study highlights and mischaracterizes" this intelligence because the author of "The Army of Madinah in Kashmir," is not identified in the intelligence report. The CIA Response states that the report "identifies the author only as 'an Afghanistan-trained British convert writing about Hindu atrocities in Kashmir.'" Notwithstanding the CIA's Response, the Committee found the intelligence report references the book, "The Army of Madinah in Kashmir," and describes the author as "a brother from England who was a Hindu and became a Muslim about six years ago" and who "got training in Afghanistan then went to fight in Kashmir." According to open sources, the 1999 book advocated "worldwide jihad" in order to bring nations "to their knees." An Internet archive search for the title of the book, "The Army of Madinah in Kashmir," found the book prominently advertised among the "Recommended Products" in 2002 on the website for the Maktabah al-Ansar bookstore (www.maktabah.net/books/images/kashmir.jpg: internet archive 2002). The website archive from 2002 states that the author "Esa al-Hindi" converted "to Islam at the age of 20" and recalls his "personal experience in occupied Kashmir fighting the Indian forces." The bookstore's website and related jihadi websites list the author of the book as "Esa Al-Hindi." CIA cables suggest it was not until June 2003 that the CIA conducted an internet search for "The Army of Madinah in Kashmir." When the search was conducted, the CIA found "it is one of the recommended reads featured" on the website of the Maktabah al-Ansar bookstore. See ALEC ██████ (052206Z JUN 03). As noted, the same information on the book was prominently listed on the same website more than a year earlier.

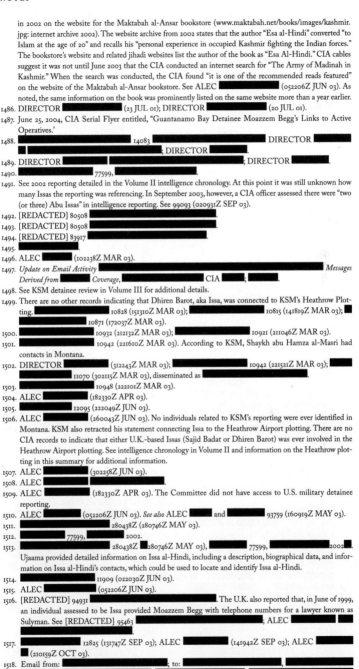

1486. DIRECTOR ██████ (23 JUL 01); DIRECTOR ██████ (20 JUL 01).

1487. June 25, 2004, CIA Serial Flyer entitled, "Guantanamo Bay Detainee Moazzem Begg's Links to Active Operatives.'

1488. ██████ 14083 ██████ DIRECTOR ██████ ██████; DIRECTOR ██████.

1489. DIRECTOR ██████ ██████; DIRECTOR ██████.

1490. ██████ 77599, ██████.

1491. See 2002 reporting detailed in the Volume II intelligence chronology. At this point it was still unknown how many Issas the reporting was referencing. In September 2003, however, a CIA officer assessed there were "two (or three) Abu Issas" in intelligence reporting. See 99093 (020931Z SEP 03).

1492. [REDACTED] 80508 ██████.

1493. [REDACTED] 80508 ██████.

1494. [REDACTED] 83917 ██████.

1495. ██████.

1496. ALEC ██████ (102238Z MAR 03).

1497. *Update on Email Activity* ██████ *Messages Derived from* ██████ *Coverage*, ██████ CIA ██████; ██████.

1498. See KSM detainee review in Volume III for additional details.

1499. There are no other records indicating that Dhiren Barot, aka Issa, was connected to KSM's Heathrow Plotting. ██████ 10828 (151310Z MAR 03); ██████ 10815 (141819Z MAR 03); ██████ 10871 (172037Z MAR 03).

1500. ██████ 10932 (212132Z MAR 03); ██████ 10921 (211046Z MAR 03).

1501. ██████ 10942 (221610Z MAR 03). According to KSM, Shaykh abu Hamza al-Masri had contacts in Montana.

1502. DIRECTOR ██████ (312243Z MAR 03); ██████ 10942 (221521Z MAR 03); ██████ 11070 (302115Z MAR 03), disseminated as ██████.

1503. ██████ 10948 (222101Z MAR 03).

1504. ALEC ██████ (182330Z APR 03).

1505. ██████ 12095 (222049Z JUN 03).

1506. ALEC ██████ (260043Z JUN 03). No individuals related to KSM's reporting were ever identified in Montana. KSM also retracted his statement connecting Issa to the Heathrow Airport plotting. There are no CIA records to indicate that either U.K.-based Issas (Sajid Badat or Dhiren Barot) was ever involved in the Heathrow Airport plotting. See intelligence chronology in Volume II and information on the Heathrow plotting in this summary for additional information.

1507. ALEC ██████ (302258Z JUN 03).

1508. ALEC ██████ ██████.

1509. ALEC ██████ (182330Z APR 03). The Committee did not have access to U.S. military detainee reporting.

1510. ALEC ██████ (052206Z JUN 03). *See also* ALEC ██████ and ██████ 93759 (160919Z MAY 03).

1511. ██████ 280438Z (280746Z MAY 03).

1512. ██████ 77599, ██████ 2002.

1513. ██████ 280438Z ██████280746Z MAY 03), ██████ 77599, ██████2002██████. Ujaama provided detailed information on Issa al-Hindi, including a description, biographical data, and information on Issa al-Hindi's contacts, which could be used to locate and identify Issa al-Hindi.

1514. ██████ 11909 (022030Z JUN 03).

1515. ALEC ██████ (052206Z JUN 03).

1516. [REDACTED] 94931 ██████. The U.K. also reported that, in June of 1999, an individual assessed to be Issa provided Moazzem Begg with telephone numbers for a lawyer known as Sulyman. See [REDACTED] 95463 ██████; ALEC ██████ ██████ ██████.

1517. ██████ 12825 (131747Z SEP 03); ALEC ██████ (141942Z SEP 03); ALEC ██████ ██████ (210159Z OCT 03).

1518. Email from: ██████; to: ██████, ██████ ██████, ██████, ██████, ██████

[REDACTED]; cc: ; subject: KSM and Khallad Issues; date: October 16, 2003, at 5:25:13 PM.

1519. 10053 .

1520. ALEC (210159Z OCT 03).

1521. Email from: ; to: , , , , , [REDACTED]; cc: ; subject: KSM and Khallad Issues; date: October 16, 2003, at 5:25:13 PM. See *also* email from: ; to: [REDACTED], [REDACTED]; cc: , , [REDACTED], [REDACTED]; subject: Some things to ping Mukie on—cable coming; date: April 11, 2003 at 5:00:12 PM; and ALEC (222153Z APR 03).

1522. ALEC (210159Z OCT 03).

1523. Draft cable included in an email from: [REDACTED]; to: and ; subject: "Abu Issa al-Hindi Targeting Study"; date: October 22, 2003, at 6:49:41 PM.

1524. ALEC .

1525. ALEC .

1526. 22359 ; 22246 . See *also* [REDACTED] email to: and others; subject: "For Immed. Coord: Al-Hindi ID Highlight"; date; June 17, 2004, at 3:06:29 PM.

1527. [REDACTED] 22406 (04 9023184 |17/JUN/2004).

1528. A June 25, 2004, CIA Serial Flyer entitled, "Guantanamo Bay Detainee Moazzem Begg's Links to Active Operatives."

1529. [REDACTED] 22406 (04 9023184 |17/JUN/2004).

1530. CIA records indicate that other detainees also identified this individual as Issa al-Hindi.

1531. See 280438Z (280746Z MAY 03) and 77599 . Ujaama provided detailed information on Issa al-Hindi, including a description, biographical data, and information on Issa al-Hindi's contacts, which could be used to locate and identify Issa al-Hindi. There are no specific CIA records of James Ujaama providing exact location data for Issaal-Hindi. As noted, however, senior CIA personnel expressed frustration that the U.K. was not sharing all known information on their investigations, writing in August 2003 that "[the FBI is] clearly working closely with the [U.K. service] on these matters and [the CIA is] at the mercy" of what it is told. As described in this summary, James Ujaama was in FBI custody.

1532. 23226 .

1533. CIA WASHINGTON DC . .

1534. 3924 ; email from: [REDACTED]; to , [REDACTED], [REDACTED]; cc: , [REDACTED], [REDACTED]; subject: DRAFT DCI SPECIAL ITEM - 14Jul04; date: July 14, 2004, at 03:48 PM. This information was obtained from sources unrelated to the CIA's Detention and Interrogation Program.

1535. 3924 ; 3889 .

1536. Email from: ; to: James Pavitt, [REDACTED], , Rodriguez, John P. Mudd, [REDACTED], , , , , [REDACTED], ; cc: , [REDACTED]; subject: Laptop docex from recent raid may yield pre-election threat information date July , 2004, at 07:35 AM.

1537. See Terrorist Threat Integration Center, Terrorist Threats to US Interests Worldwide. See *also* ; ; ; ; ; ; and .

1538. 1477 .

1539. Email from: ; to James Pavitt [REDACTED], , Rodriguez, John P. Mudd, [REDACTED], , , , , , [REDACTED], ; cc: . [REDACTED]; subject: Laptop docex from recent raid may yield pre-election threat information; date: July , 2004 at 07:35 AM.

1540. Email from: ; to: James Pavitt [REDACTED], , Rodriguez, John P. Mudd, [REDACTED], , , , , , [REDACTED],

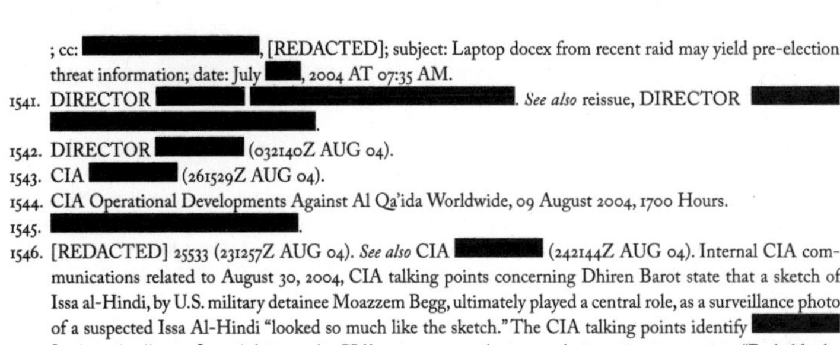

; cc: , [REDACTED]; subject: Laptop docex from recent raid may yield pre-election threat information; date: July , 2004 AT 07:35 AM.

1541. DIRECTOR . *See also* reissue, DIRECTOR .

1542. DIRECTOR (032140Z AUG 04).

1543. CIA (261529Z AUG 04).

1544. CIA Operational Developments Against Al Qa'ida Worldwide, 09 August 2004, 1700 Hours.

1545. .

1546. [REDACTED] 25533 (231257Z AUG 04). *See also* CIA (242144Z AUG 04). Internal CIA communications related to August 30, 2004, CIA talking points concerning Dhiren Barot state that a sketch of Issa al-Hindi, by U.S. military detainee Moazzem Begg, ultimately played a central role, as a surveillance photo of a suspected Issa Al-Hindi "looked so much like the sketch." The CIA talking points identify [technical collection] capabilities as the CIA's primary contribution to the investigation, stating: "Probably the most important intelligence tool we used in breaking this case was our [technical collection] enabled by the USA Patriot Act. From beginning to end [technical collection] played a role, but it was not the only tool that was used. HUMINT and SIGINT threads were followed and contributed to our understanding of the [technical collection] and in finding new [technical collection] leads. Exploitation of computers and other information obtained in the raids before and during the case also contributed significantly, as did surveillance. However, none of these tools are stand-alones. Good old fashioned hard targeting and analysis of these maddeningly vague and disparate and incomplete threads of information was the glue that put it all together." See "Capture of Al-Qa'ida Operative Abu Issa al-Hindi (aka Dhiren Barot, aka Abu Issa al-Britani)," multiple iterations of talking points, including the revised version cited, found in an email from: [REDACTED]; to [REDACTED], with multiple ccs; subject: "IMMEDIATE: al-Hindi TPs for ADCI Tuesday Briefing of Kerry/Edwards"; date: August 30, 2004, at 02:51 PM.

1547. [REDACTED] 25533 (231257Z AUG 04).

1548. [REDACTED] 25533 (231257Z AUG 04).

1549. In an email, a CIA officer commented on talking points prepared for "ADCI Tuesday Briefing of Kerry/Edwards" on Issa al-Hindi, stating that "KSM didn't decode the numbers for us (he just provided info on how he may have encoded the numbers—-which when used didn't result in valid numbers) and address with the number didn't exist; it was a dead end, and it appears KSM was protecting al-Hindi." See email from: [REDACTED]; to: [REDACTED], with multiple ccs; subject: "IMMEDIATE: al-Hindi TPs for ADCI Tuesday Briefing of Kerry/Edwards"; date: August 30, 2004, at 02:51 PM, which contains comments on previous drafts of talking points.

1550. "Capture of Al-Qa'ida Operative Abu Issa al-Hindi (aka Dhiren Barot, aka Abu Issa al-Britani)" multiple iterations of talking points, including the revised version cited, found in an email from: [REDACTED]; to: [REDACTED], with multiple ccs; subject: "IMMEDIATE: al-Hindi TPs for ADCI Tuesday Briefing of Kerry/Edwards"; date: August 30, 2004, at 02:51 PM.

1551. Disseminated intelligence product by the IICT entitled, "Homeland: Reappraising al-Qa'ida's "Election Threat," dated September 10, 2004.

1552. Disseminated intelligence product by the IICT entitled, "Homeland: Reappraising al-Qa'ida's "Election Threat," dated September 10, 2004.

1553. [REDACTED] 29759 .

1554. FBI Intelligence Assessment, "The Gas Limos Project: An al-Qa'ida Urban Attack Plan Assessment," dated December 14, 2004.

1555. Email from: [REDACTED]; to: [REDACTED] and others; subject: "Re: need answer: request for any info deemed operationally sensitive be passed to brits concerning Dhiren Barot (aka Issa al-Hindi)"; date: December 12, 2005, at 6:08:01 PM, in preparation of a document entitled, "Addendum in Respect of Disclosure - Al Hindi.pdf."

1556. See Royal Courts of Justice Appeal, Barot v. R [2007], EWCA Crim 1119 (16 May 2007). The expert assessments determined that the plotting involved "a professional-looking attempt from amateurs who did not really know what they were doing." *See also* June 15, 2007, *Bloomberg News* article entitled, "Terrorist Gang Jailed for Helping London and New York Bomb Plot."

1557. WHDC (242226Z MAR 03) (includes information acquired by the FBI on March 20, 2003).

1558. ALEC (261745Z MAR 03).

1559. ALEC (180200Z MAR 03) *See also* .

1560. Italics included in CIA Memorandum to the Office of Legal Counsel, entitled, "Effectiveness of the CIA Counterterrorist Interrogation Techniques," from March 2, 2005.

1561. From 2003 through 2009, the CIA's representations regarding the effectiveness of the CIA's enhanced interrogation techniques provided a specific set of examples of terrorist plots "disrupted" and terrorists captured that the CIA attributed to information obtained from the use of its enhanced interrogation techniques. CIA representations further asserted that the intelligence obtained from the use of the CIA's enhanced interrogation techniques was unique, otherwise unavailable, and resulted in "saved lives." Among other CIA representations, see: (1) CIA representations in the Department of Justice Office of Legal Counsel Memorandum, dated May 30, 2005, which relied on a series of highly specific CIA representations on the type of intelligence acquired from the use of the CIA's enhanced interrogation techniques to assess their legality. The CIA representations referenced by the OLC include that the use of the CIA's enhanced interrogation techniques was "necessary" to obtain "critical," "vital," and "otherwise unavailable actionable intelligence" that was "essential" for the U.S. government to detect and disrupt" terrorist threats. The OLC memorandum further states that "[the CIA] ha[s] informed [the OLC] that the CIA believes that this program is largely responsible for preventing a subsequent attack within the United States." (See Memorandum for John A. Rizzo, Senior Deputy General Counsel, Central Intelligence Agency, from Steven G. Bradbury, Principal Deputy Assistant Attorney General, Office of Legal Counsel, May 30, 2005, Re: Application of United States Obligations Under Article 16 of the Convention Against Torture to Certain Techniques that May Be Used in the Interrogation of High Value al Qaeda Detainees.) (2) CIA representations in the Department of Justice Office of Legal Counsel Memorandum dated July 20, 2007, which also relied on CIA representations on the type of intelligence acquired from the use of the CIA's enhanced interrogation techniques. Citing CIA documents and the President's September 6, 2006 speech describing the CIA's interrogation program (which was based on CIA-provided information), the OLC memorandum states: "The CIA interrogation program — and, in particular, its use of enhanced interrogation techniques — is intended to serve this paramount interest [security of the Nation] by producing substantial quantities of otherwise unavailable intelligence . . . As the President explained [on September 6, 2006], 'by giving us information about terrorist plans we could not get anywhere else, the program has saved innocent lives.'" (See Memorandum for John A. Rizzo, Acting General Counsel, Central Intelligence Agency, from Steven G. Bradbury, Principal Deputy Assistant Attorney General, Office of Legal Counsel, July 20, 2007. Re: Application of the War Crimes Act, the Detainee Treatment Act, and Common Article 3 of the Geneva Conventions to Certain Techniques that May Be Used by the CIA in the Interrogation of High Value al Qaeda Detainees.) (3) CIA briefings for members of the National Security Council in July and September 2003 represented that "the use of Enhanced Techniques of one kind or another had produced significant intelligence information that had, in the view of CIA professionals, saved lives," and warned policymakers that "[t]ermination of this program will result in loss of life, possibly extensive." (See August 5, 2003 Memorandum for the Record, Subject: Member Briefing; and September 26, 2003, Memorandum for the Record from Muller, Subject: CIA Interrogation Program.) (4) The CIA's response to the Office of Inspector General draft Special Review of the CIA program, which asserts: "Information [the CIA] received... as a result of the lawful use of enhanced interrogation techniques ('EITs') has almost certainly saved countless American lives inside the United States and abroad. The evidence points clearly to the fact that without the use of such techniques, we and our allies would [have] suffered major terrorist attacks involving hundreds, if not thousands, of casualties." (See Memorandum for: Inspector General; from James Pavitt, Deputy Director for Operations; subject: re (S) Comments to Draft IG Special Review, "Counterterrorism Detention and Interrogation Program" 2003-7123-IG; date: February 27, 2004; attachment: February 24, 2004, Memorandum re Successes of CIA's Counterterrorism Detention and Interrogation Activities.) (5) CIA briefing documents for CIA Director Leon Panetta in February 2009, which state that the "CIA assesses that the RDI program worked and the [enhanced interrogation] techniques were effective in producing foreign intelligence," and that "[m]ost, if not all, of the timely intelligence acquired from detainees in this program would not have been discovered or reported by other means." (See CIA briefing documents for Leon Panetta, entitled, "Tab 9: DCIA briefing on RDI Program- 18FEB.2009" and graphic attachment, "Key Intelligence and Reporting Derived from Abu Zubaydah and Khalid Shaykh Muhammad (KSM)," including "DCIA Briefing on RDI Program" agenda, CIA document "EITs and Effectiveness," with associated documents, "Key Intelligence Impacts Chart: Attachment," and "supporting references," to include "Background on Key Captures and Plots Disrupted.") (6) CIA document faxed to the Senate Select Committee on Intelligence on March 18, 2009, entitled, "SWIGERT and DUNBAR," located in Committee databases at DTS #2009-1258, which provides a list of "some of the key captures and disrupted plots" that the CIA had attributed to the use of the CIA's enhanced interrogation techniques, and stating: "CIA assesses that most, if not all, of the timely intelligence acquired from detainees in this program would not have been discovered or reported by any other means." See Volume II for additional CIA representations asserting that the CIA's enhanced interrogation techniques enabled the CIA to obtain unique, otherwise unavailable intelligence that "saved lives."

1562. CIA memorandum for the Record, "Review of Interrogation Program on 29 July 2003," prepared by CIA General Counsel Scott Muller, dated August 5, 2003; briefing slides entitled, "*CIA Interrogation Program,*" dated July 29, 2003, presented to senior White House officials.

1563. Italics added. CIA memorandum for the Record, "Review of Interrogation Program on 29 July 2003," prepared by CIA General Counsel Scott Muller, dated August 5, 2003; briefing slides entitled, "*CIA Interrogation Program,*" dated July 29, 2003, presented to senior White House officials.

1564. Memorandum to the Inspector General from James Pavitt, CIA's Deputy Director for Operations, dated February 27, 2004, with the subject line, "Comments to Draft IG Special Review, 'Counterterrorism Detention and Interrogation Program' (2003-7123-IG)," Attachment, "Successes of CIA's Counterterrorism Detention and Interrogation Activities," dated February 24, 2004.

1565. Memorandum to the Inspector General from James Pavitt, CIA's Deputy Director for Operations, dated February 27, 2004, with the subject line, "Comments to Draft IG Special Review, 'Counterterrorism Detention and Interrogation Program' (2003-7123-IG)," Attachment, "Successes of CIA's Counterterrorism Detention and Interrogation Activities," dated February 24, 2004.

1566. Italics added. CIA Office of Inspector General, Special Review — Counterterrorism Detention and Interrogation Program (2003-7123-IG) May 2004.

1567. The relevant sections of the Special Review were also cited in the OLC's May 30, 2005 memorandum which stated that "we understand that interrogations have led to specific, actionable intelligence," and that "[w]e understand that the use of enhanced techniques in the interrogations of KSM, Zubaydah and others . . . has yielded critical information." (see memorandum for John A. Rizzo, Senior Deputy General Counsel, Central Intelligence Agency, from Steven G. Bradbury, Principal Deputy Assistant Attorney General, Office of Legal Counsel, May 30, 2005, Re: Application of United States Obligations Under Article 16 of the Convention Against Torture to Certain Techniques that May be Used in the Interrogation of High Value Al Qaeda Detainees, p. 9 (DTS #2009-1810, Tab 11), citing *Special Review* at 86, 90-91). Like the Special Review, the OLC memorandum has been declassified with redactions.

1568. Italics added. CIA briefing documents for Leon Panetta, entitled, "Tab 9: DCIA Briefing on RDI Program-18FEB.2009" and graphic attachment, "Key Intelligence and Reporting Derived from Abu Zubaydah and Khalid Shaykh Muhammad (KSM)." The documents include "DCIA Briefing on RDI Program" agenda, CIA document "EITs and Effectiveness," with associated documents, "Key Intelligence Impacts Chart: Attachment (AZ and KSM)," "Background on Key Intelligence Impacts Chart: Attachment," and "supporting references," to include "Background on Key Captures and Plots Disrupted."

1569. CIA document faxed to the Senate Select Committee on Intelligence on March 18, 2009, at 3:46 PM, entitled, "[SWIGERT and DUNBAR]" (DTS #2009-1258).

1570. See list of CIA prepared briefings and memoranda from 2003 through 2009 with representations on the effectiveness of the CIA's enhanced interrogation techniques referenced in this summary and described in detail in Volume II.

1571. The CIA's June 2013 Response acknowledges that "we incorrectly stated or implied that KSM's information led to the investigation of Faris." Elsewhere, the CIA's June 2013 Response states that "[CIA] imprecisely characterized KSM's information as having 'led' to the investigation of Iyman Faris, rather than more accurately characterizing it as a key contribution to the investigation." As described in more detail in Volume II, the CIA and FBI had significant information on Iyman Faris prior to any reporting from KSM. The CIA's June 2013 Response also states that the CIA's inaccurate statements that KSM's reporting "led" to the investigation of Iyman Faris were only made "[i]n a few cases," and "[i]n a small number of... representations." As described in the full Committee Study, the CIA repeatedly represented that KSM's reporting "led" to the investigation of Iyman Faris, and was responsible for the "identification" and "capture" of Iyman Faris.

1572. Information provided by the FBI to the Committee on November, 30, 2010. Records do not provide an explanation for the closing of the investigation.

1573. WHDC ███ (102129Z MAR 03). *See also* ALEC ███ (180200Z MAR 03).

1574. ALEC ███ (261725Z MAR 03).

1575. Information provided to the Committee by the FBI on November, 30, 2010.

1576. ███ 13658 (050318Z MAR 03). *See* the section on the capture of Majid Khan in this summary and in Volume II.

1577. ALEC ███ (060353Z MAR 03).

1578. ALEC ███ (060353Z MAR 03).

1579. ALEC ███ (060353Z MAR 03).

1580. FBI information relayed in ALEC ███ ███.

1581. FBI information confirmed for the Committee on November, 30. 2010.

1582. 13678 (070724Z MAR 03). The cable states: "a [foreign government officer] talked quietly to [Majid Khan] alone for about ten minutes before the interview began and was able to establish an excellent level of rapport. The first hour and [a] half of the interview was a review of bio-data and information previously [reported]. When [foreign government interrogators] started putting pressure on [Majid Khan] by pulling apart his story about his 'honeymoon' in Bangkok and his attempt to rent an apartment, safehouse, for his cousin [Mansoor Maqsood, aka Iqbal, aka Talha, aka Moeen, aka Habib], at 1400, [Majid Khan] slumped in his chair and said he would reveal everything to officers...."

1583. ███ 13758 ███; FBI information later relayed in ALEC ███ ███ ███; and information provided to the Committee by the FBI on November, 30, 2010. *See* FBI case file ███.

1584. ███ 13758 ███.

1585. ███ 13758 ███.

1586. ███ 137565 ███.

1587. ███ 13785 ███.

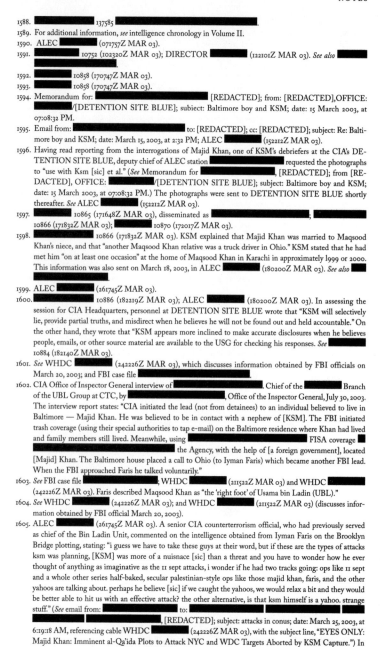

1588. 137585 .
1589. For additional information, *see* intelligence chronology in Volume II.
1590. ALEC (071757Z MAR 03).
1591. 10752 (102320Z MAR 03); DIRECTOR (122101Z MAR 03). *See also* .
1592. 10858 (170747Z MAR 03).
1593. 10858 (170747Z MAR 03).
1594. Memorandum for: [REDACTED]; from: [REDACTED],OFFICE: /[DETENTION SITE BLUE]; subiect: Baltimore boy and KSM; date: 15 March 2003, at 07:08:32 PM.
1595. Email from: to: [REDACTED]; cc: [REDACTED]; subject: Re: Baltimore boy and KSM; date: March 15, 2003, at 2:32 PM; ALEC (152212Z MAR 03).
1596. Having read reporting from the interrogations of Majid Khan, one of KSM's debriefers at the CIA's DETENTION SITE BLUE, deputy chief of ALEC station requested the photographs to "use with Ksm [sic] et al." (*See* Memorandum for , [REDACTED]; from [REDACTED], OFFICE: /[DETENTION SITE BLUE]; subject: Baltimore boy and KSM; date: 15 March 2003, at 07:08:32 PM.) The photographs were sent to DETENTION SITE BLUE shortly thereafter. *See* ALEC (152212Z MAR 03).
1597. 10865 (171648Z MAR 03), disseminated as ; 10866 (171832Z MAR 03); 10870 (172017Z MAR 03).
1598. 10866 (171832Z MAR 03). KSM explained that Majid Khan was married to Maqsood Khan's niece, and that "another Maqsood Khan relative was a truck driver in Ohio." KSM stated that he had met him "on at least one occasion" at the home of Maqsood Khan in Karachi in approximately 1999 or 2000. This information was also sent on March 18, 2003, in ALEC (180200Z MAR 03). *See also* .
1599. ALEC (261745Z MAR 03).
1600. 10886 (182219Z MAR 03); ALEC (180200Z MAR 03). In assessing the session for CIA Headquarters, personnel at DETENTION SITE BLUE wrote that "KSM will selectively lie, provide partial truths, and misdirect when he believes he will not be found out and held accountable." On the other hand, they wrote that "KSM appears more inclined to make accurate disclosures when he believes people, emails, or other source material are available to the USG for checking his responses. *See* 10884 (182140Z MAR 03).
1601. *See* WHDC (242226Z MAR 03), which discusses information obtained by FBI officials on March 20, 2003; and FBI case file .
1602. CIA Office of Inspector General interview of . Chief of the Branch of the UBL Group at CTC, by , Office of the Inspector General, July 30, 2003. The interview report states: "CIA initiated the lead (not from detainees) to an individual believed to live in Baltimore — Majid Khan. He was believed to be in contact with a nephew of [KSM]. The FBI initiated trash coverage (using their special authorities to tap e-mail) on the Baltimore residence where Khan had lived and family members still lived. Meanwhile, using FISA coverage the Agency, with the help of [a foreign government], located [Majid] Khan. The Baltimore house placed a call to Ohio (to Iyman Faris) which became another FBI lead. When the FBI approached Faris he talked voluntarily."
1603. *See* FBI case file ; WHDC (211522Z MAR 03) and WHDC (242226Z MAR 03). Faris described Maqsood Khan as "the 'right foot' of Usama bin Ladin (UBL)."
1604. *See* WHDC (242226Z MAR 03); and WHDC (211522Z MAR 03) (discusses information obtained by FBI official March 20, 2003).
1605. ALEC (261745Z MAR 03). A senior CIA counterterrorism official, who had previously served as chief of the Bin Ladin Unit, commented on the intelligence obtained from Iyman Faris on the Brooklyn Bridge plotting, stating: "i guess we have to take these guys at their word, but if these are the types of attacks ksm was planning, [KSM] was more of a nuisnace [sic] than a threat and you have to wonder how he ever thought of anything as imaginative as the 11 sept attacks, i wonder if he had two tracks going: ops like 11 sept and a whole other series half-baked, secular palestinian-style ops like those majid khan, faris, and the other yahoos are talking about. perhaps he believe [sic] if we caught the yahoos, we would relax a bit and they would be better able to hit us with an effective attack? the other alternative, is that ksm himself is a yahoo. strange stuff." (*See* email from: to: , [REDACTED]; subject: attacks in conus; date: March 25, 2003, at 6:19:18 AM, referencing cable WHDC (242226Z MAR 03), with the subject line, "EYES ONLY: Majid Khan: Imminent al-Qa'ida Plots to Attack NYC and WDC Targets Aborted by KSM Capture.") In a separate email, the senior official wrote: "again, odd. ksm wants to get 'machine tools' to loosen the bolts on bridges so they collapse? did he think no one would see or hear these yahoos trying to unscrew the bridge? that everyone would drive by and just ignore the effort to unbolt a roadway? and what about opsec: 'yup, we

were just going to recruit a few of the neighbors to help knock down the brooklyn bridge.'" *See* email from: [REDACTED]; [REDACTED] date: March 25, 2003, at 6:35:18 AM.

1606. ALEC [REDACTED] (261745Z MAR 03). During this period, the CIA was receiving updates from the FBI debriefings of Iyman Faris. *See* TRRS-03-03-0610, referenced in [REDACTED] 10984 (242351Z MAR 03). On March 20, 2003, KSM confirmed that he had tasked "the truck driver . . . to procure machine tools that would be useful to al-Qa'ida in its plan to loosen the nuts and bolts of suspension bridges," but stated he had "never divulged specific targeting information to the truck driver." (*See* [REDACTED] 10910 (202108Z MAR 03).) A CIA cable from March 24, 2003, noted that KSM's CIA interrogators were "reviewing latest [REDACTED] readout on Majid Klian debriefs [who was in foreign government custody] and FBI [intelligence reports] from debriefings of the truck driver Faris Iyman [sic]," and that the CIA team was therefore "focused entirely on sorting out the information on Majid's claim . . . as well as truck driver details on the threat." (*See* [REDACTED] 10984 (242351Z MAR 03).) According to another cable, KSM indicated that while the original plan was to sever the cables, he determined that it would be easier to acquire machine tools that would allow the operatives to "loosen the large nuts and bolts of the bridges." (*See* [REDACTED] 10985 (242351Z MAR 03).) The disseminated intelligence report from this interrogation added that KSM stated his last communication with Iyman Faris was shortly before his capture on March 1, 2003, and that he (KSM) was "severely disappointed to learn that Iyman had not yet been successful in his mission to purchase the necessary materials." (*See* DIRECTOR [REDACTED] (25111Z MAR 03).) Later, on April 10, 2003, a CIA cable stated that KSM told CIA interrogators that al-Qa'ida members had "cased" the Brooklyn Bridge and that KSM had discussed attacking suspension bridges with other senior al-Qa'ida operatives. *See* HEADQUARTERS [REDACTED] (100928Z APR 03).

1607. *See* FBI case file [REDACTED] ALEC [REDACTED] (261725Z MAR 03), and Department of Justice release dated October 28, 2003, entitled, "Iyman Faris Sentenced for Providing Material Support to Al Qaeda." During these interviews Iyman Faris provided detailed information on a variety of matters, including his ongoing relationship with Maqsood Khan; the aliases he used in Pakistan ("Mohmed Rauf and "Gura"); how he became acquainted with KSM and al-Qa'ida; as well as his interaction with the Majid Khan family. Iyman Faris further provided information on his initial meeting with UBL and how he helped Maqsood Khan obtain supplies "for usage by Usama Bin Ladin" when he was in Pakistan.

1608. ALEC [REDACTED] (022304Z APR 03); ALEC [REDACTED] (030128Z APR 03); ALEC [REDACTED] (022304Z APR 03); WHDC [REDACTED] (011857Z APR 03). *See also* ALEC (261725Z MAR 03); ALEC (010200Z APR 03); ALECBP(261933Z MAR 03).

1609. WHDC [REDACTED] 232240Z APR 03).

1610. *See* Department of Justice comments in "The Triple Life of a Qaeda Man," *Time Magazine*, June 22, 2003.

1611. *See* FBI case file [REDACTED].

1612. *See* Department of Justice release dated October 28, 2003, entitled, "Iyman Faris Sentenced for Providing Material Support to Al Qaeda."

1613. "Khalid Shaykh Muhammad's Threat Reporting — Precious Truths, Surrounded by a Bodyguard of Lies," IICT, April 3, 2003.

1614. Note on CIA records related to U.K.-based "Issas": Two United Kingdom-based al-Qa'ida associates, Dhiren Barot and Sajid Badat, were known by the same common aliases, Issa, Abu Issa, Abu Issa al-Britani ("[of] Britain") and/or Issa al-Pakistani. Both individuals were British Indians who had been independently in contact with senior al-Qa'ida leaders in Pakistan. Reporting indicated that the Issas were located in the United Kingdom and engaged in terrorist targeting of the U.K. The investigation into their true identities was a U.K.-led operation. As a result, the CIA sometimes had limited insight into U.K.-based activities to identify and locate the Issas. Senior CIA personnel expressed frustration that the U.K. was not sharing all known information on its investigations, writing in August 2003 that "[the FBI is] clearly working closely with the [U.K. service] on these matters and [the CIA is] at the mercy" of what it is told. In June 2003, the CIA informed the FBI that the CIA had "no electronic record of receiving any transcripts or summaries from your agency's interviews with [Richard] Reid, and would appreciate dissemination of summaries of questioning for the purposes of [CIA] analysis." Until the arrest of one of the Issas, Sajid Badat, on November 27, 2003, the U.S. Intelligence Community and U.K. authorities often confused the two al-Qa'ida associates. As a result, the quality and clarity of detainee reporting on the Issas (including reporting from detainees in the custody of the CIA, U.S. military, Department of Justice, and foreign services) varied. CIA personnel [REDACTED] reported in September 2003 that there were "two (or three) Abu Issas" in intelligence reporting and that because of their similarities, it was often "unclear which Issa the detainees [were] referring to at different stages." Once detained in the United Kingdom in November 2003, Sajid Badat (one of the Issas) cooperated with U.K. authorities and provided information about the other "Issa." Badat stated that "people often asked [Badat] about [the other] Issa, as they were both British Indians." According to Sajid Badat, "anyone who had been involved with jihad in Britain since the mid-90s" would know Issa al-Hindi (aka Dhiren Barot), to include Babar Ahmed, Moazzem Begg, Richard Reid, Zacarias Moussaoui, and KSM. The other Issa, Dhiren Barot, arrested on August 3, 2004, was found to have been especially well-known among the U.K.-based extremist community, having written a popular book in 1999 expounding the virtues of jihad in Kashmir under the alias, "Esa al-Hindi." CIA records include a reference to the book and a description of its author ("a brother from England who was a Hindu and became a Muslim... [who] got training in Afghanistan...") as early as December 1999 (disseminated by the CIA on 12/31/99 in [redacted] [redacted]. The [redacted] [foreign partner] would later report that Dhiren Barot "frequently" appeared "in reporting of terrorist training" and had "involvement in Jihad in occupied Kashmir, Pakistan, Afghanistan, and Malaysia, throughout the 1990s." The Committee Study is based on more than six million pages of material related to the CIA's Detention and Interrogation Program provided by the CIA. Access was not provided to intelligence databases of the CIA or any other U.S. or foreign intelligence or law enforcement agency. Insomuch as intelligence from these sources is included, it was, unless noted otherwise, found within the CIA's Detention and Interrogation Program material produced for this Study. It is likely that significant intelligence unrelated to the CIA's Detention and Interrogation Program on Sajid Badat and Dhiren Barot exists in U.S. intelligence and law enforcement records and databases. *See* intelligence chronology in Volume II, including: ALEC [redacted] (112157Z JUN 03); [redacted] 19907 (231744Z APR 04); [redacted] 99093 (020931Z SEP 03); ALEC [redacted] (212117Z AUG 03); CIA WASHINGTON DC [redacted] (162127Z JUN 03); and a series of emails between [redacted] and [redacted] (with multiple ccs)on August 22, 2003, at 9:24:43 AM.

1615. Among other documents, *see* [redacted] 19760 (251532Z JUN 02); [redacted] 80508 (081717Z AUG 02); CIA [redacted] (311736Z OCT 02), [redacted]; and [redacted] 99093 (020931Z SEP 03). The CIA's June 2013 Response states that "KSM's reporting also clearly distinguished between, and thereby focused investigations of, two al-Qa'ida operatives known as Issa al-Britani." As detailed in the KSM detainee review in Volume III, KSM did discuss the two operatives, but he did not identify either by name (or, in the case of Dhiren Barot, by his more common *kunya*, Issa al-Hindi), and provided no actionable intelligence that contributed to the eventual identification of, or locational information for, either individual.

1616. Among other documents, *see* CIA Headquarters document, entitled, "OPERATIONAL DEVELOPMENTS AGAINST GLOBAL SUNNI EXTREMIST TERRORISM," dated, "14 January 2002 1630 Hours"; CIA Headquarters document, entitled, "OPERATIONAL DEVELOPMENTS AGAINST GLOBAL SUNNI EXTREMIST TERRORISM," dated, "22 January 2002 1630 Hours"; ALEC [redacted] [redacted] (142334Z MAY 03); and [redacted] 13120 [redacted].

1617. *See* intelligence chronology in Volume II and multiple open source reports, as well as Department of Justice materials, including *United States v. Richard Reid* Indictment U.S. District Court, District of Massachusetts, January 16, 2002. According to a CIA operational update, in early December 2001, a unilateral CIA source reported that a known extremist "indicated there would be an attack on either an American or British airliner, originating in France, Germany, or Britain, with the use of explosives concealed in shoes." According to CIA records, an unclassified notice distributed to airlines concerning information from the CIA source in early December 2001 "is credited with having alerted flight crew personnel and their having reacted so swiftly to Reid's actions" aboard Flight 63. *See* intelligence chronology in Volume II, including CIA Headquarters document, entitled, "OPERATIONAL DEVELOPMENTS AGAINST GLOBAL SUNNI EXTREMIST TERRORISM," dated "9 April 2002 1630 Hours."

1618. Italics included in CIA Memorandum to the Office of Legal Counsel, entitled, "Effectiveness of the CIA Counterterrorist Interrogation Techniques," from March 2, 2005.

1619. *See* document entitled, "DCIA Talking Points: Waterboard 06 November 2007," dated November 6, 2007, with the notation the document was "sent to DCIA Nov. 6 in preparation for POTUS meeting."

1620. From 2003 through 2009, the CIA's representations regarding the effectiveness of the CIA's enhanced interrogation techniques provided a specific set of examples of terrorist plots "disrupted" and terrorists captured that the CIA attributed to information obtained from the use of its enhanced interrogation techniques. CIA representations further asserted that the intelligence obtained from the use of the CIA's enhanced interrogation techniques was unique, otherwise unavailable, and resulted in "saved lives." Among other CIA representations, see: (1) CIA representations in the Department of Justice Office of Legal Counsel Memorandum, dated May 30, 2005, which relied on a series of highly specific CIA representations on the type of intelligence acquired from the use of the CIA's enhanced interrogation techniques to assess their legality. The CIA representations referenced by the OLC include that the use of the CIA's enhanced interrogation techniques was "necessary" to obtain "critical," "vital," and "otherwise unavailable actionable intelligence" that was "essential" for the U.S. government to "detect and disrupt' terrorist threats. The OLC memorandum further states that "[the CIA] ha[s] informed [the OLC] that the CIA believes that this program is largely responsible for preventing a subsequent attack within the United States." (*See* Memorandum for John A. Rizzo, Senior Deputy General Counsel, Central Intelligence Agency from Steven G. Bradbury, Principal Deputy Assistant Attorney General, Office of Legal Counsel, May 30, 2005, Re: Application of United States Obligations Under Article 16 of the Convention Against Torture to Certain Techniques that May Be Used in the Interrogation of High Value al Qaeda Detainees.) (2) CIA representations in the Department of Justice Office of Legal Counsel Memorandum dated July 20, 2007, which also relied on CIA representations on the type of intelligence acquired from the use of the CIA's enhanced interrogation techniques. Citing CIA documents and the President's September 6, 2006, speech describing the CIA's interrogation program (which was based on CIA-provided information), the OLC memorandum states: "The CIA interrogation program—and, in particular, its use of enhanced interrogation techniques—is intended to serve this paramount interest [security of the Nation] by producing substantial quantities of otherwise unavailable intelligence.... As the President explained [on September 6, 2006], 'by giving us information about terrorist plans we could not get anywhere else, the program has saved innocent lives.'" (*See* Memorandum for John A. Rizzo, Actmg General Counsel, Central Intelligence Agency, from Steven G. Bradbury, Principal Deputy Assistant Attorney General, Office of Legal Counsel, July 20, 2007, Re: Application of the War Crimes Act, the Detainee Treatment Act, and Common Article 3 of the Geneva Conventions to Certain Techniques that May Be Used by the CIA in the Interrogation of High Value al Qaeda Detainees.) (3) CIA briefings for members of the National Security Council in July and September 2003 represented that "the use of Enhanced Techniques of one kind or another had produced significant intelligence information that had, in the view of CIA professionals, saved lives," and warned policymakers that "[t]ermination of this program will result in loss of life, possibly extensive." (*See* August 5, 2003 Memorandum for the Record from Scott Muller, Subject: Review of Interrogation Program on 29 July 2003; Briefing slides, CIA Interrogation Program, July 29, 2003; September 4, 2003, CIA Memorandum for the Record, Subject: Member Briefing; and September 26, 2003, Memorandum for the Record from Muller, Subject: CIA Interrogation Program.) (4) The CIA's response to the Office of Inspector General draft Special Review of the CIA program, which asserts: "Information [the CIA] received . . . as a result of the lawful use of enhanced interrogation techniques ('EITs') has almost certainly saved countless American lives inside the United States and abroad. The evidence points clearly to the fact that without the use of such techniques, we and our allies would [have] suffered major terrorist attacks involving hundreds, if not thousands, of casualties." (*See* Memorandum for: Inspector General; from: James Pavitt, Deputy Director for Operations; subject: re (S) Comments to Draft IG Special Review, "Counterterrorism Detention and Interrogation Program" 2003-7123-IG; date: February 27, 2004; attachment: February 24, 2004, Memorandum re Successes ofCIA's Counterterrorism Detention and Interrogation Activities.) (5) CIA briefing documents for CIA Director Leon Panetta in February 2009, which state that the "CIA assesses that the RDI program worked and the [enhanced interrogation] techniques were effective in producing foreign intelligence," and that [m]ost, if not all, of the timely intelligence acquired from detainees in this program would not have been discovered or reported by other means." (*See* CIA briefing documents for Leon Panetta, entitled, "Tab 9: DCIA Briefing on RDI Program- 18FEB.2009" and graphic attachment, "Key Intelligence and Reporting Derived from Abu Zubaydah and Khalid Shaykh Muhammad (KSM)," including "DCIA Briefing on RDI Program" agenda, CIA document "EITs and Effectiveness," with associated documents, "Key Intelligence Impacts Chart: Attachment (AZ and KSM), "Background on Key Intelligence Impacts Chart: Attachment," and "supporting references," to include "Background on Key Captures and Plots Disrupted.") (6) CIA document faxed to the Senate Select Committee on Intelligence on March 18, 2009, entitled, "[SWIGERT] and [DUNBAR]," located in Committee databases at DTS #2009-1258, which provides a list of "some of the key captures and disrupted plots" that the CIA had attributed to the use of the CIA's enhanced interrogation techniques, and stating: "CIA assesses that most, if not all, of the timely intelligence acquired from detainees in this program would not have been discovered or reported by any other means." *See* Volume II for additional CIA representations asserting that the CIA's enhanced interrogation techniques enabled the CIA to obtain unique, otherwise unavailable intelligence that "saved lives."

1621. As detailed in the intelligence chronology in Volume II, there is no evidence to support the CIA assertion in October 2007 that Sajid Badat was "preparing another attack like that attempted by 'shoe bomber' Richard Reid." A body of intelligence collected after the December 22, 2001, attempted shoe bomb attack by Richard Reid indicated that the proposed partner "backed out of the operation." This information was corroborated by signals intelligence. Once detained on November 27, 2003, Sajid Badat cooperated with U.K. authorities and described how he withdrew from the operation. See, among other CIA records, CIA Headquarters document, entitled, "OPERATIONAL DEVELOPMENTS AGAINST GLOBAL SUNNI EXTREMIST TERRORISM," dated "14 January 2002 1630 Hours."

1622. Italics added. CIA fax from CIA employee [REDACTED] to U.S. Senate Committee on Appropriations, Subcommittee on Defense, with fax cover sheet entitled, "Talking points," sent on October 26, 2007, at 5:39:48 PM; document faxed entitled, "Talking Points Appeal of the $■ Million reduction in CIA/CTC's Rendition and Detention Program." As detailed in the intelligence chronology in Volume II, there is no evidence that Sajid Badat was "preparing another attack like that attempted by 'shoe bomber' Richard Reid." All intelligence collected after the December 22, 2001, attempted shoe bomb attack by Richard Reid indicated that his proposed partner "backed out of the operation." See, for example, CIA Headquarters document, entitled, "OPERATIONAL DEVELOPMENTS AGAINST GLOBAL SUNNI EXTREMIST TERRORISM," dated,"14 January 2002 1630 Hours."

1623. Italics in original. CIA Talking Points entitled, "Talking Points for 10 March 2005 DCI Meeting PC: Effectiveness of the High-Value Detainee Interrogation (HVDI) Techniques."

1624. CIA "Briefing Notes on the Value of Detainee Reporting" faxed from the CIA to the Department of Justice on April 15, 2005, at 10:47AM. *See also* a CIA document dated December 20, 2005, and entitled, "Examples of Detainee Reporting Used by Our CT Partners to Thwart Terrorists, 2003-2005," which includes four columns:

"Detainees," "What They Told Us," "Actions Taken By Our CT Partners," and "Results." Under the heading of KSM and Ammar al-Baluchi, the document states: "What They Told Us . . ." "Provided lead information to Issa al-Britani, a.k.a. Sajid Badat in the United Kingdom, November 2003. KSM said Badat was an operative slated to launch a shoe-bomb attack simultaneously with Richard Reid in December 2001. Ammar al-Baluchi provided additional information on Badat . . . Results . . . Disrupted a shoe-bomb attack."

1625. For additional information, *see* Volume I and Volume II.

1626. There are no records of KSM identifying Sajid Badat as "Issa al-Pakistani." CIA records indicate that KSM stated he did not know Richard Reid's partner's true name, but referred to him only as "Abu Issa al-Britani" (described in CIA cables as "Abu Issa the Britain" [sic]), or as "Issa Richard." *See* intelligence chronology in Volume II, including ALEC ████ (112157Z JUN 03).

1627. CIA "Briefing Notes on the Value of Detainee Reporting" faxed from the CIA to the Department of Justice on April 15, 2005, at 10:47AM. As detailed in Volume II, there are no CIA records of KSM providing any reporting in November 2003 contributing to Sajid Badat's arrest.

1628. CIA Briefing for Obama National Security Team- "Renditions, Detentions, and Interrogations (RDI)," including "Tab 7," named "RDG Copy- Briefing on RDI Program 09 Jan. 2009": ". . . [L]eads provided by KSM and Ammar al-Baluchi in November 2003 led directly to the arrest in the United Kingdom of Sajid Badat the operative who was slated to launch a simultaneous shoe-bomb attack with Richard Reid in December 2001." Ammar al-Baluchi, while still in foreign government custody, and prior to being transferred to CIA custody and subjected to the CIA's enhanced interrogation techniques, stated that he had contacted "Abu Issa" on behalf of KSM but the CIA believed that Ammar al-Baluchi was providing inaccurate information. (*See* ALEC 206234 ████). ████ [foreign partner] authorities later indicated that they believed that Ammar al-Baluchi was providing accurate reporting on Abu Issa. (*See* ████ 10054 ████ ████. Later, in CIA custody, Ammar al-Baluchi described Issa's connection to the Richard Reid plot. The CIA credited confronting Ammar al-Baluchi with emails as "key in gaining Ammar's admissions." (*See* ALEC ████.) As detailed in Volume II, Ammar al-Baluchi, like KSM, was unable, or unwilling, to identify Sajid Badat by name.

1629. *See* list of CIA prepared briefings and memoranda from 2003 through 2009 with representations on the effectiveness of the CIA's enhanced interrogation techniques referenced in this summary and described in detail in Volume II.

1630. CIA briefing for Vice President Cheney, dated March 4, 2005, entitled, "Briefing for Vice President Cheney: CIA Detention and Interrogation Program." The briefing document states: "Shoe Bomber: Sajid Badat, an operative slated to launch a simultaneous shoe bomb attack with Richard Reid in December 2001, identified and captured. Source: Abu Zubaydah." There are no CIA records to support this statement. On August 17, 2003, Abu Zubaydah was shown a picture of Sajid Badat that a CIA officer stated "looks an awful lot like the sketches" from a detainee in foreign government custody. Abu Zubaydah stated he did not recognize the person in the photo. On August 22, 2003, sketches of Badat were shown to Abu Zubaydah, who did not recognize the individual depicted. *See* email from: ████ to: ████ (multiple ccs); subject: "Re: Meeting with ████"; date: August 17, 2003, at 1:04 PM; ████ 12679 (181124Z AUG 03); ████ 12713 (231932Z AUG 03).

1631. The CIA also credited Abu Zubaydah, who was captured in March 2002, with identifying Richard Reid, who was arrested in December 2001. This inaccurate information was presented to select National Security Council principals. Secretary of State Powell and Secretary of Defense Rumsfeld, and Assistant Attorney General Jack Goldsmith. *See* CIA briefing slides entitled, "*CIA Interrogation Program*," dated July 29, 2003, presented to senior White House officials (Memorandum for the Record; subject: CIA Interrogation Program; September 27, 2003 (OGC-FO-2003-50088); Slides, CIA Interrogation Program, 16 September 2003). The Memorandum for the Record drafted by John Bellinger refers to a "detailed handout" provided by the CIA. *See* John B. Bellinger III, Senior Associate Counsel to the President and Legal Advisor, National Security Council; Memorandum for the Record; subject: Briefing of Secretaries Powell and Rumsfeld regarding Interrogation of High-Value Detainees; date: September 30, 2003. *See also* Scott W. Muller; Memorandum for the Record; Interrogation briefing for Jack Goldsmith; date: 16 October 2003 (OGC-FO-2003-50097).

1632. ████ 13165 ████.

1633. The CIA's June 2013 Response maintains that "KSM was the first to tell [the CIA] there was a second shoe bomber and that he remained at large." The Committee found this statement to be incongruent with CIA records. There were multiple reports that Richard Reid had an unidentified partner prior to the provision of any information from KSM (captured on March 1, 2003). The CIA's June 2013 Response addresses only one of two documented efforts by the FBI in January 2002 to inform the CIA that Richard Reid had "an unidentified partner who allegedly backed out of the operation at the last minute." The CIA's June 2013 Response acknowledges that this FBI information was provided to senior CIA leadership in writing, but states that, on one of the two days the information was provided, "the Reid investigation came on page 10 of 15 pages of updates that day," and that the information did not "exist in any searchable CIA data repositories." The CIA's June 2013 Response also does not address the CIA's own source reporting on "another operative" who existed alongside Richard Reid. In April 2002, a reliable CIA source—who had warned of the Richard Reid shoe-bomb attack weeks before it occurred—reported that, in addition to Richard Reid, "another operative existed." The source stated that, instead of an airliner departing from Paris, as had Richard Reid's flight, "this attack would occur against an airliner originating from Heathrow International Airport in London." Once captured, Sajid Badat would confirm this reporting. Despite acknowledging evidence to the contrary, and without further explanation, the CIA stated in meetings with the Committee in 2013 that the CIA stands by its representations that "KSM was the first to tell [the CIA] there was a second shoe bomber and that he remained at large."

1634. *See* Volume II, including FBI WASHINGTON DC ████ (160429Z JUL 02). The CIA's June 2013 Response acknowledges that there was intelligence reporting that Sajid Badat was involved in terrorist activities and "targeting American interests," but defends its past assertions highlighting the effectiveness of the CIA's enhanced interrogation techniques in obtaining otherwise unavailable intelligence by asserting that, at the time of this reporting, there "was nothing at the time on Badat to lead [the CIA] to prioritize him over others."

1635. The CIA's June 2013 Response states: "KSM was the first person to provide—in March 2003, after having undergone enhanced interrogation techniques in CIA custody—a detailed and authoritative narrative of al-Qa'ida development of and plans to use shoe bombs operationally." The CIA's June 2013 Response does not acknowledge intelligence acquired by the Intelligence Community on these matters prior to any reporting from KSM and does not address the significant amount of fabricated reporting KSM provided. *See* Volume II for additional information.

1636. *See* Volume II for additional information.

1637. The FBI information was provided to the CIA. *See* CIA Headquarters document, entitled, "OPERATIONAL DEVELOPMENTS AGAINST GLOBAL SUNNI EXTREMIST TERRORISM," dated, "14 January 2002 1630 Hours." The CIA's June 2013 Response acknowledges the existence of this CIA document and that the information in the document was "compiled . . . for counterterrorism seniors at CIA." The CIA's 2013 Response nonetheless states that "[t]here is no reference to this possibility [of a possible second operative] in official communications between FBI and CIA, nor did it exist in any searchable CIA data repositories prior to KSM's reporting." The CIA expressed concern that the FBI was not sharing information from the debriefings of Richard Reid. Additional FBI information about Sajid Badat, including any information obtained from Richard Reid, was not available to the Committee. *See* CIA WASHINGTON DC ████ █ (162127Z JUN 03).

1638. *See* intelligence chronology in Volume II, including U.S. military detainee reporting detailed in CIA Headquarters document, entitled, "OPERATIONAL DEVELOPMENTS AGAINST GLOBAL SUNNI EXTREMIST TERRORISM," dated, "9 April 2002 1630 Hours." This CIA document included reporting from a CIA source who stated that, in addition to Richard Reid, "another operative existed" who was planning an attack "against an airliner originating from Heathrow International Airport in London." The same source had provided reporting on an "attack . . . against an airliner originating in France, Germany, or Britain, with the use of explosives concealed in shoes" just prior to Richard Reid's attempted use of explosives concealed in shoes on December 21, 2001. Despite corroborated intelligence reporting acquired prior to the provision of information from CIA detainees, the CIA represented, as late as October 2007, that "[m]ost, if not all, of the intelligence acquired from high-value detainees in [the CIA] program would likely not have been discovered or reported in any other way," crediting CIA detainees with "the discovery of an operative who was preparing another attack like that attempted by 'shoe bomber' Richard Reid." *See* CIA fax from CIA employee [REDACTED] to U.S. Senate Committee on Appropriations, Subcommittee on Defense, with fax cover sheet entitled, "Talking points," sent on October 26, 2007, at 5:39:48 PM. Document faxed entitled, "Talking Points Appeal of the $█ ███ Million reduction in CIA/CTC's Rendition and Detention Program."

1639. FBI WASHINGTON DC ████ (130706Z JUL 02).

1640. FBI WASHINGTON DC ████ (160429Z JUL 02).

1641. CIA ████ ████████; DIRECTOR ████, ████████ ███.

1642. FBI WASHINGTON DC ████ (130706Z JUL 02); FBI WASHINGTON ████ (290315Z AUG 02); ████ 13165 ████████.

1643. *See* ███ [foreign partner] summary of the Sajid Badat investigation and ████ 13165 ████.

1644. ████████ [foreign partner] authorities relayed to the CIA that there were "two (or three) Abu Issas" in terrorist threat reporting who were described as from the U.K. and engaged in suspected al-Qa'ida terrorist operations. CIA Headquarters informed ██████ in August 2003 that "there are (at least) two/two important fugitives known as Issa and carrying UK passports (those both are known at times as Issa al-Britani), and both have strong links to KSM." *See* intelligence chronology in Volume II for additional details.

1645. Among other documents, *see* ████ 19712 ████████; ████ 19744 ████ █; and ████ 19780 ████████. *See also* April 4, 2003, cable from the CIA ████ (ALEC ████████) providing information on a U.K. "Issa" in which the CIA acknowledges █ ███ investigation already underway, writing "we realize that Abu Issa is [a subject of interest] of interest [your government]." Abu Zubair al-Ha'ili is also known by the variant, Abu Zubayr al-Ha'ili. Abu Zubair al-Ha'ili was never in CIA custody.

1646. *See* intelligence chronology in Volume II.

1647. [REDACTED] 24237 [REDACTED].

1648. Email from: [REDACTED]; to: [REDACTED] (multiple ccs); subject: "Re: Meeting with [REDACTED] date: August 17, 2003, at 1:04PM. The CIA's June 2013 Response states that "[t]he fact that the [foreign partner] as late as August 2003 was only able to locate a poor quality photo of Sajid Badat belies the notion that Badat was well on his way to being identified as important and disrupted in advance of KSM's reporting. However, the Committee found when CIA officers received what they described as a "crummy" photo of Sajid Badat from the the [REDACTED], they nonetheless wrote, "it sure looks to me like Sajid is the shoe bomber Issa," noting the body of intelligence compiled to date and the fact that "the photo [of Sajid Badat] looks an awful lot like the sketches of 'Issa al-Britani/Pakistani'" the CIA had obtained from the detainee in foreign government custody, Abu Zubair al-Ha'ili. Of note to CIA officers was that al-Ha'ili "was asked, 'what is Abu Issa's most striking feature or features?'" Abu Zubair replied, "his eyes, thick frame eye glasses, and Pakistani hat." Abu Zubair stated that Issa always wore a unique, irregularly shaped checkered hat that has the front center cut out of it and is only worn in Pakistan. In a discussion of the photo of Sajid Badat, a CIA officer wrote: "Sajid appears to have the same goofy hat on that Zubair went to lengths to describe." *See* email from: [REDACTED] to: [REDACTED] (multiple ccs); subject: "Re: photo of Sajid badat, suspected as iden with Issa al-Hindi: some possible confusion"; date: August 15, 2003, at 7:20:40 PM.

1649. [REDACTED] 12679 (181124Z AUG 03). Khallad bin Attash and Abu Zubaydah were also shown the picture of Sajid Badat. Both detainees stated they did not recognize the person in the photo.

1650. Series of emails, including email from: [REDACTED]; to: [REDACTED] (multiple ccs); August 22, 2003, at 9:24:43 AM. The CIA's June 2013 Response states, "no one had suggested Badat could be a candidate for this Issa until KSM's reporting." CIA records indicate that KSM never identified Sajid Badat by name. Moreover, on March 20, 2003, while being subjected to the CIA's enhanced interrogation techniques, KSM inaccurately identified Richard Reid's U.K. associate as "Talha." (*See* [REDACTED] 10912 (202110Z MAR 03), disseminated as [REDACTED].) On May 11, 2003, a month and a half after the CIA ceased using its enhanced interrogation techniques against KSM, KSM stated that Talha was actually "Issa," and that he had provided the name Talha under pressure and had now remembered the right name — Issa — after he had time to think about the question. *See* [REDACTED] 11585 (111753Z MAY 03); DIRECTOR [REDACTED] (121729Z MAY 03).

1651. [REDACTED] 12713 (231932Z AUG 03).

1652. Ujaama had pled guilty to terrorism-related charges on April 14, 2003, and had agreed to continue cooperating with FBI officials on terrorism investigations. Earnest James Ujaama entered a guilty plea to a charge of conspiracy to provide goods and services to the Taliban on April 14, 2003. *See* U.S. Department of Justice press release dated April 14, 2003, and entitled, "Earnest James Ujaama Pleads Guilty to Conspiracy to Supply Goods and Services to the Taliban, Agrees to Cooperate with Terrorism Investigations."

1653. ALEC [REDACTED] (212117Z AUG 03). CIA records state that sometime prior to August 21, 2003, the FBI had entered Sajid Badat, with the correct identifying information, into [REDACTED] databases.

1654. [REDACTED] 99093 ([REDACTED]).

1655. DIRECTOR [REDACTED] ([REDACTED] SEP 03)/[REDACTED] [REDACTED]. *See also* CIA [REDACTED] [REDACTED] DEC 03), which includes a "Comment" that "during a 9 September 2003 interview of [Feroze Ali] Abassi at Guantanamo Bay, Abbasi identified Badat as a participant in the 'information gathering course' at al-Faruq" terrorist training camp, about which Abassi had previously provided detailed information.

1656. *See* [REDACTED] 12806 (101910Z SEP 03) and [REDACTED] 54986 (300927Z OCT 03). The CIA's June 2013 Response acknowledges that a U.S. military detainee first identified Sajid Badat, but argues that CIA representations on the effectiveness of the CIA's enhanced interrogation techniques in producing otherwise unavailable intelligence in this case were nonetheless accurate. The CIA's June 2013 Response states that KSM "did provide unique intelligence," and that "KSM's identification of Badat [in the [REDACTED] photo] was more important than others who also recognized the photograph—including one who identified the photo a day before KSM did—because only KSM at the time had characterized this Issa as a partner to Reid and as a would-be shoe bomber." As detailed in this summary and in greater detail in Volume II, the CIA's 2013 Response is incongruent with internal CIA records. After the arrest of Sajid Badat, U.K. authorities described their investigation of Sajid Badat [REDACTED]. The United Kingdom highlighted information from a [REDACTED] [specific U.K. intelligence collection on Sajid Badat] not further identified in CIA records. The U.K. record of investigation makes no reference to KSM's photo identification, but rather states: "reporting on 9 September 2003 confirmed that a U.S. military detainee had positively identified Sajid Badat as Abu Issa. We assess that Sajid Badat is identical with both Sajid and Abu Issa the shoebomber." *See* [REDACTED] 13165 [REDACTED] NOV 03); DIRECTOR [REDACTED] ([REDACTED] ([REDACTED] SEP 03) [REDACTED]; [REDACTED]; CIA [REDACTED] ([REDACTED] DEC 03). *See also* the intelligence chronology in Volume II.

1657. ALEC [REDACTED] [REDACTED]; [REDACTED] 13120 [REDACTED].

1658. ██████ 13120 ████████████.

1659. ██████ 13165 ██████ NOV 03). The ████ [foreign partner] report highlights how the "[a named foreign government] reported that on the 13 September 2001 Nizar [Trabelsi] was arrested for his alleged involvement in planning a terrorist attack against the American Embassy in Paris" and how Trabelsi was connected to a phone card "recovered from Richard Colvin Reid" but found to have been used by Sajid Badat. The report references a larger U.K. investigation, stating that Badat was found to be "a member of Babar Ahmad's group" and to have "attended a jihad training camp in Afghanistan." The ████ [foreign partner] report closes by stating: "Further reporting on 9 September 2003 confirmed that a U.S. military detainee had positively identified Sajid Badat as Abu Issa. We assess that Sajid Badat is identical with both Sajid and Abu Issa the shoebomber."

1660. Email from: ████████████; to: [REDACTED], with multiple ccs; subject: "Re: Profile on Saajid Badat for coord by 6pm, 19 October 2005; date: October 19, 2005, at 3:14:29 PM.

1661. *See* open source reporting, including "Secret Life of Shoe Bomb Saajid Badat Funded By The Taxpayer," U.K. *Telegraph*, dated April 23, 2012; "US court hears Bin Ladin testimony from UK bomb plotter," *BBC News*, dated April 24, 2012; "Operative Details Al Qaeda Plans to Hit Planes in Wake of 9/11," *CNN*, dated April 25, 2012; and "'Convention' of Convicted Terrorists at NY Trial," *NPR News*, dated April 24, 2012.

1662. *See* open source reporting, including "Secret Life of Shoe Bomb Saajid Badat Funded By The Taxpayer," U.K. *Telegraph*, dated April 23, 2012; "US court hears Bin Ladin testimony from UK bomb plotter," *BBC News*, dated April 24, 2012; "Operative Details Al Qaeda Plans to Hit Planes in Wake of 9/11," *CNN*, dated April 25, 2012; "'Convention' of Convicted Terrorists at NY Trial," *NPR News*, dated April 24, 2012; and "Man Convicted of a Terrorist Plot to Bomb Subways Is Sent to Prison for Life," *New York Times*, dated November 16, 2012.

1663. While the CIA refers to "Canary Wharf' as a potential target of KSM's plotting, intelligence records suggest the actual target was likely "One Canada Square," the tallest building in the United Kingdom at the time of the plotting, which is located in Canary Wharf, a major business district in London.

1664. *See* detailed intelligence chronology in Volume II.

1665. *See* the Karachi Plots section in this summary, as well as additional details in Volume II.

1666. Italics included in CIA Memorandum to the Office of Legal Counsel, entitled, "Effectiveness of the CIA Counterterrorist Interrogation Techniques," from March 2, 2005.

1667. From 2003 through 2009, the CIA's representations regarding the effectiveness of the CIA's enhanced interrogation techniques provided a specific set of examples of terrorist plots "disrupted" and terrorists captured that the CIA attributed to information obtained from the use of its enhanced interrogation techniques. CIA representations further asserted that the intelligence obtained from the use of the CIA's enhanced interrogation techniques was unique, otherwise unavailable, and resulted in "saved lives." Among other CIA representations, see: (1) CIA representations in the Department of Justice Office of Legal Counsel Memorandum, dated May 30, 2005, which relied on a series of highly specific CIA representations on the type of intelligence acquired from the use of the CIA's enhanced interrogation techniques to assess their legality. The CIA representations referenced by the OLC include that the use of the CIA's enhanced interrogation techniques were "necessary" to obtain "critical," "vital," and "otherwise unavailable actionable intelligence" that was "essential" for the U.S. government to "detect and disrupt" terrorist threats. The OLC memorandum further states that "[the CIA] ha[s] informed [the OLCJ that the CIA believes that this program is largely responsible for preventing a subsequent attack within the United States." (*See* Memorandum for John A. Rizzo, Senior Deputy General Counsel, Central Intelligence Agency, from Steven G. Bradbury, Principal Deputy Assistant Attorney General, Office of Legal Counsel, May 30, 2005, Re: Application of United States Obligations Under Article 16 of the Convention Against Torture to Certain Techniques that May Be Used in the Interrogation of High Value al Qaeda Detainees.) (2) CIA representations in the Department of Justice Office of Legal Counsel Memorandum dated July 20, 2007, which also relied on CIA representations on the type of intelligence acquired from the use of the CIA's enhanced interrogation techniques. Citing CIA documents and the President's September 6, 2006, speech describing the CIA's interrogation program (which was based on CIA-provided information), the OLC memorandum states: "The CIA interrogation program—and, in particular, its use of enhanced interrogation techniques—is intended to serve this paramount interest [security of the nation] by producing substantial quantities of otherwise unavailable intelligence.... As the President explained [on September 6, 2006], 'by giving us information about terrorist plans we could not get anywhere else, the program has saved innocent lives.'" (*See* Memorandum for John A. Rizzo, Acting General Counsel, Central Intelligence Agency, from Steven G. Bradbury, Principal Deputy Assistant Attorney General, Office of Legal Counsel, July 20, 2007, Re: Application of the War Crimes Act, the Detainee Treatment Act, and Common Article 3 of the Geneva Conventions to Certain Techniques that May Be Used by the CIA in the Interrogation of High Value al Qaeda Detainees.) (3) CIA briefings for members of the National Security Council in July and September 2003 represented that "the use of Enhanced Techniques of one kind or another had produced significant intelligence information that had, in the view of CIA professionals, saved lives," and warned policymakers that "[t]ermination of this program will result in loss of life, possibly extensive." (*See* August 5, 2003 Memorandum for the Record from Scott Muller, Subject: Review of Interrogation Program on 29 July 2003; Briefing slides, CIA Interrogation Program, July 29, 2003; September 4, 2003, CIA Memorandum for the Record, Subject: Member Briefing; and September 26, 2003, Memorandum for the Record from Muller, Subject: CIA Interrogation Program.) (4) The CIA's response to the Office of Inspector General draft Special Review of the CIA program, which asserts: "Information [the CIAl received . . . as a result of the lawful use of enhanced interrogation techniques ('EITs') has almost certainly saved countless American lives inside the United States and abroad. The evidence points clearly to the fact that without the use of such techniques, we and our allies would [have] suffered major terrorist attacks involving hundreds, if not thousands, of casualties." (*See* Memorandum for: Inspector General; from: James Pavitt, Deputy Director for Operations; subject: re (S) Comments to Draft IG Special Review, "Counterterrorism Detention and Interrogation Program" 2003-7123-IG; date: February 27, 2004; attachment: February 24, 2004, Memorandum re Successes of CIA's Counterterrorism Detention and Interrogation Activities.) (5) CIA briefing documents for CIA Director Leon Panetta in February 2009, which state that the "CIA assesses that the RDI program worked and the [enhanced interrogation] techniques were effective in producing foreign intelligence," and that "[m]ost, if not all, of the timely intelligence acquired from detainees in this program would not have been discovered or reported by other means." (*See* CIA briefing documents for Leon Panetta, entitled, "Tab 9: DCIA Briefing on RDI Program- 18FEB.2009" and graphic attachment, "Key Intelligence and Reporting Derived from Abu Zubaydah and Khalid Shaykh Muhammad (KSM)," including "DCIA Briefing on RDI Program" agenda, CIA document "EITs and Effectiveness," with associated documents, "Key Intelligence Impacts Chart: Attachment (AZ and KSM)," "Background on Key Intelligence Impacts Chart: Attachment," and "supporting references," to include "Background on Key Captures and Plots Disrupted.") (6) CIA document faxed to the Senate Select Committee on Intelligence on March 18, 2009, entitled, "SWIGERT and DUNBAR," located in Committee databases at DTS #2009-1258, which provides a list of "some of the key captures and disrupted plots" that the CIA had attributed to the use of the CIA's enhanced interrogation techniques, and stating: "CIA assesses that most, if not all, of the timely intelligence acquired from detainees in this program would not have been discovered or reported by any other means." *See* Volume II for additional CIA representations asserting that the CIA's enhanced interrogation techniques enabled the CIA to obtain unique, otherwise unavailable intelligence that "saved lives."

1668. This information was incorrect. CIA records indicate that by December 23, 2005, at least 38 CIA detainees had been subjected to the CIA's enhanced interrogation techniques.

1669. Italics added. "Impact of the Loss of the Detainee Program to CT Operations and Analysis," prepared to support a letter from CIA Director Goss to Stephen J. Hadley, Assistant to the President/National Security Advisor, Frances F. Townsend, Assistant to the President/Homeland Security Advisor, and Ambassador John D. Negroponte, dated December 23, 2005.

1670. Italics added. CIA memorandum to the CIA Inspector General from James Pavitt, CIA's Deputy Director for Operations, dated February 27, 2004, with the subject line, "Comments to Draft IG Special Review, 'Counterterrorism Detention and Interrogation Program' (2003-7123-IG)," Attachment, "Successes of CIA's Counterterrorism Detention and Interrogation Activities," dated February 24, 2004.

1671. *See* list of CIA prepared briefings and memoranda from 2003 through 2009 with representations on the effectiveness of the CIA's enhanced interrogation techniques referenced in this summary and described in detail in Volume II.

1672. As described in this Study, the CIA consistently represented from 2003 through 2009 that the use of the CIA's enhanced interrogation techniques resulted in "disrupted plots," listed the "Heathrow Plot" as disrupted "as a result of the EITs," and informed policymakers that the information acquired to disrupt the plotting could not have been obtained from other intelligence sources or methods available to the U.S. government. In at least one CIA representation to White House officials that highlighted the Heathrow plotting, the CIA represented that "the use of the [CIA's enhanced interrogation] techniques has produced significant results," and warned policymakers that "[t]ermination of this [CIA] program will result in loss of life, possibly extensive." The CIA's June 2013 Response states: "CIA disagrees with the *Study*'s assessment that [the CIA] incorrectly represented that information derived from interrogating detainees helped disrupt al-Qa'ida's targeting of Heathrow Airport and Canary Wharf in London, including in President Bush's 2006 speech on the Program. Detainee reporting, including some which was acquired after enhanced interrogation techniques were applied, played a critical role in uncovering the plot, understanding it, detaining many of the key players, and ultimately allowing us to conclude it had been disrupted. It is a complex story, however, and we should have been clearer in delineating the roles played by different partners." As described in this summary, past CIA representations concerning the Heathrow Airport plotting and intelligence acquired "as a result of the CIA's enhanced interrogation techniques were inaccurate. (See, among other records, the September 6, 2006, speech by President Bush, based on CIA information and vetted by the CIA, which describes the CIA's use of "an alternative set" of interrogation procedures and stating: "These are some of the plots that have been stopped because of the information of this vital program. Terrorists held in CIA custody... have helped stop a plot to hijack passenger planes and fly them into Heathrow or Canary Wharf in London.") Contrary to the CIA's June 2013 assertion, CIA records indicate that information related to the use of the CIA's enhanced interrogation techniques played no role in "detaining many of the key players" and played no role in "uncovering the [Heathrow] plot." CIA records indicate the Heathrow Airport plotting had not progressed beyond the initial planning stages when the operation was fully disrupted with the detention of Ramzi bin al-Shibh (detained on September 11, 2002), KSM (detained on March 1, 2003), Ammar-al-Baluchi (detained on April 29, 2003), and Khallad bin Attash (detained on April 29, 2003). The CIA's June 2013 Response states that "[b]y all accounts, KSM's arrest was the action that most disrupted the [Heathrow] plot." As detailed in this summary and in greater detail in Volume II, the capture of these detainees—including KSM—was unrelated to any reporting from CIA detainees. CIA records further indicate that details on al-Qa'ida's targeting of Heathrow Airport were acquired prior to any reporting from CIA detainees. For example, prior to receiving any information from CIA detainees, the CIA acquired detailed information about al-Qa'ida's targeting of Heathrow Airport, to include, but not limited to, the al-Qa'ida senior leaders involved, the method of the planned attack, the status of the operation, and the *kunyas* of two potential unwitting operatives in the United Kingdom. Finally, the CIA's June 2013 Response claims that its past CIA representations were accurate and that CIA "detainee reporting, including some which was acquired after enhanced interrogation techniques were applied, played a critical role" in providing information, "ultimately allowing [CIA] to conclude it had been disrupted." Prior to June 2013, the CIA had never represented that the use of the CIA's enhanced interrogation techniques produced information "allowing [CIA] to conclude [the Heathrow Plot] had been disrupted." Rather, as detailed in this summary and more fully in Volume II, the CIA represented that the information acquired "as a result of EITs" produced unique, otherwise unavailable "actionable intelligence" that "saved lives" and disrupted the plotting itself. As detailed, these representations were inaccurate.

1673. DIRECTOR ███ (172132Z OCT 02).
1674. DIRECTOR ███ (172132Z OCT 02).
1675. DIRECTOR ███ (172132Z OCT 02).
1676. [REDACTED] 20901 (301117Z SEP 02). *See also* ███, CIA ███ ███.
1677. CIA ███ ███. In October 2002, months prior to KSM's capture, Ramzi bin al-Shibh (RBS), who had not yet been rendered to CIA custody and therefore not yet subjected to the CIA's enhanced interrogation techniques, identified Abu Yusef and Abu Adil as potential U.K.-based Heathrow operatives. RBS described how the two English-speaking "al-Qa'ida suicide operatives" were dispatched to the United Kingdom by KSM. RBS provided a detailed description of the two potential operatives, as well as their travel. (*See* CIA ███ ███) KSM was captured on March 1, 2003. The CIA's June 2013 Response nonetheless asserts that "KSM also was responsible for helping us identify two potential operatives—known only as Abu Yusef and Abu Adil— whom al-Qa'ida had deployed to the United Kingdom by early 2002 and whom KSM wanted to tap for a role in a future Heathrow operation." U.K. investigative efforts led to the identification of Abu Yusef, who then identified Abu Adil—who was already an investigative target of the U.K. government. In February 2004, the CIA reported that no CIA detainee was able to identify a photograph of Abu Yusif. *See* ALEC ███ (262236Z FEB 04).
1678. DIRECTOR ███ (172132Z OCT 02).
1679. *See* section of this summary and Volume II on the "Capture of Ramzi bin al-Shibh." The CIA's June 2013 Response states that "the information provided by Abu Zubaydah played a key role in the capture of Ramzi Bin al-Shibh." As described in the "Capture of Ramzi bin al-Shibh" in this summary and in greater detail in Volume II, Ramzi bin al-Shibh was not captured as a result of information acquired during or after the use of the CIA's enhanced interrogation techniques against Abu Zubaydah.
1680. *See* section of this summary and Volume II on the Capture of Khalid Shaykh Mohammad (KSM). The CIA's June 2013 Response acknowledges that "[b]y all accounts, KSM's arrest was the action that most disrupted the [Heathrow] plot." The CIA's June 2013 Response asserts, however, that "[Abu] Zubaydah's reporting also contributed to KSM's arrest." As described in the "Capture of KSM" in this summary and in more detail in Volume II, the capture of KSM was not attributable to any information obtained from the CIA's Detention and Interrogation Program.
1681. As described in the section of this summary related to the "Karachi Plot(s)" and in more detail in Volume II, information from CIA detainees played no role in the arrests of Ammar al-Baluchi or Khallad bin Attash.
1682. *See* series of emails dated March 22, 2006, with the subject line, "RE: Abu Adel NTB Coord: Please Respond by 14:00 Today (3/22). *See also* series of emails dated March 22, 2006, with the subject line, "RE: Abu Adel NTB Coord: Please Respond by 14:00 Today (3/22).
1683. DIRECTOR ███ ███.
1684. Among other documents, *see* DIRECTOR ███ (172132Z OCT 02).
1685. *See* CIA WASHINGTON DC ███ (122310Z MAR 03); ███ 10883 (182127Z MAR 03); ███ ███ 10828 (151310Z MAR 03); ███ 11717 (201722Z MAY 03); ███ 10778 (121549Z MAR 03).
1686. *See* email from: [REDACTED]; to: ███; cc: ███, ███; subject: "KSM on Heathrow"; date: May 20, 2003, at 03:44 PM.
1687. ███ 222939 (031541Z JUL 04).
1688. ███ 222939 (031541Z JUL 04).
1689. In March 2003, after Ramzi bin al-Shibh had been rendered to CIA custody and subjected to the CIA's enhanced interrogation techniques, CIA officers wrote that they did "not believe [Ramzi] bin al-Shibh" was

"being completely honest" about potential Heathrow operatives. (*See* ALEC ▇▇▇ ▇▇▇▇▇▇ ▇.) A June 2003 CIA cable states that "KSM, Ammar, and Khallad remain loathe to reveal details of the Heathrow plot," and that the CIA believed the detainees were withholding information that could lead to the capture of Abu Talha al-Pakistani, noting specifically that the CIA detainees had "so far clung to such information" and "deflected questions." By this time KSM, Ammar al-Baluchi and Khallad bin Attash had all been rendered to CIA custody and subjected to the CIA's enhanced interrogation techniques. See ALEC ▇ ▇▇▇ (172242Z JUN 03) and Volume III for additional information.

1690. ALEC ▇▇▇▇ (161821Z JUL 03).

1691. ▇▇▇▇ 10787 (130716Z MAR 03). As described, the CIA represented that KSM "first repeatedly denied there was any other target than the airport," and "[o]nly after the repeated lawful use of EITs did [KSM] stop lying and admit that the sketch of a beam labeled Canary Wharf in his notebook was in fact an illustration that KSM the engineer drew himself in order to show another AQ operative that the beams in the Wharf—like those in the World Trade Center—would likely melt and collapse the building, killing all inside" (*See* CIA memorandum to the CIA Inspector General from James Pavitt, CIA's Deputy Director for Operations, dated February 27, 2004, with the subject line, "Comments to Draft IG Special Review, 'Counterterrorism Detention and Interrogation Program' (2003-7123-IG)," Attachment, "Successes of CIA's Counterterrorism Detention and Interrogation Activities," dated February 24, 2004). As described, KSM discussed the sketch the first time it was shown to him. *See* ▇▇▇▇ 10787 (130716Z MAR 03).

1692. *See* ▇▇▇▇ 14420 ▇▇▇▇▇▇ ALEC ▇▇▇▇ (192314Z MAY 03); ▇▇▇ ▇▇▇ 11717 (201222Z MAY 03 ▇▇▇▇▇ 12141 (272231Z JUN 03); ▇▇▇▇▇ 10798 (131816Z MAR 03), disseminated as ▇▇▇ ▇▇▇▇▇. The CIA's June 2013 Response asserts that Abu Talha was "the individual managing the [Heathrow] plot." Contrary to CIA assertions, CIA records indicate that Abu Talha served as an assistant to Ammar al-Baluchi and KSM and played no leadership or managerial role in the plotting. KSM reported that Abu Talha's "primary skill [was] his ability to gather information," and that Abu Talha would not have been able to take over the Heathrow plotting after the arrest of Ammar al-Baluchi and Khallad bin Attash, "stress[ing] that Talha was not well trained or particularly well connected to al-Qa'ida," did not know all of the components of the Heathrow plotting, and had no links to the unwitting Saudi operatives KSM was considering using in the plotting. KSM stated that after the arrest of Ammar al-Baluchi and Khallad bin Attash, Abu Talha "would have known that the plot was compromised and over." (*See* ▇▇▇▇▇ 12141 (272231Z JUN 03); ▇▇▇▇▇ 20525 (141731Z FEB 04). For additional information on the two potential Saudi Arabia-based operatives, Ayyub and Azmari, who were investigative targets of a foreign government prior to detainee reporting, unwitting of the Heathrow plotting, and assessed by the CIA to have been killed or detained as a result of terrorist activity unrelated to the aforementioned plotting, *see* Volume II.). The CIA's June 2013 Response further states that "CIA lacked reporting on Abu Talha prior to March 2003 and first learned of his specific role in the plot from debriefing KSM." A review of CIA records found that on March 6, 2003, prior to any reporting from KSM or any other CIA detainee, Majid Khan, in foreign government custody, discussed Ammar al-Baluchi's Karachi-based assistant, "Talha." Majid Khan provided a phone number for Talha, and used that number at the request of his captors in an effort to locate and capture Ammar al-Baluchi through Talha. (*See* ▇▇▇▇▇ 13678 (070724Z MAR 03); ▇▇▇▇▇ 13710 (081218Z MAR 03); ALEC ▇▇▇▇ (081830Z MAR 03); ▇ ▇▇▇▇ 13695 (080611Z MAR 03); ▇▇▇▇▇ 11092 ▇▇▇▇▇▇▇▇) Ammar al-Baluchi, when he was in foreign government custody, provided adescription of Talha, whom he called "Suliman," and stated that he had dispatched Talha, aka Suliman, to the United Kingdom to identify operatives "suitable for hijacking or suicide operations." Ammar al-Baluchi also identified an email address used by Talha. (*See* ▇▇▇▇▇ 14291 (021645Z May 03); ▇▇▇▇▇ 14478 ▇▇▇▇ ▇▇; ▇▇▇▇ 14420 ▇▇▇▇▇; ▇▇▇▇ 14304 ▇▇▇▇▇; ALEC ▇▇▇ (142334Z May 03).) As KSM had not yet mentioned Abu Talha, Ammar al-Baluchi's reporting prompted Deputy Chief of ALEC Station ▇▇▇ ▇▇▇ to note that KSM could be in trouble very soon." (*See* email from: ▇▇▇▇▇; to: ▇▇▇ ▇▇▇, ▇▇▇▇▇, ▇▇▇▇▇, [REDACTED], [REDACTED]; subject: action detainee branch Re: ammar and KSM).) In the context of the U.K. Urban Targets Plot, the CIA's June 2013 – Response states: "Abu Talha's arrest – a case CIA frequently cited as a success of the detainee program – would not have happened if not for reporting from CIA-held detainees." As described elsewhere in this summary, and in greater detail in Volume II, CIA records do not support this statement.

1693. DIRECTOR ▇▇▇▇ (241921Z MAR 02).

1694. Among other news sources, *see* "The Secret Mastermind Behind the Bali Horror," *The Observer,* 19 October 2002.

1695. Italics included in CIA Memorandum to the Office of Legal Counsel, entitled, "Effectiveness of the CIA Counterterrorist Interrogation Techniques," from March 2, 2005.

1696. From 2003 through 2009, the CIA's representations regarding the effectiveness of the CIA's enhanced interrogation techniques provided a specific set of examples of terrorist plots "disrupted" and terrorists captured that the CIA attributed to information obtained from the use of its enhanced interrogation techniques.

CIA representations further asserted that the intelligence obtained from the use of the CIA's enhanced interrogation techniques was unique, otherwise unavailable, and resulted in "saved lives." Among other CIA representations, see: (1) CIA representations in the Department of Justice Office of Legal Counsel Memorandum, dated May 30, 2005, which relied on a series of highly specific CIA representations on the type of intelligence acquired from the use of the CIA's enhanced interrogation techniques to assess their legality. The CIA representations referenced by the OLC include that the use of the CIA's enhanced interrogation techniques was "necessary" to obtain "critical," "vital," and "otherwise unavailable actionable intelligence" that was "essential" for the U.S. government to "detect and disrupt" terrorist threats. The OLC memorandum further states that "[the CIA] ha[s] informed [the OLC] that the CIA believes that this program is largely responsible for preventing a subsequent attack within the United States." (*See* Memorandum for John A. Rizzo, Senior Deputy General Counsel, Central Intelligence Agency, from Steven G. Bradbury, Principal Deputy Assistant Attorney General, Office of Legal Counsel, May 30, 2005, Re: Application of United States Obligations Under Article 16 of the Convention Against Torture to Certain Techniques that May Be Used in the Interrogation of High Value al Qaeda Detainees.) (2) CIA representations in the Department of Justice Office of Legal Counsel Memorandum dated July 20, 2007, which also relied on CIA representations on the type of intelligence acquired from the use of the CIA's enhanced interrogation techniques. Citing CIA documents and the President's September 6, 2006, speech describing the CIA's interrogation program (which was based on CIA-provided information), the OLC memorandum states: "The CIA interrogation program— and, in particular, its use of enhanced interrogation techniques—is intended to serve this paramount interest [security of the Nation] by producing substantial quantities of otherwise unavailable intelligence. . . . As the President explained [on September 6, 2006], 'by giving us information about terrorist plans we could not get anywhere else, the program has saved innocent lives.'" (*See* Memorandum for John A. Rizzo, Acting General Counsel, Central Intelligence Agency, from Steven G. Bradbury, Principal Deputy Assistant Attorney General, Office of Legal Counsel, July 20, 2007, Re: Application of the War Crimes Act, the Detainee Treatment Act, and Common Article 3 of the Geneva Conventions to Certain Techniques that May Be Used by the CIA in the Interrogation of High Value al Qaeda Detainees.) (3) CIA briefings for members of the National Security Council in July and September 2003 represented that "the use of Enhanced Techniques of one kind or another had produced significant intelligence information that had, in the view of CIA professionals, saved lives," and warned policymakers that "[t]ermination of this program will result in loss of life, possibly extensive." (*See* August 5, 2003 Memorandum for the Record from Scott Muller, Subject: Review of Interrogation Program on 29 July 2003; Briefing slides, CIA Interrogation Program, July 29, 2003; September 4, 2003, CIA Memorandum for the Record, Subject: Member Briefing; and September 26, 2003, Memorandum for the Record from Muller, Subject: CIA Interrogation Program.) (4) The CIA's response to the Office of Inspector General draft Special Review of the CIA program, which asserts: "Information [the CIA] received . . . as a result of the lawful use of enhanced interrogation techniques ('EITs') has almost certainly saved countless American lives inside the United States and abroad. The evidence points clearly to the fact that without the use of such techniques, we and our allies would [have] suffered major terrorist attacks involving hundreds, if not thousands, of casualties." (*See* Memorandum for: Inspector General; from: James Pavitt, Deputy Director for Operations; subject: re (S) Comments to Draft IG Special Review, "Counterterrorism Detention and Interrogation Program" 2003-7123-IG; date: February 27, 2004; attachment: February 24, 2004, Memorandum re Successes of CIA's Counterterrorism Detention and Interrogation Activities.) (5) CIA briefing documents for CIA Director Leon Panetta in February 2009, which state that the "CIA assesses that the RDI program worked and the [enhanced interrogation] techniques were effective in producing foreign intelligence," and that "[m]ost, if not all, of the timely intelligence acquired from detainees in this program would not have been discovered or reported by other means." (*See* CIA briefing documents for Leon Panetta, entitled, "Tab 9: DCIA Briefing on RDI Program- 18FEB.2009" and graphic attachment, "Key Intelligence and Reporting Derived from Abu Zubaydah and Khalid Shaykh Muhammad (KSM)," including "DCIA Briefing on RDI Program" agenda, CIA document "EITs and Effectiveness," with associated documents, "Key Intelligence Impacts Chart: Attachment (AZ and KSM)," "Background on Key Intelligence Impacts Chart: Attachment," and "supporting references," to include "Background on Key Captures and Plots Disrupted.") (6) CIA document faxed to the Senate Select Committee on Intelligence on March 18, 2009, entitled, "[SWIGERT] and [DUNBAR]," located in Committee databases at DTS #2009-1258, which provides a list of "some of the key captures and disrupted plots" that the CIA had attributed to the use of the CIA's enhanced interrogation techniques, and stating: "CIA assesses that most, if not all, of the timely intelligence acquired from detainees in this program would not have been discovered or reported by any other means." *See* Volume II for additional CIA representations asserting that the CIA's enhanced interrogation techniques enabled the CIA to obtain unique, otherwise unavailable intelligence that "saved lives."

1697. *See* May 2, 2006, Briefing for the Chief of Staff to the President: Briefing for Chief of Staff to the President Josh Bolten: CIA Rendition, Detention and Interrogation Programs.

1698. Italics added. *See* May 2, 2006, Briefing for Chief of Staff to the President Josh Bolten: CIA Rendition, Detention and Interrogation Programs. The CIA's June 2013 Response maintains that the chronology in this passage and similar representations are correct. The CIA's June 2013 Response describes the following as "standard language" and the CIA's "typical representation" of Hambali's capture: "KSM provided information about an al-Qa'ida operative, Majid Khan, who he was aware had recently been captured. KSM—possibly believing the detained operatives was 'talking' admitted to having tasked Majid with delivering a large sum of money to individuals working for another senior al-Qa'ida associate. In an example of how information from one detainee can be used in debriefing another detainee in a 'building block' process. *Khan—confronted with KSM's information about the money—acknowledged that he delivered the money to an operative named Zubair and provided Zubair's physical description and contact number*" (italics added). The CIA's June 2013 Response states that this chronology is "accurate." As detailed in this summary, and in greater detail in Volume II, this June 2013 CIA representation is inaccurate. Majid Khan—who was in foreign government custody—first provided information on the money exchange and Zubair, prior to any reporting from KSM.

1699. CIA, "Khalid Shaykh Muhammad: Preeminent Source On Al-Qa'ida," was authored by [REDACTED], CTC/UBLD/AQPO/AQLB.

1700. CIA fax to the Department of Justice, entitled, "█████, Materials on KSM and Abu Zubaydah. █████," dated 22 April 2005. For background on the intelligence product, *see* DTS #2004-3375.

1701. Italics added. CIA Directorate of Intelligence, "Khalid Shaykh Muhammad: Preeminent Source on Al-Qa'ida," dated July 13, 2004, faxed to the Department of Justice, April 22, 2005, entitled, "█████, Materials on KSM and Abu Zubaydah. █████." This report was widely disseminated in the Intelligence Community and provided to the Senate Select Committee on Intelligence on July 15, 2004.

1702. *See* www.washingtonpost.com/wp-srv/nation/documents/Khalid_Shayhk_Mohammad.pdf.

1703. *See* list of CIA prepared briefings and memoranda from 2003 through 2009 with representations on the effectiveness of the CIA's enhanced interrogation techniques referenced in this summary and described in detail in Volume II.

1704. Among other documents, *see* CIA Directorate of Intelligence, "Khalid Shaykh Muhammad: Preeminent Source on Al-Qa'ida," dated July 13, 2004, faxed the Department of Justice, April 22, 2005, fax entitled, "█████, Materials on KSM and Abu Zubaydah. █████." This Intelligence Assessment was widely disseminated in the Intelligence Community and provided to the Senate Select Committee on Intelligence on July 15, 2004. On March 31, 2009, former Vice President Cheney requested the declassification of this Intelligence Assessment, which was publicly released with redactions on August 24, 2009. *See also* CIA Memorandum for Steve Bradbury at Office of Legal Counsel, Department of Justice, dated March 2, 2005, from █████, █████ Legal Group, DCI Counterterrorist Center, subject "Effectiveness of the CIA Counterterrorist Interrogation Techniques" and Classified Statement for the Record, Senate Select Committee on Intelligence, provided by General Michael V. Hayden, Director, Central Intelligence Agency, 12 April 2007 (DTS #2007-1563).

1705. *See* intelligence chronology in Volume II for detailed information.

1706. *See* United States Court of Appeals, August Term, 2001, *U.S. v Ramzi Ahmed Yousef,* and DIRECTOR █████ (█████ JAN 02). *See also* █████ █████ CIA █████ MAR 02).

1707. December 15, 2001, CIA Briefing Document, "DCI Highlights." *See also* ALEC █████ (262150Z APR 02) and email from: REDACTED; to: REDACTED, █████, █████, █████, and others; subject: "Debriefing results of Omani al-Qa'ida cell leader yields further connections between possibly Khalid Shaykh Muhammed and the East Asia al-Qa'ida network"; date: April 16, 2002, at 9:56:34 AM. *See also* 9/11 Commission Report.

1708. *See* intelligence chronology in Volume II, including ALEC █████ (262150Z APR 02). *See also* email from: [REDACTED]; to [REDACTED], █████, █████, █████, and others; subject: "Debriefing results of Omani al-Qa'ida cell leader yields further connections between possibly Khalid Shaykh Muhammed and the East Asia al-Qa'ida network"; date: April 16, 2002, at 9:56:34 AM.

1709. DIRECTOR █████ (241921Z MAR 02).

1710. ALEC █████ (22150Z APR 02).

1711. ALEC █████ (041957Z JUN 02).

1712. █████. *See also* "Terror Informant for FBI Allegedly Targeted Agents," *Washington Post,* dated January 19, 2008, and Department of Justice documents on Mohammed Mansour Jabarah, including Jabarah's "Sentencing Memorandum."

1713. *See* section of this summary and Volume II on the "Information on the Facilitator That Led to the UBL Operation" for additional information on Abu Ahmad al-Kuwaiti. Masran bin Arshad was in the custody of the government of █████ at this time.

1714. DIRECTOR █████ (251938Z SEP 02); █████ 65903 █████ AUG 02); CIA █████ AUG 02); █████ 65903 (█████ AUG 02); █████ 65902 (█████ AUG 02).

1715. Among other open sources, *see* "The Secret Mastermind Behind the Bali Horror," *The Observer,* 19 October 2002.

1716. Among other open source reporting, *see* "The Sadness of Bali is the Sadness of the World," *The Strait Times,* dated November 16, 2002; "Jemaah Islamiyah Still Capable of Major Terrorist Attacks," Philippine *Headline News,* dated November 27, 2002; "Police Arrest 13 Linked to Bali Bombers, Uncovers Plot to Blow Up Bank," *AFP,* dated November 26, 2002; "Bali Friends Have Arabia Link," *New York Post,* dated December 2, 2002;

"Finger Is Pointed At Bomber," *AFP-Hong Kong*, dated November 26, 2002; and "Mastermind of Bali Bomb Arrested," *The Strait Times*, dated November 22, 2002.

1717. ALEC [REDACTED] (170117Z JAN 03). At this time open source reporting also placed Hambali in Thailand. See, for example, "FBI Report Pointed to Bali Bombing," *The Age*, dated January 23, 2003; "Thailand's Denial of Threat Fails to Convince," *AFP*, dated November 15, 2002; "We'll Hit You: Pre-Bali Alert," *Herald* (Australia), dated November 16, 2002; "JI Terror Group Still Major Threat Despite Arrests," *Agence France Presse (AFP)*, dated November 26, 2002; "Indonesia Arrests a Top Suspect in Southeast Asia Terror Network," *New York Times*, dated December 4, 2002; and "Inside the Bali Plot: A TIME Inquiry Unearths the Roots of the Bombings and Shows How the Masterminds Remain at Large," *Time Magazine*, dated December 9, 2002.

1718. The CIA's June 2013 Response acknowledges that the CIA "had some other information linking Zubair to al-Qa'ida's Southeast Asia network," but states "that it was KSM's information that caused us to focus on [Zubair] as an inroad to Hambali." The CIA's June 2013 Response further asserts: "KSM provided information on an al-Qa'ida operative named Zubair, we shared this information with Thai authorities, they detained Zubair, and he gave actionable intelligence information that helped us identify Hambali's location." This statement in the CIA's June 2013 Response is inaccurate. On October 25, 2013, the CIA acknowledged the inaccuracy. Confirming information in the Committee Study, the CIA stated that an additional review of CIA records by the CIA found that "No, KSM did not name Zubair in his debriefings."

1719. In May 2002, prior to the application of the CIA's enhanced interrogation techniques, Abu Zubaydah identified "Zubair" as a Malaysian national who was associated with KSM and who could be used by KSM to conduct attacks in Thailand. According to Abu Zubaydah, Zubair also "assisted Abu Zubaydah in obtaining passports from a printer facility in either Thailand or Malaysia." (*See* DIRECTOR [REDACTED] (271937Z MAY 02) [REDACTED].) In June 2002, Abu Zubaydah told an FBI interrogator that he sent a Canadian who sought to "help defend Muslims" in Indonesia to a Malaysian named Abu Zubair. (*See* [REDACTED] 10475 (141605Z JUN 02).) In July 2002, a U.S. military detainee stated that "Zubair" was a member of the Jemaah Islamiyah and was connected to Jemaah Islamiyah senior leaders. (*See* [REDACTED] 11691 (141712Z JUL 02). For other intelligence identifying "Zubair" as one of several individuals suspected of being connected to the October 2002 Bali bombings, *see* [REDACTED] 95612 (290615Z OCT 02); DIRECTOR [REDACTED] (202057Z OCT 02); and DIRECTOR [REDACTED] [REDACTED].) Open source news reports highlighted links between senior al-Qa'ida leadership—including KSM—and Jemaah Islamiyah in the context of the Bali bombings. Hambali continued to be identified as a potential mastermind of the bombing— and likely residing in Thailand. These same reports identified a Malaysian named "Zubair" as one of three individuals sought by security officials for Hambali's Bali bombings. Among other open source reporting, *see* "The Secret Mastermind Behind the Bali Horror," *The Observer*, 19 October 2002; "The Sadness of Bali is the Sadness of the World," *The Strait Times*, dated November 16, 2002; "Jemaah Islamiyah Still Capable of Major Terrorist Attacks," *Philippine Headline News*, dated November 27, 2002; "Police Arrest 13 Linked to Bali Bombers, Uncovers Plot to Blow Up Bank," *AFP*, dated November 26, 2002; "Bali Friends Have Arabia Link," *New York Post*, dated December 2, 2002; "Finger Is Pointed At Bomber," *AFP-Hong Kong*, dated November 26, 2002; "Inside the Bali Plot: A TIME Inquiry Unearths the Roots of the Bombings and Shows How the Masterminds Remain at Large," *Time Magazine*, dated December 9, 2002; and "Mastermind of Bali Bomb Arrested," *The Strait Times*, dated November 22, 2002. *See* intelligence chronology in Volume II for additional detailed information.

1720. *See* [REDACTED] 89601 (042006Z MAR 03).

1721. [REDACTED] 13678 (070724Z MAR 03). According to CIA records, "a [foreign government officer] talked quietly to [Majid Khan] alone for about ten minutes before the interview began and was able to establish an excellent level of rapport. The first hour and [a] half of the interview was a review of bio-data and information previously [reported]. When [foreign government interrogators] started putting pressure on [Majid Khan] by pulling apart his story about his 'honeymoon' in Bangkok and his attempt to rent an apartment, safehouse, for his cousin [Mansoor Maqsood, aka Iqbal, aka Talha, aka Moeen, aka Habib], at 1400, [Majid Khan] slumped in his chair and said he would reveal everything to officers . . . ."

1722. [REDACTED] 13678 (070724 MAR 03). Records indicate that this information was also disseminated in FBI channels. *See* ALEC [REDACTED] [REDACTED] [REDACTED]. For previous intelligence on Zubair's physical description, *see* [REDACTED] [REDACTED] 11715 [REDACTED] [REDACTED]. *See also* DIRECTOR [REDACTED] [REDACTED] [REDACTED]. *See* intelligence chronology in Volume II for detailed information.

1723. [REDACTED] 81553 (101010Z MAR 03). The request was approved by CIA Headquarters on March 12, 2003 (DIRECTOR [REDACTED] (March 12, 2003)).

1724. [REDACTED] 10755 (111455Z MAR 03). *See also* DIRECTOR [REDACTED] (112152Z MAR 03). ALEC Station had sent interrogators at the CIA's DETENTION SITE BLUE at least two "requirements" cables with information to use in the interrogation of KSM specially about Hambali and KSM's money transfers to Hambali. *See* ALEC [REDACTED] (072345Z MAR 03); ALEC [REDACTED] (090015Z MAR 03). KSM was rendered to CIA custody on March [REDACTED], 2003, and immediately subjected to the CIA's enhanced interrogation techniques through March 25, 2003.

1725. KSM was told the CIA had "stacks and stacks of emails," and that CIA officers were going to do a "test of his honesty" by asking him a series of questions. *See* [REDACTED] 10865 (171648Z MAR 03).

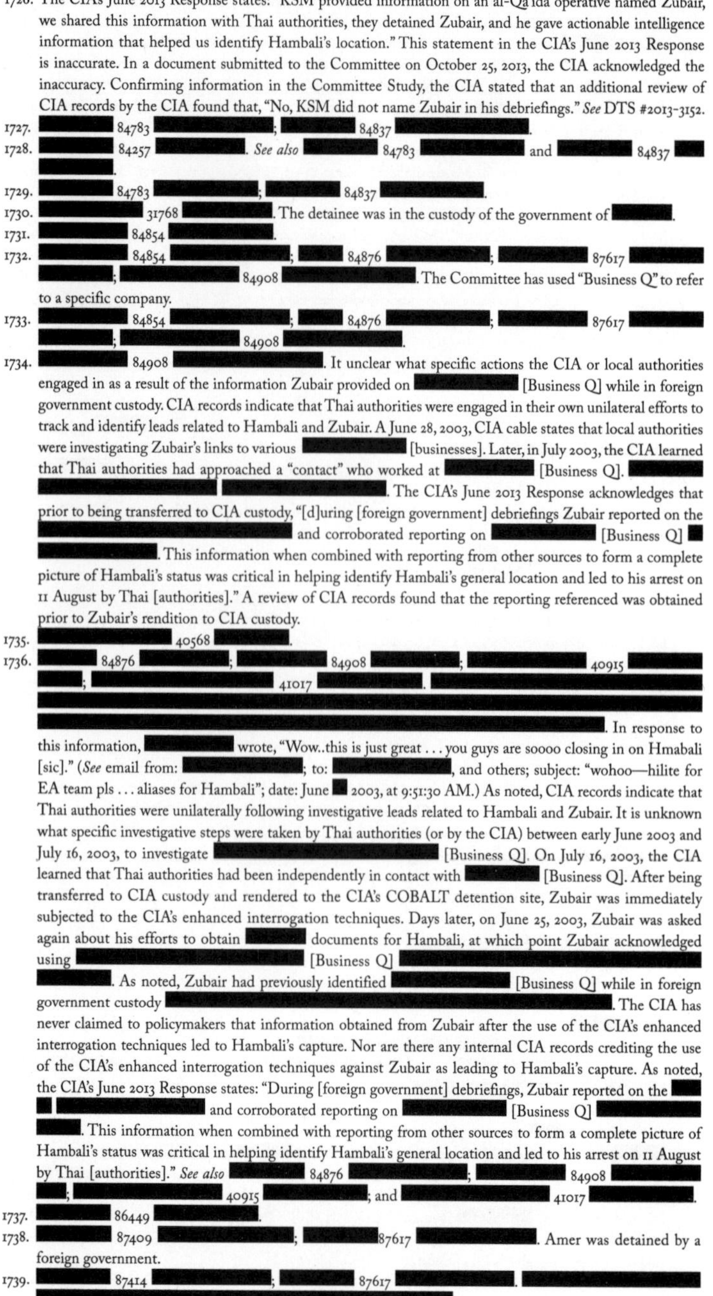

1726. The CIA's June 2013 Response states: "KSM provided information on an al-Qa'ida operative named Zubair, we shared this information with Thai authorities, they detained Zubair, and he gave actionable intelligence information that helped us identify Hambali's location." This statement in the CIA's June 2013 Response is inaccurate. In a document submitted to the Committee on October 25, 2013, the CIA acknowledged the inaccuracy. Confirming information in the Committee Study, the CIA stated that an additional review of CIA records by the CIA found that, "No, KSM did not name Zubair in his debriefings." *See* DTS #2013-3152.

1727. 84783 ; 84837 .

1728. 84257 . *See also* 84783 and 84837 .

1729. 84783 ; 84837 .

1730. 31768 . The detainee was in the custody of the government of .

1731. 84854 .

1732. 84854 ; 84876 ; 87617 ; 84908 . The Committee has used "Business Q" to refer to a specific company.

1733. 84854 ; 84876 ; 87617 ; 84908 .

1734. 84908 . It unclear what specific actions the CIA or local authorities engaged in as a result of the information Zubair provided on [Business Q] while in foreign government custody. CIA records indicate that Thai authorities were engaged in their own unilateral efforts to track and identify leads related to Hambali and Zubair. A June 28, 2003, CIA cable states that local authorities were investigating Zubair's links to various [businesses]. Later, in July 2003, the CIA learned that Thai authorities had approached a "contact" who worked at [Business Q]. . The CIA's June 2013 Response acknowledges that prior to being transferred to CIA custody, "[d]uring [foreign government] debriefings Zubair reported on the and corroborated reporting on [Business Q] . This information when combined with reporting from other sources to form a complete picture of Hambali's status was critical in helping identify Hambali's general location and led to his arrest on 11 August by Thai [authorities]." A review of CIA records found that the reporting referenced was obtained prior to Zubair's rendition to CIA custody.

1735. 40568 .

1736. 84876 ; 84908 ; 40915 ; 41017 . . In response to this information, wrote, "Wow..this is just great . . . you guys are soooo closing in on Hmabali [sic]." (*See* email from: ; to: , and others; subject: "wohoo—hilite for EA team pls . . . aliases for Hambali"; date: June 2003, at 9:51:30 AM.) As noted, CIA records indicate that Thai authorities were unilaterally following investigative leads related to Hambali and Zubair. It is unknown what specific investigative steps were taken by Thai authorities (or by the CIA) between early June 2003 and July 16, 2003, to investigate [Business Q]. On July 16, 2003, the CIA learned that Thai authorities had been independently in contact with [Business Q]. After being transferred to CIA custody and rendered to the CIA's COBALT detention site, Zubair was immediately subjected to the CIA's enhanced interrogation techniques. Days later, on June 25, 2003, Zubair was asked again about his efforts to obtain documents for Hambali, at which point Zubair acknowledged using [Business Q] . As noted, Zubair had previously identified [Business Q] while in foreign government custody . The CIA has never claimed to policymakers that information obtained from Zubair after the use of the CIA's enhanced interrogation techniques led to Hambali's capture. Nor are there any internal CIA records crediting the use of the CIA's enhanced interrogation techniques against Zubair as leading to Hambali's capture. As noted, the CIA's June 2013 Response states: "During [foreign government] debriefings, Zubair reported on the and corroborated reporting on [Business Q] . This information when combined with reporting from other sources to form a complete picture of Hambali's status was critical in helping identify Hambali's general location and led to his arrest on 11 August by Thai [authorities]." *See also* 84876 ; 84908 ; 40915 ; and 41017 .

1737. 86449 .

1738. 87409 ; 87617 . Amer was detained by a foreign government.

1739. 87414 ; 87617 . .

1740. *See* [REDACTED] 9515 [REDACTED]; [REDACTED] 87617 [REDACTED]; [REDACTED] 87414 [REDACTED] [REDACTED]; and [REDACTED] "Hambali Capture." Lillie was later rendered to CIA custody.
1741. Lillie had not yet been rendered to CIA custody. CIA Oral History Program Documenting Hambali capture, interview of [REDACTED], interviewed by [REDACTED] on November 28, 2005.
1742. [REDACTED] 1241 [REDACTED].
1743. [REDACTED] 1242 (050744Z SEP 06); 2215 (051248Z SEP 06).
1744. The CIA's June 2013 Response states: "our review showed that the *Study* failed to include examples of important information acquired from detainees that CIA cited more frequently and prominently in its representations than several of the cases the authors chose to include." This is inaccurate. The CIA's June 2013 Response provided three examples: the "Gulf shipping plot" (which is addressed in the full Committee Study and in this summary in the context of the interrogation of Abd al-Rahim al-Nashiri), "learning important information about al-Qa'ida's anthrax plotting and the role of Yazid Sufaat" (which is addressed in the full Committee Study and in this summary in the context of the interrogation of KSM), and "the detention of Abu Talha al-Pakistani" (which is addressed in the full Committee Study and in this summary in the section on the "Thwarting of the United Kingdom Urban Targets Plot and the Capture of Dhiren Barot, aka Issa al-Hindi.").
1745. For example, in the September 6, 2006, speech validated by the CIA, President George W. Bush stated that: "[Abu] Zubaydah disclosed Khalid Sheikh Mohammed, or KSM, was the mastermind behind the 9/11 attacks and used the alias Mukhtar. This was a vital piece of the puzzle that helped our intelligence community pursue KSM." *See also* CIA document dated July 16, 2006, entitled, "DRAFT Potential Public Briefing of CIA's High-Value Terrorist Interrogations Program," and "CIA Validation of Remarks on Detainee Policy" drafts supporting the September 6, 2006, speech by President George W. Bush. *See also* unclassified Office of the Director of National Intelligence release, entitled, "Summary of the High Value Terrorist Detainee Program," as well as CIA classified Statement for the Record, Senate Select Committee on Intelligence, provided by General Michael V. Hayden, Director, Central Intelligence Agency, 12 April 2007 (DTS #2007-1563).
1746. CIA classified Statement for the Record, Senate Select Committee on Intelligence, provided by General Michael V. Hayden, Director, Central Intelligence Agency, 12 April 2007; and accompanying Senate Select Committee on Intelligence hearing transcript for April 12, 2007, entitled, "Hearing on Central Intelligence Agency Detention and Interrogation Program." (*See* DTS #2007-1563 and DTS #2007-3158.) This testimony contradicted statements made in 2002 to the Joint Inquiry by [REDACTED], in which she indicated that an operative arrested in February 2002 in [REDACTED], prior to the capture of Abu Zubaydah, "provided proof... that KSM was a senior al-Qa'ida terrorist planner." (*See* interview by the Joint Inquiry of [REDACTED] [REDACTED], [REDACTED], [REDACTED], [REDACTED], [REDACTED]; subject: Khahd Shaykh Mohammad (KSM); date: 12 August 2002 (DTS #2002-4630).).
1747. Memorandum for John A. Rizzo, Senior Deputy General Counsel, Central Intelligence Agency, from Steven G. Bradbury, Principal Deputy Assistant Attorney General, Office of Legal Counsel, May 30, 2005, Re: Application of United States Obligations Under Article 16 of the Convention Against Torture to Certain Techniques that Maybe Used in the Interrogation of High Value Al Qaeda Detainees.
1748. *See* CIA Briefing Notes on the Value of Detainee Reporting, faxed to the OLC in April 2005. The "Briefing Notes" state: "Within months of his arrest, Abu Zubaydah provided details about al-Qa'ida's organization structure, key operatives, and modus operandi. It also was Abu Zubaydah, early in his detention, who identified KSM as the mastermind of 9/11." As described in detail in Volume II, this CIA document did not specifically reference the CIA's enhanced interrogation techniques; however, it was provided to the OLC to support the OLC's legal analysis of the CIA's enhanced interrogation techniques. The document included most of the same examples the CIA had previously provided as examples of the effectiveness of the CIA's enhanced interrogation techniques. There are no records to indicate that the CIA, in reviewing draft versions of the OLC memorandum, sought to correct the inaccurate OLC statements.
1749. Memorandum for John A. Rizzo, Senior Deputy General Counsel, Central Intelligence Agency, from Steven G. Bradbury, Principal Deputy Assistant Attorney General, Office of Legal Counsel, May 30, 2005, Re: Application of United States Obligations Under Article 16 of the Convention Against Torture to Certain Techniques that May be Used in the Interrogation of High Value Al Qaeda Detainees.
1750. "DCIA Talking Points: Waterboard 06 November 2007," and supporting materials, dated November 6, 2007, with the notation the document was "sent to DCIA Nov. 6 in preparation for POTUS meeting."
1751. Joint Inquiry Into the Intelligence Community Activities Before and After the Terrorist Attacks of September 11, 2001, Report of the Senate Select Committee on Intelligence and the House Permanent Select Committee on Intelligence, December 2002, pp. 325–331 (DTS #2002-5162); CIA Office of the Inspector General Report on CIA Accountability With Respect to the 9/11 Attacks, June 2005, pp. xi, 100–126 (DTS #2005-3477).
1752. Joint Inquiry Into the Intelligence Community Activities Before and After the Terrorist Attacks of September 11, 2001, Report of the Senate Select Committee on Intelligence and the House Permanent Select Committee on Intelligence, December 2002, p. 329 (DTS #2002-5162).
1753. DIRECTOR [REDACTED] ([REDACTED] SEP 98), disseminated as [REDACTED]; Office of the Inspector General Report on CIA Central Intelligence Agency Accountability Regarding Findings and

Conclusions of the Report of the Joint Inquiry Into Intelligence Community Activities Before and After the Terrorist Attacks of September 11, 2001 (DTS #2005-3477), pp. 105–107.

1754. The 9/11 Commission Report; Final Report of the National Commission on Terrorist Attacks Upon the United States, p. 277.

1755. ████ 64626 (131843Z SEP 01); ████ 64627 (131843Z SEP 01).

1756. CIA Office of the Inspector General Report on CIA Accountability With Respect to the 9/11 Attacks, June 2005, p. 113 (DTS #2005-3477).

1757. Email from: ████; to: ████; cc: ████, ████, [REDACTED], ████, [REDACTED]; subject: Re: RAMZI LEADS…; date: September 15, 2001, at 5:04:38 AM.

1758. CIA CTC internal email from: [REDACTED]; to multiple [REDACTED]; date: October 16, 2001, at 09:34:48 AM.

1759. ████; CIA ████ ████; ████; ████ 16218 ████.

1760. DIRECTOR ████ ████. The cable added "KSM is an ally of Usama bin Ladin and has been reported at facilities clearly associated with UBL."

1761. DIR████ ████ NOV 01). The cable referenced reporting that KSM, along with one other individual, "were the masterminds of the 11 September attacks."

1762. DIR ████JAN 02).

1763. For example, in the September 6, 2006, speech validated by the CIA that publicly acknowledged the CIA's Detention and Interrogation Program, President George W. Bush stated that: "[Abu] Zubaydah disclosed Khalid Shaykh Mohammed, or KSM, was the mastermind behind the 9/11 attacks and used the alias Mukhtar. This was a vital piece of the puzzle that helped our intelligence community pursue KSM."

1764. "DCIA Talking Points: Waterboard 06 November 2007," and supporting materials, dated November 6, 2007 with the notation the document was "sent to DCIA Nov. 6 in preparation for POTUS meeting."

1765. *See* Volume II, the Abu Zubaydah detainee review in Volume III, and Federal Bureau of Investigation documents pertaining "to the interrogation of detainee Zayn Al Abideen Abu Zabaidah" provided to the Senate Select Committee on Intelligence by cover letter dated July 20, 2010 (DTS #2010-2939).

1766. ████ 93972 (281153Z AUG 01). *See also* the 9/11 Commission Report: Final Report of the National Commission on Terrorist Attacks Upon the United States, p. 277. The cable was directed to the CIA's UBL Station, where it was viewed by the chief of Station and chief of targeting, and to the analytic unit responsible for UBL, where two analysts saw it. (*See* Office of the Inspector General Report on CIA Central Intelligence Agency Accountability Regarding Findings and Conclusions of the Report of the Joint Inquiry Into Intelligence Community Activities Before and After the Terrorist Attacks of September 11, 2001 (DTS #2005-3477), p. 112.) The CIA's June 2013 Response states that "[w]e continue to assess that Abu Zubaydah's information was a critical piece of intelligence." The CIA's June 2013 Response acknowledges the August 28, 2001, cable identifying KSM as "Mukhtar," but states that CIA officers "overlooked" and "simply missed" the cable.

1767. *See* President George W. Bush, Speech on Terrorism and the CIA's Detention and Interrogation Program, September 6, 2006; and CIA Validation of Remarks on Detainee Policy, Wednesday, September 6, 2006, Draft #3 (validating speech received on August 29, 2006); email from: [REDACTED]; to ████ ████; cc: [REDACTED], [REDACTED], [REDACTED], [REDACTED], [REDACTED], [REDACTED] [REDACTED], [REDACTED], [REDACTED], [REDACTED], [REDACTED], [REDACTED], ████, [REDACTED]; subject: "Speechwriter's Questions on Monday"; date: September 5, 2006, at 10:30:32 AM.

1768. Italics added. As described in this summary and in the Abu Zubaydah detainee review in Volume III, this statement was inaccurate. Abu Zubaydah provided information on al-Qa'ida activities, plans, capabilities, and relationships, in addition to information on its leadership structure, including personalities, decision-making processes, training, and tactics prior to, during, and after the utilization of the CIA's enhanced interrogation techniques. Abu Zubaydah's inability to provide information on the next attack in the United States and operatives in the United States was the basis for CIA representations that Abu Zubaydah was "uncooperative" and the CIA's determination that Abu Zubaydah required the use of the CIA's enhanced interrogation techniques to become "compliant" and reveal the information the CIA believed he was withholding—the names of operatives in the United States or information to stop the next terrorist attack. At no point during or after the use of the CIA's enhanced interrogation techniques did Abu Zubaydah provide this type of information.

1769. Italics added. *See* President George W. Bush, Speech on Terrorism and the CIA's Detention and Interrogation Program, September 6, 2006; and CIA Validation of Remarks on Detainee Policy, Wednesday, September 6, 2006, Draft #3 (validating speech received on August 29, 2006); email from: [REDACTED]; to ████ ████, ████; cc: [REDACTED], [REDACTED], [REDACTED], [REDACTED], [REDACTED], [REDACTED] [REDACTED], [REDACTED], [REDACTED], [REDACTED], [REDACTED], [REDACTED], ████, [REDACTED]; subject: "Speechwriter's Questions on Monday"; date: September 5, 2006, at 10:30:32 AM.

1770. *See* email from: [REDACTED]; to [REDACTED], [REDACTED], Mark Mansfield, Paul Gimigliano, and others; subject: "Questions about Abu Zubaydah's Identification of KSM as 'Mukhtar'"; date: September 7, 2006. A September 7, 2006, article (published September 8, 2006) in the *New York Times,* by Mark Mazzetti, entitled, "Questions Raised About Bush's Primary Claims of Secret Detention System" included comments by CIA officials defending the assertions in the President's speech: "Mr. Bush described the interrogation techniques used on the C.I.A. prisoners as having been 'safe, lawful and effective,' and he asserted that torture had not been used. ...Mr. Bush also said it was the interrogation of Mr. Zubaydah that identified Mr. bin al-Shibh as an accomplice in the Sept. 11 attacks. American officials had identified Mr. bin al-Shibh's role in the attacks months before Mr. Zubaydah's capture. A December 2001 federal grand jury indictment of Zacarias Moussaoui, the so-called 20th hijacker, said that Mr. Moussaoui had received money from Mr. bin al-Shibh and that Mr. bin al-Shibh had shared an apartment with Mohamed Atta, the ringleader of the plot. A C.I.A. spokesman said Thursday [September 7, 2006] that the agency had vetted the president's speech and stood by its accuracy. ...[CIA] spokesman, Paul Gimigliano, said in a statement... 'Abu Zubaydah not only identified Ramzi Bin al-Shibh as a 9/11 accomplice—something that had been done before—he provided information that helped lead to his capture." For additional news accounts on this subject, *see* former CIA Director Michael Hayden's interview with the *New York Times* in 2009, in which former Director Hayden "disputed an article in the *New York Times* on Saturday [4/18/2009] that said Abu Zubaydah had revealed nothing new after being waterboarded, saying that he believed that after unspecified 'techniques' were used, Abu Zubaydah revealed information that led to the capture of another terrorist, Ramzi Binalshibh." *See* "Waterboarding Used 266 Times on 2 Suspects," *New York Times,* dated April 20, 2009.

1771. CIA Testimony of [REDACTED], Transcript, Senate Select Committee on Intelligence, February 14, 2007 (DTS #2007-1337). *See also* Memorandum to the Inspector General from James Pavitt, CIA's Deputy Director for Operations, dated February 27, 2004, with the subject line, "Comments to Draft IG Special Review, 'Counterterrorism Detention and Interrogation Program' (2003-7123-IG)," Attachment, "Successes of CIA's Counterterrorism Detention and Interrogation Activities," dated February 24, 2004. Pavitt states: "Abu Zubaydah – a master al-Qa'ida facilitator – was similarly arrogant and uncooperative before the lawful use of EITs. ...His information is *singularly unique* and valuable from an intelligence point of view, but it also has produced concrete results that have helped saved lives. His knowledge of al-Qa'ida lower-level facilitators, modus operandi and safehouses, which he shared with us *as a result of the use of EITs,* for example, played a *key role* in the ultimate capture of Ramzi Bin al-Shibh" (italics added).

1772. Among other records, *see* CIA [REDACTED] ([REDACTED] SEP 02) [REDACTED]; CIA [REDACTED] ([REDACTED] SEP 02) [REDACTED]; ALEC [REDACTED] (111551Z SEP 02).

1773. *See* additional information below, as well as the Abu Zubaydah detainee review in Volume III, and Federal Bureau of Investigation documents pertaining "to the interrogation of detainee Zayn Al Abideen Abu Zabaidah" provided to the Senate Select Committee on Intelligence by cover letter dated July 20, 2010 (DTS# 2010-2939). The CIA's June 2013 Response includes the following: "...the Study states that Abu Zubaydah 'provided similar information to FBI interrogators prior to the initiation of the CIA's enhanced interrogation techniques.' This is incorrect. Abu Zubaydah's unique information concerning his contact with Hassan Gul was collected on 20 August 2002, after he had been subjected to enhanced interrogation techniques." This assertion in the CIA's June 2013 Response contains several errors: First, as described, the statement in the December 13, 2012, Committee Study pertains to Abu Zubaydah's reporting on Ramzi bin al-Shibh, not Hassan Ghul. As detailed in this summary and in other areas of the full Committee Study, while Abu Zubaydah provided information on Ramzi bin al-Shibh after the use of the CIA's enhanced interrogation techniques, he provided similar information on bin al-Shibh to FBI interrogators prior to the use and approval of the CIA's enhanced interrogation techniques. Second, as detailed in the full Committee Study, Abu Zubaydah provided considerable information on Hassan Ghul prior to the use of the CIA's enhanced interrogation techniques. (Some of this reporting has been declassified; for example, *see* the 9/11 Commission Report, specifically the Staff Report, "9/11 and Terrorist Travel," which highlights reporting by Abu Zubaydah on Hassan Ghul that was disseminated by the CIA on June 20, 2002.) Third, in referencing information that Abu Zubaydah provided on Hassan Ghul on August 20, 2002, the CIA's June 2013 Response asserts that this was "unique information." The CIA's June 2013 Response states: "Abu Zubaydah stated that if he personally needed to reach Hassan Gul, he would contact [REDACTED] [a well-known associate of Hassan Ghul]. We provided this information to Pakistani authorities, who then interviewed [the well-known associate] and [REDACTED] [a specific family member of the well-known associate]—which ultimately led them to an apartment linked to Gul." The CIA's June 2013 Response adds that the "unique information concerning his contact with Hassan Gul was collected on 20 August 2002, after [Abu Zubaydah] had been subjected to enhanced interrogation techniques." CIA records indicate, however, that the information described in the CIA's Response was not unique. Pakistani authorities had raided the home and interviewed [REDACTED] [the same well-known associate] more than a month earlier on July [REDACTED], 2002, based on similar reporting from a cooperating detainee in foreign government custody. The CIA had specific and detailed knowledge of this raid and the resulting interview of [REDACTED] [the well-known associate]. Pakistani authorities remained in contact

with [the well-known associate], the primary person interviewed, who was cooperative and sent to help Pakistani authorities identify a possible al-Qa'ida safe house—which the CIA noted was "extremely close to (if not an exact match)" for a safe house the FBI connected KSM to weeks earlier on June 18, 2002.

1774. DIRECTOR (271905Z MAY 02). *See* the Abu Zubaydah detainee review in Volume III for additional details.

1775. Federal Bureau of Investigation documents pertaining "to the interrogation of detainee Zayn Al Abideen Abu Zabaidah" and provided to the Senate Select Committee on Intelligence by cover letter dated July 20, 2010 (DTS #2010-2939).

1776. Federal Bureau of Investigation documents pertaining "to the interrogation of detainee Zayn Al Abideen Abu Zabaidah" and provided to the Senate Select Committee on Intelligence by cover letter dated July 20, 2010 (DTS #2010-2939).

1777. 10428 (071058Z JUN 02).

1778. 10424 (070814Z JUN 02).

1779. 10487 (181656Z JUN 02).

1780. *See* Abu Zubaydah detainee review in Volume III for additional details.

1781. 10644 (201235Z AUG 02) and email from: [REDACTED]; to: and [REDACTED]; subject: "Re: So it begins." Date: August 4, 2002, at 09:45:09 AM.

1782. 10654 (211318Z AUG 02); 10656 (2113149Z AUG 02).

1783. 10654 (211318Z AUG 02); 10656 (2113149Z AUG 02).

1784. 10654 (211318Z AUG 02); 10656 (2113149Z AUG 02).

1785. DIRECTOR (261338Z AUG 02).

1786. 10654 (211318Z AUG 02); 10656 (211349Z AUG 02).

1787. ALEC (222334Z SEP 01); 92557 (15SEP01).

1788. ALEC (270132Z JUL 02).

1789. ALEC (270134Z JUL 02). *See also* 97470 (281317Z MAR 02) ("In November 1998, [Muhammad] Atta, [Ramzi] Binalshibh, and [Said] Bahaji moved into the 54 Marienstrasse apartment in Hamburg that became the hub of the Hamburg cell.").

1790. ALEC (270132Z JUL 02). *See also* 62533 (information from a foreign government concerning the al-Qa'ida suicide operatives portrayed on videotapes found in Afghanistan).

1791. ALEC (292345Z AUG 02); ALEC (111551Z SEP 02).

1792. ALEC (241447Z MAR 02).

1793. ALEC (261712Z MAR 02).

1794. 17369 (131519Z APR 02).

1795. 10091 (210959Z APR 02); 10102 (230707Z APR 02); 10144 (271949Z APR 02); 10271 (151654Z MAY 02); 1295 (JAN 04); 1308 (JAN 04).

1796. 10091 (210959Z APR 02); 10102 (230707Z APR 02); 10144 (271949Z APR 02); 10271 (151654Z MAY 02); ALEC (241447Z MAR 02).

1797. DIRECTOR (1012312Z MAY 02).

1798. 10487 (181656Z JUN 2).

1799. 11746 .

1800. 11336 MAY 02).

1801. 11746 .

1802. 11746 .

1803. 11755 .

1804. 11755 . Referenced cable is ALEC (181900Z JUN 02).

1805. 11755 .

1806. *See* references to prior acquisition of passport in 12151 (301107Z AUG 02).

1807. ALEC .

1808. As noted throughout this Study, CIA produced more than six million pages of material, including records detailing the interrogation of CIA detainees, as well as the disseminated intelligence derived from the interrogation of CIA detainees. The CIA did not provide—nor was it requested to provide—intelligence records that were unrelated to the CIA's Detention and Interrogation Program. In other words, this Study was completed without direct access to reporting from CIA HUMINT assets, foreign liaison assets, electronic intercepts, military detainee debriefings, law enforcement-derived information, and other methods of intelligence collection. Insomuch as this material is included in the analysis herein, it was provided by the CIA within the context of documents directly related to the CIA Detention and Interrogation Program. As such, there is likely significant intelligence related to the terrorist plots, terrorists captured, and other intelligence matters examined in this Study that is within the databases of the U.S. Intelligence Community, but which has not been identified or reviewed by the Committee for this Study.

1809. 10091 (210959Z APR 02); 1012 (230707Z APR 02); 10144 (271949Z APR 02); 10271 (151654Z MAY 02); ALEC (2414472 MAR 02).

1810. 10487 (181656Z JUN 02).

1811. 10644 (201235Z AUG 02) and email from: [REDACTED]; to: and [REDACTED]; subject: "Re: So it begins."; date: August 4, 2002, at 09:45:09 AM.

1812. ALEC (292345Z AUG 02).

1813. 11746 . The CIA's June 2013 Response highlights the following statement in the December 13, 2012, Committee Study: "It is possible that the sourcing for CIA claims that 'as a result of the use of EITs' Abu Zubaydah provided information that 'played a key role in the ultimate capture of Ramzi Bin al-Shibh,' are related to Abu Zubaydah's information indicating that Hassan Ghul could be located through [the well-known associate]." The CIA's June 2013 Response states: "It is true that Abu Zubaydah provided no information specifically on Bin al-Shibh's whereabouts, but as the Study explicitly acknowledges, he did provide information on another al-Qa'ida facilitator that prompted Pakistani action that netted Bin al-Shibh." The Committee could find no CIA records of the CIA ever making this claim externally, or internally within the CIA, prior to the CIA's June 2013 Response. Rather, as described, the CIA claimed both before and after the President's September 2006 speech that Abu Zubaydah provided information related to bin-al-Shibh that resulted in bin al-Shibh's capture. In an email from to and , dated September 7, 2006, states: "...AZ gave us information on his recent activities that –when added into other information—helped us track him." The CIA's June 2013 Response asserts that the information Abu Zubaydah provided—that Hassan Ghul could possibly be located through [a well-known associate of Hassan Ghul]—was "unique information" and that bin al-Shibh's "capture would not have occurred" "without Abu Zubaydah's information," which was collected "after he had been subjected to the enhanced interrogation techniques." As detailed in this summary, and in greater detail in Volume II, the statement provided by Abu Zubayah was not unique, but corroborative of information already collected and acted upon by government authorities.

1814. ALEC (292345Z AUG 02).

1815. 12148 (300601Z AUG 02).

1816. 12151 (301107Z AUG 02).

1817. 12207 (050524Z SEP 02).

1818. While it is unclear from CIA records how Pakistani authorities learned [the specific family member of the well-known associate] had returned home, [the well-known associate] had sought the help of Pakistani authorities in retrieving [the specific family member of the well-known associate]. Further, the CIA in early July 2002 had requested "technical surveillance" of [the well-known associate's] telephone, and CIA records indicate that Pakistani authorities were maintaining regular contact with [the well-known associate] after the initial July 2002 raid.

1819. 12249 (091259Z SEP 02).

1820. 12249 (091259Z SEP 02).

1821. 12249 (091259Z SEP 02).

1822. 12251 (SEP 02); CIA (SEP 02) .

1823. 12251 (SEP 02); CIA (SEP 02) .

1824. 12254 (100510Z SEP 02).

1825. 33363 (111226Z SEP 02).

1826. 12251 (SEP 02); CIA (SEP 02) .

1827. ALEC (111551Z SEP 02). The CIA's June 2013 Response states that Muhammad Ahmad Ghulam Rabbani, aka Abu Badr, provided the information on the "safe houses in Karachi." This is inaccurate. Multiple CIA records state this information was provided by Abu Badr's driver, Muhammad Madni, who was cooperating with Pakistani authorities and providing information for the raids.

1828. ALEC (101749Z SEP 02).

1829. ALEC (111551Z SEP 02).

1830. CIA (SEP 02).

1831. ALEC (130206Z SEP 02). The CIA's June 2013 Response does not dispute the narrative described by the Committee, and states the "[CIA] should have more clearly explained the contribution [Abu

Zubaydah's] reporting made to this operation."

1832. 21753 .

1833. On January , 2004. Hassan Ghul was transferred to U.S. military custody. On January , 2004. Hassan Ghul was transferred to CIA custody. On August , 2006, Ghul was rendered to . On May , 2007, he was released . Hassan Ghul . *See* 21815 ; 1642 JAN 04); 2441 ; HEADQUARTERS ; 1635 ; 1712 ; HEADQUARTERS ; 1775 ; 173426 ; and Committee Notification from the CIA dated (DTS #2012-3802).

1834. Italics added. President George W. Bush, Speech on the CIA's Terrorist Detention Program, (September 6, 2006). *See also* CIA officer 's February 14, 2007, testimony to the Senate Select Committee on Intelligence in which she stated that Abu Zubaydah "really pointed us towards Khalid Shaykh Mohammad and how to find him," adding "[h]e led us to Ramzi bin al-Shibh, who in kind of [sic] started the chain of events." *See* transcript, Senate Select Committee on Intelligence, February 14, 2007 (DTS #2007-1337).

1835. CIA records provided to the Committee identify the pseudonym created by the CIA for the asset. The Study lists the asset as "ASSET X" to further protect his identity.

1836. TD INTERVIEW, CIA ORAL HISTORY PROGRAM, SEPTEMBER 14, 2004], Presentation to the CTC 14 September 2004 by . *See also* Interview of [REDACTED], by [REDACTED], 14 October 2004, CIA Oral History Program; Interview of [REDACTED], by [REDACTED], 14 September 2004, CIA Oral History Program; Interview of [REDACTED], by [REDACTED], 3 December 2004, CIA Oral History Program; Interview of [REDACTED], by [REDACTED], 30 November 2004, CIA Oral History Program; Interview of , by [REDACTED], 25 October 2004, CIA Oral History Program; Interview of [REDACTED], by [REDACTED]; 24 November & 15 December 2004, CIA Oral History Program.

1837. See, for example, the September 15, 2001, email from a CIA officer to of ALEC Station, in which the officer wrote, "I would say the percentages are pretty high that Khalid Sheikh Mohammad is involved [in the September 11, 2001, attacks]." *See* email from: ; to: ; cc: , , [REDACTED], , [REDACTED]; subject: Re: RAMZI LEADS…; date: September 15, 2001, at 5:04:38 AM). *See also* DIRECTOR (132018Z SEP 01), disseminated as .

1838. ALEC (231718Z SEP 01). Ramzi Yousef is serving a life sentence in the United States.

1839. A CIA source from 1995 reported that "all members of are acting together on behalf of a larger and well organized group." the source said, "are true terrorists and villains." (*See* WHDC OCT 95).) Reporting from 1998 indicated that "Sheikh Khalid" (KSM), along with , had "switched their allegiance" and were "part of the bin Ladin organization in Afghanistan." (*See* DIRECTOR SEP 98), disseminated as).) CIA cables describe [specific intelligence collected on KSM's]. *See* 484112 JUL 99); WHDC OCT 95); 89173 JUN 95); 90757 JUL 95); CIA APR 95); ; 91147 AUG 95); DIRECTOR FEB 96), disseminated as ; 69789 FEB 95); 85526 FEB 95); ALEC SEP 01); 70158 MAR 95); 88666 JUN 95); DIRECTOR JUL 00); ALEC APR 99).

1840. Email from: ; to: , , , [REDACTED]; subject: the yousef cohorts ; date: September 25, 2001, at 6:58:17 PM.

1841. Email from: ; to: ; cc: , ; subject: Re: ; date: October 4, 2001, at 12:52:46 PM. The CIA's June 2013 Response states that the Study "claims it was [ASSET X], not detainees, who first identified KSM's for us." This is inaccurate. The Committee Study does not claim it was ASSET X who first identified KSM's for the CIA. The Committee Study details how the CIA had extensive information on KSM's as early as 1995; and how in 2001, prior to CIA detainee reporting, ASSET X highlighted how KSM's to locating and capturing KSM.

1842. The subject of the cable from the CIA , was "possible to lead to UBL target." (*See* 73245 [spring] 01). *See also* 41495 ; Interview of [REDACTED], by [REDACTED], 14 October 2004, CIA Oral History Program.) In [spring] 2001, ASSET X would further indicate, . *See* WDC ; Interview of

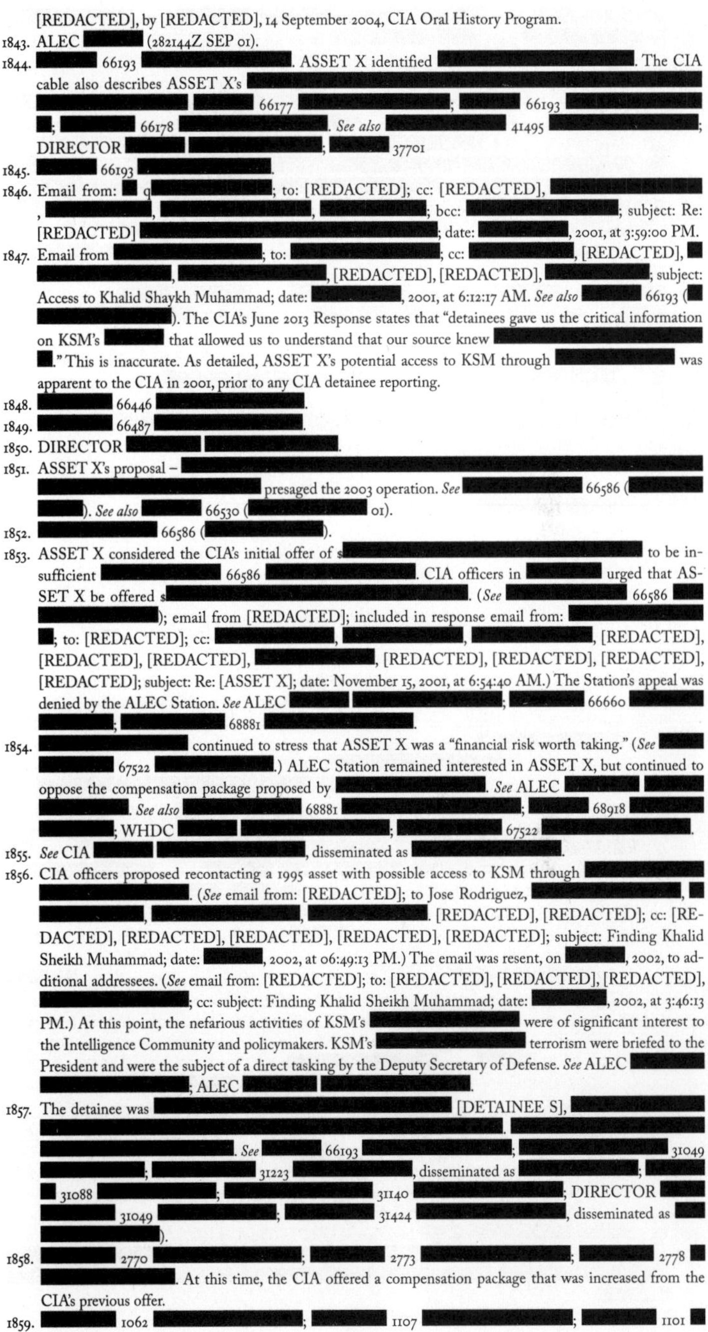

[REDACTED], by [REDACTED], 14 September 2004, CIA Oral History Program.

1843. ALEC (282144Z SEP 01).

1844. 66193 . ASSET X identified . The CIA cable also describes ASSET X's 66177 ; 66193 ; 66178 . *See also* 41495 ; DIRECTOR ; 37701

1845. 66193 .

1846. Email from: q ; to: [REDACTED]; cc: [REDACTED], , , ; bcc: ; subject: Re: [REDACTED] ; date: , 2001, at 3:59:00 PM.

1847. Email from ; to: ; cc: , [REDACTED], , , [REDACTED], [REDACTED], ; subject: Access to Khalid Shaykh Muhammad; date: , 2001, at 6:12:17 AM. *See also* 66193 ( ). The CIA's June 2013 Response states that "detainees gave us the critical information on KSM's that allowed us to understand that our source knew ." This is inaccurate. As detailed, ASSET X's potential access to KSM through was apparent to the CIA in 2001, prior to any CIA detainee reporting.

1848. 66446 .

1849. 66487 .

1850. DIRECTOR .

1851. ASSET X's proposal – presaged the 2003 operation. *See* 66586 ( ). *See also* 66530 (01).

1852. 66586 ( ).

1853. ASSET X considered the CIA's initial offer of $ to be insufficient 66586 . CIA officers in urged that ASSET X be offered $. (*See* 66586); email from [REDACTED]; included in response email from: ; to: [REDACTED]; cc: , , , [REDACTED], [REDACTED], [REDACTED], , [REDACTED], [REDACTED], [REDACTED], [REDACTED]; subject: Re: [ASSET X]; date: November 15, 2001, at 6:54:40 AM.) The Station's appeal was denied by the ALEC Station. *See* ALEC ; 66660 ; 68881 .

1854. continued to stress that ASSET X was a "financial risk worth taking." (*See* 67522 .) ALEC Station remained interested in ASSET X, but continued to oppose the compensation package proposed by . *See* ALEC . *See also* 68881 ; 68918 ; WHDC ; 67522 .

1855. *See* CIA , disseminated as .

1856. CIA officers proposed recontacting a 1995 asset with possible access to KSM through . (*See* email from: [REDACTED]; to Jose Rodriguez, , , , . [REDACTED], [REDACTED]; cc: [REDACTED], [REDACTED], [REDACTED], [REDACTED], [REDACTED], [REDACTED]; subject: Finding Khalid Sheikh Muhammad; date: , 2002, at 06:49:13 PM.) The email was resent, on , 2002, to additional addressees. (*See* email from: [REDACTED]; to: [REDACTED], [REDACTED], [REDACTED], ; cc: subject: Finding Khalid Sheikh Muhammad; date: , 2002, at 3:46:13 PM.) At this point, the nefarious activities of KSM's were of significant interest to the Intelligence Community and policymakers. KSM's terrorism were briefed to the President and were the subject of a direct tasking by the Deputy Secretary of Defense. *See* ALEC ; ALEC .

1857. The detainee was [DETAINEE S], . . *See* 66193 ; 31049 ; 31223 , disseminated as ; 31088 ; 31140 ; DIRECTOR 31049 ; 31424 , disseminated as).

1858. 2770 ; 2773 ; 2778 . At this time, the CIA offered a compensation package that was increased from the CIA's previous offer.

1859. 1062 ; 1107 ; 1101

; DIR ; 37701 ; 41495 ; Interview of [REDACTED], by [REDACTED], 14 October 2004, CIA Oral History Program; Interview of [REDACTED], by [REDACTED], 14 September 2004, CIA Oral History Program. During this time period, ASSET X reported that he had made contact with KSM's (*See* .) Also during this period, CIA officers continued to note that ASSET X had offered to locate KSM's . (*See* 2812 . 481096 .) *See* email from: ; to [REDACTED]; cc: [REDACTED], , ; subject: another for the highlights; date: , 2002, at 4:14:24 PM.

1860. 37701 ; 41495 .

1861. 37701 ; 41495 ; 2426 .

1862. Interview of [REDACTED], by [REDACTED], 14 October 2004, CIA Oral History Program. *See* 2431 ; DIRECTOR .

1863. Interview of [REDACTED], by [REDACTED], 14 October 2004, CIA Oral History Program.

1864. ASSET X had been using the same names since 2001. *See* interview of [REDACTED], by [REDACTED], 14 October 2004, CIA Oral History Program; Interview of [REDACTED], by [REDACTED], 14 September 2004, CIA Oral History Program.

1865. [TD INTERVIEW, CIA ORAL HISTORY PROGRAM, SEPTEMBER 14, 2004] Presentation to the CTC 14 September 2004.

1866. Interview of [REDACTED], by [REDACTED], 14 October 2004, CIA Oral History Program. The CIA's June 2013 Response claims that the "CIA correctly represented that detainee reporting helped us capture [KSM]." This CIA assertion is based on an indirect chain of causation purporting to connect the reporting of Abu Zubaydah to the intervention of the visiting CIA officer and the subsequent capture of KSM. This account, which the CIA represented for the first time in June 2013, is inaccurate in numerous ways: (1) The CIA represents that "information provided by Abu Zubaydah... helped lead to the capture of Ramzi Bin al-Shibh [RBS]." The inaccuracies of this representation are described in this summary and in greater detail in Volume II. (2) The CIA represents that reporting from Ramzi bin al-Shibh (who was not in CIA custody at the time) regarding Ammar al-Baluchi was key to capturing KSM. This too is inaccurate. As detailed in the Study, Ammar al-Baluchi played no role in the operation that captured KSM, which centered around ASSET X and . (3) The CIA represents that bin al-Shibh's reporting on Ammar al-Baluchi was "used... to debrief [DETAINEE R]," who was in foreign government custody, and that as a result, DETAINEE R discussed . This statement is not supported by CIA records. CIA records related to DETAINEE R's interrogation in foreign government custody indicate that DETAINEE R's reporting was prompted using a photograph and a letter. (*See* 10118 (; 10120 (; 10158 ; WASHINGT (; 10116 .) (4) The CIA represents that DETAINEE R's information on "allowed CIA to understand the value of the access [ASSET X] had to ." This is also inaccurate. As detailed in the Study, the value of ASSET X's access to KSM's was apparent to the CIA in 2001. (5) The CIA states that the visiting CIA officer who intervened to forestall the termination of ASSET X did so because, having been , he was familiar was DETAINEE R's reporting on KSM's . This representation omits the fact that the vistiting CIA officer was a member of the team that handled ASSET X while ASSET X . That team received information concerning ASSET X's stated access to KSM through . The information was provided to the team prior to the capture of DETAINEE R. (*See* 2778 ( ).) (6) The CIA asserts that DETAINEE R's reporting "helped CIA to redirect [ASSET X] in an effort to locate KSM." This is inaccurate. As detailed in the Study, ASSET X had been indicating that he had access to KSM through since 2001 and, as detailed, contacted KSM's on his own. CIA records indicate that the detainees who provided corroborating information about KSM's , DETAINEE S and DETAINEE R, were in foreign government custody at the time they provided the information. DETAINEE R would later be rendered to CIA custody and approved for the use of the CIA's enhanced interrogation techniques, although there are no CIA records indicating that he was subjected to the techniques.

1867. DIR ; Interview of [REDACTED], by [REDACTED], 14 October 2004, CIA Oral History Program; ; .

1868. Interview of [REDACTED], by [REDACTED], 14 October 2004, CIA Oral History Program; Interview of

[REDACTED], by [REDACTED], 3 December 2004, CIA Oral History Program.

1869. Interview of [REDACTED], by [REDACTED], 14 October 2004, CIA Oral History Program.

1870. Interview of [REDACTED], by [REDACTED] 14 October 2004, CIA Oral History Program; Interview of [REDACTED], by [REDACTED], 14 September 2004, CIA Oral History Program; Interview of [REDACTED], by [REDACTED]; 24 November & 15 December 2004, CIA Oral History Program; Interview of [REDACTED], by [REDACTED], 30 November 2004. *See* ███ 41034 ███.

1871. Interview of [REDACTED] by [REDACTED], 3 December 2004, CIA Oral History Program; DIRECTOR ███ ███.

1872. Interview of [REDACTED] by [REDACTED], 14 October 2004, CIA Oral History Program.

1873. Interview of [REDACTED] by [REDACTED], 14 October 2004, CIA Oral History Program; Interview of [REDACTED] by [REDACTED], 3 December 2004, CIA Oral History Program; ███ ███ 41490 ███); Interview of ███, by [REDACTED], 25 October 2004, CIA Oral History Program; Interview of [REDACTED], by [REDACTED], 14 September 2004, CIA Oral History Program.

1874. Interview of [REDACTED] by [REDACTED], 14 October 2004, CIA Oral History Program; Interview of [REDACTED] by [REDACTED], 3 December 2004, CIA Oral History Program; ███ 41490 (███).

1875. Interview of [REDACTED] by [REDACTED], 14 October 2004, CIA Oral History Program; Interview of [REDACTED] by [REDACTED], 3 December 2004, CIA Oral History Program; ███ 41490 (███).

1876. ███ 41490 (███).

1877. Interview of [REDACTED], by [REDACTED], 14 September 2004, CIA Oral History Program.

1878. ███ 41351 ███; ███ 41490 ███ ; ALEC ███ 41490 ███).

1879. *See* ███ 10983 (242321Z MAR 03); ███ 10972 (241122Z MAR 03); and the KSM detainee review in Volume III.

1880. Interview of John E. McLaughlin, by [REDACTED] and [REDACTED], Office of the Inspector General, September 5, 2003; ███, Memorandum for the Record; subject: Meeting with Deputy Chief, Counterterrorist Center Al-Qa'ida Department; date: 28 July 2003; Interview of ███, by ███, Office of the Inspector General, August 18, 2003.

1881. ███, Memorandum for the Record; subject: Meeting with Deputy Chief, Counterterrorist Center ALEC Station; date: 17 July 2003.

1882. CIA Inspector General, Special Review, Counterterrorism Detention and Interrogation Program (2003-7123-IG), January 2004.

1883. Memorandum for: Inspector General; from: James Pavitt, Deputy Director for Operations; subject: re (S) Comments to Draft IG Special Review, "Counterterrorism Detention and Interrogation Program" (2003-7123-IG); date: February 27, 2004; attachment: February 24, 2004, Memorandum re Successes of CIA's Counterterrorism Detention and Interrogation Activities.

1884. CIA Office of Inspector General, Special Review—Counterterrorism Detention and Interrogation Program, (2003-7123-IG), May 2004.

1885. Memorandum for John A. Rizzo, Senior Deputy General Counsel, Central Intelligence Agency, from Steven G. Bradbury, Principal Deputy Assistant Attorney General, Office of Legal Counsel, May 30, 2005, Re: Application of United States Obligations Under Article 16 of the Convention Against Torture to Certain Techniques that May be Used in the Interrogation of High Value Al Qaeda Detainees, pp. 10–11, citing CIA Office of Inspector General, Special Review, pp. 85–91.

1886. CIA Memorandum for the Record, "Review of Interrogation Program on 29 July 2003," prepared by CIA General Counsel Scott Muller, dated August 5, 2003; briefing slides entitled, "*CIA Interrogation Program*," dated July 29, 2003, presented to senior White House officials.

1887. *See* briefing slides entitled, "*CIA Interrogation Program*," dated July 29, 2003, presented to senior White House officials. Those attending the meeting included Vice President Richard Cheney, National Security Advisor Condoleezza Rice, White House Counsel Alberto Gonzales, Attorney General John Ashcroft, Acting Assistant Attorney General Patrick Philbin, and counsel to the National Security Council, John Bellinger.

1888. The CIA's June 2003 Response states that "CIA mistakenly provided incorrect information to the Inspector General (IG) that led to a one-time misrepresentation of this case in the IG's 2004 *Special Review*." The CIA's June 2013 Response adds that, "[t]his mistake was not, as it is characterized in the 'Findings and Conclusions' section of the *Study*, a 'repeatedly represented' or 'frequently cited' example of the effectiveness of CIA's enhanced interrogation program." The CIA's June 2013 assertion that this was a "one-time misrepresentation" is inaccurate. As described, the inaccurate information was provided numerous times to the Inspector General, in multiple interviews and in the CIA's official response to the draft Special Review. Afterwards, the CIA relied on the section of the Special Review that included the inaccurate information on the capture of Majid Khan in obtaining legal approval for the use of the CIA's enhanced interrogation techniques from the Department of Justice. This information was also provided by the CIA to the CIA's Blue Ribbon Panel for their review of the CIA's Detention and Interrogation Program. The CIA also included the inaccurate representation about the identification of Majid Khan and his family to the National Security Council principals on multiple occasions. Further, as noted, the inaccurate information in the CIA OIG Special Review was declassified and has been used in multiple open source articles and books, often as an example of the effectiveness of the CIA program.

1889. Memorandum for the Record; subject: CIA Interrogation Program; September 27, 2003 (OGC-FO-2003-50088). Slides, CIA Interrogation Program, 16 September 2003. John B. Bellinger III, Senior Associate Counsel to the President and Legal Advisor, National Security Council; Memorandum for the Record; subject: Briefing of Secretaries Powell and Rumsfeld regarding Interrogation of High-Value Detainees; date: September 30, 2003.

1890. Scott W. Muller; Memorandum for the Record; Interrogation briefing for Jack Goldsmith; date: 16 October 2003 (OGC-FO-2003-50097).

1891. For additional details, *see* Volumes II and Volume III.

1892. *See* FBI 302 on FBI case file , and 88793 .

1893. ALEC (160141Z JAN 03).

1894. 13571 (260330Z FEB 03).

1895. ALEC (040329Z MAR 03).

1896. 13658 (050318Z MAR 03); 13659 (050459Z MAR 03); DIRECTOR (050459Z MAR 03).

1897. Memorandum for: , [REDACTED]; from: [REDACTED], OFFICE: /[DETENTION SITE BLUE]; subject: Baltimore boy and KSM; date; 15 March 2003, at 07:08:32 PM.

1898. ALEC Station sent DETENTION SITE BLUE photographs for use with KSM and other detainees. They included Majid Khan, Muhammad Khan, Sohail Munir, Iyman Faris, Majid Khan's cousin (Mansour), Fayyaz Kamran, Aydinbelge, Khalid Jamil, and Aafia Siddiqui. *See* ALEC (152212Z MAR 03).

1899. 10865 (171648Z MAR 03); 10886 (182219Z MAR 03); 10870 (172017Z MAR 03).

1900. *See* "CIA Validation of Remarks on Detainee Policy," drafts supporting the September 6, 2006, speech by President George W. Bush acknowledging and describing the CIA's Detention and Interrogation Program, as well as an unclassified Office of the Director of National Intelligence release, entitled, "Summary of the High Value Terrorist Detainee Program." In October 2007 CIA officers discussed a section of the President's speech, which was based on CIA information and vetted by the CIA, related to Camp Lemonier. Addressing the section of the speech that states, "[t]errorists held in CIA custody have also provided information that helped stop the planned strike on U.S. Marines at Camp Lemonier in Djibouti," a senior CIA officer highlighted that the plotting had not been stopped, but in fact was ongoing. The officer wrote: "I have attached the cable from Guleed that was used to source the Sept '06 speech as well as a later cable from a different detainee affirming that as of mid-2004, AQ members in Somalia were still intent on attacking Camp Lemonier... As of 2004, the second detainee indicates that AQ was still working on attacking the base." The CIA officer explained that the "reasoning behind validation of the language in the speech—and remember, we can argue about whether or not 'planning' consistitutes [*sic*] a 'plot' and about whether anything is ever disrupted—was that the detainee reporting increased our awareness of attack plotting against the base, leading to heightened security." (*See* email from: ; to: ; subject: "More on Camp Lemonier"; date; October 22, 2007, at 5:33 PM). The President's reference to Camp Lemonier in the context of "this vital program" came immediately after the passage of the speech referencing the use of the CIA's enhanced interrogation techniques against KSM and immediately before statements about the thwarting of the Karachi and Heathrow Airport plots, both of which have been explicitly attributed by the CIA to the use of the CIA's enhanced interrogation techniques. The disruption of the Camp Lemonier plotting was also referenced as an intelligence success in the context of the March 2008 presidential veto of legislation that would have effectively banned the CIA's enhanced interrogation techniques. *See* "Text: Bush on Veto of Intelligence Bill," *The New York Times*, dated March 8, 2008, which states, the "main reason this program has been effective is that it allows the CIA to use specialized interrogation procedures... limiting the CIA's interrogation methods to those in the Army field manual would be dangerous...."

1901. Italics added. Unclassified Office of the Director of National Intelligence release, entitled, "Summary of the High Value Terrorist Detainee Program." CIA records indicate that the CIA had intelligence that al-Qa'ida affiliated individuals were targeting Camp Lemonier with an "explosives-laden truck" in early 2003. The CIA sought to detain Gouled because of the intelligence already collected, indicating that in 2003—at the likely behest of Abu Talha al-Sudani—Gouled was conducting casings of Camp Lemonier. Once captured, and prior to being transferred to CIA custody, Gouled confirmed that he cased Camp Lemonier for a potential terrorist attack. Despite the use of the term "revealed" in the 2006 document, the CIA's June 2013 Response states: "We did not represent that we initially learned of the plot from detainees, or that it was disrupted based solely on information from detainees in CIA custody." The CIA's June 2013 Response further states that the CIA "agree[s] with the *Study* that [the CIA] had threat reporting against Camp Lemonier prior to the March 2004 detention and rendition" of Guleed Hassan Dourad.

1902. Emphasis in original. *See* CIA Talking Points dated October 30, 2007, entitled, "DCIA Meeting with Chairman Murtha re Rendition and Detention Programs" and attachments.

1903. The CIA's June 2013 Response states: "We did not represent that we initially learned of the plot from detainees, or that it was disrupted based solely on information from detainees in CIA custody." The CIA's October 30, 2007, talking points for the chairman of the House Defense Appropriations Subcommittee, John Murtha, make no reference to the CIA receiving intelligence on the Camp Lemonier plotting from other intelligence sources prior to CIA detainee reporting. Nor do the talking points indicate that the CIA detainee initially provided information on the plotting prior to being transferred to CIA custody. In addition, as described, an Office of the Director of National Intelligence public release on the CIA's Detention and Interrogation Program from September 6, 2006, states that "the CIA designed a new interrogation program that would be safe, effective, and legal;" and that "al-Qa'ida facilitator Gouled Hassan Dourad revealed" that he had been sent to "case the US Marine base Camp Lemonier."

1904. *See* CIA Talking Points dated October 30, 2007, entitled, "DCIA Meeting with Chairman Murtha re Rendition and Detention Programs" and attachments. The talking points further state that the "Presidentially-mandated detention program is critical to our ability to protect the American homeland and US forces and citizens abroad from terrorist attack." The attachment to the document, labeled "points from CTC," further asserts that while CIA rendition activities "did yield intelligence, it did not do so in a timely, efficient, and thorough way, raising unacceptable risks," and that the CIA "experience has shown that exclusive control by CIA, in an Agency designed, built, and managed facility, allows us complete oversight and control over all aspects of detention, to include conditions of confinement, approved interrogation activities, humane standards, medical treatment, detainee engagement, security, hygiene, and infrastructure." The document references a U.S. House of Representatives Appropriations bill providing a reduction in funding for the Covert Action CT Program and states: "Had the mark been directed against the rendition and detention programs specifically, the CIA would have recommended a Presidential veto. In its appeal, CIA detailed the impact of a $███ million cut to the CA CT Program. The Agency also made it clear that it would continue the rendition and detention program because of the high value of these activities."

1905. *See* aforementioned CIA representations that: (1) "This is intelligence that cannot be found any other place. And our security depends on getting this kind of information," and (2) "Most, if not all, of the intelligence acquired from high-value detainees in this [CIA] program would likely not have been discovered or reported in any other way." As noted, the CIA's June 2013 Response states that the CIA "agree[s] with the *Study* that [the CIA] had threat reporting against Camp Lemonier prior to the March 2004 detention and rendition" of Guleed.

1906. *See* intelligence chronology in Volume II for additional information.

1907. HEADQUAR ███ ██████; ███ 1313 (041624Z MAR 04); HEADQUAR ███ (041935Z MAR 04). *See also* ██████ 15623.

1908. ███ 93364 (January 8, 2008).

1909. HEADQUAR ███ ██████; ███ 93364 (January 8, 2008).

1910. ███ 1329 ██████. The CIA's June 2013 Response states: "In March 2004, ██████ ██████, based [on] information from a clandestine source-detained and rendered to CIA custody the primary facilitator for al-Qa'ida's Camp Lemonier plot, Guleed Hassan Ahmed, who had cased the Camp on behalf of al-Qa'ida. Guleed provided details about the plot and al-Qa'ida's Somali support network, which drove CIA's targeting efforts." As described in this summary and in greater detail in Volume II, Guleed confirmed intelligence reporting already collected on his casing of Camp Lemonier prior to being rendered to CIA custody. *See* reference to material on recorded interrogations of Guleed Hassan Dourad in the cable, ███ 93364 (January 8, 2008).

1911. ███ 1543 ██████.

1912. ███ 1573 (160217Z MAR 04), later reissued as CIA ███ (021549Z APR 04)/ ██████, and used to support the president's speech on September 6, 2006.

1913. ██████. The CIA's June 2013 Response links the "disrupt[ion]" of the Camp Lemonier plotting to the CIA's Detention and Interrogation Program via the arrest of KSM, stating: "According to Khalid Shaykh Muhammad (KSM), his arrest in March 2003 (which we note in Example 12 resulted in part from information provided by Ramzi Bin al-Shibh) prevented him from transferring 30,000 euros from al-Qa'ida in Pakistan to al-Qa'ida in East Africa leaders, some of whom were plotting the Camp Lemonier attack. Funding shortages were cited repeatedly by detainees and in ██████ [technical collection] as a reason for the Camp Lemonier plot's delays." Prior to the CIA's June 2013 Response, there were no CIA records attributing the delay or disruption of the plotting to the capture or detention of KSM. While a body of intelligence reporting indicated that funding shortages contributed to delays in the targeting of Camp Lemonier, no CIA intelligence records were identified that cite any deficit of expected funds resulting from KSM's capture. As detailed in this Study, KSM was captured on March 1, 2003. Intelligence reporting indicates that Abu Talha al-Sudani sent Guleed to case the security at Camp Lemonier more than six months later, in September 2003. In early March 2004, the CIA reported that ██████ [technical collection] revealed that "Abu Talha and Guleed were working together in search of funding necessary to carry out planned operations." In late March

2004, after Guleed's detention, several associates were detained after an attack on a German aid delegation, which was suspected of being an attempt to kidnap individuals for ransom. A cable reporting this information stated that [REDACTED] [technical collection] "indicated Abu Talha continues to press forward on plans to target Western interests in Djibouti." Several days later, CIA officers surmised that the kidnapping attempt was likely an attempt" by Abu Talha to raise the operational funds for his plan to attack Camp Lemonier." (*See* intelligence chronology in Volume II, including reporting referenced in HEADQUARTERS [REDACTED] (101756Z MAR 04) and connected to [REDACTED]; ALEC [REDACTED] (222122Z MAR 04); and ALEC [REDACTED] (292353Z MAR 04)). As detailed in the section of this summary and Volume II on the Capture of Khalid Shaykh Mohammad (KSM), the capture of KSM did not result from information provided by Ramzi bin al-Shibh.

1914. [REDACTED].

1915. Draft cable in an email from: [REDACTED]; to: [REDACTED] and [REDACTED]; subject: "[REDACTED] DDO Approval to render Somali Jihadist and al-Qa'ida facilitator Ahmed Abdi Aw Mohammad to [CIA] control"; date: May 11, 2005, at 5:42:50 PM.

1916. HEADQUARTERS [REDACTED] (252044Z OCT 05).

1917. [REDACTED] 10555 (101434Z APR 07).

1918. *See* "CIA Validation of Remarks on Detainee Policy," drafts supporting the September 6, 2006, speech by President George W. Bush acknowledging and describing the CIA's Detention and Interrogation Program, as well as an unclassified Office of the Director of National Intelligence release, entitled, "Summary of the High Value Terrorist Detainee Program."

1919. *See* email from: [REDACTED]; to [REDACTED] and others; subject: "More on Camp Lemonier"; October 22, 2007, at 5:33 PM. In a reply email, a CIA officer wrote that Guleed's statement was only "that the plan was suspended while Abu Talha tried to acquire the necessary funds," and continued, "I don't want anyone to walk away from this thinking that the POTUS speech from 2006 is the only language/view we are allowed to hold, especially since most or all of us were not involved in the original coordination" of the President's September 6, 2006, speech. *See* email from: [REDACTED]; to [REDACTED] and [REDACTED]; cc: [REDACTED]; subject: "Camp Lemonier"; date: October 24, 2007, at 1:22:44 PM.

1920. [REDACTED] 1313 (041624Z MAR 04).

1921. *See* January 28, 2003, CIA Presidential Daily Brief, entitled, "Al-Qa'ida Planning Attack in Djibouti." The CIA's June 2013 Response states that the CIA "agree[s] with the *Study* that [the CIA] had threat reporting against Camp Lemonier prior to the March 2004 detention and rendition" of Guleed, but argues that the threat reporting provided to the President on January 28, 2003, had "no relation to [al-Sudani's] plot," and was "later recalled after being revealed to be a fabrication." The CIA did not provide a date for the recall. The reporting, which indicated al-Qa'ida operatives were planning "to ram an explosives-laden truck into a military base, probably Camp Lemonier," would later be corroborated by other intelligence reporting, including by Guleed in his description of al-Sudani's plotting. *See* intelligence chronology in Volume II.

1922. CIA WASHINGTON DC [REDACTED] (110056Z MAR 03). *See also* [REDACTED] 17366 (121355Z MAR 03). The CIA's June 2013 Response asserts that the March 2003 reporting was "an analytical assessment that Djibouti was a potential target given its US Military presence," was "not based on specific intelligence," and was analysis related to "a different al-Qa'ida cell." The CIA's June 2013 Response also disputes the relevance of the May 2003 reporting that al-Qa'ida affiliates were "waiting for the right time to carry out large-scale attacks, possibly involving suicide bombers, against a U.S. military base or U.S. naval ship in or near Djibouti." The CIA's June 2013 Response states that this threat reporting "was later found to be unrelated." Notwithstanding these assertions, the CIA's June 2013 Response states that the CIA "agree[s] with the *Study* that [the CIA] had threat reporting against Camp Lemonier prior to the March 2004 detention and rendition" of Guleed.

1923. ALEC [REDACTED] (021825Z OCT 03).

1924. Referenced in HEADQUAR [REDACTED] (101756Z MAR 04) and connected to [REDACTED]. *See also* [REDACTED].

1925. CIA WASHINGTON DC [REDACTED] (302034Z DEC 03) / SERIAL: [REDACTED].

1926. [REDACTED] 1313 (041624Z MAR 04).

1927. CIA classified Statement for the Record, Senate Select Committee on Intelligence, provided by General Michael V. Hayden, Director, Central Intelligence Agency, 12 April 2007; and accompanying Senate Select Committee on Intelligence hearing transcript for April 12, 2007, entitled, "Hearing on Central Intelligence Agency Detention and Interrogation Program" (DTS #2007-1563). *See also* CIA Intelligence Assessment, "Detainee Reporting Pivotal for the War Against Al-Qa'ida," June 2005, which CIA records indicate was provided to White House officials on June 1, 2005, and was broadly disseminated on June 3, 2005, as an Intelligence Assessment. On March 31, 2009, former Vice President Cheney requested the declassification of this Intelligence Assessment, which was publicly released with redactions on August 24, 2009.

1928. Italics in original. CIA Briefing for Obama National Security Team - "Renditions, Detentions, and Interrogations (RDI)" including "Tab 7," named "RDG Copy- Briefing on RDI Program 09 Jan. 2009." Referenced materials attached to cover memorandum with the title, "D/CIA Conference Room Seating Visit by President-elect Barrack [*sic*] Obama National Security Team Tuesday, 13 January 2009; 8:30 – 11:30 a.m." Expected

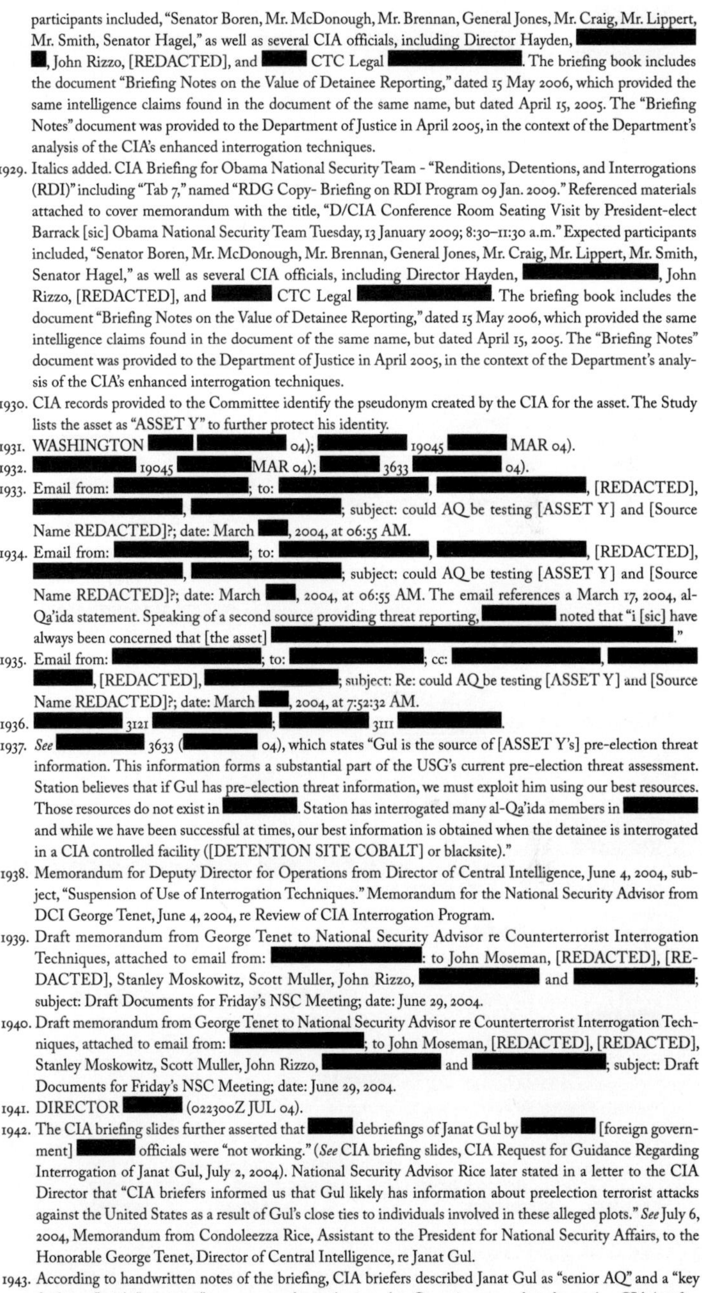

participants included, "Senator Boren, Mr. McDonough, Mr. Brennan, General Jones, Mr. Craig, Mr. Lippert, Mr. Smith, Senator Hagel," as well as several CIA officials, including Director Hayden, , John Rizzo, [REDACTED], and CTC Legal . The briefing book includes the document "Briefing Notes on the Value of Detainee Reporting," dated 15 May 2006, which provided the same intelligence claims found in the document of the same name, but dated April 15, 2005. The "Briefing Notes" document was provided to the Department of Justice in April 2005, in the context of the Department's analysis of the CIA's enhanced interrogation techniques.

1929. Italics added. CIA Briefing for Obama National Security Team - "Renditions, Detentions, and Interrogations (RDI)" including "Tab 7," named "RDG Copy- Briefing on RDI Program 09 Jan. 2009." Referenced materials attached to cover memorandum with the title, "D/CIA Conference Room Seating Visit by President-elect Barrack [sic] Obama National Security Team Tuesday, 13 January 2009; 8:30–11:30 a.m." Expected participants included, "Senator Boren, Mr. McDonough, Mr. Brennan, General Jones, Mr. Craig, Mr. Lippert, Mr. Smith, Senator Hagel," as well as several CIA officials, including Director Hayden, , John Rizzo, [REDACTED], and CTC Legal . The briefing book includes the document "Briefing Notes on the Value of Detainee Reporting," dated 15 May 2006, which provided the same intelligence claims found in the document of the same name, but dated April 15, 2005. The "Briefing Notes" document was provided to the Department of Justice in April 2005, in the context of the Department's analysis of the CIA's enhanced interrogation techniques.

1930. CIA records provided to the Committee identify the pseudonym created by the CIA for the asset. The Study lists the asset as "ASSET Y" to further protect his identity.

1931. WASHINGTON 04); 19045 MAR 04).

1932. 19045 MAR 04); 3633 04).

1933. Email from: ; to: , , [REDACTED], , ; subject: could AQ be testing [ASSET Y] and [Source Name REDACTED]?; date: March , 2004, at 06:55 AM.

1934. Email from: ; to: , , [REDACTED], , ; subject: could AQ be testing [ASSET Y] and [Source Name REDACTED]?; date: March , 2004, at 06:55 AM. The email references a March 17, 2004, al-Qa'ida statement. Speaking of a second source providing threat reporting, noted that "i [sic] have always been concerned that [the asset] ."

1935. Email from: ; to: ; cc: , , [REDACTED], ; subject: Re: could AQ be testing [ASSET Y] and [Source Name REDACTED]?; date: March , 2004, at 7:52:32 AM.

1936. 3121 ; 3111 .

1937. *See* 3633 (04), which states "Gul is the source of [ASSET Y's] pre-election threat information. This information forms a substantial part of the USG's current pre-election threat assessment. Station believes that if Gul has pre-election threat information, we must exploit him using our best resources. Those resources do not exist in . Station has interrogated many al-Qa'ida members in and while we have been successful at times, our best information is obtained when the detainee is interrogated in a CIA controlled facility ([DETENTION SITE COBALT] or blacksite)."

1938. Memorandum for Deputy Director for Operations from Director of Central Intelligence, June 4, 2004, subject, "Suspension of Use of Interrogation Techniques." Memorandum for the National Security Advisor from DCI George Tenet, June 4, 2004, re Review of CIA Interrogation Program.

1939. Draft memorandum from George Tenet to National Security Advisor re Counterterrorist Interrogation Techniques, attached to email from: : to John Moseman, [REDACTED], [REDACTED], Stanley Moskowitz, Scott Muller, John Rizzo, and ; subject: Draft Documents for Friday's NSC Meeting; date: June 29, 2004.

1940. Draft memorandum from George Tenet to National Security Advisor re Counterterrorist Interrogation Techniques, attached to email from: ; to John Moseman, [REDACTED], [REDACTED], Stanley Moskowitz, Scott Muller, John Rizzo, and ; subject: Draft Documents for Friday's NSC Meeting; date: June 29, 2004.

1941. DIRECTOR (022300Z JUL 04).

1942. The CIA briefing slides further asserted that debriefings of Janat Gul by [foreign government] officials were "not working." (*See* CIA briefing slides, CIA Request for Guidance Regarding Interrogation of Janat Gul, July 2, 2004). National Security Advisor Rice later stated in a letter to the CIA Director that "CIA briefers informed us that Gul likely has information about preelection terrorist attacks against the United States as a result of Gul's close ties to individuals involved in these alleged plots." *See* July 6, 2004, Memorandum from Condoleezza Rice, Assistant to the President for National Security Affairs, to the Honorable George Tenet, Director of Central Intelligence, re Janat Gul.

1943. According to handwritten notes of the briefing, CIA briefers described Janat Gul as "senior AQ" and a "key facilitator" with "proximity" to a suspected pre-election plot. Committee records indicate that CIA briefers told the chairman and vice chairman that, given the pre-election threat, it was "incumbent" on the CIA to

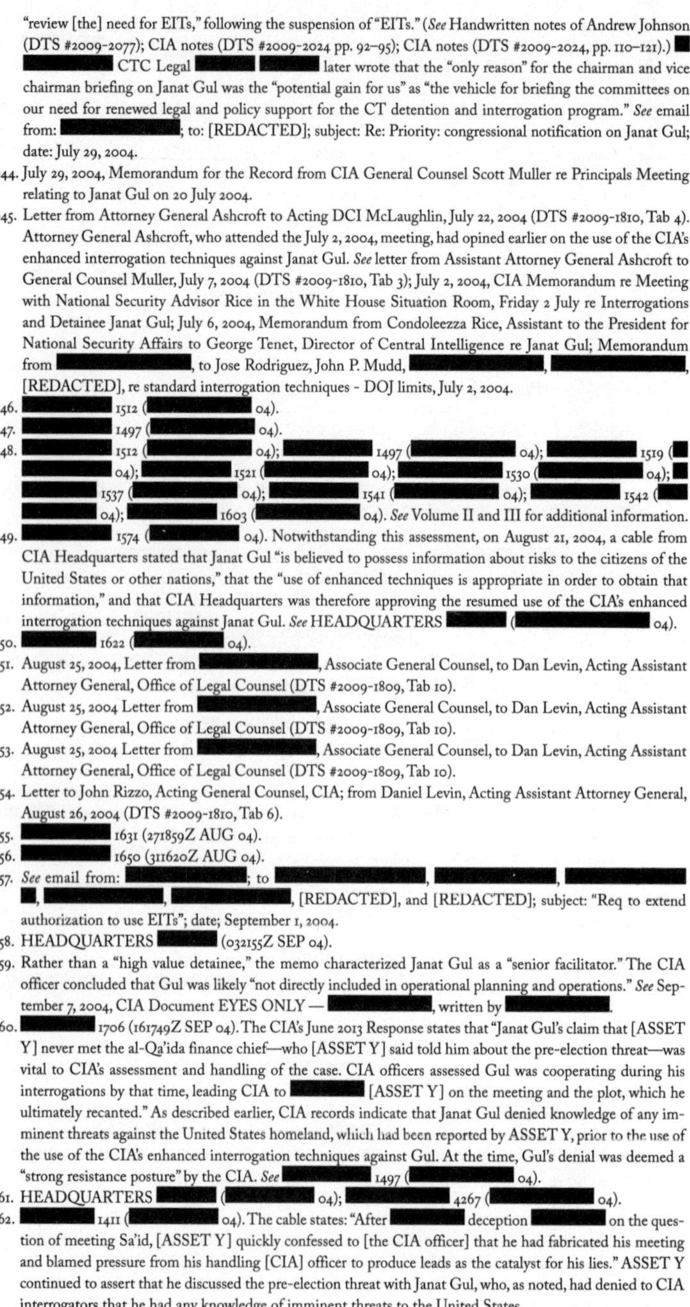

"review [the] need for EITs," following the suspension of "EITs." (*See* Handwritten notes of Andrew Johnson (DTS #2009-2077); CIA notes (DTS #2009-2024 pp. 92–95); CIA notes (DTS #2009-2024, pp. 110–121).) CTC Legal later wrote that the "only reason" for the chairman and vice chairman briefing on Janat Gul was the "potential gain for us" as "the vehicle for briefing the committees on our need for renewed legal and policy support for the CT detention and interrogation program." *See* email from: ; to: [REDACTED]; subject: Re: Priority: congressional notification on Janat Gul; date: July 29, 2004.

1944. July 29, 2004, Memorandum for the Record from CIA General Counsel Scott Muller re Principals Meeting relating to Janat Gul on 20 July 2004.
1945. Letter from Attorney General Ashcroft to Acting DCI McLaughlin, July 22, 2004 (DTS #2009-1810, Tab 4). Attorney General Ashcroft, who attended the July 2, 2004, meeting, had opined earlier on the use of the CIA's enhanced interrogation techniques against Janat Gul. *See* letter from Assistant Attorney General Ashcroft to General Counsel Muller, July 7, 2004 (DTS #2009-1810, Tab 3); July 2, 2004, CIA Memorandum re Meeting with National Security Advisor Rice in the White House Situation Room, Friday 2 July re Interrogations and Detainee Janat Gul; July 6, 2004, Memorandum from Condoleezza Rice, Assistant to the President for National Security Affairs to George Tenet, Director of Central Intelligence re Janat Gul; Memorandum from , to Jose Rodriguez, John P. Mudd, , , [REDACTED], re standard interrogation techniques - DOJ limits, July 2, 2004.
1946. 1512 (04).
1947. 1497 (04).
1948. 1512 (04); 1497 (04); 1519 (04); 1521 (04); 1530 (04); 1537 (04); 1541 (04); 1542 (04); 1603 (04). *See* Volume II and III for additional information.
1949. 1574 (04). Notwithstanding this assessment, on August 21, 2004, a cable from CIA Headquarters stated that Janat Gul "is believed to possess information about risks to the citizens of the United States or other nations," that the "use of enhanced techniques is appropriate in order to obtain that information," and that CIA Headquarters was therefore approving the resumed use of the CIA's enhanced interrogation techniques against Janat Gul. *See* HEADQUARTERS (04).
1950. 1622 (04).
1951. August 25, 2004, Letter from , Associate General Counsel, to Dan Levin, Acting Assistant Attorney General, Office of Legal Counsel (DTS #2009-1809, Tab 10).
1952. August 25, 2004 Letter from , Associate General Counsel, to Dan Levin, Acting Assistant Attorney General, Office of Legal Counsel (DTS #2009-1809, Tab 10).
1953. August 25, 2004 Letter from , Associate General Counsel, to Dan Levin, Acting Assistant Attorney General, Office of Legal Counsel (DTS #2009-1809, Tab 10).
1954. Letter to John Rizzo, Acting General Counsel, CIA; from Daniel Levin, Acting Assistant Attorney General, August 26, 2004 (DTS #2009-1810, Tab 6).
1955. 1631 (271859Z AUG 04).
1956. 1650 (311620Z AUG 04).
1957. *See* email from: ; to , , , , , [REDACTED], and [REDACTED]; subject: "Req to extend authorization to use EITs"; date; September 1, 2004.
1958. HEADQUARTERS (032155Z SEP 04).
1959. Rather than a "high value detainee," the memo characterized Janat Gul as a "senior facilitator." The CIA officer concluded that Gul was likely "not directly included in operational planning and operations." *See* September 7, 2004, CIA Document EYES ONLY — , written by .
1960. 1706 (161749Z SEP 04). The CIA's June 2013 Response states that "Janat Gul's claim that [ASSET Y] never met the al-Qa'ida finance chief—who [ASSET Y] said told him about the pre-election threat—was vital to CIA's assessment and handling of the case. CIA officers assessed Gul was cooperating during his interrogations by that time, leading CIA to [ASSET Y] on the meeting and the plot, which he ultimately recanted." As described earlier, CIA records indicate that Janat Gul denied knowledge of any imminent threats against the United States homeland, which had been reported by ASSET Y, prior to the use of the use of the CIA's enhanced interrogation techniques against Gul. At the time, Gul's denial was deemed a "strong resistance posture" by the CIA. *See* 1497 (04).
1961. HEADQUARTERS (04); 4267 (04).
1962. 1411 (04). The cable states: "After deception on the question of meeting Sa'id, [ASSET Y] quickly confessed to [the CIA officer] that he had fabricated his meeting and blamed pressure from his handling [CIA] officer to produce leads as the catalyst for his lies." ASSET Y continued to assert that he discussed the pre-election threat with Janat Gul, who, as noted, had denied to CIA interrogators that he had any knowledge of imminent threats to the United States.
1963. ALEC (092126Z NOV 04).

1964. Email from: [REDACTED]; to: , , , , subject: re ALEC ; date: November 10, 2004.
1965. *See* email from: ; to: ; subject: re Gul and Report; date: November 22, 2004, at 8:25 AM.
1966. *See* email from: ; to: ; subject: re Gul and Report; date: November 22, 2004, at 8:25 AM.
1967. CIA "Comments on Detainees," December 19, 2004, notes from DETENTION SITE BLACK. In April 2005, the chief of Base where Janat Gul was held emailed that "[Janat Gul] was never the person we thought he was. He is not the senior Al-Qa'ida facilitator that he has been labeled. He's a rather poorly educated village man with a very simple outlook on life. He's also quite lazy and it's the combination of his background and lack of initiative that got him in trouble. He was looking to make some easy money for little work and he was easily persuaded to move people and run errands for folks on our target list. While he openly admits that he helped move people, it's pretty well established that the vast majority of his work involved seeking medical care and providing housing for family members of Tahir Jan's Uzbek organization. There simply is no 'smoking gun' that we can refer to that would justify our continued holding of [Janat Gul] at a site such as [DETENTION SITE BLACK]. It should be noted, however, that [Janat Gul] has made what I think is great progress. He fingered [ASSET Y] as a fabricator and has been generally responsive to requirements though, it must be said, he never had access to most of the information we seek from him." *See* email from: [REDACTED] (COB DETENTION SITE BLACK); to: ; cc: , , ; subject: re ; date: April 30, 2005.
1968. Email from: ; to: , , , , and [REDACTED]; subject: questions from OLC for Art 16 opinion; date: April 6, 2005.
1969. Email from: ; to: , , , , and [REDACTED]; subject: questions from OLC for Art 16 opinion; date: April 12, 2005. email from: ; to: , , , , and [REDACTED]; subject: Re: questions from OLC for Art 16 opinion; date: April 14, 2005.
1970. Email from: ; to: , , , , and ; subject: response to no. 5 request from : OTA's Detainee Reporting Brief; date: April 14, 2005.
1971. Memorandum for John A. Rizzo, Senior Deputy General Counsel, Central Intelligence Agency, from Steven G. Bradbury, Principal Deputy Assistant Attorney General, Office of Legal Counsel, May 10, 2005, Re: Application of 18 U.S.C. §§ 2340-2340A to Certain Techniques That May Be Used in the Interrogation of a High Value al Qaeda Detainee.
1972. Memorandum for John A. Rizzo, Senior Deputy General Counsel, Central Intelligence Agency, from Steven G. Bradbury, Principal Deputy Assistant Attorney General, Office of Legal Counsel, May 10, 2005, Re: Application of 18 U.S.C. §§ 2340-2340A to Certain Techniques That May Be Used in the Interrogation of a High Value al Qaeda Detainee.
1973. Memorandum for John A. Rizzo, Senior Deputy General Counsel, Central Intelligence Agency, from Steven G. Bradbury, Principal Deputy Assistant Attorney General, Office of Legal Counsel, May 30, 2005, Re: Application of United States Obligations Under Article 16 of the Convention Against Torture to Certain Techniques that May be Used in the Interrogation of High Value al Qaeda Detainees.
1974. Memorandum for John A. Rizzo, Senior Deputy General Counsel, Central Intelligence Agency, from Steven G. Bradbury, Principal Deputy Assistant Attorney General, Office of Legal Counsel, May 30, 2005, Re: Application of United States Obligations Under Article 16 of the Convention Against Torture to Certain Techniques that May be Used in the Interrogation of High Value al Qaeda Detainees.
1975. Memorandum for John A. Rizzo, Senior Deputy General Counsel, Central Intelligence Agency, from Steven G. Bradbury, Principal Deputy Assistant Attorney General, Office of Legal Counsel, May 30, 2005, Re: Application of United States Obligations Under Article 16 of the Convention Against Torture to Certain Techniques that May be Used in the Interrogation of High Value al Qaeda Detainees (brackets in the original). The OLC memorandum also cited an "Undated CIA Memo, 'Janat Gul' (*'Janat Gul Memo'*). The OLC also relied on CIA representations that Janat Gul's interrogations "greatly increased the CIA's understanding of our enemy and its plans."
1976. Memorandum for John A. Rizzo, Senior Deputy General Counsel, Central Intelligence Agency, from Steven G. Bradbury, Principal Deputy Assistant Attorney General, Office of Legal Counsel, May 30, 2005, Re: Application of United States Obligations Under Article 16 of the Convention Against Torture to Certain Techniques that May be Used in the Interrogation of High Value al Qaeda Detainees.
1977. The OLC relied on CIA representations that Janat Gul had information, but that he withheld it. In describing the interrogation process, the OLC stated that Janat Gul's resistance increased as questioning moved to his "'knowledge of operational terrorist activities.'" The OLC also wrote that "Gul apparently feigned memory problems (which CIA psychologists ruled out through intelligence and memory tests) in order to avoid answering questions." The OLC further conveyed that the "CIA believes that Janat Gul continues to downplay his knowledge." *See* Memorandum for John A. Rizzo, Senior Deputy General Counsel, Central Intelligence

Agency, from Steven G. Bradbury, Principal Deputy Assistant Attorney General, Office of Legal Counsel, May 30, 2005, Re: Application of United States Obligations Under Article 16 of the Convention Against Torture to Certain Techniques that May Be Used in the Interrogation of High Value al Qaeda Detainees.

1978. As described elsewhere, on April 21, 2009, a CIA spokesperson confirmed the accuracy of the information in the OLC memorandum in response to the partial declassification of this memorandum and others.

1979. Among other documents, *see* Memorandum for: Inspector General; from: James Pavitt, Deputy Director for Operations; subject: re (S) Comments to Draft IG Special Review, "Counterterrorism Detention and Interrogation Program" (2003-7123-IG); date: February 27, 2004; attachment: February 24, 2004, Memorandum re Successes of CIA's Counterterrorism Detention and Interrogation Activities.

1980. *See* details in the intelligence chronology in Volume II.

1981. CIA memorandum to the CIA Inspector General from James Pavitt, CIA's Deputy Director for Operations, dated February 27, 2004, with the subject line, "Comments to Draft IG Special Review, 'Counterterrorism Detention and Interrogation Program' (2003-7123-IG)," Attachment, "Successes of CIA's Counterterrorism Detention and Interrogation Activities," dated February 24, 2004.

1982. [REDACTED], Memorandum for the Record; subject: Meeting with Deputy Chief, Counterterrorist Center ALEC Station; date: 17 July 2003. These representations were included in the final, and now declassified Special Review of the Inspector General, which states that KSM "provided information that helped lead to the arrests of terrorists including Sayfullah Paracha and his son Uzair, businessmen whom Khalid Shaykh Muhammad planned to use to smuggle explosives in New York." (*See* CIA Inspector General Special Review, Counterterrorism Detention and Interrogation Activities (September 2001–October 2003) (2003-7123-IG), 7 May 2004). The statements in the Special Review regarding the purported effectiveness of the program, including the reference to the Parachas, were cited by the Office of Legal Counsel in its analysis of the CIA's enhanced interrogation techniques. *See* Memorandum for John A, Rizzo, Senior Deputy General Counsel, Central Intelligence Agency, from Steven G. Bradbury, Principal Deputy Assistant Attorney General, Office of Legal Counsel, May 30, 2005, Re: Application of United States Obligations Under Article 16 of the Convention Against Torture to Certain Techniques that May Be Used in the Interrogation of High Value al Qaeda Detainees, pp. 10–11, citing IG Special Review, pp. 85–91.

1983. Email from: [REDACTED]; to: [REDACTED]; cc: [REDACTED], [REDACTED], [REDACTED], [REDACTED]; subject: re Addition on KSM/AZ and measures; date: February 9, 2004. Memorandum for: Inspector General; from: James Pavitt, Deputy Director for Operations; subject: re (S) Comments to Draft IG Special Review, "Counterterrorism Detention and Interrogation Program" (2003-7123-IG); date: February 27, 2004; attachment: February 24, 2004, Memorandum re Successes of CIA's Counterterrorism Detention and Interrogation Activities.

1984. CIA memorandum for the Record, "Review of Interrogation Program on 29 July 2003," prepared by CIA General Counsel Scott Muller, dated August 5, 2003; briefing slides entitled, "*CIA Interrogation Program,*" dated July 29, 2003, presented to senior White House officials.

1985. *See* email from: [REDACTED]; to: multiple addresses; subject: "Draft of IA on 'Detainee Reporting Pivotal to the War on Terrorism'"; date: May 16, 2005, at 2:08 PM.

1986. Italics added. CIA Intelligence Assessment, "Detainee Reporting Pivotal for the War Against Al-Qa'ida," June 2005, which CIA records indicate was provided to White House officials on June 1, 2005. The Intelligence Assessment at the SECRET//NOFORN classification level was more broadly disseminated on June 3, 2005. On March 31, 2009, former Vice President Cheney requested the declassification of this Intelligence Assessment, which was publicly released with redactions on August 24, 2009.

1987. DIRECTOR [REDACTED] (221835Z APR 02); ALEC [REDACTED] (222235Z DEC 02); DIRECTOR [REDACTED] (221835Z APR 02).

1988. ALEC [REDACTED] (222235Z DEC 02).

1989. FBI WASHINGTON DC (271623Z MAR 03); ALEC [REDACTED] (191630Z MAY 03) (cables explaining previous FBI investigative action on Paracha). On March 28, 2003, the FBI would return to the same employer and the same address, leading to the apprehension of Uzhair Paracha, who would voluntarily provide significant reporting to the FBI.

1990. CIA [REDACTED] (040123Z DEC 02)/[REDACTED]. *See also* [REDACTED].

1991. CIA [REDACTED] (040123Z DEC 02)/[REDACTED]. *See also* [REDACTED] and ALEC 222235Z DEC 02).

1992. *See* FBI investigative file [REDACTED].

1993. [REDACTED] 13890 [REDACTED]. The cable describing Majid Khan's foreign government interrogation also included Khan's reporting on how Ammar al-Baluchi intended to have Uzhair use Majid Khan's credit card to create the appearance that Majid Khan was already in the United States. As described in the full Committee Study, the cable further detailed Khan's two meetings with Uzhair and his father, and a subsequent phone call with Uzhair (following Uzhair's return to the United States), all of which were facilitated by Ammar al-Baluchi.

1994. *See* [REDACTED] 10983 (242321Z MAR 03); [REDACTED] 10972 (241122Z MAR 03); and the KSM detainee review in Volume III.

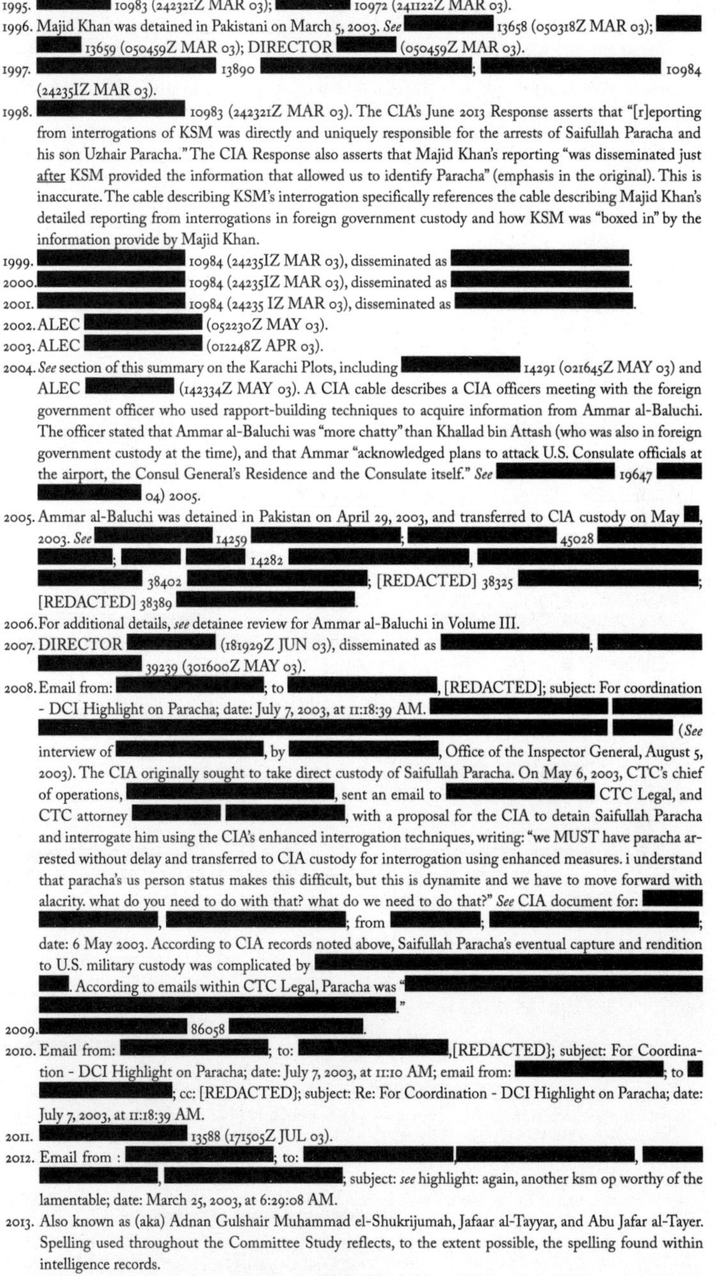

1995. 10983 (242321Z MAR 03); 10972 (241122Z MAR 03).

1996. Majid Khan was detained in Pakistani on March 5, 2003. *See* 13658 (050318Z MAR 03); 13659 (050459Z MAR 03); DIRECTOR (050459Z MAR 03).

1997. 13890 ; 10984 (24235IZ MAR 03).

1998. 10983 (242321Z MAR 03). The CIA's June 2013 Response asserts that "[r]eporting from interrogations of KSM was directly and uniquely responsible for the arrests of Saifullah Paracha and his son Uzhair Paracha." The CIA Response also asserts that Majid Khan's reporting "was disseminated just after KSM provided the information that allowed us to identify Paracha" (emphasis in the original). This is inaccurate. The cable describing KSM's interrogation specifically references the cable describing Majid Khan's detailed reporting from interrogations in foreign government custody and how KSM was "boxed in" by the information provide by Majid Khan.

1999. 10984 (24235IZ MAR 03), disseminated as .

2000. 10984 (24235IZ MAR 03), disseminated as .

2001. 10984 (24235 IZ MAR 03), disseminated as .

2002. ALEC (052230Z MAY 03).

2003. ALEC (012248Z APR 03).

2004. *See* section of this summary on the Karachi Plots, including 14291 (021645Z MAY 03) and ALEC (142334Z MAY 03). A CIA cable describes a CIA officers meeting with the foreign government officer who used rapport-building techniques to acquire information from Ammar al-Baluchi. The officer stated that Ammar al-Baluchi was "more chatty" than Khallad bin Attash (who was also in foreign government custody at the time), and that Ammar "acknowledged plans to attack U.S. Consulate officials at the airport, the Consul General's Residence and the Consulate itself." *See* 19647 04) 2005.

2005. Ammar al-Baluchi was detained in Pakistan on April 29, 2003, and transferred to CIA custody on May , 2003. *See* 14259 ; 45028 ; 14282 , 38402 ; [REDACTED] 38325 ; [REDACTED] 38389 .

2006. For additional details, *see* detainee review for Ammar al-Baluchi in Volume III.

2007. DIRECTOR (181929Z JUN 03), disseminated as ; 39239 (301600Z MAY 03).

2008. Email from: ; to , [REDACTED]; subject: For coordination - DCI Highlight on Paracha; date: July 7, 2003, at 11:18:39 AM. (*See* interview of , by , Office of the Inspector General, August 5, 2003). The CIA originally sought to take direct custody of Saifullah Paracha. On May 6, 2003, CTC's chief of operations, , sent an email to CTC Legal, and CTC attorney , with a proposal for the CIA to detain Saifullah Paracha and interrogate him using the CIA's enhanced interrogation techniques, writing: "we MUST have paracha arrested without delay and transferred to CIA custody for interrogation using enhanced measures. i understand that paracha's us person status makes this difficult, but this is dynamite and we have to move forward with alacrity. what do you need to do with that? what do we need to do that?" *See* CIA document for: , ; from ; ; date: 6 May 2003. According to CIA records noted above, Saifullah Paracha's eventual capture and rendition to U.S. military custody was complicated by . According to emails within CTC Legal, Paracha was " ."

2009. 86058 .

2010. Email from: ; to: ,[REDACTED}; subject: For Coordination - DCI Highlight on Paracha; date: July 7, 2003, at 11:10 AM; email from: ; to ; cc: [REDACTED}; subject: Re: For Coordination - DCI Highlight on Paracha; date: July 7, 2003, at 11:18:39 AM.

2011. 13588 (171505Z JUL 03).

2012. Email from : ; to: , , , ; subject: *see* highlight: again, another ksm op worthy of the lamentable; date: March 25, 2003, at 6:29:08 AM.

2013. Also known as (aka) Adnan Gulshair Muhammad el-Shukrijumah, Jafaar al-Tayyar, and Abu Jafar al-Tayer. Spelling used throughout the Committee Study reflects, to the extent possible, the spelling found within intelligence records.

2014. CIA Memorandum for Steve Bradbury at Office of Legal Counsel, Department of Justice, dated March 2, 2005, from , Legal Group, DCI Counterterrorist Center, subject

"Effectiveness of the CIA Counterterrorist Interrogation Techniques." *See also* CIA classified Statement for the Record, Senate Select Committee on Intelligence, provided by General Michael V. Hayden, Director, Central Intelligence Agency, 12 April 2007 (DTS #2007-1563). *See also* CIA Intelligence Assessment, "Detainee Reporting Pivotal for the War Against Al-Qa'ida," June 2005, which CIA records indicate was provided to White House officials on June 1, 2005. The Intelligence Assessment at the SECRET//NOFORN level was more broadly disseminated on June 3, 2005. On March 31, 2009, former Vice President Cheney requested the declassification of this Intelligence Assessment, which was publicly released with redactions on August 24, 2009. *See also* CIA graphic attachment to several CIA briefings on the CIA's enhanced interrogation techniques, entitled, "Key Intelligence and Reporting Derived from Abu Zubaydah and Khalid Shaykh Muhammad (KSM)." *See also* CIA briefing documents for Leon Panetta entitled, "Tab 9: DCIA Briefing on RDI Program- 18FEB.2009."

2015. The CIA's June 2013 Response states that "there were cases in which we either made a factual error or used imprecise language, but these mistakes were not central to our representations and none invalidates our assessment that detainee reporting provided key intelligence on this important terrorist." As one of two examples, the CIA's June 2013 Response acknowledges that the "[CIA] incorrectly stated al-Tayyar fled the United States in response to the FBI investigation, although he had in fact already departed the United States by this time." The Committee found that this inaccurate statement was central to the CIA's representations. The CIA asserted that "Ja'far al-Tayyar" fled the United States because of KSM's reporting after the use of the CIA's enhanced interrogation techniques in the context of representations that the use of the techniques "has been a key reason why al-Qa'ida has failed to launch a spectacular attack in the West."

2016. ALEC [REDACTED] (210218Z MAR 03). Extensive open source records include "Broward Man Sought as Terror Suspect," *Miami Herald*, dated March 21, 2003; "Pursuit of al-Qaeda keeps coming back to Fla.," *USA Today*, dated June 15, 2003; and "A Hunt for 'The Pilot,'" *U.S. News and World Report*, dated March 30, 2003. For context, *See also* United States District Court Southern District Florida, Case No. 02-60096, *United States of America v. Imran Mandhai and Shueyb Mossa Jokhan*, filed May 16, 2002.

2017. *See* Abu Zubaydah detainee review in Volume III and [REDACTED].

2018. [REDACTED] 10884 (182140Z MAR 03); email from: [REDACTED]; to [REDACTED]; cc: [REDACTED]; subject: Re: Reissue/Correction: CT: Comments on Khalid Shaykh Muhammad on imminent threats to U.S. targets in Thailand, Indonesia, and the Philippines; date March 12, 2003, at 9:36:57 AM; [REDACTED] 42247 (210357Z JUL 03); email from: [REDACTED]; to: [REDACTED], [REDACTED], [REDACTED], [REDACTED], [REDACTED] [REDACTED], [REDACTED], [REDACTED]; cc: [REDACTED], [REDACTED], [REDACTED], [REDACTED], [REDACTED], [REDACTED], [REDACTED]; subject: RATHER PROFOUND IMPLICATIONS... Ammar al-Baluchi's Comments on Jaffar al-Tayyar--If Ammar is Correct, then KSM Appears to Have a Focused Us on Jaffar in a Extended Deception Scheme--and His Deception Capabilities are Not Broken Down; date: 07/21/03 11:24 AM.

2019. Email from: [REDACTED]; to [REDACTED]; cc: [REDACTED]; subject: Re: REISSUE/CORRECTION: CT: CT: Comments on Khalid Shaykh Muhammad on imminent threats to U.S. targets in Thailand, Indonesia, and the Philippines; date: March 12, 2003, at 9:36:57 AM; National Counterterrorism Center, REFLECTIONS, "Ja'far al-Tayyar: An Unlikely Al-Qa'ida Operatjonal Threat," 22 December 2005; [REDACTED] 42247 (210357Z JUL 03); email from: [REDACTED]; to: [REDACTED], [REDACTED], [REDACTED], [REDACTED], [REDACTED] [REDACTED], [REDACTED], [REDACTED]; cc: [REDACTED], [REDACTED], [REDACTED], [REDACTED], [REDACTED], [REDACTED], [REDACTED]; subject: RATHER PROFOUND IMPLICATIONS... Ammar al-Baluchi's Comments on Jaffar al-Tayyar--If Ammar is Correct, then KSM Appears to Have a Focused Us on Jaffar in a Extended Deception Scheme--and His Deception Capabilities are Not Broken Down; date: 07/21/03 11:24 AM.

2020. CIA "Briefing Notes on the Value of Detainee Reporting" faxed from the CIA to the Department of Justice on April 15, 2005, at 10:47AM. For KSM's inability to identify name, *see* [REDACTED] 10741 (100917Z MAR 03); [REDACTED] 10740 (092308Z MAR 03), disseminated as [REDACTED] [REDACTED].

2021. 10787 (130716Z MAR 03); [REDACTED] 10863 (171028Z MAR 03). For example, November 6, 2006, talking points prepared for a briefing with the President stated that "KSM described Tayyar as the next Muhammad Atta." *See* CIA document entitled, "DCIA Talking Points: Waterboard 06 November 2007," dated November 6, 2007, with the notation the document was "sent to DCIA Nov, 6 in preparation for POTUS meeting."

2022. Emphasis in original document. CIA Memorandum for Steve Bradbury at Office of Legal Counsel, Department of Justice, dated March 2, 2005, from [REDACTED], [REDACTED] Legal Group, DCI Counterterrorist Center, subject "Effectiveness of the CIA Counterterrorist Interrogation Techniques."

2023. CIA Memorandum for Steve Bradbury at Office of Legal Counsel, Department of Justice, dated March 2, 2005, from [REDACTED], [REDACTED] Legal Group, DCI Counterterrorist Center, subject "Effectiveness of the CIA Counterterrorist Interrogation Techniques."

2024. CIA Briefing for Obama National Security Team - "Renditions, Detentions, and Interrogations (RDI)" including "Tab 7," named "RDG Copy- Briefing on RDI Program 09 Jan. 2009." Referenced materials attached to cover memorandum with the title, "D/CIA Conference Room Seating Visit by President-elect Barrack [sic] Obama National Security Team Tuesday, 13 January 2009; 8:30–11:30 a.m." The briefing book includes the previously mentioned "Briefing Notes on the Value of Detainee Reporting" dated 15 May 2006, which provided the same intelligence claims found in the document of the same name, but dated April 15, 2005. Expected participants included "Senator Boren, Mr. McDonough, Mr. Brennan, General Jones, Mr. Craig, Mr. Lippert, Mr. Smith, Senator Hagel," as well as several CIA officials, including Director Hayden, , John Rizzo, [REDACTED], and Legal, .

2025. Emphasis in original.

2026. The CIA's June 2013 Response states that "[i]n some of the *early* representations, we incorrectly stated al-Tayyar fled the United States in response to the FBI investigation, although he had in fact already departed the United States by this time" (italics added). As noted, this representation was made by the CIA as late as January 2009, to President-elect Obama's national security team.

2027. Emphases in original. CIA Briefing for Obama National Security Team - "Renditions, Detentions, and Interrogations (RDI)" including "Tab 7," named "RDG Copy- Briefing on RDI Program 09 Jan. 2009." Referenced materials attached to cover memorandum with the title, "D/CIA Conference Room Seating Visit by President-elect Barrack [sic] Obama National Security Team Tuesday, 13 January 2009; 8:30–11:30 a.m." The briefing book includes the previously mentioned "Briefing Notes on the Value of Detainee Reporting" dated 15 May 2006, which provided the same intelligence claims in the document of the same name, but dated April 15, 2005. *See* "RDI Key Impacts."

2028. ALEC (210218Z MAR 03). Extensive open source records include "Pursuit of al-Qaeda keeps coming back to Fla.," *USA Today*, dated June 15, 2003; "Broward Man Sought as Terror Suspect," *Miami Herald*, dated March 21, 2003; and "A Hunt for 'The Pilot,'" *U.S. News and World Report*, dated March 30, 2003. The FBI confirmed for the Committee that Adnan el-Shukrijumah departed the United States in May 2001. *See* DTS #2013- 0391.

2029. Email from: ; to: [REDACTED]; cc: , ; subject: Padilla Breaks; date: May 1, 2003, at 08:51 AM; CIA "Briefing Notes on the Value of Detainee Reporting" faxed from the CIA to the Department of Justice on April 15, 2005, at 10:47 AM; ALEC (210218Z MAR 03).

2030. ; DIRECTOR (210549Z SEP 04); 24533 (171207Z SEP 04). *See also* 14425 , describing reporting on Jaffar al-Tayyar from the interrogation of Ammar al-Baluchi in foreign government custody.

2031. 11368 . *See also* (HEADQUARTERS); .

2032. and Federal Bureau of Investigation Documents pertaining "to the interrogation of detainee Zayn Al Abideen Abu Zabaidah" and provided to the Senate Select Committee on Intelligence by cover letter dated July 20, 2010, (DTS #2010-2939). *See also* 10092 (211031Z APR 02); 10022 (121216Z APR 02); ; 10321 (231427Z MAY 02); ; .

2033. *See* HEADQUARTERS (250239Z JAN 03); ; . For example, in January 2003, a CIA cable stated that Abu Zubaydah repeated that al-Tayyar studied in the United States. The only new information provide by Abu Zubaydah was that al-Tayyar's nickname, "the pilot," did not necessarily mean that al-Tayyar could fly an airplane. Abu Zubaydah explained to CIA officers that the term "the pilot" also means someone who is righteous.

2034. ALEC (111551Z SEP 02).

2035. CIA (072303Z NOV 02). *See* "Khalid Shayk Muhammad's Threat Reporting - Precious Truths, Surrounded by a Bodyguard of Lies," IICT, April 3, 2003. For more on the letters that were seized during the September 11, 2002 raids in Pakistan, *see* ALEC (110154Z JAN 03). *See also* DIRECTOR (172117Z SEP 02).

2036. *See* 22507 ; 22508 ; 20744 .

2037. CIA (072303Z NOV 02).

2038. April 3, 2003, Intelligence Community Terrorist Threat Assessment regarding KSM threat reporting, entitled "Khalid Shaykh Muhammad's Threat Reporting—Precious Truths, Surrounded by a Bodyguard of Lies."

2039. *See* KSM detainee review in Volume III.

2040. ALEC (072215Z MAR 03).
2041. ALEC (1102097 JAN 03).
2042. ALEC (072215Z MAR 03).
2043. ALEC (072215Z MAR 03). For more on the letters that were seized during the September 11, 2002, raids in Pakistan, and Abu Zubaydah's reporting, *see* ALEC (110154Z JAN 03); DIRECTOR (172117Z SEP 02); 10092 (211031Z APR 02); 10022 (121216Z APR 02); ; 10321 (231427Z MAY 02); ; ; Federal Bureau of Investigation documents pertaining "to the interrogation of detainee Zayn Al Abideen Abu Zabaidah" and provided to the Senate Select Committee on Intelligence by cover letter dated July 20, 2010 (DTS #2010-2939).
2044. 10741 (100917Z MAR 03).
2045. 10741 (100917Z MAR 03); 10740 (092308Z MAR 03), disseminated as .
2046. Among other open source news reports, *see* "Father denies son linked to terror." *St. Petersburg Times*, published March 22, 2003.
2047. 10884 (182140Z MAR 03).
2048. 42247 (210357Z JUL 03); email from: ; to: [REDACTED], , , , , [REDACTED], [REDACTED]; cc: [REDACTED], [REDACTED], [REDACTED], [REDACTED], [REDACTED], [REDACTED], [REDACTED]; subject: RATHER PROFOUND IMPLICATIONS... Ammar al-Baluchi's Comments on Jaffar al-Tayyar--If Ammar is Correct, then KSM Appears to Have a Focused Us on Jaffar in a Extended Deception Scheme—and His Deception Capabilities are Not Broken Down; date: 07/21/03, at 11:24 AM. *See also* CIA (072303Z NOV 02) and "Khalid Shaykh Muhammad's Threat Reporting - Precious Truths, Surrounded by a Bodyguard of Lies," IICT, April 3, 2003.
2049. 10741 (100917Z MAR 03); 11377 (231943Z APR 03), disseminated as .
2050. 10778 (121549Z MAR 03), disseminated as ; 10883 (182127Z MAR 03), disseminated as 11717 (201722Z MAY 03), disseminated as .
2051. 10894 (191513Z MAR 03); 10902 (201037Z MAR 03).
2052. 10959 (231205Z MAR 03); 10950 (222127Z MAR 03).
2053. 10787 (130716Z MAR 03).
2054. 10863 (171028Z MAR 03). It is unclear if KSM made the comparison in the first instance, or if the March 13, 2003, cable provided an inaccurate account of KSM's statements. The CIA's June 2013 Response states that"KSM did not call al-Tayyar 'the next Muhammad Atta.'" The CIA's June 2013 Response characterizes the inaccuracy as "an imprecise paraphrase of KSM."
2055. Note for: [REDACTED]; from: [REDACTED], OFFICE: [DETENTION SITE BLUE]; Subject: JAFAR REQUEST; date: March 18, 2003, at 08:16:07 PM.
2056. Email from: [REDACTED]; to: [REDACTED]; subject: Re: JAFAR REQUEST; date: March 18, 2003, at 03:49:33 PM.
2057. 10902 (201037Z MAR 03); 10959 (231205Z MAR 03); 10950 (222127Z MAR 03); 11377 (231943Z APR 03), disseminated as .
2058. "Briefing Notes on the Value of Detainee Reporting" faxed from the CIA to the Department of Justice on April 15, 2005, at 10:47AM. On March 21, 2003, CIA records state that a photograph of Gulshair El Shukrijumah's son was obtained from the FBI and shown to KSM, Ramzi bin al-Shibh, and Abu Zubaydah, who all identified the photograph as that of al-Tayyar. *See* ALEC (210218Z MAR 03).
2059. Email from: ; to [REDACTED]; cc: [REDACTED]; subject: Re: REISSUE/CORRECTION: CT: COMMENTS OF KHALID SHAYKH MUHAMMAD ON IMMINENT THREATS TO U.S. TARGETS IN THAILAND, INDONESIA, AND THE PHILIPPINES; date: March 12, 2003, at 9:36:57 AM.
2060. "Khalid Shaykh Muhammad's Threat Reporting - Precious Truths, Surrounded by a Bodyguard of Lies," IICT, April 3, 2003.
2061. 42247 (210357Z JUL 03); email from: ; to: [REDACTED], , , , , [REDACTED], [REDACTED]; cc: [REDACTED], [REDACTED], [REDACTED], [REDACTED], [REDACTED], [REDACTED], [REDACTED]; subject: RATHER PROFOUND IMPLICATIONS; subject: RATHER PROFOUND IMPLICATIONS... Ammar al-Baluchi's Comments on Jaffar al-Tayyar--If Ammar is Correct, then KSM Appears to Have Focused Us on Jaffar in a Extended Deception Scheme-and His Deception Capabilities are Not Broken Down; date: 07/21/03, at 11:24 AM.
2062. National Counterterrorism Center, REFLECTIONS, "Ja'far al-Tayyar: An Unlikely Al-Qa'ida Operational

Threat," 22 December 2005. While NCTC's "mainline analytic group" disagreed with the Red Team's analytical conclusions, records do not indicate that the Red Team's account of the contrary detainee reporting was challenged Draft MEMORANDUM FOR THE DIRECTOR OF NATIONAL INTELLIGENCE from the Office of the Director of National Intelligence General Counsel; SUBJECT: [REDACTED] [REDACTED].

2063. *See* CIA memorandum to the CIA Inspector General from James Pavitt, CIA's Deputy Director for Operations dated February 27, 2004, with the subject line, "Comments to Draft IG Special Review, 'Counterterrorism Detention and Interrogation Program' (2003-7123-IG)," Attachment, "Successes of CIA's Counterterrorism Detention and Interrogation Activities, dated February 24, 2004.

2064. [REDACTED], Memorandum for the Record, subject: Meeting with Deputy Chief, Counterterrorist Center ALEC Station; date: 17 July 2003; and CIA Office of Inspector General, Special Review - Counterterrorism Detention and Interrogation Program, (2003-7123-IG), May 2004.

2065. CIA Office of Inspector General, Special Review - Counterterrorism Detention and Interrogation Program, (2003-7123-IG), May 2004.

2066. [REDACTED] 41351 [REDACTED].

2067. Information on ALI SALEH M K AL-MARRI, provided by the FBI to the Committee, March 26, 2002 (DTS 2002-1819).

2068. On July 16, 2003, informed the OIG that KSM's information "helped lead to the arrest of al-Marri. (*See* [REDACTED] [REDACTED], Memorandum for the Record; subject: Meeting with Deputy Chief, Counterterrorist Center ALEC Station; date: 17 July 2003). Two days later, [REDACTED] wrote an email with information intended for CIA leadership that stated, accurately, that al-Marri "had been detained on a material witness warrant based on information linking him to the 911 financier Hasawi." (*See* email from [REDACTED] [REDACTED]; to: [REDACTED], [REDACTED], [REDACTED], [REDACTED] [REDACTED], [REDACTED], [REDACTED], [REDACTED],[REDACTED], [REDACTED] , [REDACTED], [REDACTED]; subject: value of detainees; date: July 18, 2003, at 2:30:09 PM).

2069. The January 2004 draft OIG Special Review included the inaccurate information provided by [REDACTED] [REDACTED], that KSM "provided information that helped lead to the arrests of terrorists including . . . Saleh Almery, a sleeper operative in New York." (*See* CIA Inspector General, Special Review, Counterterrorism Detention and Interrogation Program (2003-7123-IG) January 2004). CTC's response to the draft Special Review was likewise prepared by [REDACTED], who wrote: "KSM also identified a photograph of a suspicious student in New York whom the FBI suspected of some involvement with al-Qa'ida, but against whom we had no concrete information." After describing KSM's reporting, [REDACTED] wrote, "[t]his student is now being held on a material witness warrant." (*See* email from: [REDACTED]; to: [REDACTED] [REDACTED]; cc: [REDACTED], [REDACTED], [REDACTED], [REDACTED] [REDACTED]; subject: re Addition on KSM/AZ and measures; date: February 9, 2004.) DDO Pavitt's formal response to the OIG draft Special Review included this representation, adding that the information was provided "as a result of the lawful use of EITs." Pavitt's memo to the OIG did not acknowledge that the "student now being held on a material witness warrant" had been arrested more than a year prior to the capture of KSM. Nor did it correct the inaccurate information in the OIG's draft Special Review that KSM's information "helped lead to the arrest" of al-Marri. *See* memorandum for Inspector General from James Pavitt, Deputy Director for Operations; subject: re (S) Comments to Draft IG Special Review, "Counterterrorism Detention and Interrogation Program" (2003-7123-IG); date: February 27, 2004; attachment: February 24, 2004, Memorandum re Successes of CIA's Counterterrorism Detention and Interrogation Activities.

2070. CIA Office of Inspector General, Special Review - Counterterrorism Detention and Interrogation Program, (2003-7123-IG), May 2004.

2071. In its May 30, 2005, memorandum, the OLC wrote, "we understand that interrogations have led to specific, actionable intelligence," and "[w]e understand that the use of enhanced techniques in the interrogations of KSM, Zubaydah and others . . . has yielded critical information" (Memorandum for John A. Rizzo, Senior Deputy General Counsel, Central Intelligence Agency, from Steven G. Bradbury, Principal Deputy Assistant Attorney General, Office of Legal Counsel, May 30, 2005, Re: Application of United States Obligations Under Article 16 of the Convention Against Torture to Certain Techniques that May be Used in the Interrogation of High Value Al Qaeda Detainees (DTS #2009-1810, Tab 11), citing IG Special Review at 86, 90-91.

2072. The CIA's June 2013 Response states: "CIA mistakenly provided incorrect information to the Inspector General (IG) that led to a one-time misrepresentation of this case in the IG's 2004 Special Review. The CIA's June 2013 Response states that "[t]his mistake was not, as it is characterized in the 'Findings and Conclusions' section of the Study, a 'repeatedly represented' or 'frequently cited' example of the effectiveness of CIA's interrogation program. The Committee found that, in addition to the multiple representations to the CIA OIG, the inaccurate information in the final OIG Special Review was, as noted above, provided by the CIA to the Department of Justice to support the Department's analysis of the lawfulness of the CIA's enhanced interrogation techniques. The OIG Special Review was also relied upon by the Blue Ribbon Panel evaluating the effectiveness of the CIA's enhanced interrogation techniques, and later was cited in multiple open source articles and books, often in the context of the "effectiveness" of the CIA program.

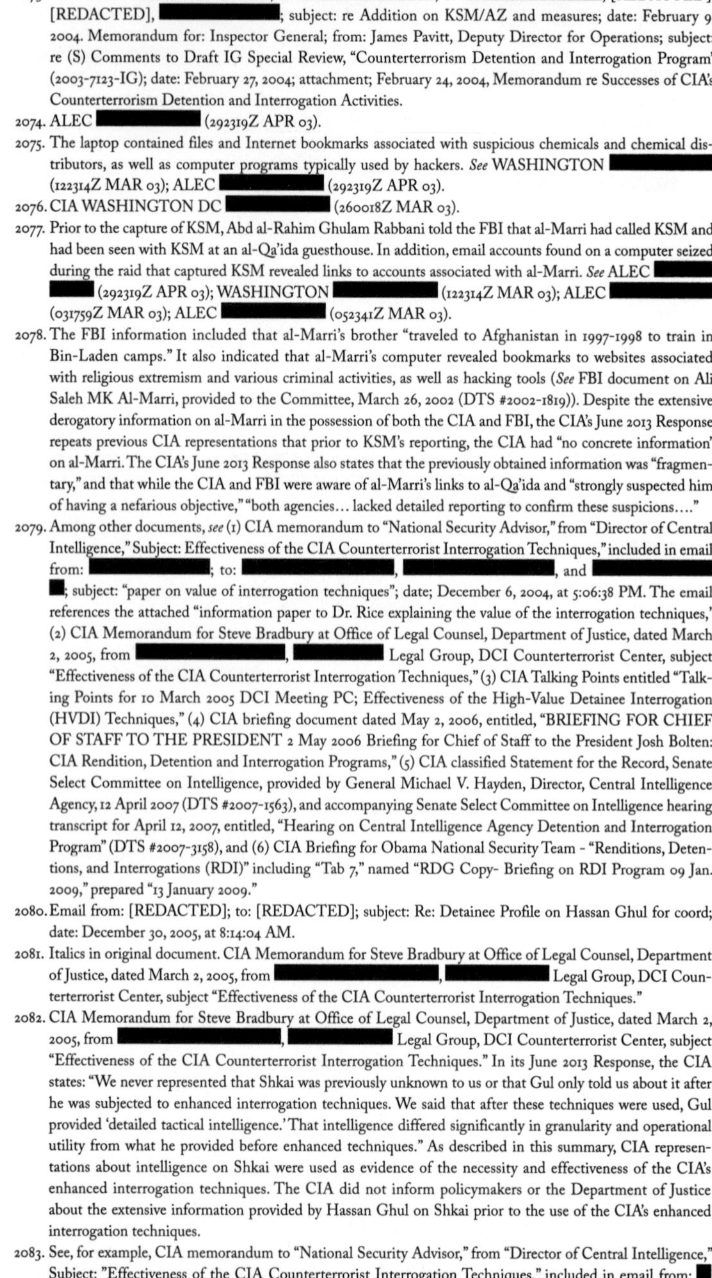

2073. Email from: ; to ; cc: , [REDACTED], [REDACTED], ; subject: re Addition on KSM/AZ and measures; date: February 9, 2004. Memorandum for: Inspector General; from: James Pavitt, Deputy Director for Operations; subject: re (S) Comments to Draft IG Special Review, "Counterterrorism Detention and Interrogation Program" (2003-7123-IG); date: February 27, 2004; attachment; February 24, 2004, Memorandum re Successes of CIA's Counterterrorism Detention and Interrogation Activities.

2074. ALEC (292319Z APR 03).

2075. The laptop contained files and Internet bookmarks associated with suspicious chemicals and chemical distributors, as well as computer programs typically used by hackers. *See* WASHINGTON (122314Z MAR 03); ALEC (292319Z APR 03).

2076. CIA WASHINGTON DC (260018Z MAR 03).

2077. Prior to the capture of KSM, Abd al-Rahim Ghulam Rabbani told the FBI that al-Marri had called KSM and had been seen with KSM at an al-Qa'ida guesthouse. In addition, email accounts found on a computer seized during the raid that captured KSM revealed links to accounts associated with al-Marri. *See* ALEC (292319Z APR 03); WASHINGTON (122314Z MAR 03); ALEC (031759Z MAR 03); ALEC (052341Z MAR 03).

2078. The FBI information included that al-Marri's brother "traveled to Afghanistan in 1997-1998 to train in Bin-Laden camps." It also indicated that al-Marri's computer revealed bookmarks to websites associated with religious extremism and various criminal activities, as well as hacking tools (*See* FBI document on Ali Saleh MK Al-Marri, provided to the Committee, March 26, 2002 (DTS #2002-1819)). Despite the extensive derogatory information on al-Marri in the possession of both the CIA and FBI, the CIA's June 2013 Response repeats previous CIA representations that prior to KSM's reporting, the CIA had "no concrete information" on al-Marri. The CIA's June 2013 Response also states that the previously obtained information was "fragmentary," and that while the CIA and FBI were aware of al-Marri's links to al-Qa'ida and "strongly suspected him of having a nefarious objective," "both agencies… lacked detailed reporting to confirm these suspicions…."

2079. Among other documents, *see* (1) CIA memorandum to "National Security Advisor," from "Director of Central Intelligence," Subject: Effectiveness of the CIA Counterterrorist Interrogation Techniques," included in email from: ; to: , , and ; subject: "paper on value of interrogation techniques"; date; December 6, 2004, at 5:06:38 PM. The email references the attached "information paper to Dr. Rice explaining the value of the interrogation techniques," (2) CIA Memorandum for Steve Bradbury at Office of Legal Counsel, Department of Justice, dated March 2, 2005, from , Legal Group, DCI Counterterrorist Center, subject "Effectiveness of the CIA Counterterrorist Interrogation Techniques," (3) CIA Talking Points entitled "Talking Points for 10 March 2005 DCI Meeting PC; Effectiveness of the High-Value Detainee Interrogation (HVDI) Techniques," (4) CIA briefing document dated May 2, 2006, entitled, "BRIEFING FOR CHIEF OF STAFF TO THE PRESIDENT 2 May 2006 Briefing for Chief of Staff to the President Josh Bolten: CIA Rendition, Detention and Interrogation Programs," (5) CIA classified Statement for the Record, Senate Select Committee on Intelligence, provided by General Michael V. Hayden, Director, Central Intelligence Agency, 12 April 2007 (DTS #2007-1563), and accompanying Senate Select Committee on Intelligence hearing transcript for April 12, 2007, entitled, "Hearing on Central Intelligence Agency Detention and Interrogation Program" (DTS #2007-3158), and (6) CIA Briefing for Obama National Security Team - "Renditions, Detentions, and Interrogations (RDI)" including "Tab 7," named "RDG Copy- Briefing on RDI Program 09 Jan. 2009," prepared "13 January 2009."

2080. Email from: [REDACTED]; to: [REDACTED]; subject: Re: Detainee Profile on Hassan Ghul for coord; date: December 30, 2005, at 8:14:04 AM.

2081. Italics in original document. CIA Memorandum for Steve Bradbury at Office of Legal Counsel, Department of Justice, dated March 2, 2005, from , Legal Group, DCI Counterterrorist Center, subject "Effectiveness of the CIA Counterterrorist Interrogation Techniques."

2082. CIA Memorandum for Steve Bradbury at Office of Legal Counsel, Department of Justice, dated March 2, 2005, from , Legal Group, DCI Counterterrorist Center, subject "Effectiveness of the CIA Counterterrorist Interrogation Techniques." In its June 2013 Response, the CIA states: "We never represented that Shkai was previously unknown to us or that Gul only told us about it after he was subjected to enhanced interrogation techniques. We said that after these techniques were used, Gul provided 'detailed tactical intelligence.' That intelligence differed significantly in granularity and operational utility from what he provided before enhanced techniques." As described in this summary, CIA representations about intelligence on Shkai were used as evidence of the necessity and effectiveness of the CIA's enhanced interrogation techniques. The CIA did not inform policymakers or the Department of Justice about the extensive information provided by Hassan Ghul on Shkai prior to the use of the CIA's enhanced interrogation techniques.

2083. See, for example, CIA memorandum to "National Security Advisor," from "Director of Central Intelligence," Subject: "Effectiveness of the CIA Counterterrorist Interrogation Techniques," included in email from: ; to: , , and ; subject:

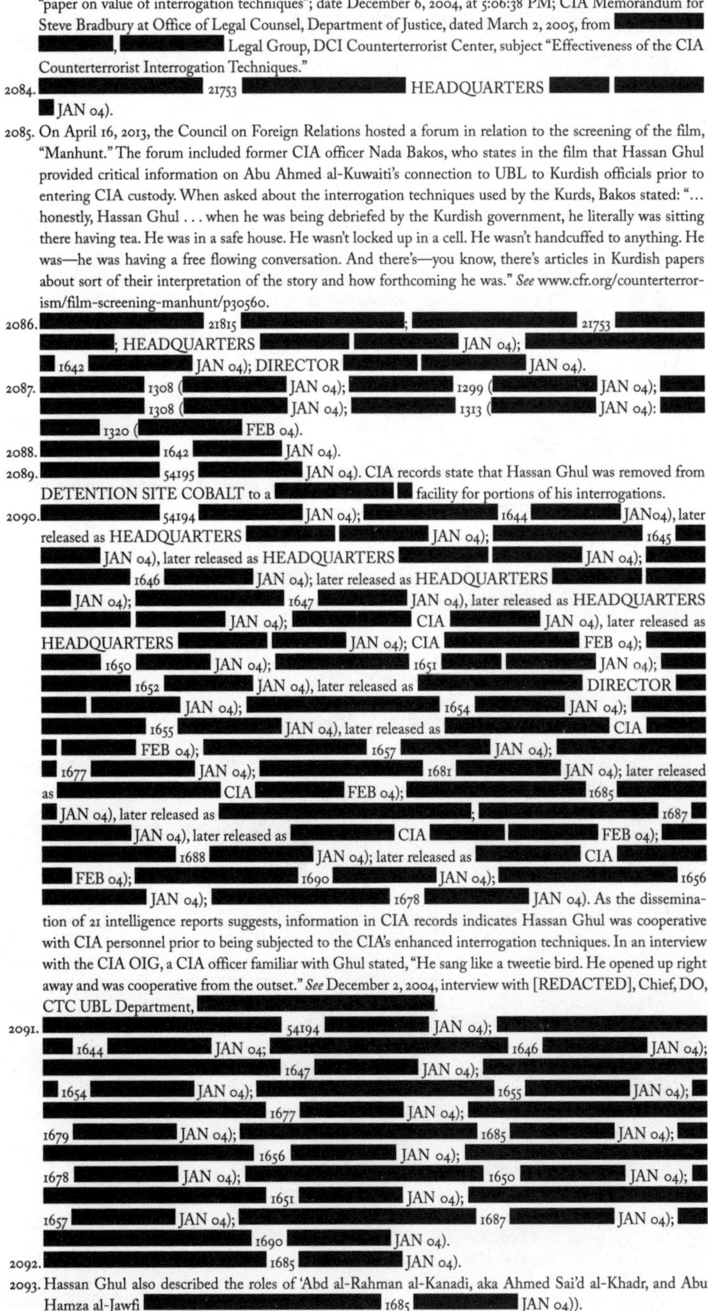

"paper on value of interrogation techniques"; date December 6, 2004, at 5:06:38 PM; CIA Memorandum for Steve Bradbury at Office of Legal Counsel, Department of Justice, dated March 2, 2005, from , Legal Group, DCI Counterterrorist Center, subject "Effectiveness of the CIA Counterterrorist Interrogation Techniques."

2084. 21753 HEADQUARTERS JAN 04).

2085. On April 16, 2013, the Council on Foreign Relations hosted a forum in relation to the screening of the film, "Manhunt." The forum included former CIA officer Nada Bakos, who states in the film that Hassan Ghul provided critical information on Abu Ahmed al-Kuwaiti's connection to UBL to Kurdish officials prior to entering CIA custody. When asked about the interrogation techniques used by the Kurds, Bakos stated: "... honestly, Hassan Ghul . . . when he was being debriefed by the Kurdish government, he literally was sitting there having tea. He was in a safe house. He wasn't locked up in a cell. He wasn't handcuffed to anything. He was—he was having a free flowing conversation. And there's—you know, there's articles in Kurdish papers about sort of their interpretation of the story and how forthcoming he was." *See* www.cfr.org/counterterrorism/film-screening-manhunt/p30560.

2086. 21815 ; 21753 ; HEADQUARTERS JAN 04); 1642 JAN 04); DIRECTOR JAN 04).

2087. 1308 (JAN 04); 1299 (JAN 04); 1308 (JAN 04); 1313 (JAN 04): 1320 (FEB 04).

2088. 1642 JAN 04).

2089. 54195 JAN 04). CIA records state that Hassan Ghul was removed from DETENTION SITE COBALT to a facility for portions of his interrogations.

2090. 54194 JAN 04); 1644 JAN04), later released as HEADQUARTERS JAN 04); 1645 JAN 04), later released as HEADQUARTERS JAN 04); 1646 JAN 04); later released as HEADQUARTERS JAN 04); 1647 JAN 04), later released as HEADQUARTERS JAN 04); CIA JAN 04), later released as HEADQUARTERS JAN 04); CIA FEB 04); 1650 JAN 04); 1651 JAN 04); 1652 JAN 04), later released as DIRECTOR JAN 04); 1654 JAN 04); 1655 JAN 04), later released as CIA FEB 04); 1657 JAN 04); 1677 JAN 04); 1681 JAN 04); later released as CIA FEB 04); 1685 JAN 04), later released as ; 1687 JAN 04), later released as CIA FEB 04); 1688 JAN 04); later released as CIA FEB 04); 1690 JAN 04); 1656 JAN 04); 1678 JAN 04). As the dissemination of 21 intelligence reports suggests, information in CIA records indicates Hassan Ghul was cooperative with CIA personnel prior to being subjected to the CIA's enhanced interrogation techniques. In an interview with the CIA OIG, a CIA officer familiar with Ghul stated, "He sang like a tweetie bird. He opened up right away and was cooperative from the outset." *See* December 2, 2004, interview with [REDACTED], Chief, DO, CTC UBL Department, .

2091. 54194 JAN 04); 1644 JAN 04; 1646 JAN 04); 1647 JAN 04); 1654 JAN 04); 1655 JAN 04); 1677 JAN 04); 1679 JAN 04); 1685 JAN 04); 1656 JAN 04); 1678 JAN 04); 1650 JAN 04); 1651 JAN 04); 1657 JAN 04); 1687 JAN 04); 1690 JAN 04).

2092. 1685 JAN 04).

2093. Hassan Ghul also described the roles of 'Abd al-Rahman al-Kanadi, aka Ahmed Sai'd al-Khadr, and Abu Hamza al-Jawfi 1685 JAN 04)).

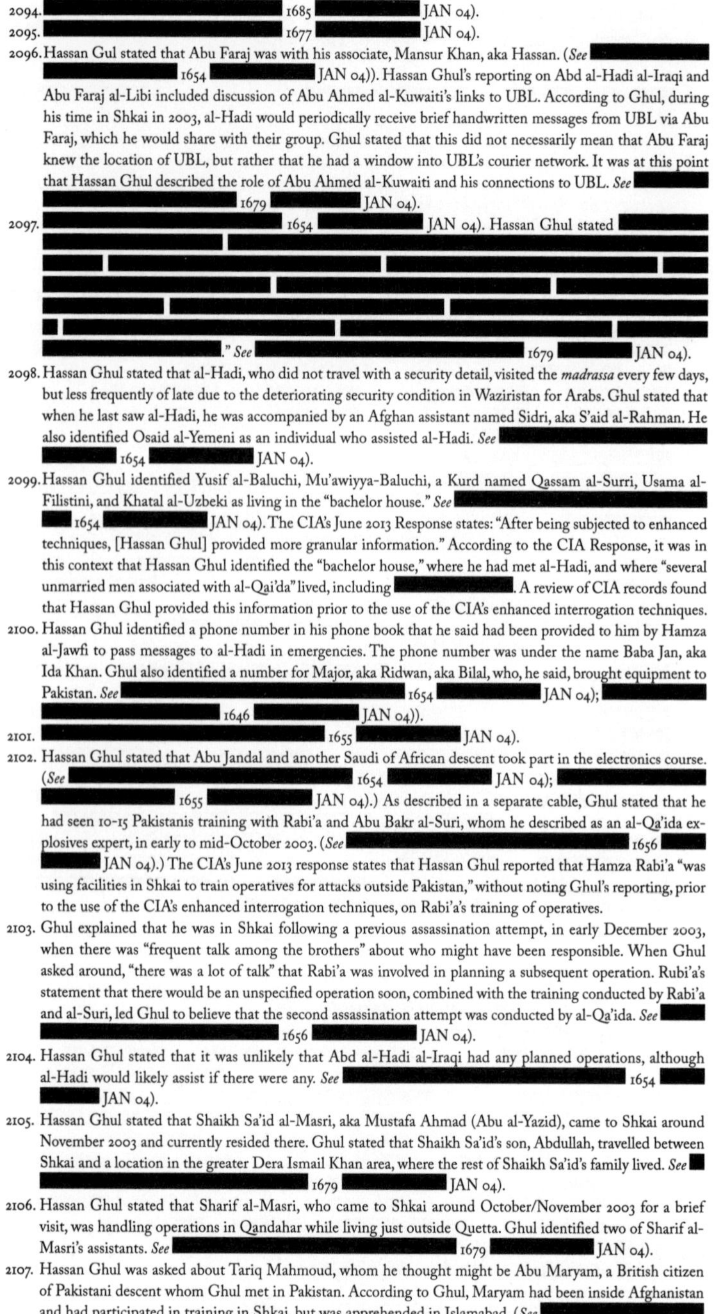

2094. 1685 JAN 04).
2095. 1677 JAN 04).
2096. Hassan Gul stated that Abu Faraj was with his associate, Mansur Khan, aka Hassan. (*See* 1654 JAN 04)). Hassan Ghul's reporting on Abd al-Hadi al-Iraqi and Abu Faraj al-Libi included discussion of Abu Ahmed al-Kuwaiti's links to UBL. According to Ghul, during his time in Shkai in 2003, al-Hadi would periodically receive brief handwritten messages from UBL via Abu Faraj, which he would share with their group. Ghul stated that this did not necessarily mean that Abu Faraj knew the location of UBL, but rather that he had a window into UBL's courier network. It was at this point that Hassan Ghul described the role of Abu Ahmed al-Kuwaiti and his connections to UBL. *See* 1679 JAN 04).
2097. 1654 JAN 04). Hassan Ghul stated ." *See* 1679 JAN 04).
2098. Hassan Ghul stated that al-Hadi, who did not travel with a security detail, visited the *madrassa* every few days, but less frequently of late due to the deteriorating security condition in Waziristan for Arabs. Ghul stated that when he last saw al-Hadi, he was accompanied by an Afghan assistant named Sidri, aka S'aid al-Rahman. He also identified Osaid al-Yemeni as an individual who assisted al-Hadi. *See* 1654 JAN 04).
2099. Hassan Ghul identified Yusif al-Baluchi, Mu'awiyya-Baluchi, a Kurd named Qassam al-Surri, Usama al-Filistini, and Khatal al-Uzbeki as living in the "bachelor house." *See* 1654 JAN 04). The CIA's June 2013 Response states: "After being subjected to enhanced techniques, [Hassan Ghul] provided more granular information." According to the CIA Response, it was in this context that Hassan Ghul identified the "bachelor house," where he had met al-Hadi, and where "several unmarried men associated with al-Qai'da" lived, including . A review of CIA records found that Hassan Ghul provided this information prior to the use of the CIA's enhanced interrogation techniques.
2100. Hassan Ghul identified a phone number in his phone book that he said had been provided to him by Hamza al-Jawfi to pass messages to al-Hadi in emergencies. The phone number was under the name Baba Jan, aka Ida Khan. Ghul also identified a number for Major, aka Ridwan, aka Bilal, who, he said, brought equipment to Pakistan. *See* 1654 JAN 04); 1646 JAN 04)).
2101. 1655 JAN 04).
2102. Hassan Ghul stated that Abu Jandal and another Saudi of African descent took part in the electronics course. (*See* 1654 JAN 04); 1655 JAN 04).) As described in a separate cable, Ghul stated that he had seen 10-15 Pakistanis training with Rabi'a and Abu Bakr al-Suri, whom he described as an al-Qa'ida explosives expert, in early to mid-October 2003. (*See* 1656 JAN 04).) The CIA's June 2013 response states that Hassan Ghul reported that Hamza Rabi'a "was using facilities in Shkai to train operatives for attacks outside Pakistan," without noting Ghul's reporting, prior to the use of the CIA's enhanced interrogation techniques, on Rabi'a's training of operatives.
2103. Ghul explained that he was in Shkai following a previous assassination attempt, in early December 2003, when there was "frequent talk among the brothers" about who might have been responsible. When Ghul asked around, "there was a lot of talk" that Rabi'a was involved in planning a subsequent operation. Rubi'a's statement that there would be an unspecified operation soon, combined with the training conducted by Rabi'a and al-Suri, led Ghul to believe that the second assassination attempt was conducted by al-Qa'ida. *See* 1656 JAN 04).
2104. Hassan Ghul stated that it was unlikely that Abd al-Hadi al-Iraqi had any planned operations, although al-Hadi would likely assist if there were any. *See* 1654 JAN 04).
2105. Hassan Ghul stated that Shaikh Sa'id al-Masri, aka Mustafa Ahmad (Abu al-Yazid), came to Shkai around November 2003 and currently resided there. Ghul stated that Shaikh Sa'id's son, Abdullah, travelled between Shkai and a location in the greater Dera Ismail Khan area, where the rest of Shaikh Sa'id's family lived. *See* 1679 JAN 04).
2106. Hassan Ghul stated that Sharif al-Masri, who came to Shkai around October/November 2003 for a brief visit, was handling operations in Qandahar while living just outside Quetta. Ghul identified two of Sharif al-Masri's assistants. *See* 1679 JAN 04).
2107. Hassan Ghul was asked about Tariq Mahmoud, whom he thought might be Abu Maryam, a British citizen of Pakistani descent whom Ghul met in Pakistan. According to Ghul, Maryam had been inside Afghanistan and had participated in training in Shkai, but was apprehended in Islamabad. (*See*

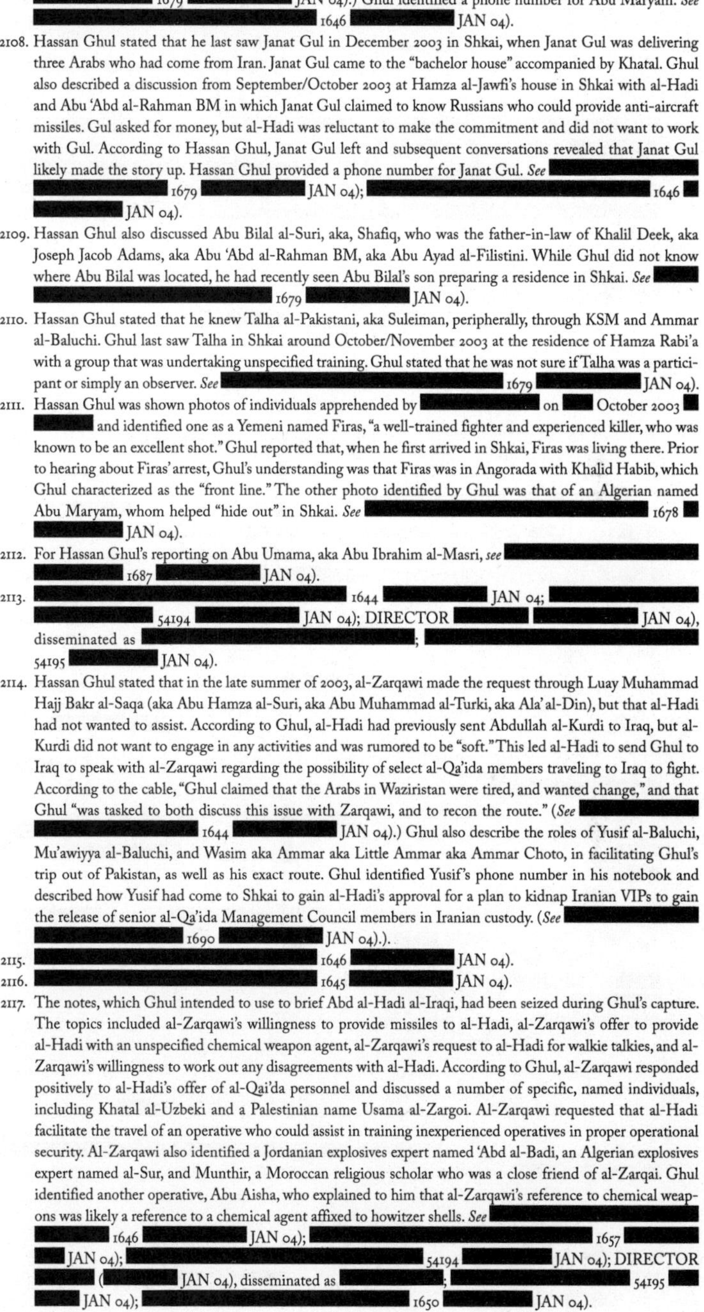

1679 JAN 04).) Ghul identified a phone number for Abu Maryam. *See* 1646 JAN 04).

2108. Hassan Ghul stated that he last saw Janat Gul in December 2003 in Shkai, when Janat Gul was delivering three Arabs who had come from Iran. Janat Gul came to the "bachelor house" accompanied by Khatal. Ghul also described a discussion from September/October 2003 at Hamza al-Jawfi's house in Shkai with al-Hadi and Abu 'Abd al-Rahman BM in which Janat Gul claimed to know Russians who could provide anti-aircraft missiles. Gul asked for money, but al-Hadi was reluctant to make the commitment and did not want to work with Gul. According to Hassan Ghul, Janat Gul left and subsequent conversations revealed that Janat Gul likely made the story up. Hassan Ghul provided a phone number for Janat Gul. *See* 1679 JAN 04); 1646 JAN 04).

2109. Hassan Ghul also discussed Abu Bilal al-Suri, aka, Shafiq, who was the father-in-law of Khalil Deek, aka Joseph Jacob Adams, aka Abu 'Abd al-Rahman BM, aka Abu Ayad al-Filistini. While Ghul did not know where Abu Bilal was located, he had recently seen Abu Bilal's son preparing a residence in Shkai. *See* 1679 JAN 04).

2110. Hassan Ghul stated that he knew Talha al-Pakistani, aka Suleiman, peripherally, through KSM and Ammar al-Baluchi. Ghul last saw Talha in Shkai around October/November 2003 at the residence of Hamza Rabi'a with a group that was undertaking unspecified training. Ghul stated that he was not sure if Talha was a participant or simply an observer. *See* 1679 JAN 04).

2111. Hassan Ghul was shown photos of individuals apprehended by on October 2003 and identified one as a Yemeni named Firas, "a well-trained fighter and experienced killer, who was known to be an excellent shot." Ghul reported that, when he first arrived in Shkai, Firas was living there. Prior to hearing about Firas' arrest, Ghul's understanding was that Firas was in Angorada with Khalid Habib, which Ghul characterized as the "front line." The other photo identified by Ghul was that of an Algerian named Abu Maryam, whom helped "hide out" in Shkai. *See* 1678 JAN 04).

2112. For Hassan Ghul's reporting on Abu Umama, aka Abu Ibrahim al-Masri, *see* 1687 JAN 04).

2113. 1644 JAN 04; 54194 JAN 04); DIRECTOR JAN 04), disseminated as ; 54195 JAN 04).

2114. Hassan Ghul stated that in the late summer of 2003, al-Zarqawi made the request through Luay Muhammad Hajj Bakr al-Saqa (aka Abu Hamza al-Suri, aka Abu Muhammad al-Turki, aka Ala' al-Din), but that al-Hadi had not wanted to assist. According to Ghul, al-Hadi had previously sent Abdullah al-Kurdi to Iraq, but al-Kurdi did not want to engage in any activities and was rumored to be "soft." This led al-Hadi to send Ghul to Iraq to speak with al-Zarqawi regarding the possibility of select al-Qa'ida members traveling to Iraq to fight. According to the cable, "Ghul claimed that the Arabs in Waziristan were tired, and wanted change," and that Ghul "was tasked to both discuss this issue with Zarqawi, and to recon the route." (*See* 1644 JAN 04).) Ghul also describe the roles of Yusif al-Baluchi, Mu'awiyya al-Baluchi, and Wasim aka Ammar aka Little Ammar aka Ammar Choto, in facilitating Ghul's trip out of Pakistan, as well as his exact route. Ghul identified Yusif's phone number in his notebook and described how Yusif had come to Shkai to gain al-Hadi's approval for a plan to kidnap Iranian VIPs to gain the release of senior al-Qa'ida Management Council members in Iranian custody. (*See* 1690 JAN 04).).

2115. 1646 JAN 04).

2116. 1645 JAN 04).

2117. The notes, which Ghul intended to use to brief Abd al-Hadi al-Iraqi, had been seized during Ghul's capture. The topics included al-Zarqawi's willingness to provide missiles to al-Hadi, al-Zarqawi's offer to provide al-Hadi with an unspecified chemical weapon agent, al-Zarqawi's request to al-Hadi for walkie talkies, and al-Zarqawi's willingness to work out any disagreements with al-Hadi. According to Ghul, al-Zarqawi responded positively to al-Hadi's offer of al-Qai'da personnel and discussed a number of specific, named individuals, including Khatal al-Uzbeki and a Palestinian name Usama al-Zargoi. Al-Zarqawi requested that al-Hadi facilitate the travel of an operative who could assist in training inexperienced operatives in proper operational security. Al-Zarqawi also identified a Jordanian explosives expert named 'Abd al-Badi, an Algerian explosives expert named al-Sur, and Munthir, a Moroccan religious scholar who was a close friend of al-Zarqai. Ghul identified another operative, Abu Aisha, who explained to him that al-Zarqawi's reference to chemical weapons was likely a reference to a chemical agent affixed to howitzer shells. *See* 1646 JAN 04); 1657 JAN 04); 54194 JAN 04); DIRECTOR (JAN 04), disseminated as ; 54195 JAN 04); 1650 JAN 04).

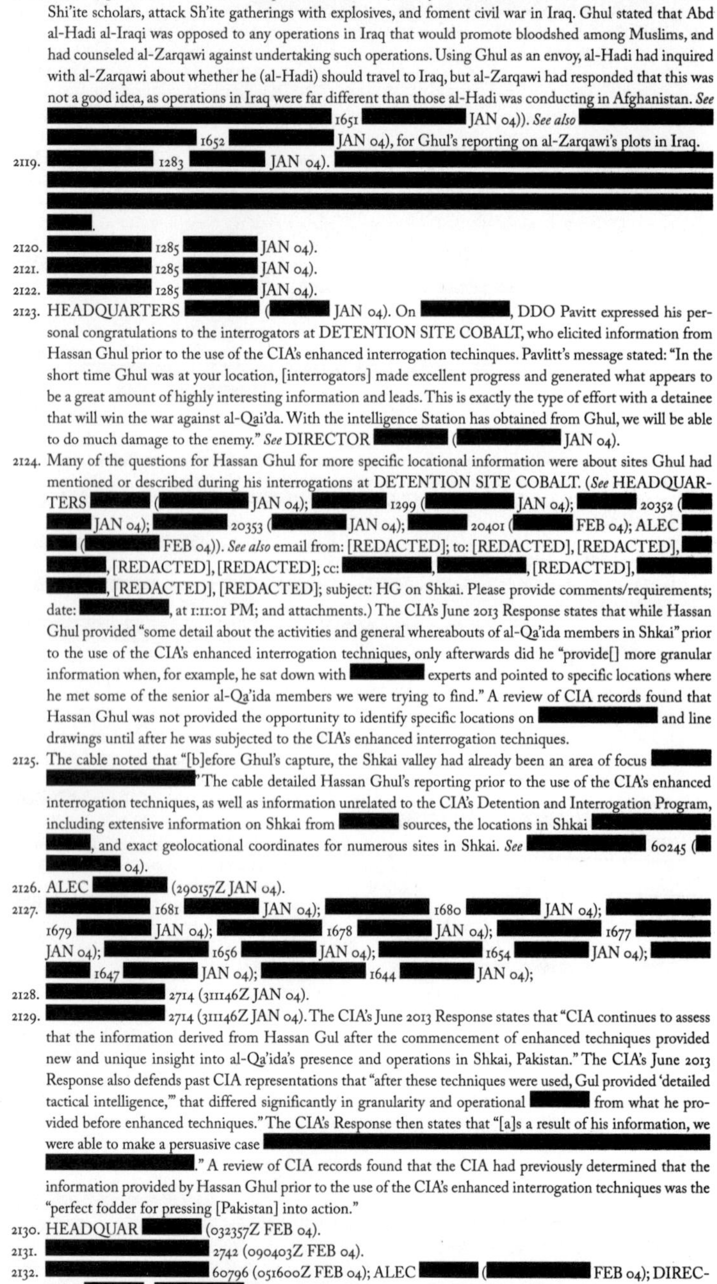

2118. According to Hassan Ghul, al-Zarqawi told Ghul in January 2004 that he intended to assassinate senior Shi'ite scholars, attack Sh'ite gatherings with explosives, and foment civil war in Iraq. Ghul stated that Abd al-Hadi al-Iraqi was opposed to any operations in Iraq that would promote bloodshed among Muslims, and had counseled al-Zarqawi against undertaking such operations. Using Ghul as an envoy, al-Hadi had inquired with al-Zarqawi about whether he (al-Hadi) should travel to Iraq, but al-Zarqawi had responded that this was not a good idea, as operations in Iraq were far different than those al-Hadi was conducting in Afghanistan. *See* 1651 JAN 04)). *See also* 1652 JAN 04), for Ghul's reporting on al-Zarqawi's plots in Iraq.

2119. 1283 JAN 04). .

2120. 1285 JAN 04).

2121. 1285 JAN 04).

2122. 1285 JAN 04).

2123. HEADQUARTERS (JAN 04). On , DDO Pavitt expressed his personal congratulations to the interrogators at DETENTION SITE COBALT, who elicited information from Hassan Ghul prior to the use of the CIA's enhanced interrogation techinques. Pavlitt's message stated: "In the short time Ghul was at your location, [interrogators] made excellent progress and generated what appears to be a great amount of highly interesting information and leads. This is exactly the type of effort with a detainee that will win the war against al-Qai'da. With the intelligence Station has obtained from Ghul, we will be able to do much damage to the enemy." *See* DIRECTOR (JAN 04).

2124. Many of the questions for Hassan Ghul for more specific locational information were about sites Ghul had mentioned or described during his interrogations at DETENTION SITE COBALT. (*See* HEADQUARTERS (JAN 04); 1299 (JAN 04); 20352 (JAN 04); 20353 (JAN 04); 20401 (FEB 04); ALEC (FEB 04)). *See also* email from: [REDACTED]; to: [REDACTED], [REDACTED], , [REDACTED], [REDACTED]; cc: , , [REDACTED], , [REDACTED], [REDACTED]; subject: HG on Shkai. Please provide comments/requirements; date: , at 1:11:01 PM; and attachments.) The CIA's June 2013 Response states that while Hassan Ghul provided "some detail about the activities and general whereabouts of al-Qa'ida members in Shkai" prior to the use of the CIA's enhanced interrogation techniques, only afterwards did he "provide[] more granular information when, for example, he sat down with experts and pointed to specific locations where he met some of the senior al-Qa'ida members we were trying to find." A review of CIA records found that Hassan Ghul was not provided the opportunity to identify specific locations on and line drawings until after he was subjected to the CIA's enhanced interrogation techniques.

2125. The cable noted that "[b]efore Ghul's capture, the Shkai valley had already been an area of focus ." The cable detailed Hassan Ghul's reporting prior to the use of the CIA's enhanced interrogation techniques, as well as information unrelated to the CIA's Detention and Interrogation Program, including extensive information on Shkai from sources, the locations in Shkai , and exact geolocational coordinates for numerous sites in Shkai. *See* 60245 (04).

2126. ALEC (290157Z JAN 04).

2127. 1681 JAN 04); 1680 JAN 04); 1679 JAN 04); 1678 JAN 04); 1677 JAN 04); 1656 JAN 04); 1654 JAN 04); 1647 JAN 04); 1644 JAN 04);

2128. 2714 (311146Z JAN 04).

2129. 2714 (311146Z JAN 04). The CIA's June 2013 Response states that "CIA continues to assess that the information derived from Hassan Gul after the commencement of enhanced techniques provided new and unique insight into al-Qa'ida's presence and operations in Shkai, Pakistan." The CIA's June 2013 Response also defends past CIA representations that "after these techniques were used, Gul provided 'detailed tactical intelligence,'" that differed significantly in granularity and operational from what he provided before enhanced techniques." The CIA's Response then states that "[a]s a result of his information, we were able to make a persuasive case ." A review of CIA records found that the CIA had previously determined that the information provided by Hassan Ghul prior to the use of the CIA's enhanced interrogation techniques was the "perfect fodder for pressing [Pakistan] into action."

2130. HEADQUAR (032357Z FEB 04).

2131. 2742 (090403Z FEB 04).

2132. 60796 (051600Z FEB 04); ALEC (FEB 04); DIRECTOR (FEB 04). The CIA's June 2013 Response states that "[s]enior US officials

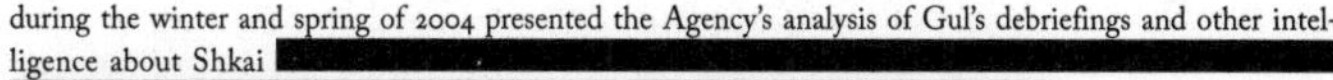

during the winter and spring of 2004 presented the Agency's analysis of Gul's debriefings and other intelligence about Shkai ." As support, the CIA Response cites two cables that relied heavily on information provided by Hassan Ghul prior to the use of the CIA's enhanced interrogation techniques, as well as information from unrelated sources. (*See* ALEC (FEB 04); DIRECTOR (FEB 04)).

2133. Directorate of Intelligence, *Al-Qa'ida's Waziristan Sanctuary Disrupted but Still Viable*, 21 July 2004 (DTS #2004-3240).

2134. Email from: [REDACTED]; to: [REDACTED]; subject: Re: Detainee Profile on Hassan Ghul for coord; date: December 30, 2005, at 8:14:04 AM.

2135. 2441 ; HEADQUARTERS ; 1635 ; 1712 ; HEADQUARTERS ; 1775 ; 173426

2136. Congressional Notification (DTS #2012-3802).

2137. In addition to classified representations to the Committee, shortly after the operation targeting UBL on May 1, 2011, there were media reports indicating that the CIA's Detention and Interrogation Program had produced "*the lead information*" that led to Abu Ahmad al-Kuwaiti, the UBL compound, and/or the overall operation that led to UBL's death. In an interview with *Time Magazine*, published May 4, 2011, Jose Rodriguez, the former CIA chief of CTC, stated that: "Information provided by KSM and Abu Faraj al-Libbi about bin Laden's courier was *the lead information* that eventually led to the location of [bin Laden's] compound and the operation that led to his death." *See* "Ex-CIA Counterterror Chief: 'Enhanced Interrogation' Led U.S. to bin Laden." *Time Magazine*, May 4, 2011 (italics added). Former CIA Director Michael Hayden stated that: "What we got, the *original lead information*— and frankly it was incomplete identity information on the couriers—*began with information from CIA detainees at the black sites*." In another interview, Hayden stated: "... the lead information I referred to a few minutes ago did come from CIA detainees, *against whom enhanced interrogation techniques* have been used" (italics added). *See* Transcript from *Scott Hennen Show*, dated May 3, 2011, with former CIA Director Michael Hayden; and interview with Fareed Zakaria, *Fareed Zakaria GPS*, CNN, May 8, 2011. See *also* "The Waterboarding Trail to bin Laden," by Michael Mukasey, *Wall Street Journal*, May 6, 2011. Former Attorney General Mukasey wrote: "Consider how the intelligence that led to bin Laden came to hand. It began with a disclosure from Khalid Sheikh Mohammed (KSM), who broke like a dam under the pressure of harsh interrogation techniques that included waterboarding. He loosed a torrent of information—including eventually the nickname of a trusted courier of bin Laden." The CIA's June 2013 Response confirms information in the Committee Study, stating: "Even after undergoing enhanced techniques, KSM lied about Abu Ahmad, and Abu Faraj denied knowing him." The CIA's September 2012 "Lessons from the Hunt for Bin Ladin," (DTS# 2012-3826) compiled by the CIA's Center for the Study of Intelligence, indicates that the CIA sought to publicly attribute the UBL operation to detainee reporting months prior to the execution of the operation. Under the heading, "The Public Roll-Out," the "Lessons from the Hunt for Bin Ladin" document explains that the CIA's Office of Public Affairs was "formally brought into the [UBL] operation in late March 2011." The document states that the "material OPA prepared for release" was intended to "describe the hunt and the operation," among other matters. The document details how, prior to the operation, "agreed-upon language" was developed for three "vital points," the first of which was "the critical nature of detainee reporting in identifying Bin Ladin's courier."

2138. CIA documents and cables use various spellings, most frequently "Abu Ahmed al-Kuwaiti" and "Abu Ahmad al-Kuwaiti." To the extent possible, the Study uses the spelling referenced in the CIA document being discussed.

2139. Testimony from the CIA to the Senate Select Committee on Intelligence and the Senate Armed Services Committee on May 4, 2011. In testimony, CIA Director Leon Panetta referenced CIA "interviews" with 12 CIA detainees, and stated that "I want to be able to get back to you with specifics... But clearly the tipoff on the couriers came from those interviews." The CIA's June 2013 Response states: "CIA has never represented that information acquired through its interrogations of detainees was either the first or the only information that we had on Abu Ahmad." Former CIA Director Michael Hayden provided similar public statements. *See* transcript of Scott Hennen talk-radio show, dated May 3, 2011. Hayden: "What we got, the *original lead information*—and frankly it was incomplete identity information on the couriers—*began with information from CIA detainees at the black sites*. And let me just leave it at that" (italics added).

2140. *See* CIA letter to the Senate Select Committee on Intelligence dated May 5, 2011, which includes a document entitled, "Background Detainee Information on Abu Ahmad al-Kuwaiti," with an accompanying six-page chart entitled, "Detainee Reporting on Abu Ahmad al-Kuwaiti" (DTS #2011-2004).

2141. The CIA's June 2013 Response states that the December 13, 2012, Committee Study "incorrectly characterizes the intelligence we had on Abu Ahmad before acquiring information on him from detainees in CIA custody as 'critical.'" This is incorrect. The Committee uses the CIA's own definition of what information was important and critical, as conveyed to the Committee by the CIA. In documents and testimony to the Committee, the CIA highlighted specific information on Abu Ahmad al-Kuwaiti that the CIA viewed as especially valuable or critical to the identification and tracking of Abu Ahmad al-Kuwaiti. For example, in May 4, 2011, CIA testimony, a CIA officer explained how "a couple of early detainees" "identi[fied]" Abu Ahmed al-Kuwaiti as someone close to UBL. The CIA officer stated: "I think the clearest way to think about this is, in 2002 a couple of early detainees, Abu Zubaydah and an individual, Riyadh the Facilitator, talked about the activities of an Abu Ahmed al-Kuwaiti. At this point we don't have his true name. And they identify him as somebody involved with AQ and facilitation and some potential ties to bin Ladin." As detailed in this summary, CIA records confirm that Riyadh the Facilitator provided information in 2002 closely linking al-Kuwaiti to UBL, but these records confirm that this information was acquired prior to Riyadh the Facilitator being rendered to CIA custody (the transfer occurred more than a year later, in January 2004). Abu Zubaydah provided no information on Abu Ahmad al-Kuwaiti in 2002. According to CIA records, Abu Zubaydah was not asked about Abu Ahmad al-Kuwaiti until July 7, 2003, when he denied knowing the name. As an additional example, *see* CIA documents and charts provided to the Committee (DTS #2011-2004) and described in this summary, in which the CIA ascribes value to specific intelligence acquired on al-Kuwaiti.

2142. In other words, the information the CIA cited was acquired from a detainee *not* in CIA custody, obtained from a CIA detainee who was not subjected to the CIA's enhanced interrogation techniques, obtained from a CIA detainee prior to the use of the CIA's enhanced interrogation techniques, or acquired from a source unrelated to detainee reporting. As described, the information contained herein is based on a review of CIA Detention and Interrogation Program records. Although the CIA has produced more than six million pages of material associated with CIA detainees and the CIA's Detention and Interrogation Program, the Committee did not have direct access to other, more traditional intelligence records, to include reporting from CIA HUMINT assets, foreign government assets, electronic intercepts, military detainee debriefings, law enforcement derived information, and other methods of collection. Based on the information found in the CIA detainee-related documents, it is likely there is significant intelligence on "Abu Ahmad al-Kuwaiti" acquired from a variety of intelligence collection platforms that the Committee did not have access to for this review.

2143. CIA record ("Call Details Incoming and Outgoing") relating to calling activity for [REDACTED] phone number #[REDACTED] A CIA document provided to the Committee on October 25, 2013, (DTS #2013-3152), states that the CIA was collecting on Abu Ahmad al-Kuwaiti's phone (#[REDACTED]) early as November 2001, and that it was collection from this time that was used to make voice comparisons to later collection targeting Abu Ahmad al-Kuwaiti.

2144. CIA [REDACTED] (03203IZ APR 02).

2145. CIA [REDACTED] (102I58Z APR02).

2146. Included in several cables and repeated in ALEC [REDACTED] [REDACTED] JUL 02).

2147. [REDACTED] 31049 ([REDACTED] 2002). The CIA's June 2013 Response downplays the importance of the email address and phone numbers collected on Abu Ahmad al-Kuwaiti, stating that the accounts were later discontinued by Abu Ahmad al-Kuwaiti and were "never linked" to bin Ladin's known locations. However, on October 25, 2013, the CIA (DTS #2013-3152) acknowledge that the "voice cuts" from Abu Ahmad al-Kuwaiti were acquired during this period (2001–2002) from the ([REDACTED]) phone number cited in the Committee Study. According to CIA records, in February 2009 and September 2009, the voice samples collected from the Abu Ahmad al-Kuwaiti ([REDACTED]) phone number (under collection in 2002) were compared to voice samples collected against [REDACTED], which led the Intelligence Community to assess that [REDACTED], who was geo-located to a specific area of Pakistan, was likely Abu Ahmad al-Kuwaiti. In August 2010, Abu Ahmad [REDACTED] and tracked to the UBL compound. *See* intelligence chronology in Volume II for additional details.

2148. ALEC [REDACTED] (240057Z AUG 02).

2149. [REDACTED] 64883 (171346Z SEP 02). This information was repeated in ALEC (302244Z SEP 02).

2150. ALEC [REDACTED] (102238Z MAR 03).

2151. [REDACTED] 19448 (101509Z JUN 02).

2152. DIRECTOR [REDACTED] (251833Z JUN 02).

2153. [REDACTED] 65902 (080950Z AUG 02); ALEC [REDACTED] (092204Z AUG 02).

2154. DIRECTOR [REDACTED] (202147Z OCT 02).

2155. *See* intelligence chronology in Volume II, specifically [REDACTED], dated 17 September 2001, [REDACTED] 60077 (09/17/2001). See *also* foreign government reporting from September 27, 2002, describing information from a detainee who was *not* in CIA custody (CIA [REDACTED] (271730Z SEP02)). That reporting is also highlighted in a CIA document, entitled, "Background Detainee Information on Abu Ahmad al-Kuwaiti," dated May 4, 2011 (DTS#2011-2004). The document highlights that "Detainee Abdallah Falah al-Dusari provided what he thought was a partial true name for Abu Ahmad—Habib al-Rahman—whom [CIA] ultimately identified as one of Abu Ahinad's deceased brothers. However, this partial true name for his brother eventually helped [CIA] map out Abu Ahmad's entire family, including the true name of Abu Ahmad himself." The CIA document did not identify that Abdallali Falah al-Dusari was *not* a CIA detainee. In June 2002, the CIA also obtained another alias for Abu Ahmad al-Kuwaiti—"Hamad al-Kuwaiti"—that included a component of his true name. This information was provided by a foreign government and was unrelated to the CIA's Detention and Interrogation Program. *See* DIRECTOR [REDACTED] (251833Z JUN 02).

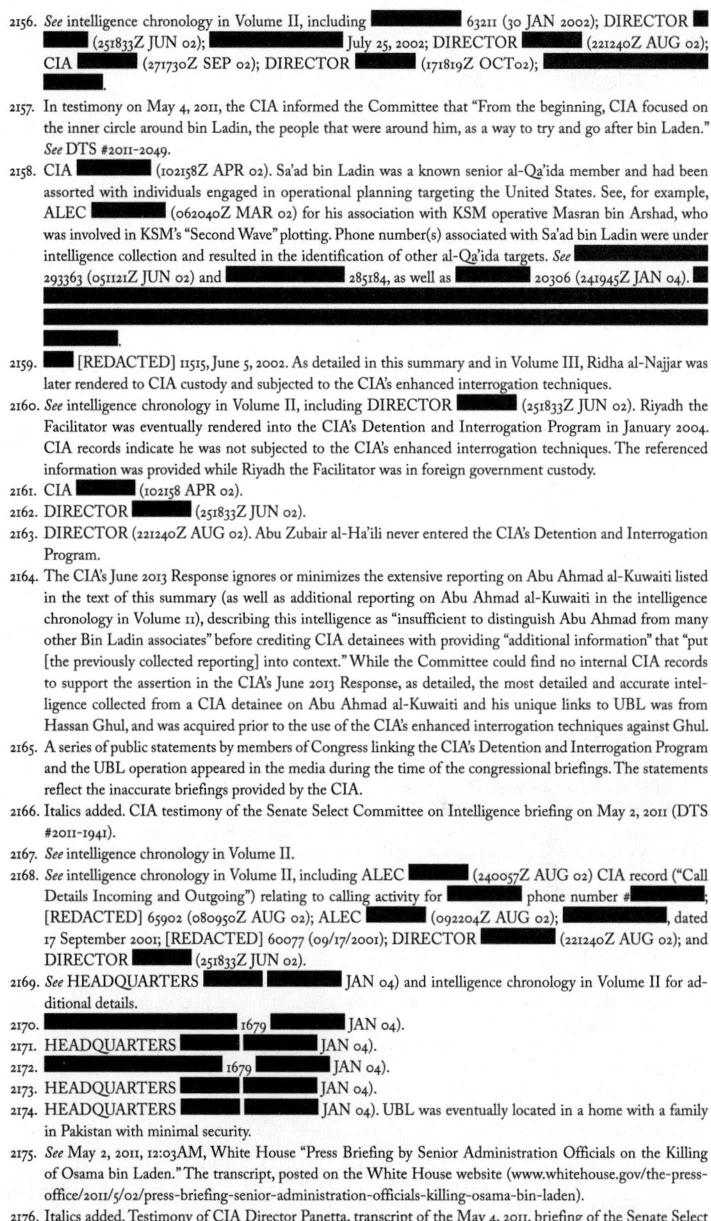

2156. *See* intelligence chronology in Volume II, including 63211 (30 JAN 2002); DIRECTOR (251833Z JUN 02); July 25, 2002; DIRECTOR (221240Z AUG 02); CIA (271730Z SEP 02); DIRECTOR (171819Z OCT02); .
2157. In testimony on May 4, 2011, the CIA informed the Committee that "From the beginning, CIA focused on the inner circle around bin Ladin, the people that were around him, as a way to try and go after bin Laden." *See* DTS #2011-2049.
2158. CIA (102158Z APR 02). Sa'ad bin Ladin was a known senior al-Qa'ida member and had been assorted with individuals engaged in operational planning targeting the United States. See, for example, ALEC (062040Z MAR 02) for his association with KSM operative Masran bin Arshad, who was involved in KSM's "Second Wave" plotting. Phone number(s) associated with Sa'ad bin Ladin were under intelligence collection and resulted in the identification of other al-Qa'ida targets. *See* 293363 (051121Z JUN 02) and 285184, as well as 20306 (241945Z JAN 04). .
2159. [REDACTED] 11515, June 5, 2002. As detailed in this summary and in Volume III, Ridha al-Najjar was later rendered to CIA custody and subjected to the CIA's enhanced interrogation techniques.
2160. *See* intelligence chronology in Volume II, including DIRECTOR (251833Z JUN 02). Riyadh the Facilitator was eventually rendered into the CIA's Detention and Interrogation Program in January 2004. CIA records indicate he was not subjected to the CIA's enhanced interrogation techniques. The referenced information was provided while Riyadh the Facilitator was in foreign government custody.
2161. CIA (102158 APR 02).
2162. DIRECTOR (251833Z JUN 02).
2163. DIRECTOR (221240Z AUG 02). Abu Zubair al-Ha'ili never entered the CIA's Detention and Interrogation Program.
2164. The CIA's June 2013 Response ignores or minimizes the extensive reporting on Abu Ahmad al-Kuwaiti listed in the text of this summary (as well as additional reporting on Abu Ahmad al-Kuwaiti in the intelligence chronology in Volume 11), describing this intelligence as "insufficient to distinguish Abu Ahmad from many other Bin Ladin associates" before crediting CIA detainees with providing "additional information" that "put [the previously collected reporting] into context." While the Committee could find no internal CIA records to support the assertion in the CIA's June 2013 Response, as detailed, the most detailed and accurate intelligence collected from a CIA detainee on Abu Ahmad al-Kuwaiti and his unique links to UBL was from Hassan Ghul, and was acquired prior to the use of the CIA's enhanced interrogation techniques against Ghul.
2165. A series of public statements by members of Congress linking the CIA's Detention and Interrogation Program and the UBL operation appeared in the media during the time of the congressional briefings. The statements reflect the inaccurate briefings provided by the CIA.
2166. Italics added. CIA testimony of the Senate Select Committee on Intelligence briefing on May 2, 2011 (DTS #2011-1941).
2167. *See* intelligence chronology in Volume II.
2168. *See* intelligence chronology in Volume II, including ALEC (240057Z AUG 02) CIA record ("Call Details Incoming and Outgoing") relating to calling activity for phone number #; [REDACTED] 65902 (080950Z AUG 02); ALEC (092204Z AUG 02); , dated 17 September 2001; [REDACTED] 60077 (09/17/2001); DIRECTOR (221240Z AUG 02); and DIRECTOR (251833Z JUN 02).
2169. *See* HEADQUARTERS JAN 04) and intelligence chronology in Volume II for additional details.
2170. 1679 JAN 04).
2171. HEADQUARTERS JAN 04).
2172. 1679 JAN 04).
2173. HEADQUARTERS JAN 04).
2174. HEADQUARTERS JAN 04). UBL was eventually located in a home with a family in Pakistan with minimal security.
2175. *See* May 2, 2011, 12:03AM, White House "Press Briefing by Senior Administration Officials on the Killing of Osama bin Laden." The transcript, posted on the White House website (www.whitehouse.gov/the-press-office/2011/5/02/press-briefing-senior-administration-officials-killing-osama-bin-laden).
2176. Italics added. Testimony of CIA Director Panetta, transcript of the May 4, 2011, briefing of the Senate Select Committee on Intelligence and the Senate Armed Services Committee (DTS #2011-2049).
2177. As described in this summary, the CIA provided documents to the Committee indicating that individuals detained in 2002 provided "Tier One" information—linking "Abu Ahmad to Bin Ladin." The document did not state when the information was provided, or when the detainee entered CIA custody. Internal CIA records indicate that no CIA detainee provided information on Abu Ahmad al-Kuwaiti in 2002. *See* CIA six-page

chart entitled, "Detainee Reporting on Abu Ahmad al-Kuwaiti," which lists 12 detainees in "CIA Custody" (DTS #2011-2004).

2178. CIA record ("Call Details Incoming and Outgoing") relating to calling activity for [REDACTED] phone number #[REDACTED]; ALEC [REDACTED] (240057Z AUG 02).

2179. *See* intelligence chronology in Volume II, including [REDACTED] 65902 (080950Z AUG 02); ALEC [REDACTED] (092204Z AUG 02); DIRECTOR [REDACTED] (221240Z AUG 02); and DIRECTOR [REDACTED] (251833Z JUN 02).

2180. *See* intelligence chronology in Volume II, including DIRECTOR [REDACTED] (251833Z JUN 02).

2181. Italics added. CIA testimony from CIA officer [REDACTED] and transcript of the Senate Select Committee on Intelligence and the Senate Armed Services Committee briefing on May 4, 2011. (*See* DTS #2011-2049.) As discussed in this summary and in greater detail in Volume II, the CIA provided additional information to the Committee on May 5, 2011, that listed Riyadh the Facilitator as a detainee in "CIA custody," who was "detained February 2002," and provided the referenced information. The CIA document omitted that Riyadh the Facilitator was not in CIA custody when he provided the referenced information in June 2002. Riyadh the Facilitator was not rendered to CIA custody until January 2004. *See* Volume III and DTS #2011-2004.

2182. The CIA's June 2013 Response does not address the Committee Study finding that Abu Zubaydah did not provide reporting on Abu Ahmad al-Kuwaiti in 2002. However, on October 25, 2013, the CIA responded in writing that the December 13, 2012, Committee Study was correct, and confirmed that the "first report from Abu Zubaydah discussing Abu Ahmad al-Kuwaiti was in 2003." (*See* DTS #2013-3152.) As described in the intelligence chronology in Volume II, on June 13, 2002, the CIA's ALEC Station sent a cable requesting that Abu Zubaydah be questioned regarding his knowledge of Abu Ahmad al-Kuwaiti, whom the CIA believed was then in Pakistan. Despite this request, CIA records indicate that Abu Zubaydah was not asked about Abu Ahmad al-Kuwaiti at this time. (*See* ALEC [REDACTED] (130117Z JUN 02).) Days later, on June 18, 2002, Abu Zubaydah was placed in isolation, without any questioning or contact. On August 4, 2002, the CIA resumed contact and immediately began using the CIA's enhanced interrogation techniques against Abu Zubaydah, including the waterboard. CIA records indicate that Abu Zubaydah was not asked about Abu Ahmad al-Kuwaiti until July 7, 2003, when he denied knowing the name. (*See* [REDACTED] 12236 (072032Z JUL 03).) As is detailed in the intelligence chronology in Volume II, on April 3, 2002, the CIA sent a cable stating that on page 8 of a 27-page address book found with Abu Zubaydah, there was the name "Abu Ahmad K." with a phone number that was found to be already under U.S. intelligence collection. *See* CIA [REDACTED] (032031Z APR 02).

2183. [REDACTED] 12236 (072032Z JUL 03).

2184. DIRECTOR [REDACTED] (251833Z JUN 02).

2185. Riyadh the Facilitator, aka Sharqawi Ah Abdu al-Hajj, was captured on February 7, 2002. (*See* [REDACTED] 10480 ([REDACTED] FEB 02).) Al-Hajj was transferred to [REDACTED] custody on February [REDACTED], 2002. (*See* [REDACTED] 18265 ([REDACTED] FEB 02).) On January [REDACTED], 2004, al-Hajj was rendered to CIA custody. *See* [REDACTED] 2335 [REDACTED].

2186. [REDACTED] 1591 [REDACTED] JAN 04). Documents provided to the Committee on "detainee reporting" related to the UBL operation (incorrectly) indicate that Riyadh the Facilitator was in CIA custody. *See* May 5, 2011, six-page CIA chart entitled, "Detainee Reporting on Abu Ahmad al-Kuwaiti"(DTS #2011-2004).

2187. DIRECTOR [REDACTED] (221240Z AUG 02). Abu Zubair al-Ha'ili never entered the CIA's Detention and Interrogation Program.

2188. Italics added. CIA testimony from CIA officer [REDACTED] and transcript of the Senate Select Committee on Intelligence and the Senate Armed Services Committee briefing on May 4, 2011 (DTS #2011-2049). The CIA subsequently provided the Committee with a letter dated May 5, 2011, which included a document entitled, "Background Detainee Information on Abu Ahmad al-Kuwaiti," with an accompanying six-page chart entitled, "Detainee Reporting on Abu Ahmad al-Kuwaiti" (DTS #2011-2004). See *also* a similar, but less detailed CIA document entitled, "Detainee Reporting on Abu Ahmad al-Kuwaiti's Historic Links to Usama Bin Laden."

2189. On May 5, 2004, the CIA provided several documents to the Committee, including a chart entitled, "Detainee Reporting on Abu Ahmad al-Kuwaiti," described in this summary. For additional details, *see* intelligence chronology in Volume II.

2190. Below are specific details on the reporting of Abu Zubaydah, KSM, Khallad bin Attash, Ammar al-Baluchi, and Abu Faraj al-Libi related to Abu Ahmad al-Kuwaiti: 1) Abu Zubaydah was captured on March 28, 2002, with a 27-page address book that included a phone number for "Abu Ahmad K," which matched a [REDACTED] mobile phone number that was already under intelligence collection by the U.S. Intelligence Community. (As early as July 2002, the CIA associated the phone number with al-Kuwaiti.) As detailed in the Study, Abu Zubaydah provided significant intelligence, primarily to FBI special agents, from the time of his capture on March 28, 2002, through June 18, 2002, when he was placed in isolation for 47 days. On June 13, 2002, less than a week before he was placed in isolation, CIA Headquarters requested that interrogators ask Abu Zubaydah about his knowledge of Abu Ahmad al-Kuwaiti, who was believed to be in Pakistan, according to the request from CIA Headquarters. There are no CIA records indicating that the interrogators asked Abu Zubaydah about al-Kuwaiti. Instead, as described, Abu Zubaydah was placed in isolation beginning on June 18, 2002, with the FBI and CIA interrogators departing the detention site. The FBI did not return. On August 4, 2002, CIA interrogators reestablished contact with Abu Zubaydah and immediately began to subject Abu Zubaydah to the non-stop use of the CIA's enhanced interrogation techniques for 17 days, which included at least 83 applications of the CIA's waterboard interrogation technique. According to CIA records, Abu Zubaydah was not asked about Abu Ahmad al-Kuwaiti until July 7, 2003, when he denied knowing the name. On April 27, 2004, Abu Zubaydah again stated that he did not recognize the name "Abu Ahmed al-Kuwaiti." In August 2005, Abu Zubaydah speculated on an individual the CIA stated might be "identifiable with Abu Ahmad al-Kuwaiti, aka Abu Ahmad al-Pakistani," but Abu Zubaydah stated the person in question was not close with UBL. 2) KSM was captured on March 1, 2003, during a raid in Pakistan. An email address associated with Abu Ahmad al-Kuwaiti was found on a laptop that was assessed to be associated with KSM. Once rendered to CIA custody on March █, 2003, KSM was immediately subjected to the CIA's enhanced interrogation techniques, which continued through March 25, 2003, and included at least 183 applications of the CIA's waterboard interrogation technique. On March 5, 2003, KSM provided information concerning a senior al-Qa'ida member named "Abu Khalid," whom KSM later called "Abu Ahmad al-Baluchi." The information KSM provided could not be corroborated by other intelligence collected by the CIA, and KSM provided no further information on the individual. On May 5, 2003, KSM provided his first information on an individual named "Abu Ahmed al-Kuwaiti" when he was confronted with reporting from a detainee not in CIA custody, Masran bin Arshad. KSM confirmed bin Arshad's reporting regarding Abu Ahmad al-Kuwaiti, specifically that bin Arshad was originally tasked by KSM to get money from Abu Ahmad al-Kuwaiti in Pakistan. KSM further relayed that Abu Ahmad al-Kuwaiti worked with Hassan Ghul helping to move families from Afghanistan to Pakistan. On May 22, 2003, KSM was specifically asked about a UBL courier named Abu Ahmed. KSM again described a courier for UBL whose name was Abu Ahmed al-Baluchi, but noted that this Abu Ahmed was more interested in earning money than in serving al-Qa'ida. According to KSM, Abu Ahmed was working with Hassan Ghul in April or May 2002, but speculated that Abu Ahmed was in Iran as of early March 2003. In July 2003, KSM stated that Abu Ahmad al-Kuwaiti worked with Abu Zubaydah's group prior to September 2001 and later with Abu Sulayman al-Jaza'iri. In September 2003, KSM was confronted with reporting from another detainee in foreign government custody on Abu Ahmad al-Kuwaiti. KSM confirmed that he had told Hambali to work with Abu Ahmad al-Kuwaiti as he transited Pakistan, but KSM downplayed al-Kuwaiti's importance, claiming to have contacted Abu Ahmad al-Kuwaiti only three to four times when he was in Peshawar and stating that Abu Ahmad worked "primarily with lower level members" and appeared to have a higher status than he actually had in al-Qa'ida because KSM relied on al-Kuwaiti for travel facilitation. In January 2004, based on statements made by Hassan Ghul—provided prior to the use of the CIA's enhanced interrogation techniques—that it was "well known" that UBL was always with al-Kuwaiti, CIA Headquarters asked CIA interrogators to reengage KSM on the relationship between al-Kuwaiti and UBL, noting the "serious disconnect" between Ghul's reporting linking UBL and Abu Ahmad al-Kuwaiti and KSM's "pithy" description of al-Kuwaiti. CIA Headquarters wrote that unlike Hassan Ghul, KSM had made "no reference to a link between Abu Ahmed and al-Qa'ida's two top leaders" and that KSM "has some explaining to do about Abu Ahmed and his support to UBL and Zawahiri." On May 31, 2004, KSM claimed that al-Kuwaiti was "not very senior, nor was he wanted," noting that al-Kuwaiti could move about freely, and might be in Peshawar. In August 2005, KSM stated that Abu Ahmad al-Kuwaiti was not a courier and that he had never heard of Abu Ahmad transporting letters for UBL. Instead, KSM claimed that al-Kuwaiti was focused on family after he married in 2002. 3) Khallad bin Attash was arrested with Ammar al-Baluchi in a unilateral operation by Pakistani authorities resulting from criminal leads on April 29, 2003. On May █ 2003, he was rendered to CIA custody and immediately subjected to the CIA's enhanced interrogation techniques from May 16, 2003, to May 18, 2003, and then again from July 18, 2003, to July 29, 2003. On June 30, 2003, bin Attash stated that al-Kuwaiti was admired among the men. On July 27, 2003, bin Attash corroborated intelligence reporting that al-Kuwaiti played a facilitation role in al-Qa'ida and that al-Kuwaiti departed Karachi to get married. In January 2004, bin Attash stated that al-Kuwaiti was not close to UBL and not involved in al-Qa'ida operations, and that al-Kuwaiti was settling down with his wife in the summer of 2003. In August 2005, bin Attash stated that Abu Ahmad al-Kuwaiti was not a courier, that he had never heard of Abu Ahmad transporting letters for UBL, and that Abu Ahmad was instead focused on family after he married in 2002. In August 2006, bin Attash reiterated that al-Kuwaiti was not a courier, but rather focused on family life. 4) Ammar al-Baluchi was arrested with Khallad bin Attash in a unilateral operation by Pakistani authorities resulting from criminal leads on April 29, 2003. Upon his arrest, Ammar al-Baluchi was cooperative and provided information on a number of topics while in foreign government custody, including information on Abu Ahmadal-Kuwaiti that the CIA disseminated prior to al-Baluchi being transferred to CIA custody on May █ 2003. After Ammar al-Baluchi was transferred to CIA custody, the CIA subjected Ammar al-Baluchi to the CIA's enhanced interrogation techniques from May 17, 2003, to May 20, 2003. On May 19, 2003, al-Baluchi stated he fabricated information while being subjected to the CIA's enhanced interrogation techniques the previous day, but in response to questioning, stated that he believed UBL was on tiie Pakistan/Afghanistan border and that a brother of al-Kuwaiti was to take over courier duties for UBL. In June 2003, al-Baluchi stated that there were rumors that al-Kuwaiti was a courier. In January 2004, al-Baluchi retracted previous reporting, stating that al-Kuwaiti was never a courier and would not have direct contact with UBL or Aymanal-Zawahiri because "unlike someone like Abu Faraj, [al-Kuwaiti] was too young and didn't have much experience or credentials to be in that position." In May 2004, al-Baluchi stated that al-Kuwaiti may have worked for Abu Faraj al-Libi. 5) Abu Faraj al-Libi was captured in Pakistan on May 2, 2005. On May ███, 2005, Abu Faraj al-Libi was rendered to CIA custody. Abu Faraj al-Libi was subjected to the CIA's enhanced interrogation techniques from May 28, 2005, to June 2, 2005, and again from June 17, 2005, to June 28, 2005. It was not until July 12, 2005, that CIA Headquarters sent a set of "Tier Three Requirements Regarding Abu Ahmad Al-Kuwaiti" to the detention site holding Abu Faraj al-Libi. Prior to this, interrogators had focused their questioning of Abu Faraj on operational plans, as well as information on senior al-Qa'ida leadership, primarily Hamza Rab'ia and Abu Musab al-Zarqawi. On July 13, 2005, Abu Faraj al-Libi denied knowledge of Abu Ahmad al-Kuwaiti, or any of his aliases. On July 15, 2005, CIA Headquarters noted they did not believe Abu Faraj was being truthful and requested CIA debriefers confront Abu Faraj again regarding his relationship with al-Kuwaiti. CIA records indicate that CIA debriefers did not respond to this request. On August 12, 2005, having received no response to its previous request, CIA Headquarters again asked Abu Faraj's debriefers to readdress the issue of Abu Ahmad al-Kuwaiti. CIA analysts noted that they "[found Faraj's] denials of even recognizing his name difficult to believe," and suggested that "one possible reason why [Faraj] lied about not recognizing Abu Ahmad's name] is [an attempt] to protect him - leading us to request that base readdress this issue with [Faraj] on a priority basis." Two days later, on August 14, 2005, after being questioned again about Abu Ahmad al-Kuwaiti, Abu Faraj al-Libi "swore to God" that he did not know al-Kuwaiti, or anybody who went by any of his aliases, insisting he would never forget anybody who worked for him. Abu Faraj did suggest, however, that an "Ahmad al-Pakistani" had worked with Marwan al-Jabbur to care for families in the Lahore, Pakistan, area, but said he (Abu Faraj) had no relationship with this al-Pakistani. On August 17, 2005, CIA Headquarters requested that debriefers reengage certain detainees on the role of Abu Ahmad al-Kuwaiti. In response, KSM and Khallad bin Attash claimed that al-Kuwaiti was not a courier and that they had never heard of Abu Ahmad transporting letters for UBL. KSM and Khallad bin Attash claimed that al-Kuwaiti was focused on family after he married in 2002. However, Ammar al-Baluchi indicated that al-Kuwaiti worked for Abu Faraj al-Libi in 2002. A September 1, 2005, CIA report states that Abu Faraj al-Libi identified an "Abu 'Abd al Khaliq Jan," as his "go-between with Bin Ladin since mid-2003," but there was no other CIA reporting to support this assertion. In May 2007, a CIA targeting study concluded that the reporting from KSM and Abu Faraj al-Libi was "not credible," and "their attempts to downplay Abu Ahmad's importance or deny knowledge of Abu Ahmad are likely part of an effort to withhold information on UBL or his close associates." A September 28, 2007, CIA report concluded that "Abu Faraj was probably the last detainee to maintain contact with UBL—possibly through Abu Ahmad," but noted that "Abu Faraj vehemently denied any knowledge of Abu Ahmad." *See* intelligence chronology in Volume II for additional details.

2191. Italics added.

2192. Italics added. For a listing of the 12 detainees, *see* CIA's six-page chart entitled, "Detainee Reporting on Abu Ahmad al-Kuwaiti," which lists 12 detainees, all of whom are listed as being in "CIA Custody" (DTS #2011-2004).

2193. Italics added. CIA records indicate that none of the three CIA detainees known to have been subjected by the CIA to the waterboard interrogation technique provided unique intelligence on Abu Ahmad al-Kuwaiti. To the contrary, there is significant evidence that two of the three detainees—Abu Zubaydah and KSM—failed to provide accurate information likely known to them about Abu Ahmad al-Kuwaiti and/or fabricated information to protect al-Kuwaiti. The third CIA detainee known to have been subjected to the CIA's waterboard interrogation technique, 'Abd al-Rahim al-Nashiri, provided no information on Abu Ahmad al-Kuwaiti. *See* intelligence chronology in Volume II for additional information.

2194. Italics added. The CIA's June 2013 Response states: "CIA has never represented that information acquired through its interrogations of detainees was either the first or the only information that we had on Abu Ahmad."

2195. Italics added. CIA testimony from CIA Director Panetta, and transcript of the Senate Select Committee on Intelligence and the Senate Armed Services Committee, May 4, 2011 (DTS #2011-2049).

2196. CIA record ("Call Details Incoming and Outgoing") relating to calling activity for ███ phone number #███ ALEC ███ (240057Z AUG 02).

2197. *See* intelligence chronology in Volume II, including CIA record ("Call Details Incoming and Outgoing") relating to calling activity for ███ phone number #███; ALEC ███ (240057Z AUG 02); [REDACTED] 65902 (080950Z AUG 02); ALEC ███ (092204Z AUG 02); ███ dated 17 September 2001; [REDACTED] 60077 (09/17/2001); DIRECTOR ███ (221240Z AUG 02); and DIRECTOR ███ (251833Z JUN 02).

2198. *See* intelligence chronology in Volume II, including DIRECTOR ███ (251833Z JUN 02). As described above, Riyadh the Facilitator was eventually rendered into the CIA's Detention and Interrogation Program in January 2004, but CIA records indicate he was not subjected to the CIA's enhanced interrogation techniques.

The referenced information was provided in June 2002, while Riyadh the Facilitator was not in U.S. custody, but in the custody of a foreign government.

2199. Senator McCain and other members requested information on the use of the CIA's enhanced interrogation techniques in the UBL operation at the previous day's hearing and the CIA committed to provide additional information to the members. Senator McCain: "I'm also interested in this whole issue of the 'enhanced interrogation,' what role it played. Those who want to justify torture seem to have grabbed hold of this as some justification for our gross violation of the Geneva Conventions to which we are signatory. I'd be very interested in having that issue clarified. I think it's really important." *See* transcript of the Senate Select Committee on Intelligence and the Senate Armed Services Committee briefing on May 4, 2011 (DTS #2011-2049).

2200. *See* CIA letter to the Senate Select Committee on Intelligence dated May 5, 2011, which includes a document entitled, "Background Detainee Information on Abu Ahmad al-Kuwaiti," with an accompanying six-page chart entitled, "Detainee Reporting on Abu Ahmad al-Kuwaiti" (DTS #2011-2004). See *also* a similar, but less detailed CIA document entitled, "Detainee Reporting on Abu Ahmad al-Kuwaiti's Historic Links to Usama Bin Laden." The CIA's September 2012 "Lessons from the Hunt for Bin Ladin," compiled by the CIA's Center for the Study of Intelligence (*See* DTS #2012-3826), appears to utilize the same inaccurate information, stating: "In sum, 25 detainees provided information on Abu Ahmad al-Kuwaiti, his al-Qa'ida membership, and his historic role as a courier for Bin Ladin. Nine of the 25 were held by foreign governments. Of the 16 held in CIA custody, all but three had given information *after* being subjected to enhanced interrogation techniques (EITs), although of the 13 only two (KSM and Abu Zubaydah) had been waterboarded" (italics added). As described, the information in this CIA "lessons" report is inaccurate.

2201. Italics added. "Lessons from the Hunt for Bin Ladin," dated September 2012, compiled by the CIA's Center for the Study of Intelligence, and provided on October 3, 2012 (DTS #2012-3826).

2202. The CIA document identified "Tier 1" intelligence as information that "linked Abu Ahmad to Bin Ladin," but inaccurately included CIA detainees under the "Tier 1" detainee reporting list who did not provide information linking "Abu Ahmad to Bin Ladin." For example, the CIA identified Abu Zubaydah and KSM as providing "Tier 1" intelligence that "linked Abu Ahmad to Bin Ladin," despite both detainees denying any significant connection between al-Kuwaiti and UBL.

2203. Riyadh the Facilitator (information on June 25, 2002 [prior to CIA custody]; CIA custody January ■, 2004), Ammar al-Baluchi (information on May 6, 2003 [prior to CIA custody]; CIA custody May ■, 2003), Ahmed Ghailani (information on August 1, 2004 [prior to CIA custody]; CIA custody September ■, 2004), Sharif al-Masri (information on September 16, 2004 [prior to CIA custody]; CIA custody September ■, 2004), and Muhammad Rahim (information on July 2, 2007 [prior to CIA custody]; CIA custody July ■, 2007). There are reports that a sixth detainee, Hassan Ghul, also provided extensive information on Abu Ahmad al-Kuwaiti prior to being transferred to CIA custody. *See* intelligence chronology in Volume II for additional information.

2204. DIRECTOR ■ (221240Z AUG 02).

2205. Ammar al-Baluchi, Hassan Ghul, Ahmad Ghallani, Sharif al-Masri, and Muhammad Rahim.

2206. Khalid Shaykh Mohammad, Khalid bin Attash, and Abu Faraj al-Libi.

2207. Khalid Shaykh Mohammad, Abu Faraj al-Libi, and Khalid bin Attash. *See* intelligence chronology in Volume II and CIA testimony from May 4, 2011. CIA officer: ". . . with the capture of Abu Faraj al-Libi and Khalid Shaykh Mohammed, these are key bin Ladin facilitators, gatekeepers if you will, and their description of Abu Ahmed, the sharp contrast between that and the earlier detainees. Abu Faraj denies even knowing him, a completely uncredible position for him to take but one that he has stuck with to this day. KSM initially downplays any role Abu Ahmed might play, and by the time he leaves our program claims that he married in 2002, retired and really was playing no role." CIA records indicate Khallad bin Attash also downplayed the role of Abu Ahmad al-Kuwaiti, stating several times that Abu Ahmad was focused on family and was not close to UBL, and that he had never heard of Abu Ahmad al-Kuwaiti serving as acourier for UBL.

2208. DIRECTOR ■ (8/25/2005). On July 7, 2003, and April 27, 2004, Abu Zubaydah was asked about "Abu Ahmed al-Kuwaiti" and denied knowing the name.

2209. *See* CIA letter to the Senate Select Committee on Intelligence dated May 5, 2011, which includes a document entitled, "Background Detainee Information on Abu Ahmad al-Kuwaiti," with an accompanying six-page chart entitled, "Detainee Reporting on Abu Ahmad al-Kuwaiti" (DTS #2011-2004). See *also* a similar, but less detailed CIA document entitled, "Detainee Reporting on Abu Ahmad al-Kuwaiti's Historic Links to Usama Bin Laden." *See* intelligence chronology in Volume II for additional details.

2210. *See* CIA letter to the Senate Select Committee on Intelligence dated May 5, 2011, which includes a document entitled, "Background Detainee Information on Abu Ahmad al-Kuwaiti," with an accompanying six-page chart entitled, "Detainee Reporting on Abu Ahmad al-Kuwaiti" (DTS #2011-2004). *See also* a similar, but less detailed CIA document entitled, "Detainee Reporting on Abu Ahmad al-Kuwaiti's Historic Links to Usama Bin Laden." The CIA's September 2012 "Lessons from the Hunt for Bin Ladin," compiled by the CIA's Center for the Study of Intelligence (DTS #2012-3826), appears to utilize the same inaccurate information, stating: "In sum, 25 detainees provided information on Abu Ahmad al-Kuwaiti, his al-Qa'ida membership, and his historic role as a courier for Bin Ladin. Nine of the 25 were held by foreign governments. Of the 16 held in CIA custody, all but three had given information *after* being subjected to enhanced interrogation techniques

(EITs) . . ." (italics added). As described, the information in this CIA "Lessons Learned" report is inaccurate.

2211. Ridha al-Najjar/al-Tunisi, who was detained in May 2002, first provided intelligence on al-Kuwaiti on June 4/5 2002, and was subsequently transferred to CIA custody on June █, 2002; and subjected to the CIA's enhanced interrogation techniques in October 2002. Hambali, who was detained on August 11, 2003, first provided information on al-Kuwaiti on August 13, 2003. Later, Hambali was rendered to CIA custody on August █, 2003. *See* intelligence chronology in Volume II, including 63211 (30 JAN 2002).

2212. *See* intelligence chronology in Volume II, including █ 63211 (30 JAN 2002).

2213. DIRECTOR █ (221240Z AUG 02).

2214. *See* intelligence chronology in Volume II, including reporting from Riyadh the Facilitator, Ammar al-Baluchi, Ahmad Ghailani, Sharif al-Masri, Muhammad Rahim, Ridha al-Najjar/al-Tunisi, and Hambali. As detailed, a former CIA officer stated publicly that Hassan Ghul provided reporting on Abu Ahmad al-Kuwaiti prior to being transferred to CIA custody.

2215. "Lessons from the Hunt for Bin Ladin," dated September 2012, compiled by the CIA's Center for the Study of Intelligence, and provided on October 3, 2012 (DTS #2012-3826).

2216. *See* intelligence chronology in Volume II, including reporting from Ammar al-Baluchi, Ahmad Ghailani, Sharif al-Masri, Muhammad Rahim, Ridha al-Najjar/al-Tunisi, Hambali, and Hassan Ghul.

2217. Khalid Shaykh Mohammad, Khalid bin Attash, Abu Yasir al-Jaza'iri, Samir al-Barq, and Abu Faraj al-Libi.

2218. Khalid Shaykh Mohammad, Abu Faraj al-Libi, and Khalid bin Attash. *See* intelligence chronology in Volume II and CIA testimony from May 4, 2011. CIA officer: ". . . with the capture of Abu Faraj al-Libi and Khalid Shaykh Mohammed, these are key bin Ladin facilitators, gatekeepers if you will, and their description of Abu Ahmed, the sharp contrast between that and the earlier detainees. Abu Faraj denies even knowing him, a completely uncredible position for him to take but one that he has stuck with to this day. KSM initially downplays any role Abu Ahmed might play, and by the time he leaves our program claims that he married in 2002, retired and really was playing no role." CIA records indicate Khallad bin Attash also downplayed the role of Abu Ahmad al-Kuwaiti, stating several times that Abu Ahmad was focused on family and was not close to UBL, and that he had never heard of Abu Ahmad al-Kuwaiti serving as a courier for UBL.

2219. Abu Yasir ai-Jaza'iri provided corroborative information in July 2003 that Abu Ahmad al-Kuwaiti was associated with KSM, was best known in Karachi, and appeared to be Pakistani. (*See* DIRECTOR █ (111632Z JUL 03).) Samir al-Barq provided information in September 2003 that al-Kuwaiti had provided al-Barq with $1000 to obtain a house in Karachi that al-Qa'ida could use for a biological weapons lab. (*See* █47409 (191324Z NOV03), as well as the detainee review of Samir al-Barq in Volume III that details al-Barq's various statements on al-Qa'ida's ambition to establish a biological weapons program.) Neither of these reports is cited in CIA records as providing unique or new information. In October 2003, both detainees denied having any information on the use of Abbottabad as a safe haven for al-Qa'ida. *See* █ 10172 (160821Z OCT 03); 48444 (240942Z OCT 03).

2220. DIRECTOR (8/25/2005). On July 7, 2003, and April 27, 2004, Abu Zubaydah was asked about "Abu Ahmed al-Kuwaiti" and denied knowing the name.

2221. "Lessons from the Hunt for Bin Ladin," dated September 2012, compiled by the CIA's Center for the Study of Intelligence, and provided on October 3, 2012 (DTS #2012-3826).

2222. In addition to "Abu Ahmad K." being included in Abu Zubaydah's address book, there was additional reporting indicating that Abu Zubaydah had some knowledge of Abu Ahmad al-Kuwaiti. For example, on October 12, 2004, another CIA detainee explained how he met al-Kuwaiti at a guesthouse that was operated by Ibn Shaykh al-Libi and Abu Zubaydah in 1997. *See* intelligence chronology in Volume II.

2223. *See* DIRECTOR █ (252024Z AUG 05) and the intelligence chronology in Volume II.

2224. *See* intelligence chronology in Volume II, including ALEC █ (102238Z MAR 03); HEADQUARTERS █ (█ JAN 04); █ 29986 (171741Z AUG 05); █ 5594 (201039Z MAY 07).

2225. As the dissemination of 21 intelligence reports suggests, information in CIA records indicates Hassan Ghul was cooperative with CIA personnel prior to being subjected to the CIA's enhanced interrogation techniques. In an interview with the CIA Office of Inspector General, a CIA officer familiar with Ghul stated, "He sang like a tweetie bird. He opened up right away and was cooperative from the outset." (*See* December 2, 2004, interview with [REDACTED], Chief, DO, CTC UBL Department, █) The CIA's September 2012 "Lessons from the Hunt for Bin Ladin," compiled by the CIA's Center for the Study of Intelligence (DTS #2012-3826), states that: "Ghul's tantalizing lead began a systematic but low profile effort to target and further identify Abu Ahmad." On April 16, 2013, the Council on Foreign Relations hosted a forum in relation to the screening of the film, "Manhunt." The forum included former CIA officer Nada Bakos, who states in the film that Hassan Ghul provided the critical information on Abu Ahmed al-Kuwaiti to Kurdish officials prior to entering CIA custody. When asked about the interrogation techniques used by the Kurds, Bakos stated: ". . . honestly, Hassan Ghul . . . when he was being debriefed by the Kurdish government, he literally was sitting there having tea. He was in a safe house. He wasn't locked up in a cell. He wasn't handcuffed to anything. He was—he was having a free flowing conversation. And there's—you know, there's articles in Kurdish papers about sort of their interpretation of the story and how forthcoming he was." *See*

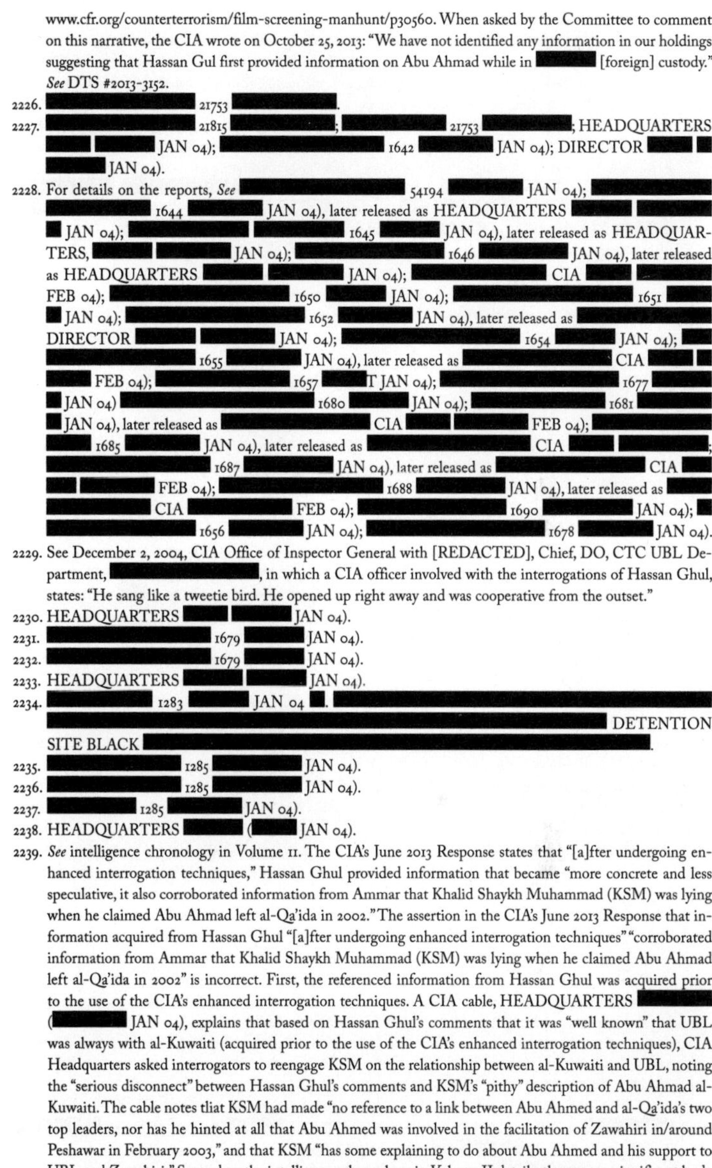

www.cfr.org/counterterrorism/film-screening-manhunt/p30560. When asked by the Committee to comment on this narrative, the CIA wrote on October 25, 2013: "We have not identified any information in our holdings suggesting that Hassan Gul first provided information on Abu Ahmad while in [foreign] custody." *See* DTS #2013-3152.

2226. 21753 .

2227. 21815 ; 21753 ; HEADQUARTERS JAN 04); 1642 JAN 04); DIRECTOR JAN 04).

2228. For details on the reports, *See* 54194 JAN 04); 1644 JAN 04), later released as HEADQUARTERS JAN 04); 1645 JAN 04), later released as HEADQUARTERS, JAN 04); 1646 JAN 04), later released as HEADQUARTERS JAN 04); CIA FEB 04); 1650 JAN 04); 1651 JAN 04); 1652 JAN 04), later released as DIRECTOR JAN 04); 1654 JAN 04); 1655 JAN 04), later released as CIA FEB 04); 1657 T JAN 04); 1677 JAN 04) 1680 JAN 04); 1681 JAN 04), later released as CIA FEB 04); 1685 JAN 04), later released as CIA ; 1687 JAN 04), later released as CIA FEB 04); 1688 JAN 04), later released as CIA FEB 04); 1690 JAN 04); 1656 JAN 04); 1678 JAN 04).

2229. See December 2, 2004, CIA Office of Inspector General with [REDACTED], Chief, DO, CTC UBL Department, , in which a CIA officer involved with the interrogations of Hassan Ghul, states: "He sang like a tweetie bird. He opened up right away and was cooperative from the outset."

2230. HEADQUARTERS JAN 04).

2231. 1679 JAN 04).

2232. 1679 JAN 04).

2233. HEADQUARTERS JAN 04).

2234. 1283 JAN 04 . DETENTION SITE BLACK .

2235. 1285 JAN 04).

2236. 1285 JAN 04).

2237. 1285 JAN 04).

2238. HEADQUARTERS (JAN 04).

2239. *See* intelligence chronology in Volume II. The CIA's June 2013 Response states that "[a]fter undergoing enhanced interrogation techniques," Hassan Ghul provided information that became "more concrete and less speculative, it also corroborated information from Ammar that Khalid Shaykh Muhammad (KSM) was lying when he claimed Abu Ahmad left al-Qa'ida in 2002." The assertion in the CIA's June 2013 Response that information acquired from Hassan Ghul "[a]fter undergoing enhanced interrogation techniques" "corroborated information from Ammar that Khalid Shaykh Muhammad (KSM) was lying when he claimed Abu Ahmad left al-Qa'ida in 2002" is incorrect. First, the referenced information from Hassan Ghul was acquired prior to the use of the CIA's enhanced interrogation techniques. A CIA cable, HEADQUARTERS (JAN 04), explains that based on Hassan Ghul's comments that it was "well known" that UBL was always with al-Kuwaiti (acquired prior to the use of the CIA's enhanced interrogation techniques), CIA Headquarters asked interrogators to reengage KSM on the relationship between al-Kuwaiti and UBL, noting the "serious disconnect" between Hassan Ghul's comments and KSM's "pithy" description of Abu Ahmad al-Kuwaiti. The cable notes tliat KSM had made "no reference to a link between Abu Ahmed and al-Qa'ida's two top leaders, nor has he hinted at all that Abu Ahmed was involved in the facilitation of Zawahiri in/around Peshawar in February 2003," and that KSM "has some explaining to do about Abu Ahmed and his support to UBL and Zawahiri." Second, as the intelligence chronology in Volume II details, there was a significant body of intelligence well before Hassan Ghul's pre-enhanced interrogation techniques reporting in January 2004 indicating that KSM was providing inaccurate information on Abu Alimad al-Kuwaiti. *See* detailed information in Volume II intelligence chronology. Third, as detailed in CIA-provided documents (DTS #2011- 2004), the CIA described Hassan Ghul's reporting as "speculat[ive]" both during and after the use of the CIA's enhanced interrogation techniques. Finally, as noted earlier, the CIA's June 2013 Response ignores or minimizes a large body of intelligence reporting in CIA records—and documented in the Committee Study—that was acquired from sources and methods unrelated to the use of the CIA's enhanced interrogation techniques. Nonetheless, the CIA's June 2013 Response asserts: "It is impossible to know in hindsight whether we could have obtained from Ammar, Gul, and others the same information that helped us find Bin Ladin *without using enhanced techniques*, or whether we eventually would have acquired other intelligence that allowed us to successfully pursue the Abu Ahmad lead or some other lead without the information we acquired from detainees in CIA custody" (italics added). As detailed in this summary, the most accurate intelligence from a detainee on Abu Ahmad al-Kuwaiti was acquired prior to the use of the CIA's enhanced interrogation techniques, and CIA detainees subjected to the CIA's enhanced interrogation techniques provided inaccurate and fabricated information on al-Kuwaiti. *See* detailed information in the Volume II intelligence chronology.

2240. ██████ 2441 ██████; HEADQUARTERS ██████ ██████; ██████ 1635 ██████; ██████ 1712 ██████; HEADQUARTERS ██████ ██████ ██████; ██████ 1775 ██████; ██████ 173426 ██████.

2241. *See* Committee Notification from the CIA dated ██████ (DTS #2012-3802).

2242. *See* CIA letter to the Senate Select Committee on Intelligence dated May 5, 2011, which includes a document entitled, "Background Detainee Information on Abu Ahmad al-Kuwaiti," with an accompanying six-page chart entitled, "Detainee Reporting on Abu Ahmad al-Kuwaiti" (DTS #2011-2004). See *also* a similar, but less detailed CIA document entitled, "Detainee Reporting on Abu Ahmad al-Kuwaiti's Historic Links to Usama Bin Laden."

2243. Significant information was acquired on Abu Ahmad al-Kuwaiti independent of CIA detainees. *See* intelligence chronology in Volume II.

2244. Italics added. CIA analysis entitled, "Overcoming Challenges To Capturing Usama Bin Ladin, 1 September 2005." CIA records indicate that Abu Faraj al-Libi fabricated information relating to "'Abd al Khaliq Jan."

2245. Italics added. As detailed, the reporting that Abu Ahmad al-Kuwaiti "worked closely with KSM" and was "one of a few close associates of Usama bin Ladin," who "traveled frequently" to "meet with Usama bin Ladin," was acquired in 2002, from sources unrelated to the CIA's Detention and Interrogation Program.

2246. Italics added. ██████ 5594 (201039Z MAY 07). Reporting from CIA detainees Ammar al-Baluchi and Khallad bin Attash—both subjected to the CIA enhanced interrogation techniques —included similar inaccurate information. Khallad bin Attash was arrested with Ammar al-Baluchi in a unilateral operation by Pakistani authorities resulting from criminal leads on April 29, 2003. On May ██, 2003, bin Attash was rendered to CIA custody and immediately subjected to the CIA's enhanced interrogation techniques from May 16, 2003, to May 18, 2003, and then again from July 18, 2003, to July 29, 2003. On June 30, 2003, bin Attash stated that al-Kuwaiti was admired among the men. On July 27, 2003, bin Attash corroborated intelligence reporting that al-Kuwaiti played a facilitation role in al-Qa'ida and that al-Kuwaiti departed Karachi to get married. In Januaiy 2004, bin Attash stated that al-Kuwaiti was not close to UBL and not involved in al-Qa'ida operations, and that al-Kuwaiti was settling down with his wife in the summer of 2003. In August 2005, bin Attash stated that Abu Ahmad al-Kuwaiti was not a courier, that he had never heard of Abu Ahmad transporting letters for UBL, and that Abu Ahmad was instead focused on family after he married in 2002. In August 2006, bin Attash reiterated that al-Kuwaiti was not a courier, but rather focused on family life. Ammar al-Baluchi was arrested with Khallad bin Attash in a unilateral operation by Pakistani authorities resulting from criminal leads on April 29, 2003. Upon his arrest in Pakistan, Ammar al-Baluchi was cooperative and provided information on a number of topics to foreign government interrogators, including information on Abu Ahmad al-Kuwaiti that the CIA disseminated prior to al-Baluchi being transferred to CIA custody on May ██, 2003. After Ammar al-Baluchi was transferred to CIA custody, the CIA subjected Ammar al-Baluchi to the CIA's enhanced interrogation techniques from May 17, 2003, to May 20, 2003. On May 19, 2003, al-Baluchi admitted to fabricating information while being subjected to the CIA's enhanced interrogation techniques the previous day, and in response to questioning, stated that he believed UBL was on the Pakistan/Afghanistan border and that a brother of al-Kuwaiti was to take over courier duties for UBL. In June 2003, al-Baluchi stated that there were rumors that al-Kuwaiti was a courier. In early 2004, al-Baluchi acknowledged that al-Kuwaiti may have worked for Abu Faraj al-Libi, but stated that al-Kuwaiti was never a courier and would not have direct contact with UBL. *See* intelligence chronology in Volume II and detainee reviews of Khallad bin Attash and Ammar al-Baluchi for additional information.

2247. *See* CIA CTC "Al-Qa'ida Watch," dated November 23, 2007.

2248. *See* CIA CTC "Al-Qa'ida Watch," dated November 23, 2007.

2249. ██████ 3808 (211420Z JAN 08); HEADQUARTERS ██████ (232217Z JAN 08); ██████ 9044 (240740Z JAN 08); ██████ 5568 (081633Z FEB 08).

2250. Italics added. ██████ 9044 (240740Z JAN 08).

2251. HEADQUARTERS ██████ (011334Z MAY 08).

2252. ██████ 5594 (201039Z MAY 07).

2253. ██████ 5594 (201039Z MAY 07).

2254. See information in Volume II intelligence chronology for additional details.

2255. On October 28, 2013, the CIA informed the Committee that "CIA policy is to conduct background briefings using unclassified or declassified information" (DTS #2013-3152).

2256. Email from: ██████; to: [REDACTED], ██████, [REDACTED],

[REDACTED]; cc: ; subject: CIA at War; date: January 20, 2004, at 11:13 AM; email from: ; to: ; cc: [REDACTED], [REDACTED], , [REDACTED]; subject: Re: CIA at War; date: January 21, 2004; at 02:11 PM; email from: ; to Scott W. Muller, John A. Rizzo, ; cc: ; subject: Re: CIA at War; date: January 21, 2004, at 02:27 PM.

2257. Email from John A. Rizzo; to: ; cc: , Scott W. Muller, , [REDACTED]; subject: Re: CIA at War; date: January 22, 2004, at 09:28 AM.

2258. "Rule Change Lets C.I.A. Freely Send Suspects Abroad to Jails," by Douglas Jehl and David Johnston, *The New York Times*, March 6, 2005; email from: ; to: ; cc: , ; subject: Question on 06 March New York Times revelations; date: April 22, 2005, at 1:38 PM; email from: ; to: ; cc: , , , , ; subject: Re: Question on 06 March New York Times revelations; date: April 28, 2005, at 8:12:46 am.

2259. Email from: ; to: ; cc: , ; subject: Re: Question on 06 March New York Times revelations; date: April 28, 2005, at 8:25:23 AM.

2260. *The CIA at War*, Ronald Kessler, St. Martin's Press, New York, 2003. As detailed elsewhere, Iyman Faris was already under investigation and Majid Khan, who was then in foreign government custody, had discussed Faris, prior to any mention of Faris by KSM. Likewise, the capture of Khallad bin Attash in April 2003 was unrelated to the reporting from KSM or any other CIA detainee. Kessler's book also stated that Abu Zubaydah "soon began singing to the FBI and CIA about other planned plots," and that "intercepts and information developed months earlier after the arrest of Ramzi Binalshibh . . . allowed the CIA to trace [KSM]." (*See* Ronald Kessler, *The CIA at War*, St. Martin's Press, New York, 2003.) As detailed elsewhere, Abu Zubaydah did not provide intelligence on al-Qa'ida "planned plots," and KSM's capture was unrelated to information provided by Ramzi bin Al-Shibh. Finally, Kessler's book stated that KSM "told the CIA about a range of planned attacks—on U.S. convoys in Afghanistan, nightclubs in Dubai, targets in Turkey, and an Israeli embassy in the Middle East. Within a few months the transcripts of his interrogations were four feet high." These statements were incongruent with CIA records.

2261. "Rule Change Lets C.I.A. Freely Send Suspects Abroad," by Douglas Jehl and David Johnston, *The New York Times*, March 6, 2005.

2262. Email from: ; to: [REDACTED], , , [REDACTED], [REDACTED], [REDACTED], , [REDACTED], , [REDACTED], , [REDACTED], [REDACTED]; cc: , ; subject: FOR IMMEDIATE COORDINATION: Summary of impact of detainee program; date: April 13, 2005, at 5:21:37 PM.

2263. Sametime communication, between John P. Mudd and , April 13, 2005, from 19:23:50 to 19:56:05.

2264. As detailed in this summary, this exchange occurred the day before an anticipated Committee vote on a proposed Committee investigation of the CIA's Detention and Interrogation Program.

2265. Sametime communication, between John P. Mudd and , April 13, 2005, from 19:23:50 to 19:56:05.

2266. Sametime communication, between John P. Mudd and , April 13, 2005, from 19:23:50 to 19:56:05.

2267. Sametime communication, between John P. Mudd and , April 13, 2005, from 19:23:50 to 19:56:05.

2268. Email from: , Chief of Operations, ALEC Station; to , , [REDACTED], [REDACTED], [REDACTED], , , [REDACTED], [REDACTED], , , ; [REDACTED], [REDACTED], , , ; cc: , ; subject: Brokaw interview: Take one; date: April 13, 2005, at 6:46:59 PM; email from: ; to: ; cc: , [REDACTED], [REDACTED], , [REDACTED], , , [REDACTED], , [REDACTED], [REDACTED], , , , , , [REDACTED], ; subject: Re: Brokaw interview: Take one; date: April 13, 2005; at 6:50:28 PM; email from: ; to: , [REDACTED], ; cc: John A. Rizzo, , , , [REDACTED]; subject: Re: Brokaw interview: Take one; date: April 13, 2005, 7:24:50 PM.

2269. Email from: ; to: ; cc: [REDACTED], , [REDACTED], John A. Rizzo, , , ; subject: Re: Brokaw interview: Take one; date: April 14, 2005, at 9:22:32 AM.

2270. Email from: ; to: , ; cc: [REDACTED], , [REDACTED], , ; subject: Re: Brokaw interview: Take one; date: April

14, 2005, at 8:08:00 AM.

2271. Email from: ; to: ; subject: Brokaw interview: Take one; date: April 15, 2005, at 1:00:59 PM. The CIA's June 2013 Response states that "[w]ith regard to information related to covert action, authorization [to disclose information to the media] rests with the White House." CIA records made available to the Committee, however, do not indicate White House approval for the subsequent media disclosures. In the summer of 2013, the Committee requested the CIA provide any such records should they exist. No records were identified by the CIA.

2272. *See* "The Long War; World View of War on Terror," *Dateline NBC*, June 24, 2005. In April 2005, Mudd stated that the program would likely be aired in June. *See* email from: John P. Mudd; to: ; subject: Re: Brokaw interview: Take one; date: April 18, 2005, at 08:31 AM.

2273. "The frightening evolution of al-Qaida; Decentralization has led to deadly staying power," *Dateline NBC*, June 24, 2005.

2274. "The frightening evolution of al-Qaida; Decentralization has led to deadly staying power," *Dateline NBC*, June 24, 2005; "Al-Qaida finds safe haven in Iran," *Dateline NBC*, June 24, 2005. Notwithstanding this content, the CIA's June 2013 Response states that "[a] review of the NBC broadcast, cited by the *Study*, shows that it contained no public disclosures of classified CIA information; indeed, *the RDI program was not discussed*"(emphasis in the original). In addition to the information described above included in the online articles associated with the broadcast, the broadcast itself described the role of a CIA asset in the capture of KSM and the capture of Abu Faraj al-Libi in "joint US/Pakistani actions" ("The Long War; World View of War on Terror," *Dateline NBC*, June 24, 2005).

2275. As described elsewhere in this summary and in more detail in the full Committee Study, the captures of KSM and Khallad bin Attash were unrelated to the capture and interrogation of Ramzi bin al-Shibh.

2276. Email from: ; to: ; cc: [REDACTED], , , , ; bcc: ; subject: Re: Interrogation Program--Going Public Draft Talking Points--Comments Due to me by COB TODAY. Thanks.; date: April 20, 2005, at 5:58:47 PM.

2277. *See* email from: ; to: ; cc: [REDACTED], , [REDACTED]; subject: Re: Interrogation Program--Going Public Draft Talking Points--Comments Due to me by COB TODAY. Thanks.; date: April 21, 2005, at 07:24 AM. was referring to the assault case against David Passaro. The Committee Study does not include an analysis of the accuracy of declarations to U.S. courts by senior CIA officials.

2278. Email from: ; to: ; cc: , , , [REDACTED], , [REDACTED]; subject: Re: Interrogation Program--Going Public Draft Talking Points—Comments Due to me by COB TODAY. Thanks.; date: April 25, 2005, at 11:41:07 AM.

2279. Email from: ; to: , John A. Rizzo, , , [REDACTED], Robert L. Grenier; subject: Doug Jehl - Comprehensive Story on the Capture of Abu Zubaydah and Conception of EITs; date: December 15, 2005, at 02:04 PM.

2280. Email from: ; to: , John A. Rizzo, , , [REDACTED], Robert L. Grenier; subject: Doug Jehl - Comprehensive Story on the Capture of Abu Zubaydah and Conception of EITs; date: December 15, 2005, at 02:04 PM.

2281. Email from: ; to: [REDACTED], [REDACTED], , , [REDACTED], ; cc: [REDACTED], [REDACTED], ; subject: Doug Jehl - Comprehensive Story on the Capture of Abu Zubaydah and Conception of EITs; date: December 15, 2005, at 02:10 PM. Another CIA officer added "I don't like so much talk about EIT's, but that particular horse has long left the barn . . . ." *See* email from: ; to: ; cc: [REDACTED], [REDACTED], [REDACTED], [REDACTED], , [REDACTED], , ; subject: Re: Doug Jehl - Comprehensive Story on the Capture of Abu Zubaydah and Conception of EITs; date: December 15, 2005, at 03:03 PM.

2282. Email from: ; to: [REDACTEDı; cc: , , , , , ; subject: Re: Doug Jehl - Comprehensive Story on the Capture of Abu Zubaydah and Conception of EITs; date: December 15, 2005, at 8:50:36 PM.

2283. Email from: Mark Mansfield; to: , ; cc: , Paul Gimigliano, ; subject: We Can't Let This Go Unanswered; date: September 7, 2006, at 01:12 PM.

2284. Email from: Mark Mansfield; to: ; cc: , [REDACTED], , , , ; subject: Re: Immediate re Abu Zubaydah – Re: Fw: We Can't Let This Go Unanswered; date: September 7, 2006, at 3:14:53 PM.

2285. "At a Secret Interrogation, Dispute Flared Over Tactics," *New York Times*, David Johnston, September 10, 2006.

2286. *See* Abu Zubaydah detainee review in Volume III and sections on CIA claims related to the "Capture of Ramzi bin al-Shibh" in this summary and Volume II.

2287. CY 2005 & CY 2006 CTC Media Leaks; September 21, 2006. The document described "the more serious CTC media leaks that occurred in CY 2005 and 2006."

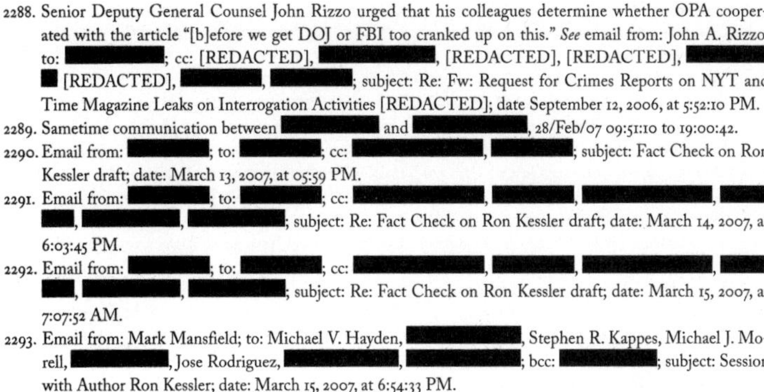

2288. Senior Deputy General Counsel John Rizzo urged that his colleagues determine whether OPA cooperated with the article "[b]efore we get DOJ or FBI too cranked up on this." *See* email from: John A. Rizzo; to: ; cc: [REDACTED], , [REDACTED], [REDACTED], [REDACTED], , ; subject: Re: Fw: Request for Crimes Reports on NYT and Time Magazine Leaks on Interrogation Activities [REDACTED]; date September 12, 2006, at 5:52:10 PM.
2289. Sametime communication between and , 28/Feb/07 09:51:10 to 19:00:42.
2290. Email from: ; to: ; cc: , ; subject: Fact Check on Ron Kessler draft; date: March 13, 2007, at 05:59 PM.
2291. Email from: ; to: ; cc: , , , , , ; subject: Re: Fact Check on Ron Kessler draft; date: March 14, 2007, at 6:03:45 PM.
2292. Email from: ; to: ; cc: , , , , , ; subject: Re: Fact Check on Ron Kessler draft; date: March 15, 2007, at 7:07:52 AM.
2293. Email from: Mark Mansfield; to: Michael V. Hayden, , Stephen R. Kappes, Michael J. Morell, , Jose Rodriguez, , ; bcc: ; subject: Session with Author Ron Kessler; date: March 15, 2007, at 6:54:33 PM.
2294. Kessler's changes repeated the representation made in the president's September 6, 2006, speech, which was based on CIA information and vetted by the CIA, that Abu Zubaydah and Ramzi bin al-Shibh "provided information that would help in the planning and execution of the operation that captured Khalid Sheikh Mohammed." With regard to the Second Wave plotting, Kessler stated that "'[i]f it had not been for coercive interrogation techniques used on Abu Zubaydah, CIA officials suggest, the second wave of attacks might have occurred and KSM could be free and planning more attacks." As detailed in this summary, and in greater detail in Volumes II and III, the thwarting of the Second Wave plotting and the capture of KSM were unrelated to reporting from Abu Zubaydah. Kessler's changes also included statements about the training and expertise of CIA interrogators, the Department of Justice review of the CIA's interrogation techniques, and congressional oversight of the CIA's Detention and Interrogation Program. For example, Kessler wrote, "[b]efore confronting a terrorist, each interrogator was given 250 hours of specialized training." This statement is incongruent with the history of the CIA program. Email from: Ronald Kessler; to: Mark Mansfield; subject: follow-up; date: March 16, 2007, at 10:52:05.
2295. Email from: Ronald Kessler; to: Mark Mansfield; subject: follow-up; date: March 16, 2007, at 10:52:05.
2296. Memorandum for John Rizzo, Acting General Counsel, Central Intelligence Agency, from Jay Bybee, Assistant Attorney General, Office of Legal Counsel, August 1, 2002, Interrogation of al Qaeda Operative (DTS #2009-1810, Tab 1). Also on August 1, 2002, OLC issued an unclassified, but non-public, opinion, from Deputy Assistant Attorney General John Yoo to White House Counsel Alberto Gonzales analyzing whether certain interrogation methods violate 18 U.S.C. §§ 2340-2340A.
2297. Memorandum for John Rizzo, Acting General Counsel, Central Intelligence Agency, from Jay Bybee, Assistant Attorney General, Office of Legal Counsel, August 1, 2002, Interrogation of al Qaeda Operative (DTS #2009-1810. Tab 1).
2298. Memorandum for John Rizzo, Acting General Counsel, Central Intelligence Agency, from Jay Bybee, Assistant Attorney General, Office of Legal Counsel, August 1, 2002, Interrogation of al Qaeda Operative (DTS #2009-1810, Tab 1). During a 2008 hearing of the Senate Select Committee on Intelligence, then-Acting Assistant Attorney General Steven Bradbury stressed that the OLC's opinions relied on factual representations made by the CIA. As Bradbury testified, "all of our advice addressing the CIA's specific interrogation methods has made clear that OLC's legal conclusions were contingent on a number of express conditions, limitations and safeguards adopted by the CIA and designed to ensure that the program would be administered by trained professionals with strict oversight and controls, and that none of the interrogation practices would go beyond the bounds of the law." When asked whether information could be elicited from detainees using techniques authorized by the Army Field Manual, Bradbury responded, "I will have to defer, because on those kinds of questions in terms of the effectiveness and the information obtained I have to rely on the professional judgment of the folks involved at the agency, and General [Michael] Hayden I think has spoken to this issue before this Committee." (*See* transcript of hearing of the Senate Select Committee on Intelligence, June 10, 2008 (DTS #2008-2698).) General Hayden's representations to the Committee are described elsewhere in this summary and in greater detail in Volume II.
2299. Memorandum for John Rizzo, Acting General Counsel, Central Intelligence Agency, from Jay Bybee, Assistant Attorney General, Office of Legal Counsel, August 1, 2002, Interrogation of al Qaeda Operative (DTS #2009-1810, Tab 1).
2300. Email from: ; to: with multiple cc's; subject: AZ information; date: July 10, 2002, at 1:18:52 PM. This claim was included in subsequent OLC memoranda. *See* Memorandum for John A. Rizzo, Senior Deputy General Counsel, Central Intelligence Agency, from Steven G. Bradbury, Principal Deputy Assistant Attorney General, Office of Legal Counsel, May 30, 2005, Re: Application of United States Obligations Under Article 16 of the Convention Against Torture to Certain Techniques that May be

Used in the Interrogation of High Value Al Qaeda Detainees (DTS #2009-1810, Tab 11).

2301. CIA Intelligence Assessment, August 16, 2006, "Countering Misconceptions About Training Camps in Afghanistan, 1990-2001."

2302. Memorandum for John Rizzo, Acting General Counsel, Central Intelligence Agency, from Jay Bybee, Assistant Attorney General, Office of Legal Counsel, August 1, 2002, Interrogation of al Qaeda Operative (DTS #2009-1810, Tab 1). This claim was included in subsequent OLC memoranda. *See* Memorandum for John A. Rizzo, Senior Deputy General Counsel, Central Intelligence Agency, from Steven G. Bradbury, Principal Deputy Assistant Attorney General, Office of Legal Counsel, May 30, 2005, Re: Application of United States Obligations Under Article 16 of the Convention Against Torture to Certain Techniques that May be Used in the Interrogation of High Value Al Qaeda Detainees (DTS #2009-1810, Tab 11).

2303. Memorandum for John Rizzo, Acting General Counsel, Central Intelligence Agency, from Jay Bybee, Assistant Attorney General, Office of Legal Counsel, August 1, 2002, Interrogation of al Qaeda Operative (DTS #2009-1810, Tab 1).

2304. Memorandum for John Rizzo, Acting General Counsel, Central Intelligence Agency, from Jay Bybee, Assistant Attorney General, Office of Legal Counsel, August 1, 2002, Interrogation of al Qaeda Operative (DTS #2009-1810, Tab 1).

2305. 10496 (162014Z FEB 03).

2306. Memorandum for John Rizzo, Acting General Counsel, Central Intelligence Agency, from Jay Bybee, Assistant Attorney General, Office of Legal Counsel, August 1, 2002, Interrogation of al Qaeda Operative (DTS #2009-1810, Tab l).

2307. [REDACTED] 73208 (231043Z JUL 02); email from: to: [REDACTED], [REDACTED], , subject: Addendum from [DETENTION SITE GREEN], [REDACTED] 73208 (231043Z JUL 02); July 23, 2004, at 07:56:49 PM. See *also* email from: [REDACTED]; to: [REDACTED]; subject: Re: [SWIGERT and DUNBAR]; date: August 8, 21, 2002, at 10:21 PM.

2308. Letter from Assistant Attorney General Jack L. Goldsmith III to Director Tenet, June 18, 2004 (DTS #2004-2710). In an August 2003 interview with the OIG, CTC Legal, , stated that "every detainee interrogated is different in that they are outside the opinion because the opinion was written for Zubaydah." The context for 's statement was the legality of the waterboarding of KSM. *See* interview of by [REDACTED], [REDACTED], and [REDACTED], Office of the Inspector General, August 20, 2003.

2309. Memorandum for John Rizzo, Acting General Counsel, Central Intelligence Agency, from Jay Bybee, Assistant Attorney General, Office of Legal Counsel, August 1, 2002, Interrogation of al Qaeda Operative (DTS #2009-1810, Tab 1).

2310. Department of Justice Office of Professional Responsibility; Report, Investigation into the Office of Legal Counsel's Memoranda Concerning Issues Relating to the Central Intelligence Agency's Use of 'Enhanced Interrogation Techniques' on Suspected Terrorists, July 29, 2009, pp. 140–41 (DTS #2010-1058).

2311. Memorandum for John Rizzo, Acting General Counsel, Central Intelligence Agency, from Jay Bybee, Assistant Attorney General, Office of Legal Counsel, August 1, 2002, Interrogation of al Qaeda Operative (DTS #2009-1810, Tab I).

2312. 1396 ; 1299 (JAN 04); 1308 (JAN04) 1312 (JAN 04); 1530 (04).

2313. Memorandum for John Rizzo, Acting General Counsel, Central Intelligence Agency, from Jay Bybee, Assistant Attorney General, Office of Legal Counsel, August 1, 2002, Interrogation of al Qaeda Operative (DTS #2009-1810, Tab 1).

2314. 10536 (151006Z JUL 02); ALEC (182321Z JUL 02). After the use of the CIA's enhanced interrogation techniques on Abu Zubaydah, reported that "[d]uring the most aggressive portions of[Abu Zubaydah's] interrogation, the combination of a lack of hygiene, sub-optimal nutrition, inadvertent trauma to the wound secondary to some of the stress positions utilized at that stage and the removal of formal, obvious medical care to further isolate the subject had an overall additive effect on the deterioration of the wound." See 10679 (250932Z AUG 02).

2315. *See* Volume III, including detainee reviews of Abu Hazim and Abd al-Karim.

2316. As described later, the CIA sought OLC approval for these techniques on July 30, 2004, almost two years after the August 1, 2002, memorandum. *See* letter from CTC Legal to Acting Assistant Attorney General Levin, July 30, 2004 (DTS #2009-1809).

2317. Letter from Assistant Attorney General Jack L. Goldsmith, III to Director George Tenet, June 18, 2004 (DTS #2004-2710). As described above, the CIA's presentation to the NSC principals undercounted the frequency with which KSM and Abu Zubaydah were subjected to the waterboard.

2318. Letter from Assistant Attorney General Goldsmith to CIA General Counsel Scott Muller, May 27, 2004.

2319. CIA Office of Inspector General, Special Review - Counterterrorism Detention and Interrogation Program, (2003-7123-IG), May 2004.

2320. May 25, 2004, Talking Points for DCI Telephone Conversation with Attorney General: DOJ's Legal Opinion Re: CIA's Counterterrorist Program (CT) Interrogation. This position was confirmed in a June 10, 2004, letter

(Letter from Assistant Attorney General Jack L. Goldsmith III, to Scott Muller, General Counsel, Central Intelligence Agency, June 10, 2004).

2321. May 24, 2004, Memorandum for the Record from [REDACTED], [REDACTED] Legal Group, DCI Counterterrorism Center, Subject: Memorandum of Meeting with the DCI Regarding DOJ's Statement that DOJ has Rendered No Legal Opinion on Whether the CIA's Use of Enhanced Interrogation Techniques would meet Constitutional Standards; email from: [REDACTED], C/RDG; to: [REDACTED]; cc: Jose Rodriguez, [REDACTED], [REDACTED], [REDACTED], [REDACTED], [REDACTED]; subject: Interim Guidance for Standard and Enhanced Interrogations; date: May 25, 2004.

2322. June 4, 2004, Memorandum for Deputy Director for Operations from Director of Central Intelligence Re: Suspension of Use of Interrogation Techniques. On June 2, 2004, George Tenet informed the President that he intended to resign from his position on July 11, 2004. The White House announced the resignation on June 3, 2004

2323. Janat Gul's interrogation is detailed in Volume III and more briefly in this summary.

2324. Letter from Assistant Attorney General Ashcroft to General Counsel Muller, July 7, 2004 (DTS #2009-1810, Tab 3); July 2, 2004, CIA Memorandum re Meeting with National Security Advisor Rice in the White House Situation Room, Friday 2 July Re: Interrogations and Detainee Janat Gul; July 6, 2004, Memorandum from Condoleezza Rice, Assistant to the President for National Security Affairs, to George Tenet, Director of Central Intelligence, Re: Janat Gul.

2325. July 29, 2004, Memorandum for the Record from CIA General Counsel Scott Muller Re: Principals Meeting relating to Janat Gul on 20 July 2004.

2326. The one-paragraph letter did not provide legal analysis or substantive discussion of the interrogation techniques. (*See* letter from Attorney General John Ashcroft to Acting DCI John McLaughlin, July 22, 2004 (DTS #2009-1810, Tab 4).).

2327. Letter from [REDACTED] CTC Legal [REDACTED] Acting Assistant Attorney General Daniel Levin, July 30, 2004 (DTS #2009-1809).

2328. OMS GUIDELINES ON MEDICAL AND PSYCHOLOGICAL SUPPORT TO DETAINEE RENDITION, INTERROGATION, AND DETENTION, May 17, 2004, OMS Guidelines on Medical and Psychological Support to Detainee Interrogations, First Draft, March 7, 2003. The evolution of OMS Guidelines is described in Volume III of the Committee Study.

2329. Interview Report, 2003-7123-IG, Review of Interrogations for Counterterrorism Purposes, [REDACTED] [REDACTED], April 14, 2003.

2330. Email from: [REDACTED] ([REDACTED]); to: [REDACTED]; subject: Memo; date; March 15, 2004. *See* detainee reviews of Abu Hudhaifa and Muhammad Umar 'Abd al-Rahman aka Asadallah.

2331. OMS Guidelines on Medical and Psychological Support to Detainee Interrogations, "First Draft," March 7, 2003; [REDACTED] 28246 [REDACTED]; Interview Report, 2003-7123-IG, Review of Interrogations for Counterterrorism Purposes [REDACTED], April 5, 2003; Interview Report, 2003-7123-IG, Review of Interrogations for Counterterrorism Purposes [REDACTED], April 30, 2003; Memorandum for [REDACTED] from [REDACTED] [REDACTED], November [REDACTED], 2002, Subject: Legal Analysis of [REDACTED] Personnel Participating in Interrogation at the CIA Detention Facility in [REDACTED] "[DETENTION SITE COBALT]"). For example, Ridha al-Najjar was reported to have undergone "hanging," described as "handcuffing one or both of his wrists to an overhead horizontal bar" for 22 hours each day for two consecutive days. *See* Memorandum for [REDACTED], November [REDACTED], 2002, Subject: Legal Analysis of [REDACTED] Personnel Participating in Interrogation at the CIA Detention Facility in [REDACTED] (aka "[DETENTION SITE COBALT]". See *also* [REDACTED] 10171 (101527Z JAN 03), indicating that Abd al-Rahim al-Nashiri "remained in the standing position, with hands tied overhead, overnight."

2332. [REDACTED] interview of [REDACTED] [CIA OFFICER 1], December 19, 2002; CIA Interrogation Program Draft Course Materials, March 11, 2003, pg. 28; CTC/RDG Interrogation Program, December 15, 2003, pg. 10. DIRECTOR [REDACTED] (251609Z JUL 02). See *also* "Standard Interrogation Techniques," attachment to email from: [REDACTED]; to: Scott W. Muller, John Rizzo, [REDACTED], [REDACTED] [REDACTED]; subject: revised interrogation discussion; date: July 19, 2004.

2333. August 11, 2004, Letter from [REDACTED], Assistant General Counsel, to Dan Levin, Acting Assistant Attorney General, Office of Legal Counsel; August 27, 2004, Memorandum for the Record from [REDACTED] Re: Meeting with Department of Justice Attorneys on 13 August, 2004, Regarding Specific Interrogation Techniques, Including the Waterboard.

2334. As described in this summary, and in more detail in the Committee Study, the source later admitted to fabricating information related to the "pre-election" threat.

2335. Letter from [REDACTED], Associate General Counsel, CIA, to Dan Levin, Acting Assistant Attorney General, August 25, 2004 (DTS #2009-1809). For Gul's rendition, *See* [REDACTED] 1512 ([REDACTED] 04). According to an August 16, 2004, cable, a CIA interrogator did "not believe that escalation to enhanced measures will increase [Gul's] ability to produce timely accurate locational and threat information." (*See* [REDACTED] [REDACTED] 1567 [REDACTED] 04).) On August 19, 2004, a cable from DETENTION SITE BLACK noted that the interrogation team "does not believe [Gul] is withholding imminent threat information." *See* 1574 (04).

2336. Letter to John Rizzo, Acting General Counsel, CIA; from Daniel Levin, Acting Assistant Attorney General, August 26, 2004 (DTS #2009-1810, Tab 6). In May 2005, the OLC again accepted the CIA's representations that a psychological assessment found that Gul was "alert and oriented and his concentration and attention were appropriate," that Gul's "thought processes were clear and logical; there was no evidence of a thought disorder, delusions, or hallucinations," and that there "were not significant signs of depression anxiety or other mental disturbance." *See* memorandum for John A. Rizzo, Senior Deputy General Counsel, Central Intelligence Agency, from Steven G. Bradbury, Principal Deputy Assistant Attorney General, Office of Legal Counsel, May 10, 2005, Re: Application of 18 U.S.C. Sections 2340-2340A to Certain Techniques That May be Used in the Interrogation of a High Value al Qaeda Detainee (DTS #2009-1810, Tab 9).

2337. 1530 (081633Z AUG 04); 1541 (101228Z AUG 04).

2338. 1567 (161730Z AUG 04).

2339. 1574 (191346Z AUG 04).

2340. Letter to John Rizzo, Acting General Counsel, CIA; from Daniel Levin, Acting Assistant Attorney General, August 26, 2004 (DTS #2009-1810, Tab 6).

2341. Letter from , Associate General Counsel, CIA, to Dan Levin, Acting Assistant Attorney General, August 25, 2004 (DTS #2009-1809).

2342. Email from: ; to: , , [REDACTED], , ; subject: could AQ be testing [ASSET Y] and [Source Name REDACTED]?; date: March , 2004, at 6:55 AM; email from: ; to ; cc: , , [REDACTED], ; subject: Re: could AQ be testing [ASSET Y] and [Source Name REDACTED]?; date: March , 2004, at 7:52:32 AM. The fabricated source reporting is described elsewhere in this summary.

2343. 1411 (04).

2344. Email from [REDACTED]; to: , , , ; subject: re ALEC ; November 10, 2004.

2345. CIA "Comments on Detainees," December 19, 2004, Notes from a CD from [DETENTION SITE BLACK].

2346. Email from: [REDACTED] (COB DETENTION SITE BLACK); to: ; cc: , , ; subject: re ; date: April 30, 2005.

2347. Email from: ; to: , , , , and [REDACTED]; subject: questions from OLC for Art 16 opinion; date: April 12, 2005; email from: ; to: , , , , and [REDACTED]; subject: Re: questions from OLC for Art 16 opinion; date: April 14, 2005.

2348. April 15, 2005, fax to DOJ Command Center, for , Office of Legal Counsel, U.S. Department of Justice, from . Legal Group, DCI Counterterrorist Center, re: Janat Gul.

2349. Memorandum for John A. Rizzo, Senior Deputy General Counsel, Central Intelligence Agency, from Steven G. Bradbury, Principal Deputy Assistant Attorney General, Office of Legal Counsel, May 10, 2005, Re: Application of 18 U.S.C. Sections 2340-2340A to Certain Techniques That May Be Used in the Interrogation of a High Value al Qaeda Detainee.

2350. Memorandum for John A. Rizzo, Senior Deputy General Counsel, Central Intelligence Agency, from Steven G. Bradbury, Principal Deputy Assistant Attorney General, Office of Legal Counsel, May 30, 2005, Re: Application of United States Obligations Under Article 16 of the Convention Against Torture to Certain Techniques that May be Used in the Interrogation of High Value Al Qaeda Detainees (DTS #2009-1810, Tab 11).

2351. Memorandum for John A. Rizzo, Senior Deputy General Counsel, Central Intelligence Agency, from Steven G. Bradbury, Principal Deputy Assistant Attorney General, Office of Legal Counsel, May 30, 2005, Re: Application of United States Obligations Under Article 16 of the Convention Against Torture to Certain Techniques that May be Used in the Interrogation of High Value Al Qaeda Detainees (DTS #2009-1810, Tab 11), citing *Janat Gul Memo* pp. 1–2. *See* April 15, 2005, fax to DOJ Command Center, for , Office of Legal Counsel, U.S. Department of Justice, from , Legal Group, DCI Counterterrorist Center, re: Janat Gul.

2352. Letter to John A. Rizzo, Acting General Counsel, CIA; from Daniel Levin, September 6, 2004 (DTS #2009-1810, Tab 7); Letter to John A. Rizzo, Acting General Counsel, CIA; from Daniel Levin, September 20, 2004 (DTS #2009-1810, Tab 8).

2353. 1411 (04).

2354. [REDACTED] 3221 ; [REDACTED] 3242 (04).

2355. Letter from , Associate General Counsel, CIA, to Steve Bradbury, Acting Assistant Attorney General, Office of Legal Counsel, May 4, 2005. Multiple interrogation plans for CIA detainees called for "uncomfortably" cool temperatures along with sleep deprivation. *See* 10361 ; 1758 ; 10654 (030904Z MAR 03).

2356. Letter from , Associate General Counsel, CIA, to Steve Bradbury, Acting Assistant Attorney General, Office of Legal Counsel, May 4, 2005. The CIA had subjected detainees to cold water baths during

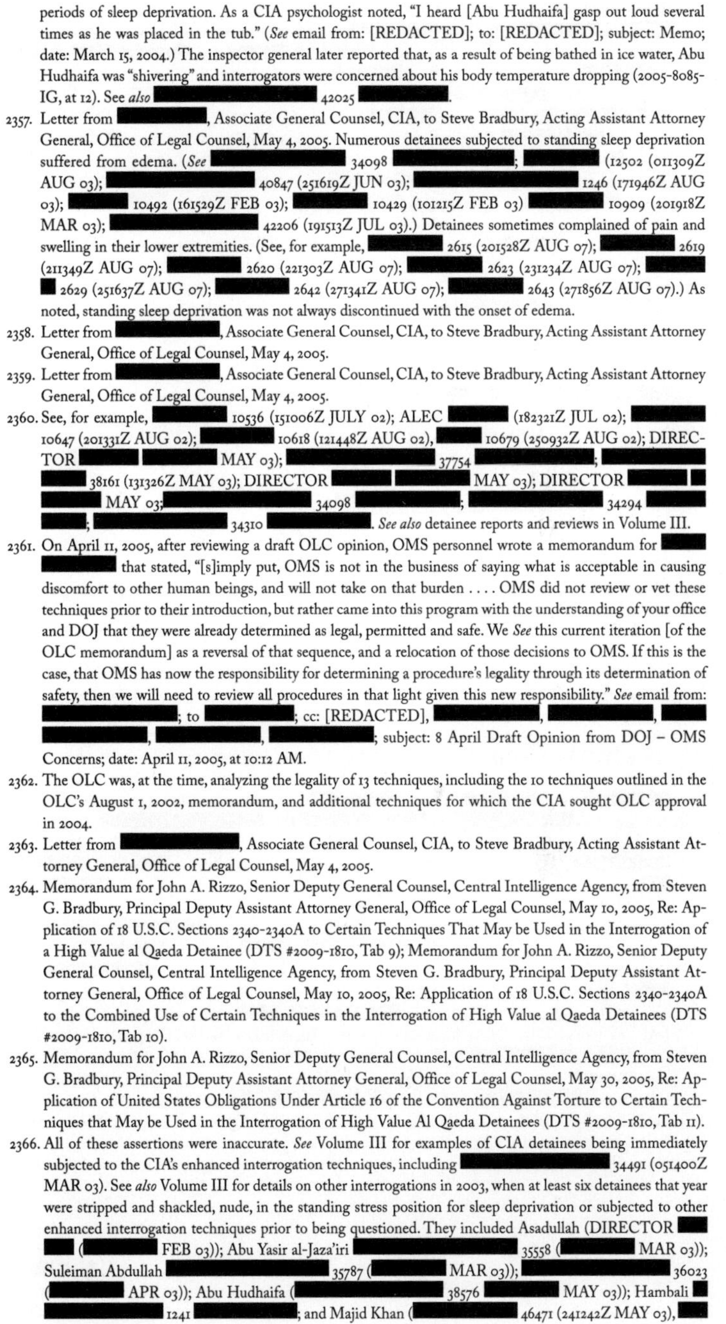

periods of sleep deprivation. As a CIA psychologist noted, "I heard [Abu Hudhaifa] gasp out loud several times as he was placed in the tub." (*See* email from: [REDACTED]; to: [REDACTED]; subject: Memo; date: March 15, 2004.) The inspector general later reported that, as a result of being bathed in ice water, Abu Hudhaifa was "shivering" and interrogators were concerned about his body temperature dropping (2005-8085-IG, at 12). See *also* ▇▇▇ 42025 ▇▇▇.

2357. Letter from ▇▇▇, Associate General Counsel, CIA, to Steve Bradbury, Acting Assistant Attorney General, Office of Legal Counsel, May 4, 2005. Numerous detainees subjected to standing sleep deprivation suffered from edema. (*See* ▇▇▇ 34098 ▇▇▇; ▇▇▇ (12502 (011309Z AUG 03); ▇▇▇ 40847 (251619Z JUN 03); ▇▇▇ 1246 (171946Z AUG 03); ▇▇▇ 10492 (161529Z FEB 03); ▇▇▇ 10429 (101215Z FEB 03) ▇▇▇ 10909 (201918Z MAR 03); ▇▇▇ 42206 (191513Z JUL 03).) Detainees sometimes complained of pain and swelling in their lower extremities. (See, for example, ▇▇▇ 2615 (201528Z AUG 07); ▇▇▇ 2619 (211349Z AUG 07); ▇▇▇ 2620 (221303Z AUG 07); ▇▇▇ 2623 (231234Z AUG 07); ▇▇▇ 2629 (251637Z AUG 07); ▇▇▇ 2642 (271341Z AUG 07); ▇▇▇ 2643 (271856Z AUG 07).) As noted, standing sleep deprivation was not always discontinued with the onset of edema.

2358. Letter from ▇▇▇, Associate General Counsel, CIA, to Steve Bradbury, Acting Assistant Attorney General, Office of Legal Counsel, May 4, 2005.

2359. Letter from ▇▇▇, Associate General Counsel, CIA, to Steve Bradbury, Acting Assistant Attorney General, Office of Legal Counsel, May 4, 2005.

2360. See, for example, ▇▇▇ 10536 (151006Z JULY 02); ALEC ▇▇▇ (182321Z JUL 02); ▇▇▇ 10647 (201331Z AUG 02); ▇▇▇ 10618 (121448Z AUG 02), ▇▇▇ 10679 (250932Z AUG 02); DIRECTOR ▇▇▇ ▇▇▇ MAY 03); ▇▇▇ 37754 ▇▇▇; ▇▇▇ 38161 (131326Z MAY 03); DIRECTOR ▇▇▇ ▇▇▇ MAY 03); DIRECTOR ▇▇▇ ▇▇▇ MAY 03; ▇▇▇ 34098 ▇▇▇; ▇▇▇ 34294 ▇▇▇; ▇▇▇ 34310 ▇▇▇. *See also* detainee reports and reviews in Volume III.

2361. On April 11, 2005, after reviewing a draft OLC opinion, OMS personnel wrote a memorandum for ▇▇▇ that stated, "[s]imply put, OMS is not in the business of saying what is acceptable in causing discomfort to other human beings, and will not take on that burden . . . . OMS did not review or vet these techniques prior to their introduction, but rather came into this program with the understanding of your office and DOJ that they were already determined as legal, permitted and safe. We *See* this current iteration [of the OLC memorandum] as a reversal of that sequence, and a relocation of those decisions to OMS. If this is the case, that OMS has now the responsibility for determining a procedure's legality through its determination of safety, then we will need to review all procedures in that light given this new responsibility." *See* email from: ▇▇▇; to ▇▇▇; cc: [REDACTED], ▇▇▇, ▇▇▇, ▇▇▇, ▇▇▇, ▇▇▇; subject: 8 April Draft Opinion from DOJ – OMS Concerns; date: April 11, 2005, at 10:12 AM.

2362. The OLC was, at the time, analyzing the legality of 13 techniques, including the 10 techniques outlined in the OLC's August 1, 2002, memorandum, and additional techniques for which the CIA sought OLC approval in 2004.

2363. Letter from ▇▇▇, Associate General Counsel, CIA, to Steve Bradbury, Acting Assistant Attorney General, Office of Legal Counsel, May 4, 2005.

2364. Memorandum for John A. Rizzo, Senior Deputy General Counsel, Central Intelligence Agency, from Steven G. Bradbury, Principal Deputy Assistant Attorney General, Office of Legal Counsel, May 10, 2005, Re: Application of 18 U.S.C. Sections 2340-2340A to Certain Techniques That May be Used in the Interrogation of a High Value al Qaeda Detainee (DTS #2009-1810, Tab 9); Memorandum for John A. Rizzo, Senior Deputy General Counsel, Central Intelligence Agency, from Steven G. Bradbury, Principal Deputy Assistant Attorney General, Office of Legal Counsel, May 10, 2005, Re: Application of 18 U.S.C. Sections 2340-2340A to the Combined Use of Certain Techniques in the Interrogation of High Value al Qaeda Detainees (DTS #2009-1810, Tab 10).

2365. Memorandum for John A. Rizzo, Senior Deputy General Counsel, Central Intelligence Agency, from Steven G. Bradbury, Principal Deputy Assistant Attorney General, Office of Legal Counsel, May 30, 2005, Re: Application of United States Obligations Under Article 16 of the Convention Against Torture to Certain Techniques that May be Used in the Interrogation of High Value Al Qaeda Detainees (DTS #2009-1810, Tab 11).

2366. All of these assertions were inaccurate. *See* Volume III for examples of CIA detainees being immediately subjected to the CIA's enhanced interrogation techniques, including ▇▇▇ 34491 (051400Z MAR 03). See *also* Volume III for details on other interrogations in 2003, when at least six detainees that year were stripped and shackled, nude, in the standing stress position for sleep deprivation or subjected to other enhanced interrogation techniques prior to being questioned. They included Asadullah (DIRECTOR ▇▇▇ (▇▇▇ FEB 03)); Abu Yasir al-Jaza'iri ▇▇▇ 35558 (▇▇▇ MAR 03)); Suleiman Abdullah ▇▇▇ 35787 (▇▇▇ MAR 03)); ▇▇▇ 36023 (▇▇▇ APR 03)); Abu Hudhaifa (▇▇▇ 38576 ▇▇▇ MAY 03)); Hambali ▇▇▇ 1241 ▇▇▇; and Majid Khan (▇▇▇ 46471 (241242Z MAY 03), ▇▇▇

39077 (271719Z MAY 03)).

2367. Letter from CTC Legal to Acting Assistant Attorney General Levin, December 30, 2004 (DTS #2009-1809). See, for example, 31118 ; , 31429 (161303Z DEC 02); 10006 (070902Z DEC 02); [REDACTED] 33962 (211724Z FEB 03); 34031 (231242Z FEB 03); 34575 ; 34354 MAR 03); DIRECTOR MAR 03). Email to: ; from: [REDACTED]; subject: Medical Evaluation/Update (047); date: March , 2004. Email to ; from: [REDACTED]; subject: Medical Evaluation/Update (047); date: March 8, 2004. Email to: ; from: [REDACTED]; subject: Medical Evaluation/ Update (047); date: March 9, 2004. 2347 (300624Z MAY 05); 1797 (021612Z DEC 05).

2368. See, for example, 10909 (201918Z MAR 03); 2622 (230851Z AUG 07).

2369. According to a CIA cable, cells at DETENTION SITE COBALT were "blacked out at all times using curtains plus painted exterior windows. And double doors. The lights are never turned on." (*See* 28246 .) Upon finding Ramzi bin al-Shibh "cowering in the corner, shivering" when the light in his cell burned out, interrogators decided to use darkness as an interrogation technique. He was then placed in sleep deprivation "standing, shackled feet and hands, with hands over his head, naked, in total darkness." *See* 10521 (191750Z FEB 03); 10525 (200840Z FEB 03).

2370. interview of [CIA OFFICER 1], December 19, 2002. CIA Interrogation Program Draft Course Materials, March 11, 2003, p. 28. CTC/RDG Interrogation Program, December 15, 2003. DIRECTOR (251609Z JUL 02). See *also* "Standard Interrogation Techniques," attachment to email from: ; to: Scott W. Muller, John Rizzo, [REDACTED], ; subject: revised interrogation discussion; date: July 19, 2004.

2371. Letter from CTC Legal to Acting Assistant Attorney General Levin, December 30, 2004 (DTS #2009-1809).

2372. Memorandum for John A. Rizzo, Senior Deputy General Counsel, Central Intelligence Agency, from Steven G. Bradbury, Principal Deputy Assistant Attorney General, Office of Legal Counsel, May 10, 2005, Re: Application of 18 U.S.C. Sections 2340-2340A to Certain Techniques That May be Used in the Interrogation of a High Value al Qaeda Detainee (DTS #2009-1810, Tab 9); Memorandum for John A. Rizzo, Senior Deputy General Counsel, Central Intelligence Agency, from Steven G. Bradbury, Principal Deputy Assistant Attorney General, Office of Legal Counsel, May 10, 2005, Re: Application of 18 U.S.C. Sections 2340-2340A to the Combined Use of Certain Techniques in the Interrogation of High Value al Qaeda Detainees (DTS #2009-1810, Tab 10); Memorandum for John A. Rizzo, Senior Deputy General Counsel, Central Intelligence Agency, from Steven G. Bradbury, Principal Deputy Assistant Attorney General, Office of Legal Counsel, May 30, 2005, Re: Application of United States Obligations Under Article 16 of the Convention Against Torture to Certain Techniques that May be Used in the Interrogation of High Value Al Qaeda Detainees (DTS #2009-1810, Tab 11).

2373. 10643 AUG 02); 10644 (201235Z AUG 02).

2374. *See* email from: ; to: ; cc: ; subject: More; date: April 10, 2003, at 5:59: 27 PM.

2375. 10644 (201235Z AUG 02); email from: [REDACTED]; to: and [REDACTED]; subject: Re: So it begins; date: August 4, 2002, at 09:45:09 AM; 10803 (131929Z MAR 03).

2376. *See* Abu Zubaydah and KSM detainee reviews in Volume III, including 10803 (131929Z MAR 03). *See* email from: , OMS; to: and [REDACTED]; subject: Re: Departure; date: March 6, 2003, at 7:11:59 PM; email from: , OMS; to [REDACTED] and [REDACTED]; subject: Re: Acceptable lower ambient temperatures; date: March 7, 2003, at 8:22 PM; email from , OMS: to: [REDACTED] and [REDACTED]; subject: Re: Talking Points for review and comment; date: August 13, 2004, at 10:22 AM; email from: to: [REDACTED], [REDACTED], [REDACTED], [REDACTED], and [REDACTED]; subject: Re: Discussion with Dan Levin- AZ; date: October 26, 2004, at 6:09 PM.

2377. Letter from CTC Legal to Acting Assistant Attorney General Dan Levin, August 19, 2004 (DTS# 2009-1809). The OLC, having been informed by the CIA that 40 seconds was the maximum length of a single waterboard application, noted that "you have informed us that this maximum has rarely been reached." This is inaccurate. KSM was subjected to 40-second exposure at least 19 times.

2378. Memorandum for John A. Rizzo, Senior Deputy General Counsel, Central Intelligence Agency, from Steven G. Bradbury, Principal Deputy Assistant Attorney General, Office of Legal Counsel, May 10, 2005, Re: Application of 18 U.S.C. Sections 2340-2340A to Certain Techniques That May be Used in the Integration of a High Value al Qaeda Detainee (DTS #2009-1810, Tab 9). As described in this summary, when CTC Legal, insisted that CTC Legal vet and review the background of CIA personnel involved in the CIA's interrogations, he directly linked this review to the legality of the CIA's enhanced interrogation techniques. ███ wrote: "we will be forced to DISapprove [sic] the participation of specific personnel in the use of enhanced techniques unless we have ourselves vetted them and are satisfied with their qualifications and suitability for what are clearly unusual measures that are lawful only when practiced correctly by personnel whose records clearly demonstrate their suitability for that role." The chief of CTC, Jose Rodriguez, objected to this proposal. *See* email from: ███, ███CTC/LGL; to: [REDACTED]; cc: Jose Rodriguez, [REDACTED], [REDACTED], ███; subject: EYES ONLY; date: November ███, 2002, at 03:13:01 PM; email from: Jose Rodriguez, to ███ ███, ███CTC/LGL; cc: [REDACTED],[REDACTED], [REDACTED], [REDACTED], ███ ███; subject: EYES ONLY; date: November ███, 2002, at 04:27 PM.

2379. The training to conduct the CIA's enhanced interrogation techniques required only approximately 65 hours of classroom and operational instruction. December 4, 2002, Training Report, High Value Target Interrogation and Exploitation (HVTIE) Training Seminar 12-18 Nov 02 (pilot running).

2380. Among other abuses. ███ "Russian Roulette" with a detainee. (*See* Memorandum for Chief, Staff and Operations Branch from [REDACTED], ███ April 3, 1980, subject: ███ ███; ███ 1984, Memorandum for Inspector General from [REDACTED], Inspector, via Deputy Inspector General, re ███, IG-███84.) [CIA OFFICER 2], who threatened 'Abd al-Rahim al-Nashiri with a gun and power drill, ███ ███. He was sent home short of tour twice—once for ███ and again, a few months before interrogating al-Nashiri, for engaging in ███ ███ [REDACTED] ███ 91638 ███ ███, from [REDACTED], ███ ███60500███; DIRECTOR ███ ███; ███ 59478 ███: ███ 59479 ███ [REDACTED] ███ [REDACTED] ███.) *See also* Report to CIA Headquarters, ███ ███ [REDACTED] ███ ███[REDACTED], ███, by [REDACTED] ███ ███[REDACTED], ███ ███ *See* email from: [REDACTED]; to [REDACTED], [REDACTED], [REDACTED], and [REDACTED]; subject: ███ ███[REDACTED] ███ ███[REDACTED] ███ ███. For more information, *See* Volume III.

2381. Fax to Acting Assistant Attorney General Levin from ███ January 4, 2005 (DTS #2009-1809).

2382. *See* detainee reviews for Suleiman Abdullah and Janat Gul in Volume III for additional information.

2383. *See* detainee review for Rafiq bin Bashir bin Halul Al-Hami in Volume III for additional information.

2384. *See* detainee review for Ridha Ahmad al-Najjar in Volume III for additional information.

2385. *See* detainee reviews for Tawfiq Nasir Awad al-Bihani and Arsala KJian in Volume III for additional information.

2386. Letter from ███CTC Legal ███ to Acting Assistant Attorney General Bradbury, May 23, 2006 (DTS #2009-1809).

2387. Memorandum for John A. Rizzo, Acting General Counsel, Central Intelligence Agency, from Steven G. Bradbury, Principal Deputy Assistant Attorney General, Office of Legal Counsel, July 20, 2007, Re: Application of the War Crimes Act, the Detainee Treatment Act, and Common Article 3 of the Geneva Conventions to Certain Techniques that May Be Used by the CIA in the Interrogation of High Value al Qaeda Detainees (DTS #2009-1810, Tab 14).

2388. ███ 6439 (███); ███ 7516 (███ ███). Muhammad Rahim entered CIA custody on July ███, 2007.

2389. CIA Memorandum for Steve Bradbury at the Department of Justice, dated March 2, 2005, from ███ ███ ███, ███ Legal Group, DCI Counterterrorist Center, subject "Effectiveness of the CIA

Counterterrorist Interrogation Techniques."

2390. Interview of [REDACTED], by [REDACTED] and [REDACTED], Office of the Inspector General, May 15, 2003; Interview of [REDACTED], by [REDACTED] and [REDACTED], Office of the Inspector General, October 22, 2003; [REDACTED] 11715 (201047Z MAY 03); Sametime Communication, [REDACTED] and [REDACTED] 15/Aug/06, 10:28:38 to 10:58:00; Interview of [REDACTED] by [REDACTED] and [REDACTED], Office of the Inspector General, April 3, 2003; Sametime Communication [REDACTED] and [REDACTED], 02/May/05, 14:51:48 to 15:17:39; Interview of by [REDACTED], [REDACTED], and [REDACTED], Office of the Inspector General, August 20, 2003.

2391. Emphasis in the original.

2392. *See* list of 20 CIA representations included in this summary and additional details in Volume II. Representations regarding Abu Talha al-Pakistani, which were less frequent, are also described this summary and in greater detail in Volumes II and III.

2393. April 15, 2005,10:47AM, fax to DOJ Command Center for [REDACTED] Office of Legal Counsel, U.S. Department of Justice, from [REDACTED], [REDACTED] Legal Group, DCI Counterterrorist Center. Cover note: "[REDACTED], Answers to some of your questions," with attachment titled "Briefing Notes on the Value of Detainee Reporting."

2394. Memorandum for John A. Rizzo, Senior Deputy General Counsel, Central Intelligence Agency, from Steven G. Bradbury, Principal Deputy Assistant Attorney General, Office of Legal Counsel, May 30, 2005, Re: Application of United States Obligations Under Article 16 of the Convention Against Torture to Certain Techniques that May be Used in the Interrogation of High Value Al Qaeda Detainees.

2395. *See* specific CIA examples of the "Results" of using the "CIA's use of DOJ-approved enhanced interrogation techniques" in March 2, 2005, Memorandum for Steve Bradbury from [REDACTED], [REDACTED] Legal Group, DCI Counterterrorist Center, "Effectiveness of the CIA Counterterrorist Interrogation Techniques." The specific representations in the "Briefing Notes" document were similar to those in the CIA's "Effectiveness Memo" and included references to detainee reporting on Jose Padilla, Hambali, Dhiren Barot, Sajid Badat, Iyman Faris, Jaffar al-Tayyar, the Heathrow Airport plotting, and the Karachi plotting.

2396. For example, as detailed elsewhere in this review, Hassan Gul provided detailed information on al-Qa'ida's presence in Shkai, Pakistan, prior to the use of the CIA's enhanced interrogation techniques.

2397. Memorandum for John A. Rizzo, Senior Deputy General Counsel, Central Intelligence Agency, from Steven G. Bradbury, Principal Deputy Assistant Attorney General, Office of Legal Counsel, May 30, 2005, Re: Application of United States Obligations Under Article 16 of the Convention Against Torture to Certain Techniques that May be Used in the Interrogation of High Value Al Qaeda Detainees.

2398. The OLC memorandum stated that "[b]oth KSM and Zubaydah had 'expressed their belief that the general US population was 'weak,' lacked resilience, and would be unable to 'do what was necessary' to prevent the terrorists from succeeding in their goals.'" As described elsewhere in this summary, and in more detail in the full Committee Study, CIA records indicate that KSM and Abu Zubaydah did not make these statements. The memorandum also repeated CIA representations about KSM's comment, "Soon, you will know," and Abu Zubaydah's reported statements about being "permitted by Allah" to provide information. As described in this summary, these representations are not supported by CIA records.

2399. Memorandum for John A. Rizzo, Senior Deputy General Counsel, Central Intelligence Agency, from Steven G. Bradbury, Principal Deputy Assistant Attorney General, Office of Legal Counsel, May 30, 2005, Re: Application of United States Obligations Under Article 16 of the Convention Against Torture to Certain Techniques that May be Used in the Interrogation of High Value Al Qaeda Detainees.

2400. Memorandum for John A. Rizzo, Senior Deputy General Counsel, Central Intelligence Agency, from Steven G. Bradbury. Principal Deputy Assistant Attorney General, Office of Legal Counsel, May 30, 2005, Re: Application of United States Obligations Under Article 16 of the Convention Against Torture to Certain Techniques that May be Used in the Interrogation of High Value Al Qaeda Detainees, pp. 10–11, citing IG Special Review, pp. 85–91.

2401. The Detainee Treatment Act passed on December 30, 2005. Letter from Senior Deputy General Counsel John Rizzo to Acting Assistant Attorney General Bradbury, December 19, 2005 (DTS #2009-1809).

2402. April 19, 2006, Fax from [REDACTED], [REDACTED] Legal Group, CIA Counterterrorism Center to DOJ Command Center for Steve Bradbury (DTS #2009-1809).

2403. Email from: [REDACTED] to: [REDACTED]; cc: [REDACTED], John Rizzo; subject: FW: Summary of *Hamdan* Decision; date; June 30, 2006, at 4:44 PM.

2404. Department of Justice Office of Professional Responsibility; Report, Investigation into the Office of Legal Counsel's Memoranda Concerning Issues Relating to the Central Intelligence Agency's Use of 'Enhanced Interrogation Techniques' on Suspected Terrorists, July 29, 2009. (DTS #2010-1058).

2405. Letter from Senior Deputy General Counsel John Rizzo to Acting Assistant Attorney General Bradbury, December 19, 2005 (DTS #2009-1809). January 25, 2006, Letter to Steve Bradbury Acting Assistant Attorney General, Office of Legal Counsel, Department of Justice, from [REDACTED] CTC Legal, CIA (DTS #1809-2009).

2406. See, for example, [REDACTED] 31369 (151028Z DEC 02); [REDACTED] 10361 [REDACTED] HEADQUARTERS [REDACTED] (151955Z SEP 05); HEADQUARTERS [REDACTED] (212005Z JUN 05); HEADQUARTERS (202036Z JUN 05).

2407. As one example, CIA records indicate that in the CIA interrogation of Ramzi bin al-Shibh, the "the Blues Brothers rendition of 'Rawhide' [was] played." CIA records state that bin al-Shibh's reaction to hearing the song was evidence of his conditioning, as bin al-Shibh "knows when he hears the music where he is going and what is going to happen." (*See* [REDACTED] 10602 (262020Z FEB 03); [REDACTED] 10591 (252002Z FEB 03); [REDACTED] 1889 (091823Z MAR 03); [REDACTED] 1924 (151729Z MAR 04) [REDACTED] 10361 [REDACTED].) "Loud noise" was also used to "prevent concentrating, planning, and derailing of the exploitation/interrogation process with interrogation countermeasures (resistance)." See, for example, detainee reviews detailing the detention and interrogations of Lillie and Hambali in Volume III.

2408. See, for example, [REDACTED] 2505 (272059Z JUN 05). The amenities described by the CIA to the OLC were not available to detainees during earlier iterations of the program.

2409. April 23, 2006, Fax from [REDACTED], [REDACTED] Legal Group, CIA Counterterrorism Center to DOJ Command Center for Steve Bradbury (DTS #2009-1809).

2410. May 2006, Letter to Steven G. Bradbury, Acting Assistant Attorney General, Office of Legal Counsel, from [REDACTED], [REDACTED] CTC Legal, CIA, re: Request for Information on Security Measures (DTS #2009-1809).

2411. Memorandum for John Rizzo, Acting General Counsel, Central Intelligence Agency, from Steven G. Bradbury, Acting Assistant Attorney General, Office of Legal Counsel, August 31, 2006, Re: Application of the Detainee Treatment Act to Conditions of Confinement at Central Intelligence Agency Detention Facilities (DTS #2009-1810, Tab 13).

2412. Letter for John Rizzo, Acting General Counsel, Central Intelligence Agency, from Steven G. Bradbury, Acting Assistant Attorney General, Office of Legal Counsel, August 31, 2006 (DTS #2009-1810, Tab 12).

2413. The OLC did not apply the Detainee Treatment Act or Common Article 3 to the use of shaving or other conditions of confinement in terms of their use as an interrogation technique. The OLC stated that while "the primary purpose of the conditions of confinement we consider here is to maintain the security of the CIA's detention facilities . . . [m]any of these conditions may also ease the obtaining of crucial intelligence information from the detainees." Nonetheless, the OLC concluded that "the security rationale alone is sufficient to justify each of the conditions of confinement in question." *See* memorandum for John Rizzo, Acting General Counsel, Central Intelligence Agency, from Steven G. Bradbury, Acting Assistant Attorney General, Office of Legal Counsel, August 31, 2006, Re: Application of the detainee Treatment Act to Conditions of Confinement at Central Intelligence Agency Detention Facilities (DTS #2009-1810, Tab 13).

2414. Memorandum for John Rizzo, Acting General Counsel, Central Intelligence Agency, from Steven G. Bradbury, Acting Assistant Attorney General, Office of Legal Counsel, August 31, 2006, Re: Application of the Detainee Treatment Act to Conditions of Confinement at Central Intelligence Agency Detention Facilities (DTS #2009-1810 Tab 13).

2415. For additional detailed information, *See* Volume I and Volume III.

2416. April 23, 2006, Fax to DOJ Command Center for Steve Bradbury, Office of Legal Counsel, from [REDACTED], [REDACTED] Legal Group, CIA Counterterrorism Center.

2417. CIA Intelligence Assessment, August 16, 2006, "Countering Misconceptions About Training Camps in Afghanistan, 1990-2001." For additional details, *See* the Abu Zubaydah detainee review in Volume III.

2418. Memorandum for John A. Rizzo, Acting General Counsel, Central Intelligence Agency, from Steven G. Bradbury, Principal Deputy Assistant Attorney General, Office of Legal Counsel, July 20, 2007, Re: Application of the War Crimes Act, the Detainee Treatment Act, and Common Article 3 of the Geneva Conventions to Certain Techniques that May Be Used by the CIA in the Interrogation of High Value al Qaeda Detainees (DTS #2009-1810, Tab 14).

2419. Memorandum for John A. Rizzo, Acting General Counsel, Central Intelligence Agency, from Steven G. Bradbury, Principal Deputy Assistant Attorney General, Office of Legal Counsel, July 20, 2007, Re: Application of the War Crimes Act, the Detainee Treatment Act, and Common Article 3 of the Geneva Conventions to Certain Techniques that May be Used by the CIA in the Interrogation of High Value Al Qaeda Detainees (DTS #2009-1810, Tab 14).

2420. Although all 119 known CIA detainees had entered CIA custody by July 20, 2007, Muhammad Rahim, the last detainee, had not yet been subjected to the CIA's enhanced interrogation techniques by the time of the OLC memorandum. Muhammad Rahim was rendered to CIA custody on July [REDACTED], 2007. (*See* [REDACTED] 6439 ([REDACTED]); [REDACTED] 7516 ([REDACTED]).) Interrogators began using the CIA's enhanced interrogation techniques on Rahim on July 21, 2007; the day after the OLC Memorandum was issued. *See* [REDACTED] 2467 (211341Z JUL 07).

2421. Memorandum for John A. Rizzo, Acting General Counsel, Central Intelligence Agency, from Steven G. Bradbury, Principal Deputy Assistant Attorney General, Office of Legal Counsel, July 20, 2007, Re: Application of the War Crimes Act, the Detainee Treatment Act, and Common Article 3 of the Geneva Conventions to Certain Techniques that May be Used by the CIA in the Interrogation of High Value Al Qaeda Detainees

(DTS #2009-1810, Tab 14).

2422. Integrators had asked CIA Headquarters for the assessments supporting the decision to subject Asadullah to the CIA's enhanced interrogation techniques, noting that "it would be of enormous help to the interrogator to know what is concrete fact and what is good analysis." (See 33963 ; see *also* 34098 ; 34812 .) In response, ALEC Station acknowledged that "[t]o be sure our case that Asadullah should have a good sense of bin Ladin's location is circumstantial." (*See* ALEC .) The following day, interrogators commented that "it may be that he simply does not know the [locational information on AQ leaders]." *See* 34310 .

2423. Following al-Hawsawi's first interrogation session, Chief of Interrogations asked CIA Headquarters for information on what al-Hawsawi actually "knows," saying: "he does not appear to the [sic] be a person that is a financial mastermind. However, we lack facts with which to confront [al-Hawsawi]. What we need at this point is substantive information vice supposition." *See* 34757 (101742Z MAR 03).

2424. Although CIA records include no requests or approval cables, Abu Hudhaifa was subjected to ice water baths and 66 hours of standing sleep deprivation. He was released because the CIA discovered he was likely not the person he was believed to be. *See* WASHINGTON DC T; 51303 .

2425. CIA Headquarters initially resisted approving Arsala Khan's capture because of a lack of information confirming that he was a "continuing threat." (*See* 169986 ; email from: ; to: , and [REDACTED]; subject: Denial of Approval to Capture Arsala Khan; date:). Despite doubts that Arsala Khan was the individual sought by the CIA, interrogators subjected him to the CIA's enhanced interrogation techniques "to make a better assessment regarding [his] willingness to start talking, or assess if our subject is, in fact the man we are looking for." *See* 1373 .

2426. The true names of these detainees have been replaced with the capitalized pseudonyms AL-MAGREBI and AL-TURKI. At the time the two detainees were rendered to CIA custody, the CIA was aware that they were then working for a foreign partner government. (*See* ALEC [REDACTED]; [REDACTED] 43773 [REDACTED].) They were subjected to sleep deprivation and dietary manipulation until the CIA confirmed that the detainees had been trying to contact the CIA for weeks to inform the CIA of what they believed were pending al-Qa'ida terrorist attacks. (*See* 22227 [REDACTED]; T 2233 [REDACTED] 2185[REDACTED]; HEADQUARTERS [REDACTED] 2232 [REDACTED].) After the CIA had determined that AL-MAGREBI and AL-TURKI should not be in CIA custody, the two detainees were held for additional months before they were released. *See* [REDACTED] 2025 [REDACTED].

2427. The case of Janat Gul is described above in the context of OLC advice in 2004 and afterwards. As Gul's interrogators noted, "Team does not believe [Gul] is withholding imminent threat information, however team will continue to press [Gul] for that during each session." *See* 1574 (04).

2428. The CIA's assessment of Ghailani's knowledge of terrorist threats was speculative. As one official noted, "[al]though Ghailani's role in operational planning is unclear, his respected role in al-Qa'ida and presence in Shkai as recently as October 2003 may have provided him some knowledge about ongoing attack planning against the United States homeland, and the operatives involved." *See* email from: , CTC/UBLD (formerly ALEC); to: [REDACTED], [REDACTED], [REDACTED], [REDACTED]; subject: derog information for ODDO on Talha, Ghailani, Hamza Rabi'a and Abu Faraj; date: August 10, 2004.

2429. As noted above, the credibility of the source implicating Sharif al-Masri, Janat Gul, and Ghailani's connections to a pre-election plot was questioned by CIA officials prior to the application of the CIA's enhanced interrogation techniques against them. The source was later determined to have fabricated the information.

2430. Five days after interrogators began using enhanced interrogation techniques against Sayyid Ibrahim, interrogators cabled CIA Headquarters requesting information that would "definitely link [Ibrahim] to nefarious activity or knowledge by [Ibrahim] of known nefarious activities of al-Qa'ida members, if this is possible." (*See* 1324 FEB 04). Without receiving a response, they continued to subject Ibrahim to the CIA's enhanced interrogation techniques. CIA Headquarters, which rejected an assessment from two debriefers that Ibrahim was, "at best . . . a low-level facilitator," would later indicate that it was "uncertain" he would meet the requirements for U.S. military or detention. *See* HEADQUARTERS ; HEADQUARTERS .

2431. The OLC further stated that "enhanced techniques would be used only as less harsh techniques fail or as interrogators ran out of time in the face of an imminent threat, so that it would be unlikely that a detainee would be subjected to more duress than is reasonably necessary to elicit the information sought." *See* Memorandum for John A. Rizzo, Acting General Counsel, Central Intelligence Agency, from Steven G. Bradbury, Principal Deputy Assistant Attorney General, Office of Legal Counsel, July 20, 2007, Re: Application of the War Crimes Act, the Detainee Treatment Act, and Common Article 3 of the Geneva Conventions to Certain Techniques that May be Used by the CIA in the Interrogation of High Value Al Qaeda Detainees (DTS #2009-1810, Tab 14).

2432. *See* Volume III for additional details.

2433. Memorandum for John A. Rizzo, Acting General Counsel, Central Intelligence Agency, from Steven G. Bradbury, Principal Deputy Assistant Attorney General, Office of Legal Counsel, July 20, 2007, Re: Application of the War Crimes Act, the Detainee Treatment Act, and Common Article 3 of the Geneva Conventions to Certain Techniques that May be Used by the CIA in the Interrogation of High Value Al Qaeda Detainees (DTS #2009-1810, Tab 14).

2434. Memorandum for John A. Rizzo, Acting General Counsel, Central Intelligence Agency, from Steven G. Bradbury, Principal Deputy Assistant Attorney General, Office of Legal Counsel, July 20, 2007, Re: Application of the War Crimes Act, the Detainee Treatment Act, and Common Article 3 of the Geneva Conventions to Certain Techniques that May be Used by the CIA in the Interrogation of High Value Al Qaeda Detainees (DTS #2009-1810, Tab 14).

2435. Memorandum for John A. Rizzo, Acting General Counsel, Central Intelligence Agency, from Steven G. Bradbury, Principal Deputy Assistant Attorney General, Office of Legal Counsel, July 20, 2007, Re: Application of the War Crimes Act, the Detainee Treatment Act, and Common Article 3 of the Geneva Conventions to Certain Techniques that May be Used by the CIA in the Interrogation of High Value Al Qaeda Detainees (DTS #2009-1810, Tab 14).

2436. Memorandum for John A. Rizzo, Acting General Counsel, Central Intelligence Agency, from Steven G. Bradbury, Principal Deputy Assistant Attorney General, Office of Legal Counsel, July 20, 2007, Re: Application of the War Crimes Act, the Detainee Treatment Act, and Common Article 3 of the Geneva Conventions to Certain Techniques that May be Used by the CIA in the Interrogation of High Value Al Qaeda Detainees (DTS #2009-1810, Tab 14).

2437. Memorandum for John A. Rizzo, Acting General Counsel, Central Intelligence Agency, from Steven G. Bradbury, Principal Deputy Assistant Attorney General, Office of Legal Counsel, July 20, 2007, Re: Application of the War Crimes Act, the Detainee Treatment Act, and Common Article 3 of the Geneva Conventions to Certain Techniques that May be Used by the CIA in the Interrogation of High Value Al Qaeda Detainees (DTS #2009-1810, Tab 14).

2438. This is a reference to the CIA's representation that KSM, "as a result of EITs," provided critical and unique reporting on Iyman Faris and Majid Khan. As described briefly in this summary, and in greater detail in the full Committee Study, Iyman Faris was already under investigation, and Majid Khan was already in custody, before KSM mentioned them. Khan himself revealed a discussion about poisoning reservoirs prior to his rendition to CIA custody. (*See* ALEC [REDACTED] (210015Z MAR 03).) When Faris, who was likewise not in CIA custody, discussed a plot against the Brooklyn Bridge, the former chief of CTC's Bin Ladin Unit described it as "half-baked," and "more of a nuisnance [sic] than a threat." *See* WHDC [REDACTED] (242226Z MAR 03) and email from: [REDACTED]; to: [REDACTED], [REDACTED] [REDACTED], [REDACTED], [REDACTED], [REDACTED]; subject: attacks in conus; date: March 25, 2003, at 6:19:18 AM).

2439. Memorandum for John A. Rizzo, Acting General Counsel, Central Intelligence Agency, from Steven G. Bradbury, Principal Deputy Assistant Attorney General, Office of Legal Counsel, July 20, 2007, Re: Application of the War Crimes Act, the Detainee Treatment Act, and Common Article 3 of the Geneva Conventions to Certain Techniques that May be Used by the CIA in the Interrogation of High Value Al Qaeda Detainees (DTS #2009-1810, Tab 14).

2440. Memorandum for John A. Rizzo, Acting General Counsel, Central Intelligence Agency, from Steven G. Bradbury, Principal Deputy Assistant Attorney General, Office of Legal Counsel, July 20, 2007, Re: Application of the War Crimes Act, the Detainee Treatment Act, and Common Article 3 of the Geneva Conventions to Certain Techniques that May be Used by the CIA in the Interrogation of High Value Al Qaeda Detainees (DTS #2009-1810, Tab 14).

2441. Email from: [REDACTED]; to [REDACTED] [REDACTED]; cc: [REDACTED], [REDACTED], [REDACTED], [REDACTED], [REDACTED], [REDACTED]; [REDACTED], [REDACTED], [REDACTED], [REDACTED], [REDACTED], [REDACTED], [REDACTED]; subject: Briefing for Senator John S. McCain (R-AZ); date: September 11, 2006, at 5:51 PM ("[Senator McCain] asked if I thought 'sleep deprivation' was torture. I responded that I did not and he then added that he had talked with a Marine Colonel friend of his and the Colonel had indicated it was and he believed his friend"). In another exchange, the officer who briefed Senator McCain was asked about the Senator's position. CIA officer [REDACTED]: "so, is the senator onboard? . . ." CIA officer [REDACTED]: "not totally." [REDACTED]: "if he's moved in our direction at all, you are a miracle worker . . . was it painful?" [REDACTED]: "Very much so." [REDACTED]: "is the issue the EITs still?" [REDACTED]: "Yep." (*See* Sametime communication between [REDACTED] and [REDACTED], 11/Sep/06, 15:47:27 to 18:43:29.) The OLC specifically cited statements from Senator McCain that the Military Commissions Act "will allow the CIA to continue interrogating prisoners within the boundaries established in the bill." Memorandum for John A. Rizzo, Acting General Counsel, Central Intelligence Agency, from Steven G. Bradbury, Principal Deputy Assistant Attorney General, Office of Legal Counsel, July 20, 2007, Re: Application of the War Crimes Act, the Detainee Treatment Act, and Common Article 3 of the Geneva Conventions to Certain Techniques that May be Used by the CIA in the Interrogation of High Value Al Qaeda Detainees (DTS #2009-1810, Tab 14). The OLC did not mention that McCain had specifically objected to the use of sleep deprivation.

2442. Letter from Senator Dianne Feinstein to Director Hayden, September 27, 2006 (DTS #2006-3717).

2443. Transcript of hearing of the Senate Select Committee on Intelligence, September 6, 2006 (DTS #2007-1336).

2444. Letter from Senator Russ Feingold to Director Hayden, May 1, 2007 (DTS #2007-1858).

2445. Letter from Senators Chuck Hagel, Dianne Feinstein and Ron Wyden, May 11, 2007 (DTS #2007-2102).

2446. Transcript of Senate Select Committee on Intelligence staff briefing, November 13, 2001 (DTS #2002-0629).

2447. "We're not going to engage in torture. But, that said, how do I deal with somebody I know may know right now that there is a nuclear weapon somewhere in the United States that is going to be detonated tomorrow, and I've got the guy who I know built it and hid it? I don't know the answer to that." (*See* transcript of Senate Select Committee on Intelligence MON briefing, November 7, 2001 (DTS #2002-0611); *See also* transcript of Senate Select Committee on Intelligence staff briefing, December 11, 2001 (DTS #2002-0615).

2448. Email from: [REDACTED], SSCI Staff; to: [REDACTED] Cleared SSCI staff; subject: Meeting yesterday with CIA lawyers on [REDACTED]; date February 26, 2002 (DTS #2002-0925).

2449. CIA responses to Questions for the Record (hearing, March 6, 2002), April 18, 2002 (DTS #2002-1800).

2450. Email from: [REDACTED]; to: [REDACTED]; subject: Issues for SSCI and HPSCI bi-weekly update on CT; date: April 9, 2002; Transcript of "Update on War on Terrorism," April 24, 2002 (DTS #2002-1993). Committee notifications of the capture of 'Abd al-Rahim al-Nashiri likewise omitted reference to his location and the use of the CIA's enhanced interrogation techniques. (*See* Congressional Notification, November 20, 2002 (DTS #2002- 4910).) On November [REDACTED], 2002, the CIA notified the Committee of the death of Gul Rahman at a "detention facility in [Country [REDACTED]] operated by the [Country [REDACTED] government] and funded by CIA." This description, as well as subsequent representations to the Committee, understated the role of the CIA in managing DETENTION SITE COBALT. *See* Congressional Notification, November [REDACTED] 2002 (DTS #2002-5015); Responses to [REDACTED] Counterterrorism Questions for the Record, Question 3 (DTS #2002-5059).

2451. Congressional Notification, April 15, 2002 (DTS #2002-1710); CIA responses to Questions for the Record (hearing, March 6, 2002), April 18, 2002 (DTS #2002-1800).

2452. Transcript of "Update on War on Terrorism," April 24, 2002 (DTS #2002-1993).

2453. Email from: John Moseman; to: Stanley Moskowitz, et al.; subject: Abu Zubaydah Interrogation; date: August 3, 2002, at 11:34:13 AM.

2454. Email from: [REDACTED]; to [REDACTED]; bcc: Jose Rodriguez; subject: Re: immediate coord; date: September 6, 2002. *See also* ALEC [REDACTED] (101607Z SEP 02).

2455. Email from: Jose Rodriguez; to: [REDACTED]; subject: Re: immediate coord; date: September 6, 2002, at 2:52 PM.

2456. DIRECTOR [REDACTED] (252018Z OCT02).

2457. Email from: Stanley Moskowitz; to: John Moseman, Scott Muller, James Pavitt; subject: Graham request for oversight into interrogation; date: December 4, 2002, at 05:58:06 PM; Stanley Moskowitz, Memorandum for the Record, February 4, 2003, "Subject: Sensitive Notification." *See also* email from: Scott W. Muller; to: John A. Rizzo; cc: [REDACTED]; date: December 19, 2002.

2458. Email from: [REDACTED]; to: [REDACTED] and [REDACTED]; subject: Sensitive Matters for the SSCI Quarterly CA Briefing; date: November 19, 2002. This email included the text of the CIA cables documenting the September 4, 2002, briefing to HPSCI leadership. *See* ALEC [REDACTED] (101607Z SEP 02), and the September 27, 2002, briefing to SSCI leadership, DIRECTOR [REDACTED] (252018Z OCT02).

2459. Email from: Stanley Moskowitz; to: John Moseman, Scott Mueller, James Pavitt; subject: Graham request for oversight into interrogation; date: December 4, 2002, at 05:58:06 PM; email from: Stanley Moskowitz; to: John H. Moseman; cc: Scott Muller and James Pavitt; subject: [attached document] Re: Graham request on interrogations; date: December 9, 2002, at 05:46:11 PM.

2460. Memorandum of December 26, 2002; FOR: Director of Central Intelligence; FROM: Scott W. Muller, General Counsel; SUBJECT: Disposition of Videotapes.

2461. Memorandum to: Stanley Moskowitz; from: Steven A. Cash; subject: Briefing; Interrogation and Debriefing of individuals in custody related to counterterrorism operations, January 2, 2003 (DTS #2003-0266); Lotus Notes dated January 2 – January 3 between OCA, ODDO, CTC personnel; email correspondences between [REDACTED], [REDACTED], [REDACTED]; subject: "SSCI's Request for Staff

Briefing on Terrorism Interrogation/Debriefing Techniques."

2462. Moskowitz Memorandum for the Record, February 4, 2003, "Subject: Sensitive Notification."

2463. Moskowitz Memorandum for the Record, February 4, 2003, "Subject: Sensitive Notification." For information on Senator Roberts's objections, *See* "Destroying C.I.A. Tapes Wasn't Opposed, Memos Say," by Scott Shane, *The New York Times,* dated February 22, 2010.

2464. Transcript of CIA briefing for the Senate Select Committee on Intelligence, March 5, 2003 (DTS #2003-1156); Transcript of "Intelligence Update," April 30, 2003 (DTS #2003-2174); Transcript of Senate Select Committee on Intelligence briefing, September 3, 2003 (DTS #2004-0288); email from: [REDACTED] to: [REDACTED]; subject: Re: EYES ONLY Re: Question Regarding Interrogations from SSCI Member Briefing on KSM Capture; date: March 17, 2003.

2465. CIA Interrogation Program: DDO Talking Points, 04 September 2003.

2466. For example, the talking points included inaccurate data on the waterboarding of Abu Zubaydah and KSM; stated that two unauthorized techniques were used with a detainee, whereas 'Abd al-Rahim al-Nashiri was subjected to numerous unauthorized techniques; and inaccurately stated that the offending officers were removed from the site. The talking points also stated that the use of the CIA's enhanced interrogation techniques "has produced significant results," and that the "[i]nformation acquired has saved countless lives . . . ." *See* CIA Interrogation Program: DDO Talking Points, 04 September 2003.

2467. Because the Committee was not informed of the CIA detention site at Guantanamo Bay, Cuba, no member of the Committee was aware that the U.S. Supreme Court decision to grant certiorari in the case of *Rasul v. Bush,* which related to the *habeas corpus* rights of detainees at Guantanamo Bay, resulted in the transfer of CIA detainees from the CIA detention facility at Guantanamo Bay to other CIA detention facilities. *See* HEADQUARTERS [REDACTED] [REDACTED], subject "RESTRICTED ACCESS TO [DETENTION SITE COBALT] AND [DETENTION SITE ORANGE]"; email from: [REDACTED] [REDACTED]; to [REDACTED]; cc: Jose Rodriguez, [REDACTED], [REDACTED] [REDACTED], [REDACTED], [REDACTED], [REDACTED], [REDACTED]; subject: guidance to [REDACTED]gitmo; date: May 14, 2004; forwarding final cable: HEADQUARTERS [REDACTED] (141502Z MAY 04), subject "Possible Brief to US Senator"; email from: Stanley Moskowitz; to: [REDACTED]; cc: [REDACTED]; subject: Re: guidance to [REDACTED]gitmo; date: May 14, 2004; CIA responses to Questions for the Record, March 13, 2008 (DTS #2008-1310); "CODEL Roberts to Miami/Guantanamo, 7-8 July 2005," dated 5 July, [REDACTED] 902860.

2468. Transcript of hearing. May 12, 2004 (DTS #2004-2332); Transcript of hearing, September 13, 2004 (DTS #2005-0750).

2469. Transcript of Senate Select Committee on Intelligence hearing, May 12, 2004 (DTS #2004-2332). Muhammad Rahim, the CIA's last detainee, was transferred to U.S. military custody on March 13, 2008. *See* [REDACTED] [REDACTED] 3445 [REDACTED]; [REDACTED] 9754 [REDACTED] [REDACTED]; [REDACTED] 8405 [REDACTED]; [REDACTED] 8408 [REDACTED].

2470. Handwritten notes of SSCI Minority Staff Director Andrew Johnson (DTS #2009-2077); CIA notes (DTS #2009-2024, pp. 92–95); CIA notes (DTS #2009-2024, pp. 110–121).

2471. Email from: [REDACTED]; to: [REDACTED]; subject: Re: Priority: congressional notification on Janat Gul; date: July 29, 2004.

2472. Handwritten notes of SSCI Minority Staff Director Andrew Johnson (DTS #2009-2077); CIA notes (DTS #2009-2024, pp. 92–95); CIA notes (DTS #2009-2024, pp. 110–121).

2473. February 3, 2005, letter from Senator Rockefeller to Senator Roberts on "the Committee's upcoming agenda," (letter incorrectly dated February 3, 2004).

2474. Sametime message discussion between [REDACTED] and [REDACTED], March 3, 2005.

2475. The notes indicate that CIA briefers provided inaccurate information. For example, the notes indicate that "[w]e screen carefully all people who might have contact with detainees" (emphasis in the Vice Chairman's notes) and that "positive incentives" are used prior to "coercive measures." In a reference to the waterboard, the notes state, the detainee "thinks he's drowning, even though they are breathing." *See* handwritten notes of then-Committee Minority Staff Director Andrew Johnson (DTS #2009-2077, Image 1) and handwritten notes of Senator Rockefeller.

2476. Letter to Senator Roberts from minority SSCI members, March 10, 2005 (DTS #2005-1126); Letter to Vice President Cheney from Vice Chairman Rockefeller and Representative Harman, March 11, 2005; Letter from Senator Rockefeller, March 11, 2005.

2477. Sametime communication, between John P. Mudd and [REDACTED], April 13, 2005, from 19:23:50 to 19:56:05.

2478. *See* email from: CIA Inspector General John Helgerson; to: [REDACTED]; subject: this afternoon's briefing; date: April 13, 2005. There is no Committee transcript of the briefing. CIA records state that the briefing covered "updates on the half dozen key abuse cases," ghost detainees, and renditions. The notes do not reference the CIA's enhanced interrogation techniques. In response to a question from Vice Chairman Rockefeller, Helgerson explained that the CIA was "preparing a comprehensive briefing" on detention and interrogation activities for the Committee.

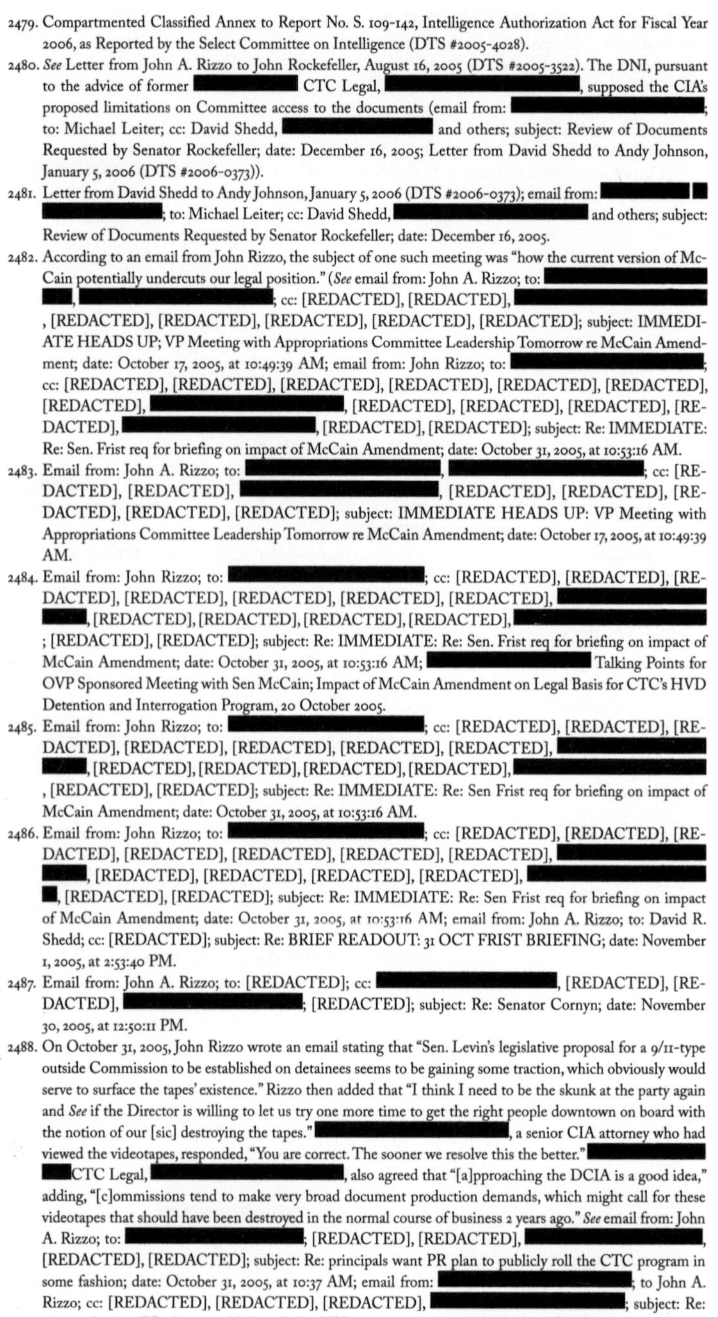

2479. Compartmented Classified Annex to Report No. S. 109-142, Intelligence Authorization Act for Fiscal Year 2006, as Reported by the Select Committee on Intelligence (DTS #2005-4028).

2480. *See* Letter from John A. Rizzo to John Rockefeller, August 16, 2005 (DTS #2005-3522). The DNI, pursuant to the advice of former ████ CTC Legal, ████, supposed the CIA's proposed limitations on Committee access to the documents (email from: ████; to: Michael Leiter; cc: David Shedd, ████ and others; subject: Review of Documents Requested by Senator Rockefeller; date: December 16, 2005; Letter from David Shedd to Andy Johnson, January 5, 2006 (DTS #2006-0373)).

2481. Letter from David Shedd to Andy Johnson, January 5, 2006 (DTS #2006-0373); email from: ████ ████; to: Michael Leiter; cc: David Shedd, ████ and others; subject: Review of Documents Requested by Senator Rockefeller; date: December 16, 2005.

2482. According to an email from John Rizzo, the subject of one such meeting was "how the current version of McCain potentially undercuts our legal position." (*See* email from: John A. Rizzo; to: ████, ████; cc: [REDACTED], [REDACTED], ████, [REDACTED], [REDACTED], [REDACTED], [REDACTED], [REDACTED]; subject: IMMEDIATE HEADS UP; VP Meeting with Appropriations Committee Leadership Tomorrow re McCain Amendment; date: October 17, 2005, at 10:49:39 AM; email from: John Rizzo; to: ████; cc: [REDACTED], [REDACTED], [REDACTED], [REDACTED], [REDACTED], [REDACTED], [REDACTED], ████, [REDACTED], [REDACTED], [REDACTED], [REDACTED], ████, [REDACTED], [REDACTED]; subject: Re: IMMEDIATE: Re: Sen. Frist req for briefing on impact of McCain Amendment; date: October 31, 2005, at 10:53:16 AM.

2483. Email from: John A. Rizzo; to: ████, ████; cc: [REDACTED], [REDACTED], ████, [REDACTED], [REDACTED], [REDACTED], [REDACTED], [REDACTED]; subject: IMMEDIATE HEADS UP: VP Meeting with Appropriations Committee Leadership Tomorrow re McCain Amendment; date: October 17, 2005, at 10:49:39 AM.

2484. Email from: John Rizzo; to: ████; cc: [REDACTED], [REDACTED], [REDACTED], [REDACTED], [REDACTED], [REDACTED], [REDACTED], ████, [REDACTED], [REDACTED], [REDACTED], [REDACTED], ████; [REDACTED], [REDACTED]; subject: Re: IMMEDIATE: Re: Sen. Frist req for briefing on impact of McCain Amendment; date: October 31, 2005, at 10:53:16 AM; ████ Talking Points for OVP Sponsored Meeting with Sen McCain; Impact of McCain Amendment on Legal Basis for CTC's HVD Detention and Interrogation Program, 20 October 2005.

2485. Email from: John Rizzo; to: ████; cc: [REDACTED], [REDACTED], [REDACTED], [REDACTED], [REDACTED], [REDACTED], [REDACTED], ████, [REDACTED], [REDACTED], [REDACTED], [REDACTED], ████, [REDACTED], [REDACTED]; subject: Re: IMMEDIATE: Re: Sen Frist req for briefing on impact of McCain Amendment; date: October 31, 2005, at 10:53:16 AM.

2486. Email from: John Rizzo; to: ████; cc: [REDACTED], [REDACTED], [REDACTED], [REDACTED], [REDACTED], [REDACTED], [REDACTED], ████, [REDACTED], [REDACTED], [REDACTED], [REDACTED], ████, [REDACTED], [REDACTED]; subject: Re: IMMEDIATE: Re: Sen Frist req for briefing on impact of McCain Amendment; date: October 31, 2005, at 10:53:16 AM; email from: John A. Rizzo; to: David R. Shedd; cc: [REDACTED]; subject: Re: BRIEF READOUT: 31 OCT FRIST BRIEFING; date: November 1, 2005, at 2:53:40 PM.

2487. Email from: John A. Rizzo; to: [REDACTED]; cc: ████, [REDACTED], [REDACTED], ████; [REDACTED]; subject: Re: Senator Cornyn; date: November 30, 2005, at 12:50:11 PM.

2488. On October 31, 2005, John Rizzo wrote an email stating that "Sen. Levin's legislative proposal for a 9/11-type outside Commission to be established on detainees seems to be gaining some traction, which obviously would serve to surface the tapes' existence." Rizzo then added that "I think I need to be the skunk at the party again and *See* if the Director is willing to let us try one more time to get the right people downtown on board with the notion of our [sic] destroying the tapes." ████, a senior CIA attorney who had viewed the videotapes, responded, "You are correct. The sooner we resolve this the better." ████ CTC Legal, ████, also agreed that "[a]pproaching the DCIA is a good idea," adding, "[c]ommissions tend to make very broad document production demands, which might call for these videotapes that should have been destroyed in the normal course of business 2 years ago." *See* email from: John A. Rizzo; to: ████; [REDACTED], [REDACTED], ████, [REDACTED], [REDACTED]; subject: Re: principals want PR plan to publicly roll the CTC program in some fashion; date: October 31, 2005, at 10:37 AM; email from: ████; to John A. Rizzo; cc: [REDACTED], [REDACTED], [REDACTED], ████; subject: Re: principals want PR plan to publicly roll the CTC program in some fashion; date: October 31, 2005, at 12:32

PM; email from: [REDACTED]; to: John A. Rizzo; cc: [REDACTED], [REDACTED], [REDACTED], [REDACTED], [REDACTED]; subject: Re: principals want PR plan to publicly roll the CTC program in some fashion; date: October 31, 2005, at 11:45 AM. *See also* interview of [REDACTED], by [REDACTED] and [REDACTED], Office of the Inspector General, June 17, 2003.

2489. *See* Senate Roll Call Vote #00309, November 8, 2005, 5:37pm, on Amendment #2430.

2490. [REDACTED] 27089 (090627Z NOV 05).

2491. A review of the Committee record of this briefing indicates much of the information provided by the CIA was inaccurate. For example, according to the Committee's Memorandum for the Record, CIA briefers stated "the plan divorces questioning from coercive measures." CIA records indicate, however, that questioning and the use of the CIA's enhanced interrogation techniques were combined in practice. According to Committee records, CIA officials stated that Khalid al-Masri had and maintained connections to al-Qa'ida, and that he was released "when the CIA reached a point in debriefings that required [foreign government] assistance," which was not forthcoming. The CIA Inspector General would later determine that when CIA officers questioned al-Masri, "they quickly concluded that he was not a terrorist," and that there was "insufficient basis to render and detain al-Masri." CIA officers referenced the captures of Hambali, Sajid Badat, Jose Padilla, and Iyman Faris, as well as the disruption of the West Coast/Second Wave plotting, the Heathrow Airport plotting, and the Karachi plotting. As detailed in this summary, the CIA consistently provided inaccurate representations regarding the plotting and the capture of the referenced individuals. CIA briefers also compared the program to U.S. military custody, stating that "the CIA can bring far more resources – debriefers, analysts, psychologists, etc. – per detainee than is possible at large scale facilities such as Guantanamo Bay, Cuba." As described, the chief of Base at DETENTION SITE BLACK complained of "problem, underperforming" and "totally inexperienced" debriefers almost a year prior to this briefing. As further described, an inspector general audit completed three months after the briefing described the lack of debriefers at CIA detention facilities as "an ongoing problem." (Senate Select Committee on Intelligence, Memorandum for the Record, "CIA Briefing on Detention Program," March 8, 2006 (DTS #2006-1182).).

2492. Senate Select Committee on Intelligence, Memorandum for the Record, "CIA Briefing on Detention Program" March 8, 2006 (DTS #2006-1182).

2493. By the time of the briefing, press disclosures had resulted in widespread public discussion about some of the CIA's reported enhanced interrogation techniques, including the waterboard. Goss was thus asked by a member of the Committee whether the CIA had undertaken a "technique by technique" analysis of the effectiveness of the program. Goss responded that the problem with such an analysis is that the techniques were used "in combination." Asked by the member for a comparison of "waterboarding versus sleep deprivation," Goss responded that "waterboarding is not used in conjunction with anything else." As detailed elsewhere, this testimony was inaccurate. Goss then referred to sleep deprivation, dietary manipulation, and "environment control" as "alleged techniques." *See* transcript of Senate Select Committee on Intelligence briefing, March 15, 2006 (DTS #2006- 1308).

2494. Director Goss stated: "I've had to seriously consider whether passage of the McCain amendment was a congressional disapproval of the CIA use of EITs. I don't think it was, and I don't think that was the message you sent me. But I have to at least get that assurance, that that's not what you were saying to me." *See* transcript of Senate Select Committee on Intelligence briefing, March 15, 2006 (DTS #2006-1308).

2495. Transcript of Senate Select Committee on Intelligence briefing, March 15, 2006 (DTS #2006-1308).

2496. Transcript of Senate Select Committee on Intelligence briefing, March 15, 2006 (DTS #2006-1308).

2497. Transcript of Senate Select Committee on Intelligence briefing, March 15, 2006 (DTS #2006-1308).

2498. Transcript of Senate Select Committee on Intelligence briefing, March 15, 2006 (DTS #2006-1308).

2499. Letter from Vice Chairman Rockefeller to Director Goss, containing Questions for the Record, May 10, 2006 (DTS #2006-1949); Letter from Chairman Roberts to Director Goss, May 4, 2006 (DTS #2006-1876).

2500. Classified Annex to Report No. S. 109-259, the Intelligence Authorization Act for Fiscal Year 2007 (DTS #2006-2208). Compartmented annex (DTS #2006-2209).

2501. Hayden stated that *Hamdan v. Rumsfeld* had effectively prohibited the use of the CIA's enhanced interrogation techniques. He then described an "action" that would define Common Article 3 according to the Detainee Treatment Act, which was in turn "anchored" in the Convention Against Torture to "which the Senate express[ed] reservation." As described, two months later, the President sought Congressional approval of the Military Commissions Act. Based on handwritten notes by the Committee minority staff director.

2502. Transcript of Senate Select Committee on Intelligence briefing, September 6, 2006 (DTS #2007-1336).

2503. As described above, the CIA had sought the Department of Justice's opinion on the application of the Detainee Treatment Act to the CIA's enhanced interrogation techniques. The draft memorandum was withdrawn after the U.S. Supreme Court case in *Hamdan v. Rumsfeld.*

2504. Transcript of Senate Select Committee on Intelligence briefing, September 6, 2006 (DTS#2007-1336). The transcript includes the following exchange: Senator Feingold: "...you make it tougher on me and the members of the Committee by the decision to not allow staff access to a briefing like this. Was it your recommendation to deny staff access to this hearing?" CIA Director Hayden: "It was."

2505. Memorandum for John A. Rizzo, Acting General Counsel, Central Intelligence Agency, from Steven G.

Bradbury, Principal Deputy Assistant Attorney General, Office of Legal Counsel, July 20, 2007, Re: Application of the War Crimes Act, the Detainee Treatment Act, and Common Article 3 of the Geneva Conventions to Certain Techniques that May be Used by the CIA in the Interrogation of High Value Al Qaeda Detainees (DTS #2009-1810, Tab 14).

2506. Email from: ; to ; cc: , [REDACTED], [REDACTED], [REDACTED], [REDACTED], ; [REDACTED], [REDACTED], [REDACTED], [REDACTED], [REDACTED], [REDACTED], [REDACTED]; subject: Briefing for Senator John S. McCain (R-AZ); date: September 11, 2006, at 5:51 PM.

2507. Letter from Senator Feinstein to Director Hayden, September 27, 2006 (DTS #2006-3717).

2508. Letter from Senator Feingold to Director Hayden, May 1, 2007 (DTS #2007-1858); Letter from Senators Feinstein, Wyden and Hagel to Director Hayden, May 11, 2007 (DTS #2007-2102).

2509. As in the September 6, 2006, briefing, only two staff members were permitted to attend.

2510. Director Hayden testified that detainees were never provided fewer than 1,000 calories a day. This is inaccurate. There were no calorie requirements until May 2004, and draft OMS guidelines from March 2003 indicated that "[b]rief periods in which food is withheld (1-2 days), as an adjunct to interrogations are acceptable." (*See* OMS GUIDELINES ON MEDICAL AND PSYCHOLOGICAL SUPPORT TO DETAINEE RENDITION, INTERROGATION, AND DETENTION, May 17, 2004; OMS Guidelines on Medical and Psychological Support to Detainee Interrogations, First Draft, March 7, 2003.) Director Hayden testified that detainees were "not paraded [nude] in front of anyone," whereas a CIA interrogator told the inspector general that nude detainees were "kept in a center area outside the interrogation room," and were "'walked around' by guards." (*See* Interview Report, . April 14, 2003.) testified that standing sleep deprivation is discontinued when swelling or "any abnormality" appears. This was inaccurate. For example, KSM's standing sleep deprivation continued, notwithstanding pedal edema and abrasions on his ankles, shins and wrists, as well as the back of his head. (*See* 10916 (210845Z MAR 03); 10909 (201918Z MAR 03).) Director Hayden testified that "mental conditions that would be of normal concern do not present themselves until a person has experienced more than 100 hours of sleep deprivation," however at least three detainees experienced hallucinations after being subjected to fewer than 96 hours of sleep deprivation. *See* 1393 (201006Z OCT 03); 48122 ; 1299 (JAN 04); 1312 (JAN 04); 1530 (04); 3221 ; 3241 (04).

2511. Transcript of Senate Select Committee on Intelligence hearing, November 16, 2006 (DTS #2007-1422).

2512. This testimony included inaccurate information. For example, testified that KSM "identified sleeper cells inside the U.S., [and] the information allowed the FBI to identify that and take action." She further testified that KSM "identified the second wave of attacks against the U.S. that were planned after 9/11," that Abu Zubaydah "really pointed us towards [KSM] and how to find him," and that Abu Zubaydah "led us to Ramzi bin al-Shibh." *See* transcript of Senate Select Committee on Intelligence hearing, February 14, 2007 (DTS #2007-1337). Additional information on the testimony is included in the full Committee Study.

2513. Transcript of Senate Select Committee on Intelligence hearing, February 14, 2007 (DTS #2007-1337).

2514. DIRECTOR (152227Z MAR 07).

2515. Senate Select Committee on Intelligence, Transcript of hearing, April 12, 2007 (DTS #2007-3158).

2516. For example, the Statement for the Record claimed that Abu Zubaydah was "an up-and-coming lieutenant of Usama Bin Ladin (UBL) who had intimate knowledge of al-Qa'ida's current operations, personnel and plans." It also stated that "[a]fter the use of these techniques, Abu Zubaydah became one of our most important sources of intelligence on al-Qa'ida, and he himself has stated that he would not have been responsive or told us all he did had he not gone through these techniques." The Statement claimed that CIA interrogators were "carefully chosen and screened for demonstrated professional judgment and maturity," and that "they must complete more than 250 hours of specialized training before they are allowed to come face-to-face with a terrorist." Claims made in the Statement refuting the abuses identified by the ICRC were repeated by Director Hayden during the hearing, and are described in an appendix to this summary. The Statement for the Record also included inaccurate information about past congressional oversight, claiming that "[a]s CIA's efforts to implement [new interrogation] authorities got underway in 2002, the majority and minority leaders of the Senate, the speaker and the minority leader of the House, and the chairs and ranking members of the intelligence committees were fully briefed on the interrogation program." See Witness Statement for the Senate Select Committee on Intelligence from CIA Director Hayden, for April 12, 2007, hearing (DTS #2007-1563).

2517. The Statement for the Record included claims of effectiveness similar to those made in other contexts by the CIA, related to the captures of Hambali (on which Director Hayden elaborated during the hearing), Issa al-Hindi ("KSM also provided the first lead to an operative known as 'Issa al-Hindi'"), Sajid Badat ("[l] eads provided by KSM in November 2003 led directly to the arrest of [Badat]"), Jose Padilla ("Abu Zubaydah provided information leading to the identification of alleged al-Qa'ida operative Jose Padilla"), and Iyman

Faris ("[s]oon after his arrest, KSM described an Ohio-based truck driver whom the FBI identified as Iyman Faris, already under suspicion for his contacts with al-Qa'ida operative Majid Khan"). The statement also described the "thwarting" and "disrupting" of the "West Coast Airliner Plot" (aka, the Second Wave plotting), the "Heathrow Airport plot," the "Karachi plots," and "Plots in the Saudi Peninsula." *See* Witness Statement for the Senate Select Committee on Intelligence from CIA Director Hayden, for April 12, 2007, hearing (DTS #2007-1563).

2518. Witness Statement for the Senate Select Committee on Intelligence from CIA Director Hayden, for April 12, 2007, hearing (DTS #2007-1563).

2519. Senate Select Committee on Intelligence, Transcript of hearing, April 12, 2007 (DTS #2007-3158).

2520. The Committee had asked for specifics related to the assertion in Director Hayden's written statement that the CIA program was effective in gaining intelligence after detainees successfully resisted interrogation under U.S. military detention. The CIA's response referenced only one detainee, Abu Ja'far al-Iraqi, stating that he was "unwilling to become fully cooperative given the limitations of the U.S. military's interrogation and detention regulations." The CIA's response to Committee questions then asserted that "[i]t was not until Abu Jaf'ar was subjected to EITS that he provided detailed information [about] his personal meetings with Abu Mus'ab al-Zarqawi and Zarqawi's advisors," and that "[i]n addition, Abu Jaf'ar provided information on al-Qa'ida in Iraq (AQI) finances, travel, and associated facilitation activities." The provided information was inaccurate. CIA records indicate that, while still in U.S. military custody, Abu Ja'far described multiple meetings with al-Zarqawi, other members of al-Qa'ida in Iraq, and individuals who were to serve as al-Zarqawi's connection to senior al-Qa'ida leadership. Abu Ja'far also provided insights into al-Zarqawi's beliefs and plans. *See* ██████ 32732 (██████ OCT 05); ██████ 32707 (██████ OCT 05); ██████ 32726 (██████ OCT 05); ██████ 32810 (██████ OCT 05); ██████ 32944 (██████ OCT 05).

2521. CIA Response to Senate Select Committee on Intelligence Questions for the Record, June 18, 2007 (DTS #2007-2564).

2522. For example, the director of CTC, ██████, testified that detainees "are given ample opportunity to provide the information without the use of EITs" (Senate Select Committee on Intelligence, Transcript of hearing, August 2, 2007 (DTS #2007-3641). As detailed in this Study, numerous detainees were subjected to the CIA's enhanced interrogation techniques immediately upon being questioned.

2523. Senate Select Committee on Intelligence, Transcript of hearing, August 2, 2007 (DTS #2007-3641).

2524. Transcript, Committee of Conference on the Intelligence Authorization Act for Fiscal Year 2008, December 5, 2007 (DTS #2009-1279).

2525. "C.I.A. Destroyed Tapes of Interrogations," *The New York Times*, December 6, 2007 (published in the December 7, 2007, edition of the newspaper).

2526. Press Release, entitled, "Chairman Rockefeller Says Intel Committee Has Begun Investigation Into CIA Detainee Tapes; Senator Expresses Concern that CIA Continues to Withhold Key Information," Office of Senator Rockefeller, December 7, 2007.

2527. Transcript of Senate Select Committee on Intelligence hearing, November 16, 2006 (DTS #2007-1422). The CIA's June 2013 Response states only that "[w]e acknowledge that DCIA did not volunteer past information on CIA's process of videotaping the interrogation sessions or of the destruction of the tapes . . . ." The Committee review found that in testimony to the Committee in November 2006, CIA witnesses responded to questions about videotaping in terms of current practice, while avoiding any reference to past practice. This was similar to what was conveyed in June 2003, to David Addington of the Office of the Vice President, by CIA General Counsel Scott Muller. In June 2003, the CIA's General Counsel Scott Muller traveled to Guantanamo Bay, Cuba, with White House Counsel Alberto Gonzales, the Vice President's counsel David Addington, Department of Defense General Counsel Jim Haynes, Patrick Philbin from the Department of Justice, and NSC Legal Advisor John Bellinger. According to CIA records, during the trip, White House officials asked CIA General Counsel Muller about the CIA Inspector General's concerns regarding the waterboard technique and whether the CIA videotaped interrogations, as David Addington had heard tapes existed of the CIA's interrogations of Abu Zubaydah. In an email to CIA colleagues providing details on the trip, Muller wrote: "(David Addington, by the way, asked me if were [sic] taping interrogations and said he had heard that there were tapes of the Zubaydah interrogations. I told him that tapes were not being made)." *See* email from: Scott Muller; to: John Rizzo, ██████, and ██████; subject: Report from Gitmo trip (Not proofread as usual); date: June ██, 2003, at 5:47 PM.

2528. Senate Select Committee on Intelligence, Transcript of hearing, December 11, 2007 (DTS #2007-4904). In the spring of 2008, after the Committee agreed on a bipartisan basis to continue investigating the destruction of the interrogation tapes, Chairman Rockefeller and Vice Chairman Bond pressed the CIA to provide the operational cables promised by Director Hayden. *See* April 21, 2008, letter from Chairman Rockefeller and Vice Chairman Bond, to Director Hayden (DTS #2008-1798). See *also* May 8, 2008, letter from Chairman Rockefeller and Vice Chairman Bond, to Director Hayden (DTS #2008-2030).

2529. Senate Select Committee on Intelligence, Transcript of hearing, February 5, 2008 (DTS #2008-1140).

2530. U.S. Senate vote to adopt the conference report on February 13, 2008, 4:31 PM. H.R. 2082 (Intelligence Authorization Act for Fiscal Year 2008).

2531. The President's veto message to the House of Representatives stated that "[t]he CIA's ability to conduct a separate and specialized interrogation program for terrorists who possess the most critical information in the war on terror has helped the United States prevent a number of attacks, including plots to fly passenger airplanes into the Library Tower in Los Angeles and into Heathrow Airport or buildings in downtown London" (Message to the House of Representatives, President George W. Bush, March 8, 2008). The president also explained his veto in his weekly radio address, in which he referenced the "Library Tower," also known as the "Second Wave" plot, and the Heathrow Airport plot, while representing that the CIA program "helped us stop a plot to strike a U.S. Marine camp in Djibouti, a planned attack on the U.S. consulate in Karachi . . . ." (*See* President's Radio Address, President George W. Bush, March 8, 2008). As detailed, CIA representations regarding the role of the CIA's enhanced interrogation techniques with regard to the Second Wave, Heathrow Airport, Djibouti, and Karachi plots were inaccurate.

2532. U.S. House of Representatives Roll Call Vote 117 of the 110th Congress, Second Session, March 11, 2008, 7:01 PM.

2533. CIA Responses to Questions for the Record from the 6 March 2008 SSCI Covert Action Hearing, May 22, 2008 (DTS #2008-2234).

2534. Transcript of Senate Select Committee on Intelligence briefing, March 15, 2006 (DTS #2006-1308).

2535. Memorandum for John A. Rizzo, Acting General Counsel, Central Intelligence Agency, from Steven G. Bradbury, Principal Deputy Assistant Attorney General, Office of Legal Counsel, July 20, 2007, Re: Application of the War Crimes Act, the Detainee Treatment Act, and Common Article 3 of the Geneva Conventions to Certain Techniques that May be Used by the CIA in the Interrogation of High Value Al Qaeda Detainees (DTS #2009-1810, Tab 14).

2536. The CIA response stated that during sleep deprivation, the detainee is "typically . . . handcuffed in front of his body," and "will not be permitted to hang from [the handcuffs]," despite the practice of detainees being subjected to the technique with their hands above their heads, and reports of detainees hanging from their wrists at DETENTION SITE COBALT. The response stated that "adult diapers and shorts [are] for sanitary purposes," and that "caloric intake will always be at least 1,000 kcal/day," although CIA records indicate that the purpose of the diapers in several cases was humiliation and there were no caloric requirements until May 2004. The response stated that "[n]o sexual abuse or threats of sexual abuse are permitted," despite an insinuation that a family member of a detainee would be sexually abused. The response stated that "[t]he detainee may not be intentionally exposed to detention facility staff," even though detainees at DETENTION SITE COBALT were walked around nude by guards. The response stated that during water dousing, water "cannot enter the detainee's nose, mouth, or eyes," but did not acknowledge detainees being immersed in water. Finally, the CIA response described limitations on the use of the waterboard that were exceeded in the case of KSM. (See Response to Congressionally Directed Actions cited in the Compartmented Annex to Report 110-75, June 16, 2008 (DTS #2008-2663).) This response was provided notwithstanding the presidential veto of this legislation on March 8, 2008.

2537. The Committee had been provided four copies of the memoranda for a limited time. *See* Senate Select Committee on Intelligence, Transcript of hearing, June 10, 2008 (DTS #2008-2698).

2538. [REDACTED] CTC Legal repeated the representation that during sleep deprivation, detainees' hands were shackled "about chin to chest level," and stated that "[i]f there is any indication, such as the legs begin to swell, or things of that nature, that may terminate the sleep deprivation." [REDACTED] CTC Legal also stated, inaccurately, that "we cannot begin to implement any of the measures, absent first attempting to get information from the individual in an up front and non-coercive way." He added, also inaccurately, that "if the individual cooperates and begins to talk to you, you never go into the interrogation program."

2539. Senate Select Committee on Intelligence, Senate Select Committee on Intelligence, Transcript of hearing, June 10, 2008 (DTS #2008-2698).

2540. Questions for the Record submitted to CIA Director Michael Hayden, September 8, 2008, with a request for a response by October 10, 2008 (DTS #2008-3522).

2541. *See* CIA document prepared in response to "Questions for the Record" submitted by the Senate Select Committee on Intelligence on September 8, 2008. The Committee had inquired why information provided by Abu Zubaydah about Jose Padilla was included in the CIA's "Effectiveness Memo" for the Department of Justice, given that Abu Zubaydah provided the information to FBI Special Agents prior to being subjected to the CIA's enhanced interrogation techniques. The CIA response, prepared but never sent to the Committee, stated that the CTC attorney who prepared the CIA "Effectiveness Memo," [REDACTED], "simply inadvertently reported this wrong." The unsent CIA response added that "Abu Zubaydah provided information on Jose Padilla while being interrogated by the FBI," and cited a specific CIA cable, [REDACTED] 10991. In contrast to the CIA's unsent response to Committee questions in 2008, the CIA's June 2013 Response states: "[t]he Study also claims Abu Zubaydah had already provided [Jose Padilla's] 'Dirty Bomb' plot information to FBI interrogators prior to undergoing CIA interrogation, but this is based on an undocumented FBI internal communication and an FBI officer's recollection to the Senate Judiciary Committee seven years later." The CIA's June 2013 Response also represents that "[w]hile we have considerable information from FBI debriefings of Abu Zubaydah, we have no record that FBI debriefers acquired information about such an al-Qa'ida threat." As detailed in this summary, this is inaccurate. The CIA's June 2013 Response further states that "CIA correctly represented Abu Zubaydah's description of Jose Padilla as an example of information provided after an individual had been subjected to enhanced interrogation techniques." The CIA's unsent response to Committee questions in 2008 acknowledged that "[d]uring the initial timeframe Abu Zubaydah (AZ) was waterboarded the interrogation team believed that AZ was compliant and was not withholding actionable threat information," but ALEC Station "had additional information they felt linked AZ with more planned attacks," and that "[a]s a result, the interrogation team was instructed to continue with the waterboarding based on ALEC Station's belief." Finally, the unsent responses acknowledged that notwithstanding CIA representations to the Department of Justice regarding amenities available to CIA detainees, "[t]he amenities of today evolved over the first year and a half of the program," and that Abu Zubaydah was not initially provided those amenities.

2542. CIA Letter to Chairman John D. Rockefeller, IV, October 17, 2008 (DTS #2008-4131).

2543. Letter from Chairman John D. Rockefeller, IV to CIA Director Michael Hayden, October 29, 2008 (DTS #2008-4217).

2544. Letter from Senator Feinstein to CIA Director Michael Hayden, October 30, 2008 (DTS #2008-4235).

2545. *See* Committee business meeting records and transcript from February 11, 2009 (DTS #2009-1420).

2546. Senate Select Committee on Intelligence, Transcript of hearing, December 11, 2007 (DTS #2007-4904). In the spring of 2008, after the Committee agreed on a bipartisan basis to continue investigating the destruction of the interrogation tapes, Chairman Rockefeller and Vice Chairman Bond pressed the CIA to provide the operational cables promised by Director Hayden. *See* letter from Chairman Rockefeller and Vice Chairman Bond, to Director Hayden, April 21, 2008 (DTS #2008-1798); letter from Chairman Rockefeller and Vice Chairman Bond, to Director Hayden, May 8, 2008 (DTS #2008-2030).

2547. Senate Select Committee on Intelligence, Transcript, business meeting, February 11, 2009 (DTS #2009-1420).

2548. Senate Select Committee on Intelligence, Transcript, business meeting, February 11, 2009 (DTS #2009-1420).

2549. Senator Ron Wyden (D-OR). Senate Select Committee on Intelligence, Transcript, business meeting, February 11, 2009 (DTS #2009-1420).

2550. Transcript, business meeting, February 24, 2009 (DTS #2009-1913).

2551. Transcript, business meeting, March 5, 2009 (DTS #2009-1916).

2552. After the receipt of the CIA's June 27, 2013, Response to the Committee Study of the CIA's Detention and Interrogation Program, and subsequent meetings between the CIA and the Committee in the summer of 2013, the full Committee Study was updated. The final Committee Study of the CIA's Detention and Interrogation Program exceeds 6,700 pages and includes approximately 38,000 footnotes.

2553. Transcript at DTS #2007-3158. The CIA's June 2013 Response states: "We disagree with the *Study's* conclusion that the Agency actively impeded Congressional oversight of the CIA Detention and Interrogation Program... As discussed in our response to Conclusion 9, we also disagree with the assessment that the information CIA provided on the effectiveness of the program was largely inaccurate. Finally, we have reviewed DCIA Hayden's testimony before SSCI on 12 April, 2007 and do not find, as the *Study* claims, that he misrepresented virtually all aspects of the program, although a few aspects were in error . . . . The testimony contained some inaccuracies, and the Agency should have done better in preparing the Director, particularly concerning events that occurred prior to his tenure. However, there is no evidence that there was any intent on the part of the Agency or Director Hayden to misrepresent material facts." The CIA's June 2013 Response states that the CIA has "identified a number of broad lessons learned" and includes eight recommendations. The CIA's only recommendation related to Congress was: "Recommendation 8: Improve recordkeeping for interactions with Congress. Direct the Director of the Office of Congressional Affairs (OCA) and the Chief Information Officer to develop a concrete plan to improve recordkeeping on CIA's interactions with Congress. OCA's records going forward should reflect each interaction with Congress and the content of that interaction. OCA should work with the oversight committees to develop better access to transcripts of CIA testimony and briefings. This plan should be completed within 90 days of the arrival of a new Director of OCA."

2554. *See* intelligence reporting charts in Abu Zubaydah detainee review in Volume III, as well as a CIA paper entitled, "Abu Zubaydah," dated March 2005. Similar information was included in, "Abu Zubaydah Bio," a CIA document "Prepared on 9 August 2006."

2555. *See* Abu Zubaydah detainee review in Volume III.

2556. *See* Volume I, including ██████ 178955 (012236Z APR 02); April 1, 2002 email from [REDACTED] to [REDACTED], re: Please coord on cable attached; and email from [REDACTED] to [REDACTED], cc: ██████████, April 1, 2002, re: POC for [SWIGERT]- consultant who drafted Al-Qa'ida resistance to interrogation backgrounder (noting that CTC/LGL would contact SWIGERT).

2557. *See* Abu Zubaydah detainee review in Volume III.

2558. *See* Volume I for additional details.

2559. Email from: [REDACTED] (outgoing Chief of Base at DETENTION SITE GREEN): to: [REDACTED] subject: "Assessment to Date" of AZ; date: 10/06/2002, at 05:36:46 AM.

2560. CIA Intelligence Assessment, August 16, 2006, "Countering Misconceptions About Training Camps in Afghanistan, 1990-2001."

2561. *See* Abu Zubaydah detainee review in Volume III, including monthly intelligence reporting charts.

2562. Letter from Assistant Attorney General Goldsmith to CIA General Counsel Scott Muller, May 27, 2004. For more information on the SERE program, *See* the Senate Armed Services Committee Inquiry into the Treatment of Detainees in U.S. Custody, December 2008. See *also* statement of Senator Carl Levin relating to the inquiry, December 11, 2008: "In SERE school, our troops who are at risk of capture are exposed in a controlled environment with great protections and caution - to techniques adapted from abusive tactics used against American soldiers by enemies such as the Communist Chinese during the Korean War. SERE training techniques include stress positions, forced nudity, use of fear, sleep deprivation and, until recently, the Navy SERE school used the waterboard. These techniques were designed to give our students a taste of what they might be subjected to if captured by a ruthless, lawless enemy so that they would be better prepared to resist. The techniques were never intended to be used against detainees in U.S. custody."

2563. [REDACTED] 73208 (231043Z JUL 02).

2564. The August 1, 2002, OLC memorandum addressed 10 interrogation techniques. The May 10, 2005, OLC memorandum addressed 13 techniques.

2565. "Our advice is based upon the following facts, which you have provided to us. We also understand that you do not have any facts in your possession contrary to the facts outlined here, and this opinion is limited to these facts. If these facts were to change, this advice would not necessarily apply." (*See* Memorandum for John Rizzo, Acting General Counsel, Central Intelligence Agency, from Jay Bybee, Assistant Attorney General, Office of Legal Counsel, August 1, 2002, Interrogation of al Qaeda Operative (DTS #2009-1810, Tab 1).) CIA records indicate that it was not until July 29, 2003, that the Attorney General stated that the legal principles of the August 1, 2002, memorandum could be applied to other CIA detainees. (*See* June 18, 2004, letter from Assistant Attorney General Jack L. Goldsmith III to Director Tenet (DTS #2004-2710).) In a subsequent interview with the OIG, however, ▇▇▇ CTC Legal, ▇▇▇, stated that "every detainee interrogated is different in that they are outside the opinion because the opinion was written for Zubaydah." The context for ▇▇▇'s statement was the legality of the waterboarding of KSM. See Interview of ▇▇▇, by [REDACTED], [REDACTED], and [REDACTED], Office of the Inspector General, August 20, 2003.

2566. Other CIA attendees at the hearing included John Rizzo, ▇▇▇ and ▇▇▇. ▇▇▇, former ▇▇▇ CTC Legal, attended for the ODNI.

2567. Memorandum for John Rizzo, Acting General Counsel, Central Intelligence Agency, from Jay Bybee, Assistant Attorney General, Office of Legal Counsel, August 1, 2002, Interrogation of al Qaeda Operative (DTS #2009-1810, Tab 1).

2568. ▇▇▇ 10496 (162014Z FEB 03). On July 25, 2002, a CIA Headquarters cable stated that Abu Zubaydah was the "author of a seminal al-Qa'ida manual on resistance to interrogation techniques." (*See* DIRECTOR ▇▇▇ (251609Z JUL 02)). As a result of an ACLU lawsuit, in April 2010, the CIA released a document stating that Abu Zubaydah was the "author of a seminal al-Qa'ida manual on resistance to interrogation techniques." (*See* ACLU release entitled, "CIA Interrogation of AZ Released 04-15-10.") No CIA records could be identified to support this CIA assessment.

2569. ▇▇▇ 10496 (162014Z FEB 03).

2570. The CIA's June 2013 Response states that "[w]e concede that prior to promulgation of DCI guidance on interrogation in January 2003 and the establishment of interrogator training courses in November of the same year, not every CIA employee who debriefed detainees had been thoroughly screened or had received formal training. After that time, however - the period with which DCIA Hayden, who came to the Agency in 2005, was most familiar - the statement is accurate." CIA records indicate that the first interrogator training course was established in November 2002. General Hayden became the CIA Director on May 30, 2006. After this time two CIA detainees entered CIA custody, one of whom was subjected to the CIA's enhanced interrogation techniques.

2571. Email from: ▇▇▇, ▇▇▇/CTC/LGL; to: [REDACTED]; cc: Jose Rodriguez, [REDACTED], [REDACTED], ▇▇▇; subject: EYES ONLY; date: November ▇▇▇, 2002, at 03:13:01 PM. As described above, Gul Rahman likely froze to death at DETENTION SITE COBALT sometime in the morning of November ▇▇▇, 2002. ▇▇▇ ▇▇▇'s email, however, appears to have been drafted before the guards had found Gul Rahman's body and before that death was reported to CIA Headquarters. See [REDACTED] 30211 ▇▇▇ ▇▇▇, describing the guards observing Gul Rahman alive in the morning of November ▇▇▇, 2002. Gul Rahman's death appeared in cable traffic at least ▇▇▇ after ▇▇▇ ▇▇▇'s email. No records could be identified to provide the impetus for ▇▇▇'s email.

2572. In addition, ▇▇▇, Former Chief, ▇▇▇ ▇▇▇, CTC, testified: "First off, we have thirteen interrogators and, of that thirteen, eleven are contract employees of ours, and they've all been through the screening process, they've all been through our vetting process, and they are certainly more than qualified. They are probably some of the most mature and professional people you will have in this business."

2573. Email from: Jose Rodriguez; to: ▇▇▇, ▇▇▇CTC/LGL; cc: [REDACTED], [REDACTED], [REDACTED], [REDACTED], ▇▇▇; subject: EYES ONLY; date:

November ■■, 2002, at 04:27 PM.

2574. For additional detailed information, *See* Volume III.

2575. December 4, 2002 Training Report, High Value Target Interrogation and Exploitation (HVTIE) Training Seminar 12-18 Nov 02, (pilot running).

2576. DIRECTOR ■■■■■ ■■■■■ APR 03).

2577. Interrogator Selection, Training, Qualification, and Certification Process; approximately January 29-February 4, 2003.

2578. *See* ■■■■■ 10604 (091624Z AUG 02) and ■■■■■ 10607 (100335Z AUG 02). In an email, the former SERE psychologists on contract with the CIA, who largely devised the CIA enhanced interrogation techniques, wrote that Abu Zubaydah stated he was "ready to talk" the first day after they used the CIA's techniques. Speaking specifically of the waterboard technique, they wrote, "As for our buddy; he capitulated the first time. We chose to expose him over and over until we had a high degree of confidence he wouldn't hold back. He said he was ready to talk during the first exposure." *See* email from: [REDACTED]; subject: "Re: [SWIGERT and DUNBAR]"; date: August 21, 2002, at 10:21 PM.

2579. ■■■■■ 10607 (100335Z AUG 02).

2580. Email from: Jose Rodriguez; to: [REDACTED]; subject: "[DETENTION SITE GREEN]," with attachment of an earlier email from: [REDACTED]; to: [REDACTED]; date: August 12, 2002. *See also* the section on Abu Zubaydah's interrogation in this summary and the Abu Zubaydah detainee review in Volume III.

2581. Email from: [REDACTED]; to: ■■■■■; cc: ■■■■■ ■■■■■; subject: Re: MEDICAL SITREP 3/10; date: March 11, 2003, at 8:10:39 AM.

2582. Email from: [REDACTED]; to: ■■■■■; cc: ■■■■■ ■■■, ■■■■■, Jose Rodriguez; subject: re: Eyes Only – Legal and Political Quand[] ry; date: March 13, 2003, at 11:28:06 AM.

2583. Email from: ■■■■■; to: [REDACTED]; cc: Jose Rodriguez, ■■■■■ ■■■■■, ■■■■■, ■■■■■, ■■■■■ ■■■■■; subject: EYES ONLY - Use of Water Board; date: March 13, 2003, at 08:28 AM.

2584. Email from: [REDACTED]; to: ■■■■■; cc: ■■■■■; subject: Re: State cable; date: March 13, 2003, at 1:43:17 PM. The previous day, the medical officer had written that "I am going the extra mile to try to handle this in a non confrontational manner." *See* email from: [REDACTED]; to: ■■■■■; cc: ■■■■■; subject: Re: MEDICAL SITREP 3/10; date: March 12, 2003, at 5:17:07 AM.

2585. See, *for example,* the report of investigation of the Inspector General: "By mid-2002, Headquarters and [DETENTION SITE BLUE] were at odds regarding [DETENTION SITE BLUE]'s assessment on Al-Nashiri and how to proceed with his interrogation or debriefing. On several occasions throughout December 2002, [DETENTION SITE BLUE] reported via cables and secure telephone calls that Al-Nashiri was not actively resisting and was responding to questions directly. Headquarters disagreed with [DETENTION SITE BLUE]'s assessment because Headquarters analysts thought Al-Nashiri was withholding imminent threat information." *See* Report of Investigation, Office of the Inspector General, Unauthorized Interrogation Techniques at [DETENTION SITE BLUE] (2003-7123-IG), 29 October 2003, p. 18 (DTS #2003-4897).

2586. Special Review, Office of the Inspector General, Counterterrorism Detention and Interrogation Activities (September 2001–October 2003) (2003-7123-IG), 7 May 2004, p. 35 (DTS #2004-2710).

2587. Special Review, Office of the Inspector General, Counterterrorism Detention and Interrogation Activities (September 2001–October 2003) (2003-7123-IG), 7 May 2004, p. 40 (DTS #2004-2710).

2588. Email from: [REDACTED]; to: ■■■■■, [REDACTED]; subject: Re: Monday; date: August 5, 2002, at 05:35 AM.

2589. Email from: [REDACTED]; to: [REDACTED], ■■■■■, [REDACTED]; subject: Update; date: August 8, 2002, at 06:50 AM.

2590. Email from: [REDACTED]; to: [REDACTED], ■■■■■, [REDACTED]; subject: Update; date: August 8, 2002, at 06:50 AM.

2591. Email from: [REDACTED]; to: [REDACTED], [REDACTED]; subject: Re: 9 August Update; date: August 9, 2002, at 10:44 PM.

2592. Email from: [REDACTED]; to: ■■■■■, [REDACTED]; subject: Greetings; date: August 11, 2002, at 09:45 AM.

2593. Email from: Jose Rodriguez; to: [REDACTED]; subject: [DETENTION SITE GREEN]; date: August 12, 2002.

2594. Interview Report, 2003-7123-IG, Review of Interrogations for Counterterrorism Purposes, Scott W. Muller, September 5, 2003.

2595. Interview Report, 2003-7123-IG, Review of Interrogations for Counterterrorism Purposes, ■■■■■ ■■■, April 7, 2003.

2596. Report of Investigation, Office of the Inspector General, Unauthorized Interrogation Techniques at [DETENTION SITE BLUE] (2003-7123-IG), 29 October 2003, p. 24 (DTS #2003-4897).

2597. *See* Volume III for details.

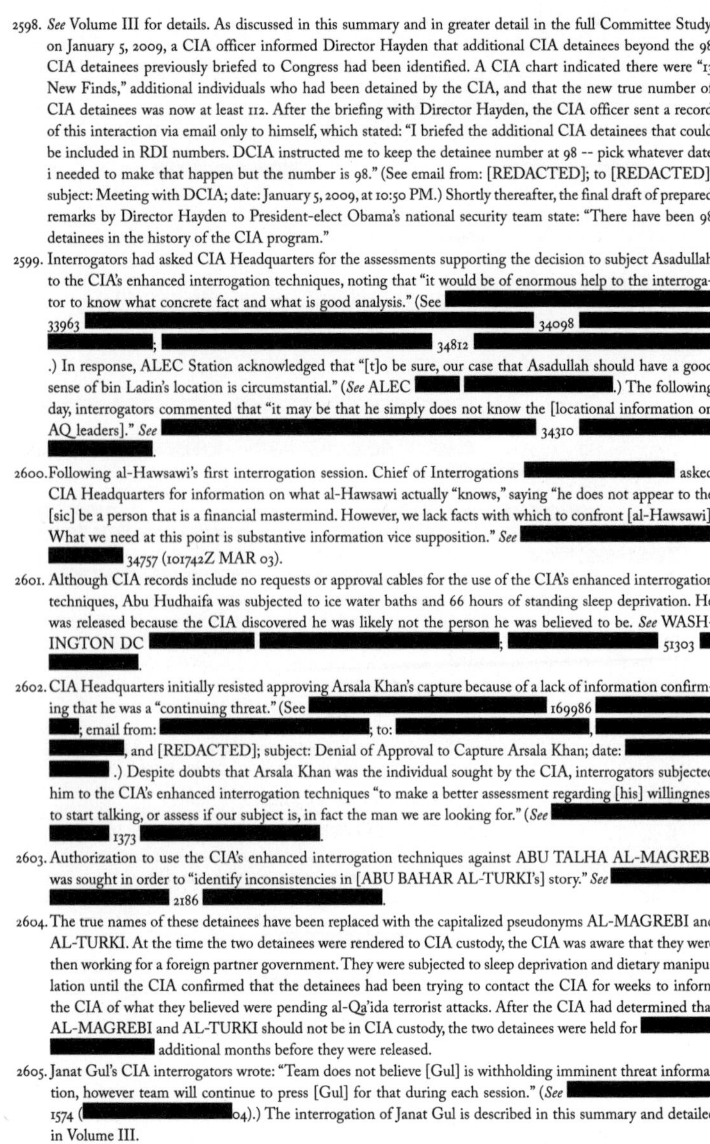

2598. *See* Volume III for details. As discussed in this summary and in greater detail in the full Committee Study, on January 5, 2009, a CIA officer informed Director Hayden that additional CIA detainees beyond the 98 CIA detainees previously briefed to Congress had been identified. A CIA chart indicated there were "13 New Finds," additional individuals who had been detained by the CIA, and that the new true number of CIA detainees was now at least 112. After the briefing with Director Hayden, the CIA officer sent a record of this interaction via email only to himself, which stated: "I briefed the additional CIA detainees that could be included in RDI numbers. DCIA instructed me to keep the detainee number at 98 -- pick whatever date i needed to make that happen but the number is 98." (See email from: [REDACTED]; to [REDACTED]; subject: Meeting with DCIA; date: January 5, 2009, at 10:50 PM.) Shortly thereafter, the final draft of prepared remarks by Director Hayden to President-elect Obama's national security team state: "There have been 98 detainees in the history of the CIA program."

2599. Interrogators had asked CIA Headquarters for the assessments supporting the decision to subject Asadullah to the CIA's enhanced interrogation techniques, noting that "it would be of enormous help to the interrogator to know what concrete fact and what is good analysis." (See 33963 34098 ; 34812 .) In response, ALEC Station acknowledged that "[t]o be sure, our case that Asadullah should have a good sense of bin Ladin's location is circumstantial." (*See* ALEC .) The following day, interrogators commented that "it may be that he simply does not know the [locational information on AQ leaders]." *See* 34310 .

2600. Following al-Hawsawi's first interrogation session. Chief of Interrogations asked CIA Headquarters for information on what al-Hawsawi actually "knows," saying "he does not appear to the [sic] be a person that is a financial mastermind. However, we lack facts with which to confront [al-Hawsawi]. What we need at this point is substantive information vice supposition." *See* 34757 (101742Z MAR 03).

2601. Although CIA records include no requests or approval cables for the use of the CIA's enhanced interrogation techniques, Abu Hudhaifa was subjected to ice water baths and 66 hours of standing sleep deprivation. He was released because the CIA discovered he was likely not the person he was believed to be. *See* WASHINGTON DC ; 51303 .

2602. CIA Headquarters initially resisted approving Arsala Khan's capture because of a lack of information confirming that he was a "continuing threat." (See 169986 ; email from: ; to: , , and [REDACTED]; subject: Denial of Approval to Capture Arsala Khan; date: .) Despite doubts that Arsala Khan was the individual sought by the CIA, interrogators subjected him to the CIA's enhanced interrogation techniques "to make a better assessment regarding [his] willingness to start talking, or assess if our subject is, in fact the man we are looking for." (*See* 1373 .

2603. Authorization to use the CIA's enhanced interrogation techniques against ABU TALHA AL-MAGREBI was sought in order to "identify inconsistencies in [ABU BAHAR AL-TURKI's] story." *See* 2186 .

2604. The true names of these detainees have been replaced with the capitalized pseudonyms AL-MAGREBI and AL-TURKI. At the time the two detainees were rendered to CIA custody, the CIA was aware that they were then working for a foreign partner government. They were subjected to sleep deprivation and dietary manipulation until the CIA confirmed that the detainees had been trying to contact the CIA for weeks to inform the CIA of what they believed were pending al-Qa'ida terrorist attacks. After the CIA had determined that AL-MAGREBI and AL-TURKI should not be in CIA custody, the two detainees were held for additional months before they were released.

2605. Janat Gul's CIA interrogators wrote: "Team does not believe [Gul] is withholding imminent threat information, however team will continue to press [Gul] for that during each session." (*See* 1574 (04).) The interrogation of Janat Gul is described in this summary and detailed in Volume III.

2606. The CIA's assessment of Ghailani's knowledge of terrorist threats was speculative. As one CIA official noted, "[a]lthough Ghailani's role in operational planning is unclear, his respected role in al-Qa'ida and presence in Shkai as recently as October 2003 may have provided him some knowledge about ongoing attack planning against the United States homeland, and the operatives involved." *See* email from: , CTC/UBLD (formerly ALEC); to: [REDACTED], [REDACTED], [REDACTED], [REDACTED]; subject: derog information for ODDO on Talha, Ghailani, Hamza Rabi'a and Abu Faraj; date: August 10, 2004.

2607. As noted above, the credibility of the source implicating Sharif al-Masri, Janat Gul, and Ghailani's connection to a pre-election plot was questioned by CIA officials prior to the application of the CIA's enhanced interrogation techniques against the detainees. The source was later determined to have fabricated the information.

2608. Five days after interrogators began using the CIA's enhanced interrogation techniques against Sayyid Ibrahim, interrogators cabled CIA Headquarters requesting information that would "definitively link [Ibrahim] to nefarious activity or knowledge by [Ibrahim] of known nefarious activities of al-Qa'ida members, if this is possible." (*See* 1324 FEB 04).) Without receiving a response, they continued using the CIA's enhanced interrogation techniques against Ibrahim. CIA Headquarters, which rejected an assessment from two CIA debriefers that Ibrahim was, "at best . . . a low-level facilitator," would later indicate that it was "uncertain" he would meet the requirements for U.S. military or foreign government detention. (See HEADQUARTERS ; HEADQUARTERS .) Other detainees, Abd al-Karim and Abu Hazim, were subjected to the CIA's enhanced interrogation techniques "in an attempt to more rapidly assess [their] knowledge of pending attacks, operational planning, and whereabouts of UBL." See 36843 ; 36908 .

2609. The OLC defined a High-Value Detainee as "a detainee who, until time of capture, we have reason to believe: (1) is a senior member of al-Qai'da or an al-Qai'da associated terrorist group (Jemaah Islamiyyah, Eqyptian[sic] Islamic Jihad, al-Zarqawi Group, etc.); (2) has knowledge of imminent terrorist threats against the USA, its military forces, its citizens and organizations, or its allies; or that has/had direct involvement in planning and preparing terrorist actions against the USA or its allies, or assisting the al-Qai'da leadership in planning and preparing such terrorist actions; and (3) if released, constitutes a clear and continuing threat to the USA or its allies" (Memorandum for John A. Rizzo, Senior Deputy General Counsel, Central Intelligence Agency, from Steven G. Bradbury, Principal Deputy Assistant Attorney General, Office of Legal Counsel, May 10, 2005, Re: Application of 18 U.S.C. Sections 2340-2340A to Certain Techniques That May Be Used in the Interrogation of a High Value al Qaeda Detainee (DTS #2009-1810, Tab 9); Memorandum for John A. Rizzo, Senior Deputy General Counsel, Central Intelligence Agency, from Steven G. Bradbury, Principal Deputy Assistant Attorney General, Office of Legal Counsel, May 30, 2005, Re: Application of United States Obligations Under Article 16 of the Convention Against Torture to Certain Techniques that May be Used in the Interrogation of High Value Al Qaeda Detainees (DTS #2009-1810, Tab 11)). Memorandum for John A. Rizzo, Acting General Counsel, Central Intelligence Agency, from Steven G. Bradbury, Principal Deputy Assistant AttorneyGeneral, Office of Legal Counsel, July 20, 2007, Re: Application of the War Crimes Act, the Detainee Treatment Act, and Common Article 3 of the Geneva Conventions to Certain Techniques that May Be Used by the CIA in the Interrogation of High Value al Qaeda Detainees (DTS #2009-1810, Tab 14) ("The CIA informs us that it currently views possession of information regarding the location of Osama bin Laden or Ayman al-Zawahiri as warranting application of enhanced techniques, if other conditions are met.").

2610. Ridha Ahmad al-Najjar (11542 ; ALEC ; Ghairat Bahir 31118 ; 'Umar 'Abd al-Rahman aka Asadullah (CIA ; 40471 ; 10673 ; DIRECTOR ; 10673 ; 10732 ; Adnan al-Libi 1478 ; 1758 ; Majid Bin Muhammad Bin Sulayman Khayil aka Arsala Khan 1370 ; Sayyid Ibrahim (1294 .

2611. Similar representations had been made by Director Hayden on September 6, 2006. Senator Bayh: "I was impressed by your statement about how effective the [CIA's enhanced interrogation] techniques have been in eliciting important information to the country, at one point up to 50 percent of our information about al-Qa'ida. I think you said 9000 different intelligence reports?" Director Hayden: "Over 8000, sir." Senator Bayh: "And yet this has come from, I guess, only thirty individuals." Director Hayden: "No, sir, 96, all 96" (Senate Select Committee on Intelligence, Briefing by the Director, Central Intelligence Agency, on the Central Intelligence Agency Detention, Interrogation and Rendition Program, September 6, 2006 (DTS #2007-1336)).

2612. See, for example, , Memorandum for the Record; subject: Meeting with Deputy Chief, Counterterrorist Center ALEC Station; date: 17 July 2003; Memorandum for: Inspector General; from: James Pavitt, Deputy Director for Operations; subject: re (S) Comments to Draft IG Special Review, "Counterterrorism Detention and Interrogation Program" (2003-7123-IG); date: February 27, 2004; attachment: February 24, 2004, Memorandum re Successes of CIA's Counterterrorism Detention and Interrogation Activities; CIA briefing slides entitled, "*CIA Interrogation Program.*" dated July 29, 2003, presented to senior White House officials; Hearing of the Senate Select Committee on Intelligence, February 14, 2007 (DTS #2007-1337). For additional details, *See* Volume II.

2613. ALEC (170117Z JAN 03).

2614. *See* intelligence chronology in Volume II.

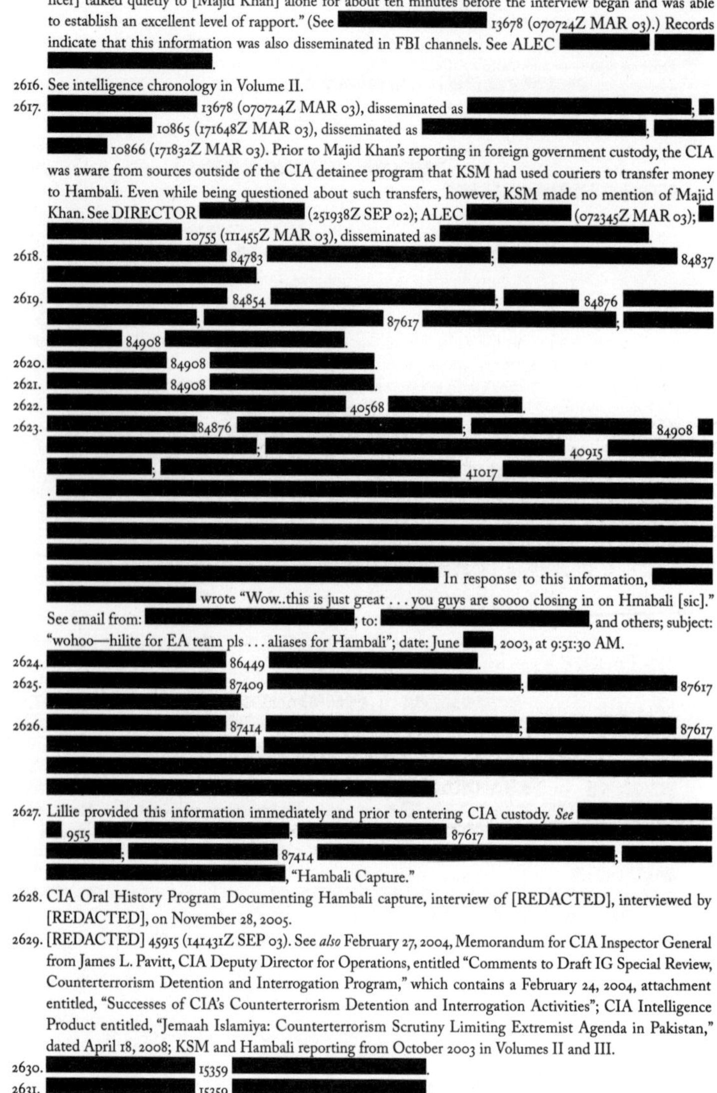

2615. A cable describing the foreign government interrogation of Majid Khan stated, "[a foreign government officer] talked quietly to [Majid Khan] alone for about ten minutes before the interview began and was able to establish an excellent level of rapport." (See 13678 (070724Z MAR 03).) Records indicate that this information was also disseminated in FBI channels. See ALEC .

2616. See intelligence chronology in Volume II.

2617. 13678 (070724Z MAR 03), disseminated as ; 10865 (171648Z MAR 03), disseminated as ; 10866 (171832Z MAR 03). Prior to Majid Khan's reporting in foreign government custody, the CIA was aware from sources outside of the CIA detainee program that KSM had used couriers to transfer money to Hambali. Even while being questioned about such transfers, however, KSM made no mention of Majid Khan. See DIRECTOR (251938Z SEP 02); ALEC (072345Z MAR 03); 10755 (111455Z MAR 03), disseminated as .

2618. 84783 ; 84837 .

2619. 84854 ; 84876 ; 87617 ; 84908 .

2620. 84908 .

2621. 84908 .

2622. 40568 .

2623. 84876 ; 84908 ; 40915 ; 41017 . In response to this information, wrote "Wow..this is just great . . . you guys are soooo closing in on Hmabali [sic]." See email from: ; to: , and others; subject: "wohoo—hilite for EA team pls . . . aliases for Hambali"; date: June , 2003, at 9:51:30 AM.

2624. 86449 .

2625. 87409 ; 87617 .

2626. 87414 ; 87617 . .

2627. Lillie provided this information immediately and prior to entering CIA custody. *See* 9515 ; 87617 ; 87414 ; , "Hambali Capture."

2628. CIA Oral History Program Documenting Hambali capture, interview of [REDACTED], interviewed by [REDACTED], on November 28, 2005.

2629. [REDACTED] 45915 (141431Z SEP 03). See *also* February 27, 2004, Memorandum for CIA Inspector General from James L. Pavitt, CIA Deputy Director for Operations, entitled "Comments to Draft IG Special Review, Counterterrorism Detention and Interrogation Program," which contains a February 24, 2004, attachment entitled, "Successes of CIA's Counterterrorism Detention and Interrogation Activities"; CIA Intelligence Product entitled, "Jemaah Islamiya: Counterterrorism Scrutiny Limiting Extremist Agenda in Pakistan," dated April 18, 2008; KSM and Hambali reporting from October 2003 in Volumes II and III.

2630. 15359 .

2631. 15359 .

2632. *See* the intelligence chronology in Volume II, including [REDACTED] 45953 (151241Z SEP 03) [REDACTED] 1323 (161749Z SEP 03).

2633. 1142 (301055Z NOV 03).

2634. See intelligence chronology in Volume II. Although NSA signals intelligence was not provided for this Study, an April 2008 CIA intelligence report on the Jemaah Islamiya noted that the al-Ghuraba group "consisted of the sons of JI leaders, many of whom completed basic militant training in Afghanistan and Pakistan while enrolled at Islamic universities in Karachi," and that this assessment was based on "signals intelligence and other reporting." *See* CIA Intelligence Product entitled, "Jemaah Islamiya: Counterterrorism Scrutiny Limiting Extremist Agenda in Pakistan," dated April 18, 2008.

2635. *See* intelligence chronology in Volume II.
2636. [REDACTED] 10223 (221317Z OCT 03); [REDACTED].
2637. WASHINGTON DC [REDACTED] (272113Z OCT 06).
2638. CIA Intelligence Product entitled, "Jemaah Islamiya: Counterterrorism Scrutiny Limiting Extremist Agenda in Pakistan," dated April 18, 2008.
2639. Numerous detainees were stripped and shackled, nude, in the standing stress position for sleep deprivation or subjected to other enhanced interrogation techniques prior to being questioned by an interrogator. *See* for example KSM [REDACTED] 34491 (051400Z MAR 03); Asadullah (DIRECTOR [REDACTED] ([REDACTED] FEB 03)); Abu Yasir al-Jaza'iri [REDACTED] 35558 ([REDACTED] MAR 03)); Suleiman Abdullah ([REDACTED] 35787 ([REDACTED] MAR 03); [REDACTED] 36023 ([REDACTED] APR 03)); Abu Hudhaifa [REDACTED] 38576 ([REDACTED] MAY 03)); Hambali [REDACTED] 1241 [REDACTED]; and Majid Khan ([REDACTED] 46471 (241242Z MAY 03); [REDACTED] 39077 (271719Z MAY 03).
2640. [REDACTED] 10016 (120509Z APR 02); [REDACTED] 10594 (061558Z AUG 02).
2641. See detainee reviews in Volume III for additional information.
2642. For example, on May 15 and May 16, 2003, the FBI hosted a conference on KSM and investigations resulting from KSM's reporting. The agenda included al-Qa'ida recruitment efforts in the U.S., a topic on which KSM had provided significant fabricated information. (See Memorandum from: [REDACTED]; for: [REDACTED], [REDACTED], [REDACTED], [REDACTED], [REDACTED], [REDACTED], [REDACTED], [REDACTED], [REDACTED] [REDACTED], [REDACTED], [REDACTED], [REDACTED], [REDACTED], [REDACTED], [REDACTED], [REDACTED], [REDACTED], [REDACTED], [REDACTED], [REDACTED], [REDACTED], [REDACTED], [REDACTED], [REDACTED], REDACTED], [REDACTED], [REDACTED], [REDACTED], [REDACTED], [REDACTED], [REDACTED], [REDACTED]; date: 8 May 2003.) See *also* Email from: [REDACTED]; to: [REDACTED], [REDACTED], [REDACTED], [REDACTED]; cc: [REDACTED], [REDACTED]; subject: Thanks from FBI; date: May 17, 2003, at 7:25:15 PM; [REDACTED] 12095 (222049Z JUN 03); [REDACTED] 12558 (041938Z AUG 03); [REDACTED] 31148 (171919Z DEC 05); [REDACTED] 31147 (171919Z DEC 05), disseminated as [REDACTED].
2643. [REDACTED] 10942 (221610Z MAR 03), disseminated as [REDACTED]; [REDACTED] 10948 (222101Z MAR 03), disseminated as [REDACTED].
2644. [REDACTED] 12095 (222049Z JUN 03).
2645. The CIA captured and detained two individuals whom KSM had identified as the protectors of his children. KSM later described his reporting as "all lies." *See* [REDACTED] 34569 (061722Z MAR 03); [REDACTED] 1281 (130801Z JUN 04).
2646. The CIA has referred only to Abu Zubaydah in the context of this representation. *See* Memorandum for John A. Rizzo, Senior Deputy General Counsel, Central Intelligence Agency, from Steven G. Bradbury, Principal Deputy Assistant Attorney General, Office of Legal Counsel, May 30, 2005, Re: Application of United States Obligations Under Article 16 of the Convention Against Torture to Certain Techniques that May be Used in the Interrogation of High Value Al Qaeda Detainees. The OLC document states: "As Zubaydah himself explained with respect to enhanced techniques, 'brothers who are captured and interrogated are permitted by Allah to provide information when they believe they have 'reached the limit of their ability to withhold it' in the fact of psychological and physical hardships."
2647. While there are no records of CIA detainees making these statements, the Deputy Chief of ALEC Station, [REDACTED], told the Inspector General on July 17, 2003, that the "best information [the CIA] received on how to handle the [CIA] detainees came from a walk-in [a source [REDACTED] to volunteer information to the CIA] after the arrest of Abu Zubaydah. He told us we were underestimating Al-Qa'ida. The detainees were happy to be arrested by the U.S. because they got a big show trial. When they were turned over to [foreign governments], they were treated badly so they talked. Allah apparently allows you to talk if you feel threatened. The [CIA] detainees never counted on being detained by us outside the U.S. and being subjected to methods they never dreamed of." See [REDACTED], Memorandum for the Record; subject: Meeting with Deputy Chief, Counterterrorist Center ALEC Station; date: 17 July 2003.
2648. [REDACTED] 10262 (151138Z MAR 02).
2649. [REDACTED] 10262 (151138Z MAR 02).
2650. [REDACTED] 10496 (162014Z FEB 03).
2651. [REDACTED] 10496 (162014Z FEB 03).
2652. [REDACTED] 10496 (162014Z FEB 03).

2653. In addition, CIA officer [REDACTED] testified at the April 12, 2007, Committee hearing: "I spoke with Zubaydah. I was at one of these facilities for several months and I spent around 18 hours a day with Abu Zubaydah. At the conclusion of my time, as I was leaving the facility, he spoke with me, and he said there is something I need you to understand – to go back to the question that came earlier about walling and a collar. He looked at the plywood wall in the cell and said I want to thank you for that. I've had a lot of time to sit and reflect, and I understand why that's there. That's there so I don't get hurt. In terms of the totality of the experience, his advice was I may have been the first person, but you need to continue to do this because I need to be able to live with who I am and I will continue to be the religious believing person I am, but you had to get me to the point where I could have absolution from my god to cooperate and deal with your questions. So he thanked us for bringing him to that point, beyond which he knew his religious beliefs absolved him from cooperating with us." There are no CIA records to support this testimony.

2654. According to the Inspector General Special Review, a debriefer threatened al-Nashiri by saying "[w]e could get your mother in here," and, "[w]e can bring your family in here." In addition, one of KSM's interrogators told the inspector general that the psychologist/interrogators told KSM that, if anything happens in the United States, "[w]e're going to kill your children." (*See* Special Review, pp. 42–43; interview of [REDACTED] [REDACTED], by [REDACTED] and [REDACTED], Office of the Inspector General, 30 April 2003; interview of [REDACTED] by [REDACTED] and [REDACTED], Office of the Inspector General, 22 October 2003; [REDACTED] 10757 (111505Z MAR 03).) According to a CIA cable, a case officer "used [Abu Zubaydah's] 'family card' to apply more psychological pressure on [Abu Zubaydah]." The cable stated that the case officer "advised [Abu Zubaydah] that even if [Abu Zubaydah] did not care about himself…[Abu Zubaydah] should at least care about his family and keep in mind their welfare; the insinuation being [that] something might happen to them." *See* [REDACTED] 10095 (220713Z APR 02).

2655. [REDACTED] 10507 [REDACTED]. CIA leadership, including CIA General Counsel Scott Muller and DDO James Pavitt, were also alerted to allegations that rectal exams were conducted with "excessive force" on two detainees at DETENTION SITE COBALT. *See* email from [REDACTED]; to [REDACTED]; cc: [REDACTED], [REDACTED], [REDACTED]; subject: ACTIONS from the GC Update this Morning, date: [REDACTED] 12:15 PM; Email from [REDACTED]; to: [REDACTED]; cc: [REDACTED], [REDACTED], [REDACTED], [REDACTED], subject: ACTIONS from the GC Update this Morning; date: [REDACTED] 1:23:31 PM; Email from [REDACTED]; to: [REDACTED]; cc: [REDACTED] [REDACTED], [REDACTED]; subject: Re: ACTIONS from the GC Update this Morning REQUEST FOR STATUS UPDATE; date: [REDACTED], at 10:47:32 AM. [REDACTED] 3223 [REDACTED]; HEADQUARTERS [REDACTED] [REDACTED].

2656. [REDACTED] 10070 [REDACTED].

2657. [REDACTED] 3868 (291534Z DEC 04); [REDACTED] 3868 (291534Z DEC 04). *See also* HEADQUARTERS [REDACTED] (302114Z NOV 04).

2658. [REDACTED] 34491 (051400Z MAR 03); Interview of [REDACTED] [REDACTED], by [REDACTED] and [REDACTED], Office of the Inspector General, 27 March 2003. [REDACTED] [REDACTED], [REDACTED] the Office of Medical Services (OMS), described the rectal rehydration of KSM as helping to "clear a person's head" and effective in getting KSM to talk.

2659. *See* [REDACTED] 2563 [REDACTED]; email from: [REDACTED]; to: [REDACTED] [REDACTED], [REDACTED], [REDACTED], [REDACTED], [REDACTED]; subject: Re: TASKING – Fw: [REDACTED] [REDACTED]; date; March 30, 2007; DTS #2007-1502.

2660. As described in the context of the rectal feeding of al-Nashiri, Ensure was infused into al-Nashiri "in a forward-facing position (Trendlenberg) with head lower than torso." *See* [REDACTED] 1203 (231709Z MAY 04).

2661. According to CIA records, Majid Khan's "lunch tray," consisting of hummus, pasta with sauce, nuts, and raisins was "pureed" and rectally infused. See [REDACTED] (231839Z SEP 04).

2662. *See* Volume III for additional information.

2663. The CIA's June 2013 Response states, "DCIA Hayden stated that 'punches' and 'kicks' were not authorized techniques and had never been employed and that CIA officers never threatened a detainee or his family." The CIA's June 2013 Response adds: "Part of that assertion was an error. The DCIA would have been better served if the Agency had framed a response for him that discussed CIA's policy prohibiting such conduct, and how the Agency moved to address unsanctioned behavior which had occurred (including punches and kicks) and implement clear guidelines."

2664. Memorandum for Deputy Director of Operations, from [REDACTED], January 28, 2003, Subject: Death Investigation – Gul RAHMAN, pp. 21–22.

2665. CIA Inspector General report, "Report of Investigation, Death of a Detainee [REDACTED]," (2003-7402-IG), April 27, 2005, at 38.

2666. [REDACTED] 37493 [REDACTED].

2667. ALEC [REDACTED] (182321Z JUL 02). According to the CIA attorney who reviewed the videotapes of the interrogation of Abu Zubaydah, "the person he assumed was a medical officer was dressed completely in black from head to toe, and was indistinguishable from other [interrogation] team members." *See* June 18, 2003, Interview Report of [REDACTED], Office of General Counsel Assistant General Counsel.

2668. Abu Ja'far al-Iraqi was subjected to nudity, dietary manipulation, insult slaps, abdominal slaps, attention grasps, facial holds, walling, stress positions, and water dousing with 44 degree Fahrenheit water for 18 minutes. He was shackled in the standing position for 54 hours as part of sleep deprivation, and experienced swelling in his lower legs requiring blood thinner and spiral ace bandages. He was moved to a sitting position, and his sleep deprivation was extended to 78 hours. After the swelling subsided, he was provided with more blood thinner and was returned to the standing position. The sleep deprivation was extended to 102 hours. After four hours of sleep, Abu Ja'far al-Iraqi was subjected to an additional 52 hours of sleep deprivation, after which CIA Headquarters informed interrogators that eight hours of sleep was the minimum. In addition to the swelling, Abu Ja'far al-Iraqi also experienced an edema on his head due to walling, abrasions on his neck, and blisters on his ankles from shackles. *See* ████ 1810 (████ DEC 05); ████ 1813 (████ DEC 05); ████ 1819 (████ DEC 05); ████ 1847 (████ DEC 05); ████ 1848 (████ DEC 05); HEADQUARTERS ████ (████ DEC 05). *See* additional information on Abu Ja'far al-Iraqi in Volume III.

2669. ████ 10536 (151006Z JULY 02); ALEC ████ (182321Z JUL 02).

2670. ████ 10536 (151006Z JULY 02).

2671. ████ 10607 (100335Z AUG 02).

2672. ████ 10647 (201331Z AUG 02); ████ 10618 (121448 AUG 02); ████ 10679 (250932Z AUG 02).

2673. ████ 11026 (070729Z OCT 02).

2674. ████ 44147 ████; ████ 36862 (181352Z APR 03); DIRECTOR ████ ████; ████ 44147 ████; DIRECTOR ████ ████.

2675. ████ 36908 ████; ████ 36862 (181352Z APR 03). The interrogator requested approval to use sleep deprivation, the facial slap, attention grasp, abdominal slap and water dousing. To accommodate Abu Hazim's and Abd al-Karim's injuries, the cable stated that, rather than being shackled standing during sleep deprivation, the detainees would be "seated, secured to a cell wall, with intermittent disruptions of normal sleeping patterns." For water dousing, the detainees' injured legs would be "wrapped in plastic." The request was approved. *See* DIRECTOR ████ ████; DIRECTOR ████ ████.

2676. ████ 37121 (221703Z APR 03); ████ 37152 (231424Z APR 03).

2677. ████ 37508 (021305Z MAY 03); ████ 37202 (250948Z APR 03).

2678. ████ 37152 (231424 APR 03).

2679. DIRECTOR ████ ████.

2680. ████ 37410 (291828Z APR 03); ████ 37509 (021309Z MAY 03).

2681. DIRECTOR ████ ████ MAY 03); ████ 37754 ████.

2682. ████ 38161 (131326Z MAY 03); DIRECTOR ████ ████ MAY 03); DIRECTOR ████ ████ MAY 03).

2683. ████ 39582 (041743Z JUN 03); ████ 39656 (060955Z JUN 03).

2684. ████ 38365 (170652Z MAY 03).

2685. Asadullah was also placed in a "small isolation box" for 30 minutes, without authorization and without discussion of how the technique would affect his ankle. See ████ 34098 ████; ████ 34294 ████; ████ 34310 ████.

2686. In May 2002, ████ stated that variety was introduced into Abu Zubaydah's diet; in addition to his daily intake of two cups of kidney beans, one cup of rice, Ensure, and juice, Abu Zubaydah was given a piece of fried chicken, Coke, and several cups of hot tea. *See* ████ 10327 (240624Z MAY 02).

2687. Email from: [REDACTED]; to: ████ and [REDACTED]; date: August 4, 2002, at 09:45:09 AM.

2688. ████ 10961 (260650Z SEP 02).

2689. *See* detainee reviews in Volume III.

2690. Email from: [REDACTED]; to: ; cc: ; subject: Re: Sitrep as of AM 3/15; date: March 15, 2003, at 3:52:54 AM; Interview of , by [REDACTED] and [REDACTED], Office of the Inspector General, May 15, 2003. See *also* interview of , by [REDACTED] and [REDACTED], Office of the Inspector General, May 15, 2003.

2691. Email from: ; to: ; cc: ; subject: More; date: April 10, 2003, at 5:59:27 PM.

2692. 10800 (131909Z MAR 03); 10801 (131918Z MAR 03); 10802 (131921Z MAR 03); 10803 (131929Z MAR 03).

2693. CIA record entitled, "Aggressive Interrogation Phase Synopsis," Abu Zubaydah, August 2002.

2694. Similarly, participants in the interrogation of Abu Zubaydah wrote that Abu Zubaydah "probably reached the point of cooperation even prior to the August institution of 'enhanced' measures –a development missed because of the narrow focus of the questioning. In any event there was no evidence that the waterboard produced time-perishable information which otherwise would have been unobtainable." *See* CIA Summary and Reflections of Medical Services on OMS participation in the RDI program, at 41.

2695. Interview of , by [REDACTED] and [REDACTED], Office of the Inspector General, May 15, 2003.

2696. Interview of , by [REDACTED] and [REDACTED], Office of the Inspector General, October 22, 2003.

2697. 11715 (201047Z MAY 03). In August 2006, wrote in a Sametime communication that KSM and Abu Zubaydah "held back" despite the use of the CIA's enhanced interrogation techniques, but added "I'm ostracized whenever I suggest those two did not tell us everything." *See* Sametime Communication, and , 15/Aug/06, 10:28:38 to 10:58:00.

2698. Interview of , by [REDACTED] and [REDACTED], Office of the Inspector General, April 3, 2003. also wrote in a 2005 Sametime communication that "we broke KSM . . . using the Majid Khan stuff . . . and the emails." *See* Sametime Communication, and [REDACTED], 02/May/05, 14:51:48 to 15:17:39.

2699. Interview of , by [REDACTED], [REDACTED], and [REDACTED], Office of the Inspector General, August 20, 2003.

2700. Email from: , OMS; to: [REDACTED] and [REDACTED], subject: Re: Acceptable lower ambient temperatures; date: March 7, 2003; email from: , OMS; to: [REDACTED] and [REDACTED]; subject: Re: Talking Points for review and comment; date: August 13, 2004; email from ; to: [REDACTED], [REDACTED], [REDACTED], [REDACTED], and [REDACTED]; subject: Re: Discussion with Dan Levin – AZ; date: October 26, 2004.

2701. 1396 ; 1299 (JAN 04); 1308 (JAN 04); 1312 (JAN 04); 1530 (04).

2702. 10429 (101215Z FEB 03).

2703. 10916 (210845Z MAR 03).

2704. Swelling of the feet.

2705. 10909 (201918Z MAR 03).

2706. Memorandum for Deputy Director of Operations, from , January 28, 2003, Subject: Death Investigation – Gul RAHMAN, pp. 21–22. *See* Volume III for additional injuries resulting from CIA interrogations.

2707. ALEC .

2708. August 21, 2003, Interview Report of James Pavitt, (pursuant to 2003-7123-IG), Deputy Director of Operations.

2709. 29520 ; email dated November , 2002, from CIA interrogator to , CTC/LGL Officer with the subject line, "Another example of field interrogation using coercive techniques without authorization."

2710. 29909 ; ALEC .

2711. Report of Investigation, Death of a Detainee (2003-7402-IG), 27 April 2005, p. 23 (DTS #2005-1957).

2712. In the short chain position, a detainee's hands and feet are shackled together by a short chain.

2713. [REDACTED] 29520 .

2714. January 27, 2003, Memorandum from [REDACTED], Chief, Counterintelligence Evaluation Branch, Counterespionage Group Counterintelligence Center, to Deputy Director for Operations, Subject: Death Investigation - Gul Rahman.

2715. January 27, 2003, Memorandum from [REDACTED], Chief, Counterintelligence Evaluation Branch, Counterespionage Group Counterintelligence Center, to Deputy Director for Operations, Subject: Death Investigation - Gul Rahman. The circumstances surrounding Gul Rahman's death are described in detail in both reports prepared by the Counterintelligence Center and a 2005 report prepared by the Inspector General. See April 27, 2005, CIA Inspector General, Report of Investigation, Death of a Detainee (DTS #2005-1957).

2716. FINAL AUTOPSY FINDINGS, by [REDACTED], MD, CASE #: OMS A-01-02.

2717. 28246 ; Interview Report, 2003-7123-IG, Review of Interrogations for Counterterrorism Purposes, , April 5, 2003; Interview Report, 2003-7123-IG. Review of Interrogations for Counterterrorism Purposes, , April 30, 2003; Memorandum for [REDACTED] from [REDACTED] November 2002, Subject: Legal Analysis of [REDACTED] Personnel Participating in Interrogation at the CIA Detention Facility in (aka "[DETENTION SITE COBALT]").

2718. Memorandum for [REDACTED] from [REDACTED] November 2002, Subject: Legal Analysis of [REDACTED] Personnel Participating in Interrogation at the CIA Detention Facility in (aka "[DETENTION SITE COBALT]").

2719. Email from: [DETENTION SITE BLUE] COB ; to: ; subject: EYES ONLY - [ ] ONLY -- MEMO FOR ADDO/DDO; date: January 22, 2003.

2720. 1285 .

2721. 34491 (051400Z MAR 03); 10654 (030904Z MAR 03); 10752 (102320Z MAR 03).

2722. 10487 (181656Z JUN 02); 10393 (020543Z JUN 02).

2723. OMS GUIDELINES ON MEDICAL AND PSYCHOLOGICAL SUPPORT TO DETAINEE INTERROGATIONS, "First Draft," March 7, 2003.

2724. PowerPoint presentation, Options of Incarcerating Abu Zubaydah, March 27, 2002.

2725. Email from: Scott W. Muller; to: , [REDACTED]; cc: [REDACTED]; subject: Detainees in Gitmo; date: January 2004; email from Scott W. Muller; to: [REDACTED] subject: DCI Meeting with Rice; date: January 2004; email from: Scott Muller; to: James Pavitt; ; cc: George Tenet, John McLaughlin, [REDACTED], [REDACTED], , [REDACTED], ; subject: CIA Detainees at GITMO; date: February 2004.